Lecture Notes in Computer Science   11858

More information about this series at http://www.springer.com/series/7412

Zhouchen Lin · Liang Wang ·
Jian Yang · Guangming Shi ·
Tieniu Tan · Nanning Zheng ·
Xilin Chen · Yanning Zhang (Eds.)

Pattern Recognition and Computer Vision

Second Chinese Conference, PRCV 2019
Xi'an, China, November 8–11, 2019
Proceedings, Part II

Springer

Editors
Zhouchen Lin
School of EECS
Peking University
Beijing, China

Jian Yang
Nanjing University of Science
and Technology
Nanjing, China

Tieniu Tan
Institute of Automation
Chinese Academy of Sciences
Beijing, China

Xilin Chen
Chinese Academy of Sciences
Beijing, China

Liang Wang
Institute of Automation
Chinese Academy of Sciences
Beijing, China

Guangming Shi
Xidian University
Xi'an, China

Nanning Zheng
Institute of Artificial Intelligence
Xi'an Jiaotong University
Xi'an, China

Yanning Zhang
Northwestern Polytechnical University
Xi'an, China

ISSN 0302-9743   ISSN 1611-3349   (electronic)
Lecture Notes in Computer Science
ISBN 978-3-030-31722-5   ISBN 978-3-030-31723-2   (eBook)
https://doi.org/10.1007/978-3-030-31723-2

LNCS Sublibrary: SL6 – Image Processing, Computer Vision, Pattern Recognition, and Graphics

This Springer imprint is published by the registered company Springer Nature Switzerland AG
The registered company address is: Gewerbestrasse 11, 6330 Cham, Switzerland

Preface

Welcome to the proceedings of the Second Chinese Conference on Pattern Recognition and Computer Vision (PRCV 2019) held in Xi'an, China!

PRCV merged from CCPR (Chinese Conference on Pattern Recognition) and CCCV (Chinese Conference on Computer Vision), which are both the most influential Chinese conferences on pattern recognition and computer vision, respectively. Pattern recognition and computer vision are closely inter-related and the two communities are largely overlapping. The goal of merging CCPR and CCCV into PRCV is to further boost the impact of the Chinese community in these two core areas of artificial intelligence and further improve the quality of academic communication. Accordingly, PRCV is co-sponsored by four major academic societies of China: the Chinese Association for Artificial Intelligence (CAAI), the China Computer Federation (CCF), the Chinese Association of Automation (CAA), and the China Society of Image and Graphics (CSIG).

PRCV aims at providing an interactive communication platform for researchers from academia and from industry. It promotes not only academic exchange, but also communication between academia and industry. In order to keep track of the frontier of academic trends and share the latest research achievements, innovative ideas, and scientific methods in the fields of pattern recognition and computer vision, international and local leading experts and professors are invited to deliver keynote speeches, introducing the latest advances in theories and methods in the fields of pattern recognition and computer vision.

PRCV 2019 was hosted by Northwestern Polytechnical University and was co-hosted by Xi'an Jiaotong University, Xidian University, and Shaanxi Normal University. We received 412 full submissions. Each submission was reviewed by at least three reviewers selected from the Program Committee and other qualified researchers. Based on the reviewers' reports, 165 papers were finally accepted for presentation at the conference, including 18 oral and 147 posters. The acceptance rate is 40%. The proceedings of the PRCV 2019 are published by Springer.

We are grateful to the keynote speakers, Prof. Kyros Kutulakos from the University of Toronto in Canada, Prof. Licheng Jiao from Xidian University, Prof. Tinne Tuytelaars from the University of Leuven in Belgium, and Prof. Kyoung Mu Lee from Seoul National University in South Korea.

We give sincere thanks to the authors of all submitted papers, the Program Committee members and the reviewers, and the Organizing Committee. Without their contributions, this conference would not be a success. Special thanks also go to all of the sponsors and the organizers of the special forums; their support made the conference a success. We are also grateful to Springer for publishing the proceedings and especially to Ms. Celine (Lanlan) Chang of Springer Asia for her efforts in coordinating the publication.

We hope you find the proceedings enjoyable and fruitful.

November 2019

Tieniu Tan
Nanning Zheng
Xilin Chen
Yanning Zhang
Zhouchen Lin
Liang Wang
Jian Yang
Guangming Shi

Organization

Steering Committee Chair

Tieniu Tan — Institute of Automation, Chinese Academy of Sciences, China

Steering Committee

Xilin Chen — Institute of Computing Technology, Chinese Academy of Sciences, China

Chenglin Liu — Institute of Automation, Chinese Academy of Sciences, China

Long Quan — The Hong Kong University of Science and Technology, SAR China

Yong Rui — Lenovo, China

Hongbin Zha — Peking University, China

Nanning Zheng — Xi'an Jiaotong University, China

Jie Zhou — Tsinghua University, China

Steering Committee Secretariat

Liang Wang — Institute of Automation, Chinese Academy of Sciences, China

General Chairs

Tieniu Tan — Institute of Automation, Chinese Academy of Sciences, China

Nanning Zheng — Xi'an Jiaotong University, China

Xilin Chen — Institute of Computing Technology, Chinese Academy of Sciences, China

Yanning Zhang — Northwestern Polytechnical University, China

Program Chairs

Zhouchen Lin — Peking University, China

Liang Wang — Institute of Automation, Chinese Academy of Sciences, China

Jian Yang — Nanjing University of Science and Technology, China

Guangming Shi — Xidian University, China

Organizing Chairs

Jianru Xue	Xi'an Jiaotong University, China
Peng Wang	Northwestern Polytechnical University, China
Wei Wei	Northwestern Polytechnical University, China

Publicity Chairs

Shiguang Shan	Institute of Computing Technology, Chinese Academy of Sciences, China
Qiguang Miao	Xidian University, China
Zhaoxiang Zhang	Institute of Automation, Chinese Academy of Sciences, China

International Liaison Chairs

Jingyi Yu	ShanghaiTech University, China
Jiwen Lu	Tsinghua University, China
Zhanyu Ma	Beijing University of Posts and Telecommunications, China

Publication Chairs

Xiang Bai	Huazhong University of Science and Technology, China
Tao Yang	Northwestern Polytechnical University, China

Special Issue Chairs

Ming-Ming Cheng	Nankai University, China
Weishi Zheng	Sun Yat-sen University, China

Tutorial Chairs

Deyu Meng	Xi'an Jiaotong University, China
Yuxin Peng	Peking University, China
Feiping Nie	Northwestern Polytechnical University, China

Workshop Chairs

Huchuan Lu	Dalian University of Technology, China
Yunhong Wang	Beihang University, China
Qingshan Liu	Nanjing University of Information Science and Technology, China

Sponsorship Chairs

Tao Wang	iQIYI, China
Jinfeng Yang	Civil Aviation University of China, China
Xinbo Zhao	Northwestern Polytechnical University, China

Demo Chairs

Huimin Ma	Tsinghua University, China
Runping Xi	Northwestern Polytechnical University, China

Competition Chairs

Nong Sang	Huazhong University of Science and Technology, China
Wangmeng Zuo	Harbin Institute of Technology, China
Hanlin Yin	Northwestern Polytechnical University, China

PhD Forum Chairs

Junwei Han	Northwestern Polytechnical University, China
Xin Geng	Southeast University, China
Si Liu	Beihang University, China

Web Chairs

Guofeng Zhang	Zhejiang University, China
Di Xu	Northwestern Polytechnical University, China

Financial Chairs

Jinqiu Sun	Northwestern Polytechnical University, China
Lifang Wu	Beijing University of Technology, China

Registration Chairs

Yu Zhu	Northwestern Polytechnical University, China
Shizhou Zhang	Northwestern Polytechnical University, China

Area Chairs

Xiang Bai	Huazhong University of Science and Technology, China
Songcan Chen	Nanjing University of Aeronautics and Astronautics, China
Jian Cheng	Chinese Academy of Sciences, China

Ming-Ming Cheng	Nankai University, China
Junyu Dong	Ocean University of China, China
Jianjiang Feng	Tsinghua University, China
Shenghua Gao	ShanghaiTech University, China
Xin Geng	Southeast University, China
Huiguang He	Institute of Automation, Chinese Academy of Sciences, China
Qinghua Hu	Tianjin University, China
Shuqiang Jiang	Institute of Computing Technology, China Academy of Science, China
Yu-Gang Jiang	Fudan University, China
Lianwen Jin	South China University of Technology, China
Xiaoyuan Jing	Wuhan University, China
Liping Jing	Beijing Jiaotong University, China
Xi Li	Zhejiang University, China
Zhouchen Lin	Peking University, China
Guangcan Liu	Nanjing University of Information Science and Technology, China
Qingshan Liu	Nanjing University of Information Science and Technology, China
Huchuan Lu	Dalian University of Technology, China
Jiwen Lu	Tsinghua University, China
Deyu Meng	Xi'an Jiaotong University, China
Qiguang Miao	Xidian University, China
Yadong Mu	Peking University, China
Yuxin Peng	Peking University, China
Yu Qiao	Shenzhen Institutes of Advanced Technology, Chinese Academy of Sciences, China
Nong Sang	Huazhong University of Science and Technology, China
Hongbin Shen	Shanghai Jiao Tong University, China
Linlin Shen	Shenzhen University, China
Mingli Song	Zhejiang University, China
Zhenan Sun	Chinese of Academy of Sciences, China
Kurban Ubul	Xinjiang University, China
Hanzi Wang	Xiamen University, China
Jingdong Wang	Microsoft, China
Lifang Wu	Beijing University of Technology, China
Yihong Wu	Institute of Automation, Chinese Academy of Sciences, China
Guisong Xia	Wuhan University, China
Yong Xia	Northwestern Polytechnical University, China
Shiming Xiang	Chinese Academy of Sciences, China
Xiaohua Xie	Sun Yat-sen University, China
Junchi Yan	Shanghai Jiao Tong University, China

Jinfeng Yang	Civil Aviation University of China, China
Xucheng Yin	University of Science and Technology Beijing, China
Xiaotong Yuan	Nanjing University of Information Science and Technology, China
Zhengjun Zha	University of Science and Technology of China, China
Changshui Zhang	Tsinghua University, China
Daoqiang Zhang	Nanjing University of Aeronautics and Astronautics, China
Zhaoxiang Zhang	Chinese Academy of Sciences, China
Weishi Zheng	Sun Yat-sen University, China
Wangmeng Zuo	Harbin Institute of Technology, China

Additional Reviewers

Peijun Bao	Jiaqing Fan	Rui Huang
Jiawang Bian	Qingnan Fan	Sheng Huang
Jinzheng Cai	Jianjiang Feng	Rongrong Ji
Ziyun Cai	Wei Feng	Kui Jia
Xiangyong Cao	Jingjing Fu	Ming Jiang
Yang Cao	Xueyang Fu	Shuqiang Jiang
Boyuan Chen	Chenqiang Gao	Tingting Jiang
Chusong Chen	Jin Gao	Yu-Gang Jiang
Dongdong Chen	Lin Gao	Liang Jie
Juncheng Chen	Shaobing Gao	Lianwen Jin
Songcan Chen	Shiming Ge	Xin Jin
Tianshui Chen	Xin Geng	Jianhuang Lai
Xilin Chen	Guoqiang Gong	Chenyi Lei
Yingcong Chen	Shuhang Gu	Chunguang Li
Jingchun Cheng	Xiaojie Guo	Kai Li
Ming-Ming Cheng	Yiwen Guo	Shijie Li
Li Chi	Yulan Guo	Stan Li
Yang Cong	Zhenhua Guo	Wenbo Li
Peng Cui	Chunrui Han	Xiangyang Li
Daoqing Dai	Hu Han	Xiaoxiao Li
Yuchao Dai	Tian Han	Xin Li
Cheng Deng	Yahong Han	Yikang Li
Weihong Deng	Huiguang He	Yongjie Li
Chao Dong	Fan Heng	Yufeng Li
Jiangxin Dong	Qibin Hou	Zechao Li
Weisheng Dong	Tingbo Hou	Zhanqing Li
Xiwei Dong	Changhui Hu	Zhizhong Li
Lijuan Duan	Lanqing Hu	Wei Liang
Lixin Duan	Qinghua Hu	Minghui Liao
Bin Fan	Xiaowei Hu	Zicheng Liao
Dengping Fan	Qingqiu Huang	Shuoxin Lin

Weiyao Lin
Zhouchen Lin
Bing Liu
Bo Liu
Chenchen Liu
Chenglin Liu
Dong Liu
Guangcan Liu
Jiawei Liu
Jiaying Liu
Liu Liu
Mengyuan Liu
Miaomiao Liu
Nian Liu
Qingshan Liu
Risheng Liu
Sheng Liu
Shuaicheng Liu
Si Liu
Siqi Liu
Weifeng Liu
Weiwei Liu
Wentao Liu
Xianglong Liu
Yebin Liu
Yiguang Liu
Yu Liu
Yuliang Liu
Yun Liu
Xihui Liu
Yaojie Liu
Mingsheng Long
Cewu Lu
Jiang Lu
Sihui Luo
Bingpeng Ma
Chao Ma
Huimin Ma
Lin Ma
Zhanyu Ma
Zheng Ma
Lin Mei
Deyu Meng
Qiguang Miao
Weiqing Min
Yue Ming

Yadong Mu
Feiping Nie
Yuzhen Niu
Gang Pan
Jinshan Pan
Yu Pang
Xi Peng
Yuxin Peng
Xiaojuan Qi
Yu Qiao
Jianfeng Ren
Jimmy Ren
Min Ren
Peng Ren
Wenqi Ren
Nong Sang
Mingwen Shao
Dongyu She
Shuhan Shen
Tianwei Shen
Lu Sheng
Boxin Shi
Jian Shi
Yukai Shi
Zhenwei Shi
Tianmin Shu
Dongjin Song
Xinhang Song
Jian Sun
Ke Sun
Qianru Sun
Shiliang Sun
Zhenan Sun
Ying Tai
Mingkui Tan
Xiaoyang Tan
Yao Tang
Youbao Tang
Yuxing Tang
Jun Wan
Changdong Wang
Chunyu Wang
Dong Wang
Guangrun Wang
Hanli Wang
Hanzi Wang

Hongxing Wang
Jian Wang
Le Wang
Liang Wang
Limin Wang
Lingjing Wang
Nannan Wang
Qi Wang
Tao Wang
Weiqun Wang
Wenguan Wang
Xiaosong Wang
Xinggang Wang
Xintao Wang
Yali Wang
Yilin Wang
Yongtao Wang
Yunhong Wang
Zilei Wang
Hongyuan Wang
Xiushen Wei
Junwu Weng
Kwanyee Wong
Yongkang Wong
Baoyuan Wu
Fei Wu
Jianlong Wu
Jianxin Wu
Lifang Wu
Shuzhe Wu
Xiaohe Wu
Xinxiao Wu
Yihong Wu
Guisong Xia
Fanyi Xiao
Xiaohua Xie
Xianglei Xing
Peixi Xiong
Yu Xiong
Xiangyu Xu
Yongchao Xu
Yuanlu Xu
Zheng Xu
Jianru Xue
Shipeng Yan
Sijie Yan

Hao Yang
Jufeng Yang
Meng Yang
Shuang Yang
Wei Yang
Yang Yang
Jingwen Ye
Ming Yin
Dongfei Yu
Gang Yu
Jiahui Yu
Tan Yu
Yang Yu
Zhenbo Yu
Ganzhao Yuan
Jiabei Zeng
Dechuan Zhan
Daoqiang Zhang
Hc Zhang
Juyong Zhang
Lei Zhang

Lin Zhang
Runze Zhang
Shanshan Zhang
Shengping Zhang
Shiliang Zhang
Tianzhu Zhang
Wei Zhang
Xiangyu Zhang
Xiaoyu Zhang
Yongqiang Zhang
Yu Zhang
Zhaoxing Zhang
Feng Zhao
Jiaxing Zhao
Kai Zhao
Kaili Zhao
Qian Zhao
Qijun Zhao
Qilu Zhao
Tiesong Zhao
Ya Zhao

Yue Zhao
Haiyong Zheng
Wenming Zheng
Guoqiang Zhong
Yiran Zhong
Chunluan Zhou
Hao Zhou
Jiahuan Zhou
Xinzhe Zhou
Yipin Zhou
Siyu Zhu
Chao Zhu
Guangming Zhu
Tyler (Lixuan) Zhu
Xiaoke Zhu
Yaohui Zhu
Liansheng Zhuang
Nan Zhuang
Dongqing Zou
Qi Zou
Wangmeng Zuo

Contents – Part II

Image/Video Processing and Analysis

Multiscale Entropy Analysis of EEG Based on Non-uniform Time

Hongxia Deng[1], Jinxiu Guo[1], Xiaofeng Yang[1], Jinxiu Hou[1],
Haoqi Liu[2], and Haifang Li[1(✉)]

[1] Taiyuan University of Technology, Taiyuan 030024, China
lihaifang@tyut.edu.cn
[2] North China Electric Power University, Beijing 102206, China

Abstract. To address the problem of loss of time series information when taking the mean value of the average signal from EEG data, a variance index is used to reconstruct the time series, and a multi-scale entropy method based on a non-uniform time window is proposed. The effectiveness of the method is verified in two data sets. The results show that the use of the variance of multi-scale time series can extract more effective features compared with average indicators. Compared with coarse-grained methods, the fine-grained method has better accuracy, but its time complexity is also higher. The uniform time window method has not only better accuracy, but also reduced time complexity.

Keywords: Non-uniform time window · Multi-scale entropy ·
Coarse-grained · Fine-grained · EEG

1 Introduction

Traditional methods to measure the complexity of physiological signals include time domain analysis, frequency domain analysis, and time-frequency analysis. Following the discovery of non-linear features in physiological signals, a nonlinear dynamics approach was introduced to analyze the kinematic complexity of time series. The relevant dimensions [1], including the largest Lyapunov index [2], are used to analyze the physiological signal. Since entropy theory was proposed in 1865, it has become one of the most widely used and most useful methods in the field of physiological signals. The sample entropy [3, 4] proposed by Richman and Moorman in 2000 is the most commonly used entropy owing to its robustness to noise.

However, the traditional sample entropy method measures the complexity of time series on a single scale and fails to measure the relationship between time series complexity and long-range temporal correlation. In 2002, Costa et al. [5, 6] introduced a multi-scale entropy (MSE) method based on sample entropy, which solves the problem based on signal entropy in multiple time scales [7, 8]. However, although the MSE(multi-scale entropy) method has been proved to be very successful in many fields, it still has shortcomings when used with short time series. Therefore, in 2013, Wu et al. [9] proposed a modified multi-scale entropy method. This method uses a fine-grained approach. The fine-grained method uses a sliding time window method, taking the average of each time window to reconstruct the time series at each scale, and then

© Springer Nature Switzerland AG 2019
Z. Lin et al. (Eds.): PRCV 2019, LNCS 11858, pp. 3–17, 2019.
https://doi.org/10.1007/978-3-030-31723-2_1

extracts the sample entropy values on different scales of the time series. This fine-grained method essentially reconstructs the time series to be consistent with the length of the original time series, especially when the time series is very long. In addition, Amoud et al. [10] proposed that the multi-scale entropy method in 2007 cannot reflect the existence of high-frequency components in physiological signals. They combined multi-scale reconstruction with empirical mode decomposition and proposed intrinsic mode entropy method for nonlinear discriminant analysis. The algorithm was applied to stability test data, and made a good distinction between elderly individuals and a normal control group. In 2011 Labate et al. [11] proposed a multi-resolution method based on wavelet analysis. Based on this, in 2012, Hu et al. [12] put forward the adaptive multiscale entropy (AME) method and further improved the multi-scale entropy algorithm in the frequency domain.

As the name implies, the multi-scale entropy method searches for the best eigen-values to interpret the complexity of time series at multiple time scales. The coarse-grained and fine-grained methods are the two most commonly used multi-scale tech-niques. The fine-grained method is an improvement on the coarse-grained method; however, although its accuracy and efficiency are higher than those of the coarse-grained method, its time complexity is much greater. Lehmann et al. [17] proposed the idea of non-uniform segmentation based on spatial trends, which can be divided into several non-uniform segments according to the hidden spatial information of the time series (especially physiological signals). Combining this method with the multi-scale method [18, 19] is believed to improve the accuracy of the coarse-grained method and reduce the time complexity of the fine-grained method.

The research presented in this article has two main aspects. (1) Using coarse-grained and fine-grained methods, the time series of each scale is reconstructed by combining the average value and the variance index, and the sample entropy value is extracted from the time series of each scale, so as to analyze the efficiency of various multi-scale entropy methods. (2) A new method to reconstruct time series is introduced, using non-uniform segmentation based on spatial trends. This method is combined with the mean and variance indices to extract the sample entropy of the reconstructed time series. The accuracy and time complexity of this method are compared with those of the coarse-grained and fine-grained methods.

2 Method

2.1 Entropy Method

At present, there are many entropy algorithms commonly used, such as the method of approximation entropy proposed by Pincus et al. [20], the method of sample entropy proposed by JSRichman et al., fuzzy entropy [21], and mode entropy [22] and variance entropy [23] and so on. However, some of the disadvantages of entropy algorithms are also obvious. The shortcomings of approximate entropy lie in: In the calculation, it has a great relationship with the length of the input time series and noise. And the approximate entropy is a biased statistic, it calculates the amount of self-matching [9, 24, 25]. and it is not suitable for analyzing EEG signals. Fuzzy entropy uses the exponential function instead of the binarization function in the sample entropy, which improves the time complexity. The advantages of sample entropy lie in: ① Sample entropy can be used in shorter time series and has better robustness to noise; ② The theory of random time series is theoretically better than the approximate entropy and can maintain the relative consistency [24]. Do not use the approximate entropy algorithm in the match, thus reducing the bias. Therefore, this paper chooses the sample entropy to compare and analyze the proposed multi-scale entropy method.

The sample entropy *SampEn* is calculated as follows:

$$SmapEn(m, r, N) = -ln\frac{B^{m+1}(r)}{B^m(r)} \tag{1}$$

2.2 Multi-scale Method

(1) Coarse-grained method

As shown in Fig. 1, the coarse-grained approach divides the original time series into multiple time scales and reconstructs the time series at each scale using the average metric to extract eigenvalues at each scale, when the scale s = 1 in the figure, the size of the time window selected by the coarse-grained method is 1, so the time series is still the original sequence, when s = 2, the coarse-grained method selects non-overlapping time windows of length 2 and reconstructs the time series using averages. Similarly, when s = 3, the length of time window selected is 3.

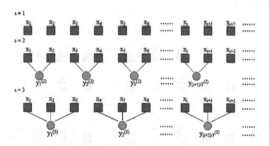

Fig. 1. Coarse-grained method process diagram

The algorithm steps for the coarse-grained method are as follows:

Given a given time series $\{x_1, x_2, \ldots, x_N\}$, you can construct a coarse-grained time series with scale s:

① Starting from the first element of the sequence, take a time window of length s, that is $\{x_1, x_2, \ldots, x_s\}$, The average of the sequences in the time window is $y_1^{(s)}$, Taking s = 2 in Fig. 1 as an example, the selected time window is $\{x_1, x_2\}$, and the result is obtained $y_1^{(2)} = (x_1 + x_2)/2$;

② move the time window forward s data length, the time window is $\{x_{s+1}, x_{s+2}, \ldots, x_{2*s}\}$ Averaging the sequence in the time window is $y_2^{(s)}$, In this case, when s = 2 the selected time window is $\{x_3, x_4\}$ and the result is obtained $y_2^{(2)} = (x_3 + x_4)/2$;

③ The time window according to the above rules, traverse the entire time series, you can get a sequence $\left\{y_1^{(s)}, y_2^{(s)}, \ldots, y_j^{(s)}\right\}$. The value of j is $[1, \lfloor N/s \rfloor]$. When s = 2, the new time series obtained is $\left\{y_1^{(2)}, y_2^{(2)}, \ldots, y_{\lfloor N/2 \rfloor}^{(2)}\right\}$.

The elements of each coarse-grained sequence can be defined as:

$$y_j^{(s)} = \frac{1}{s} \sum_{i=(j-1)*s+1}^{j*s} x_i, \; 1 \leq j \leq \left\lfloor \frac{N}{s} \right\rfloor \tag{2}$$

Where, s is the scale factor.

(2) Fine-grained method

Figure 2 shows the process diagram for the fine-grained method. As for the coarse-grained method, the time length of the fine-grained method is 1 when the scale s = 1 and the reconstructed time series is still the original sequence. When s = 2, the fine-grained method uses an overlapping time of length 2. The window and the time window each have a sliding step length of 1, and the average is used to reconstruct the sequence. When s = 3, the time window length is 3 and the sliding overlap window with the length of 1 remains.

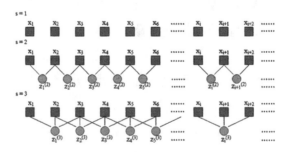

Fig. 2. Fine-grained method process diagram

The algorithm steps for the fine-grained method are as follows.

Given a given time series $\{x_1, x_2, \ldots, x_N\}$, a fine-grained time series can be constructed with scale s $\{z^{(s)}\}$ by the following steps.

① Take a time window of length s, that is, $\{x_1, x_2, \ldots, x_s\}$. The average of the sequences in the time window is $z_1^{(s)}$, Taking s = 3 as in Fig. 2 as an example, the selected time window is $\{x_1, x_2, x_3\}$, and $z_1^{(3)} = (x_1 + x_2 + x_3)/3$ is obtained.

② Move the time window forward a data length; the time window is $\{x_2, x_3, \ldots, x_{s+1}\}$. Averaging the sequence in the time window gives $z_2^{(s)}$. At this time, when s = 3, the time window is $\{x_2, x_3, x_4\}$, and $z_2^{(3)} = (x_2 + x_3 + x_4)/3$ is obtained.

③ The time window according to the above rules, traversing the entire time series $\{x_1, x_2, \ldots, x_N\}$, and then we can obtained $\{z^{(s)}\}$. Figure can be obtained when s = 3, the time series of reconstruction $\left\{z_1^{(3)}, z_2^{(3)}, \ldots, z_{\lfloor N/3 \rfloor}^{(3)}\right\}$.

The elements of the time series after each fine-grained method reconstruction can be defined as:

$$z_j^{(s)} = \frac{1}{s} \sum_{i=j}^{j+s-1} x_i, 1 \leq j \leq N - s + 1 \tag{3}$$

where s is the scale factor.

This work examines the use of the variance instead of the average for sequence reconstruction in both coarse-grained and fine-grained methods, and compares the accuracies and effectiveness of different multi-scale entropy methods in epilepsy and schizophrenia data sets.

In the coarse-grained method, the elements of each coarse-grained sequence can be defined as:

$$y_j^{(s)} = \frac{1}{s} \sum_{i=(j-1)*s+1}^{j*s} (x_i - \bar{X})^2, \quad \bar{X} = \frac{1}{s} \sum_{i=(j-1)*s+1}^{j*s} x_i, 1 \leq j \leq \left\lfloor \frac{N}{s} \right\rfloor \tag{4}$$

In the fine-grained approach, when reconstructing a sequence using variance indicators, the elements of each coarse-grained sequence can be defined as:

$$z_j^{(s)} = \frac{1}{s} \sum_{i=j}^{j+s-1} (xi - \bar{X})^2, \quad \bar{X} = \frac{1}{s} \sum_{i=j}^{j+s-1} x_i, 1 \leq j \leq N - s + 1 \tag{5}$$

(3) Non-uniform time window method

We introduce the trend of dividing non-uniform time window method to effectively improve the accuracy of the coarse-grained method and reduce the time complexity of the fine-grained method inspired by the division of micro-state based on the spatial trend proposed by Lehmann et al. The algorithm is as follows.

Assume that the EEG time series matrix is A(N, n), where N is the total number of channels and n is the time series length.

① Calculate the total field power (global field power; GFP), namely:

$$GFP = [\frac{1}{N}\sum_{i=1}^{N}(x_i - \bar{x})^2]^{\frac{1}{2}} \qquad (6)$$

where N is the total number of channels, x_i is the voltage measured on the ith channel, and $\bar{x}$ is the average of all channel voltages.

② Using the curve of the time series GFP with time, calculate all the maximum points of the curve and record the maximum value corresponding to the time point. That is, a maximum value sequence is obtained: the maximum GFP value sequence $\{y_1, y_2, \ldots, y_j, \ldots, y_m\}$ and the corresponding time point sequence $\{t_1, t_2, \ldots, t_j, \ldots, t_m\}$, where m is the maximum number of the curve that is the maximum number of GFP, y_j is the maximum point on the curve. t_j for the maximum y_j corresponding to the point in time.

③ Using the time point sequence $\{t_1, t_2, \ldots, t_j, \ldots, t_m\}$ corresponding to the original time series, find the maximum GFP corresponding to the original time series matrix $B(N, m)$, where N is the total number of channels, and m is the maximum value of GFP.

④ Find the maximum voltage MAX and the minimum voltage MIN at each time point corresponding to the maximum GFP, find their corresponding positions in the channel profile, and connect the two channels.

⑤ Based on the results of step ④, the maximum GFP values corresponding to the time points of the channel connection trends are divided, the same trend in the connection within a time window, or in another time window.

⑥ From step ⑤ the sub-results returned to the original time series, according to the time point of the window will be the original time series is divided into a number of non-uniform time window.

We used the Kolmogorov-Smirnov (KS) test to calculate the p-values.

3   Data and Results

3.1   Data

In this paper, two data sets were used to verify the accuracy and efficiency of various multi-scale entropy algorithms.

(1) Epilepsy data

Data of children with epilepsy were obtained from the MIT-BIH database. The data were collected at Boston Children's Hospital using an international standard 10–20 electrode. A total of 23 epilepsy subjects were included in the data set. All participants stopped using the drug one week prior to their seizures and collected data continuously for 916 h. Following analysis and diagnosis by epilepsy experts, the data sets were clearly marked with the beginning, end, and duration of each epileptic seizure. Owing to individual variation, the number of seizures and the duration of seizure were different for each subject. EEG signals were recorded for multiple seizures in different subjects, with a total of 198 epileptic seizures. In this experiment, 18 subjects (four males, 3–22 years of age; 14 females, 1.5–19 years of age) were used for data integrity reasons. Data sampling rates were 256 Hz; interictal 23 channel EEG data were collected for epileptic seizures in the 18 subjects.

(2) Schizophrenia data

The scoring data consisted of multi-channel EEG time series collected from Beijing Huilongguan Hospital from normal subjects and schizophrenia patients. EEG data were collected from 76 patients and 208 normal subjects. The participants wore a Neuroscan electrode cap for collection of the EEG data, as shown in Fig. 8. The data sampling rate was 500 Hz. The experimental paradigm used for data acquisition consisted of only one experimental task, which beeped at 10 s and 10.5 s, respectively. During the experiment, each subject participated in three sessions, each of which consisted of 20 trials. Each trial involved an experimental task, and a total of 630 s of data were collected. Owing to individual differences among participants and some unavoidable objectivity, in this paper, we used 25 trials of patients and 16 trials of six normal subjects, that is, a total of 6300 data points were analyzed.

3.2 Experimental Results and Analysis

3.2.1 Entropy Value Analysis of Different Subjects

(1) Analysis of the difference of entropy between seizure and episode in epileptic seizures.

Following studies by Leonidas [27] and Bai [28], we applied sample entropy to epilepsy. The time series were reconstructed using the coarse-grained method, the fine-grained method, the non-uniform time window method, and the average and variance, respectively. The entropy of the sample was extracted on the new-scale time series. Finally, the average entropy of samples on all channels (23 channels) for all subjects (18 subjects) at all scales was calculated, and the differences in entropy under the two states of epileptic seizure and interictal seizure were analyzed. The results are shown in Figs. 3, 4 and 5.

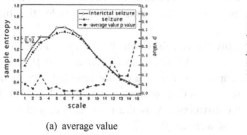
(a) average value

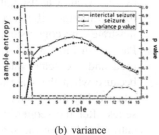
(b) variance

Fig. 3. Sample entropy under the coarse-grained approach

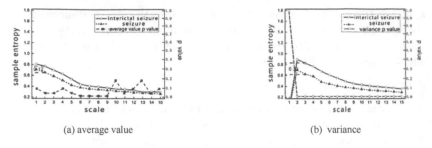

(a) average value   (b) variance

Fig. 4. Sample entropy under the fine-grained approach

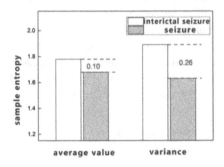

Fig. 5. Sample entropy under non-uniform time window method

① Part (a) in Figs. 3 and 4 shows the calculated sample entropy values when using the average indicator, whereas part (b) shows the sample entropy when using the variance indicator. As can be seen from Fig. 3, when using the variance indicator, the maximum entropy difference between the two states of the epileptic seizure and the seizure reached 0.18, while when the mean was used, the maximum difference between the two remained at about 0.10; therefore, the difference between the two states was more significant when using the variance indicator than using the average indicator. The same conclusion can be drawn from Fig. 4(a) and (b). In Fig. 5, the abscissa is the selected index and the ordinate is the sample entropy. When the average value was used, the difference in entropy between the two states was 0.10, while the difference between the two entropies was 0.26; this further illustrates the conclusion.

② Part (b) in Figs. 3 and 4 show the results when the variance indicator was used and the scale value was 1. All the entropy values are 0; this was because when the scale factor was 1, the size of the selected time window when using the variance reconstruction sequence was also 1, so the time series after the sequence reconstruction was the 0 sequence, and thus the entropy values of the samples were all 0.

③ Comparing Figs. 3 and 4, it can be seen that with the coarse-grained method, the differences between the entropy values of the two states decreased gradually with increasing scale. For scale values higher than 3–5

(Fig. 3), the changes in entropy values in the two states were essentially the same. In the case of the fine-grained method, there was always a difference between the two; this was due to the significant reduction in the length of the time series reconstructed by the coarse-grained method;

④ Comparing Figs. 3, 4, and 8, it can be seen that the coarse-grained method of multi-scale Fig. 3 in the epileptic seizure and the onset of the two states of the entropy difference is not as obvious as Fig. 4 using the fine-grained method. This also shows, on the one hand, that the fine-grained method is superior to the coarse-grained method in accuracy. As shown in Fig. 5, although the entropy difference between the two states was not as good as that of the fine-grained method under the mean index, the variance of the entropy differed significantly between the coarse-grained and fine-grained methods. This also shows that the non-uniform time window method can well characterize the difference between the two states.

(2) Entropy difference analysis of schizophrenia subjects and normal subjects

The time series were reconstructed using the coarse-grained method, the fine-grained method, the non-uniform time window method, and the mean and variance, respectively. The entropy of the sample was extracted into the new-scale time series. Finally, the average entropy of samples on all channels (64 channels) of all subjects in each category at each scale (26 subjects in the precision test and 15 subjects in the normal test) was calculated. The differences in entropy between the alcohol abuse test subjects and the normal subjects were analyzed; the results are shown in Figs. 6, 7 and 8.

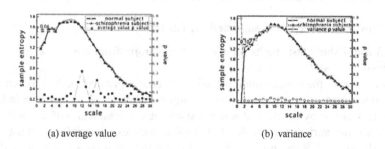

(a) average value   (b) variance

Fig. 6. Sample entropy under coarse-grained approach

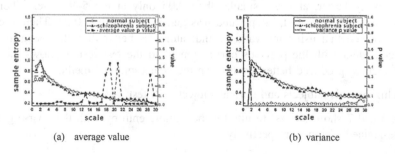

(a)   average value   (b) variance

Fig. 7. Sample entropy under the fine-grained approach

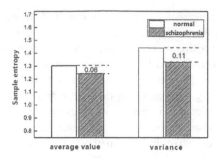

Fig. 8. Sample entropy under non-uniform time window method

Comprehensive comparison of the data obtained from the three maps was performed, and consistent conclusions were reached for the epilepsy and alcoholic data. ① Variance indicators gave better results than average indicators. ② Fine-grained method compared to coarse-grained methods, the difference between the entropy values of the two types of subjects was even greater. ③ The non-uniform time window method showed large differences between entropy values under the variance index.

Comparing the analysis of Figs. 3, 4, 5, 6, 7 and 8, we can find that in the coarse-grained and fine-grained methods, the difference in entropy between the two types of subjects tends to be non-stable or tend to be stable with the increase of the scale, so the scale factor selected when analyzing the EEG signals by the coarse-grained method or the fine-grained method may be 2–10.

3.2.2   Different Test States KS Test Verification

(1) Epilepsy subjects episode and interictal KS test

Figures 3 and 4 show test results for the sample entropy from the coarse-grained and fine-grained methods, respectively.

Figure 3 shows the p-value obtained using the coarse-grained method to extract the entropy of samples. As can be seen from the figure, when using the average indicator, the p-value obtained by the KS test was not stable; it was less than 0.05 when the scale was 6–8, and the variance of the KS test p-value was less than 0.05 on most scales. Figure 8 shows the KS test p-value obtained using the fine-grained method under the same calculation conditions; when using the average index, the p-value of each scale was obviously larger, and was smaller than 0.05 only at the 5–9 scale. When the variance indicator was used, the p-value was generally less than 0.05. Therefore, the KS test showed that using the variance indicator was better than the using average value, consistent with the previous conclusion. And the test results shows the fine-grained method produced better results than the coarse-grained method.

(2) Schizophrenic subjects and normal subjects KS test

Figures 6 and 7 show the test results for the sample entropy with the coarse-grained and fine-grained methods, respectively.

Figure 6 shows the result of KS tests for the two kinds of indices when using the coarse-grained method and normal subjects. When using the average index, the KS test p-value was large at most scales and did not meet requirements, while the variance index satisfied the condition of a p-value less than 0.05 at most scales. Figure 7 shows the results of the KS test using the fine-grained method under the same conditions; the results obtained by the coarse-grained method were the same. When the mean value was used, the p-value obtained from the KS test was larger at some scales, while the p-value obtained by the KS test met the requirements under the variance index.

(3) KS Test in two data sets by non-uniform time window method

Consistent with the results above for the coarse-grained and fine-grained methods, the mean entropy values of all samples on each channel were calculated and the KS test was performed on the entropy of two samples or two types of subjects. Table 1 shows the KS test results obtained using the non-uniform time window method for the two data sets.

Table 1. Non-uniform time window method sample entropy value KS test p value

	Epilepsy data	Schizophrenia data
Average value	0.00754	0.00705
variance	0.00001	0.00001

As can be seen from Table 1, the KS test results on the two data sets were generally less "well-behaved" when using the mean indicators than when using the variance indicators; their values were also more stable than those obtained using the coarse-grained approach and the fine-grained approach.

3.2.3   Different Participant State SVM Classification

After the original EEG signals were reconstructed, the scales and the eigenvalues of the subjects were extracted into the support vector machine (SVM) classifier. The status of both epilepsy subjects and normal subjects, schizophrenic subjects and normal subjects were classified. Table 2 shows the classification results when using various multi-scale methods and indicators and sample entropy. In the above analysis of the entropy difference, it is concluded that the scale factor range can be selected as 2–10 when analyzing the data in the two data sets. Therefore, the results shown in the Table 2 are the better values among the classification results when the scale factor range is 2–10 under various methods.

From Table 2, we can draw the following conclusions.

① Comparing the second row with the third row in Table 2, we can see that the classification accuracy obtained using the variance index for various multi-scale methods was markedly higher than that obtained using the average index. This shows that using the variance indicator is more effective than using the average indicator.

② compared with the coarse-grained method, an improved classification accuracy was obtained using the fine-grained method and the non-uniform time window method; the fine-grained method and the non-uniform time window method were not very different in classification accuracy. This shows that the fine-grained approach and the non-uniform time window approach outperform the coarse-grained approach when the time complexity is not considered.

Table 2. Sample entropy classification accuracy of average and variance

	Epilepsy data			Schizophrenia data		
	Coarse-grained approach	Fine-grained approach	Non-uniform time window	Coarse-grained approach	Fine-grained approach	Non-uniform time window
Average value	94.22% (scale 5)	95.65% (scale 4)	96.45%	94.39% (scale 5)	96.47% (scale 5)	94.33%
variance	95.62% (scale 4)	98.98% (scale 3)	98.73%	96.85% (scale 4)	98.94% (scale 5)	98.26%

3.3 Multi-scale Method of Time Complexity Analysis

The time complexity of the sample entropy algorithm is $O(n^2)$, where n is the time series length. In the coarse-grained method, when the sample entropy is calculated on each scale s, the time series length is N/s, so the time complexity at each scale is $O((N/s)^2)$. The time complexity of calculating the sample entropy in the coarse-grained method is:

$$T_1(s) = \sum_s O\left((N/s)^2\right) \tag{7}$$

Similarly, in the fine-grained approach, the time complexity of calculating the sample entropy is:

$$T_2(s) = \sum_s O\left((N - s + 1)^2\right) \tag{8}$$

The time complexity of calculating the sample entropy in the non-uniform segmentation method is:

$$T_3(s) = O(k^2) \tag{9}$$

where, k is the original time series segmentation number.

In this case, in contrast to $T_1(s), T_2(s), T_3(s)$, we can conclude that $T_2(s) > T_1(s) > T_3(s)$.

Based on this analysis, the following conclusions can be made. ① Of the coarse-grained methods, the fine-grained method and the non-uniform time window method, the non-uniform time window algorithm has the lowest time complexity, followed by the coarse-grained method; the fine-grained method has the highest temporal complexity. ② Using the variance indicator instead of the average results in greater time complexity. Table 3 shows the time it takes the algorithm to calculate the actual data.

Table 3. Epilepsy data in a variety of multi-scale entropy method in the calculation of the actual time

	Coarse-grained approach	Fine-grained approach	Non-uniform time window
Average value	3'02"	15'32"	1'20"
variance	3'57"	17'36"	1'54"

Table 3 shows EEG signal data from epilepsy subjects during epileptic seizures, including the original EEG, obtained using a variety of multi-scale entropy algorithms for multi-scale, sequence reconstruction, and feature extraction three steps spent in the actual time. Given the above selection of a scale factor of 2–10, the factor determining the time spent, for both the coarse-grained and the fine-grained method, is the time needed to reconstruct and extract the eigenvalues at the 2–10 scale. The time is also related to the efficiency of the computer itself, here for reference. Based on the data in the table, the various algorithms in practice have essentially the same time complexity as that of the theoretical analysis. However, the choice of a suitable algorithm for the diagnosis of brain diseases depends on the actual situation.

4 Conclusions

Based on the validation of epilepsy and schizophrenic data sets in this work, the following conclusions can be drawn. (1) For EEG signals, when the sample entropy is extracted after reconstructing the time series using the variance indicator instead of the average value, the difference in the eigenvalues between the two groups of subjects was relatively large. Correspondingly, the p-value of the KS test was smaller, and the accuracy of classification for both types of subject was higher; this would be beneficial in the diagnosis of patients with brain diseases. (2) The use of fine-grained methods to reconstruct sequences resulted in more accurate results on the whole compared with coarse-grained methods. However, fine-grained methods have the disadvantage of high time complexity. (3) A combination of the non-uniform segmentation method based on spatial trends and the multi-scale entropy concept is suitable to analyze EEG signals, and can effectively reduce the time complexity of the fine-grained method to improve its accuracy and potential applications.

Acknowledgments. This study was supported by research grants from the National Natural Science Foundation of China (61472270, 61672374, 61741212), Natural Science Foundation of Shanxi Province (201601D021073, 201801D121135), and Scientific and Technological Innovation Programs of Higher Education Institutions in Shanxi (2016139).

References

1. Zou, X., Lei, M.: Model recognition of surface EMG signals based on multi-scale maximum Lyapunov exponents. Chin. J. Biomed. Eng. **31**(1), 7–12 (2012)
2. Zhao, L., Liang, Z., Wu, W., et al.: Analysis of EEG-related dimension changes in patients with epilepsy after biofeedback training. Chin. J. Biomed. Eng. **29**(1), 71–76 (2010)
3. Richman, J.S., Moorman, J.R.: Physiological time-series analysis using approximate entropy and sample entropy. Am. J. Physiol. Heart Circ. Physiol. **278**(6), H2039–H2049 (2000)
4. Richman, J.S.: Sample entropy statistics and testing for order in complex physiological signals. Commun. Stat. - Theory Methods **36**(5), 1005–1019 (2007)
5. Costa, M., Goldberger, A.L., Peng, C.K.: Multiscale entropy analysis of complex physiologic time series. Phys. Rev. Lett. **89**(6), 068102 (2002)
6. Costa, M., Goldberger, A.L., Peng, C.K.: Multiscale entropy analysis of biological signals. Phys. Rev. E **71**(2), 021906 (2005)
7. Heisz, J.J., Shedden, J.M., McIntosh, A.R.: Relating brain signal variability to knowledge representation. Neuroimage **63**(3), 1384–1392 (2012)
8. da Silva, F.L.: EEG and MEG: relevance to neuroscience. Neuron **80**(5), 1112–1128 (2013)
9. Wu, S.D., Wu, C.W., Lee, K.Y., et al.: Modified multiscale entropy for short-term time series analysis. Physica A **392**(23), 5865–5873 (2013)
10. Amoud, H., Snoussi, H., Hewson, D., et al.: Intrinsic mode entropy for nonlinear discriminant analysis. IEEE Signal Process. Lett. **14**(5), 297–300 (2007)
11. Labate, D., Foresta, F.L., Inuso, G., et al.: Multiscale entropy analysis of artifactual EEG recordings. Front. Artif. Intell. Appl. **234**, 170–177 (2011)
12. Hu, M., Liang, H.: Adaptive multiscale entropy analysis of multivariate neural data. IEEE Trans. Biomed. Eng. **59**(1), 12–15 (2012)
13. Hu, M., Liang, H.: Variance entropy: a method for characterizing perceptual awareness of visual stimulus. Appl. Comput. Intell. Soft Comput. **2012**, 1 (2012)
14. Costa, M.D., Goldberger, A.L.: Generalized multiscale entropy analysis: application to quantifying the complex volatility of human heartbeat time series. Entropy **17**(3), 1197–1203 (2015)
15. Yin, Y., Shang, P., Feng, G.: Modified multiscale cross-sample entropy for complex time series. Appl. Math. Comput. **289**, 98–110 (2016)
16. Wu, Y., Shang, P., Li, Y.: Multiscale sample entropy and cross-sample entropy based on symbolic representation and similarity of stock markets. Commun. Nonlinear Sci. Numer. Simul. **56**, 49–61 (2018)

17. Lehmann, D., Ozaki, H., Pal, I.: EEG alpha map series: brain micro-states by space-oriented adaptive segmentation. Electroencephalogr. Clin. Neurophysiol. **67**(3), 271–288 (1987)
18. Liu, Z., Huang, J., Feng, X.: Construction of multi-scale depth convolution neural network behavior recognition model. Editorial Office Opt. Precis. Eng. **25**(3), 799–805 (2017)
19. Yang, Q., Li, S., Zhang, Y., et al.: Time-frequency analysis algorithm for multi-particle motion segmentation. J. Comput.-Aided Des. Comput. Graph. **29**(12) (2017)
20. Pincus, S.M.: Approximate entropy (ApEn) as a complexity measure. Chaos **5**, 110–117 (1995)
21. Kosko, B.: Fuzzy entropy and conditioning. Inf. Sci. **40**(2), 165–174 (1986)
22. Wang, J., Ning, X., Li, J., et al.: ECG multi-scale entropy analysis. In: Cutting-Edge Science Conference Papers (2004)
23. Ebrahimi, N., Maasoumi, E., Soofi, E.S.: Ordering univariate distributions by entropy and variance. J. Econometrics **90**(2), 317–336 (1999)
24. Okazaki, R., Takahashi, T., Ueno, K., et al.: Changes in EEG complexity with electroconvulsive therapy in a patient with autism spectrum disorders: a multiscale entropy approach. Front. Hum. Neurosci. **9**, 106 (2015)
25. Humeau-Heurtier, A., Mahé, G., Abraham, P.: Modified multiscale sample entropy computation of laser speckle contrast images and comparison with the original multiscale entropy algorithm. J. Biomed. Opt. **20**(12), 121302 (2015)
26. Diao, L., Wang, L., Lu, Y., et al.: Method of calculating text similarity threshold. J. Tsinghua Univ. (Sci. Technol.) **43**(1), 108–111 (2003)
27. Bai, D., Qiu, T., Li, X.: Sample entropy and its application in EEG seizure detection. J. Biomed. Eng. **24**(1), 200–205 (2007)
28. Iasemidis, L.D., Sackellares, J.C., Zaveri, H.P., Williams, W.J.: Phase space topography and the Lyapunov exponent of electrocorticograms in partial seizures. Brain Topogr. **2**(3), 187–201 (1990)

Recurrent Deconvolutional Generative Adversarial Networks with Application to Video Generation

Hongyuan Yu[1,2], Yan Huang[1,2], Lihong Pi[3], and Liang Wang[1,2,4(✉)]

[1] University of Chinese Academy of Sciences (UCAS), Beijing, China
hongyuan.yu@cripac.ia.ac.cn
[2] Center for Research on Intelligent Perception and Computing (CRIPAC),
National Laboratory of Pattern Recognition (NLPR), Beijing, China
{yhuang,wangliang}@nlpr.ia.ac.cn
[3] The Institute of Microelectronics, Tsinghua University (THU), Beijing, China
plh17@mails.tsinghua.edu.cn
[4] Chinese Academy of Sciences Artificial Intelligence Research (CAS-AIR),
Beijing, China

Abstract. This paper proposes a novel model for video generation and especially makes the attempt to deal with the problem of video generation from text descriptions, i.e., synthesizing realistic videos conditioned on given texts. Existing video generation methods cannot be easily adapted to handle this task well, due to the frame discontinuity issue and their text-free generation schemes. To address these problems, we propose a recurrent deconvolutional generative adversarial network (RD-GAN), which includes a recurrent deconvolutional network (RDN) as the generator and a 3D convolutional neural network (3D-CNN) as the discriminator. The RDN is a deconvolutional version of conventional recurrent neural network, which can well model the long-range temporal dependency of generated video frames and make good use of conditional information. The proposed model can be jointly trained by pushing the RDN to generate realistic videos so that the 3D-CNN cannot distinguish them from real ones. We apply the proposed RD-GAN to a series of tasks including conventional video generation, conditional video generation, video prediction and video classification, and demonstrate its effectiveness by achieving well performance.

Keywords: Video generation · RD-GAN · GAN

1 Introduction

Image generation has drawn much attention recently, which focuses on synthesizing static images from random noises or semantic texts. But video generation, i.e., synthesizing dynamic videos including sequences of static images with temporal dependency inside, has not been extensively studied. In this work, we wish

---

Student first author.

Z. Lin et al. (Eds.): PRCV 2019, LNCS 11858, pp. 18–28, 2019.
https://doi.org/10.1007/978-3-030-31723-2_2

to push forward this topic by generating better videos and dealing with a rarely investigated task of text-driven video generation.

The task here can be defined as follows: given a text describing a scene in which someone is doing something, the goal is to generate a video with similar content. This is challenging since it involves language processing, visual-semantic association and video generation together. A straightforward solution is to generalize the existing video generation models for this task. But it is not optimal due to the following reasons: (1) conventional video generation directly generates videos from noises but not from semantic texts as our case, and (2) existing video generation models mostly suffer from the visual discontinuity problem, since they either directly ignore the modeling of temporal dependency of generated videos, or simply consider it in a limited range with 3D deconvolution.

In this paper, we propose a recurrent deconvolutional generative adversarial network (RD-GAN) for conditional video generation. The proposed RD-GAN first represents given semantic texts as latent vectors with skip-thoughts [8], and exploits a generator named recurrent deconvolutional network (RDN) to generate videos in a frame-by-frame manner based on the latent vectors. The RDN can be regarded as a deconvolutional version of conventional recurrent neural network by replacing all the full connections with weight-sharing convolutional and deconvolutional ones. Accordingly, its hidden states now are 2D feature maps rather than 1D feature vectors, which efficiently facilitates the modeling of spatial structural patterns. After the generation, the generated videos are then fed into a discriminator which uses 3D convolutional neural network (3D-CNN) to distinguish from non-generated real videos. The generator and discriminator in RD-GAN can be jointly trained with the goal to generate realistic videos that can confuse the discriminator. To demonstrate the effectiveness of our proposed RD-GAN, we perform various experiments in terms of conventional and conditional video generation, video prediction and classification.

Our contributions are summarized as follows. To the best of our knowledge, we make the attempt to study the problem of sentence-conditioned video generation, which is a rarely investigated but very important topic for the current research interest on generative models. We propose a novel model named recurrent deconvolutional generative adversarial networks to deal with the task, which is demonstrated to achieve good performance in a wide range of both generative and discriminative tasks.

2   Related Work

Image Generation. With the fast development of deep neural networks, the generative models have made great progress recently. As we know, Tijmen [19] proposed capsule networks to generate images and Dosovitskiy et al. [2] generated 3D chairs, tables and cars with deconvolutional neural networks. There are also some other works [15,26] using supervised methods to generate images. Recently, the unsupervised methods, such as variational auto-encoder (VAE) [7] and generative adversarial network (GAN) [3] have attracted much attention. Gregor et al. [4] found that they can generate simple images by imitating human painting based on the recurrent variational autoencoder and the attention mechanism. The autoregressive models proposed by Oord et al. [21] modeled the conditional distribution of the pixel space and also achieved good experimental results. Compared with other methods, GAN has a relatively better performance on such tasks and various models [1,18,24,25] based on GAN generated appealing synthetic images. Beside that, conditional image generation has also been extensively studied. At first, simple variables, attributes or class labels [9,12] were used to generate specific images. Furthermore, researchers try to use unstructured text to do this work. For instance, Reed et al. [14] used the text descriptions and object location constraints to generate images with conditional PixelCNN. The later works [13,27] built upon conditional GAN yielded 64 × 64 or larger scale images of birds and flowers from text descriptions successfully.

Video Generation. Before we go into our video generation model, it is essential to review the recent advance related to video prediction and generation. [6,28] inspired us in terms of video continuity. Compared with video prediction, there is no context information in the video generation task. Vondrick et al. [22] first came up with a "violence" generative model which can directly yield fixed length videos from 3D deconvolution. However, the 3D deconvolution causes more serious loss of information than 1D and 2D deconvolution. In order to fix this problem, Saito et al. [16] proposed TGAN which tried to find all the latent vectors of continuous frames with the thought that videos are composed of images. And they used 1D and 2D deconvolution to generate video frame by frame. Unfortunately, their results do not have good continuity as they expected. MoCoGAN [20] decomposing motion and content for video generation, but their model lack understanding of semantics. In this work, we propose recurrent deconvolutional generative adversarial network (RD-GAN) including a recurrent deconvolutional network (RDN) to handle the current problems in video generation and well exploit the conditional constraints.

3   Recurrent Deconvolutional Generative Adversarial Network

The architecture of our proposed recurrent deconvolutional generative adversarial network for generating videos with text condition is shown in Fig. 1. The RD-GAN is built upon the conventional generative adversarial network (GAN), which has two sub-networks: a generator and a discriminator. The generator is a recurrent deconvolutional network (RDN) which tries to generate more realistic videos, whose input is sequential concatenated vectors of noise sampled from Gaussian distribution and text embedding by skip-thoughts [8]. While the discriminator is a 3D convolutional neural network (3D-CNN) which tries to distinguish input videos between two classes: "real" and "fake". During the binary classification, it also exploits the text embedding that concatenated with video feature maps in the discriminator. These two sub-networks are jointly trained by playing a non-cooperative game, in which the generator RDN tries to fool the discriminator 3D-CNN while the discriminator aims to make few mistakes. Such

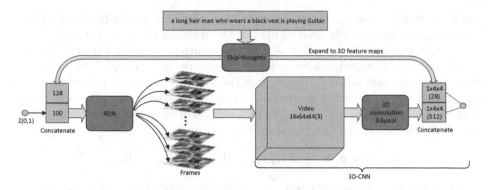

Fig. 1. The proposed recurrent deconvolutional generative adversarial network (RD-GAN) for generating videos with text condition. The sentence is encoded into an 28-dimensional vector by skip-thoughts [8] and linear operation. In the generator, the text vector and an 100-dimensional vector sampled from Gaussian distribution are concatenated as input. Then the text vector is copied 4 times and the same 16 text vectors are stacked as $28 \times 1 \times 4 \times 4$ feature maps before being fed into the penultimate layer of discriminator.

a competitive scheme has been demonstrated to be effective for training generative models [3]. In the following, we will present the generator and discriminator in details.

3.1 Recurrent Deconvolutional Network as Generator

The task of video generation based on semantic texts mainly encounters two challenges. One is how to extract suitable information from texts and associate it with the content of generated videos. It can be solved by exploiting recent advances in areas of natural language processing and multimodal learning. The other one is how to well model both long-range and short-range temporal dependencies of video frames, which focus on global slow-changing and local fast-changing patterns, respectively. The exist methods either just consider the local fast-changing ones with 3D convolutions or directly ignore the modeling of temporal dependency by treating each frame generation as a separate procedure.

To well model the long-term temporal dependency during video generation, we propose a recurrent deconvolutional network (RDN) as shown in Fig. 2. The RDN has a deep spatio-temporal architecture, whose input is a combination of noise and the vector extracted from the given text and the output is a sequence of generated video frames. Weight sharing is widely used in the temporal and the spatial direction, which can effectively reduce the number of parameters and contribute to model stability.

The whole network can be regarded as a nonlinear mapping from semantic texts to desired videos. In particular, in the spatial direction, there is a deep deconvolution network at each timestep for frame-wise generation. Between adjacent levels of feature maps, deconvolution, batch normalization and ReLU activation are successively used to upscale the frame size by a factor of 2.

In the temporal direction, it is a broad recurrent convolution network, in which pairwise feature maps at adjacent timesteps are connected by convolutions. It means that when predicting one video frame, the result can be directly modulated by its previous frame and recursively depends on other previous frames in a long temporal range. The formulation of inferring feature maps $H_{i,t}$ at the i-th level and the t-th timestep is:

$$H_{i,t} = a(b(H_{i-1,t} \mathbin{\hat{*}} W_{i-1,t} + H_{i,t-1} * U_{i,t-1} + B_{i,t})) \qquad (1)$$

where $*$ and $\hat{*}$ represent temporal convolution and spatial deconvolution operations, respectively. $U_{i,t-1}$ and $W_{i-1,t}$ contain the filter weights of temporal convolution and spatial deconvolution, respectively. $B_{i,t}$ denotes the bias weights. $a(\cdot)$ and $b(\cdot)$ are ReLU activation function and batch normalization operation, respectively. Due to the recurrent scheme, our RDN can flexibly produces videos with any length.

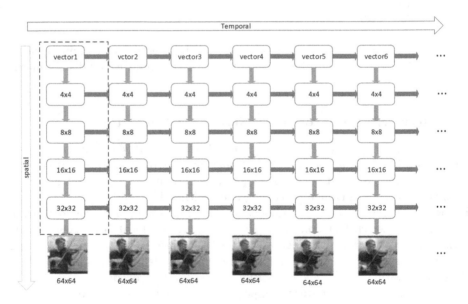

Fig. 2. The proposed recurrent deconvolutional network as the generator. The input is vector1 and all vectors in the top level are 1D vectors connected by linear transformation. The rest are 2D feature maps connected by convolutions and we use blue arrows to represent them. While green arrows refer to deconvolution, which enlarges the scale of images in the spatial direction. The sizes of images and feature maps are annotated in the figure. All the different parameters are in the dashed box, and the rest are consistent with these parameters. (Best viewed in color)

3.2   Modified 3D Convolutional Neural Network as Discriminator

The role of a discriminator is to identify the authenticity by classifying a given video into two classes: "real" and "fake". Considering that 3D convolutional neural network (3D-CNN) performs very well in the task of video classification, so we directly exploit it as our discriminator.

We make a few changes to the 3D-CNN as follows: (1) the last two linear layers are replaced by one 3D convolution layer, (2) the original sizes of some layers are reduced as the size of our video frame is 64×64, (3) 3D batch normalization, leakyReLU activation function and 3D max-pooling are used after each 3D convolution, and (4) the text embedding by skip-thoughts is combined in the penultimate layer.

3.3   Learning

The weights of both generator and discriminator can be jointly trained by using the following objective:

$$
\min_{\theta_G} \max_{\theta_D} \mathbb{E}_{x \sim p_{data}(x)}[\log D(x|t; \theta_D)] + \\
\mathbb{E}_{z \sim p_z(z)}[\log(1 - D(G(z; \theta_G)|t; \theta_D))]
$$
(2)

where θ_G and θ_D represent the parameters of generator and discriminator, respectively. $p_{data}(x)$ is the distribution of real videos x. z denotes the noise which is sampled from Gaussian distribution and t is the text condition. The object will reach the global optimum when $p_{G(z)} = p_{data}$. However, it is usually infeasible to obtain the global optimum, so we usually use gradient-based methods such as stochastic gradient descent (SGD) [11] to find a good local equilibrium.

All the network weights are initialized by sampling from a Gaussian distribution with a mean of 0 and standard deviation of 0.02. We use the ADAM solver to optimize all the parameters, in which the learning rate is 0.0002 and the momentum is 0.5. To speed up the training procedure, we first use all the images in video segments to train an image-based GAN, which has the same architecture in the spatial direction as the proposed RD-GAN. Then we use the learned weights as pretrained weights for the RD-GAN and fine-tune all the weights on videos. In fact, we can alternatively remove such a pretraining step with a longer training time.

4   Experiments

4.1   Dataset and Implementation Details

The UCF-101 [17] dataset is used during the training process. It contains 13,320 videos belonging to 101 different classes of human actions. Because there are many classes of videos in the UCF-101, it is very difficult for our model to learn such a complex data distribution. As a result, we use videos belonging to the same class to train a separate network every time. Note that the whole UCF-101 dataset is used when we evaluate the representations taken from the discriminator.

To enlarge our training dataset, we divide each video into multiple video segments containing 16 consecutive frames. For example, frames 1 to 16 make up the first video segment, the second video segment consists of frames 2 to 17 and the third video segment consists of frames 3 to 18, and so on. So a single class of video can get about 20,000 video segments and the included frames are all resized to the size of 64 × 64.

For the semantic texts associated with videos, we make the attempt to give different human-written text descriptions for different videos. For example, "a cute little boy who wears a red headband and a black shirt is playing Violin" or "a curly young man who wears a black T-shirt is playing Guitar". Videos with similar content and background are put into the same class and named with the same text description because those videos in the UCF-101 are divided from the same long video.

Fig. 3. Results of conditional video generation.

Fig. 4. Results of conditional video generation with "unfamiliar" sentence.

4.2   Video Generation from Sentence

Generating a specific video from human-written texts is equivalent to imagining a scene by our brain when we look at a novel. To adapt our model to the task of text-driven video generation, we exploit text information for both generator and discriminator as shown in Fig. 1. We use skip-thoughts [8] to encode a given text into a 4800-dimensional vector, and then map the vector from 4800 to 28 dimensions. After that, we concatenate the 28-dimensional text vector with an 100-dimensional vector that is sampled from Gaussian distribution, then the new 128-dimensional vector is used as the input of the generator. We also feed the same concatenated vector to the discriminator, which was extended to 3D data before combining with the penultimate layer of the 3D-CNN.

To simply annotate video data, we just gather similar videos into the same class and give them the same text descriptions. Firstly, we generate videos from already known texts as shown in Fig. 3. From this figure we can see that our model is able to generate semantic-related videos. For example, when given the text: "a long hair man who wears a black vest is playing Guitar", our model can accordingly generate video with attributes: "long hair", "man" and "black vest". Then we try to change some attributes in sentence and send these "unfamiliar" sentences to our model. Figure 4 shows our model can generate new samples with the corect attributes. The result is not clear because the amount of data is not enough. In other words there is the problem of lack of continuous mapping between the semantic space and the image space.

Table 1. Accuracy of unsupervised methods on the UCF-101 dataset.

Method	Accuracy
Chance	0.9%
STIP Features [17]	43.9%
Temporal Coherence [5]	45.4%
Shuffle and Learn [10]	50.2%
VGAN + Logistic Reg [22]	49.3%
VGAN + Fine Tune [22]	52.1%
TGAN + Linear SVM [16]	38.7%
Ours + Convolution Softmax	**53.3%**
Ours + Linear Softmax	**55.7%**
ImageNet Supervision [23]	91.4%

4.3   Video Classification

Considering that the features in our discriminator are learned without supervision, we want to quantitatively analyze the capacity of discrimination on the task of video classification. Since the discriminator was originally used for binary

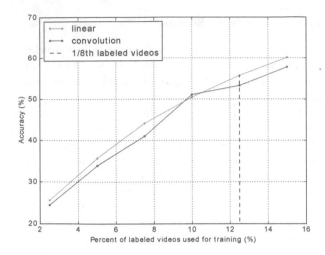

Fig. 5. Ratio of labeled training videos vs Accuracy.

classification, we have to replace its last layer with the softmax classifier for multi-class classification. All the videos in the UCF-101 dataset are used in this experiment. By segmenting all the videos into 16-frame segments, we can obtain totally 6 million video segments. The class for each video segment is in consistent with the class of its original video.

We first use the same softmax and dropout as [22] in the last two layers, which uses convolution to make the last feature maps transform into an 101-dimensional vector. We follow them and use 1/8 labeled videos to train the softmax classifier. Table 1 shows that our model improves the accuracy by 1.2%. Considering that linear operation can also convert the last feature maps into an 101-dimensional vector for classification, we use liner operation to replace the previously used convolution. To our surprise, this liner operation further improves our performance by 2.4%. Note that both convolution and linear operations have the same number of parameters. Obviously, models that leverage external supervision are still much better than unsupervised methods. In Fig. 5, the performances of convolution softmax and linear softmax are also compared by using different numbers of labeled videos, and we can observe that the more number of training data, the higher the accuracy. On the whole, linear softmax produces more discirminative results than convolution softmax.

5 Conclusions and Future Work

We have proposed a recurrent deconvolutional generative adversarial network that generates videos based on semantic texts. Its generator is a deconvolutional version of recurrent neural network, which is able to well exploit the text information and efficiently models the long-range temporal dependency during video generation. We have performed various experiments in terms of conventional video generation, video generation driven by text, video prediction and video classification. The experimental results have demonstrated the effectiveness of our model.

Note that this is just an initial work on video generation, and it might have the following drawbacks. The proposed model based on GAN becomes unstable if trained with too many frames and currently cannot well generate clear videos of a larger size and a longer length. The processing of given text only involves simple steps of feature extraction. This might not be optimal to associate it with diverse video contents. In the future, we will consider to train the RDN with more frames and extend our model to generate videos with a larger size and a longer length in a cascade manner. Furthermore, we plan to expand the annotated videos in details for better text-driven video generation.

Acknowledgments. This work is jointly supported by National Key Research and Development Program of China (2016YFB1001000), National Natural Science Foundation of China (61525306, 61633021, 61721004, 61420106015, 61806194), Capital Science and Technology Leading Talent Training Project (Z181100006318030), Beijing Science and Technology Project (Z181100008918010) and CAS-AIR.

References

1. Bin, H., Weihai, C., Xingming, W., Chun-Liang, L.: High-quality face image SR using conditional generative adversarial networks. arXiv preprint arXiv:1707.00737 (2017)
2. Dosovitskiy, A., Tobias Springenberg, J., Brox, T.: Learning to generate chairs with convolutional neural networks. In: CVPR (2015)
3. Goodfellow, I., et al.: Generative adversarial nets. In: NeurIPS (2014)
4. Gregor, K., Danihelka, I., Graves, A., Rezende, D., Wierstra, D.: Draw: a recurrent neural network for image generation. In: ICML (2015)
5. Hadsell, R., Chopra, S., LeCun, Y.: Dimensionality reduction by learning an invariant mapping. In: CVPR (2006)
6. Kalchbrenner, N., et al.: Video pixel networks. arXiv:1610.00527 (2016)
7. Kingma, D.P., Welling, M.: Auto-encoding variational bayes. arXiv:1312.6114 (2013)
8. Kiros, R., et al.: Skip-thought vectors. In: NeurIPS (2015)
9. Mirza, M., Osindero, S.: Conditional generative adversarial nets. arXiv:1411.1784 (2014)
10. Misra, I., Zitnick, C.L., Hebert, M.: Shuffle and learn: unsupervised learning using temporal order verification. In: Leibe, B., Matas, J., Sebe, N., Welling, M. (eds.) ECCV 2016. LNCS, vol. 9905, pp. 527–544. Springer, Cham (2016). https://doi.org/10.1007/978-3-319-46448-0_32
11. Nemirovski, A., Yudin, D.: On Cezari's convergence of the steepest descent method for approximating saddle point of convex-concave functions. In: Soviet Math. Dokl (1978)
12. van den Oord, A., Kalchbrenner, N., Espeholt, L., Vinyals, O., Graves, A., et al.: Conditional image generation with PixelCNN decoders. In: NeurIPS (2016)
13. Reed, S., Akata, Z., Yan, X., Logeswaran, L., Schiele, B., Lee, H.: Generative adversarial text to image synthesis. In: ICML (2016)

14. Reed, S., van den Oord, A., Kalchbrenner, N., Bapst, V., Botvinick, M., deFreitas, N.: Generating interpretable images with controllable structure. Technical report (2016)
15. Reed, S.E., Zhang, Y., Zhang, Y., Lee, H.: Deep visual analogy-making. In: NeurIPS (2015)
16. Saito, M., Matsumoto, E., Saito, S.: Temporal generative adversarial nets with singular value clipping. In: ICCV (2017)
17. Soomro, K., Zamir, A.R., Shah, M.: UCF101: a dataset of 101 human actions classes from videos in the wild. arXiv:1212.0402 (2012)
18. Tan, W.R., Chan, C.S., Aguirre, H., Tanaka, K.: Improved ArtGAN for conditional synthesis of natural image and artwork. arXiv preprint arXiv:1708.09533 (2017)
19. Tieleman, T.: Optimizing neural networks that generate images. Ph.D. thesis (2014)
20. Tulyakov, S., Liu, M.Y., Yang, X., Kautz, J.: MoCoGAN: decomposing motion and content for video generation. In: CVPR (2018)
21. Van DenOord, A., Kalchbrenner, N., Kavukcuoglu, K.: Pixel recurrent neural networks. In: ICML (2016)
22. Vondrick, C., Pirsiavash, H., Torralba, A.: Generating videos with scene dynamics. In: NeurIPS (2016)
23. Wang, L., Xiong, Y., Wang, Z., Qiao, Y.: Towards good practices for very deep two-stream ConvNets. arXiv:1507.02159 (2015)
24. Wang, X., Gupta, A.: Generative image modeling using style and structure adversarial networks. In: Leibe, B., Matas, J., Sebe, N., Welling, M. (eds.) ECCV 2016. LNCS, vol. 9908, pp. 318–335. Springer, Cham (2016). https://doi.org/10.1007/978-3-319-46493-0_20
25. Wu, H., Zheng, S., Zhang, J., Huang, K.: GP-GAN: towards realistic high-resolution image blending. arXiv preprint arXiv:1703.07195 (2017)
26. Yang, J., Reed, S.E., Yang, M.H., Lee, H.: Weakly-supervised disentangling with recurrent transformations for 3D view synthesis. In: NeurIPS (2015)
27. Zhang, H., et al.: StackGAN: text to photo-realistic image synthesis with stacked generative adversarial networks. In: ICCV (2017)
28. Zhou, Y., Berg, T.L.: Learning temporal transformations from time-lapse videos. In: Leibe, B., Matas, J., Sebe, N., Welling, M. (eds.) ECCV 2016. LNCS, vol. 9912, pp. 262–277. Springer, Cham (2016). https://doi.org/10.1007/978-3-319-46484-8_16

Functional Brain Network Estimation Based on Weighted BOLD Signals for MCI Identification

Huihui Chen[✉]

School of Mathematics, Liaocheng University, Liaocheng 252000, China
chenhuihui94@126.com

Abstract. Functional brain network (FBN) provides an important way to reveal the inherent organization of the brain and explore informative biomarkers of neurological disorders. Due to its increasing potential in clinical applications, many methods, such as Pearson's correlation and sparse representation, have been proposed in the recent years for FBN estimation. In practice, before the FBN estimation, a complex data preprocessing pipeline is involved to improve the quality of the data (i.e., fMRI signals in this paper), in which the scrubbing is an optional scheme for removing some "bad" time points (or volumes) from the fMRI signals according to a hard threshold related to, for example, the frame-wise displacement (FD). However, on one hand, the direct removal of time points may cause the loss of some useful information in data, and, on the other hand, the remaining time points may be not clean enough. In addition, with a fixed threshold, different numbers of volumes are generally scrubbed for different subjects, resulting in a bias or inconsistency in the estimated FBNs. To address these issues, in this paper, we develop a motion-dependent FBN estimation scheme by weighting the fMRI signals according to the values of FD. As a result, the proposed method can not only reduce the difficulty of threshold selection involved in the traditional scrubbing scheme, but also provide a more flexible framework that scrubs the data in the subsequent FBN estimation model. To verify the effectiveness of the proposed approach, we conduct experiments to identify subjects with mild cognitive impairment (MCI) from normal controls on a publicly available dataset. The experimental results show that our newly estimated FBNs can significantly improve the final classification accuracy.

Keywords: Functional brain network · Resting-state functional magnetic resonance imaging (rs-fMRI) · Scrubbing · Pearson's correlation · Sparse representation · Mild cognitive impairment (MCI)

1 Introduction

Functional magnetic resonance imaging (fMRI), by detecting the change of cerebral blood oxygen saturation degree, achieves the goal of noninvasive "observation" of the brain activity (Brunetti et al. 2006; Jin et al. 2010; Whittingstall et al. 2008). However,

---

The first author of this student paper.

© Springer Nature Switzerland AG 2019
Z. Lin et al. (Eds.): PRCV 2019, LNCS 11858, pp. 29–40, 2019.
https://doi.org/10.1007/978-3-030-31723-2_3

it is hard to identify patients from normal controls (NC) by a direct comparison of the fMRI data (i.e., time courses), since the spontaneous brain activities are random and asynchronous across subjects. In contrast, functional brain network (FBN), as a measure of the dependency between the fMRI time series, can provide a more reliable way of exploring the inherent organization of the brain and identifying neurological or psychiatric disorders, such as autism spectrum disorder (Gotts et al. 2012; Theijea et al. 2011), Alzheimer's disease (Huang et al. 2009; Liu et al. 2013; Supekar et al. 2008), and its early stage, namely mild cognitive impairment (MCI) (Fan and Browndyke 2010; Wee et al. 2012; Yu et al. 2016).

Due to the increasing potential in clinical applications, many methods, mainly including Pearson's correlation (PC) (Smith et al. 2013), sparse representation (SR) (Peng et al. 2009; Rosa et al. 2013; Yamashita et al. 2008; Zhou et al. 2014), Bayesian network (Ramsey et al. 2010) and dynamic casual modelling (Biswa et al. 2016; Friston et al. 2003), etc., have been proposed towards a better FBN estimation. In this paper, we only focus on correlation-based methods, especially PC and SR, due to their simplicity and empirical effectiveness. In fact, a recent review (Smith et al. 2011) has verified, on simulated data, that the PC and SR are more sensitive than some complex higher-order methods.

Although many methods have been proposed in recent years, how to estimate a "good" FBN is still an extremely challenging problem, due to our limited understanding (prior knowledge) of the brain and the heavy noises/artifacts in the fMRI data. In practice, on one hand, some priors are generally introduced into the FBN estimation models, including sparsity (Zhou et al. 2014), group-sparsity (Wee et al. 2014; Yu et al. 2016), scale-free (Li et al. 2017) and modularity (Qiao et al. 2016), and most of which can be encoded by a regularized learning framework (Qiao et al. 2016). On the other hand, a sophisticated preprocessing pipeline is also quite important to improve the quality of data before FBN estimation (Poldrack et al. 2011), in which the scrubbing is often used to remove some "bad" time points (or volumes) from the fMRI signals according to a given threshold related to the frame-wise displacement (FD), DVARS (D means temporal derivative of time courses, VARS means RMS variance over voxels) or other measurements (Yan et al. 2013).

Despite its seeming appeal to clean the data, the scrubbing scheme still causes some controversies or problems for FBN estimation (Dijk et al. 2012; Murphy et al. 2013; Power et al. 2012; Yan et al. 2013; Yang et al. 2005). In particular, there is no principle way of determining the threshold, and it is hard to guarantee the removed volumes are completely useless to the FBN estimation (Yan et al. 2013). Additionally, a fixed threshold always results in different length of the fMRI time series for different subjects, which can reduce the statistical power and cause biases in the estimated FBNs.

To address the above issues, in this paper, we develop a new FBN estimation strategy by weighting the fMRI time series (instead of the direct removal of time points) according to the values of FD. As a result, the proposed method can not only reduce the difficulty of threshold selection involved in the traditional scrubbing scheme, but also provide a framework that conducts more flexible data "scrubbing" in the subsequent FBN estimation. Finally, the experimental results illustrate that the proposed approach can achieve better classification accuracy than the baseline.

The rest of this paper is organized as follows. In **Materials and methods** section, we introduce the material and methods. In **Experiment** section, we evaluate our proposed method with experiments. In **Discussion** section, we discuss our findings based on the experimental results. In **Conclusion** section, we conclude the whole paper with a brief discussion.

2 Introduction

2.1 Data Acquisition Preprocessing

In this paper, we validate the proposed method by identifying subjects with MCI from NCs based on a publicly available dataset from Alzheimer's Disease Neuroimaging Initiative (ADNI). Specifically, 88 participants, including 44 MCIs and 44 NCs, are adopted in our experiment. The observed rs-fMRI images were scanned by 3.0T Philips scanners with the following parameters: TR/TE is 3,000/30 mm, flip angle is 80°, imaging matrix size is 64 × 64 with 48 slices and 140 volumes, and voxel thickness is 3.3 mm.

The acquired rs-fMRI data was processed by SPM8 toolbox[2] based on the well-accepted pipeline. The first three volumes of each subject were removed for signal stabilization. Then, the remaining 137 volumes were corrected for different slice acquisition timing and head motion. To further reduce the influences of nuisance signals, regression of ventricle and white matter signals as well as six head-motion profiles were conducted. Based on the Automated Anatomical Labeling (AAL) template atlas, pre-processed Blood Oxygen Level Dependent (BOLD) time series signals were partitioned into 116 ROIs. Prior to FBN estimation, the mean rs-fMRI time series of each ROI was bandpass filtered from 0.01 to 0.08 Hz. Finally, the time series was put into a data matrix $\mathbf{X} \in R^{137 \times 116}$ for FBN estimation.

Despite the above preprocessing pipeline, the fMRI series may be not clean enough due to, for example, head micromovements (Poldrack et al. 2011). In order to eliminate the influence of the instantaneous head motion, one option is to entirely remove the current time points when the subject moved during the scan. This approach is referred to as scrubbing (also often called volume censoring or spike removal). In practice, the scrubbing operation applies a threshold of FD to determine time points that are to be removed, where FD is a measure of movement and is calculated by combining motion parameters estimated during motion correction (Power et al. 2012) as follows:

$$FD_t = |x_{t-1} - x_t| + |y_{t-1} - y_t| + |z_{t-1} - z_t| + \frac{50\pi}{180} \times (|\alpha_{t-1}| + |\beta_{t-1}| + |\gamma_{t-1}|)$$

where $x, y, z, \alpha, \beta, \gamma$ are six head motion parameters, and 50 (with the unit of mm) denotes the assumed radius of the head (Power et al. 2014). The threshold applied to the FD crucially determines the extent of the clean-up achieved by scrubbing. The commonly used threshold is FD > 0.5 mm (more lenient) or FD > 0.2 mm (more stringent). In this paper, we employ the more lenient value of the threshold, meaning that we remove the time points if FD > 0.5 mm.

2.2   Functional Brain Network Estimation

With the preprocessing fMRI data, the crucial step in what follows is FBN estimation. As a baseline, we first review several representative FBN estimation models in **Related Works**. Then, we develop our new FBN estimation scheme in **The Proposed Method**.

2.3   Related Work

To start with, we assume that each brain has been parcellated into N ROIs, each of which corresponds to an observed time series $x_i \in R^T$, $i = 1, \cdots, N$. Then, the edge weight matrix W of PC-based FBN can be defined as follows:

$$W_{ij} = \frac{(\mathbf{x}_i - \bar{\mathbf{x}}_i)^T (\mathbf{x}_j - \bar{\mathbf{x}}_j)}{\sqrt{(\mathbf{x}_i - \bar{\mathbf{x}}_i)^T (\mathbf{x}_i - \bar{\mathbf{x}}_i)} \sqrt{(\mathbf{x}_j - \bar{\mathbf{x}}_j)^T (\mathbf{x}_j - \bar{\mathbf{x}}_j)}} \tag{1}$$

where $\bar{\mathbf{x}}_i$ is the mean vector corresponding to $\mathbf{x}_i$. Without loss of generality, we define a new $\mathbf{x}_i \triangleq (\mathbf{x}_i - \bar{\mathbf{x}}_i)/\sqrt{(\mathbf{x}_i - \bar{\mathbf{x}}_i)^T(\mathbf{x}_i - \bar{\mathbf{x}}_i)}$. Then, PC-based FBN can be simplified to $W_{ij} = \mathbf{x}_i^T \mathbf{x}_j$. Further, we suppose $\mathbf{X} = [\mathbf{x}_1, \mathbf{x}_2, \cdots, \mathbf{x}_N] \in R^{T \times N}$, and thus we have the estimated FBN $\mathbf{W} = \mathbf{X}^T \mathbf{X}$, which is the solution of the following optimization problem:

$$min_{\mathbf{W}} \|\mathbf{W} - \mathbf{X}^T \mathbf{X}\|_F^2 \tag{2}$$

where $\| \cdot \|_F$ denotes the F-norm of a matrix.

Different from PC that measures the full correlation between ROIs, SR is one of the statistical methods for modeling the partial correlation by regressing out the confounding effect from other ROIs. The model of SR is shown as follows:

$$min_{\mathbf{W}} \sum_{i=1}^{N} \left(\left\| \mathbf{x}_i - \sum_{j \neq i} W_{ij} \mathbf{x}_j \right\|^2 + \lambda \sum_{j \neq i} |W_{ij}| \right) \tag{3}$$

or equivalently, it can be expressed as the following matrix form:

$$min_{\mathbf{W}} \|\mathbf{X} - \mathbf{X}\mathbf{W}\|_F^2 + \lambda \|\mathbf{W}\|_1 \\ s.t. W_{ii} = 0, \ \forall i = 1, \cdots, N \tag{4}$$

where $\| \cdot \|_1$ is the L_1-norm of a matrix, and $W_{ii} = 0$ is employed for avoiding the trivial solution.

2.4   The Proposed Method

As we mentioned earlier, the observed fMRI data commonly contain noises or artifacts, and thus may lead to a poor FBN estimation. Different from the traditional scrubbing that entirely removes the "noisy" time points (or volumes) based on a hard threshold, we develop a more flexible scheme by introducing a weight p_t for the tth time point, where the p_t is defined as follows:

$$p_t = \frac{1}{|N_k(t)|} \sum_{j \in N_k(t)} e^{-\frac{x_j^2}{(d_{tj}+1)^2}}, \quad t = 1, 2, \cdots, T \tag{5}$$

where x_j is the FD value associated with the jth time point, $N_k(t)$ is a set of k neighbors of the tth time point, and $d_{tj} = |t - j|$ is the distance or interval between the tth and jth time points. Note that, p_t is inversely proportional to the value of FD, that is, when a point has a large FD, the time points will contribute less for the FBN estimation.

Further, we define $\mathbf{P} = diag(p_1, p_2, \ldots, p_T) \in R^{T \times T}$ as a diagonal matrix. Then, the improved PC based on the weighted time series can be formulated as follows:

$$min_{\mathbf{W}} \sum_{i=1}^{N} \sum_{t=1}^{T} \left(\mathbf{W}_{ij} - (\mathbf{Px}_i)^T (\mathbf{Px}_j) \right)^2 \tag{6}$$

For simplicity, we rewrite Eq. (6) into the following matrix form:

$$min_{\mathbf{W}} \left\| \mathbf{W} - (\mathbf{PX})^T (\mathbf{PX}) \right\|_F^2 \tag{7}$$

Especially when $\mathbf{P}$ is an identity matrix (meaning that $p_t = 1$ for all $t = 1, 2, \cdots, T$), Eq. (7) reduces to the original PC-based FBN estimation model given in Eq. (2). Obviously, the optimal solution of Eq. (7) is $\mathbf{W} = (\mathbf{PX})^T (\mathbf{PX}) = \mathbf{X}^T \mathbf{P}^2 \mathbf{X}$.

Similarly, we can introduce the weighted matrix $\mathbf{P}$ into SR, and propose a new FBN estimation model as follows:

$$min_{\mathbf{W}} \sum_{i=1}^{N} \sum_{t=1}^{T} p_t \left(x_i^{(t)} - \sum_{j \neq i}^{n} W_{ij} x_j^{(t)} \right)^2 + \lambda \|\mathbf{W}\|_1 \tag{8}$$

where $x_i^{(t)}$ is the tth time point of the fMRI series associated with the ith ROI. Further, we rewrite Eq. (8) into the following matrix form:

$$min_{\mathbf{W}} \|\mathbf{PX} - \mathbf{PXW}\|_F^2 + \lambda \|\mathbf{W}\|_1 \tag{9}$$

Note that the objective function in Eq. (9) is non-differentiable due to the L_1-norm regularizer. Therefore, we employ the proximal method (Combettes and Pesquet 2011) to solve Eq. (9) in this paper. In particular, we first differentiate the data-fitting term $\|\mathbf{PW} - \mathbf{PXW}\|_F^2$, and get its gradient of $2(\mathbf{X}^T \mathbf{P}^T \mathbf{PXW} - \mathbf{X}^T \mathbf{P}^T \mathbf{PX})$. As a result, we have the following update formula according to the gradient descent criterion:

$$\mathbf{W}_k = \mathbf{W}_{k-1} - \alpha_k (\mathbf{X}^T \mathbf{P}^T \mathbf{PXW} - \mathbf{X}^T \mathbf{P}^T \mathbf{PX}) \tag{10}$$

where α_k denotes the step size of the gradient descent. Then, the current $\mathbf{W}_k$ is "projected" onto the feasible region by the proximal operator of regularization term $\lambda \|W\|_1$, which is defined as follows:

$$prox_{\lambda\|\cdot\|_1}(\mathbf{W}) = \left[sgn(\mathbf{W}_{ij}) \times \max\left(abs(\mathbf{W}_{ij}) - \lambda, 0\right)\right]_{N \times N} \tag{11}$$

where $sgn(\mathbf{W}_{ij})$ and $abs(\mathbf{W}_{ij})$ return the sign and absolute value of $\mathbf{W}_{ij}$, respectively. Finally, we get a simple algorithm as follows (Table 1):

Table 1. Algorithm of SR-based FBN estimation with weighted BOLD signals.

Input: $\mathbf{X}$, $\mathbf{P}$ //observed data and weighted matrix for fMRI signals
Output: $\mathbf{W}$ //functional brain network
Initialize $\mathbf{W}$;
while *not converge*;
$\mathbf{W}_k \leftarrow \mathbf{W}_{k-1} - \alpha_k(\mathbf{X}^T\mathbf{P}^T\mathbf{P}\mathbf{X}\mathbf{W} - \mathbf{X}^T\mathbf{P}^T\mathbf{P}\mathbf{X})$;
$\mathbf{W} \leftarrow prox_{\lambda\|\cdot\|_1}(\mathbf{W}) = [sgn(\mathbf{W}_{ij}) \times \max(abs(\mathbf{W}_{ij}) - \lambda, 0)]_{N \times N}$;
end

3 Experiment

3.1 Experimental Setting

Once we obtain all FBNs, the subsequent work is to identify subjects with MCI form NCs based on the estimated FBNs. It is well known that differently selected features and classifiers tend to have a significant influence on the final classification accuracy. As a result, it is hard to determine whether the estimated FBN itself or the ensuing classification pipeline contribute more to the final performance. Therefore, we only use the simple t-test with default $p \leq 0.05$ for selecting features and then the most popular linear SVM with default parameter C=1 as the classifier in our experiment.

Duo to limited samples, we test our methods by the leave-one-out cross validation (LOOCV) strategy, in which only one subject is left for testing while the others are used to train the models. For determining the optimal value of parameters, an inner LOOCV is further conducted on the training data by a linear search. For regularized parameter λ involved in SR, the candidate values range in $[2^{-5}, 2^{-4}, \cdots, 2^0, \cdots, 2^4, 2^5]$. Different SR, PC-based FBN model is parameter-free. For improving its flexibility and conducting fair comparison, we introduce a thresholding parameter in PC by preserving a proportion of strong edge weights. To be consistent with SR-based method, we also use 11 candidate values $[1\%, 10\%, \cdots, 90\%, 100\%]$.

3.2 Visualization of Function Brain Network

After obtaining the preprocessed fMRI data, we estimate FBNs based on two kinds of methods (i.e., PC and SR) and their variants, including PC-scrubbing, SR-scrubbing, and our proposed PC-weighted and SR-weighted.

As we know, the FBN methods can be broadly divided into voxel-based and node-based methods (Bijsterbosch 2017). For voxel-based methods, the visualization is relatively straightforward, as the results from these methods can typically be visualized by spatial maps. For node-based methods, however, the visualization is more challenging, because we are generally interested in the connections between regions (nodes), not in the nodes themselves. Therefore, there are many options available for visualizing node-based results, including anatomical graph, connective graph, network matrix, functional cloud, etc. Each of these options tends to show different aspects of the FBN. Please refer to Sect. 6.3.2 in a recent book (Bijsterbosch 2017) that summarizes different schemes for visualizing voxel-based and node-based functional connectivity results.

Note that, in this paper, we only focus on the node-based functional connectivity methods, and, thus, the typical spatial maps used in voxel-based methods are not suitable for visualizing the estimated FBNs. Actually, we can visualize the "spatial map" of the FBN by plotting an anatomical graph on top of the brain. However, due to the three-dimensional nature of the brain and the large number of connections (even via sparsification), it is hard to see individual edges in such a layout. Therefore, in this paper, we use the network matrix (i.e., adjacency matrix of FBN) for visualizing FBN.

In Fig. 1, we show the adjacency matrices of FBNs constructed by six different methods. It can be observed that the FBN estimated by PC has a topology highly different from those estimated by SR-based methods, since they use different data fitting terms. For both PC and SR, we note that the traditional scrubbing scheme affect the network structure significantly, while the proposed weighted method can preserve the original network structure well. Especially for the FBN estimated by SR-weighted, it removes some possibly noisy connections to make the adjacency matrix clearer, and meanwhile keep the original hub and sparsity structure, as shown in Fig. 1(f). In contrast, the hub structure of the FBN does not exist in the traditional scrubbing method, as shown in Fig. 1(e).

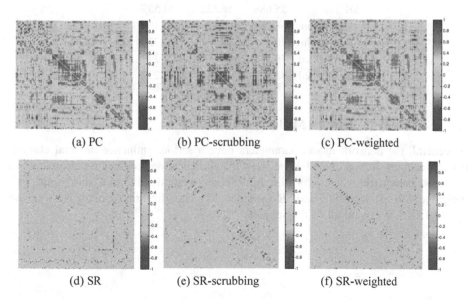

(a) PC   (b) PC-scrubbing   (c) PC-weighted

(d) SR   (e) SR-scrubbing   (f) SR-weighted

Fig. 1. The FBN adjacency matrices of a certain subject, constructed by different methods. (a) PC, (b) PC-scrubbing, (c) PC-weighted, (d) SR, (e) SR-scrubbing and (f) SR-weighted.

3.3 Classification Performance

There are a set of quantitative measurements, including accuracy, sensitivity and specificity, which are generally used to estimate the classification performance of different methods. Their mathematical definitions are given as follows:

$$Accuracy = \frac{TP + TN}{TP + FP + TN + FN}$$

$$Sensitivity = \frac{TP}{TP + FN}$$

$$Specificity = \frac{TN}{TN + FP}$$

where TP, TN, FP and FN indicate true positive, true negative, false positive and false negative, respectively.

Specifically, the classification results corresponding to these methods on ANDI dataset are given in Table 2.

Based on the results, we observe that our proposed methods achieve the best performance. This illustrates that our data weighted strategy can significantly improve the classification performance of both PC and SR.

Table 2. Classification results corresponding to methods.

Method	Accuracy	Sensitivity	Specificity
PC	53.41%	52.27%	54.55%
SR	55.68%	56.82%	54.55%
PC-scrubbing	68.18%	65.91%	70.45%
SR-scrubbing	70.45%	68.18%	72.73%
PC-weighted	76.14%	75.00%	77.27%
SR-weighted	78.41%	79.54%	77.27%

3.4 Sensitivity to Network Modeling Parameters

In general, the network model parameters have a serious influence on final classification accuracy. In Figs. 2 and 3, we show the classification accuracy corresponding to different parametric values for the 6 different methods, PC, PC-scrubbing, PC-weighted, SR, SR-scrubbing and SR-weighted. The classification accuracy is computed by the LOOCV test on all of the subjects.

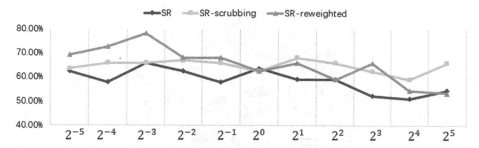

Fig. 2. Classification accuracy for SR-based method by three methods of 11 regularized parameters.

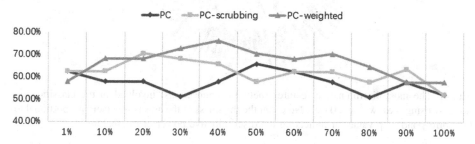

Fig. 3. Classification accuracy for PC-based method by three methods of 11 regularized parameters.

4 Discussion

In this paper, we propose a new FBN estimation scheme based on weighted BOLD signals. The experiments show that our methods can achieve better classification accuracy on ADNI dataset. According to the experimental results, we have the following discussions:

(1) In this study, we adopt the edge weights of estimated FBNs as features for identifying subjects with MCI from NC. Therefore, a main problem is which features contribute to the final classification accuracy. In particular, after constructing FBNs by the proposed models, we apply t-test to select discriminative features in order of their p-values (<0.001). Consequently, we obtain 58 most discriminative features for MCI identification task, and visualize the features (i.e., connections) in Fig. 4. Note that the thickness of the arcs is inversely proportional to the corresponding p-value for indicating the discriminative power of the features, and the color of each arc in Fig. 4 is randomly assigned only for visualized purpose. From Fig. 4, we found that the brain regions associated with top discriminative features include the middle temporal gyrus, precuneus, supramarginal gyrus, hippocampus, parahippocampus, etc. These findings are consistent with the previous neuroimaging biomarker reports and the pathology studies on MCI (Mckhannab et al. 2011; Michael 2008).

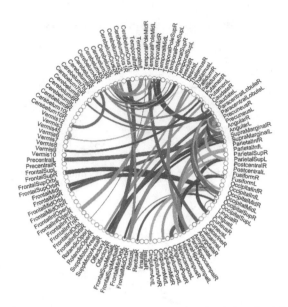

Fig. 4. The most discriminative features (network connections) involved in the classification tasks by using t-test with p < 0.001. Note that the thickness of the arcs is inversely proportional to the corresponding p-value for indicating the discriminative power of the features.

(2) Currently, although many FBN estimation methods have been developed, due to some inevitable factors, such as micro head motion or non-resting functional disturbing, may usually cause various noises or artifacts in observed fMRI time series, thus leading to a poor estimation of FBN. In this paper, based on PC and SR, we develop FBN estimation schemes by reweighting the fMRI signals according to the values of FD, which is expected to alleviate the influence of noises and artifacts. Experimental results show that our methods are significantly better than the baseline methods (i.e., PC and SR). However, it is currently still an open problem to estimate biologically meaningful and statistically robust brain networks due to our limited understanding of the human brain as well as complex noises in the observed data. In the future, we plan to employ our proposed weighted scheme in other FBN estimation models, and evaluate it on higher quality data with more subjects.

5   Conclusion

FBN has been an increasingly important way of exploring our brain and some neurological disorders. Pearson's correlation and sparse representation are the most commonly used methods in estimating FBNs duo to their simplicity and empirical effectiveness. However, the quality of estimated FBN may be not reliable, since the observed fMRI signals usually contain various noises or artifacts. In practice, the scrubbing is one of options to clean the data by directly removing some "noisy" time points. Unfortunately, the direct removal of time points tends to cause the loss of some useful information in data. On the hand, we cannot guarantee the remaining time points are necessarily helpful. In this paper, we develop a new scheme for FBN estimation by weighting the fMRI signals according to the FD values. Finally, we use our methods to identify subjects with MCI from NCs, and found that the weighted scheme can significantly improve the baseline methods.

Acknowledgement. We thank Lishan Qiao, Yining Zhang, Weikai Li and Limei Zhang for the help in this paper.

References

Biswa, S., Friston, K.J., Penny, W.D.: Gradient-based MCMC samplers for dynamic causal modelling. Neuroimage **125**, 1107–1118 (2016)

Brunetti, M., et al.: Human brain activation elicited by the localization of sounds delivering at attended or unattended positions: an fMRI/MEG study. Cogn. Process. **7**, 116–117 (2006)

Combettes, P.L., Pesquet, J.C.: Proximal splitting methods in signal processing. In: Bauschke, H., Burachik, R., Combettes, P., Elser, V., Luke, D., Wolkowicz, H. (eds.) Fixed-Point Algorithms for Inverse Problems in Science and Engineering, vol. 49, pp. 185–212. Springer, New York (2011). https://doi.org/10.1007/978-1-4419-9569-8_10

Dijk, K.R.A.V., Sabuncu, M.R., Buckner, R.L.: The influence of head motion on intrinsic functional connectivity MRI. Neuroimage **59**, 431–438 (2012)

Fan, Y., Browndyke, J.N.: MCI diagnosis via manifold based classification of functional brain networks. Alzheimers & Dementia J. Alzheimers Assoc. **6**, S16–S16 (2010)

Friston, K.J., Harrison, L., Penny, W.: Dynamic causal modelling. Neuroimage **19**, 1273–1302 (2003)

Gotts, S.J., Simmons, W.K., Milbury, L.A., Wallace, G.L., Cox, R.W., Martin, A.: Fractionation of social brain circuits in autism spectrum disorders. Brain **135**, 2711–2725 (2012)

Huang, S., et al.: Learning brain connectivity of Alzheimer's disease from neuroimaging data. In: Advances in Neural Information Processing Systems 22: Conference on Neural Information Processing Systems 2009. Proceedings of a Meeting Held, Vancouver, British Columbia, Canada, 7–10 December 2009, pp. 808–816 (2009)

Bijsterbosch, J., Smith, S.M., Beckmann, C.F.: Introduction to Resting State fMRI Functional Connectivity (2017)

Jin, H.L., et al.: Global and local fMRI signals driven by neurons defined optogenetically by type and wiring. Nature **465**, 788 (2010)

Li, W., Wang, Z., Zhang, L., Qiao, L., Shen, D.: Remodeling Pearson's correlation for functional brain network estimation and autism spectrum disorder identification. Front. Neuroinform. **11**, 55 (2017)

Liu, F., Wee, C.-Y., Chen, H., Shen, D.: Inter-modality relationship constrained multi-task feature selection for AD/MCI classification. In: Mori, K., Sakuma, I., Sato, Y., Barillot, C., Navab, N. (eds.) MICCAI 2013. LNCS, vol. 8149, pp. 308–315. Springer, Heidelberg (2013). https://doi.org/10.1007/978-3-642-40811-3_39

Mckhannab, G.M., et al.: The diagnosis of dementia due to Alzheimer's disease: recommendations from the National Institute on Aging-Alzheimer's Association workgroups on diagnostic guidelines for Alzheimer's disease (2011)

Michael, G.: Resting-state functional connectivity in neuropsychiatric disorders. Curr. Opin. Neurol. **21**, 424–430 (2008)

Murphy, K., Birn, R.M., Bandettini, P.A.: Resting-state FMRI confounds and cleanup. Neuroimage **80**, 349–359 (2013)

Peng, J., Wang, P., Zhou, N., Zhu, J.: Partial correlation estimation by joint sparse regression models. J. Am. Stat. Assoc. **104**, 735–746 (2009)

Poldrack, R.A., Mumford, J.A., Nichols, T.E.: Handbook of Functional MRI Data Analysis. Cambridge University Press, Cambridge (2011)

Power, J.D., Barnes, K.A., Snyder, A.Z., Schlaggar, B.L., Petersen, S.E.: Spurious but systematic correlations in functional connectivity MRI networks arise from subject motion. Neuroimage **63**, 999 (2012)

Power, J.D., Mitra, A., Laumann, T.O., Snyder, A.Z., Schlaggar, B.L., Petersen, S.E.: Methods to detect, characterize, and remove motion artifact in resting state fMRI. Neuroimage **84**, 320–341 (2014)

Qiao, L., Han, Z., Kim, M., Teng, S., Zhang, L., Shen, D.: Estimating functional brain networks by incorporating a modularity prior. Neuroimage **141**, 399–407 (2016)

Ramsey, J.D., Hanson, S.J., Hanson, C., Halchenko, Y.O., Poldrack, R.A., Glymour, C.: Six problems for causal inference from fMRI. Neuroimage **49**, 1545–1558 (2010)

Rosa, M.J., Portugal, L., Shawe-Taylor, J., Mourao-Miranda, J.: Sparse network-based models for patient classification using fMRI. In: 2013 3rd International Workshop on Pattern Recognition in Neuroimaging, (PRNI 2013), vol. 105, pp. 66–69 (2013)

Smith, S.M., et al.: Network modelling methods for FMRI. Neuroimage **54**, 875–891 (2011)

Smith, S.M., et al.: Functional connectomics from resting-state fMRI. Trends Cogn. Sci. **17**, 666–682 (2013)

Supekar, K., Menon, V., Rubin, D., Musen, M., Greicius, M.D.: Network analysis of intrinsic functional brain connectivity in Alzheimer's Disease. PLoS Comput. Biol. **4**, e1000100 (2008)

Theijea, C.G.M.D., Silva, S.L.D., Kamphuis, P.J., Garssen, J., Korte, S.M., Kraneveld, A.D.: Pathways underlying the gut-to-brain connection in autism spectrum disorders as future targets for disease management. Eur. J. Pharmacol. **668**, S70–S80 (2011)

Wee, C.Y., et al.: Identification of MCI individuals using structural and functional connectivity networks. Neuroimage **59**, 2045–2056 (2012)

Wee, C.Y., Yap, P.T., Zhang, D., Wang, L., Shen, D.: Group-constrained sparse fMRI connectivity modeling for mild cognitive impairment identification. Brain Struct. Funct. **219**, 641–656 (2014)

Whittingstall, K., et al.: Correspondence of visual evoked potentials with FMRI signals in human visual cortex. Brain Topogr. **21**, 86 (2008)

Yamashita, O., Sato, M.A., Yoshioka, T., Tong, F., Kamitani, Y.: Sparse estimation automatically selects voxels relevant for the decoding of fMRI activity patterns. Neuroimage **42**, 1414–1429 (2008)

Yan, C.G., et al.: A comprehensive assessment of regional variation in the impact of head micromovements on functional connectomics. Neuroimage **76**, 183–201 (2013)

Yang, S., Ross, T.J., Zhang, Y., Stein, E.A., Yang, Y.: Head motion suppression using real-time feedback of motion information and its effects on task performance in fMRI. Neuroimage **27**, 153–162 (2005)

Yu, R., Zhang, H., An, L., Chen, X., Wei, Z., Shen, D.: Correlation-weighted sparse group representation for brain network construction in MCI classification. In: Ourselin, S., Joskowicz, L., Sabuncu, M.R., Unal, G., Wells, W. (eds.) MICCAI 2016. LNCS, vol. 9900, pp. 37–45. Springer, Cham (2016). https://doi.org/10.1007/978-3-319-46720-7_5

Zhou, L., Wang, L., Ogunbona, P.: Discriminative sparse inverse covariance matrix: application in brain functional network classification. In: Computer Vision and Pattern Recognition, pp. 3097–3104 (2014)

ESNet: An Efficient Symmetric Network for Real-Time Semantic Segmentation

Yu Wang[1], Quan Zhou[1(✉)], Jian Xiong[1], Xiaofu Wu[1], and Xin Jin[2,3]

[1] National Engineering Research Center of Communications and Networking,
Nanjing University of Posts and Telecommunications,
Nanjing, People's Republic of China
quan.zhou@njupt.edu.cn

[2] Beijing Electronic Science and Technology Institute,
Beijing, People's Republic of China

[3] State Key Laboratory of Virtual Reality Technology and Systems,
Beihang University, Beijing, People's Republic of China

Abstract. The recent years have witnessed great advances for semantic segmentation using deep convolutional neural networks (DCNNs). However, a large number of convolutional layers and feature channels lead to semantic segmentation as a computationally heavy task, which is disadvantage to the scenario with limited resources. In this paper, we design an efficient symmetric network, called (*ESNet*), to address this problem. The whole network has nearly symmetric architecture, which is mainly composed of a series of factorized convolution unit (FCU) and its parallel counterparts. On one hand, the FCU adopts a widely-used 1D factorized convolution in residual layers. On the other hand, the parallel version employs a transform-split-transform merge strategy in the designment of residual module, where the split branch adopts dilated convolutions with different rate to enlarge receptive field. Our model has nearly 1.6M parameters, and is able to be performed over 62 FPS on a single GTX 1080Ti GPU. The experiments demonstrate that our approach achieves state-of-the-art results in terms of speed and accuracy trade-off for real-time semantic segmentation on CityScapes dataset.

Keywords: Real-time semantic segmentation · DCNNs · Factorized convolution

1 Introduction

Semantic segmentation plays a significant role in image understanding [1–3]. From the perspective of computer vision, the task here is to assign a semantic label for each image pixel, which thus can be also considered as a dense prediction problem. Unlike conventional approaches that handle this challenge task by designing hand-craft features, deep convolutional neural networks (DCNNs)

The first author is student.

© Springer Nature Switzerland AG 2019
Z. Lin et al. (Eds.): PRCV 2019, LNCS 11858, pp. 41–52, 2019.
https://doi.org/10.1007/978-3-030-31723-2_4

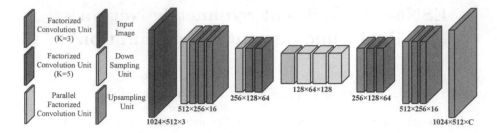

Fig. 1. Overall symmetric architecture of the proposed ESNet. The entire network is composed by four components: down-sampling unit, upsampling unit, factorized convolution unit and its parallel version. (Best viewed in color)

have shown their impressive capabilities in terms of end-to-end segmentation with full image resolution. The first prominent work in this field is fully convolutional networks (FCNs) [4], which are composed by a series of convolutional and max-pooling layers. After that, vast number of FCN-based network architectures [5–7] have been proposed and the remarkable progress have been achieved within segmentation accuracy. However, multiple stages of spatial pooling and convolution stride significantly reduce the dimension of feature representation, thereby losing much of the finer image structure. In order to address this problem, a more deeper architecture, named encoder-decoder network [8–10], has become a trend, where the encoder network is utilized to abstract image features and the decoder counterpart is employed to sequentially recover image details. In the designment of network architecture, the residual network (ResNet) [2] has been commonly adopted in recent years, where the residual layer allows to stack large amounts of convolutional layers, leading to the great improvement for both image classification [1,2,11] and semantic segmentation [12–14].

In spite of achieving impressive results, these accurate DCNNs neglect the implementing efficiency, which is a significant factor in limited resources scenarios. Considering running DCNNs on the mobile platforms (e.g., drones, robots, and smartphones), the designed networks are not only required to perform reliably (stability), but also required to conduct fast (real-time), suitable for embedded devices with space and memory constraints (compactness), and have low power consumption due to limited energy overhead (energy-saving). With this in mind, some preliminary research work [15–18] have been proposed to design lightweight networks that aim to develop efficient architectures for real-time semantic segmentation. However, these approaches usually focus on accelerating inference speed by aggressively reducing network parameters, which highly detriments segmentation performance. Therefore, pursuing the best performance with a good trade-off between accuracy and efficiency still remains an open research issue for the task of real-time semantic segmentation.

In this paper, we design a novel lightweight network called ESNet, adopting a nearly symmetric encoder-decoder architecture to address above problems. As shown in Fig. 1, our ESNet is based on ResNet [2], which consists of four basic components, including down-sampling unit, upsampling unit, factorized convolution unit (FCU) and its parallel version. The core element of our architecture is parallel factorized convolution unit (PFCU), where a novel transform-split-transform-merge strategy is employed in the designment of residual layer, approaching the representational power of large and dense layers, but at a considerably lower computational complexity. More specifically, the PFCU leverages the identity mappings and multi-path factorized convolutions with 1D filter kernels. While the identity mappings allow the convolutions to learn residual functions that facilitate training, the multi-path factorized convolutions allow a significant reduction of the convolutional layers. On the other hand, in contrast to previous lightweight networks [8,17,19] that abstract feature representation with fixed filter kernel size, the FCUs adopt the 1D factorized convolutions with different kernel size, where the receptive fields are adaptive to capture object instances with different scales. The FCUs and PFCUs are symmetrically stacked to construct our encoder-decoder architecture, producing semantic segmentation output end-to-end in the same resolution as the input image. Although the focus of this paper is the task of semantic segmentation, the proposed FCUs and PFCUs is directly transferable to any existing network that makes use of residual layers, including both classification and segmentation architectures. In summary, our contributions are three-folds: (1) The symmetrical architecture of ESNet leads to the great reduction of network complexity, accelerating the entire inference process; (2) Using multiple branch parallel convolutions in the residual layer leverages network size and powerful feature representation, still resulting in the whole network can be trained end-to-end. (3) We evaluate the performance of ESNet on CityScapes dataset [20], and the experimental results show that compared with recent mainstream lightweight networks, it achieves the best available trade-off in terms of accuracy and efficiency.

The remainder of this paper is organized as follows. After a brief discussion of related work in Sect. 2, a fast and compact architecture named ESNet is proposed in Sect. 3. The proposed network has been evaluated on CityScapes dataset, where the benchmark is constructed on a single NVIDIA GTX 1080Ti GPU. These experiments can be found in Sect. 4. Finally, the conclusion remarks and future work are given in Sect. 5.

2   Related Work

Recent success in DCNNs has brought significant progress on semantic segmentation in the past few years [3–6]. As a pioneer work, Farabet et al. [21] utilized DCNNs to abstract hierarchical feature representation for semantic segmentation. In [4], Long et al. first proposed an end-to-end segmentation based on VGG-16 network, where the fully connected layers in traditional DCNNs are replaced by convolutional layers to upsample feature maps. So far, a large amount of FCN-based networks [5–7,22,23] have been designed to deal with semantic segmentation challenge. To enlarge receptive fields, the dilated convolution [24] or atrous convolution [5,23] is also employed in FCN to capture large scale context. Due to continuous pooling, however, the resolution of feature maps are significant reduced and directly adapting FCNs always leads to the poor estimation outputs. To refine predict results, the encoder-decoder networks [8–10, 12] are commonly-used to develop FCN architecture by sequentially recovering fine image details. For instance, Noh et al. employ deconvolution to upsample low resolution feature responses [10]. SegNet [8] reuses the recorded pooling indices to upsample feature maps, and learns extra deconvolutional layers to densify the feature responses. Through adding skip connections, U-Net [25] designs an elegant symmetric network architecture, which stacks convolutional features from the encoder to the decoder activations. More recently, more attention have been paid to RefineNets [9, 12, 26, 27], which adopt ResNet [2] in encoder-decoder structure, and have been demonstrated very effective on several semantic segmentation benchmarks [20, 28].

In spite of achieving promising performance, these advances are at the sacrifice of running time and speed. In order to overcome this problem, many lightweight networks, initially designed for image classification task [29–33], have been designed to balance the segmentation accuracy and implementing efficiency [15–18, 34, 35]. ENet [17] is the first work that considers the efficiency issue, where the point-wise convolution is adopted in the residual layer. Apart from this initial designment, some recent work always employ convolution factorization principle [11, 29, 36] in their network architecture, where the 2D standard convolution is replaced by depthwise separable convolution. For example, Zhao et al. [35] investigate the high-level label cues to improve performance. ERFNet [19] leverages skip connections and 1D convolutions in residual block design, greatly reducing network parameters while maintaining high efficiency. In [18], Mehta et al. design an efficient spatial pyramid convolution network for semantic segmentation. Some similar networks also use symmetrical encoder-decoder architecture [8, 18, 19, 37], while the other approaches take the contextual clues into account [15, 34] to balance performance and efficiency. Unlike these lightweight networks, our ESNet utilizes multiple branch parallel factorized convolution, achieving real-time inference and higher accuracy.

3   ESNet

In this section, we first introduce the whole architecture of ESNet, and then elaborate on the designed details of each unit.

3.1   Network Overview

As shown in Table 1 and illustrated in Fig. 1, our ESNet has a symmetric encoder-decoder architecture, where an encoder produces downsampled feature maps, and a decoder upsamples the feature maps to match input resolution. The entire network is composed of 18 convolution layers, where the residual module is adopted as our core element. As shown in Table 1, the encoder and decoder has nearly same number of convolution layers, and utilize similar convolution type.

Table 1. The architecture of ESNet. "Size" denotes the dimension of output feature maps, C is the number of classes.

Stage	Name	Layer	Type	Size
Encoder	Block 1	1	**Down-sampling Unit**	$512 \times 256 \times 16$
		2–4	$3\times$ **FCU** ($K = 3$)	$512 \times 256 \times 16$
	Block 2	5	**Down-sampling Unit**	$256 \times 128 \times 64$
		6–7	$2\times$ **FCU** ($K = 5$)	$256 \times 128 \times 64$
	Block 3	8	**Down-sampling Unit**	$128 \times 64 \times 128$
		9–11	$3\times$ **PFCU** (dilated $r_1 = 2, r_2 = 5, r_3 = 9$)	$128 \times 64 \times 128$
Decoder	Block 4	12	**Up-sampling Unit**	$256 \times 128 \times 64$
		13–14	$2\times$ **FCU** ($K = 5$)	$256 \times 128 \times 64$
	Block 5	15	**Up-sampling Unit**	$512 \times 256 \times 16$
		15–17	$2\times$ **FCU** ($K = 3$)	$512 \times 256 \times 16$
	Full Conv	18	**Up-sampling Unit**	$1024 \times 512 \times C$

For instance, both Block 1 and Block 5 employ FCU with $K = 3$, while Block 2 and Block 4 also employ FCU with $K = 5$. As illustrated in Fig. 1, the input image first undergoes a down-sampling unit to form initial feature maps, which are fed into the subsequent residual layers. Downsampling enables more deeper network to gather context, while at the same time helps to reduce computation. Additionally, two types of residual convolution module, called FCU and PFCU are employed, where the first one uses factorized convolution to extract low-level features, and the second one utilizes multi-branch dilated convolution to enlarge receptive fields to capture high-level semantics. In [17,19,37], the designed networks are began with sustained downsampling, however, such kind of operation may be harmful to feature abstraction, which highly detriment segmentation accuracy. In order to address this problem, our ESNet postpones downsampling operation in encoder, with the similar spirit of [36]. In the following, we will describe how to design FCU and PFCU, which focus on solving the efficiency limitation that is essentially present in the residual layer.

3.2   FCU Module

To reduce computation budget, the pointwise convolutions [17,31,33] and factorized convolutions [19,37] are widely used to take place of traditional standard convolution in residual layer. Essentially, pointwise convolution (e.g., 1×1) speeds up computation by reducing the number of convolutional channels, which thus can be also considered as dimensionality reduction of feature maps. On the other hand, factorized convolution attempts to perform convolution with smaller filter kernel size. As a result, the recent years have witnessed multiple successful instances of lightweight residual layer [17,29], such as Non-bottleneck (Fig. 2(a)), Bottleneck (Fig. 2(b)), and Non-bottleneck-1D (Fig. 2(c)). More specifically, the Bottleneck module comes from the standard residual layer of ResNet [2], which requires less computational resources with respect to Non-bottleneck module.

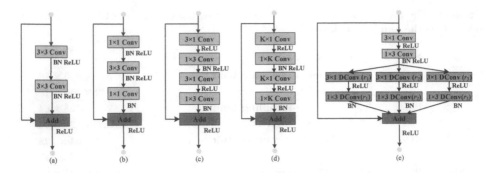

Fig. 2. Comparison of different residual layer modules. From left to right are (a) Non-bottleneck [2], (b) Bottleneck [17], (c) Non-bottleneck-1D [19], (d) FCU and (e) PFCU module. "DConv" denotes the dilated convolution, where r_1, r_2, and r_3 are dilated rates for each split branch, respectively.

Although it is commonly adopted in state-of-the-art networks [17,18,29], the performance descend drastically when network goes deeper. Another outstanding residual module is Non-bottleneck-1D [19], which can be considered as a special case of our FCU with $K = 3$. In this module, a standard 3×3 convolution in the bottleneck is decomposed into two 1D convolutions (e.g., 3×1 and 1×3), yet the fixed kernel size of factorized convolution limits the field-of-view, leading to the decrease of performance.

As shown in Fig. 2(d), we again employ Non-bottleneck-1D module [19,37] to design our FCU, as this is helpful for greatly reducing the number of parameters and accelerating the training and inference process. Unlike previous approaches [19,37], however, the size of convolutional kernel is unfixed, allowing FCU to adaptively broaden receptive fields. For example, in the encoder, the shallow layers (Block 1 in Table 1) prefer to use smaller kernel size ($K = 3$) to abstract low-level image features, while deeper layers (Block 2 in Table 1) resort to larger kernel size ($K = 5$) for capturing wide-scale context. Conversely, in the decoder, the shallow layers (Block 4 in Table 1) utilize a larger kernel size ($K = 5$) to gather long-ranged information to enhance prediction accuracy, while deeper layers (Block 5 in Table 1) symmetrically employ smaller kernel size ($K = 3$) to recover image details by smoothing filter responses of short-ranged neighborhood pixels.

3.3 PFCU Module

We focus on solving the accuracy and efficiency trade-off as a whole, without sitting on only one of its sides. To this end, this section introduces PFCU, as depicted in Fig. 2(e). Motivated from [30,36], a *transform-split-transform-merge* strategy is employed in the designment of our PFCU, where each branch employs dilated convolution with different rate to broaden receptive fields. The dilated convolutions with parallel multiple branch are adaptive to capture objects within

Table 2. Comparison of weights used in different type of residue blocks. Three parameters of "Size" are number of layers, feature channels and convolutional kernels in corresponding residue block, respectively.

Method		Encoder			Decoder			#Para
ERFNet [19]	Type	Non-bt-1D	–	Non-bt-1D	Non-bt-1D	Non-bt-1D		17,688
	Size	$5 \times 64 \times 12$	–	$8 \times 128 \times 12$	$2 \times 64 \times 12$	$2 \times 16 \times 12$		
ESNet	Type	FCU(K = 3)	FCU(K = 5)	PFCU	FCU(K = 5)	FCU(K = 3)		15,296
	Size	$3 \times 16 \times 12$	$2 \times 64 \times 20$	$3 \times 128 \times 24$	$2 \times 64 \times 20$	$2 \times 16 \times 12$		

different scales, approaching the representational power of large and dense layers, but at a considerably lower computational complexity. At the beginning of each PFCU, the input is first transferred by a set of specialized 1D filters (e.g., 1×3 and 3×1), and the convolutional outputs pass through three parallel dilated convolution with rates $r_1 = 2$, $r_2 = 5$, and $r_3 = 9$, respectively. To facilitate training, finally, the outputs of three convolutional branches are added with input through the branch of identity mapping. After merging, the next PFCU begins. It is clear that our PFCU is not only efficient, but also accurate. Firstly, the powerful representation ability of PFCU allows us to use less convolution layers. Secondly, in PFCU, each branch shares the same convolutional feature maps. This can be regarded as a kind of feature reuse, which to some extent enlarges network capacity without significantly increasing complexity.

3.4 Comparison of Network Complexity

In this section, we analyze the network complexity of our ESNet and compare with recent state-of-the-art ERFNet [19]. In addition, we also compare our new implementation of the residual layer that makes use of the parallel 1D factorization to accelerate and reduce the parameters. Table 2 summarizes the total dimensions of the weights on the convolutions of every residual block. As shown in Fig. 2, Non-Bottleneck-1D has the simplest structure and fewest parameters. Since the standard 3×3 convolution has been decomposed into 1×3 and 3×1 convolution, the number of convolutional kernels is only 12 in each residual layer. As our FCU (K = 3) module also adopts 1D factorized convolution, it has the same number of kernels with respect to Non-Bottleneck-1D. On the other hand, FCU (K = 5) and PFCU involve larger kernel size or more factorized convolution, leading to the increase of convolutional kernels (20 for FCU (K = 5), and 24 for PFCU) used in corresponding residual layers. However, the total weights are not only decided by filter kernel size, but also depend on the number of feature channels and convolution layers. Due to the parallel design of PFCU that facilitates the reduction of convolution layers, the entire size of ESNet is still smaller than ERFNet [19]. For example, in contrast to ERFNet [19] that contains 8 layers of dilated convolution ($8 \times 128 \times 12 = 12,288$), our ESNet only has 3 layers of PFCU, resulting in more fewer parameters ($3 \times 128 \times 24 = 9,216$) while achieving higher accuracy. As for the total parameters, our ESNet design

Table 3. Comparison with the state-of-the-art approaches in terms of segmentation accuracy and implementing efficiency.

Method	Cla(%)	Cat(%)	Time(ms)	Speed(Fps)	Para(M)
SegNet [8]	57.0	79.1	67	15	29.5
ENet [17]	58.3	80.4	13	**77**	**0.36**
ESPNet [18]	60.3	82.2	18	54	1.5
CGNet [15]	64.8	85.7	20	50	0.50
ERFNet [19]	66.3	86.5	21	48	2.10
ICNet [35]	69.5	86.4	33	30	7.80
Ours	**70.7**	**87.4**	16	63	1.66

is clearly more benefited, by receiving a direct 13.5% reduction, and thus greatly accelerates its execution. This is also consistent with the results of Table 3.

4   Experiments

In this section, we carry on the experiments to demonstrate the potential of our segmentation architecture in terms of accuracy and efficiency trade-off.

4.1   Dataset

The widely-used CityScapes dataset [20], including 19 object classes and one additional background, is selected to evaluate our ESNet. Beside the images with fine pixel-level annotations that contain 2,975 training, 500 validation and 1,525 testing images, we also use the 20K coarsely annotated images for training.

4.2   Implementation Details

To show the advantages of ESNet, we selected 6 state-of-the-art lightweight networks as baselines, including SegNet [8], ENet [17], ERFNet [19], ICNet [35], CGNet [15], and ESPNet [18]. We adopt mean intersection-over-union (mIOU) averaged across all classes and categories to evaluate segmentation accuracy, while running time, inference speed (FPS), and model size (number of parameters) to measure implementing efficiency. For fair comparison, all the methods are conducted on the same hardware platform of DELL workstation with a single GTX 1080Ti GPU. We favor a large minibatch size (set as 4) to make full use of the GPU memory, where the initial learning rate is 5×10^{-4} and the 'poly' learning rate policy is adopted with power 0.9, together with momentum and weight decay are set to 0.9 and 10^{-4}, respectively.

4.3   Evaluation Results

In Tables 3 and 4, we have reported the quantitative results compared with state-of-the-art baselines. The results demonstrate that ESNet achieves the best available trade-off in terms of accuracy and efficiency. Without data augmentation, our ESNet obtains comparable results with respect to ICNet [35] (only slight 0.4% drop of class mIOU, but 0.4% improvement of category mIOU). After augmented with 20K additional data with coarse annotations, our ESNet yields 70.7% class mIOU and 87.4% category mIOU, respectively, where 16 out of the 19 categories obtains best scores. Regarding to the efficiency, ESNet is nearly 4× faster and 18× smaller than SegNet [8]. Although ENet [17], an anther efficient network, is nearly 1.2× efficient, and has 5× less parameters than our ESNet, but delivers poor segmentation accuracy of 12.4% and 7% drops in terms of class and category mIOU, respectively. Another interesting results is the comparison with CGNet [15] in Table 3, where it has 3× fewer parameters, while performs slightly slower than our ESNet. This is probably because that ESNet has more simpler architecture and less convolution layers, yielding more efficient in inference process. Figure 3 shows some visual examples of segmentation outputs on the CityScapes validation set. It is demonstrated that, compared with baselines,

Table 4. Individual category results on the CityScapes test set in terms of class and category mIOU scores. Methods trained using both fine and coarse data are marked with superscript '†'. The best performance for each individual class is marked with bold-face number.

Method	Roa	Sid	Bui	Wal	Fen	Pol	TLi	TSi	Veg	Ter	Cla
SegNet [8]	96.4	73.2	84.0	28.4	29.0	35.7	39.8	45.1	87.0	63.8	57.0
ENet [17]	96.3	74.2	75.0	32.2	33.2	43.4	34.1	44.0	88.6	61.4	58.3
ESPNet [18]	97.0	77.5	76.2	35.0	36.1	45.0	35.6	46.3	90.8	63.2	60.3
CGNet [15]	95.5	78.7	88.1	40.0	43.0	54.1	59.8	63.9	89.6	67.6	64.8
ERFNet [19]	97.2	80.0	89.5	41.6	45.3	56.4	60.5	64.6	91.4	**68.7**	66.3
ICNet [35]	97.1	79.2	89.7	43.2	48.9	**61.5**	60.4	63.4	91.5	68.3	69.5
Ours	97.1	78.5	90.4	46.5	48.1	60.1	60.4	70.9	91.1	59.9	69.1
Ours†	**98.1**	**80.4**	**92.4**	**48.3**	**49.2**	61.5	**62.5**	**72.3**	**92.5**	61.5	**70.7**

Method	Sky	Ped	Rid	Car	Tru	Bus	Tra	Mot	Bic		Cat
SegNet [8]	91.8	62.8	42.8	89.3	38.1	43.1	44.1	35.8	51.9		79.1
ENet [17]	90.6	65.5	38.4	90.6	36.9	50.5	48.1	38.8	55.4		80.4
ESPNet [18]	92.6	67.0	40.9	92.3	38.1	52.5	50.1	41.8	57.2		82.2
CGNet [15]	92.9	74.9	54.9	90.2	44.1	59.5	25.2	47.3	60.2		85.7
ERFNet [19]	94.2	76.1	**56.4**	92.4	45.7	60.6	27.0	48.7	61.8		86.5
ICNet [35]	93.5	74.6	56.1	92.6	51.3	72.7	51.3	**53.6**	70.5		86.4
Ours	93.2	74.3	51.8	92.3	61.0	72.3	51.0	43.3	70.2		86.8
Ours†	**94.4**	**76.6**	53.2	**94.4**	**62.5**	**74.3**	**52.4**	45.5	**71.4**		**87.4**

our ESNet not only correctly classifies object with different scales (especially for very small object instance, such as "traffic sign" and "traffic light"), but also produces consistent qualitative results for all classes.

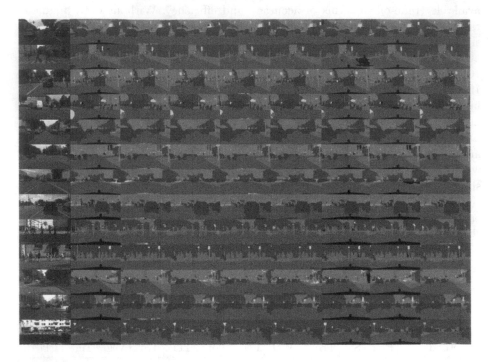

Fig. 3. The visual comparison on CityScapes val dataset. From left to right are input images, ground truth, segmentation outputs from our ESNet, SegNet [8], ENet [17], ERFNet [19], ESPNet [18], ICNet [35], and CGNet [15]. (Best viewed in color)

5 Conclusion Remark and Future Work

This paper has proposed an architecture that achieves accurate and fast pixel-wise semantic segmentation. In contrast to top-accurate networks that are computationally expensive with complex and deep architectures, our ESNet focuses more on developing the core elements of network architecture: the convolutional blocks. The transform-split-transform-merge scheme is adopted to redesign the commonly-used residual layers, leading to the multi-branch parallel 1D decomposed convolution, which is more efficient while retaining a similar learning performance. As this design can be directly used in existing encoder-decoder networks, we propose an ESNet that completely leverages its benefits to reach state-of-the-art segmentation accuracy and efficiency. The experimental results show that our ESNet achieves best available trade-off on CityScapes dataset in terms of segmentation accuracy and implementing efficiency. The future work includes incorporating contextual branch, as well as [15,34] does, to further improve performance while remaining few parameters.

Acknowledgments. The authors would like to thank all the anonymous reviewers for their valuable comments and suggestions. This work was partly supported by the National Natural Science Foundation of China (Grant No. 61876093, 61701258, 61701252, 61671253), Natural Science Foundation of Jiangsu Province (Grant No. BK20181393, BK20170906), Natural Science Foundation of Guizhou Province (Grant No. [2017] 1130), and Huawei Innovation Research Program (HIRP2018).

References

1. Krizhevsky, A., Sutskever, I., Hinton, G.E.: ImageNet classification with deep convolutional neural networks. In: NIPS, pp. 1097–1105 (2012)
2. He, K., Zhang, X., Ren, S., Sun, J.: Deep residual learning for image recognition. In: CVPR, pp. 770–778 (2016)
3. Girshick, R., Donahue, J., Darrell, T., Malik, J.: Rich feature hierarchies for accurate object detection and semantic segmentation. In: CVPR, pp. 580–587 (2014)
4. Long, J., Shelhamer, E., Darrell, T.: Fully convolutional networks for semantic segmentation. IEEE TPAMI **39**, 640–651 (2017)
5. Chen, L.C., Papandreou, G., Kokkinos, I., Murphy, K., Yuille, A.L.: Deeplab: semantic image segmentation with deep convolutional nets, atrous convolution, and fully connected CRFs. IEEE TPAMI **40**, 834–848 (2018)
6. Zhao, H., Shi, J., Qi, X., Wang, X., Jia, J.Y.: Pyramid scene parsing network. In: CVPR, pp. 6230–6239 (2016)
7. Xiaoxiao, L., Zhiwei, L., Ping, L., Chenchange, L., Xiaoou, T.: Not all pixels are equal: difficulty-aware semantic segmentation via deep layer cascade. In: CVPR, pp. 6459–6468 (2017)
8. Badrinarayanan, V., Alex, K., Roberto, C.: SegNet: a deep convolutional encoder-decoder architecture for image segmentation. arXiv preprint arXiv:1511.00561 (2015)
9. Guosheng, L., Anton, M., Chunhua, S., Reid, I.: RefineNet: multi-path refinement networks for high-resolution semantic segmentation. In: CVPR, pp. 5168–5177 (2017)
10. Noh, H., Hong, S., Han, B.: Learning deconvolution network for semantic segmentation. In: ICCV, pp. 1520–1528 (2015)
11. Szegedy, C., et al.: Going deeper with convolutions. In: CVPR, pp. 1–9 (2015)
12. Peng, C., Xiangyu, Z., Gang, Y., Guiming, L., Jian, S.: Large kernel matters: improve semantic segmentation by global convolutional network. In: CVPR, pp. 1743–1751 (2017)
13. Lin, G.S., Shen, C.H., Van, D.H., Reid, I.: Exploring context with deep structured models for semantic segmentation. IEEE TPAMI **40**, 1352–1366 (2018)
14. Cong, D., et al.: Can: contextual aggregating network for semantic segmentation. In: ICASSP (2019, accepted)
15. Wu, T.Y., Tang, S., Zhang, R., Zhang, Y.D.: CGNet: a light-weight context guided network for semantic segmentation. arXiv preprint arXiv:1811.08201v1 (2018)
16. Treml, M., et al.: Speeding up semantic segmentation for autonomous driving. In: NIPS Workshop, pp. 1–7 (2016)

17. Paszke, A., Chaurasia, A., Kim, S., Culurciello, E.: ENet: a deep neural network architecture for real-time semantic segmentation. arXiv preprint arXiv:1606.02147 (2016)
18. Mehta, S., Rastegari, M., Caspi, A., Shapiro, L., Hajishirzi, H.: ESPNet: efficient spatial pyramid of dilated convolutions for semantic segmentation. arXiv preprint arXiv:1803.06815v3 (2018)
19. Romera, E., Alvarez, J.M., Bergasa, L.M., Arroyo, R.: ERFNet: efficient residual factorized convnet for real-time semantic segmentation. IEEE TITS **19**, 263–272 (2018)
20. Cordts, M., et al.: The cityscapes dataset for semantic urban scene understanding. In: CVPR, pp. 3213–3223 (2016)
21. Farabet, C., Couprie, C., Najman, L., LeCun, Y.: Learning hierarchical features for scene labeling. IEEE TPAMI **35**, 1915–1929 (2013)
22. Panqu, W., et al.: Understanding convolution for semantic segmentation. In: WACV, pp. 1451–1460 (2018)
23. Chen, L.C., Papandreou, G., Schroff, F., Adam, H.: Rethinking atrous convolution for semantic image segmentation. arXiv:1706.05587 (2017)
24. Yu, F., Koltun, V.: Multi-scale context aggregation by dilated convolutions. arXiv preprint arXiv:1511.07122 (2015)
25. Ronneberger, O., Fischer, P., Brox, T.: U-Net: convolutional networks for biomedical image segmentation. In: Navab, N., Hornegger, J., Wells, W.M., Frangi, A.F. (eds.) MICCAI 2015. LNCS, vol. 9351, pp. 234–241. Springer, Cham (2015). https://doi.org/10.1007/978-3-319-24574-4_28
26. Pohlen, T., Hermans, A., Mathias, M., Leibe, B.: Full-resolution residual networks for semantic segmentation in street scenes. In: CVPR, pp. 3309–3318 (2017)
27. Islam, M.A., Rochan, M., Bruce, N.D.B., Wang, Y.: Gated feedback refinement network for dense image labeling. In: CVPR, pp. 4877–4885 (2017)
28. Everingham, M., Eslami, S.A., Van Gool, L., Williams, C.K., Winn, J., Zisserman, A.: The pascal visual object classes challenge: a retrospective. IJCV **111**, 98–136 (2015)
29. Howard, A.G., et al.: MobileNets: efficient convolutional neural networks for mobile vision applications. arXiv preprint arXiv:1704.04861 (2017)
30. Rastegari, M., Ordonez, V., Redmon, J., Farhadi, A.: XNOR-Net: imagenet classification using binary convolutional neural networks. In: Leibe, B., Matas, J., Sebe, N., Welling, M. (eds.) ECCV 2016. LNCS, vol. 9908, pp. 525–542. Springer, Cham (2016). https://doi.org/10.1007/978-3-319-46493-0_32
31. Zhang, X., Zhou, X., Lin, M., Sun, J.: ShuffleNet: an extremely efficient convolutional neural network for mobile devices. In: CVPR, pp. 6848–6856 (2018)
32. Wu, J., Leng, C., Wang, Y., Hu, Q., Cheng, J.: Quantized convolutional neural networks for mobile devices. In: CVPR, pp. 5168–5177 (2016)
33. Xie, X., Girshick, R., Dollar, P., Tu, Z.W., He, K.M.: Aggregated residual transformations for deep neural networks. In: CVPR, pp. 5987–5995 (2017)
34. Changqian, Y., Jingbo, W., Chao, P., Changxin, G., Gang, Y., Nong, S.: BiSeNet: bilateral segmentation network for real-time semantic segmentation. arXiv preprint arXiv:1808.00897 (2018)
35. Zhao, H.S., Qi, X.J., Shen, X.Y., Shi, J.P., Jia, J.Y.: ICNet for real-time semantic segmentation on high-resolution images. arXiv preprint arXiv:1704.08545v2 (2018)
36. Szegedy, C., Vanhoucke, V., Ioffe, S., Shlens, J., Wojna, Z.: Rethinking the inception architecture for computer vision. In: CVPR, pp. 2818–2826 (2016)
37. Zhang, X., Cheny, Z., Wu, Q.M.J., Cai, L., Lu, D., Li, X.: Fast semantic segmentation for scene perception. IEEE TII (2019, accepted)

Assignment Problem Based Deep Embedding

Ruishen Zheng, Jin Xie, Jianjun Qian, and Jian Yang[✉]

PCA Lab, Key Lab of Intelligent Perception and Systems for High-Dimensional Information of Ministry of Education, and Jiangsu Key Lab of Image and Video Understanding for Social Security, School of Computer Science and Engineering, Nanjing University of Science and Technology, Nanjing 210094, China
{zrs,csjxie,csjqian,csjyang}@njust.edu.cn

Abstract. How to measure the similarity of samples is a fundamental problem in many computer vision tasks such as retrieval and clustering. Due to the rapid development of deep neural networks, deep metric learning has been widely studied. Some studies focus on the hard sample mining strategy for triplet loss. We observe that hard mining strategies are also vital for contrastive loss. But the hardest mining strategy for contrastive loss is sensitive to outliers. In this paper, based on combinatorial information of sample pairs, we propose a novel linear assignment problem based hard sample mining strategy for contrastive loss to learn feature embeddings. Specifically, our method can assign 0/1 weight to sample pairs for the hard sample selection by maximizing a linear assignment loss and ensure that each sample is only included by one pair for the optimization. Our method can obtain the state-of-the-art performance on the CUB-200-2011, Cars196, and In-shop datasets with the GoogLeNet network.

Keywords: Metric learning · Combinatorial optimization · Contrastive loss

1 Introduction

With the rapid development of deep learning in recent years, deep metric learning has played an increasingly important role in the field of computer vision and has been widely used in many tasks such as image retrieval [17], clustering [16], and recognition [2,18]. In these tasks, one key problem is how to employ the neural network to learn a nonlinear transformation, so that the complex high-dimensional input data can be mapped to a low-dimensional embedding space where the intra-class distance between embedding features can be reduced and the inter-class distance can be enlarged. Once the transformation is learned, many tasks such as retrieval and classification can be performed by a simple K-nearest neighbor algorithm in the embedding space.

This is a student paper.

© Springer Nature Switzerland AG 2019
Z. Lin et al. (Eds.): PRCV 2019, LNCS 11858, pp. 53–65, 2019.
https://doi.org/10.1007/978-3-030-31723-2_5

In general, the goal of metric learning is to learn a semantic feature embedding where there is sufficient discrimination between the intra-class sample pairs and inter-class sample pairs, which are called positive/negative pairs.

Benefited from the powerful nonlinear representation of deep neural networks, the major task of deep metric learning is to design a loss function to learn a better semantic feature embedding. In deep metric learning, commonly used loss functions include contrastive loss [1,3] and triplet loss [15,22]. The contrastive loss constrains the absolute distance of positive/negative pairs while the triplet loss constrains the relative distance of positive/negative pairs – just impels the distance of the positive pair being closer than the negative pair. Moreover, based on the global structure of the embedding space, Song et al. [16] proposed a structured facility location loss to learn a deep embedding function. By estimating two distributions of similarities of positive and negative pairs, Ustinova et al. [20] proposed a histogram loss to learn deep embeddings, where the probability of the similarity of negative pair is smaller than that of the positive pair.

For triplet loss, the space complexity of constructing triplets is $O(n^3)$, n is the number of samples in a batch, which will cause the explosion of the number of triplets. In order to figure out this problem, several hard sample mining strategies have been proposed to mine a part of hard triplets from all triplets, such as the hardest negative sample mining strategy [4], the semi-hard negative sample mining strategy [14] and the lifted negative sample mining with smooth bound [17].

For original contrastive loss, the pairs used for optimization are randomly sampled, which usually leads to inefficiency. In fact, to make full use of information in a batch, the contrastive loss often sums loss values of all pairs which means all possible positive/negative pairs in a batch will be used to optimize the model in an iteration.

However, the imbalanced positive/negative pairs in a batch usually lead to biased embeddings. Moreover, one sample is shared by multiple pairs to pulled closer or pushed away to different directions, which will make the optimization difficult.

We have observed that the hardest sample mining strategy for contrastive loss are effective. But it is sensitive to outliers and cannot mathematically guarantee that each sample has an independent optimization direction. Therefore, it is desirable to propose a hard mining strategy that reduces the number of repeatedly calculated samples, meanwhile ensures the constraint ability of loss function.

Inspired by global structure information considered metric learning method [16], in this paper, based on the combinatorial information of the sample pairs, we propose a novel linear assignment problem based hard sample mining strategy for contrastive loss, where 0/1 weights are assigned to positive and negative pairs as a selection mask matrix to select proper hard pairs. The mask matrix is generated by maximizing the linear assignment loss of positive and negative pairs and ensure that for each sample, one pair is only used for optimization. The deep feature embeddings are then learned by minimizing the selected contrastive loss.

We evaluate our proposed method for the retrieval and clustering tasks on the CUB-200-2011 [21], CARS196 [8] and In-Shop [11] Clothes Retrieval datasets. The experiment results demonstrate that our linear assignment problem based hard mining strategy is effective.

2   Related Work

Contrastive Loss [1] is presented to learn the similarity metric for pairwise data $\{x_i, x_j\}$. For each pair, if they are from the same class, the pair is called the positive pair; otherwise, it is called the negative pair. The main goal of the contrastive loss is to minimize the distance between the samples in positive pairs and maximize the distance between samples in negative pairs with a fixed margin α. In general, the loss function is defined as:

$$Loss = \frac{1}{N} \sum_{i,j} y_{ij} d_{ij}^2 + (1 - y_{ij}) \max(\alpha - d_{ij}^2, 0) \tag{1}$$

where the N is the number of pairs, $d_{ij} = \|f(x_i) - f(x_j)\|_2$, $f(\cdot)$ is the embedding function from the neural network, and y_{ij} indicates whether the pair is positive or not. For positive pairs, $y_{ij} = 1$; otherwise, $y_{ij} = 0$.

Triplet Loss [15,22] is different from contrastive loss. It constructs the triplet $\{x_{anchor}, x_{positive}, x_{negative}\}$ instead of constraining the absolute distance between pairs. The $\{x_{anchor}, x_{positive}\}$ have the same label and the $\{x_{anchor}, x_{negative}\}$ have different labels. The triplet loss encourages the network to learn an embedding where the distance between the positive pairs is smaller than the negative pairs with a fixed margin α. Precisely, the loss can be defined as:

$$Loss = \frac{1}{N} \sum \max\left(d_{ap}^2 + \alpha - d_{an}^2, 0\right) \tag{2}$$

where the N is the number of triplets used in a batch, $d_{ap} = \|f(x_{anchor}) - f(x_{positive})\|_2$ and $d_{an} = \|f(x_{anchor}) - f(x_{negative})\|_2$, $f(\cdot)$ is the embedding function.

In practice, the triplet sampling strategy highly influences the performance. A common strategy is the hardest negative mining. It selects the nearest negative sample with an anchor. However, the too hard sample will result in the bad local optima. In FaceNet [14] a new online hard negative mining strategy called semi-hard negative mining is proposed. This strategy selects the negative sample whose distance is farther than positive but still hard.

Lifted Structured Feature Embedding [17] is proposed to mine the hard negative sample from two directions of positive pairs and make full use of information in a batch. It uses the log-sum-exp operation to replace the $max(\cdot)$ operation to optimize a smooth upper bound, preventing the model converges to a bad local optimum. The loss function is defined as:

$$Loss = \frac{1}{2N} \sum_{i,j} \left[\log \left(\sum_{i,k} \exp\{\alpha - d_{ik}\} \right. \right.$$
$$\left. \left. + \sum_{j,l} \exp\{\alpha - d_{jl}\} \right) + d_{ij} \right]_+^2 \tag{3}$$

where the N is the number of positive pairs in a batch and the $[\cdot]_+$ is the hinge function $\max(0, \cdot)$.

Histogram Loss [20] is proposed by Evgeniya to solve the problem that the performance of many deep metric learning methods highly depends on the hyper-parameters such as the fixed margin α. It estimates two discrete distributions of similarities for positive and negative sample pairs by kernel density estimation and then computes the probability that the similarity of negative pairs is larger than that of the positive pairs as a loss. The histogram loss has no parameters that need to be manually tuned.

Precisely, denoting Φ_r^+ is the cumulative density function of discrete distribution of similarities for positive pair $p^+(x)$, h_r^- is the value of the r_{th} bin of discrete distribution (histogram) of similarities for negative pair $p^-(x)$,

$$Loss_{histogram} = \sum_{r=1}^{R} h_r^- \Phi_r^+ \tag{4}$$

3   Linear Assignment Problem Based Hard Mining

In this section, we present our linear assignment based hard sample mining method for the construction of the contrastive loss.

Given a batch of m-dimensional embedding features $\boldsymbol{X} = [\boldsymbol{x}_1; \boldsymbol{x}_2; \cdots ; \boldsymbol{x}_n] \in \mathbb{R}^{n \times m}$ from the output of the network, we can construct a pairwise distance matrix $\boldsymbol{D}$:

$$\boldsymbol{D} = (\boldsymbol{X} \circ \boldsymbol{X}) \, \mathbf{1}_n \, \mathbf{1}_n^\mathsf{T} - 2\boldsymbol{X}\boldsymbol{X}^\mathsf{T} + ((\boldsymbol{X} \circ \boldsymbol{X}) \, \mathbf{1}_n \, \mathbf{1}_n^\mathsf{T})^\mathsf{T} \tag{5}$$

where $D_{ij} = \|f(x_i) - f(x_j)\|_2^2$, the $\circ$ operation is the Hadamard product, $f(\cdot)$ is the embedding function from the output of the network. For the pairwise distance matrix $\boldsymbol{D}$, we can define the following loss matrix $\boldsymbol{L}$ of positive pairs and negative pairs based on the contrastive loss form:

$$\boldsymbol{L} = \{L_{i,j} = y_{ij}D_{ij} + (1 - y_{ij})\max(\alpha - D_{ij}, 0)\} \tag{6}$$

where y_{ij} is the label indicating the pair is positive or not and α is the margin. For positive pairs, $y_{ij} = 1$, otherwise $y_{ij} = 0$.

For loss matrix L, an intuitive approach is to sum loss values of all pairs as the total loss:

$$Loss_{contrastive} = \frac{1}{N} \sum \dot{L}_{i,j} \qquad (7)$$

Though this approach makes full use of information in a batch, it often makes optimization difficult due to one sample shared by multiple pairs being pulled closer or pushed away to different directions. If the batch size is n, each sample is comprised in $n-1$ positive/negative pairs that need to be optimized to different directions. Figure 1 shows two basic failure cases in the two-dimensional embedding space.

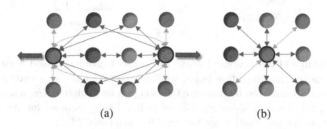

(a)   (b)

Fig. 1. Two basic failure cases of the contrastive loss in the two-dimensional embedding space. Different color represent samples with different classes. The yellow arrow means positive pairs which need to be pulled closer and the purple arrow means negative pairs which need to be pushed away. Figure (a) shows that two black-edged red samples need to be close but cannot be correctly optimized due to the heterogeneous samples in the middle. Figure (b) shows that the black-edged red sample cannot be optimized due to the conflict of optimization directions caused by surrounding samples. (Color figure online)

Therefore, how to reduce the number of repeatedly calculated samples and ensure the constraint ability of the loss is important. To achieve this goal, we take into account global combinational information of sample pairs to propose a hard sample mining method.

Based on the defined loss matrix L, we formulate the following selected loss function according to the linear assignment problem:

$$J = \max_{\gamma} \langle \gamma, L \rangle$$

$$s.t. \quad \gamma_{i,j} \in \{0,1\}, \quad \sum_i \gamma_{i,\cdot} = 1_n, \quad \sum_j \gamma_{\cdot,j} = 1_n^\mathsf{T} \qquad (8)$$

where the $\gamma_{i,j}$ is the element of the selection matrix γ.

In the proposed method, we generate the selection matrix γ by maximizing the linear assignment loss J. The sample pairs with a large loss value are usually viewed as hard pairs. By maximizing the linear assignment loss, we can mine the hard pairs in all possible pairs, which play an important role in training with the stochastic gradient descent method.

We can use the Hungarian algorithm [10] in the combinational optimization theory to solve the selection matrix γ. The time complexity of the Hungarian algorithm is $O(n^3)$. Since the batch size n is small in the actual training, the time-overhead of the Hungarian algorithm is acceptable.

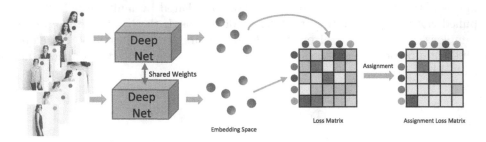

Fig. 2. The pipeline of the proposed linear assignment problem based deep embedding method. For positive and negative pairs, we first construct the loss matrix. The Hungarian algorithm is employed to generate 0/1 weights for constructing a selection mask by maximizing the linear assignment loss of pairs. Then, we use the mask matrix to select the contrastive loss matrix for learning feature embeddings.

Once the selection matrix γ is generated, we can minimize a selected contrastive loss J to train the network for feature embeddings by stochastic gradient descent method.

Since the matrix D constructed by Eq. 5 is a symmetric matrix (i.e., $D_{ij} = D_{ji}$), half of the pairs in the matrix is redundant. In the actual implementation, to further increase the amount of information in the loss matrix, we sample two batches X_1, X_2 to construct an asymmetric matrix D:

$$D = (X_1 \circ X_1)\, 1_n\, 1_n^{\mathsf{T}} - 2X_1 X_2^{\mathsf{T}} + ((X_2 \circ X_2)\, 1_n\, 1_n^{\mathsf{T}})^{\mathsf{T}} \tag{9}$$

Figure 2 illustrates the pipeline of our proposed method. In the proposed method, the hard positive/negative pairs can be selected and easy pairs can be ignored. Please note that our loss matrix is constructed from the contrastive loss matrix, where one element in each row and column is only selected. It ensures that each sample is only contained by one pair to be optimized in an iteration.

4   Experiment

4.1   Dataset

To verify the effectiveness of our proposed method, we conduct experiments on the CUB-200-2011, Cars196 and In-shop Clothes Retrieval datasets and compare the results with the state-of-the-art deep metric learning methods.

CUB-200-2011 is a dataset of birds [21], which includes 11,788 images of 200 classes of birds. As in [16,17], we use the first 100 classes for training and the remaining 100 classes (8,131 images) for testing.

Cars196 dataset [8] consists of 16,185 images of 196 classes of cars. The first 98 classes (8,054 images) are used for training and the remaining 98 classes (8,131 images) for testing.

In-shop Clothes Retrieval dataset [11] is a subset of DeepFashion [11] and contains 52,712 images of 7,982 classes clothing items. The In-shop Clothes Retrieval dataset is a typical application scenario for commodity retrieval. We follow the settings in [11] to use the 25,882 images of 3,997 classes for training and 28,760 images of 3,985 classes for testing. The test set is divided into the query set and gallery set, where the query set consists of 14,218 images of 3,985 classes and the gallery set includes 12,612 images of 3,985 classes.

The CUB-200-2011 and Cars196 datasets include different subclasses of birds and cars, respectively. Since the images in the datasets are semantically similar, both of them are quite challenging for learning embedded features, where there are only fine-grained differences.

In order to CUB-200-2011 and Cars196, during testing, each image is used in turn as the query while the remaining images are used as the gallery set. For the In-shop Clothes Retrieval dataset, all images in the query set are used for retrieval in the gallery set.

4.2 Implementation Details

Our experiments are implemented by Pytorch [13] platform. For the network architecture, we use the GoogLeNet [19] network for embedding. The network is pre-trained on the ImageNet [9] dataset. The ℓ_2-normalization is applied on all embedding vectors in our proposed method.

We use stochastic gradient descent to fine-tune the network on our datasets with an Adam [7] optimizer. All input images in a batch are resized to 256 $\times$ 256 and cropped to 224 $\times$ 224. We use a random crop for training and center crop for testing. For data augmentation, training images are randomly flipped horizontally after being cropped.

When constructing a batch, we firstly sample several classes. And for each sampled class, we randomly sample several images to ensure enough positive pairs in a batch.

For generate the selection matrix γ, we use the Hungarian algorithm [10] to solve Eq. 8. The implementation of the Hungarian algorithm is from Scipy [6], which is an open source scientific toolbox for Python.

For CUB-200-2011, Cars196 and In-shop datasets, the iteration times are set to 5K, 10K and 10 K respectively. For all the experiments, the learning rate is set to 1.0×10^{-5} except ones on the In-shop dataset. For In-shop dataset, the learning rate is set to 1.0×10^{-4} in the first 5 K iterations and is decreased to 1.0×10^{-5} in remaining iterations.

4.3   Results

We compare our method with the following deep metric learning methods: (1) original contrastive loss [1], (2) triplet loss with semi-hard negative mining strategy [14], (3) lifted structured feature embedding [17], (4) histogram loss [20]. In addition, the output of the pool5 layer in the pre-trained GoogLeNet as the learned feature is also compared.

The mean average precision(mAP) [24] and Recall@K [5] are used to evaluate the retrieval quality of our embeddings. For the Recall@K, the query image is used to retrieve the k-nearest images from the testing set, using the Euclidean distance between the embedding features. If any of the k-nearest neighbors are of the same class, the query is assigned to a score of 1; otherwise, the score is 0. Recall@K is average of all query scores. For the mAP, we calculate the average precision which is the area under the Precision-Recall curve for per query. The clustering quality is evaluated by NMI metrics. If the set of clusters is denoted as $\Omega = \{\omega_1, \cdots, \omega_K\}$, and the set of ground truth classes is denoted as $\mathbb{C} = \{c_1, \cdots, c_K\}$, the NMI is defined as $NMI(\Omega, \mathbb{C}) = \frac{I(\Omega; \mathbb{C})}{2(H(\Omega) + H(\mathbb{C}))}$ [12], where $I(\Omega; \mathbb{C})$ is mutual information of clusters and labels, $H(\Omega)$ and $H(\mathbb{C})$ are the entropy of clusters and the entropy of labels, respectively. In practice, we cluster embedding features by the k-means method with different random seeds for 5 times and calculate the average NMI.

Table 1. Retrieval performance with different embedding dimensions for our method on In-shop dataset.

Embedding dim	64	128	256	512
mAP	0.5388	0.5374	0.5366	0.5387

Table 1 shows the mAP metrics of our method with respect to embedding dimensionality on the In-shop dataset. The result shows that within the scope of the experiment, the embedding dimensionality has little impact on performance. In the following evaluation, we fix embedding dimensionality to 128 for all experiments.

Tables 2, 3 and 4 show the experimental results of our method and other deep metric embedding methods on the CUB-200-2011 [21], Cars196 [8], and In-shop Clothes Retrieval [11] datasets. We report Recall@K, mAP metrics and NMI scores for the CUB-200-2011 and Cars196 datasets to evaluate the retrieval performance and clustering quality of the embedding. For the In-Shop dataset, following the setting in [23], for a fair comparison, we only report the Recall@K and mAP metrics to evaluate the retrieval performance of embeddings.

As shown in the tables, our method has achieved the best performance for all metrics across all datasets. In our proposed method, we select hard pairs by maximizing linear assignment loss and make full use of information of all samples to train the network and avoid possible optimization direction conflicts caused

Table 2. Retrieval and clustering performance on CUB-200-2011@5K iterations.

	R@1	R@2	R@4	mAP	NMI
GoogLeNet [19]	38.96	51.60	63.71	13.37	48.40
Contrastive [1]	46.20	58.20	69.01	22.17	54.73
Triplet [14]	47.74	60.08	71.05	21.55	56.39
Lifted struct [17]	47.52	59.57	70.81	21.67	56.91
Histogram [20]	49.14	61.24	72.45	24.06	58.64
Ours	**52.75**	**64.10**	**74.27**	**26.08**	**60.11**

by a sample being used by multiple pairs. Therefore, compared to original contrastive loss, triplet loss and lifted structured feature embedding, our proposed loss can yield better performance in terms of different criteria. For example, in terms of R@1, on the CUB-200-2011 dataset, our proposed method can obtain the accuracy of 52.75% while the original contrastive loss, triplet loss and lifted structured feature embedding can achieve the accuracies of 46.20%, 47.74%, and 47.52%, respectively. Figure 3 shows some queries according to our embedding and corresponding results sorted by distances in the embedding space.

Table 3. Retrieval and clustering performance on Cars196@10K iterations.

	R@1	R@2	R@4	mAP	NMI
GoogLeNet [19]	36.23	48.08	59.50	06.86	35.22
Contrastive [1]	51.56	63.18	73.47	21.10	53.73
Triplet [14]	63.09	73.85	81.85	22.50	56.01
Lifted struct [17]	60.28	71.85	80.37	22.11	55.54
Histogram [20]	60.88	71.81	81.27	22.29	54.92
Ours	**66.30**	**76.80**	**84.92**	**25.25**	**58.67**

In addition, we also evaluate the mAPs of the proposed method, original contrastive loss, triplet loss, lifted structured feature embedding and histogram loss in terms of different iteration steps. Figure 4 shows the variation of the retrieval performance according to iterations for different methods on the In-Shop dataset. From this figure, one can see that our proposed method can significantly perform better than the other deep metric embedding methods in terms of training stability and performance. Especially, we can also find that our method converges significantly faster than the compared method.

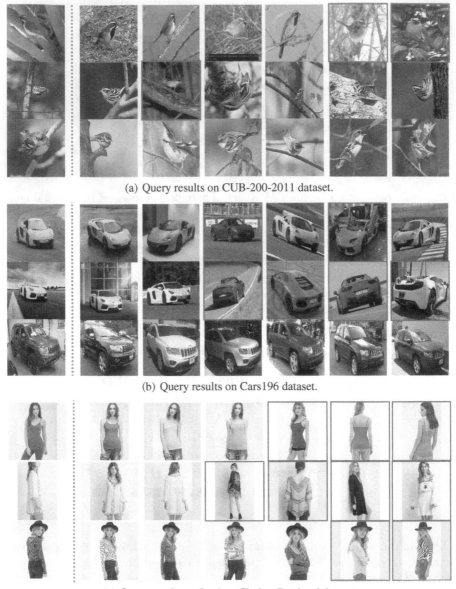

(a) Query results on CUB-200-2011 dataset.

(b) Query results on Cars196 dataset.

(c) Query results on In-shop Clothes Retrieval dataset.

Fig. 3. Some queries examples using on the GoogLeNet model trained by our proposed method. The images in the first column are query samples, and the remaining is retrieval result which is sorted by the distance. The images marked with a red outline are incorrect query results. (Color figure online)

Table 4. Retrieval performance on In-shop Clothes Retrieval@10K iterations.

	R@1	R@10	R@20	R@30	mAP
GoogLeNet [19]	18.27	37.28	44.02	48.16	09.07
Contrastive [1]	54.91	81.97	86.69	89.20	42.96
Triplet [14]	61.43	86.50	90.78	92.67	46.36
Lifted struct [17]	63.81	87.96	91.79	93.45	48.76
Histogram [20]	62.75	86.00	89.89	91.69	48.10
Ours	**67.63**	**89.22**	**92.33**	**93.59**	**53.74**

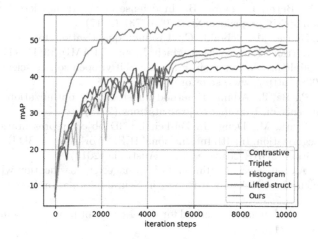

Fig. 4. The mAPs of different methods in the case of different iterations on In-shop dataset.

5   Conclusion

In this paper, we proposed a novel linear assignment problem based hard pairs mining strategy for contrastive loss of deep embedding method. In the proposed method, we first generated a selection mask for all pairs in a contrastive loss matrix by maximizing the linear assignment loss of pairs. Then, we used the mask matrix to select hard pairs from contrastive loss matrix to train the neural network learning feature embedding. Our experimental results on the CUB-200-2011, Cars196, and In-shop Clothes Retrieval datasets demonstrate that our proposed method can yield good performance on the image retrieval and clustering tasks.

In the future, we will expand our method to a three-dimensional linear assignment problem for triplet loss. In addition, we will also consider how to learn binary feature embeddings with the proposed method.

References

1. Chopra, S., Hadsell, R., LeCun, Y.: Learning a similarity metric discriminatively, with application to face verification. In: Proceedings of the IEEE Conference on Computer Vision and Pattern Recognition (2005)
2. Dai, J., Li, Y., He, K., Sun, J.: R-FCN: object detection via region-based fully convolutional networks. In: Advances in Neural Information Processing Systems 29 (2016)
3. Hadsell, R., Chopra, S., Lecun, Y.: Dimensionality reduction by learning an invariant mapping. In: Proceedings of the IEEE Conference on Computer Vision and Pattern Recognition (2006)
4. Hermans, A., Beyer, L., Leibe, B.: In defense of the triplet loss for person re-identification. arXiv preprint arXiv:1703.07737 (2017)
5. Jegou, H., Douze, M., Schmid, C.: Product quantization for nearest neighbor search. IEEE Trans. Pattern Anal. Mach. Intell. (TPAMI) **33**(1), 117–128 (2011)
6. Jones, E., Oliphant, T., Peterson, P., et al.: SciPy: open source scientific tools for Python (2001). http://www.scipy.org/
7. Kingma, D.P., Ba, J.: Adam: a method for stochastic optimization. In: International Conference on Learning Representations (2015)
8. Krause, J., Stark, M., Deng, J., Fei-Fei, L.: 3D object representations for fine-grained categorization. In: 4th International IEEE Workshop on 3D Representation and Recognition (3DRR 2013), Sydney, Australia (2013)
9. Krizhevsky, A., Sutskever, I., Hinton, G.E.: ImageNet classification with deep convolutional neural networks. In: Advances in Neural Information Processing Systems 25 (2012)
10. Kuhn, H.W.: The hungarian method for the assignment problem. Naval Res. Logistics Q. **2**, 83–97 (1955)
11. Liu, Z., Luo, P., Qiu, S., Wang, X., Tang, X.: DeepFashion: powering robust clothes recognition and retrieval with rich annotations. In: Proceedings of the IEEE Conference on Computer Vision and Pattern Recognition (2016)
12. Manning, C.D., Raghavan, P., Schütze, H.: Introduction to Information Retrieval. Cambridge University Press, New York (2008)
13. Paszke, A., et al.: Automatic differentiation in pytorch. In: NIPS-W (2017)
14. Schroff, F., Kalenichenko, D., Philbin, J.: FaceNet: a unified embedding for face recognition and clustering. In: Proceedings of the IEEE Conference on Computer Vision and Pattern Recognition (2015)
15. Schultz, M., Joachims, T.: Learning a distance metric from relative comparisons. In: Advances in Neural Information Processing Systems 16 (2004)
16. Song, H.O., Jegelka, S., Rathod, V., Murphy, K.: Deep metric learning via facility location. In: Proceedings of the IEEE Conference on Computer Vision and Pattern Recognition (2017)
17. Song, H.O., Xiang, Y., Jegelka, S., Savarese, S.: Deep metric learning via lifted structured feature embedding. In: Proceedings of the IEEE Conference on Computer Vision and Pattern Recognition (2016)
18. Sun, Y., Chen, Y., Wang, X., Tang, X.: Deep learning face representation by joint identification-verification. In: Advances in Neural Information Processing Systems 27 (2014)
19. Szegedy, C., et al.: Going deeper with convolutions. In: Proceedings of the IEEE Conference on Computer Vision and Pattern Recognition (2015)

20. Ustinova, E., Lempitsky, V.: Learning deep embeddings with histogram loss. In: Advances in Neural Information Processing Systems 29 (2016)
21. Wah, C., Branson, S., Welinder, P., Perona, P., Belongie, S.: The caltech-UCSD birds-200-2011 dataset. Technical report, CNS-TR-2011-001, California Institute of Technology (2011)
22. Weinberger, K.Q., Blitzer, J., Saul, L.K.: Distance metric learning for large margin nearest neighbor classification. In: Advances in Neural Information Processing Systems 18 (2006)
23. Yuan, Y., Yang, K., Zhang, C.: Hard-aware deeply cascaded embedding. In: 2017 IEEE International Conference on Computer Vision. IEEE (2017)
24. Zheng, L., Shen, L., Tian, L., Wang, S., Wang, J., Tian, Q.: Scalable person re-identification: a benchmark. In: Proceedings of the IEEE International Conference on Computer Vision (2015)

Auto Data Augmentation for Testing Set

Wanshun Gao[1] and Xi Zhao[2,3]($\boxtimes$) (iD)

[1] School of Electronic and Information Engineering,
Xi'an Jiaotong University, Xi'an 710049, China
g-wanshun@stu.xjtu.edu.cn
[2] School of Management, Xi'an Jiaotong University, Xi'an 710049, China
zhaoxi@ieee.org
[3] The Key Lab of the Ministry of Education for Process Control & Efficiency
Engineering, Xi'an 710049, China

Abstract. Testing phase augmentation is a fast way to further improve
the performance of image classification when CNN (Convolutional Neural Network) is already trained for hours. Limited attempts have been
made to find the best augmentation strategy for testing set. We propose
a reinforcement learning based augmentation strategy searching method
for testing phase augmentation. With the augmentation strategy, we augment each testing image and integrate features of its augmented images
into one feature. The reinforcement learning method searches the best
parameters in the augmentation strategy which is formed as a matrix in
this paper. Using the proposed method, we achieve competitive accuracies on image classification and face verification.

Keywords: Image augmentation · Deep reinforcement learning ·
Face verification

1 Introduction

Data augmentation is a method which introduces unobserved data or features to
help CNNs (Convolutional Neural Networks) achieve higher accuracy on image
classification [2,3]. Data augmentation contains training phase and testing phase
augmentation. Training phase augmentation transforms each training image to
another image and feeds the transformed image to a CNN for training. Compared to training phase augmentation, testing phase augmentation is composed
of image transformation [8,12,17,20] and feature fusion [4,8,11,12,17]. Image
transformation transforms a testing image to multiple images for feature extraction. The features of these images are then merged to one feature with feature

Wanshun Gao is a student. This work is supported by the National Natural Science
Foundation of China (Grant No. 91746111, Grant No.71702143), Ministry of Education & China Mobile Joint Research Fund Program (No. MCM20160302), Shaanxi
provincial development and reform commission (No. SFG2016789), Xi'an Science and
Technology Bureau (No. 2017111SF/RK005-(7)), the Fundamental Research Funds for
the Central Universities, Tang Zhongying Foundation for Zhongying Young Scholars.

© Springer Nature Switzerland AG 2019
Z. Lin et al. (Eds.): PRCV 2019, LNCS 11858, pp. 66–78, 2019.
https://doi.org/10.1007/978-3-030-31723-2_6

fusion. If the CNN is trained already, testing phase augmentation may further increase the classification accuracy.

In testing phase augmentation, recent researches apply limited image transformations [8,12,17,20] on testing images. Jia *et al.* and Parkhi *et al.* [8,17] crop each testing image into four corners, the center, and their mirrored versions from image size 256×256 to 224×224. In total, 10 patches are cropped from the testing image. Such cropping augmentation achieves higher accuracy than flipping augmentation [2]. DeepFace [20] transforms every testing image to its 3D aligned image, the gray-level image plus image gradient magnitude and orientation, and the 2D-aligned image. Masi *et al.* [12] transform the testing facial image to multipose facial images to produce identity preserving transformations. Above image transformations usually come from the experience of researchers. Other image transformations, such as auto contrast and rotation which are proven to increase the classification accuracy in training phase augmentation, are unexplored in existing testing phase augmentation works. Typically, an augmentation method comprises several image transformations and their magnitudes. There are many possibilities when finding a best augmentation method. Especially, for different testing sets, the best augmentation strategy may be different. For example, flipping augmentation strategy achieves more performance improvement on face identification [4] than it achieves on image classification [2]. Finding the best augmentation method from many image transformations, for the specific testing set, is still an unsolved problem.

In this paper, we propose a reinforcement learning method composed of an augmentation environment and a controller model to find the best testing phase augmentation strategy. The augmentation strategy comprises image transformations, their magnitudes and the type of feature fusion. The proposed method samples an augmentation strategy from the controller model as an action of the augmentation environment which invokes a state-of-the-art CNN model and outputs an evaluation score. The controller model takes in the evaluation score as a reward of the augmentation strategy, and updates itself with a batch of rewards. To directly use the state-of-the-art CNN whose deep learning framework may be incompatible with the controller model, we implement the reinforcement learning method to run on two deep learning frameworks which are coordinated to each other. The comparison between traditional methods and the proposed method is depicted as Fig. 1.

Our testing phase augmentation method achieves state-of-the-art performance on image classification datasets (CIFAR-10, CIFAR-100) and face verification datasets (LFW, CFP-FP and Age-DB30). Our contributions are:

- To the best of our knowledge, it is the first auto testing phase augmentation method. We design the augmentation strategy of testing phase, and search the best augmentation strategy using a reinforcement learning method.
- We implement the components of the proposed method to run on different learning frameworks.
- Competitive accuracies are achieved on image classification and face verification.

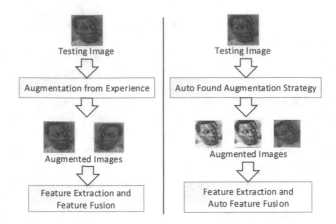

Fig. 1. Comparison of traditional methods (Left) with the proposed method (Right). The traditional methods augment testing images by experience. Using augmentation strategy which is found automatically, we augment testing images to more types, and combine the features of augmented images with the feature fusion found automatically.

Rest of this paper is organized as follows. Section 2 reviews recent works on image augmentation and parameter optimization. The differences between the proposed method and other works are demonstrated. Section 3 shows the framework and three parts of the proposed method. The details of the augmentation environment and the controller model are shown in each subsections of Sect. 3. Experimental results are list in Sect. 4.

2   Related Work

Image augmentation is widely used for image classification [8], emotion classification [24], semantic segmentation [10], face recognition [12], person re-identification [14] etc. In training phase augmentation, the early augment method is random corp, rotation, flip and so on. MixUp [6,21,23] augment examples and labels on convex combination of them. It reduces the effect of corrupt labels and stabilizes the training network. The augmentation method tries to increase the classification difficulty of permanent identities. It is interesting that, although they used strong in-plane augmentation at training time, improved recognition at test-time if face imagery is aligned with a 2D similarity transformation using detected face landmarks [13]. Autoaugment [3] designs its augmentation strategy as selecting possible image processing functions in order, and transforming an image with selected functions and their magnitudes. Such augmentation strategy lacks feature fusion, which is critical to testing phase augmentation. In testing phase augmentation, both feature pooling [4,8,12,17] and feature concatenation [11] are utilized to fuse features of augmented testing images. Inspired by Autoaugment, we design a matrix-like augmentation strategy for testing phase augmentation. For a testing set, we describe the augmentation strategy as a matrix. Each element in the matrix represents an operation, which is comprised of an image transformation function and the magnitude of the function. Elements in a row form an augmentation where features of transformed images are concatenated. Further more, we pool these concatenated features of all rows to one augmented feature, corresponding to a testing image.

In machine learning, hyper-parameters are predefined parameters before model training. Hyper-parameter optimization will result in the best performance when training a model. There are large amount of parameter optimization methods, such as Random Search, Bayesian Parameter Optimization, DRL (Deep Reinforcement Learning) etc. Bergstra [1] proposed a meta-modeling approach to optimize hyper-parameter automatically. Bayesian optimization is employed to optimize Expected Improvement (EI). It is first proven useful for optimizing hundreds of hyper-parameters. These methods [1,15] are able to optimize non fixed length hyper-parameters. Compared to them, Zoph and Le [25] proposed a more general and flexible method, which used a Recurrent Neural Network (RNN) interact with a child neural network and searched the hyper-parameters of the child neural network. The method is further extended to search more powerful neural architectures [18,26]. We inherit the idea of Zoph and Le [25] to automatically searching a testing phase augmentation strategy.

3   Methods

We decompose this section to three parts: augmentation environment, controller model θ_c and compatible implementation. Augmentation environment takes in an augmentation strategy and returns a reward to controller model. Controller model outputs augmentation strategy samples, and updates its weights with rewards. Compatible implementation helps augmentation environment running with independent deep learning framework, which may be different with controller model.

3.1   Augmentation Environment

Augmentation environment is to evaluate the performance of augmentation strategies that sampled from the controller model, by calling a trained CNN model θ_t. The evaluation score will return to controller model for weights updating. Based on the task of augmentation environment, the evaluation score can be classification accuracy or verification accuracy.

Existing image transformation functions in testing phase augmentation only contains crop, flip and grey-level. We extend it to all 19 image transformation functions in Python Imaging Library, which are "shearX/Y", "translateX/Y", "rotate", "color", "posterize", "solarize", "contrast", "sharpness", "brightness", "autocontrast", "equalize", "invert", "flipLR/UD", "blur" and "smooth". Additionally, we add "cutout" [5], and "identity". The identity function means none of any image processing is done. It is important to keep original image in augmented images, and also convenient when doing non-augmentation evaluation.

To make image transformations functions accompany with two types of feature fusion, we formulize a testing phase augmentation strategy as an augmentation matrix T (Fig. 2). Each element $T_{i,j}$ represents an image that is augmented by an image transformation function and the magnitude of the function. We discrete the range of the magnitude to 10 values uniformly. $T_{i,:}$ or T_i (elements in row) represents concatenated augmentation, which means features of these augmented images are concatenated. $[T_1; T_2; ...; T_n]$ represent pooling augmentation which means all concatenated features are pooling to one feature, which is used for classification or verification. That is, in an augmentation matrix, one element has 210 options. If an augmentation matrix has 6 elements, it will be $210^6 \approx 8.58 \times 10^{13}$ options, which is very large.

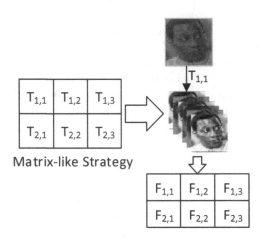

Fig. 2. Matrix-like augmentation strategy.

3.2   Controller Model

In the augmentation matrix T, concatenated augmentation T_i and pooling augmentation $[T_1; T_2; ...; T_n]$ are sequential. RNN (Recurrent Neural Network) is designed for the sequential data, which is appropriate to our augmentation method. In this paper, we adopt LSTM (Long Short Term Memory) as an implementation of RNN. To predict m elements in concatenated augmentation T_i, we set the size of initial input to m. Every time step in m time steps, a new softmax layer takes in the hidden state of LSTM, and predicts an elements in T_i. After m time steps, controller model predicts one concatenated augmentation T_i. With n times repetition above, controller model generates pooling augmentation $[T_1; T_2; ...; T_n]$. If $m = 1, n > 1$, controller model just generates pooling augmentation. The same with concatenated augmentation when $n = 1, m > 1$. The details are depicted as Fig. 3.

Generally, the reward is the accuracy of dataset. We try to maximize the reward to get higher accuracy. The purpose mainly focus on the maximization of the augmentation performance. So we exclude the bias of CNN performance, by minus the accuracy of raw images. The difference of augmented images and raw images is the reward to update controller. PPO (Proximal Policy Optimization) algorithm is used to update the weights of controller model.

It's the best to search the augmentation strategy on whole testing set. But it costs too much time to calculate a accuracy of whole testing set, even when the size of testing set is large. So we sample a mini-dataset from testing set for searching the test testing phase augmentation. The controller model aims to maximize the expected reward $\mathbb{E}_{a \sim \pi(a|C;\theta)}[r(a|C)]$. Here, the reward $r(a|C)$ is the accuracy on training images with a CNN model C. Several augmentation strategy a are sampled from the strategy $\pi(a|C;\theta)$. We apply the Adam optimizer to update the controller parameters θ.

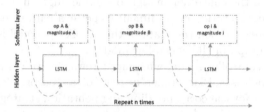

Fig. 3. The controller model. For each LSTM cell, we can sample an action from its softmax layer at the first step. The action represents an image operation and the magnitude of the operation. The next step, the last hidden layer and the action sample are inputs of the same LSTM cell. The output is the updated hidden layer and softmax layer. We sample a new action from the updated softmax layer. After m steps, we can obtains m sequential actions, which are applied for augment an image to another image. By repeat n times, we can obtains n augmented images.

The gradient is:

$$\nabla J(\theta) = \frac{1}{N} \sum_{i=1}^{N} [\nabla_\theta \log \pi(a_i|C;\theta)(r(a_i|C) - b_i)] \tag{1}$$

where, N is the number of samples in every controller step. Baseline b_i is a moving average of historical rewards. Augmentation strategy a_i is that augment a image to several images.

After training, we choose the augmentation strategies with high rewards during training. Then we test them on testing set with trained CNN models.

3.3 Compatible Implementation

Generally, DRL (Deep Reinforcement Learning) runs on single DLF (deep learning framework). In our case, both the controller model and the augmentation environment are deep neural networks. The augmentation environment invokes a state-of-the-art CNN model to evaluate augmentation strategies, while the CNN model is implemented with its own DLF which may not be the same with the DLF of the controller model. If migrating the DLF of the CNN model to the same DLF of the controller model, it will spend much time on CNN migration and CNN training. Also, it often exists differences when compared with the original CNN model, because of parameters tuning.

To use the state-of-the-art CNN directly, we implement the proposed DRL method with compatible mode. The controller model is implemented on TensorFlow which is widely used in academic and industrial circle. The concept of TensorFlow is building graph and running the graph to get results. Once the graph is built, it cannot be modified any more. Therefore, when the state-of-the-art CNN model in augmentation environment is ran on TensorFlow, we build the graphs of the controller model and the augmentation environment first. Then we run the graph of the controller model to sample augmentation strategy, and the graph of the augmentation environment to get evaluation result of the input augmentation strategy. When the state-of-the-art CNN model is ran on Mxnet, we only build the graph of the controller model.

To update the controller model with input rewards, we define the reward of the controller model as a Placeholder instead of a Tensor. Besides, we define another Placeholder for the corresponding augmentation strategy of the reward. We feed both the reward and its corresponding augmentation strategy to the controller model.

TensorFlow tends to allocate full GPU memory if not configured. We configure the GPU allocation of TensorFlow based on the framework of augmentation environment. When the augmentation environment runs on TensorFlow, we allocate the full GPU memory. When the augmentation environment runs on Mxnet, we allocate the GPU memory to minimal percent. In the experiment section, we allocate forty percent of whole GPU memory for TensorFlow.

4 Experiments

We evaluate the testing phase augmentation method by searching the best augmentation strategy on image classification dataset CIFAR-10 and three face verification datasets. Then, we evaluate the transferability of augmentation strategy by applying the best augmentation strategy of CIFAR-10 to CIFAR-100. Final, we evaluate the effective of compatible mode by demonstrating the GPU resource allocation under compatible mode and single mode. All experiments are ran on a Titan Xp GPU with 12GB GPU memory. When training the controller model, the learning rate is 0.35. The controller model samples 10 augmentation strategies in every training step, and samples 2000 augmentation strategies in total. The best augmentation strategy is selected from historical strategies which has the highest train accuracy.

4.1   Datasets

CIFAR-10 [9] has 10 classes with totally 50000 training images and 10000 testing images. To search the best augmentation strategy on testing images, we randomly divide 10000 testing images to 2048 images and 7936 images. 2048 images are used to training controller model, and 7936 images are used to test the best augmentation strategy that controller model has found.

CIFAR-100 [9] has 100 classes. Each class contains 500 training images and 100 testing images. Total 10000 testing images are used on the experiment of transferability of augmentation strategy.

Three face verification datasets are LFW [7], CFP-FP [19] and Age-DB30 [16]. The same as we did on CIFAR-10, we randomly separate 2048 pairs from original testing pairs of images for training controller model, and the rest of original testing pairs for testing.

4.2   Searching Augmentation Strategy on CIFAR-10

To evaluate the effective of the proposed method, we search the best augmentation strategy in six searching spaces with the possibilities from 210 to 8.58×10^{13}. In the augmentation matrix, the possibilities of searching space is $210^{m \times n}$, where m, n is the length of columns and rows. Theoretically, the proposed method supports unlimited size of the augmentation matrix. But, with the size increasing, the searching space is exponentially growing. It also needs more time to process testing images and find the best strategy. We limit the row length of the augmentation matrix no more than 6. The CNN in augmentation environment is trained with training set augmented by Autoaugment [3]. The architecture of CNN is Wide-ResNet 28 10 [22]. We apply pooling augmentation on the softmax layer of Wide-ResNet-28-10. The column length of the augmentation matrix can only be one. The results are demonstrated in Table 1.

As Table 1 shown, pooling augmentation is always effective, when the number of rows increase from 2 to 6. If we only transform original testing images without pooling augmentation (1 row), the accuracy of transformed images is no better than the accuracy on the original testing images. As the rows grows, the improved accuracy between training and testing becomes closer. Although the searching space is exponentially growing, we can easily find effective augmentation strategy in relatively small searching steps.

4.3   Searching Augmentation Strategy on Face Verification Datasets

We demonstrate the accuracies of the best augmentation strategy on three face verification datasets in Table 2. The CNN model (L50E-IR) in augmentation environment is trained by Arcface [4]. Compared with usual flipping augmentation, the proposed method can find better augmentation strategy on all three datasets. On CFP-FP, we increase the accuracy higher than other two datasets. It may because current alignment method is not suitable for profile-front face verification (Fig. 4).

Table 1. Evaluation of pooling augmentation with the number of rows growing.

	Train Mean (STD)	Test Mean (STD)
None	97.22	97.32
1 row	97.33 ± 0.07	97.22 ± 0.12
2 rows	97.58 ± 0.11	97.50 ± 0.18
3 rows	97.48 ± 0.11	97.34 ± 0.25
4 rows	97.55 ± 0.08	97.50 ± 0.10
5 rows	97.62 ± 0.08	97.61 ± 0.13
6 rows	97.59 ± 0.07	97.60 ± 0.09

Table 2. The improvement on three datasets with L50E-IR.

Dataset	Augmentation strategy	Acc.
LFW	None	99.70
LFW	[4]	99.80
LFW	Ours	99.82
CFP-FP	None	92.01
CFP-FP	[4]	92.76
CFP-FP	Ours	93.06
Age-DB30	None	97.60
Age-DB30	[4]	97.70
Age-DB30	Ours	97.80

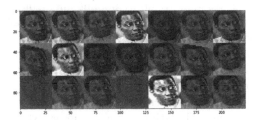

Fig. 4. The augment result on a facial images.

4.4   The Transferability of Testing Phase Augmentation Strategy

To evaluate the transferability of testing phase augmentation strategy found on CIFAR-10 with the CNN Wide-ResNet-28-10, we calculate the accuracy of the best augmentation strategy on testing set by replacing CIFAR-10 with CIFAR-100 or replacing Wide-ResNet-28-10 with Shake-Shake. Further, we calculate the accuracy by replacing both CIFAR-10 and Wide-ResNet-28-10 with CIFAR-100 and Shake-Shake. These results are shown in Tables 3, 4 and 5.

From Table 3, we can tell that the best augmentation strategy found on CIFAR-10 is transferable to CIFAR-100 which has the similar distribution with CIFAR-10. The accuracy increases more than it increases on CIFAR-10.

Table 3. Evaluate the transferability of testing phase augmentation strategy on CIFAR-100.

	Mean Accuracy (STD)
None	83.27
1 row	83.20 ± 0.31
2 rows	84.01 ± 0.37
3 rows	83.67 ± 0.42
4 rows	84.00 ± 0.26
5 rows	84.20 ± 0.23
6 rows	84.30 ± 0.13

Table 4 demonstrates that, we increase the accuracy on all Shake-Shake models. Although Autoaugment [3] already augment training set for training Shake-Shake models, we can also get a higher accuracy by using the best augmentation strategy found on CIFAR-10 with Wide-ResNet-28-10.

Table 4. Evaluate the transferability of testing phase augmentation strategy with Shake-Shake.

Test Aug	Shake-Shake 32	Shake-Shake 96
None	97.54	98.01
6 rows	97.74	98.39

When we replace both CIFAR-10 and Wide-ResNet-28-10 that used during controller model training, the best augmentation strategy also shows its effective. As Table 4 shows, the accuracy is higher than it on testing set without augmentation.

Table 5. Evaluate the transferability of testing phase augmentation strategy on CIFAR-100 with Shake-Shake.

Test Aug	Shake-Shake 32	Shake-Shake 96
None	82.88	84.89
6 rows	83.55	85.92

4.5   Compatibility of Controller Model and Augmentation Environment

To evaluate the compatibility of controller model and augmentation environment, we demonstrate the GPU resource allocation under compatible mode and single mode. In the experiment section, we employed two DL (deep learning) frameworks, TensorFlow and Mxnet. For CIFAR-10 and CIFAR-100, the DL frameworks of controller model and augmentation environment both are Tensor-Flow. For LFW, CFP_FF and AgeDB30, the DL framework of controller model is TensorFlow and augmentation environment is Mxnet (Table 6).

Table 6. Compatible of controller model and augmentation environment.

Environment	GPU resource
None	4919 M
TensorFlow	10775 M
Mxnet	10667 M

5   Conclusion

This paper proposed an auto testing phase augmentation method. It is effective to find the best augmentation strategy on the testing set, even the CNN model is trained using augmented training set. The best augmentation strategy also can be used on other datasets which has the similar distribution with the dataset where the best augmentation strategy was found on.

In further work, we will analysis the difference between training phase augmentation and testing phase augmentation, and design the parallelization of image transformations to speed the image processing time.

References

1. Bergstra, J., Yamins, D., Cox, D.D.: Making a science of model search: hyperparameter optimization in hundreds of dimensions for vision architectures. JMLR (2013)
2. Chatfield, K., Simonyan, K., Vedaldi, A., Zisserman, A.: Return of the devil in the details: delving deep into convolutional nets. In: British Machine Vision Conference (2014)
3. Cubuk, E.D., Zoph, B., Mane, D., Vasudevan, V., Le, Q.V.: Autoaugment: learning augmentation policies from data. arXiv preprint arXiv:1805.09501 (2018)
4. Deng, J., Guo, J., Xue, N., Zafeiriou, S.: Arcface: additive angular margin loss for deep face recognition. arXiv preprint arXiv:1801.07698 (2018)
5. DeVries, T., Taylor, G.W.: Improved regularization of convolutional neural networks with cutout. arXiv preprint arXiv:1708.04552 (2017)

6. Guo, H., Mao, Y., Zhang, R.: Mixup as locally linear out-of-manifold regularization. arXiv preprint arXiv:1809.02499 (2018)
7. Huang, G.B., Ramesh, M., Berg, T., Learned-Miller, E.: Labeled faces in the wild: a database for studying face recognition in unconstrained environments. Technical report 07–49, University of Massachusetts, Amherst, October 2007
8. Jia, Y., et al.: Caffe: convolutional architecture for fast feature embedding. arXiv preprint arXiv:1408.5093 (2014)
9. Krizhevsky, A., Hinton, G.: Learning multiple layers of features from tiny images. Technical report. Citeseer (2009)
10. Liu, S., Zhang, J., Chen, Y., Liu, Y., Qin, Z., Wan, T.: Pixel level data augmentation for semantic image segmentation using generative adversarial networks. arXiv preprint arXiv:1811.00174 (2018)
11. Liu, W., Wen, Y., Yu, Z., Li, M., Raj, B., Song, L.: Sphereface: deep hypersphere embedding for face recognition. In: The IEEE Conference on Computer Vision and Pattern Recognition (CVPR) (2017)
12. Masi, I., Hassner, T., Tran, A.T., Medioni, G.: Rapid synthesis of massive face sets for improved face recognition. In: 2017 12th IEEE International Conference on Automatic Face & Gesture Recognition (FG 2017), pp. 604–611. IEEE (2017)
13. Masi, I., Wu, Y., Natarajan, T.H.P.: Deep face recognition: a survey. In: Conference on Graphics, Patterns and Images (SIBGRAPI), October 2018
14. McLaughlin, N., Del Rincon, J.M., Miller, P.: Data-augmentation for reducing dataset bias in person re-identification. In: 2015 12th IEEE International Conference on Advanced Video and Signal Based Surveillance (AVSS), pp. 1–6. IEEE (2015)
15. Mendoza, H., Klein, A., Feurer, M., Springenberg, J.T., Hutter, F.: Towards automatically-tuned neural networks. In: Workshop on Automatic Machine Learning, pp. 58–65 (2016)
16. Moschoglou, S., Papaioannou, A., Sagonas, C., Deng, J., Kotsia, I., Zafeiriou, S.: AgeDB: the first manually collected, in-the-wild age database. In: Proceedings of the IEEE Conference on Computer Vision and Pattern Recognition Workshops, pp. 51–59 (2017)
17. Parkhi, O.M., Vedaldi, A., Zisserman, A.: Deep face recognition. In: British Machine Vision Conference (2015)
18. Pham, H., Guan, M.Y., Zoph, B., Le, Q.V., Dean, J.: Efficient neural architecture search via parameter sharing. In: ICML (2018)
19. Sengupta, S., Chen, J.C., Castillo, C., Patel, V.M., Chellappa, R., Jacobs, D.W.: Frontal to profile face verification in the wild. In: IEEE Conference on Applications of Computer Vision, February 2016
20. Taigman, Y., Yang, M., Ranzato, M., Wolf, L.: Deepface: closing the gap to human-level performance in face verification. In: Proceedings of the IEEE Conference on Computer Vision and Pattern Recognition, pp. 1701–1708 (2014)
21. Verma, V., et al.: Manifold mixup: learning better representations by interpolating hidden states. Stat **1050**, 4 (2018)
22. Zagoruyko, S., Komodakis, N.: Wide residual networks. arXiv preprint arXiv:1605.07146 (2016)
23. Zhang, H., Cisse, M., Dauphin, Y.N., Lopez-Paz, D.: Mixup: beyond empirical risk minimization. arXiv preprint arXiv:1710.09412 (2017)

24. Zhu, X., Liu, Y., Li, J., Wan, T., Qin, Z.: Emotion classification with data augmentation using generative adversarial networks. In: Phung, D., Tseng, V.S., Webb, G.I., Ho, B., Ganji, M., Rashidi, L. (eds.) PAKDD 2018. LNCS (LNAI), vol. 10939, pp. 349–360. Springer, Cham (2018). https://doi.org/10.1007/978-3-319-93040-4_28
25. Zoph, B., Le, Q.V.: Neural architecture search with reinforcement learning. arXiv preprint arXiv:1611.01578 (2016)
26. Zoph, B., Vasudevan, V., Shlens, J., Le, Q.V.: Learning transferable architectures for scalable image recognition. In: Proceedings of the IEEE Conference on Computer Vision and Pattern Recognition, pp. 8697–8710 (2018)

Dense Activation Network for Image Denoising

Yan Shen, Liao Zhang, Shuqin Lou$^{(\boxtimes)}$ (iD), and Zhongli Wang

School of Electronic and Information Engineering, Beijing Jiaotong University,
Beijing, China
{sheny,17120033,shqlou,zlwang}@bjtu.edu.cn

Abstract. Although deep convolutional neural networks (CNNs) have
received great attention in image denoising, most CNN-based methods
do not take full account of the hierarchical features of the original low-
quality images, including the spatial feature information within channels,
which decreases the representational capacity of the network. To solve
this problem, we propose a dense activation network (DAN) with a dense
activation block (DAB) consisting of a dense information fusion (DIF)
net and a spatial activation (SA) net. Specifically, DIF takes into account
both local feature information in the current block and global feature
information across blocks to enhance the propagation of feature information, and it adopts dilated convolution to enlarge the receptive field
of a network. Furthermore, we focus on the intra-channel spatial relationships and propose a novel SA net that adaptively recalibrates features
by considering the spatial relationships within channels. Experiments on
benchmark datasets show that our DAN models achieve favorable performance against state-of-the-art methods.

Keywords: Image denoising · Deep learning · Attention mechanism

1 Introduction

Image denoising is a classical and long-standing problem in low-level computer
vision, aiming to estimate an latent clean image from its degraded observation.
Various methods, including model-based methods [4,5,11] and discriminative
learning methods [16,24,25], have been proposed for image denoising in the past
few decades. With the great progress made by convolutional neural networks
(CNNs) in high-level computer vision, such as image classification and object
detection, CNN-based methods [14,20,24,25] have achieved notable improvements over model-based methods in image denoising [16,24,25]. Among them,
Zhang et al. [24] proposed a denoising convolutional neural network (DnCNN),

---

This work has been supported in part by National Natural Science Foundation of
China under Grants 61702032, 61573057, 61771042; by Fund 6140001030213; by Fund
2017JBZ002.

Z. Lin et al. (Eds.): PRCV 2019, LNCS 11858, pp. 79–90, 2019.
https://doi.org/10.1007/978-3-030-31723-2_7

which successfully introduced residual learning and batch normalization (BN) to improve denoising performance. A very deep residual encoder-decoder network (RED) [16] adopted symmetric skip connections to alleviate training difficulty. In [25], dilated convolution [23] was introduced to tackle low-level vision tasks, thus enlarging the receptive field of a network without the sacrifice of computational cost.

Although they achieve excellent performance, most CNN-based methods still have some drawbacks. Firstly, most of the current methods described above simply stack convolution layers in a sequence without considering the relationships between the feature information of different layers, which reduces the utilization of features in the network. Secondly, all of these methods neglect the spatial attention mechanism, which can be used to exploit the intra-channel spatial relationships to reduce the unnecessary computing burden and improve the expression ability of the whole network.

To address these drawbacks, we propose a novel dense activation network (DAN) (Fig. 1) that introduces a dense activation block (DAB) to implement pixel-wise activation of a feature map. The feature extraction block (FEB), at the start of the DAN, can extract shallow features from the input low-quality image. Multiple DABs are then stacked to progressively implement feature information fusion and activation. Finally, a reconstruction block (RB) consisting of one convolutional layer is adopted to aggregate the feature information from all previous blocks and output the restored image. Experiments on benchmark datasets clearly show that our proposed DAN models achieve sound performance against state-of-the-art methods for image denoising.

DAB, a critical component of our proposed DAN, contains a dense information fusion (DIF) net and a spatial activation (SA) net. Local feature information in the current block is combined with the global feature information across blocks in DIF, which enhances the feature propagation and enables the maximal utilization of image features during training. Dilated convolution is used to enlarge the receptive field of DAN, which allows the DAN model to capture more spatial context information. Inspired by squeeze-and-excitation (SE) [7], we propose a novel SA net to introduce the spatial attention mechanism in low-level computer vision. SA net adaptively recalibrates features through modeling the intra-channel spatial relationships. Such a spatial attention mechanism encourages the network to focus on informative and important features, which further enhances the representational ability of the network. More details will be provided in Sect. 3.

The main contributions of this work are the following:

- We propose a novel DAN for image denoising, which achieves better performance than previous state-of-art CNN-based methods.
- We propose DIF net to combine local feature information in the current block with global feature information across blocks to enhance the feature propagation, which assures maximum flow of the feature information in the DAN.

– We propose SA net to introduce a spatial attention mechanism into image denoising, which adaptively recalibrates features by considering the spatial relationships within channels.

2 Related Work

2.1 Image Denoising

Recently, CNNs have been extensively studied in image denoising. Zhang et al. first introduced residual learning and BN into a DnCNN model [24], which achieved great improvement in image denoising. Skip connections [16] and dilated cvonvolution [25] have also been suggested to improve the denoising performance. In [20], a recursively branched deconvolutional network (RBDN) was proposed to obtain rich multi-scale image representation at low cost. Liu et al. [14] suggested utilizing the high-level computer vision information to improve the denoising performance. In [15], a novel multilevel wavelet CNN (MWCNN) model was proposed to expand the receptive field for better tradeoff between the efficiency and restoration performance. In [26], FFDNet was proposed to use noise map as an input to the model, resulting in a single model which can process multi-level noise. Liu et al. [13] proposed non-local recurrent network (NLRN), which introduced non-local operations into the recurrent neural network to allow relevant information to flow between adjacent states. However, most of these methods just stack convolution layers using the chained mode, and they also neglect the intra-channel spatial relationships of the feature map, which reduces the utilization of features in the network.

2.2 Attention Mechanism

The human visual system selectively pays attention to salient parts of the whole image [12] for more detailed information and ignores other less useful information. The attention mechanism can be considered a guide to allocate computation efficiency [7,12,19]. Recently, the attention mechanism has been applied to image classification [7,22], understanding in images [2,9], sequence-based models [1,18], etc. Wang et al. [22] proposed a residual attention network to introduce a powerful trunk-and-mask attention mechanism for image classification. Hu et al. [7] proposed squeeze-and-excitation (SE) block to exploit inter-channel relationships by performing feature recalibration on the feature map. However, few works have investigated the impact of the spatial attention mechanism for image denoising. To handle this case, we propose a novel SA net to exploit the intra-channel spatial relationships to selectively emphasize those informative features and suppress less important ones. Our proposed model will be detailed in the next section.

3   Proposed Method

3.1   Network Structure

The proposed DAN mainly consists of three parts: feature extraction block (FEB), multiple stacked dense activation blocks (DABs) and the reconstruction block (RB), as shown in Fig. 1. Let x and y be the input and output of the DAN, respectively. For the FEB, two convolutional layers are firstly utilized to extract the shallow features from the input noisy image,

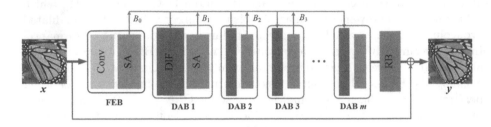

Fig. 1. The architecture of our proposed dense activation network (DAN).

$$B_{-1} = F_{ex}(x), \tag{1}$$

where F_{ex} denotes the feature extraction function and B_{-1} represents the shallow features and serves as the input to the following SA net. Therefore, the FEB can be formulated as

$$B_0 = F_{FEB}(x) = F_{SA}(F_{ex}(x)), \tag{2}$$

where F_{FEB} denotes the feature extraction block function and F_{SA} denotes the operation of the SA net. Suppose there are M DABs, and each DAB contains a DIF net and an SA net. The output B_m of the m-th DAB can be obtained as follows:

$$\begin{aligned} B_m &= F_{DAB}^m([B_0, \cdots, B_{m-1}]) \\ &= F_{SA}^m(F_{DIF}^m([B_0, \cdots, B_{m-1}])), \end{aligned} \tag{3}$$

where F_{DAB}^m denotes the operation of the m-th DAB, which contains F_{DIF}^m and F_{SA}^m operations of the m-th DIF and m-th SA, respectively. $[B_0, \cdots, B_{m-1}]$ indicate the concatenation of the feature maps, which are the output of the FEB and DABs. Local feature information generated by DIF is activated via SA and then used as the input for each subsequent DAB. The SA process selectively allows salient features of the feature map to be preserved and transferred to the next several DABs, which improves the expressional ability of the network. SA will be detailed in Sect. 3.3.

Finally, the DAN comes to the RB, a convolution layer without BN and rectified linear unit (ReLU), denoted as the F_{RB} function. Therefore, the DAN can be formulated as

$$y = F_{DAN}(x)$$
$$= F_{RB}\left(F_{DAB}^{m}\left(\cdots\left(F_{DAB}^{1}\left(F_{FEB}(x)\right)\right)\cdots\right)\right) + x, \qquad (4)$$

where F_{DAN} denotes the complete operation of the DAN model.

3.2 Dense Information Fusion Net

The proposed DIF net can enhance the feature transferring among blocks and improve the ability of each block to capture more spatial context information, as shown in Fig. 2.

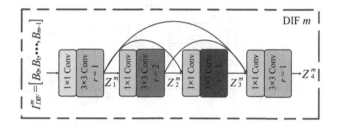

Fig. 2. Dense information fusion (DIF) architecture.

Global information fusion is introduced to exploit the global feature information across blocks by integrating the features from all previous blocks. The input of the m-th DIF, I_{DIF}^{m}, is composed of the concatenation of all the historical blocks $[B_0, \cdots, B_{m-1}]$. Therefore, the output of the first layer of the m-th DIF, Z_1^m, can be formulated as

$$Z_1^m = F_{GIF}^m\left([B_0, B_1, \cdots, B_{m-1}]\right), \qquad (5)$$

where F_{GIF}^m is a composite function of 1×1 convolution and 3×3 convolution in the m-th DIF. Each convolution layer in DIF outputs $k = 64$ feature maps, where k is the growth rate mentioned in DenseNet [8].

Local information fusion is then applied to integrate local feature information in the current block, which can be implemented by adopting a 1×1 convolution layer in front of each 3×3 convolution layer. Meanwhile, the 1×1 convolution can be used to reduce the number of feature maps and improve the computational efficiency. Therefore, we have

$$Z_i^m = \delta\left(W_i^2 * \delta\left(W_i^1 * \left[Z_1^m, \cdots, Z_{i-1}^m\right]\right)\right), \qquad (6)$$

where $*$ and δ represent the operation of convolution and ReLU activation function, respectively; $Z_i^m (2 \leq i \leq 4)$ denotes the output feature map of the i-th convolutional layer in the m-th DIF; and $\left[Z_1^m, \cdots, Z_{i-1}^m\right]$ refer to the concatenation of feature maps produced by the previous layers in the m-th DIF. W_i^1 and W_i^2 are the weights of the i-th convolution layer with kernel sizes of 1×1

and 3×3, respectively, where the bias term is omitted. BN and ReLU activation are also omitted in Fig. 2 for simplicity.

Dilated convolution is introduced here to enlarge the receptive field of each DIF, which enables the network to learn more extensive features without introducing additional parameters. We propose adopting dilated convolution for the second and third convolution layer with the dilation rates $r = 2$ and $r = 3$, respectively. Consequently, it can be seen that the receptive field of DIF is 15×15, while the receptive field of DIF will be just 9×9 if we use the traditional 3×3 convolution. Experimental results in Sect. 5 also demonstrate the effectiveness of our proposed DIF.

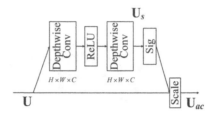

Fig. 3. Spatial activation (SA) architecture.

3.3   Spatial Activation Net

Inspired by SE [7], we propose the SA net (Fig. 3) for image denoising to consider the spatial relationships within channels to realize a better attention mechanism than SE for image denoising.

We propose generating the spatial statistics within channels $\mathbf{U}_s \in \mathbb{R}^{H \times W \times C}$ by using a set of depthwise convolution layers. Assum the feature map $I_{DIF}^m = [B_0, B_1, \cdots, B_{m-1}]$, $I_{DIF}^m \in \mathbb{R}^{H \times W \times C'}$ that passes through DIF net to generate output feature map $\mathbf{U} \in \mathbb{R}^{H \times W \times C}$. The generate $\mathbf{U}$ combines the spatial and channel information of I_{DIF}^m through convolution layers and nonlinearities. $\mathbf{U} = [u_1, u_2, \cdots, u_C]$ is constituted by channels from u_1 to u_C, where $u_i \in \mathbb{R}^{H \times W \times 1}$ refers to the feature map of the i-th channel. So

$$u_{s,i} = F_{sa}(u_i, v) = v_i^2 * \delta(v_i^1 * u_i), \tag{7}$$

where v refers to the 2D spatial convolution filter with a kernel size of 3×3. Considering the output of traditional convolution is produced by a summation through all channels, we adopt the depthwise convolution to overcome the entanglement between spatial relationship and channel correlation introduced by the traditional convolution. Equation (7) indicates that the i-th convolution filter v_i only acts on the corresponding i-th channel of $\mathbf{U}$, which completes the modeling of the spatial relationships within channels.

As discussed in [7], since we expect that the multiple spatial locations can be emphasized opposed to one-hot activation, the output map $\mathbf{U}_s$ is passed through a sigmoid layer $\sigma\left(\cdot\right)$ to obtain activation values, which are used to recalibrate or activate the feature map $\mathbf{U}$,

$$\mathbf{U}_{ac} = F_{activate}\left(\mathbf{U}, \sigma\left(\mathbf{U}_s\right)\right) = \mathbf{U} \cdot \sigma\left(\mathbf{U}_s\right), \tag{8}$$

where $F_{activate}$ denotes element-wise multiplication. SA assigns a learned activation value to each feature value of the input $\mathbf{U}$. The high activation values are allocated to the features with abundant spatial information, by which the detailed features of images can be restored with better visual effect.

4 Discussions

Difference to SE. SE [7] is applied in high-level computer vision tasks (e.g., image classification), while our SA net is proposed for image denoising. SE proposes a structural unit to model the interdependencies between channels and achieves adaptive recalibration of channel-wise features. Unlike the channel-wise relationships considered in SE, we chose to exploit the spatial relationships within channels, which is considered more important and even better than the channel-wise relationships, especially for low-level computer vision tasks. Furthermore, SE [7] adopts a global average pooling layer to generate channel-wise statistics, then uses adaptive recalibration to the feature map to capture channel-wise interdependencies. However, in this work, SA adopts a set of depth-wise convolution layers to exploit the intra-channel spatial relationships, which is different from SE. The experimental results in Sect. 5 also proves that our proposed SA net is more effective than SE in image denoising.

Difference to DenseNet. DenseNet [8] is proposed for high-level computer vision tasks (e.g., object recognition), while our proposed DAN is designed to solve image denoising problems. For image denoising, we changed the operational order of BN-ReLU-Conv in the original structure to Conv-BN-ReLU in DIF. Dense connection was adopted to transfer local feature information in a dense block [8]. However, our proposed DAN combines local feature information in the current block with global feature information across blocks, which further enhances the propagation of feature information and greatly improves the expressional ability of the model. In addition, the proposed DAN introduces dilated convolution to enlarge the receptive field of each DIF and thus enable the network to capture more extensive feature information, which is different from DenseNet using the pooling layer. DIF is guaranteed to expand the receptive field without increasing the computational burden and introducing additional network parameters, which helps to reconstruct corrupted pixels in image denoising.

5 Experimental Results

5.1 Settings

For image denoising, we follow [24] and use 400 images with a size of 180×180 from the Berkeley Segmentation Dataset (BSD) [17] to generate clean image

Table 1. Ablation investigation of DIF, SE, and SA. We observe the denoising performance (PSNR) on the BSD68 dataset.

Noise	15	25	50
DnCNN	31.73	29.23	26.23
DAN-D-N	31.98	29.50	26.52
DAN-D-SE	32.07	29.56	26.61
DAN-D-SA	**32.16**	**29.71**	**26.76**

patches as the training set. Data augmentation is used in the training set to improve the training results. We downscale images with factors of 1, 0.9, 0.8 and 0.7, and then crop images into 128×1772 patches with a size of 40×40. Each patch is flipped or rotated randomly. During training, Gaussian noise with three different noise levels ($\sigma = 15, 25, 50$) is added to clean patches to generate corresponding noisy patches.

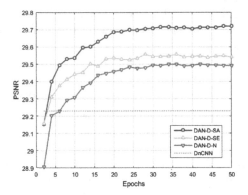

Fig. 4. Convergence analysis of DIF, SE, and SA. The denoising results are evaluated on the BSD68 dataset with noise level $\sigma = 25$.

The proposed network for image denoising, called DAN here, is composed of one FEB, three DABs and one RB. The Adam optimizer [10] is used to minimize the L_2 loss function with parameters $\beta_1 = 0.9$, $\beta_2 = 0.999$, $\alpha = 0.01$ and $\varepsilon = 1e-8$. Adam uses a default setting for the other hyper-parameters. We use the batch size of 128 for image denoising. The kernel weights are initialized using the method in [6], and the biases are initialized to zero. The parameter of epoch is set as 50 for DAN. The learning rate is initialized to 0.0001, which is divided by 10 at 40% and 80% of the training epochs. The proposed networks are implemented with the Tensorflow framework running on a PC with Intel(R) Xeon(R) E5-2650V4 CPU 2.2GHz and an Nvidia GTX1080Ti GPU. It takes one day to train DAN.

5.2 Ablation Investigation

Table 1 shows the ablation investigation on the effects of DIF, SE [7] and our proposed SA. For image denoising, the baseline network DAN-D-N (DAN without activation) is obtained by removing the SA activation net in the DAN-D. It can be seen that DAN-D-N achieves a notable peak signal-to-noise ratio (PSNR) gain compared with DnCNN. This demonstrates that our proposed DIF is a more effective network structure in image denoising, which assures maximum flow of the feature information in the network.

Table 2. Average PSNR(dB)/SSIM results of the competing methods for image denoising with noise levels $\sigma = 15$, 25 and 50 on datasets Set12 and BSD68. Red color indicates the best performance.

Dataset	Noise	BM3D [4]	TNRD [3]	DnCNN [24]	IRCNN [25]	MemNet [21]	MWCNN [15]	DAN
Set12	15	32.37/0.8952	32.50/0.8962	32.86/0.9027	32.77/0.9008	-	33.15/0.9088	33.41/0.9105
	25	29.97/0.8505	30.05/0.8515	30.44/0.8618	30.38/0.8601	-	30.79/0.8711	31.08/0.8743
	50	26.72/0.7676	26.82/0.7677	27.18/0.7827	27.14/0.7804	27.38/0.7931	27.74/0.8056	27.96/0.8061
BSD68	15	31.08/0.8722	31.42/0.8822	31.73/0.8906	31.63/0.8881	-	31.86/0.8947	32.16/0.8968
	25	28.57/0.8017	28.92/0.8148	29.23/0.8278	29.15/0.8249	-	29.41/0.8360	29.71/0.8390
	50	25.62/0.6869	25.97/0.7021	26.23/0.7189	26.19/0.7171	26.35/0.7294	26.53/0.7366	26.76/0.7367

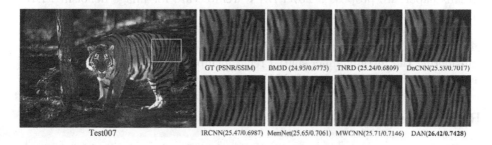

Fig. 5. *Image denoising* results of "Test007" (BSD68) with noise level 50.

We replace the SA with the SE activation in the proposed DAN networks for image denoising, resulting in DAN-D-SE. As shown in Table 1, DAN-D-SE only slightly outperforms DAN-D-N by 0.09, 0.06 and 0.09dB under the noise levels of 15, 25 and 50, respectively. Therefore, it can be validated that the activation net indeed improves the performance of the baseline networks for image denoising.

We further compare the performance of the SE activation with the proposed SA, called DAN-D-SA (DAN). For image denoising, DAN-D-SA can improve the PSNR values higher than DAN-D-SE by 0.09, 0.15 and 0.15dB under the noise levels of 15, 25 and 50, respectively. We also visualize the convergence process of the above models in Fig. 4. One can see that our proposed methods achieve the best performance in image denoising, which also proves the proposed DAN with novel SA net can greatly improve the representational power of the network and the performance for image denoising.

5.3   Comparisons with State-of-the-Arts

The proposed DAN is compared with six state-of-the-art methods: BM3D [4], TNRD [3], DnCNN [24], IRCNN [25], MemNet [21] and MWCNN [15]. We use two standard benchmark datasets, Set12 [24] and BSD68 [17], to evaluate the denoising methods. Table 2 shows the average PSNR and structural similarity (SSIM) of the competing methods on those two datasets. When compared with all previous methods, our proposed DAN obtains the best performance on all the datasets according to different noise levels. When the noise level increases (e.g., $\sigma = 50$), our proposed DAN outperforms DnCNN by about 0.5dB on Set12, and 0.7dB on BSD68. Compared with other methods, DAN can still maintain a considerable margin. Figure 5 shows the denoising results of image Test007 from BSD68 under the noise level $\sigma = 50$. One can see that BM3D is blurry; TNRD still contains noise; and DnCNN, IRCNN, MemNet and MWCNN have lost minor details of the stripes. Our DAN, on the other hand, has shown great performance in restoring image details and structures and can achieve better visual results than the competing methods.

6   Conclutions

In this paper, we propose a novel DAN architecture for image denoising. DIF combines local feature information in the current block with global feature information across blocks, which can greatly boost the representational power of the network. Furthermore, we propose SA net to adaptively recalibrate features by considering the intra-channel spatial relationships. Extensive experiments have demonstrated the superiority of DAN over state-of-the-art methods.

References

1. Bluche, T.: Joint line segmentation and transcription for end-to-end handwritten paragraph recognition. In: Advances in Neural Information Processing Systems (2016)
2. Cao, C., et al.: Look and think twice: capturing top-down visual attention with feedback convolutional neural networks. In: Proceedings of the International Conference on Computer Vision (ICCV) (2015)
3. Chen, Y., Pock, T.: Trainable nonlinear reaction diffusion: a flexible framework for fast and effective image restoration. IEEE Trans. Pattern Anal. Mach. Intell. **39**(6), 1256–1272 (2016)
4. Dabov, K., Foi, A., Katkovnik, V., Egiazarian, K.: Image denoising by sparse 3-D transform-domain collaborative filtering. IEEE Trans. Image Process. **16**(8), 2080–2095 (2007)
5. Gu, S., Zhang, L., Zuo, W., Feng, X.: Weighted nuclear norm minimization with application to image denoising. In: Proceedings of the Conference on Computer Vision and Pattern Recognition (CVPR) (2014)
6. He, K., Zhang, X., Ren, S., Sun, J.: Delving deep into rectifiers: surpassing human-level performance on ImageNet classification. In: Proceedings of the International Conference on Computer Vision (ICCV) (2015)

7. Hu, J., Shen, L., Sun, G.: Squeeze-and-excitation networks. In: Proceedings of the Conference on Computer Vision and Pattern Recognition (CVPR) (2018)
8. Huang, G., Liu, Z., Weinberger, K.Q., van der Maaten, L.: Densely connected convolutional networks. In: Proceedings of the Conference on Computer Vision and Pattern Recognition (CVPR) (2017)
9. Jaderberg, M., Simonyan, K., Zisserman, A., Kavukcuoglu, K.: Spatial transformer networks. In: Advances in Neural Information Processing Systems (2015)
10. Kingma, D., Ba, J.: Adam: a method for stochastic optimization. In: Proceedings of the International Conference on Learning Representations (ICLR) (2015)
11. Lan, X., Roth, S., Huttenlocher, D., Black, M.J.: Efficient belief propagation with learned higher-order Markov random fields. In: Leonardis, A., Bischof, H., Pinz, A. (eds.) ECCV 2006. LNCS, vol. 3952, pp. 269–282. Springer, Heidelberg (2006). https://doi.org/10.1007/11744047_21
12. Larochelle, H., Hinton, G.E.: Learning to combine foveal glimpses with a third-order Boltzmann machine. In: Advances in Neural Information Processing Systems (2010)
13. Liu, D., Wen, B., Fan, Y., Loy, C.C., Huang, T.S.: Non-local recurrent network for image restoration. In: Advances in Neural Information Processing Systems (2018)
14. Liu, D., Wen, B., Liu, X., Wang, Z., Huang, T.S.: When image denoising meets high-level vision tasks: a deep learning approach. arXiv preprint arXiv:1706.04284 (2017)
15. Liu, P., Zhang, H., Zhang, K., Lin, L., Zuo, W.: Multi-level wavelet-CNN for image restoration. In: Proceedings of the Conference on Computer Vision and Pattern Recognition (CVPR) Workshops (2018)
16. Mao, X., Shen, C., Yang, Y.: Image restoration using very deep convolutional encoder-decoder networks with symmetric skip connections. In: Advances in Neural Information Processing Systems (2016)
17. Martin, D., Fowlkes, C., Tal, D., Malik, J.: A database of human segmented natural images and its application to evaluating segmentation algorithms and measuring ecological statistics. In: Proceedings of the Conference on Computer Vision and Pattern Recognition (CVPR) (2001)
18. Miech, A., Laptev, I., Sivic, J.: Learnable pooling with context gating for video classification. arXiv:1706.06905 (2017)
19. Mnih, V., Heess, N., Graves, A., Kavukcuoglu, K.: Recurrent models of visual attention. In: Advances in Neural Information Processing Systems (2014)
20. Santhanam, V., Morariu, V.I., Davis, L.S.: Generalized deep image to image regression. In: Proceedings of the Conference on Computer Vision and Pattern Recognition (CVPR) (2017)
21. Tai, Y., Yang, J., Liu, X., Xu, C.: MemNet: a persistent memory network for image restoration. In: Proceedings of the International Conference on Computer Vision (ICCV) (2017)
22. Wang, F., et al.: Residual attention network for image classification. In: Proceedings of the Conference on Computer Vision and Pattern Recognition (CVPR) (2017)
23. Yu, F., Koltun, V.: Multi-scale context aggregation by dilated convolutions. arXiv:1511.07122 (2015)

24. Zhang, K., Zuo, W., Chen, Y., Meng, D., Zhang, L.: Beyond a Gaussian denoiser: residual learning of deep cnn for image denoising. IEEE Trans. Image Process. **26**(7), 3142–3155 (2016)
25. Zhang, K., Zuo, W., Gu, S., Zhang, L.: Learning deep CNN denoiser prior for image restoration. In: Proceedings of the Conference on Computer Vision and Pattern Recognition (CVPR) (2017)
26. Zhang, K., Zuo, W., Zhang, L.: FFDNet: toward a fast and flexible solution for cnn-based image denoising. IEEE Trans. Image Process. **27**(9), 4608–4622 (2018)

The Optimal Graph Regularized Sparse Coding with Application to Image Representation

Zhenqiu Shu[1,2], Xiaojun Wu[2(✉)], Zhen Liu[2], Congzhe You[1], and Honghui Fan[1]

[1] School of Computer Engineering,
Jiangsu University of Technology, Changzhou 231001, China
shuzhenqiu@163.com
[2] Jiangsu Provincial Engineering Laboratory of Pattern Recognition and
Computational Intelligence, Jiangnan University, Wuxi 214122, China
wu_xiaojun@jiangnan.edu.cn

Abstract. Sparse representation has shown its superiority and effectiveness in many real applications in recent years. However, it is still an open problem to effectively preserve the intrinsic geometric structure of data in new representation space. In this paper, we propose a novel method, called the Optimal Graph regularized Sparse Coding (OGSC), to deal with the high dimensional data. Specifically, we impose a rank constraint on the Laplacian matrix of the graph model, and thus can learn the optimal graph to preserve the manifold structure of data in each iteration. Additionally, the optimization scheme for our proposed method is also provided in this paper. The experimental results on three benchmark datasets have shown that our proposed OGSC method outperforms other stat-of-the-art methods.

Keywords: Sparse representation · Geometric structure · Rank constraint · Laplacian matrix · Optimal graph

1 Introduction

Data representation techniques play an important role in many classification and clustering tasks. Over the past few decades, many data representation techniques have been proposed to learn the latent semantic information embedded in high dimensional data. Recently, sparse coding based data representation methods have shown an attractive performance in many real applications, such as image classification [1–3], image super-resolution [4], image processing [5,6], etc.

The goal of sparse coding method is to represent the query sample using few atoms that are selected from an overcomplete dictionary. To achieve the

This work was supported by the National Natural Science Foundation of China [Grant No. 61603159, 61672265, U1836218], Natural Science Foundation of Jiangsu Province [Grant No. BK20160293] and Excellent Key Teachers of QingLan Project in Jiangsu Province.

© Springer Nature Switzerland AG 2019
Z. Lin et al. (Eds.): PRCV 2019, LNCS 11858, pp. 91–101, 2019.
https://doi.org/10.1007/978-3-030-31723-2_8

sparseness of the coefficients, some constraints, such as l_0-norm, $l_{2,0}$-norm, etc., are imposed on the representation coefficients. Many variants of the sparse representation techniques have been developed in recent years. Wright et al. [7] proposed a novel method, called Sparse Representation Classification (SRC), for the classification problems. It uses the minimal residual to predict the class label of a query sample. Up to now, the SRC method has shown a very promising performance in many applications. However, traditional sparse representation methods neglect the intrinsic geometric hidden in data. Therefore, Zhang et al. [8] proposed a graph regularized sparse coding (GSC) method for data presentation. In order to preserve the manifold structure hidden in high-dimensional data, it enforces the graph regularization term constraint on the model of the sparse coding method. However, GSC only considers the local affinity of data, and neglects the distant repulsion property of data. Therefore, a structure preserving sparse coding method [9] is developed by imposing these two properties of data, simultaneously. To preserve both local and global structure information of data, Shu et al. [10] proposed a local and global graph regularized sparse coding (LGSC) using the regularization technology. However, the graph-based learning methods mentioned above need to predefine a fixed neighborhood number of the graph model. Therefore, it cannot learn the optimal affinity matrix in practice. To solve this issue, Nie et al. [11] proposed a Constrained Laplacian Rank (CLR) algorithm for graph-learning clustering. CLR imposes the rank constraint on the Laplacian matrix of the graph model to learn a new data similarity matrix. Therefore, it can guarantee exactly k connected components, and thus is a block diagonal matrix that is benefit for clustering.

In this paper, we propose a novel method, called the Optimal Graph regularized Sparse Coding (OGSC), to effectively discover the intrinsic geometric structure of data. Specifically, the rank constraint is imposed on the Laplacian matrix of the given nearest neighbor graph, and then the graph model is updated iteratively in optimization process. Therefore, it leads to learn more optimal graph than traditional graph based sparse representation methods. Thus, our proposed method can effectively discover the hidden feature information among data, and is more suitable for clustering tasks. Experimental results on three benchmark datasets have shown that our proposed OGSC method achieves better performance than other state-of-the-art methods.

The paper is organized as follows. We briefly review the sparse coding method in Sect. 2. In Sect. 3, we introduce our proposed OGSC method, and then derive its optimization scheme. Finally, we empirically evaluate the proposed OGSC method in Sect. 4 and conclude in Sect. 5.

2   The Relative Work

In this section, we briefly describe the model of the sparse coding method. The sparse coding method seeks a sparse coefficient $V \in R^{k \times n}$ to represent the query samples $X \in R^{m \times n}$ under a overcomplete dictionary $D \in R^{m \times k}$. Therefore, the sparse coding problem can be formulated as

$$\min_{D,V}\|X - DV\|_F^2 + \alpha \sum_{i=1}^{m} \|v_i\|_0, \quad s.t. \ \|d_j\|^2 \leq C \tag{1}$$

where $\|\cdot\|_0$ stands for the l_0-norm of a vector, and its goal is to guarantee the sparseness of the coefficient vector. α and C denote the regularization parameter and the given constant, respectively. However, the l_0-norm constraint in Eq. (1) leads to an NP-hard problem, and thus its optimization procedure is computationally expensive. Fortunately, it can be approximated by the l_1-norm constraint if the matrix satisfies some particular constraints [12]. Therefore, we can reformulate the Eq. (1) as the following problem:

$$\min_{D,V}\|X - DV\|_F^2 + \alpha \sum_{i=1}^{m} \|v_i\|_1 \quad s.t. \ \|d_j\|^2 \leq C \tag{2}$$

where $\|\cdot\|_1$ denotes the l_1-norm of a vector. It is worth noting that the l_1-norm based minimization optimization problem can be efficiently solved by some existing software packages [13,14].

3 The Proposed Method

3.1 Motivation

Traditional graph regularized sparse coding methods model the geometric structure of data by constructing a fixed nearest neighbor graph. However, it cannot effectively discover the intrinsic manifold structure hidden in data using the fixed graph regularizer in the same case. Therefore, in this paper, we construct an initial nearest neighbor graph model, and then iteratively update the graph model by imposing the rank constraint on its Laplacian matrix. Therefore, we can learn a optimal graph model to explore the manifold structure of data. Thus, the optimal graph regularizer can be further constructed, and then added into the model of sparse coding. Here, we first introduce the model of CLR proposed in reference [11].

3.2 Constrained Laplacian Rank (CLR)

Using the l_2-norm to measure the approximation error between the initial affinity matrix W and the learned similarity matrix A, the constrained Laplacian rank for graph-based clustering is expressed as the solution to the following problem:

$$J_{CLR_{l_2}} = \min_{\sum_j a_{ij}=1, a_{ij} \geq 0, rank(L_A)=n-k} \|A - W\|_F^2 \tag{3}$$

Here, L_A denotes the Laplacian matrix of the matrix A. Denote $\sigma_i(L_A)$ as the i-th smallest eigenvalue of L_A. Noting that $\sigma_i(L_A) > 0$ because the Laplacian matrix L_A is positive semidefinite. Therefore, the Eq. (3) can be rewritten as the following problems for a large enough value of λ:

$$J_{CLR_{l_2}} = \min_{\sum_j a_{ij}=1, a_{ij} \geq 0} \|A - W\|_F^2 + 2\lambda \sum_{i=1}^{k} \sigma_i(L_A) \tag{4}$$

According to Ky Fans Theorem, we have

$$\sum_{i=1}^{k} \sigma_i(L_A) = \min_{V \in^{n \times k}, V^T V = I} Tr(V^T L_A V)\} \tag{5}$$

Therefore, the Eq. (5) can be further rewritten to the following problem:

$$\min_{A} \|A - W\|_F^2 + \lambda Tr(V L_A V^T)$$
$$s.t.\, VV^T = I, A1 = 1, A \geq 0, A \in R^{n \times n} \tag{6}$$

3.3   The Objective Function of the Proposed Method

By imposing the Laplacian rank constraint on the Laplacian matrix of the graph model, the objective function of the proposed OGSC method is given as follows:

$$\min_{D,V} \|X - DV\|_F^2 + \alpha \sum_{i=1}^{m} \|v_i\|_1$$
$$+ \beta \|A - W\|_F^2 + \lambda Tr(V L_A V^T)$$
$$s.t. \|d_j\|^2 \leq C, VV^T = I, A1 = 1, A \geq 0, A \in R^{n \times n} \tag{7}$$

The first term of Eq. (7) is the reconstruction error. The second term aims to guarantee the sparseness of the coding coefficient. The rest two terms of Eq. (7) are used to learn the optimal graph model. The α, β and λ denote the regularization parameters balancing reconstruction error, sparsity and graph regularizer.

Representation Coefficient Learning. With fixed the dictionary D and the graph A, the subproblem of Eq. (7) is reformulated as the following optimization problem:

$$\min_{D,V} \|X - DV\|_F^2 + \alpha \sum_{i=1}^{m} \|v_i\|_1 + \lambda Tr(V L_A V^T) \tag{8}$$

It is easy to know that the problem (8) cannot be solved using the standard unconstrained optimization methods. Here, we adopt an optimization algorithm based upon coordinate descent to solve the problem (8). In addition, we can get the global minimum of Eq. (8) due to its convexity.

To optimize over each v_i, we can reformulate the Eq. (8) as the following vector form:

$$\min_{D,V} \sum_{i=1}^{m} \|x_i - Dv_i\|^2 + \alpha \sum_{i=1}^{m} \|v_i\|_1 + \lambda \sum_{i,j=1}^{m} L_{A_{ij}} v_i^T v_j \tag{9}$$

Here, $\{v_i\}_{j\neq i}$ is alternately updated while fixed the other vectors. Therefore, we rewrite Eq. (9) as follows:

$$\min_{D,V} \|x_i - Dv_i\|^2 + \alpha \sum_{i=1}^{k} \left| v_i^{(j)} \right| + \lambda L_{ij} v_i^T v_i + v_i^T h_i \tag{10}$$

where $h_i = 2\eta(\sum_{j\neq i} L_{Aij} v_j)$ and $v_i^{(j)}$ denotes the j-th element of v_i. It is easy to solve Eq. (10) by adopting the feature-sigh search algorithm proposed in reference [15].

Dictionary Learning. In this step, we solve the dictionary D with fixed A and V. Therefore, Eq. (7) can be formulated as the following problem:

$$\min_{D,V} \|X - DV\|_F^2$$

$$s.t. \|d_j\|^2 \leq c \tag{11}$$

It is clear to see that Eq. (7) is a least squares problem with quadratic constraints. Therefore, we can adopt the Lagrangian dual method to solve this problem.

Let $\eta = [\eta_1, \eta_2, ..., \eta_k]$, and η_k be the Lagrange multiplier associated with i-th inequality constrained $\|d_i\|^2 - c \leq 0$. Therefore, the problem (11) can be rewritten as follows:

$$g(\eta) = \inf_D (L(D, \eta))$$

$$= \inf_D (\|X - DV\|_F^2 + \sum_{i=1}^{m} \eta_i (\|v_i\|^2 - c)) \tag{12}$$

By setting the first order derivative of $L(D, \eta)$ to zero, we can derive the optimal solution D^* as

$$D^* = XV^T (VV^T + \Delta)^{-1} \tag{13}$$

By substituting (13) into (12), the problem Eq. (12) can be presented as follows:

$$g(\eta) = Tr(X^T X) - Tr(XV^T(VV^T + \Delta)^{-1}VX^T)$$

$$- cTr(\Delta) \tag{14}$$

Thus, the Lagrange dual function of problem (14) can be derived as follows:

$$\min_{\Delta} r(XV^T(VV^T + \Delta)^{-1}VX^T) - cTr(\Delta)$$

$$s.t. \eta_i \geq 0, i = 1, ..., k \tag{15}$$

Here, the Newtons or conjugate gradient methods can be used to optimize the problem (15). Let Δ^* be the optimal solution, then the optimal $D^* = XV^T pinv(VV^T + \Delta^*)$, where $pinv(.)$ denotes the pseudo-inverse of a matrix.

The Optimal Graph Learning. By updating A with fixed D, V, we have

$$\min_{A}(\beta \|A - W\|_F^2 + \lambda Tr(V L_A V^T))$$
$$s.t.\, a_i^T 1 = 1, 0 \leq a_i \leq 1, A \in R^{n \times n} \tag{16}$$

Then we rewrite the Eq. (16) as the following problem:

$$\min_{a_i \geq 0, a_i 1 = 1} \beta \sum_{i,j=1} (a_{ij} - w_{ij})^2 + \frac{\lambda}{2} \sum_{i,j=1} \|v_i - v_j\|_2^2 \, a_{i,j}$$
$$s.t. \sum_{j} a_{ij} = 1, A \geq 0 \tag{17}$$

It is worth noting that the problem (17) is independent for different i values, and thus can be written in the vector form as

$$\min_{a_i \geq 0, a_i 1 = 1} \left\| \beta a_i - (\beta w_i - \frac{\lambda}{2} u_i) \right\|_2^2 \tag{18}$$

where $u_{ij} = \|v_i - v_j\|_2^2$ and u_i denotes a vector with the jth element equal to u_{ij}. Obviously, we can get a closed form solution of the problem (18). Here, an alternative approach for solving the Eq. (18) adopts an efficient iterative algorithm [16].

4   Experimental Results

In this section, we compare our proposed OGSC method with other state-of-the-art methods, such as K-means, Principal Component Analysis (PCA), NMF, Sparse Coding (SC) and GSC, on the Yale, ORL and Ferent face datsets. In our experiments, we use two common metrics, such as Accuracy (AC) and Normalized Mutual Information (NMI), to measure the quantitative performances of data representation methods.

4.1   Yale Face Dataset

The Yale face dataset includes 165 image samples from 15 individuals. In this experiment, we randomly sampled P categories images as the experimental sub-dataset to evaluate our proposed OGSC method. Each experiment was run ten times, and their average values were reported as the final results. Table 1 shows the results of five data representation methods on the Yale face dataset. It can be observed that our proposed OGSC method can achieve the best performance among all methods. The main reason is that our proposed OGSC method can capture the intrinsic structure of data by imposing the optimal graph regularizer on the model of sparse coding (Fig. 1).

Fig. 1. Some image samples from the Yale dataset

Table 1. The clustering performances on the Yale face dataset

P	AC						NMI					
	K-means	PCA	NMF	SC	GSC	OGSC	K-means	PCA	NMF	SC	GSC	OGSC
8	0.440	0.434	0.488	0.261	0.359	**0.489**	0.394	0.387	0.423	0.190	0.343	**0.430**
9	0.454	0.446	0.428	0.280	0.317	**0.469**	0.416	0.412	0.405	0.210	0.316	**0.428**
10	0.427	0.412	0.414	0.285	0.370	**0.455**	0.430	0.402	0.401	0.240	0.290	**0.437**
11	0.404	0.421	0.424	0.347	0.333	**0.444**	0.407	0.430	0.424	0.324	0.341	**0.455**
12	0.381	0.413	0.412	0.339	0.281	**0.437**	0.403	0.419	0.423	0.327	0.326	**0.458**
13	0.377	0.411	0.436	0.337	0.288	**0.450**	0.406	0.447	0.455	0.330	0.337	**0.475**
14	0.396	0.410	0.381	0.371	0.293	**0.425**	0.427	0.450	0.420	0.370	0.345	**0.458**
15	0.375	0.381	0.383	0.366	0.273	**0.428**	0.427	0.441	0.442	0.387	0.335	**0.466**
AVG	0.407	0.416	0.421	0.323	0.314	**0.450**	0.414	0.424	0.424	0.297	0.329	**0.451**

4.2 ORL Face Dataset

The ORL face dataset includes a total of 400 image samples from 40 individuals. Here, we adopted the similar experimental scheme to evaluate the proposed OGSC method. All methods were run ten times in each experiment, and then their average performances were recorded as the final results. The performances of different data representation methods on the ORL dataset are shown in Table 2. We can see that the AC and NMI of SC are superior to these of GSC. The results have demonstrated that the fixed graph regularization method cannot discover the intrinsic geometric structure in this dataset. It is worth noting that the proposed OGSC method consistently outperforms the other methods regardless of the values of samples classes P. The main reason is that our proposed OGSC method can effectively explore the geometric structure of data by constructing the optimal graph (Fig. 2).

Fig. 2. Some image samples from the ORL dataset

Table 2. The clustering performances on the ORL face dataset

P	AC						NMI					
	K-means	PCA	NMF	SC	GSC	OGSC	K-means	PCA	NMF	SC	GSC	OGSC
20	0.589	0.595	0.560	0.468	0.263	**0.605**	0.707	0.713	0.694	0.564	0.399	**0.719**
22	0.581	0.577	0.580	0.449	0.248	**0.588**	0.712	0.715	0.711	0.545	0.404	**0.725**
24	0.513	0.534	0.515	0.440	0.245	**0.543**	0.676	0.687	0.680	0.554	0.407	**0.695**
26	0.573	0.570	0.549	0.464	0.260	**0.621**	0.722	0.719	0.704	0.586	0.435	**0.731**
28	0.541	0.557	0.524	0.447	0.232	**0.592**	0.707	0.710	0.699	0.596	0.425	**0.719**
30	0.533	0.540	0.508	0.472	0.245	**0.560**	0.698	0.704	0.692	0.616	0.438	**0.707**
32	0.538	0.527	0.514	0.489	0.211	**0.561**	0.714	0.713	0.695	0.651	0.413	**0.719**
34	0.505	0.514	0.515	0.530	0.216	**0.547**	0.691	0.699	0.698	0.669	0.432	**0.714**
36	0.528	0.536	0.521	0.522	0.214	**0.567**	0.708	0.713	0.709	0.685	0.438	**0.717**
38	0.487	0.511	0.512	0.526	0.212	**0.546**	0.700	0.700	0.694	0.694	0.441	**0.710**
40	0.498	0.527	0.488	0.520	0.204	**0.533**	0.694	0.711	0.689	0.684	0.440	**0.712**
AVG	0.533	0.544	0.526	0.484	0.232	**0.569**	0.703	0.708	0.697	0.622	0.425	**0.715**

4.3 FERENT Face Dataset

The initial goal of the FERET face database is used for facial recognition system evaluation. It includes a total of 1400 face samples from 200 different individuals. Similarly, we carried out above experimental setting to evaluate all methods. The experimental results of all methods are shown in Table 3. Noting that the AC and NMI of the GSC method are 19.9% and 60.2%, respectively, and the AC and NMI of the SC method are 25.8% and 63.4%, respectively. It is clear that GSC cannot show the more superior performance in comparison to SC. This is because that the GSC method cannot explore the intrinsic structure information of data using the fixed graph regularizer on the FERENT dataset. Additionally, we can see that our proposed OGSC method achieves the best performance among all method, and thus has demonstrated its effectiveness (Fig. 3).

Fig. 3. Some image samples from the FERENT dataset

Table 3. The clustering performances on the FERENT face dataset

P	AC						NMI					
	K-means	PCA	NMF	SC	GSC	OGSC	K-means	PCA	NMF	SC	GSC	OGSC
80	0.285	0.281	0.270	0.282	0.207	**0.286**	0.600	0.610	0.599	0.614	0.571	**0.617**
100	0.271	0.272	0.262	0.280	0.199	**0.277**	0.604	0.612	0.601	0.626	0.577	**0.618**
120	0.260	0.246	0.257	0.25	0.203	**0.281**	0.613	0.619	0.602	0.625	0.593	**0.635**
140	0.262	0.265	0.247	0.259	0.206	**0.267**	0.617	0.627	0.611	0.638	0.611	**0.639**
160	0.254	0.257	0.232	0.247	0.196	**0.265**	0.621	0.632	0.612	0.638	0.612	**0.644**
180	0.247	0.248	0.240	0.243	0.195	**0.255**	0.626	0.632	0.623	0.647	0.623	**0.648**
200	0.254	0.253	0.233	0.245	0.184	**0.258**	0.640	0.649	0.628	0.649	0.626	**0.658**
AVG	0.262	0.260	0.259	0.258	0.199	**0.270**	0.617	0.626	0.611	0.634	0.602	**0.637**

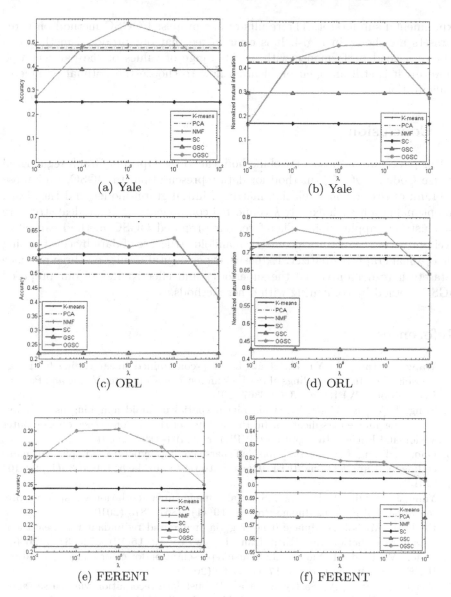

Fig. 4. The performances of all methods varied with different values of the parameter λ

4.4   The Analysis of the Parameters

Our proposed OGSC method includes three parameters λ, α and β. According to previous studies, we empirically set the values of the sparse term parameter α and β as 0.1 and 1, respectively. Therefore, we only carried out the experiments to investigate the impact of the regularization parameters λ due to space limitation. Specifically, we randomly selected 8, 30, 120 categories samples as the experimental subdataset. The results of our proposed OGSC method on three datasets are shown in Fig. 4. It is clear to see that our proposed method can achieve a good performance with a wide range of values of the parameter λ. However, it is still an open problem on how to choose the optimal parameter configuration.

5   Conclusion

In this paper, we propose a novel method, called the Optimal Graph regularized Sparse Coding (OGSC), method for data representation. In OGSC, we impose the rank constraint on Laplacian matrix of initial graph model, and thus learn an optimal graph with exactly k connected components. It is an ideal structure for clustering applications. Therefore, our proposed OGSC method can effectively preserve the intrinsic geometric manifold structure of data by constructing the optimal graph regularizer. Extensive experimental results on three real face datasets have demonstrated the superiority and effectiveness of our proposed OGSC method by comparing with other methods.

References

1. Wang, J., Yang, J., Yu, K., et al.: Locality-constrained linear coding for image classification. In: Proceedings of IEEE Conference on Computer Vision and Pattern Recognition (CVPR), pp. 3360–3367 (2010)
2. Yang, J., Yu, K., Gong, Y., et al.: Linear spatial pyramid matching using sparse coding for image classification. In: Proceedings of IEEE Conference on Computer Vision and Pattern Recognition (CVPR), pp. 1794–1801 (2009)
3. Gao, S., Tsang, I., Chia, L.: Laplacian sparse coding, hypergraph Laplacian sparse coding, and applications. IEEE Trans. Pattern Anal. Mach. Intell. **35**(1), 92–104 (2013)
4. Yang, J., Wright, J., Huang, T.S., et al.: Image super-resolution via sparse representation. IEEE Trans. Image Process. **19**(11), 2861–2873 (2010)
5. Elad, M., Michal, A.: Image denoising via sparse and redundant representations over learned dictionaries. IEEE Trans. Image Process. **15**(12), 3736–3745 (2006)
6. Julien, M., Elad, M., Sapiro, G.: Sparse representation for color image restoration. IEEE Trans. Image Process. **17**(1), 53–69 (2008)
7. Wright, J., Yang, A., Sastry, S., et al.: Robust face recognition via sparse representation. IEEE Trans. Pattern Anal. Mach. Intell. **31**(2), 210–227 (2009)
8. Zheng, M., Bu, J., Chen, C., et al.: Graph regularized sparse coding for image representation. IEEE Trans. Image Process. **20**(5), 1327–1336 (2011)
9. Shu, Z., Wu, X., Hu, C.: Structure preserving sparse coding for data representation. Neural Process. Lett. **48**, 1–15 (2018)
10. Shu, Z., Zhou, J., Huang, P., et al.: Local and global regularized sparse coding for data representation. Neurocomputing **198**(29), 188–197 (2016)
11. Nie, F., Wang, X., Jordan, M.I., et al.: The constrained Laplacian rank algorithm for graph-based clustering. In: Thirtieth AAAI Conference on Artificial Intelligence. AAAI Press (2016)

12. Donoho, D.L.: For most large underdetermined systems of equations, the minimal 1-norm near-solution approximates the sparsest near-solution. Commun. Pure Appl. Math **59**(6), 797–829 (2006)
13. Cands, E., Romberg, J.: L1-magic: a collection of matlab routines for solving the convex optimization programs central to compressive sampling (2006). www.acm.caltech.edu/l1magic/
14. Saunders, M.: PDCO: primal-dual interior method for convex objectives (2002). http://www.stanford.edu/group/SOL/software/pdco.html
15. Lee, H., Battle, A., Raina, R., et al.: Efficient sparse coding algorithms. In: Proceedings of the Advances Neural Information Processing Systems, vol. 20, pp. 801–808 (2007)
16. Huang, J., Nie, F., Huang, H.: A new simplex sparse learning model to measure data similarity for clustering. In: Proceedings of the 24th International Conference on Artificial Intelligence, pp. 3569–3575 (2015)

Robust Embedding Regression
for Face Recognition

Jiaqi Bao[1], Jianglin Lu[1(✉)], Zhihui Lai[1,2], Ning Liu[1], and Yuwu Lu[1]

[1] College of Computer Science and Software Engineering, Shenzhen University,
Shenzhen 518060, China
1419465415@qq.com
[2] Institute of Textiles & Clothing, Hong Kong Polytechnic University,
Kowloon, Hong Kong

Abstract. Classical subspace learning methods such as spectral regression (SR) and its sparse extensions are all two-step ways, which will lead to a suboptimal subspace for feature extraction. Another potential drawback is that these methods are not robust to the outliers and the variations of data because they use Frobenius norm as the basic distance metric. To address these problems, a novel face recognition method called robust embedding regression (RER) is proposed, which performs low-dimensional embedding and jointly sparse regression simultaneously. By this way, the optimal subspace can be obtained. Besides, we not only emphasize $L_{2,1}$-norm minimization on both loss function and regularization terms, but also use $L_{2,1}$-norm as the basic distance metric. Therefore, we can obtain jointly sparse projections in the regression process and more stable and robust low-dimensional reconstruction in the embedding process. Moreover, we use a more generalized constraint to improve the generalization of RER. The corresponding optimal solution can be computed by generalized eigen-decomposition via an iterative optimization algorithm. Theoretical analysis and experimental results prove the convergence of RER. Extensive experiments show the proposed RER has a better performance than other related methods on four well-known datasets.

Keywords: Robust low-dimensional embedding · Jointly sparse projection · Subspace learning · Face recognition

1 Introduction

In the past few decades, a family of linear subspace learning methods were proposed for face recognition. The traditional methods include principal component analysis (PCA) [1], linear discriminant analysis (LDA) [2], locality preserving projection (LPP) [3], neighborhood preserving embedding (NPE) [4] and marginal fisher analysis (MFA) [5]. However, these classical methods usually involve eigen-decomposition of dense matrix, which is time-consuming in face recognition task. To address this problem, spectral regression (SR) [6] was proposed for efficient regularized subspace learning, which casts the problem of learning the projection functions into a regression framework and thus avoid expensive computational consumption.

© Springer Nature Switzerland AG 2019
Z. Lin et al. (Eds.): PRCV 2019, LNCS 11858, pp. 102–113, 2019.
https://doi.org/10.1007/978-3-030-31723-2_9

Recently, sparse subspace learning methods, which imposes L_1-norm penalty (or elastic net penalty [7]) on the regularization, have attracted great attention in pattern recognition. The representative methods include sparse PCA (SPCA) [8], sparse discriminant analysis (SDA) [9] and sparse linear embedding (SLE) [10]. A unified sparse method called unified sparse subspace learning (USSL) [11] is also proposed, which extends SR to sparse case by exploiting elastic net penalty. The remarkable advantage of sparse subspace learning is that most of elements of the learned projection matrix are zero. Therefore, the sparse projection can provide interpretability on which feature are more significant for face recognition.

However, the projections learned by L_1-norm penalty are not jointly sparse, which indicates that the selected features are independent and generally different for each dimension of the subspace [12]. To this end, a larger number of $L_{2,1}$-norm based methods were proposed, such as robust feature selection (RFS) [13], joint feature selection and subspace learning (FSSL) [12], minimum redundancy spectral feature selection (MRSF) [14], global and local structure preservation feature selection (GLSPFS) [15] and joint embedding learning and sparse regression (JELSR) [16]. Nevertheless, there is a potential drawback of these $L_{2,1}$-norm based methods. That is, they all use Frobenius norm as the basic distance metric to preserve the low-dimensional intrinsic structure. As it is mentioned in [17], using $L_{2,1}$-norm as the basic metric can enhance the robustness. Therefore, some related methods are proposed, such as robust discriminant regression (RDR) [17], low-rank linear embedding (LRLE) [18] and generalized robust regression (GRR) [19].

As mentioned above, SR is an efficient method for subspace learning. Although its sparse extension USSL can obtain sparse projection, they are both two-step methods and not robust to outliers and the variations of data. In this paper, a novel face recognition method called robust embedding regression (RER) is proposed, which solves the problems in SR and its sparse extensions. The main contributions of this paper include: (1) Motivated by RDR, we proposed a novel robust subspace learning method for face recognition, which performs robust low-dimensional embedding and jointly sparse projection learning simultaneously by exploiting $L_{2,1}$-norm as the basic distance metric and the regularization penalty. An iterative algorithm corresponding to the proposed method is also presented, (2) Theoretical analysis proves the convergence of RER and experimental result indicates that the iterative algorithm converges fast, (3) Extensive experiments show that the proposed method has a significantly better performance than other related methods on four well-known datasets.

2   Notation and Definition

In this section, we first give some notations and definitions used in this paper. Then we will briefly review some related works including SR, USSL and JELSR, and then discuss the potential drawbacks of these works which inspire us to develop RER approach.

In this paper, the matrix $X = [x_1, x_2, \ldots, x_n]^T \in \mathbb{R}^{nxd}$ is defined as the data matrix including all training samples in its rows, where n is the number of training samples and d is the feature dimension. In real world task, d is usually very high which leads to high computational and memory consumption. To this end, dimensionality reduction methods are designed to find an optimal projection matrix $W = [w_1, w_2, \ldots, w_d]^T \in \mathbb{R}^{dxc}$ so as to transform the original data into a c dimensional subspace, where $c \ll d$.

Let ϕ_{ij} denotes the element in the ith row and jth column of matrix $\Phi \in \mathbb{R}^{n \times d}$, and ϕ^i denotes the ith row vector of Φ, then the definition of $L_{2,1}$-norm of matrix Φ is defined as

$$\|\Phi\|_{2,1} = \sum_{i=1}^{n} \sqrt{\sum_{j=1}^{d} \phi_{ij}^2} = \sum_{i=1}^{n} \|\phi^i\|_2 \tag{1}$$

3   Robust Embedding Regression

In this section, a novel face recognition method called robust embedding regression (RER) is first proposed and its optimal solution is also presented. Then, theoretical analysis on the convergence of RER is discussed.

3.1   Motivation

As discussed above, the projections learned by SR are not sparse. Hence, it cannot provide the interpretability on which feature is more important for recognition tasks. Subsequently, the sparse extension of SR, i.e. USSL, is proposed for unified sparse subspace learning. Although USSL can provide sparse projections for interpretability, it is also a two-step method. Therefore, these two methods both separate the low-dimensional embedding and projection learning, which will lead to bigger approximation error [10] and the performance is largely determined by the effectiveness of graph construction [16]. To this end, a joint method, i.e. JELSR, is proposed to jointly perform the low-dimensional embedding and sparse regression. However, a potential drawback of JELSR is that only the regularization term uses $L_{2,1}$-norm for sparse projection, while the low-dimensional embedding and regression terms still use Frobenius norm as the basic distance metric. Therefore, JELSR is not robust to outliers and data's variations. To address these problems, we propose a novel method in the next section.

3.2   The Objective Function of RER

In this section, we would like to propose a more robust method for face recognition. First, we construct a neighborhood graph $G\{S, X\}$ as in SR, where X denotes the training data and S denotes the similarity of each pair data. Motivated by RFS [20], which imposes $L_{2,1}$-norm penalty on both regression and regularization terms to get robust projections, we take the following optimization problem into consideration:

$$\min_{Y,W} \sum_{i \neq j} \left\| y_i - y_j \right\|_2^2 S_{ij} + \alpha \| Y - XW \|_{2,1} + \beta \| W \|_{2,1} \quad s.t. \, Y^T Y = I \qquad (2)$$

where α and β are two balance parameters, $Y = [y_1, y_2, \cdots, y_n]^T \in \mathbb{R}^{n \times c}$ is the low-dimensional representation of original data X, W is the projection matrix, I denotes the identity matrix, and $\| \bullet \|_{2,1}$ denotes the $L_{2,1}$-norm as defined in Sect. 2.

Apparently, the low-dimensional embedding term of (2) still uses Frobenius norm of Euclidean distance as the basic distance metric, which will increase the impact of outliers and data's variations in the embedding process. Inspired by [17], we exploit the merits of $L_{2,1}$-norm to lower the impact of outliers when perform low-dimensional reconstruction. Therefore, we obtain the following optimization problem:

$$\min_{Y,W} \sum_{i \neq j} \left\| y_i - y_j \right\|_{2,1} S_{ij} + \alpha \| Y - XW \|_{2,1} + \beta \| W \|_{2,1} \quad s.t. \, Y^T Y = I \qquad (3)$$

Furthermore, we consider using a more generalized constrains for face recognition. Then, the objective function of the proposed RER can be presented as

$$\min_{Y,W} \sum_{i \neq j} \left\| y_i - y_j \right\|_{2,1} S_{ij} + \alpha \| Y - XW \|_{2,1} + \beta \| W \|_{2,1} \quad s.t. \, Y^T DY = I \qquad (4)$$

where D is a diagonal matrix as defined in Sect. 3.3. As such, with the generalized constraint, the manifold structure and the data's distribution in each neighborhood can be fully considered for low-dimensional embedding.

As we can see from (4), the first term is designed for robust low-dimensional embedding to preserve the intrinsic local geometric structure of original data. The second term aims at projection learning via linear approximation to the nonlinear mappings and the last term is to get the jointly sparse projections by imposing $L_{2,1}$-norm penalty. As there are two variables in (4), it is difficult to obtain the optimal solution directly. Therefore, we provide an iterative algorithm to optimize the above objective function, which is represented in the next section.

3.3 The Optimal Solution

According to the definition of $L_{2,1}$-norm, we first define three diagonal matrices U_1, U_2 and U_3 as

$$U_1^{ij} = 1/(2 \| y_i - y_j \|_2 + \xi), \, U_2^{ii} = 1/(2 \| (Y - XW)^i \|_2 + \xi), \, U_3^{ii} = 1/(2 \| B^i \|_2 + \xi)$$
$$(5)$$

where $(\Theta)^i$ denotes the ith column of Θ and ξ is a very small constant to avoid the case where the denominator is zero. Then the optimization problem (4) can be reformulated as follows:

$$\min_{Y^T D^p Y=I,W} \sum_{i \neq j} tr(y_i - y_j)^T U_1 S_{ij}(y_i - y_j) + tr\{\alpha[(Y - XW)^T U_2(Y - XW)] + \beta(W^T U_3 W)\}$$

$$\Leftrightarrow \min_{Y^T D^p Y=I,W} \sum_{i \neq j} tr(y_i^T U_1 S_{ij} y_i - 2y_j^T U_1 S_{ij} y_i + y_j^T U_1 S_{ij} y_j)$$

$$+ tr\{\alpha(Y^T U_2 Y - 2W^T X^T U_2 Y + W^T X^T U_2 XW) + \beta(W^T U_3 W)\} \tag{6}$$

Let $F = U_1 \odot S$ and diagonal matrix $D_{ii} = \sum_j F_{ij}$, where $\odot$ denotes the matrix element wise multiplication. Then (6) can be rewritten as

$$\min_{Y^T D^p Y=I,W} tr[Y^T(2D - 2F + \alpha U_2)Y - 2\alpha W^T X^T U_2 Y + W^T(\alpha X^T U_2 X + \beta U_3)W]$$

$$\Leftrightarrow \min_{Y^T D^p Y=I,W} tr[Y^T GY - 2\alpha W^T X^T U_2 Y + W^T(\alpha X^T U_2 X + \beta U_3)W] \tag{7}$$

where $G = 2D - 2F + \alpha U_2$.

For given matrix Y, take the derivative of (7) with respect to W and set it to zero, then we obtain:

$$W = \alpha(\alpha X^T U_2 X + \beta U_3)^{-1} X^T U_2 Y = \alpha A^{-1} X^T U_2 Y \tag{8}$$

where $A = \alpha X^T U_2 X + \beta U_3$.

For given matrix W, substitute (8) back to (7), then we get the following problem:

$$\min_{Y^T D^p Y=I} tr[Y^T GY - 2\alpha^2 Y^T U_2 XA^{-1} X^T U_2 Y + \alpha^2 Y^T U_2 XA^{-1} X^T U_2 Y]$$

$$\Leftrightarrow \min_{Y^T D^p Y=I} tr[Y^T(G - \alpha^2 U_2 XA^{-1} X^T U_2)Y] \tag{9}$$

It is easy to see that, the minimization problem (9) is equivalent to the following maximum problem:

$$\max_Y tr[Y^T(\alpha^2 U_2 XA^{-1} X^T U_2 - G)Y] \quad s.t. \, Y^T DY = I \tag{10}$$

Apparently, the optimal value of the optimization problem (10) can be obtained by addressing the following generalized eigen problem:

$$(\alpha^2 U_2 XA^{-1} X^T U_2 - G)y = \lambda Dy \tag{11}$$

The eigenvectors corresponding to the first c largest eigenvalues are selected and used as the optimal solution of Y. Details of the iterative algorithm can be seen in Table 1.

3.4   Convergence

In this section, we give the proof of the convergence of our RER method. Before the proof, we have the following lemma:

Lemma 1. [20] For any nonzero vectors a and b, the following inequality holds:

$$\|a\| - \|a\|^2/2\|b\| \le \|b\| - \|b\|^2/2\|b\| \tag{12}$$

From Lemma 1, we have the following theorem.

Theorem 1. The iterative algorithm in Table 1 will decrease the value of objective function (7) monotonically and provide a local optimal solution.

Proof. For convenience, we denote the tth iteration of (7) as $G(W^t, Y^t, U_1^t, U_2^t, U_3^t)$. Since $W^{t+1} = \alpha A^{-1} X^T U_2 Y^t$ minimizes the objective function value, we have

$$G(W^{t+1}, Y^t, U_1^t, U_2^t, U_3^t) \le G(W^t, Y^t, U_1^t, U_2^t, U_3^t) \tag{13}$$

Since Y^{t+1} is the optimal value of the eigenfunction (11), we further have

$$G(W^{t+1}, Y^{t+1}, U_1^t, U_2^t, U_3^t) \le G(W^t, Y^t, U_1^t, U_2^t, U_3^t) \tag{14}$$

For convenience, we further denote $m_{ij} = y_i - y_j$ and $N = Y - XW$, then we have

$$\sum_{i \neq j} tr\left(m_{ij}^{t+1^T} U_1^t S_{ij} m_{ij}^{t+1} \right) + tr\left[\alpha \left(N^{t+1^T} U_2^t N^{t+1} \right) + \beta \left(W^{t+1^T} U_3^t W^{t+1} \right) \right]$$

$$\le \sum_{i \neq j} tr\left(m_{ij}^{t^T} U_1^t S_{ij} m_{ij}^t \right) + tr\left[\alpha \left(N^{t^T} U_2^t N^t \right) + \beta \left(W^{t^T} U_3^t W^t \right) \right] \tag{15}$$

That is,

$$\sum_{i \neq j} \frac{\left\| \sqrt{S_{ij}} m_{ij}^{t+1} \right\|_2^2}{2 \left\| \sqrt{S_{ij}} m_{ij}^t \right\|_2} + \alpha \sum_i \frac{\|N_i^{t+1}\|_2^2}{2\|N_i^t\|_2} + \beta \sum_i \frac{\|W_i^{t+1}\|_2^2}{2\|W_i^t\|_2} \le \sum_{i \neq j} \frac{\left\| \sqrt{S_{ij}} m_{ij}^t \right\|_2^2}{2 \left\| \sqrt{S_{ij}} m_{ij}^t \right\|_2} + \alpha \sum_i \frac{\|N_i^t\|_2^2}{2\|N_i^t\|_2} + \beta \sum_i \frac{\|W_i^t\|_2^2}{2\|W_i^t\|_2}$$
$$\tag{16}$$

From lemma 1, we have

$$\sum_{i \neq j} \left(\left\| \sqrt{S_{ij}} m_{ij}^{t+1} \right\|_2 - \frac{\left\| \sqrt{S_{ij}} m_{ij}^{t+1} \right\|_2^2}{2 \left\| \sqrt{S_{ij}} m_{ij}^t \right\|_2} \right) + \alpha \sum_i \left(\|N_i^{t+1}\|_2 - \frac{\|N_i^{t+1}\|_2^2}{2\|N_i^t\|_2} \right) + \beta \sum_i \left(\|W_i^{t+1}\|_2 - \frac{\|W_i^{t+1}\|_2^2}{2\|W_i^t\|_2} \right)$$

$$\le \sum_{i \neq j} \left(\left\| \sqrt{S_{ij}} m_{ij}^t \right\|_2 - \frac{\left\| \sqrt{S_{ij}} m_{ij}^t \right\|_2^2}{2 \left\| \sqrt{S_{ij}} m_{ij}^t \right\|_2} \right) + \alpha \sum_i \left(\|N_i^t\|_2 - \frac{\|N_i^t\|_2^2}{2\|N_i^t\|_2} \right) + \beta \sum_i \left(\|W_i^t\|_2 - \frac{\|W_i^t\|_2^2}{2\|W_i^t\|_2} \right)$$
$$\tag{17}$$

According to (16) and (17), we get the following inequality:

$$\sum_{i \neq j} \left\| \sqrt{S_{ij}} m_{ij}^{t+1} \right\|_{2,1} + \sum_{i} \left(\alpha \left\| N_i^{t+1} \right\|_{2,1} + \beta \left\| W_i^{t+1} \right\|_{2,1} \right)$$
$$\leq \sum_{i \neq j} \left\| \sqrt{S_{ij}} m_{ij}^{t} \right\|_{2,1} + \sum_{i} \left(\alpha \left\| N_i^{t} \right\|_{2,1} + \beta \left\| W_i^{t} \right\|_{2,1} \right)$$

(18)

That shows the following result:

$$G(W^{t+1}, Y^{t+1}, U_1^{t+1}, U_2^{t+1}, U_3^{t+1}) \leq G(W^t, Y^t, U_1^t, U_2^t, U_3^t)$$

(19)

The inequality (19) demonstrates our algorithm decreases monotonically and since $G(W^t, Y^t, U_1^t, U_2^t, U_3^t)$ is bounded, it will converge to the local optimal solution. ∎

Table 1. The iterative algorithm of RER

Input: Training samples X, affinity matrix W, the dimension of subspace c, parameters α and β, the maximum number of the iterations $Step$.

Output: Projection matrix B.

Step 1: Initialize Y, U_1 randomly, set W as a zero matrix, U_2, U_3, I as an identity matrix

Step 2: While $ite < Step$

　　　　-Set $ite = ite + 1$

　　　　-Update F using $F = U_1 \odot S$.

　　　　-Update D using $D_{ii} = \sum_j F_{ij}$.

　　　　-Compute W using $W = \alpha (\alpha X^T U_2 X + \beta U_3)^{-1} X^T U_2 Y$.

　　　　-Compute Y **by solving the generalized eigenproblem (11).**

　　　　-Update U_1 using $U_1^{ij} = 1/(2\|y_i - y_j\|_2 + \xi)$.

　　　　-Update U_2 using $U_2^{ii} = 1/(2\|(Y - XW)^i\|_2 + \xi)$.

　　　　-Update U_3 using $U_3^{ii} = 1/(2\|B^i\|_2 + \xi)$.

　　End

---

4 Experiments

In this section, we test the proposed method on several well-known face datasets and the experimental results are presented. For comparison, the classical manifold-learning based methods LPP [3], NPE [4], the $L_{2,1}$-norm based methods UDFS [21], RDR [17], JELSR [16], RIPCA [22], the Uncorrelated Regression with Adaptive graph for unsupervised Feature Selection (URAFS) [23] method and the low-rank linear embedding (LRLE) [18] method are selected to compare with the proposed RER method. For all the manifold-learning based methods, the affinity matrix S was constructed by an unsupervised method and the number of nearest neighbor points was set to the same.

(a)   (b)   (c)   (d)

Fig. 1. Face Samples on (a) YaleB, (b) FERET, (c) AR, (d) PIE datasets

4.1 Details of Face Datasets

The **YaleB** dataset contains 16,128 images of 38 individuals. We select a subset of the YaleB dataset with frontal pose and different illumination. By this way, there are 2414 images in total and each image is cropped to 32*32 pixels. A subset of the **FERET** dataset used in our experiments includes 1400 images of 200 individuals. Each image in FERET dataset is cropped to 40*40 pixels. The subset of **AR** dataset has 2400 images of 120 individuals. Each image in AR dataset is resized to 50*40 pixels. The **PIE** dataset contains 41,368 images of 68 individuals and we choose a subset (C29) which includes 1632 images in our experiments. Each image in PIE dataset is resized to 32*32 pixels. Figure 1(a), (b), (c) and (d) show the sample images from these datasets.

4.2 Experimental Setting and Results

In our experiments, L samples of each class were selected randomly for training and the test samples were collected as the test set. In YaleB, FERET, AR and PIE datasets, $L = 20$, $L = 3, 4$, $L = 3, 4$ and $L = 8$, respectively. To obtain the stable and reliable results, all the experiments were independently performed ten times and the nearest neighbor classifier was used for classification. Then we obtained and presented the best average recognition rates. For computational efficiency, we first projected the original samples into the PCA subspace. The dimension in the low-dimensional subspace varied from 5 to 50 in FERET dataset, and from 5 to 100 in YaleB, AR and PIE datasets.

Table 2. Recognition accuracy (%), Standard Deviation, Dimension on FERET dataset

L	LPP	NPE	UDFS	RDR	JELSR	RIPCA	URAFS	LRLE	RER
3	62.85	63.35	72.75	68.13	73.55	73.66	74.49	73.55	**75.76**
	3.91	4.00	7.02	4.65	5.68	5.70	9.32	5.71	**7.36**
	50	50	50	50	50	50	50	50	**35**
4	77.22	77.73	82.07	79.02	81.97	82.17	82.90	82.12	**84.32**
	3.23	3.08	4.67	3.32	3.79	3.79	6.40	3.85	**4.96**
	50	50	50	50	45	45	50	45	**45**

Table 3. Recognition accuracy (%), Standard Deviation, Dimension on YaleB dataset

L	LPP	NPE	UDFS	RDR	JELSR	RIPCA	URAFS	LRLE	RER
20	76.04	63.68	64.14	66.59	64.08	64.30	81.84	64.35	**85.38**
	22.58	14.23	15.02	17.87	14.86	14.79	18.35	14.99	**17.85**
	100	100	100	100	100	100	100	100	**90**

The experimental results are reported in Tables 2, 3 and 4. Figure 2(a)–(d) show the variation of the average recognition rate versus the dimension in the subspace for all the methods. From the results, we know that the performance of RER obtains about 1.2%–21.7% improvements against other eight methods on four datasets. The reason is that RER performs robust low-dimensional embedding and jointly sparse projection alternately by exploiting $L_{2,1}$-norm as the basic distance metric and the regularization penalty. Therefore, the approximate error can be further reduced and the robustness of RER can be further improved. Besides, RER uses a more generalized constraint, by which the generalization performance can be further enhanced. Moreover, we can see from the Tables that all the sparse learning methods such as JELSR, LRLE obtain significantly higher recognition rates than non-sparse learning methods such as LPP, NPE on FERET and AR datasets. However, it is interesting that LPP has a better performance than these sparse learning methods except RER and URAFS on YaleB and PIE datasets.

As proved by theoretical analysis in previous section, the convergence of our algorithm is also verified in the experiments. Figure 3(c) shows the curve of the objective function value of RER on AR dataset. Apparently, our algorithm converges very fast, which indicates that RER is not a time-consuming method for face recognition (Table 5).

Table 4. Recognition accuracy (%), Standard Deviation, Dimension on AR dataset

L	LPP	NPE	UDFS	RDR	JELSR	RIPCA	URAFS	LRLE	RER
3	66.78	68.85	75.13	71.62	75.77	75.78	74.56	77.85	**83.85**
	10.71	12.14	12.44	8.53	8.38	8.41	16.76	8.99	**10.87**
	100	85	100	100	100	100	100	100	**70**
4	74.06	78.05	80.29	75.86	80.51	80.54	75.65	81.48	**87.39**
	9.70	9.64	9.27	7.67	7.88	7.88	15.50	8.57	**10.67**
	100	95	100	100	100	100	100	100	**85**

Table 5. Recognition accuracy (%), Standard Deviation, Dimension on PIE dataset

L	LPP	NPE	UDFS	RDR	JELSR	RIPCA	URAFS	LRLE	RER
8	89.33	89.36	86.03	87.75	86.18	86.24	90.96	86.28	**93.42**
	12.29	9.71	8.05	10.10	7.66	7.68	10.68	7.78	**8.04**
	100	100	100	100	100	100	100	100	**80**

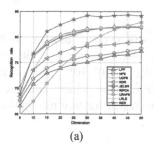
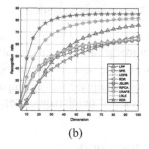

(a)   (b)

Fig. 2. Experimental results on the (a) FERET dataset (L = 4), (b) YaleB dataset (L = 20)

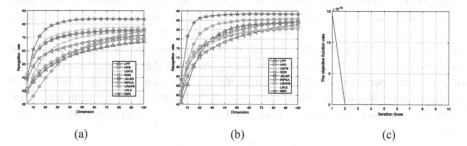

(a)   (b)   (c)

Fig. 3. Experimental results on the (a) AR dataset (L = 3), (b) PIE dataset (L = 8), (c) the objective function value versus the number of iterations on AR dataset

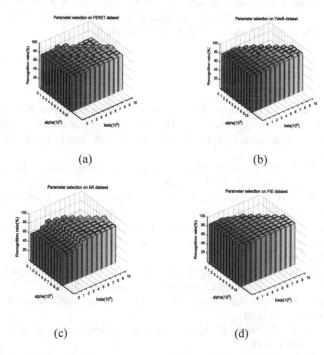

(a)   (b)

(c)   (d)

Fig. 4. The 2-D grid search of parameters α and β on (a) FERET dataset, (b) YaleB dataset, (c) AR dataset, (d) PIE dataset

4.3   Parameters Selection

In the literature, how to obtain the optimal parameter is still an open question. We find the optimal parameters empirically. Figure 4 shows the average recognition rate when the two balance parameters are both in the rage $\{10^0, 10^1, \cdots, 10^9, 10^{10}\}$. It is obvious that each parameter has an impact on the performance of RER, which indicates the regression and regularization terms in RER are both important for face recognition.

5   Conclusion

In this paper, a novel face recognition method called robust embedding regression (RER) is proposed, which integrates the advantages of manifold learning and jointly sparsity. Different from the two-step methods such as SR and its sparse extensions, RER performs robust low-dimensional embedding and jointly sparse projection simultaneously. Moreover, by exploiting the $L_{2,1}$-norm as the basic distance metric, the robustness and performance of RER can be further improved. Theoretical analysis and experimental results indicate the convergence of the proposed optimization algorithm. Extensive experiments on some well-known datasets show the superior performance of RER.

Acknowledgments. This work was supported in part by the Natural Science Foundation of China under Grant 61573248, Grant 61802267 and Grant 61732011, and in part by the Shenzhen Municipal Science and Technology Innovation Council under Grant JCYJ20180305124834854 and JCYJ20160429182058044, in part by the Natural Science Foundation of Guangdong Province (Grant 2017A030313367 and Grant 2016114162135515).

References

1. Turk, M., Pentland, A.: Eigenfaces for recognition. J. Cogn. Neurosci. **3**(1), 71–86 (1991)
2. Belhumeur, P., Hespanha, J., Kriengman, D.: Eigenfaces vs Fisherfaces: recognition using class specific linear projection. IEEE Trans. Pattern Anal. Mach. Intell. **19**(7), 711–720 (1997)
3. He, X., Yan, S., Hu, Y., Niyogi, P., Zhang, H.: Face recognition using Laplacianfaces. IEEE Trans. Pattern Anal. Mach. Intell. **27**(3), 328–340 (2005)
4. He, X., Cai, D., Yan, S., Zhang, H.: Neighborhood preserving embedding. In: 10th IEEE International Conference on Computer Vision, pp. 1208–1213 (2005)
5. Yan, S., Xu, D., Zhang, B., Zhang, H., Yang, Q., Lin, S.: Graph embedding and extensions: a general framework for dimensionality reduction. IEEE Trans. Pattern Anal. Mach. Intell. **29**(1), 40–51 (2007)
6. Cai, D., He, X., Han, J.: Spectral regression for efficient regularized subspace learning. In: 11th International Conference on Computer Vision, pp. 1–8 (2007)
7. Zou, H., Hastie, T.: Regularization and variable selection via the elastic net. J. R. Stat. Soc. Ser. B **67**(2), 301–320 (2005)
8. Zou, H., Hastie, T., Tibshirani, R.: Sparse principal component analysis. J. Comput. Graph. Stat. **15**(2), 265–286 (2006)

9. Clemmensen, L., Hastie, T., Witten, D., Ersbøll, B.: Sparse discriminant analysis. Technometrics **53**(4), 406–413 (2011)
10. Lai, Z., Wong, W., Xu, Y., Yang, J., Zhang, D.: Approximate orthogonal sparse embedding for dimensionality reduction. IEEE Trans. Neural Netw. Learn. Syst. **27**(4), 723–735 (2016)
11. Cai, D., He, X., Han, J.: Spectral regression: a unified approach for sparse subspace learning. In: 7th IEEE International Conference on Data Mining, pp. 73–82 (2007)
12. Gu, Q., Li, Z., Han, J.: Joint feature selection and subspace learning. In: International Joint Conference on Artificial Intelligence, pp. 1294–1299 (2011)
13. Nie, F., Huang, H., Cai, X., Chris, D.: Efficient and robust feature selection via joint L2,1 norms minimization. In: 23th Neural Information Processing Systems, pp 1813–1821 (2010)
14. Zheng, Z., Lei, W., Huan, L.: Efficient spectral feature selection with minimum redundancy. In: 24th AAAI Conference on Artificial Intelligent, pp 1–6 (2010)
15. Liu, X., Wang, L., Zhang, J., Yin, J., Liu, H.: Global and local structure preservation for feature selection. IEEE Trans. Neural Netw. Learn. Syst. **25**(6), 1083–1095 (2014)
16. Hou, C., Nie, F., Li, X., Yi, D., Wu, Y.: Joint embedding learning and sparse regression: a framework for unsupervised feature selection. IEEE Trans. Cybern. **44**(6), 793–804 (2014)
17. Lai, Z., Mo, D., Wong, W., Xu, Y., Miao, D., Zhang, D.: Robust discriminant regression for feature extraction. IEEE Trans. Cybern. **48**(8), 2472–2484 (2018)
18. Chen, Y., Lai, Z., Wong, W., Shen, L., Hu, Q.: Low-rank linear embedding for image recognition. IEEE Trans. Multimed. **20**(12), 3212–3222 (2018)
19. Lai, Z., Mo, D., Wen, J., Shen, L., Wong, W.: Generalized robust regression for jointly sparse subspace learning. IEEE Trans. Circuits Syst. Video Technol. **29**(3), 756–772 (2019)
20. Nie, F., Huang, H., Cai, X., Ding, C.: Efficient and robust feature selection via joint $\ell 2, 1$-norms minimization. In: Neural Information Processing Systems (2010)
21. Yang, Y., Shen, H., Ma, Z., Huang, Z., Zhou, X.: L2,1-norm regularized discriminative feature selection for unsupervised learning. In: International Joint Conference on Artificial Intelligence (2011)
22. Lai, Z., Xu, Y., Yang, J., Shen, L., Zhang, D.: Rotational invariant dimensionality reduction algorithms. IEEE Trans. Cybern. **47**(11), 3733–3746 (2017)
23. Li, X., Zhang, H., Zhang, R., Liu, Y., Nie, F.: Generalized uncorrelated regression with adaptive graph for unsupervised feature selection. IEEE Trans. Neural Netw. Learn. Syst. **30**, 1–9 (2018)

Deep Feature-Preserving Based Face Hallucination: Feature Discrimination Versus Pixels Approximation

Xiaoyu Zheng[1], Heng Liu[1(✉)], Jungong Han[2], and Shudong Hou[1]

[1] Anhui University of Technology, Maanshan, Anhui, China
zhengxiaoyu51888@163.com, hengliusky@aliyun.com, ice--book@163.com
[2] Lancaster University, Lancashire LA1 4YW, UK
jungonghan77@gmail.com

Abstract. Face hallucination aims to produce a high-resolution (HR) face image from an input low-resolution (LR) face image, which is of great importance for many practical face applications, such as face recognition and face verification. Since the structure features of face image is complex and sensitive, obtaining a super-resolved face image is more difficult than generic image super-resolution (SR). To address these limitations, we present a novel GAN (Generative adversarial network) based feature-preserving face hallucination approach for very low resolution (16 × 16 pixels) faces and large scale upsampling (8×). Specifically, we design a new residual structure based face generator and adopt two different discriminators - an image discriminator and a feature discriminator, to encourage the model to acquire more realistic face features rather than artifacts. The evaluations based on both PSNR and visual result reveal that the proposed model is superior to the state-of-the-art methods.

Keywords: GAN · Face hallucination · Feature discrimination

1 Introduction

Face hallucination, another name for face super-resolution, intended to restore a HR face image from a LR input face image, has attracted great interest in the past few years. Unlike a generic image SR, face hallucination is more difficult because of the complex structures and sensitive appearances in human face.

For single image super-resolution (SISR) task, the LR observed image y is usually generated from a HR x based on a degradation model, which can be formulated as follows:

$$y = (x * k) \downarrow_s + n, \tag{1}$$

The first autor is a postgraduate student.

© Springer Nature Switzerland AG 2019
Z. Lin et al. (Eds.): PRCV 2019, LNCS 11858, pp. 114–125, 2019.
https://doi.org/10.1007/978-3-030-31723-2_10

where k denotes a blur kernel (low pass filter), $*$ denotes the convolution operator, $\downarrow_s$ is a decimating (down-sampling) operator with factor s, n represents the noise model. Therefore, face hallucination is an inverse problem of face image degradation process, that is, given an input LR face image y, face hallucination aims at estimating the original HR face image x. It is actually an ill-posed problem because of the non-unique solution.

Most existing face hallucination approaches [5,8,12,13,17] are all based on deep Convolutional Neural Network (CNN), and these approaches try to minimize the MSE loss to push the hallucinated face close to the HR faces during the training phase. However, these approaches tend to generate blurry faces without high-frequency details. Several recent efforts [4,6,7,19–21,23] have been developed to deal with this issue by using generative adversarial network (GAN).

While GAN-based methods show significant improvements in perceived quality relative to previous methods, they typically produce meaningless high frequency noise in super-resolution images. Briefly, the face images produced by GAN contain a lot of artifacts.

In this work, we proposed a novel method (see in Fig. 1), which super-resolve a LR face to its 8× larger without taking other information into account. Our method consists of 4 connected components: a generator, a discriminator, an encoder, and a second discriminator. Our generative network comprises residual block and pixel-shuffle layer. It can upsample the resolutions of the feature maps by pixel-shuffle layer, at the same time, the details of the feature maps are restored by the residual blocks. Similar to [6,7,21], we not only employ the MSE loss between the hallucinated faces and the HR faces, but also use the adversarial loss. In order to overcome the limitation of previous GAN-based methods, we employ other discriminative network to distinguish SR faces from HR faces based on the feature map extracted from the encoder network. In this manner, the artifacts are greatly reduced and the SR faces are more realistic.

In summary, our contributions are:

- We propose a new GAN based deep architecture for super-resolving a very LR face to its 8× larger without using any prior information.
- We analysis in detail the effect of feature discrimination loss and pixels approximation loss on the performance of face hallucination, from both objective signal-to-noise ratio and subjective visual perception.
- Our proposed model achieves the state-of-the-art performance in PSNR and SSIM when compared to current existing methods.

2   Related Works

Face hallucination was originally proposed by Baker et al. [1]. Based on face image samples learning, Baker proposed to use multi-level Gaussian image pyramid model to predict the high-frequency components of the HR image. The basic idea of face samples learning based algorithm assumes there is a mathematical transformation or mapping between the LR and HR images of the faces and the purpose of training is just to mine the mapping function or transformation from the LR face samples to the HR face samples. Once the mapping function is acquired from the learning, it can be applied into the test LR face images to reconstruct the super-resolved face images.

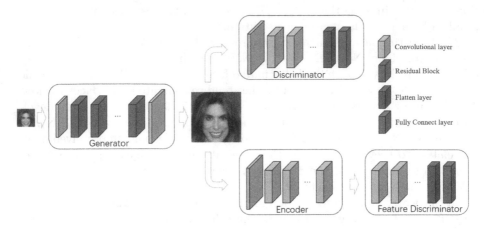

Fig. 1. Our proposed method contains 4 parts: the first is a residual-based super-resolution network, second is a discriminator used to distinguish between the hallucinated and the original HR faces. The third network is an encoder network used to encode the hallucinated and the original HR faces. The last network is a feature discriminator used to encourager the generator to produce more structural details rather than artifacts.

The recent work of [21] take GANs to get perceptually realistic face hallucination images, which can ultra-resolve a very low-resolution face image of size 16×16 pixels to its $8\times$ larger version. Based on boundary equilibrium generative adversarial networks (BEGAN [2]), Huang *et al.* [4] propose a new face hallucination method, named face conditional generative adversarial network (FCGAN). They claimed that without any facial prior information, their method can generate HR face images based on the corresponding LR images input.

Noting that the specific facial prior information will be beneficial to face SR, Bulat *et al.* [6] propose the first deep model to address face SR and face alignment at the same time, which can be called as Super-FAN. At the same time, Chen *et al.* [7] propose a novel end-to-end trainable face SR network (FSRNet) to super-resolve very low-resolution (LR) face images without alignment requirement.

Since the existing face hallucination methods do not consider the pose and the expression details, their super-resolved face images will always contain ambiguity semantic. To address these issues, in [20], Yu *et al.* propose a new model for face hallucination, which fully utilize facial attributes to preserve face detail features. In [23], the same authors proposed a two-step decoder-encoder-decoder network, it combines spatial transformer network to remove translation, scale and rotation misalignments. In [19], Yu *et al.* argue that most of the previous methods never consider facial structure and will lose effect when facing large pose variations.

They propose a new face SR method guided by facial component heatmaps (called FSRFCH). Their method uses not only low-level (image pixels) but also middle-level information (facial structure) to achieve better face hallucination results.

3   Proposed Method

In this section, we describe the proposed architecture comprising of 4 connected networks: the first network is a super-resolution network used to super-resolve the LR faces. The second network is a discriminator used to distinguish between the hallucinated and the original HR faces. The third network is an encoder network used to encode the hallucinated and the original HR faces. The last network is a feature discriminator used to encourage the generator to produce more structural details rather than artifacts. Note that only the generator is used at test time.

3.1   Super-Resolution Network

In this section, we propose a new residual-based super-resolution network which is inspired by [14] and [16], our network as shown in Fig. 2. Following recent work [7, 19–21, 23], the resolution of input faces and output faces are 16×16 and 128×128, respectively. Compare to [14], our super-resolution network uses 10 residual blocks, 3 pixel shuffle layers to obtain $8\times$ larger faces. And the big difference with [14] is that our network only learns the residual image by adding the bicubic interpolation of LR faces to the network's output. Following [14], applying this approach could help us stabilize training and reduce color shift during the training phase.

Another difference with [14] is that we change the order of residual blocks and pixel shuffle layers. In [14], Ledig et al. first use 16 residual blocks work at the input faces resolution (i.e. 16×16), then they use 2 pixel shuffle layers to get

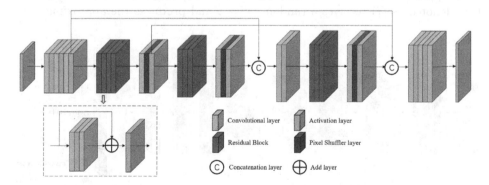

Fig. 2. Our super-resolution network which only learns the residual knowledge between the bicubic interpolation of LR faces and the corresponding HR faces.

4× larger hallucinated faces. But we first use 4 residual blocks and a pixel shuffle layer to obtain 2× larger residual features. Then we apply 3 residual blocks and another pixel shuffle layer, finally we apply other 3 residual blocks and third pixel shuffle layer to get the 8× larger residual faces. The motivation of our decision is that using 2 pixel shuffle layers after 16 residual blocks is infeasible, and cannot get a sharp detail for hallucinated faces.

Pixel-Wise ℓ_2 Loss. Given a LR face I_{LR} and its corresponding HR face I_{HR}, we use the MSE loss to minimize the distance between the hallucinated face and the HR face. The loss function of MSE loss is denoted as:

$$\ell_{mse} = \mathbb{E}_{I_{LR} \sim P_L(l), I_{HR} \sim P_H(h)} ||G(I_{LR}) - I_{HR}||_F^2, \tag{2}$$

where $|| \cdot ||_F^2$ means the Frobenius norm, $P_L(l)$ represents the distribution of the LR face images, $P_H(h)$ represents the distribution of the real HR face image, and $G(I_{LR})$ is the generated HR face image by our super-resolution network.

Perceptual Loss. Following [6,7,14,22], we also use perceptual loss to obtain a sharp detail for super-resolved ultrasound images. Different to MSE loss, we first map $G(I_{LR})$ and I_{HR} into feature space by using a function $\phi(\cdot)$, then we calculate the distance between them. So, the loss function of perceptual loss is denoted as:

$$\ell_{vgg} = \mathbb{E}_{I_{LR} \sim P_L(l), I_{HR} \sim P_H(h)} ||\phi(G(I_{LR})) - \phi(I_{HR})||_F^2, \tag{3}$$

For the function $\phi(\cdot)$, we use a combination of the first, second and third convolution layers from the popular VGG-19 [18] network. Thus, we can get both low-level and high-level feature.

3.2 Discriminative Network

Recently, with great success in high-level face recognition task, deep learning methods, especially generative adversarial networks (GANs [9]), have also been applied to low-level face hallucination. In the original GAN, the generator (denoted as G) receives a random noise z and produces the approximation

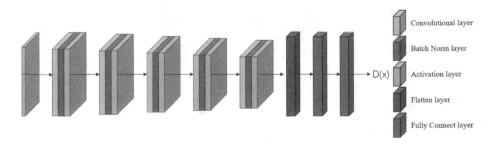

Fig. 3. Our discriminative network is inspired by [23], and is made up of convolutional layer, batch normalization layer and fully connect layer.

image of the real data, denoted as $G(z)$. The discriminator D tries to distinguish the real data from the synthesized data, and the generator G tries to fool the discriminator.

In our work, we did not try to improve GAN itself, we just applied the latest GAN architecture (RSGAN [11]) to our model. Our discriminative network is inspired by [23], but we did not use max pooling layer. The discriminative network is shown in Fig. 3.

Adversarial Loss. Following [11], our super-resolution network tries to minimize:

$$\ell_{adv} = -\mathbb{E}_{I_{LR} \sim P_L(l), I_{HR} \sim P_H(h)}[log(sigmoid(D(G(I^{LR})) - D(I^{HR})))], \quad (4)$$

where the discriminator minimizes:

$$\ell_{dis} = -\mathbb{E}_{I_{LR} \sim P_L(l), I_{HR} \sim P_H(h)}[log(sigmoid(D(I^{HR}) - D(G(I^{LR}))))]. \quad (5)$$

3.3   Encoder Network

Typically, we use MSE loss, perceptual loss and adversarial loss to force the generated faces to approximate high-resolution faces at the pixel levels. However, this will lose some detailed features in the generated faces, and even generate wrong faces. To address this problem, we employ an encoder network, which aims to improve perceptual quality, and also to force the generated faces and high-resolution faces to be consistent at the feature level.

In our work, we just employ a simple network, which is the encoder of a Face Autoencoder (FAE). The encoder network is shown in Fig. 4.

Encoder Loss. Given a LR face I_{LR} and its corresponding HR face I_{HR}, we use the MSE loss to minimize the feature distance between the hallucinated face and the HR face. The loss function of encoder loss is denoted as:

$$\ell_{enc} = \mathbb{E}_{I_{LR} \sim P_L(l), I_{HR} \sim P_H(h)}||E(G(I_{LR})) - E(I_{HR})||_F^2, \quad (6)$$

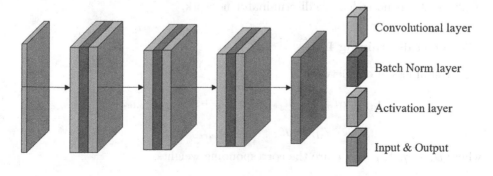

Fig. 4. Our encoder network has only 3 convolution layers, its role is to extract the features from the HR and the hallucinated faces.

where $E(\cdot)$ denotes encoder network.

3.4   Feature Discriminative Network

The conventional GAN architecture is made up of a generator and a discriminator, but we use 2 discriminators: an image discriminator and a feature discriminator. The feature discriminator receives feature maps from the encoder network, and its main role is to generate more feature details on the super-resolution faces rather than noisy artifacts. The feature discriminator network is shown in Fig. 5.

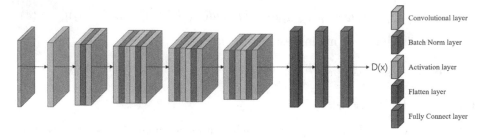

Fig. 5. Our feature discriminative network is modified from SRGAN [14], which receives the feature inputs from the encoder network.

Feature Adversarial Loss. Following [11], our super-resolution network tries to minimize:

$$\ell_{feature\_adv} = -\mathbb{E}_{I_{LR} \sim P_L(l), I_{HR} \sim P_H(h)}[log(sigmoid(FD(G(I^{LR})) - FD(I^{HR})))], \tag{7}$$

where the discriminator minimizes:

$$\ell_{feature\_dis} = -\mathbb{E}_{I_{LR} \sim P_L(l), I_{HR} \sim P_H(h)}[log(sigmoid(FD(I^{HR}) - FD(G(I^{LR}))))]. \tag{8}$$

where $FD(\cdot)$ denotes feature discriminator network.

3.5   Overall Training Loss

The overall loss of our network is

$$\mathcal{L}_G = \alpha \ell_{mse} + \beta \ell_{perc} + \gamma \ell_{adv} + \lambda \ell_{feature\_adv}, \tag{9}$$

$$\mathcal{L}_D = \mu \ell_{dis} + \nu \ell_{feature\_dis}. \tag{10}$$

where α, β, γ, λ, μ and ν are the corresponding weights.

4   Experiments

We trained our model using rmsprop with the learning rate of 0.0002, and it spend about 3 h for all methods with the machine which have one NVIDIA TITAN X GPU. We report results for the method of [7,10,21], called FSRGAN, UR-DGN and Wavelet-SRNet, respectively, and for the standard baseline based on bicubic interpolation. The source code and the model can be downloaded at Github.[1]

4.1   Training Protocol

Dataset. We trained our model on the celebrity face attributes (CelebA) dataset [15]. There are more than 200k images in this dataset, but only 20k images are used. We first crop faces from all 20k images, then resize them to 128×128 pixels. The first 18k face images are used for training and another 2k images are actually used for performance testing.

Faces Setting. We downsample the HR faces to 16×16 pixels. The input and output image were 16×16 pixels and 128×128 pixels, respectively. Same as [4,6,7,21], the RGB images are used during the training and inference phase.

Model Variants. Here, we present a number of model variant networks, in which the different components used are listed in Table 1. The equations involved in the variants are described in the following.

Table 1. The information of the component used by variant networks.

Network	Generator	Discriminator	Encoder	Feature discriminator
Our-generator	✓			
Our-GAN	✓	✓		
Our-GAN-encoder	✓	✓	✓	
Our-full	✓	✓	✓	✓

– Our-generator: this is the super-resolution network of Subsect. 3.1 trained with the pixel loss of Eq. 1.
– Our-GAN: this improves upon generator by adding the perceptual loss and adversarial loss of Eqs. 2, 3 and 4.
– Our-GAN-Encoder: this improves upon GAN by adding the encoder loss of Eq. 5.
– Our-full: this improves upon GAN-Encoder by adding the feature adversarial loss of Eqs. 6 and 7.

---

[1] https://github.com/hengliusky/Feature-preserving-Based-Face-Hallucination.

Table 2. The information of the component used by variant networks.

Method	Bicubic	UR-DGN	FSRGAN	Wavelet-SRNet	Our-generator	Our-GAN	Our-GAN-Encoder	Our-full
PSNR	23.3289	24.7250	25.2000	25.7428	**26.5810**	25.8682	25.8196	25.7506
SSIM	0.6652	0.6926	0.7023	0.7492	**0.7666**	0.7298	0.7297	0.7253

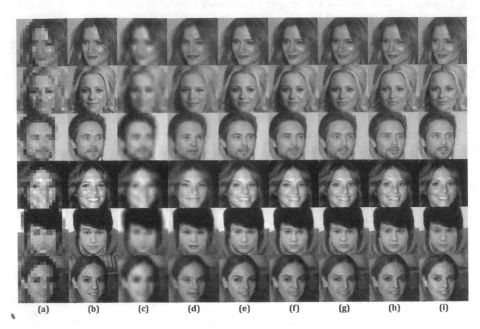

(a)   (b)   (c)   (d)   (e)   (f)   (g)   (h)   (i)

Fig. 6. The visual results on CelebA. (a) The LR faces. (b) The HR faces. (c) Bicubic interpolation. (d) Results of UR-DGN. (e) Results of Wavelet-SRNet. (f) Results of our-generator. (g) Results of our-GAN. (h) Results of our-GAN-Encoder. (i) Results of our-full.

5   Experimental Results and Analysis

In this section, we compare our methods with the state-of-the- art face SR methods. We now report the visual results in Fig. 5, and the quantitative results in Table 2.

In terms of PSNR and SSIM, the best results are achieved by Our-generator method. From these numbers, it is hard to conclude which method is the best. Visually inspecting the super-resolution images through Fig. 6 clearly shows that the shaper and more realistic faces are produced by Our-full method.

When only MSE is used as our loss function, as shown in Fig. 6(f), the faces generated by Our-generator are too blurry. However, when the adversarial loss is added, as shown in Fig. 6(d), the model generates more artifacts.

In terms of image quality, the difference between Fig. 6(g) and (h) is not large. This is because the network structure of Ours-GAN and Ours-GAN-Encoder is very similar. The former uses VGG-19 to extract the features from hallucinated face and HR face and calculate the perceptual loss. The latter we use Encoder network to extract features and Calculating Encoder loss, from this point of view, Encoder loss is also a perceptual loss.

As shown in Fig. 6(i), our feature adversarial loss suppresses noisy high frequencies, while generating perceptually plausible structured textures. In other words, our results have naturally synthesized sharp details without blurriness or high-frequency artifacts thanks to our feature adversarial loss.

6   Conclusion and Future Work

In this paper, we have proposed a novel face super-resolution method with $8\times$ upscaling factors. Our method is an end-to-end framework, and it is employed by 2 discriminators: an image discriminator and a feature discriminator. Especially, the image discriminator encourages the hallucinated faces close to the HR faces in pixel space, and the feature discriminator encouragers the generator to produce more structural details rather than artifacts. We also proposed an improved residual-based network for face super-resolution. Experiment show that our model generates more attractive faces than the state-of-the-art.

However, there are several problems need to deal with in the future. First, we found our method is not sensitive to the face wearing the thin frame glasses. Second, we believe that applying the GAN to feature maps may also be useful to other problems such as image deblur. Finally, It is clear that joint learning two tasks [3, 6, 7] could greatly improve the performance of both SR and face aligned (or face recognition) from. Thus, designing a multi-task learning network may be a promising and useful research direction for face hallucination.

Acknowledgments. This work is supported by the Major Project and Key Project of Natural Science of Anhui Provincial Department of Education (Grant No. KJ2015ZD09 and KJ2018A0043). It is also partly supported by Anhui Provincial Natural Science Foundation (Grant No. 1608085MF129, 1808085QF210) and by the Innovation Foundation of Key Laboratory of Intelligent Perception and Systems for High Dimensional Information of Ministry of Education (Grant No. JYB201705).

References

1. Baker, S., Kanade, T.: Hallucinating faces. In: FG 2000, pp. 83–88 (2000)
2. Berthelot, D., Schumm, T., Metz, L.: Began: boundary equilibrium generative adversarial networks. arXiv preprint arXiv:1703.10717 (2017)
3. Bhat, A.: Makeup invariant face recognition using features from accelerated segment test and eigen vectors. Int. J. Image Graph. **17**(01), 1750005 (2017)
4. Bin, H., Weihai, C., Xingming, W., Chun-Liang, L.: High-quality face image SR using conditional generative adversarial networks. arXiv preprint arXiv:1707.00737 (2017)
5. Bruna, J., Sprechmann, P., LeCun, Y.: Super-resolution with deep convolutional sufficient statistics. arXiv preprint arXiv:1511.05666 (2015)

6. Bulat, A., Tzimiropoulos, G.: Super-FAN: integrated facial landmark localization and super-resolution of real-world low resolution faces in arbitrary poses with GANs. In: Proceedings of the IEEE Conference on Computer Vision and Pattern Recognition, pp. 109–117 (2018)

7. Chen, Y., Tai, Y., Liu, X., Shen, C., Yang, J.: FSRNet: end-to-end learning face super-resolution with facial priors. In: Proceedings of the IEEE Conference on Computer Vision and Pattern Recognition, pp. 2492–2501 (2018)

8. Dong, C., Loy, C.C., He, K., Tang, X.: Image super-resolution using deep convolutional networks. IEEE Trans. Pattern Anal. Mach. Intell. **38**(2), 295–307 (2016)

9. Goodfellow, I., et al.: Generative adversarial nets. In: Proceedings conference and Workshop on Neural Information Processing Systems, pp. 2672–2680 (2014)

10. Huang, H., He, R., Sun, Z., Tan, T.: Wavelet-SRNet: a wavelet-based CNN for multi-scale face super resolution. In: Proceedings of the IEEE International Conference on Computer Vision, pp. 1689–1697 (2017)

11. Jolicoeur-Martineau, A.: The relativistic discriminator: a key element missing from standard GAN. arXiv preprint arXiv:1807.00734 (2018)

12. Kim, J., Kwon Lee, J., Mu Lee, K.: Accurate image super-resolution using very deep convolutional networks. In: Proceedings of the IEEE Conference on Computer Vision and Pattern Recognition, pp. 1646–1654 (2016)

13. Kim, J., Kwon Lee, J., Mu Lee, K.: Deeply-recursive convolutional network for image super-resolution. In: Proceedings of the IEEE Conference on Computer Vision and Pattern Recognition, pp. 1637–1645 (2016)

14. Ledig, C., et al.: Photo-realistic single image super-resolution using a generative adversarial network. In: Proceedings of the IEEE Conference on Computer Vision and Pattern Recognition, pp. 4681–4690 (2017)

15. Liu, Z., Luo, P., Wang, X., Tang, X.: Deep learning face attributes in the wild. In: Proceedings of the IEEE International Conference on Computer Vision, pp. 3730–3738 (2015)

16. Sajjadi, M.S., Scholkopf, B., Hirsch, M.: EnhanceNet: single image super-resolution through automated texture synthesis. In: Proceedings of the IEEE International Conference on Computer Vision, pp. 4491–4500 (2017)

17. Shi, W., et al.: Real-time single image and video super-resolution using an efficient sub-pixel convolutional neural network. In: Proceedings of the IEEE Conference on Computer Vision and Pattern Recognition, pp. 1874–1883 (2016)

18. Simonyan, K., Zisserman, A.: Very deep convolutional networks for large-scale image recognition. arXiv preprint arXiv:1409.1556 (2014)

19. Yu, X., Fernando, B., Ghanem, B., Porikli, F., Hartley, R.: Face super-resolution guided by facial component heatmaps. In: Ferrari, V., Hebert, M., Sminchisescu, C., Weiss, Y. (eds.) ECCV 2018. LNCS, vol. 11213, pp. 219–235. Springer, Cham (2018). https://doi.org/10.1007/978-3-030-01240-3_14

20. Yu, X., Fernando, B., Hartley, R., Porikli, F.: Super-resolving very low-resolution face images with supplementary attributes. In: Proceedings of the IEEE Conference on Computer Vision and Pattern Recognition, pp. 908–917 (2018)

21. Yu, X., Porikli, F.: Ultra-resolving face images by discriminative generative networks. In: Leibe, B., Matas, J., Sebe, N., Welling, M. (eds.) ECCV 2016. LNCS, vol. 9909, pp. 318–333. Springer, Cham (2016). https://doi.org/10.1007/978-3-319-46454-1_20

22. Yu, X., Porikli, F.: Face hallucination with tiny unaligned images by transformative discriminative neural networks. In: Thirty-First AAAI Conference on Artificial Intelligence (2017)
23. Yu, X., Porikli, F.: Hallucinating very low-resolution unaligned and noisy face images by transformative discriminative autoencoders. In: Proceedings of the IEEE Conference on Computer Vision and Pattern Recognition, pp. 3760–3768 (2017)

Lung Parenchymal Segmentation Algorithm Based on Improved Marker Watershed for Lung CT Images

Ying Chen and Ding Wang$^{(\boxtimes)}$

Nanchang Hangkong University, Nanchang 330063, Jiangxi, China
nchu_wd@163.com

Abstract. Watershed algorithm is the basic method of digital image processing. and the most important segmentation technology. The lung CT images of human thoracic cross-section are segmented by watershed algorithm and edge detection in this paper. 400 CT images of human lung contour will be picked from Related data set to label artificially. Then the segmentation results are compared with those randomly selected labeled images to evaluate the performance using with Jaccard Index, dice coefficients and Correlation coefficients. At the same time, by comparing the accuracy between the image of lung segmentation and lung connection, the former reached to 99% and the latter is 98%. The real details can be preserved after segmentation by this segmentation.

Keywords: CT scans · Watershed algorithm · Image segmentation

1 Introduction

Lung cancer is considered to be a group of diseases caused by uncontrolled cell growth. It is one of the major public health problems in the world. Besides Lung cancer is an invasive disease. It is difficultly to be detected for its rapid development. According to relevant data, the 5-year survival rate of lung cancer is only 17.7% [1]. However, mortality can be reduced by early detection and treatment. Fortunately, the survival rate can be improved to 52% by the early discovery and positioning of the nodule [2]. But only 15% of cases are diagnosed in the early stage [3]. About 20% of all nodular cases are lung cancer [4]. Therefore, the advancement can be improved and more lives can be saved by diagnosis of pulmonary nodules.

Computed Tomography (CT) is an early discovery of nodules which is one of imaging studies. As can be seen form screening results in lung cancer screening test LCST (Lung Cancer Screening Trials), CT screening is decreased by about 20% compared with X-ray chest X-ray in 5 years [5]. Other studies have shown that CT has a higher detection rate in nodules than simulated radiology [6]. The best imaging technology in CT imaging is a reliable cancer diagnosis by which every suspicious and unsuspected lung cancer nodule can be got [7]. However, cancer cells will be labeled difficultly [8], because of intensity change in the CT scan images and anatomical structures, as well as misjudgment to structures by doctors and radiologists. In recent

© Springer Nature Switzerland AG 2019
Z. Lin et al. (Eds.): PRCV 2019, LNCS 11858, pp. 126–137, 2019.
https://doi.org/10.1007/978-3-030-31723-2_11

years, the accuracy of detecting cancer with radiologists and doctors has been improved by using computer-aided diagnosis.

The basis for the detection and diagnosis of lung cancer is the segmentation of the lung CT images. We can get the region of interest (ROI) in the lungs. In addition the next step can be processed to the ROI. Therefore, the quality of lung CT image segmentation plays an important role in the diagnosis or detection lung cancer. The common method used in lung segmentation mainly is threshold segmentation of the lung tissue according its HU (Hounsfield Unit) value, which is followed by taking a further process by using mathematical morphology. Although good result can be achieved to a certain extent by these methods, these methods also have serious shortcoming that many tissues are neither lungs nor ROI. Moreover, CT images in which the left and right lungs are connected, cannot be accurately segmented. The preferred method of separating the convex features in the image is called watershed segmentation. The effect of directly applying the watershed segmentation algorithm is often not good. If the foreground and background objects are marked differently in the image before applying the watershed algorithm, a better segmentation effect can be got. To solve these problem, a lung parenchyma segmentation algorithm based on improved marker watershed algorithm for lung CT images is proposed in this paper.

2   Related Work

So far, there has several algorithms effectively solving the problem of lung CT image segmentation. They can be roughly divided into two types of methods, (1) lung CT images based on non-machine learning methods, (2) lung parenchymal segmentation based on machine learning.

Non-machine learning methods for processing lung CT image segmentation mainly includes edge-based, region-based, model-based, watershed-based segmentation, and clustering-based methods. The first step of edge-based image segmentation is using the edge detection operator to detect the edge of the ROI. In addition segment the ROI is segmented. Traditional edge detection operators include Laplacian operator, Sobel operator, Robert operator, Canny operator etc. An edge detection method based on Sobel technology and generalized fuzzy logic system is proposed by Suzuki et al. in [9]. The relatively complex CT images under the condition of prior probability can be proposed by the region-based segmentation method. However these algorithms have the tendency of under-segmentation or over-segmentation. In addition, the algorithm calculation is more complicated. Image features that are in contact with each other can be effectively separated by watershed segmentation. Xue et al. in [10] proposed a multi-threshold and marker watershed fusion algorithm together to segment the lung CT image. The algorithm steps are as follows: Initially, the CT image of the lung is roughly segmented by multi-threshold method. Furthermore the left and right bronchus are removed by mathematical morphology. Finally the segmentation is performed by the marker watershed method. Model-based methods are consisted of segmentation methods based on local priors (eg, graph cuts) and global priors (eg, active contour models). A systematic description of the graph cutting method is proposed by Songtao et al. [11]. A comprehensive description of the segmentation method based on active contour model is proposed by Dingna et al. in [12]. The cluster-based method has a long running time, and the segmentation result is related to the location of the cluster center. An algorithm combining Fast Fuzzy C-Means clustering (FFCM) with threshold to segment low-dose CT images of the lungs is proposed by Doganay et al. in [13].

With the rapid development of medical image processing technology, the current segmentation algorithms based on machine learning are also emerging one after another. A lung CT image segmentation algorithm using U-NET network structure is proposed by Skourt et al. in [14]. U-NET network structure is one of the most common structures used for learning image segmentation. A segmentation algorithm based on improved U-NET network is proposed by Tong et al. in [15]. Initially, the CT image is transformed and normalized, and the lung parenchyma is obtained by a simple and effective morphological method. Besides the U-NET network is improved. In summary, as shown in Table 1, these methods have advantages and disadvantages in applicability, performance and so on. Most these methods are time consuming and responding differently to different patients. They usually produce excessive self-regulation. In addition the blurring of the lung boundaries can produce less than ideal results. Thus, a lung parenchyma segmentation algorithm based on improving marker watershed for lung CT images is proposed in this paper.

Table 1. Segmentation algorithm summary

Methods	Advantages	Disadvantages
Edge-based	Fast speed and easy to operate	Edges are often disconnected
Region-based	The method is simple. Multiple stop criteria can be chosen	The choice of seeds is important and critical. Sensitive to noise
Model-based	Finds certain-shaped regions	The regions need to fit a certain mode
Watershed	The boundaries of each region are continuous. No seed is needed. Resulting regions are connected	Sensitive to noise and non-homogeneity. The algorithm is time-consuming and over-segmentation problem
Clustering-based	Fuzzy set is a rule-based segmentation and takes into account the uncertainty and fuzziness	Affected by the number of initial clusters
Machine learning	Stable, different lesion characteristics can be incorporated by feature extraction	Long training time; over-fitting problem; test images should come from the same platform as the training images

3 Proposed Segmentation Approach

In this paper, the lung segmentation algorithm based on improved watershed lung image segmentation algorithm is used to solve the segmentation problem. The algorithm is roughly divided into four steps: original CT scan image loading, conversion (Hounsfield Units) HU value, generation marker and lung segmentation. The specific steps are shown in Fig. 1.

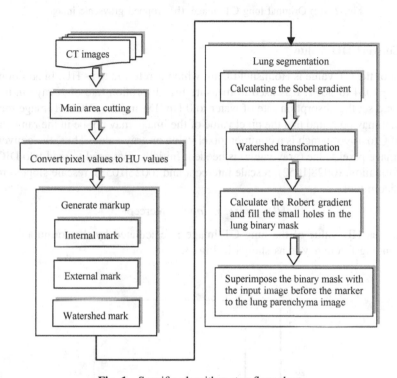

Fig. 1. Specific algorithm step flow chart

3.1 Original Lung CT Image Loading Processing

Each lung CT scan image is provided by multiple two-dimensional slice DICOM formats. The Dicom file will be read randomly first. Since the original CT image has some useless annotation information for processing the image. The intensity value is updated from −2000 to 0 by the image after read by the pydicom toolkit. Because there are some pixels of the boundary over the scanner scanning, so the main portion will be cropped. As shown in Fig. 2. (a) is the original CT image, (b) is the cropped grayscale image, so that the CT grayscale image of the central main region is obtained.

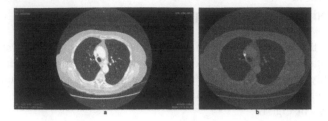

Fig. 2. (a) Original lung CT image, (b) cropped grayscale image

3.2 Convert HU Value

The unit of the CT value is Hounsfield Unit, which is referred to as HU. In addition, the range is −1024 to 3071. It is used to measure the absorption rate of X-rays in human tissues and set the absorption rate of water to 0 Hu. During the DICOM image reading process, it may be found that the pixel value of the image may not be in the range but in range of 0 to 4096, which is a common pixel value or gray value. Thus, the conversion of the image pixel value (gray value) is needed. Initially, We need to read two DICOM Tag information, (0028|1052): rescale intercept and (0028|1053): rescale slope through the pydicom tool.

$$HU = pixel * slope + \text{intercept} \tag{1}$$

Then the HU value of the lung CT image is calculated by the formula 1 and its corresponding frequency is as shown in Fig. 3.

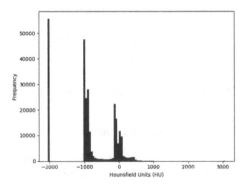

Fig. 3. HU value of lung CT image and its corresponding frequency

3.3 Generate Markup

In the lung CT image, the foreground and background objects will be labeled to make a distinction. Furthermore the watershed will be used to achieve better segmentation. The marker is composed of an internal tag inside each ROI object and an external tag in the background of image. Therefore, this paper uses the marker to divide the left and right lung tissue by watershed. The specific steps are as follows:

(1) According to the gray value of the lung ROI, a threshold value of −400 HU is selected for internal labeling, which is obtained according to the HU value distribution map of the previous lung CT image conversion. Besides the boundary is cleared and the connected area is marked. Finally the largest area is selected to get the internal mark.

(2) The internal mark is quickly expanded by 10 and 55 iterations respectively. Furthermore the expanded result is XORed to obtain an external mark.

(3) The internal marker and the external marker is superimposed to obtain the watershed marker.

The CT image of the mark is shown in Fig. 4.

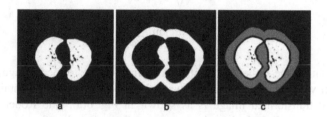

Fig. 4. (a) Internal marker image, (b) external marker image, (c) watershed marker image

3.4 Segmentation of Lung Parenchyma

In the CT scan image of the lung, the actual feature overlap may occur, or the particles on the surface may contact each other due to aggregation, which leads to that feature is not individually identified, counted or measured. The preferred method of separating the convex features which are in contact with each other in the image is called watershed segmentation, a classical algorithm in the morphological segmentation method. The image is viewed as a topographically water-covered natural landscape. The gray value of each pixel in the image indicates the altitude of the point. In addition each local minimum and its affected area become a collecting basin. Besides the boundary of the collecting basin is a watershed. The range that affects each very small area is the corresponding collecting basin corresponding to the area in the image; the boundary where the water flows from different areas meet is the expected watershed which is the edge of the corresponding area. The watershed transformation can ensure the continuity and closure of the segmentation area. To suppress the over-segmentation phenomenon, a multi-scale gradient map is obtained for the input CT image.

This Sobel operator used in this paper for gradient calculation is mainly used for edge detection. It is a discrete difference operator which is used to calculate the approximation of the gray level of the image brightness function. A corresponding gray vector or its normal vector can be produces by Using this operator at any point in the image. As shown in Fig. 5, the G_x direction and the G_y direction which are related template of the Sobel operator are shown.

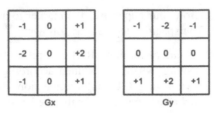

Fig. 5. Sobel operator G_x direction and G_y direction related template

The lateral and longitudinal gradient approximation of each pixel in the image can be calculated by Eq. 2 below. In addition the gradient direction is calculated as shown in Eq. 3 below.

$$G = \sqrt{G_x^2 + G_y^2} \tag{2}$$

$$\Theta = \arctan(\frac{G_x}{G_y}) \tag{3}$$

After obtaining the Sobel gradient, to obtain the transformed image, watershed transformation was performed with the watershed markers which is obtained before. The watershed transformed image is as shown in Fig. 6(a). The Roberts crossover operator will be used to calculate the image gradient after that the watershed transformation result is obtained. Furthermore the holes are filled in the lung image by using binary mask. The image of the lung boundary Obtained by the above steps is shown in Fig. 6(b). The Roberts crossover operator template is shown in Fig. 7.

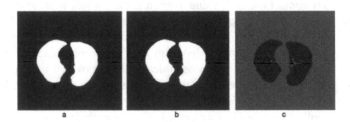

Fig. 6. (a) The watershed transformed image, (b) the Roberts operator gradient calculation and the mask-filled image, and (c) the mask overlay to segment the lung parenchyma image

The gradient width of the image $f(x,y)$ is as shown in Eq. 4, and the result is obtained according to the template as shown in Eq. 5.

$$G(x,y) = |G_x| + |G_y| \tag{4}$$

$$G(x,y) = |G_x| + |G_y| = |f(x,y) - f(x+1,y+1)| + |f(x+1,y) - f(x,y+1)| \tag{5}$$

Finally, a lung parenchymal image is obtained by superimposing the edge image obtained in the previous step and the input image. The result is shown in Fig. 6(c).

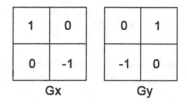

$$Gx \qquad\qquad Gy$$

Fig. 7. Roberts cross operator template

4 Experimental and Analysis

4.1 Lung CT Image Data Set and Experimental Environment Description

In this text, a LIDC-IDRI (lung image database consortium-Image Database Resource Initiative) data set of LIDC (lung image database consortium) was used for testing, which is composed of a chest medical image file (for instance CT, The X-ray film) and the corresponding diagnostic lesions result which are labeled. The data was collected by the National Cancer Institute (NCI) for studying, training, and evaluating the early cancer detection and diagnosis in high-risk populations using spiral CT [16]. In this test, ten cases were selected. Each of them contains more than 100 CT images of lung slices, from which 400 CT images were randomly selected for artificial lung marking. The artificial marking could be viewed by using the labelmc image tagging software to label and name the background using _lung_ for lung parenchyma and _background_ for _background_. After the markup is completed, it will be saved in the json format file. Then the Python tool will be used to parse the labeled CT image. In addition the final image will be converted into a PNG format image of 512 * 512 pixels. The experimental platform for this experiment is: Ubuntu 16.04 LTS operating system, CPU Intel i5 processor, running memory 12 GB, programming software Pycharm.

4.2 Performance

In order to verify the quality of CT image segmentation, the algorithm proposed in this paper is compared with other algorithms. The experiment adapt three indicators including Jaccard Index [17], dice coefficient [17] and Correlation coefficient (CC) to analyze the result. These indices are shown as follows:

The Jaccard Index is very popular which is used as a similarity index for binary data, which is shown in Eq. 6 below.

$$J(OA) = \frac{A \cap B}{A \cup B} \tag{6}$$

Where OA is the overlap region, A is the binarized image, and B is the real value image.

The definition of dice coefficient is shown in Eq. 7 below:

$$D(A, B) = \frac{2|A \cap B|}{|A| + |B|} \tag{7}$$

The dice coefficient is usually used to measure the performance of the segmentation. Its value is between 0 and 1, which means 0 no overlap and 1 completely consistent.

The Correlation coefficient (CC) is used to measure the similarity between the segmented image and the ground truth value and their respective pixel intensities. CC is defined as shown in the following Eq. 8:

$$CC = \frac{\sum_i \sum_j (A_{ij} - mean(A))(B_{ij} - mean(B))}{\sqrt{\left(\sum_i \sum_j (A_{ij} - mean(A))^2\right)\left(\sum_i \sum_j (B_{ij} - mean(B))^2\right)}} \tag{8}$$

The subscript indices i and j represent the positions of the pixels in the image.

4.3 Experimental Results and Discussion

An improved watershed-based lung CT image segmentation algorithm is proposed in this paper to extract lung parenchyma images from lung slice scanning CT images. The overall accuracy rate is close to 99%. In this paper, two CT images and marker images were randomly selected from the lung CT image series of 10 cases. In addition the above three evaluation indicators are combined. It can be seen that high accuracy values for all measurements are achieved by the proposed method. The relevant data is shown in Table 2.

Table 2. Using the Jaccard Index, dice coefficient, and correlation coefficient, the calculated values of the lung segmentation results proposed by this method are used.

Im.	Jaccard Index	Dice coefficient	CC
1	0.989181	0.963280	0.969869
2	0.990779	0.969745	0.975336
3	0.993396	0.980450	0.984635
4	0.983581	0.954698	0.964902
5	0.994613	0.981521	0.984786
6	0.991249	0.969177	0.974372
7	0.995456	0.978046	0.980619
8	0.989856	0.957505	0.963066
9	0.992790	0.981323	0.986194
10	0.990388	0.971911	0.978189
11	0.993167	0.981590	0.986058

(continued)

Table 2. (*continued*)

Im.	Jaccard Index	Dice coefficient	CC
12	0.990737	0.974983	0.981063
13	0.992183	0.976440	0.981360
14	0.992214	0.976226	0.981125
15	0.990257	0.958990	0.964367
16	0.991718	0.965363	0.970101
17	0.994033	0.975452	0.978889
18	0.991210	0.962715	0.967679
19	0.995075	0.972838	0.975576
20	0.995429	0.976886	0.979432

Based on the advantages of the improved watershed algorithm in this paper, the lung CT images in which the left and right lungs are connected, are compared with the labeled images. As can be seen in the Fig. 8, an ideal effect can be achieved in the precise segmentation of the area, in which the left and right lung are connected.

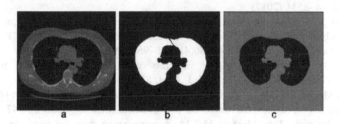

Fig. 8. (a) Original image (b) artificially labeled contour image (c) segmented lung parenchyma image

Next, Table 3 is shown below, which presents a comparison between the method of this paper and the results of other methods. Furthermore, for instance the features of the works, data sets, algorithms used for segmentation in addition to the accuracy of the segmentation are also shown. It can be seen from Table 3 that the proposed method is better than the other methods on the same or different data sets. And the overall accuracy is 99%. That the improved watershed segmentation method can effectively reduce over-segmentation, effectiveness, robustness can be proved by comparison in this paper. In addition, this algorithm can deal with uncertainty and uncertainty in CT images.

Table 3. Comparison of the proposed method with other existing lung segmentation methods

Author	Year	Data set	Average accuracy
Skourt et al. [14]	2018	LIDC	95.02%
Wenli et al. [18]	2018	LIDC	96.0%
Siyuan et al. [19]	2018	LIDC	96.9%
Proposed approach	2019	LIDC	99.02%

5 Summary

This paper proposes a hybrid segmentation method that uses watershed algorithm and edge detection to automatically segment lung parenchyma from chest CT images. Experiment shows that the proposed method can deal with uncertainty better. It can reduce over-segmentation and has good precision and performance for non-uniform and noisy images. The overall accuracy obtained from the proposed method is almost better. The further diagnosis and treatment planning are contributed to by this result. In future, the improved watershed segmentation method will be applied to a large number of CT images to evaluate its performance by us in plan.

References

1. Jemal, A., Siegel, R., Xu, J., et al.: Cancer statistics. CA Cancer J. Clin. **60**(5), 277–300 (2010)
2. Henschke, C.I.: Early lung cancer action project: overall design and findings from baseline screening. Cancer **89**(S11), 2474–2482 (2000)
3. Siegel, R., Ma, J., Zou, Z., et al.: Early estimates of SEER cancer incidence, 2014. Cancer **123**(13), 2524–2534 (2017)
4. Takashima, S., Sone, S., Li, F., et al.: Small solitary pulmonary nodules (≤ 1 cm) detected at population-based CT screening for lung cancer: reliable high-resolution CT features of benign lesions. Am. J. Roentgenol. **180**(4), 955–964 (2003)
5. Abraham, J.: Reduced lung cancer mortality with low-dose computed tomographic screening. Community Oncol. N. Engl. J. Med. **8**(10), 441–442 (2011)
6. Awai, K., Murao, K., Ozawa, A., et al.: Pulmonary nodules at chest CT: effect of computer-aided diagnosis on radiologists' detection performance. Radiology **230**(2), 347–352 (2004)
7. Gindi, A., Attiatalla, T.A., Mostafa, M.S.M.: A comparative study for comparing two feature extraction methods and two classifiers in classification of early stage lung cancer diagnosis of chest X-ray images. J. Am. Sci. **10**(6), 13–22 (2014)
8. Suzuki, K., Kusumoto, M., Watanabe, S., et al.: Radiologic classification of small adenocarcinoma of the lung: radiologic-pathologic correlation and its prognostic impact. Ann. Thorac. Surg. **81**(2), 413–419 (2006)
9. Gonzalez, C.I., Melin, P., Castro, J.R., et al.: An improved sobel edge detection method based on generalized type-2 fuzzy logic. Soft. Comput. **20**(2), 773–784 (2016)
10. Xue, X., Heng, G., Zhong, C.: Segmentation method of CT lung image based on multi-threshold and marker watershed algorithm. Lasernal **9**, 74–78 (2014)
11. Songtao, L., Fuliang, Y.: The basic principle and its new advances of image segmentation methods based on graph cuts. Acta Autom. Sin. **38**(6), 911–922 (2012)
12. Dingna, D., Huan, Z., Chenhui, Q., et al.: A survey of image segmentation algorithms based on active contour model. Chin. J. Biomed. Eng. **34**(4), 445–454 (2015)
13. Doganay, E., Kart, L., Özcelik, H.K., et al.: A robust lung segmentation algorithm using fuzzy C-means method from HRCT scans. Eur. Respir. J. **48**(suppl 60), PA750 (2016)
14. Skourt, B.A., El Hassani, A., Majda, A.: Lung CT image segmentation using deep neural networks. Procedia Comput. Sci. **127**, 109–113 (2018)
15. Tong, G., Li, Y., Chen, H., et al.: Improved U-NET network for pulmonary nodules segmentation. Optik **174**, 460–469 (2018)

16. Armato, S.G., McLennan, G., Bidaut, L., et al.: The lung image database consortium (LIDC) and image database resource initiative (IDRI): a completed reference database of lung nodules on CT scans. Med. Phys. **38**(2), 915–931 (2011)
17. Anter, A.M., Hassenian, A.E.: Computational intelligence optimization approach based on particle swarm optimizer and neutrosophic set for abdominal CT liver tumor segmentation. J. Comput. Sci. **25**, 376–387 (2018)
18. Wenli, Z., Xiaoqi, L., Yu, G., et al.: Segmentation of diseased lung parenchyma based on Freeman chain code. Comput. Eng. Des. **39**(10), 195–198+227 (2018)
19. Siyuan, T., Min, Y., Yue, M., et al.: CT image segmentation of lungs with regional growth and horizontal integration. Electron. Technol. Appl. **44**(5), 129–133 (2018)

Fine Grain Lung Nodule Diagnosis Based on CT Using 3D Convolutional Neural Network

Qiuli Wang[1], Jiajia Zhang[1], Sheng Huang[1], Chen Liu[2], Xiaohong Zhang[1], and Dan Yang[1(✉)]

[1] School of Big Data and Software Engineering, Chongqing University, Chongqing 400032, China
{wangqiuli,gagazhang,huangsheng,xhongzh,dyang}@cqu.edu.cn
[2] Radiology Department, The First Affiliated Hospital of Army Medical University, Chongqing 400032, China
cqliuchen@foxmail.com

Abstract. As the core step of lung nodule analysis, lung nodule diagnosis comprises two important tasks: False Positive Reduction (FPR) and Malignancy Suspiciousness Estimation (MSE). Many studies tackle these two tasks separately. However, these two tasks share a lot of similarities and have connections with each other, since MSE is the successive step of FPR, and both tasks can be deemed as the lung nodule labeling problems. In this paper, we split the label 'real nodule' defined in FPR into two new finer grain labels, namely 'low risk' and 'high risk', which are defined in MSE. In such way, we merge these two separated issues into a unified fine grain lung nodule classification problem. Finally, a novel Attribute Sensitive Multi-Branch 3D CNN (ASMB3DCNN) is proposed for performing the fine grain lung nodule classification. We evaluate our model on LIDC-IDRI and LUNA2016 datasets. Experiments demonstrate that ASMB3DCNN can efficiently address the two tasks above in a joint way and achieve the promising performances in comparison with the state-of-the-arts.

Keywords: Joint learning · Lung nodule diagnosis · Convolutional Neural Network · Computed tomography (CT) · Computer-aided detection and diagnosis (CAD)

1 Introduction

Each year, there are 8.2 million deaths caused by cancer in the worldwide. Lung cancer accounts for the highest number of mortalities i.e. 1.59 million [1]. However, according to statistics, most patients diagnosed with lung cancer today already have advanced disease (40% are stage IV, 30% are stage III), and the current 5-year survival rate is only 16% [2], which indicates that early diagnosis and treatment can effectively improve survival chance of lung cancer patients. As the

© Springer Nature Switzerland AG 2019
Z. Lin et al. (Eds.): PRCV 2019, LNCS 11858, pp. 138–149, 2019.
https://doi.org/10.1007/978-3-030-31723-2_12

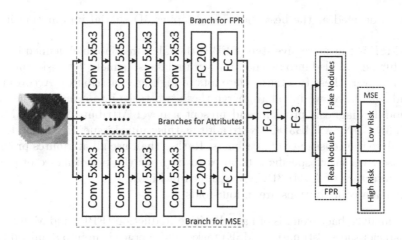

Fig. 1. Architecture of ASMB3DCNN

core step of lung nodule analysis, classifying a large number of detected nodules by the radiologists, which includes False Positive Reduction (FPR) and Malignancy Suspiciousness Estimation (MSE), can be very time-consuming. Small nodules are very difficult to be found and can be confused with normal tissues. Long time reading work can also cause the fatigue of the radiologists and reduce the work efficiency. Thus, developing a fast, robust and accurate CAD system to perform automated diagnosis of lung nodules is meaningful and important [3], many CAD systems have been designed to help the radiologists like [4–7]. To the best of our knowledge, most studies considered FPR and MSE as two totally separated problems.

In the task of FPR, Dou et al. [8] designed a multilevel contextual 3D Convolutional Neural Networks (3D CNN) to encode richer spatial information and extract more discriminative representations via the hierarchical architecture trained with 3D samples. In the task of MSE, Shen et al. [9] exploited CNN to differentiate lung nodules and proposed a Multi-crop CNN network structure. Hussein [10] used multi-task learning model based on 3D CNN, which showed that information of high-level attributes can help to improve the performance of the model. Wu [11] designed PN-SAMP, which can also provide related evidences and segmentation information to radiologists. Study in [12] is very instructive, they use the attributes information to predict the malignancy level. Their model HSCNN share weights between first two convolutional layers, then splits into a few branches to finish tasks of predicting attributes and feeds predictions of attributes into dense layers to predict malignancy level. Causey et al. [6] proposed NoduleX. In NoduleX, they leveraged a deep CNN (more than 10 CNN layers) to tackle FPR and MSE tasks separately, and they also proved that these two tasks are similar. Extensive studies show that 3D CNN is a powerful approach for addressing both MSE and FPR issues in a separated way [6,8,13,14], since it is deemed as the best choice for keeping 3D spatial information in the CT scans [15].

As MSE is the successive step of FPR, the label 'real nodule' defined in FPR can be further divided into two new finer grain labels, namely 'low risk' and 'high risk'. Moreover, these two tasks share lots of high-level attributes. According to the findings above, we intent to merge these two tasks into a unified fine grain lung nodule diagnosis problem and present a novel Attribute Sensitive Multi-Branch 3D CNN (ASMB3DCNN) to address this unified issue. In this model, we also analyse the sensitivity of attributes. Rather than use all attributes provided by dataset, we select specific attributes to improve the performance of model. The architecture of ASMB3DCNN is shown in Fig. 1.

Our main contributions are in four-folds:

(1) We analyze backgrounds of False Positive Reduction (FPR) and Malignancy Suspiciousness Estimation (MSE) tasks, and merge them into a unified task.
(2) We measure the sensitivities of attributes and select the most reliable attributes to yield an attribute sensitive version of 3D CNN for fine grain lung nodule diagnosis.
(3) We design a method of normalization to capture different sizes of inputs according to the slices-thickness and pixel-spacing which has been empirically proved that such strategy can improve accuracy of classification and reduce the burden of calculation.
(4) Beyond FPR and MSE, we extend the proposed approach to predict nodule attributes, which could potentially assist radiologists in evaluating malignancy uncertainty.

The rest of paper is organized as follows: Sect. 2 introduces the methodology of our works; experiments are presented in Sect. 3; the conclusion is finally summarized in Sect. 4.

2   Method

Since Malignancy Suspiciousness Estimation (MSE) is the successive task of False Positive Reduction (FPR) in the lung nodule diagnosis, MSE essentially performs a further classification on the positive samples labeled by FPR. In such way, we can further categorize the positive samples into two finer categories, namely 'low risk' and 'high risk', and these two tasks can be unified as a fine grain lung nodule classification issue. In this paper, we present a novel 3D CNN named Attribute Sensitive Multi-Branch 3D CNN (ASMB3DCNN) to address such issue and then the tasks of FPR and MSE can be jointly tackled.

We firstly analyse the sensitivity of all attributes and select attributes which are more sensitive to the malignancy level. Then we use a normalization method to resize nodules in CT scans into the same scale and feed them into different branches to predict level of different attributes. The last step is to train all branches jointly to perform the unified fine grain lung nodule diagnosis classification.

2.1   Sensitivity Analysis of Attributes

The study in [10] indicates that the attributes can facilitate the solution of MSE. There are 8 attributes, namely 'subtlety', 'internal-Structure', 'calcification', 'sphericity', 'margin', 'lobulation', 'spiculation' and 'texture', and all attributes are classified into 6 levels by radiologists in LIDC-IDRI. However, not all attributes are sensitive to (or strongly correlated to) the level of malignancy suspiciousness of lung nodules. Thus, here we intend to analyse the sensitivities of attributes to malignancy suspiciousness level via measure the variance of the proportion of high risk lung nodules under different levels of attributes as follows:

$$\mathcal{S} = \frac{1}{n-1} \sum_{i=1}^{n} (X_i - \bar{X})^2 \tag{1}$$

where n is the number of score levels, X_i is the proportion of malignant nodules, $\bar{X}$ is the average of proportion.

We measure the sensitivity of these attributes in LIDC-IDRI, rank them by their sensitivities and tabulate the results in Table 1. We find the top 2 sensitive attributes are 'internalStructure' and 'calcification' whose sample distributions are extremely unbalanced as shown in Table 2. In category of 'internalStructure', 99.8% of nodules are in level 1 and 2. In category of 'calcification', 99.8% of nodules are in level 3, 4, 5 and 6. This makes us very hard to train the reliable predictors for these two attributes via using the training samples, and the unreliably predicted attributes may corrupt the performance of the lung nodule diagnosis system. Thus, we choose 'subtlety', 'lobulation', 'spiculation' (their ranks are from 3 to 5) as complementary information for lung nodule classification. In order to prove that our selection of attributes can actually help the model, we also train the model with 'subtlety', 'lobulation', 'spiculation', 'sphericity', 'margin' and 'texture', and results shown in Table 3 prove that model with 3 selected attributes is better than model with 6 attributes. The architecture of each branch will be discussed later in Sect. 2.3. Examples of nodules with different level attributes are shown in Table 2, nodules framed with red rectangles

Table 1. Proportion of malignant nodules in each level

Attributes category	Attribute rate						Sensitivity (variance)	Rank
	1	2	3	4	5	6		
subtlety	2.56%	5.92%	5.53%	17.23%	44.61%	-	0.030	5
internal-Structure	18.90%	47.62%	50.00%	0.00%	0.00%	-	0.060	1
calcification	0.00%	0.00%	0.00%	1.80%	10.81%	21.88%	0.057	2
sphericity	0.00%	17.28%	23.00%	20.79%	8.60%	-	0.009	6
margin	20.56%	23.83%	28.36%	21.80%	9.78%	-	0.004	7
lobulation	6.77%	26.67%	54.55%	56.12%	13.79%	-	0.052	3
spiculation	7.47%	31.39%	58.70%	57.39%	41.94%	-	0.045	4
texture	11.56%	20.35%	20.86%	23.57%	18.41%	-	0.002	8

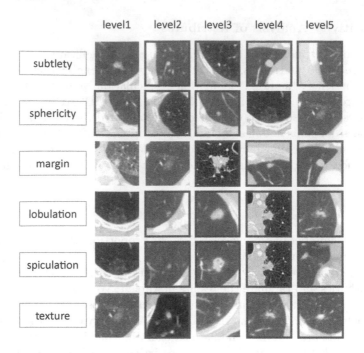

Fig. 2. Nodules with different level attributes (nodules framed with red rectangles are high risk nodules) (Color figure online)

are high risk nodules. We can clearly see that nodules with high level attributes like 'lobulation' are more likely to be malignant.

2.2   Normalization

The slice-thickness ranges from 0.6 mm to 5.0 mm, the pixel-spacing ranges from 0.4609375 mm to 0.9765625 mm. Shen et al. [9] normalized images using spline interpolation to have a fixed resolution with 0.5 mm/voxel along all three axes, all images will be re-sampled before cropping nodules, which is time-consuming. Moreover, coordinates of nodules will be affected during re-sampling.

To reduce the burden of computation, we adjust the input size according to slice-thickness and pixel-spacing and resize the input after cropping. The length, width and height of inputs are set to 30 mm [1]. Fewer slices are needed if the slice-thickness gets larger. The coordinates of nodules are not affected. Then we resize the input into $20 \times 20 \times 10$ using spline interpolation since ASMB3DCNN needs a size-fixed input. Each input cubic contains a nodule in its center. Figure 3 shows that after normalization, the accuracy of six branches are improved in LIDC-IDRI dataset, accuracy of branch margin drops 1.09%, and accuracy of FPR is still the same.

---

[1] In clinical, nodules larger than 30 mm in diameter are called lung masses and will not be discussed here

Table 2. Number of nodules in each level

Attributes category	Attributes rate					
	1	2	3	4	5	6
subtlety	117	321	506	1097	594	-
internal-Structure	2609	21	2	2	1	-
calcification	3	2	187	111	74	2258
sphericity	5	191	613	1419	407	-
margin	107	277	342	1101	808	-
lobulation	1433	855	220	98	29	-
spiculation	1647	704	138	115	31	-
texture	173	113	139	488	1722	-

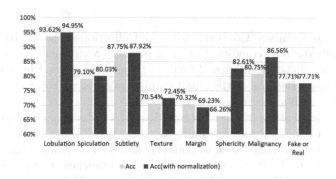

Fig. 3. Comparison of accuracy after normalization

2.3   Architecture of ASMB3DCNN

There are eight branches in the proposed Attribute Sensitive Multi-Branch 3D CNN (ASM3DCNN), follow the study [7], our model is split at the very first, and all branches share the same architecture as shown in Fig. 1. Like model in [8], we use kernels with size of $5 \times 5 \times 3$, $1 \times 1 \times 1$ and adjust the architecture according to the results of experiments. Each branch consists of four 3D convolutional layers (the kernel sizes are $5 \times 5 \times 3$, $5 \times 5 \times 3$, $5 \times 5 \times 3$, $1 \times 1 \times 1$, and the number of kernels are 64, 128, 256, 256 respectively), two fully-connected layers, and one softmax layer for giving an initial binary prediction to a specific attribute or a category. Between CNN layers, we use ReLU as activation function. In these eight branches, there are two branches used for predicting false positive (FPR) and malignancy suspiciousness (MSE) of a lung nodule respectively, and the other six branches are used for predicting the selected attributes, which have been empirically verified to be helpful for lung nodule diagnosis [10]. We select the attributes based on the sensitivity analysis of attributes. We fuse the outputs of these branches via two fully-connected layers and present the final classification via a softmax layer. In the training phase, we adopt the pre-training +

fine-tuning strategy to train our network. Branches are trained separately to predict 6 attributes, MSE and FPR. After pre-training, the branches are combined with the fusion layers to perform a fine-tuning. We have tried different kinds of combination: (1) ASMB3DCNN (MSE/FPR) has only one branch for MSE or FPR; (2) ASMB3DCNN (MSE/FPR+6 Attributes) contains one branch for MSE/FPR and all 6 attributes; (3) ASMB3DCNN (MSE/FPR+3 Attributes) contains one branch for MSE/FPR and 3 selected attributes; (4) ASMB3DCNN (ALL) contains branches for MSE, FPR and 3 attributes; (5) ASMB3DCNN (Attributes only) contains branches only for attributes. Why we try these different combination will be discussed latter in Sect. 3.

3   Experiments and Results

3.1   Datasets

The Lung Image Database Consortium Image Collection (LIDC-IDRI) [16], is a public-available dataset, consisting of 1010 patients with chest CT scans. This dataset provides 36378 nodules and 2635 of them are analyzed by four experienced radiologists. Because of the small number of data, we rotate nodules 90°, 180°, and 270° within the transverse plane.

Lung Nodule Analysis 2016 (LUNA2016) [17] is a challenge for lung nodules detection and FPR. Its dataset is built based on LIDC-IDRI, while it removes nodules which are less than 3 mm in diameter and provides more than 700 thousand fake nodules for FPR. Since then, we train the branches of six attributes and MSE using LIDC-IDRI dataset while train the branch of FPR using LUNA2016 dataset (samples from LIDC-IDRI dataset + fake nodule samples).

3.2   Nodule Attributes Prediction Results

In branches of attribute predictions, we binarize the levels of attributes. More specifically, we label the nodules with level equal to or higher than 3 as 'high', and the ones with level lower than 3 as 'low'. Therefore, each branch of attribute prediction can be considered as a naive binary classifier. Figure 3 presents the classification performance for each of the attribute-branches. We achieved mean accuracy (with normalization) of 94.95%, 80.03%,87.92%, 72.45%, 69.23%, 82.61% for lobulation, spiculation, subtlety, texture, margin, sphericity, respectively. As mentioned in [10], nodule attributes can facilitate the solution of MSE, so we combine predictions of attributes with MSE. Moreover, we find that these attributes information can actually help to improve FPR, since real nodules trend to have more obvious features and fake nodules trend have less obvious features. Finally, we combine attributes branches with FPR and MSE to perform both tasks together. Meanwhile, we provide attributes information for radiologists and it will assist radiologists in evaluating the nodule classification result.

3.3 Malignancy Suspiciousness Estimation

Following the study [6,9], we exclude the nodules whose average malignancy scores are equal to 3. We respectively label the nodules whose average malignancy scores higher than 3 as 'high risk nodules' and label the nodules whose average malignancy score lower than 3 as 'low risk nodules'.

Table 3 shows the performances of different versions of ASMB3DCNN in comparison with the state-of-the-arts. ASMB3DCNN (MSE), which uses the MSE branches only, is actually degraded as an ordinary single steam 3D CNN. It obtains 86.6% in accuracy and 84.5% in AUC score respectively, while ASMB3DCNN (MSE+3 Attributes) obtains 11.2% and 11.1% gains in accuracy and AUC score, these observations verify that the high-level attributes can indeed bring a boost in the performance of MSE.

Compared to ASMB3DCNN (MSE+3 Attributes), ASMB3DCNN (MSE+6 Attributes) obtains 93.8% in accuracy. As shown in Table 1, attributes like texture, have a low variance of the proportion, which means branches of these attributes cannot provide useful features and information for decision process of MSE and corrupts the performances of the model. We also train ASMB3DCNN (Attributes only), it obtains only 67.6% in accuracy, it verifies that branch of MSE learn something more complex than combination of attributes.

ASMB3DCNN (ALL) performs less worse than ASMB3DCNN (MSE+3 Attributes) but gets a similar performance to NoduleX. It is not hard to understand this phenomenon, since FPR performs a superclass labeling instead of a simple classification from the perspective of the MSE task. More specifically, the category 'real nodule' in FPR, which can be seen as a superclass, includes all two categories of MSE, namely 'low risk' and 'high risk'. In such way, the output of FPR branch actually has not offered any useful information for discriminating the 'high risk' and the 'low risk' data, and even corrupts the performances a little bit.

Table 3. Comparison with other studies for MSE

Methods	Accuracy	Sensitivity	Specificity	AUC score
ASMB3DCNN (ALL)	0.961	0.900	0.991	0.965
ASMB3DCNN (MSE+6 Attributes)	0.938	0.845	0.979	0.942
ASMB3DCNN (MSE+3 Attributes)	**0.978**	**0.957**	0.993	**0.976**
ASMB3DCNN (MSE)	0.866	0.696	**0.999**	0.845
ASMB3DCNN (Attributes only)	0.676	0.395	0.798	0.602
NoduleX [6]	0.932	0.879	0.985	0.971
Fuse-TSD [18]	0.895	0.842	0.920	0.966
MC-CNN [9]	0.871	0.77	0.93	0.93
HSCNN [12]	0.842	0.705	0.889	0.856

Study in [12] is very instructive, they also use the attributes information to predict the malignancy level, but HSCNN obtains 84.2% in accuracy. In order

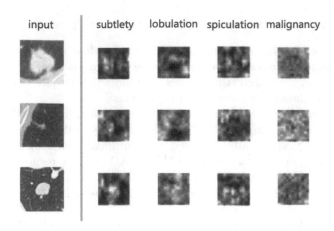

Fig. 4. Feature maps of convolutional layers for different attributes

to explain this phenomenon, we examine the feature maps of the second convolutional layer for different attributes and find that convolutional kernels pay attention to different part of nodules in different branches. As shown in Fig. 4, 'subtlety' pays more attention to the center of nodules, 'lobulation' and 'spiculation' pay more attention to the edge of nodules, and 'malignancy' pay attention to the whole view. Feature maps are conflict between attributes, so joint learning at first two convolutional layers may lead to interaction between branches and reduce the accuracy.

3.4   False Positive Reduction

We conduct experiments via following the same experimental settings for nodule labeling in Sect. 3.3. As Table 4 shows, ASMB3DCNN (FPR) obtains 77.7% in accuracy and 75.3% in AUC score respectively, while the ones of ASMB3DCNN (FPR+3 Attributes) are 96.9% and 96.9%, which shows the significant improvement over ASMB3DCNN (FPR). This phenomenon also indicates that the high-level attributes can benefit the solution of FPR problem. Another interesting

Table 4. Comparison with other studies for FPR

Methods	Accuracy	Sensitivity	Specificity	AUC score
ASMB3DCNN (ALL)	**0.974**	0.935	0.992	0.967
ASMB3DCNN (FPR+3 Attributes)	0.969	0.898	0.996	0.969
ASMB3DCNN (FPR)	0.777	0.697	**0.997**	0.753
Multilevel 3D-CNN [8]	-	0.827	-	-
UACNN (ccanoespinosa)	-	0.824	-	-
NoduleX (CNN47+RF) [6]	0.946	**0.948**	0.943	**0.984**

observation is that ASMB3DCNN (ALL) outperforms ASMB3DCNN (FPR+3 Attributes) particularly in accuracy and sensitivity. The gains of ASMB3DCNN (ALL) over the FPR+Attributes version are 0.5% and 3.7% respectively. This verifies that the labels in a finer grain level is helpful to the solution of a classification task in a coarse level of labels. It also confirms the reasonability of our idea that these two separated issues can be merged into a unified fine grain lung nodule classification problem for better solving them together. Moreover, our proposed approaches have higher accuracy and specificity than other compared approaches. Although our approaches get slightly lower scores in comparison with NoduleX in sensitivity and AUC, NoduleX suffers from a heavier computation burden due to its deeper architecture. NoduleX has more than ten convolutional layers and max-pooling layers, while our models have only 4 convolutional layers.

3.5   Fine Grain Lung Nodule Diagnosis

We conduct experiments via extracting 7000 'fake nodules' from LUNA2016 and 'real nodules' from LIDC-IDRI as the dataset (1:1 fake nodules to real nodules). As Table 5 shows, the fine grain ASMB3DCNN (ALL) obtains 95.7% in the accuracy of classifying Fake Nodules (FN), while the accuracy of ASMB3DCNN (ALL) in Sect. 3.4 is 99.2%. This is because the FPR branch is not trained with the 'real nodule' in LIDC-IDRI, thus this branch has difficulty in classifying 'low risk nodule' and 'fake nodule', which has side effects on system. On the other hand, ASMB3DCNN (ALL) in Sect. 3.3 obtains 99.1% in the accuracy of classifying Low Risk Nodules (LR) and 90.0% in the accuracy of classifying High Risk nodules (HR), while the fine grain ASMB3DCNN (ALL) improve 0.5% and 2.3% in accuracy of classifying LR and HR respectively over ASMB3DCNN (ALL) in MSE, which means the FPR can help to make a distinction between 'low risk nodules' and 'high rick nodules'. In general, the results confirm our idea about FPR and MSE are actually similar tasks and these two separated issues can be merged into a unified fine grain lung nodule classification problem.

Table 5. Results of ASMB3DCNN (ALL)

Method	Acc of FN	Acc of LR	Acc of HR
Fine grain	0.957	0.996	0.923
FPR	0.992	-	-
MSE	-	0.991	0.900

4   Conclusions

In this paper, we propose ASMB3DCNN which can merge two tasks: False Positive Reduction (FPR) and Malignancy Suspiciousness Estimation (MSE) into a unified task: fine grain lung nodule diagnosis. Label 'real nodule' defined in FPR can be split into two new finer grain labels, namely 'low risk' and 'high risk' defined in MSE. We analyse the sensitivity of attributes and choose three attributes to improve the performance of the model. Moreover, we design a method of normalization to improve the performance of each branch and reduce the burden of computation. Experiments show that our model can achieve promising results in FPR, MSE and the task of fine grain lung nodule diagnosis, what's more, our method provides nodule attributes prediction to assist radiologists in evaluating malignancy uncertainty.

We find that this classification system for nodules (1–6 levels and 8 attributes) is problematic. For extremely unbalanced attributes, we should adjust different evaluation criterion. Since attributes have conflict information, sharing high level semantic information may bring negative effects to CNN models. Because of the strong learning ability of CNN and small number of dataset, all models for nodules classification have a risk of over-fitting. Moreover, few models use information of patients like smoking history and family history, which is different from diagnosis process in clinical. Our future work will also focus on fusing information of patients with CNN models to improve ability of generalization, and overcome the problems of predicting unbalance attributes.

Acknowledgment. This work was partially supported by the Chongqing Major Thematic Projects (Grant no. cstc2018jszx-cyztzxX0017).

References

1. Wild, C.P.: International agency for research on cancer. In: Encyclopedia of Toxicology, vol. 133, no. 9, pp. 1067–1069 (2014)
2. Bach, P.B., et al.: Benefits and harms of CT screening for lung cancer: a systematic review. JAMA, J. Am. Med. Assoc. **307**(22), 2418 (2012)
3. Greenspan, H., Van Ginneken, B., Summers, R.M.: Guest editorial deep learning in medical imaging: overview and future promise of an exciting new technique. IEEE Trans. Med. Imaging **35**(5), 1153–1159 (2016)
4. Rajpurkar, P., et al. CheXNet: radiologist-level pneumonia detection on chest X-rays with deep learning. arXiv preprint arXiv:1711.05225 (2017)
5. Wang, X., Peng, Y., Lu, L., Lu, Z., Summers, R.M.: TieNet: text-image embedding network for common thorax disease classification and reporting in chest X-rays. In: Proceedings of the IEEE Conference on Computer Vision and Pattern Recognition, pp. 9049–9058 (2018)
6. Causey, J.L., et al.: Highly accurate model for prediction of lung nodule malignancy with CT scans. Sci. Rep. **8**(1), 9286 (2018)
7. Park, J., Shen Y., Huang, Z., Zorin, M., Wu, N., Phang, J., et al.: Deep neural networks improve radiologists' performance in breast cancer screening. arXiv preprint arXiv:1903.08297v1 (2019)
8. Dou, Q., Chen, H., Yu, L., Qin, J., Heng, P.A.: Multilevel contextual 3-D CNNs for false positive reduction in pulmonary nodule detection. IEEE Trans. Bio-Med. Eng. **64**(7), 1558–1567 (2016)
9. Shen, W., et al.: Multi-crop convolutional neural networks for lung nodule malignancy suspiciousness classification. Pattern Recogn. **61**(61), 663–673 (2017)

10. Hussein, S., Cao, K., Song, Q., Bagci, U.: Risk stratification of lung nodules using 3D CNN-based multi-task learning. In: Niethammer, M., et al. (eds.) IPMI 2017. LNCS, vol. 10265, pp. 249–260. Springer, Cham (2017). https://doi.org/10.1007/978-3-319-59050-9_20

11. Wu, B., Zhou, Z., Wang, J., Wang, Y.: Joint learning for pulmonary nodule segmentation, attributes and malignancy prediction. In: IEEE International Symposium on Biomedical Imaging, pp. 1109–1113 (2018)

12. Shen, S., Han, S.X., Aberle, D.R., Bui, A.A., Hsu, W.: An interpretable deep hierarchical semantic convolutional neural network for lung nodule malignancy classification. Expert Syst. Appl. **128**, 84–95 (2019)

13. Shen, W., Zhou, M., Yang, F., Yang, C., Tian, J.: Multi-scale convolutional neural networks for lung nodule classification. In: Ourselin, S., Alexander, D.C., Westin, C.-F., Cardoso, M.J. (eds.) IPMI 2015. LNCS, vol. 9123, pp. 588–599. Springer, Cham (2015). https://doi.org/10.1007/978-3-319-19992-4_46

14. Kang, G., Liu, K., Hou, B., Zhang, N.: 3D multi-view convolutional neural networks for lung nodule classification. PLoS ONE **12**(11), 12–22 (2017)

15. Yorozu, T., Hirano, M., Oka, K., Tagawa, Y.: Electron spectroscopy studies on magneto-optical media and plastic substrate interface. IEEE Transl. J. Magn. Jpn. **2**(8), 740–741 (1987)

16. Armato, S., et al.: The lung image database consortium (LIDC) and image database resource initiative (IDRI): a completed public database of CT scans for lung nodule analysis. Med. Phys. **37**(Part 6), 3416–3417 (2010)

17. Setio, A.A.A., et al.: Validation, comparison, and combination of algorithms for automatic detection of pulmonary nodules in computed tomography images: the LUNA16 challenge. Med. Image Anal. **42**, 1–13 (2016)

18. Xie, Y., Zhang, J., Xia, Y., Fulham, M., Zhang, Y.: Fusing texture, shape and deep model-learned information at decision level for automated classification of lung nodules on chest CT. Inf. Fusion **42**, 102–110 (2017)

Segmentation Guided Regression Network for Breast Cancer Cellularity

Yixuan Wang, Li Yu[⊠], and Shengwei Wang

School of Electronic Information and Communications,
Huazhong University of Science and Technology (HUST), Wuhan, China
{yixuanwang,hustlyu,kadinwang}@hust.edu.cn

Abstract. Evaluation and diagnosis of breast cancer will be more and more vital in medical field. A general solution to breast cancer cellularity is to modify output of a state-of-the-art classification backbone to prediction a score between 0 and 1. However, this solution does not take clinical meaning of cancer cellularity which defined as proportion of cancer cells over image patches into consideration. In this paper, a segmentation guided regression network is proposed for breast cancer cellularity, adding more semantic detailed features for regression task. Consequently, the proposed method can not only take advantage of global context features from classification backbone, but also position feature and texture feature from segmentation network. A powerful segmentation network with 0.8438 mean Intersection-over-Union is obtained on extremely class imbalanced datasets. The proposed method with Resnet101 as regression backbone gets PK value of 0.9260 and L1 loss of 0.0719.

Keywords: Cancer cellularity · Image segmentation · Non-linear regression

1 Introduction

Breast cancer has become a general and vital problem for women around the world [1,2]. To carry out medical diagnosis and inspection on breast cancer, clinician usually utilize tissue slice as golden ground truth to judge cancer state and what treatment can be executed on the patients and the cancer cellularity is defined as percentage area of cancer cell within a tissue section [3]. Specifically, medical doctors obtain whole slide images (WSI) of breast histological sections by the microscope firstly. Then hematoxylin and eosin are stained on pathological slides. Finally, a caner cellularity or score is given out according to observation on growing state and complicated cell structures of cancer cell within each image patches cropped from a tissue section [4]. The cancer cellularity can be seen as a score between 0 and 1 to describe how severe the tumor condition is. To

Y. Wang—Currently working toward the Master degree in the School of Electric Information and Communications, HuaZhong University of Science and Technology.

help patients get diagnosis results in time, automated methods for breast cancer cellularity are in great demand.

Breast cancer cellularity challenge can be formulated as a non-linear regression problem: using stained image patches cropped from WSI, a cancer score ranging from 0 to 1 is predicted to represent severity of breast cancer. Previous methods utilize traditional segmentation method to get categories of each pixel and machine learning method for regression [5]. Recently, adopting a classification network and modify the last layer of fully connected layer from 1000 categories to a single output together with sigmoid activation function might be a basic solution. Nonetheless, those solution are not end-to-end or do not take the realistic physical significance of cancer cellularity into account. And the features extracted by classification backbone lose high level detailed semantic information. CNNs features are translation invariant and scale invariant to get robust performance in various image instances within a specific category in image classification task, thus features contain global abstract context information and detailed structure or position spatial information might be lost. However, for image segmentation task, appearance and spatial geographic information will be preserved to output a high-resolution map with precise features on each pixel. A segmentation guided regression network is proposed to fuse segmentation features and classification features for regression in this paper.

The designed network is composed of segmentation part which derives from DeepLabv3+ model and regression part which stems from typical classification models like Resnet101. The devised network is trained in two steps sequentially: segmentation network and the whole network for regression. In segmentation task, class imbalance problem is figured out by weighted cross entropy loss and focal loss [15] techniques. The designed model utilizes encoder weights of DeepLabv3+ as initial parameters of segmentation module. And the whole network is updated with L1 loss for regression. The proposed cancer cellularity model is compared with multiple state-of-the-art classification backbones such as Resnet101, Resnet152 [19], Resnext [20], SENet [21] and NASNet [22] on regression task. While all typical backbone with stride of convolution stage1 changed to 2 for computationally efficiency. Experimental results show that the proposed network based on Resnet101 performs better than merely single regression networks with typical CNNs as backbones.

2   Related Works

Deep convolutional neural networks (CNNs) have made great progress in medical image processing [6,7] recently. CNNs are composed of a series of basic components such as two-dimension convolution operation, batch normalization layers, activation function and spatial pooling layers [12]. CNNs have been widely utilized in various vision task such as image classification, image segmentation, object detection and many other high-level tasks in computer vision due to its strong ability for feature extraction.

2.1 CNNs in Semantic Segmentation

State-of-the-art image segmentation methods based on CNNs [8–11] work well on both natural image and medical image. Typical segmentation networks are composed of two modules: encoder module and decoder module. Encoder module performs convolutional operations and max pooling layers for down sampling to obtain a low resolution, rich semantic feature map. Several spatial pooling layers in encoder module are to increase the receptive field of convolutional kernels to get plentiful semantic information. Decoder module adopts the output feature maps of encoder module as input, and executes up-sampling to gain a high-resolution output with abundant categories information for semantic segmentation. General methods of up-sampling are deconvolution operation and bilinear interpolation. Previous improvements on segmentation networks always concentrate on decoder module. To be specific, UNet brings in skip connection in the way like FPN [13] to get high level, high resolution feature maps for better performance. SegNet [14] reuses indices in the max pooling step of encoder module at corresponding decoding layers for more precise up sampling. DeepLabv3+ improves encoder parts of segmentation architecture. DeepLabv3+ focuses on enrichment of encoder module and introduces atrous spatial pyramid pooling layers to extract robust semantic features. DeepLabv3+ model also shows that the design of encoder module is much more significant than decoder module, thus it is believable that the encoder module of segmentation network is responsible for extracting rich semantic features and the decoder part is just used for up sampling. The output stride of segmentation network refers to the ratio of the resolution of input images to feature maps output by the encoder module. The output stride usually equals 16 in segmentation networks.

2.2 CNNs in Image Classification

The fundamental tasks in computer vision are image classification, object detection and semantic segmentation. High level complex tasks such as scene text recognition, automatic driving and image captioning and so on. The most basic task is image classification and all other task adopts CNN parts of image classification model as base network or backbone. Deep learning method outperforms traditional image processing method in computer vision task mostly due to the strong feature extraction ability of convolutional networks. CNNs frameworks in image classification are composed of two parts: CNNs part for extracting convolutional features and fully connected layers used as classifier. CNNs consist of a sequence of two-dimension convolution operations, batch normalization layers, activation functions and max pooling layers. Fully connected layers are made up of linear connected and activation functions.

The main development of classification model focus on CNNs part. From VGGNet [16] to GoogLenet [17], the development in image classification indicates that the increasing depth and width of convolutional layers within CNNs can improve the feature representation ability of CNNs for attaining global context features. By normalizing the input feature maps for each convolutional stage, batch normalization operation is presented to regulating each feature map generated by corresponding convolutional kernel within a batch size, that is, normalizing output values along batch size and spatial dimension in CNNs. Batch normalization in fully connected layers operates in batch size and node dimension. The loss function can get convergence stably and the internal covariate shift is solved by adding batch normalization. However, increasing the depth of CNNs without limitation can lead gradient vanishing problem and gradient exploding problem. Resnet shows that the CNNs can be designed deeper by adding skip connections. Residual blocks within Resnet performs element wise summation between input features maps and output convolutional feature maps. The gradient from upstream is propagated to the input feature maps if the convolutional stage of current residual block is unimportant, thus avoiding gradient accumulation. Attention mechanism is applied in the design of CNNs backbone to guide CNNs to concentrate more on learning meaningful features related to specific task. SENet introduces channel-wise attention information by utilizing squeeze-and-excitation module. Non local neural network [18] performs attention operation on convolutional feature map directly on both channel dimension and spatial dimension.

3   Segmentation Guided Regression Network

The overview of the proposed network is presented in Fig. 1. It is made up of two submodules: segmentation module and regression module. The segmentation module is derived from the encoder part of DeepLabv3+ which can obtain high level and semantic feature map with high resolution. The regression module can be any classification backbones and can acquire global context features. Feature maps from two submodules are fused to be one feature map as input to prediction layers. The fused feature maps which contain rich semantic features and texture information on each pixel can offer corresponding message about cancer cell areas on input images, which makes output results of prediction layers more reasonable and trustworthy. Cancer cells always have significant difference from normal cells in textures and edges, so it is extremely helpful if high-level semantic features or appearance details could be taken into account when scoring input images. Consequently, the prediction procedure of the proposed network is more similar to the realistic clinical meaning of cancer cellularity, that is, the percentage areas of cancer cell within an image patch.

3.1   The Architecture of Segmentation Guided Regression Network

Segmentation Module. Segmentation dataset is adopted to train a DeepLabv3+ network which is pretrained on ImageNet classification task with the guidance of transfer learning. The output stride in encoder part of segmentation network equals 16 to get $32 \times 32 \times 256$ feature maps for $512 \times 512 \times 3$ input images. Output stride is formulated as the ratio of input image resolution to feature map in the last convolutional layer. The segmentation module of the proposed method is identical to encoder part of DeepLabv3+.

Regression Module. Regression network can be arbitrary classification backbones. Given the fact that general classification networks need input of 224 × 224 × 3 and the standard resolution of image patches in classification datasets is 512 × 512 × 3, the stride in first convolutional stage is changed from 1 to 2 in all classification backbones for computational efficiency.

Segmentation Guided Regression Network. A DeepLabv3+ model is trained on segmentation dataset at first. Then the encoder part of DeepLabv3+ segmentation network and regression module in the proposed method are trained simultaneously, while weights in first step are applied as initial parameters for segmentation network encoder part and regression network adopts kaiming normal initialization. The output of DeepLabv3+ encoder is concatenated with the outputs of convolution stage2 of regression network in channel dimension, and both output stride equal 16. To obtain better merged feature map, 3 × 3 and 1 × 1 convolution layers are applied after concatenation of two feature maps from segmentation module and regression module for smoothing. Global average pooling is operated on 8 × 8 feature maps with output stride 64. Finally, fully connected layers and sigmoid activation function are used for score regression.

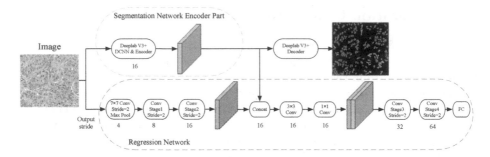

Fig. 1. Network architecture of the proposed segmentation guided regression network for breast cancer cellularity.

3.2   Training

The dataset adopted in this paper is from 2019 MICCAI grand challenge on breast cancer cellularity at http://spiechallenges.cloudapp.net/competitions/14. In this challenge, for regression, there are 2394 training images and 185 validation images with resolution of 512 × 512 in RGB color space, and regression scores are given for both two batches of images. For additional segmentation dataset, only cell nucleus points coordinate ground truth are given for 154 images with various spatial resolutions. That is, the pixel points that are cell nucleus points are marked as a specific category and other pixels are viewed as background points.

Segmentation Ground Truth Generation. Given that only cell nucleus points coordinate ground truth are given for segmentation task, to get cancer cell areas in image patches, ground truth mask should contain information about not only cancer nucleus but also a completed cell area. Therefore, ground truth masks about completed cells are generated with some prior knowledge and traditional algorithms in image processing. Specifically, watershed algorithm is adopted to acquire cell edges and contours, then fill each contour with categories-specific color labels using points coordinate given by experts as center points. Initial image, contours given by watershed algorithm and the generated cell segmentation ground truth are demonstrated in Fig. 2 from left to right, while black/red/blue/green indicates background/malignant cells/normal cells/lymphocyte cells respectively. While center points given by experts are shown as small circles centered on that pixel points for better visualization in the middle column.

Fig. 2. Generation of segmentation ground truth via a set of labeled pixel points. Initial image is on the left. Contours and edges are produced by watershed algorithm via a list of labels points indicated cell nucleus of each categories. Each contour is filled with center categories by a threshold to obtain segmentation ground truth. (Color figure online)

Class Imbalanced in Segmentation. Segmentation dataset is grouped into two parts randomly: 146 training images and 8 images for validation. DeepLabv3+ model with output stride 16 is adopted. In training sets, the number of four categories pixel points are: 71338338, 819834, 1848719, 11644755 which indicates background, lymphocyte cells, normal cells, malignant cells respectively. As a result, severe class imbalance problems should be faced with. Weighted cross entropy and focal loss are adopted to figure out this problem. Small weights are distributed to the categories that have large frequency and a log smooth item is employed to balance weights magnitude. However, experiments show that weighted loss is not too effective to perform well on lymphocyte cells for the reason that lymphocyte category is extremely less in training set. Consequently, focal loss technique which obtain perfect performance in object detection filed is added to force training optimizer pay more attention to hard pixel points.

$$w_i = \frac{1}{\log\left(1.10 + f_i\right)} \tag{1}$$

where f_i is the frequency of specific category cell pixels. Equation (1) shows the method of calculating weights of each categories pixels within a batch size.

Regression Task. The encoder weights of well-trained DeepLabv3+ network are initial parameters value of segmentation module in the proposed network. When training the whole network for regression task, the regression module is initialized with kaiming normal. The whole network with Resnet101 as CNNs backbone is updated using L1 loss.

4   Experimental Results

4.1   Training Strategy

Segmentation Training. When training DeepLabv3+, various augmentation strategies are exploited, such as: scale with ratios from 0.8 to 1.2 randomly, crop a fixed size 256×256 randomly, flip vertically and horizontally randomly. Through contrast experiments, it can be found that it is better to use pretrained parameters on ImageNet classification task as initial weights of the feature extraction networks of segmentation network. SGD optimizer with an initial learning rate 0.01 and batch size 50 is used and the learning rate is decayed every 3000 epochs for total 7000 epochs.

The Whole Network Training. For data augmentation: First rotate images randomly with 0, 90, 180, 270°. Then randomly flip images horizontally and vertically. Finally, shift brightness, contrast, saturation and hue randomly. Adam optimizer is used with start learning rate 0.003 and decay rate 0.1 every 300 epochs for total 900 epochs with batch size 64 on the regression dataset.

4.2   Metrics and Results

Segmentation Results. Tables 1 and 2 shows segmentation MIOU on segmentation validation dataset and training dataset with various γ value in focal loss equation respectively. For the reason that 8 validation images are randomly chosen from segmentation dataset and the number of Lymphocyte pixels is extremely less, so segmentation result on training set is given as a reference. Those process aims to acquire best training strategy on segmentation task, consequently, all data is utilized to obtain an overfitting model to learn high-level complicate semantic features of different kinds of cells. MIOU indicates mean Intersection-over-Union of all categories. PA means pixel accuracy on a specific category and it is formulated as the number of true predictions of that category divides all pixels of that category.

It is obvious that γ equals 1 might be better for class imbalance problem. Tables 3, 4 and 5 demonstrate the results of confusion matrix on validation dataset on different γ values respectively. Confusion matrix is a typical metric in classification problems. The summation of each row equals the number of ground truth samples of specific category and elements of main diagonal are true positive of each category. Take Table 3 for example: the second row, the first column indicates that 225 pixels which are lymphocyte are predicted as background. It is evident that normal pixels and lymphocyte pixels can be distinguished clearly for the reason that there are no normal pixels being predicted as lymphocyte wrongly and vise versa. The mispredicted pixels for foreground categories are always being predicted as background. It might be that the number of background pixels is extremely large and the model tends to predict any pixels that it cannot determinate correct categories as background to minimize the risk (Fig. 3).

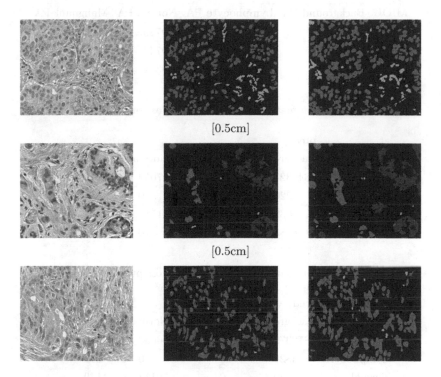

[0.5cm]

[0.5cm]

Fig. 3. Segmentation result with γ equals 1 in focal loss. Initial images are on the first column. Ground truths generated by watershed algorithm are on the second column and predictions by segmentation network are on the last column.

Regression Results. Resnet101, Resnet152, Resnext, SEnet, NASNet and the proposed regression network based on Resnet101 are all trained with L1 loss for non-linear regression. PK value for predicting probability is formulated in [23]. The experiment results express that the proposed segmentation guided regression network gets more excellent performance than any other regression network based on typical classification networks either on PK value or L1 loss. The experimental results also indicate that all state-of-the-art classification backbone get very close performance with regression module merely. The classifi-

Table 1. Segmentation results of different γ in focal loss on validation set.

γ	MIOU	Background PA	Lymphocyte PA	Normal PA	Malignant PA
1	0.6449	0.9467	0.6432	0.9257	0.8608
2	0.6461	0.9421	0.5298	0.9430	0.8824
5	0.6233	0.9344	0.6009	0.9047	0.8902

Table 2. Segmentation results of different γ in focal loss on training set.

γ	MIOU	Background PA	Lymphocyte PA	Normal PA	Malignant PA
1	0.8438	0.9625	0.9663	0.9725	0.9681
2	0.8254	0.9588	0.9631	0.9743	0.9674
5	0.6310	0.9017	0.8044	0.9322	0.8449

Table 3. Confusion matrix of $\gamma = 1$ in focal loss on validation set.

gt	pred			
	Background	Lymphocyte	Normal	Malignant
Background	1840327	7883	17059	58244
Lymphocyte	226	10575	0	2
Normal	1632	0	51512	0
Malignant	8483	51	0	258342

Table 4. Confusion matrix of $\gamma = 2$ in focal loss on validation set.

gt	pred			
	Background	Lymphocyte	Normal	Malignant
Background	1812079	4916	26636	79882
Lymphocyte	4828	5723	0	252
Normal	1890	0	50114	1140
Malignant	31020	356	0	235500

Table 5. Confusion matrix of $\gamma = 5$ in focal loss on validation set.

gt	pred			
	Background	Lymphocyte	Normal	Malignant
Background	1797263	7707	30056	88487
Lymphocyte	4278	6492	0	33
Normal	3304	0	48079	1761
Malignant	28313	1000	0	237563

cation backbone can extract global abstract features without detailed texture features. Consequently, the regression layers cannot distinguish which category each pixels belong to and cannot get area of cancer cell in image patches which generate accurate prediction score for cancer cellularity. The proposed segmentation guided regression network utilizes both semantic features from segmentation module and global context features from regression module to obtain rich features for better regression performance (Table 6).

Table 6. Evaluation of different network on regression validation dataset.

Model	Resnet101	Resnet152	Resnext	SEnet	NASnet	The proposed
PK	0.9229	0.9206	0.9228	0.9232	0.9237	0.9260
L1 distance	0.0779	0.07231	0.0778	0.0735	0.0748	0.0719

5   Conclusion

In this paper, a segmentation guided regression network was proposed to fuse segmentation feature and classification feature to extract more detailed abstract semantic features for regression task. Segmentation features are usually with high resolution and well-preserved geometric information to get better understanding of local pixels, while classification features contain global context. The final prediction score is based on the fused feature map which contains high level semantic features and global context information. The main idea behind the proposed network is to combine segmentation features and classification features to gain higher performance on scoring task.

The segmentation guided regression network is trained by two steps sequentially. First, a completed DeepLabv3+ model is trained with multi-categories cross entropy and focal loss on segmentation dataset with backbone weights initialized on ImageNet classification task. Next, the whole network is trained with L1 loss for regression. And the segmentation module of network is initialized by encoder part of DeepLabv3+ in the first step. Resnet101 is used as base network in network with kaiming normal initialization. Experimental results indicate that the proposed segmentation guided regression network performs better than using a regression network merely.

References

1. Siegel, R.L., Miller, K.D., Jemal, A.: Cancer statistics. CA Cancer J. Clin. **65**(1), 5–29 (2015)
2. Symmans, W.F., et al.: Measurement of residual breast cancer burden to predict survival after neoadjuvant chemotherapy. J. Clin. Oncol. **25**(28), 4414–4422 (2007)
3. Thompson, A.M., Moulder-Thompson, S.L.: Neoadjuvant treatment of breast cancer. Ann. Oncol. **23**, x231–x236 (2012)

4. Hermanek, P., Wittekind, C.: Residual tumor (R) classification and prognosis. In: Seminars in Surgical Oncology (1994)
5. Peikari, M., Salama, S., Nofech-Mozes, S., et al.: Automatic cellularity assessment from post-treated breast surgical specimens. Cytom. Part A **91**(11), 1078–1087 (2017)
6. Wang, Z., Liu, C., Cheng, D.: Automated detection of clinically significant prostate cancer in mp-MRI images based on an end-to-end deep neural network. IEEE Trans. Med. Imaging **37**, 1127–1139 (2018)
7. Mehta, S., Mercan, E., Bartlett, J.: Y-Net: joint segmentation and classification for diagnosis of breast biopsy images. CoRR, abs/1806.01313 (2018)
8. Long, J., Shelhamer, E., Darrell, T.: Fully convolutional networks for semantic segmentation. In: The IEEE Conference on Computer Vision and Pattern Recognition (2015)
9. Ronneberger, O., Fischer, P., Brox, T.: U-Net: convolutional networks for biomedical image segmentation. CoRR abs/1505.04597 (2015)
10. Chen, L.-C., Zhu, Y.: Encoder-decoder with atrous separable convolution for semantic image segmentation. arXiv:1802.02611 (2018)
11. Chen, L.-C., Papandreou, G., Schroff, F.: Rethinking atrous convolution for semantic image segmentation. CoRR, abs/1706.0558 (2017)
12. Ioffe, S., Szegedy, C.: Batch normalization: accelerating deep network training by reducing internal covariate shift. CoRR, abs/1502.03167 (2015)
13. Lin, T.-Y., et al.: Feature pyramid networks for object detection. In: Proceedings of the IEEE Conference on Computer Vision and Pattern Recognition (2017)
14. Badrinarayanan, V., Kendall, A., Cipolla, R.: SegNet: a deep convolutional encoder-decoder architecture for image segmentation. IEEE Trans. Pattern Anal. Mach. Intell. **39**(12), 2481–2495 (2017)
15. Lin, T.-Y., Goyal, P.: Focal loss for dense object detection. IEEE Trans. Pattern Anal. Mach. Intell. (2018)
16. Simonyan, K., Zisserman, A.: Very deep convolutional networks for large-scale image recognition. arXiv preprint arXiv:1409.1556 (2014)
17. Szegedy, C., et al.: Going deeper with convolutions. In: Proceedings of the IEEE Conference on Computer Vision and Pattern Recognition (2015)
18. Wang, X., Girshick, R., Gupta, A., He, K.: Non-local neural networks. In: Proceedings of the IEEE Conference on Computer Vision and Pattern Recognition, pp. 7794–7803 (2018)
19. He, K., Zhang, X.: Deep residual learning for image recognition. In: Proceedings of the IEEE Conference on Computer Vision and Pattern Recognition, pp. 770–778 (2016)
20. Xie, S., Girshick, R., Dollár, P., Tu, Z., He, K.: Aggregated residual transformations for deep neural networks. In: Computer Vision and Pattern Recognition (2017)
21. Jie, H., Li, S.: Squeeze-and-excitation networks. arXiv preprint arXiv:1709.01507 (2017)
22. Zoph, B., Vasudevan, V., Shlens, J.: Learning transferable architectures for scalable image recognition. arXiv preprint arXiv:1707.07012 (2017)
23. Smith, W.D., Dutton, R.C., Smith, N.T.: A measure of assosication for assessing prediction accuracy that is a generalization of non-parameteric ROC area. Stat. Med. **15**(11), 1199 (1996)

Automatic Inspection of Yarn Locations by Utilizing Histogram Segmentation and Monotone Hypothesis

Yu Han and Ling Luo[✉]

Shenzhen Key Laboratory of Advanced Machine Learning and Applications,
College of Mathematics and Statistics, Shenzhen University,
Shenzhen 518060, China
hany@szu.edu.cn, luoling2018@email.szu.edu.cn

Abstract. We present an automatic method for the estimation of yarn locations in fabric images. The proposed method is based on histogram segmentation and a so-called monotone hypothesis which is a nonparametric statistical approach. In this method, accumulated partial derivatives histograms are statistically unimodal, which indicate the periodic structures of fabric images. Then, the monotone hypothesis is applied to divide the histograms into several segments. According to the maximum value and the minimum value of the histograms in each segment, the locations of yarn boundaries and yarn centers can be correspondingly estimated. The method reduces the influence of yarn random texture noise that comes from yarn hairiness, improving the accuracy of detection. Furthermore, compared with classical method based on image smoothing, the proposed method can avoid over-smoothing of the edges of yarns.

Keywords: Yarn density · Weave mode · Fabric image · Nonparametric estimation · Image segmentation

1 Introduction

Yarn locations contribute a lot in fabric producing processes, such as real-time monitoring fabric woven processes, and it refers to the process of locating each yarn in a fabric image. Since it is laborious to count yarn manually, textile researchers tend to focus on some automatic methods for estimating yarn locations and numbers in fabric images. Then, the yarn localization problem becomes an important research topic in the field of fabric image processing.

As patterns woven by warp and weft yarn have a certain periodicity, a fabric image is usually transformed into its frequency/time-frequency domain, where the higher frequency coefficients in the domain relate to yarn boundary details. Many researchers tend to select Fourier transform to estimate yarn numbers in the fabric image [1–3].

For example, based on Fourier transform, Pan et al. [1] propose a new method to determine the locations and numbers of weft and warp yarn. In the method, according to the amplitude spectrum of a fabric image, a new image which indicates boundaries of yarn is reconstructed by thresholding lower frequency coefficients. The model is

© Springer Nature Switzerland AG 2019
Z. Lin et al. (Eds.): PRCV 2019, LNCS 11858, pp. 161–172, 2019.
https://doi.org/10.1007/978-3-030-31723-2_14

suitable to deal with clear boundary fabric images. However, as pointed out by the work in [2], some incorrect results can be generated from Pan's model for some high tightness fabric. Then, Pan et al. [2] use the relation of yarn location structure in twill and satin fabric to estimate yarn numbers in high-density fabric images.

Similarly, the wavelet transform method can also be a way to extract the boundaries of the yarn and reconstruct a fabric image [4–7]. And compared with Fourier transform, wavelet transform has lower computation complexity and higher efficient. Jing et al. [4] apply decomposition and reconstruction filters, generated from spline Biorthogonal wavelet 3.7, to obtain the outline of each yarn in a fabric image and locate them via Bernsen algorithm and smooth processing. With the help of Gabor filter, Aldemir et al. [6] detect the edge of the yarn in a fabric image and extract its texture structure, and then count the number of local peaks of the gray line profile, obtained from Gray Line Profile method, to determine the number of yarn in the image.

Besides the methods mentioned above, gray projection method [8–12] is used to estimate the yarn counts and yarn locations in a fabric image. After detecting the skew angle in a fabric image by Hough transform, Pan et al. [8] project the pixels along the skew-direction, obtaining the projection curve. Then, the local maximum and local maximum, representing the position and the edge of yarn, respectively, are used to locate each yarn in a fabric image. Although the method is effective for solid color fabrics, it seems that it is unsuitable for the fabric image with more than two colors. Zhang et al. [9] introduce a Otsu algorithm-based projection method to inspect yarn locations. An optical system of SMZ 140-N2LED is used to generate a transmission image from a fabric image, which can reduce the effect of color difference on density detection.

Additionally, for yarn-dyed fabrics, Pan et al. [10] apply Fuzzy C-clustering Method (FCM) to segment the colors in CIELAB color space, which can partition a fabric image into different color regions. Then, the position of yarn in different regions can be determined by the gray-projection method and correlation coefficient. Yet, the approach is unsuitable for fabric images with scattered color regions or containing some similar colors and it is difficult to select the initial clustering centers which will affect the clustering results. Meanwhile, the nonlinear deformation of the yarn is not considered, when using Hough transform to detect the skew angle. Hence, Zheng et al. [12] utilize lightness gradient projection method to obtain the projection curve. And the structure–texture decomposition method is used to enhance the accuracy of detection.

While these approaches can successfully estimate the yarn density and position in different fabric images, some procedures in these methods are relatively complicated. To overcome the difficulty, in this paper we propose a new yarn locating method which is based on the histogram segmentation. The new method can estimate the number as well as the locations of both weft and warp yarn in plain-weave fabric images automatically. It is worth noting that, originally, the histogram segmentation algorithm is used to achieve image segmentation and color extraction in [13–15]. However, in this paper we generate the algorithm to dealing with our yarn localization problem. Firstly, instead of applying *rgb2gray* function in Matlab, we convert the color plain-weave fabric image into the grayscale images with the method in [16], which can extract the boundaries of the yarn with higher accuracy. Secondly, propose to apply monotone hypothesis [14] to segment the accumulated histograms. Contrasted with the smoothing based method, the estimation of yarn numbers and the locations of each yarn are better preserved in our method.

2   Our Method

2.1   Calculating Accumulated Partial Derivatives

Firstly, given a color image of size $H \times W$, we convert the image into its grayscale image g by the method in [16], where $g(x,y)$ is the grayscale value of the pixel (x,y). For determining the boundary of the yarn, the modulus of discrete partial derivatives in warp and weft directions are selected to indicate the periodic structures of fabric images. The definitions at (x,y) is

$$\begin{cases} \nabla g_x = |g(x,y) - g(x+1,y)| \\ \nabla g_y = |g(x,y) - g(x,y+1)| \end{cases} \tag{1}$$

Then, we project the modulus of discrete partial derivatives in two directions, respectively, to get accumulated partial derivatives histograms. Here, $d(x)$ is the accumulated partial derivatives in the warp direction and $d(y)$ is the one in the weft direction.

$$\begin{cases} d(x) = \sum_y \nabla g_x \\ d(y) = \sum_x \nabla g_y \end{cases} \tag{2}$$

2.2   Histogram Segmentation

Ideally, from yarn centers to yarn boundaries, accumulated partial derivatives histograms are increasing, while from boundaries to centers of yarns, the values of histograms tend to decrease. It means that in accumulated partial derivatives histograms, peaks (local maximum) correspond to yarn boundaries, and valleys (local minimum) correspond to yarn centers. Thus, because of the periodic structures of fabric image, the accumulated partial derivative histogram can be divided into several intervals, and the distribution of each interval is unimodal.

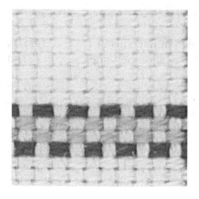 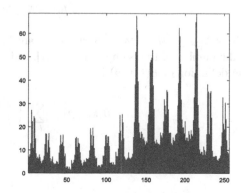

Fig. 1. The accumulated partial derivatives histogram of plain-weave fabric image.

However, influenced by yarn hairiness and color pattern [22], the accumulated partial derivatives histogram is "statistically unimodal" [14]. For example, a plain-weave fabric images and its accumulated partial derivatives histograms is shown in Fig. 1. In Fig. 1(b), the accumulated partial derivatives histogram is likely unimodal.

Hence, not all local maximums and local minimums indicate yarn locations. To find right peaks and valleys, the monotone hypothesis [14] is used to segment histograms, and yarn locations are estimated by the maximum and minimum in each segment.

Monotone Hypothesis. As introduced by Desolneux et al. [21], the test statistic in monotone hypothesis is the number of false alarms (NFA) [17–19]. Under an assumption that the distribution of an object is monotonically decreasing/increasing, if the NFA is more than a given parameter ε, the objects can be grouped together.

After obtaining a horizontal/vertical accumulated partial derivatives histogram $d = \{d(x_i)\}_{i=1,2,\ldots,M}$ from a fabric image, there are T samples on M bins $M \in \{H, W\}$. Here, T is the total number of pixels in the fabric image, $T = H \times W$.

Let $d(x_i)$ be the value of histogram d in the i-th bin ($i = 1, 2, \ldots, M$), and $d(x_i)$ follows that:

$$\sum_{i=1}^{M} d(x_i) = T. \tag{3}$$

Assume that $P(M)$ is the space of normalized probability distributions on $\{1, 2, \ldots, M\}$ and $I(M)$ be the space of increasing densities on $\{1, 2, \ldots, M\}$.

In interval $[x_a, x_b]$ $(1 \leq a, b \leq M), r(a, b) \in P(M)$ is the proportion of points in T

$$r(a, b) = \frac{1}{T} \sum_{i=a}^{b} d(x_i). \tag{4}$$

Then, monotone hypothesis H_0 in interval $[x_a, x_b]$ is that the histogram d obeys the Bernoulli distribution with the parameter $p(a, b) \in I(M)$, and the discussion about the decreasing is similar.

In [18, 19], under the Bernoulli distribution with the parameter $p(a, b)$, the definition of NFA is

$$NFA([a, b]) = N_{test} B(k_t, v_t, p(a, b)). \tag{5}$$

where $N_{test} = (M + 1)M/2$ means there are N_{test} different intervals in $\{1, 2, \ldots, M\}$, k_t is the number of true samples in $[x_a, x_b]$, and v_t is the total of the samples, $v_t = T$, and the definition of $B(k, v, p)$ is

$$B(k, v, p) = \sum_{i=k}^{v} \binom{v}{i} p^i (1 - p)^{v-i}. \tag{6}$$

If $r(a,b) \geq p(a,b)$, the probability that at least $Tr(a,b)$ samples are included in $[x_a, x_b]$ is $B(Tr(a,b), T, p(a,b))$, then we have $k_t = Tr(a,b)$ and

$$NFA([a,b]) = \frac{M(M+1)}{2} B(Tr(a,b), T, p(a,b)). \tag{7}$$

If $r(a,b) \leq p(a,b)$, the probability that less than $Tr(a,b)$ samples are included in $[x_a, x_b]$ is $B(0, Tr(a,b), p(a,b)) = B(T(1 - r(a,b)), T, 1 - p(a,b))$, then we have $k_t = T(1 - r(a,b))$ and

$$NFA([a,b]) = \frac{M(M+1)}{2} B(T(1 - r(a,b)), T, 1 - p(a,b)). \tag{8}$$

Therefore, the hypothesis H_0 is rejected when $NFA < \varepsilon$ and accepted when $NFA \geq \varepsilon$. However, the calculation of NFA is complicated. We can use the sufficient condition of $NFA < \varepsilon$ to decide whether H_0 is rejected.

Theorem 1. In interval $[x_a, x_b]$, there are two Bernoulli distributions with the parameter $r(a, b)$ and $p(a, b)$ respectively. If relative entropy

$$KL(r(a,b) \| p(a,b)) > \frac{1}{T} \log \frac{M(M+1)}{2\varepsilon}, \tag{9}$$

we have $NFA([a,b]) < \varepsilon$, where

$$KL(r(a,b) \| p(a,b)) = r(a,b) \log \frac{r(a,b)}{p(a,b)} + (1 - r(a,b)) \log \frac{1 - r(a,b)}{1 - p(a,b)}. \tag{10}$$

Hence, relative entropy $KL(r \| p)$ can be selected as the test statistic in H_0. If relative entropy $KL(r \| p)$ satisfies the inequality (9), hypothesis H_0 is rejected, owervise H_0 is accepted.

In addition, since relative entropy $KL(r \| p)$ can measure the difference between two probability distributions $r(a,b)$ and $p(a,b)$, we use $\tilde{p}(a,b) \in I(M)$ that minimizes $KL(r \| p)$ as the parameter in H_0

$$\tilde{p}(a,b) = \arg \min_{p(a,b) \in I(M)} KL(r(a,b) \| p(a,b)). \tag{11}$$

It has been proven [20] that $\tilde{p}(a, b)$ can be derived from $r(a, b)$ by an algorithm called "Pool Adjacent Violators". Figure 2 shows the result obtained from Pool Adjacent Violators Algorithm.

We perform monotone hypothesis on all the intervals of the histogram d and combine the intervals where the hypothesis H_0 is accepted. Then, we obtain n monotonically increasing and m monotonically decreasing intervals. The maximum and minimum in each segment are used to estimate yarn locations in a fabric image. The yarn localization method is described as Algorithm 1.

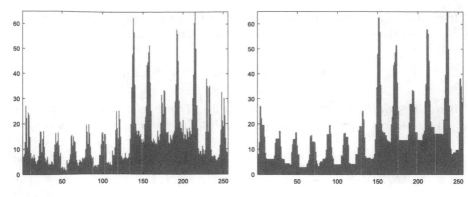

Fig. 2. The results obtained from Pool Adjacent Violators Algorithm, where (a) is the accumulated partial derivatives histogram of a plain-weave fabric image, (b) is the histogram obtained from the Pool Adjacent Violators Algorithm.

Algorithm 1. Nonparametric Histogram Segmentation for Yarn Localization

---

Input: A color plain-weave fabric image

Pre-process: Convert the color fabric image into a grayscale image g, and generate accumulated partial derivatives histograms d.

Require: Parameter ε and step size h

Initialization:

Select the set $s = \{s_1, ..., s_m\}$, containing the position of all the peaks and troughs in the histogram, as the finest segmentation of the histogram.

Repeat:

In $[s_i, s_{i+h}]$, calculate $r(s_i, s_{i+h})$ of histograms d and $p(s_i, s_{i+1})$ by Pool Adjacent Violators Algorithm where i from 1 to length(s)-h.

Perform monotone hypothesis on the interval $[s_i, s_{i+h}]$ (i =1,2,..., length(s)-h).

Compute relative entropy $KL(r \| p)$, if $KL(r \| p)$ satisfies the inequality (9), hypothesis H_0 is rejected, overwise H_0 is accepted.

Then, combine the intervals where H_0 hypothesis is accepted.

Update s

Stop when s is no longer changes.

Output: the abscissa of the peak in each segment is the yarn boundaries in the fabric image, and the abscissa of the midpoint in two peaks is the yarn centers.

---

3   Numerical Results

In this section, we inspect the yarn counts in several typical plain-weave fabric images to illustrate the effectiveness of our proposed method and compare our method with the smoothing based method. Both methods are implemented in MATLAB R2017a on a 1.86-GHz Intel dual-core computer. All testing fabric images are provided from the

GAMA Lab of the Hong Kong Polytechnic University, including the single-yarn structure and the double yarn structure, with 96 DPI and RGB true color mode. We fix the size of the images to be 256 × 256.

3.1 Automatic Selection of Parameter

The value of the parameter ε can influence the position and number of yarns in an image. Let $e = -\log\varepsilon$, and the smaller the value of e, the finer the histogram is divided. Since the width of each yarn is substantially the same, the length of each segment should be similar.

Let t_i be the length of the i-th segmentation interval, and then we select the e that minimizes the variance $\sigma^2(t_i)$ as a parameter in the histogram segmentation. Thereby the locations of each weft and warp yarn are determined adaptively. In Fig. 3(b) and (c) show the effect of the parameter e on the yarn localization and the result obtained by our automatic method is displayed in (d).

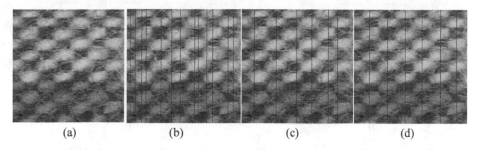

     (a)   (b)   (c)   (d)

Fig. 3. The estimate results of the location of each warp yarn with different e, where (a) is the original image (256 × 256 pixels), and (b)–(d) are the position and number of yarn with different e, and $e = 1$ in (b), $e = 100$ in (c) and $e = 28$ in (d).

3.2 Detection of the Warp and Weft Yarn

In this section, we make use of several fabric samples to evaluate the proposed method and compare it with a classical yarn localization method which is based on image smoothing [23]. Here, in the smoothing based method, color bilateral filter is used to reduce the influence of yarn hairiness and color pattern on detection.

Figure 4 displays the detection results in a plain-weave fabric images, which obtained by our method and the smoothing based method, respectively, where (a) shows the input image, (b) shows the results of histogram segmentation in vertical and horizontal detections, (c) and (d) show the locations of each warp and weft yarn obtained from the smoothing based method and the our method, respectively.

However, from Figs. 5 and 6, contrast with our method, it shows that there are misjudgments and missed judgment of the locations of warp and weft yarn by the smoothing based method, while it can get the correct estimation results by our method. Furthermore, we estimate the number of the warp and weft yarn in five different fabric images with these two methods and the results of yarn counts are shown in Table 1.

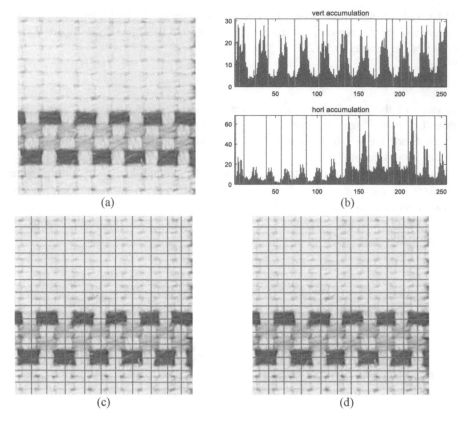

Fig. 4. The location of each yarn obtained from different methods, where (a) is the input fabric image (256 × 256 pixels), (b) is the segmentation results of vertical and horizontal accumulated histograms, (c) and (d) show the locations of each warp and weft yarn obtained from the smoothing based method and the our method, respectively.

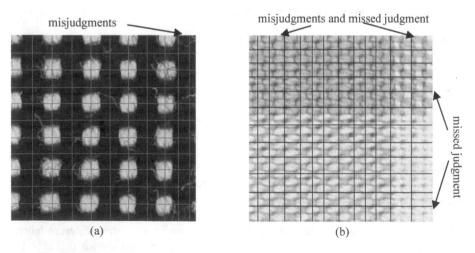

Fig. 5. The detection results of yarn obtained from the smoothing based method.

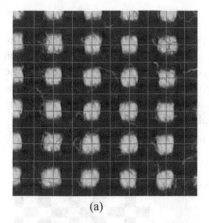
(a)

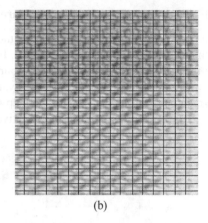
(b)

Fig. 6. The detection results of yarn obtained from our method.

Table 1. Vertical and horizontal yarn number of different fabric images

Image name	Vertical and horizontal number (our method)	Vertical and horizontal number (the smoothing based method)	Actual number
GAAD-59017b-S1_1	**(13, 25)**	(13, 12)	(13, 25)
GAAD-54760b-S1_1	**(17, 26)**	(12, 11)	(17, 26)
GAAK-00963-S1_1	**(18, 26)**	(9, 13)	(18, 26)
GAAK-01348-S1_4	**(11, 11)**	(10, 11)	(11, 11)
GAAK-01338-S1_1	**(10, 13)**	(10, 13)	(10, 13)

Compared with the smoothing based method, our method generates better results. This is because that in the smoothing based method, parameters are not easily to be determined, which may cause yarns in fabric images to be over-smoothed. Then, few weak edge details of yarns are preserved by the smoothing based method. Furthermore, the method is unsuitable for fabric images with dark color yarns [22].

We detect yarn location of 120 fabric images in GAMA Lab, and the accuracy in both weft and warp directions and is as high as 90% (Table 2).

Table 2. The accuracy of yarn localization

	Vertical direction for original image	Horizontal direction for original image
The accuracy	90.20%	96.40%

3.3 Detection of the Fabric Structure

Our detection method can be applied to the detection of the plain-weave fabric structure with multiple color effects. For example, Fig. 7(c) displays the structure detection result for the plain-weave fabric image by our method. Additionally, in Fig. 7(b), it also shows the representative color for each yarn patch, which is obtained by calculating the average color of the patch, with the help of our method. More examples are shown in Fig. 8, which further confirm the effectiveness of our approach.

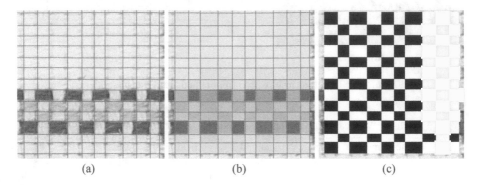

Fig. 7. The detection result of the double yarn structure, where (a) shows fabric boundary grid, (b) shows the representative color for each yarn patch, and (c) shows the detection result.

Fig. 8. The structure detection results in different fabric images with the single-yarn structure and the double yarn structure.

4   Conclusion

In this paper, a new method for automatically locating each yarn and calculating the yarn counts based on histogram segmentation is proposed. The approach can inspect the location and the numbers of the weft and warp yarn in the plain-weave fabric images automatically, and it suitable for the fabric images with different structure, including the single-yarn structure and the double yarn structure. The key step of the method is based on a nonparametric monotone hypothesis, which is utilized to segment the accumulated partial derivatives histogram in a plain-weave image. The segment results determine the numbers and locations of yarn. The experiments indicate that the accuracy for the detecting the yarn numbers in the fabric image is above 90%, and our detection method can also be used to detect the plain-weave fabric structure.

Acknowledgements. This work was supported in part by the National Natural Science Foundation of China (Grants 61872429, 61402290, 61472257 and 61772343); in part by the Natural Science Foundation of Guangdong (Grant 1714050003822); and in part by the Natural Science Foundation of Shenzhen (Grants JCYJ20170818091621856).

References

1. Pan, R., Gao, W., Li, Z., Gou, J., Zhang, J., Zhu, D.: Measuring thread densities of woven fabric using the Fourier transform. Fibres Text. East. Eur. **23**(1), 35–40 (2015)
2. Pan, R., Zhang, J., Li, Z., Gao, W., Xu, B., Li, W.: Applying image analysis for automatic density measurement of high-tightness woven fabrics. Fibres Text. East. Eur. **24**(2), 66–72 (2016)
3. Zhang, J., Pan, R., Gao, W.: Automatic inspection of density in yarn-dyed fabrics by utilizing fabric light transmittance and Fourier analysis. Appl. Opt. **54**(4), 966 (2015)
4. He, F., Li, L., Xu, J.: Woven fabric density measure based on adaptive wavelets transform. J. Text. Res **28**(2), 32–35 (2007)
5. Jing, J., Liu, S., Li, P., Li, Q., Liu, S., Jiang, M.: Automatic density detection of woven fabrics via wavelet transform. J. Inf. Comput. Sci. **11**(8), 2559–2568 (2014)
6. Technikova, L., Tunak, M.: Weaving density evaluation with the aid of image analysis. Fibres Text. East. Eur. **98**(2), 74–79 (2013)
7. Pan, R., Gao, W., Liu, J., Wang, H.: Automatic inspection of woven fabric density of solid colour fabric density by the Hough transform. Fibres Text. East. Eur. **81**(4), 46–51 (2010)
8. Zhang, J., Gao, W., Pan, R.: A backlighting method for accurate inspection of woven fabric density. Ind. Textila **68**(1), 31–36 (2017)
9. Pan, R., Liu, J., Gao, W.: Measuring linear density of threads in single system melange color fabrics with FCM algorithm. Color Res. Appl. **38**(6), 456–462 (2013)
10. Zhang, J., Pan, R., Gao, W., Zhu, D.: Automatic inspection of yarn-dyed fabric density by mathematical statistics of sub-images. J. Text. Inst. **106**(8), 823–834 (2015)
11. Zheng, D., Wang, L.: Multi-scale density detection for yarn-dyed fabrics with deformed repeat patterns. Text. Res. J. **87**(20), 2524–2540 (2017)
12. Aldemir, E., Özdemir, H., Sarı, Z.: An improved gray line profile method to inspect the warp–weft density of fabrics. J. Text. Inst. **110**(1), 105–116 (2019)
13. Delon, J., Desolneux, A., Lisani, J.L., Petro, A.B.: Automatic color palette. In IEEE International Conference on Image Processing 2005, vol. 2, pp. II–706. IEEE (2005)

14. Delon, J., Desolneux, A., Lisani, J.L., Petro, A.B.: A nonparametric approach for histogram segmentation. IEEE Trans. Image Process. **16**(1), 253–261 (2007)
15. Delon, J., Desolneux, A., Lisani, J.L., Petro, A.B.: Automatic color palette. Inverse Probl. Imaging **1**(2), 265–287 (2007)
16. Lu, C., Xu, L., Jia, J.: Real-time contrast preserving decolorization. In: SIGGRAPH Asia 2012 Posters, p. 161. ACM, Singapore (2012)
17. Eduardo, B.C., Jan-Olof, E.: Progress in Pattern Recognition, Image Analysis, Computer Vision, and Applications, p. 967. Springer, Heidelberg (2009). https://doi.org/10.1007/978-3-642-10268-4
18. Le Hegarat-Mascle, S., Aldea, E., Vandoni, J.: Efficient evaluation of the number of false alarm criterion. EURASIP J. Image Video Process. **2019**(1), 35 (2019)
19. Rajaei, B., von Gioi, R.G., Morel, J.: From line segments to more organized gestalts. In: 2016 IEEE Southwest Symposium on Image Analysis and Interpretation (SSIAI), pp. 137–140. IEEE (2016)
20. Miriam, A., Brunk, H.D., Ewing, G.M., Reid, W.T., Edward, S.S.: An empirical distribution function for sampling with incomplete information. Ann. Math. Stat. **26**(4), 641–647 (1955)
21. Desolneux, A., Moisah, L., Morel, J.M.: A grouping principle and four applications. IEEE Trans. Pattern Anal. Mach. Intell. **25**(4), 508–513 (2003)
22. Pan, R., Gao, W., Liu, J., Wang, H., Zhang, X.: Automatic detection of structure parameters of yarn-dyed fabric. Text. Res. J. **80**(17), 1819–1832 (2010)
23. Zheng, D.: A new method for automatic separation of fabric color. Text. Res. J. **85**(14), 1520–1538 (2015)

Membranous Nephropathy Identification Using Hyperspectral Microscopic Images

Xueling Wei[1], Tianqi Tu[2], Nianrong Zhang[2], Yue Yang[2], Wenge Li[2], and Wei Li[1,3(✉)]

[1] Beijing University of Chemical Technology, Beijing 100029, China
[2] China-Japan Friendship Hospital, Beijing 100029, China
[3] Beijing Institute of Technology, Beijing 100081, China
liwei089@ieee.org

Abstract. In clinical diagnosis of membranous nephropathy (MN), separating hepatitis B virus-associated membranous nephropathy (HBV-MN) and primary membranous nephropathy (PMN) is an important step. Currently, most diagnostic technique is to conduct immunofluorescence on kidney biopsy samples with high false positive probability. In this paper, an automatic MN identification approach using medical hyperspectral microscopic images is developed. The proposed framework, denoted as local fisher discriminant analysis-deep neural network (LFDA-DNN), firstly constructs a subspace with well separability for HBV-MN and PMN through projection, and then obtains high-level features that are beneficial for final classification via a DNN-based network. To evaluate the effectiveness of LFDA-DNN, experiments are implemented on a real MN dataset, and the results confirm the superiority of LFDA-DNN for recognising HBV-MN and PMN precisely.

Keywords: Hyperspectral microscopic images · MN Identification · Deep neural network

1 Introduction

Nowadays, chronic kidney disease (CKD) has become a prevalent global health issue that harms people's fitness seriously [18]. If CKD develops into chronic renal failure uremia, patients and their families will bear a lot of economic and psychological burdens. Among CKDs, membranous nephropathy (MN) is one of the most common pathological types of adult nephrotic syndrome [1], of which the characteristic pathological changes are immune complex deposition in the glomerular capillaries epithelium, accompanied by glomerular base membrane (GBM) diffuse thickening. Depending on the causes of the disease, MN could be divided into primary membranous nephropathy (PMN) and secondary

This work was supported by Beijing Natural Science Foundation (4172043), Beijing Nova Program (Z171100001117050), and in part by the Research Fund for Basic Researches in Central Universities under Grant PYBZ1831.

© Springer Nature Switzerland AG 2019
Z. Lin et al. (Eds.): PRCV 2019, LNCS 11858, pp. 173–184, 2019.
https://doi.org/10.1007/978-3-030-31723-2_15

membranous nephropathy (SMN), and hepatitis B virus-associated membranous nephropathy (HBV-MN) is a popular variety of SMN. To be specific, HBV-MN is a nephropathy that secondary to hepatitis B virus (HBV) infection of the immune complex mediated.

In practical diagnosis, differentiating HBV-MN and PMN is a crucial procedure of making accurate diagnosis for MN. Clinically, there are three primary methods based on renal biopsy for MN detection: light microscopy, immunofluorescence or immunohistochemistry, and electron microscopy. Actually, subjected to price and other factors, hospitals usually regard the second as the most commonly used detection technique [4]. However, methods based on immunofluorescence or immunohistochemistry have a certain probability of false positives and consume many human resources. Hence, computer-based automatic identification methods for MN, which have been drawn attention, are essential to be explored to provide verification and supplementation for the immunofluorescence results and relieve the burden of doctors.

Conventional bi-dimensionality images acquired by optical microscopes just utilize the morphological information of samples, while hyperspectral image (HSI) possesses abundant spatial and spectral information simultaneously [11,20]. HSI technique was originally explored in remote sensing fields and applied into biomedical fields gradually, such as disease diagnosis [14], and cell identification [2,12]. Wang et al. has successfully combined HSI skillfulness with microscopic imaging for classifying five-type white blood cells [16]. Furthermore, the value of integrating HSI technique with microscopy was highlighted [3] in the journal of Science. Generally, different material compositions would lead to discrepancies in spectral curves, which is beneficial for recognising HBV-MN and PMN precisely, this is because the immune complex components of HBV-MN and PMN are different due to their diverse pathogenesis.

Although the spectral curves of HBV-MN and PMN own differences, the curves also have high similarity since both of HBV-MN and PMN's pathological changes are immune complex deposition, which increases the challenge of identifying HBV-MN and PMN. Therefore, projection transformation is employed to dispose the problem aforementioned. As a typical variety of dimensionality reduction paradigms, projection transformation is advantageous for acquiring an optimal reduced subspace with highly separability for features. Moreover, HSI data often has redundant information as its hundreds of spectral channels are regularly with high correlation, hence dimensionality reduction methods have become a prevalent preprocessing step for utilizing HSI data. Common projection transformation techniques contain unsupervised approaches, such as principal component analysis (PCA) and independent component analysis (ICA), associated with supervised approaches, such as Fisher's linear discriminant analysis (LDA) [19]. An obvious disadvantage of paradigms like PCA, ICA and LDA is that all of them are only suitable for processing data with gaussian distribution [13]. However, in most practical circumstances, the distribution of data is not gaussian. Moreover, the dimension of the reduced subspace for LDA technique is upper restricted to $c - 1$ (c is the number of varieties for classification objects).

In the recent decade, artificial neural network (ANN) experienced rapid development and has grown up to be a powerful technique in image processing field. Among ANNs, as the representative of deep learning (DL) algorithms, deep convolutional neural network (CNN) has superiority to image processing tasks for its capability of acquiring deep and high-grade features in data. Furthermore, compared with fully connected networks, CNN has fewer parameters, which enhances computational efficiency. Particularly, CNN models have been successfully applied in HSI data classification missions broadly and obtained superior performance [17].

In this paper, an effective projection transformation technique that is originated from LDA and not subjected to the limitations of gaussian distribution, named as local Fisher's discriminant analysis (LFDA) [10], is first employed as preprocessing procedure. In doing so, a reduced subspace with high separability and low redundant information of medical HSI data is obtained, which has advantages of preserving essential structure and desirable information of HSI data with multi-modal non-gaussian distribution. And then, a deep neural network (DNN) is adopted as a powerful deep feature extractor and classifier to gain intrinsic and high-level features. To the best of our knowledge, it is the first time to integrate HSI technology with microscopy for identifying MN automatically in the medical field. Practically, due to the influence of external environment, imaging is often accompanied by noise that lowers the image quality, hence the common but effective mean filtering technique is applied before projection transformation procedure. Based on the aforementioned work, an automatic MN identification framework, denoted as LFDA-DNN, is developed. To evaluate the effectiveness of LFDA-DNN, experiments on a real MN dataset captured with the China-Japan Friendship Hospital are implemented.

2   Membranous Nephropathy Hyperspectral Data

As illustrated in Fig. 1, the imaging system for experimental data is composing an American portable hyperspectral imaging device SOC-710 and a biological microscope UB203i. Specifically, for SOC-710, the wavelength of it ranges from 400 nm to 1000 nm and the spectral resolution is up to 1.3 nm; the microscope UB203i is produced by Chongqing Aopu Photoelectric Technology Cooperation.

Renal biopsy tissue slices used for imaging operation were made by specialists in nephrology of China-Japan Friendship Hospital. Furthermore, classification objectives (immune complexes) are labeled under the guidance and help of experts. The MN hyperspectral dataset includes 30 HBV-MN images and 24 PMN images, involving 10 HBV-MN patients and 9 PMN patients totally; generally, collecting three images from one patient's renal biopsy sample. Each hyperpsectral data is a three-dimensional image cube, including spatial and spectral dimensions, the size of spatial dimension is 696×520 and spectral dimension contains 128 channels. To visualize the data and map of MN samples, a HBV-MN sample (17002-1) and a PMN sample (16466-1) are chosen to show, Fig. 2 displays the data and map of selected HBV-MN and PMN samples, and white pixels in maps are labeled immune complex points, which are regarded as samples to differentiate HBV-MN and PMN.

Fig. 1. The system for hyperspectral microscopic imaging procedure.

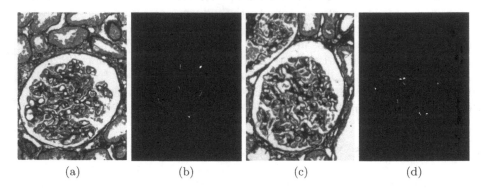

Fig. 2. (a) and (c) are the data of the 17002-1 and 16466-1 respectively; (b) and (d) are the corresponding ground truth maps, here white color represents the area of labeling, and the black color depicts the area of backgrounds.

3   Membranous Nephropathy Identification Framework

The sufficient spectral information of HSI data offers a novel solution for classifying HBV-MN and PMN accurately, while both of HBV-MN and PMN's pathological changes are immune complex deposition, which results in the spectral curves of HBV-MN and PMN still have relatively high similarities, hence projection transformation technique is employed as a critical preprocessing procedure to seek for an optimal reduced subspace with well separability for features of HBV-MN and PMN, and decrease redundant spectral information. Furthermore, a powerful DNN-based architecture is employed to extract high-level features and complete the final classification task.

3.1   Filtering Preprocessing

The medical HSI data is often affected by imaging system noise, thus a simple while effective mean filtering noise reduction algorithm is applied to reduce the influences of noise. The main principle of mean filtering is replacing the center pixel's value with the average value of pixels' in the local window centered on the center point. Mathematically, mean filtering can be illustrated as $D(i,j) = \sum_{(m,n) \in R_{i,j}} S(m,n)/HW$, where $S(m, n)$ is the value of pixels in the window $(i = 0,1...H - 1; j = 0,1...W - 1)$, W and H represent width and height of filtering window respectively, $R(i, j)$ depicts a series of pixels in the filtering window, $D(i, j)$ illustrates the value of center pixel in the filtering window and HW describes the total number of pixels in the local filtering window.

To confirm the significance of filtering procedure, the original image and the processed image of the 10th channel in 17221-2 are depicted in (a) and (b) of Fig. 3 respectively. Obviously, mean filtering technique has excellent abilities for decreasing the noise of practical MN data.

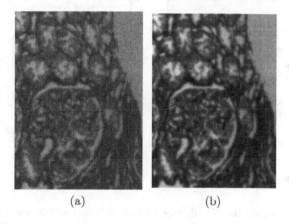

(a)   (b)

Fig. 3. (a) and (b) illustrate the original image and the processed image of the 10th channel in 17221-2, respectively.

3.2   Projection Transformation

Although HSI data contains affluent spectral information, it is also prone to suffer from the drawback of information redundancy. Projection transformation algorithms have capabilities for seeking for a reduced subspace with optimal separability of features as well as reducing the dimensionality of spectral dimensions for hyperspectral data without losing intrinsic information. As an optimized extension of LDA, LFDA fuses the advantages of LDA and locality-preserving projections (LPP) [6]. As is known, LPP has capabilities for retaining local structure of samples. Therefore, LFDA has benefits of acquiring a subspace with well inter-class separability and maintaining intra-class local structure in the process of projection.

Conventional LDA regards all samples in a class have identical contribution weights and forces distant data pairs of the same class to be adjacent in the procedure of estimating scatter matrices, while LFDA views samples of one class or mode as independent individuals and qualifies them with data-dependent contribution weights. Therefore, LFDA is not upper bounded with $c - 1$ (c is the number of classes) and has advantages of preserving the local structures, which is beneficial for obtaining the intrinsic features and preserving desirable connection between samples in the process of projection. Based on the aforementioned properties, LFDA could be expected to acquire features with high separability.

Aiming at visualizing the effectiveness of LFDA for acquiring a subspace with better separability, the distribution of testing samples' features before and after projection process are illustrated in (a) and (b) of Fig. 4, respectively, the results confirm the potentiality of LFDA for seeking for a subspace with high separability for features.

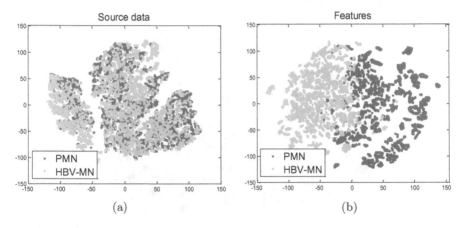

(a)   (b)

Fig. 4. (a) and (b) depict the distribution of testing samples' features before and after projection procedure respectively. Note that blue points indicate HBV-MN features and red points represent PMN features.

3.3 Deep Neural Network Feature Extractor

In this paper, DNN is further applied into identifying glomerular disease in microscopic hyperspectral images for the first time, providing a verification and supplementation for the results of immunofluorescence or immunohistochemistry manners.

DNN-based network is utilized to extract high-grade features of glomerular image and complete the final classification mission of HBV-MN and PMN, associated with aforementioned procedures of filtering and projection transformation, an automatic MN identification architecture is formulated, as depicted in Fig. 5. The DNN-based model is mainly composed of input layer, convolutional layer, max pooling layer, fully connected layer and softmax layer, taking

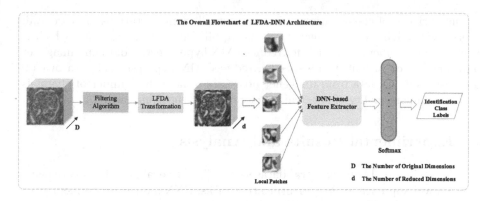

Fig. 5. The overall flowchart of the proposed LFDA-DNN architecture.

the VGG-based model as an example: an input layer, 16 convolutional layers, five max pooling layers, two fully connected layers and a softmax layer, the detailed configuration of VGG-based model is illustrated in Fig. 6.

For acquiring well performance, several optimizing operations were utilized when constructing the DNN-based model: firstly, applying Leaky ReLU activation function after each convolutional layer to solve the problem of gradient vanishing and accelerate the fitting speed, meanwhile, avoiding the ReLU function's drawback of dying easily; secondly, exploring batch normalization (BN) strategy behind some convolutional layers as a regularizer to simplify the tuning process and lower initialization requirement; thirdly, utilizing dropout technique to avoid over-fitting issue, and the dropout rate is set to 0.5.

In the process of training, the number of batch size is set to 64, the patch size is set to 11×11, and the parameters of two FC layers are both set to 128

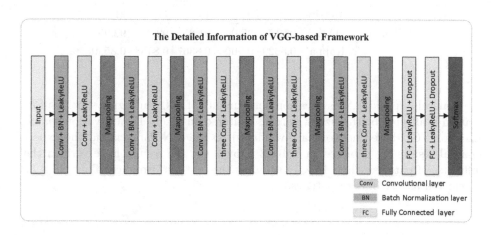

Fig. 6. The detailed information of VGG-based architecture. Note that the input is a local patch centered at a pixel.

as the varieties of classification objects are small. Some notations are essential: pretrained weights from imagenet are not applied in our experiments, which is because the number of channels for reduced MN hyperspectral data and imagenet data are not consistent, to be specific, reduced MN hyperpsectral data owns 9 dimensions while data from imagenet possesses 3, here the number of channels and the dimensionality of spectral space represent the same meaning.

4   Experimental Results and Analysis

In this section, real hyperspectral dataset is utilized to evaluate the effectiveness of the novel approach for MN identification tasks. CNN models are implemented in *Tensorflow*[1] with advanced *Keras*[2] API. For acquiring better performance, LFDA-DNN and other DL techniques are all trained for 500 epoches. Adam [8] is chosen as the optimizing strategy and the initial learning rate is set to 0.0001.

4.1   Parameter Tuning

Applying LFDA as a preprocessing procedure has two critical benefits: (1) obtaining a subspace with well separability for features, and (2) decreasing the influence of redundant information. To explore the impact of dimension of reduced subspace, experiments with different dimensions of reduced subspace for VGG-based network are employed as comparisons. Results on the MN dataset are expressed in Table 1, where the first row indicates the number of dimension. It can be seen that the dimension of nine provides the best classification performance.

Table 1. Comparisons with different dimensions of reduced subspace for LFDA.

	Metrics	5	9	13	17	21
MN dataset	OA(%)	93.17	95.04	91.87	92.27	92.95
	Kappa	0.8629	0.9006	0.8367	0.8458	0.8590

Generally speaking, classification performance of CNNs utilizing spatial information is affected by the size of patches centered on pixels. Hence, various patch sizes for VGG-based network are validated on the MN dataset and the experimental results are depicted in Table 2. Obviously, the results have verified the influence of patch size and 11×11 acquires the best performance. Thus, 11×11 is selected as size of data patches.

---

[1] http://tensorflow.org/.
[2] https://github.com/fchollet/keras.

Table 2. The classification performance of various patch sizes.

	Metrics	9×9	11×11	13×13	15×15
MN dataset	OA(%)	93.13	95.04	92.43	94.36
	Kappa	0.8629	0.9006	0.8485	0.8872

4.2 Classification Performance and Analysis

To acquire better performance, different manners including classic machine learning algorithms and off-the-shelf DL models are implemented on the MN dataset, to be specific, support vector machine (SVM), extreme learning machine (ELM) [7], Alexnet [9], Resnet20 [5] and VGG19 [15], as well as techniques with preprocessing steps. Specifically, to guarantee the justification of experimental comparison, training and testing samples for all methods are exactly consistent. Note that data of patient 17002 and 16466, to be specific, a total of 1414 labeled samples, are utilized for training samples, and the rest data are viewed as testing samples.

Table 3 elaborates the experimental results of different methods for identifying HBV-MN and PMN. Here several prevalent metrics of overall accuracy (OA), average accuracy (AA) and Kappa Coefficient are employed to assess the performance of diverse algorithms. As shown in Table 3, DNN models are more competitive than conventional classifiers. Moreover, LFDA-DNNs acquire better results than algorithms without filtering and projection transformation preprocessing, which confirms the effectiveness of preprocessing procedures, among LFDA-DNNs, LFDA-VGG19 reflects superiority in recognizing HBV-MN and PMN precisely, to be specific, the OA of LFDA-VGG19 paradigm is 3.85% and 5.50% higher than that of LFDA-SVM and LFDA-ELM, and 0.95% and 0.85% higher that of LFDA-Alexnet and LFDA-Resnet20. Particularly, although LFDA-Resnet20 and LFDA-Alexnet gain the highest accuracy for HBV-MN and PMN respectively, LFDA-VGG19 obtains more balanced and relatively high classification results for two kinds of targets and has optimal results for metrics of OA, AA and Kappa Coefficient.

For MN identification task, training data and testing data are strictly separated. The reason is due to that training samples are from a HBV-MN (ID:17002) and a PMN (ID:16466) patients, and samples from other patients are regarded as testing data. Promising the complete separability of training and testing samples for classification application is a challenging task, which requires model owns strong generalization capability, while this situation is more in line with realistic application need.

In the process of implementing experiments, a special phenomenon about the accuracy of single glomerular image caught our attention. To express more clearly, the classification results of all glomerular images using LFDA-VGG19 are listed in Tables 4 and 5. There exists several glomerular images' accuracies are relatively low, such as 17559-1, 18055-1 and 16295-1, while the other images from the same patient acquire better performance. The phenomenon aforemen-

Table 3. The classification performance of the LFDA-DNN and the baselines using the *MN dataset.*

Comparisons	HBV-MN	PMN	OA(%)	AA(%)	Kappa
SVM	65.20	68.27	66.80	66.74	0.3347
ELM	61.85	71.62	66.94	66.74	0.3356
Alexnet	65.16	69.01	67.16	67.09	0.3418
Resnet20	80.17	68.31	73.99	74.24	0.4819
VGG19	79.70	85.72	82.84	82.71	0.6554
LFDA-SVM	94.28	88.35	91.19	91.31	0.8239
LFDA-ELM	94.92	84.58	89.54	89.75	0.7913
LFDA-Alexnet	92.00	**96.00**	94.09	94.00	0.8814
LFDA-Resnet20	**96.88**	91.72	94.19	94.30	0.8839
LFDA-VGG19	95.67	94.45	**95.04**	**95.06**	**0.9006**

Table 4. The classification accuracy (%) of the single glomerular image of HBV-MN.

ID	Accuracy	ID	Accuracy	ID	Accuracy	ID	Accuracy
17072-1	100.00	17198-2	100.00	17276-3	100.00	**17559-1**	**56.08**
17072-2	100.00	17198-3	100.00	17325-1	100.00	17559-2	100.00
17072-3	100.00	17221-1	100.00	17325-2	100.00	17559-3	97.20
17136-1	100.00	17221-2	100.00	17325-3	100.00	**18055-1**	**50.00**
17136-2	100.00	17221-3	100.00	17472-1	100.00	18055-2	90.91
17136-3	100.00	17276-1	100.00	17472-2	94.84	18055-3	80.98
17198-1	100.00	17276-2	100.00	17472-3	100.00		

Table 5. The classification accuracy (%) of the single glomerular image of PMN.

ID	Accuracy	ID	Accuracy	ID	Accuracy	ID	Accuracy
15684-1	100.00	16367	100.00	16442-3	96.46	16485-3	100.00
15684-2	90.02	16389-1	100.00	16480-1	100.00	17516-1	100.00
15684-3	75.32	16389-2	78.59	16480-2	100.00	17516-2	100.00
16295-1	**62.21**	16389-3	85.05	16480-3	100.00		
16295-2	100.00	16442-1	100.00	16485-1	100.00		
16295-3	100.00	16442-2	100.00	16485-2	100.00		

tioned brings us some inspiration: whether it is more reasonable to refer several glomerular images from the same patient in the process of diagnosing, which may become a critical principle for the auxiliary diagnosis in our future work.

5   Conclusion

Aiming at providing a novel approach as verification and supplement of conventional immunofluorescence technique for MN identification mission, a hyperspectral imaging-based architecture consists of filtering, projection transformation, high-level feature extractor and softmax classifier was employed. The main contributions of this explorative method can be summarized as follows: firstly, degrading the influence of noise through mean filtering operation; secondly, seeking for a reduced subspace with high separability for features via projection transformation to identify HBV-MN and PMN more precisely; thirdly, extracting high-grade and intrinsic features that are beneficial for final classification procedure. Experiments are implemented on a real MN hyperspectral dataset with 54 glomerular images to evaluate the effectiveness of the automatic MN recognition framework, and experimental results demonstrate that the proposed LFDA-DNN possesses superiority for identifying MN accurately.

References

1. van den Brand, J.A.J.G., Hofstra, J.M., Wetzels, J.F.M.: Low-molecular-weight proteins as prognostic markers in idiopathic membranous nephropathy. Clin. J. Am. Soc. Nephrol. **6**(12), 2846–2853 (2011)
2. Chang, L., Li, W., Li, Q.: Guided filter-based medical hyperspectral image restoration and cell classification. J. Med. Imaging Health Inform. **8**(4), 825–834 (2018)
3. Cheng, J.X., Xie, X.S.: Vibrational spectroscopic imaging of living systems: an emerging platform for biology and medicine. Science **350**(6264), aaa8870 (2015)
4. Dong, H., et al.: Retrospective study of phospholipase A2 receptor and IgG subclasses in glomerular deposits in chinese patients with membranous nephropathy. PLoS One **11**(5), 1–12 (2016)
5. He, K., Zhang, X., Ren, S., Sun, J.: Deep residual learning for image recognition. In: Proceedings of the IEEE Conference on Computer Vision and Pattern Recognition, pp. 770–778 (2016)
6. He, X., Niyogi, P.: Locality preserving projections. In: Advances in Neural Information Processing Systems, pp. 153–160 (2004)
7. Huang, G., Zhou, H., Ding, X., Zhang, R.: Extreme learning machine for regression and multiclass classification. IEEE Trans. Syst. Man Cybern. Part B (Cybern.) **42**(2), 513–529 (2012)
8. Kingma, D., Ba, J.: Adam: a method for stochastic optimization. In: International Conference on Learning Representations (2014)
9. Krizhevsky, A., Sutskever, I., Hinton, G.E.: Imagenet classification with deep convolutional neural networks. In: International Conference on Neural Information Processing Systems, pp. 1097–1105 (2012)
10. Li, W., Prasad, S., Fowler, J.E., Bruce, L.M.: Locality-preserving dimensionality reduction and classification for hyperspectral image analysis. IEEE Trans. Geosci. Remote Sens. **50**(4), 1185–1198 (2012)
11. Li, W., Wu, G., Du, Q.: Transferred deep learning for anomaly detection in hyperspectral imagery. IEEE Geosci. Remote Sens. **14**(5), 597–601 (2017)
12. Li, W., Wu, L., Qiu, X., Ran, Q., Xie, X.: Parallel computation for blood cell classification in medical hyperspectral imagery. Meas. Sci. Technol. **27**(9), 095102 (2016)

13. Martinez, A.M., Kak, A.C.: PCA versus LDA. IEEE Trans. Pattern Anal. Mach. Intell. **23**(2), 228–233 (2001)
14. Pike, R., Lu, G., Wang, D., Zhuo, G.C., Fei, B.: A minimum spanning forest based method for noninvasive cancer detection with hyperspectral imaging. IEEE Trans. Biomed. Eng. **63**(3), 653–663 (2016)
15. Simonyan, K., Zisserman, A.: Very deep convolutional networks for large-scale image recognition. In: International Conference on Learning Representations (2015)
16. Wang, Q., Chang, L., Zhou, M., Li, Q., Liu, H., Guo, F.: A spectral and morphologic method for white blood cell classification. Opt. Laser Technol. **84**, 144–148 (2016)
17. Xu, X., Li, W., Ran, Q., Du, Q., Gao, L., Zhang, B.: Multisource remote sensing data classification based on convolutional neural network. IEEE Trans. Geosci. Remote Sens. **56**(2), 937–949 (2018)
18. Yang, Y., Zhang, Z., Zhuo, L., Chen, D., Li, W.: The spectrum of biopsy-proven glomerular disease in china: a systematic review. Chin. Med. J. **131**(6), 731–735 (2018)
19. Zhang, L., Zhong, Y., Huang, B., Gong, J., Li, P.: Dimensionality reduction based on clonal selection for hyperspectral imagery. IEEE Trans. Geosci. Remote Sens. **45**(12), 4172–4186 (2007)
20. Zhang, M., Li, W., Du, Q.: Diverse region-based CNN for hyperspectral image classification. IEEE Trans. Image Process. **27**(6), 2623–2634 (2018)

A Level Set Method Combined with Gaussian Mixture Model for Image Segmentation

Xin Lu, Xuewu Zhang$^{(\boxtimes)}$, Min Li, Zhuo Zhang, and Haiyan Xu

College of Internet of Things Engineering,
Hohai University, Changzhou 213022, China
lx_zjwf1218@hhu.edu.cn, lab_112@126.com

Abstract. Chan-Vese (CV) model promotes the evolution of level set curve based on the gray distribution inside and outside the curve. It has a better segmentation effect on images with intensity homogeneity and obvious contrast. However, when the gray distribution of image is uneven, the evolution speed of the curve will be significantly slower, and the curve will be guided to the wrong segmentation result. To solve this problem, a method to improve CV model by using of Gaussian mixture model (GMM) is proposed. We use the parameters of the Gaussian submodels to correct the mean value of grayscale inside and outside the curve in the energy function. The target region can be quickly segmented in the images with complex background gray distribution. Experimental results show that the proposed algorithm can significantly reduce the number of iterations and enhance the robustness to noise. The level set curve can quickly evolve into target region in the images with intensity inhomogeneity.

Keywords: Image segmentation · Level set · Chan-Vese model · Gaussian mixture model

1 Introduction

Level set method is an important research direction in the field of image segmentation in recent years, and has been widely used in various fields, such as medicine [1] and remote sensing, etc. It has an important research value. The Level set method based on contour evolution, such as Snake model and Geometric Active Contour (GAC) model [2], makes curve gradually approach the edge of target by minimizing the energy function of the closed curve [3]. However, such models only use local edge information of image and do not have a good segmentation effect on the images with blurred or discrete edges [4].

For images with weak edges and discontinuous boundaries, Mumford and Shah proposed a new curve evolution model (M-S model), which mainly used

---

A student paper.

© Springer Nature Switzerland AG 2019
Z. Lin et al. (Eds.): PRCV 2019, LNCS 11858, pp. 185–196, 2019.
https://doi.org/10.1007/978-3-030-31723-2_16

the foreground and background gray information of image to realize image segmentation by solving the minimum value of energy function. However, M-S model is over-ideal and computationally complex. On this basis, Chan and Vese simplified the original model and put forward CV model, making the level set curve evolve without depending on the image gradient. They introduced image grayscale information and successfully applied the model in the remote sensing satellite cloud image segmentation [5], nuclear magnetic resonance image segmentation [6], and CT image segmentation [7], etc. However, CV model requires high uniformity of image gray distribution. In practical applications, if background gray distribution is complex, or the grayscale difference between foreground and background is not obvious, the segmentation effect of CV model will all reduce and even lead to wrong segmentation results. Li [8] introduced penalty terms into the original CV model and tackled the problem of model initialization, reducing the influence of uneven gray distribution during the evolution of level set. However, in each evolution process, the average of foreground and background grayscale is determined by the gray distribution inside and outside the curve. If the two values can be optimized, the evolution speed of level set will be greatly accelerated.

In terms of the optimization and application of CV model, Liu [9] proposed an improved method, which introduced local information to the images with uneven gray distribution after Gaussian filtering, and constructed a CV model that is more suitable for the uneven background. Zhang [10] defined an energy function of the entire image region, and combined it with bias field, level set function and real image signals, proposing a CV model that can segment the images with uneven gray distribution. Li et al. [11] used watershed algorithm to extract useful information of image regions and boundaries for pre-segmentation of image, and then used CV model for further segmentation, verifying the efficiency and accuracy of the algorithm in magnetic resonance images.

The paper introduces the Gaussian mixture model (GMM) to optimize the average of grayscale inside and outside the level set curve. For images with noise and intensity inhomogeneity, a single value is not enough to represent the gray distribution of image's foreground and background. While the distribution of intensity inside and outside the curve can be represented by a GMM. The parameters of model are updated with the evolution of the curve, and a changing foreground and background value can be obtained for every pixel point in the image respectively. It makes the CV model more adaptable to complex background. Through experiments, we find that although the algorithm in this paper increases the complexity of operations, it significantly reduces the number of iterations. And the model can segment images with intensity inhomogeneity faster and more effectively, with better noise suppression effect.

2   Related Works

For images with uneven gray distribution, the traditional CV model only guides curve evolution through the weighted mean of grayscale inside and outside the curve, which is slow in evolution and easy to get wrong segmentation results. A GMM is formed by combining multiple Gaussian functions of multiple probability distributions, it can be used to describe complex changes of grayscale. During the evolution of level set curve, we use GMM's parameters to optimize energy function, and the mean gray value in the function changes according to different points inside and outside the curve. It makes the curve more adaptive to the changes in complex background.

2.1 The CV Model

The energy function of CV model is:

$$F(C, c_1, c_2) = \lambda_1 \int_{inside(C)} |u_0(x,y) - c_1|^2 dxdy +$$

$$\lambda_2 \int_{outside(C)} |u_0(x,y) - c_2|^2 dxdy + \mu L(C) + \nu A(C), \tag{1}$$

where C refers to the evolution curve of level set, $L(C)$ is the length of the contour line, $A(C)$ means the area of the region within the curve. μ and ν are the coefficients of two terms, and $u_0(x,y)$ is the gray value of a point in the image. c_1 represents the mean gray value of the points inside the curve, and c_2 represents the mean gray value of the points outside the curve. The first two terms of the whole energy function are regularization terms, which are used to regulate evolution curve. The last two are fidelity terms, which are responsible for guiding level set curve to evolve on the target contour.

According to level set method, we replace the evolution curve C in energy function with the level set function $\phi(x,y)$. If point (x,y) is on the curve, then $\phi(x,y) = 0$. If the point (x,y) is outside the curve $\phi(x,y) < 0$ while inside the curve $\phi(x,y) > 0$. By solving the Euler-Lagrange equation, the energy function can be minimized, and the corresponding evolution function of CV model is:

$$\frac{\partial \phi}{\partial t} = \delta(\phi) \left\{ \mu div(\frac{\nabla \phi}{|\nabla \phi|}) - \nu - \lambda_1 [u_0(x,y) - c_1]^2 + \lambda_2 [u_0(x,y) - c_2]^2 \right\}. \tag{2}$$

Where the calculation method of the contour's inside and outside mean gray value is:

$$c_1 = \frac{\int u_0(x,y) H(\phi) dxdy}{\int H(\phi) dxdy}, \tag{3}$$

$$c_2 = \frac{\int u_0(x,y)[1 - H(\phi)] dxdy}{\int [1 - H(\phi)] dxdy}. \tag{4}$$

Where $H(\phi)$ and $\delta(\phi)$ are the regular forms of Heviside function and Delta function respectively, and the corresponding calculation method is:

$$H(\phi) = \frac{1}{2} \left[1 + \frac{2}{\pi} arctan\left(\frac{\phi}{\varepsilon}\right) \right], \tag{5}$$

$$\delta(\phi) = H'(\phi) = \frac{\varepsilon}{\pi} * \frac{1}{\phi^2 + \varepsilon^2}, \tag{6}$$

in the formula ε is a constant.

It can be inferred from the evolution function that the internal and external mean gray values change with the evolution of curve. In turn, it affects the evolution of level set curve, and the final result of evolution depends on the image gray distribution. If the distribution is uneven, both internal and external mean gray values cannot reflect both foreground and background gray distribution well. It is easy to lead the level set curve to the wrong segmentation result.

2.2   Improved CV Model

In respect of the issues above, the paper introduces GMM into the process of curve evolution, optimizing the average grayscale inside and outside the curve in the energy function. The method improves the anti-interference ability of the evolution curve, and guides the level set curve to achieve correct segmentation effect. When describing an image, a gray histogram can generally be used to describe the distribution of each gray level in the image. When the gray distribution of an image is complex, combining multiple Gaussian functions with different weights to form a multiple probability distribution can represent the images gray distribution well.

Image Modeling. For the images with intensity inhomogeneity, choosing a single gray value as the average grayscale inside and outside the curve cannot represent the gray distribution characteristics of the foreground and background regions. The evolution curve is easy to be led to wrong results. Hence, the GMM is introduced to describe the gray distribution inside and outside the curve, and the parameters of GMM are used to optimize the average grayscale in the CV model's evolution function.

Parameter Estimation. The paper learns the method of parameters calculation from the Expectation Maximization (EM) algorithm [12], but the results of each iteration are calculated by the level set evolution function. The parameters update depending on the grayscale distribution inside and outside the curve after each evolution. Firstly, the evolution curve of level set is initialized, and we use the K-means algorithm to divide the regions inside and outside the curve into k parts. After segmentation, the gray distribution of each part can be approximated by a Gaussian function. According to k parts of initial segmentation, the internal GMM $G_{inside}(\pi_k, \mu_k, \sigma_k)$ and the external GMM $G_{outside}(\pi_k, \mu_k, \sigma_k)$ of the curve are constructed. Parameters of the model are:

$$\mu_k = \frac{\sum_{i=1}^{N_k} u_i}{N_k}, \quad k = 1, 2, ..., K, \tag{7}$$

$$\sigma_k^2 = \frac{\sum_{i=1}^{N_k} (u_i - \mu_k)^2}{N_k}, \quad k = 1, 2, ..., K, \tag{8}$$

$$\pi_k = \frac{N_k}{\sum_{k=1}^{K} N_k}, \quad k = 1, 2, ..., K. \tag{9}$$

Where μ_k represents the mean gray value of each submodel, σ_k is the grayscale variance of each submodel, and π_k is the proportion of each submodel in the entire GMM. N_k denotes the number of elements in each submodel, and u_i is the grayscale value of a certain point in the submodel.

Construction of GMM. According to the mean and other parameters calculated above, a GMM can be built for the images inside and outside the curve:

$$P(u_i|\theta) = \sum_{k=1}^{K} \pi_k \frac{1}{\sqrt{2\pi}\sigma_k} exp\left[-\frac{(u_i - \mu_k)^2}{2\sigma_k^2} \right], \tag{10}$$

where the coefficient $\pi_k \geq 0$ and $\sum_{k=1}^{K} \pi_k = 1$, $\theta_k = (\mu_k, \sigma_k^2)$ represents the mean and variance of each Gaussian submodel. Figure 1(a) illustrates the level set curve initialized in an image, (b) and (c) demonstrate the probability density functions of each Gaussian submodel inside and outside the curve respectively:

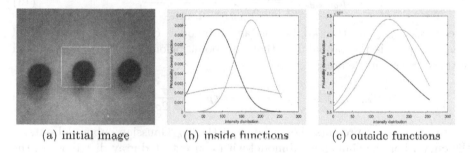

(a) initial image   (b) inside functions   (c) outside functions

Fig. 1. Probability density function of Gaussian submodel

It should be noted that the number of submodels should be adjusted according to the complexity of the image's gray distribution. Generally, images with a single gray distribution only need three or less submodels, while images with a complex gray distribution need more than five submodels to describe its distribution well.

GMM Optimized CV Model

Model Improvement. According to prior knowledge, no matter how complex the background gray distribution is, the gray distribution of target region and background region always maintain significant differences. Under this condition, we can use the GMM of curve's outside region to screen out the most likely submodel of the target region from the internal model:

$$m_{fore} = \arg\max_i \sum_{k=1}^{K} \pi_{outside,k}(\mu_{inside,i} - \mu_{outside,k})^2. \tag{11}$$

Where $\mu_{outside,k}$ and $\pi_{outside,k}$ denote the mean value and coefficient of the k_{th} Gaussian submodel outside the curve, and $\mu_{inside,i}$ represents the mean value of the i_{th} Gaussian submodel inside the curve. By calculating the weighted difference between the mean value of each Gaussian submodel inside the curve and that of the external GMM, the i_{th} internal region submodel with the largest difference from the background is obtained, and the average grayscale of this submodel $\mu_{m_{fore}}$ is used to represent the gray distribution of the foreground region.

When calculating the energy function, by calculating the responsiveness $\gamma_{outside,k}$ of the k_{th} external Gaussian submodel to the point with gray value of u, a dynamic external mean gray value can be obtained for different pixel points. The responsiveness $\gamma_{outside,k}$ and the external average grayscale $\mu_{outside}$ are respectively defined as:

$$\gamma_{outside,k} = \frac{\pi_{outside,k}\varphi(u|\theta_{outside,k})}{\sum_{k=1}^{K}\pi_{outside,k}\varphi(u|\theta_{outside,k})}, \quad i = 1, 2, ..., N; \ k = 1, 2, ..., K \tag{12}$$

$$\mu_{outside} = \frac{\sum_{k=1}^{K}\gamma_{outside,k}\mu_{outside,k}}{\sum_{k=1}^{K}\gamma_{outside,k}}, \tag{13}$$

where $\theta_{outside,k}$ is the k_{th} Gaussian submodel outside the curve, and $\varphi(u|\theta_{outside,k})$ is the probability that the point belongs to the k_{th} submodel of the curve's outside area:

$$\varphi(u|\theta_{outside,k}) = \frac{1}{\sqrt{2\pi}\sigma_{outside,k}}exp\left[-\frac{(u - \mu_{outside,k})^2}{2\sigma_{outside,k}^2}\right], \tag{14}$$

where, $\sigma_{outside,k}$ represents the variance of the k_{th} Gaussian submodel outside the curve. For the Gaussian submodel with concentrated gray distribution, the variance $\sigma_{outside,k}$ is small, so the responsiveness of the submodel to the points belonging to it may be much greater than other models. In order to ensure that each submodel has an impact on the mean gray value and avoid mistaking foreground pixels for background, the value of responsiveness can be smoothed as:

$$\gamma_{outside,k} = \frac{\gamma_{outside,k} + \frac{a}{\sqrt{\sigma_{outside,k}}}}{1 + \frac{a}{\sqrt{\sigma_{outside,k}}}}. \tag{15}$$

Where, a denotes smooth coefficient, and the smoothing term is inversely proportional to the standard deviation of submodel. When $\sigma_{outside,k}$ is small, the data distribution of submodel is concentrated, and the smoothing term at this time is larger, which reduces the response of the submodels' point to the model. The response generated by the points outside model is increased, so that the calculated external mean value is affected by the Gaussian submodel in which the point is located, and is not excessively close to the grayscale mean of the submodel.

After optimization with GMM, the energy value of each point can be calculated, and a new level set evolution result is obtained. The improved model's energy function is:

$$F(\phi, c_1, c_2) = \lambda_1 \int_{inside(\phi)} |u_0(x,y) - \mu_{m_{fore}}|^2 H(\phi)dxdy +$$

$$\lambda_2 \int_{outside(\phi)} |u_0(x,y) - \mu_{outside}|^2 [1 - H(\phi)] dxdy + \quad (16)$$

$$\mu \int \delta(\phi)| \bigtriangledown \phi|dxdy + \nu \int H(\phi)dxdy.$$

The level set evolution function corresponding to each point is:

$$\frac{\partial \phi}{\partial t} = \delta(\phi) \left\{ \mu div(\frac{\bigtriangledown \phi}{|\bigtriangledown \phi|}) - \nu - \lambda_1[u_0(x,y) - \mu_{m_{fore}}]^2 + \right.$$

$$\left. \lambda_2 [u_0(x,y) - \mu_{outside}]^2 \right\}, \quad (17)$$

The fidelity term from the equation which guides curve evolution is extracted, and the gray value of any pixel point $u_0(x,y)$ in the image is analyzed: $f(u) = -\lambda_1 [u_0(x,y) - \mu_{m_{fore}}]^2 + \lambda_2 [u_0(x,y) - \mu_{outside}]^2$. Without considering the influence of coefficient, set λ_1, λ_2 as 1. If a certain point belongs to foreground, the grayscale of that point will be significantly different from the background gray value. At this time, u is closer to the optimal submodel's mean gray value m_{fore} within the curve (with the largest difference from the gray value outside the curve). And when m_{fore} completely represents the foreground region's gray distribution, the difference between u and $\mu_{m_{fore}}$ is close to 0. At this time $|u - \mu_{m_{fore}}| < |u - \mu_{outside}|$, the result $f(u)$ is positive and the point evolves into the interior of the curve. If a point belongs to background, its gray value has high responsiveness to the Gaussian submodel which contains it. At this time, the submodel has a greater influence on the calculation result of the external mean gray value, and the value $|u - \mu_{outside}|$ of this point is smaller, which satisfies $|u - \mu_{m_{fore}}| > |u - \mu_{outside}|$. At this time, the result of $f(u)$ is negative and the point evolves to the outside of the curve.

Algorithm Procedure. Through above improvement, the CV model combined with GMM can produce a good segmentation effect on the images with complex gray distribution and noise. The specific algorithm steps are as follows:

Algorithm 1. Curve Evolution Based on The Proposed Model

Input: Image I
Output: Level set curve $\phi(x,y)$
Initialize level set curve, divide the region inside and outside the curve into k blocks by K-means algorithm;
Build interior and exterior GMMs and calculate (π_k, μ_k, σ_k);
Calculate $\mu_{m_{fore}}$ and $\mu_{outside}$ for the points in the image;
Update the curve according to the calculation result of evolution function $\partial \phi / \partial t$;
Continue iteration until the level set curve no longer converge.

---

3   Experiments and Analysis

The experiments select images with noise and uneven gray distribution to perform segmentation test. By comparing the segmentation effects of traditional CV model, Local Binary Fitting (LBF) model [13], Chan Vese-Geometric Active Contour (CV-GAC) model [14], Variational Level Set (VLS) model [15], Distance Regularized LS Evolution Method (DRLSE) model [16], Saliency Driven Region-Edge-based Top Down Level Set Evolution (SDREL) model [17] and CV model in this paper, we verify the superiority of our algorithm. The experimental environment is Intel(R)Core(TM)i7-8700 CPU @ 3.20 GHz clock/16.0 GB memory/MATLAB R2014b. In the experiment, the model parameters are listed as follows: $\lambda_1 = \lambda_2 = 1$, $\nu = 0.03 \times 255^2$, $\mu = 1$.

In the experiments, we first discuss final evolution results with different submodel numbers. We mentioned above that according to different initial positions of level set curve and different gray distributions, the number of Gaussian submodels inside and outside should be set differently as well. This operation helps us segment target area faster and more accurately. As experimental results shown in Fig. 2, we set different number of Gaussian submodels for images with different gray distributions and get evolution results after iterating 10 times. The gray distribution of the first image is relatively simple. When we set $k_{inside} = 3$ and $k_{outside} = 2$, the level set curve evolves to target area more accurately. While gray distribution of the second image is more complex, thus more submodels are needed to characterize gray distribution for a better segmentation effect. However, an excess of submodels will increase time-consuming of a single iteration, thus extending convergence time. Although results of Fig. 2(g) and (h) are similar, the latter's time-consuming is 1.23 s longer.

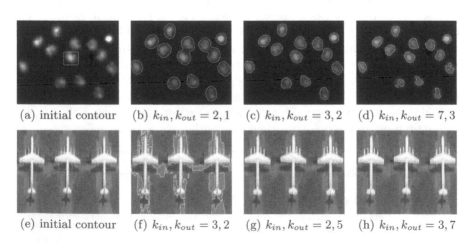

(a) initial contour   (b) $k_{in}, k_{out} = 2, 1$ (c) $k_{in}, k_{out} = 3, 2$ (d) $k_{in}, k_{out} = 7, 3$

(e) initial contour   (f) $k_{in}, k_{out} = 3, 2$ (g) $k_{in}, k_{out} = 2, 5$ (h) $k_{in}, k_{out} = 3, 7$

Fig. 2. Results of 10 iterations with different numbers of submodels

In Fig. 3, we compare different models' anti-noise performance by images with Gaussian noise (zero mean and standard deviation $\sigma = 0.05$). It can be seen from the results that CV model, CV-GAC model, and LBF model do not have a good segmentation effect on such images. While SDREL model, VLS model, and our model have a better resolving ability for target region and noise, with a better evolution result.

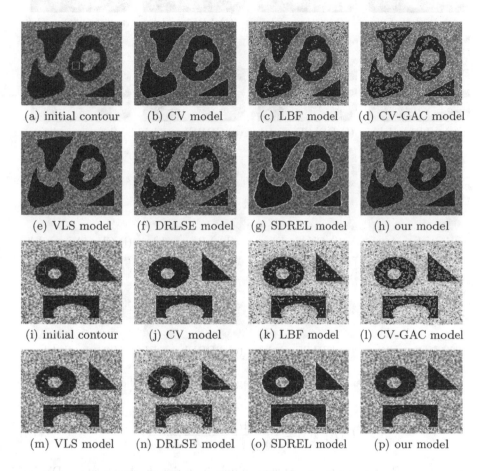

(a) initial contour   (b) CV model   (c) LBF model   (d) CV-GAC model

(e) VLS model   (f) DRLSE model   (g) SDREL model   (h) our model

(i) initial contour   (j) CV model   (k) LBF model   (l) CV-GAC model

(m) VLS model   (n) DRLSE model   (o) SDREL model   (p) our model

Fig. 3. Segmentation results of noisy images

As shown in Fig. 4, the gray distribution of images is uneven. The level set curves of some models tend to misjudge noise as small targets in the process of evolution, or mistake some foreground regions as background, thus form a segmentation gap. After several iterations, the evolution of level set curve stopped gradually. It can be seen that our model has superiority in segmenting images with uneven gray distribution.

Besides, we use the Dice Similarity Coefficients (DSC) to compare segmentation effect of different models. DSC represents the difference between segmentation result R_1 and the ground truth R_2. It can be defined as:

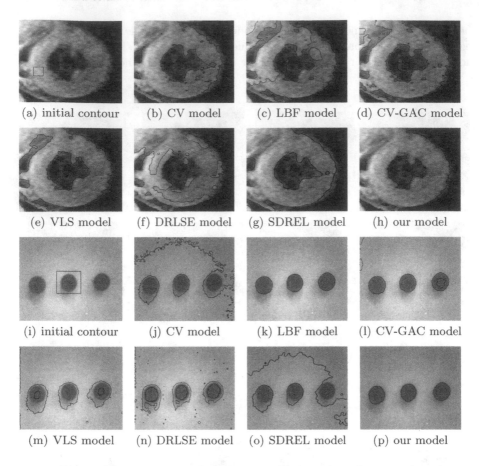

(a) initial contour   (b) CV model   (c) LBF model   (d) CV-GAC model

(e) VLS model   (f) DRLSE model   (g) SDREL model   (h) our model

(i) initial contour   (j) CV model   (k) LBF model   (l) CV-GAC model

(m) VLS model   (n) DRLSE model   (o) SDREL model   (p) our model

Fig. 4. Segmentation results of images with intensity inhomogeneity

$$D\left(R_1, R_2\right) = \frac{2 Area\left(R_1 \cap R_2\right)}{Area\left(R_1\right) + Area\left(R_2\right)}, \tag{18}$$

where $Area\left(R\right)$ denotes the number of pixels in region R. The average DSC of different models' segmentation results in our dataset is calculated and shown in Table 1. As the larger DSC value indicates a better segmentation result, it demonstrates the advantage of our algorithm quantitatively.

For images with complex gray distribution, the number of iterations and the time consumed of different models have a great difference. It can be seen from the Fig. 5 that although the time our model consuming in a single iteration increases slightly, the total number of iterations is smaller and the total time required for convergence is less than the other models.

Table 1. Quantitative analysis of different models' segmentation results

Models	CV	LBF	CV-GAC	VLS	DRLSE	SDREL	Our
DSC	0.7435	0.7293	0.7620	0.8964	0.7818	0.8255	0.9319

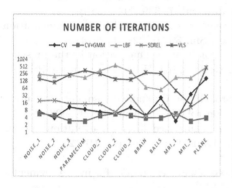
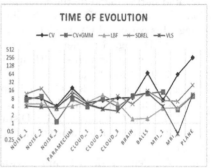

Fig. 5. Iteration number and evolution time of different models

4   Conclusion

In this paper, a level set method combined with GMM for image segmentation is proposed. The GMM is used to describe gray distribution characteristics inside and outside the curve. The improved model optimizes the mean gray value inside and outside the curve in the energy function, which makes the overall segmentation effect of CV model greatly improved.

Experimental results show that the improved CV model can not only segment target regions from the images with intensity inhomogeneity, but also reduce iteration number and evolution time, improving the anti-noise capability of the model. By analysis, we prove that the proposed model has superiority over general CV model. However, it depends too much on the curve's initial position, and requires images with contrasting foreground and background. To overcome these shortcomings is the next research direction.

Acknowledgement. This project is supported by National Key R&D Program of China (2016YFC0401606) and National Natural Science Foundation of China (61671202, 61573128, 61701169).

References

1. Devraj, M., Amitava, C., Madhubanti, M.: Robust medical image segmentation using partical swarm optimization aided level set based global fitting energy active contour approach. Eng. Appl. Artif. Intell. **35**, 199–214 (2014)
2. Ren, J.J., He, M.Y.: Level set method of image segmentation based on improved CV model of 3-D histogram. Infrared Millim. Waves **27**(1), 72–76 (2008)

3. Chen, B., Zhang, M., Chen, W., Pan, B., Li, L.C., Wei, X.: A novel adaptive segmentation method based on legendre polynomials approximation. In: Lai, J.H., et al. (eds.) PRCV 2018. LNCS, vol. 11256, pp. 297–308. Springer, Cham (2018). https://doi.org/10.1007/978-3-030-03398-9_26

4. Fu, J.M., Xu, M.Y.: An improved C-V level set image segmentation model based on rapid narrow-band method. Metall. Min. Ind. **7**, 339–344 (2015)

5. Song, Y., Wu, Y.Q., Bi, S.B.: Satellite remote sensing cloud image segmentation using edge corrected CV model. Acta Opt. Sin. **34**(9), 22–29 (2014)

6. Li, C.M., Huang, R.: A level set method for image segmentation in the presence of intensity inhomogeneities with application to MRI. IEEE Trans. Image Process. **20**(7), 2007–2016 (2011)

7. Juneja, P., Kashyap, R.: Optimal approach for CT image segmentation using improved energy based method. Int. J. Control Theory Appl. **9**, 599–608 (2016)

8. Li, C.M., Xu, C.Y., Gui, C.F.: Distance regularized level set evolution and its application to image segmentation. IEEE Trans. Image Process. **19**(12), 3243–3254 (2010)

9. Liu, S.G., Peng, Y.L.: A local region-based Chan-Vese model for image segmentation. Pattern Recogn. **45**, 2769–2779 (2012)

10. Zhang, K.H., Zhang, L.: A level set approach to image segmentation with intensity inhomogeneity. IEEE Trans. Cybern. **46**(2), 546–557 (2016)

11. Li, N., Liu, M.M., Li, Y.F.: Image segmentation algorithm using watershed transform and level set method. In: IEEE International Conference on Acoustics, Speech and Signal Processing, ICASSP 2007, Honolulu, pp. 613–616 (2007)

12. Hayit, G., Amit, R., Jacob, G.: Constrained Gaussian mixture model framework for automatic segmentation of MR brain images. IEEE Trans. Med. Imaging **25**(9), 1233–1245 (2006)

13. Li, C., Kao, C., Gore, J.C., Ding, Z.: Implicit active contours driven by local binary fitting energy. In: 2007 IEEE Conference on Computer Vision and Pattern Recognition, pp. 1–7. IEEE, Minneapolis (2007)

14. Lin, Y., Tong, L.: Level set image segmentation of CV-GAC model. In: 2018 13th International Conference on Computer Science and Education (ICCSE), pp. 1–5. IEEE, Colombo (2018)

15. Wang, L.L., Hu, L., Wang, X.Y.: A bias correction variational level set image segmentation model combining structure extraction. In: 2017 2nd International Conference on Image, Vision and Computing (ICIVC), pp. 327–331. IEEE, Chengdu (2017)

16. Wang, X.C., Shan, J.X., Niu, Y.M., Tan, L.W., Zhang, S.X.: Enhanced distance regularization for re-initialization free level set evolution with application to image segmentation. Neurocomputing **141**, 223–235 (2014)

17. Zhi, X.H., Shen, H.B.: Saliency driven region-edge-based top down level set evolution reveals the asynchronous focus in image segmentation. Pattern Recognit. **80**, 241–255 (2018)

Nonstandard Periodic Gait Energy Image for Gait Recognition and Data Augmentation

Kejun Wang[1(✉)], Liangliang Liu[1], Yilong Lee[1], Xinnan Ding[1], and Junyu Lin[2]

[1] College of Automation, Harbin Engineering University, Harbin, China
{wangkejun,liuliangliang,xuyibo,
dingxinnan}@hrbeu.edu.cn
[2] Institute of Information Engineering, Chinese Academy of Sciences,
Beijing 100093, China
linjunyu@iie.ac.cn

Abstract. The method for synthesizing Gait Energy Image (GEI) is to use the silhouettes overlay of a pedestrian gait cycle, whereas, it is difficult to obtain the silhouettes of a pedestrian gait cycle in practical applications, due to many factors such as pedestrian occlusion and pedestrian direction change, etc. In addition, the existing gait cycle detection methods suffer from limitations. Therefore, a Nonstandard Periodic Gait Energy Image (NP-GEI) is proposed in this paper, which is synthesized without gait cycle detection. And it is verified that the CNN trained by NP-GEI can achieve the same recognition accuracy as that by CP-GEI in most cases. Moreover, we also verify that the CNN, trained by various NP-GEIs which is synthesized by different frame-number silhouettes, can recognize the GEI with robustness in single-view and multi-view scenarios. Finally, a data augmentation method is developed based on NP-GEI, and an experiment is provided to verify the effectiveness of this proposed method.

Keywords: Nonstandard periodic GEI · Data augmentation · Gait recognition · Gait cycle detection

1 Introduction

Gait recognition is a new biometric technology, which uses the unique gesture of pedestrians to complete pedestrian identification. This technology has the characteristics of easy information collection, non-contact, difficult to hide and difficult to camouflage. More importantly, compared with other existing biometric recognition methods, gait recognition is a better way to recognize pedestrian identity information in the long distance without pedestrian cooperation [1]. Therefore, gait recognition has good prospects for application in many fields such as safety monitoring, human-computer interaction and entrance guard.

Recent gait recognition methods can be divided into two main categories. The first one is to use 3D-CNN [14] or 2D-CNN and LSTM [15] to extract and classify the gait information from image sequence directly. The second one is to synthesize Gait Energy Image (GEI) [2] by using pedestrian silhouettes sequence and then extract and classify

© Springer Nature Switzerland AG 2019
Z. Lin et al. (Eds.): PRCV 2019, LNCS 11858, pp. 197–208, 2019.
https://doi.org/10.1007/978-3-030-31723-2_17

gait information in GEI by using 2D-CNN, so as to realize identification or authentication [3–5]. The GEI was proposed by Han et al. [2], which is an image superimposed by a sequence of pedestrian silhouettes. These silhouettes are derived from a gait cycle of the pedestrian and need to be normalized. In this way, GEI contains both static and dynamic feature information of pedestrians. Compared with using images directly, using the GEI training model can effectively reduce the scale of the model and reduce the amount of calculation. Therefore, GEI has been widely used in gait recognition.

Existing gait recognition methods need to obtain a complete gait outline of pedestrians when using GEI. However, in reality, it is difficult to obtain these images as follows:

- Existing gait cycle detection methods are sensitive to viewing angles. These periodic detection methods tend to effective only at specific angles, but in other angles the accuracy drops sharply. The gait cycle detection methods are described in detail in Sect. 2.1.
- Due to the different frame rates of different cameras, the number of frames in the same gait cycle may vary greatly across cameras. Because the images taken by cameras are discrete, it is difficult to ensure that a set of image sequences accurately contain the complete gait cycle of pedestrians.
- Pedestrian walking status also affects gait cycle detection. In reality, it is difficult to ensure that pedestrians walk straight and evenly at a constant speed.
- In some cases, the camera obtains a limited number of pedestrian contours due to obstacles or other pedestrian occlusions. These contour maps do not contain a complete gait cycle.

In view of the above problems, we propose a Non-standard Periodic Gait Energy Image (NP-GEI), which can be synthesized directly by any number of frames without gait cycle detection. Therefore, compared to Complete Periodic gait Energy Image (CP-GEI), NP-GEI is easier to synthesize and has a wider range of applications. At the same time, the model trained by NP-GEI also has good recognition performance.

In this paper, we make the following contributions:

- We propose a gait energy image based on Nonstandard gait periodic pedestrian silhouettes, which is named NP-GEI. Furthermore, we verify the effectiveness of using NP-GEI to train CNN for gait recognition.
- It is verified that, in most cases, using NP-GEI training CNN to identify CP-GEI in both single-view and multi-view scenarios is robust.
- In this paper, a NP-GEI based-data augmentation method is presented. This method is especially suitable for the case of insufficient silhouettes.

In the remaining part of this paper, Sect. 2 presents more related works on gait periodicity detection and Gait recognition using GEI. And then Sect. 3 describes the proposed method in detail. Some experimental evaluations are conducted on the CASIA-B gait database and results are shown in Sect. 4. Finally, conclusions are drawn in Sect. 5.

2 Related Work

2.1 Gait Cycle Detection

Gait is a kind of periodic movement when walking. Gait cycle detection uses the method of periodic analysis to determine the start and end frames of the silhouettes, and then to determine a gait cycle. The existing gait cycle detection method is mainly based on the periodic variation of the height and width of the human body region in the silhouettes. Culter et al. [8] calculated the similarity of the pedestrian contour with time by similarity matrix to detect pedestrian gait cycle, but the algorithm has a large amount of computation. Collins et al. [12] proposed to use the height and width of the silhouettes to detect the pedestrian gait cycle. But if the distance between the pedestrian and the camera changes during walking, the size of the silhouettes will change greatly. So this method is difficult to apply to the existing security system. Wang et al. [13] proposed a gait cycle detection method based on the aspect ratio of silhouette, which effectively solved this problem. But it still affected by covariates such as pedestrian clothing. Wang et al. [17] proposed a method of using the average width of the specific area of lower limbs to realize gait cycle detection. Ben et al. [18] proposed a method of double ellipse fitting to achieve gait cycle detection. Lee et al. [19] proposed a gait cycle detection method by using the normalized image width method. However, these methods tend to have higher detection accuracy only for the side view profile, but there is a large error for other view profile detection. Gait cycle even cannot be achieved from some specific perspectives.

2.2 Gait Recognition Method Based on GEI

It is effective to use CNN in image feature extracting, researchers often use CNN to extract gait features from GEI for identity recognition. Shiraga et al. [3] used GEI directly input CNN to extract the gait features in the images for identification. Wu et al. [6] used the idea of metric learning to build a variety of convolutional neural network frameworks. Each framework combines different levels of features and can be applied to authentication tasks. Yu et al. [7] proposed a GAN to eliminate identity-independent covariates in GEI. The model includes three parts: converter, true/false discriminator and identity discriminator. The converter is an Autoencoder implemented by CNN, which inputs the original GEI and generates a covariate GEI with a 90° viewing angle. True/false discriminators are used to verify the authenticity of the generated GEI, and identity authenticators are used to verify whether the generated GEI is completed and retain the identity information of the original GEI.

However, because of the definition in document [2], GEI is superimposed by a standard gait periodic silhouettes, so these methods all adopt CP-GEI. Although Maryam et al. [16] proposed ITCNet, this model can transform the GEI synthesized by fewer frame contours layer-by-layer through encoding-decoding, and finally generate a full cycle GEI. However, this method needs a large number of complete cycle GEI as training samples. In addition, this method only considers the GEI from 90° perspective.

2.3   Data Augmentation

Image processing refers to the use of image flipping, rotation, zooming, clipping, translation, adding noise and other ways to expand the number of training samples in order to improve the robustness of model recognition. And sample generation methods mostly use GAN [10] to generate the required samples under certain constraints. Existing Data Augmentation methods for gait recognition are limited. Charalambous et al. [11] proposed a method to generate GEI using motion capture and human 3D model reconstruction. But this method needs special equipment, so it is difficult to use it directly.

3   Method

3.1   Overview

Due to the lack of research on the sensitivity of GEI to the number of frames in the silhouettes, and the existing gait cycle detection methods have some shortcomings. we proposed NP-GEI. We tried to verify that the CNN based-model trained by NP-GEI can also accomplish the gait recognition task.

We build a gait recognition model based on CNN. The structure of the model is described in detail in Sect. 3.2. The overall process is shown in Fig. 1. First, we synthesize the gait silhouettes into NP-GEI and then use these NP-GEIs to train models. The recognition accuracy of the model on the test set is evaluated after the training was completed. We also use the same model and evaluation method to evaluate the effectiveness of our data augmentation method based on NP-GEI.

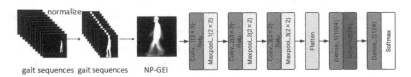

Fig. 1. Experimental flow chart for evaluating the effectiveness of NP-GEI

3.2   Synthesis of NP-GEI

NP-GEI is synthesized from pedestrian profiles with multiple frames. For example, NP-GEI-5 is synthesized by 1–5 frames of the profiles; NP-GEI-10 is synthesized by 1–10 frames of the profiles, etc. The method of synthesizing NP-GEI is similar to the generation of GEI. Firstly, the specific number of pedestrian images are taken and the highest and the lowest points of the images are obtained. Then, the images are clipped according to the aspect ratio of each original images. And then the pedestrian symmetry axis of every clipped image is obtained. Finally, NP-GEI can be obtained by aligning the images with the symmetry axis and superimposing them according to Eq. 1.

$$E_{GEI}(x,y) = \frac{1}{N}\sum_{n=1}^{N} B(x,y,n) \tag{1}$$

In the equation, N is the total number of images taken; (x, y) is the pixel coordinates of the silhouette; n is the nth image.

Some examples of NP-GEI are shown in Fig. 2. Observing Fig. 2 and comparing it with the CP-GEI in Fig. 3 we can see that there are some differences between NP-GEI-5, NP-GEI-10, and CP-GEI. While for NP-GEI-15 to NP-GEI-50, the differences between NP-GEI and CP-GEI are difficult to observe directly.

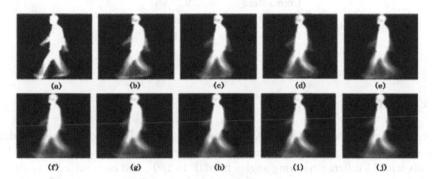

Fig. 2. Some examples of NP-GEINetwork Architectures. (a) an example of NP-GEI-5, (b) an example of NP-GEI-10, (c) an example of NP-GEI-15, (d) an example of NP-GEI-20, (e) an example of NP-GEI-25, (f) an example of NP-GEI-30, (g) an example of NP-GEI-35, (h) an example of NP-GEI-40, (i) an example of NP-GEI-45, (j) an example of NP-GEI-50.

Fig. 3. An example of CP-GEI

3.3 Network Architectures

CNN is the most commonly used structure in gait recognition research in recent years. In this paper, we examine the general effects of various NP-GEIs on CNN prediction. Therefore, for universality, the model we build does not contain special structures. It is only a multi-layer CNN with convolutional layers, pooling layers, and fully connected layers. The first six layers of the model consist of convolutional layers with convolution core size of 3 × 3 and maximum pooling size of 2 × 2 alternately, which are used to extract gait features in GEIs. Then the feature map is flattened to one-dimensional vector, and the feature is classified by the full connection layer with 1024 nodes, and the Dropout of 0.5 is added to eliminate the over-fitting. Finally, Softmax is used to output all kinds of probability values. In addition, all activation functions are Relu, except for the output layer. The detailed architecture of the network is listed in Table 1.

Table 1. Detailed architecture of the network

Layer	Output shape
Conv3-Relu	128,128,24
Maxpool	64,64,24
Conv3-Relu	62,62,48
Maxpool	31,31,48
Conv3-Relu	29,29,96
Maxpool	14,14,96
FC-Relu-Dropout	1024
FC-Softmax	124

4 Experiments

We conduct experiments on CASIA-B dataset [9], which is one of the most widely used multi-view datasets for gait recognition. The CASIA-B data set contains 124 subjects with 11 different viewing angles from 0° to 180°, and each subject has 10 sets of gait sequences. Among them, nm-01 to nm-06 are normal walking, bg-01 and bg-02 are walking with backpacks, cl-01 and cl-02 are walking in coats. In the experiment, NP-GEIs are synthesized by using different frame number silhouettes from nm-01 to nm-06, respectively, and named it NP-GEI-x (where x is the number of silhouettes)

In this section, **Experiment 1** is designed to verify that gait recognition can be accomplished directly by NP-GEI without gait cycle detection. Meanwhile, we explored the relationship between the number of silhouettes to synthetic NP-GEI and the recognition accuracy. **Experiment 2** is to study the recognition rate of the model for CP-GEI under different frame number NP-GEI registration. At the same time, the robustness of CNN for cross-frame GEI recognition was verified. **Experiment 3** is to verify that NP-GEI can be used in multi-view gait recognition and that the increase in training set samples can improve the recognition accuracy of the model. And, **Experiment 4** is to verify the effectiveness of our proposed data enhancement method based on Experiment 1 and Experiment 2.

4.1 Experiment 1: Effectiveness of NP-GEI for Gait Recognition

In Experiment 1, we use NP-GEI-x synthesized from nm-01 to nm-04 as training sets. And NP-GEI-x synthesized by nm-05 and nm-06 was used as test sets.

Firstly, the model is trained by the NP-GEI-5 training set and test by the NP-GEI-5 test set to evaluate recognition accuracy. Then NP-GEI-10 is utilized to train and test model, etc. Finally, we use CP-GEI to train and test model as a comparison. The experimental results were listed in Table 2.

Table 2. Performances of models on each NP-GEI and CP-GEI test sets.

NP-GEI-	5	10	15	20	25	30	35	40	45	50	CP-GEI
Acc	0.81	0.86	0.93	0.96	0.96	0.96	0.98	0.96	0.96	0.98	0.98
Err	0.17	0.12	0.05	0.02	0.02	0.02	0	0.02	0.02	0	0

In the table, Acc represents the accuracy of the model on every test set, while Err represents the difference of the accuracy between the model trained by NP-GEI and by CP-GEI on the respective test set.

From the analysis of the data above, we can find that when the model trained by NP-GEI which was synthesized by less than 15 frames silhouettes, there is a big gap in recognition accuracy between the model trained by NP-GEI with by CP-GEI.

Analyzing a sequence of silhouettes of a synthetic CP-GEI, it can be find the silhouettes of a complete gait cycle are about 20–25 (as listed in Table 3). The NP-GEI synthesized with fewer frames contains limited gait information, which makes the recognition accuracy relatively lower. NP-GEI basically contains the same gait information as CP-GEI when the number of frames is 20–25. NP-GEI contains some redundant information when the number of frames is more than 25. Due to CNN's powerful feature extraction capabilities, the model still has a high recognition accuracy.

Table 3. A sequence of silhouettes of a synthetic CP-GEI

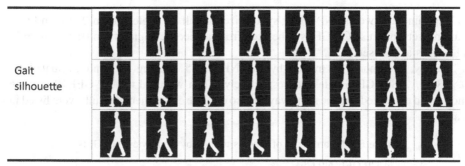

Gait silhouette

4.2 Experiment 2: Robustness of CNN to GEI Recognition of Cross-Frame Number from a Single Perspective

In Experiment 2, we use NP-GEI-x synthesized from nm-01 to nm-06 at 90° as the training set, and use CP-GEI synthesized from nm-01 to nm-06 as the test set. The view angle is the same as training set.

Firstly, the model is trained by the NP-GEI-5 training set and test by the CP-GEI test set to evaluate recognition accuracy. Then the model is trained by the NP-GEI-10 training set and test by the CP-GEI test set, etc. Finally, the CP-GEI training and testing model is used as a comparison. The experimental results are listed in Table 4.

Table 4. Performances of models on CP-GEI test set.

NP-GEI-	5	10	15	20	25	30	35	40	45	50	CP-GEI
Acc	0.59	0.76	0.80	0.92	0.95	0.97	0.96	1.00	0.99	0.99	1.00
Err	0.41	0.24	0.20	0.08	0.05	0.03	0.04	0	0.01	0.01	0

The definition of Acc and Err are the same as those in experiment 1. From the analysis of the data above, we can find that when the number of silhouettes of the synthesized NP-GEI is less than the number of silhouettes of the synthesized CP-GEI, the difference in number is larger, the accuracy of recognition is lower. On the contrary condition, the recognition accuracy is high, and there is little correlation between the accuracy and the number of frames.

Similar to the analysis of Experiment 1. The NP-GEI with fewer silhouettes contains limited identity information, while the NP-GEI with more silhouettes contains redundant information. However, CNN can extract gait features from redundant information. It should be noted that all kinds of GEI used in this experiment are contour map synthesis from 90 angle of view. If the GEI perspective of training set is different from that of testing set, the prediction will decrease greatly. Of course, even though CP-GEI is used in training set and test set, when these CP-GEI are taken from different angles, it is difficult to get accurate identity prediction using general CNN.

4.3   Experiments 3: Robustness of CNN to GEI Recognition of Cross-Frame Number in Multi-view

In Experiment 3, we use NP-GEI-x synthesized by all 11 angles of nm-01 to nm-06 as training sets, and use CP-GEI synthesized from a specific angle of nm-01 to nm-06 in 11 angles as test set.

Firstly, the model is trained by the NP-GEI-5 training set, and evaluated by $0°, 18°, \ldots, 180°$ CP-GEI test set respectively. Then we used the NP-GEI-10 training model and evaluated it in the same way, and so on. The experimental results were listed in Table 5.

Table 5. Performances of models trained by multi-view NP-GEIs

Angle of CP-GEI	NP-GEI-									
	5	10	15	20	25	30	35	40	45	50
0°	0.85	0.97	0.99	1.00	1.00	1.00	0.99	0.97	0.97	1.00
18°	0.89	0.98	0.99	1.00	1.00	0.99	0.99	0.97	0.97	1.00
36°	0.75	0.92	0.96	1.00	1.00	0.99	0.95	0.93	1.00	0.99
54°	0.53	0.84	0.95	0.99	1.00	0.99	0.97	0.90	0.97	0.99
72°	0.91	0.99	1.00	1.00	1.00	1.00	0.99	0.99	0.98	1.00
90°	0.90	0.97	1.00	1.00	1.00	1.00	1.00	0.99	1.00	0.99
108°	0.86	0.97	0.99	1.00	1.00	1.00	0.99	0.99	0.99	1.00
126°	0.87	0.98	0.99	1.00	1.00	1.00	1.00	1.00	1.00	1.00
144°	0.73	0.94	0.97	1.00	1.00	1.00	1.00	0.99	0.99	0.99
162°	0.74	0.93	0.98	1.00	1.00	1.00	1.00	1.00	0.99	0.99
180°	0.90	0.97	0.99	1.00	1.00	1.00	0.99	1.00	0.99	1.00
Mean	0.81	0.95	0.98	1.00	1.00	1.00	0.99	0.98	0.96	1.00

Comparing the data in Table 5 with it in Table 4, we can find that the accuracy can be greatly improved by using NP-GEI with 11 perspectives training the model simultaneously. Moreover, the model can well recognize CP-GEI of various angles when the number of image of synthetic NP-GEI is more than 10 frames.

Analyzing results, it can be found that the training set data in Experiment 3 was 11 times as much as that in experiment 2. Although NP-GEIs has big difference in appearance from different angles, all of them contain the gait information. Adequate gait information enables CNN to extract the gait characteristics of samples more accurately for recognition and classification.

4.4 Experiments 4: Experiments on the Effectiveness of Data Augment Based on NP-GEI

Inspired by the results of experiment 3, we propose a method of data augmentation based on NP-GEI. Assuming that limited number of images are obtained, we can synthesize various NP-GEIs from these images as a training set. Because abundant NP-GEIs provide abundant gait information, and that information extract by CNN to enhance the recognition accuracy.

The model which we trained by NP-GEI-5 training set in Experiment 1 had poor recognition accuracy. So we consider expanding the NP-GEI-5 training set.

Firstly, we synthesize NP-GEI from 1–3 frames and 1–5 frames in nm-01 to nm-04 and name this training set as Mix_1_1. Then we synthesize various NP-GEIs in 1–5 frames from nm-01 to nm-04 in all combinations $(1-2, 1-3, \ldots, 4-5)$ along with the 5-frame images together as a training set, name it as Mix_all_1. Subsequently, models are trained by Mix_1_1 and Mix_all_1 separately. The trained model is tested on NP-GEI-5 test set (NP-GEI-5 synthesized from nm-05 to nm-06). The experimental results are listed in Table 6.

Table 6. Performances of models trained by Mix on condition of Experiment 1

Training set	Mix_1_1	Mix_all_1
Acc	0.82	0.95

We compared the data in Tables 2 and 6 and arranged them as Fig. 4. It can be seen from Fig. 4. Although Mix_1_1 is doubled in data volume compared to the NP-GEI-5 training set in Experiment 1, the model recognition accuracy is only increased by 2%. Obviously, only adding 1–3 frames of silhouettes synthesis NP-GEI can provide additional gait information is limited. However, using the Mix_all_1 training model can greatly improve the accuracy of model recognition. The accuracy of model recognition can reach 95%, which is close to the recognition accuracy obtained by the training set NP-GEI-20 training the model.

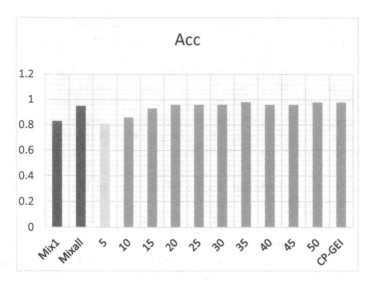

Fig. 4. The accuracy of the models trained by Mix_1 and Mix_all (red) is comparing with the result of the experimental 1 (yellow, blue). (Color figure online)

In addition, we remix mix_1_1 and mix_all_1 using the first 5 frames from nm-01 to nm-06 and named them mix_1_2 and mix_all_2. We used these two training sets to train the models separately and tested the models on the CP-GEI test set in Experiment 2. The experimental results are shown in Table 7. Compared with NP-GEI-5 training set, the recognition accuracy of mix_1_2 and mix_all_2 models is improved by 3% and 15%. The results show that this data augment method is also effective for training model recognition of cross-frame GEI.

Table 7. Performances of models trained by Mix on condition of Experiment 2

Training set	Mix_1_2	Mix_all_2
Acc	0.62	0.74

5   Conclusion

In this paper, a Nonstandard Periodic Gait Energy Image has been proposed And some experiments, have been provided to draw a conclusion that in most cases, the CNN trained by NP-GEI can achieve the same recognition accuracy as that by CP-GEI. Moreover, By utilizing NP-GEI, the system based on GEI has no longer the need of gait cycle detection, which both simplifies the system structure and improves the efficiency of the system. It has been analyzed that NP-GEI is easier to be implemented in practice as compared with CP-GEI. In addition, the robustness of the CNN trained by various NP-GEIs for GEI recognition has been validated in single-view and multi-view scenarios. Finally, the experiments have demonstrated that the proposed NP-GEI based-Data Augmentation method can effectively improve the accuracy of model recognition.

References

1. Phillips, P.J.: Human identification technical challenges. In: 2002 International Conference on Image Processing, pp. 49–52. IEEE, Rochester (2002)
2. Han, J., Bhanu, B.: Individual recognition using gait energy image. IEEE Trans. Pattern Anal. Mach. Intell. **28**(2), 316–322 (2006)
3. Shiraga, K., Makihara, Y., Muramatsu, D., Echigo, T., Yagi, Y.: GEINet: view-invariant gait recognition using a convolutional neural network. In: 2016 International Conference on Biometrics, pp. 1–8. IEEE, Halmstad (2016)
4. Zhang, C., Liu, W., Ma, H., Fu, H.: Siamese neural network based gait recognition for human identification. In: 2016 International Conference on Acoustics, pp. 2832–2836. IEEE, Shanghai (2016)
5. Yeoh, T.W., Aguirre, H.E., Tanaka, K.: Clothing-invariant gait recognition using convolutional neural network. In: 2016 International Symposium on Intelligent Signal Processing and Communication Systems, pp. 1–5. ISPACS, Phuket (2016)
6. Wu, Z., Huang, Y., Wang, L., Wang, X., Tan, T.: A comprehensive study on cross-view gait based human identification with deep CNNs. IEEE Trans. Pattern Anal. Mach. Intell. **39**(2), 209–226 (2016)
7. Yu, S., Chen, H., Reyes, G., Edel, B., Poh, N.: GaitGAN: invariant gait feature extraction using generative adversarial networks. In: 2017 IEEE Conference on Computer Vision and Pattern Recognition Workshops, pp. 532–539. IEEE, Honolulu (2017)
8. Cutler, R., Davis, L.S.: Robust real-time periodic motion detection, analysis, and applications. IEEE Trans. Pattern Anal. Mach. Intell. **22**(8), 781–796 (1999)
9. Yu, S., Tan, D., Tan, T.: A framework for evaluating the effect of view angle, clothing and carrying condition on gait recognition. In: 18th International Conference on Pattern Recognition, pp. 441–444. IEEE, Hong Kong (2006)
10. Goodfellow, I.J., Pouget-Abadie, J., Mirza, M., Xu, B., Warde-Farley, D., Ozair, S., et al.: Generative adversarial networks. Adv. Neural. Inf. Process. Syst. **3**, 2672–2680 (2014)
11. Charalambous, C.C., Bharath, A.A.: A data augmentation methodology for training machine/deep learning gait recognition algorithms. arXiv preprint. arXiv:1610.07570 (2016)
12. Collins, R.T., Gross, R., Shi. J.: Silhouette-based human identification from body shape and gait. In: 5th IEEE International Conference on Automatic Face and Gesture Recognition, pp. 366–372. IEEE, Washington (2002)
13. Wang, L., Tan, T., Ning, H., Hu, W.: Silhouette analysis-based gait recognition for human identification. IEEE Trans. Pattern Anal. Mach. Intell. **25**(12), 1505–1518 (2003)
14. Wolf, T., Babaee, M., Rigoll, G.: Multi-view gait recognition using 3D convolutional neural networks. In: 2016 IEEE International Conference on Image Processing, pp. 4165–4169. IEEE, Phoenix (2016)
15. Feng Y., Li Y., Luo J.: Learning effective gait features using LSTM. In: 2016 23rd International Conference on Pattern Recognition, pp. 325–330. ICPR, Cancun (2016)
16. Babaee, M., Li, L., Rigoll, G.: Person identification from partial gait cycle using fully convolutional neural networks. Neurocomputing **338**, 116–125 (2019)

17. Wang, C., Zhang, J., Wang, L., Pu, J., Yuan, X.: Human identification using temporal information preserving gait template. IEEE Trans. Pattern Anal. Mach. Intell. **34**(11), 2164–2176 (2012)
18. Ben, X., Meng, W., Yan, R.: Dual-ellipse fitting approach for robust gait periodicity detection. Neurocomputing **79**(3), 173–178 (2012)
19. Lee, C.P., Tan, A.W.C., Tan, S.C.: Gait recognition with transient binary patterns. Vis. Commun. Image Represent. **33**(C), 69–77 (2015)

A Temporal Attentive Approach for Video-Based Pedestrian Attribute Recognition

Zhiyuan Chen[✉], Annan Li, and Yunhong Wang

School of Computer Science and Engineering, Beihang University, Beijing, China
{dechen,liannan,yhwang}@buaa.edu.cn

Abstract. In this paper, we first tackle the problem of pedestrian attribute recognition by video-based approach. The challenge mainly lies in spatial and temporal modeling and how to integrating them for effective and dynamic pedestrian representation. To solve this problem, a novel multi-task model based on the conventional neural network and temporal attention strategy is proposed. Since publicly available dataset is rare, two new large-scale video datasets with expanded attribute definition are presented, on which the effectiveness of both video-based pedestrian attribute recognition methods and the proposed new network architecture is well demonstrated. The two datasets are published on http://irip.buaa.edu.cn/mars_duke_attributes/index.html.

Keywords: Video-based pedestrian attribute recognition ·
Convolutional neural networks · Temporal attention

1 Introduction

Pedestrian attribute, such as gender, age and clothing characteristics, has drawn a great attention recently due to its wide range of applications in intelligent surveillance system. It can be used for retrieving pedestrian and assisting other computer vision tasks, such as human detection [1], person re-identification [2–8] etc.

In the past years, a lot of effort has been made to pedestrian attribute recognition. Layne et al. [2], Deng et al. [9] and Li et al. [3] use support vector machines to recognize pedestrian attribute, while AdaBoost is utilized by Zhu et al. [10]. Recently, Convolutional Neural Networks (CNN) have been adopted. Sudowe et al. [11] propose a jointly-trained holistic CNN model, while Li et al. [12] investigate CNN for both individual and group attributes. Liu et al. [13] introduce attention model to CNN-based pedestrian attribute recognition. Wang et al. [14], use recurrent learning for modeling the attribute correlations. Zhao et al. [15] further improve such approach by analyzing intra-group and

---

Z. Chen—Student first author.

© Springer Nature Switzerland AG 2019
Z. Lin et al. (Eds.): PRCV 2019, LNCS 11858, pp. 209–220, 2019.
https://doi.org/10.1007/978-3-030-31723-2_18

Fig. 1. Comparison between image and video based pedestrian attribute recognition. (a) Backpack is invisible in the frontal view, but can be clearly observed in other image of a sequence. (b) For a woman in dark color, it is difficult to classify whether she is wearing a skirt or shorts using one single image of limited resolution. However, the difficulty can be mitigated with the swinging of skirt. (c) The act of bowing head may makes it impossible to recognize the hair length attribute of the pedestrain from one single image, while video data contains richer motion information. (d) Quality problems like occlusion may highly affected the recognition progress of some specific attributes in still-images.

inter-group correlations. Since clothing attribute is highly relevant to spatial location, Zhang et al. [16] and Li et al. [17] use pose estimation for assistance.

Although demonstrated good performance, the above-mentioned methods are all based on static image. They are trained and evaluated on datasets with only one image per instance [9, 18–23]. However, in a real-world surveillance scenario, consecutive image sequence is available. As can, be seen from Fig. 1(a), a single shot of pedestrian (dashed rectangle) is not necessarily the most representative one for a specific attribute. Besides that sequential data can also provide strong temporal cues (see Fig. 1(b)), which are overlook in existing image-based approaches. What's more, as shown in Fig. 1(c) and (d), video data shows clear superiority in handling some special cases and quality problems. It is reasonable that pedestrian attribute recognition should be tackled by video-based approach.

In this paper, a novel deep learning approach for video-based pedestrian attribute recognition is proposed. To our knowledge, it is the first one tackling pedestrian attribute recognition by video. Lack of data is the possible reason why existing approaches are limited to static image. To address this problem, we annotate two large-scale datasets of pedestrian image sequences with rich attribute. Experimental results clearly demonstrate that the proposed approach is very effective. Detailed contributions of this paper include:

- Two large-scale pedestrian video datasets with rich attribute annotation are presented.
- A novel multi-task model based conventional neural network and temporal attention strategy is proposed for pedestrian attribute recognition.

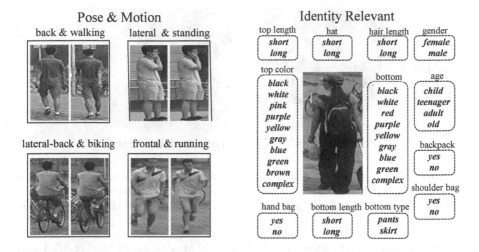

Fig. 2. Exemplar attribute annotation. (Color figure online)

– Extensive experiments are conducted and the results clearly show the superiority of video-based pedestrian attribute recognition.

The rest of this paper is organized as follows. The next section describes the annotated datasets. Then, Sect. 3 introduces the proposed video-based pedestrian attribute recognition approach. Experimental results are shown in Sect. 4 and conclusion is drawn in Sect. 5.

2   Dataset

Existing datasets for pedestrian attribute recognition such as PETA [9], RAP [18] and Market-1501 [19,24] are mainly image-based. Fortunately, with the progress in video-based person re-identification (ReID), large-scale dataset of pedestrian image sequence becomes available. The Motion Analysis and Re-identification Set (MARS) [25] and DukeMTMC-VideoReID [26] are newly released datasets, MARS consists of 20,478 tracklets from 1,261 people captured by six cameras, while DukeMTMC-VideoReID dataset contains 4,832 tracklets from 1,402 different pedestrians captured by eight cameras. MARS is an extension of Market-1501, they share the same identity, DukeMTMC-VideoReID is also an extension of DukeMTMC-ReID which also follows the same identity rules. Although Lin et al. [24] provides identity-level attribute annotation for Market-1501 and DukeMTMC-ReID, these annotations cannot be directly adopted to MARS and DukeMTMC-VideoReID for two reasons: Firstly, instance correspondences between the imaged-based dataset and the video-based dataset are not one-to-one; Secondly, as can be seen from Fig. 3, due to some temporal changes, even for the same people in different tracklets, some attribute appears while some

Subject A   Subject B

Tracklets#1 Tracklets#2   Tracklets#1 Tracklest#2

Fig. 3. Examples of attribute change over time in MARS. A man puts on a backpack (left) and woman takes off her cardigan (right). Using the attributes annotated on a single image sequence for all the video instances of a pedestrian may incorporate errors.

attribute disappears. Therefore the identity-level annotation of Market-1501 and DukeMTMC-ReID is inaccurate for MARS and DukeMTMC-VideoReID.

To address the above-mentioned problem, we build new datasets by re-annotating MARS and DukeMTMC-VideoReID using an extended attribute definition based on Lin et al. [24]. As shown in Fig. 2, there are 16 kinds of attributes are labeled for each tracklets in MARS dataset: motion (walking, standing, running, biking, various), pose (frontal, lateral-frontal, lateral, lateral-back, back, various), gender (male, female), length of hair (long, short), length of tops/sleeve (long, short), length of bottoms (long, short), type of bottoms (pants, dress), wearing hat (yes, no), carrying shoulder bag (yes, no), carrying backpack (yes, no), carrying handbag (yes, no), nine bottom colors (black, white, red, purple, yellow, gray, blue, green, complex), ten top colors (black, white, pink, purple, yellow, gray, blue, green, brown, complex) and four kinds of ages (child, teenager, adult, old) which results in a total attribute number of 52. The DukeMTMC-VideoReID dataset is also re-annotated with the same expanded attribute definition rule.

The attributes can be divided into two categories: identity-relevant and behavior-relevant. Prior arts only focus on the former one since their main purpose is retrieving people from surveillance video. However, as can be seen from Fig. 2 (left column), behavior-relevant factors can greatly influence the appearance of a pedestrian. We argue that identifying such attributes is not only useful for comprehensive pedestrian understanding but also beneficial for ID-relevant attribute recognition itself. Because excluding the distraction caused by behavior can improve the focus on salient frame that containing identical attribute feature.

3   Approach

In this section, we first describe the overall architecture of our pedestrian attribute recognition network. Then we give a detailed introduction of the temporal attention strategy of the architecture.

3.1   Network Architecture

The overall architecture of our proposed model is illustrated in Fig. 4. At the beginning of the network, we choose ResNet-50 [27] as the backbone model, and the outputs of last flatten layer are used as the frame-level spatial feature, then the network is separated into two channels: i.e. the motion & pose channel and the ID-relevant channel respectively. The reason why we separate the classifiers into two channels is that motion & pose attributes are ID-irrelevant and its classifier would focus on different parts of the spatial features compared with the id-relevant attributes, so directly sharing the same spatial features among all the id-irrelevant and id-relevant attribute classifiers will lead to a feature-compete situation, which means both the id-irrelevant classifiers and id-relevant classifiers would restrain each other in the training progress. The effectiveness of this separation will be validated in the experiments.

Let $I = \{I_1, I_2, ..., I_n\}$ be an input image sequence or a tracklet, where n, w and h are the frame number, image width and height respectively, and we choose $n = 6, w = 112, h = 224$ in practice. Using the spatial feature extractor Resnet-50, each frame is represented by a tensor sized $2048 \times 4 \times 7$. Then the spatial feature vector is respectively processed by the convolution + pooling units in the two channels. Consequently, the $n \times 3 \times w \times h$ tensor is converted into a two-dimensional matrix $S = \{S_1, S_2, ..., S_n\}, S \in \mathbb{R}^{n \times 2048}$.

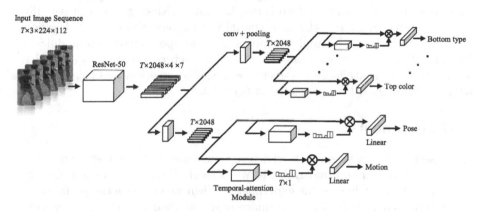

Fig. 4. Overall architecture of the proposed model. For an input pedestrian image sequence, frame-level spatial feature is first extracted by using the ResNet-50 network, then the spatial features is processed by two separated channels, one is the motion & pose attribute recognition channel which processed the spatial features by an unique convolution + pooling unit then put pooled features into single attribute recognition classifiers, the other channel shares similar architecture with the first one but takes the responsibility for recognizing ID-relevant attributes such as top color, gender or bottom type. Each single attribute recognition classifier contains a temporal-attention module which is used to generate temporal attention for the single attribute recognition process.

Then the pooled spatial feature vector is processed by the attribute classifiers. Firstly the temporal-attention module in each attribute classifier would take the spatial feature vector as input and generate a temporal attention vector A sized $n \times 1$ which represents the importance of each frame in recognizing the specific attribute. Then the temporal attention vector is used to weight the spatial feature of each frame, and a final feature vector of the image sequence for recognizing a specific attribute would be generated $F = A^T \times S$. Lastly the final feature vector would be fed into fully connected layer to achieve the attribute classification results.

We evaluate the influence of both the separated channel strategy and the temporal attention strategy in term of attributes recognition accuracy in Sect. 4, and the results shows that the corresponding strategies are the best choices for video-based pedestrian attributes recognition.

3.2 Temporal-Attention Strategy

Although ResNet-50 is able to capture effective spatial information from each single frame, however, we find that the importance of each frame in recognizing different attributes may vary. In other words, some frames may be greatly helpful in recognizing one attribute but may be harmful to another. As can be seen from Figs. 1 and 2, the recognition of different attributes may rely on different key frames, therefore each single attribute classifier is equipped with a temporal-attention module, which is also helpful in reducing the negative influence introduced by sharing the same spatial feature vector among the classifiers.

As shown in Fig. 5, by applying independent temporal-attention modules on different classifiers, various temporal attention vectors would be generated to be adaptive to the attribute classifier it serves. The superiority of this temporal attention strategy will be presented in Sect. 4.3.

4   Experiments

In this section, firstly we give a brief description about the train/test set partition of the annotated MARS and DukeMTMC-VideoReID datasets as well as some training/testing settings in the experiments. Then we compare the performance of the proposed method with the image-based method as well as other video analysis model such as 3DCNN [28] and CNN-RNN model [29], which demonstrates the superiority of our multi-task architecture in video-based pedestrian attribute recognition. Lastly ablation study shows the effectiveness of the separated channel strategy and temporal-attention strategy.

4.1   Settings

We follow the original train/test set partition rule of MARS [25] and DukeMTMC-VideoReID [26]. The training set of MARS consists of 8,298 tracklets from 625 people, while the rest 8,062 tracklets corresponding to 626 pedestrians make up the test set, the average frame number among these tracklets is

60. DukeMTMC-VideoReID has a smaller tracklets number but a larger average frame number which is 169. Both two datasets shares no identity in its train and test sets due to the peculiarity of the person re-identification task.

In the training progress, to form a training batch, firstly we random select $K = 64$ tracklets from the train set, then $n = 6$ frames is randomly sampled from each tracklets, so each training batch is formed by $K \times n$ frames, random sampling strategy is more suitable to temporal attention models for it increases the variance among the sampled frames compared with consecutive sampling strategy. In the testing process, for each testing tracklets which contains F frames, these frames would be randomly split into $\lfloor \frac{F}{n} \rfloor$ groups, and the testing attribute prediction result is the average prediction result among these groups. Cross Entropy Loss is chosen as the loss function and Adam with a learning rate 0.0003 is selected as the optimizer in training.

Table 1. Comparisons of recognition accuracy and F1 measure on MARS datasets (%).

Attribute	Image-based baseline		3DCNN		CNN-RNN		Ours	
	acc	F1	acc	F1	acc	F1	acc	F1
motion	91.08	39.39	90.34	33.64	**92.12**	**43.92**	**92.12**	43.69
pose	72.03	56.91	62.51	47.69	72.40	58.36	**73.65**	**61.36**
top color	**74.73**	**72.72**	68.04	65.63	71.90	69.28	73.43	71.44
bottom color	68.27	**44.63**	65.44	40.39	65.77	39.68	**69.45**	43.98
age	83.44	38.87	81.70	36.22	84.28	39.93	**84.71**	**40.21**
top length	94.21	58.72	93.63	56.37	**94.60**	65.18	94.47	**71.61**
bottom length	92.69	92.29	89.96	89.35	93.70	93.33	**94.22**	**93.90**
shoulder bag	80.39	72.57	71.82	61.30	82.70	75.89	**83.48**	**76.08**
backpack	89.37	85.95	82.60	76.58	90.18	87.17	**90.59**	**87.62**
hat	96.91	57.57	96.53	57.69	**97.90**	77.74	97.51	**77.84**
hand bag	85.71	62.82	83.88	59.90	**88.07**	71.68	87.61	**73.55**
hair	88.61	86.91	85.12	82.77	88.78	87.11	**89.54**	**88.17**
gender	91.32	90.89	86.49	85.75	92.77	92.44	**92.83**	**92.50**
bottom type	93.12	81.69	89.19	72.86	93.67	84.16	**94.60**	**86.62**
Average	85.85	67.28	81.95	61.87	86.35	70.42	**87.01**	**72.04**

4.2   Comparison with Other Approaches

The key contribution of this work is the introduction of video-based approach to pedestrian attribute recognition. To demonstrate its superiority, an imaged-based baseline ResNet-50 model with multi-classification head trained on the

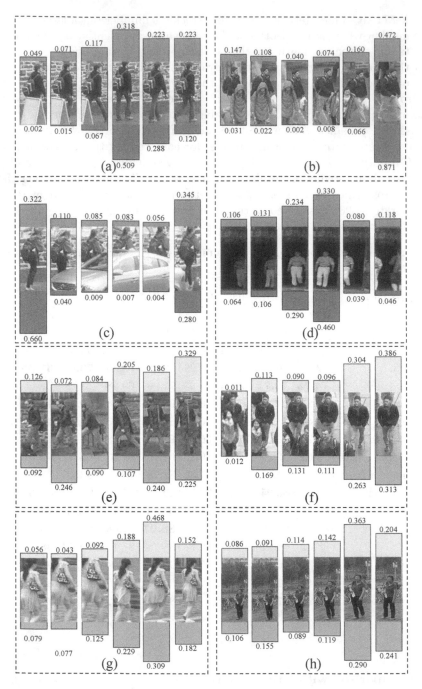

Fig. 5. Examples of temporal attention. The blue/brown/yellow/green bars represent the temporal attention vector generated by the *backpack/bottom color/shoulder bag/boots* attribute classifier respectively. (Color figure online)

Table 2. Comparisons of recognition accuracy and F1 measure on DukeMTMC-VideoReID dataset (%).

Attributes	Image-based baseline		3DCNN		CNN-RNN		Ours	
	acc	F1	acc	F1	acc	F1	acc	F1
motion	97.65	19.76	97.68	21.37	**97.76**	26.65	97.65	**27.68**
pose	72.46	62.63	69.46	59.95	74.36	66.26	**75.31**	**67.73**
backpack	87.41	86.12	81.05	77.59	89.78	87.95	**90.05**	**88.37**
shoulder bag	86.15	**77.90**	83.14	64.28	87.35	75.33	**87.88**	76.47
hand bag	**94.95**	56.34	94.34	51.09	94.34	57.82	94.42	**64.67**
boots	94.12	92.57	83.59	78.97	94.72	93.25	**94.95**	**93.52**
gender	89.57	89.49	82.49	82.47	90.35	90.28	**90.85**	**90.78**
hat	93.02	88.26	87.54	76.12	93.32	88.45	**93.73**	**89.41**
shoes color	**93.32**	83.35	88.07	69.76	93.05	84.65	93.13	**85.18**
top length	91.54	78.10	89.14	69.28	92.25	80.06	**92.52**	**81.06**
bottom color	76.82	47.25	75.92	48.19	78.85	51.66	**79.95**	**55.95**
top color	76.25	42.57	78.39	56.14	79.98	57.20	**81.28**	**58.07**
Average	87.77	68.70	84.24	62.93	88.84	71.63	**89.31**	**73.24**

framc images in the two datasets is also proposed in this paper, as shown in Tables 1 and 2, except for several attributes which is highly-relied on the spatial feature, the proposed model and CNN-RNN model achieves better results in most attributes, which demonstrates both the effectiveness of the proposed multi-task architecture and the superiority of video-based approach in recognizing pedestrian attribute.

We also introduce two deep-based video analysis models 3DCNN and CNN-RNN model into this video-based pedestrian attribute recognition task. As shown in the results, 3DCNN is not suitable for this task, which may imply that the 3D convolution operation would lost many important spatial clues in the tracklets. CNN-RNN model works even better than our model in recognizing the motion attribute, that's because recognizing the motion attribute relies on finding important temporal clues from the tracklets which can not be achieved by only temporal attention strategy, but our model still works better in the rest attributes, this phenomenon is consistent with the observations shown in Figs. 1 and 5, it shows that temporal feature would also cause spatial information loss, and highlighting the representativeness of key frames needs necessary spatial cues. The pedestrian attributes annotated in our dataset can be relevant to any part of the body (see Fig. 2). In other words, a region important to some attributes is not necessarily the same important to others. It is reasonable that emphasizing some specific spatial region might lead to detail loss. That is the possible explanation why temporal attention strategy outperforms RNN in recognizing most of the pedestrian attributes.

4.3 Ablation Study

Since we introduce the separated channel strategy and temporal attention strategy into our multi-task architecture, a series of ablation experiments are conducted to illustrate the effectiveness of these strategies. As shown in Table 3, both the two strategies can improve the recognition performance, and the temporal attention strategy contributes more observed from their results in both two metrics, that's mainly because that the temporal attention strategy can not only pick the discriminative frames out from the input tracklets, but also can ease the feature-compete phenomenon described in Sect. 3.1.

Table 3. Ablation study on two datasets (%).

Model	DukeMTMC-VID		MARS	
	Aver. acc	Aver. F1	Aver. acc	Aver. F1
Temporal pooling baseline	86.25	69.80	87.86	70.36
Baseline + separated channels strategy	86.84	71.38	88.97	71.70
Baseline + temporal attention strategy	86.93	70.59	89.09	72.40
Proposed Method	**87.01**	**72.04**	**89.31**	**73.24**

The channel separation strategy solves the feature-compete problem in physical, it physically splits the attributes into two channels, and applying separated convolution + pooling operation on the same spatial features vector, which could directly restrain the feature competition between id-relevant attributes and id-irrelevant attributes. While temporal attention strategy handles this problem latently, since each attribute classifier contains a temporal-attention module, so in the backward progress, the temporal-attention module can help smooth the backward gradients passed to bottom layers, which can also play the similar role as the Separated channel strategy.

It can be observed from Tables 1, 2 and 3 that even the video-based temporal pooling baseline can outperform the image-based method, this also illustrates the superiority of video-based approach in recognizing pedestrian attribute.

5   Conclusion

In this paper, we first study pedestrian attribute recognition with video-based approach. Two new large-scale datasets for video-based pedestrian attribute recognition is presented. We also proposed a novel multi-task architecture based on the conventional neural network and temporal attention strategy. Experiments show that video-based approach is better than image-based method in recognizing pedestrian attribute and the proposed architecture is very effective.

Acknowledgment. This work was supported by The National Key Research and Development Plan of China (Grant No. 2016YFB1001002).

References

1. Tian, Y., Luo, P., Wang, X., Tang, X.: Pedestrian detection aided by deep learning semantic tasks. In: IEEE Conference on Computer Vision and Pattern Recognition, pp. 5079–5087 (2015)
2. Layne, R., Hospedales, T.M., Gong, S.: Person re-identification by attributes. In: British Machine Vision Conference (2012)
3. Li, A., Liu, L., Wang, K., Liu, S., Yan, S.: Clothing attributes assisted person re-identification. IEEE Trans. Circuits Syst. Video Technol. **25**(5), 869–878 (2015)
4. Zhu, J., Liao, S., Yi, D., Lei, Z., Li, S.Z.: Multi-label CNN based pedestrian attribute learning for soft biometrics. In: International Conference on Biometrics, pp. 535–540. IEEE (2015)
5. Matsukawa, T., Suzuki, E.: Person re-identification using CNN features learned from combination of attributes. In: International Conference on Pattern Recognition, pp. 2428–2433 (2016)
6. Su, C., Yang, F., Zhang, S., Tian, Q., Davis, L.S., Gao, W.: Multi-task learning with low rank attribute embedding for multi-camera person re-identification. IEEE Trans. Pattern Anal. Mach. Intell. **40**(5), 1167–1181 (2018)
7. Wang, J., Zhu, X., Gong, S., Li, W.: Transferable joint attribute-identity deep learning for unsupervised person re-identification. In: IEEE Conference on Computer Vision and Pattern Recognition, pp. 2275–2284 (2018)
8. Chang, X., Hospedales, T.M., Xiang, T.: Multi-level factorisation net for person re-identification. In: IEEE Conference on Computer Vision and Pattern Recognition (2018)
9. Deng, Y., Luo, P., Loy, C.C., Tang, X.: Pedestrian attribute recognition at far distance. In: ACM International Conference on Multimedia, pp. 789–792 (2014)
10. Zhu, J., Liao, S., Lei, Z., Yi, D., Li, S.Z.: Pedestrian attribute classification in surveillance: database and evaluation. In: IEEE International Conference on Computer Vision Workshops, pp. 331–338 (2013)
11. Sudowe, P., Spitzer, H., Leibe, B.: Person attribute recognition with a jointly-trained holistic CNN model. In: IEEE International Conference on Computer Vision Workshops, pp. 329–337 (2015)
12. Li, D., Chen, X., Huang, K.: Multi-attribute learning for pedestrian attribute recognition in surveillance scenarios. In: Asian Conference on Pattern Recognition, pp. 111–115 (2015)
13. Liu, X., et al.: HydraPlus-Net: attentive deep features for pedestrian analysis. In: IEEE International Conference on Computer Vision, pp. 350–359 (2017)
14. Wang, J., Zhu, X., Gong, S., Li, W.: Attribute recognition by joint recurrent learning of context and correlation. In: IEEE International Conference on Computer Vision, pp. 531–540 (2017)
15. Zhao, X., Sang, L., Ding, G., Guo, Y., Jin, X.: Grouping attribute recognition for pedestrian with joint recurrent learning. In: International Joint Conference on Artificial Intelligence, pp. 3177–3183 (2018)
16. Zhang, N., Paluri, M., Ranzato, M., Darrell, T., Bourdev, L.: PANDA: pose aligned networks for deep attribute modeling. In: IEEE Conference on Computer Vision and Pattern Recognition (2014)
17. Li, D., Chen, X., Zhang, Z., Huang, K.: Pose guided deep model for pedestrian attribute recognition in surveillance scenarios. In: IEEE International Conference on Multimedia and Expo, pp. 1–6 (2018)

18. Li, D., Zhang, Z., Chen, X., Ling, H., Huang, K.: A richly annotated dataset for pedestrian attribute recognition. arXiv preprint arXiv:1603.07054 (2016)
19. Zheng, L., Shen, L., Tian, L., Wang, S., Wang, J., Tian, Q.: Scalable person re-identification: a benchmark. In: IEEE International Conference on Computer Vision (2015)
20. Cheng, H.U., Chen, L., Zhang, X., Sun, S.Y.: Pedestrian attribute recognition based on convolutional neural network in surveillance scenarios. In: Modern Computer (2018)
21. Sarfraz, M.S., Schumann, A., Wang, Y., Stiefelhagen, R.: Deep view-sensitive pedestrian attribute inference in an end-to-end model (2017)
22. He, K., Wang, Z., Fu, Y., Feng, R., Jiang, Y.-G., Xue, X.: Adaptively weighted multi-task deep network for person attribute classification. In: ACM International Conference on Multimedia (2017)
23. Sun, C., Jiang, N., Zhang, L., Wang, Y., Wu, W., Zhou, Z.: Unified framework for joint attribute classification and person re-identification. In: Kůrková, V., Manolopoulos, Y., Hammer, B., Iliadis, L., Maglogiannis, I. (eds.) ICANN 2018. LNCS, vol. 11139, pp. 637–647. Springer, Cham (2018). https://doi.org/10.1007/978-3-030-01418-6_63
24. Lin, Y., Zheng, L., Zheng, Z., Wu, Y., Yang, Y.: Improving person re-identification by attribute and identity learning. arXiv preprint arXiv:1703.07220 (2017)
25. Zheng, L., et al.: MARS: a video benchmark for large-scale person re-identification. In: Leibe, B., Matas, J., Sebe, N., Welling, M. (eds.) ECCV 2016. LNCS, vol. 9910, pp. 868–884. Springer, Cham (2016). https://doi.org/10.1007/978-3-319-46466-4_52
26. Wu, Y., Lin, Y., Dong, X., Yan, Y., Ouyang, W., Yang, Y.: Exploit the unknown gradually: one-shot video-based person re-identification by stepwise learning. In: IEEE Conference on Computer Vision and Pattern Recognition (2018)
27. He, K., Zhang, X., Ren, S., Sun, J.: Deep residual learning for image recognition. In: IEEE Conference on Computer Vision and Pattern Recognition, pp. 770–778 (2016)
28. Ji, S., Xu, W., Yang, M., Yu, K.: 3D convolutional neural networks for human action recognition. IEEE Trans. Pattern Anal. Mach. Intell. 35, 221–231 (2013)
29. McLaughlin, N., del Rincon, J.M., Miller, P.: Recurrent convolutional network for video-based person re-identification. In: IEEE Conference on Computer Vision and Pattern Recognition (2016)

An Effective Network with ConvLSTM for Low-Light Image Enhancement

Yixi Xiang, Ying Fu[✉], Lei Zhang, and Hua Huang

Beijing Institute of Technology, Beijing, China
fuying@bit.edu.cn

Abstract. Low-light image enhancement is a fundamental problem in computer vision. The artifact, noise, insufficient contrast and color distortion are common challenging problems in low-light image enhancement. In this paper, we present a convolutional Long Short-Term Memory (ConvLSTM) network based method to directly restore a normal image from a low-light image, which can be learned in an end-to-end way. Specifically, our base network employs the encoder-decoder structure. Meanwhile, considering that a normal image may correspond to low-light images of different illuminance levels, we adopt a multi-branch structure combined with ConvLSTM to solve this problem. The extensive experiments on two low-light datasets show that our method outperforms the state-of-the-art traditional and deep learning based methods vertified by both quantitative and qualitative evaluation.

Keywords: Low-light image enhancement · ConvLSTM

1 Introduction

When the camera sensor receives a small amount of light during taking a photo, the image, namely low-light image would have the poor-quality appearance. A typical scenario is to capture the images in the very dark environment, as well as the manipulation of camera lighting and exposure is not proper, whereupon the quality of the captured images might be seriously affected with the reduced saturation and contrast and the increased noise. This kind of poor-quality images can also affect the performance of other processing. Thus, low-light image enhancement is a very important problem.

A lot of low-light image enhancement methods have been proposed in recent years [6,14,15,30,32,33], which can be roughly classified into two categories: traditional methods [6,14] and deep learning based methods [15,30,32,33]. As for the traditional methods, the histogram equalization (HE) and its variance focus on increasing the image contrast by stretching the non-linearity to redistribute pixel values, while the retinex based methods assume that the observed image is composed of reflectance and illumination. Deep learning based methods have

---

Y. Xiang—The first author is a master student.

Z. Lin et al. (Eds.): PRCV 2019, LNCS 11858, pp. 221–233, 2019.
https://doi.org/10.1007/978-3-030-31723-2_19

also been widely used in the low-light image enhancement [15,30,32,33]. Unfortunately, due to the lack of datasets based on real scenes, most of the learning based methods have to be trained on synthetic datasets. Although a small number of works are done on real datasets, there is still much room for improving the quality of the low-light image enhancement.

In this paper, we present a novel network by building an encoder-decoder architecture for the low-light image enhancement, by which we can solve the common problems such as the artifact, noise, insufficient contrast and color distortion in the low-light image enhancement task. Since a bright image corresponds to low illumination images of different intensities, we propose to use a multi-branch scheme by incorporating the convolutional Long Short-Term Memory (ConvLSTM) [29], where the useful information in the previous branch can be utilized for the current branch. The experiments show that the proposed method achieves state-of-the-art results on both synthetic and real datasets.

2   Related Work

In this section, we briefly review the related work in the low-light image enhancement, typically including traditional methods and deep learning based methods.

2.1   Traditional Methods

The histogram equalization [31] is the simplest and straightforward method to enhance the contrast of an image by directly adjusting pixel values in the low-light image. The dynamic histogram equalization (DHE) [1] technique partitions the image histogram based on local minima and assigns specific gray level ranges for each partition before equalizing them separately.

The retinex theory assumes that the observed image is composed of the reflectance and the illumination, whereupon SSR [11] performs the decomposition and takes the reflectance component as the final result. Because of the characteristics of the Gaussian function selected in SSR, the large compression of dynamic range has to be the trade-off of the contrast of the enhanced images. MSR [23] is developed based on SSR, which has the advantage of maintaining high image fidelity and compressing the dynamic range of images. On the basis of MSR, MSRCR [24] adds a color recovery factor to adjust the defect of color distortion caused by the contrast enhancement of the local area of images. Recently, LIME [6] estimates the illumination of each pixel individually by finding the maximal value in the R, G, and B channels. And by imposing a structure prior on it, the final illumination map can be obtained as well as the enhanced image. Li *et al.* [14] present a robust retinex model by adding a noise term to handle the low-light image enhancement in the case of intensive noise. These methods have the obvious limitation on the fitting ability of the low-light image model because the model is actually very complex and has an adverse effect of noise.

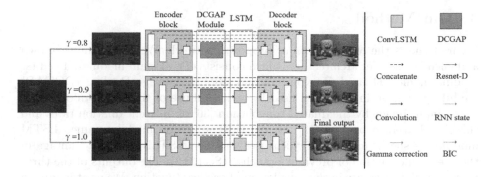

Fig. 1. The overview of our network based on a multi-branch and an encoder-decoder architecture. In the Encoder block, the Resnet-D structure is used to implement the downsampling operation, while in the Decoder block, the Bilinear Interpolation and Convolution(BIC) is used to implement the upsampling operation. There are another two main modules in our network: the Dilated Convolution and Global Average Pooling (DCGAP) module and the LSTM module. The outputs of the three branches all participate in the calculation of the loss function. We use the branch with $\gamma = 1.0$ as our final target image.

2.2 Deep Learning Based Methods

Driven by a large amount of data and the increasing computing power, deep neural networks have been widely used in various computer vision tasks [3,7,9,16,25,37], and also in the low-light image enhancement task. LLNet [17] trains a variance of the stacked sparse autoencoder from various synthetic examples to enhance the naturally low-light and degraded images. LLCNN [30] proposes a low-light image enhancement method based on CNN that is a variance of the LLNet. Liang et al. [15] prove that the multi-scale retinex is equivalent to a feedforward convolutional neural network with different Gaussian convolution kernels and construct a network (MSR-Net) to directly learn the mapping between dark and bright images. Wang et al. [32] propose a global illumination-aware and detail-preserving network (GLADNet), where the details of images can be preserved in enhancing the brightness of the images. Lv et al. [18] extract rich features up to different levels, then fuse the features via multiple subnets to finally achieve the good low-light image enhancement effect. These methods have achieved appealing results, but a big problem is that they are all trained based on synthetic datasets that are more or less different from natural images.

Fortunately, Wei et al. [33] provide the **LO**w **L**ight dataset (LOL) that contains low/normal-light image pairs and propose a deep Retinex-Net learned on this dataset to decompose images into the components of reflectance and illumination. But the visual effect of the images decomposed by Retinex-Net is not very good. SID [2] also collects a real dataset and does some experiments on it, but it can only process the RAW data without the application for sRGB format images.

3   Our Method

Figure 1 shows the overview of our proposed network. We take a multi-branch and encoder-decoder architecture, which consists of two main modules. The first module, named **D**ilated **C**onvolution and **G**lobal **A**verage **P**ooling (DCGAP) module (as shown in Fig. 3), is used to make full use of the global information of the input image by the dilated convolution [36] of different dilation rates and the global average pooling [19] (Sect. 3.1). The second module, named LSTM module (as shown in Fig. 3), which uses the ConvLSTM to take advantage of the useful information of previous branches (Sect. 3.2). The outputs of the three branches all participate in the calculation of the loss function. We use the branch with $\gamma = 1.0$ as our final target image since it corresponds to the original input. We will explain the details of our network in the sequel.

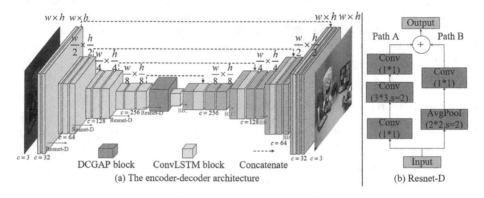

Fig. 2. An illustration of the encoder-decoder architecture and Resnet-D. In the encoder part, we use the Resnet-D structure for downsampling. In the decoder part, we use the Bilinear Interpolation and Convolution (BIC) for upsampling. w and h denote the width and height of the input image, and c denotes the number of channels in the convolution layer.

3.1   Base Network

Encoder-Decoder Architecture. The encoder-decoder architecture is illustrated in Fig. 2. In the encoder block, the size of the feature map decreases gradually to obtain the context information. There are 8 convolutional layers, each of which uses kernels of size 3×3, stride of 1 and a Leaky ReLU activation function [20]. A downsampling operation is performed after every two convolutions, considering that three-quarters of the information will be lost in the max pooling, we use a Resnet-D [8] structure (Fig. 2) to implement the downsampling operation. The model tweak ResNet-D contains two paths, i.e., Path A and Path B where no information is ignored in Path A and Path B because

Path A uses a kernel size 3 × 3 in the second convolution and Path B uses a 2 × 2 average pooling. In the decoder block, the feature maps are enlarged by upsampling. Similarly to the U-net [28], a skip-connection is used to concatenate the features in the encoder part to obtain more information. Two convolutional layers are followed after a concatenation with kernels of size 3 × 3, stride of 1 and a Leaky ReLU activation function. We use **B**ilinear **I**nterpolation followed by a **C**onvolution (BIC) [4] to implement upsampling in the decoder part instead of the deconvolution, which can effectively eliminate checkerboard artifacts [22]. The DCGAP and ConvLSTM blocks are used in the bottleneck layer.

Dilated Convolution and Global Average Pooling (DCGAP) Module. Although the receptive field in the bottleneck layer has increased a lot, it is insufficient to utilize the global information of the input image. So we use the dilated convolution with different dilation rates to obtain the features of different sizes of receptive fields while more information can be available, no more parameters are added. We use the global average pooling to extract the global features of size $1 \times 1 \times c$ (c denotes the number of channels in the convolution layer) simultaneously, and then duplicate $h/16 \times w/16$ (h and w represent the height and width of the input image respectively) copies. We also use a 1×1 convolution to get the features of the smallest receptive field. By concatenating the feature maps obtained before, we can make full use of the global information. Figure 3 shows the details of the DCGAP block.

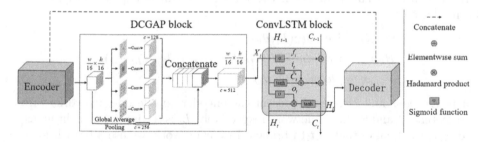

Fig. 3. An illustration of our Dilated Convolution and Global Average Pooling (DCGAP) block and ConvLSTM block. In the DCGAP block, we use different dilation rates to obtain the different size of receptive fields, Global Average Pooling is used to get global information. The ConvLSTM block is used to utilize the useful information in the previous branches. w and h denote the width and height of the input image, c denotes the number of channels in the convolution layer.

3.2   LSTM Module

Since a bright image may correspond to low-light images with the illumination of different degrees, in order to deal with this situation, we use the gamma correction to do different preprocessing of input images and to get the input of different branches. By using the ConvLSTM (Fig. 3) in the bottleneck layer, the useful information in previous branches can be utilized in the current branch to better enhance the image.

ConvLSTM. LSTM [10] can effectively remember the historical information and use the previous information in the current task. ConvLSTM [29] is established by adding the convolution operation in LSTM, which can be expressed as follows:

$$
\begin{aligned}
i_t &= \sigma\left(W_{xi} * X_t + W_{hi} * H_{t-1} + b_i\right) \\
f_t &= \sigma\left(W_{xf} * X_t + W_{hf} * H_{t-1} + b_f\right) \\
\tilde{C}_t &= \tanh\left(W_{xc} * X_t + W_{hc} * H_{t-1} + b_c\right) \\
C_t &= f_t \circ C_{t-1} + i_t \circ \tilde{C}_t \\
o_t &= \sigma\left(W_{xo} * X_t + W_{ho} * H_{t-1} + b_o\right) \\
H_t &= o_t \circ \tanh\left(C_t\right)
\end{aligned}
\tag{1}
$$

where X_t is the input of the t-th branch in our network that means the input image of different illuminance, H_{t-1} and C_{t-1} represent the output information of the t-1-th branch, H_t and C_t are with the same meaning, W is the convolutional kernel and b is the bias. σ is the sigmoid function defined by $\sigma(x) = 1/(1 + e^{-x})$, $*$ represents the convolution operation, and $\circ$ denotes the element-wise multiplication.

Multi-branch Structure. The network structure can be expressed by the following formula:

$$
\begin{aligned}
X_t &= Encoder(L_t; \theta_E) \\
H_t, C_t &= ConvLSTM(X_t, H_{t-1}, C_{t-1}; \theta_{ConvLSTM}) \\
o_t &= Decoder(C_t; \theta_D)
\end{aligned}
\tag{2}
$$

where $Encoder$ and $Decoder$ represent the encoder and decoder networks with parameters θ_E and θ_D in our network respectively. L_t is the input low-light image and o_t is the final output in t-th branch. In our network, we use 3 branches.

3.3   Loss Function

The loss function is composed of the L_1 loss and the SSIM loss. Here, the L_1 loss is defined by

$$
L_{L_1} = \frac{1}{hw} \sum_{i=1}^{w} \sum_{j=1}^{h} |o_{ij} - y_{ij}|
\tag{3}
$$

where o means the output of one branch in our network, y means the corresponding ground truth, h and w are the height and width of the output. i and j define the position of a pixel in the image.

The SSIM loss is defined by

$$
L_{SSIM} = 1 - \frac{2\mu_o\mu_y + C_1}{\mu_o^2 + \mu_y^2 + C_1} \cdot \frac{2\sigma_{oy} + C_2}{\sigma_o^2 + \sigma_y^2 + C_2}
\tag{4}
$$

where μ_o and μ_y represent the pixel value average of the output o and ground truth y, σ_o^2 and σ_y^2 represent the variances, σ_{oy} represents the covariance, and C_1 and C_2 are the constants to prevent the denominator to be zero. So the loss function of the t-th branch is as follows:

$$L_t = L_{L_1} + \beta L_{SSIM} \tag{5}$$

The corresponding final loss function is:

$$L = \frac{1}{n} \sum_{t=1}^{n} L_t \tag{6}$$

where we set β to be 0.07, n to be 3, and n denotes the numbers of branches which means we take the output of all three branches into the calculation of the loss function.

The L_1 loss minimizes the difference between the output and the ground truth on the single pixel value. It preserves the color and brightness information in the processing. The SSIM loss not only compares the contrast and brightness, but also the structural similarity. It takes the global structure and the connection between different parts of an image into account to make the visual quality better.

4   Experiment

4.1   The Datasets

Although the problem of low-light image enhancement has been studied for a long time, most methods are based on the synthetic data [15,17,18,30,32]. This is mainly because learning-based methods require a large number of pairs of images and it is very tedious to collect images that satisfy the conditions in the low-light image enhancement. Fortunately, Wei et al. [33] construct a new dataset that has two categories: real photography pairs and synthetic pairs from raw images.

The dataset is the so-called **LOw Light** paired dataset (LOL), which contains 500 low/normal-light image pairs. We randomly select 485 pairs as the training set and another 15 ones for evaluation. The size of the images is 400×600. The synthesized SYN dataset has 1000 pairs and the size is 384×384. We choose 950 pairs for training and the remaining 50 for the evaluation.

4.2   Implementation Details

Since the number of training sets is not sufficient, we randomly crop smaller patches for training, to ensure the richness of the training set. Especially, we first use the patches of size 96×96 and the batch size of 16 to train 2000 epochs, and then use 192×192 patches to train up to 4000 epochs. Due to the larger size of the training patches, the more likely the over-fitting may occur. So we

(a) Inputs   (b) LDR   (c) LIME   (d) SRIE   (e) SRLLIME

(f) MSR-Net   (g) GLADNet   (h) Retinex-Net   (i) Ours   (j) Ground truth

Fig. 4. The enhancement results by different methods on the LOL and SYN datasets. The first two rows show the results based on the LOL dataset, and the last two rows show the results based on the SYN dataset.

only increase the patch size to 192×192. We use ADAM optimizer [12] with learning rate of $lr = 1e - 4$, $\beta_1 = 0.9$, $\beta_2 = 0.999$ and $\varepsilon = 1e - 8$. The learning rate is reduced to $1e - 5$ after 1500 epochs. We use the gamma correction for the preprocessing, the value of γ is set to 1.0, 0.9, 0.8 respectively. Our network has about 28 million parameters. Its training needs 10 h with a Nvidia TITAN X GPU, and its testing on a 400*600 image is about 0.4 s.

4.3 The Results

We compare our method with several traditional methods [5,6,13,14] and learning-based methods in recent years [15,32,33], and make the statistics on values of the Peak Signal-to-Noise Ratio (PSNR) and Structural Similarity (SSIM). To better demonstrate the experimental results on the LOL and SYN datasets, Fig. 4 selects some typical examples, where the recovery ability of traditional methods is very limited. They cannot be applied to various scenarios, because there will be a color shift and many other issues. The learning based methods are not sufficiently good. MSR-Net is prone to the over-enhancement problem. Retinex-Net can cleverly decompose images into the reflectance and illumination components, but like GLADNet, the visual quality of the enhanced images is not very good that has a certain difference with the ground truth with a lot of noise. Compared with other methods, our method enhances the visual quality of images well and eliminates artifacts and noise on the basis of ensuring a good contrast. Tables 1 and 2 show that our method performs better on both LOL and SYN datasets than other methods in terms of PSNR and SSIM.

4.4 The Ablation Study

The Effect of BIC. In the decoding process (Sect. 3.1), we use the bilinear interpolation (BIC) to replace deconvolution. In order to better understand the effect of this setting, we compare the results obtained by BIC and deconvolution respectively with other parameters and settings unchanged. As shown in Fig. 5 and Table 3, the checkerboard artifacts can be effectively suppressed by replacing the deconvolution with BIC.

Table 1. The statistics on PSNR and SSIM values on the LOL dataset.

	LDR	LIME	SRIE	SRLLIME	MSR-Net	GLADNet	Retinex-Net	Ours
PSNR	17.484	11.414	12.440	13.629	17.940	**20.314**	17.780	23.076
SSIM	0.634	0.333	0.549	0.706	0.732	**0.739**	0.425	0.860

The Effect of DCGAP. We have explained in Sect. 3.1 that by means of DCGAP, we can make full use of the global information of the image and effectively eliminate other artifacts. To verify this point, we train our network with and without DCGAP. Figure 5 and Table 3 show the results, where it can be seen that DCGAP is an indispensable component.

Table 2. The statistics on PSNR and SSIM values based on the SYN dataset.

	LDR	LIME	SRIE	SRLLIME	MSR-Net	GLADNet	Retinex-Net	Ours
PSNR	13.187	14.318	14.478	16.873	**17.004**	16.761	16.286	25.024
SSIM	0.591	0.554	0.639	0.714	0.759	**0.797**	0.779	0.929

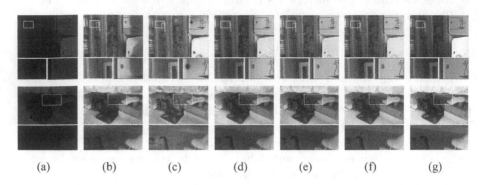

(a)   (b)   (c)   (d)   (e)   (f)   (g)

Fig. 5. The results in the ablation study. From left to right, (a) Input. (b) w/o DCGAP. (c) w/o BIC. (d) w/o SSIM loss. (e) Multi-scale. (f) Ours. (g) Ground truth.

Table 3. The statistics on PSNR and SSIM values in the ablation study.

	w/o BIC	w/o DCGAP	w/o SSIM loss	Multi-scale	Ours
PSNR	19.024	18.929	21.241	**21.505**	23.076
SSIM	0.811	0.828	0.830	**0.851**	0.860

The Effect of SSIM Loss. As mentioned in Sect. 3.3, SSIM loss can keep the connection between the various parts of the image and make the visual quality better. We train our network with and without th SSIM loss respectively. It can be seen from Fig. 5 that the images look more natural and the noise is significantly eliminated after adding the SSIM loss. Table 3 shows the PSNR and SSIM values.

Multi-scale or Same-Scale. In this paper, we use a multi-branch network structure. Actually, the similar structure has also been used in many other low-level visual problems [21,27,34,35]. But they all use a multi-scale approach, which means the input size of each branch is different, and the corresponding problem is solved by a coarse-to-fine way. We also try this multi-scale approach at the beginning. As you can see from Table 3, the results obtained in this way are not very good. The reason is that the input and the output differ a lot in their appearances. So it can not be completely generalized with other low-level visual problems. Finally, we follow our idea of using the same scale as the input just like [26] and achieve the desired results.

5   Conclusion

In this paper, we deal with the low-light image enhancement task by using an encoder-decoder structure network, which is good at eliminating the common artifacts, color distortion noise and other problems in the low-light image enhancement. By taking advantage of multi-branch structure and ConvLSTM, the problem of different illuminance in low-light images is resolved. Experiments are done on both the real scene dataset and synthetic dataset. The results show that our method can produce better quality results than state-of-the-arts in terms of both quantitative and qualitative evaluations.

Although we have achieved pleasant results in the task of low-light image enhancement, there still exists some limitations. The first is that the learning-based methods can only be applied to some specific distributed data that are in accordance with the training data. The second is that we need paired data to train, but there are few existing datasets for providing paired images. If we can use unpaired images to training the network, we can significantly reduce the difficulty of this task. Our future work aims at unpaired training, and we hope our idea can also be applied to solve other low-level visual problems. Besides, we will investigate a lighter network to achieve real-time processing in future.

Acknowledgements. This work was supported by the National Natural Science Foundation of China under Grants No. 61425013 and No. 61672096.

References

1. Abdullah Al-Wadud, M., Kabir, M.H., Dewan, M.A.A., Chae, O.: A dynamic histogram equalization for image contrast enhancement. IEEE Trans. Consum. Electron. **53**(2), 593–600 (2007)
2. Chen, C., Chen, Q., Xu, J., Koltun, V.: Learning to see in the dark. In: Proceedings of Conference on Computer Vision and Pattern Recognition (CVPR) (2018)
3. Chen, J., Chen, J., Chao, H., Yang, M.: Image blind denoising with generative adversarial network based noise modeling. In: Proceedings of Conference on Computer Vision and Pattern Recognition (CVPR), pp. 3155–3164 (2018)
4. Dong, C., Loy, C.C., He, K., Tang, X.: Image super-resolution using deep convolutional networks. IEEE Trans. Pattern Anal. Mach. Intell. **38**(2), 295–307 (2016)
5. Fu, X., Zeng, D., Huang, Y., Zhang, X.P., Ding, X.: A weighted variational model for simultaneous reflectance and illumination estimation. In: Proceedings of Conference on Computer Vision and Pattern Recognition (CVPR), pp. 2782–2790 (2016)
6. Guo, X., Li, Y., Ling, H.: LIME: low-light image enhancement via illumination map estimation. IEEE Trans. Image Process. **26**(2), 982–993 (2017)
7. Han, W., Chang, S., Liu, D., Yu, M., Witbrock, M., Huang, T.S.: Image super-resolution via dual-state recurrent networks. In: Proceedings of Conference on Computer Vision and Pattern Recognition (CVPR), pp. 1654–1663 (2018)
8. He, T., Zhang, Z., Zhang, H., Zhang, Z., Xie, J., Li, M.: Bag of tricks for image classification with convolutional neural networks. arXiv preprint arXiv:1812.01187 (2018)

9. He, Z., Patel, V.M.: Densely connected pyramid dehazing network. In: Proceedings of Conference on Computer Vision and Pattern Recognition (CVPR), pp. 3194–3203 (2018)

10. Hochreiter, S., Schmidhuber, J.: Long short-term memory. Neural Comput. **9**(8), 1735–1780 (1997)

11. Jobson, D.J., Rahman, Z., Woodell, G.A.: Properties and performance of a center/surround retinex. IEEE Trans. Image Process. **6**(3), 451–62 (1997)

12. Kingma, D., Ba, J.: Adam: a method for stochastic optimization. arXiv preprint arXiv:1412.6980 (2014)

13. Lee, C., Lee, C., Kim, C.S.: Contrast enhancement based on layered difference representation of 2D histograms. IEEE Trans. Image Process. **22**(12), 5372–5384 (2013)

14. Li, M., Liu, J., Yang, W., Sun, X., Guo, Z.: Structure-revealing low-light image enhancement via robust retinex model. IEEE Trans. Image Process. **27**(6), 2828–2841 (2018)

15. Liang, S., Yue, Z., Fan, F., Quan, C., Jie, M.: MSR-net: low-light image enhancement using deep convolutional network. arXiv preprint arXiv:1711.02488 (2017)

16. Liu, W., et al.: SSD: single shot multibox detector. In: Proceedings of European Conference on Computer Vision (ECCV), pp. 21–37 (2016)

17. Lore, K.G., Akintayo, A., Sarkar, S.: LLNet: a deep autoencoder approach to natural low-light image enhancement. Pattern Recogn. **61**, 650–662 (2017)

18. Lv, F., Lu, F., Wu, J., Lim, C.: MBLLEN: low-light image/video enhancement using CNNs. In: Proceedings of Conference on British Machine Vision Conference (BMVC) (2018)

19. Lin, M., Chen, Q., Yan, S.: Network in network. arXiv preprint arXiv:1312.4400 (2013)

20. Maas, A.L., Hannun, A.Y., Ng, A.Y.: Rectifier nonlinearities improve neural network acoustic models. In: Proceedings of International Conference on Machine Learning (ICML), vol. 30, p. 3 (2013)

21. Nah, S., Kim, T.H., Lee, K.M.: Deep multi-scale convolutional neural network for dynamic scene deblurring. Proc. of Conference on Computer Vision and Pattern Recognition (CVPR) pp. 3883–3891 (2017)

22. Odena, A., Dumoulin, V., Olah, C.: Deconvolution and checkerboard artifacts. Distill (2016). https://doi.org/10.23915/distill.00003. http://distill.pub/2016/deconv-checkerboard

23. Rahman, Z.U., Jobson, D.J., Woodell, G.A.: Multi-scale retinex for color image enhancement. In: Proceedings of IEEE International Conference on Image Processing (ICIP), vol. 3, pp. 1003–1006. IEEE (1996)

24. Rahman, Z.U., Woodell, G.A.: A multiscale retinex for bridging the gap between color images and the human observation of scenes. IEEE Trans. Image Process. **6**(7), 965–976 (2002)

25. Redmon, J., Divvala, S., Girshick, R., Farhadi, A.: You only look once: unified, real-time object detection. In: Proceedings of Conference on Computer Vision and Pattern Recognition (CVPR), pp. 779–788 (2016)

26. Ren, D., Zuo, W., Hu, Q., Zhu, P., Meng, D.: Progressive image deraining networks: a better and simpler baseline. In: IEEE Conference on Computer Vision and Pattern Recognition (2019)

27. Ren, W., et al.: Gated fusion network for single image dehazing. In: Proceedings of Conference on Computer Vision and Pattern Recognition (CVPR), pp. 3253–3261, June 2018

28. Ronneberger, O., Fischer, P., Brox, T.: U-Net: convolutional networks for biomedical image segmentation. In: International Conference on Medical Image Computing and Computer-Assisted Intervention, pp. 234–241 (2015)
29. Shi, X., Chen, Z., Hao, W., Yeung, D.Y., Wong, W., Woo, W.: Convolutional LSTM network: a machine learning approach for precipitation nowcasting. In: Proceedings of Conference on Neural Information Processing Systems (NIPS), pp. 802–810 (2015)
30. Tao, L., Zhu, C., Xiang, G., Li, Y., Jia, H., Xie, X.: LLCNN: a convolutional neural network for low-light image enhancement. In: 2017 IEEE Visual Communications and Image Processing (VCIP), pp. 1–4. IEEE (2017)
31. Trahanias, P.E., Venetsanopoulos, A.N.: Color image enhancement through 3-D histogram equalization. Proceedings of International Conference on Pattern Recognition (ICPR), pp. 545–548 (1992)
32. Wang, W., Chen, W., Yang, W., Liu, J.: GLADNet: low-light enhancement network with global awareness. In: 2018 13th IEEE International Conference on Automatic Face & Gesture Recognition, FG 2018, pp. 751–755. IEEE (2018)
33. Wei, C., Wang, W., Yang, W., Liu, J.: Deep retinex decomposition for low-light enhancement. In: Proceedings of Conference on British Machine Vision Conference (BMVC). British Machine Vision Association (2018)
34. Xia, L., Wu, J., Lin, Z., Hong, L., Zha, H.: Recurrent squeeze-and-excitation context aggregation net for single image deraining. Proc. of European Conference on Computer Vision (ECCV), pp. 254–269 (2018)
35. Xin, T., Gao, H., Yi, W., Shen, X., Wang, J., Jia, J.: Scale-recurrent network for deep image deblurring. In: Proceedings of Conference on Computer Vision and Pattern Recognition (CVPR), pp. 8174–8182 (2018)
36. Yu, F., Koltun, V.: Multi-scale context aggregation by dilated convolutions. arXiv preprint arXiv:1511.07122 (2015)
37. Zhang, Y., Tian, Y., Yu, K., Zhong, B., Yun, F.: Residual dense network for image super-resolution. In: Proceedings of Conference on Computer Vision and Pattern Recognition (CVPR), pp. 2472–2481 (2018)

Self-Calibrating Scene Understanding Based on Motifnet

Xiangyu Yin[✉][iD]

Beijing University of Posts and Telecommunications,
Beijing 100876, Haidian, China
yxy197091426@outlook.com

Abstract. Scene understanding has made significant progress recently that motivates the development of practical applications and accelerates the prosperity of general artificial intelligence. As one of the most important tools in scene understanding, scene graph generation inspires abundant researches focusing on the reasoning of different relationships among objects. However, as one of the basic concepts constructing physical hierarchies of our world, mutual promotion and calibration within different perceptual contexts are sparsely considered in current work. In this paper, we introduce the Self-Calibrating Scene Understanding Model based on the combination between Motifnet and Wasserstein GAN [1], which emulates the methodologies people cognize the world and brings out an idea that scene understanding, recognized as one of the core technologies towards general artificial intelligence, should be fused with calibrating mechanism.

Keywords: Scene understanding · Scene graph generation · Generative Adversarial Network

Fig. 1. At the first glance of this picture, we would consider it as a man wearing a cap because of our subconsciousness on similar scenes under normal conditions. Henceforce, such cognition should be calibrated by combined self-correcting mechanisms.

X. Yin—Undergraduate first author.

© Springer Nature Switzerland AG 2019
Z. Lin et al. (Eds.): PRCV 2019, LNCS 11858, pp. 234–240, 2019.
https://doi.org/10.1007/978-3-030-31723-2_20

1   Introduction

Scene understanding refers to a concept to analyze and predict what entities in pictures are doing, why these plots are happening, what are going to happen next and what should observers do to handle their situations [9], it always goes far beyond individual objects [6] and concentrates on structural and semantic interactions [7,13] in different context stages under large-scale scenarios. Researching in current related work, we conclude that transformation from recognition to cognition plays an important role for the development of scene understanding and general artificial intelligence. As one of the most powerful tool in visual understanding recently, scene graph generation attracts a large amount of outstanding implementations, which concatenate high-level vision problem, such as image captioning, visual commensense reasoning (VCR) and low-level vision challenges like object detection, semantic segmentation so that plays a significant role in tackling with vision difficulties. According to this, how to contribute to the improvement of models on scene graph generation and unify such two levels of structural information has gradually become indispensable in current related work.

Currently, corresponding work related to scene graph generation always include two general models, which in our opinions, are seperated as *parallel reasoning* [3,5,8,11,12] and *sequential reasoning* [10]. Parallel reasoning focus on the fusion of object features, spatial features, semantic labels, contextual features etc, trying to utilize the interaction among all of these entities and predict their dependence. They achieve great performance in determining the predicates between objects with plenty of outstanding perceptual models deriving from this in the past few years, such as Multi-level Scene Description Network (MSDN) proposed by Yikang Li, et al., which aligns objects, phrases and caption regions with a dynamic graph based on their spatial and semantic connections, and an interpretable model to generate scene graph built by Ji Zhang, et al., effectively combining three features and showing what each feature contributes to the final prediction and how much the prediction is. Sequential reasoning, on the other hand, burgeones recently and achieves excellent results. Such as Stacked Motif Network (Motifnet), the representative of sequential reasoning, captures higher order structures and global interactions which obtains significant improvements over already baseline. Also, some practical applications extend from this, such as mobile apps based on Civic Issue Graph [4] and so on, making breakthroughs in certain fields. However, mutual promotion and calibration of different contextual stages are rarely considered in current work, they corrects visual confusion and cognitive deviation according to our commonsense.

In this paper, We emulate such mechanism and develop a self-correcting scene understanding model combining Motifnet [10] and Wasserstein GAN [1], which makes improvement on the baseline in some aspects.

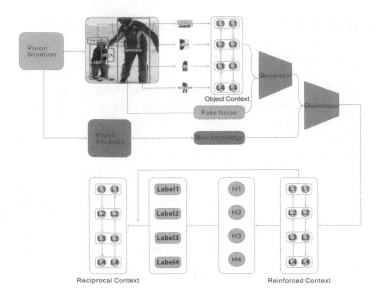

Fig. 2. This is a flowchart showing our Self-Correcting Scene Understanding Model, which derives from Motifnet and is calibrated by WasserteinGAN. It is constructed by three stages, which is object context, reinforced context and reciprocal context. Different from previous work it extends, we add an extra processing step within Wasserstein GAN adjusted by real knowledge in order to offset the impact of scene's fake noise. Then reinforced context is assigned at the second stage to enhance information we obtain, which is necessary due to the fluctuation of cognition after adjustment from the first stage. Similar to edge context raised in Motifnet, we pass object features, reinforced context along with object labels into reciprocal context to define final outputs.

2   Model

Take a look at Fig. 1 on page 1. Having the first glance at this man, we would consider him wearing a hat, not a lamp-chimney based on our subconsciousness towards similar vision situations. This phenomenon is quite common in our daily life, which is also universal in computer vision and can cause unnecessary mistakes refering to scene understanding. However, after self-calibration between global object context and our knowledge "library", we could always avoid this confusion to some extent and obtain reasoning answers more precisely according to self-correcting mechanism in reality. Following this assumption, we extend from Stacked Motif Network and combine it with Generative Adversarial Network in order to remedy such deficiencies.

As shown in Fig. 2, similar to the previous work we derived from, we tackle with vision situations, consisting of object classes, bounding boxes calculated by Faster R-CNN performed on Visual Genome dataset and seperate scene graph detection and classification procedures into three interactive stages, which are *Object Context*, *Reinforced Context* and *Reciprocal Context*. To be convenient, they are represented as *ObjC*, *ReinC* and *ReciC* in the following sections.

Also, each of these stages execute *AlternatingHighwayLSTM* and *DecoderRNN*, *Encoder* and *Decoder* are adopted as the abbreviation of them, which are the same approaches connecting semantic representations and word embeddings as Zellar et al. implemented in Motifnet [10]. Additionally, we add an extra calibrating structure between *ObjC* and *ReinC*, which as we illustrate above, is Generative Adversarial Network. Different from previous related work demonstrated by generating lifelike faces, we believe that to some extent, GAN is not only an framework to generate pictures, but also a concept to tackle with challenges in calibrating task and modulate the self-calibrating mechanism in cognition.

The core of our model mainly utilize feature maps of images with RoIs, object labels, bounding boxes priors, object context, reinforced context, reciprocal context, noise produced by CRF from scenes and fake noise, which can be represented as **objF**, **objL/objP**, **Bpri**, **objC**, **reinC**, **reciC**, **CRFN**, **N** and in the following sections. Also, due to extending from Motifnet, there are four approaches to rearrange different bounding boxes, including **LeftRight**, **Confidence**, **Size** and **Random**. Due to **LeftRight**'s higher performance after testing within different evaluation metrics in Motifnet and its better functionalities, we only utilize *Confidence* as our method to reorder different regions of interest.

$$objC = Encoder(objF, objL, Bpri) \tag{1}$$

$$N = G(objC, CRFN) \tag{2}$$

$$objP_{fake} = Decoder(N, objL) \tag{3}$$

$$objP = D(objP_{fake}, objL) \tag{4}$$

As Eqs. (1)–(4) illustrated above, we process such information using *Encoder* in the first context region, *ObjC*, based on vision situations giving *objF*, *objL* and *Bpri*. This object context performs the same functionalities as Motifnet. However, as we talked above, they are unstable and inclined to have mistakes in scene recognition and understanding. Then we mix them with some fake noise generated from the input images and their features using *CRF* (Conditional Random Field) [14] and obtain materials for next step of *Generator* (represented as **G** in the following sections) in Wasserstein GAN to produce fake object context. Sequentially, *Decoder* is implemented next to calculate object labels for bounding boxes in permutations. Also in parallel, concluding from the changing state of our vision situations, which delivers a message that previous understanding is deviant from our knowledge database accumulated in observations and in need of calibrating, we introduce real knowledge along with *objP_{fake}* to *Discriminator* (represented as **D**) in order to distinguish between each of them.

$$reinC = Encoder(objF, objP, Bpri) \tag{5}$$

$$reinP = Decoder(reinC, objP) \tag{6}$$

Next, after execution from the first stage of our model, we move into the following step, *ReinC*, which is raised considering the unstable state of predictions and context generated from last step. As shown in Eqs. (5) (6), we pass *objF*, *objP* and *Bpri* to *Encoder* to produce the **reinC** using the same approach in *ObjC*. However, we extends *objP* calculated from the first stage and deliver it to *Decoder* to generate **reinP**. This part plays an important role in our whole model, which enhances the comprehension after previous fluctuating impact of Wasserstein GAN.

$$reciC = Encoder(objF, reinP, Bpri) \qquad (7)$$

At the last stage in Self-Calibrating Scene Understanding model, we set one *Encoder* to produce **reciC**, which is present in Eq. (7). Similar with Eqs. (1) and (5), we deal with three inputs, *objF*, *reinP* and *Bpri* here to calculate context information in this layer. After all the operations shown above, we obtain the final context and send it to scene graph generation procedure.

3   Experiment

Based on the combination of Stacked Motif Network (Motifnet) and Wasserstein GAN, our experimental methodologies derive from them and make improvements on previous results. As mentioned above, there are four approaches to rearrange different bounding boxes, including *LeftRight*, *Confidence*, *Size* and *Random*. In the experiment, we choose *LeftRight* as our evaluation mode, which has the best performance among all of the other four approaches rearranging bounding regions.

Firstly, object context needs to be constructed to leverage *objL*, *objF* and *Bpri* from input resources. Extended from Stacked Neural Network (Motifnet), we adopt *AlternatingHighwayLSTM* and *DecoderRNN* to modulate encoding and decoding operation in object layers. We set object layers to **2** in this experiment. After processing procedure of such recurrent neural network, we update what we tackle with at the beginning of object layers and put them into next step, where we apply Wasserstein GAN.

Within the procedure of Wasserstein GAN which calibrates *objP* obtained from the first stage, we take *objC* with **512** dimensions and fake noise generated by *CRF* (Conditional Random Field) as our input, then we can map these concatenated data to hidden dimensions, trying to deceive *D*. However, there are some difference between our model and common structures of GAN. Before delivering two inputs to Discriminator individually, we execute one step more on *G*, which is the transmission from *objC* to *objP* through *Decoder*. The reason to perform such operation is matching global context with real knowledge.

After previous data processing and correcting, we obtain basic context information. However, it is still unformed and indetermined, like people will hesitate between scene recognition and cognition. So we set a reinforced context of **4** layers to enhance model's judgement, which is also supported by *AlternatingHighwayLSTM* and *DecoderRNN*.

On the last stage of our model, We encode *Reciprocal Context*, which is a 2-layer structure. It extends from edge context in Stacked Motif Network given labels information and *Reinforced Context*.

As Table 1 shows below, we make some improvement according to scene graph generation and scene graph classification. R@20, R@50 and R@100 are selected as our evaluation modes extended from Motifnet [10]. In our experimental results, **SelfCali-LeftRight** model achieves better performance using R@20, R@100 in *Sgcls* and R@50, R@100 in *PredCls* respectively.

Table 1. We compute our model, Self-Calibrating Scene Understanding Model on three different evaluation modes, which are R@20, R@50 and R@100 and compare the result with previous work [2,8,10].

Model	SgCls			PredCls		
	R@20	R@50	R@100	R@20	R@50	R@100
Message Passing [8]		21.7	24.4		44.8	53.0
Associate Embed [15]	18.2	21.8	22.6	47.9	54.1	55.4
Motifnet-LeftRight	32.9	35.8	36.5	58.5	65.2	67.1
SelfCali-LeftRight	**33.8**	35.7	**37.6**	**58.9**	**66.4**	**68.4**

4   Conclusion

Scene graph generation, as one of the most significant tools to build basic structures of different scenes, plays an indispensable role in scene understanding task. In this paper, we summerize and seperate previous work for scene graph generation as *Parallel Reasoning* and *Sequential Reasoning*. Then we modulate human's cognition activity in self-correcting mechanisms. To the best of our knowledge, this is the first attempt to solve vision confused problem in scene graph generation. We extends from Stacked Motif Network to build the self-calibrating model combined with Wasserstein GAN, which diminishes vision confusion based on real knowledge.

Although same demands for large datasets like Visual Genome and COCO are needed to train scene graph models, *Sequential Reasoning* is more suitable and scalable compared to *Parallel Reasoning* based on human cognition commonsense. Thus, deeper demonstration in discrepancy of divergence speed or other evaluation settings could be raised in subsequent work. Also, new approaches of scene understanding calibration should be considered.

References

1. Arjovsky, M., Chintala, S., Bottou, L.: Wasserstein GAN (2017)
2. Armeni, I., Sax, S., Zamir, A.R., Savarese, S.: Joint 2D-3D-semantic data for indoor scene understanding (2017)

3. Herzig, R., Raboh, M., Chechik, G., Berant, J., Globerson, A.: Mapping images to scene graphs with permutation-invariant structured prediction (2018)

4. Kumar, S., Atreja, S., Singh, A., Jain, M.: Adversarial adaptation of scene graph models for understanding civic issues (2019)

5. Li, Y., Ouyang, W., Zhou, B., Wang, K., Wang, X.: Scene graph generation from objects, phrases and caption regions (2017)

6. Liu, Y., Liu, L., Rezatofighi, H., Do, T.T., Shi, Q., Reid, I.: Learning pairwise relationship for multi-object detection in crowded scenes (2019)

7. Lu, C., Krishna, R., Bernstein, M., Fei-Fei, L.: Visual relationship detection with language priors. In: Leibe, B., Matas, J., Sebe, N., Welling, M. (eds.) ECCV 2016. LNCS, vol. 9905, pp. 852–869. Springer, Cham (2016). https://doi.org/10.1007/978-3-319-46448-0_51

8. Xu, D., Zhu, Y., Choy, C.B., Fei-Fei, L.: Scene graph generation by iterative message passing (2017)

9. Yatskar, M., Zettlemoyer, L., Farhadi, A.: Situation recognition: visual semantic role labeling for image understanding. In: Computer Vision & Pattern Recognition (2016)

10. Zellers, R., Yatskar, M., Thomson, S., Choi, Y.: Neural motifs: scene graph parsing with global context (2017)

11. Zhang, J., Shih, K., Tao, A., Catanzaro, B., Elgammal, A.: An interpretable model for scene graph generation (2018)

12. Zhang, R., Lin, L., Wang, G., Wang, M., Zuo, W.: Hierarchical scene parsing by weakly supervised learning with image descriptions. IEEE Trans. Pattern Anal. Mach. Intell. **PP**(99), 1 (2017)

13. Zhao, Y., Zhu, S.C.: Scene parsing by integrating function, geometry and appearance models (2013)

14. Lafferty, J., McCallum, A., Pereira, F.C.N.: Conditional random fields: probabilistic models for segmenting and labeling sequence data (2001)

15. Newell, A., Deng, J.: Pixels to graphs by associative embedding (2017)

BDGAN: Image Blind Denoising Using Generative Adversarial Networks

Shipeng Zhu[1], Guili Xu[1(✉)], Yuehua Cheng[1], Xiaodong Han[2],
and Zhengsheng Wang[1]

[1] College of Automation Engineering,
Nanjing University of Aeronautics and Astronautics,
Nanjing 211106, China
`guilixu@nuaa.edu.cn`
[2] China Academy of Space Technology, Beijing 100081, China

Abstract. In this paper, we present an end-to-end method for image blind denoising based on a conditional generative adversarial network (GAN). Discriminative learning-based methods, such as DnCNN, can achieve state-of-the-art denoising results but these methods usually focus on establishing noise model that resembles natural noisy images, thus neglecting to recover clean images from noisy images. Non-blind denoising methods are also limited since a precise noise level is hard to be obtained in the real world. Using multiple modified methods, we propose a novel end-to-end architecture which could directly generate clean images. A range of experiments have been done to show the convenience and superiority of our approach in image blind denoising.

Keywords: Image blind denoising · Generative adversarial networks · U-Net · Loss function

1 Introduction

Image blind denoising is a necessary low-level vision task but it has issues that remain unresolved. Image blind denoising aims to recover a clean image x from its observation of y which follows a degradation model $y = x + v$. However, the source of noise v is unavailable because the complex environmental and image sensor issues present the real world. This paper seeks to address how to solve this blind denoising problem.

Over the past decades, many traditional denoising models have been utilized using image priors and nonlocal self-similarity, such as BM3D [1], EPLL [2] and WNNM [6]. These methods are not always equipped to deal with complex noise sources. Furthermore, model-based methods usually spend a considerable amount of time on denoising but perform poorly with blind noise. With the development of deep learning, data-based methods have received significant attention

---

The first author is a student.

© Springer Nature Switzerland AG 2019
Z. Lin et al. (Eds.): PRCV 2019, LNCS 11858, pp. 241–252, 2019.
https://doi.org/10.1007/978-3-030-31723-2_21

due to their adaptability and high performance. As an import category, discriminative learning methods aim to learn the noise model using inference procedures [3], such as CNN [5]. Nevertheless, existing discriminative methods still lack flexibility, and the trained model is usually tailored to a fixed noise level.

Generative adversarial networks (GANs) have been shown to possess significant capacity for preserving image details and creating strong mapping relationship between two complicated distributions. Inspired by recent work on image super-resolution [19] and style transfer [13], we considered denoising as a case of conditional image-to-image translation and therefore have attempted to resolve it under supervised learning. We propose BDGAN, an end-to-end approach to blind denoising task based on conditional generative adversarial networks [22] and featuring several improvements.

To evaluate different models, the general consensus is that v can be instead of additive white Gaussian noise (AWGN) with a given noise level. In this paper, we adopt AWGN with zero mean in order to achieve fair comparison between the different methods. In addition, we use a real-noisy dataset to measure real denoising ability of BDGAN. Our main quantitative indexes are Peak Signal to Noise Ratio (PSNR) and structural similarity index (SSIM) which are widely used in image enhancement. On the other hand, we employ Precision, Recall and F1-Measure to evaluate the visual object detection performance on images, which allows us to restore image quality across a range of methods.

We revisit the basic concept of CGAN and improve the property of blind denoising in three areas. Firstly, we improve the architecture of network by adopting a modified U-Net as our generator and utilizing techniques which enhance training stability and obtain improved image quality such as removing the Batch Normalization (BN) layers of generator for realistic details. Then we use a multi-scale discriminator, which proved to be more capable than a single-scale. Finally, we utilize a combined loss function, which consists of four components including perceptual loss [23], in order to obtain high image quality.

2   Related Work

2.1   Blind Image Denoising

As touched on above, there are two major denoising camps: model denoising methods and learning based denoising methods. The former is independent on training data since the image prior information can be constructed to deal with unknown noise. Nevertheless, there are still two major dilemmas that we have to face when using model-based method. Firstly, image prior and noise modeling only make use of human experience and knowledge, which may not recover the raw information or true distribution. Secondly, these methods can only extract the internal information from one single image ignoring the common external information from a large dataset thereby weakening the overall performance of the method. On the other hand, the advent of deep learning has promoted the development of learning-based methods. These methods generally utilize the powerful perceptron capability of networks and extract abundant feature information from images. Notably, in 2016, Zhang et al. suggest DnCNN [16] could outperform traditional model denoising methods. This model aimed to extract real noise distribution with residual learning in deep networks, which is a technique avoiding destroying images' structure. Henceforth, the major methods now prefer to exploit more realistic noise information, such as FFDNet [17] and CBDNet [18], which can also achieve promising results.

2.2 Generative Adversarial Networks

The use of generative adversarial networks (GANs), proposed by Ian Goodfellow [7] in 2014, has become increasingly popular in generative problems. The framework of GAN contains a generative model and a discriminative model. The former is designed to capture the distribution of real sample data in order to produce more realistic data, the latter is trained to judge whether the input is real or not. Although the original GAN did not have stable training processes or the ability to perform complex distribution, there are several recent methods which can improves the performance of GAN. DCGAN [10] introduced the concept of convolution and many additional useful tricks. LSGAN [11] raises more mathematically rigorous loss instead of cross-entropy and rectifies the lack of image diversity. CGAN presents the concept of condition and learns mapping via the following game problem, which is widely used in transfer tasks.

$$\min_G \max_D \mathcal{L}_G (G, D) \tag{1}$$

And the loss function is given by:

$$\mathcal{L}_G (G, D) = \mathbb{E}_{x_r} [\log D (x_r)] + \mathbb{E}_{x_f} [\log (1 - D (G (x_f)))] \tag{2}$$

where G represents the generative network and D represents the discriminative network. x_r stands for the input image of generative network, and x_f stands for a natural image. In this paper, we intend to enhance CGAN by utilizing an effective loss function and introducing some training tricks which solve the current blind denoising problem.

2.3 Pretrained Models

VGGNet [12], widely used in the field of image classification, attempts to explore the relationship between the depth and the performance of a network. These systems build deep convolutional neural networks with stacking 3×3 kernel and 2×2 max-pooling kernels. Further research shows that VGGNet can extract precise multi-scale pattern information alongside good generalization.

Object Detection is one of the most advanced areas of computer vision and has great potential in the field of autonomous driving. Among current multitudinous learning-based approaches YOLO [4], and its improved versions [30], are considered to be the most applicable. They have been demonstrated to have stable and powerful object detection abilities across a range of applications. In this paper, we use the newest YOLO v3, which was pretrained on MSCOCO dataset [28], to evaluate the effect of image quality on object detection.

3   The Proposed Method

Our method aims to recover sharp images from noisy images with no prior information provided. In this section, we introduce the network architecture and detail the improvements made to the discriminator. Finally, we discuss the components of loss function which are used to maintain image quality and structural integrity [29].

3.1   Network Architecture

We aim to learn mapping relationship via the equation $x = F(y)$ to produce clean, high-quality images, where $y = x + v$. As shown in our architecture in Fig. 1, we take three structural approaches: (1) employ U-Net [24] as the backbone of generator G; (2) remove all BN and Max-Pooling layers of G and replace RELU with Leakey-RELU; (3) adopt multi-scale discriminators instead of a single discriminator.

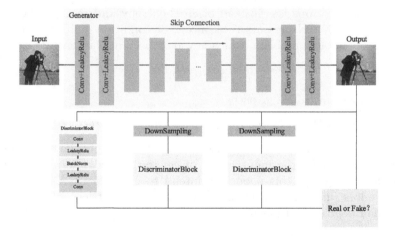

Fig. 1. The architecture of our proposed BDGAN. The generator is formed by a U-Net without BN layers. The multi-scale discriminators consist of three discriminator blocks.

Researchers usually utilize residual networks as the backbone of generator to resolve PSNR-related tasks and achieve commendable performance. Nevertheless, all information has been stored in each layer of residual network during training and leaded to errors easily. Hence, we employ U-Net, which was initially presented to deal with biomedical image segmentation, as our backbone of generator G. U-Net places an emphasis on image contour for reference and efficiently transmitting less error-prone information between nonadjacent layers with skip connections.

BN layers are designed to normalize the features in a batch with mean and variance, which are widely used in image recognition [25] for their improvement of gradient diffusion. However, BN layers tend to monopolize much computing resources and memory usage in order to accelerate training process. BN layers also attempt to limit the generalization performance when the training and testing datasets are radically different [27]. Especially, we find that complicated GAN framework might be affected by BN layers, which cause indelible artifacts and interference in image generation during training. Based on the above reasons, we have removed all BN layers from the generator in order to increase the stability of the generated images and reduce overall computational complexity. Max-Pooling layers are supposed to reduce sample feature maps. However, these layers usually cause latent feature information losses which reduce image quality. Therefore, we have removed all Max-Pooling layers to obtain high performance. Lastly, we observed that Leakey-RELU promotes the training stability and rate of convergence better than standard RELU, so we initiated the replacement.

3.2 Multi-scale Discriminators

Recovering a high-quality image from a perceptible noise poses a challenge. To effectively differentiate between real from synthesized fake images, we attempted to enlarge the receptive field of our discriminator, which usually require a more complicated network or larger convolutional kernels. However, these methods would result in overfitting and require greater memory usage, which would limit the training batch size for image generation. Therefore, we present multi-scale discriminators with three single discriminator blocks D_1, D_2, D_3. Specifically, clean images and synthesized images are down sampled based different size factors to build an image pyramid of three scales. The three identical discriminator blocks (shown in Fig. 1.) are then trained to discriminate whether input is real or not at different scales. This hierarchical structure encourages the generator to produce both fine details and consistent image integrity. In making these alterations, we also observed that multi-scale discriminators helped decrease the presence of artifacts [30].

3.3 Loss Function

To acquire an improved generative capacity, we propose an improved loss function based on LSGAN, which consists of four losses. The formula is defined as:

$$\mathcal{L}_{total} = \sum_{k=1,2,3} \mathcal{L}_G^{D_k} + \lambda \sum_{k=1,2,3} \mathcal{L}_{Feat}^{D_k} + \eta \sum_{k=1,2,3} \mathcal{L}_1 + \mu \mathcal{L}_{vgg} \tag{3}$$

where $\mathcal{L}_G$ means adversarial loss, $\mathcal{L}_{Feat}$ represents feature matching loss, $\mathcal{L}_1$ represents L1 loss and $\mathcal{L}_{Percep}$ is the perceptual loss. Here, λ, η, μ control the influence of four terms. In this paper, we set them into 20, 40, 2.

Adversarial Loss. Researchers usually use vanilla GAN objective [15] as the loss function in CGAN-related tasks. However, vanilla GAN relies on cross entropy, a process which refuses to optimize the generative image that is recognized as real one, thereby resulting in an unsatisfactory performance. We propose an alternative way of using LSGAN. And the whole formula is given by:

$$\min_{D} \sum_{k=1,2,3} \mathcal{L}_D (D_k, G) = \min_{D} \sum_{k=1,2,3} \frac{1}{2} \mathbb{E}_{x_f} \left[(D_k (x_f) - 1)^2 \right]$$
$$+ \frac{1}{2} \mathbb{E}_{x_r} \left[(D_k (G (x_r)))^2 \right] \tag{4}$$

$$\min_{G} \sum_{k=1,2,3} \mathcal{L}_G (D_k, G) = \min_{G} \sum_{k=1,2,3} \frac{1}{2} \mathbb{E}_{x_r} \left[(D_k (G (x_r)) - 1)^2 \right] \tag{5}$$

Feature Matching Loss. To enhance the robustness of training and structural consistency, we tend to extract image information from the three discriminator blocks and match these representations between real and generative images by 1-norm. The feature matching loss is defined as:

$$\sum_{k=1,2,3} \mathcal{L}_1 = \sum_{k=1,2,3} \mathbb{E}_{x_r} || (G (x_r))_{downsamp_k} - (x_f)_{downsamp_k} ||_1 \tag{6}$$

where D_k^i represents the ith-layer of discriminator block D_k. T is the number of total layers and N_i is the number of elements within each layer.

L1 Loss. To strengthen the content quantity of synthetic images, we utilize mean absolute error (MAE) loss to learn the content information from multiple scales for the generator. The loss is expressed as:

$$\mathcal{L}_{Feat}^{D_k} = \mathbb{E}_{(x_r, x_f)} \sum_{i=1}^{M} \frac{1}{N_i} \left[||D_k^i (x_r, x_f) - D_k^i (x_r, G (x_f)) ||_1 \right] \tag{7}$$

where $downsamp_k$ represents the kth down sample from real and generative images.

Perceptual Loss. To the best of our knowledge, single L1 Loss could lead to the presence of artifacts due to the average pixel-level, thus we have employed perceptual loss to compare the global feature information between synthetic and ground-truth clean image. These features can be extracted from a powerful pre-trained CNN. In this paper, we have obtained our feature information from the multi-depth layers presented in the VGG19 pre-trained model. The perceptual loss is as the following:

$$\mathcal{L}_{percep} = \mathbb{E}_{(x_r, x_f)} \sum_{i=1}^{N} \omega_i ||VGG (x_r) - VGG (x_f) ||_2 \tag{8}$$

where VGG^i presents the ith-layer of VGG19 and ω_i are the weights for multi-scales. We set ω_i to $\frac{1}{32}, \frac{1}{16}, \frac{1}{8}, \frac{1}{4}, 1$ specifically.

4   Training Details

We deploy our work with using PyTorch framework. Both of training and test are implemented on a single NVIDIA GTX 1080Ti GPU. We obtain the noisy and clean image in pairs by adding AWGN with zero mean from natural clean images using the scikit-image package with randomly cropped of size in 256×256. To train our blind denoising GAN, we set the range of noise level as $\sigma \in [0, 60]$.

For the training process, we alternated between training the generator and discriminator. The learning rate was initialized as 1×10^{-4} with 400 iterations and gradually decreases over next 100 iterations. Both models are trained with a batch 16, which empirically promoted performance. We utilized Adam [14] as an optimization solver with $\beta_1 = 0.9, \beta_2 = 0.999$.

5   Experiments

5.1   Dataset

For training, we use the BSD500 [20] and Waterloo exploration dataset [21], which are widely used for image intensification. The former consists of 500 high-quality images and the latter consists of 4,744 images, depicting a range of subjects including people, buildings and scenery. We remove 68 images from the BSD500 for testing and then mix the remainder of the BSD500 with the Waterloo exploration dataset and randomly cut out 40k 256×256 images from them since a larger training dataset only has a negligible impact on performance. Furthermore, we randomly cut out 10k images from RENOIR [29] as the real noisy images and test real-noise denoising abilities of different data sources versions of BDGAN on DND [26] dataset.

We tend to train our models both in RGB and gray channels in order to appraise color restoration ability and structure stability. We evaluate PSNR and SSIM for our models on BSD68 as well as 12 widely-used testing images (Set12). In order to assess the visualized quality of denoising we also evaluate 200 images from MSCOCO through a pre-trained YOLO v3 model.

5.2   Evaluation

Compared Methods. We compare the BDGAN method with several state-of-the-art models, including Non-Blind methods: BM3D, WNNM and Blind methods: Multiscale [8], DnCNN-B (blind denoising model of DnCNN) and GCBD [9]. Specifically, we made some ablation investigations on studying the effects of each component in the proposed BDGAN including BN removal, Multi-scale Discriminators, et al. The overall comparison is illustrated in Table 3.

Quantitative Results. Four comparisons are made to evaluate all models. On the one hand, we focus on AWGN denoising task in order to measure different methods quantitatively. Specifically, non-blind models are provided with noise levels. Different models are applied to the BSD68 dataset and the average PSNR and SSIM results are shown in Table 1. Based on these results, although no noise level is offered, our model outperforms other methods. This result is incredible because DnCNN-B and GCBD tend to extract noise distribution and obtain clean images from input by subtracting noise while BDGAN is an end-to-end method which generates sharp images directly. Table 2 lists different PSNR results of competing methods on the Set12 dataset. The best result for each image is highlighted in bold. To be specific, BDGAN achieves impressive performance and outperforms competing methods on most images. Denoising images from test on BSD68 and Set12 dataset are shown on Fig. 2 and 3. Meanwhile, we make some ablation investigations of BDGAN on Set12 and BSD68 and showed results of them in Table 3. According to it, the trend of results is incrementally improved and each component plays role in denoising task. In particular, the perceptual loss and feature matching loss focus more on structure and L1 loss places emphasis on image feature, BN and Max-pooling removal help to increase denoising stability. The multi-discriminator significantly improved model performance due to its wide perception domain. On the other hand, the results in Table 4 show the average PSNR and SSIM on DND real noise dataset. Although the best results belong to CBDNet, our model achieve high SSIM performance and great PSNR compared with others. In fact, the model trained by synthetic data is influenced by unreal information and limits the effect. However, the model trained by real mixed data obtain remarkable results. In consideration of special architecture of CBDNet, which consists of noise estimation and non-blind denoising subnetworks, our BDGAN shows strong capacities in feature extraction and Image structure preservation.

Table 1. The average PSNR (dB)/SSIM results on BSD68

Method	BM3D	TNRD	WNNM	Multiscales		DnCNN-B	GCBD	BDGAN
/	/	/	/	scale = 1	scale = 2	/	/	/
$\sigma = 15$	31.07/0.87	31.42/0.88	31.37/-	30.48/-	29.72/-	31.61/0.88	31.59/0.86	**32.12/0.91**
$\sigma = 25$	28.57/0.80	28.92/0.82	28.83/-	27.58/-	27.58/-	29.16/0.82	29.15/0.82	**29.82/0.86**
$\sigma = 50$	25.62/0.69	25.97/0.70	25.67/-	-/-	-/-	26.23/0.71	26.19/0.70	**26.78/0.76**

Object Detection. In order to test object detection, we selected 200 images from MSCOCO dataset as the object detection test clean data and got noisy images by adding AWGN. This approach corresponds to real vision tasks and encourages us to intuitively understand the denoising result. The quantitative indexes consist of precision, recall and F1-measure, which are able to comprehensively measure the influence of image quality on object detection.

Our results are shown in Table 5 and Fig. 4, illustrating the visual results of different methods. The results for natural clean images are recognized as ground truth. To be specific, Fig. 4 shows that the result of BDGAN is more reliable than that of DnCNN due to its low false detection rate. As shown, BDGAN significantly outperforms the competitor in most fields.

Table 2. The PSNR (dB) results of different models on Set12

Images	C.man	House	Peppers	Starfish	Monar	Airpl	Parrot	Lena	Barbara	Boat	Man	Couple	Ave
Level						$\sigma = 15$							
BM3D	31.91	34.93	32.69	31.14	31.85	31.07	31.37	34.26	33.1	32.13	31.92	32.1	32.372
WNNM	32.17	**35.13**	**32.99**	31.82	32.71	31.39	31.62	34.27	**33.6**	32.27	32.11	31.93	32.667
DnCNN-B	32.1	34.93	33.15	32.02	**32.94**	**31.56**	31.63	**34.56**	32.09	32.35	**32.41**	32.41	32.679
BDGAN	**33.09**	34.57	32.66	**32.68**	32.38	30.97	**32.65**	34.17	32.77	**32.66**	32.11	**32.46**	**32.764**
Level						$\sigma = 25$							
BM3D	29.45	32.85	30.16	28.56	29.25	28.42	28.93	32.07	30.71	29.9	29.61	29.71	29.969
WNNM	29.64	33.22	30.42	29.03	29.84	28.69	29.15	32.24	**31.24**	30.03	29.76	29.82	30.257
DnCNN-B	29.94	33.05	30.84	29.34	30.25	**29.09**	29.35	32.42	29.69	**30.2**	**30.09**	30.1	30.363
BDGAN	**30.81**	**33.28**	**30.88**	**30.31**	**30.49**	28.7	**30.41**	**32.77**	29.95	30.14	29.63	**30.95**	**30.693**
Level						$\sigma = 50$							
BM3D	26.13	29.69	26.68	25.04	25.82	25.1	25.9	29.05	27.22	26.78	26.81	26.46	26.722
WNNM	26.45	30.33	26.95	25.44	26.32	25.42	26.14	29.25	**27.79**	26.97	26.94	26.64	27.052
DnCNN-B	27.03	30.02	27.39	**26.83**	25.89	25.87	26.48	29.38	26.38	27.23	27.23	26.91	27.206
BDGAN	**27.78**	**30.61**	**27.79**	26.54	**27.46**	**26.51**	**27.34**	**29.54**	26.34	**27.93**	**27.62**	**27.66**	**27.76**

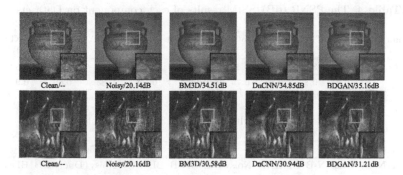

Fig. 2. Denoising results from the BSD68 dataset with noise level 25 by different methods

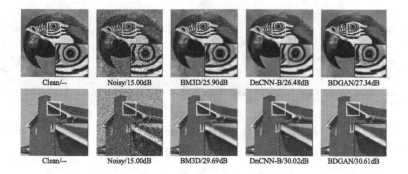

Fig. 3. Denoising results from the Set12 dataset with noise level 50 by different methods

Table 3. The PSNR (dB)/SSIM results of each component on Datasets

	Level	PSNR/ SSIM	PSNR/ SSIM	PSNR/ SSIM	PSNR/ SSIM	PSNR/ SSIM	PSNR/ SSIM	PSNR/ SSIM
BN	/	Yes	No	No	No	No	No	No
Max-pooling	/	Yes	Yes	No	No	No	No	No
Multi_D	/	No	No	No	Yes	Yes	Yes	Yes
Perceptual	/	No	No	No	No	Yes	Yes	Yes
Feature Matching	/	No	No	No	No	No	Yes	Yes
L1	/	No	No	No	No	No	No	Yes
Set12	$\sigma = 15$	29.97/0.88	30.02/0.88	30.07/0.88	31.14/0.90	31.54/0.90	32.32/0.90	**32.77/0.93**
	$\sigma = 25$	27.99/0.77	28.09/0.79	28.11/0.80	29.05/0.83	29.31/0.83	29.77/0.85	**30.70/0.89**
	$\sigma = 50$	26.16/0.74	26.18/0.74	26.36/0.77	26.92/0.79	27.33/0.79	27.59/0.79	**27.76/0.81**
BSD68	$\sigma = 15$	28.05/0.82	28.17/0.83	28.00/0.83	30.22/0.88	31.20/0.89	31.53/0.89	**32.12/0.91**
	$\sigma = 25$	26.94/0.76	27.00/0.76	27.10/0.78	28.75/0.83	29.25/0.84	29.78/0.84	**29.82/0.86**
	$\sigma = 50$	24.47/0.61	24.49/0.62	24.59/0.64	26.03/0.72	26.21/0.74	26.40/0.74	**26.78/0.76**

Table 4. The PSNR (dB)/SSIM results of each component on Datasets

Method	EPLL	NCSR	TNRD	BM3D	DnCNN-B	FFDNet	CBDNet	BDGAN (Syn)	BDGAN (Real)	BDGAN (All)
PSNR	33.51	34.05	33.65	34.51	32.43	34.39	**38.06**	33.11	35.11	35.83
SSIM	0.83	0.83	0.83	0.85	0.79	0.85	**0.94**	0.83	0.89	0.91

Table 5. The Results of YOLO v3 object detection

Method	$\sigma = 15$			$\sigma = 40$			$\sigma = 50$		
Method	Noisy	DncNN-B	BDGAN	Noisy	DncNN-B	BDGAN	Noisy	DncNN-B	BDGAN
Prec	0.787	**0.805**	0.751	0.755	**0.751**	0.679	0.333	0.476	**0.528**
Recall	0.521	0.621	**0.722**	0.281	0.538	**0.58**	0.069	0.327	**0.401**
F1	0.303	0.658	**0.691**	0.217	0.505	**0.569**	0.042	0.415	**0.538**

Original   Detection   Noisy   DnCNN   BDGAN

Fig. 4. Object detection before and after denoising with noise level 40 by different methods

6   Conclusion

We have described an end-to-end learning-based approach to image blind denoising and introduced BDGAN, a much-improved conditional GAN. Our process has made use of a wide range of new methods, including a result-oriented evaluation technique which shows that BDGAN achieves favorable blind denoising performance as well as improving visual object detection.

Acknowledgement. This project is supported by the National Natural Science Foundation of China (61473148), 13th Five-Year equipment pre research project (30501050403) and GraduateInnovation Base LabOpen Fund of Nanjing University of Aeronautics and Astronautics (No. kfjj20180316).

References

1. Dabov, K., Foi, A., Katkovnik, V., Egiazarian, K.: Image denoising by sparse 3-D transform-domain collaborative filtering. IEEE Trans. Image Proces. **16**(8), 2080–2095 (2007)
2. Zoran, D., Weiss, Y.: From learning models of natural image patches to whole image restoration. In: 2011 International Conference on Computer Vision. IEEE (2011)
3. Chen, Y., Pock, T.: Trainable nonlinear reaction diffusion: a flexible framework for fast and effective image restoration. IEEE Trans. Pattern Anal. Mach. Intell. **39**(6), 1256–1272 (2017)
4. Redmon, J., et al.: You only look once: unified, real-time object detection. In: Proceedings of the IEEE Conference on Computer Vision and Pattern Recognition (2016)
5. Jain, V., Seung, S.: Natural image denoising with convolutional networks. In: Advances in Neural Information Processing Systems, pp. 769–776 (2009)
6. Gu, S., Zhang, L., Zuo, W., Feng, X.: Weighted nuclear norm minimization with application to image denoising. In: IEEE Conference on Computer Vision and Pattern Recognition, pp. 2862–2869 (2014)
7. Goodfellow, I.J., et al.: Generative adversarial nets. In: Advances in Neural Information Processing Systems, vol. 3, pp. 2672–2680 (2014)
8. Lebrun, M., Colom, M., Morel, J.M.: Multiscale image blind denoising. IEEE Trans. Image Process. Publ. IEEE Sig. Process. Soc. **24**(10), 3149–61 (2015)
9. Chen, J., et al.: Image blind denoising with generative adversarial network based noise modeling. In: Proceedings of the IEEE Conference on Computer Vision and Pattern Recognition (2018)
10. Radford, A., Metz, L., Chintala, S.: Unsupervised representation learning with deep convolutional generative adversarial networks. Comput. Sci. (2015)
11. Mao, X., et al.: Least squares generative adversarial networks (2016)
12. Simonyan, K., Zisserman, A.: Very deep convolutional networks for large-scale image recognition. arXiv preprint arXiv:1409.1556 (2014)
13. Huang, X., et al.: Multimodal unsupervised image-to-image translation. In: Proceedings of the European Conference on Computer Vision (ECCV) (2018)
14. Kingma, D.P., Ba, J.: Adam: a method for stochastic optimization. arXiv preprint arXiv:1412.6980 (2014)

15. Nah, S., Hyun, T., Kyoung, K., Lee, M.: Deep multi-scale convolutional neural network for dynamic scene deblurring (2016)
16. Zhang, K., et al.: Beyonda Gaussian denoiser: residual learning of deep CNN for image denoising. IEEE Trans. Image Process. **26**(7), 3142–3155 (2017)
17. Zhang, K., et al.: FFDNet: toward a fast and flexible solution for CNN based image denoising. IEEE Trans. Image Process. **27**, 4608–4622 (2018)
18. Guo, S., et al.: Toward convolutional blind denoising of real photographs. arXiv preprint arXiv:1807.04686 (2018)
19. Ledig, C., et al.: Photo-realistic single image super-resolution using a generative adversarial network. ArXiv e-prints, September 2016
20. Arbelaez, P., et al.: Contour detection and hierarchical image segmentation. IEEE Trans. Pattern Anal. Mach. Intell. **33**(5), 898–916 (2011)
21. Ma, K., et al.: Waterloo exploration database: new challenges for image quality assessment models. IEEE Trans. Image Process. **PP**(99), 1 (2016)
22. Mirza, M., Osindero, S.: Conditional generative adversarial nets. arXiv preprint arXiv:1411.1784 (2014)
23. Johnson, J., Alahi, A., Fei-Fei, L.: Perceptual losses for real-time style transfer and super-resolution. In: Leibe, B., Matas, J., Sebe, N., Welling, M. (eds.) ECCV 2016. LNCS, vol. 9906, pp. 694–711. Springer, Cham (2016). https://doi.org/10.1007/978-3-319-46475-6_43
24. Ronneberger, O., Fischer, P., Brox, T.: U-Net: convolutional networks for biomedical image segmentation. In: Navab, N., Hornegger, J., Wells, W.M., Frangi, A.F. (eds.) MICCAI 2015. LNCS, vol. 9351, pp. 234–241. Springer, Cham (2015). https://doi.org/10.1007/978-3-319-24574-4_28
25. He, K., et al.: Deep residual learning for image recognition. In: Proceedings of the IEEE Conference on Computer Vision and Pattern Recognition (2016)
26. Plotz, T., Roth, S.: Benchmarking denoising algorithms with real photographs. In: IEEE Conference on Computer Vision and Pattern Recognition (2017)
27. Wang, X., et al.: ESRGAN: enhanced super-resolution generative adversarial networks. In: Proceedings of the European Conference on Computer Vision (ECCV) (2018)
28. Lin, T.-Y., et al.: Microsoft COCO: common objects in context. In: Fleet, D., Pajdla, T., Schiele, B., Tuytelaars, T. (eds.) ECCV 2014. LNCS, vol. 8693, pp. 740–755. Springer, Cham (2014). https://doi.org/10.1007/978-3-319-10602-1_48
29. Redmon, J., Farhadi, A.: YOLOV3: an incremental improvement. arXiv preprint arXiv:1804.02767 (2018)
30. Anaya, J., Barbu, A.: RENOIR - a benchmark dataset for real noise reduction evaluation. Comput. Sci. **51**, 144–154 (2014)

Single Image Reflection Removal Based on Deep Residual Learning

Zhixin Xu, Xiaobao Guo, and Guangming Lu[✉]

Harbin Institute of Technology, Shenzhen, China
{xuzhixin,guoxiaobao}@stu.hit.edu.cn,
luguangm@hit.edu.cn

Abstract. We present a deep residual learning approach to address the single image reflection removal problem. Specifically, residual learning exploits the mapping between the observed image and its comparatively simple reflection information, which is then removed to obtain a clear background. Different from other methods that roughly eliminating the reflections and producing the images with remanent sticking, a novel generative adversarial framework is proposed, where the generator is embedded with the deep residual learning, significantly boosting the performance without impairing the intactness of the background by adversarial training. Moreover, a multi-part balanced loss is introduced with comprehensive consideration on the measure of feature similarity as well as the discriminating ability of GAN. It produces the result of high quality by learning the reflection and the background feature simultaneously. Experiments show that the proposed method achieves a state-of-the-art performance.

Keywords: Reflection removal · Residual learning · GAN

1 Introduction and Related Work

Along with the rapid advancement and application of the digital camera, photographing is becoming increasingly prevailing and indispensable in our daily life. However, the image would be corrupted by some additional undesirable parts when is taken in the reflective surroundings such as glass, water, and windows, which exerts considerable degradation on the visual perceptual quality. As shown in Fig. 1, the reflection in the images tends to distract our eyes from the scenes behind the glass. Furthermore, reflection, as a typical kind of noise, would impede both human and computer vision programs from better understanding the scene. Therefore, single image reflection removal is the active and essential research in computer vision community.

Student First Author

The work is supported by the NSFC fund (61332011), Shenzhen Fundamental Research fund (JCYJ20170811155442454, JCYJ20180306172023949), China Postdoctoral Science Foundation (2019TQ0316), and Medical Biometrics Perception and Analysis Engineering Laboratory, Shenzhen, China.

© Springer Nature Switzerland AG 2019
Z. Lin et al. (Eds.): PRCV 2019, LNCS 11858, pp. 253–266, 2019.
https://doi.org/10.1007/978-3-030-31723-2_22

Fig. 1. Captured image samples with reflection in the real world.

Years of studies on solving the reflection removal problem have made some achievements especially on eliminating reflection from non-metallic surfaces by adjusting the assembled component in the camera, e.g. rotating a polarized lens [3,4], moving focus [5], and using a flash [6]. Yet, hardware-based method is usually constrained by the lack of adaptability and flexibility when dealing with various background scenes and tricky reflection sources. In comparison, algorithms that tackle the reflection removal issue are more practical. Conventionally, prior knowledge and hand-crafted features [1,2,7] are utilised to learn the representation or mapping between the input image and the clear background scene. Li *et al.* [7] introduce gradient histogram for the image to construct long tail distribution, assuming that the relative smoothness for reflection and background are different, by which to determine and separate reflection. However, we can not tell the reflection is always smooth in the real case. Arvanitopoulos *et al.* [8] try to solve the problem by suppressing the reflection instead of getting rid of it by manually adjusting the thresholds of Laplacian data fidelity term and an l_0 gradient sparsity term on the output, which is a trade-off between suppressing reflection artifacts and image details. Therefore, it probably causes a degradation on important image details. Although traditional algorithms could basically solve the problem, they still suffer great limitations on coping with challenging situations. Deep learning based methods have greatly mitigated the illogicality between the robustness and adaptiveness compared with traditional methods. CEILNet [9] is the first to address the reflection removal problem with a deep convolutional network, where two cascaded sub-networks are combined, one for edge prediction and the other for image reconstruction. However, features are too many in input images and two-cascaded structure is complicated.

Under the same the precondition that other methods use [7,9], our method is also conducted on the basis of the assumption that the observed image is a compound of a reflection image and a clear background image. This assumption is rational and valid in practice since the reflective source or objects are usually observed and known when people take pictures of a scene. However, they usually focus on reflection removal by suppressing reflection artifacts to restore the background scene only, the learning and separation of the reflection are ignored, which causes a degradation on the result. It is substantial to learn both reflection information and the background scene jointly as they are intertwined in a single observed image.

To alleviate the aforementioned problems, a deep residual learning based single image reflection removal method is proposed. Instead of predicting the background image layer from the observed image directly, the proposed method learns a mapping between the observed image and its reflection layer since the background image is usually intractable for a generator [10] to learn while the reflection is relatively consistent in terms of luminance and color. Intuitively, residual learning is embedded into the proposed generative adversarial framework which provides an effective approach that decouples the reflection information from the entangled observed image [17, 18]. Simultaneously, the discriminator is trained to encourage the generated background image, the observed one without residual reflection information, to be more similar to the real background image. Unlike other deep reflection removal network, each part in our proposed method aims at a different target that jointly contributes to solving the reflection removal problem. To make it feasible in practice, the excogitation of loss function is supposed to be balanced, taking both feature similarity and discriminatory ability into consideration. Therefore, the proposed multi-part balanced loss comprises the content loss which measures the similarity between the learned residual information and the real reflection information, a perceptual loss that encourage the feature of the decoupled image to be more consistent with the real background image, and an adversarial loss for improving the discriminating ability of the discriminator. Through experiments, the multi-part balanced loss is proved to be beneficial to eliminating the gradient vanishing and exploding during training while the residual learning with the generative adversarial network is of great ability for both modeling the reflection information and the background image feature.

Our main contributions are as follows:

- A deep residual learning approach is proposed to solve the single image reflection removal problem. It exploits the mapping between the observed image and its reflection information, repressing the intractable issue of learning the complicated feature of the background image directly. Residual learning provides an effective method for deep reflection removal framework, yielding a faster convergence for training the model as well as an enhancement on its performance.
- The design of a novel generative adversarial network is utilized in this task, where the generator is embedded with the residual learning strategy and the discriminator is assigned to distinguish the generated background image from the real background image. The proposed generative adversarial framework for single image reflection removal demonstrates an exceeding performance by keeping the intactness of the background image through adversarial training.
- A multi-part balanced loss as the objective function is proposed, which is composed of the content loss, the perceptual loss, and the adversarial loss. It is of comprehensive consideration on both the measure of feature similarity and the description of the discriminating ability, which entails the network

to produce the background image of high quality by learning the reflection information and the background feature simultaneously.

The experiment results show the effectiveness of the proposed method for single image reflection removal task.

2   Deep Residual Learning Network with GAN

2.1   The Generative Adversarial Framework

The proposed generative adversarial framework is shown in Fig. 2, which can be rendered into two parts, one is a generator embedded with deep residual learning while the other is a discriminator to distinguish the generated background image and its corresponding real one. The captured image is first input into the generator, then the generator is trained to produce its reflection image through residual learning. The difference between the generated reflection image and the real reflection (ground-truth) will be formulated as the content loss which is a part of the objective function for the network. The discriminator is then trained to discriminate the generated background image and the real background (ground-truth), which in turn acts on the generator to produce a reflection image layer that is largely identical to the reality. Hence, residual learning and adversarial training are implemented in the generative adversarial framework. For the target of acquiring a clear background image without any reflection remanent, the features of both generated background image and real background image are extracted from several layers of a pretrained VGG-19 network [12], being reinforced to be similar by introducing a perceptual loss. By learning the mapping of the input image and its reflection information, together with modeling the distribution of the background image, the proposed method enjoys a high efficiency and quality for single image reflection removal. The implementations and details of the proposed method can be referred in the following parts in this paper.

2.2   Residual Learning

Reflection in an observed image usually presents a high intensity of light, emerging in part or full area in the image, pretty confusing when entangled with the background objects. Therefore, it imposes restrictions upon the network to learn the subtle features of the background image, which is normally the reason why extracting the background image directly would not be a favorable solution. Residual learning aims at learning the reflection information from the input image. It is a roundabout method that enables more effective learning to separate the reflection layer from the entangled image without impairing the background scene.

Let G be the trained network for residual learning. I represents the input image while I_b and I_r represent the real background image and the real reflection

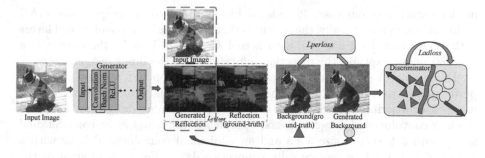

Fig. 2. Overview of the proposed generative adversarial framework. Generator is embedded with deep residual learning to produce reflection image (left). The content loss is conducted between two images in grey dashed box. The generated background image (yellow point) is produced (red dashed box) to be discriminated with the real background image (red triangle) by Discriminator (right). The perceptual loss is also acted as shown. (Color figure online)

image. Let O_b and O_r represent the generated background image and generated reflection image, respectively.

The assumption mentioned above can be interpreted as:

$$I = I_b + I_r \tag{1}$$

And residual learning can be formulated as:

$$O_r = G(I, \theta) \tag{2}$$

where θ is the parameter in the network G.

Combine (1) and (2), we have:

$$O_r = G(I_b, I_r, \theta) \tag{3}$$

Under the assumption mentioned above, the generated background image is formulated by following equation:

$$O_b = I - G(I_b, I_r, \theta) \tag{4}$$

As shown in Fig. 3, a captured image is sent to the network, which learns a mapping between it and its reflection information. The output is a generated reflection image, which is further used to get the generated background image. Experiments reveal that residual learning effectively improves the quality of reflection removal. More details can be found in Sect. 3.

2.3 Design of GAN for Single Image Reflection Removal

The network design of generator of our proposed GAN is shown in Fig. 3. Firstly, a captured image is directly passed into the network with padding in each layer to keep the scale invariant. In the first block, a 9×9 convolutional kernel is adopted to enlarge receptive field so as to acquire as much as valuable information. The following two convolutional layers utilize kernels of size 3×3. Then its output passes through a series of residual blocks [11], as shown in Fig. 3, which enable the network being extended or squeezed without gradient vanishing and to learn more powerful representation by stacking a different number of them. In the implementation of our case, 36 residual blocks are used in the proposed GAN architecture. Symmetrically, the output is then passed to two convolutional layers with kernel size 3×3 and one with kernel size 9×9. Finally, the output is a residual image captures the reflection information of the input image.

Discriminator plays an important role in the proposed method since the performance, to a large extent, depends on the gradient from it. However, the network of discriminator does not require much complex design but simply a stack of convolutional network layers. Specifically, we adopt eight convolutional layers with a kernel of size 3×3 and an additional convolutional layer with a kernel of size 1×1 to replace fully connection layer. For each interval of the convolutional layer, a batch normalization layer [15] is inserted to normalize the network. Adversarial training is conducive to model the distribution of the generated background image and the real background image when the generator is embedded with residual learning strategy. It is conceivable that the generated background image stems from the captured image without reflection information, which shares a great similarity to the real background image. Therefore, for the latter stages of discriminator training, the challenging cases will dramatically enhance the discriminating ability of discriminator, further providing effective gradient information to instruct generator and the entire model to learn better feature and generate more vivid details coherently.

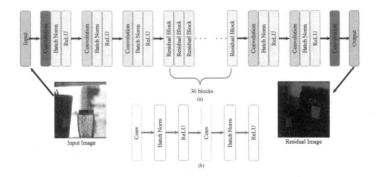

Fig. 3. Network design of generator in proposed GAN.

2.4   Multi-part Balanced Loss

Based on deep residual learning and designed network for single image reflection removal task, an objective function called multi-part balanced loss is proposed. To ensure the gradient information exist both in training the generator and the discriminator, the objective function should balance the network for each part to achieve a different purpose as contributing to the general goal. A content loss measures the similarity between the learned residual information and real reflection information. To encourage the feature of the generated background image to be more consistent with the real background image, a perceptual loss is exploited. Features for perceptual loss is sampled from several layers from a deep pretrained convolutional network, VGG-19 [12]. Along with an adversarial loss which keeps the detail information in the images by improving the discriminating ability of the discriminator, the proposed multi-part balanced loss is composed of the three parts above, instructing the network to produce an image of high quality. Specifically, let G be the generator in our proposed GAN and D be the discriminator. The rest representations are the same as those in Sect. 2.2. For each sample in one mini-batch, the content loss between I_r and O_r can be formulated as:

$$L_{content}(I_r, O_r) = Avg \sum_{i=1}^{w} \sum_{j=1}^{h} MSE(t_{i,j}, o_{i,j}), \qquad (5)$$

where w, h represents the weight and height for each sample, $t_{i,j}$ and $o_{i,j}$ represent the target and the predicted value for each pixel, respectively.

Perceptual loss is calculated between the features of I_b and O_b, we indicate perceptual loss by $L_{perceptual}$:

$$L_{perceptual}(I_b, O_b) = \sum_{i=k}^{n} (I_{b,k} - O_{b,k})^2, \qquad (6)$$

where k indicate each convolutional layer from the total selected n layers while $I_{b,k}$ and $O_{b,k}$ represent the features for I_b and O_b, respectively.

To implement adversarial training, we adopt binary cross entropy loss for the discriminator as the objective function:

$$L_{adversarial}(I_b, O_b) = log[D(I_b)] + log[D(1 - O_b)], \qquad (7)$$

For each time updating discriminator in a mini-batch, the loss is the average of the summation of (6) and (7). The loss for generator is the average of (5) and the second term in (7).

The objective function in the proposed method can be interpreted as:

$$L_{multi-part\ balanced}(G, D) = \min_{G} \max_{D} (L_{content} + L_{perceptual} + L_{adversarial}) \quad (8)$$

3 Experiment

In this section, several experiments are conducted on both synthetic and real-world datasets to demonstrate the superiority of the proposed method. On the one hand, we set experiments to show the effectiveness of each component in the proposed method and further analyse the model in terms of quality and quantitative results. On the other, a comparison between the proposed method and state-of-the-art methods is conducted on both synthetic and real-world images. SSIM [14] and PSNR [13] are exploited as metrics to evaluate the generated images.

Background   Reflection   Input Image

Fig. 4. Synthetic dataset samples. The background scene, the reflection image layer, and the synthetic image (from left to right).

3.1 Dataset

On account of the difficulty of labelling the real-world images, we handcraft a synthetic dataset using the images from PASCAL VOC2012 [16], which is widely adopted by current methods. Based on the valid assumption that the observed image is a compound of the reflection image layer and the clear background image layer, we synthesis one image by adding a reflection layer to a background image. In practice, to make the reflection image more consistent with the true case, a random Gaussian blur is first imposed on it. Subsequently, a clear background image and a randomly selected reflection image are added as an input image. As shown in Fig. 4, the clear background images show more details compared with the reflection images that transmit the moderate light. The synthetic images demonstrate a striking similarity to the real world cases. The synthetic dataset contains 11453 images in total and 500 from which is assigned as a test dataset.

In addition, we test our model on both the synthetic images and real-world images from CEIL dataset [9]. The CEIL real-world image test dataset contains 45 images in total with different degrees of reflection on various background scenes.

3.2 Implementation and Analysis

We implement training the model by deep learning platform PyTorch. It runs on the GPU of NVIDIA Tesla M40 of memory size 24 GB with CUDA version 8.0.44 and CUDNN version 5. The model was trained using Adam optimizer with each mini-batch of 10 and a learning rate of 0.0001. The maximum epoches was set to be 50. The model was tested on 500 pictures from the synthetic dataset.

Table 1. Ablation experiment results on the synthetic test dataset.

Model	SSIM	PSNR
RL	0.8564	22.71
GAN+P	0.8545	23.17
RL+P	0.8841	23.95
RL+GAN+P	**0.8924**	**24.84**

Input Image   RL   GAN+P   RL+P   RL+GAN+P

Fig. 5. Qualitative results of ablation experiment with different settings.

To verify the effectiveness of each component in the proposed method. We conduct several ablation experiments in terms of SSIM and PSNR metrics. As shown in Table 1, RL indicates that the model is implemented by residual learning while GAN means the model is trained by adversarial learning in the proposed GAN framework. Letter P represents that the features of predicted and real background images are measured by the perceptual loss function. Simply applying residual learning gains 0.8564 in SSIM and 22.17 in PSNR on average respectively. Comparing the second and the last experiment settings, it shows that deep residual learning contributes to the final results by 0.0379 in SSIM and 1.67 in PSNR, leading a prominent enhancement. In addition, it can be noticed that the proposed GAN is conducive to the performance by comparing the third and the last settings. Perceptual loss evaluates the features of the generated background images and the real background images, which directly benefits the network to produce images of high quality. Therefore, from the results of the first and the third settings, it improves the performance by 0.0277 in SSIM and 1.24 in PSNR averagely.

The qualitative results are shown in Fig. 5, where the visual perception of the proposed method transcends all other settings, which further proves the significance of the deep residual learning and the proposed method.

3.3   Comparison to State-of-the-art Methods

Several experiments are conducted to show both qualitative and quantitative superiorities compared with state-of-the-art methods. Figure 7 compares the visual results on our synthetic datasets, where the proposed method turns out to tackle different complex scenes. As shown in Fig. 8, the proposed method also shows better performance on the images provided by CEILNet [9], where more

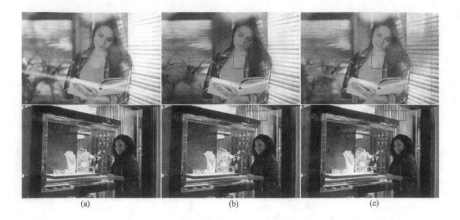

Fig. 6. Comparison of the real-world image with CEILNet.

image details are preserved after reflection removal while other methods leave some remanet artifacts. From top to down, images (a) to (g) show remarkable differences in the marked boxes. The results of the proposed method precede the rest images with clearer background and least reflection remaining.

Samples of real-world image dataset in Fig. 6 further illustrate the exceeding performance especially on fidelity and less distortion of background scene. As we can see, the tone of the objects on the image suffers a degeneration after the process of CEILNet [9], while the result of the proposed method is capable of preserving better color authenticity. From box of the second image, it can be found that the proposed method could deal with the reflection even if it is shown on the confusing background scene. Please zoom in for better view.

Table 2. Quantitative comparison to state-of-the-art methods on images (a) to (g) corresponding to each column in Figs. 7 and 8.

Image	SSIM				PSNR			
	Li [7]	Nikolaos [8]	CEILNet [9]	Ours	Li [7]	Nikolaos [8]	CEILNet [9]	Ours
(a)	0.7379	0.9008	0.9499	**0.9702**	19.7754	23.2607	24.9851	**28.5102**
(b)	0.7497	0.8579	0.8912	**0.9142**	21.4570	20.9500	21.4921	**22.6718**
(c)	0.6434	0.8987	0.9458	**0.9602**	18.0398	21.2330	24.0125	**24.3933**
(d)	0.8359	0.9305	0.9098	**0.9344**	21.6833	22.4701	26.0067	**27.6002**
(e)	0.7261	0.9303	0.9028	**0.9311**	20.0862	23.4430	24.2102	**26.2652**
(f)	0.5784	0.8672	0.9088	**0.9169**	13.2471	22.2741	23.9800	**24.7217**
(g)	0.5522	0.9231	0.8312	**0.9429**	12.8058	25.2152	23.8229	**26.0204**

Table 2 compares the SSIM and PSNR of the images (a) to (g) corresponding to each column in Figs. 7 and 8. Out of fairness, we set the hyperparameters for Nikolaos method [8] to its best adaptiveness for each picture. It is obvious that

(a)   (b)   (c)   (d)

Fig. 7. Reflection removal comparison of the synthetic dataset in this paper with Li, Nikolaos, CEILNet and the proposed method from top to bottom (original images are on the first line).

the evaluation figures of the proposed method outstrip the rest methods, yielding 0.9385 and 25.7404 on average in terms of SSIM and PSNR respectively, which further demonstrates the excellent performance of our proposed method.

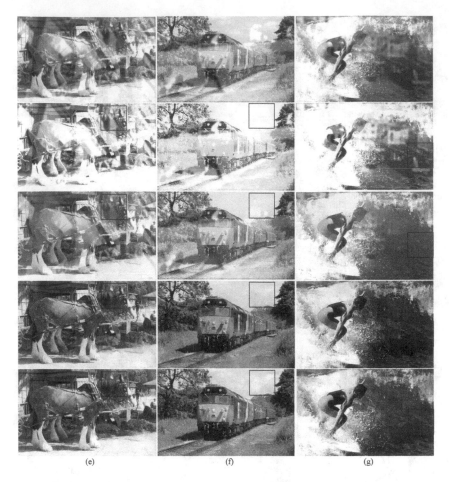

(e)   (f)   (g)

Fig. 8. Comparison of the synthetic images in CEILNet with Li, Nikolaos, CEILNet and the proposed method from top to bottom (original images are on the first line).

4 Conclusion

In this paper, a deep residual learning approach is proposed to address the single image reflection removal problem. Instead of eliminating or suppressing the reflection information from the observed images directly, the proposed method first exploits the mapping between the observed image and its reflection information which is comparatively simple, and then removed it to obtain a clear background image. A novel generative adversarial framework is also proposed that dramatically improves the performance through deep residual learning and adversarial training. Furthermore, a multi-part balanced loss is introduced by considering both the reflection information learning and the background feature similarity measurement simultaneously. The proposed method entails a great performance by keep the intactness of the background scene. Experiments compared with several state-of-the-art methods reveal a significant meaning of deep residual learning and effectiveness of the proposed method on the single image reflection removal task.

References

1. Levin, A., Weiss, Y.: User assisted separation of reflections from a single image using a sparsity prior. IEEE Trans. Pattern Anal. Mach. Intell. **29**(9), 1647–1654 (2007)
2. Han, B.J., Sim, J.Y.: Reflection removal using low-rank matrix completion. In: Proceedings of the IEEE Conference on Computer Vision and Pattern Recognition, pp. 5438–5446 (2017)
3. Kong, N., Tai, Y.-W., Shin, S.Y.: A physically-based approach to reflection separation. In: 2012 IEEE Conference on Computer Vision and Pattern Recognition (CVPR), pp. 9–16. IEEE (2012)
4. Schechner, Y.Y., Shamir, J., Kiryati, N.: Polarization-based decorrelation of transparent layers: the inclination angle of an invisible surface. In: Proceedings of the Seventh IEEE International Conference on Computer Vision (ICCV), vol. 2, pp. 814–819. IEEE (1999)
5. Schechner, Y.Y., Kiryati, N., Basri, R.: Separation of transparent layers using focus. Int. J. Comput. Vis. **39**(1), 25–39 (2000)
6. Agrawal, A., Raskar, R., Nayar, S.K., Li, Y.: Removing photography artifacts using gradient projection and flash-exposure sampling. ACM Trans. Graph. (TOG) **24**(3), 828–835 (2005)
7. Li, Y., Brown., M.S.: Single image layer separation using relative smoothness. In: 2014 IEEE Conference on Computer Vision and Pattern Recognition (CVPR), pp. 2752–2759. IEEE Computer Society (2014)
8. Arvanitopoulos, N., Achanta, R., Susstrunk, S.: Single image reflection suppression. In: Proceedings of the IEEE Conference on Computer Vision and Pattern Recognition, pp. 4498–4506 (2017)
9. Fan, Q., Yang, J., Hua, G., Chen, B., Wipf, D.: A generic deep architecture for single image reflection removal and image smoothing. In: 2017 IEEE International Conference on Computer Vision (ICCV), pp. 3238–3247 (2017)
10. Goodfellow, I., et al.: Generative adversarial nets. In: Advances in Neural Information Processing Systems, pp. 2672–2680 (2014)
11. He, K., Zhang, X., Ren, S., Sun, J.: Deep residual learning for image recognition. In: Proceedings of the IEEE Conference on Computer Vision and Pattern Recognition, pp. 770–778 (2016)
12. Simonyan, K., Zisserman, A.: Very deep convolutional networks for large-scale image recognition. arXiv preprint arXiv:1409.1556 (2014)
13. Huynh-Thu, Q., Ghanbari, M.: Scope of validity of PSNR in image/video quality assessment. Electron. Lett. **44**(13), 800–801 (2008)
14. Wang, Z., Bovik, A.C., Sheikh, H.R., Simoncelli, E.P.: Image quality assessment: from error visibility to structural similarity. IEEE Trans. Image Process. **13**(4), 600–612 (2004)
15. Ioffe, S., Szegedy, C.: Batch normalization: accelerating deep network training by reducing internal covariate shift. arXiv preprint arXiv:1502.03167 (2015)

16. Everingham, M., Eslami, S.A., Van Gool, L., Williams, C.K., Winn, J., Zisserman, A.: The pascal visual object classes challenge: a retrospective. Int. J. Comput. Vis. **111**(1), 98–136 (2015)
17. Li, J., et al.: A probabilistic hierarchical model for multi-view and multi-feature classification. In: Thirty-Second AAAI Conference on Artificial Intelligence (2018)
18. Li, J., et al.: Generative multi-view and multi-feature learning for classification. Inf. Fusion **45**, 215–226 (2019)

An Automated Method with Attention Network for Cervical Cancer Scanning

Lijuan Duan[1], Fan Xu[1], Yuanhua Qiao[2(✉)], Di Zhao[3], Tongtong Xu[2], and Chunli Wu[1]

[1] College of Computer Science, Beijing University of Technology,
Beijing 100124, China
[2] College of Mathematics and Physics, Beijing University of Technology,
Beijing 100124, China
qiaoyuanhua@bjut.edu.cn
[3] Computer Network Information Center, Chinese Academy of Sciences,
Beijing 100190, China

Abstract. Cervical cancer is a major threat to women's health and there is a huge population suffering from it in the world. Colposcopy screening is one of the important methods for early diagnosis of cervical cancer. In this paper, we propose a method based on deep learning for colposcopy images recognition, which could be used for early screening of cervical cancer. The method is mainly composed of two parts, the segmentation of the diseased tissue in the colposcopy image and the classification of the image. In our method, the U-Net is used to extract the ROI of images and a deep convolutional neural network is designed to extract features for classification of the ROI. In addition, we introduce the spatial attention mechanism to make the neural network pay more attention to the diseased tissue in images. Experiments demonstrate that the proposed method has a good performance on the colposcopy images, and even achieve nearly test accuracy of 68.03%, which is better than others by ~6%.

Keywords: Cervical cancer · Digital colposcopy · Transformation zone · Attention neural network

1 Introduction

Cervical cancer is a common malignant tumor of the cervix and the fourth most common disease in the world [2]. It is also the major disease in underdeveloped regions and the second most common cause of death among women worldwide, accounting for 12% of all cancers [6]. Fortunately, it is the only malignant tumor that can be prevented and cured. Therefore, the early screening of cervical cancer is important for the prevention of cervical cancer. As the necessary way of cervical cancer screening, colposcopy is a vital measure to help women escape from cervical cancer. It can help reduce the number of unnecessary blinded biopsies and conization procedures as well as the frequency of cauterization therapy

© Springer Nature Switzerland AG 2019
Z. Lin et al. (Eds.): PRCV 2019, LNCS 11858, pp. 267–278, 2019.
https://doi.org/10.1007/978-3-030-31723-2_23

for cervical erosions. It also can help identify abnormal lesions and assist doctors to take proper diagnosis and treatment, which lead to a beneficial reduction in the incidence of cervical cancer [15]. The transformation zone (TZ) is the area of cervical canceration [5]. TZ imaging is of great significance for doctors to diagnose cervical cancer and colposcopy is one of the important means of TZ imaging [24]. International Federation for Cervical Pathology and Colposcopy divides TZ into 3 types: Type1, Type2, and Type3 [20] and here are some example images in Fig. 1. Different types of transition zones correspond to different degrees of tissue lesions. Therefore, correct identification of the type of TZ is an important step in the early screening of cervical cancer. However, only experienced doctors can correctly determine the TZ type based on colposcopy images [16]. So early screening of cervical cancer is extremely difficult in areas with inadequate healthcare resources. In addition, the doctor's diagnosis results are subjective, and long-term work may lead to misdiagnosis. Therefore, it is very important for early screening of cervical cancer to use computer-aided diagnosis (CAD) techniques to help determine the type of TZ. In this paper, we propose a novel method based on deep convolution attention network for TZ type recognition of colposcopy images, which can be used to distinguish the type of colposcopy images. The method is mainly composed of two parts: segmentation of diseased tissue in raw images and classification of diseased tissue. As shown in Fig. 1, because the raw colposcopy images collected by the doctor have many unrelated backgrounds like medical instruments, we use an algorithm to segment the diseased tissue in the raw colposcopy image. Then, we design a deep convolutional neural network (ConvNet) to recognize the segmented images and determine the TZ type of images. In addition, considering the small difference between colposcopy images with different TZ types, we introduce a spatial attention mechanism to enhance the feature extraction power of convolutional neural networks, so that the network can concentrate more on the lesions in the image, which help increase the classification accuracy of our method. In order to get better results, our ConvNet is pre-trained on Imagenet-1K dataset [4] for transfer learning.

The paper is organized as follows: In Sect. 2, related research is introduced; In Sect. 3, details about our method are given. In Sect. 4, experiments are done to demonstrate the effect of our method. In Sect. 5, conclusions are shown.

2   Related Work

Recently, many automatic or semi-automatic image analysis algorithms have been applied to cancer detection and diagnosis [18,30,31]. As for the CAD of cervical cancer, because the raw colposcopy images collected by the doctor have many unrelated backgrounds like medical instruments, automatic detection of the region of interest (ROI) which contains the relevant information like tissue is of critical importance for more accurate disease classification [21]. ROI can be detected by color features [11,19,29] and texture features [13,23,27]. Gaussian Mixture Model can also be used for the purpose of ROI detection [32].

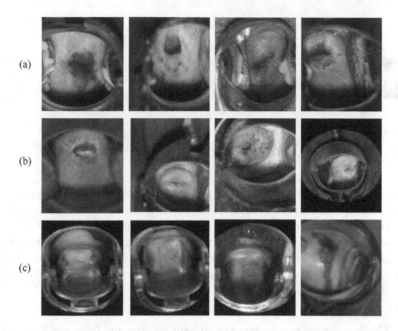

Fig. 1. Some example images with different TZ types. (a) Type 1, (b) Type 2, (c) Type 3.

Edward [8] utilizes nearly 1000 annotated cervigram images to automatically locate the ROI of the cervix, where both color features and texture features are extracted from the ROI on cervigram images and a classifier is used to verify results of the algorithm on cervigram images, and it achieves compared results to an experienced expert. Das [3] proposes a novel humanitarian technology for ROI extraction and specular region removal (SR), in which HSV space is considered for extracting the cervix boundary in the colposcopy image. [22] proposes an algorithm based on K-means clustering in one chromaticity layer from LAB color space for automatic ROI segmentation. With the development of deep learning, many artificial neural networks (ANN) has been applied for detecting cervical cancer. Different ANN architecture and their performance are given and analyzed Table 2. The early diagnosis of cervical cancer is achieved by LeNet [7], VGG16, and VGG19 with transfer learning [14], equipped with a classifier such as random forest [12,28], softmax classifier, and SVM. Haidar [1] found that logistic regression and random forest usually misclassify CIN1 (a kind of cervix precancerous lesion) as normal with the segments of one image for testing and the rest for training.

3   Methodology

The architecture of the proposed method for the recognition of the colposcopy images' TZ type is shown in Fig. 2. It mainly consists of five steps: segmentation

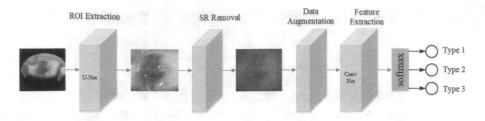

Fig. 2. The architecture of our proposed method.

of diseased tissue, removal of specular reflections (SR), data augmentation, feature extraction, and feature classification. Firstly, the U-Net network is used to extract the diseased tissue in the colposcopy image. Secondly, a specific algorithm is applied to remove the SR from the image. Thirdly, some data augmentation techniques are utilized to reduce overfitting. Fourthly, a convolutional neural attention network is designed to extract the features of images. Finally, features are classified by a softmax classifier.

Data. The dataset we use for our experiment is obtained from the Kaggle competition in 2017[1]. It contains three types of cervix images: Type 1, Type 2 and Type 3. All images were released in two stages. The first stage dataset consists of 249 images of Type 1, 781 images of Type 2 and 450 images of Type 3, and the second stage dataset consists of 1187 images of Type 1, 639 images of Type 2 and 1972 images of Type 3. However, according to the official introduction, the data from the second stage contains images of the same patients and images of high noise, and it is suggested that the second stage dataset would result in poor training [14]. Therefore, images from the second stage are not selected for our experiment. Finally, 20% of the first stage data are randomly selected as the test set and the rest is for the training set, and the final distribution of dataset is exhibited in Table 1.

Table 1. The distribution of dataset for our experiment.

Cervix type	Type1	Type2	Type3	Total
Train	199	617	356	1172
Test	50	155	89	294

Image Segmentation. The raw colposcopy images (shown as (a) in Fig. 3) contain superfluous features such as vaginal sidewalls and speculums, which greatly affects the recognition of colposcopy images. Therefore, they should be removed

---

[1] https://www.kaggle.com/c/intel-mobileodt-cervical-cancer-screening/data.

from images for higher recognition accuracy. In this part, we use U-net to extract ROI of images. The U-net stands out with absolute superiority in 2015 ISBI competition of cell edge detection. It consists of a contraction path and an expansion path to obtain context information and accurate location of cell edge respectively [7]. Firstly, we use the bounding boxes labeled by professional doctors to train the network, and then the trained network is applied to extract the ROI of images. The result is shown in Fig. 3.

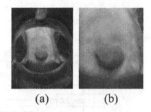

(a)   (b)

Fig. 3. (a) The raw image. (b) the image after ROI extraction

Specular Reflections Removal. The appearance of SR is due to the exposure of light to the liquid during colposcopy scanning, which appears as a bright white spot on colposcopy images [17]. So, after extracting the ROI, the SR should also be removed from images for better performance. In this part, we use the strategy mentioned in [3] to remove the SR in images. The specific operation process is shown in Fig. 4. The first step is to convert an image into a grayscale image and then top hat filtering is applied. After that, the image is converted to a binary image, which acts as a mask, and then it is applied to the original image to obtain the image which the SR is already removed from. Finally, the SR region is filled according to the surrounding pixels to get final images.

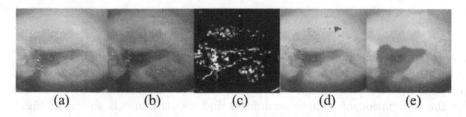

(a)   (b)   (c)   (d)   (e)

Fig. 4. The process of SR detection and removal. (a) the original image, (b) the grayscale image of the original one, (c) the binary mask, (d) the image without SR, (e) the final image.

Data Augmentation. Due to the limited experimental data, in particular, there are only about 400 images per class for training, which is totally not enough for training a neural network, we use data enhancement technology to expand the training data to prevent over-fitting after extracting the ROI from the raw image. The main operations include random cropping, vertical and horizontal flipping, random rotation. Finally, the experimental training data is increased by four times.

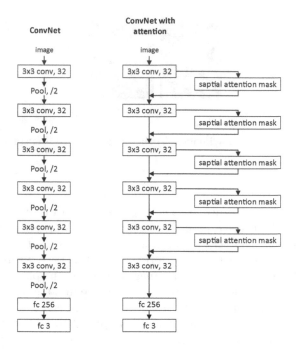

Fig. 5. The architecture of the proposed ConvNet (left) and ConvNet with attention (right, pooling layers are omitted for simplify).

Deep Convolution Neural Network. Because the training data is too less to train a mainstream deep convolutional neural network with too many parameters, like vgg16 [26] and resnet [9], we design a deep convolutional neural network for the recognition of colposcopy images and its structure is shown in Fig. 5. We also compare the performance of our proposed network and ResNet on our dataset in the experimental section. The main idea of our network is that the downsampling operation should be performed after each convolutional layer so that the network can extract features quickly and efficiently with fewer parameters. The size of all convolutional filters is 3×3. After 6 convolutional layers and 6 downsampling layers, we get feature maps of 4×4 for an input size of 256×256. Then two fully connected layers and the softmax function are applied to classify the extracted features. In addition, to prevent over-fitting, we add a dropout operation between fully connected layers, which is set to 0.5.

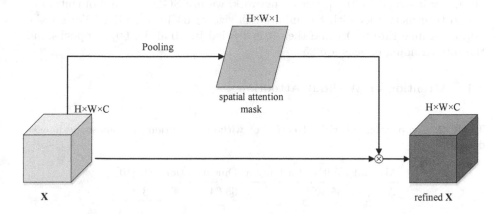

Fig. 6. The architecture of the spatial attention model.

Attention Neural Network. From Fig. 1, we observe that the lesion tissue of colposcopy images is mostly in the center of images and the surrounding area is mostly normal tissue. Moreover, the lesion tissue is key features for distinguishing different TZ types. For that reason, we introduce attention mechanism to make the network pay more attention to the lesion area in images and suppress those background areas, which would boost the feature extraction power and help improve the recognition accuracy of our network.

According to [4], pooling operations along the channel axis can be an effective way to highlight informative regions, so the structure of our attention module is shown in Fig. 6. For the given input $\mathbf{X}$, the spatial attention is computed as:

$$\mathbf{M} = \sigma(Avgpool(\mathbf{X})), \tag{1}$$

where σ denotes the sigmoid function. Then we have the following way to refine the input $\mathbf{X}$:

$$\tilde{\mathbf{X}} = \mathbf{M} \otimes \mathbf{X}, \tag{2}$$

where $\otimes$ denotes element-wise multiplication and $\tilde{\mathbf{X}}$ is refined feature maps by attention mask $\mathbf{M}$. Because the spatial attention model is very light, we add it to all the convolutional layers to build the attention neural network and its structure is shown in Fig. 7.

4   Experiments

Training Details. All images are resized to 256 * 256 and the per-pixel value of images is scaled to [0, 1]. For all network, we use SGD with a momentum of 0.9 to train networks with the mini-batch size of 64 in one GPU. We set the initial learning rate to 0.1 and then it is divided by 10 at 30, 60, 90 epochs and the total training epochs are 95.

4.1   Attention or Without Attention

Table 2. Comparisons of with attention or without attention on colposcopy images dataset.

Method	Without attention	Our attention	SE [10]
Acc (%)	65.30	65.64	63.2

Firstly, we use experiments to illustrate the impact of the spatial attention mechanism in our proposed network and the experimental results are shown in Table 2. We can see that the ConvNet with attention achieves a better result than the ConvNet without attention on the test set by 0.34% and we also found that our approach achieves better results than other attention mechanisms such as SE [10]. SE even lead to worse results. Maybe SE [10] brings additional parameters, which makes it difficult to be well trained while ours does not bring additional parameters. The experiment shows that the spatial attention mechanism can enhance the performance of our proposed network. In addition, we use the Method [25] to visualize the results of the network and they are shown in Fig. 7. We can see that spatial attention allows the network to focus on lesions in the images.

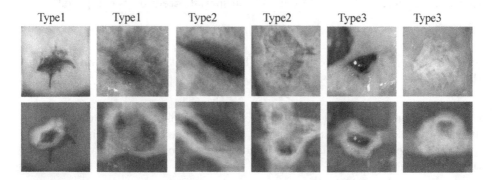

Fig. 7. Grad-CAM [25] visualization results of attention network. The grad-CAM visualization is calculated for the last convolutional outputs.

4.2   Comparison of Different Classification Networks.

In this part, we compared the performance of our proposed network with other baseline networks on colposcopy images dataset and results are shown in Table 3. We can see that our proposed network has better performance than other networks, and what is more, the test accuracy rate of our network is higher than resnet18 by 0.7%. Because our network has fewer layers than others, it can achieve better performance when the dataset is small.

Table 3. Comparisons of test accuracy rates (%) on colposcopy images dataset. The best result is shown in bold.

Network	Param	Acc (%)
Resnet18 [9]	11.69M	64.62
Resnet34 [9]	21.8M	63.90
VGG16 [26]	165M	52.71
Ours	0.33M	**65.30**

4.3   The Result of Transfer Learning

Since the dataset is too small, we also introduce transfer learning to further enhance the performance of our network. Firstly, we pre-train our network on the Imagenet dataset [4] and then fine-tune the pre-trained network on the cervical cancer dataset. The experimental results are shown in Table 4. We can see that when all networks adopt transfer learning, our network can still achieve best results with fewer parameters.

Table 4. Comparisons of different networks when transfer learning is introduced. "TL" means transfer learning.

Network	Param	Acc (%)
Resnet34 + TL	21.8M	67.68
VGG16 + TL	165M	67.34
Ours (with attention) + TL	0.33M	**68.03**

4.4   Comparison with Other Methods

Finally, we compare the performance of our proposed method with other methods on colposcopy images dataset. The results are shown in Table 5. Note that all the methods use the same dataset from the kaggle competition and different methods adopt different image processing technology. We can see that our method achieve ~6% higher accuracy than [14] while we all use deep learning.

Table 5. Comparisons of different methods on colposcopy images dataset.

Method	Navdeep Kaur [14]	Ours
Acc (%)	62.15	68.03

5 Conclusion

In this paper, we propose a method based on deep learning for cervical TZ type classification, which can be used for early screening of cervical cancer. The method is mainly composed of two parts, the segmentation of the diseased tissue in the colposcopy image and the classification of the image. In our method, the U-Net is used to extract the ROI of images and a deep convolutional neural network is designed to extract features for classification of the ROI. In addition, we introduce the spatial attention mechanism to make the neural network can pay more attention to the diseased tissue in images and We also introduce transfer learning to overcome the overfitting of our network because of too little training data. Experiments demonstrate that the proposed method has a good performance on the cervical cancer dataset. In addition, we also find that the spatial attention mechanism can improve the classification performance of the convolutional neural network. We hope that our proposed method will assist in the early screening of cervical cancer.

Acknowledgement. This research is partially sponsored by National Natural Science Foundation of China (No. 61572004,61672070), the Project of Beijing Municipal Education Commission (No. KZ201910005008,KM201911232003), the Research Fund from Beijing Innovation Center for Future Chips (No. KYJJ2018004).

References

1. Almubarak, H.A., et al.: Convolutional neural network based localized classification of uterine cervical cancer digital histology images. Proc. Comput. Sci. **114**, 281–287 (2017)
2. Asiedu, M.N., et al.: Image processing and machine learning techniques to automate diagnosis of Lugol's iodine cervigrams for a low-cost point-of-care digital colposcope. In: Optics and Biophotonics in Low-Resource Settings IV, vol. 10485, p. 1048508. International Society for Optics and Photonics (2018)
3. Das, A., Choudhury, A.: A novel humanitarian technology for early detection of cervical neoplasia: ROI extraction and SR detection. In: 2017 IEEE Region 10 Humanitarian Technology Conference (R10-HTC), pp. 457–460. IEEE (2017)
4. Deng, J., Dong, W., Socher, R., Li, L.J., Li, K., Fei-Fei, L.: ImageNet: a large-scale hierarchical image database. In: 2009 IEEE Conference on Computer Vision and Pattern Recognition, pp. 248–255. IEEE (2009)
5. Elson, D.A., Riley, R.R., Lacey, A., Thordarson, G., Talamantes, F.J., Arbeit, J.M.: Sensitivity of the cervical transformation zone to estrogen-induced squamous carcinogenesis. Cancer Res. **60**(5), 1267–1275 (2000)

6. Ferlay, J., et al.: Cancer incidence and mortality worldwide: IARC CancerBase. In: GLOBOCAN 2012 v10, vol. 11 (2012)
7. Fernandes, K., Chicco, D., Cardoso, J.S., Fernandes, J.: Supervised deep learning embeddings for the prediction of cervical cancer diagnosis. Peer J. Comput. Sci. **4**, e154 (2018)
8. Gordon, S., Zimmerman, G., Long, R., Antani, S., Jeronimo, J., Greenspan, H.: Content analysis of uterine cervix images: initial steps toward content based indexing and retrieval of cervigrams. In: Medical Imaging 2006: Image Processing, vol. 6144, p. 61444U. International Society for Optics and Photonics (2006)
9. He, K., Zhang, X., Ren, S., Sun, J.: Deep residual learning for image recognition. In: Proceedings of the IEEE Conference on Computer Vision and Pattern Recognition, pp. 770–778 (2016)
10. Hu, J., Shen, L., Sun, G.: Squeeze-and-excitation networks. In: The IEEE Conference on Computer Vision and Pattern Recognition (CVPR), June 2018
11. Hu, Z., Tang, J., Wang, Z., Zhang, K., Zhang, L., Sun, Q.: Deep learning for image-based cancer detection and diagnosis- a survey. Pattern Recogn. **83**, 134–149 (2018)
12. Jaiswal, M., et al.: Characterization of cervigram image sharpness using multiple self-referenced measurements and random forest classifiers. In: Optics and Biophotonics in Low-Resource Settings IV, vol. 10485, p. 1048507. International Society for Optics and Photonics (2018)
13. Ji, Q., Engel, J., Craine, E.: Classifying cervix tissue patterns with texture analysis. Pattern Recogn. **33**(9), 1561–1573 (2000)
14. Kaur, N., Panigrahi, N., Mittal, A.: Automated cervical cancer screening using transfer learning. In: Proceedings of International Conference on Recent Advances in Engineering Science and Management, pp. 2110–2119 (2017)
15. Kessler, T.A.: Cervical cancer: prevention and early detection. In: Seminars in Oncology Nursing, vol. 33, pp. 172–183. Elsevier (2017)
16. Khan, M.J., et al.: Asccp colposcopy standards. role of colposcopy, benefits, potential harms, and terminology for colposcopic practice. J. Lower Genital Tract Dis. **21**(4), 223–229 (2017)
17. Kudva, V., Prasad, K., Guruvare, S.: Detection of specular reflection and segmentation of cervix region in uterine cervix images for cervical cancer screening. IRBM **38**(5), 281–291 (2017)
18. Lee, H., Chen, Y.P.P.: Image based computer aided diagnosis system for cancer detection. Expert Syst. Appl. **42**(12), 5356–5365 (2015)
19. Li, W., Gu, J., Ferris, D., Poirson, A.: Automated image analysis of uterine cervical images. In: Medical Imaging 2007: Computer-Aided Diagnosis, vol. 6514, p. 65142P. International Society for Optics and Photonics (2007)
20. Luyten, A., et al.: Utility and reproducibility of the international federation for cervical pathology and colposcopy classification of transformation zones in daily practice: a multicenter study of the german colposcopy network. J. Lower Genital Tract Dis. **19**(3), 185–188 (2015)
21. Naganawa, S., Sato, C., Kumada, H., Ishigaki, T., Miura, S., Takizawa, O.: Apparent diffusion coefficient in cervical cancer of the uterus: comparison with the normal uterine cervix. Eur. Radiol. **15**(1), 71–78 (2005)
22. Obukhova, N.A., Motyko, A.A., Kang, U., Bae, S.J., Lee, D.S.: Automated image analysis in multispectral system for cervical cancer diagnostic. In: 2017 20th Conference of Open Innovations Association (FRUCT), pp. 345–351. IEEE (2017)

23. Reuzé, S., et al.: Prediction of cervical cancer recurrence using textural features extracted from 18f-FDG PET images acquired with different scanners. Oncotarget **8**(26), 43169 (2017)

24. Saslow, D., et al.: American cancer society, American society for colposcopy and cervical pathology, and American society for clinical pathology screening guidelines for the prevention and early detection of cervical cancer. CA: Cancer J. Clin. **62**(3), 147–172 (2012)

25. Selvaraju, R.R., Cogswell, M., Das, A., Vedantam, R., Parikh, D., Batra, D.: Grad-CAM: visual explanations from deep networks via gradient-based localization. In: Proceedings of the IEEE International Conference on Computer Vision, pp. 618–626 (2017)

26. Simonyan, K., Zisserman, A.: Very deep convolutional networks for large-scale image recognition. arXiv preprint arXiv:1409.1556 (2014)

27. Srinivasan, Y., Nutter, B., Mitra, S., Phillips, B., Sinzinger, E.: Classification of cervix lesions using filter bank-based texture mode. In: 19th IEEE Symposium on Computer-Based Medical Systems, CBMS 2006, pp. 832–840. IEEE (2006)

28. Sun, G., Li, S., Cao, Y., Lang, F.: Cervical cancer diagnosis based on random forest. Int. J. Perform. Eng. **13**(4), 446–457 (2017)

29. Xue, Z., Antani, S., Long, L.R., Jeronimo, J., Thoma, G.R.: Comparative performance analysis of cervix ROI extraction and specular reflection removal algorithms for uterine cervix image analysis. In: Medical Imaging 2007: Image Processing, vol. 6512, p. 65124I. International Society for Optics and Photonics (2007)

30. Yang, Z., Yang, D., Dyer, C., He, X., Smola, A., Hovy, E.: Hierarchical attention networks for document classification. In: Proceedings of the 2016 Conference of the North American Chapter of the Association for Computational Linguistics: Human Language Technologies, pp. 1480–1489 (2016)

31. Zhang, J., Xia, Y., Wu, Q., Xie, Y.: Classification of medical images and illustrations in the biomedical literature using synergic deep learning. CoRR abs/1706.09092 (2017)

32. Zimmerman-Moreno, G., Greenspan, H.: Automatic detection of specular reflections in uterine cervix images. In: Medical Imaging 2006: Image Processing, vol. 6144, p. 61446E. International Society for Optics and Photonics (2006)

Graph-Based Scale-Aware Network for Human Parsing

Beibei Yang(iD), Changqian Yu(iD), Jiahui Liu(iD), Changxin Gao(✉)(iD), and Nong Sang(iD)

Key Laboratory of Ministry of Education for Image Processing and Intelligent Control, School of Artificial Intelligence and Automation, Huazhong University of Science and Technology, Wuhan, China
{m_bbyang,changqian_yu,ljh_auto,cgao,nsang}@hust.edu.cn

Abstract. Recent work has made considerable progress in exploring contextual information for human parsing with the Fully Convolutional Network framework. However, there still exist two challenges: (1) inherent relative relationships between parts; (2) scale variation of human parts. To tackle both problems, we propose a Graph-Based Scale-Aware Network for human parsing. First, we embed a Graph-Based Part Reasoning Layer into the backbone network to reason the relative relationship between human parts. Then we construct a Scale-Aware Context Embedding Layer, which consists of two branches to capture scale-specific contextual information, with different receptive fields and scale-specific supervisions. In addition, we adopt an edge supervision to further improve the performance. Extensive experimental evaluations demonstrate that the proposed model performs favorably against the state-of-the-art human parsing methods. More specifically, our algorithm achieves 53.32% (mIoU) on the LIP dataset.

Keywords: Human parsing · Segmentation · Graph-based reasoning · Scale-aware embedding

1 Introduction

Understanding the fine-grained semantic parts of a human image in the wild is one of the most fundamental tasks in computer vision. It plays a crucial role in higher-level application domains, such as human behavior analysis [10, 15], fine-grained recognition [8], pose estimation [25], and fashion synthesis [30].

Recent approaches have made considerable success in the human parsing task directly based on the semantic segmentation methods [1, 4, 19]. However, most of them are less optimal for human parsing by ignoring the specific challenges of this task. Compared to general semantic segmentation, the human parsing task still has two challenges: (1) Inherent relative relationship between human parts. For example, as shown in Fig. 1(a), the head is on the top, next to the torso, while the feet at the bottom. This relationship helps the network to make correct

© Springer Nature Switzerland AG 2019
Z. Lin et al. (Eds.): PRCV 2019, LNCS 11858, pp. 279–290, 2019.
https://doi.org/10.1007/978-3-030-31723-2_24

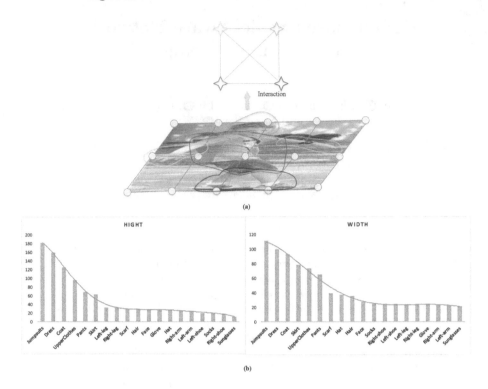

Fig. 1. (a) There is an inherent relative relationship between human parts, implying the interaction between human parts. (b) There is a scale variation in human parts, for example, sunglasses are too small, relative to jumpsuits, to be segment precisely in pixel level.

recognition. (2) Scale variation of human parts. As shown in the statistics of Fig. 1(b), the height and width of different parts vary dramatically, which makes the network hard to segment correctly. For example, sunglasses are too small, relative to jumpsuits, to be segmented precisely in pixel level. Therefore, different scale of part requires different scale of receptive field, which needs consideration in the network architecture design.

To address the above-mentioned problems, we propose a novel Graph-Based Scale-Aware Network (GSNet) for human parsing. It mainly has the Graph-based Part Reasoning Layer (GPLayer) to reason the relative dependence between human parts and the Scale-aware Context Embedding Layer (SCLayer) to capture the scale-specific contextual information. The GPLayer first maps the feature space learned by the convolutional network to the interaction space. Then the GPLayer constructs one graph based on the interaction space, some nodes of which represents the part of the human. According to the information propagation between nodes, we can model the inherent relative relationship, which can capture the long-range information easily. In addition, the SCLayer adopts a two-branch architecture, which has different receptive fields at each branch with the scale-specific supervisions. According to the scale distribution of different parts, we divide the ground truth of human parts to different groups as the scale-specific supervisions. Moreover, we employ an attention mechanism to embed the scale-specific context captured by the SCLayer.

Our main contributions are summarized as follows:

- We propose a novel Graph-based Scale-Aware Network (GSNet) for human parsing.
- We present a Graph-Based Part Reasoning Layer (GPLayer) to model the inherent relative relationships between human parts.
- We design a Scale-Aware Context Embedding Layer (SCLayer) to address the problem of scale variation of human parts.
- Extensive experimental evaluations demonstrate that the proposed model performs favorably against the state-of-the-art approaches. More specifically, our algorithm achieves 53.32% (mIoU) on the LIP dataset.

2 Related Work

2.1 Semantic Segmentation

As human parsing is a representative branch of semantic segmentation, the methods applied to semantic segmentation are parallel to human parsing. Recently, Fully Convolutional Networks (FCN) [19] are popular configurations for semantic segmentation. Thereupon, many researches have made effort based on FCN (e.g., [3,13,20]). Typically, DeepLab [5] proposed atrous convolution (a.k.a. dilated convolution) to dilate the receptive fields in fully convolutional networks, and obtained a high performance in the human parsing task, and the spatial pyramid structures [5,17,28], to learn the multi-scale contextual information, are popular in the semantic segmentation networks.

Although the semantic segmentation methods have remarkable power to have a high performance in human parsing, they are less optimal to boost the performance, aiming to specific human parsing, for ignoring the specific challenges of this task. In this work, our goal is to design a human parsing specific network to figure out some challenges that we have mentioned in this task.

2.2 Human Parsing

As to human parsing, a fine-grained semantic segmentation task, has attracted mass attention due to the more and more popular applications about people. Ordinarily, there are two main directions to deal with the human parsing task. One is employing extra human pose information, such as human pose [25] and human attributes [21], to generate hierarchical parse graph to assist the human parsing task. The other one is training an end-to-end network with the semantic information [17,24,26]. For the reason that extra human pose information is another expense, we develop an end-to-end network in an efficient and concise way.

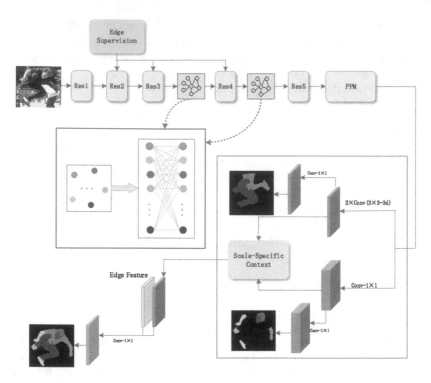

Fig. 2. Graph-based Scale-Aware Network (GSNet). Graph-Based Part Reasoning Layer (as shown in red frame) is inserted after Res3 and Res4 of the baseline model PSPNet. Then Scale-Aware Context Embedding Layer (as shown in green frame) is after the Pyramid Pooling Module (PPM), which consists of a small-scale branch, a large-scale branch, and a scale-specific context module to promote the features. Eventually, feature maps of edge supervision module are integrated together to refine the final parsing result. (Color figure online)

There are more and more researchers shift attention to human parsing from semantic segmentation, with the two mentioned directions. A Co-CNN [16] architecture integrates the local and global context, semantic edge context, cross super-pixel neighborhood context and within-super-pixel context into a unified framework. An attention-based model [6] is proposed to softly weight the multi-scale features at each pixel location and deal with the multi-scale problem of a whole image in the dataset of human parsing. A novel self-supervised structure-sensitive learning approach [11] is proposed to impose human pose structures on the parsing results. Following previous work, JPPNet [14] incorporates the human parsing and pose estimation task into a unified network. Although these human parsing methods have taken into account the characteristics of human parsing, they are still limited in various ways. Co-CNN and attention-to-scale model do not explore human structure information just like general semantic segmentation methods. Moreover, the jointed method takes full advantage of human structure, but extra labeled data is needed and the coupled optimization problems may appear. In this paper, we develop a novel human parsing specific network in an efficient and concise way.

3 Graph-Based Scale-Aware Network

The architecture of the proposed Graph-based Scale-Aware Network (GSNet) is shown in Fig. 2, Graph-Based Part Reasoning Layer (GPLayer) is inserted after Res3 and Res4 of the baseline model PSPNet [28]. Then Scale-Aware Context Embedding Layer (SCLayer) is after the Pyramid Pooling Module (PPM) [28], in which there are small-scale branch and large-scale branch, and a scale-specific context module to promote the features. Eventually, feature maps of edge supervision module are integrated together to refine the final parsing result.

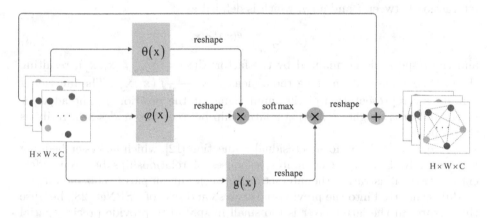

Fig. 3. Graph-Based Part Reasoning Layer (GPLayer). The nodes in different represent different parts of human. ⊗ denotes matrix multiplication, and ⊕ denotes element-wise sum.

3.1 Graph-Based Part Reasoning Layer

Inherent relative relationship between human parts is an important point to make correct recognition for human parsing. Draw on the previous work [2, 7,23], we develop a Graph-Based Part Reasoning Layer (GPLayer) to reason the relative dependence between human parts as shown in Fig. 3. The GPLayer maps the feature space learned by the convolutional network to the interaction space, to capture the location dependencies of human parts more simply. Then reasoning the relative relationship between human parts is simplified to model the correlation between human parts in the interaction space, which is defined as:

$$\mathbf{z}_i = W_z \mathbf{y}_i + \mathbf{x}_i, \tag{1}$$

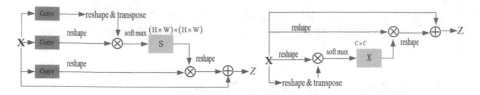

Fig. 4. Scale-specific context module to promote features across spatial dimensions (left) and channel dimensions (right) simultaneously.

$$y_i = \frac{1}{\mathcal{C}(\mathbf{x})} \sum_{\forall j} f(\mathbf{x}_i, \mathbf{x}_j) g(\mathbf{x}_j),$$ (2)

where i is the index of an output position in space and j is the index that enumerates all possible positions of feature map. A pairwise function f computes interaction between i and all j, which is defined as

$$f(\mathbf{x}_i, \mathbf{x}_j) = e^{\theta(\mathbf{x}_i)^T \phi(\mathbf{x}_j)},$$ (3)

and the response is normalized by the factor: $\mathcal{C}(\mathbf{x}) = \sum_{\forall j} f(\mathbf{x}_i, \mathbf{x}_j)$, resulting the softmax computation along the dimension j: $\frac{1}{\mathcal{C}(x)} f(\mathbf{x}_i, \mathbf{x}_j)$. The function g computes a representation of the input signal at the position j. The adjacent matrix f learns weights reflecting relationship between two nodes arbitrarily as shown in Fig. 1.

In Eq. 1, $\mathbf{y}_i$ and $+\mathbf{x}_i$ form a residual connection [12], which allows embedding Eq. 2 exactly. Equation 2 computes responses of relationships between different locations, illustrating the interaction between human parts. This interaction module is inserted into the previous layers res3 and res4 of PSPNet [28], because the features in the latter layer is too small in spatial to provide precise spatial information, and in former layer contain too less semantic information.

3.2   Scale-Aware Context Embedding Layer

It is widespread that the scales of object instances vary in a wide range, which undermines the performance of segmentation, especially for very large objects. In view of this problem, we develop a Scale-Aware Context Embedding Layer (SCLayer) as shown in Fig. 2 to cope with the scale variation problem. As is known to all, due to convolution strides, the receptive field is extended significantly. Whereas inefficient computation issue appears, if convolutions are stacked too much. Enlightened by atrous convolution [5], which doesn't give rise to additional parameters, we incorporate multi-branch structure with different dilation and different number of layers.

As shown in the Fig. 2, our SCLayer consists of a multi-branch structure with scale-specific supervisions and a scale-specific module. In multi-branch structure, the small-scale branch is composed of a 1×1 convolution, and the large-scale branch is composed of two 3×3 convolutions with dilation rate of 3. Specifically, a dilated 3×3 convolution could have the same receptive field as the convolution with kernel size of $3 + 2(dilation\ rate - 1)$. Besides, we divide the ground truth of human parts to different groups as the scale-specific supervisions.

Only by concatenating to integrate the features from multi-branch structure, the result is too coarse. Therefore we should employ something to optimize the result. In order to promote the intrinsic information of human structure and inspired by [6,9], a scale-specific context is designed into SCLayer to promote rich contextual dependencies and emphasize interdependent feature maps.

As shown in Fig. 4, the matrix S of module A, whose dimension is $(H \times W) \times (H \times W)$, is the spatial attention map. The result feature Z in module A is a weighted sum of the features at all positions and original features, which selectively aggregates contexts according to the spatial attention map. Moreover, the matrix X of module B, whose dimension is $C \times C$, is the channel attention map. The result feature Z in module B is a weighted sum of the features at all channels and original features, which emphasizes class-dependent feature maps and helps to boost feature discriminability.

3.3 Edge Module

There is a common problem between segmentation task and human parsing. The pixels around boundary are usually confused with different categories because of their contradictory locations that they are adjacent spatially to more than one category. Therefore, we need to enhance the distinction of features, namely inter-class distinction [27]. For this purpose, we adopt an edge module [18] aimed at learning the contour of human to further sharp and refine the prediction, as illustrated in Fig. 2. Moreover, to extract the accurate semantic boundary, we apply the explicit supervision of semantic boundary.

4 Experiments

4.1 Data

We evaluate our algorithm on the public human parsing dataset, Look into Person (LIP) [11], which contains 50,462 images with fine-grained annotations at pixel-level with 19 semantic human part labels (hat, hair, gloves, sunglasses, upper-clothes, dress, coat, socks, pants, jumpsuits, scarf, skirt, face, left-arm, right-arm, left-leg, right-leg, left-shoe, and right-shoe) and one background label. The images of LIP are collected from the real-world scenarios containing people appearing with challenging poses, viewpoints, heavy occlusions, various appearances and in wide range of resolutions. Moreover, the background of images of LIP is also more complex and diverse than the one in previous counterparts. All those challenges give rise to more difficulties for semantic segmentation.

4.2   Implementation Details

Loss Function. Our network is an end-to-end system, and the outputs consist of scale-branches results, attention module results, edge prediction and parsing result. Hence, the loss can be formulated as:

$$L = L_{parsing} + L_{scale} + L_{attention} + L_{edge}, \tag{4}$$

$$L_* = -\log \hat{y}_i(l) \tag{5}$$

Training Detail. We implement the proposed framework in PyTorch [22], and adopt PSPNet [28] as the baseline network. We utilize the stochastic gradient descent (SGD) solver with batch size 12, momentum 0.9 and weight decay 0.0005. Inspired by the semantic segmentation optimization [5,28], we use the poly learning rate policy $\left(1 - \frac{iter}{\max iter}\right)^{power}$. We set the base learning rate as 0.001. As for the input image size, we resize it to 384×384. The networks are fine-tuned for approximately 150 epochs. For data augmentation, we apply the random scaling (from 0.5 to 1.5), cropping and left-right flipping during training.

Table 1. Comparison of our network in various module settings on the validation set on LIP. The results are obtained without left-right flipping except for the last row. GP means Graph-Based Part Reasoning Layer. SC_o means Scale-aware Context Embedding Layer without scale-specific context module. SC means Scale-aware Context Embedding Layer.

Method	Pixel acc	Mean acc	mIoU
PSP [28]	86.01	60.56	49.55
PSP+GP	85.94	61.73	49.96
PSP+GP+SC_o	86.34	62.82	51.17
PSP+GP+SC	86.55	63.18	51.48
PSP+GP+SC+Edge	86.90	64.08	52.55
PSP+GP+SC+Edge+Flip (ours)	**87.28**	**65.03**	**53.32**

4.3   Experimental Results

To prove the effectiveness of each module, the result of each module is reported in Table 1. The baseline model includes no proposed modules, which the final result is extracted from PSPNet and is 1/16 to the input size.

Table 2. Comparison of performance on the validation set of LIP with state-of-arts methods.

Method	Pixel acc	Mean acc	mIoU
Deeplab [5] (VGG-16)	82.66	51.64	41.64
Attention [6]	83.43	54.39	42.92
Deeplab (ResNet-101)	84.09	55.62	44.80
SS-NAN [29]	87.59	56.03	47.92
JPPNet [14]	86.39	62.32	51.37
our	**87.28**	**65.03**	**53.32**

Graph-Based Part Reasoning Layer. To evaluate the effectiveness of each module, we first conduct experiments by introducing GPLayer. As shown in Table 1, we can find it brings about 0.41% improvement on mIoU, which demonstrates that the interaction information between human parts can assist the fine-grained parsing. The reason for no massive improvement like other modules, is that the baseline model is powerful enough, that no many labels of parts are confused spatially nonsensically just as shown in the baseline model result in Fig. 5(a). The right-leg is mislabeled as right-arm on account of their adjoining positions and absence of interaction between human parts.

Scale-Aware Context Embedding Layer. To figure out the importance of matching receptive field, we conduct experiments by further introducing Scale-aware Context Embedding Layer without scale-specific context module, namely multi-branch structure. From Table 1, nearly 1.21% improvement can be found owing to matching receptive field by multi-branch structure. Oversized receptive field is dispensable for small parts, and even undermine their performances. Moreover, too small receptive field is certain to ruin the performances of large parts as shown in the baseline model result in Fig. 5(b) and (c). Part of dress is mislabeled as upper-clothes, more seriously, the dress is cut apart into a dress with upper-clothes outside. The reason of this phenomenon is that the receptive field is too small to cover the entire coat, which is a large part.

In order to optimize the result from multi-branch structure, we further introduce a scale-specific context module, namely the entire SCLayer. We report the performance of 51.48% after adding the scale-specific context module to from the entire SCLayer in Table 1. The response of result is heightened by the weighted sum of features, especially available for those pixels that are so small that are drowned by the surrounding pixels and mislabeled as shown in Fig. 5(d). Right-arm is drowned completely in the baseline model result.

Edge Module. Based on all above modules, appending edge module still brings nearly 1% boost. Its the reason that the contours of the parts are constraints when separating a human body into semantic parts. Furthermore, the features from multiple branches, which include various details of parts, would further promote parts prediction as shown in the baseline model result in Fig. 5(e). Finally, fusing with the flipped images has 0.77% gain.

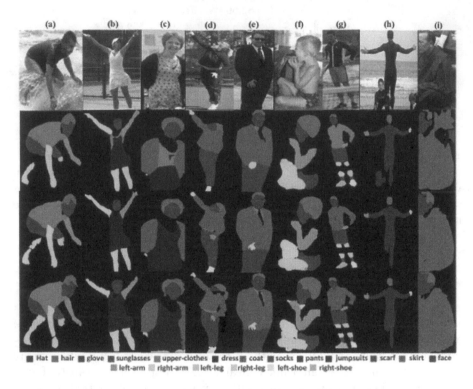

Fig. 5. Visual comparison among baseline model and our network. In each column, from top to bottom, the pictures input image, result of baseline model, result of our model, and ground truth.

Comparison with State-of-the-Arts. We evaluate the performance of our network on the validation dataset of LIP and compare it with other state-of-the-art methods, as reported in Table 2. We notice that the mIoU of our network significantly outperforms other approaches. Specially, that our network outperform SS-NAN [29], demonstrates the multi-branch structure is light but extremely efficient. Moreover, JPPNet [14] achieves the performance of 51.37% by adding extra pose into the network. Nevertheless, our network is simple and have no extra pose information, but have archived a better performance. The improvements over the state-of-the-art methods prove the effectiveness of our network for human parsing. There are another some typical visual examples demonstrating superiority of our network over the baseline model shown in Fig. 5. Arms, legs and shoes, that are divided into the left side and right side, crossing together, makes the parsing more difficult as shown in Fig. 5(f). Some categories have so similar characteristics, that they are mislabeled mutually, as the coat is mislabeled as upper-clothes shown in Fig. 5(g). When there are more than one person appearing in the image, the segmentation target tend to be disturbed by other people, as shown in Fig. 5(h). In the wild, there are a lot of time, the background is relatively complex to be extracted clearly as many similar pixels of background are regarded as coat of human in Fig. 5(i). Stated thus, our proposed network have substantially realized superiority over powerful baseline model.

5   Conclusion

In this paper, we propose a novel Graph-based Scale-Aware Network (GSNet) to address two problems, namely inherent relative relationships between part and scale variation of human parts. We design a Graph-Based Part Reasoning Layer into the backbone network to reason the relative relationships between different human parts. Then we construct a Scale-Aware Context Embedding Layer, which consists of a multi-branch truture to capture scale-specific feature, with different receptive fields and scale-specific supervisions, and a scale-specific context module to promote the feature maps. Finally, feature maps of edge supervision module are integrated together to refine the final parsing result. Our experiments show that our method improves the performance of the baseline models significantly and are helpful for further research on human parsing.

Acknowledgements. This work was supported by the Project of the National Natural Science Foundation of China (No. 61876210), and Natural Science Foundation of Hubei Province (No. 2018CFB426).

References

1. Badrinarayanan, V., Kendall, A., Cipolla, R.: SegNet: a deep convolutional encoder-decoder architecture for image segmentation. TPAMI **39**(12), 2481–2495 (2017)
2. Buades, A., Coll, B., Morel, J.-M.: A non-local algorithm for image denoising. In: CVPR (2005)
3. Chen, L.-C., Barron, J.T., Papandreou, G., Murphy, K., Yuille, A.L.: Semantic image segmentation with task-specific edge detection using CNNs and a discriminatively trained domain transform. In: CVPR (2016)
4. Chen, L.-C., Papandreou, G., Kokkinos, I., Murphy, K., Yuille, A.L.: Semantic image segmentation with deep convolutional nets and fully connected CRFs. In: ICLR (2015)
5. Chen, L.-C., Papandreou, G., Kokkinos, I., Murphy, K., Yuille, A.L.: DeepLab: semantic image segmentation with deep convolutional nets, atrous convolution, and fully connected CRFs. TPAMI **40**(4), 834–848 (2017)
6. Chen, L.-C., Yang, Y., Wang, J., Xu, W., Yuille, A.L.: Attention to scale: scale-aware semantic image segmentation. In CVPR (2016)
7. Chen, Y., Rohrbach, M., Yan, Z., Yan, S., Kalantidis, Y.: Graph-based global reasoning networks. In: CVPR (2019)

8. Fu, J., Zheng, H., Mei, T.: Look closer to see better: recurrent attention convolutional neural network for fine-grained image recognition. In: CVPR (2017)
9. Fu, J., Liu, J., Tian, H., Fang, Z., Lu, H.: Dual attention network for scene segmentation. In: CVPR (2019)
10. Gan, C., Lin, M., Yang, Y., de Melo, G., Hauptmann, A.G.: Concepts not alone: exploring pairwise relationships for zero-shot video activity recognition. AAAI Press (2016)
11. Gong, K., Liang, X., Zhang, D., Shen, X., Lin, L.: Look into person: self-supervised structure-sensitive learning and a new benchmark for human parsing. In: CVPR (2017)
12. He, K., Zhang, X., Ren, S., Sun, J.: Deep residual learning for image recognition. In: CVPR (2016)
13. Jégou, S., Drozdzal, M., Vazquez, D., Romero, A., Bengio, Y.: The one hundred layers tiramisu: fully convolutional densenets for semantic segmentation. In: CVPR (2017)
14. Liang, X., Gong, K., Shen, X., Lin, L.: Look into person: joint body parsing & pose estimation network and a new benchmark. TPAMI **41**(4), 871–885 (2018)
15. Liang, X., Lin, L., Wei, Y., Shen, X., Yang, J., Yan, S.: Proposal-free network for instance-level object segmentation. TPAMI **40**(12), 2978–2991 (2017)
16. Liang, X., et al.: Human parsing with contextualized convolutional neural network. In: ICCV (2015)
17. Lin, G., Milan, A., Shen, C., Reid, I.: RefineNet: multi-path refinement networks for high-resolution semantic segmentation. In: CVPR (2017)
18. Liu, T., et al.: Devil in the details: towards accurate single and multiple human parsing. In: AAAI (2019)
19. Long, J., Shelhamer, E., Darrell, T.: Fully convolutional networks for semantic segmentation. In: CVPR (2015)
20. Mostajabi, M., Yadollahpour, P., Shakhnarovich, G.: Feedforward semantic segmentation with zoom-out features. In: CVPR (2015)
21. Park, S., Nie, B.X., Zhu, S.-C.: Attribute and-or grammar for joint parsing of human pose, parts and attributes. TPAMI **40**(7), 1555–1569 (2017)
22. Paszke, A., et al.: Automatic differentiation in PyTorch. In: NIPS (2017)
23. Wang, X., Girshick, R., Gupta, A., He, K.: Non-local neural networks. In: CVPR (2018)
24. Xia, F., Wang, P., Chen, X., Yuille, A.L.: Joint multi-person pose estimation and semantic part segmentation. In: CVPR (2017)
25. Xia, F., Zhu, J., Wang, P., Yuille, A.L.: Pose-guided human parsing by an and/or graph using pose-context features. In: AAAI (2016)
26. Yu, C., Wang, J., Peng, C., Gao, C., Yu, G., Sang, N.: BiSeNet: bilateral segmentation network for real-time semantic segmentation. In: ECCV (2018)
27. Yu, C., Wang, J., Peng, C., Gao, C., Yu, G., Sang, N.: Learning a discriminative feature network for semantic segmentation. In: CVPR (2018)
28. Zhao, H., Shi, J., Qi, X., Wang, X., Jia, J.: Pyramid scene parsing network. In: CVPR (2017)
29. Zhao, J., et al.: Self-supervised neural aggregation networks for human parsing. In: CVPR (2017)
30. Zhu, S., Urtasun, R., Fidler, S., Lin, D., Change Loy, C.: Be your own prada: fashion synthesis with structural coherence. In ICCV (2017)

Semi-supervised Lesion Detection with Reliable Label Propagation and Missing Label Mining

Zhuo Wang[1,2], Zihao Li[1,2], Shu Zhang[3], Junge Zhang[1,2], and Kaiqi Huang[1,2(✉)]

[1] CRISE, Institute of Automation, Chinese Academy of Sciences, Beijing, China
{wangzhuo2017,lizihao2018}@ia.ac.cn, {jgzhang,kqhuang}@nlpr.ia.ac.cn
[2] University of Chinese Academy of Sciences, Beijing, China
[3] Deepwise AI Lab, Beijing, China
zhangshu@deepwise.com

Abstract. Annotations for medical images are very hard to acquire as it requires specific domain knowledge. Therefore, performance of deep learning algorithms on medical image processing is largely hindered by the scarcity of large-scale labeled data. To address this challenge, we propose a semi-supervised learning method for lesion detection from CT images which exploits a key characteristic of the volumetric medical data, i.e. adjacent slices in the axial axis resemble each other, or say they bear some kind of continuity. Specifically, by exploiting such a prior, a semi-supervised scheme is adopted to propagate bounding box annotations to adjacent CT slices to obtain more training data with fewer false positives and more true positives. Furthermore, considering that the NIH DeepLesion dataset has many missing labels, we develop a missing ground truth mining process by considering the continuity (or appearance-consistency) of multi-slice axial CT images. Experimental results on the NIH DeepLesion dataset demonstrate the effectiveness our methods for both semi-supervised label propagation and missing label mining.

Keywords: Semi-supervised learning · Label propagation · Lesion detection · Data distillation

1 Introduction

Recently, Convolutional neural networks (CNN) based deep learning algorithms have shown impressive results on various visual recognition tasks, e.g. image classification [1–4], object detection [5–9], image segmentation [10–12], etc. These progresses are mainly nourished by the improved network architecture, increased computing power, and availability of large amounts of labeled scale training data.

A student paper.

However, such successes is not easy to be replicated to medical fields. In most medical scenario, collecting a large-scale dataset could be particularly difficult with the concern of ethical and privacy problem. What's more, the labeling procedure is remarkably time-consuming due to the complexity of medical images, and requires experts with professional domain knowledge. The insufficiency of large-scale labeled data significantly hinders the deep learning methods from going further.

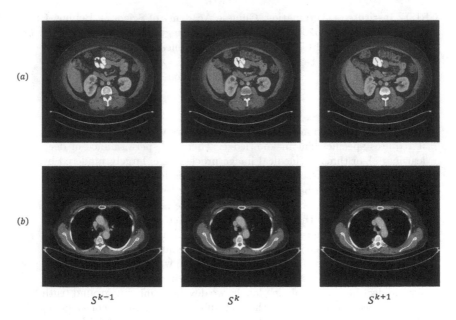

Fig. 1. A CT scan can be seen as a series of continuous slices, with intervals ranging from tenths of a millimeter to a few millimeters. Lesions can be observed among multiple slices. The liver lesion in key slice S^k is labeled by human experts manually, it also appears in adjacent slices S^{k+1}, S^{k-1} with different appearance.

Many approaches [13,14] have explored the data-insufficient problem using weakly-supervised learning methods to train a lesion detector. These methods successfully reduce the demand of comprehensive labels, however, the performances are relatively not satisfied with image-level supervision only. In clinical practice, it's common to only mark the partial of lesions which are most representative for disease diagnosis, and the trivial lesions are ignored for tedious. This is also a time-cost trade-off for lesion labeling between weakly-supervised and fully-supervised learning. However, it further brings the missing label problem, which is harmful to the training procedure.

To tackle this problem, we adapt missing ground truth mining method to find lost annotations automatically. Our method bases is based on the observation of lesion continuity: given a sample consisted of a labeled 2D CT slice with extra unlabeled slices as 3D context, a lesion would appear crossing multiple adjacent slices simultaneously, as is shown in Fig. 1.

Such characteristic of CT images brings us a availability to retrieve the missing labels. We first make predictions on multiple slices with a pre-trained model, and then adapt a cross-slice-fusion (CSU) module to integrate generate reliable missing labels.

Besides, to address the data-hunger problem, semi-supervised learning (SSL) method [15] finds another way to utilize large unlabeled datasets with few labeled data as a starting point.

Inspired by SSL, we develop a slice-level label propagation method to fully exploit the knowledge of limited labeled data.

More specifically, with the consideration of lesion continuity, we propagate pseudo labels to adjacent slices, so as to get more labeled samples for further training.

To sum up, our contributions can be summarized as follows: (1) We identify an important characteristic of CT images and propose a novel semi-supervised label propagation approach to generate reliable labels for adjacent CT slices. The proposed approach reduces the risk of overfitting and helps to easy the data-hunger problem for medical image analysis. (2) Exploiting the same characteristic, we also develop a missing annotation mining approach to learn from partially-annotated medical data. (3) Our method is model-agnostic and easy to be transformed for other tasks without tedious human labor, which is meaningful for medical image processing.

2   Related Work

Automated lesion detection has gained a lot of attention in computer-aided medical image processing. However, deep learning based methods suffer from the insufficiency of labeled data. To address this, Cai et al. [13] proposed a weakly-supervised approach to generate pseudo mask for lesion segmentation. Lee et al. [14] adopt data augmentation for weakly-labeled liver lesion detection. Recently, DeepLesion [16], a large-scale CT dataset was proposed, filled the gap of data sizes in universal lesion detection task. In ULDOR [13], a auxiliary supervision with pseudo masks was explored to boost detection task with Mask-RCNN [12]. Yan et al. [17] modeled 3D Context Enhanced R-CNN(3DCE) which ensembles multiple 2D slices as 3D context, and achieved the state-of-the-art performance. In this paper, we choose 3DCE as basic detection framework.

Weakly-supervised detection learns to classify and locate objects from image-level annotations. Class activation maps [18] is an intuitive way to get localization information from a pre-trained classification network. [19] further employed adversarial complementary learning to obtain localizations in an end-to-end CNN. Although many impressive approaches have been proposed, there's still a large performance gap between WSL and FSL methods.

Semi-supervised methods provides another thinking to utilize a large amount of unlabeled data with a small set of fully-labeled data. Among them, self-training [15] and its follow-up work explored a way to predict pseudo labels

---

Algorithm 1. Slice-Level Label Propagation

Input: D, Y: Images and annotations of original dataset; θ: Random initialized network; τ: IOU threshold;
Output: $\widetilde{D}$: Augmented dataset with label propagation.
1: Train θ on original dataset $D = \{x_i\}_{i=1}^{N}$ with labels $Y = \{y_i\}_{i=1}^{N}$;
2: Set Images $\widetilde{D^+} = \{\widetilde{x}_i\}_{i=1}^{N}$ and pseudo labels $\widetilde{Y^+} = \{\widetilde{y}_i\}_i^{N}$ for upper adjacent slices
3: **for** i in N **do**
4:     Get slice $\widetilde{x}_i$ which is adjacent to x_i, initialize $\widetilde{y}_i = \{\}$
5:     Get ground-truth $g_i = \{g_{ik}\}_{k=1}^{O}$ of CT slice x_i
6:     Get predicted bounding-boxes $B_i = \{b_{ij}\}_{j=1}^{M}$ with θ on slice $\widetilde{x}_i$
7:     **for** j in M **do**
8:         **for** k in O **do**
9:             **if** $IOU(b_{ij}, g_{ik}) > \tau$ **then**
10:                 Append b_{ij} into $\widetilde{y}_i$.
11:             **end if**
12:         **end for**;
13:     **end for**;
14: **end for**;
15: Follow 2 to 14 to generate $\widetilde{D^-}$ and $\widetilde{Y^-}$ for lower slices
16: $\widetilde{D} = \widetilde{D^+} \cup \widetilde{D^-}$
17: $\widetilde{Y} = \widetilde{Y^+} \cup \widetilde{Y^-}$

---

of unlabeled data, and then retrain itself. [20] ensemble various of transformations on unlabeled data to generate reliable annotations. Huang et al. further [21] extended data distillation as well as model distillation to medical tasks.

Object detection from partially-annotated data is another problem different from the two methods above. In such case, only part of objects in images are labeled, while others are ignored. Open Images Dataset v4 [22] present a large-scale detection dataset with severe missed annotations. [23] attempted to alleviate the effect of partially-annotated data through several practices.

3   Method

In this paper, we explore a post-processing method with consideration of lesion continuity to tackle problems mentioned above. In Sect. 3.1, we will introduce a novel data augmentation approach implemented by semi-supervised label propagation. In Sect. 3.2, based on the few instance-level annotations, we develop a missing ground truth mining procedure to automatically find the high-quality pseudo bounding-boxes for the unlabeled instances.

3.1   Slice-Level Label Propagation

CT datasets consist of a series of axial images. In most cases, only key slices with the maximum cross-sectional area or the most distinctive feature of lesion are labeled by human experts. The other slices can also contain part of lesions,

Algorithm 2. Missing Ground-Truth Mining

Input: D, Y: Images and annotations of original dataset; θ: Random initialized network; τ: IOU threshold; α: score threshold;

Output: $\widehat{Y}$: Augmented dataset with missing labels.

1: Train θ on original dataset $D = \{x_i\}_{i=1}^N$ with labels $Y = \{y_i\}_{i=1}^N$;
2: **for** i in N **do**
3:    Get key slice x_i^k as well as its upper slice x_i^{k+1}, lower slice x_i^{k-1}
4:    Get predicted bounding-boxes $B_i^k = \{b_{ij}^k\}_{j=1}^O$ for x_i^k
5:    Get predicted bounding-boxes $B_i^{k+1} = \{b_{ij}^{k+1}\}_{j=1}^P$ and $B_i^{k+1} = \{b_{ij}^{k+1}\}_{j=1}^Q$ for adjacent slices x_i^{k+1} ,x_i^{k-1}, respectively
6:    Get ground-truth $G_i = \{g_{ik}\}_{k=1}^M$ of CT slice x_i
7:    Get predicted score $S(b^k)$ for bounding-boxes b^k
8:    **for** b^k in B_i^k **do**
9:       **if** $S(b^k) > \alpha$ **then**
10:          **if** b^k has $IOU(b^k, \cdot) > \tau$ with any boxes in $B_i^{k+1} \cup B_i^{k-1}$ **then**
11:             Append b_{ij} into $\widehat{y}_i$.
12:          **end if**
13:       **end if**
14:    **end for**;
15:    **for** b^{k+1} in B_i^{k+1} **do**
16:       **if** b^{k+1} has $IOU(b^{k+1}, b^{k-1}) > \tau$ with any boxes b^{k-1} in B_i^{k-1} and
17: b^{k+1} has $IOU(b^{k+1}, \cdot) = 0$ with any boxes in B_i^k **then**
18:          **if** $S(b^k + 1) > \alpha$ and $S(b^k - 1) > \alpha$ **then**
19:             Calculate average coordinate $\widetilde{b} = AVG(b^{k+1}, b^{k-1})$
20:             Append $\widetilde{b}$ into $\widehat{y}_i$.
21:          **end if**
22:       **end if**
23:    **end for**;
24:    **for** b in $\widehat{y}_i$ **do**
25:       **if** b has $IOU(b, \cdot) > 0$ with any boxes in G_i **then**
26:          Delete b from $\widehat{y}_i$.
27:       **end if**
28:    **end for**;
29:    $\widehat{y}_i = \widehat{y}_i \cup G_i$
30: **end for**;

---

while they are usually ignored for deficiency of annotations [16]. A naive way to utilize these information is to take multiple 2D slices as 3D context. In this section, a label propagation algorithm is used to generate annotations for those unlabeled slices, so as to get more available data for training.

First, we follow the method proposed in [17] to train an initial model on the original dataset. After training, we make predictions for slices adjoin to labeled slices in training set. Then, for each predicted bounding box p_i, we calculate Intersection over Union (IOU) with all ground-truth boxes $B_i = \{b_{ij}\}_{j=1}^M$. Once higher than a threshold τ, we regard it as corresponding area of lesion in this slice, and preserve it as pseudo labels. The algorithm is summarized in Algorithm 1.

3.2   Missing Ground-Truth Mining

A simple way to deal with missing labels is taking the predicted results of training set as pseudo ground truth bounding-boxes, and re-train the detection network. However, the achieved bounding-boxes are quite low-quality for the existing of noise. [20] ensemble multiple image transformations to generate reliable results. Similar with [20], we use multi-scale testing and horizontal flipping to get predictions on labeled slices and its adjacent slices in training set, and a False Positive Reduction procedure is applied to mine accurate pseudo labels with the consideration of lesion continuity.

Specifically, for predicted bounding-boxes in arbitrary slice among the three adjoin slices, we calculate IOU with boxes in the adjoin slices. If a box has more than one corresponding box with IOU higher than τ, and it's predicted score is higher than α, we take the box of middle slice as mined ground truth. The corresponding boxes may appear in both upper and lower slices, while missing in the key slice, in this case, we take the average of coordinate the two predicted boxes as a final pseudo label. The algorithm is summarized in Algorithm 2.

4   Experiments

4.1   Experimental Setup

Dataset. The DeepLesion dataset [16] is mined from annotations stored in hospitals picture archiving and communication systems (PACS) which is marked by radiologists during their daily work to highlight significant image findings that may serve as reference for later studies. It is composed of 32,735 lesions in 32,120 bookmarked CT slices from 10,594 studies of 4427 unique patients. Each study contains multiple volumes (series) that are scanned at the same time point but differs in image filters, contrast phases, etc. The slice intervals of the CT studies in the dataset range between 0.25 and 22.5 mm, among which 48.3% are 1 mm and 48.9% are 5 mm. The diameter of the lesions ranges from 0.42 to 342.5 mm for long diameter and 0.21 to 212.4 mm for short diameter. In all experiments, we follow the settings used in [8], to divide the dataset into training (70%), validation (15%) and test (15%) sets.

Implementation Details. We re-implement the method [17] using Faster R-CNN with FPN [24] in Pytorch. In all experiments, ResNet-50 is used as backbone. Parameters in backbone are initialized with ImageNet pre-trained model, and all the other layers are randomly initialized. We rescaled the 12-bit CT intensity range to floating-point numbers in [0, 255]. It uses a single windowing (-1024-3071 HU) that covers the intensity ranges of the lung, soft tissue, and bone. Intervals of all volumes are interpolated in the z-axis to 2 mm manually. Five anchor scales (32, 64, 128, 256, 512) and three anchor ratios (1:1, 1:2, 2:1) are used in FPN. We use a weight decay of 0.0001 and a momentum of 0.9. The learning rate is 0.02 for the first 30k mini-batches and reduced by a factor of 10 after the 34k and 36k mini-batches. In Missing Ground-Truth Mining method, the score threshold α is 0.9. The IOU threshold τ used in this paper is 0.5.

4.2   Results and Discussion

A predicted box was regarded as correct if its intersection over union (IOU) with a ground-truth box is larger than 0.5.

In this paper, FPN–3DCE indicates our re-implementation of 3DCE (9 slices) using Faster R-CNN with FPN. We use FPN-3DCE as our baseline.

The results in Table 1 show our baseline is better than ULDOR [13] and 3DCE (9 slices) [17].

Data Distillation [20] is a kind of semi-supervised learning, which can ensemble predictions from multiple transformations of unlabeled data, using a single model, to automatically generate new training annotations.

We use FPN–3DCE to implement Data Distillation method. A threshold of score 0.9 is used to filter reliable annotations for unlabeled slices.

In Table 1, Data Distillation method gets higher sensitivity than baseline with 4 and 8 false positives (FPs) per image, suggesting Data Distillation method is effective to generate labels for unlabeled slices in training set. Data Distillation method gets lower sensitivity than baseline with 2 or less false positives (FPs) per image, suggesting that only use score threshold to filter reliable annotations for unlabeled slices brings some false annotations.

To demonstrate the effectiveness our method, first we use Missing Ground-Truth Mining method to deal with missing labels in labeled slices, then we use Slice-level Label Propagation method to generate annotations for unlabeled slices in training set. The IOU threshold (τ) used in our method is 0.5. Table 1 shows our method is better than baseline and Data Distillation method. Our method achieves a sensitivity of 89.15 with 4 false positives (FPs) per image, which obtains an absolute improvement of 1.57% from previous state-of-the-art.

Table 1. Sensitivity (%) at various FPs per image on the testing set of DeepLesion. FPN–3DCE indicates our re-implementation of 3DCE using Faster R-CNN with FPN.

FPs per image	0.5	1	2	4	8
ULDOR [13]	52.86	64.80	74.84	84.38	87.17
3DCE, 9 slices [17]	59.32	70.68	79.09	84.34	87.81
FPN–3DCE (baseline)	64.56	75.29	82.49	86.87	89.92
Data distillation	61.05	72.54	81.58	87.58	91.65
Ours	**66.02**	**76.87**	**84.61**	**89.15**	**92.00**

4.3   Ablation Study

To demonstrate the effectiveness of our method for both Slice-level Label Propagation (LP) and Missing Ground-Truth Mining (MM), we conduct the following experimental comparisons. The results are presented in Table 2.

Table 2. Ablation study of our approach on the DeepLesion dataset.

FPN–3DCE	LP	MM	FPs@0.5	FPs@1.0	FPs@2.0	FPs@4.0	FPs@8.0
✓			64.56	75.29	82.49	86.87	89.92
✓		✓	65.49	75.71	83.27	87.83	90.82
✓	✓		65.70	76.23	84.14	88.70	91.75
✓	✓	✓	66.02	76.87	84.61	89.15	92.00

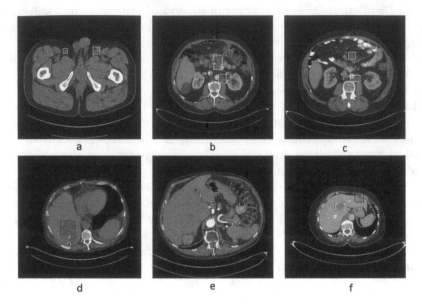

Fig. 2. The results of MM method. a, b, c, d, e, f are labeled slices in training set with human annotations (red boxes). Yellow boxes in a, b, c, d, e, f represent missing labels in labeled slices of training set. The MM method generated missing labels (yellow boxes) in labeled slices. (Color figure online)

(1) FPN–3DCE (Baseline): We train FPN–3DCE on the official training set of DeepLesion dataset.

(2) FPN–3DCE + MM: First we use MM method to deal with missing labels in labeled slices of training set. Then we retrain FPN–3DCE on the augmented training set with missing labels.

In Fig. 2, red boxes stand for labels in labeled slices. Yellow boxes represent missing labels in labeled slices of training set. The MM method generated missing labels (yellow boxes) in labeled slices.

In Table 2, results of FPN–3DCE with MM method are better than that of FPN–3DCE, suggesting the effectiveness of MM method.

(3) FPN–3DCE + LP: First we use LP method to generate high-quality labels for unlabeled slices in training set. Then we retrain FPN–3DCE on the augmented training set with label propagation.

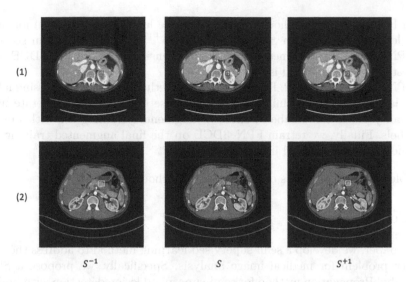

Fig. 3. The results of LP method. Row (1) and Row (2) stand for adjacent slices. Slices in Column S are labeled slices with human annotations (red boxes) in training set. Slices in Column S^{-1} and Column S^{+1} are unlabeled slices in training set. The LP method generated reliable labels (yellow boxes) for unlabeled slices in Column S^{-1} and Column S^{+1}. (Color figure online)

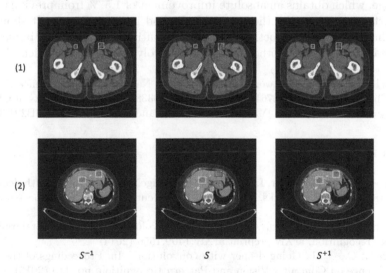

Fig. 4. The results for LP and MM method. Row (1) and Row (2) stand for adjacent slices. First we use MM method to deal with missing labels in labeled slices (slices in column S) of training set. Then we use LP method to generate high-quality labels for unlabeled slices (slices in column S^{-1} and column S^{+1}) in augmented training set with missing labels. (Color figure online)

In Fig. 3, The LP method generated reliable labels (yellow boxes) for unlabeled slices in Column S^{-1} and Column S^{+1}. In Table 2, we can see that FPN–3DCE with LP method gets higher sensitivity than FPN–3DCE, suggesting the LP method is useful.

(4) FPN–3DCE+MM+LP: First we use MM method to deal with missing labels in labeled slices of training set. Then we use LP method to generate high-quality labels for unlabeled slices in augmented training set with missing labels. Finally, we retrain FPN–3DCE on the final augmented training set. The results are showed in Fig. 4.

In Table 2, the effectiveness of LP and MM method is verified.

5   Conclusion

In this paper, we develop a semi-supervised learning method to address the data scarcity problem for medical image analysis. Specifically, we propose a Slice-level Label Propagation method for semi-supervised lesion detection with limited training data. By exploiting the continuity of the adjacent slices in volumetric medical data, we develop a semi-supervised learning method that can simultaneously acquire reliable label propagation and complete the missing annotations. The proposed method achieves a sensitivity of 89.15% with four false positives per image, which obtains an absolute improvement of 1.57% from previous state-of-the-art, suggesting that the proposed method is very effective. It should be noted that the proposed method, which is intuitive and simple to implement, can be easily extended to other tasks which involve volumetric medical data.

Acknowledgements. This work is funded by the National Natural Science Foundation of China (Grant No. 61876181, 61721004, 61403383), and the Projects of Chinese Academy of Sciences (Grant QYZDB-SSW-JSC006 and Grant 173211KYSB20160008).

References

1. Krizhevsky, A., Sutskever, I., Hinton, G.E.: ImageNet classification with deep convolutional neural networks. In: Advances in Neural Information Processing Systems, pp. 99–110 (2016)
2. Simonyan, K., Zisserman, A.: Very deep convolutional networks for large-scale image recognition. arXiv preprint arXiv:1409.1556 (2014)
3. Szegedy, C., et al.: Going deeper with convolutions. In: Proceedings of the IEEE Conference on Computer Vision and Pattern Recognition, pp. 1–9 (2015)
4. He, K., Zhang, X., Ren, S., Sun, J.: Deep residual learning for image recognition. In: Proceedings of the IEEE Conference on Computer Vision and Pattern Recognition, pp. 770–778 (2016)
5. Girshick, R., Donahue, J., Darrell, T., Malik, J.: Rich feature hierarchies for accurate object detection and semantic segmentation. In: Proceedings of the IEEE Conference on Computer Vision and Pattern Recognition, pp. 580–587 (2014)
6. Girshick, R.: Fast R-CNN. In: Proceedings of the IEEE International Conference on Computer Vision, pp. 1440–1448 (2015)

7. Ren, S., He, K., Girshick, R., Sun, J.: Towards real-time object detection with region proposal networks. In: Advances in Neural Information Processing Systems, pp. 91–99 (2015)
8. Redmon, J., Divvala, S., Girshick, R., Farhadi, A.: You only look once: unified, real-time object detection. In: Proceedings of the IEEE Conference on Computer Vision and Pattern Recognition, pp. 779–788 (2016)
9. Liu, W., et al.: SSD: single shot multibox detector. In: Leibe, B., Matas, J., Sebe, N., Welling, M. (eds.) ECCV 2016. LNCS, vol. 9905, pp. 21–37. Springer, Cham (2016). https://doi.org/10.1007/978-3-319-46448-0_2
10. Long, J., Shelhamer, E., Darrell, T.: Fully convolutional networks for semantic segmentation. In: Proceedings of the IEEE Conference on Computer Vision and Pattern Recognition, pp. 3431–3440 (2015)
11. Chen, L.C., Papandreou, G., Kokkinos, I., et al.: DeepLab: semantic image segmentation with deep convolutional nets, atrous convolution, and fully connected CRFs. IEEE Trans. Pattern Anal. Mach. Intell. 40(4), 834–848 (2018)
12. He, K., Gkioxari, G., Girshick, R.: Mask R-CNN. In: Proceedings of the IEEE International Conference on Computer Vision, pp. 2961–2969 (2017)
13. Tang, Y., Ke, Y., Tang, Y., Liu, J., Xiao, J., Summers, R.M.: ULDor: a universal lesion detector for CT scans with pseudo masks and hard negative example mining. arXiv preprint arXiv:1901.06359 (2019)
14. Lee, S., Bae, J.S., Kim, H., Kim, J.H., Yoon, S.: Liver lesion detection from weakly-labeled multi-phase CT volumes with a grouped single shot multibox detector. In: Frangi, A.F., Schnabel, J.A., Davatzikos, C., Alberola-López, C., Fichtinger, G. (eds.) MICCAI 2018. LNCS, vol. 11071, pp. 693–701. Springer, Cham (2018). https://doi.org/10.1007/978-3-030-00934-2_77
15. Rosenberg, C., Hebert, M., Schneiderman, H.: Semi-supervised self-training of object detection models. In: 2005 Seventh IEEE Workshops on Applications of Computer Vision, pp. 29–36 (2005)
16. Yan, K., et al.: Deep lesion graphs in the wild: relationship learning and organization of significant radiology image findings in a diverse large-scale lesion database. In: Proceedings of the IEEE Conference on Computer Vision and Pattern Recognition, pp. 9261–9270 (2018)
17. Yan, K., Bagheri, M., Summers, R.M.: 3D context enhanced region-based convolutional neural network for end-to-end lesion detection. In: Frangi, A.F., Schnabel, J.A., Davatzikos, C., Alberola-López, C., Fichtinger, G. (eds.) MICCAI 2018. LNCS, vol. 11070, pp. 511–519. Springer, Cham (2018). https://doi.org/10.1007/978-3-030-00928-1_58
18. Zhou, B., Khosla, A., Lapedriza, A., Oliva, A., Torralba, A.: Learning deep features for discriminative localization. In: Proceedings of the IEEE Conference on Computer Vision and Pattern Recognition, pp. 2921–2929 (2016)
19. Zhang, X., Wei, Y., Feng, J., Yang, Y., Huang, T.S.: Adversarial complementary learning for weakly supervised object localization. In: Proceedings of the IEEE Conference on Computer Vision and Pattern Recognition, pp. 1325–1334 (2018)
20. Radosavovic, I., Girshick, R., Gkioxari, G., He, K.: Data distillation: towards omni-supervised learning. In: Proceedings of the IEEE Conference on Computer Vision and Pattern Recognition, pp. 4119–4128 (2018)
21. Huang, R., Noble, J.A., Namburete, A.I.L.: Omni-supervised learning: scaling up to large unlabelled medical datasets. In: Frangi, A.F., Schnabel, J.A., Davatzikos, C., Alberola-López, C., Fichtinger, G. (eds.) MICCAI 2018. LNCS, vol. 11070, pp. 572–580. Springer, Cham (2018). https://doi.org/10.1007/978-3-030-00928-1_65

22. Kuznetsova, A., et al.: The open images dataset V4: unified image classification, object detection, and visual relationship detection at scale. arXiv preprint arXiv:1811.00982 (2018)
23. Gao, Y., et al.: Solution for large-scale hierarchical object detection datasets with incomplete annotation and data imbalance. arXiv preprint arXiv:1810.06208 (2018)
24. Lin, T.-Y., Girshick, R., He, K., Hariharan, B., Belongie, S.: Feature pyramid networks for object detection. In: Proceedings of the IEEE Conference on Computer Vision and Pattern Recognition, pp. 2117–2125 (2017)

Image Aesthetic Assessment Based on Perception Consistency

Weining Wang, Rui Deng, Lemin Li, and Xiangmin Xu$^{(\boxtimes)}$

South China University of Technology, Guangzhou, China
{wnwang,xmxu}@scut.edu.cn, rui.deng94@gmail.com, lminscut@gmail.com

Abstract. Automatically assessing the aesthetic quality of images that is consistent with humans is a challenging task. Previous works based on Convolution Neural Network (CNN) lacks of perception consistency in two aspects. First, they mainly extract features from the entire image without distinguishing between the foreground and background. Second, they classify images with highly-compressed semantic feature. In this paper, we proposed a visual perception network (VP-Net) to support perception consistency learning. It was designed as a double-subnet network which can learn from subject region feature and multi-level features. In addition, a subject region search algorithm was proposed to find out a composed of multiple subject regions. Experimental results on a large scale aesthetic dataset (AVA) have demonstrated the superiority of our approach.

Keywords: Perception consistency · Subject region · Adaptive aggregation · Multi-level feature

1 Introduction

Automatically assessing the aesthetic quality of images that is consistent with humans is widely used in some subjective tasks. For example, a intelligent photography assistant can help non-professional photographers take a high aesthetic quality photo, and a good image recommendation or retrieval system will regard aesthetic quality as an important ranking indicator so that users will be more satisfied with the recommendation or search results.

There have been numbers of works on image aesthetic assessments considering extracting basic image attributions or high-level semantic information from images [2,3,11,13,15,24,25]. Different from these works, we think about what makes a photo look beautiful in human perception. Some related work has been published in [1,14,16]. Luo *et al.* [16] extracted the subject region from a photo, and then designed a number of high-level semantic features based on foreground and background division. But the algorithm they used can only roughly identify the focus subject region. In recent years, convolution neural network (CNN) [4,8,9,22,26] is introduced to assess image aesthetic. To learn fine-gained

© Springer Nature Switzerland AG 2019
Z. Lin et al. (Eds.): PRCV 2019, LNCS 11858, pp. 303–315, 2019.
https://doi.org/10.1007/978-3-030-31723-2_26

details from images, which is crucial to assess aesthetic, Lu *et al.* [14] proposed a deep multi-patch aggregation network. Their key idea is to represent the original high-resolution input image using multiple randomly-cropped patches. Inspired by Lu *et al.* [14], Chen *et al.* [1] also extracted patches and fed them into CNN. But they represent image using multiple patches computed based on visual word, such as car or sky. While they don't consider the uncommon subjects and the relationship among patches.

The two mainly problems with existing methods is that they compute feature from the entire image and only use the high-compressed semantic feature to represent the image. Both of them limited the performance of the aesthetic model since a good photo takes care of the whole and the details. Professional photographers not only consider the overall harmony of subject and composition but also pay attention to details. While it is a big challenge to find out the subject region from a image. Since the subject region is hard to define and the aesthetic dataset don't contain semantic label.

Starting from these two problems, we propose a two independent network structure to explore effective approaches that applys the principle of perception consistency to CNN. We combine these two parts and call the whole architecture as the Visual Perception Network (VP-Net). It contains two subnets, to be specifically, a Subject-Focused Subnet and a Detail-Oriented Subnet. The former subnet adaptively aggregate the features of the subject regions, and the latter one enriches the image representation ability by combining shallow fine-grained features and deep semantic features. In addition, following the visual perception mechanism, we develop a subject region search algorithm by measuring the semantics, saliency, size and overlap of regions and ranking them with the quantized score. Our contribution is as follow:

- Proposed a novel architecture to assess image aesthetic by applying the principle of perception consistency.
- Designed two subnets that focus on overall harmony and fine-gained details of images.
- Developed a subject region search algorithm by measuring the quantized visual properties of local regions.
- Verified the superiority of our approach by experimenting on large-scale aesthetic dataset AVA [19].

2 Related Work

In this section we review the studies which are closely related to our work. Studies on perceptually aesthetic modeling try to discover various visual patterns which are consistency with human perception. These studies have attempted to proposed approaches from the holistic or fine-gained details perspective.

2.1 Holistic Perspective

From a holistic perspective, image can be treat as a whole region or a combination of multiple local regions. We introduce them separately.

Most of works extracted feature from the entire images [5,6,17,27]. Mai et al. [17] observed the fixed-size restriction on CNN may damage the composition of the image, so they propose a composition-preserving model that uses an adaptive spatial pooling layer to adopt arbitrary size image as input. Kairanbay et al. [5] propose two efficient deep-learning approaches for image aesthetic by using image content and additional attribute information.

Some works pay more attention to the foreground and extracted meaningful features from these regions [1,13,14,16]. Luo et al. [16] extracted the subject region from a photo with a blur detection method. But the hand-craft features they designed are too delicate and ideal to adapt to large data sets which contains a variety of images. Chen et al. [1] proposed an Aesthlet-Based model based on image attributions. They extracted patches to obtain a bag-of-words representation with lots of auxiliary images downloaded from Flickr. But in this way, the patches are too small and scattered to represent the original images.

Differently from the aforementioned methods, we focus on subject regions, considering their semantic, saliency, size and the correlation between them. In addition, our approach does not require auxiliary data and manual labeling to learn the meaningfully and overlapped subject regions, which make it practical in many application.

2.2   Fine-Gained Details Perspective

From a fine-gained details perspective, many works use multiple inputs based on different purposes and use multi-columns CNN to learn from these features.

Lu et al. [13] proposed an architecture based on double-columns CNN (DCNN) which supports two heterogenous inputs. They use the features extracted from the entire image and a randomly cropped region to represent the global and local information. To get fine-gained information, Lu et al. [14] developed an architecture based on multi-columns CNN (DMA-Net). In this scheme, five patches are randomly cropped from the image and then fed into a five-columns CNN to extracts fine-gained features. Both of the two methods utilize multiple inputs to obtain fine-gained details and have achieved a good results.

In [10,12,29], researchers computed features from low-level and intermediate-level layer to detect small objects. It has been demonstrated that as the network goes deeper, with more stride or pooling layers added, some features will disappear. For example, the output feature size of the last convolution layer is usually only 1/32 of the original image, which potentially loss the detail of image.

In this paper, the key idea is to represent the input image with shallow fine-gained and deep semantic features and carry out separately training to avoid cross interference. It is worth noting that separation training is important to guide the gradient propagation correctly.

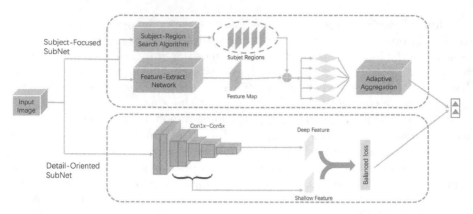

Fig. 1. The architecture of the VP-Net. More details will be shown in Figs. 2 and 3.

3 Our Method

3.1 Overview

The architecture of our proposed VP-Net is shown in Fig. 1. In the following part, we will describe the specific details of the two subnets, Subject-Focused Subnet and Detailed-Oriented Subnet.

3.2 Subject-Focused Subnet

Network Structure. According to the studies of photography, the foreground region where subject appear can convey more semantic and emotional information, and thus can draw more attention. Therefore we heuristically design the search subject region algorithm based on the image content. After extracting features from subject regions, we conduct the aggregation of these features by employing an adaptive aggregation layer. The network is shown in Fig. 2.

Subject Region Search Algorithm. Unlike the random-cropping representation in [14] and bag-of-words representation in [1]. We want to find more informative and relational regions for effective learning. So it should have the following properties:

- *Strong Semantics & Highly Salient:* be consistency with human perception and contain meaningful subjects.
- *Classes-Agnostic:* have good generalization ability to identify subject with unknown categories.
- *Size & Overlapped:* have enough receptive filed and maybe overlap with each other but convert various information.

We achieve this by employing the object detection algorithm and saliency detection algorithm. There are two problems need to be addressed. First, the

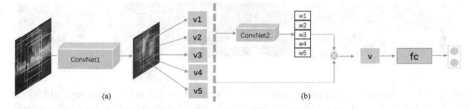

Fig. 2. The architecture of proposed Subject-Focused Subnet. (a) Subject region features extracting (b) Adaptive aggregation layer.

object detection algorithm can not detect uncommon object due to lack of supervise signal. Second, the saliency detection algorithm cannot provide a clear region boundary. So we develop a new algorithm to find subject region set, which include three parts as following:

i. *Priority Knowledge of Image Spatial Composition:* To acquire spatial composition of images, we utilize bounding boxes detected by [21] and salience map detected by [20], as shown in Fig. 3b and c. We combine the centers of bounding boxes and centers of the connected domains in binary salience map to a center set as prior knowledge, respectively C_{BB} and C_{SAL}. It should be note that about 46% images in AVA [19] can not be detected any boxes with class confidence of 50%. The final center set $\{C_j\}_{j \in [1, n_1 + n_2]}$ can be formulated as following:

$$\{C_j\}_{j \in [1, n_1 + n_2]} = \{\{C_{BBi}\}_{i \in [1, n_1]}; \{C_{SALi}\}_{i \in [1, n_2]}\} \tag{1}$$

where n_1 and n_2 are the length of C_{BB} and C_{SAL}.

ii. *Subject Region Representation:* After finding the center set $\{C_j\}_{j \in [1, n_1 + n_2]}$, we introduce anchor mechanism to locate the subject regions. Given a center point C_j, we assign k anchor boxes with different sizes and aspect ratios centered on C_j. The candidate subject regions $\{p_j\}_{j \in [1, k*(n_1 + n_2)]}$ can be represented by these $k*(n_1 + n_2)$ anchor boxes, as shown in Fig. 3d.

iii. *Region Ranking:* Finally, we rank regions by assessing their semantic, salience and size. We search the optimal combination of M subject regions from $\{p_j\}_{j \in [1, k*(n_1 + n_2)]}$, and define the optimal combination is $\{p_j^*\}_{j \in [1, M]}$, so that the solution can be calculated by the following cost function:

$$L = \alpha * \sum_{i=1}^{M} |\frac{S(p_i)}{w_i * h_i}| + \beta * \sum_{i=1}^{M} |w_i * h_i| - \gamma * \sum_{i,j=1.i \neq j}^{M} H(p_i, p_j) \tag{2}$$

$$s.t. \ \alpha > 0, \beta > 0, \gamma > 0$$

where p_i is a subject region, h_i and w_i are the height and width of p_i. $S(p_i)$ is the sum of the saliency values in this region. $H(x_1, x_2)$ is a constraint function which uses to control the overlap between a pair of regions (p_i, p_j). α, β, γ are the weights related to each part of the cost function. A series of

(a)   (b)   (c)   (d)   (e)

Fig. 3. The procedure of subject region search algorithm. (a) original image (b) object detection result (c) saliency detection result (d) candidate subject regions (e) optimal subject regions discovered by the algorithm.

semantic and representative regions can be searched by maximizing this cost function. The final result is shown in Fig. 3e.

Adaptive Aggregation Layer. As shown in Fig. 2, given an image $I^{(i)}$ and its subject region $P^{(i)}$, the feature vector set $\boldsymbol{F}^{(i)}$ is cropping from the output of last convolution layer in CNN.

$$\boldsymbol{F}^{(i)} = \mathcal{G}(I^{(i)}, P^{(i)}) = \{f_m^{(i)}\}_{m\in[0,M-1]} \tag{3}$$

where $\mathcal{G}(\cdot)$ is the feature extraction function which adopts $I^{(i)}$ and $P^{(i)}$ as input and calculates the corresponding feature vector $\boldsymbol{F}^{(i)}$ for each subject region in $P^{(i)}$. M is the number of subject regions.

Then we utilize a small neural network to compute a weight score vector for $\boldsymbol{F}^{(i)}$. The network contains one global average pooling and two 256-D hidden layers. Finally, we aggregate $\boldsymbol{F}^{(i)}$ according to the weight score. The aggregated feature $\boldsymbol{F}_{agg}^{(i)}$ can be formulated as follow:

$$\boldsymbol{\theta}^{(i)} = \mathcal{H}(\boldsymbol{F}^{(i)}), \boldsymbol{\theta} \in \mathbb{R}^{M\times 1} \tag{4}$$

$$\boldsymbol{F}_{agg}^{(i)} = \sum_{m=0}^{M-1} \theta_m^{(i)} * f_m^{(i)} \tag{5}$$

where $\mathcal{H}$ represents the map function of neural network, and $\boldsymbol{\theta}^{(i)}$ is the weight score vector.

This method is different from multi-columns CNN method in [1,14], we only use one CNN to extract feature map from the original image, and crop feature vectors $F^{(i)}$ from the feature map. In this way, we can reduce the amount of computation and improve the efficiency of training.

3.3   Detail-Oriented Subnet

Network Structure. To utilize different features, existing work usually concatenate them. However, these concatenated-based models will not only cause a negative cross interference between features, but also greatly increase the computational burden, which may cause overfitting. Unlike previous work, our proposed network combine the multi-scale features learned from different with balance loss. Our network is shown in Fig. 4.

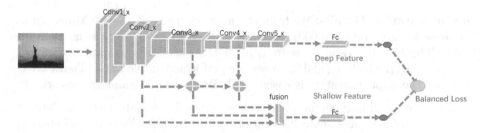

Fig. 4. The architecture of Detail-Oriented Subnet.

Feature Extraction. In this section, we will explain the details of our proposed Detail-Oriented Subnet. We choose ResNet50 [4] as the backbone network. We connect the side output of the three bottom blocks to represent the shallow feature. Besides, since the scale of each block is different, we add two other convolution layers in each side output to encode them into the same shape. We denote the side output from the last layer of Block2, Block3 and Block4 as f_{b2}, f_{b3}, f_{b4}, and the corresponding encoded version is $f'_{b2}, f'_{b3}, f'_{b4}$. The shallow feature is given by:

$$f'_{b2} = \sigma(W'_{b2} * \psi(W_{b2} * f_{b2})), f'_{b2} \in \mathbb{R}^{H' \times W' \times C'} \tag{6}$$

$$f'_{b3} = \sigma(W'_{b3} * \psi(W_{b3} * f_{b2})), f'_{b3} \in \mathbb{R}^{H' \times W' \times C'} \tag{7}$$

$$f'_{b4} = \sigma(W'_{b4} * \psi(W_{b4} * f_{b3})), f'_{b4} \in \mathbb{R}^{H' \times W' \times C'} \tag{8}$$

$$f_{shallow} = \{f'_{b2}; f'_{b3}; f'_{b4}\}, f_{shallow} \in \mathbb{R}^{H' \times W' \times 3C'} \tag{9}$$

where the height H' and width W' is 14, and the number of channel C' is 256. In the mean time, we use the output of Block5 as deep feature which is given by:

$$f_{deep} = f_{b5}, f_{deep} \in \mathbb{R}^{H'' \times W'' \times C''} \tag{10}$$

where the height H'' and width W'' is 7, and the number of channel C'' is 2048.

Network Training. We train each feature independently without concatenation since the nature of shallow and deep feature are very different. The shallow one is high-resolution but redundant and the deep one is more distinguishing but highly compressed. Our loss function can be define by:

$$\mathcal{L}(y, \hat{y}) = \lambda_s * \mathcal{L}_s(y, \hat{y}) + \lambda_d * \mathcal{L}_d(y, \hat{y}) \tag{11}$$

where $\mathcal{L}_s$ and $\mathcal{L}_d$ are the loss of shallow and deep features. λ_s and λ_d are the balance weight to leverage these two features.

Standard back propagation algorithm was used for training. In our design, the useful gradient is passed directly to the lower convolutional layer, which can help to alleviate gradient disappearance in very deep networks.

4   Experimental Result

4.1   Experimental Setting

Implementation Details: We train the network using SGD-with-Momentum. The base learning rate is 0.0001, the weight decay is 2e−4, and the momentum is 0.9. The learning rate drops to 1/10 of the base learning rate per 14,000 iterations. All the training and inference are performed on the 12 GB TianX GPU card and the implementation is based on PyTorch deep learning framework.

Dataset: We evaluate our proposed scheme on a large scale aesthetic dataset AVA [19]. AVA contains about 250,000 images downloaded from images sharing website www.dpchallenge.com. Each image is scored by 78 to 549 users rated from 1 to 10. The rating criterion is based on the average score, and those above 5 are of high aesthetic quality, others are low aesthetic. Following the previous work [13,14,23,28]. We randomly selected 230,000 images as the training set and 20,000 images as the test set.

4.2   Experimental Result on Subject-Focus Subnet

Visualize the Result of Subject Region Search Algorithm. The purpose of subject region search algorithm is to find out the optimal combination of subject regions which draw human's attention. An empirical opinion is that the distribution of the subject region is various, which depends on the content of image. We visualized the search results given by the algorithm when the number of regions M = 5. The results are shown in Fig. 5.

(a)   (b)   (c)   (d)

Fig. 5. The result of our subject region search algorithm, which can adaptively select the combination pattern according to the images content. For close-up images, as shown in (a) and (b), this algorithm can find the region contains local salience subject, such as human face and animal head. For panoramic images, as shown in (c) and (d), the algorithm pays more attention to the global information.

Step-by-Step Analyze. We decouple the two components in Subject-Focused Subnet to assess their ability. We carried out two experiments. First, we used random cropping to replace the subject region search algorithm while keep adaptive aggregation. Second, we used the average aggregation feature to replace the

Table 1. Results on step-by-step analyze.

Method	Accuracy
Random Crop+Adap-Agg	77.4%
Subject Region+Avg-Agg	78.3%
Subject-Focused	**79.8%**

Table 2. Comparison with patch-based aesthetic models.

Method	Accuracy
DCNN-VGG16 [13]	76.23%
DMA-Net-VGG16 [14]	76.40%
Aesthlet-Based Net [1]	77.86%
Subject-Focused-VGG16	78.8%
Subject-Focused-Resnet50	**79.8%**

proposed adaptive aggregation while keep using subject region. The experimental results are shown in Table 1.

As Table 1 shows that the two components do boost the performance of aesthetic model. This is because the selected subject regions with high semantic and salience can express image aesthetic better. In addition, adaptive aggregation consider the relationship among subject regions, which can learn various patterns based on images content and get better performance compared with average aggregation.

Compare with Patch-Based Multi-column Aesthetic Model. As described in Sect. 2, there are several patch-based methods with either holistic or fine-gained details view [1,13,14]. During the comparison study, we choose VGG16 [22] as backbone network to reimplement DCNN [13] and DMA-Net [14]. We do not use Resnet50 [4] because we observed a memory overflow even if the batch size is 1 in DMA-Net. For the Aesthlet-based model in [1], we found that both the source codes and auxiliary Flicker dataset collected by them are unavailable, so we report their best results without considering backbone.

We present the experience results in Table 2. We can see that our Subject-Focused Subnet outperforms other methods with the same backbone. Furthermore, due to the feature-sharing strategy, we can use more advanced network architecture to achieve better performance without worrying about the memory burden.

4.3   Experimental Result on Detail-Oriented Subnet

In this section, we evaluate the performance of Detail-Oriented Subnet. In order to evaluate the relative importance of deep features and shallow features, we tune the weight ratio of (λ_s, λ_d) and observe their effects. We fix the parameter $\lambda_d = 1$, and tune λ_s among [0, 0.5, 0.75, 1.0, 1.5, 2.0]. Specially, $\lambda_s = 0$ is equivalent to not using the shallow feature. The results are shown in Fig. 6.

We can observe that all results are better than the baseline (78.83%) when $\lambda_s = 0$. With the increase of λ_s, the performance of the model gets better at first and then becomes worse. It achieves best performance when $\lambda_s = 1.0$ at 80.30%, indicating that high-level abstract information and fine-grained informa-

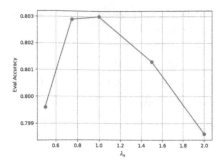

Fig. 6. Performance comparison of Detail-Oriented Subnet with different λ_s when $\lambda_d = 1$.

Table 3. Performance comparison with other methods.

Method	Accuracy
Mai [17]	76.63%
Kong [7]	77.33%
MTRLCNN [6]	79.06%
AesAttCNN [5]	78.62%
MLANs [18]	79.38%
AesCNN-W [27]	78.87%
Subject-Focused Subnet	79.8%
Detail-Oriented SubNet	80.30%
VP-Net	**80.55%**

tion are both important for assess aesthetic. Finally, the Detail-Oriented Subnet is improved by 1.47% compared with the baseline model.

4.4   VP-Net Experience Result

Compare with Other Methods. In this section, we compare our method with several representative approaches. We observe these approaches have different experimental settings. For a fair comparison, we report the best performance they have achieved, as shown in Table 3.

It can be seen that the two subnets can be used individually and still have a good performance, but get the best performance when they combined. This result proves that both of our approaches to achieve perceptual consistency are useful, either from the subject region or fine-gained details view. To summarize, Subject-Focus Subnet is highly interpretable with extractable intermediate result and decomposable sub-modules. It means that the overall performance can be improved by improving the performance of the sub-modules, but its disadvantage is that the model is more complex. While the Detail-Oriented Subnet is relatively simple which can be trained end-to-end and has better performance than others. But its disadvantages are poor interpretability and difficult to get more improve.

Experimental Result on AVA Dataset. In order to have a more intuitive understanding of VP-Net, we show some randomly selected images that are misclassified by the baseline model but can be correctly classified by VP-Net, as shown in Fig. 7.

It can be observed that VP-Net can distinguish the aesthetic from the holistic and fine-gained details. For example, the rainbow photo in Fig. 7a which is overall harmony but has rough details, or the celebrations photo in Fig. 7b which has delicate details but looks messy if it is resized to square and fed into CNN.

(a)

(b)

Fig. 7. Images misclassified by baseline model but correctly classified by VP-Net. (a) Low aesthetic examples. (b) High aesthetic examples.

5   Conclusion

In this paper, we propose a novel Visual Perception Net (VP-Net) architecture for image aesthetic assessment, which learn from subject region feature and multi-level deep-shallow features. In addition, we developed a subject region search algorithm to find out a composed region set from image. The experimental results demonstrate the superiority of our method. Future work can extend the principle of perceptual consistency to other abstract visual tasks, i.e., emotion classification or style classification.

References

1. Chen, Y., Hu, Y., Zhang, L., Li, P., Zhang, C.: Engineering deep representations for modeling aesthetic perception. IEEE Trans. Cybern. **48**(11), 3092–3104 (2018)
2. Datta, R., Joshi, D., Li, J., Wang, J.Z.: Studying aesthetics in photographic images using a computational approach. In: Leonardis, A., Bischof, H., Pinz, A. (eds.) ECCV 2006. LNCS, vol. 3953, pp. 288–301. Springer, Heidelberg (2006). https://doi.org/10.1007/11744078_23
3. Datta, R., Li, J., Wang, J.Z.: Algorithmic inferencing of aesthetics and emotion in natural images: an exposition. In: 2008 15th IEEE International Conference on Image Processing, ICIP 2008, pp. 105–108. IEEE (2008)
4. He, K., Zhang, X., Ren, S., Sun, J.: Deep residual learning for image recognition. In: Proceedings of the IEEE Conference on Computer Vision and Pattern Recognition, pp. 770–778 (2016)
5. Kairanbay, M., See, J., Wong, L.K., Hii, Y.L.: Filling the gaps: reducing the complexity of networks for multi-attribute image aesthetic prediction. In: 2017 IEEE International Conference on Image Processing (ICIP), pp. 3051–3055. IEEE (2017)
6. Kao, Y., He, R., Huang, K.: Deep aesthetic quality assessment with semantic information. IEEE Trans. Image Process. **26**(3), 1482–1495 (2017)

7. Kong, S., Shen, X., Lin, Z., Mech, R., Fowlkes, C.: Photo aesthetics ranking network with attributes and content adaptation. In: Leibe, B., Matas, J., Sebe, N., Welling, M. (eds.) ECCV 2016. LNCS, vol. 9905, pp. 662–679. Springer, Cham (2016). https://doi.org/10.1007/978-3-319-46448-0_40
8. Krizhevsky, A., Sutskever, I., Hinton, G.E.: ImageNet classification with deep convolutional neural networks. In: Advances in Neural Information Processing Systems, pp. 1097–1105 (2012)
9. LeCun, Y., Bengio, Y., Hinton, G.: Deep learning. Nature **521**(7553), 436 (2015)
10. Lin, T.Y., Dollár, P., Girshick, R.B., He, K., Hariharan, B., Belongie, S.J.: Feature pyramid networks for object detection. In: 2017 IEEE Conference on Computer Vision and Pattern Recognition (CVPR), pp. 936–944 (2017)
11. Liu, L., Chen, R., Wolf, L., Cohen-Or, D.: Optimizing photo composition. In: Computer Graphics Forum, vol. 29, pp. 469–478. Wiley (2010)
12. Liu, W., et al.: SSD: single shot multibox detector. In: Leibe, B., Matas, J., Sebe, N., Welling, M. (eds.) ECCV 2016. LNCS, vol. 9905, pp. 21–37. Springer, Cham (2016). https://doi.org/10.1007/978-3-319-46448-0_2
13. Lu, X., Lin, Z., Jin, H., Yang, J., Wang, J.Z.: RAPID: rating pictorial aesthetics using deep learning. In: Proceedings of the 22nd ACM International Conference on Multimedia, pp. 457–466. ACM (2014)
14. Lu, X., Lin, Z., Shen, X., Mech, R., Wang, J.Z.: Deep multi-patch aggregation network for image style, aesthetics, and quality estimation. In: Proceedings of the IEEE International Conference on Computer Vision, pp. 990–998 (2015)
15. Luo, W., Wang, X., Tang, X.: Content-based photo quality assessment. In: 2011 IEEE International Conference on Computer Vision (ICCV), pp. 2206–2213. IEEE (2011)
16. Luo, Y., Tang, X.: Photo and video quality evaluation: focusing on the subject. In: Forsyth, D., Torr, P., Zisserman, A. (eds.) ECCV 2008. LNCS, vol. 5304, pp. 386–399. Springer, Heidelberg (2008). https://doi.org/10.1007/978-3-540-88690-7_29
17. Mai, L., Jin, H., Liu, F.: Composition-preserving deep photo aesthetics assessment. In: Proceedings of the IEEE Conference on Computer Vision and Pattern Recognition, pp. 497–506 (2016)
18. Meng, X., Gao, F., Shi, S., Zhu, S., Zhu, J.: MLANs: image aesthetic assessment via multi-layer aggregation networks. In: 2018 Eighth International Conference on Image Processing Theory, Tools and Applications (IPTA), pp. 1–6. IEEE (2018)
19. Murray, N., Marchesotti, L., Perronnin, F.: AVA: a large-scale database for aesthetic visual analysis. In: 2012 IEEE Conference on Computer Vision and Pattern Recognition (CVPR), pp. 2408–2415. IEEE (2012)
20. Pan, J., Sayrol, E., Giro-i Nieto, X., McGuinness, K., O'Connor, N.E.: Shallow and deep convolutional networks for saliency prediction. In: Proceedings of the IEEE Conference on Computer Vision and Pattern Recognition, pp. 598–606 (2016)
21. Ren, S., He, K., Girshick, R., Sun, J.: Faster R-CNN: towards real-time object detection with region proposal networks. In: Advances in Neural Information Processing Systems, pp. 91–99 (2015)
22. Simonyan, K., Zisserman, A.: Very deep convolutional networks for large-scale image recognition. arXiv preprint arXiv:1409.1556 (2014)
23. Wang, Z., Liu, D., Chang, S., Dolcos, F., Beck, D., Huang, T.: Image aesthetics assessment using Deep Chatterjee's machine. In: 2017 International Joint Conference on Neural Networks (IJCNN), pp. 941–948. IEEE (2017)
24. Xie, S., Tu, Z.: Holistically-nested edge detection. In: Proceedings of the IEEE International Conference on Computer Vision, pp. 1395–1403 (2015)

25. Yeh, M.C., Cheng, Y.C.: Relative features for photo quality assessment. In: 2012 19th IEEE International Conference on Image Processing (ICIP), pp. 2861–2864. IEEE (2012)
26. Zeiler, M.D., Fergus, R.: Visualizing and understanding convolutional networks. In: Fleet, D., Pajdla, T., Schiele, B., Tuytelaars, T. (eds.) ECCV 2014. LNCS, vol. 8689, pp. 818–833. Springer, Cham (2014). https://doi.org/10.1007/978-3-319-10590-1_53
27. Zhang, C., Zhu, C., Xu, X., Liu, Y., Xiao, J., Tillo, T.: Visual aesthetic understanding: sample-specific aesthetic classification and deep activation map visualization. Sig. Process. Image Commun. **67**, 12–21 (2018)
28. Zhang, J., Du, J., Dai, L.: Multi-scale attention with dense encoder for handwritten mathematical expression recognition. arXiv preprint arXiv:1801.03530 (2018)
29. Zhou, X., et al.: EAST: an efficient and accurate scene text detector. In: 2017 IEEE Conference on Computer Vision and Pattern Recognition (CVPR), pp. 2642–2651 (2017)

Image De-noising by an Effective SURE-Based Weighted Bilateral Filtering

Jian Ji[(⊠)], Sitong Li, Guofei Hou, Fen Ren, and Qiguang Miao

School of Computer Science and Technology,
Xidian University, Xi'an 710071, China
jji@xidian.edu.cn

Abstract. The weighted bilateral filtering has been widely used in image de-noising, and there have been numerous improved bilateral filters. When dealing with the images with different noise levels, however, they may get de-noising results that are not robust and cannot remove salt and pepper (s&p) noise effectively. In this paper, we propose a new weighted bilateral filter, which preserves edge information and improves robustness, for image de-noising. The new filter introduces a new pseudo-median bilateral filter (NMBF) combined with a robust bilateral filter (RBF) in a weighted way for removing additive Gaussian and s&p noise. In addition, given the edge preserving, a robust estimation kernel function is applied in NMBF. Besides, to get optimal parameters, the modified filter involves the Stein's unbiased risk estimate (SURE) method. A diversity of images polluted by various degrees of Gaussian, s&p, and mixed noise were used to evaluate the performance of this new bilateral filter.

Keywords: Bilateral filtering · Image de-noising · Robust estimation · Edge preserving

1 Introduction

Tomasi and Manduchi by considering photometric distance in Gaussian filter propose the bilateral filter (BF) [1]. They preserve the edges as well as smooth the images by weighting the neighboring pixels based on their similarity and spatial distance. However, with the noise level increasing, the performance of the BF for image de-noising degrades quickly. Due to the BF can lead to staircase effect and gradient reversal which introduction of false edges in the image. Therefore, here our goal is computing BF's kernel function accurately to make it robust and preserve edges. This plays an important role in image de-noising.

There are several filters, such as fast bilateral filter, adaptive bilateral filter described in [2–5]. Good summaries on bilateral filter, interpretations, improvements and extensions are given in [6]. [7] recasted bilateral filtering in the framework of robust statistics. It turned out that the bilateral filtering is an estimator that considers the outliers over edges and the involved anisotropic diffusion. However, when dealing with the images with different noise levels, it has no robust de-noising results. To make bilateral filter more effective and robust for image de-noising, many improved filters have been proposed. Some variants of original bilateral filter replaced the combination

© Springer Nature Switzerland AG 2019
Z. Lin et al. (Eds.): PRCV 2019, LNCS 11858, pp. 316–327, 2019.
https://doi.org/10.1007/978-3-030-31723-2_27

of two or more bilateral filters, called weighted bilateral filter (WBF). There is a weighted bilateral filter [8] can perform as a detail information-preserving smoothing and Gaussian noise removing filter like the BF, also it can remove the impulse noise as Order-Statistic Filter (OSF) or nonlinear filter do. [9] proposed a self-intersections bilateral filtering algorithm, so that it can achieve good results on large noise, but this algorithm is relatively complex and computationally intensive. However, it has to be considered that a real image not only with Gaussian noise but salt and pepper noise (s&p) possibly. It was proved that above filters have no obvious advantages when the noise is mixed noise.

To overcome above problems, [10] proposed an adaptive median filter to remove impulse noise. [11] etc. have a better effect mainly for the removal of mixed noise. The Double Bilateral Filtering (DBF) [12] was proposed by a median filter integrated into a second bilateral filter for image mixed noise removal. However, due to the neglect of edge preservation and mean squared error (MSE), it makes the ability of noise suppression decrease at large noise levels. [13] brought up an adaptive median bilateral filtering algorithm, which analyze the bilateral filter mainly in the efficiency of noise suppression and the robustness. Thus, the weighted bilateral filters can actively direct mixed noise with good robustness, however it need to encounter the problem of choosing a filtering optimal parameter.

The above-mentioned filter can achieve promising performance on removing the different levels of noise and mixed noise. But it also needs to balance the parameters of the filter kernel function and the weight values or size of the filter window. Recently, a constant time implementation of the bilateral filter [14] has been proposed by Chaudhury et al., which based on SURE-optimal [15] raised-cosine range kernel approximate the Gaussian so that facilitate fast implementation of the bilateral filter. MSE can be calculated without the information of the clean image, because SURE is a useful surrogate of the MSE. In consequence, literatures [16] and [17] taking linear combination of estimators and adjusting the weights to get the optimal SURE. [18] proposed a fast algorithm for the optimized weighted filtering (OWBF) by combining standard bilateral filter (SBF) and RBF in a weighted way. Although the OWBF filter perform well in removing additive noise at modest level, its de-noising performance decreases at large level noise and s&p noise owing to the drawbacks of SBF.

In this paper, we propose a new SURE and edge-preserving weighted bilateral filter, which with edge preservation and outstanding robustness, for image noise removal, also called SEWBF. We introduce a new pseudo-median bilateral filter (NMBF), a Tukey's kernel function is applied to pseudo-median bilateral filter (PMBF) for edge preserving. Afterward, we incorporate the modified NMBF and robust bilateral filter (RBF) by weighting function, in which the RBF employed Gaussian kernel. Besides, we obtain optimal parameters of these filters and the estimate of the MSE according to the Stein's unbiased risk estimate (SURE) method.

This paper is organized as follows. In Sect. 2, we introduce the robust estimation, and employ the Tukey's kernel in a new pseudo-median bilateral filter. In Sect. 3, we propose the new weighted bilateral filter with edge preserving and robust filtering framework. In Sect. 4, we obtain de-noising results used some similar filter on test images, which demonstrate that the SEWBF perform better in visual effect and PSNR.

2 New Pseudo-Median Bilateral Filtering with Edge Preserving

In this section, we introduce a new pseudo-median bilateral filter with edge preserving, and also analyze the robustness of kernel functions.

2.1 Robust Estimators of Kernel Functions

In order to pursue the edge preserving when image de-noising, here we introduce several robust edge-stopping functions as follow:

$$Tukey\, g_\sigma(x) = \begin{cases} \frac{1}{2}\left[1 - (x/\sigma)^2\right]^2 & |x| \leq \sigma \\ 0, & otherwise \end{cases}, Huber\, g_\sigma(x) = \begin{cases} \frac{1}{\sigma} & |x| \leq \sigma \\ \frac{1}{|x|}, & otherwise \end{cases},$$

$$Lorentz\, g_\sigma(x) = \frac{2}{2 + \frac{x^2}{\sigma^2}}, \; Gaussian\, g_\sigma(x) = e^{-\frac{x^2}{2\sigma^2}}.$$

The "edge-stopping" function in the gray-scale weight equation is closely related to the error norm and influence function (shown in Fig. 1(a)) in the robust estimation framework. Shown in Fig. 1(b), outliers are influenced by the Huber mini-max constantly, and the Lorentz estimator gives them more importance than, say, the Gaussian estimator. The Tukey is the purely re-descending function we show and its outliers are thus completely ignored.

This connection leads to a new "edge-stopping" function based on Tukey's kernel robust estimator that preserves sharper boundaries than previous formulations and improves the automatic stopping of the diffusion [13]. It proved to be that Tukey's kernel influence function is more robust to outliers and have better edge-preserving.

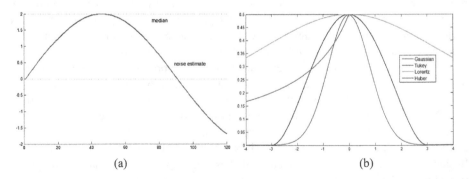

Fig. 1. (a) Shows the noise influence function. (b) Plots a variety of robust influence functions.

2.2   New Pseudo-Median Bilateral Filtering with Tukey's Kernel

The bilateral filter proposed in [1] involves a photometric weight as a factor of the spatial weight. From the original image I, the result of the bilateral filter of pixel p can be formulated as follows:

$$BF_1[I]_p = \frac{\sum\limits_{q \in S} G_{\sigma_d}(\|p - q\|)G_{\sigma_r}(\left|I_p - I_q^M\right|)I_q^M}{\sum\limits_{q \in S} G_{\sigma_d}(\|p - q\|)G_{\sigma_r}(\left|I_p - I_q^M\right|)} \qquad (1)$$

where

$$G_{\sigma_d}(\|p - q\|) = e^{\frac{-[(x-u)^2 + (y-v)^2]}{2\sigma_d^2}}, \; G_{\sigma_r}(\left|I_p - I_q^M\right|) = e^{\frac{-(I_p - I_q^M)^2}{2\sigma_r^2}} \qquad (2)$$

$BF[I]$ is an abbreviation of pseudo-median bilateral filtering (PMBF), the left of formula (1) is the pixel value after filtering. Our goal is to find an estimation of the clean image from the polluted samples. S is a collection of $(2N+1) \times (2N+1)$ neighborhood center pixels. I_q^M is gray-scale values of S. The domain and range similarity factor are defined by Gaussian kernels function in (2), respectively. σ_d is Gaussian kernels function's corresponding standard deviation for weight value adjustment of pixels whose space distances are large, and σ_r is Gaussian kernels function's corresponding standard deviation for weight value adjustment of pixels whose discrepancies are conspicuous. They are artificially set, according to the experience.

In PMBF approach, pixel values are averaged upon neighborhoods, whose size and shape depend on local image variation that is measured at every point. According to the analysis in Sect. 2.1, we consider that apply the robust estimation Tukey's kernel in pseudo median bilateral filtering. Therefore, we can obtain the new G'_{σ_d} and G'_{σ_r}, they are respectively:

$$G'_{\sigma_d}(\|p - q\|) = \frac{1}{2}\left[1 - (\|p - q\|/\sigma_d^2)\right]^2 \qquad (3)$$

$$G'_{\sigma_r}(\left|I_p - I_q^M\right|) = \frac{1}{2}\left[1 - \left(\left|I_p - I_q^M\right|/\sigma_r^2\right)\right]^2 \qquad (4)$$

Plugging (3) and (4) into (1), we obtain the new pseudo-median bilateral filtering (NMBF) formulate. Although the pseudo median bilateral filtering suppresses s&p noise, it causes the image lose edge detail information when suppress mixed noise, so that the de-noised images are blurred. However, the new pseudo-median bilateral filter (NMBF) not only suppresses mixed noise, but also preserves edge details well.

3   Weighted Bilateral Filtering with SURE-Robust Estimation

3.1   Robust Bilateral Filter

Our goal is to make the new weighted filter robust, so we introduce the robust bilateral filter (RBF) here. Firstly, the goal is to find a de-noised estimate $\widehat{I}_p$ of the corrupted samples. The de-noised image should bear a resemblance to the clean image visually. We use the MSE to quantify the resemblance:

$$MSE = \frac{1}{N} \sum_{q \in I} \left(\widehat{I}_p - I_p \right)^2 \tag{5}$$

where N denotes the total number of the pixels in the image I. Here, we propose the improved bilateral filtering RBF formula:

$$BF_2[I]_p = \frac{\sum\limits_{q \in S} G_{\sigma_d}(\|p - q\|) G_{\sigma_r}\left(|\bar{I}_q - \bar{I}_p|\right) I_q}{\sum\limits_{q \in S} G_{\sigma_d}(\|p - q\|) G_{\sigma_r}\left(|\bar{I}_q - \bar{I}_p|\right)} \tag{6}$$

where $\bar{I}_q = \frac{1}{(2L+1)^2} \sum\limits_{q \in S} I_p$, L controlled by the smoothing mechanism window size, a large number of experiments show that the optimal settings are $L = 1$ and window size is 3×3.

3.2   SURE-Optimally Bilateral Filtering

To smooth an image optimally with bilateral filter in the presence of noise, it need choose the parameters optimally as well. Here, SURE is introduced to calculate the optimal parameters of the RBF. The results are shown in Fig. 2. SURE in (b) infinitely approximates the MSE in (a). Meanwhile, SURE estimator for the RBF get the PSNR (b) match closely. So, the optimal parameters of MSE and SURE proved to be the same. This makes SURE a useful surrogate for the MSE. We can compute it without the information of the clean image.

Because SURE is an unbiased estimation of the MSE, the optimal parameters in the minimum MSE sense can be approximated by minimizing SURE. The RBF utilizes Lemma 1 [19] to the expression of MSE. The formula (7) for SURE RBF is obtained:

$$SURE(I) = \frac{1}{|I|} \sum_{p \in I} \left(BF[I]_p - I_p \right)^2 - \sigma^2 + \frac{2\sigma^2}{|I|} \sum_{p \in I} \frac{\partial BF[I]_p}{\partial I_p} \tag{7}$$

SURE for the RBF can be expressed by substituting:

$$\frac{\partial BF[I]_p}{\partial I_p} = \sum_{p \in I} \frac{1}{W_p} \left(\sum_{q \in S} \frac{\partial(\|p - q\|)\left(|I_p - I_q|\right)}{\partial I_p} I_q + 1 - BF[I]_p \sum_{q \in S} \frac{\partial(\|p - q\|)\left(|I_p - I_q|\right)}{\partial I_p} \right) \tag{8}$$

where $W_p = \sum_{q \in S} G_{\sigma_d}(\|p - q\|)G_{\sigma_r}(|I_p - I_q|)$. The meaning of σ_d and σ_r here are similar to those in Sect. 2.2. Through the above formula (8), we can get the optimal and sure parameters for robust bilateral filtering, and then improve the filtering result.

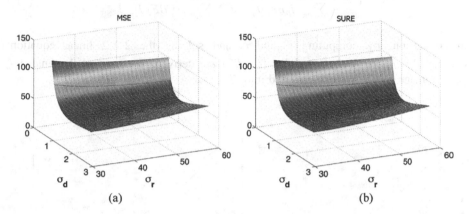

(a)   (b)

Fig. 2. Comparison of the MSE and SURE plots for Lena image: (a) and (b) correspond to the robust bilateral filter.

3.3   SURE and Edge-Preserving Weighted Bilateral Filtering

Through robust bilateral filtering, Gaussian noise can be effectively suppressed. The de-noising results that obtained by using a standard bilateral filter (SBF), median bilateral filter (MBF) and robust bilateral filter (RBF) upon a pair of test images are displayed in Fig. 3. At low noise levels the RBF makes more blurring compared to MBF and SBF, which lowers the overall signal-to-noise ratio. However, note that the RBF in PSNR is regularly as large as 9 dB in the case of large noise. These results indicate that it depends on the type of the image whether the RBF perform better exceed a certain noise level. The noise image has been a relatively clean image when the noise is small.

On one hand, we should consider the robustness of the bilateral filter. On the other hand, we also need try to maintain more edge detail information. According to above analysis, thus, we use the edge-preserving NMBF combined with the SURE-RBF to obtain a final normalization weighted filtering (SEWBF) formula:

$$BF[I]_p = \alpha BF_1[I]_p + \beta BF_2[I]_p \tag{9}$$

where α, β are weight values for balancing these two bilateral filters. The optimal weights in (9) are proposed to find by minimizing SURE. On substituting (9) in (7), we see that SURE is quadratic in α and β. Thus, by convexity, a necessary and sufficient condition for optimality is that the gradient of (7) must vanish at the optimal weights. The resulting gradient equations can be described as $C(\alpha^{\#}, \beta^{\#}) = c$, where

$$C = \begin{pmatrix} \sum_{p \in I} BF_1[I]_p^2 & \sum_{p \in I} BF_1[I]_p BF_2[I]_p \\ \sum_{p \in I} BF_1[I]_p BF_2[I]_p & \sum_{p \in I} BF_2[I]_p^2 \end{pmatrix}, \tag{10}$$

$$c = \begin{pmatrix} \sum_{p \in I} I_p BF_1[I]_p - \sigma^2 & \sum_{p \in I} \partial_p BF_1[I]_p \\ \sum_{p \in I} I_p BF_2[I]_p - \sigma^2 & \sum_{p \in I} \partial_p BF_2[I]_p \end{pmatrix} \tag{11}$$

In conclusion, by computing C and c, and solving the 2×2 linear equation $C(\alpha^{\#}, \beta^{\#}) = c$, the optimal weights $(\alpha^{\#}, \beta^{\#})$ are derived. We can get the final de-noised image by the weights inserted into (7).

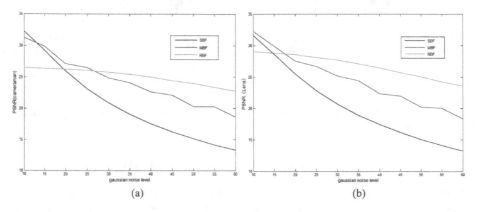

Fig. 3. Comparison the PSNR value of the SBF, MBF and RBF at Gaussian noise standard deviation $\sigma = 10, 15, 20, 25, 30, 35, 40, 45, 50, 55, 60$.

4   Experiments

To verify the performance of the new edge-preserving weighted bilateral filter—SEWBF method, we use several images (Butterfly, Lena, Cameraman, House with $size = 256 \times 256$) contaminated with Gaussian noise and mixed noise. We compared the de-noising results in several algorithms in terms of both visual effect and the peak signal-to-noise ratios (PSNR) of de-noised images.

4.1   Weighted Kernel Function

We verify that two bilateral filters can be weighted by observing the sensitivity of weighted parameters of Gaussian's and Tukey's kernel functions (expressed as w_G and w_T respectively). We first researched the sensitivity of parameter of the kernel functions, to the de-noised results in PSNR while keeping $\sigma_r = \sigma_r'$ of NMBF and RBF, on image added additive Gaussian noise with $\sigma = 10, 20, 30, 100$ for Lena. The abscissa represents the weighting parameter of the Gaussian kernel function, and the ordinate is the PNSR of de-noising results under different noise conditions. As shown in Fig. 4, it is not difficult to find that achieve the better performance under small noises by SEWBF method, which with larger Tukey's kernel weight value. On the other hand, larger w_G were beneficial for moderately and seriously degraded images in the case of large noise (such as $\sigma = 100$). As a result, combining the two kernel functions is beneficial to the de-noising effect of combining two bilateral filters.

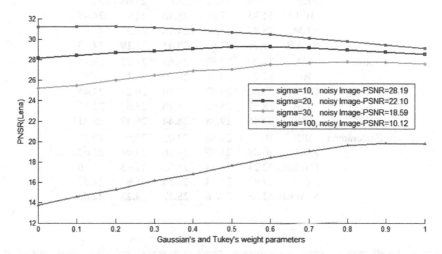

Fig. 4. Sensitivity analyses in PSNR of parameters w_G and w_T in restoring image corrupted by different degrees of additive Gaussian noise using the proposed weighted bilateral filter. The abscissa represents is w_G from 0 to 1, increasing by 0.1 (w_T from 1 to 0). And the different-color curves represent the PSNR of the de-noised Lena image at different noise levels $\sigma = 10, 20, 30, 100$. (Color figure online)

4.2 Experiments with Additive Gaussian Noise

De-noising Result. To validate the ability of de-noising additive Gaussian noise, we compared SEWBF filtering method with the OWBF, RBF, MBF, and Non-local means filter (NLM) on a series of noisy images. Note that the de-noised image that obtained by using the SEWBF method looks much sharper than that OWBF's, and has a markedly higher PSNR value. As is shown in Table 1, we compare the de-noising performance of the SEWBF method at different noise levels. We can see that this new algorithm has extent advantages over other algorithms, it has larger PSNR values than other algorithms overall.

Table 1. Comparison of the MBF, RBF, OWBF, NLM and SEWBF at different noise levels

Images	Method	$\sigma = 10$	$\sigma = 30$	$\sigma = 40$	$\sigma = 50$	$\sigma = 60$
Butterfly	MBF	29.99	24.95	22.54	20.54	18.74
	RBF	29.14	27.38	26.16	24.63	23.17
	OWBF	**31.79**	27.52	26.05	24.48	23.20
	NLM	28.22	23.54	22.83	22.27	21.66
	SEWBF	31.74	**27.77**	**26.29**	**24.83**	**23.45**
Lena	MBF	29.62	25.42	22.99	20.86	19.16
	RBF	29.09	27.72	28.09	25.08	24.42
	OWBF	**31.83**	27.86	28.10	24.93	24.45
	NLM	28.87	24.90	24.16	23.37	22.72
	SEWBF	31.79	**27.98**	**28.41**	**25.19**	**24.63**
House	MBF	31.74	23.69	23.65	21.22	19.35
	RBF	31.71	29.80	28.09	26.18	24.42
	OWBF	**33.60**	29.82	28.10	26.29	24.45
	NLM	28.97	25.02	24.26	23.63	22.82
	SEWBF	33.46	**29.98**	**28.44**	**26.49**	**25.31**
Cameraman	MBF	30.78	23.88	23.03	20.95	19.16
	RBF	26.48	25.75	24.86	23.98	22.62
	OWBF	32.21	26.34	25.05	24.05	22.66
	NLM	27.90	23.14	22.54	21.82	21.32
	SEWBF	**32.25**	**26.76**	**25.27**	**24.23**	**22.83**

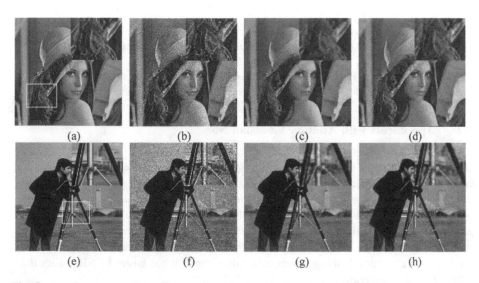

(a)   (b)   (c)   (d)

(e)   (f)   (g)   (h)

Fig. 5. (a) The Lena original image. (b) Noisy image ($\sigma = 30$). (c) OWBF (PSNR = 29.23) (d) SEWBF (PSNR = 29.81). (e) The Cameraman original image. (f) Noisy image ($\sigma = 30$). (g) OWBF (PSNR = 26.34). (h). SEWBF (PSNR = 26.76). It is obvious that the new filter remains more edge detail in the black wireframe.

Edge Preserving. To understand the ability of edge preserving when removing additive Gaussian noise, we compared SEWBF with the OWBF on noisy images. Figure 5 illustrates the restoration results of image Lena and Cameraman corrupted by additive Gaussian noise with $\sigma = 30$ using the OWBF and SEWBF method. From the following two comparisons of Lena and Cameraman (in Fig. 5), the SEWBF de-noising results of hair filament in Lena image has clearer performance while the OWBF's is relatively fuzzy. In the Cameraman image, the former performance is more real of the camera support rod details. It is indicated that comparing with the OWBF methods SEWBF can removes quantities of noise and preserves edges sharpness simultaneously, e.g., the hair and camera support rod.

4.3 Experiments on Mixed Noise

For the sake of completeness, we research the performance of the NMBF in restoring images by a various of mixed noise. Table 2 shows the restoration result of Monarch images corrupted by a mix of Gaussian noise with $\sigma = 10$, 20, 30 and s&p noise with s&p = 10% using Double BF (DBF), entropy-based bilateral filtering (EBF) [20], and NMBF methods (proposed in Sect. 2) respectively. It is observed that a certain amount of noise was suppressed, and boundaries tiny details are preserved. The NMBF out-performed the DBF and EBF, and its visual quality was more excellent.

Table 2. Comparison of the DBF, EBF and NMBF at different noise levels

Image	Method	$\sigma = 10$	$\sigma = 20$	$\sigma = 30$
		s&p = 10%		
Monarch	DBF	24.92	24.49	22.89
	EBF	26.36	25.32	23.72
	NMBF	**27.58**	**26.48**	**24.52**

At last, we compared the NMBF with other filters in de-noising Monarch, Lena, House and Cameraman images contaminated by mixed noise with different levels of Gaussian noise ($\sigma = 10$ and 20) and s&p (s&p = 10%). Although MBF and Dou-ble BF can suppress the mixed noise better, the more loss of the edge details causes the image very fuzzy. As illustrated in Fig. 6, the PSNR values of the NMBF were quite higher than other methods in all experiments. Furthermore, the original bilateral fil-tering algorithm has no ability to suppress the s&p noise completely.

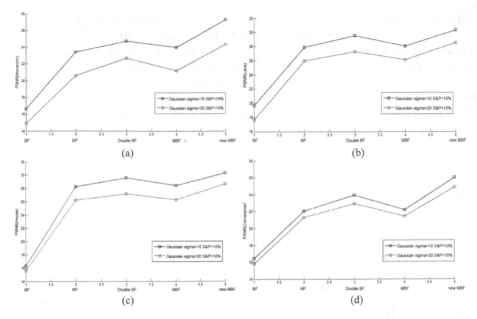

Fig. 6. Comparison of restoration results in PSNR respectively on Monarch, Lena, House and Cameraman, images corrupted by mixes of different degrees of additive Gaussian noise ($\sigma = 10$ and 20.) and a constant s&p noise (s&p = 10%).

5   Conclusion

The SEWBF algorithm is a weighted filtering algorithm, which possesses the comprehensive advantages of PMBF and RBF, can achieve robustness and maintain the edge details. Moreover, the inhibitory effect of Gaussian noise and s&p noise and other noise types are very good. In this paper, a novel robust kernel function is proposed, which is then applied to the pseudo median bilateral filter which can effectively remove s&p noise. At the same time, the robust bilateral filter is introduced, which involves the estimation of the mean square error (MSE), and then the SURE estimation method is used to define the robust bilateral filtering de-noising model to obtain the optimal parameters. Finally, the optimal weight factor is calculated by SURE, and the SEWBF algorithm is obtained by weighted mean of improved pseudo median bilateral filter and robust bilateral filter. Multiple sets of experiments verified the effectiveness of SEWBF.

References

1. Tomasi, C., Manduchi, R.: Bilateral filtering for gray and color images. In: 6th International Conference on Computer Vision, pp. 839–846 (1998)
2. Guo, J., Chen, C., Xiang, S., Ou, Y., Li, B.: A fast bilateral filtering algorithm based on rising cosine function. Neural Comput. Appl. **31**, 1–12 (2019)

3. Joseph, J., Periyasamy, R.: An image driven bilateral filter with adaptive range and spatial parameters for denoising magnetic resonance images. Comput. Electr. Eng. **69**, 782–795 (2018)
4. Yuan, M., Zhang, X.: Bilateral filter acceleration based on weighted variable projection. Electron. Lett. **54**(6), 352–353 (2018)
5. Mathiyalagan, P., Suvitha, N.: Image fusion using convolutional neural network with bilateral filtering. In: 2018 9th International Conference on Computing, Communication and Networking Technologies, pp. 1–11 (2018)
6. Paris, S., Kornprobst, P., Tumblin, J., Durand, F.: Bilateral filtering: theory and applications. Found. Trends Comput. Graph. Vis. **1**(4), 1–74 (2016)
7. Durand, F., Dorsey, J.: Fast bilateral filtering for the display of high-dynamic-range images. ACM Trans. Graph. **21**(3), 257–266 (2002)
8. Shen, C., Lu, Z.: Weighted Bilateral Filter - a new image filter for noise removing and detail information preserving. In: 2012 IEEE Global High Tech Congress on Electronics, pp. 1–5 (2012)
9. Chang, H., Chu, W.C.: Double bilateral filtering for image noise removal. In: 2009 WRI World Congress on Computer Science and Information Engineering, pp. 451–455 (2009)
10. Kumar, A., Datta, A.: Adaptive edge discriminated median filter to remove impulse noise. In: 2016 International Conference on Computing, Communication and Automation, pp. 1409–1413 (2016)
11. Xiong, C., Chen, L., Pang, Y.: An adaptive bilateral filtering algorithm and its application in edge detection. In: 2010 International Conference on Measuring Technology and Mechatronics Automation, pp. 440–443 (2010)
12. Liu, Y.H., Gao, K., Ni, G.Q.: An improved trilateral filter for Gaussian and impulse noise removal. In: The 2nd International Conference on Industrial Mechatronics and Automation, pp. 385–388 (2010)
13. Balasubramanian, G., Chelvan, A.C., Vijayan, S., Gowrison, G.: Adaptive averaging of multiresolution bilateral and median filtering for image denoising. In: 2012 International Conference on Emerging Trends in Science, Engineering and Technology, pp. 154–158 (2012)
14. Chaudhury, N., Sage, D., Unser, M.: Fast $O(1)$ bilateral filtering using trigonometric range kernels. IEEE Trans. Image Process. **20**(12), 3376–3382 (2011)
15. Blu, T., Luisier, F.: The SURE-LET approach to image denoising. IEEE Trans. Image Process. **16**(11), 2778–2786 (2007)
16. Kishan, H., Seelamantula, C.S.: SURE-fast bilateral filters. In: 2012 IEEE International Conference on Acoustics, Speech and Signal Processing, pp. 1129–1132 (2012)
17. Guglani, D., Katyal, N.K.: Noise removal using double density Complex Dual Tree Transform with NeighShrink SURE and median filter. In: 1st International Conference on Next Generation Computing Technologies, pp. 995–998 (2015)
18. Chaudhury, K.N., Rithwik, K.: Image de-noising using optimally weighted bilateral filters: a sure and fast approach. In: IEEE International Conference on Image Processing, Quebec City, pp. 108–112 (2015)
19. Black, M.J., Sapiro, G., Marimont, D.H., Heeger, D.: Robust anisotropic diffusion. IEEE Trans. Image Process. **7**(3), 421–432 (1998)
20. Dai, T., Lu, W., Wang, W., Wang, J., Xia, S.T.: Entropy-based bilateral filtering with a new range kernel. Sig. Process. **137**, 223–234 (2017)

Automatic Detection of Pneumonia in Chest X-Ray Images Using Cooperative Convolutional Neural Networks

Kun Wang[1] , Xiaohong Zhang[1,2]([✉]), Sheng Huang[1], and Feiyu Chen[1]

[1] School of Big Data and Software Engineering, Chongqing University,
Chongqing 401331, China
{kun.wang,xhongz,huangsheng,fchen}@cqu.edu.cn
[2] Key Laboratory of Dependable Service Computing in Cyber Physical Society,
Ministry of Education, Chongqing University, Chongqing 400044, China

Abstract. Chest X-ray images are currently the best available visual media for diagnosing pneumonia, which plays a crucial role in clinical care. Medical images diagnosing can be error-prone for inexperienced radiologists, while tedious and time-consuming for experienced radiologists. To address these issues, we study automatically detect pneumonia in Chest X-ray images. However, this task exists several challenges. First, abnormal regions of pneumonia are difficult to identify due to the noise interference from other tissue and lesions. Second, the features of lung regions are usually essential information for diagnosis. With the pneumonia disease happens in lung areas, only training CNNs using global image may be affected by the irrelevant noisy regions. Third, the appearance of pneumonia in X-ray images is often vague, can overlap with other diagnoses. To cope with these challenges, we first introduce a lung segmentation network, which segments the lung from the original images. Then, develop a feature extraction model, which incorporates global and local features for pneumonia classification. Finally, build a cooperative learning framework, which merges bounding boxes (localization of pneumonia) from two cooperative models. We demonstrate the effectiveness of our proposed methods on the Kaggles RSNA Pneumonia Detection Challenge dataset and reaches excellent performance with the level of the top 1% in this competition.

Keywords: Pneumonia detection · Chest X-ray images ·
Deep learning · Convolutional Neural Networks

This work was partially supported by the Chongqing Major Thematic Projects (Grant no. cstc2018jszx-cyztzxX0017). Xiaohong Zhang is the corresponding author of the article.

Z. Lin et al. (Eds.): PRCV 2019, LNCS 11858, pp. 328–340, 2019.
https://doi.org/10.1007/978-3-030-31723-2_28

1   Introduction

Pneumonia accounts for over 15% of all deaths of children under five years old internationally. In 2015, 920,000 children under the age of 5 died from the disease. In the United States, pneumonia accounts for over 500,000 visits to emergency departments [23] and over 50,000 deaths in 2015 [15], keeping the ailment on the list of top 10 causes of death in the country. Chest X-ray images are currently the best available visual media for diagnosing pneumonia [17], playing a crucial role in clinical care. However, detecting pneumonia in Chest X-rays is a challenging task that relies on the availability of expert radiologists. For less-experienced radiologists, especially those working in the rural area where the quality of healthcare is relatively low, diagnosing medical-imaging is hard.

For experienced radiologists reading a lot of medical images is tedious and time-consuming. China has the world's largest population (1.42 billion), followed by India (1.35 billion), a radiologist may need to read hundreds of radiology images per day, which occupies most of their working time. In summing, for both inexperienced and experienced medical professionals, diagnosing Chest X-ray images is an effortful task.

This motivates us to investigate whether it is possible to detect pneumonia in Chest X-ray images automatically. Several challenges need to be addressed.

First, how to localize the lung region and identify the area of pneumonia are challenging. We solve these problems by introducing the lung segmentation network, which effectively positions the region of the lung and removes noise interference from other tissue and lesions.

Second, how to effectively combine the global and local regions of images. With the pneumonia disease happens in lung areas, only training CNNs using global image may be affected by the irrelevant noisy areas. A radiologist first generally will combine the global images and the local of lung regions, then analyze and diagnose the results. Similar like that, we feed the segmented lung image together with the original image to the CNNs, so that the feature extracted by the model can complement and contrast each other.

Third, it is difficult for radiologists to detect pneumonia in Chest X-ray images. The appearance of pneumonia in X-ray images is often vague, can overlap with other diagnoses, and can mimic many other benign abnormalities. These differences have led to considerable differences in the diagnosis of pneumonia by radiologists [7,16,17]. In the actual diagnosis process, multiple radiologists work together to diagnose the patient, which will improve accuracy. We address this advantage by building a novel cooperative learning task framework, which treats the detection task of Chest X-ray images as a cooperative learning task.

Overall, the main contributions of our work are:

- We introduce a lung segmentation network, which can segment the lung from the original images. Input the original image and the segmented image into our model, which combines global and local features to improve the detection effect of pneumonia.

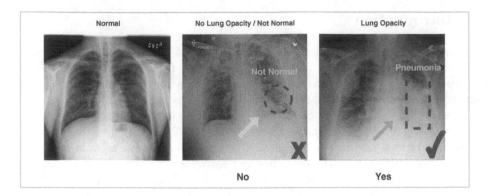

Fig. 1. Examples of the dataset [1]. (left) Normal Lung, (mid) No Lung Opacity/Not Normal (no pneumonia), (right) Lung Opacity (pneumonia).

- We build a cooperative learning framework, and merges bounding boxes from two cooperative models, which improves the accuracy of the localization of pneumonia.
- We perform extensive experiments on the Kaggles RSNA Pneumonia Detection Challenge dataset (see Fig. 1). The experiment results show that the effectiveness of our proposed methods and achieves promising performance with the level of the top 1% in this competition.

2 Related Works

Medical Disease Diagnosis with Deep Learning. Deep Learning methods have applied to disease classification [2], sensitive area localization [18,22] and tissue segmentation [11,14]. With the development of pulmonary tuberculosis classification [10] and pulmonary nodule detection [8] algorithms, more and more attention paid to the automatic diagnosis of chest X-ray images. Islam et al., [9] explore various CNN architectures and find that single CNN does not perform well across all abnormalities. Therefore, they leverage the model ensemble to improve classification accuracy. Wang et al. [25] released chest X-ray-14, an order of magnitude larger than previous datasets of its kind, and also benchmarked different convolutional neural network architectures pre-trained on ImageNet. Rajpurkar et al. [17], developed an algorithm called Chexnet, which is a 121-layer neural network that solves the problem of multi-label classification.

This paper unlike the previous methods in that we use a cooperative learning framework and fuse the global and local information to detection(localization) pneumonia.

General Object Detectors. In recent years, the use of deep neural network (DNN) frameworks has made significant progress in object detection. The most advanced DNN detectors can be divided into two categories: (1) two-stage methods, including [3,20] and (2) one-stage methods, including [19,24]. In general, one-stage methods are faster, but two-stage methods are more accurate. However, in [13], the authors suggest that the dense anchor boxes create a considerable imbalance between positive and negative anchor boxes during training. This imbalance causes the training to be inefficient and hence the performance to be suboptimal. They propose a new loss, Focal Loss, to dynamically adjust the weights of each anchor box and show that their one-stage detector can outperform the two-stage detectors. Inspired by this, our method also adopts a modified RetinaNet [13] as pneumonia detectors.

3 Methods

In this section, we describe the proposed automatic detection of pneumonia in Chest X-ray images (CXRs) using Cooperative Convolutional Neural Networks (Co-CNN). We will first interpret the architecture of Co-CNN in Sect. 3.1. Second, we present the implementation process of Co-CNN in Sect. 3.2. Finally, introduce the dataset we used in Sect. 3.3.

3.1 Network Architecture of Co-CNN

The architecture of Co-CNN is presented in Fig. 2. It has three major branches, i.e., the lung segmentation processing branch, pneumonia classification branch, and pneumonia detection (localization) branch. We develop a network with CNN architecture that avoids the classical handcrafted features extraction step, by processing features extraction and detection lesion at one time within the two detections neural network and consequently provide a diagnosis automatically.

Processing of Lung Segmentation Branch. The U-Net [21] neural network, which was used to predict the confidence of each pixel associated with the lung. Then we multiply the original image matrix by the lung localization matrix to get the lung segmentation (Fig. 3). Both the original image and the segmented image were fed into our Co-CNN to provide a hypothesis for lung localization.

Pneumonia Classification Branch. The pneumonia classification branch predicts the probability of object presence at each spatial position for each of the A anchor and object classes. The parameters for this subnet are shared across all pyramid leves. The subnet obtains an input feature map with a $C(C = 256)$ channel from a given pyramid level, applying four 3×3 conv layers, each with a C filter and each followed by ReLU activation, then it is followed by a 3×3 with KA filters. Finally, connect sigmoid activation to output the KA binary prediction for each spatial location.

.

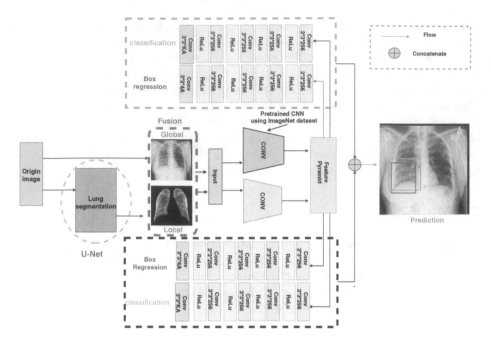

Fig. 2. The overall framework of the Cooperative Convolutional Neural Networks (Co-CNN). We show an example with ResNet50 and ResNet101 as a base network (a) lung segmentation processing branch (b) pneumonia classification branch (c) pneumonia detection (localization) branch. A represents the number of anchors and K represents the object classes. We used $K = 2$ and $A = 9$ in our experiments.

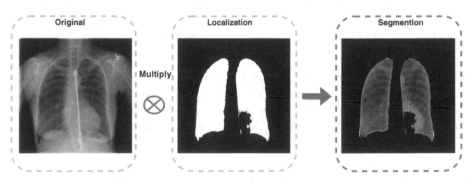

Fig. 3. (Left) The original input image, (Mid) Predicted lung location, (Right) Segmented lung. This task used a pre-trained 2D lung segmentation U-Net (https://github.com/hahnicity/pytorch-lung-segmentation) to carry out.

Pneumonia Localization Branch. In parallel with the pneumonia classification subnet. The design of the box regression subnet is same to the classification subnet except that it terminates in $4A$ linear outputs at each spatial location.

For each spatial location of each anchors A, these 4 outputs predict the relative offset between the ground truth box and the anchor.

3.2 Implementation Process of Co-CNN

Data Augmentation. In our implementation, before being fed the images into the network, the original image resized from 1024×1024 pixels down to 224×224 pixels. Normalize each pixel of the image by subtracting the average and dividing by the standard deviation at that location, allowing us to make training on hardware more efficient. We also augmented the training data with rotating, translating, scaling and horizontal flipping.

Network Structure. The ResNet-50 and ResNet-110 [6] was pre-trained on ImageNet as our base network. The Feature Pyramid Network (FPN) from [12] was adopt as the backbone network for Co-CNN. We used Non-Maximum Suppression (NMS) to eliminate any overlapping bounding boxes for each detection network. Then got the weighted average of over the overlapping bounding boxes from them.

Network Parameters Setting. We randomly split the dataset into training (95%), validation (5%). The network was trained applying stochastic gradient descent (SGD) with Nesterov momentum. A low initial learning rate of 0.01 that is delayed by a factor of 1e−4 for each epoch and with momentum 0.9 used. We training for 25 epochs with 3000 steps per epoch and batch size of 8.

Model Selection. The model snapshot was saved after each epoch. We calculated bounding boxes, and the score threshold was providing the maximum *Youden* index on the validation dataset. We calculated *sensitivity* and *specificity* concerning images, not bounding boxes it was necessary for the system to classify whether an image as a whole was positive or negative for pneumonia. The model snapshots that performed best on the leaderboard were ones with the highest *Youden* index, which is the best candidate for the cooperative model.

Loss Function. Denote the ground truth bounding box of a target pneumonia by (G_x, G_y, G_w, G_h) and the bounding box of an anchor by (A_x, A_y, A_w, A_h), where x, y, w, and h denote the box's center coordinates and its width and height. Intersection over Union (IoU) is used to determine the label of each anchor box. Anchor boxes whose IoU with the target pneumonia larger than 0.5 and smaller than 0.02 are treated as positive and negative samples, respectively. Others are neglected in the training process. For bounding box regression, we adopt the parameterizations of the four coordinates following:

$$d_x = (G_x - A_x)/A_w \tag{1}$$

$$d_y = (G_y - A_y)/A_h \tag{2}$$

$$d_w = log(G_w/A_w) \tag{3}$$

$$d_h = log(G_h/A_h) \tag{4}$$

The corresponding predictions are $\hat{d}_x, \hat{d}_y, \hat{d}_w, \hat{d}_z$ respectively. The total regression loss is defined by:

$$L_{reg} = \sum_{k \in x,y,w,h} S(d_k, \hat{d}_x) \tag{5}$$

Where the loss metric is a smoothed L1-norm function:

$$S(d, \hat{d}) = \begin{cases} 0.5|d - \hat{d}|, & \text{if } |d - \hat{d}| < 1, \\ |d - \hat{d}| - 0.5. & \text{otherwise.} \end{cases} \tag{6}$$

Focal loss [13] is mainly to solve the severe imbalance of positive and negative sample proportion in one-stage target detection. The loss function reduces the weight of a large number of simple negative samples in training. The focal loss is a modification based on cross-entropy loss function and $p \in [0, 1]$ is the model's estimated probability for the class with label $y = 1$. In practice, adding balance factor α to balance the positive and negative samples were not the proportion of itself:

$$L_{cls} = \begin{cases} -\alpha(1-p)^\gamma, & y = 1, \\ -(1-\alpha)p^\gamma log(1-p). & y = 0. \end{cases} \tag{7}$$

In general α should be decreased slightly as γ is increased (for $\gamma = 2$, $\alpha = 0.25$ works best). The loss function for each anchor box is defined by

$$L = L_{cls} + mL_{reg} \tag{8}$$

The term mL_{reg} means the regression loss is activated only for positive anchors ($m = 1$) and is disabled otherwise ($m = 0$). The overall loss function is the mean of loss function for some selected anchor boxes.

Bounding Box Prediction. Finally, predictions generated by the cooperative of two of models trained on the entirety of the training set. To reduce false negatives, which might occur if any one of the two models did not get out a bounding box, We used a relatively low bounding box confidence. First, bounding boxes from two models were clustered such that those with a $IoU \geq 0.25$ were grouped. We took the two bounding boxes which contributed to the resulting regions in the intersected image. We used the score of the boxes from each network as the weight. So the final predicted bounding boxes are:

$$Box_{pred} = (w_1 box_{pred1} \oplus w_2 box_{pred2})\sigma \tag{9}$$

Where $\oplus$ represents the array concatenate. The Box_{pred} is the final predicted bounding boxes of Co-CNN, box_{pred1} and box_{pred2} represent the result of each network bounding boxes. w_1, w_2 represents the weight of each network and σ represents the scaling factor(set to 0.18).

3.3   Dataset

Our dataset from Kaggles RSNA Pneumonia Detection Challenge 2018 [1]. All provided images are in DICOM format. The dataset consists of approximately 26,000 training images and 3,000 test images. In the training set, 6,000 CXRs were patients with pneumonia, and 20,000 CXRs were patients without pneumonia, some of which with other medical conditions. The testing set contained CXRs with no pneumonia, with pneumonia, and with other medical conditions. There are three types of labels for each patient that are found in the dataset (Normal, No Lung Opacity/Not Normal, Lung Opacity).

4   Results

Figure 4a, b and c respectively shows the classification results of a single model in the validation dataset. As shown in the graph, A model is in the 22 epoch, B model is in the 18 epoch, and the C model is in the 25 epoch, which the *Youden* index is the largest, and in (Fig. 4d) shows the mean score of every single model. Table 1 shows the results of the best model's classification and localization of pneumonia in the validation set. The experimental results using a single detection model and cooperative detection models on the RSNA Pneumonia Detection test dataset in Table 2. The results of different input images for comparison in Table 3. Table 4 shows the performance of the top 5 teams in the competition. PEEP [1] is the champion team and gets the score is 0.2547 in this competition. We provide examples of bounding box predictions from the test dataset in Fig. 5. The top row shows successful predictions and the bottom row displays the mismatch between ground truth annotations and predictions.

Table 1. The best model choices are A_{22}, B_{18}, C_{25}, and the subscript represents the epoch of the model. The results of classification and localization pneumonia in the validation dataset.

Training model	Base network	Youden	Sensitivity	Specificity	Score
A_{22}	ResNet50	0.6606	0.8937	0.7669	0.2204
B_{18}	ResNet101	0.6618	**0.9036**	0.7582	0.2187
C_{25}	ResNet152	**0.6757**	0.8904	**0.7853**	**0.2256**

5   Discussion

Our Co-CNN models outperformed single models (see Table 2). We illustrate that our proposed cooperative learning framework is effective. We used the residual network as a base network, and also tried other base networks (such as VGGNet),

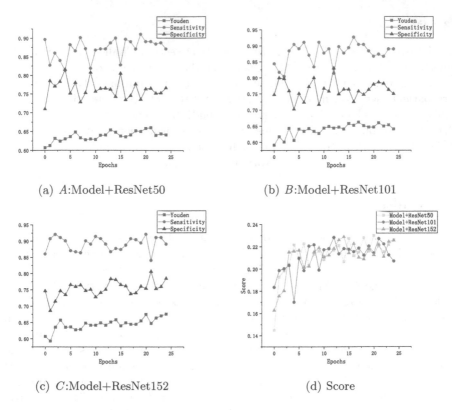

(a) A:Model+ResNet50

(b) B:Model+ResNet101

(c) C:Model+ResNet152

(d) Score

Fig. 4. Main result of the model in the validation dataset at each epoch ($Youden, sensitivity$ and $specificity$). (a) A: Model+ResNet50 (b) B: Model+ResNet101 (c) C: Model+ResNet152 (d) the mean score of each model (A, B, C). Where ($Youden = sensitivity + specificity - 1$).

Table 2. Main results for Kaggles RSNA Pneumonia Detection Challenge in the test dataset, prediction of a single detection model (upper part). Prediction of cooperative detection models (lower part). We use VGG-16-FPN as baseline for our experiment.

Method	Backbone	Score
Single-CNN$_{(22)}$	ResNet-50-FPN	**0.2123**
cre Single-CNN$_{(18)}$	RcsNet-101-FPN	0.2107
Single-CNN$_{(25)}$	ResNet-152-FPN	0.2108
Single-CNN (baseline)	VGG-16-FPN	0.1570
Mask R-CNN [5]	ResNet-101-FPN	0.2170
Co-CNN$_{(22,25)}$	ResNet50+ResNet152+FPN	0.2398
Co-CNN$_{(18,25)}$	ResNet101+ResNet152+FPN	0.2267
Co-CNN$_{(22,18)}$	ResNet50+ResNet101+FPN	**0.2409**

Table 3. Different input images, respectively, original images (Global), lung area images (Local), fusion images (Global+Local). We use single model for comparison.

Base network	Global	Local	Fusion
Resnet50	0.2033	0.1455	**0.2123**
Resnet101	0.1986	0.1434	0.2107
Resnet152	0.2016	0.1446	0.2108

Table 4. The performance of the top 5 teams in the competition (1,499 teams in total). Our model (Co-CNN) reaches the 3rd place.

Top 5 teams [1]	Score
1. PEEP	**0.2547**
2. Dmytro poplavskiy [ods.ai]	0.2478
3. Phillip Cheng	0.2391
4. 16bit.ai/layer6	0.2390
5. JRS_HP	0.2381
Co-CNN (top 1%)	0.2409

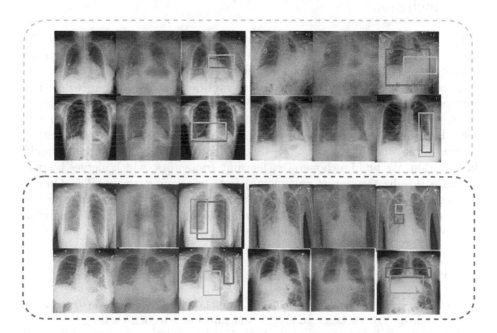

Fig. 5. Example results from our Co-CNN on the test dataset, the top row represents the prediction correct samples and the bottom row displays errors. Red represents the ground truth of pneumonia, green indicates the result of network prediction. (Color figure online)

but the result slightly not well. The single model with ResNet50 has better localization of pneumonia than the model with ResNet101 or ResNet152. The shallow neural network is responsible for detecting and identifying some superficial features, and deeper networks calculate and identify more specific features through these superficial features. The x-ray findings of pneumonia are airspace opacity, interstitial opacities. There is usually considerable overlap. These features may require more edge information learning in shallow networks. The fusion of multiple feature learning is beneficial to the complementarity of information and makes the detection network more robust. In our experiment, the cooperative model of ResNet50 and ResNet101 combined reached the best score of 0.2409. From Table 3, we find that the fusion of global features and local features of the lungs significantly improve the detection of pneumonia.

However, there are still many challenges left for us to solve. (1) We also tried to add some collaboration models on this basis, but at the cost of training and testing time. To resolve this problem, we can compress the model by involving some model compression techniques [4]. (2) In the actual diagnosis of pneumonia, the radiologist will combine the CXRs and medical report to comprehensively judge the disease. When we are aware of some recent advance ways in this area [26]. We expect to improve the accuracy of the diagnosis of pneumonia.

6 Conclusion

In this paper, we study how to automatically detect pneumonia in Chest X-ray images (CXRs), with the goal to help radiologists diagnose pneumonia more accurately and efficiently. Our proposed methods address three major challenges: (1) how to ease up the interference of irrelevant noisy areas, (2) how to use the features of lung areas, (3) how to localize pneumonia regions and produce accurate results. To deal with these challenges, we introduce a lung segmentation network that can segment the lung from the original images. We develop a feature extraction model, which incorporates global and local features for pneumonia classification. We build a cooperative learning framework, which merges bounding boxes (localizationtion of pneumonia) from two cooperative models. On the Kaggles RSNA Pneumonia Detection Challenge dataset, we demonstrate the effectiveness of our proposed methods and achieves excellent performance with the level the top 1% in this competition.

References

1. RSNA pneumonia detection challenge. Radiological Society of North America (2018). https://www.kaggle.com/c/rsna-pneumonia-detection-challenge
2. Esteva, A., et al.: Dermatologist-level classification of skin cancer with deep neural networks. Nature **542**(7639), 115 (2017)
3. Girshick, R.: Fast R-CNN. In: Proceedings of the IEEE International Conference on Computer Vision, pp. 1440–1448 (2015)

4. Han, S., Pool, J., Tran, J., Dally, W.: Learning both weights and connections for efficient neural network. In: Advances in Neural Information Processing Systems, pp. 1135–1143 (2015)

5. He, K., Gkioxari, G., Dollár, P., Girshick, R.: Mask R-CNN. In: Proceedings of the IEEE International Conference on Computer Vision, pp. 2961–2969 (2017)

6. He, K., Zhang, X., Ren, S., Sun, J.: Deep residual learning for image recognition. In: Proceedings of the IEEE Conference on Computer Vision and Pattern Recognition, pp. 770–778 (2016)

7. Hopstaken, R., Witbraad, T., Van Engelshoven, J., Dinant, G.: Inter-observer variation in the interpretation of chest radiographs for pneumonia in community-acquired lower respiratory tract infections. Clin. Radiol. $59(8)$, 743–752 (2004)

8. Huang, P., et al.: Added value of computer-aided CT image features for early lung cancer diagnosis with small pulmonary nodules: a matched case-control study. Radiology $286(1)$, 286–295 (2017)

9. Islam, M.T., Aowal, M.A., Minhaz, A.T., Ashraf, K.: Abnormality detection and localization in chest X-rays using deep convolutional neural networks. arXiv preprint arXiv:1705.09850 (2017)

10. Lakhani, P., Sundaram, B.: Deep learning at chest radiography: automated classification of pulmonary tuberculosis by using convolutional neural networks. Radiology $284(2)$, 574–582 (2017)

11. Liang, T.-T., Sun, M., Gao, L., Lu, J.-J., Tsutsui, S.: APNet: semantic segmentation for pelvic MR image. In: Lai, J.-H., et al. (eds.) PRCV 2018. LNCS, vol. 11257, pp. 259–272. Springer, Cham (2018). https://doi.org/10.1007/978-3-030-03335-4_23

12. Lin, T.Y., Dollár, P., Girshick, R., He, K., Hariharan, B., Belongie, S.: Feature pyramid networks for object detection. In: Proceedings of the IEEE Conference on Computer Vision and Pattern Recognition, pp. 2117–2125 (2017)

13. Lin, T.Y., Goyal, P., Girshick, R., He, K., Dollár, P.: Focal loss for dense object detection. In: Proceedings of the IEEE International Conference on Computer Vision, pp. 2980–2988 (2017)

14. Long, J., Shelhamer, E., Darrell, T.: Fully convolutional networks for semantic segmentation. In: Proceedings of the IEEE Conference on Computer Vision and Pattern Recognition, pp. 3431–3440 (2015)

15. Murphy, S.L., Xu, J., Kochanek, K.D., Curtin, S.C., Arias, E.: Deaths: final data for 2015 (2017)

16. Neuman, M.I., et al.: Variability in the interpretation of chest radiographs for the diagnosis of pneumonia in children. J. Hosp. Med. $7(4)$, 294–298 (2012)

17. Rajpurkar, P., et al.: CheXNet: radiologist-level pneumonia detection on chest X-rays with deep learning. arXiv preprint arXiv:1711.05225 (2017)

18. Rakhlin, A., Shvets, A., Iglovikov, V., Kalinin, A.A.: Deep convolutional neural networks for breast cancer histology image analysis. In: Campilho, A., Karray, F., ter Haar Romeny, B. (eds.) ICIAR 2018. LNCS, vol. 10882, pp. 737–744. Springer, Cham (2018). https://doi.org/10.1007/978-3-319-93000-8_83

19. Redmon, J., Farhadi, A.: YOLO9000: better, faster, stronger. In: Proceedings of the IEEE Conference on Computer Vision and Pattern Recognition, pp. 7263–7271 (2017)

20. Ren, S., He, K., Girshick, R., Sun, J.: Faster R-CNN: towards real-time object detection with region proposal networks. In: Advances in Neural Information Processing Systems, pp. 91–99 (2015)

21. Ronneberger, O., Fischer, P., Brox, T.: U-Net: convolutional networks for biomedical image segmentation. In: Navab, N., Hornegger, J., Wells, W.M., Frangi, A.F. (eds.) MICCAI 2015. LNCS, vol. 9351, pp. 234–241. Springer, Cham (2015). https://doi.org/10.1007/978-3-319-24574-4_28
22. Roth, H.R., et al.: Improving computer-aided detection using convolutional neural networks and random view aggregation. IEEE Trans. Med. Imaging **35**(5), 1170–1181 (2016)
23. Rui, P., Kang, K.: National hospital ambulatory medical care survey: emergency department summary tables (2015)
24. Shrivastava, A., Gupta, A., Girshick, R.: Training region-based object detectors with online hard example mining. In: Proceedings of the IEEE Conference on Computer Vision and Pattern Recognition, pp. 761–769 (2016)
25. Wang, X., Peng, Y., Lu, L., Lu, Z., Bagheri, M., Summers, R.M.: ChestX-ray8: hospital-scale chest X-ray database and benchmarks on weakly-supervised classification and localization of common thorax diseases. In: Proceedings of the IEEE Conference on Computer Vision and Pattern Recognition, pp. 2097–2106 (2017)
26. Wang, X., Peng, Y., Lu, L., Lu, Z., Summers, R.M.: TieNet: text-image embedding network for common thorax disease classification and reporting in chest X-rays. In: Proceedings of the IEEE Conference on Computer Vision and Pattern Recognition, pp. 9049–9058 (2018)

Siamese Spatial Pyramid Matching Network with Location Prior for Anatomical Landmark Tracking in 3-Dimension Ultrasound Sequence

Jishuai He[1,2], Chunxu Shen[1,2], Yibin Huang[3], and Jian Wu[2(✉)]

[1] Tsinghua University, Beijing 100084, China
{hjs18,scx16}@mails.tsinghua.edu.cn
[2] Graduate School at Shenzhen, Tsinghua University, Shenzhen 518055, China
wuj@sz.tsinghua.edu.cn
[3] Shenzhen Traditional Chinese Medicine Hospital, Shenzhen 518034, China
huangyb2004@126.com

Abstract. Accurate motion tracking of the liver target is crucial in image-guided intervention therapy. Compared with other imaging modalities, ultrasound is appealing choice as it provides accurate and real-time anatomical information surrounding lesions. Besides, compared with 2-dimensional ultrasound (2DUS) image, 3-dimensional ultrasound (3DUS) image shows the spatial structure and real lesion motion pattern in patient so that it is an ideal choice for image-guided intervention. In this work, we develop Siamese Spatial Pyramid Matching Network (SSPMNet) to track anatomical landmark in 3DUS sequences. SSPMNet mainly consists of two parts, namely feature extraction network and decision network. Feature extraction network with fully convolutional neural (FCN) layers is employed to extract the deep feature in 3DUS image. Spatial Pyramid Pooling (SPP) layer is connected to the end of feature extraction network to generate multiple-level and robust anatomical structure features. In decision network, three fully connected layers are used to compute the similarity between features. Moreover, with the prior knowledge of physical movement, we elaborately design a temporal consistency model to reject outliers in tracking results. Proposed algorithm is evaluated on the Challenge of Liver Ultrasound Tracking (CLUST) across 16 3DUS sequences, yielding 1.89 ± 1.14 mm mean compared with manual annotations. Moreover, extensive ablation study proves that the leading tracking result can benefit from hierarchical feature extraction by SPP. Besides proposed algorithm is not sensitive to sampled sub-volume size. Therefore, proposed algorithm is potential for accurate anatomical landmark tracking in ultrasound-guided intervention.

Keywords: Landmark tracking · Spatial Pyramid Pooling · Ultrasound-guided intervention

---

J. He and C. Shen—The first two authors contribute equally, and the first author is student.

© Springer Nature Switzerland AG 2019
Z. Lin et al. (Eds.): PRCV 2019, LNCS 11858, pp. 341–353, 2019.
https://doi.org/10.1007/978-3-030-31723-2_29

1 Introduction

In liver interventional therapy, accurate motion tracking of target is crucial for minimizing damage to healthy tissues surrounding lesions. However, due to breathing,
heartbeat, and drift of patients, anatomical landmark tracking in liver is full of challenges. Conventional approaches, such as respiratory gating technology [1] and
anesthesia [2] are usually used to alleviate these uncertainties. Nevertheless, these
methods are potential to increase treatment time and even cause additional damage to
healthy tissues.

With the emergence of medical image-based motion correction approach [3],
image-guided tracking for the anatomical landmark attracts wide attention. Compared
with other types of medical images, such as computed tomography (CT) and magnetic
resonance imaging (MRI), ultrasound (US) imaging is a more appealing choice as it is
non-invasive, affordable, portable and real-time. Moreover, compared with two-
dimensional ultrasound (2DUS), three-dimensional ultrasound (3DUS) can show 3D
anatomical structure and more real landmark motion pattern in liver. Therefore, 3DUS
image is an ideal imaging modality for estimating liver motion pattern and tracking
anatomical landmark.

Over the last decade, several approaches that utilize 3DUS for the anatomical
landmark tracking have been proposed. Mageras et al. [4] first propose to utilize 3DUS
sequence to model the respiratory movement of the abdomen. However, 3DUS
sequence is only used for preoperative modeling, so it does not solve the problem of
intraoperative liver motion tracking. Further Vijayan et al. [2] employ 3DUS to capture
anatomical landmark movement pattern in operation. While their algorithm achieves a
high landmark location accuracy, high complexity limited its clinical application. To
reduce the complexity, Banerjee et al. [5] propose an outliers rejection method based on
morphological and geometrical constraints, and then they achieve more robust tracking
results. However, Banerjee et al. only validate the tracking performance in multiple
single breathing cycle. Additionally, Royer et al. [6] propose a method by combining
robust dense motion estimation and mechanical model simulation, which can effectively simulate the actual liver motion pattern. Though this approach achieves
impressive tracking performance, both low processing speed and substantial parameter
tuning bother followers.

Therefore, we propose an end-to-end Siamese network based on patch-wise
matching to achieve state-of-the-art anatomical landmark tracking results in 3DUS
sequences. In proposed network, CNNs are employed to extract the deep features of
sub-volumes, and the decision network based on fully-connected layers is employed to
learn the pairwise similarity. Utilizing deep features is potential to alleviate the impact
of low spatial resolution and low SNR of 3DUS. Moreover, Spatial Pyramid Pooling
(SPP) [7] that removes the fixed-size constraint of the network and extracts anatomical
structure features is introduced to proposed network. Besides, based on prior knowledge, temporal consistency model is introduced into this work to reject outliers in
tracking results.

In this work, our contributions mainly focus on two aspects: Firstly, proposed
algorithm is evaluated on the Challenge of Liver Ultrasound Tracking (CLUST) across

16 3DUS sequences, yielding 1.89 ± 1.14 mm mean comparing with manual annotations. Secondly, extensive ablation study proves that the leading tracking result benefits from hierarchical feature extraction by SPP, and proposed algorithm is not sensitive to sampled sub-volume size. Further, it proves that proposed algorithm is robust and is potential to meet the clinical need to track targets of different sizes. Therefore, proposed algorithm is potential for accurate anatomical landmark tracking in ultrasound-guided intervention.

2   Methods

2.1   End-to-End Siamese Spatial Pyramid Matching Network

Inspired by MatchNet [8], proposed network, namely Siamese Spatial Pyramid Network (SSPMNet), consists of two parts, namely feature extraction network, and decision network. Furthermore, SPP layer is connected to the end of feature extraction network. We implement SSPMNet as depicted in Fig. 1 and the details of network are shown in Table 1. Firstly, we utilize CNNs in feature extraction network to extract deep features by coding a number of clinical ultrasound sub-volume pairs, i.e. landmark-centered sub-volume in previous frame and candidate sub-volumes in current frame. Then SPP layer is employed to generate multi-level and robust structure features which are fixed-length. Finally, the decision network computes the similarity between features and discriminates the candidate sub-volume as target or not. Furthermore, as the loss function is optimized, the output value of the network would be closer to the actual label.

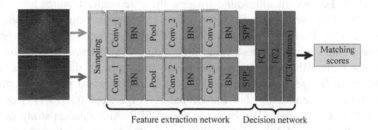

Fig. 1. The architecture of Siamese Spatial Pyramid Matching Network.

Feature Extraction Network: Three convolutional layers (Conv) are employed in feature extraction network. Batch normalization (BN) [9] is inserted immediately after every convolutional layer. And, we use Rectified Linear Units (ReLU) as non-linearity for the convolution layers. Meanwhile, Maxpooling is employed after the first convolutional layer to reduce the size of feature maps.

Decision Network: The decision network based on three fully connected (FC) layers is used to model the similarity between extracted features. ReLU is the activation function of the first two fully-connected (FC) layers, and Softmax is the activation function of the last FC layer. Two nodes of the last FC layer output two values between [0, 1], and the output of the second node is the probability value of two sub-volumes match.

Table 1. The details of SSPMNet. $S \times S \times S$ is the size of feature maps after Conv_3. n and $\lfloor \cdot \rfloor$ denote pyramid level and floor operations. Besides, C denotes convolution, MP denotes Maxpooling, AP denotes Averagepooling, FC denotes fully-connected, and—means that there is no such property.

Layers	Support	Type	Stride	Padding
Conv_1	$3 \times 3 \times 3 \times 24$	C	$1 \times 1 \times 1$	Valid
Pool	$3 \times 3 \times 3 \times 24$	MP	$2 \times 2 \times 2$	Valid
Conv_2	$3 \times 3 \times 3 \times 32$	C	$1 \times 1 \times 1$	Valid
Conv_3	$3 \times 3 \times 3 \times 48$	C	$1 \times 1 \times 1$	Valid
SPP	1-level	AP	$\lfloor S/n \rfloor$	—
	2-level	MP		
FC1	128	FC	—	—
FC2	128	FC	—	—
FC3	2	FC	—	—

SPP Layer: We employ SPP layer after the third Convolutional layer to generate the feature which is fixed-length and is the input of decision network. Because 3DUS suffers from low signal-to-noise ratio and low spatial resolution, voxel in ultrasound images is unreliable [10]. Extracting the semantic features of 3DUS by Convolutional Neural Network is potential to alleviate the impact of low spatial resolution and low SNR of 3DUS. Further, in ultrasound images, these semantic features are similar to local anatomical features, and SPP can effectively extract multi-level anatomical structure features. Therefore, we introduce SPP to proposed network to generate hierarchical features which proposed algorithm would benefit from. In addition, due to SPP, proposed algorithm can track anatomical structures of different size without scaling the input image. The process of 2-level spatial pyramid pooling is shown in Fig. 2. It is worth mentioning that the Global Average Pool (GAP) [11] or Global Maximum Pool (GMP) may play the same role as SPP. And ablation study shows the different results obtained by utilizing different methods we mentioned above. For convenience, we call this layer as the bottleneck layer.

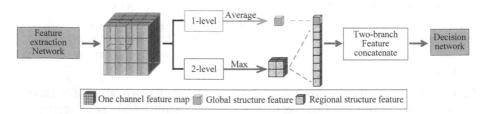

Fig. 2. The process of 2-level spatial pyramid pooling on 3D feature maps.

Loss Function: We utilize Cross-entropy loss as the loss function of proposed network, and we obtain the optimal network by minimizing loss. Below is the formula form of Cross-entropy loss.

$$L = -\frac{1}{n}\sum_{i=1}^{n} [y_i \log(\widehat{y}_i) + (1 - y_i) \log(1 - \widehat{y}_i)] \tag{1}$$

Where, y_i is the 0/1 label of the input pair x_i and 1 indicates match. $\widehat{y}_i$ is the value computed by the Softmax and indicates the probability of match or matching score. The calculation method of $\widehat{y}_i$ is as follows:

$$\widehat{y}_i = \frac{e^{v_1(x_i)}}{e^{v_0(x_i)} + e^{v_1(x_i)}} \tag{2}$$

Where, $\widehat{y}_i$ is the output of the second node in the last FC layer. Besides, in this work, Adam [12] with a learning rate of 0.001 and a batch size of 600 is used to minimize the loss. By using Adam, the convergence speed of the network is obviously improved. Once the proposed end-to-end network is trained well, state-of-the-art tracking results can be achieved without optimizing a large number of parameters, so that the complexity of our model is low.

2.2 Patch-Based Matching Based Tracking

The goal for patch-based matching is to compute the matching scores of paired sub-volumes. In this work, there are two types of sub-volumes, one centered on the landmark and the other not centered on the landmark, but centered on surrounding anatomical structure around landmark.

In training, landmark-centered sub-volume from the previous frame and landmark-centered sub-volume from current frame make up positive samples. Landmark-centered sub-volume from the previous frame and non-landmark-centered sub-volumes from current frame make up negative samples. Positive and negative samples are inputted in batches to train proposed network. Besides, like the common Siamese network, paired sub-volumes go through the same feature encoding before computing a similarity by sharing parameters between two branches.

In tracking, the target sub-volume which is landmark-centered is extracted from the first frame, and the candidate sub-volumes which are in search range are extracted one by one from current frame. Target and candidate sub-volumes go through the proposed network to compute the matching scores. The position of the landmark in current frame is the position of the sub-volume with the highest matching score.

2.3 Temporal Consistency Model for Landmark Tracking

Although proposed network has learned the similarity computing method well, there are also individual outliers in tracking results. However, it is unavoidable for algorithms that only use local spatial information. Therefore, with the prior knowledge of physical movement, we introduce the temporal consistency model which employs the temporal information to reject outliers in tracking results. The formula is as follows.

$$C'_t = (1 - S_{joint})C'_{t-1} + S_{joint}C_t \tag{3}$$

$$S_{jiont} = e^{-\frac{\left[s'_{joint}\hat{\Sigma}^{-1}\left(s'_{joint}\right)^T\right]}{2}} \tag{4}$$

$$S'_{joint} = (1 - S_{match}, 1 - S_{dis}) \tag{5}$$

$$S_{dis} = e^{-\frac{d^2}{2\times(1.5\times\bar{d})^2}} \tag{6}$$

Where, C'_t/C_t is new/old coordinate of landmark in current frame, and C'_{t-1} is the coordinate of the landmark in the previous frame. All tracking results are corrected one by one from the second frame. S_{joint} is composed of matching score S_{match} and distance score S_{dis} as shown in Eq. (4). And S'_{joint} is the vector containing S_{match} and S_{dis}. $\hat{\Sigma}$ represents the covariance matrix, which assigns two different weights to S_{match} and S_{dis}. In Eq. (6), d is the displacement of the current frame landmark and the previous frame landmark. And $\bar{d}$ is the average displacement between all corrected adjacent landmarks. Through Eq. (6), we obtain the S_{dis} whose value is between [0, 1]. It can be understood as the reliability of the displacement between the current frame and the previous frame before correction. The smaller the displacement, the higher S_{dis}. Furthermore, using the form similar to the normalized two-dimensional Gauss distribution function as shown in Formula 4, the joint score of the tracked landmark coordinates, namely the reliability of tracking result, can be obtained, and then the current tracking results can be corrected. Therefore, outliers in tracking results are rejected due to their low displacement scores and matching scores.

3   Experiment and Result

In this work, the CLUST 2015 challenge dataset [13], including 16 sets of 3DUS landmark sequences, is used to train and evaluate proposed algorithm. The ground truth of landmark is established using manual annotations by the radiologist. The summary of this data is shown in Table 2 and Fig. 3.

Table 2. Summary of data

Source	Objects	Volume size	Resolution (mm)	Frame rate (Hz)	Scanner
EMC	6	$192 \times 246 \times 117$	$1.14 \times 0.59 \times 1.19$	6	Philips iU22
ICR	1	$480 \times 120 \times 120$	$0.31 \times 0.51 \times 0.67$	24	Siemens SC2000
SMT	9	$227 \times 227 \times 229$	$0.70 \times 0.70 \times 0.70$	8	GE E9

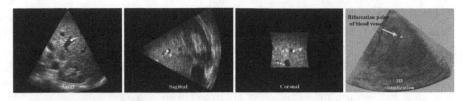

Fig. 3. Sample image is from the first frame in SMT-03_2. The tracking anatomical structure is the bifurcation point of blood vessel.

3.1 Implementation Details

The size of sub-volumes is $19 \times 19 \times 19$. For decision network, the size of the first two fully connected layers is $\{128 \times 128, 128 \times 128\}$. 2-level pyramid pooling $\{1 \times 1 \times 1, 2 \times 2 \times 2\}$ is used in this work. The number of parameters in proposed network is 190,866. For temporal consistency model, the value of $\widehat{\Sigma}$ is shown below, and $\bar{d}$ is initialized to 4 mm.

$$\widehat{\Sigma} = \begin{pmatrix} 0.4 & 0 \\ 0 & 1.4 \end{pmatrix} \tag{7}$$

In training, sampling plays an important role, as the matching (1) and non-matching pairs (0) are highly unbalanced. In order to avoid all samples being predicted as negative samples and based on prior knowledge of human tissue movement [5], we augment positive samples by rotating the landmark-center sub-volumes in pair around three axes and rotating to $\{-2, -1.75, -1.5, -1.25, -1, -0.75, -0.5, -0.25, 0.5, 0.5, 0.75, 1.25, 1.5, 1.75, 2\}$ degrees. Besides, the central points of non-landmark-centered sub-volume are generated by using three-dimensional Gauss random sampling with coordinates of landmarks as mean, and the Euclidean distance between these central points and the landmark is from $\sqrt{2}$ to $\sqrt{6}$ in pixel. Finally, we select nearly 9% of all frames to train our network and the data of ICR-01_1 sequence do not participate in training.

Proposed algorithm is developed in Keras [14]. All experiments with fixed parameters are conducted on a computer with Intel Core i7-8700 at 3.2 GHz and a single NVIDIA GTX 1060 6 GB GPU. •

3.2 Performance Evaluation and Results Analysis

Euclidean distance is employed to evaluate tracking performance between each manual annotation and the output of proposed algorithm. The evaluation criteria are: mean, standard deviation (SD), 95%ile and maximum error. Table 3 shows the tracking performance of proposed algorithm on CLUST dataset.

Table 3. Tracking performance of proposed algorithm on CLUST dataset in millimeters

Landmark	Objects	Mean	SD	95%ile	Max
EMC-01	1	0.68	0.68	1.60	1.75
EMC-02	4	1.30	1.14	3.03	4.74
EMC-03	1	3.02	4.45	13.64	14.13
ICR-01	1	2.44	0.82	3.80	4.45
SMT-01	3	1.29	1.17	3.47	6.23
SMT-02	3	1.22	1.09	2.39	11.18
SMT-03	2	1.11	0.81	2.58	5.81
SMT-04	1	9.14	3.65	16.52	21.24
Results	16	1.89	1.41	4.40	21.24

Table 4. Tracking performance comparison of another research on the same dataset in millimeter

Landmark	Mean	SD	95%ile	Max
Banerjee et al. [15]	3.26	2.62	9.20	16.49
Proposed algorithm	**1.89**	**1.41**	**4.40**	21.24

As shown in Table 4, compared with the tracking results of Banerjee et al. [15], our tracking result achieves an improvement in mean 1.37 mm (approximately 42.02%), standard deviation of 1.21 mm (approximately 46.18%) and 95%ile error 4.80 mm (approximately 52.17%).

3.3 Ablation Study

Although the algorithm achieves state-of-the-art results, the contribution of each part to proposed algorithm is uncertain. Moreover, the number of convolution layer, the size of sub-volume and the type of bottleneck layer may have a significant impact on the performance of the algorithm. Therefore, the effect of sub-volume size changing, the number of convolutional layer, and the type of bottleneck layer for the tracking performance are investigated in this section. Table 5 shows the tracking performance when the network is trained by different sub-volume sizes with using SPP layer and keeping the number of convolutional layer fixed. Table 6 shows the performance of the network with different the number of convolutional layer with keeping the sub-volume size fixed and using SPP layer. Table 7 shows the performance of the network with different types of bottleneck layer keeping the sub-volume size and the number of convolutional layer fixed.

Table 5. Change the sub-volume size with keeping the number of convolutional layers fixed and using SPP layer in millimeters. Num-Conv denotes the number of convolutional layer

Sub-volume size	Num-Conv	Bottleneck	Mean	SD	95%ile	Max
15 × 15 × 15	3	SPP ($1^3, 2^3$)	2.61	2.46	7.11	29.13
17 × 17 × 17	3	SPP ($1^3, 2^3$)	1.92	1.88	5.45	25.61
19 × 19 × 19	3	SPP ($1^3, 2^3$)	1.89	1.41	4.40	21.21
21 × 21 × 21	3	SPP ($1^3, 2^3$)	2.17	1.85	5.43	21.59

Table 6. Change the number of convolutional layer with keeping the sub-volume size fixed and using SPP layer in millimeters. Num-Conv denotes the number of convolutional layer

Sub-volume size	Num-Conv	Bottleneck	Mean	SD	95%ile	Max
19 × 19 × 19	1	SPP ($1^3, 2^3$)	6.77	3.28	11.08	24.82
19 × 19 × 19	2	SPP ($1^3, 2^3$)	2.82	2.68	6.07	25.97
19 × 19 × 19	3	SPP ($1^3, 2^3$)	1.89	1.41	4.40	21.24
19 × 19 × 19	4	SPP ($1^3, 2^3$)	2.08	3.26	3.86	27.25

Table 7. Change the type of bottleneck layer (means that the network does not converge) with keeping the sub-volume size and the number of convolutional layers fixed in millimeters. Num-Conv denotes the number of convolutional layer

Sub-volume size	Num-Conv	Bottleneck	Mean	SD	95%ile	Max
19 × 19 × 19	3	GMP	3.08	4.64	7.91	30.26
19 × 19 × 19	3	GAP	2.78	2.22	6.48	31.68
19 × 19 × 19	3	SPP ($1^3, 2^3$)	1.89	1.41	4.40	21.24
19 × 19 × 19	3	FC layer (128)	/	/	/	/

Table 5 supports proposed algorithm is not sensitive to sampled sub-volume size, because it shows that when the sub-volume size is 19 × 19 × 19, proposed algorithm achieves the best tracking performance, further increasing or decreasing sub-volume size does not lead to significantly different in tracking performance. Therefore, it proves that the proposed algorithm is potential to meet clinical need to track anatomical targets of different sizes. Besides, Convolutional features are conducive to improve the performance of the algorithm, comparing to the tracking results of Banerjee et al. [14]. However, Table 6 shows that too few the number of convolutional layer leads to degradation of tracking performance and an increase in the number of convolution layers does not always lead to an improvement in tracking performance. It is because multiple convolution operations lead to the reduction of target location accuracy, which is similar to the research of Lin et al. [16]. Table 7 shows that using SPP layer leads to the best tracking performance. Further, it proves that a leading tracking result can benefit from hierarchical features extracted by SPP. Besides, employing FC layer as the bottleneck layer lead to non-convergence of proposed network. It is proved that feature extraction based on ultrasound pixels is unreliable, which is consistent with the results of Yang et al. [10]. By contrast, the best benefits cannot also be achieved by only utilizing global structural features. Generally, ablation research supports that the algorithm can get the greatest benefit from the hierarchical features extracted by SPP.

4 Conclusion and Discussion

In this paper, we propose an algorithm which is consist of an end-to-end network, namely Siamese Spatial Pyramid Matching Network and a temporal consistency model to track anatomical landmarks in 3DUS sequences. Further, the proposed algorithm with tied parameters has lower complexity and obtains the state-of-the-art result. Comparing with other published work, i.e. Banerjee et al. [14], the tracking results of our algorithm achieve improvement in mean 1.37 mm (approximately 42.02%), SD of 1.21 mm (approximately 46.18%) and 95%ile error 4.80 mm (approximately 52.17%). Further, extensive ablation study proves that a leading tracking result can benefit from hierarchical feature extracted by SPP. And proposed algorithm is not sensitive to sampled sub-volume size. Therefore, proposed algorithm is potential for anatomical landmarks tracking in liver.

Considering 3DUS suffers from low signal-to-noise ratio and low spatial resolution so that voxel in ultrasound images are unreliable. And traditional similarity measurement methods in sub-volume matching, such as normalized cross correlation (NCC) [5] et al., is affected by this leading to matching error. Therefore, instead of matching in the original data space, we encode the US image into the feature space through Convolutional neural network (CNNs). Through proper training, CNNs can extract effective features and filter out noise like ultrasound shadow to a certain extent. Besides, ablation study supports that too many or too few the number of convolutional layers would degrade tracking performance.

For the bottleneck layer, we utilize SPP to generate hierarchical features. Ablation study proves that SPP plays the most important role in the network. Essentially, this is because SPP makes the network pays attention to global and regional structural features instead of voxel features which is unreliable. Besides, SPP makes proposed algorithm robust to slight deformations.

For decision network, three FC layers are employed to compute the similarity of hierarchical features. And the tracking performance of the algorithm proves that the decision network learns the compute method well. In addition, our work also proves that Siamese network is also applicable to the tracking anatomical landmarks in 3DUS sequences. Finally, based on all improvements or innovations which is mentioned above, proposed algorithm with tied parameters has lower complexity and obtains the state-of-the-art results.

The purpose of the proposed algorithm is to track the target accurately, so as to guide doctors to perform more accurate interventional therapy. Compared with other research results [14], it is proved that the proposed algorithm further improves the accuracy of target tracking. Moreover, mean error in the results of proposed algorithm is in line with the clinical requirements. Therefore, the proposed algorithm is potential for further reducing the injury of interventional surgery for healthy tissues. In addition, the robustness of target tracking is also very important in interventional surgery.

Extensive ablation study proves that proposed algorithm is not sensitive to sampled sub-volume size, so that proposed algorithm can guarantee the tracking robustness of targets that are different sizes and types. In general, the proposed algorithm further solves the tracking problem of anatomical landmarks in 3DUS and is potential for guiding liver interventional therapy.

However, as shown in Table 3, there are large errors in the tracking results. And Fig. 4 shows that when the tracking target undergoes tremendous deformation, the proposed algorithm does not perform well. Referring to the previous work of others, i.e. [5], using global information is helpful to solve this problem.

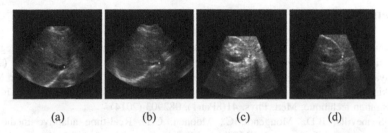

    (a)   (b)   (c)   (d)

Fig. 4. (a) and (b) are axial sections of the first and 42-th frame of EMC-03_1 sequence. At time point of 42, the tracking error is 14.13 mm. (c) and (d) are axial sections of the first and 23-th frame of SMT-04_1 sequence. At time point of 23, the tracking error is 21.24 mm. Figure 4 shows that when the tracking target undergoes tremendous deformation, the proposed algorithm does not perform well.

Besides, due to the small field of view (FOV) of ultrasound, when the sub-volume is too large, the ultrasound boundary will appear in the sub-volume. As a strong edge, the ultrasound boundary shown in Fig. 5, would decrease the tracking performance. Because, the ultrasound boundary is very easy to appear in the sub-volume, the data from ICR-01_1 sequence do not participate in training. However, if the sub-volume is too small, some anatomical structures would not be completely covered which will also affect the tracking performance. For this problem, attention mechanism [17] may be a reasonable choice.

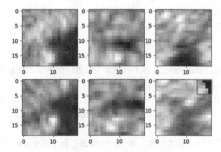

Fig. 5. Three-section image of landmark-centered sub-volume from two adjacent frames. The results show that when the sub-volume is too large, the ultrasonic boundary as shown in the red box will appear in the sub-volume (Color figure online)

In the future, global information and attention mechanisms will be introduced into our research. Besides, convolutional long short-term memory (LSTM) [18] will be introduced to utilize spatial and temporal information for anatomical landmark tracking.

Acknowledgement. This work is supported in part by Knowledge Innovation Program of Basic Research Projects of Shenzhen under Grant JCYJ20160428182053361, in part by Guangdong Science and Technology Plan under Grant 2017B020210003 and in part by National Natural Science Foundation of China under Grant 81771940, 81427803.

References

1. Mageras, G.S., Yorke, E.: Deep inspiration breath hold and respiratory gating strategies for reducing organ motion in radiation treatment. Semin. Radiat. Oncol. **14**(1), 65–75 (2004)
2. Vijayan, S., Klein, S., Hofstad, E.F., Lindseth, F., Ystgaard, B., Langø, T.J.M.: Motion tracking in the liver: validation of a method based on 4D ultrasound using a nonrigid registration technique. Med. Phys. **41**(8Patr1), 082903 (2014)
3. De Senneville, B.D., Mougenot, C., Moonen, C.T.: Real-time adaptive methods for treatment of mobile organs by MRI-controlled high-intensity focused ultrasound. Magn. Reson. Med. Off. J. Int. Soc. Magn. Reson. Med. **57**(2), 319–330 (2007)
4. Dürichen, R., Davenport, L., Bruder, R., Wissel, T., Schweikard, A., Ernst, F.: Evaluation of the potential of multi-modal sensors for respiratory motion prediction and correlation. In: 2013 35th Annual International Conference of the IEEE Engineering in Medicine and Biology Society (EMBC), pp. 5678–5681. IEEE (2013)
5. Banerjee, J., Klink, C., Peters, E.D., Niessen, W.J., Moelker, A., van Walsum, T.: Fast and robust 3D ultrasound registration–block and game theoretic matching. Med. Image Anal. **20**(1), 173–183 (2015)
6. Royer, L., Krupa, A., Dardenne, G., Le Bras, A., Marchand, E., Marchal, M.: Real-time target tracking of soft tissues in 3D ultrasound images based on robust visual information and mechanical simulation. Med. Image Anal. **35**, 582–598 (2017)
7. He, K., Zhang, X., Ren, S., Sun, J.: Spatial pyramid pooling in deep convolutional networks for visual recognition. IEEE Trans. Pattern Anal. Mach. Intell. **37**(9), 1904–1916 (2015)
8. Han, X., Leung, T., Jia, Y., Sukthankar, R., Berg, A.C.: MatchNet: unifying feature and metric learning for patch-based matching. In: Proceedings of the IEEE Conference on Computer Vision and Pattern Recognition (CVPR), pp. 3279–3286. IEEE (2015)
9. Ioffe, S., Szegedy, C.J.: Batch normalization: accelerating deep network training by reducing internal covariate shift. In: International Conference on Machine Learning (ICML), pp. 448–456. ACM (2015)
10. Yang, H., Shan, C., Kolen, A.F., de With, P.H.: Catheter detection in 3D ultrasound using triplanar-based convolutional neural networks. In: 2018 25th IEEE International Conference on Image Processing (ICIP), pp. 371–375. IEEE (2018)
11. Lin, M., Chen, Q., Yan, S.J.: Network in network. arXiv preprint arXiv:1312.4400 (2014)
12. Kingma, D.P., Ba, J.: Adam: a method for stochastic optimization. arXiv preprint arXiv: 1412.6980 (2014)
13. Luca, V., et al.: The 2014 liver ultrasound tracking benchmark. Phys. Med. Biol. **60**(14), 5571–5599 (2015)
14. Chollet, F.: Keras. GitHub (2015). https://github.com/fchollet/keras

15. Banerjee, J., Klink, C., Vast, E., Niessen, W.J., Moelker, A., van Walsum, T.: A combined tracking and registration approach for tracking anatomical landmarks in 4D ultrasound of the liver. In: MICCAI Workshop: Challenge on Liver Ultrasound Tracking, pp. 36–43 (2015)
16. Lin, T., Dollar, P., Girshick, R.B., He, K., Hariharan, B., Belongie, S.J.: Feature pyramid networks for object detection. In: Proceedings of the IEEE Conference on Computer Vision and Pattern Recognition (CVPR), pp. 936–944. IEEE (2017)
17. Min, S., Chen, X., Zha, Z.-J., Wu, F., Zhang, Y.: A two-stream mutual attention network for semi-supervised biomedical segmentation with noisy labels. arXiv preprint arXiv:1807.11719 (2019)
18. Zhao, C., Zhang, P., Zhu, J., Wu, C., Wang, H., Xu, K.: Predicting tongue motion in unlabeled ultrasound videos using convolutional LSTM neural network. arXiv preprint arXiv:1902.06927 (2019)

Local Context Embedding Neural Network for Scene Semantic Segmentation

Junxia Li[1(✉)], Lingzheng Dai[2], Yu Ding[1], and Qingshan Liu[1]

[1] B-DAT and CICAEET, Nanjing University of Information Science and Technology,
Nanjing 210044, China
junxiali99@163.com
[2] School of Computer Science and Engineering,
Nanjing University of Science and Technology, Nanjing 210094, China

Abstract. This paper presents a novel and effective architecture for scene semantic segmentation, named Local Context Embedding (LCE) network. Unlike previous work, in this paper we characterize local context by exploiting the content of image patches to improve the discrimination of features. Specifically, LCE passes spatially varying contextual information both horizontally and vertically across each small patch derived from fully convolutional feature maps, through the use of Long Short-Term Memory (LSTM) network. Using the sequences of local patches from different directions can extensively characterize the spatial context. Therefore, this embedding based network enables us to utilize more meaningful information for segmentation in an end-to-end fashion. Comprehensive evaluations on CamVid and SUN RGB-D datasets well demonstrate the effectiveness and robustness of our proposed architecture.

Keywords: Scene semantic segmentation · Local context embedding · Deep learning

1 Introduction

Scene semantic segmentation, which refers to the problem of predicting pixel-wise label for input image, has drawn much attention in recent years. A reliable segmentation result is highly desirable for many higher-level computer vision applications, including image caption, autonomous driving, advanced driver assistance system and robotics. So far, it is still a challenging problem because it requires combining dense pixel-level accuracy with multi-scale contextual reasoning and thus current computer vision technique cannot recognize and segment objects in an image as human beings [2,4].

Many research works have been devoted to exploring various convolutional neural networks (CNNs) for semantic object segmentation [1,3,5]. Long *et al.* [1]

© Springer Nature Switzerland AG 2019
Z. Lin et al. (Eds.): PRCV 2019, LNCS 11858, pp. 354–366, 2019.
https://doi.org/10.1007/978-3-030-31723-2_30

propose an end-to-end solution, *i.e.*, fully convolutional network (FCN), for segmenting semantic objects. This network produces a score map with the size proportional to the input image, where each pixel represents a classifier of objects. Despite the ease of usage, FCN is often not capable of capturing the detailed structures of object (*e.g.*, the boundary). To this end, DeconvNet [5] further enhances the segmentation performance by learning a multi-layer deconvolution network. DeconvNet is a much deeper network and the training stage needs large amount of samples. Recently, Badrinarayanan *et al.* [3] presents a SegNet framework, which investigates the unsampling use for network and achieves the state-of-the-art results. In these CNNs based methods, the context is captured limitedly via only leveraging the convolutional filters.

Some recent works, on the other hand, began to investigate the role of context in segmentation [9,11]. To enhance the feature representation, their strategy is mainly to exploit long-range dependencies by directly augmenting the intermediate features. Most of them characterize the contextual information from all pixels with multi-dimensional Long Short-Term Memory (LSTM). In this way, the long-range dependencies of all pixels can be memorized, making the global contextual information be incorporated to enhance the segmentation performance. However, the pixel representation mainly depends on its local neighboring ones. First, the faraway neighbors of the pixel in general have few or very limited influence on the representation of that pixel. Second, local contextual information is proven to be significant in hand-crafted image features, which seek to describe one pixel by considering its neighbors. These indicate that exploiting the local context information of neighboring pixels is essential to improve the discriminative of features. Third, since targets in the road scene (*e.g.*, bicyclist, signsymbol) are typically small, it is desirable to make the input size small, which reduces the search field of the network naturally. All these motivate us to make full use of local contextual information for each image patch in the feature representation process.

In this paper, we develop a local context embedding (LCE) network that characterizes the meaningful information of neighboring pixels extensively, and demonstrate its superiority on the scene semantic segmentation. To gather local context which plays an important role in visual recognition, we employ LSTMs as tool and propose a novel multi-direction feature fusion strategy for computing this information. The LSTMs layers are appended to the last layer derived from a deep CNNs to enhance visual features. These LSTMs pass spatially varying context both horizontally and vertically across each small patch of the feature map. Specifically, we have four independent LSTMs that move in four directions to make full use of pair-wise pixels of each patch, instead of learning features only from local convolutional kernels as done in previous methods. In this way, the sequences of pixels from different directions are fully utilized to capture the contextual information in a fusion way. We explicitly increase the capabilities of features and train networks in an end-to-end process in this work, instead of employing separate processing steps.

The main contributions of this paper can be summarized in the following. (i) A novel LCE network is presented to improve the discriminative ability of features. It passes spatially both horizontally and vertically across each small patch feature maps and thus can utilize more meaningful information of local patches in a fusion way; (ii) The proposed LCE layers are incorporated into fully convolutional networks to enable an end-to-end computer architecture. Besides, LCE network is general and other network structures can be incorporated to learn the feature representation for segmentation tasks; (iii) We apply the proposed LCE network in scene semantic segmentation, and demonstrate its superiority by comprehensive comparisons on two challenging segmentation datasets.

2   Related Work

Semantic Object Segmentation: There are many CNNs works in the semantic segmentation problem. FCN *et al.* [1] converts an existing CNN framework constructed for classification to an effective architecture for segmenting semantic objects. In FCN, the network builds on several convolutional layers and a deconvolutional layer for pixel-level labeling. However, the detailed structures of an object are often smoothed, since the map generated from convolutions is too coarse and the procedure of deconvolutional layer is overly simple, which is implemented as bilinear interpolation. Based on FCN, DeconvNet [5] further learns a multi-layer deconvolution network which contains deconvolution, unpooling, and rectified linear unit layers. This strategy can improve the segmentation performance benefiting from much deeper network and large amount of training samples. But, the training stage is very time-consuming. Furthermore, it is expensive and changeable to produce accurate region proposals for an input image. Chen *et al.* [7] use the dense pixel-level CRF as the post-processing step after CNN-based pixel-wise prediction. Badrinarayanan *et al.* [3] investigates the upsampling usage for network and propose an encoder-decoder architecture, *i.e.*, SegNet. This network only stores the max-pooling indices of feature maps to guide the decoder procedure. Moreover, it achieves state-of-the-art scene semantic segmentation performance without the aid of region proposals for inference. Thus, we use this method as one of the baselines to evaluate our method.

Spatial RNNs: Recurrent Neural Networks (RNNs) have been originally introduced for sequence prediction tasks [12,13] and have many forms. For example, bidirectional RNNs [14] process the sequences left-to-right and right-to-left in parallel; [16] extends it to a full multi-dimensional form and uses it to address the handwriting recognition. Recently, LSTM networks have been devoted to exploring the 2D images [8–10,15]. Grid LSTM [10] extended LSTM cells to allow the multi-dimensional communication across the LSTM cells. As an alternative strategy, [9] explores running a LSTM spatial over a feature map in place of convolutions for sematic segmentation. In their models, LSTM is used to characterize the sequence information of pixels derived from images. Specifically, the long-range dependencies can be memorized by sequentially functioning on

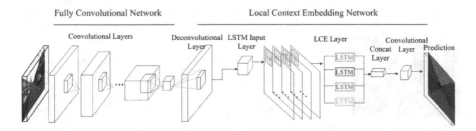

Fig. 1. Illustration of the proposed network architecture for scene semantic segmentation. LCE network integrates several LSTM layers into the CNN architecture for pixel-wise labeling. First, an input image component passes through several convolutional layers and a deconvolutional layer to generate the feature map. Then, the obtained LCE layers are appended to continuously characterize the local contextual information. By concating the derived features, the 1×1 convolutional layer produces the final scene semantic segmentation result.

more pixels due to the powerful memorization of LSTMs. Most related to our framework, the ION [8] applies RNNs to compute contextual features for object detection. However, our network differs from ION in that we leverage LSTMs to characterize only the local context derived from neighboring pixels, leading us to extract this extensive information using a fusion strategy. In this way, the length of each sequence of LSTMs is the number of neighboring pixels in each small patch.

3 Local Context Embedding Network

3.1 Network Architecture

The proposed LCE network aims to assign a semantic label for each image pixel. Figure 1 illustrates the designed network architecture based on LCE network. Our network takes several image components from an entire image as input. The network first processes the input component with several convolutional (conv), max pooling layers and a deconvolutional (deconv) layer to produce the feature map. We use the VGG-16 [30] as the basic convolutional neural network. Each input component is of fixed size 227×227. Then the proposed LCE layers are incorporated to exploit upon the deconv feature maps for better prediction. Specifically, at the top of the deconv layer, a $2 \times$ stacked 4-directional LSTMs compute context features that describe each image patch locally. The derived context features have the same dimensions as "deconvolution". This is done once per input data.

To make full use of FCN network [1], which is previously trained on PASCAL VOC [19], we adopt all its parameters to initialize the filters of the convolutional layers of LCE. In practice, to preserve its existing layer shapes and make the training stage easier, we trained our architecture in an end-to-end fashion for scene semantic segmentation, without concatenating each feature along

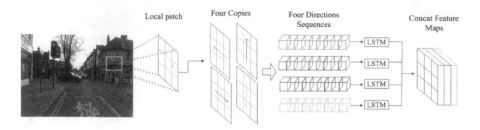

Fig. 2. Illustration of the proposed local contextual embedding architecture. LCE network integrates several LSTM layers into the previous generated feature map for meaningful information fusion. For each local patch from generated feature map, four independent LSTMs are placed upon it to move in four directions respectively. Finally, the derived features are concatenated to generate the fused feature maps.

the channel axis from FCN convolutions (*e.g.*, conv3, conv4, conv5). To match the required shape of feature maps, we directly use the deconvolution data to form the LSTM input. The outputs of LCE are concatenated and then pass conv layer (1×1 conv) to produce a probability confidence map. The confidence map indicates the probability of each pixel that belongs to one of the predefined classes.

In ION [8], they place an RNN along each row and along each column of the image. Different from it, we focus on charactering the local contextual information and each sequence is implemented upon local neighboring of its input feature map. Furthermore, compared with ION, the architecture of our model is easy to train and is good at modeling local contexture information, without concatenating multiple pooled features from different convs.

3.2   Local Contextual Information Embedding

Figure 2 shows more details of our architecture for computing context features in LCE network. To make full use of local context, LSTM is utilized to move along each row and each column of the local patch respectively as a sequence. To this end, on the top of the last deconv layer, we place 4 LSTMs that move across each small region in 4 cardinal directions: right, left, down, up, and then concatenate them to build the output feature map. To enable an end-to-end computing fashion, the LSTMs sit on the top of deconv and produce an output with the same shape as deconv feature map.

Specifically, as we need to predict 9 locations from each local field of deconv feature map, we get 9 features x_t ($t = 1, \ldots, 9$) corresponding to the predefined labels, where $x_t \in \mathbb{R}^d$ and d is the length of each deconv feature. These features are used as inputs to a LSTM structure with 9 time steps. The order of the sequence follows the default definition in feature map location which is ordered as 4 different directions. This makes sure that the pixels from the neighboring areas are always close to each other. Hidden units of traditional RNN are replaced by the so-called memory blocks in LSTM. Each memory block contains self-connected memory cells and three multiplicative units - the input, output and forget gates. These gates control the behavior of the memory block. The three gates of LCE network for each patch are denoted as: the input gate i_t, the forget gate f_t and the output gate o_t respectively, at each time step t. Let c_t be the sum of inputs at each time step t and its previous time step activations. The hidden and memory states by the LCE can be updated as follows:

$$
\begin{aligned}
i_t &= \sigma(W_{xi}x_t + W_{hi}h_{t-1} + W_{ci}c_{t-1} + b_i), \\
f_t &= \sigma(W_{xf}x_t + W_{hf}h_{t-1} + W_{cf}c_{t-1} + b_f), \\
c_t &= i_t \cdot \tanh(W_{xc}x_t + W_{hc}h_{t-1} + b_c) + f_t c_{t-1}, \\
o_t &= \sigma(W_{xo}x_t + W_{ho}h_{t-1} + W_{co}c_t + b_o),
\end{aligned}
\tag{1}
$$

where σ and tanh denote the element-wised sigmoid and tanh activation function respectively, and x_t is the input at time step t. W is the weight matrix specified for input features. h_{t-1} is the hidden state vector of the previous time step and b denotes the input bias vector.

Finally, the output of the memory cell is delivered by $h_t = o_t \cdot \tanh(c_t)$. For convenience, we mark $h_t = S^1(x_t)$, where $S^1(\cdot)$ is constructed by above functions from x_t to h_t. Totally, k such LSTM networks are stacked as a deep LSTM to map the deconv feature to the predefined object classes: $\mathbf{S}_t = S^k(S^{k-1} \cdots (S^1(x_t)))$, where $\mathbf{S}_t$ is the estimated prediction at time step t. All the patches are concatenated and fed into 1×1 conv layer to produce a probability confidence map that indicates probability of each pixel that belongs to one of the predefined classes.

4   Experiments

Datasets: We comprehensively evaluate the performance of LCE on two different benchmarks: CamVid road scenes dataset [17] and SUN RGB-D indoor scenes dataset [18] which contain images under complex scenarios.

Evaluation Metrics: Two standard pixel-wise accuracy metrics: class-wise average accuracy (class avg.) which calculates the mean of the predictive accuracy over all categories in the dataset and intersection-over-union (I/U) criterion are adopted for evaluation on these datasets. Compared with class avg., the mean I/U metric penalizes false positive predictions and is the more strict metric.

Implementation Details: Our network is trained in an end-to-end fashion and it can be jointly optimize all the weights in the architecture using an efficient weight update technique. The network is implemented by extending the Caffe framework [20]. The scale of each input image component is fixed as 227×227 for training networks by preserving the existing layer shapes of FCN. After obtaining feature maps that pass from the previous conv and deconv layers, the LSTM predicts the hidden and memory states of 100 and 60 of first and second layer, respectively. Since it consumes more computation resources by using more LSTMs, we only use two LSTM layers for all models in this work. We train all

Table 1. Comparison of scene semantic segmentation with state-of-the-art methods on CamVid road scenes dataset.

Method	Building	Tree	Sky	Car	Sign-Symbol	Road	Pedestrian	Fence	Column-Pole	Side-walk	Bicyclist	Class avg.	Mean I/U
Local Label Descriptors [22]	80.7	61.5	88.8	16.4	n/a	**98.0**	1.09	0.05	4.13	12.4	0.07	36.3	n/a
Super Parsing [23]	87.0	67.1	**96.9**	62.7	30.1	95.9	14.7	17.9	1.7	70.0	19.4	51.2	n/a
Boosting-Detectors-CRF [25]	81.5	76.6	96.2	78.7	40.2	93.9	43.0	47.6	14.3	81.5	33.9	62.5	n/a
Neural Decision Forests [24]						n/a						56.1	n/a
SegNet-Basic	80.6	72.0	93.0	78.5	21.0	94.0	**62.5**	31.4	36.6	74.0	42.5	62.3	46.3
SegNet-Basic (layer-wise training) [26]	75.0	84.6	91.2	**82.7**	36.9	93.3	55.0	37.5	**44.8**	74.1	16.0	62.9	n/a
SegNet [3]	88.0	**87.3**	92.3	80.0	29.5	97.6	57.2	**49.4**	27.8	84.8	30.7	65.9	50.2
LCE (Ours)	**91.9**	80.7	93.6	77.2	**43.8**	96.6	51.1	45.4	8.8	**85.6**	**52.4**	**66.1**	**57.3**

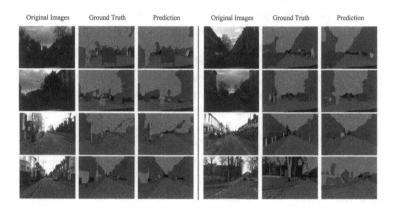

Fig. 3. Qualitative results by our method on the CamVid road scenes database.

the models using stochastic gradient descent (SGD) [21] with a batch size of 1 image, momentum of 0.99, and weight decay of 0.0005. For training based on the pre-trained FCN on PASCAL dataset, it takes about 2 days for CamVid road scene dataset and 7 days for SUN RGB-D indoor scenes dataset. All networks are trained on a single NVIDIA K80 GPU with 12 GB memory.

4.1   Result Comparisons

CamVid Road Scenes Dataset. This dataset consists of 367 training, 101 validation and 233 testing RGB images (day and dusk scenes) at 360 × 480 resolution. There are 11 classes including road, bicyclist, building, side-walks, cars, pedestrians, signs, etc. We compare our method with the state-of-the-art work SegNet [3] with the same size training set. We use their public available results for the fair comparison. We also compare our method with the well-known Local Label Descriptors [22], Neural Decision Forests [24], Super Parsing [23] and Boosting-Detectors-CRF [25]. Note that SegNet has two other versions: a small version SegNet-Basic which has 4 encoders and 4 decoders and SegNet-Basic (layer-wise training) [26] trained in a layer-wise way using L-BFGS [27]. For fair comparison with SegNet (the version presented in the paper [3]) and FCN, the 367 training images are used to train our network. This enables us to compare our method with the SegNet directly.

Table 1 presents the comparison of the proposed LCE with the state-of-the-arts using two evaluation metrics. We directly use their published results on CamVid dataset for fair comparison. LCE obtains competitive results with the state-of-the-art method SegNet. The results of SegNet achieve 65.9% and 50.2% in class avg. and mean I/U metric. Meanwhile, our LCE is superior over this baseline, *i.e.*, 66.1% vs 65.9% in class avg. and 57.3% vs 50.2% in mean I/U metric, using the same size training set. The most interesting result is the 7.1% performance improvement in the hardest metric mean I/U. Correspondingly, the qualitative result of LCE is clearly superior to the rest of the methods. Table 1 also provides further detailed comparisons in two metrics over 11 classes, where our method performs best in 4 categories. All the comparisons verify the effectiveness of our LCE to extract the local contexture information from the input image and map it to accurate and smooth class segment labels.

Figure 3 visualizes some qualitative results by our LCE network on the CamVid dataset. It can be observed that the proposed LCE network performs well in predicting the objects with a smooth segmentation. The scene segmentations of LCE are consistent with the annotation under complex scenes, *e.g.*, road, building, pedestrian, side-walks, cars, are visually distinguished. These visualization results further show the effectiveness of the proposed LCE to extract objects explicitly from road images.

Table 2. Quantitative results of scene semantic segmentation with state-of-the-art methods on SUN RGB-D indoor secnes dataset. The methods that do not use the depth channel are listed below RGB.

	Method	Class avg.	Mean I/U
RGB-D	Liu *et al.* [28]	10.0	n/a
	Ren *et al.* [29]	36.3	n/a
RGB	Liu *et al.* [28]	9.3	n/a
	SegNet [3]	35.6	22.1
	ENet [6]	32.6	19.7
	LCE (ours)	**37.3**	**28.8**

SUN RGB-D Indoor Scenes Dataset. SUN RGB-D indoor scenes dataset contains 10335 images, including 5285 training and 5050 testing images, which come from very complex indoor scenes. The images of indoor scenes contain 37 classes such as window, bookshelf, curtain, bed, etc., that are much more difficult to characterize than outdoor classes such as sky, car and road. Note that, we

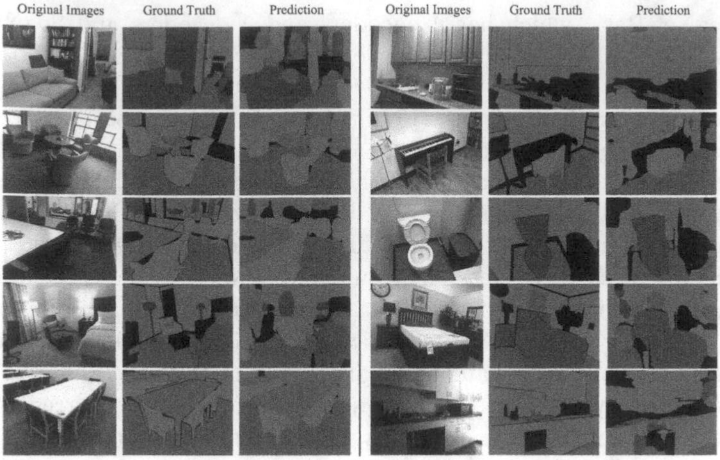

Fig. 4. Some predictions examples of our method on the SUN RGB-D indoor scenes database.

only focus on using the RGB modality for our training and testing, following the benchmark on this dataset used in SegNet. Using depth for segmentation merits a separate body of work is not in the scope of this paper.

We compare our proposed method with other four state-of-the-art approaches including Liu *et al.* [28], Ren *et al.* [29], SegNet [3] and ENet [6]. Table 2 presents the comparison results of the proposed LCE with the four methods in terms of two evaluation metrics on the SUN RGB-D dataset. The proposed method performs better than the state-of-the-art method SegNet, using the same RGB training set. From the results, we can see that compared with ENet, our method can obtain better segmentation results in terms of two evaluation metric, *i.e.*, 37.3% vs 32.6% in class avg. and 28.8% vs 19.7% in mean I/U. The result of SegNet achieves 35.6% and 22.1% in class avg. and mean I/U metric. From the experimental results, we can see that our LCE is superior over this baseline, *i.e.*, 37.3% vs 35.6% in class avg. and 28.8% vs 22.1% in mean I/U metric. Furthermore, the methods that leverage the depth channel (*e.g.*, [28,29]), listed below as (RGB-D), are also reported in Table 2. The state-of-the-art [29] that relies on the depth and low-level image features (*e.g.*, color, gradients and surface normal) achieves better class avg. metric than SegNet. It first describes super-pixel with these features and then improves their labels using a CRF. Our method is superior over this method, *i.e.*, 37.3% vs 36.3% in class avg. This experiment well demonstrates that LCE can utilize more meaningful information, and then improve the segmentation results. Figure 4 visualizes some qualitative results of our LCE network on the SUN RGB-D dataset. It can be observed that the proposed LCE performs well in predicting the objects with heavy occlusion, large background clutters and complex scenes.

Table 3. Quantitative results of scene semantic segmentation of our method with variants on CamVid road scenes and SUN RGB-D indoor scenes datasets.

Method	CamVid		SUN RGB-D	
	Class avg.	Mean I/U	Class avg.	Mean I/U
LCE (noDir)	63.4	53.3	36.1	26.8
LCE (1Dir)	62.2	54.0	34.5	27.2
LCE (4Dir)	**66.1**	**57.3**	**37.3**	**28.8**

4.2 Ablations Studies of Our Network

To further evaluate the effectiveness of the important components of our model, *i.e.*, the LCE network, in this section we compare our whole framework with two versions, including the no local context embedding framework and the one of embedding local context from less directions. The performance by all variants is reported in Table 3.

Is LCE Effect? To justify the necessity of using the local context embedding strategy, we evaluate the performance of segmenting image with setting no local context embedding in our architecture. In this way, this approach degenerates into the standard FCN model, denoted as "LCEnoDir" in this work. Meanwhile, the model that incorporates 4 directions contextual information embedding is denoted as "LCE4Dir". The comparison results of these two versions both on CamVid road scenes dataset and SUN RGB-D indoor scenes dataset are reported in Table 3. From this table, we can see that LCE4Dir leads to 2.7% increase in class avg. and 4% increase in mean I/U metric on the CamVid dataset, compared with LCEnoDir. Meanwhile, the increase of LCE4Dir on the SUN RGB-D dataset is 1.2% and 2% in class avg. and mean I/U metrics, respectively. Intuitively, the better result can be obtained by integrating more local contextual information. This comparison result verifies well that LCE4Dir can lead better object segmentation, indicating that the local context embedding in LSTM is a reasonable strategy.

More Directions Embedding? To further illustrate the effectiveness of local context embedding with more directions, we also extensively evaluate the performance of LCE based on only one direction embedding, referred as "LCE1Dir". Specifically, LCE1Dir denotes the case where LSTM moves in the right direction in this paper. The comparisons are shown in Table 3. Compared with LCE1Dir, LCE4Dir improves class avg. by 3.9% and 2.8%, mean I/U metric by 3.3% and 1.6% on CamVid and SUN RGB-D datasets, respectively. These comparison results indicate that embedding more local contextual information is critical to obtain the final segmentation result. Besides, the superiority of LCE4Dir over the LCE1Dir demonstrates that LCE has the capability of fusing more reasonable local context for predicting segmentation. We also observe that LCE1Dir can only achieve comparable results with LCEnoDir. The main reason may be that just using the information from only one direction is possibly not sufficient to guarantee a better performance.

Do We Need More Training Data? The performance of a good scene semantic segmentation network should be improved when supplied with more training data. Here we augment the CamVid train set with its validation set, a total of 468 images, to evaluate the performance of LCE. Enlarging the training on this data improves class avg. on CamVid test set from 66.1% to 67.5%, and mean I/U metric from 57.3% to 57.5%. From the results, we can clearly see that our proposed LCE network can improve the segmentation performance when more images are used in the training.

5   Conclusions and Future Work

To capture and utilize the contextual information of an image for semantic segmentation task, we propose a novel Local Context Embedding (LCE) network, which uses LSTMs to describe the relationship between local pixels. By incorporating LCE and FCN, the obtained feature representation has high discriminative power and hence benefits semantic segmentation. LCE network is general and others networks can be also incorporated to learn the feature representation for many computer vision tasks. Comprehensive evaluations on CamVid and SUN RGB-D datasets well demonstrate the effectiveness of the proposed method. Furthermore, to make our approach more robust, in our future work we will seek a scheme to adaptively determine the number of directions and which directions should be used in LCE.

Acknowledgments. This work was supported by the National Natural Science Foundation of China under Grant Numbers 61702272, 61773219, 61771249 and 61802199, the Startup Foundation for Introducing Talent of NUIST (2243141701034, 2243141701023), and the Natural Science Foundation of the Jiangsu Higher Education Institutions of China (17KJB535002).

References

1. Long, J., Shelhamer, E., Darrell, T.: Fully convolutional networks for semantic segmentation. In: CVPR, pp. 3431–3440 (2015)
2. Wang, X., Girshick, R., Gupta, A., He, K.: Non-local neural networks. In: CVPR (2018)
3. Badrinarayanan, V., Kendall, A., Cipolla, R.: SegNet: a deep convolutional encoder-decoder architecture for scene segmentation. IEEE Trans. Pattern Anal. Mach. Intell. **PP**(99), 2481–2495 (2017)
4. Yu, C., Wang, J., Peng, C., Gao, C., Yu, G., Sang, N.: BiSeNet: bilateral segmentation network for real-time semantic segmentation. In: ECCV, pp. 325–341 (2018)
5. Noh, H., Hong, S., Han, B.: Learning deconvolution network for semantic segmentation. In: ICCV, pp. 1520–1528 (2015)
6. Paszke, A., Chaurasia, A., Kim, S., Culurciello, E.: ENet: a deep neural network architecture for real-time semantic segmentation. arXiv preprint arXiv: 1606.02147 (2016)

7. Chen, L.C., Papandreou, G., Kokkinos, I., Murphy, K., Yuille, A.L.: DeepLab: semantic image segmentation with deep convolutional nets, atrous convolution, and fully connected CRFs. IEEE Trans. Pattern Anal. Mach. Intell. **40**(4), 834–848 (2018)
8. Bell, S., Zitnick, C.L., Bala, K., Girshick, R.: Inside-outside net: detecting objects in context with skip pooling and recurrent neural networks. In CVPR, pp. 2874–2883 (2016)
9. Byeon, W., Breuel, T.M., Raue, F., Liwicki, M.: Scene labeling with LSTM recurrent neural networks. In: CVPR, pp. 3547–3555 (2015)
10. Kalchbrenner, N., Danihelka, I., Graves, A.: Grid long short-term memory. Comput. Sci. (2016)
11. Oord, A.V.D., Kalchbrenner, N., Kavukcuoglu, K.: Pixel recurrent neural networks. arXiv preprint arXiv: 1601.06759 (2016)
12. Sutskever, I., Vinyals, O., Le, Q.V.: Sequence to sequence learning with neural networks. In: NIPS (2014)
13. Xu, K., et al.: Show, attend and tell: neural image caption generation with visual attention. In: ICML (2015)
14. Schuster, M., Paliwal, K.K.: Bidirectional recurrent neural networks. IEEE Trans. Sig. Process. **45**(11), 2673–2681 (1997)
15. Liu, Q., Zhou, F., Huang, R., Yuan, X.-T.: Bidirectional-convolutional LSTM based spectral-spatial feature learning for hyperspectral image classification. Remote Sens. **9**(12), 1330 (2017)
16. Graves, A., Schmidhuber, J.: Offline handwriting recognition with multidimensional recurrent neural networks. In: NIPS (2009)
17. Brostow, G., Fauqueur, J., Cipollal, R.: Semantic object classed in video: a high-definition ground truth database. Pattern Recogn. Lett. **30**(2), 88–97 (2009)
18. Song, S., Lichtenberg, S., Xiao, J.: SUN RGB-D: A RGB-D scene understanding benchmark suite. In: CVPR, pp. 567–576 (2015)
19. Everingham, M., Gool, L.V., Williams, C.K., Winn, J., Zisserman, A.: The pascal visual object classes (VOC) challenge. Int. J. Comput. Vis. **88**(2), 303–338 (2010)
20. Jia, Y., et al.: Caffe: convolutional architecture for fast feature embedding. arXiv preprint arXiv: 1408.5093 (2014)
21. Bottou, L.: Large-scale machine learning with stochastic gradient descent. In: Lechevallier, Y., Saporta, G. (eds.) Proceedings of COMPSTAT 2010, pp. 177–186. Springer, Cham (2010). https://doi.org/10.1007/978-3-7908-2604-3_16
22. Yang, Y., Li, Z., Zhang, L., Murphy, C., Ver Hoeve, J., Jiang, H.: Local label descriptor for example based semantic image labeling. In: Fitzgibbon, A., Lazebnik, S., Perona, P., Sato, Y., Schmid, C. (eds.) ECCV 2012. LNCS, vol. 7578, pp. 361–375. Springer, Heidelberg (2012). https://doi.org/10.1007/978-3-642-33786-4_27
23. Tighe, J., Lazebnik, S.: SuperParsing: scalable nonparametric image parsing with superpixels. Int. J. Comput. Vis. **101**(2), 329–349 (2013)
24. Bulo, S.R., Kontschieder, P.: Neural decision forests for semantic image labelling. In: CVPR, pp. 81–88 (2014)
25. Ladický, L., Sturgess, P., Alahari, K., Russell, C., Torr, P.H.S.: What, where and how many? Combining object detectors and CRFs. In: Daniilidis, K., Maragos, P., Paragios, N. (eds.) ECCV 2010. LNCS, vol. 6314, pp. 424–437. Springer, Heidelberg (2010). https://doi.org/10.1007/978-3-642-15561-1_31
26. Badrinarayanan, V., Kendall, A., Cipolla, R.: SegNet: a deep convolutional encoder-decoder architecture for robust semantic pixel-wise labelling. CoRR, vol.abs/1505.07293 (2015)

27. Nocedal, J., Wright, S.J.: Numerical Optimization. 2nd edn, New York (2006)
28. Liu, C., Yuen, J., Torralba, A., Sivic, J., Freeman, W.T.: SIFT flow: dense corre-
    spondence across different scenes. In: Forsyth, D., Torr, P., Zisserman, A. (eds.)
    ECCV 2008. LNCS, vol. 5304, pp. 28–42. Springer, Heidelberg (2008). https://doi.
    org/10.1007/978-3-540-88690-7_3
29. Ren, X., Bo, L., Fox, D.: RGB-(D) scene labeling: features and algorithms. In:
    CVPR, pp. 2759–2766 (2012)
30. Simonyan, K., Zisserman, A.: Very deep convolutional networks for large-scale
    image recognition. arXiv preprint arXiv: 1409.1556 (2014)

Retinex Based Flicker-Free Low-Light Video Enhancement

Juanjuan Tu, Zongliang Gan$^{(\boxtimes)}$, and Feng Liu

Jiangsu Provincial Key Lab of Image Processing and Image Communication,
Nanjing University of Posts and Telecommunications, Nanjing 210003, China
{1217012310,ganzl,liuf}@njupt.edu.cn

Abstract. Videos captured in low light environment tend to be poor visual effect. To get better visual experience, a video enhancement algorithm based on improved center-surrounded Retinex and optical flow is proposed in this paper, which contains intra-frame brightness enhancement and inter-frame brightness continuity. In intra-frame brightness enhancement, reflection of each frame is estimated by adjusting the illumination using a weight factor, so that bright illumination is compressed to obtain a reflection with approximately uniform illumination. Then logarithmic image processing subtraction (LIPS) is adopted to enhance its contrast. To maintain inter-frame brightness continuity, the background and brightness changes of adjacent frames are measured using optical flow and just noticeable difference (JND) threshold, respectively. If the background and average brightness change little, their reflection brightness is almost the same, so LIPS parameter of previous frame is applied to current frame. Otherwise, current frame will be updated by calculating its own parameter. Experimental results demonstrate that proposed algorithm performs well in brightness continuity and detail enhancement.

Keywords: Video enhancement · Retinex ·
Logarithmic image processing subtraction (LIPS) ·
Brightness continuity

1 Introduction

Affected by the environment, equipment and human factors, images/videos are often of low quality, which significantly reduces the performance of some application fields such as remote sensing image, biomedical image, surveillance video, computer vision. In order to obtain images/videos with better visual effects, various enhancement technologies have emerged. From the aspects of brightness, contrast, color fidelity and naturalness, researchers at home and abroad have made countless contributions to the study of image/video enhancement.

The work was supported by the National Nature Science Foundation P.R. China No. 61471201; The first author is a student.

© Springer Nature Switzerland AG 2019
Z. Lin et al. (Eds.): PRCV 2019, LNCS 11858, pp. 367–379, 2019.
https://doi.org/10.1007/978-3-030-31723-2_31

Over the past decades, many algorithms based on image histogram or Retinex theory have been proposed. Histogram equalization is an efficient way to stretch contrast, but it is prone to over enhancement. To solve this problem, Chen [2] divides image histogram into several ranges, and perform histogram equalization in the separated histogram. Stark [3] performs histogram equalization by clipping image histogram and interpolating cumulative distribution function (CDF) of blocks. However, the extremely narrow histogram of dark areas spreads out too much would result in over-saturation in bright areas. To improve the problem, optimization-based histogram equalization is proposed in [4].

Center-surrounded Retinex algorithms aim to separate the illumination component from input image, and then perform logarithmic transformation to enhance the dynamic range of reflectance component [5–7]. However, estimating illumination with low-pass filter usually generates halo near edges, and enhanced image tends to disturb color information due to the independent process in each color channel. Hence, various improved algorithms have been put forward.

Kimmel [8] first proposes a variation-based method, estimating illumination by solving a quadratic programming optimal problem. Besides, Li [9] proposes an algorithm by introducing a noise term and a gradient term in variational model, so that structure is maintained while noise suppression. Nevertheless, variation Retinex methods usually have high computational complexity. Thus, some scholars prefer to estimate illumination with a filter to acquire enhancements more effectively. Xu [10] proposes perceptual contrast enhancement with adaptive luminance estimation, which uses different filter parameters at different contrast edges. Moreover, Wang [12] presents a naturalness preserved method using priori multi-layer lightness statistics, and gains quite excellent enhancements.

Different from single image enhancement, video enhancement needs to consider the continuity between adjacent frames. Dong [13] enhances video by applying an optimized de-haze algorithm on the inverted video and expediting the calculation of key parameter utilizing temporal correlations between subsequent frames. Huang [14] applies adaptive gamma correction with weighting distribution (AGCWD) to low-illumination video, which uses same gamma mapping curve for similar scenes. Ko [15] enhances video brightness by accumulating similar blocks in adjacent frames. To reduce color distortion and avoid artifacts, they improve color assignment and fuse image using the guide map in [16].

However, Retinex based enhancement algorithms are rarely applied to video, and it is easy to generate brightness flicker when each frame is enhanced independently, because the correlation between adjacent frames is not taken into consideration. To solve this problem, this paper proposes a flicker-free video enhancement algorithm. Main contributions are as follows:

(i) A video enhancement framework based on Retinex is proposed, which consists of two parts: intra-frame brightness enhancement and inter-frame brightness continuity maintenance. Improved center-surrounded Retinex is used to estimate the reflection component of each frame, and its brightness is enhanced by logarithmic image processing subtraction (LIPS).

(ii) A method to maintain brightness continuity is proposed, which is to determine the LIPS parameter of each frame according to background and brightness change. Same parameter is taken for adjacent frames with little change of background and brightness because their reflection brightness is similar. Otherwise, parameter is updated. Where background and brightness changes are measured using optical flow and just noticeable difference (JND) threshold, respectively.

The remainder of this paper is organized as follows. Related theories adopted in the proposed algorithm are introduced in Sect. 2. The proposed method is described in detail in Sect. 3. Experimental results and performance comparison are presented in Sect. 4. At last, conclusions are drawn in Sect. 5.

2   Related Works

2.1   Center-Surrounded Retinex Based Enhancement Method

Retinex theory is first proposed by Land [17], which holds that image S we see is the product of illuminance component L and reflection component R.

$$S = L \times R \tag{1}$$

Since the real scene illumination cannot be measured, L is always obtained by estimation. Single-Scale Retinex (SSR) [5], based on the assumption that illumination changes slowly, estimates illumination with Gaussian filter. To preserve information at different scales, Rahman proposes Multi-Scale Retinex (MSR) [6] that weights the reflection components of different scales (Eq. (2)). N takes 3, ω_n and σ_n are the weight and scale parameter. Where ω_n generally takes $\frac{1}{3}$.

$$\log R(x, y) = \sum_{n=1}^{N} \omega_n \{\log S(x, y) - \log [F_{\sigma_n}(x, y) * S(x, y)]\} \tag{2}$$

However, it is pathological to solve the problem based on Retinex model. And the inaccuracy of illumination estimation often leads to halo, noise amplification and color distortion. To improve the visibility of enhanced image, Li [9] and Guo [18] adjust the illumination with global gamma correction, and the enhanced result E is expressed as (3) rather than only reflection component R in (2).

$$E = L^\gamma \times R \tag{3}$$

Equation (3) adjusts the illuminance component in real domain, while Xu [10] adjusts illumination adaptively in logarithmic domain with control factor to suppress noise. Our previous work [1] also adjusts illumination with adaptive factor, but uses bilateral filter instead of gaussian to estimate illumination, which ensures the edge details while making the illumination as smooth as possible.

2.2   Optical Flow

Optical flow is defined as the apparent motion in an image sequence, that is, the object motion on image plane can be detected with it. The basic principle of optical flow detection for moving objects is that a velocity vector is assigned to each pixel in the image to form a motion field. Since objects generally move in a relatively continuous manner in space, the image projected onto a two-dimensional plane should change continuously. If the pixel (x, y) in a video frame at time t is $I(x, y, t)$, the optical flow $w = (u, v)$ with horizontal $u(x, y)$ and vertical $v(x, y)$ moving components at that point are

$$u(x, y) = \frac{dx}{dt}, v(x, y) = \frac{dy}{dt} \tag{4}$$

Thus, the constraint equation of optical flow can be expressed as

$$-\frac{\partial I}{\partial t} = \frac{\partial I}{\partial x} \cdot u + \frac{\partial I}{\partial y} \cdot v \tag{5}$$

In order to determine the solution (u, v), extra constraints must be attached to (5). Lucas-Kanade (LK) optical flow proposed by Lucas [19] introduces a local smoothness constraint, assuming that the motion vector is constant over a small space, which is mainly used to calculate sparse optical flow field.

3   Proposed Method

3.1   Algorithm Introduction

To enhance low-light video without brightness flicker, this paper proposes an algorithm based on improved center-surrounded Retinex and optical flow. Algorithm framework is illustrated in Fig. 1. For each incoming frame, improved center-surrounded Retinex is used to estimate its reflection. If the incoming frame is the first frame of a scene, its reflection brightness is enhanced with LIPS by calculating parameter adaptively. Otherwise, the background change is judged by counting the proportion of motion pixels in background. If there is no change, then determine whether the scene brightness mutation. If not, the LIPS parameter of previous frame is used to enhance current frame. As long as the background or average brightness change significantly, LIPS parameter and first frame number of the new scene are updated. Where the background is estimated with P-frames before current frame using optical flow.

3.2   Intra-frame Brightness Enhancement

This paper proposes a bright illumination adjustment and reflection contrast enhancement method to enhance each frame. The processing is performed on V channel without affecting hue (H) and saturation (S). Based on center-surrounded Retinex, adaptive weight factor is used to adjust illumination estimated by bilateral filter. And the contrast of reflection is enhanced with LIPS.

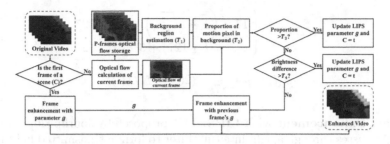

Fig. 1. Framework of video enhancement algorithm.

Bright Illumination Adjustment. Videos acquired at night are often of uneven illumination due to complex lighting. So it is necessary to adjust the illumination image to make it nearly uniform for enhancement. This paper adds a weight factor to adjust illumination in the logarithmic domain, which is defined in (6). Where V is the brightness of original frame and R' is the estimated reflection component. Bilateral filter is selected as $F_{\sigma_n}(x, y)$ in this paper.

$$\log R'(x, y) = \sum_{n=1}^{N} \omega_n \{\log V(x, y) - \beta \cdot \log [F_{\sigma_n}(x, y) * V(x, y)]\} \qquad (6)$$

Aimed to eliminate halo, adaptive scale parameters are adopted in [10]. Inspired by it, brightness standard deviation of bilateral filter is locally set. Edge position is detected by *Canny* operator, and parameter σ_n at weak contrast edge is large, while a little smaller one $0.6\sigma_n$ at high edge. In addition, the average of three scale filtered images is used as background illumination.

By converting (6) to the real domain (Eq. (7)), we find that adjusting illumination with β in logarithmic domain is similar to $1 - \beta$ correcting illumination in real domain. Image enhancement with globally fixed β improves the brightness but contrast is insufficient. Obviously, adaptive β is better. To obtain a approximately uniform illumination, $1 - \beta$ decreasing with illumination is needed to improve the brightness in low-illumination area (lower than 127), while gradually increasing $1 - \beta$ is for bright-illumination region (larger than 127). That is β first increases and then decreases, with 127 as the turning point.

$$R' = e^{\log V - \beta \log L} = \frac{V}{L^{\beta}} = \frac{L \cdot R}{L^{\beta}} = L^{1-\beta} \cdot R \qquad (7)$$

From the just noticeable difference (JND) [23] defined in Eq. (8), we find that it is negatively correlated with the value of β. Taking into account the naturalness and contrast of frames, the adaptive β is set in conjunction with the JND threshold. In Eq. (9), q controls the floating range of β, p determines the starting position of β, and l is the background luminance. The larger the q, the wider the range of β and the greater the contrast of enhancement. The larger the p, the larger the β, the more the reflection brightness is compressed, and the brighter the enhanced frame. In this paper, p is 0.25 and q is 0.1.

$$JND(l) = \begin{cases} 17 \times \left(1 - \sqrt{\frac{l}{127}}\right) + 3 & l \le 127 \\ \frac{3}{128} \times (l - 127) + 3 & l > 127 \end{cases} \tag{8}$$

$$\beta(l) = p + \frac{q}{17} \times (20 - JND(l)) \tag{9}$$

Contrast Enhancement with LIPS. LIP, proposed by Jourlin [20], considers that light passes through a light intensity filter to form a transmitted light image that enters human eyes. In fact, the image is represented by an absorption filter function, which is defined as gray tone function f. For an 8-bit image I, its gray tone function is expressed as $f = M - I$ ($M = 256$). Moreover, LIP model redefines addition, subtraction and scalar multiplication. Where, LIPS is denoted as Eq. (10), and $g = M - J$ is a gray tone function of image J.

$$f \ominus g = M \cdot \frac{f - g}{M - g} \tag{10}$$

In this paper, subtraction is used to improve the reflection brightness. Enhancement E is equivalent to reflection R' multiplied by luminance $M/(M - g)$ in (11). Analysis in (12–13) reveals that as g increases, brightness m_E and contrast σ_E^2 of reflection also increase. Where m_E and $m_{R'}$ are average brightness of enhancement and reflection; σ_E^2 and $\sigma_{R'}^2$ are the variance of enhancement and reflection, respectively.

$$E = M - f \ominus g = M - \frac{M - R' - g}{1 - \frac{g}{M}} = \frac{M}{M - g} \cdot R' \tag{11}$$

$$m_E = E\left(\frac{M}{M - g} \cdot R'\right) = \frac{M}{M - g} \cdot E(R') = \frac{M}{M - g} \cdot m_{R'} \tag{12}$$

$$\sigma_E^2 = E\left(\left(\frac{M \cdot R'}{M - g}\right)^2\right) - m_E^2 = \left(\frac{M}{M - g}\right)^2 \cdot \sigma_{R'}^2 \tag{13}$$

From Fig. 2(a) we know that pixels of reflection are mainly concentrated in a narrow brightness range. To maximize the brightness of enhanced frame without exceeding $[0, M)$, parameter g should select within $(0, M - R'_{max})$. And the brightness and contrast are the maximum when g is $M - R'_{max}$. However, maximum of reflection may deviate far from the brightness range of most pixels. Obviously, it is better to ignore those scattered bright spots in the reflection.

In Fig. 2(b), CDF grows sharply in $(0, T)$, while the flat portion exceeding T is scattered with a few bright spots. If an error e is set, the intensity T corresponding to CDF less than $1 - e$ could be taken as the maximum of reflection, that is $R'_{max} = T$. The value of e in this paper is $0.08\,\mu$, where μ is the average brightness of input frame. Next, calculate LIPS parameter according to (14). As a result, enhanced frame can be obtained by substituting (14) into (12).

$$g = M - R'_{max} = M - T \tag{14}$$

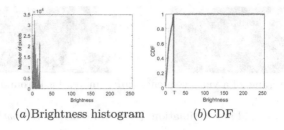

(a)Brightness histogram   (b)CDF

Fig. 2. Brightness histogram of reflection component and its CDF.

3.3   Inter-frame Brightness Continuity

Video scenes are complex and variable, independent enhancement of each frame ignores the correlation of adjacent frames. Especially for dynamic video with almost invariable or slowly changing background, the brightness continuity of adjacent frames should be guaranteed while improving brightness.

It is clear that frame enhancement in Sect. 3.2 is affected by two adaptive parameters (β and g). LIPS parameter g has a greater impact on final brightness. To ensure the inter-frame brightness continuity, we choose g of previous frame to enhance current frame for invariant or gradual scenes. Because one gray-level increase of g will cause the average brightness of enhanced frame to differ by several gray-levels when g is large. While frames with abrupt scene are enhanced by calculating g adaptively. In this section, the scene change is judged by calculating the motion pixel ratio in the background area with optical flow method.

Background Estimation. For a video with invariant or gradual background, the optical flow amplitude of the background is small, while the optical flow amplitude of foreground part is large. In order to estimate the background area more accurately, we record the part whose magnitude is greater than a threshold T_1 as the foreground by accumulating the optical flow (of) of P frames before current frame, and the rest is background area.

$$OF = \sum_{p=1}^{P} of_{t-p} \tag{15}$$

where t is the frame number of current frame. $t - p = max(C, t - p)$, and C is the first frame number of current scene. OF is the cumulative optical flow amplitude. In this paper, when $T_1 = 10$ and $P = 5$, estimated background is shown in Fig. 3.

Motion Pixel Statistics in the Background. In the previously estimated background region (Number of pixels is N_{bg}), the number of motion pixels (N_{of}) in current frame is counted, whose optical flow amplitude is greater than a

(a)One frame of a video sequence (b)Estimated background area

Fig. 3. Background area estimation. (Non-white area is the background.)

threshold T_2 in this region. When the background changes little with respect to previous frame, optical flow amplitude in the background larger than T_2 is less, and the proportion (N_{of}/N_{bg}) of moving pixels in the background is smaller.

In this paper, T_2 is set to 2 and the proportional threshold T_3 is set to 0.55. When the threshold T_3 is exceeded, it is considered that the background of current frame has a sudden change relative to the previous frame. Thus, parameter g of current frame should be recalculated and the frame number of current frame is record as the first frame of new scene $(C = t)$.

Except for the frames with sudden scene change, those with brightness variation that is perceptible to human eyes but scene remains unchanged also need to re-estimated LIPS parameter g to prevent improper brightness enhancement. The brightness difference threshold T_4 of adjacent frames is calculated with (16), where μ_{t-1} is the previous frame's average brightness, and $JND(\mu_{t-1})$ is the visibility threshold. Brightness difference between adjacent frames greater than this threshold indicates that original video has a discontinuous brightness here. Parameter g should be updated. At the same time, the first frame of the new scene also needs to be updated, that is $C = t$. Finally, enhanced video is obtained by connecting the enhanced frame sequence into a video.

$$T_4 = JND(\mu_{t-1}) \tag{16}$$

4   Experimental Results and Analysis

All the experiments are carried out on a PC with 2.50 GHz CPU and 8G RAM. Performance of proposed method is compared with five algorithms including AGCWD [14], video enhancement proposed by Jiang [21], LIME [18], naturalness preserved image enhancement by Wang [12] and deep Retinex decomposition RetinexNet [22] in subjective and objective assessments. The first two are video enhancement algorithms, while the last three independently enhance each frame.

4.1   Subjective Assessment

Figure 4 presents one video sequence and its enhanced result using our method. It can be seen that video brightness is effectively improved. Nine frames with the size of 960×404 from three movie videos are shown in Fig. 5, which are the sequences that contain invariant, gradual and abrupt scenes. Horizontally,

Jiang and Wang's algorithm, LIME and RetinexNet improve the brightness of each frame. However, over-saturation and noise amplification cause the frames unnatural. AGCWD increases the contrast, but bright areas are prone to over-exposure and low contrast frame enhancement is insufficient. Our results are not as bright as those of other algorithms, but the details in bright area preserves well. As a result, enhanced frames look more natural. Vertically, whether the scene changes or not, our algorithm performs better for each frame.

4.2 Objective Assessment

This section selects one quality metric to evaluate enhanced frames, namely colorfulness-based patch-based contrast quality index CPCQI [24]. CPCQI calculates the perceived distortion, and value greater than 1 indicates quality enhancement, while the more it is less than 1, the more serious degradation is.

Table 1 shows the average CPCQI of three video sequences (100 frames of each video). It can be found that indexes of our method are ranked in the top one. And average CPCQI of ours is greater than 1, suggesting that frame quality is improved. While indexes of other algorithms are smaller than 1 in video 3, which means enhanced frame quality decreased. Especially the CPCQI of Jiang's algorithm and RetinexNet is smaller in three videos, indicating that the distortion is serious. AGCWD and Wang's algorithm improves the frame quality for video 1, 2, but failed in high contrast sequence (video 3). LIME produces distortion in video 1, 3, because it works better for very dark frames (video 2).

In addition, the average running speed of our method and five algorithms is also compared in Table 2. Except for RetinexNet with Python, other algorithms are processed by Matlab. Our algorithm ranked fourth in processing speed because bilateral filtering takes a long time. AGCWD and Jiang's algorithm and LIME process faster, while Wang's algorithm and RetinexNet process each frame independently at very slow speeds.

4.3 Flickering-Artifact Assessment

In order to visually demonstrate the brightness continuity, we compare the average brightness and flickering score of three videos. Their results are shown in Fig. 6. When the average brightness trend of enhanced video is consistent with that of original video and the average brightness difference between adjacent frames is not large, it is considered that no flicker occurs. Moreover, flickering score [11] defined in (17) is to evaluate the degree of brightness flicker.

$$FS = \frac{1}{M} \sum_{m=1}^{M} \frac{\left| \hat{f}_t(m) - \hat{f}_{t-1}(m) \right| + \alpha}{\left| f_t(m) - f_{t-1}(m) \right| + \alpha} \tag{17}$$

where f and $\hat{f}$ are frames before and after enhancement, and M is the number of blocks (4×4). Constant α is 1, $\|f_t(m) - f_{t-1}(m)\|_2^2 < \theta, \theta$ is 10. Flickering score close to 1 means that video is more flickering free.

In Fig. 6, from top to bottom are results of video sequence with invariant, gradual and abrupt scene respectively. For sequences with invariant or gradual scene in first two lines, brightness change of ours are consistent with original sequence, while AGCWD and Wang's algorithm produce noticeable brightness flicker. Other algorithms have no obvious brightness flicker in average brightness, but their flickering scores are higher due to the amplified noise. Sudden change of average brightness in the third line of Fig. 6(a) indicates that the scene changes, corresponding to the peak in flickering score. In Fig. 6(b), our algorithm has the lowest score in the first and third lines, suggesting no brightness flicker. Score in the second line is higher because of the noise, but there is still no flicker.

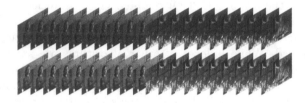

Fig. 4. Enhanced result of video sequence 3. (The first line is original video sequence and the second line is enhanced video sequence.)

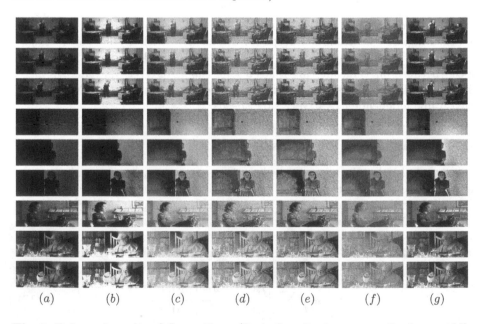

(a) (b) (c) (d) (e) (f) (g)

Fig. 5. Enhanced results of three videos. (Each three lines represent the first, middle and last frames of the video sequence. (a) Input frame, (b) AGCWD [14], (c) Jiang [21], (d) LIME [18], (e) Wang [12], (f) RetinexNet [22], (g) Proposed.)

Table 1. Average CPCQI of different algorithms for three enhanced video sequences.

Video	AGCWD [14]	Jiang [21]	LIME [18]	Wang [12]	RetinexNet [22]	Proposed
1	1.0134	0.9337	0.9954	1.0180	0.9339	**1.1093**
2	1.0324	0.9652	1.0428	1.0220	0.9487	**1.0535**
3	0.9225	0.7561	0.9163	0.9642	0.7984	**1.0528**

Table 2. Comparison of average running speed (frames/second).

	AGCWD [14]	Jiang [21]	LIME [18]	Wang [12]	RetinexNet [22]	Proposed
Speed	5.2713	0.7842	0.4926	0.0309	0.0735	0.3309

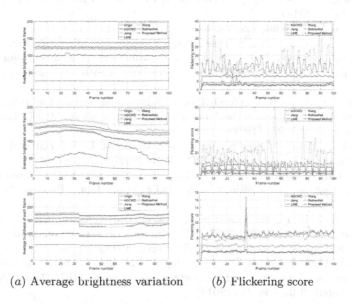

(a) Average brightness variation   (b) Flickering score

Fig. 6. Comparison of brightness continuity for three videos.

5 Conclusion

In this paper, we propose an improved Retinex-based video enhancement algorithm. Weight factor is calculated to adjust illumination, so that reflection is compressed into a dark image with approximately uniform illumination. Then same LIPS parameter is adopted for frames with similar scene to ensure continuous brightness, while updated parameter for abrupt frames. Experiments show that our method has less distortion as well as no brightness flicker. Next, we'll focus on reducing processing time and adjusting LIPS parameter for gradual scene to improve the enhanced quality of frames farther from the first frame.

References

1. Pan, W., Gan, Z., Qi, L., Chen, C., Liu, F.: Efficient retinex-based low-light image enhancement through adaptive reflectance estimation and LIPS postprocessing. In: J-H, L., et al. (eds.) PRCV 2018. LNCS, vol. 11256, pp. 335–346. Springer, Cham (2018). https://doi.org/10.1007/978-3-030-03398-9_29
2. Chen, S.D., Ramli, A.R., Chiu, Y.S.: Contrast enhancement using recursive mean-separate histogram equalization for scalable brightness preservation. IEEE Trans. Consum. Electron. **49**(4), 1301–1309 (2003)
3. Stark, J.A.: Adaptive image contrast enhancement using generalizations of histogram equalization. IEEE Trans. Image Process. **9**(5), 889–896 (2000)
4. Gu, K., Zhai, G., Yang, X., Zhang, W., Chen, C.: Automatic contrast enhancement technology with saliency preservation. IEEE Trans. Circ. Syst. Video Technol. **25**(9), 1480–1494 (2015)
5. Jobson, D.J., Rahman, Z., Woodell, G.A.: Properties and performance of a center/surround retinex. IEEE Trans. Image Process. **6**(3), 451–462 (1997)
6. Rahman, Z., Jobson, D.J., Woodell, G.A.: Multiscale retinex for color rendition and dynamic range compression. In: Proceedings of SPIE, vol. 2847, pp. 183–191 (1996)
7. Jobson, D.J., Rahman, Z., Woodell, G.A.: A multiscale retinex for bridging the gap between color images and the human observation of scenes. IEEE Trans. Image Process. **6**(7), 965–976 (1997)
8. Kimmel, R., Elad, M., Shaked, D., Keshet, R., Sobel, I.: A variational framework for retinex. Int. J. Comput. Vis. **52**(1), 7–23 (2003)
9. Li, M., Liu, J., Yang, W., Sun, X., Guo, Z.: Structure-revealing low-light image enhancement via robust retinex model. IEEE Trans. Image Process. **27**(6), 2828–2841 (2018)
10. Xu, K., Jung, C.: Retinex-based perceptual contrast enhancement in images using luminance adaptation. In: 2017 IEEE International Conference on Acoustics, Speech and Signal Processing (ICASSP), pp. 1363–1367 (2017)
11. Yang, H., Park, J., Moon, Y.: Flickering effect reduction based on the modified transformation function for video contrast enhancement. IEIE Trans. Smart Process. Comput. **3**(6), 358–365 (2014)
12. Wang, S., Luo, G.: Naturalness preserved image enhancement using a priori multilayer lightness statistics. IEEE Trans. Image Process. **27**(2), 938–948 (2018)
13. Dong, X., et al.: Fast efficient algorithm for enhancement of low lighting video. In: 2011 IEEE International Conference on Multimedia and Expo, pp. 1–6 (2011)
14. Huang, S.C., Cheng, F.C., Chiu, Y.S.: Efficient contrast enhancement using adaptive gamma correction with weighting distribution. IEEE Trans. Image Process. **22**(3), 1032–1041 (2013)
15. Ko, S., Yu, S., Kang, W., Kim, D., Paik, J.: Flicker-free low-light video enhancement using patch-similarity and adaptive accumulation. In: 2016 IEEE International Conference on Consumer Electronics (ICCE), pp. 215–216 (2016)
16. Ko, S., Yu, S., Kang, W., Park, C., Lee, S., Paik, J.: Artifact-free low-light video enhancement using temporal similarity and guide map. IEEE Trans. Ind. Electron. **64**(8), 6392–6401 (2017)
17. Land, E.H.: The retinex theory of color vision. Sci. Am. **237**(6), 108–129 (1977)
18. Guo, X., Li, Y., Ling, H.: LIME: low-light image enhancement via illumination map estimation. IEEE Trans. Image Process. **26**(2), 982–993 (2017)

19. Lucas, B., Kanade, T.: An iterative image registration technique with an application to stereo vision. In: Image Understanding Proceedings of a Workshop, vol. 81, pp. 121–130 (1981)
20. Jourlin, M., Pinoli, J.C.: A model for logarithmic image processing. J. Microsc. **149**(1), 21–35 (1988)
21. Jiang, X., Yao, H., Zhang, S., Lu, X., Zeng, W.: Night video enhancement using improved dark channel prior. In: 2013 IEEE International Conference on Image Processing, pp. 553–557 (2013)
22. Chen, W., Wang, W., Yang, W., Liu, J.: Deep retinex decomposition for low-light enhancement. In: British Machine Vision Conference (2018)
23. Jayant, N.: Signal compression: technology targets and research directions. IEEE J. Sel. Areas Commun. **10**(5), 796–818 (1992)
24. Gu, K., Tao, D., Qiao, J., Lin, W.: Learning a no-reference quality assessment model of enhanced images with big data. IEEE Trans. Neural Netw. Learn. Syst. **29**(4), 1301–1313 (2018)

Transfer Learning for Rigid 2D/3D Cardiovascular Images Registration

Shaoya Guan[1], Cai Meng[2,3(✉)], Kai Sun[2], and Tianmiao Wang[1,3]

[1] School of Mechanical Engineering and Automation, Beihang University,
Beijing 100083, China
guanshaoya@163.com
[2] School of Astronautics, Beihang University, Beijing 100083, China
tsai@buaa.edu.cn
[3] Beijing Advanced Innovation Center for Biomedical Engineering,
Beihang University, Beijing 100083, China
itm@buaa.edu.cn

Abstract. Cardiovascular image registration is an essential approach to combine the advantages of preoperative 3D computed tomography angiograph (CTA) images and intraoperative 2D X-ray/ digital subtraction angiography (DSA) images together in minimally invasive vascular interventional surgery (MIVI). Recent studies have shown that convolutional neural network (CNN) regression model can be used to register these two modality vascular images with fast speed and satisfactory accuracy. Because of the large differences in the vascular architecture of different patients, a CNN regression model trained on one patient often cannot be applied to another. To overcome this challenge, we proposed a transfer learning based CNN regression model which can be transferred from one patient to another with only tiny modifications. The registration error of our proposed method can reach less than 1 mm or 1° when a trained model is fine-tuned with only 200 images of the target patient in about 150 s. We tested the transfer ability of our method with images from various patients suffering different cardiovascular disease and confirm the effectiveness of our method. Deformation of cardiac vessels was not considered in this rigid registration model and non-rigid cardiovascular registration model will be developed in our future work to improve the registration accuracy of t_z.

Keywords: 2D/3D registration · Transfer learning · Convolutional neural network · Rigid and non-rigid registration · Vascular deformatio

1 Introduction

Minimally invasive vascular intervention (MIVI), which is safe and easy for recovery, has been the state-of-the-art therapy for aortic diseases. In MIVI, the pre-

Supported by the National Natural Science Foundation of China (Grants No. 61533016, 61873010).

operative data are often three dimensional (3D) CTA images, while the intra-operative data are mostly two dimensional (2D) X-ray (fluoroscopy) images. Consequently, 2D/3D medical image registration [13] is a significant approach to take advantages of both the ability to display vessels in real time of 2D X-ray images and the complete vascular spatial topology of 3D CT images. 2D/3D registration is usually to match the pre-operative 3D data and the intra-operative 2D data by finding an optimal transformation that best aligns these two modality images.

The efficiency of machine learning in image processing has been proved in recent years [6,12]. Machine learning methods are also gradually being used for registration of medical images [8]. Several researchers proposed a new direction that treats 2D/3D registration as a regression problem in which a network was trained by using intensity or structural features from X-ray images to estimate the 3D transformation parameters directly. Chou et al. [4] trained linear regressors by using the residual between the DRR and X-ray images as a feature to estimate the transformation parameters. However, linear regression tends to yield unreliable results when the mapping from residuals to transformation parameters is highly nonlinear. Many researchers have made some explorations on the application of highly nonlinear convolutional neural networks in registration [5,14,15]. Most of these machine learning and deep learning methods are used to register objects that do not deform with different patients. Vascular structure and location of vascular lesions varies greatly of different patients. Therefore, a trained regression model may perform perfectly on patient A, but present poor results on patient B. Also, training a regression model often requires tens of thousands of images, which is difficult for clinical application. So whether we can train a common model, with a small amount of data on different patients to make minor modifications to the model, we can get satisfactory registration results suit for various patients. Transfer learning is a proper solution for this problem.

Transfer learning techniques are relatively new in medical image processing and have shown great success in computer-aided classification and detection of medical images [2,3,7,16]. Transfer learning has also been used for medical image segmentation, such as brain tissue, white matter lesion, hippocampus segmentation [1] and brain tumor retrieval [17]. However, these approaches focus on feature-transfer between datasets for image or pixel classification, while we investigate a transfer learning approach which focus on the difference of vascular structures and lesion positions. Regression model for registration depends severely on vascular characteristics, such as vascular diameters, vascular lengths and vascular shapes. It is scarcely possible to transfer a model trained on one patient to other patients. As a result that we have to train different models for different patients, which will spend a lot of time and hinder the clinical application of our model. Transfer learning is a proper way to solve these problems.

In this paper, we combine transfer learning with our previous proposed regression model to obtain a new approach to register 2D and 3D images of cardiac vessels using a extensively small dataset in a relatively short time. As far as we know, this is the first application of transfer learning in vascular image registration. We just focus on transfer learning for rigid cardiovascular registration in this paper.

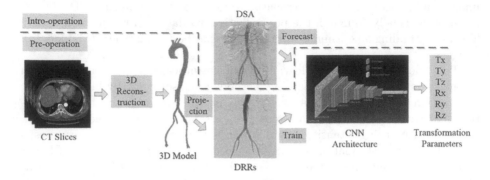

Fig. 1. Framework of 2D/3D registration by CNN regression.

2 Methods

2.1 2D/3D Registration

The purpose of 2D/3D vascular image registration is to find the optimal transformation parameters from a pre-operative 3D vascular model to an intra-operative 2D DSA images by comparing the similarity of the DSA image and 2D projections, often digitally reconstructured radiograph images (DRR), of the 3D model (see Fig. 1). Accordingly, the inputs of our 2D/3D registration framework include: (1) annotated projections of a 3D vascular model reconstructed from the pre-operative CT slices, (2) an intro-operative DSA image with unknown transformation parameters, and (3) initial transformation parameters (set to zero in this paper).

2.2 Registration with Transfer Learning

Rigid CNN regression model as shown in Fig. 2 consists of 9 convolution layers followed by 2 fully connected layers. As we all know that convolutional layers of CNNs are designed to extract features of input images. Features of cardiac vessels such as vascular lengths, vascular diameters and vascular locations are similar in different patients. Accordingly, our hypothesis on CNN parameter transfer learning is the following: despite the disparity among CTA and DSA images obtained from different equipment in different clinics, CNN trained on one large scale well-annotated data set of any patient may still be transferred to make registration tasks of other patients effective. Collecting and annotating large number of medical images still pose significant challenges. Also, the deep

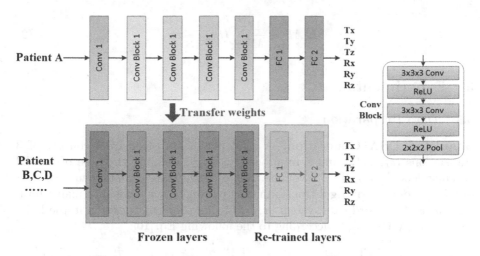

Fig. 2. Rigid CNN regression model for 2D-3D vascular image registration with transfer learning.

CNN architectures contain tens of millions of free parameters to train, and thus require sufficient large number of labeled vascular images and long training time.

Rigid models were pre-trained by large number of cardiovascular images of a certain patient without deformation. Then the convolutional layers of rigid models were frozen and the last two fully connected layers were retrained at smaller learning rates as the fine-tuning step. Weights were transferred from the pre-trained model to the retrained ones.

2.3   Evaluation of Image Registration Accuracy

Target registration error (TRE) is a widely used evaluation criteria of 2D-3D registration accuracy [11]. A mean target registration error (mTRE) as described in (1) is a gold standard used to measure the quality of registration results.

$$mTRE(P, T_{reg}, T_{gold}, T_{proj}) = \frac{1}{k} \sum_{i=1}^{k} ||T_{proj} T_{reg} p_i - T_{proj} T_{gold} p_i|| \qquad (1)$$

As shown in Eq. (1), T_{gold} is a 4×4 gold standard transformation matrix representing the 3D vascular model transformation from the initial position to the final position aligned with 2D DSA images exactly; T_{reg} represents the transformation parameters that is obtained from our 2D/3D CNN regression model; T_{proj} indicates the projective matrix from a 3D volume space to a 2D image space. P stands for a fixed feature point set containing k feature points extracted from 3D volume. The mean absolute error (MAE) of six transformation parameters is another criterion to assess errors between the ground truth t_{gold} and the predicted registration result $\hat{t}$. MAE among M test images can be expressed as:

$$MAE = \frac{1}{M} \sum_{i=1}^{M} (t_{gold} - \hat{t}) \qquad (2)$$

3   Experiments

3.1   Data Preparation

Simulated DSA Generation. A rigid 6DOF transformation consists of 3 translations (t_x, t_y, t_z) and 3 rotations (r_x, r_y, r_z) defining the pose of the 3D vascular model in a 3D CT volume. A projective transformation matrix $T_{3\times4}$ obtained from the six rigid transformation parameters is defined to map a position in the CT coordinate system (x, y, z) to its projected position in the DRR coordinate system (u, v) according to the following Eq. [10]:

$$c \begin{bmatrix} u \\ v \\ 1 \end{bmatrix} = T_{3\times4} \begin{bmatrix} x \\ y \\ z \\ 1 \end{bmatrix} = \begin{bmatrix} z_s & 0 & x_s & 0 \\ 0 & z_s & y_s & 0 \\ 0 & 0 & 1 & 0 \end{bmatrix} \begin{bmatrix} & & & T_x - x_s \\ & R_{3\times3}(r_x, r_y, r_z) & & T_y - y_s \\ & & & T_z - z_s \\ 0 & 0 & 0 & 1 \end{bmatrix} \begin{bmatrix} x \\ y \\ z \\ 1 \end{bmatrix} \qquad (3)$$

where c is a constant to normalize the third element of the 2D position vector and (x_s, y_s, z_s) represents the light source position. According to this formula, we obtain a series of DRR projections of the vascular model by ray casting method []. The synthetic DSA images are obtained by mixing the obtained DRR images with backgrounds stripped from real DSA images as described in the following formula:

$$I = I_{BG} + \gamma \cdot G_\sigma * I_{DRR} + N(a, b) \qquad (4)$$

where I_{BG} is the background from real DSA images before injecting contrast agent, I_{DRR} represents the DRR image, G_σ denotes a Gaussian smoothing kernel with a standard deviation σ simulating the noises caused by the patients' breathing and heartbeat, $*$ represents the convolution procedure, and $N(a, b)$ is a random noise uniformly distributed between $[a, b]$. The empirical parameters (γ, σ, a, b) of each patient are adjusted to make the appearance of the synthetic DSA images as realistic as the real DSA images. Figure 3 shows three synthetic DSA images compared with three real DSA images.

Simulated DSA images of six patients from three clinics with different aorta diseases, i.e., aortic dissection (AD), thoracic aortic aneurysm (TAA) and abdominal aortic aneurysm (AAA) are selected to validate the correctness and robustness of our method at different stages. DRRs generated to simulate the real DSA images are all with the dimension of 1024 × 1024 and the pixel spacing of 0.5 mm consistent with that of real DSA images. Transformation parameters for generating these DRRs are randomly and uniformly sampled in the extent of ±20 mm and ±5°.

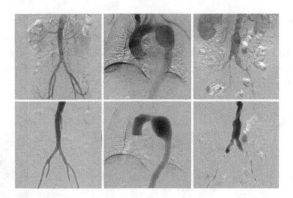

Fig. 3. Synthetic DSA images compared with real DSA images. From left to right: patient with AD, TAA and AAA.

3.2 Experimental Environment

We conducted the regression experiments on a workstation with Intel(R) Xeon(R) CPU E5-2620 2.4 GHz × 12, 32 GB RAM and Nvidia GeForce GTX 980 GPU. An open-source deep learning framework is used to implement the neural network with cuDNN acceleration, Caffe [9]. For traditional methods, the similarity measures are implemented using Matlab 2014a, while the computational DRR render processes are implemented in C++ and executed in a single CPU core. All the intensity-based methods are conducted on a PC with Intel(R) Core(TM) i7-6820HQ CPU @ 2.70 GHz, 16 GB RAM.

3.3 Rigid Registration Without Transfer Learning

It is hard for the rigid CNN regression model to transfer from one patient to another. To confirm this, we first trained the model using a data set with 1×10^4 labeled images of patients suffering TAA, AD and AAA disease separately. After training 5×10^4 times, the trained models were tested not only for images of the same patients as training, but also those from patients different from the training ones but suffering the same disease with them. We also combined the training datasets of patient A, B and C with different disease and fed them (3×10^4 images) to our rigid CNN model. Then we tested the combined model using 1×10^3 images from six patients with the same or different disease. The registration result and accuracy was evaluated by MAE and mTRE.

3.4 Rigid Registration with Transfer Learning

Firstly, we trained our rigid CNN regression model on any patient and transfer the trained model to other patients. Then, we froze the convolution layers of the trained model to re-train the fully connected layers using images of the target patient. Re-train times and the size of re-train dataset affected registration accuracy and efficiency severely. The optimal parameters help to obtain satisfactory results with the shortest time of the least data, which is especially important to clinical applications. Therefore, a series of models were trained in different re-train times and re-train data sizes. The test dataset containing 1×10^3 images from target patient, different from images used for training, is permanent when re-train parameters change.

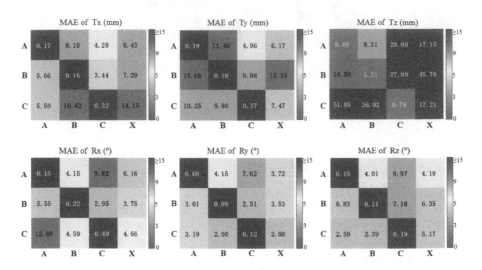

Fig. 4. Registration results of six transformation parameters, without transfer learning, for patients with different cardiovascular disease (A, B and C with TAA, AD and AAA separately). The top row is translation errors (errors of T_x, T_y and T_z) and the second line is rotation errors (errors of R_x, R_y and R_z). Three datasets (rows) are used for training and six datasets (columns, X represents different patients for different training datasets, i.e., when training images from patient A, X represents another patient suffering the same disease as A.) are used for testing. Diagonal elements show training and testing datasets are from the same patient, others show training and testing datasets are from different patients.

4   Results

4.1   Rigid Registration Without Transfer Learning

Figure 4 illustrates the result of patients with different cardiovascular disease for rigid registration, without using transfer learning. A, B and C represent a patient with three different cardiovascular diseases TAA, AD and AAA separately. The diagonal elements are almost all smaller than 1 mm or 1° representing that our rigid registration model perform well if both the training and testing datasets are from the same patients. However, if images using for testing and training are from different patients, even suffering the same cardiovascular disease (Lesions are similar in location.), the registration result will be inaccurate. Other elements

Table 1. Mean absolute errors and mean target registration errors of our rigid CNN registration model. Training set synthesizes data of patient A, B and C. Testing sets are from not only patient A, B and C, but also patient D, E and F not included in the training set.

Train	Test	Disease	T_x/mm	T_y/mm	T_z/mm	R_x/°	R_y/°	R_z/°	$mTRE$/mm
	A	TAA	1.99	1.09	9.10	2.10	0.75	0.80	1.23
	B	AD	1.11	0.97	7.84	2.72	0.38	0.99	1.01
ABC	C	AAA	1.82	3.10	12.33	2.40	1.38	1.61	1.74
	D	TAA	3.47	15.13	8.65	4.97	1.89	3.61	2.74
	E	AD	4.15	16.84	39.41	4.96	2.28	3.40	4.18
	F	AAA	11.54	6.95	9.95	4.68	2.17	8.26	2.86

in Fig. 4 except the diagonal ones are too large to obtain wrong registration results. MAEs of T_z are even larger than 20 mm, which means that the vascular diameters of the testing images vary a lot comparing with the testing ones.

Table 1 shows the registration result of the rigid model trained by combined dataset from patient A, B and C, but tested by images from six patients suffering three kinds of cardiovascular disease (TAA, AD and AAA). The first three rows represent that the testing images are from the same patients (A, B and C) contained in the combined training dataset, while the last three rows demonstrate three other patients (D, E and F) who do not participate in training. Every two of the six patients had the same cardiovascular disease. Although patient A, B and C participate in training, most of their translation and rotation errors are larger than 1 mm or 1°, much worse than the result training with single patient. Training with combined dataset also increase the errors of T_z which are extremely sensitive to the difference of vascular diameter between three patients. The poorer test results of other patients (D, E and F) show that the model trained with the combined data is also difficult to migrate to other patients.

4.2 Optimal Parameter Selection with Transfer Learning

We now examine the performance of rigid CNN regression model with transfer learning. As shown in Fig. 5, variations of translation and rotation errors are recorded when the number of iterations increases or the size of dataset changes. The top two line charts in Fig. 5 illustrate the variation on six transformation parameters as the number of iteration times increase. MAEs show downward trend when the number of iterations increases from 1000 to 10000. Surprisingly, after 5000 iterations almost all MAEs of translation errors are less than 1 mm and rotation errors less than 1° except that of T_z, because errors of T_z are sensitive to vascular diameters change. Then MAEs of all six transformation parameters remain unchanged when iterations increase. Considering the registration accuracy as well as re-training time and robustness, we choose 10000 as the optimal

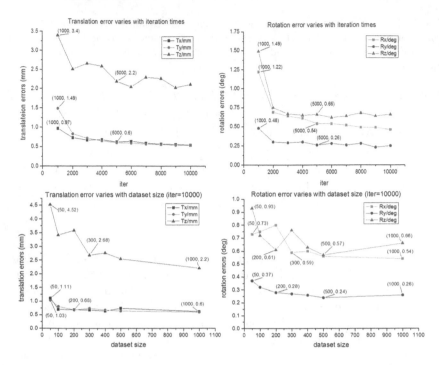

Fig. 5. The top row is the variation of translation and rotation errors as the iteration times increase from 1000 to 10000. The bottom row shows the varied translation and rotation errors with different dataset sizes (50, 100, 200, 300, 400, 500 and 1000)

number of iterations. The 10000 iterations of re-training took less than three minutes, about 150 s.

The bottom two charts in Fig. 5 demonstrate changes of translation and rotation errors with different dataset sizes. The size of dataset is set to 50, 100, 200, 300, 400, 500 and 1000 in each experiment. The overall trend of this two charts verified that registration errors decrease as dataset size improves. Errors of T_x, T_y together with three rotation parameters are all less than 1 mm or 1° when the dataset size is larger than 200. For clinical application, we tend to choose the smallest dataset to get a satisfactory result. Registration errors less than 1 mm or 1° are accurate enough to fulfill the need of clinical applications. So we chose 10000 as the optimal iterations, 200 as the optimal size of dataset in subsequent experiments.

4.3   Transfer Learning for Different Patients

After selecting the optimal number of iterations and dataset sizes, we tested the transferable ability of our approach between different patients. We compared the registration result with and without transfer learning to verify that transfer learning was capable to improve the registration accuracy. As shown in Table 2, the model was pre-trained with the dataset of D, so the registration result of D is more accurate than others. Also, by comparing the experiment results with and without transfer learning, we can conclude that models after transfer learning are able to obtain more accurate registration results, MAEs of which are even less than 1 mm or 1° except that of T_z. We will design a non-rigid model in our future work to reduce sensitivity of our model to vascular diameters to minimize the registration error of T_z.

Table 2. Comparison of registration result of different patients with and without transfer learning. The transfer model was pre-trained by the dataset of D and fine-tuned by the target dataset of A, B and C separately. TL means transfer learning in this table.

Patient	Disease	With or without TL	T_x/mm	T_y/mm	T_z/mm	$R_x/°$	$R_y/°$	$R_z/°$	$mTRE$/mm
D	TAA	–	0.16	0.19	0.69	0.15	0.07	0.14	0.11
A	TAA	Without	8.42	17.15	16.74	6.16	3.71	4.19	4.25
A	TAA	With	0.69	0.68	3.58	0.80	0.28	0.61	0.49
B	AD	Without	8.10	9.31	11.46	2.34	4.14	4.01	3.32
B	AD	With	0.80	0.98	3.38	0.81	0.27	0.58	0.52
C	AAA	Without	4.27	4.96	28.9	9.82	7.62	8.97	3.83
C	AAA	With	0.60	0.71	3.45	1.16	0.29	0.60	0.48

5   Discussion and Conclusion

We presented a method for 2D/3D multimodal cardiovascular image registration using transfer learning which generalizes well to datasets acquired from different patients. Our method solved the problem that our previous proposed regression model must be trained again faced with different patients. We discuss the selection of optimal parameters, number of iterations and dataset sizes. The experiment results of patients with different cardiovascular disease verify the efficiency of our method despite the relatively high registration errors of t_z. Our future work will focus on non-rigid cardiovascular image registration to improve the robustness of our model against the variation of vascular diameters, position as well as shapes of different patients.

References

1. Annegreet, V.O., Hakim, C.A., Vernooij, M.W., de Bruijne, M.: Convolutional neural networks for medical image analysis: full training or fine tuning? IEEE Trans. Med. Imaging **38**(1), 213–224 (2019)
2. Cheplygina, V., de Bruijne, M., Pluim, J.P.W.: Not-so-supervised: a survey of semi-supervised, multi-instance, and transfer learning in medical image analysis. Med. Image Anal. **54**, 1–24 (2018)

3. Cheplygina, V., Pino, I., Pedersen, J., Lynch, D., Sørensen, L., de Bruijne, M.: Transfer learning for multicenter classification of chronic obstructive pulmonary disease. IEEE J. Biomed. Health Inform. **22**(5), 1486–1496 (2018)
4. Chou, C.R., Frederick, B., Mageras, G., Chang, S., Pizer, S.: 2D/3D image registration using regression learning. Comput. Vis. Image Underst. **117**(9), 1095 (2013)
5. Guan, S., Meng, C., Xie, Y., Wang, Q., Sun, K., Wanga, T.: Deformable cardiovascular image registration via multi-channel convolutional neural network. IEEE Access **7**, 17524–17534 (2019)
6. Hinton, G.E., Osindero, S., Teh, Y.W.: A fast learning algorithm for deep belief nets. Neural Comput. **18**(7), 1527–1554 (2006)
7. Shin, H.C., Roth, H.R., Gao, M., Lu, L., Xu, Z.: Deep convolutional neural networks for computer-aided detection: Cnn architectures, dataset characteristics and transfer learning. IEEE Trans. Med. Imaging **35**(5), 1285–1298 (2016)
8. Hu, Y., Modat, M., Gibson, E., et al.: Label-driven weakly-supervised learning for multimodal deformable image registration. In: IEEE 15th International Symposium on Biomedical Imaging (ISBI 2018), pp. 1070–1074. IEEE, Washington, DC (2018)
9. Jia, Y., Shelhamer, E., Donahue, J., et al.: Caffe: convolutional architecture for fast feature embedding. In: Proceedings of the 22nd ACM International Conference on Multimedia, pp. 675–678. ACM, Florida (2014)
10. Ketcha, M.D., et al.: Multi-stage 3D–2D registration for correction of anatomical deformation in image-guided spine surgery. Phys. Med. Biol. **62**(11), 4604 (2017)
11. Kraats, E.B.V.D., Penney, G.P., Tomazevic, D., Walsum, T.V., Niessen, W.J.: Standardized evaluation methodology for 2-D-3-D registration. IEEE Trans. Med. Imaging **24**(9), 1177–1189 (2005)
12. Krizhevsky, A., Sutskever, I., Hinton, G.E.: ImageNet classification with deep convolutional neural networks. In: Advances in Neural Information Processing Systems, pp. 1097–1105. MIT Press, Lake Tahoe (2012)
13. Markelj, P., Tomazevic, D., Likar, B., Pernus, F.: A review of 3D/2D registration methods for image-guided interventions. Med. Image Anal. **16**(3), 642–661 (2012)
14. Miao, S., Wang, Z., Liao, R.: A CNN regression approach for real-time 2D/3D registration. IEEE Trans. Med. Imaging **35**(5), 1352–1363 (2016)
15. Miao, S., Wang, Z.J., Liao, R.: Real-time 2D/3D registration via CNN regression. Optoelectron. Adv. Mater.-Rapid Commun. **4**(3), 636–648 (2015)
16. Nima, T., et al.: Convolutional neural networks for medical image analysis: full training or fine tuning? IEEE Trans. Med. Imaging **35**(5), 1299–1312 (2016)
17. Swati, Z., et al.: Content-based brain tumor retrieval for MR images using transfer learning. IEEE Access **7**, 17809–17822 (2019)

Temporal Invariant Factor Disentangled Model for Representation Learning

Weichao Shen, Yuwei Wu[(⊠)], and Yunde Jia

Beijing Laboratory of Intelligent Information Technology,
School of Computer Science, Beijing Institute of Technology, Beijing 100081, China
{shenweichao,wuyuwei,jiayunde}@bit.edu.cn

Abstract. This paper focuses on disentangling different kinds of underlying explanatory factors from image sequences. From the temporal perspective, we divide the explanatory factors into the temporal-invariant factor and the temporal-variant factor. The temporal-invariant factor corresponds to the categorical concept of objects in an image sequence while the temporal-variant factor describes the object appearance changing. We propose a disentangled model to disentangle from an image sequence the temporal-invariant factor that is used as an object representation insensitive to appearance changes. Our model is built upon the variational auto-encoder (VAE) and the recurrent neural network (RNN) to independently approximate the posterior distributions of the factor in an unsupervised manner. Experimental results on the HeadPose image database show the effectiveness of the proposed method.

Keywords: Representation learning · Disentangled model ·
Unsupervised learning · Temporal invariant factor

1 Introduction

Data representation is a fundamental problem in machine learning and pattern recognition. Most of representation learning methods are designed for certain specific tasks based on a supervised learning framework [7,9,10]. For example, the VGG network trained on the ImageNet dataset learns a powerful representation for image classification [14]. With the guidance of labels, the data are transformed into a task-corresponding representation space in which robust features are extracted. While good performance is achieved in a specific task, the representation learned with supervision may be over-fitting to the label space. Therefore, to some extent, such a representation is weak in disentangling the general underlying explanatory factors in the observed data. Bengio *et al.* [1] pointed out that the general underlying explanatory factors are important for an AI system to understand the world around us. They also argued that regardless of the demand for specific tasks, a good representation should express general priors about the world around us, which is helpful for the relevant but unknown tasks. The temporal coherence of sequence data, as one of the general priors,

Z. Lin et al. (Eds.): PRCV 2019, LNCS 11858, pp. 391–402, 2019.
https://doi.org/10.1007/978-3-030-31723-2_33

supports that a good representation of consecutive nearby observations leads to a move on the surface of the high-density manifold, and the categorical attributes of the interesting object are supposed to be temporal invariant or changing very slowly. Thus, it is necessary to exploit the temporal invariant information from sequence data for generating an interpretable and general representation.

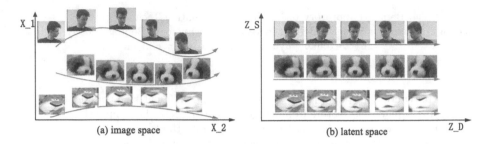

Fig. 1. Three sequences of different kinds of targets (a person, a dog, and a tiger) with the same action (shaking). The left shows the image sequences in image space, and the right illustrates them with the temporal invariant factors Z^S and temporal variant factors Z^D in the disentangled latent space. In the disentangled latent space, the same appearance change leads to the same temporal variant factor Z^D and the different temporal invariant factor Z^S indicates the different categorical concept.

What are the temporal invariant and variant information of an image sequence? As shown in the first sequence of Fig. 1(a), a person is shaking his head. In this sequence, the temporal invariant information is the noun 'person' involving attributes about what a person looks like. The temporal variant information is the verb 'shaking' which describes temporal appearance changes. We assume that the temporal invariant information and the temporal variant information are independent, as if the definition of "person" does not matter whether his/her action is "shaking" or "running", and the description of "shaking" does not need to consider whether the object is a "person" or a "dog". Following this assumption, we can disentangle two kinds of latent factors from an image sequence independently: *temporal invariant factor* and *temporal variant factor*. As the two kinds of latent factors are independent, no appearance changing information is encoded into the temporal invariant factor, so that the temporal invariant factor disentangled from the image sequence can be used as an object representation insensitive to the appearance changes.

To disentangle the temporal invariant factor from an image sequence, we propose a temporal invariant factor disentangled model (TIFDM) to approximate the posterior distribution of temporal invariant and temporal variant factors independently. As the posterior distribution is often intractable, we introduce the variational inference and build the TIFDM based on a convolutional variational auto-encoder framework. The temporal invariant factor is disentangled from the image sequence with a temporal invariant constraint, and the temporal variant factor is encoded using the long-short term memory (LSTM) [8]. We test our model on the HeadPose database and achieve satisfactory experimental results.

2   Related Work

In recent years, many researchers focused on learning a disentangled representation with labeled data. Yang *et al.* [15] designed a recurrent latent variant model that generates a sequence of latent factor transformations. Zhu *et al.* [16] developed a multi-view perceptron to separate face identity and view point. These methods generate disentangled representations with the guidance of labels. These representations are weak in disentangling the general underlying explanatory factors in observed data.

The disentangled representation can be generated with unsupervised methods. InfoGAN [2] learns the saliency factors using an induced latent code by injecting a mutual information constraint into the generative adversarial network. Chen *et al.* [3] produced a representation with VAE combining with the autoregressive models, and controlled over what the representation can learn in a lossy fashion. Different from these methods over static datasets, our work focus on how to exploit the temporal information in sequence data.

There has been some work on exploitation of the temporal information. Zou *et al.* [17] incorporated the temporal coherence penalty with a training criterion for unsupervised representation learning. Pan *et al.* [13] presented the local temporal relationship of adjacent frames and the graph structure of video to learn a deep intrinsic video representation. In contrast with these methods, we interpret sequence data using both the temporal invariant and variant factors.

3   Temporal Invariant Factor Disentangled Model

In this section, we elaborate the formulation of our representation learning model in a generative model framework. From the perspective of generative models, learning a representation is meant to derive the posterior distribution of the latent variable Z given observed data X. To formulate the posterior distribution, we give the generative model of X with the latent variable Z firstly.

To exploit the temporal information, we focus on generative models for sequence data. Given sequence data $X = \{x_1, x_2, ..., x_T\}$, it can be interpreted with a set of corresponding latent variable $Z = \{z_1, z_2, ..., z_T\}$. T is the number of frames. We thus formulate the generative model with a joint distribution

$$p_\theta(x_{\leq T}, z_{\leq T}) = \prod_{t=1}^{T} p_\theta(x_t|x_{<t}, z_{\leq t})p_\theta(z_t|x_{<t}, z_{<t}). \tag{1}$$

The first term is the likelihood distribution of current observed data x_t given the current latent variables z_t. The second term is the prior distribution of latent variables z_t on the historical observed information and historical latent ones.

According to our assumption about temporal invariant and variant information, the latent variable Z can be divided into temporal invariant factors Z^S and temporal varient factors Z^D. The joint distribution is defined as

$$p_\theta(x_{\leq T}, z^D_{\leq T}, z^S_{\leq T}) = \prod_{t=1}^{T} p_\theta(x_t | x_{<t}, z^D_{\leq t}, z^S_{\leq t}) p_\theta(z^D_t, z^S_t | x_{<t}, z^D_{<t}, z^S_{<t}). \quad (2)$$

This formulation presents the generation process of X with the latent factors Z^D and Z^S which are sampled from a prior distribution. With this generative model, the representation learning problem is transformed into inferring the posterior distribution of both the latent variables Z^D and Z^S given observed historical data $x_{\leq T}$.

$$[Z^D, Z^S] \sim p_\theta(z^D_{\leq T}, z^S_{\leq T} | x_{\leq T}), \quad (3)$$

where θ denotes model parameters.

Inferring the posterior distribution in Eq. (3) gives us an encoding model to project the original data X into two different kinds of latent factors Z^S and Z^D. A challenging problem is that the latent variable Z^S and Z^D are unobservable, so that the parameters of this distribution cannot be resolved by the maximum likelihood method directly. One popular solution is variational inference [11] which learns a distribution q_ϕ by minimizing the Kullback-Leibler divergence between p_θ and q_ϕ,

$$q_\phi^*(z^D_{\leq T}, z^S_{\leq T} | x_{\leq T}) = \arg\min \mathrm{KL}\left[q_\phi(z^D_{\leq T}, z^S_{\leq T} | x_{\leq T}) || p_\theta(z^D_{\leq T}, z^S_{\leq T} | x_{\leq T})\right]. \quad (4)$$

With a small KL divergence, the inferred distribution q_ϕ^* can be treated as a suitable approximatetion for the true posterior distribution p. Thus our representation learning is transformed into calculating the optimal inferred distribution q_ϕ^* by optimizing Eq. (4). However, when q_ϕ^* disentangle two different kinds of the latent factors Z^S and Z^D, it can not guarantee that the information encoded by Z^S is temporal invariant.

To make sure that q_ϕ^* encodes temporal invariant information into Z^S, we introduce a temporal invariant constraint into Eq. (4). As a temporal invariant descriptor, Z^S should change within a small range in a sequence. We measure the temporal variance of $z^S_{\leq T}$ using $\mathbb{V}(z^S_{\leq T}) = \sum_{i=1}^{T} \sum_{j=i+1}^{T} \mathbb{D}(z^S_i, z^S_j)$, where $\mathbb{D}$ is a distance matric. Imposing this constraint into Eq. (4), we have

$$q_\phi^*(z^D_{\leq T}, z^S_{\leq T} | x_{\leq T}) = \arg\min \left\{ \mathrm{KL}[q_\phi(z^D_{\leq T}, z^S_{\leq T} | x_{\leq T}) || p_\theta(z^D_{\leq T}, z^S_{\leq T} | x_{\leq T})] + \mathbb{V}(z^S_{\leq T}) \right\}. \quad (5)$$

Thus, our representation learning problem can be defined as getting a inferred posterior distribution q_ϕ^* by minimizing Eq. (5).

3.1 Calculating $\mathrm{KL}[q_\phi \| p_\theta]$

Unfolding the $\mathrm{KL}[q_\phi \| p_\theta]$ in Eq. (5) and applying the Bayes rule to $p_\theta(z^D_{\leq T}, z^S_{\leq T} | x_{\leq T})$, we have

$$\log p(X_{\leq T}) - \mathrm{KL}\left[q_\phi(z^D_{\leq T}, z^S_{\leq T} | x_{\leq T}) \| p_\theta(z^D_{\leq T}, z^S_{\leq T} | x_{\leq T})\right]$$
$$= \mathbb{E}_{q(z^D_{\leq T}, z^S_{\leq T} | x_{\leq T})}\left[\log p(x_{\leq T} | z^D_{\leq T}, z^S_{\leq T})\right] - \mathrm{KL}\left[q(z^D_{\leq T}, z^S_{\leq T} | x_{\leq T}) \| p(z^D_{\leq T}, z^S_{\leq T})\right], \tag{6}$$

where $\mathbb{E}$ denotes the expectation and $p(z^D_{\leq T}, z^S_{\leq T})$ is the prior distribution of latent factors. For simplicity, we omit the subscript ϕ and θ in the following discussion. Equation (6) is the evidence lower bound on the original log-marginal likelihood [12], which is known as the negative free energy $\mathcal{E}(q)$. As the distribution of X is fixed, we treat $\log p(X_{\leq T})$ as a constant, thus

$$\min \mathrm{KL}[q_\phi(z^D_{\leq T}, z^S_{\leq T} | x_{\leq T}) \| p_\theta(z^D_{\leq T}, z^S_{\leq T} | x_{\leq T})]) = \min -\mathcal{E}(q)$$
$$= \min -\{\mathbb{E}_{q(z^D_{\leq T}, z^S_{\leq T} | x_{\leq T})} \log p(x_{\leq T} | z^D_{\leq T}, z^S_{\leq T}) - \mathrm{KL}[q(z^D_{\leq T}, z^S_{\leq T} | x_{\leq T}) \| p(z^D_{\leq T}, z^S_{\leq T})]\} \tag{7}$$

As discussed in [5], we choose the auto-regressive form for the inferred posterior distribution q,

$$q(z^D_{\leq T}, z^S_{\leq T} | x_{\leq T}) = \prod_{t=1}^T q(z^D_t, z^S_t | z^D_{<t}, z^S_{<t}, x_{\leq t}). \tag{8}$$

With this setting, the total negative free energy can be rewritten as the sum of per step energies,

$$\mathcal{E}(q) = \sum_{t=1}^T \mathbb{E}_{q(z^D_{<t}, z^S_{<t} | x_{<t})}[\mathcal{E}_t(q)], \tag{9}$$

$$\mathcal{E}_t(q) = \mathbb{E}_{q(z^D_t, z^S_t | x_{\leq t}, z^D_{<t}, z^S_{<t})}\left[\log p(x_t | z^D_{\leq t}, z^S_{\leq t}, x_{<t})\right]$$
$$- \mathrm{KL}\left[q(z^D_t | z^D_{<t}, z^S_{\leq t}, x_{\leq t}) \| p(z^D_t | z^D_{<t}, z^S_{\leq t}, x_{<t})\right]$$
$$- \mathrm{KL}\left[q(z^S_t | z^D_{<t}, z^S_{<t}, x_{\leq t}) \| p(z^S_t | z^D_{<t}, z^S_{<t}, x_{<t})\right]. \tag{10}$$

This formulation can be optimized using the Monte Carlo method. The expectations in Eqs. (9) and (10) are able to be calculated efficiently using the reparameterization trick [11]. The Kullback-Leibler divergence is calculated analytically when the distributions q and p are given.

3.2 Calculating $\mathbb{V}(z^S_{\leq T})$

We simply set distance matric $\mathbb{D}$ as Euclidean distance, then $\mathbb{V}(z^S_{\leq T})$ is given by

$$\mathbb{V}(z^S_{\leq T}) = \sum_{i=1}^T \sum_{j=i+1}^T \|z^S_i - z^S_j\|^2. \tag{11}$$

Since Eq. (11) requires traversing all the binary combination in the sequence, the computational complexity is still considerable. In practice, we just compute the mean center of all points in Z^S and sum up the distance between the mean center and each point as the total change in a sequence.

3.3   Final Formulation

Substituting Eqs. (9) and (11) into Eq. (5), we get our final optimization function written in a per-step form,

$$q_\phi^*(z_{\leq T}^D, z_{\leq T}^S | x_{\leq T}) = \arg\min\left\{ -\sum_{t=1}^{T} \mathbb{E}_{q(z_{<t}^D, z_{\leq t}^S | x_{<t})}[\mathcal{E}_t(q)] + \sum_{\substack{i=1, \\ j=i+1}}^{T} ||z_i^S - z_j^S||^2 \right\}. \tag{12}$$

4   Optimization

We propose to design a deep neural network to derive an optimal inferred posterior distribution q_ϕ^*, in which Eq. (12) is used as a loss function. To calculate the Kullback-Leibler divergence in $\mathcal{E}_t(q)$, we need to further give the prior distributions and inferred posterior distribution in Eq. (10).

4.1   Prior Distribution

We define the prior distribution of z^D and z^S as the Gaussian distribution,

$$p(z_t^D | z_{<t}^D, z_{\leq t}^S, x_{<t}) = \mathcal{N}(z_t^D | f_{z^D}^\mu(z_{<t}^D, z_{\leq t}^S, x_{<t}), f_{z^D}^\sigma(z_{<t}^D, z_{\leq t}^S, x_{<t})), \tag{13}$$

$$p(z_t^S | z_{<t}^D, z_{<t}^S, x_{<t}) = \mathcal{N}(z_t^S | f_{z^S}^\mu(z_{<t}^D, z_{<t}^S, x_{<t}), f_{z^S}^\sigma(z_{<t}^D, z_{<t}^S, x_{<t})). \tag{14}$$

The parameters of the distribution are defined by different functions historical latent factors. f_z^μ and f_z^σ are the prior parameter functions which compute the means and variances of the prior Gaussian distributions.

As assumed previously, the temporal invariant factor Z^S is independent to the temporal variant factor Z^D. We thus simplify the prior distribution of temporal variant factor as $p(z_t^D | z_{<t}^D, z_{\leq t}^S, x_{<t}) = p(z_t^D | z_{<t}^D, x_{<t})$. Then we introduce a hidden-state variable h_t to store the historical information of $z_{<t}^D$ and $x_{<t}$. h_t updates every time step using a transition function $h_t = f_h(h_{t-1}, z_t^D, x_t)$, which can be parameterised by the recurrent neural network (e.g., LSTM).

The independence constraint between temporal invariant and variant factors make $p(z_t^S | z_{<t}^D, z_{<t}^S, x_{<t}) = p(z_t^S | z_{<t}^S, x_{<t})$. Since z^S encodes the temporal invariance information, its prior distribution does not change in a training sequence, which means that $p(z_t^S | z_{<t}^S, x_{<t}) = \cdots = p(z_k^S | z_{<k}^S, x_{<k}) = \cdots = p(z_1^S)$. Learning $p(z_k^S)$ from the dataset can be solved by the traditional VAE [11]. Here we give the prior distribution of $p(z_k^S)$ as the same as VAE, i.e., setting it as a normal Gaussian distribution.

In summary, the final prior distribution of temporal invariant factor and temporal variant factor are formulated as

$$p(z_t^D|z_{<t}^D, z_{\leq t}^S, x_{<t}) = \mathcal{N}\big(z_t^D|f_{z^D}^\mu(h_{t-1}), f_{z^D}^\sigma(h_{t-1})\big), \tag{15}$$

$$p(z_t^S|z_{<t}^D, z_{<t}^S, x_{<t}) = p(z_K^S) = \mathcal{N}(0,1). \tag{16}$$

The prior parameter function $f_{z^D}^\mu$ and $f_{z^D}^\sigma$ can be computed with deep neural networks.

4.2   Inferred Posterior Distribution

We define the inferred posterior distributions q_ϕ in Eq. (10) as a Gaussian distribution for both temporal invariant factor and temporal variant factor,

$$q(z_t^D|z_{<t}^D, z_{\leq t}^S, x_{\leq t}) = \\ \mathcal{N}\big(z_t^D|g_q^\mu(x_{\leq t}, z_{<t}^D, z_{\leq t}^S), g_q^\sigma(x_{\leq t}, z_{<t}^D, z_{\leq t}^S)\big) = \mathcal{N}\big(z_t^D|g_q^\mu(x_t, h_{t-1}), g_q^\sigma(x_t, h_{t-1})\big), \tag{17}$$

$$q(z_t^S|z_{<t}^D, z_{<t}^S, x_{\leq t}) = \\ \mathcal{N}\big(z_t^S|g_q^\mu(x_{\leq t}, z_{<t}^D, z_{\leq t}^S)g_q^\sigma(x_{\leq t}, z_{<t}^D, z_{\leq t}^S)\big) = \mathcal{N}\big(z_t^S|g_q^\mu(x_t), g_q^\sigma(x_t)\big), \tag{18}$$

where g_z^μ and g_z^σ are the posterior parameter functions computing the means and variances of the Gaussian posterior distributions. With the independence constraint and the hidden-state variable h formulating the historical information of $z_{<t}^D$ and $x_{<t}$, the posterior distribution of temporal invariant factors can be rewritten into the second equality in Eq. (17). h updates itself with the transition function $h_t = f_h(h_{t-1}, z_t^D, x_t)$ parameterized by the same LSTM used in the prior distribution. For the temporal invariant factor, we deprive its ability of encoding temporal variant information, so that we can simplify the $q(z_t^S|z_{<t}^D, z_{\leq t}^S, x_{\leq t})$ into the second equality in Eq. (18).

The posterior parameter functions g_z^μ and g_z^σ are different from temporal invariant and temporal variant factors. However, it does not mean these two functions can be effectively learned separately using two independent networks. Separately learning g_z^μ and g_z^σ would project the observed data into two different latent spaces independently and there is no relationship between two latent spaces. We expect that our latent factors Z^S and Z^D are "divided" directly from an "universal latent factors" of X, so that the combination of Z^S and Z^D encodes all the observed information, and less overlapped information exists in both kinds of factors. Therefore, we rewrite the posterior parameter function g_z as

$$g_{z^D} = m_{z^D}(l^-(x), h) \quad g_{z^S} = m_{z^S}(l^+(x)) \quad s.t. \quad [l^+(x), l^-(x)] = l(x). \tag{19}$$

where $l(x)$ is shared for g_{z^D} and g_{z^S} until it can be divided into $l^+(x)$ and $l^-(x)$. m_{z^D} and m_{z^S} are task-specific function for Z^D and Z^S, respectively. Then the Z^S and Z^D can be regarded as divided from $l(x)$ directly if the function complexity of m_{z^D} and m_{z^S} is small enough. $l(x)$, m_{z^D} and m_{z^S} can be computed with a deep neural network.

4.3   Implementation with Deep Neural Networks

We design a deep neural network (TIFDM) to learn functions mentioned in the previous sections (*i.e.*, $f_{z^D}^\mu$, $f_{z^D}^\sigma$, f_h, $l(x)$, m_{z^D} and m_{z^S}). The network is composed of two modules: the posterior inference module and the generative module. The posterior inference module consists of the posterior temporal invariant and variant factors learning modules. The detailed network architecture is shown in Fig. 2.

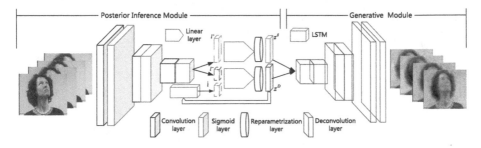

Fig. 2. The TIFDM model consists of a posterior inference module and a generative module. The inference module uses a convolution network to extract a deep code l. The code is split into l^+ and l^-, which is fed into different modules to generate different factors. The green solid cube represents temporal invariable factors Z^S and the mazarine cube denotes temporal changing factors. The LSTM updates itself with Z^D. The generative module works on deconvolution network. (Color figure online)

By using the proposed network (TIFDM), the first item $\mathbb{E}_{q(z_t^D, z_t^S | x_{\leq t}, z_{<t}^D, z_{<t}^S)}$ in Eq. (10) can be calculated by $\mathbb{D}_t(x_t, \overline{x}_t) = ||x_t - \overline{x}_t||^2$ [4], where $\overline{x}_t$ is sampled from the generative distribution $p(x_t | z_{\leq t}^D, z_{\leq t}^S, x_{<t})$ approximated by the generative module.

5   Experiments

In this section, we evaluate if our model can disentangle the temporal invariant factors and temporal variant factors. With the generative module, we use the control variates method to test the influence of different kinds of factors on generated sequences.

5.1   Dataset

We conduct our validation experiments on an adjustment dataset based on Head Pose Image Database [6]. This dataset contains the temporal variant information (*i.e.*, shaking in different tilt angles) and the temporal invariant information (*i.e.*, the salient attributes distinguishing different persons), which is suitable for the validation of our model. The original head pose database is a benchmark of 2790 monocular face images of 15 persons with variations of pan and tilt angles from −90 to +90°. We reorganize the dataset and construct 2 sequences for each person. Each sequence contains 93 face images of with continuous variations of the pan angles from −90 to +90.

5.2   Training Details

Our network is trained end-to-end with Mini-batches equalling to 6. We set the number of both the temporal invariant factor and the temporal variant factor to 32. The prior and posterior LSTM contain 10 cells. The learning rate starts at 0.001 and decays 1% every 10 epochs.

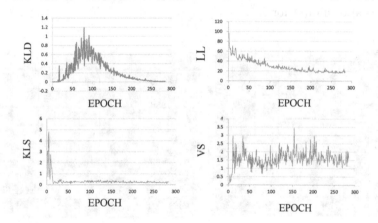

Fig. 3. The qualitative evaluation values of our model during the training process. KLD item, LL item, KLS item and VS item are presented from top to bottom, left to right. The horizontal axis represents the epoch.

5.3   Evaluations

Extensive evaluations are performed to test if our model can disentangle the temporal invariant factors and the temporal variant factors from sequence data. For qualitative analysis, we test what kind of information is encoded in different kinds of factors by using the generative module. Different kinds of factors lead to different kinds of changes in the generated sequence. If our model disentangles the factors successfully, varying the values of temporal invariant factor Z^S leads to generating different persons, while different temporal variant factor Z^D generates different appearance of a same target.

We utilize the likelihood item (LL), the variance of Z^S item (VS), the KLS item and the KLD item to evaluate the performance. The LL item represents the reconstruction error of the generated output. A low LL value means that the latent factors encode important information enough for reconstructing the observed data. The VS item computes the total variances of the temporal invariant factors in a sequence. A smaller VS denotes that the information stored in temporal invariant factors is more temporal invariant.

The KLS (or KLD) item measures the number of bits of additional information needed to represent the inferred posterior distribution of temporal invariant factors (or temporal variant factors) using the prior distribution. Compared with the posterior distribution (*e.g.*, $q(z_t^D|h_{<t}, x_t)$), the prior distribution (*e.g.*, $p(z_t^D|h_{<t})$) does not encode the information from current observed data, so KLD indicates how much information our model gathers from current observed data to reconstruct it. A low KLD denotes that most of the information used for reconstructing the current data comes from $z_{<t}^D$, which means that the valuable information is encoded into Z^D by inferred posterior distribution q. This analysis is also suitable for Z^S.

Fig. 4. The Qualitative results of our model. The left shows the results when we fix the temporal variant factor but change temporal invariant factor. We can see that different temporal invariant factor generates different person. The right shows the results when we fix the temporal invariant factor but change temporal variant factor. Each row shows a generated sequence with a fixed temporal invariant factor computed from the first image. We can see that all frames of each sequence correspond to the same temporal invariant factor and a different value of temporal variant factors relates to a different appearance of the same target.

5.4   Quantitative Analysis

Figure 3 shows the evaluation values of our model during training process. The values of the VS converge to a very small value after several epochs, which means that our temporal invariant factor has a little fluctuation within a training sequence. Our model also achieves a good convergence on KLD and KLS. With a small VS and a small LL, the low KLD illustrates that most of the temporal variant information is stored into temporal variant factor which can be well described with the LSTM. The low KLS shows that the temporal invariant information is encoded into temporal invariant factor well.

5.5   Qualitative Analysis

Figure 4 shows the sequence data generated by our model to exam if the temporal invariant and variant information is separately learned into corresponding factors. To test the validity of temporal invariant factor, we fix the value of the temporal variant factor and change the value of temporal invariant factor at a time. The initial value of temporal variant factor Z^D is given by encoding any image in the dataset. Z^S is randomly sampled from an uniform Gaussian distribution. The left of Fig. 4 depicts some generated images. We can see that when we vary the values of temporal invariant factor, different persons are generated. This demonstrates that the disentangled temporal invariant factor are associated with the categorical concepts of the target in the dataset. Then we fix the temporal invariant factor and vary the value of temporal variant factor Z^D to test what kinds of information are stored in different kinds of factors. We generated 9 sequences with our generative module. For each sequence, the Z^S is given by our posterior inference module and fixed over the whole sequence. The Z^D is generated by the prior LSTM. The right of Fig. 4 shows the generated results. Each row is a sequence with the same Z^S. We can see that most frames of each sequence describe the appearance change of the same target, which proves that our temporal invariant factor is insensitive to the appearance change of the target. The appearance changes in a sequence demonstrate that the temporal variant factor Z^D encodes the temporal variant information.

6   Conclusion

In this paper, we have presented the interpretation of sequence data by using temporal invariant and variant factors. The temporal invariant factors disentangled model (TIFDM) can encode the temporal invariant and variant factors in representation learning of sequence data. The model allows to obtain a non-task-specific, temporal variance robust representation via the general temporal invariant constraint. Without the guidance of labeled information, our representation learning model can avoid over-fitting to the label space, which strengthens the ability to disentangle the underlying explanatory factors.

Acknowledgement. This work was supported in part by Beijing Municipal Natural Science Foundation under Grant No. L172027, and the Natural Science Foundation of China (NSFC) under Grants No. 61702037 and No. 61773062, and Beijing Institute of Technology Research Fund Program for Young Scholars.

References

1. Bengio, Y., Courville, A., Vincent, P.: Representation learning: a review and new perspectives. IEEE Trans. Pattern Anal. Mach. Intell. **35**(8), 1798–1828
2. Chen, X., et al.: InfoGAN: interpretable representation learning by information maximizing generative adversarial nets. In: Advances in Neural Information Processing Systems 29, pp. 2172–2180 (2016)
3. Chen, X., et al.: Variational lossy autoencoder. In: International Conference on Learning Representations (ICLR) (2017)
4. Doersch, C.: Tutorial on variational autoencoders. arXiv e-prints, June 2016
5. Gemici, M., et al.: Generative temporal models with memory (2017)
6. Gourier, N., Hall, D., Crowley, J.L.: Estimating face orientation from robust detection of salient facial structures. In: FG Net workshop on Visual Observation of Deictic Gestures (2004)
7. He, R., Wu, X., Sun, Z., Tan, T.: Learning invariant deep representation for NIR-VIS face recognition (2017)
8. Hochreiter, S., Schmidhuber, J.: Long short-term memory. Neural Comput. **9**(8), 1735–1780 (1997)
9. Ke, Q., Bennamoun, M., An, S., Sohel, F., Boussaid, F.: A new representation of skeleton sequences for 3D action recognition. In: IEEE Conference on Computer Vision and Pattern Recognition (CVPR), July 2017
10. Khasanova, R., Frossard, P.: Graph-based isometry invariant representation learning. In: Proceedings of the 34th International Conference on Machine Learning, vol. 70, pp. 1847–1856, 6–11 August 2017
11. Kingma, D.P., Welling, M.: Auto-encoding variational Bayes. In: Proceedings of the 2nd International Conference on Learning Representations (ICLR), No. 2014 (2013)
12. Paisley, J., Blei, D.M., Jordan, M.I.: Variational Bayesian inference with stochastic search. In: Proceedings of the 29th International Conference on Machine Learning, ICML 2012, pp. 1363–1370 (2012)
13. Pan, Y., Li, Y., Yao, T., Mei, T., Li, H., Rui, Y.: Learning deep intrinsic video representation by exploring temporal coherence and graph structure. In: Proceedings of the Twenty-Fifth International Joint Conference on Artificial Intelligence, IJCAI 2016, pp. 3832–3838. AAAI Press (2016)
14. Simonyan, K., Zisserman, A.: Very deep convolutional networks for large-scale image recognition. CoRR abs/1409.1556 (2014)
15. Yang, J., Reed, S.E., Yang, M.H., Lee, H.: Weakly-supervised disentangling with recurrent transformations for 3D view synthesis. In: Advances in Neural Information Processing Systems 28, pp. 1099–1107 (2015)
16. Zhu, Z., Luo, P., Wang, X., Tang, X.: Multi-view perceptron: a deep model for learning face identity and view representations. In: Advances in Neural Information Processing Systems 27, pp. 217–225 (2014)
17. Zou, W.Y., Ng, A.Y., Yu, K.: Unsupervised learning of visual invariance with temporal coherence. In: Neural Information Processing Systems (NIPS) Workshop on Deep Learning and Unsupervised Feature Learning (2011)

A Multi-frame Video Interpolation Neural Network for Large Motion

Wenchao Hu[1,2] and Zhiguang Wang[1,2(✉)]

[1] Department of Computer Science and Technology,
China University of Petroleum, Beijing, China
wenchaohu94@gmail.com, cwangzg@cup.edu.cn
[2] Beijing Key Laboratory of Petroleum Data Mining,
China University of Petroleum, Beijing, China

Abstract. Video frame interpolation algorithms typically estimate optical flow to guide the synthesis of intermediate frame(s) between two consecutive input frames. However, the estimation of optical flow is easily affected by large motion. To tackle this problem, we combine multi-scale optical flow network PWC-Net and optimized network UNet++ to form our multi-frame interpolation neural network, which can be trained end-to-end. Specifically, we first use PWC-Net to estimate bidirectional optical flows between two input frames and linearly combine the flows at each time step to obtain the approximate flows for generating the intermediate frames. Next, we use a modified UNet++ to refine the approximate flows and avoid the effects of occlusion. Finally, guided by the accurate flows, two input frames are warped and linearly fused to form each intermediate frame. Experiments show that our network outperforms representative state-of-the-art methods, especially in large motion scenarios.

Keywords: Multi-frame interpolation · Large motion · Bidirectional optical flows · Deep learning

1 Introduction

Video frame interpolation is one of the basic techniques for video processing. It is used to generate one or more plausible video frames from two consecutive input frames. In general, video frame interpolation relies on optical flow estimation [1, 2]. Optical flow is the distribution of apparent velocities of movement of brightness pattern in an image. Therefore, one solution for frame interpolation is to assume constant velocity in motion and generate an interpolated frame by warping. Video frame interpolation technology has high research value. For example, data compression can be achieved by actively dropping video frames at the emitting end and recovering them via interpolation on the receiving end [3]. Increasing video frame-rate also directly allows to improve visual quality or to obtain an artificial slow-motion effect [2, 4].

Student as first author.

© Springer Nature Switzerland AG 2019
Z. Lin et al. (Eds.): PRCV 2019, LNCS 11858, pp. 403–415, 2019.
https://doi.org/10.1007/978-3-030-31723-2_34

The quality of frame interpolation results heavily depends on optical flow estimation, which can be roughly divided into two steps: optical flow estimation and pixel synthesis [1, 5]. In fact, the estimation of optical flow is very difficult. For example, when suffering from occlusion, blur, and abrupt brightness change, it is difficult to estimate optical flow due to the loss of corresponding moving pixel points. In recent years, deep neural networks have made great breakthroughs in many problems of computer vision. Compared with traditional methods, video frame interpolation based on neural networks [6–8] has significantly improved video frame interpolation in some difficult scenarios. However, the frame generated by these methods is poor when facing large displacements caused by fast motion or camera panning. We call this large displacement of objects large motion. Van et al. [9] proposed a video frame interpolation method combining multi-scale feature estimation and adversarial training. Although this method can effectively solve the large motion problem, it is poor in occlusion. As reported in recent work, many frame interpolation methods estimate bidirectional optical flows between two input frames and use the obtained flows to handle inaccuracies of motion estimation and occlusion [5, 10]. Actually, there are still problems with blurred edges of moving objects and inaccuracies of optical flow.

Those methods we discussed above are all single frame interpolation methods, which generate a single frame at intermediate time between two input frames. However, in scenarios such as slow motion and frame rate conversion, the interpolation of a single video frame is often insufficient to meet the demand. Jiang et al. [11] first proposed an efficient multi-frame interpolation network Super-SloMo, which significantly improved the accuracy of bidirectional optical flows estimation and performed well in a variety of complex scenarios. But the range of motion is limited by the filter size in their flow estimation network, the quality of the generated frames will be greatly reduced in the face of large motion problems.

In this paper, we propose a multi-frame interpolation convolutional neural network which combines bidirectional optical flows estimation with a state-of-the-art optical flow estimation network to solve the problem in large motion scenarios. Following the main idea of Super-SloMo, we warp the input two video frames to specific time step, and adaptively fuse the two warped frames to generate the intermediate frames, where the motion interpretation and occlusion reasoning are modeled in a single end-to-end trainable network. Specifically, our network consists of two subnetworks: Flow Compute Network and Flow Refine Network. Firstly, Flow Compute Network uses a multi-scale optical flow estimation network PWC-Net [12] to estimate bidirectional optical flows between two input frames in an unsupervised way. PWC-Net significantly improves the accuracy of optical flow estimation in large motion scenarios while at the same time being computationally efficient. Next, we obtain approximate optical flows for generating intermediate frames by linearly fusing the bidirectional optical flows. Since the approximate optical flows are not accurate, we use Flow Refine Network with encoder-decoder structure to optimize the approximate optical flows and simultaneously generate parameters to exclude the contribution of occlusion. Compared with various encoder-decoder structure, we find that structure of U-Net++ [13] works best. Finally, we use the outputs of Flow Refine Network and adaptively fuse the two warped images to generate the intermediate frames. Experiments show that our method

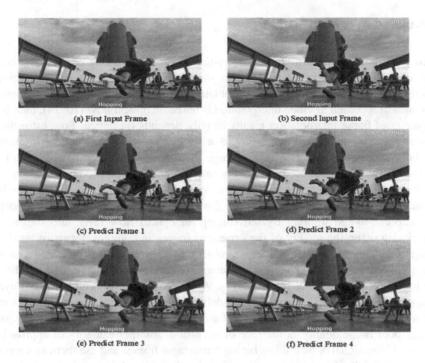

(a) First Input Frame

(b) Second Input Frame

(c) Predict Frame 1

(d) Predict Frame 2

(e) Predict Frame 3

(f) Predict Frame 4

Fig. 1. A challenging example, which contains two input video frames (a, b) and four predicted frames (c, d, e, f). We can observe a significant leg movement between the (a) and (b). As is shown in the four predicted frames, our method can handle this movement very well.

can generate high-quality multiple intermediate frames in the face of complex scenarios such as large motion, an example of the experimental results is shown in Fig. 1.

Contribution: The main contributions of this paper can be summarized as follows:

(a) We propose a multi-frame interpolation method for large motion, which uses PWC-Net, a multi-scale optical flow algorithm to estimate the bidirectional flows in an unsupervised way.

(b) By comparing various encoder-decoder structure, we use a modified U-NET++ as an optimized network to improve optical flow accuracy, which significantly improves the quality of generated frames.

We organize the rest of the paper as follows. In Sect. 2, we discuss previous work on frame interpolation and optical flow methods. In Sect. 3, we describe our method in more detail. In Sect. 4, a comparison with state-of-the-art methods is presented, as well as the analysis of our method. Finally, we make a conclusion of this paper in Sect. 5.

2   Related Work

Video Frame Interpolation. Frame interpolation for video is one of the basic computer vision and video processing techniques. It is a special case of image-based rendering where middle frames are interpolated from temporally neighboring frames. The classical approach to video interpolation is based on optical flow [10, 14], therefore the quality of frame interpolation results heavily depends on optical flow estimation. However, the estimation of optical flow is a very complicated and difficult problem, especially in complex scenarios such as large motion, occlusion and blur. It is still an unsolved problem to generate high quality intermediate frames in complex scenarios. Various approaches have been developed to handle the inaccuracies and missing information from optical flow results. The flow-based frame interpolation networks [2, 6] realize end-to-end training by introducing an optical flow layer into the neural network. However, the quality of the generated frames in complex scenarios needs to be improved. To solve the large motion problem, Mathieu et al. [15] proposed a multi-scale architecture, with an adversarial training method, and an image gradient difference loss function to predict future frames. Amersfoort et al. [9] combined the pyramidal structure of classical optical flow modeling with spatial transformer networks and used a perceptual training loss [16] for frame interpolation, but these methods still produce poor frame quality in the face of occlusion. Another category of approaches estimates bidirectional optical flows between two input frames and use them to improve the accuracy and infer missing motion information caused by occlusion [10, 17]. However, their performance is sometimes limited by the subsequent interpolation step that blends the pre-warped frames to produce the final result.

Unlike flow-based frame interpolation methods, Meyer et al. [4] proposed a phase-based method to accommodate large motion by propagating phase information across oriented multi-scale pyramid levels using a bounded shift correction strategy, but the estimable motion amplitude of the method is still small. Niklaus et al. [7, 8] proposed a convolution-based video interpolation method, which combines motion estimation and pixel synthesis into one step, and directly obtains the interpolation frame by using the convolution kernel. However, due to the size of the convolution kernel, the network is not suitable for large motion scenarios.

Optical Flow. Inspired by the successes of deep learning in high-level vision tasks, Dosovitskiy et al. [18] proposed two CNN models for optical flow, i.e., FlowNetS and FlowNetC, and introduce a paradigm shift. Ilg et al. [19] further used the FlowNetS and FlowNetC as building blocks to design a larger network, FlowNet2, to achieve much better performance. The proposed networks [12, 20] which use the multi-scale pyramid structure to estimate optical flow further improves the accuracy of optical flow estimation in large motion scenarios.

In addition to the supervised methods, Long et al. [21] proposed an unsupervised optical flow estimation method. The main idea is to warp an input frame to another input frame by using the predicted optical flow, and then the reconstruction error can be a supervision signal to train the network.

3   Our Proposed Method

Given two input frames I_0 and I_1, our goal is to predict the intermediate frame $\widehat{I}_t$ at time $t \in (0,1)$. We can synthesize the intermediate frames $\widehat{I}_t$ as follows:

$$\widehat{I}_t = w * g(I_0, F_{t\to0}) + (1 - w) * g(I_1, F_{t\to1}) \tag{1}$$

where $F_{t\to0}$ and $F_{t\to1}$ denote the optical flow from I_t to I_0 and I_t to I_1, $g(\cdot,\cdot)$ is a backward warping function [2, 17], $*$ denotes elementwise multiplication, w controls the temporal consistency and occlusion reasoning.

As shown in Fig. 2, we first estimate the bidirectional optical flows $F_{0\to1}$ and $F_{1\to0}$ between two input frames through the Flow Compute Network. Then, we obtain the approximate optical flows $\widehat{F}_{t\to0}$ and $\widehat{F}_{t\to1}$ at time t by linear combination of $F_{0\to1}$ and $F_{1\to0}$. We also get $g\left(I_0, \widehat{F}_{t\to0}\right)$ and $g\left(I_1, \widehat{F}_{t\to1}\right)$ by warping input frames I_0 and I_1, and make them become one of the inputs to the Flow Refine Network. Next, we use U-NET++ with encode-decoder structure as the Flow Refine Network to optimize the approximate optical flows at time t. Flow Refine Network computes approximate errors $\Delta F_{t\to0}$ and $\Delta F_{t\to1}$ to get accurate optical flows $F_{t\to0}$ and $F_{t\to1}$, it also generates visibility maps [11] $V_{t\leftarrow0}$ and $V_{t\leftarrow1}$ to solve the occlusion problem. Finally, the frame $\widehat{I}_t$ is generated by linearly fusing. We will introduce the estimation of approximate optical flows in Sect. 3.1, Flow Refine Network in Sect. 3.2, and the training loss in Sect. 3.3.

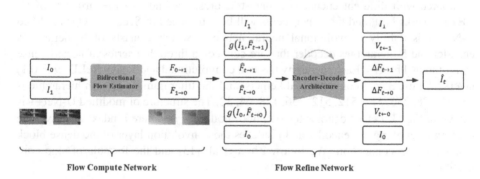

Fig. 2. Network architecture of our approach. Our network is divided into two parts: Flow Compute Network and Flow Refine Network. The Bidirectional Flow Estimator uses a multi-scale flow estimation network to expand the range of motion estimation. The Encoder-Decoder structure is used to optimize the approximate optical flows and reduce the occlusion effect. Implementation details are described in Sect. 3.

3.1   Estimation of Approximate Optical Flows

Since the synthesized frame $\widehat{I}_t$ is not the input frames, it is difficult to directly estimate the optical flows $F_{t\to0}$ and $F_{t\to1}$. To overcome this difficulty and obtain the approximate optical flows $\widehat{F}_{t \to 0}$ and $\widehat{F}_{t \to 1}$, same as Super-SloMo, we linearly fuse the bidirectional optical flows $F_{0 \to 1}$ and $F_{1 \to 0}$ at time t:

$$\widehat{F}_{t \to 0} = -(1 - t)tF_{0 \to 1} + t^2 F_{1 \to 0} \tag{2}$$

$$\widehat{F}_{t \to 1} = -(1 - t)^2 F_{0 \to 1} - t(1 - t)F_{1 \to 0} \tag{3}$$

Therefore, the quality of the bidirectional optical flows $F_{0 \to 1}$ and $F_{1 \to 0}$ directly affects the estimation of approximate optical flows. In order to obtain accurate bidirectional optical flows $F_{0 \to 1}$ and $F_{1 \to 0}$, we compare various optical flow estimation networks (experimental comparisons will be introduced in Sect. 4.2) and finally adopt PWC-Net network structure. PWC-Net uses a multi-scale feature pyramid combined with warping and cost volumes, which can effectively expand the range of motion estimation and obtain accurate bidirectional optical flows $F_{0 \to 1}$ and $F_{1 \to 0}$. To realize the end-to-end training, we use the unsupervised way to train the PWC-Net. Guided by predicted optical flow, we warp the input video frame I_0 to another frame I_1. The reconstruction error can be a supervision signal to train the network.

The approximate optical flows at time t can be estimated by a linear combination, but this method has a poor effect on the motion boundary. In the next section, we will use the optimization method [11] which uses a network with the encode-decoder structure to reduce the effects of approximate optical flows and occlusion.

3.2 Flow Refine Network

Compared with different encode-decoder structures, we find that the structure of U-NET++ works best, and the experiments will be introduced in Sect. 4.2. Our modified U-Net++ is a fully convolutional neural network, which consists of 6 hierarchies encoder and 5 hierarchies decoder that are connected through a series of nested dense convolutional blocks. Each hierarchy has two convolutional and Leaky ReLU ($\alpha = 0.1$) layers. We use 3×3 convolutional kernels, and the filter number of each hierarchie is 32, 64, 128, 256, 512, 512, 512, 256, 128, 64, 32. The structure of modified U-Net++ is shown in Fig. 3. Let $x^{i,j}$ denotes the output of node $X(i,j)$, where i indexes the average pooling layer along the encoder and j indexes the convolution layer of the dense block along the skip connection. We follow Zhou et al. [13] and the formula of skip connection is:

$$x^{i,j} = \begin{cases} \mathcal{H}(x^{i-1,j}), & j = 0 \\ \mathcal{H}([[x^{i,k}]_{k=0}^{j-1}, \mathcal{U}(x^{i+1,j-1})]), & j > 0 \end{cases} \tag{4}$$

Where function $\mathcal{H}(\cdot)$ is a convolution operation followed by an activation function Leaky ReLU ($\alpha = 0.1$), $\mathcal{U}(\cdot)$ denotes a bilinear upsampling layer, and $[\cdot]$ denotes the concatenation layer.

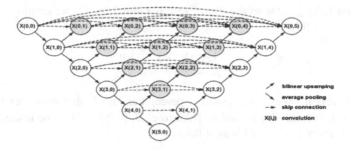

Fig. 3. The Flow Refine Network in Fig. 2, adapted from the U-Net++ structure.

We make the input frames, approximate optical flows and the wrapped frames as the input of our Flow Refine Network, then we can get the flow error $\Delta F_{t\rightarrow 0}$, $\Delta F_{t\rightarrow 1}$ and visibility maps $V_{t\leftarrow 0}$, $V_{t\leftarrow 1}$. The accurate optical flows $F_{t\rightarrow 0}$ and $F_{t\rightarrow 1}$ can be synthesized as:

$$F_{t\rightarrow 0} = \widehat{F}_{t\rightarrow 0} + \Delta F_{t\rightarrow 0} \tag{5}$$

$$F_{t\rightarrow 1} = \widehat{F}_{t\rightarrow 1} + \Delta F_{t\rightarrow 1} \tag{6}$$

Proposed in Super-SloMo, the formula (1) can be extended by using accurate optical flows and visibility maps:

$$\widehat{I}_t = \frac{1}{Z} * \left((1-t)V_{t\leftarrow 0} * g(I_0, F_{t\rightarrow 0}) + tV_{t\leftarrow 1} * g(I_1, F_{t\rightarrow 1}) \right) \tag{7}$$

Where $Z - (1-t)V_{t\rightarrow 0} + tV_{t\rightarrow 0}$ is a normalization factor.

By using formula (7), we can synthesize the intermediate frame $\widehat{I}_t$ at each time step.

3.3 Training Loss

Given two consecutive input frames I_0, I_1 and a set of ground truth intermediate frames $\{I_{t_i}\}_{i=1}^N$, we can train our network by reducing the training loss which measures the difference between ground truth intermediate frames $\{I_{t_i}\}_{i=1}^N$ and synthetic intermediate frames $\left\{\widehat{I}_{t_i}\right\}_{i=1}^N$. Our loss function l is weighted by three parts: color-based loss l_c, perceptual loss l_p and Warping loss l_w:

$$l = \lambda_c l_c + \lambda_p l_p + \lambda_w l_w \tag{8}$$

Where $\lambda_c = 0.8$, $\lambda_p = 0.005$, $\lambda_w = 0.2$.

Color-Based Loss l_c. Due to the blurry results caused by $\ell2$, we employ a $\ell1$-based loss function as follows:

$$l_c = \frac{1}{N}\sum\nolimits_{i=1}^{N}\left\|\widehat{I}_{t_i} - I_{t_i}\right\|_1 \tag{9}$$

Perceptual Loss l_p. We also consider a perceptual loss l_p that measures perceptual difference [16]. Specifically, we follow Niklaus et al. [7, 8] and use the features $\emptyset$ of the relu4_4 layer from VGG-19 [22] as follows:

$$l_p = \frac{1}{N}\sum\nolimits_{i=1}^{N}\left\|\emptyset\left(\widehat{I}_{t_i}\right) - \emptyset(I_{t_i})\right\|_2 \tag{10}$$

Warping Loss l_w. We also introduce the warping loss l_w to measure the quality of our multi-scale optical flow estimation network PWC-Net and the approximate optical flows.

$$l_w = \sum\nolimits_{i=1}^{M} 2^{i-1}\left\|L^i\left(\widehat{I}_0\right) - L^i(I_0)\right\|_1 + \sum\nolimits_{i=1}^{M} 2^{i-1}\left\|L^i\left(\widehat{I}_1\right) - L^i(I_1)\right\|_1 + \frac{1}{N}\sum\nolimits_{i=1}^{N}\left\|I_{t_i} - g\left(I_0, \widehat{F}_{t_i\to0}\right)\right\|_1$$
$$+ \frac{1}{N}\sum\nolimits_{i=1}^{N}\left\|I_{t_i} - g\left(I_1, \widehat{F}_{t_i\to1}\right)\right\|_1 \tag{11}$$

Where M is the number of scales in PWC-Net, $\widehat{I}_0$ is $g\left(I_1, \widehat{F}_{0\to1}\right)$, $\widehat{I}_1$ is $g\left(I_0, \widehat{F}_{1\to0}\right)$, $L^i(\cdot)$ is the input frame in different scale i.

4 Experiments

4.1 Implementation Details and Datasets

We used PyTorch to implement our convolutional neural network, with a GTX 1080Ti GPU. Our network is trained by using the Adam optimizer [23] for 300 epochs, the learning rate is initialized to be 0.0001 and the batch_size is 2. The more intermediate frames we predict during training, the better the model is [11]. Following this training principle, we use 12 consecutive frames as a group from our datasets and remain one-third of groups for testing. We then select 9 consecutive frames from the other two-thirds groups for training and use the middle 7 frames as ground truth. To better compare with the multi-frame interpolation network Super-SloMo, we use the same training dataset Adobe240-fps [24] to train our first model. But Adobe240-fps dataset does not contain large motion videos. So, we have collected some large motion video clips from internet and named the videos as Large-Motion Dataset, as shown in Fig. 4. Our full model is trained by using Adobe240-fps and our Large-Motion dataset.

Then we test our model on several datasets, including Adobe240-fps, our Large-Motion and UCF101 [25]. For Adobe240-fps and Large-Motion datasets, we use the first and eighth video frames as input and interpolate intermediate 7 frames. For

Fig. 4. Snapshot of our Large-Motion Dataset, including racing car, breaking, running, etc. Large-Motion Dataset has 228 video clips and 137620 video frames. The resolution is 720p.

UCF101, the first and third video frames are used as input to predict the second frame. In order to evaluate, we report Peak Signal-to-Noise Ratio (PSNR) and Structural Similarity Index (SSIM) scores [26] between predictions and ground-truth in-between video frames.

4.2 Ablation Experiments

In this section, we first compare a few design choices in the Flow Compute Network and the Flow Refine Network. We then discuss how the different loss functions affect the interpolation results. We randomly sampled two-thirds of videos from Adobe240-fps and our Large-Motion dataset for training and the remaining 12 ones for testing.

Table 1. Different performance of Flow Compute Network on test dataset.

	Adobe240-fps		Large-Motion	
	PSNR	SSIM	PSNR	SSIM
PWC-Net	**31.56**	**0.928**	**30.17**	**0.908**
FlowNet2	31.34	0.925	30.11	0.905
SpyNet	31.21	0.919	30.06	0.901

Flow Compute Network. Keeping U-NET++ as the Flow Refine Network, we compare different flow estimation networks which can handle large motion. Two different optical flow estimation networks FlowNet2 [19], SpyNet [20] are used as alternative networks for PWC-Net. As shown in Table 1, Both FlowNet2 and SpyNet perform less well than PWC-Net on test datasets.

Flow Refine Network. Keeping PWC-Net as the Flow Compute Network, we also use two encoder-decoder structures GridNet [27] and U-NET [28] as alternative networks for U-NET++. For fair comparisons, we all use the same encoder-decoder structure that consists of 6 hierarchies encoder and 5 hierarchies decoder for training. As shown in Table 2, U-NET++ perform well than GridNet and U-NET on test datasets.

Table 2. Different performance of Flow Refine Network on test dataset.

	Adobe240-fps		Large-Motion	
	PSNR	SSIM	PSNR	SSIM
U-NET++	**31.56**	**0.928**	**30.17**	**0.908**
GridNet	31.44	0.920	29.99	0.903
U-NET	31.28	0.913	29.81	0.894

Loss Functions. We consider three different loss functions to train our frame synthesis neural network, as detailed in Sect. 3.3. As shown in Table 3, warping loss is the most important one and adding perceptual loss can make the frames further improved in some details.

Table 3. Effect of different loss function on test dataset.

	Adobe240-fps		Large-Motion	
	PSNR	SSIM	PSNR	SSIM
w/o warping loss	30.83	0.911	28.78	0.889
w/o perceptual loss	31.49	0.926	30.11	0.903
Full model	**31.56**	**0.928**	**30.17**	**0.908**

4.3   Comparison with State-of-the-Art Methods

In this section, we compare our approach with state-of-the-art methods including Phase-Based interpolation [4], SepConv [8] and Super-SloMo [11] on Adobe240-fps, Large-Motion and UCF101 dataset. As is shown in Sect. 4.1, we use UCF101 dataset for single-frame interpolation, the Adobe240-fps and Large-Motion dataset for multi-frame interpolation. We report PSNR and SSIM scores of all above methods in Table 4. For Adobe240-fps and UCF101, our network is slightly better than other methods. However, when dealing with large motion problems, our network shows an extraordinary advantage. We also have collected some examples of visual results and selected one intermediate frame for better display. The examples can be obtained in Fig. 5.

First Input Frame   Second Input Frame   Ground Truth   PhaseBased   SepConv   Super-SloMo   Ours

Fig. 5. Visual results. The first column and second column are input frames. The third column is the ground truth. The other columns are the predicted frames of different method. The first line is the frames that come from our Large-Motion dataset. We can see that our method produces the best results in the yellow roadblock area. Caused by the limited estimation of large motion, other methods have a poor quality of predicted frame. The second line is the frames that come from UCF101 dataset. Our model can not only handle large motion but also produce less artifacts and sharper edge in the hand area. (Color figure online)

Table 4. Performance of all above methods on test datasets.

	Adobe240-fps		Large-Motion		UCF101	
	PSNR	SSIM	PSNR	SSIM	PSNR	SSIM
Phase-Based	30.75	0.903	25.10	0.782	32.35	0.924
SepConv	31.17	0.915	27.97	0.833	33.02	0.935
Super-SloMo	31.19	0.918	28.37	0.859	33.14	0.938
Ours(Adobe240-fps)	31.43	0.925	29.52	0.893	33.18	**0.941**
Ours	**31.56**	**0.928**	**30.17**	**0.908**	**33.21**	0.940

In summary, our approach achieves state-of-the-art results on all testing datasets. Especially for large motion, our method significantly improves the quality of predicted frames.

5 Conclusion

In this paper, we propose a multi-frame interpolation network for large motion. Firstly, we use a state-of-the-art optical flow network to estimate the bidirectional optical flow between two input frames. Secondly, we get approximate optical flows by linear combination of the bidirectional optical flows and use Flow Refine Network to optimize the approximate optical flows. Finally, the two input frames are warped and linearly fused to form each intermediate frame. As demonstrated in our experiments, our method can produce high-quality video frame interpolation results and outperform state-of-the-art methods especially in large motion scenarios.

Acknowledgement. This work is supported by National Science & Technology Major Project (no. 2017ZX05018-005).

References

1. Baker, S., Scharstein, D., Lewis, J.P., Roth, S., Black, M.J., Szeliski, R.: A database and evaluation methodology for optical flow. Int. J. Comput. Vision **92**(1), 1–31 (2011)
2. Liu, Z., Yeh, R.A., Tang, X., Liu, Y., Agarwala, A.: Video frame synthesis using deep voxel flow. In: Proceedings of the IEEE International Conference on Computer Vision, pp. 4463–4471 (2017)
3. Sekiguchi, S., Idehara, Y., Sugimoto, K., Asai, K.: A low-cost video frame-rate up conversion using compressed-domain information. In: IEEE International Conference on Image Processing, vol. 2, p. II–974. IEEE (2005)
4. Meyer, S., Wang, O., Zimmer, H., Grosse, M., Sorkine-Hornung, A.: Phase-based frame interpolation for video. In: Proceedings of the IEEE Conference on Computer Vision and Pattern Recognition, pp. 1410–1418 (2015)
5. Yu, Z., Li, H., Wang, Z., Hu, Z., Chen, C.W.: Multi-level video frame interpolation: exploiting the interaction among different levels. IEEE Trans. Circuits Syst. Video Technol. **23**(7), 1235–1248 (2013)
6. Samsonov, V.: Deep frame interpolation. arXiv preprint arXiv:1706.01159 (2017)
7. Niklaus, S., Mai, L., Liu, F.: Video frame interpolation via adaptive convolution. In: Proceedings of the IEEE Conference on Computer Vision and Pattern Recognition, pp. 670–679 (2017)
8. Niklaus, S., Mai, L., Liu, F.: Video frame interpolation via adaptive separable convolution. In: Proceedings of the IEEE International Conference on Computer Vision, pp. 261–270 (2017)
9. Van Amersfoort, J., et al.: Frame interpolation with multi-scale deep loss functions and generative adversarial networks. arXiv preprint arXiv:1711.06045 (2017)
10. Herbst, E., Seitz, S., Baker, S.: Occlusion reasoning for temporal interpolation using optical flow. Department of Computer Science and Engineering, University of Washington, Technical report UW-CSE-09-08-01 (2009)
11. Jiang, H., Sun, D., Jampani, V., Yang, M.H., Learned-Miller, E., Kautz, J.: Super SloMo: high quality estimation of multiple intermediate frames for video interpolation. In: Proceedings of the IEEE Conference on Computer Vision and Pattern Recognition, pp. 9000–9008 (2018)
12. Sun, D., Yang, X., Liu, M.Y., Kautz, J.: PWC-Net: CNNs for optical flow using pyramid, warping, and cost volume. In: Proceedings of the IEEE Conference on Computer Vision and Pattern Recognition, pp. 8934–8943 (2018)
13. Zhou, Z., Rahman Siddiquee, M.M., Tajbakhsh, N., Liang, J.: UNet++: a nested U-Net architecture for medical image segmentation. In: Stoyanov, D., et al. (eds.) DLMIA 2018, ML-CDS 2018. LNCS, vol. 11045, pp. 3–11. Springer, Cham (2018). https://doi.org/10.1007/978-3-030-00889-5_1
14. Barron, J.L., Fleet, D.J., Beauchemin, S.S.: Performance of optical flow techniques. Int. J. Comput. Vis. **12**(1), 43–77 (1994)

15. Mathieu, M., Couprie, C., LeCun, Y.: Deep multi-scale video prediction beyond mean square error. arXiv preprint arXiv:1511.05440 (2015)
16. Johnson, J., Alahi, A., Fei-Fei, L.: Perceptual losses for real-time style transfer and super-resolution. In: Leibe, B., Matas, J., Sebe, N., Welling, M. (eds.) ECCV 2016. LNCS, vol. 9906, pp. 694–711. Springer, Cham (2016). https://doi.org/10.1007/978-3-319-46475-6_43
17. Zhou, T., Tulsiani, S., Sun, W., Malik, J., Efros, A.A.: View synthesis by appearance flow. In: Leibe, B., Matas, J., Sebe, N., Welling, M. (eds.) ECCV 2016. LNCS, vol. 9908, pp. 286–301. Springer, Cham (2016). https://doi.org/10.1007/978-3-319-46493-0_18
18. Dosovitskiy, A., et al.: Flownet: learning optical flow with convolutional networks. In: Proceedings of the IEEE International Conference on Computer Vision, pp. 2758–2766 (2015)
19. Ilg, E., Mayer, N., Saikia, T., Keuper, M., Dosovitskiy, A., Brox, T.: FlowNet 2.0: evolution of optical flow estimation with deep networks. In: Proceedings of the IEEE Conference on Computer Vision and Pattern Recognition, pp. 2462–2470 (2017)
20. Ranjan, A., Black, M.J.: Optical flow estimation using a spatial pyramid network. In: Proceedings of the IEEE Conference on Computer Vision and Pattern Recognition, pp. 4161–4170 (2017)
21. Long, G., Kneip, L., Alvarez, J.M., Li, H., Zhang, X., Yu, Q.: Learning image matching by simply watching video. In: Leibe, B., Matas, J., Sebe, N., Welling, M. (eds.) ECCV 2016. LNCS, vol. 9910, pp. 434–450. Springer, Cham (2016). https://doi.org/10.1007/978-3-319-46466-4_26
22. Simonyan, K., Zisserman, A.: Very deep convolutional networks for large-scale image recognition. arXiv preprint arXiv:1409.1556 (2014)
23. Kingma, D.P., Ba, J.: Adam: a method for stochastic optimization. arXiv preprint arXiv: 1412.6980 (2014)
24. Su, S., Delbracio, M., Wang, J., Sapiro, G., Heidrich, W., Wang, O.: Deep video deblurring for hand-held cameras. In: Proceedings of the IEEE Conference on Computer Vision and Pattern Recognition, pp. 1279–1288 (2017)
25. Soomro, K., Zamir, A.R., Shah, M.: A dataset of 101 human action classes from videos in the wild. Center for Research in Computer Vision (2012)
26. Wang, Z., Bovik, A.C., Sheikh, H.R., Simoncelli, E.P.: Image quality assessment: from error visibility to structural similarity. IEEE Trans. Image Process. 13(4), 600–612 (2004)
27. Fourure, D., Emonet, R., Fromont, E., Muselet, D., Tremeau, A., Wolf, C.: Residual conv-deconv grid network for semantic segmentation. arXiv preprint arXiv:1707.07958 (2017)
28. Ronneberger, O., Fischer, P., Brox, T.: U-Net: convolutional networks for biomedical image segmentation. In: Navab, N., Hornegger, J., Wells, W., Frangi, A. (eds.) MICCAI 2015. LNCS, vol. 9351, pp. 234–241. Springer, Cham (2015). https://doi.org/10.1007/978-3-319-24574-4_28

One-Shot Video Object Segmentation Initialized with Referring Expression

XiaoQing Bu[1], Jianming Wang[2,5], Jiayu Liang[2], Kunliang Liu[2], Yukuan Sun[4], and Guanghao Jin[2,3](✉)

[1] School of Electronic and Information Engineering, Tianjin Polytechnic University, Tianjin, China
[2] School of Computer Science and Technology, Tianjin Polytechnic University, Tianjin, China
jinguanghao@tjpu.edu.cn
[3] Tianjin International Joint Research and Development Center of Autonomous Intelligence Technology and Systems, Tianjin Polytechnic University, Tianjin, China
[4] Center for Engineering Internship and Training, Tianjin, China
[5] Tianjin Key Laboratory of Autonomous Intelligence Technology and Systems, Tianjin Polytechnic University, Tianjin, China

Abstract. One-Shot Video Object Segmentation (OSVOS) is a CNN architecture to tackle the problem of semi-supervised video object segmentation, which performs the separation of an object from the background in a frame-independent way with the aid of one manually-segmented frame. However, in the scenarios of real applications, the requirement of one manually-segmented frame would do harm to user-friendliness of a system. To tackle the problem above, we propose a video object segmentation based on referring expression (named as REVOS), which obtains the segmented frame by a referring expression (a noun phrase whose function is to identify on specific object). The main task of our method is to select the target from all candidate objects which have the highest matching score with the referring expression by using the language analysis module. Then generate the annotation of the first frame and continue to segment all the remaining frames with OSVOS. The results of experiment show that our method can achieve similar accuracy to OSVOS and more convenient and flexible for system design.

Keywords: Video segmentation · Referring expression · DAVIS dataset

1 Introduction

The task of video object segmentation is to accurately segment the objects in all frames of the video by given one or a few frames annotated with segmentation

The first author of this paper is a student. This work was supported by National Natural Science Foundation of China (No. 61373104, No. 61405143) and the Excellent Science and Technology Enterprise Specialist Project of Tianjin (No. 18JCTPJC59000) and the Tianjin Natural Science Foundation (No. 16JCYBJC42300).

© Springer Nature Switzerland AG 2019
Z. Lin et al. (Eds.): PRCV 2019, LNCS 11858, pp. 416–428, 2019.
https://doi.org/10.1007/978-3-030-31723-2_35

masks of a particular object instance. This task is a well-researched problem in the computer vision and has many high-level vision applications, including activity understanding, 3D scene analysis and targeted content replacement.

In recent years, some methods have been proposed to research this field, including unsupervised techniques and semi-supervised techniques. They are all contributed to solving the problem of video segmentation. However, those methods must have the object mask annotated by the user of the first frame. Only in this way can it segment the object in the remaining frames, which is unrealistic in practical applications. For instance, If the user wants to segment multiple objects in the video, then the user is required to manually label the segmentation mask of the objects in the first frame. Thus, those methods have limitations because the cost of manual segmentation is high.

In this paper, we proposed a video object segmentation based on referring expression (REVOS), which can automatically mark the segmentation of the key frame and correctly segment the object in the video by referring expression instead of manually segmenting the object. The existing methods required the mask of the first frame to segment the video, which was annotated by the user. In contrast, our method can generate segmented mask automatically by the referring expression, which makes users to segment video more convenient and flexible. Our method can contribute a lot to video analysis and understanding as it can reduce the cost of segmentation and make it possible to perform the segmentation from any frame without manual segmentation for the first frame. Figure 1 summarizes the difference between the existing stat-of-art method(a) with our method(b). This paper evaluated our method with the existing method on the DAVIS video dataset. The experimental result shows that our method simplifies the video segmentation process and is more effective for users than the existing methods.

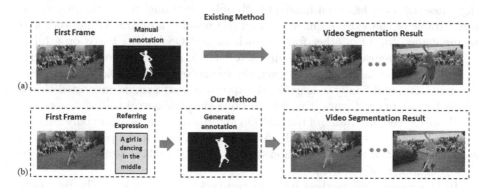

Fig. 1. Example result of our technique: (a) is existing method of video segmentation, and (b) is ours. Input the referring expression, and our model will automatically segment the object in the entire video

The main contribution of this paper is that we proposed a novel method for video object segmentation by only using referring expression. It does not require manual marking, which reduces the workload and easer to start segmentation at any frame. REVOS can processes each frame of the video independently, and realizes segmentation of the video object from the super pixel level without considering the timing information between sequential frames.

2   Related Work

Semi-supervised Video Object Segmentation: Deep learning techniques for semi-supervised video object segmentation(VOS), the first frame or key frames are user labelled and the object is segmented in the remaining frames, have gained attention in the research community during the recent years. However, most of the current literature on semi-supervised VOS enforces temporal consistency in video sequences to propagate the initial mask into the following frames. For example, in order to reduce the computational complexity some works make use of superpixels [5,7], patches [3,6], or even object proposals [20]. Moreover, an optimization using one of the previous aggregations of pixels is usually performed; which can consider the full video sequence [16], a subset of frames [7], or only the results in frame n to obtain the mask in $n + 1$ [3,5,6]. As part of their pipeline, some of other methods include the computation of optical flow [3,7], which considerably reduces speed.

Unlike those methods, REVOS is a simpler pipeline that separates each frame independently. It makes the method more convenient and produces more accurate results, while also significantly improves speed.

One-Shot Framework of VOS: For segmentation without temporal modeling, one-shot VOS has been handled with online learning, where the first annotated frame of the video sequence is used to fine-tune a pretrained network and segment the objects in other frames, such as OSVOS [4]. It's based on a fully-convolutional neural network architecture that is able to successively transfer generic semantic information, learned on ImageNet to the task of foreground segmentation, and finally to learning the appearance of a single annotated object of the test sequence (hence it is called as one-shot framework).

However, the first frame of the OSVOS algorithm requires a manually annotation of the object, which is difficult to implement in human-computer interaction scenarios, and the mask acquisition cost is too high, which would do harm to user-friendliness of a system.

In this paper, our method REVOS can tackle this problem. The user only needs to give a referring expression, and our model can automatically generate the annotation of the first frame according to the expression.

Referring Expression Comprehension(REC): The task of referring expression comprehension is to localize a region described by a given referring expression. To address this problem, some recent work [15,26] uses CNNLSTM structure to model and looks for the object o maximizing the probability. Other recent work uses joint embedding model [9,14,22,23] to compute matching score directly. In a hybrid of both types of approaches, [25] proposed a joint speaker-listener-reinforcer model that combined CNN-LSTM (speaker) with embedding model (listener) to achieve state-of-the-art results. Most of the above treat comprehension as bounding box localization, but object segmentation from referring expression has also been studied in some recent work [8,13]. Most of the above treat comprehension as bounding box localization, but object segmentation from referring expression has also been studied in some recent work, such as MAttNet [27] which takes a natural language expression as input and softly decomposes it into three phrase embeddings. MAttNet learns to parse expressions automatically through a soft attention based mechanism, instead of relying on an external language parser [12,18]. Our method is based on MAttNet, given the first frame and a set of candidates o_i, we run Mask R-CNN to extract their region representations. Then select the specific target described by the user based on the referring expression.

3   Proposed Method

In this section, we introduce our segmentation model. Given a referring expression, it should output the segmentation of the first frame. Then our goal is to propagate foreground tags throughout the video. Compared with the unsupervised methods [10,11] that rely on motion and object suggestions and process the entire video offline in batch mode, the proposed method is to automatically track and segment objects while retain the quality of result.

3.1   The Framework of Our Method

Referring expressions are natural language utterances that indicate particular objects within a scene. Referring expression comprehension can be typically formulated as selecting the best region from a set of objects $O = \sum_{i=1}^{N} o_i$ in the first frame, given an input expression r. We need to pick out the object o_j with the highest match between O and r. At the very beginning, we find all candidate objects in the first frame and determine whether there are multiple objects in the first frame. If not, then generate a hint to the user, telling the user to input only one keyword. If the first frame contains multiple objects, then we need to further determined whether the target subject overlaps with other objects. If there is no overlap, the user is prompted to input the format of the subject and location. If there is overlap, indicating that the two objects are related, the user is prompted to input the subject, the object and the relationship between them. These tips can help the user accurately describe the subject in the video, thereby improving the accuracy of the segmentation.

After the user gives the expression, we parse referring expression into three phrase embeddings, which are input to three visual modules that process the described visual region in different ways and compute individual matching scores. The overview of this task is shown as Fig. 2. After getting annotation, we can continue to segment all the remaining frames with OSVOS.

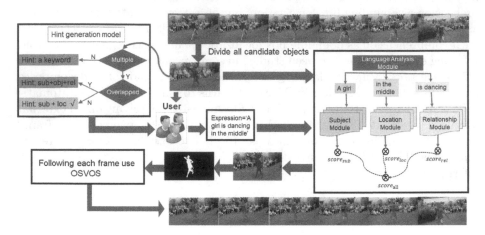

Fig. 2. The framework of our method: Divide all candidate objects in the first frame and determine if it is a multi-object. If return NO, the user only needs to input a keyword. If return YES, then further determine if there is overlap relationship between the two objects. After the user gives the expression, we parse it into three phrase embeddings to compute individual matching scores. An overall score is then computed as a weighted combination of the module scores. Finally, we segment each frame by using OSVOS.

3.2   Referring Expression for Semantic Segmentation

Before processing each frame of video, we first use the referring expression to mark the object in the first frame (or other key frame) in the video so that our model can learn the features of the segmented object. In order to achieve our goal, we need to do some preparatory work. We have tagged 50 videos in the DAVIS dataset. Each video corresponds to a related expression. There are three principles for generating referring expressions. (1) If there is only a single object in the video, we use a keyword to describe it. Such as 'bear','dog','cow' and so on. (2) If there are more than two objects in the video, we can describe the subject and its location or action. (3) If there are double objects in the video and they are related to each other, then we can describe the relationship between the subject and other objects. The generation mechanism of referring expressions is shown in the Fig. 3.

Instead of using an external language parser [1,2,12] or pre-defined templates [17] to parse the expression, our method is to learn the relevant words

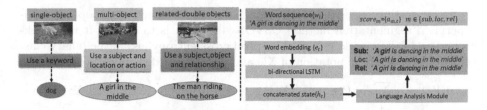

Fig. 3. The principles of generating referring expressions and Language Analysis Module

automatically for each module, similar to MAttNet [27]. For a given expression $r = \sum_{i=1}^{N} w_i$, we use a bi-directional LSTM to encode the context for each word. We first embed each word w_i into a vector e_t using an one-hot word embedding, then a bidirectional LSTM-RNN is applied to encode the whole expression. The final hidden representation for each word is the concatenation of the hidden vectors in both directions:

$$e_t = embedding(w_i) \tag{1}$$

$$\overrightarrow{h_t} = \overrightarrow{LSTM}(e_t, \overrightarrow{h_{t-1}}) \tag{2}$$

$$\overleftarrow{h_t} = \overleftarrow{LSTM}(e_t, \overleftarrow{h_{t+1}}) \tag{3}$$

$$h_t = [\overrightarrow{h_t}, \overleftarrow{h_t}] \tag{4}$$

Given $H = \sum_{t=1}^{T} h_t$, we apply three trainable vectors f_m where $m \in sub, loc, rel$, computing the score of each module:

$$a_{m,t} = \frac{exp(f_m^T h_t)}{\sum_{k=1}^{T} exp(f_m^T h_k)} \tag{5}$$

3.3 Semi-supervised Video Object Segmentation

After having correct referring expression, we start to segment the first frame. We define the video segmentation function S_n:

$$S_n = F(S_1, I_n) \tag{6}$$

$$S_1 = Seg(r_{exp}, I_1) \tag{7}$$

Where S_n is the segmentation result of the current frame I_n. $F(\cdot)$ is the mathematical model of our REVOS algorithm. S_1 is the segmentation result of the first frame. We can obtain S_1 via inputing r_{exp} and I_1. Formally, during the training of MAttNet, it defines a multi-task loss as $L = L_{cls} + L_{mask} + L_{obj}$. The classification loss L_{cls} is identical as those defined in [21] R. Girshick and defines L_{mask} as the average binary cross-entropy loss. L_{obj} is defined as the cross-loss entropy of the object that is related to the expression.

After getting referring expression and annotation, we adopted semi-supervised segmentation method OSVOS [4], which is to classify it into background and foreground. The pixel-by-pixel cross-entropy loss in the binary classification (we keep the notation of Xie and TU [24]) is defined in this case as:

$$\vartheta(W) = -\sum_{j} log P(y_j = 1 \mid X; W) + (1 - y_j) log(1 - P(y_j = 1 \mid X; W))$$

$$= -\sum_{j \in Y_+} log P(y_j = 1 \mid X; W) - \sum_{j \in Y_-} log P(y_j = 0 \mid X; W) \qquad (8)$$

where W are the standard trainable parameters of a CNN, X is the input image, $y_j \in 0, 1, j = 1, ..., Y_+$ and Y_- are the positive and negative labeled pixels. $P(\cdot)$ is obtained by applying a sigmoid to the activation of the final layer.

4   Experimental Validation

Our main experiment was carried out in the recently released DAVIS dataset [19], which consists of 50 full HD video sequences. We artificially divide it into three categories. The first type samples are a video with only a single object, there are 27 samples; the second type samples are a video containing multiple objects, there are 11; the third type samples are a video of related-double objects, there are 12. As mentioned above, we use a keyword to describe single object videos, use the subject and its location or action to describe multiple objects videos and use the relationship between the subject and other objects to describe related-double objects videos.

4.1   Evaluation of Results on DAVIS Dataset

There are three types of referring expressions, which correspond to three types of video frame sequences. For single-object video, no matter which expression we choose, the final accuracy is similar, as it is shown in the Table 1, so we choose the simplest way, only use a *keyword*. Through experiments we can conclude that for multi-object video, the best way is to choose *subject + location*. For related-double objects, the best way is to choose *subject + relationship + object*.

Table 1. Choose three types of referring expressions and accuracy

Referring expression	Single-object	Multi-object	Related-double objects
A keyword	0.836 ✓	0.207	0.513
Subject+location	0.835	0.792 ✓	0.609
Subject+relationship+object	0.832	0.621	0.784 ✓

We ran all of the video sequences on the DAVIS dataset and evaluated them using two ways for metric segmentation accuracy on the DAVIS dataset:

(1) **Region Similarity:** The region similarity is the Intersection over $Union$ function between the mask M and the ground truth G. The calculation formula is: $IoU = \frac{M \cap G}{M \cup G}$

(2) **Contour Accuracy:** Thinking the mask as a collection of closed contours and compute a contour-based F metric, a function of accuracy and recall. Its calculation formula is: $P = \frac{M \cap G}{M}, R = \frac{M \cap G}{G}$, so the F is calculated with $F = \frac{a^2 + 1}{a^2} \times \frac{P \times R}{P + R}$, which P is the accuracy rate, R is the recall rate, and a is the weight. It can be seen that the F metric is the weighted harmonic average of the accuracy rate and the recall rate. When the weight $a = 1$, the F metric becomes the common $F_1 = \frac{2 \times P \times R}{P + R}$, that is, the recall rate is as important as the accuracy rate in this case (the weight a can be adjusted according to specific needs by users). The final statistical results are shown in the following Table 2:

Table 2. DAVIS Validation: REVOS versus the state of the art, and practical quality.

Measure		OURS	OSVOS	OFL	BVS	HVS	SEA
Region similarity	Mean	79.6	79.8	68.0	60.0	54.6	50.4
	Recall	93.7	93.6	75.6	66.9	61.4	53.1
Contour accuracy	Mean	80.3	80.6	63.4	58.8	52.9	48.0
	Recall	92.5	92.6	70.4	67.9	61.0	46.3

To show more details, we randomly selected 20 video sequences in the DAVIS data set, calculated their average IoU values, and compared them with the other five methods. The results are shown in Fig. 4.

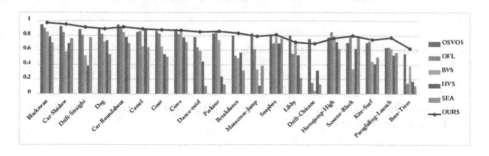

Fig. 4. DAVIS Validation: Per-sequence results of region similarity

4.2   The Effect of Mark Accuracy to Segmentation Results

In order to obtain a better segmentation result, we hope that the annotation of the first frame is as accurate as possible, which facilitates subsequent migration and segmentation. To this end, we did an experiment, using the Crystallize operation in photoshop to change the accuracy of the annotation. This operation can agglomerate some pixels as a polygon. We set five crystallize levels, which is divided into 0%, (Original innotation) 20%, 40%, 60%, 80%, as is shown in Fig. 5, and take it as an annotation and then perform the segmentation operation to count the final results.

Table 3 shows the average IoU values of the randomly selected 5 video frames at different annotation accuracy, and the results confirm our view.

(a) Crystallize0%   (b) Crystallize20%   (c) Crystallize40%   (d) Crystallize60%   (e) Crystallize80%

Fig. 5. Impact of different accuracy on subsequent segmentation

Table 3. The mean IoU value of segmentation with different accuracy

Crystallize	0%	20%	40%	60%	80%
Dance-Twirl	0.85	0.801	0.774	0.684	0.557
Boat	0.824	0.795	0.724	0.642	0.598
Parkour	0.86	0.817	0.792	0.613	0.573
Breakdance	0.83	0.785	0.717	0.593	0.526
Camel	0.89	0.826	0.784	0.634	0.551

4.3   Training Iterations and Timing

To evaluate how much annotated data are needed to train REVOS network, Table 4 shows the performance of REVOS when using a subset of the DAVIS training set. Then discuss the relation between the training iterations and quality(IoU value) of REVOS.

Table 4. Amount of training data

Training images	100	500	1000	2000
Quality(IoU)	74.6	76.9	77.2	77.4

The computational efficiency of video object segmentation is important to the algorithms to be usable in practice. REVOS can adapt to different timing requirements, providing progressively better results the more time we can afford, by letting the fine-tuning algorithm at test time do more or fewer iterations. To show this behavior, Fig. 6 shows the quality of the result with respect to the time it takes to process each 480p frame. REVOS time can be divided into fine-tuning time plus the time to process each frame independently. We conducted four experiments, as it is shown in Fig. 6, and trained 100 times (in blue), 500 times (in orange), 1000 times (in gray) and 2000 times (in yellow). It can be seen from the figure that the IoU of training 2000 times is obviously improved. We further experiment by modifying the time of processing each frame independently. The final experimental results show that the more times the training is performed and the longer the processing time per frame, the higher the accuracy it gets. On the other side, there is also a limitation of maximum. Once this method reached this maximum, the accuracy does not change with time and training iterations.

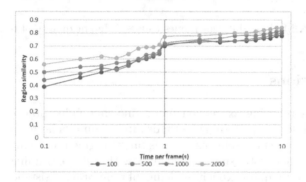

Fig. 6. Quality versus timing (Color figure online)

4.4   Improve Accuracy by Annotating Different Frames

In some cases, the user may feel that the segmentation is not good, such as a frame is segmented out of a large area beyond the target object. In this case, the user can easily choose other frames in the video to restart the program without manual segmentation by our method. One of the principles of restarting can be detection of the IOU value of objects. When the IOU value drops significantly, it can restart REVOS from this frame. Another principle is to detect the overlapping by using the classification or segmentation methods like Mask R-CNN. When the mask of the object is overlapped by the mask of other objects, it indicates that there is occlusion in this frame, then it can restart REVOS from this frame.

Through the experiments, we found that if it marks different frames (such as marking the frame 0, or marking the frame 11), it can get different segmentation quality. Thus, the user can also choose the better one than the first frame of

REVOS. Figure 7 shows the examples of this process, where the user annotates frame 0 and a dog is visible as it shows in (a). In frame 35, REVOS also segments the some parts of the tree which blocking the dog as it shows in (b). This can be solved as it is shows in (f) by annotating another two frames like the frame 14 in (c) or 11 in (e), which allows REVOS to learn the difference between those two similar objects, even without taking temporal consistency into account.

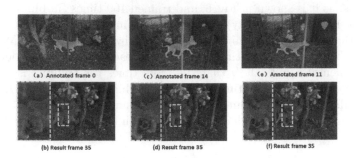

Fig. 7. Marking different frames causes different quality of results

5   Conclusions

We proposed a referring expression based one-shot video object segmentation (REVOS) method. Deep learning methods often require a large amount of training data to solve specific problems, such as target segmentation in video. Instead, human observers can solve similar challenges with a single training example. Our approach does not require explicit modeling of temporal consistency using optical flow algorithms or temporal smoothing, so it does not suffer from error propagation (drift) over time. Instead, our model processes each frame of the video independently and produces highly accurate and time-consistent segments. Furthermore, we demonstrate the ability to reproduce the difficulty of first frame annotation by referring expression. Compared with the existing methods, our model is not only more convenient in practical applications, but also can realize the segmentation of any one video with much lower cost. As a future work, we will focus on how to control the restart of segmentation to get higher quality result. This will be about the relationship between refereeing expression, annotation of the starting frame and following segmentation.

References

1. Andreas, J., Rohrbach, M., Darrell, T., Dan, K.: Learning to compose neural networks for question answering (2016)
2. Andreas, J., Rohrbach, M., Darrell, T., Klein, D.: Neural module networks. In: IEEE Conference on Computer Vision and Pattern Recognition (2015)

3. Avinash Ramakanth, S., Venkatesh Babu, R.: SeamSeg: video object segmentation using patch seams. In: Proceedings of the IEEE Conference on Computer Vision and Pattern Recognition, pp. 376–383 (2014)
4. Caelles, S., Maninis, K.K., Pont-Tuset, J., Leal-Taixé, L., Cremers, D., Van Gool, L.: One-shot video object segmentation. In: Proceedings of the IEEE Conference on Computer Vision and Pattern Recognition, pp. 221–230 (2017)
5. Chang, J., Wei, D., Fisher, J.W.: A video representation using temporal super-pixels. In: Proceedings of the IEEE Conference on Computer Vision and Pattern Recognition, pp. 2051–2058 (2013)
6. Fan, Q., Zhong, F., Lischinski, D., Cohen-Or, D., Chen, B.: JumpCut: non-successive mask transfer and interpolation for video cutout. ACM Trans. Graph. **34**(6), Article No. 195 (2015)
7. Grundmann, M., Kwatra, V., Han, M., Essa, I.: Efficient hierarchical graph-based video segmentation. In: 2010 IEEE Conference on Computer Vision and Pattern Recognition (CVPR), pp. 2141–2148. IEEE (2010)
8. Hu, R., Rohrbach, M., Darrell, T.: Segmentation from natural language expressions. In: Leibe, B., Matas, J., Sebe, N., Welling, M. (eds.) ECCV 2016. LNCS, vol. 9905, pp. 108–124. Springer, Cham (2016). https://doi.org/10.1007/978-3-319-46448-0_7
9. Kan, C., Kovvuri, R., Nevatia, R.: Query-guided regression network with context policy for phrase grounding (2017)
10. Lee, Y.J., Kim, J., Grauman, K.: Key-segments for video object segmentation. In: 2011 IEEE International Conference on Computer Vision (ICCV), pp. 1995–2002. IEEE (2011)
11. Li, F., Kim, T., Humayun, A., Tsai, D., Rehg, J.M.: Video segmentation by tracking many figure-ground segments. In: Proceedings of the IEEE International Conference on Computer Vision, pp. 2192–2199 (2013)
12. Li, J., Mu, L., Zan, H., Zhang, K.: Research on Chinese parsing based on the improved compositional vector grammar. In: Lu, Q., Gao, H. (eds.) Chinese Lexical Semantics. LNCS (LNAI), vol. 9332, pp. 649–658. Springer, Cham (2015). https://doi.org/10.1007/978-3-319-27194-1_64
13. Liu, C., Zhe, L., Shen, X., Yang, J., Xin, L., Yuille, A.: Recurrent multimodal interaction for referring image segmentation (2017)
14. Liu, J., Liang, W., Yang, M.H.: Referring expression generation and comprehension via attributes. In: IEEE International Conference on Computer Vision (2017)
15. Mao, J., Huang, J., Toshev, A., Camburu, O., Yuille, A., Murphy, K.: Generation and comprehension of unambiguous object descriptions (2016)
16. Märki, N., Perazzi, F., Wang, O., Sorkine-Hornung, A.: Bilateral space video segmentation. In: Proceedings of the IEEE Conference on Computer Vision and Pattern Recognition, pp. 743–751 (2016)
17. Mitchell, M., Deemter, K.V., Reiter, E.: Natural reference to objects in a visual domain. In: INLG - Sixth International Natural Language Generation Conference (2010)
18. Paraboni, I., Galindo, M.R., Iacovelli, D.: Stars2: a corpus of object descriptions in a visual domain. Lang. Resour. Eval. **51**(2), 1–24 (2016)
19. Perazzi, F., Pont-Tuset, J., McWilliams, B., Van Gool, L., Gross, M., Sorkine-Hornung, A.: A benchmark dataset and evaluation methodology for video object segmentation. In: Proceedings of the IEEE Conference on Computer Vision and Pattern Recognition, pp. 724–732 (2016)

20. Perazzi, F., Wang, O., Gross, M., Sorkine-Hornung, A.: Fully connected object proposals for video segmentation. In: Proceedings of the IEEE International Conference on Computer Vision, pp. 3227–3234 (2015)
21. Ren, S., He, K., Girshick, R., Sun, J.: Faster R-CNN: towards real-time object detection with region proposal networks. In: Advances in Neural Information Processing Systems, pp. 91–99 (2015)
22. Rohrbach, A., Rohrbach, M., Hu, R., Darrell, T., Schiele, B.: Grounding of textual phrases in images by reconstruction. In: Leibe, B., Matas, J., Sebe, N., Welling, M. (eds.) ECCV 2016. LNCS, vol. 9905, pp. 817–834. Springer, Cham (2016). https://doi.org/10.1007/978-3-319-46448-0_49
23. Wang, L., Yin, L., Lazebnik, S.: Learning deep structure-preserving image-text embeddings. In: Computer Vision and Pattern Recognition (2016)
24. Xie, S., Tu, Z.: Holistically-nested edge detection. In: Proceedings of the IEEE International Conference on Computer Vision, pp. 1395–1403 (2015)
25. Yu, L., Hao, T., Bansal, M., Berg, T.L.: A joint speaker-listener-reinforcer model for referring expressions (2016)
26. Yu, L., Poirson, P., Yang, S., Berg, A.C., Berg, T.L.: Modeling context in referring expressions. In: Leibe, B., Matas, J., Sebe, N., Welling, M. (eds.) ECCV 2016. LNCS, vol. 9906, pp. 69–85. Springer, Cham (2016). https://doi.org/10.1007/978-3-319-46475-6_5
27. Yu, L., Zhe, L., Shen, X., Yang, J., Berg, T.L.: MAttNet: modular attention network for referring expression comprehension (2018)

Scalable Receptive Field GAN: An End-to-End Adversarial Learning Framework for Crowd Counting

Yukang Gao and Hua Yang[✉]

Institution of Image Communication and Network Engineering,
Shanghai Jiao Tong University, Shanghai, China
hyang@sjtu.edu.cn

Abstract. Crowd counting is challenging for unrestricted open outdoor and diverse scenes. To address large variety of perspective, density distribution and clutter problems, a novel end-to-end deep generative adversarial framework with scalable receptive field (SRFGAN) is proposed for obtaining high quality density estimation in this paper. Specifically, our generator adopts an encoder-decoder network with residual blocks to achieve multi-scale features due to scalable receptive fields which adapts to different scale crowd distribution. We also explore a spatial global pooling layer to acquire image-level prior representation which helps to tackle severe perspective distortion and background clutter. Besides, feature matching loss and adversarial loss are combined via a joint training scheme, which helps to improve the quality of generated density map. Experiment results on ShanghaiTech and UCF_CC_50 datasets illustrate the superior effectiveness.

Keywords: Crowd counting · Scalable receptive field · Image-level prior · Adversarial network

1 Introduction

Along with the process of urbanization, crowd analysis plays an increasing role in society security and intelligent city management. As an essential part, crowd counting, however, remains a challenging problem due to serious occlusion, various perspective and non-uniform distribution.

In the literature of crowd counting, methods [12,23] used a detection-based framework to estimate the number of pedestrians, while methods [2,16] regressed the count by training with the extracted low-level feature. But both kinds of algorithms fail to solve the challenges mentioned above.

Recent CNN-based methods for crowds counting estimation [17,25] have made great progress via changing the counting task to density map generation task, which contains crowd distribution information. However, most of previous

---

The first author is a student.

© Springer Nature Switzerland AG 2019
Z. Lin et al. (Eds.): PRCV 2019, LNCS 11858, pp. 429–440, 2019.
https://doi.org/10.1007/978-3-030-31723-2_36

methods focus on making receptive field of the network correspond to the size of people/head with multi-column structure. From another point of view, multi-scale information is captured to generate density maps. But such framework is high redundant and scale-limited, with tedious work training the network if more scalable features are needed (e.g. multi-column CNN (MCNN) [25]). The algorithms proposed by [17,20,25] split each image into several patches to augment the dataset and use them for classification by the crowd density level. In this way, they can solve the challenges brought by arbitrary perspective and different density levels. However, it is observed that small patches cropped from the whole image would lose global contextual information between patches. Moreover, we find that larger receptive field is essential for avoiding the confusion of foreground and background like trees, clothing and dense crowds. On the other hand, more downsampling layers are frequently used to enlarge the receptive field, as adopted in methods [11,19], which lose a number of information during the downsampling process. It is difficult to restore the details in the decoder part.

(a)   (b)   (c)

Fig. 1. Representative samples from ShanghaiTech Part_A dataset [25]. (a) large scale variation in head size due to perspective effect. (b)(c) complicated background including crowd-like trees and fence. Thus, the network should have large receptive field to capture global information.

To address these issues, in this paper, we propose a new end-to-end framework called SRFGAN. We introduce GAN [4,7] based scheme to generate higher quality density map and deploy an encoder-decoder structure to enlarge the receptive field with less downsampling layers. Residual blocks [5] extract multi-scale features which is of the essence in tackling cross-scale counting problem. In order to make up for the insufficient receptive field, global pooling layer is exploited to capture global priors information.

Rather than L2 Euclidean distance widely used as loss function before, our proposed loss function combines L1 Euclidean distance with least square adversarial loss. The L1 Euclidean distance helps to enhance the robustness of the model, and adversarial loss highlights the high-frequency parts. We use the discriminator called "PatchGAN" [7] which models high frequency and classify the image by scanning the local patch and help to generate density map with more details. Our approach takes the whole image as input and outputs the desired density map. As a result, our model is much easier to train and avoids the problems of patched-based methods mentioned above.

To summarize, contributions of this paper are summarized in three main aspects as follows:

1. We introduce a deeper encoder-decoder framework with residual blocks to achieve scalable receptive field. Different from multi-column structure adopted by previous works, our framework could achieve scalable and larger receptive field with less downsampling layers.
2. Generative adversarial framework is adopted by combining the traditional L1 Euclidean loss with least square adversarial loss to generate high quality density maps. Traditional Euclidean loss tends to capture features at low frequency and thus the generated density map is blurring. As a result we use adversarial loss to generate high quality density maps with more high frequency features.
3. We apply global pooling layer to provide global priors. The priors provide the global contextual information and make up for insufficient receptive field, which is essential in complex background.

2   Related Work

Many works have been proposed to estimate the number of crowds. Recent years CNN-based approaches make great success in crowd counting and outperform most of traditional methods.

Pioneering work Zhang et al. [24] proposed a CNN-based method to regress both density map and crowd count. Shang et al. [18] then proposed an end-to end network, in which they used GoogLeNet to extract features and regress the local counts and global counts via LSTM decoder. Later, Zhang et al. [25] estimated the number of individuals in dense crowds based on Multi-column CNN architecture (MCNN), three columns with filters of different kernel size were used to adapt to different size of people heads, and a 1×1 convolutional layer fused the three columns. However, they pay more attention to make the network wider rather than deeper, which results in limited scale receptive field for tackling large scale crowd density levels.

Switching-CNN [17] built the framework on [25] and added a switching architecture as a switching architecture and preclassifier to decide which one of the three CNN regressors corresponding to the input patch. Contextual Pyramid CNN (CP-CNN) [20] achieved lower count errors by estimating contexts at various levels, they split the dataset into 5 classes by density levels and fused global and local contexts. In this hybrid CP-CNN, density levels of the whole image are used as global contextual knowledge and extra labels and classifiers are needed. Both Switching-CNN and CP-CNN adopt 2-stage framework: classification stage and regression stage, rather than end-to-end framework. Therefore, It makes the training process more complicated and difficult.

Recently, Shen et al. [19] adopted "PatchGAN" [7] as discriminator to improve the quality of output density maps, combined with L2 loss function.

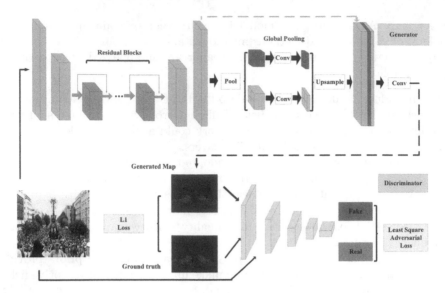

Fig. 2. Overview of our proposed SRFGAN. The feature maps of the last conventional layer pass through the global pyramid pooling module to get the image-level priors, which are then concatenated with the original ones and fed into the final convolutional layer to generate the predicted density map. The whole framework is optimized by L1 loss and least square adversarial loss.

Multi-scale information was processed by the parent-patch network and the child-patch network. However, the structure of generator limit the size of the input image, collaborative learning between parent network and child network makes the training process more complicated and time-consuming.

3   Proposed Method

The core idea of our framework is to extract multi-scale features via residual-based CNN model in generator part because of its powerful multi-column-style structure [22]. In addition, we apply the global pooling technique to capture global contextual information. The adversarial architecture is adopted with deeper receptive field which is helpful both in generating more delicate density maps and converging faster. In this part, we introduce our SRFGAN framework and make a full discussion.

3.1   SRFGAN Framework

As shown in Fig. 2, our framework consists of two full convolutional network: generator G and discriminator D. For G, the input and output are respectively the crowd image and generated density map. For D, the input is a pair of crowd image and generated/ground truth density map.

Based on the framework proposed by [8], our generator G first uses two stride-2 convolutional layers to downsample the input image. Then 9 residual blocks [5] are applied, followed by two deconvolution layers to decode and upsample. After we get the feature maps of the last conventional layer, global average pooling pyramid then extract effective global contextual priors for our framework. Finally the priors are concatenated with the original feature maps and pass through the last conventional layer to get the final output. The detailed architecture parameters of generator are shown in Table 1.

Our discriminator D uses a PatchGAN structure introduced by [7], which is composed of 4 downsampling layers and one extra convolutional layer, illustrated in Fig. 2. Each pixel in the output of D is corresponding to $N \times N$ patch of the input, where N is the receptive field of D, set as 70 in this paper.

3.2   Residual Structure for Crowd Counting

Residual connections proposed by He *et al.* [5] use a skip connection between the two conventional layers to train very deep networks. Further study [22] points out that residual networks can be seen as a collection of paths of different lengths. Since network with different depths has different receptive field, the residual structure helps to gather features at different scales corresponding to different size of people in the crowd image. It is a more efficient way to capture multi-scale information of the crowd than previous works. We use the same design of residual blocks as [8,9], each residual block consists of two convolutional layers and one skip connection from the head to the end.

Table 1. Network architectures of the generator. Layers 4–12 are corresponding to 9 residual blocks.

Layer	G	Layer	G	Layer	G
1	Conv7-64-1	4–12	Conv3-256-1	14	Decv3-64-1/2
2	Conv3-128-2		Conv3-256-1	15	Conv1-16-1
3	Conv3-256-2	13	Decv3-128-1/2	16	Decv7-3-1

3.3   Image-Level Prior

Global average pooling has been commonly used in image classification tasks [5, 21]. Recent works [3,13,26] show it's effective in semantic image segmentation. Since there is strong response in the head area of high-level feature maps, global average pooling will help to capture global contextual information including density level. Another benefit is that it cost few parameters and computations.

We first seperate the feature map of the output of the last residual blocks to $N \times N$ sub-regions, and form pooled feature, then we use 1×1 conventional layer to reduce the number of feature maps to 1/4 of original number, followed by upsampling layer using bilinear interpolation to keep the output same size as input feature map. Our pyramid pooling module is a two-level one with bin sizes of 1×1, 2×2, which means that the kernels cover the whole and half of the image.

(a)   (b)

Fig. 3. Different receptive fields corresponding to different CNN architectures. Red, green, blue, and yellow boxes respectively represent theoretical receptive field defined by Zhang *et al.* [24], MCNN [25], CP-CNN [20] and our proposed network structure. Clearly small receptive field is not large enough to capture global context and distinguish background from crowds. (Color figure online)

3.4 Comparison on Receptive Field

Previous works [17,25] pay more attention to make the receptive field adaptive to head/human size, causing bad performance in complex background. As illustrated in Fig. 3, small receptive field makes it difficult to make a clear distinction between the crowd and dark background which has some similarities with crowd. Compared with previous works, our generator has larger receptive field, hence it could capture more global contextual information.

However, although the receptive field of our network can be up to 157×157, for a 1024×1024 image with no cropping or resizing, it's still not enough to avoid mistakes like counting the background as a crowd. As a result, we address the issue by introducing global average pooling as image-level prior representation as mentioned above.

3.5 Loss Function

Our objective combines both feature matching loss and adversarial loss. We choose L1 loss for our pixel matching loss rather than L2 loss used by most of previous works, since we find L1 loss can help to make the training process more stable and estimate the counts of crowds more accurately. Adversarial loss could make up for shortcomings of L1 loss that generate low quality density map. As mentioned in Sect. 1, "PatchGAN" [7] aims to model the high frequencies of the density map, which is corresponding to the extreme dense area in the image. The role of L1 distance is to restrict generated images close to the distribution of the ground truth. Otherwise when generator find a "shortcut" that could easily fooled the discriminator, it would be optimized in a wrong way.

Pixel Matching Loss. The pixel matching loss is L1 distance between generated density map from G and ground-truth density map. Given a $C \times W$ image, the pixel matching loss can be defined as

$$L_{l1} = \frac{1}{CW}||F(I) - F^{GT}(I)||_1 \tag{1}$$

where I is the input image; $F(I)$ represents estimated density map by the generator; $F^{GT}(I)$ represents ground truth density map.

Adversarial Loss. Conditional GANs aim to model the conditional distribution of target image via min-max game. Given the input crowd image as c_i and ground-truth density map as d_i, the objective function $L_{GAN}(G, D)$ is given by

$$L_{GAN}(G, D) = \mathbb{E}_{c \sim p_{data}(c,d)}[logD(c, d)] + \mathbb{E}_{c \sim p_{data}(c)}[log(1 - D(G(c), c))] \tag{2}$$

However, in some cases original GAN loss function may make training process unstable and difficult to converge [1]. We replace the negative log likelihood objective by a least square loss [14]. This loss can also help to generate higher quality results than original GAN loss. The new loss is defined as:

$$L_{LSGAN}(G, D) = \mathbb{E}_{c \sim p_{data}(c,d)}[(D(c, d) - 1)^2] + \mathbb{E}_{c \sim p_{data}(c)}[(1 - D(G(c), c))^2] \tag{3}$$

Our full objective combine both pixel matching loss and adversarial loss as:

$$G = argmin_G max_D L_{LSGAN}(G, D) + \lambda L_{l1}(G) \tag{4}$$

where λ is fixed at 10 for all experiments.

Such structure can focus on local patches and model high-frequency structure which traditional L2 and L1 loss fail to. For the crowd problem, crowd distribution is usually consistent and dense, appropriate size patch can provide more local contextual information and help to improve the quality of density map.

4   Experiments

We evaluate our approach on two public datasets [6, 25]. In this section, we introduce our implementation details, ablation study results on ShanghaiTech dataset Part_A [25] and comparisons with state-of-the-art methods in all datasets. The implementation of our model is based on the Pytorch framework.

4.1   Evaluation Metric

We evaluate our method against the state-of-the-art crowd counting methods with Mean Absolute Error (MAE) and Mean Squared Error (MSE) following previous work, which are defined as follows:

$$MAE = \frac{1}{N} \sum_{i=1}^{N} |C_i - C_i^{GT}| \tag{5}$$

$$MSE = \sqrt{\frac{1}{N} \sum_{i=1}^{N} |C_i - C_i^{GT}|^2} \tag{6}$$

where N is the number of test images; C_i represents the estimated count which is the sum of the density map pixels generated by generator and C_i^{GT} represents the ground truth count.

4.2   Implementation Details

Data Augmentation. The training dataset is augmented by cropping and flipping randomly. For datasets of both gray and colored images, we make the input image grayscale randomly at a low rate to increase the diversity of datasets.

Training Procedures. Global average pooling used in generative models might hurt convergence speed [15], so we first pretrain the model without global priors information at the learning rate of 0.0001. Then we modify the last conventional layer of the generator to concatenate feature maps with the global priors. Finally we fine-tune all the parameters at the learning rate of 0.00002. We do not add any noise like dropout as the condition of the generator since the task is to generate specific density map rather than a diversity of images. We set 150 epoches for pretraining and 50 epoches for fine-tuning. Adam optimizer is applied to train the whole framework.

Density Map Generation. There are two major configurations for generating density maps. The one uses fixed Gaussian kernels [10], while the other uses geometry-adaptive kernels to make the spread parameter in the Gaussian kernel base on the size of each person's head in the image [25]. For datasets having great variation in head's size, we use geometry-adaptive kernels with the same configuration as [25]. Fixed Gaussian kernel is adopted for datasets with a relatively fixed perspective.

4.3   Ablation Study

To evaluate SRFGAN, we conduct experiments on ShanghaiTech Part_A dataset [25] which is a challenging but representative dataset, to show the effect of receptive field, adversarial loss and global priors.

Table 2. Ablation study on ShanghaiTech dataset.

Settings	Filter size			Global prior		Loss function			
	3×3	5×5	7×7	w/o	w/	L2	L2+GAN	L1	L1+GAN
MAE	80.0	74.5	**71.3**	73.1	**71.3**	94.0	97.1	100.8	**71.3**
MSE	140.9	133.5	**126.9**	131.2	**126.9**	154.4	159.2	178.0	**126.9**

Effect of Receptive Field. We carry experiments to adjust receptive field size by modifying only the first and the last convolutional filter size of the generator. The larger filter size represents the larger receptive field size. Seen from the comparison shown in the first column of Table 2, there is a close relation between receptive field size and network performance.

Effect of Global Priors. An example is shown the effect of global priors in Fig. 4. It could be seen that the image-level contextual information extracted by pyramid pooling module is a simple but valuable prior to reduce errors when meeting with complicated background, thus improves the performance as shown in the second column Table 2.

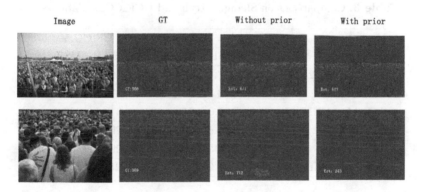

Fig. 4. Effect of global priors. The priors help to avoid the confusion of crowd-style background.

Comparison of Loss Function. We compare our combined loss with the traditional Euclidean loss, and verify the validity of our proposed joint loss. The result is presented in the third column of Table 2. The joint adversarial loss yields the best performance and outperform the single L2 loss baseline. In addition, L1 loss is less sensitive to outliers than the L2 loss and hence more robust in the training process, which is of great importance to GANs for their training and optimization challenges, also confirmed by the comparison results.

4.4   Evaluation and Comparison

ShanghaiTech. ShanghaiTech dataset is created by [25], consisting of two parts: Part_A including 482 images of different resolution and high-density which randomly crawled from the Internet, and Part_B including 716 images of sparse crowd scenes taken from the busy streets in Shanghai. We use geometry-adaptive kernels for Part_A dataset and fixed Gaussian kernel with variance $\sigma = 15$ for Part_B dataset. We compare our method with previous state-of-art methods and present our results in Table 3. The proposed method achieves superior performance than previous works especially in dataset Part_B, of which the MAE is put down to 8.7 significantly. It illustrates the effectiveness and feasibility of our algorithm in surveillance videos.

UCF_CC_50. The UCF_CC_50 dataset [6] is a quite challenging dataset including 50 images from the internet with large variation on the number of individuals per frame. The head counts range from 94 to 4543. Limited number of frames also increase the difficulty. We perform 5-fold cross-validation to keep same as previous works. As shown in Table 3, our proposed method still has good performance in extreme crowd scenes.

Table 3. Comparisons on ShanghaiTech and UCF_CC_50 datasets.

Method	Part_A		Part_B		UCF_CC_50	
	MAE	MSE	MAE	MSE	MAE	MSE
Zhang *et al.* [24]	181.8	277.7	32.0	49.8	467.0	498.5
MCNN [25]	126.5	173.5	23.8	33.1	377.6	509.1
Switching-CNN [17]	90.4	135.0	21.6	33.4	318.1	439.2
CP-CNN [20]	73.6	106.4	20.1	30.1	295.8	**320.9**
ACSCP [19]	75.7	**102.7**	17.2	27.4	291.0	404.6
SRFGAN (ours)	**71.3**	126.9	**8.7**	**13.5**	**280.8**	350.2

5   Conclusions

In this paper, we propose a novel end-to-end deep generative adversarial framework with scalable receptive field. We use residual connections to capture multiscale features and adversarial loss to generate higher quality density maps. In order to capture global contextual information, we use global average pooling pyramid module as the image-level prior extractor. The proposed method can adapt to crowds of different scales and perspectives more efficiently. Extensive experiments show that our framework could improve the performance remarkably in major datasets.

Acknowledgements. This work was supported in part by National Natural Science Foundation of China (NSFC, Grant No. 61771303 and 61671289), Science and Technology Commission of Shanghai Municipality (STCSM, Grant Nos. 17DZ1205602, 18DZ1200-102, 18DZ2270700), SJTUYitu/Thinkforce Joint laboratory for visual computing and application, and National Engineering Laboratory for Public Safety Risk Perception and Control by Big Data (PSRPC).

References

1. Arjovsky, M., Chintala, S., Bottou, L.: Wasserstein GAN. arXiv preprint arXiv:1701.07875 (2017)
2. Chan, A.B., Vasconcelos, N.: Bayesian Poisson regression for crowd counting. In: 2009 IEEE 12th International Conference on Computer Vision, pp. 545–551. IEEE (2009)
3. Chen, L.C., Papandreou, G., Schroff, F., Adam, H.: Rethinking atrous convolution for semantic image segmentation. arXiv preprint arXiv:1706.05587 (2017)
4. Goodfellow, I., et al.: Generative adversarial nets. In: Advances in Neural Information Processing Systems, pp. 2672–2680 (2014)
5. He, K., Zhang, X., Ren, S., Sun, J.: Deep residual learning for image recognition. In: Proceedings of the IEEE Conference on Computer Vision and Pattern Recognition, pp. 770–778 (2016)
6. Idrees, H., Saleemi, I., Seibert, C., Shah, M.: Multi-source multi-scale counting in extremely dense crowd images. In: 2013 IEEE Conference on Computer Vision and Pattern Recognition (CVPR), pp. 2547–2554. IEEE (2013)
7. Isola, P., Zhu, J.Y., Zhou, T., Efros, A.A.: Image-to-image translation with conditional adversarial networks. In: CVPR (2017)
8. Johnson, J., Alahi, A., Fei-Fei, L.: Perceptual losses for real-time style transfer and super-resolution. In: Leibe, B., Matas, J., Sebe, N., Welling, M. (eds.) ECCV 2016. LNCS, vol. 9906, pp. 694–711. Springer, Cham (2016). https://doi.org/10.1007/978-3-319-46475-6_43
9. Ledig, C., et al.: Photo-realistic single image super-resolution using a generative adversarial network. arXiv preprint (2016)
10. Lempitsky, V., Zisserman, A.: Learning to count objects in images. In: Advances in Neural Information Processing Systems, pp. 1324–1332 (2010)
11. Li, Y., Zhang, X., Chen, D.: CSRNet: dilated convolutional neural networks for understanding the highly congested scenes. In: Proceedings of the IEEE Conference on Computer Vision and Pattern Recognition, pp. 1091–1100 (2018)
12. Lin, Z., Davis, L.S.: Shape-based human detection and segmentation via hierarchical part-template matching. IEEE Trans. Pattern Anal. Mach. Intell. **32**(4), 604–618 (2010)
13. Liu, W., Rabinovich, A., Berg, A.C.: ParseNet: looking wider to see better. arXiv preprint arXiv:1506.04579 (2015)
14. Mao, X., Li, Q., Xie, H., Lau, R.Y., Wang, Z., Smolley, S.P.: Least squares generative adversarial networks. In: 2017 IEEE International Conference on Computer Vision (ICCV), pp. 2813–2821. IEEE (2017)
15. Radford, A., Metz, L., Chintala, S.: Unsupervised representation learning with deep convolutional generative adversarial networks. arXiv preprint arXiv:1511.06434 (2015)

16. Ryan, D., Denman, S., Fookes, C., Sridharan, S.: Crowd counting using multiple local features. In: Digital Image Computing: Techniques and Applications, DICTA 2009, pp. 81–88. IEEE (2009)
17. Sam, D.B., Surya, S., Babu, R.V.: Switching convolutional neural network for crowd counting. In: Proceedings of the IEEE Conference on Computer Vision and Pattern Recognition, vol. 1, p. 6 (2017)
18. Shang, C., Ai, H., Bai, B.: End-to-end crowd counting via joint learning local and global count. In: 2016 IEEE International Conference on Image Processing (ICIP), pp. 1215–1219. IEEE (2016)
19. Shen, Z., Xu, Y., Ni, B., Wang, M., Hu, J., Yang, X.: Crowd counting via adversarial cross-scale consistency pursuit. In: Proceedings of the IEEE Conference on Computer Vision and Pattern Recognition, pp. 5245–5254 (2018)
20. Sindagi, V.A., Patel, V.M.: Generating high-quality crowd density maps using contextual pyramid cnns. In: 2017 IEEE International Conference on Computer Vision (ICCV), pp. 1879–1888. IEEE (2017)
21. Szegedy, C., et al.: Going deeper with convolutions. In: CVPR (2015)
22. Veit, A., Wilber, M.J., Belongie, S.: Residual networks behave like ensembles of relatively shallow networks. In: Advances in Neural Information Processing Systems, pp. 550–558 (2016)
23. Wang, M., Wang, X.: Automatic adaptation of a generic pedestrian detector to a specific traffic scene. In: 2011 IEEE Conference on Computer Vision and Pattern Recognition (CVPR), pp. 3401–3408. IEEE (2011)
24. Zhang, C., Li, H., Wang, X., Yang, X.: Cross-scene crowd counting via deep convolutional neural networks. In: 2015 IEEE Conference on Computer Vision and Pattern Recognition (CVPR), pp. 833–841. IEEE (2015)
25. Zhang, Y., Zhou, D., Chen, S., Gao, S., Ma, Y.: Single-image crowd counting via multi-column convolutional neural network. In: Proceedings of the IEEE Conference on Computer Vision and Pattern Recognition, pp. 589–597 (2016)
26. Zhao, H., Shi, J., Qi, X., Wang, X., Jia, J.: Pyramid scene parsing network. In: IEEE Conference on Computer Vision and Pattern Recognition (CVPR), pp. 2881–2890 (2017)

Lightweight Video Object Segmentation Based on ConvGRU

Rui Yao[1]([✉]), Yikun Zhang[2], Cunyuan Gao[1], Yong Zhou[1], Jiaqi Zhao[1], and Lina Liang[1]

[1] School of Computer Science and Technology,
China University of Mining and Technology, Xuzhou 221116, China
ruiyao@cumt.edu.cn
[2] School of Computer Science and Engineering,
Southeast University, Nanjing 211189, China

Abstract. As one of the key tasks of video processing, video object segmentation technology is the foundation of high-level computer vision application. The spatio-temporal context information in the video is of great significance for video object segmentation. Existing algorithms usually introduce spatio-temporal context information with pre-trained models such as optical flow for segmentation, which will result in sub-optimal solution and huge computational resource consumption. To address the above problem, this paper proposes an end-to-end lightweight video object segmentation model based on ConvGRU. A convolutional neural network is used to extract the visual features of each frame, and recursive neural network is used to extract the spatio-temporal context information of the whole video. The ConvGRU is used to achieve the deep fusion of visual features and spatial-temporal context information. The MobileNet-based lightweight algorithm can meet the demand for practical application and solve the problem of high consumption for computing resources. Experiments on DAVIS2016 dataset show that our method is competitive with similar state-of-the-art methods.

Keywords: Video object segmentation · Spatio-temporal context · Lightweight · ConvGRU

1 Introduction

Video object Segmentation (VOS) is essentially a pixel-level classification task. As one of the key tasks of computer vision, video object segmentation has many applications, such as video editing, video surveillance, video abstraction, video retrieval, video semantics and human interaction understanding [1, 2]. The goal of VOS is to distinguish the object of interest from background in the video sequences at the pixel level.

Previous studies are largely limited by the lack of data sets for video object segmentation. The performance of video object segmentation improves significantly after the benchmark data set DAVIS (Densely Annotated Video Segmentation) [3] is available. Existing VOS algorithms can be divided into two categories based on

© Springer Nature Switzerland AG 2019
Z. Lin et al. (Eds.): PRCV 2019, LNCS 11858, pp. 441–452, 2019.
https://doi.org/10.1007/978-3-030-31723-2_37

whether or not utilizing spatio-temporal context information: VOS without spatio-temporal context information and VOS with spatio-temporal context information.

The general practice of VOS without spatio-temporal context information is to extract rough appearance features of the object by training a convolutional neural network (CNN) model and then achieve satisfactory segmentation mask by filtering or fine-tuning the extracted appearance features through some other constraints. OSVOS (One-Shot Video Object Segmentation) [4] is a representative algorithm. First, OSVOS differentiates general foreground objects by offline training a foreground-background segmentation network. Then, during testing, the first frame data is used to fine-tune the network so that it quickly focuses on a specific object. Caelles [5] et al. then further introduce semantic prior knowledge to guide segmentation to make up for the lack of temporal information, and achieve better results. Yang [6] et al. reduce the online fine-tuning time by 70 times by second meta neural network named modulator to adjust the middle layer of appearance network. These algorithms can achieve satisfactory performance through some prior constraints. However, because the vital spatio-temporal context information is ignored, when the appearance and position of the object in video change too much, the information from the first frame is not enough to complete the segmentation of the whole video.

Existing VOS methods with spatio-temporal context information generally rely on the pre-trained model such as optical flow or motion segmentation to achieve the tracking of pixels or super-pixels in temporal dimension and extract the spatio-temporal context information. Then the features are utilized to guide the segmentation of the whole video. MaskTrack segment object with the temporal information from adjacent video frames. In [7], Perazzi et al. also proposes the variant of MaskTrack, which significantly improves the precision of segmentation with optical flow. Li [8] et al. use optical flow technology in motion prediction in order to solve the problem that traditional segmentation algorithm has drifted and cannot deal with large scale motion, and prevent missing object through adaptive object re-recognition. Wang [9] proposed an unsupervised video segmentation method based on the super trajectory representation. The long-term motion information, local spatio-temporal information and the diversity and compactness of video captured by the super trajectory are very valuable for object segmentation. Many studies have noticed the application of spatio-temporal context information in VOS, but on the whole, these methods are not mature enough. Due to the dependence on other pre-trained models, the captured spatio-temporal context features are sub-optimal, and the computation is complex.

To address the above problem, this paper proposes a lightweight model based on ConvGRU to achieve end-to-end video object segmentation. The main contributions of this paper are as follows: (i) We suggest a lightweight model based on MobileNet to extract visual features to save computing resources and meet practical application needs. (ii) The video object segmentation method based on ConvGRU perfectly fuses visual features and spatio-temporal context information into a framework, improving the segmentation accuracy. (iii) The end-to-end segmentation method solves the problem of suboptimal solution.

2 Related Work

2.1 Convolutional Gated Recurrent Unit

The traditional fully connected recurrent neural network (RNN) [10] uses the fully connected layer in state transitions. However, in these transitions, the spatial information is not encoded, so there are certain limitations in the processing of spatio-temporal data. Convolutional neural network (CNN) is not well adapted to sequence data, and the traditional recurrent neural network lacks competitive image description ability. Shi [11] et al. proposed a convolutional recurrent neural network for precipitation prediction, which well combines the convolutional neural network and the traditional neural network.

The convolutional recurrent neural network, especially ConvGRU, perfectly combines the advantages of RNN and CNN. Compared with the traditional recurrent neural network, ConvGRU expands the input and output, reset and update gate, hidden state to a three-dimensional tensor, and the latter two dimensions are the spatial information (row and column). The updated formula of ConvGRU is as follows:

$$
\begin{aligned}
z_t &= sigmoid(X_t * W_{xz} + H_{t-1} * W_{hz} + b_z) \\
r_t &= sigmoid(X_t * W_{xr} + H_{t-1} * W_{hr} + b_r) \\
\hat{H}_t &= \tanh(X_t * W_{x\hat{h}} + r_t H_{t-1} * W_{h\hat{h}} + b_{\hat{h}}), \\
H_t &= (1 - z_t)H_{t-1} + z_t \hat{H}_t
\end{aligned}
\tag{1}
$$

where "$*$" represents the convolution operation.

2.2 MobileNet

MobileNet is a convolutional neural network framework for mobile vision applications proposed in [12]. The core idea of MobileNet is depthwise separable convolution, which is a kind of factorized convolution. In MobileNet, a standard convolution is replaced by a depthwise convolution and a pointwise convolution (1×1 convolution). The depthwise convolution filters on each channel separately without increasing the number of channels. The pointwise convolution combines the output of the depthwise convolution through 1×1 convolution, and it can expand the channels.

As shown in Fig. 1, given the input feature maps F with the size of $D_F \times D_F \times M$, the output feature maps G with the size of $D_F \times D_F \times N$ and the kernels with the size of $D_K \times D_K$, the computational cost of a standard convolution is:

$$
D_K \cdot D_K \cdot M \cdot N \cdot D_F \cdot D_F,
\tag{2}
$$

and the depthwise separable convolution cost is:

$$
D_K \cdot D_K \cdot M \cdot D_F \cdot D_F + M \cdot N \cdot D_F \cdot D_F.
\tag{3}
$$

The ratio of (3) to (2) is:

$$\frac{D_K \cdot D_K \cdot M \cdot D_F \cdot D_F + M \cdot N \cdot D_F \cdot D_F}{D_K \cdot D_K \cdot M \cdot N \cdot D_F \cdot D_F} = \frac{1}{N} + \frac{1}{D_K^2}. \qquad (4)$$

It can be seen that depthwise separable convolution has the effect of drastically reducing computation and model size from formula (4).

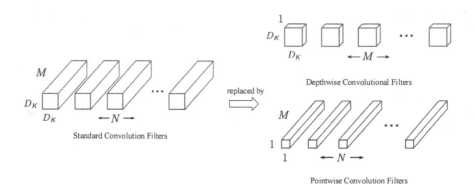

Fig. 1. Comparison between the standard convolution and depthwise separable convolution.

3 Method

3.1 Problem Formulation

After introducing spatio-temporal context information, video object segmentation can be formulated as a sequence-to-sequence problem. Given the video sequences $\{x_0, x_1, \ldots, x_{T-1}\}$, the goal of VOS is looking for a sequence $\{\hat{y}_1, \hat{y}_2, \ldots, \hat{y}_{T-1}\}$ that approximates ground-truth sequence $\{y_1, y_2, \ldots, y_{T-1}\}$ as closely as possible. Then the video object segmentation task is formulated as follow:

$$\hat{y}_t = \arg\max_{\forall \bar{y}_t} \mathbb{P}(\bar{y}_t \mid x_0, x_1, \ldots, x_t, y_0), \qquad (5)$$

where $x_t \in \mathbb{R}^{H \times W \times 3}$ is the RGB image of the t video frame, $y_t \in \mathbb{R}^{H \times W}$ is the corresponding binary ground-truth.

3.2 Network Architecture

The end-to-end video object segmentation model proposed is shown in the Fig. 2. We adopt the framework of "Encoder-Decoder" to deal with the video object segmentation problem of "sequence to sequence". The proposed model borrows from the framework in [13], what is different from it is that we pursue a lightweight model. Firstly, in the selection of convolutional recurrent neural network, we suggest ConvGRU with almost the same performance but fewer parameters and less computational resources instead of

ConvLSTM. Secondly, the VGG16 [14] model is used for both the initialization network and the encoder and decoder network in [13], while we utilize convolutional layers based on MobileNet instead. Our initialization network has only four down-sampling layers with channels are 64, 128, 256 and 512 respectively. In the choose of encoder network, we adopt the simplified lightweight model based on MobileNet, as shown in Fig. 3. In order to better extract image features, the structure and channel are adjusted to a certain degree. The decoder is a five-layers network with channels are 512, 256, 128, 64 and 1 respectively. The first four are up-sample layers with 3×3 kernels, followed by a convolution layer with 1×1 kernel suitable for the pixel-level classification task. And assign a sigmoid activation function for the output of decoder network.

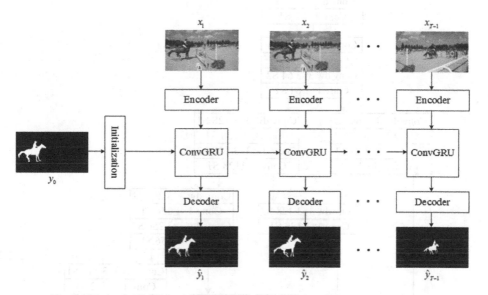

Fig. 2. End-to-end video object segmentation framework based on ConvGRU.

The encoder network based on MobileNet is shown in Fig. 3. First, the final pooling layers and the fully connected layers are removed. Skip connections are suggested to extract the different levels of information from different stages. Then the feature maps are fused linearly and the final binary segmentation mask is obtained by the sigmoid function. As a lightweight model, MobileNet reduces the parameter scale to 4.2M when the input image is $224 \times 224 \times 3$, compared with the 138 M parameters of VGG16. The lightweight models such as MobileNet [15], SqueezeNet [16], CondenseNet [17], ShuffleNet [18, 19], IGCV [20] and so on can effectively reduce the consumption of training resource and time.

3.3 Training Details

Data Augment. As the end-to-end training requires a large scale of data for fitting, the DAVIS2016 dataset is augmented by the combination of mirroring and scaling. As shown in the Fig. 4, the dataset is expanded to 6 times of the original dataset.

The video sequences of DAVIS2016 varies from 25 to 104 frames, so there's a huge difference in length. In order to better fit the end-to-end segmentation model, in

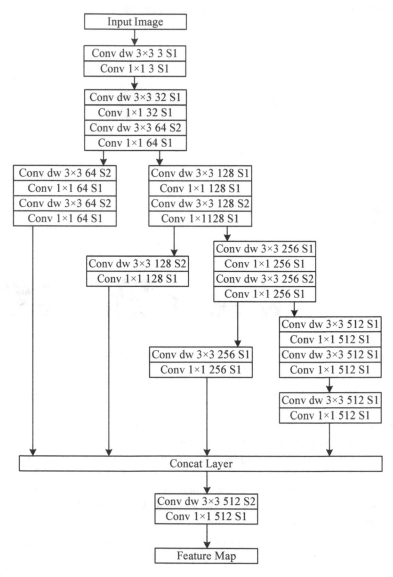

Fig. 3. The encoder network based on MobileNet.

addition to the technique of data augment, each video sequence is divided into multiple groups with 25 frames each group in experiment, and the last group is completed forward when it is less than 25 frames. Because the length of video sequences in DAVIS2016 varies greatly, this trick is more conducive to the model convergence during end-to-end training than the zero padding. The proposed algorithm takes 25 frames as a fixed processing length for object segmentation until the whole video is processed.

Offline and Online Training. We adopt two stages with offline and online for training. Offline training learns the general end-to-end foreground and background segmentation with spatio-temporal context information. Online training enables the convolutional network to focus on a specific object appearance. The ConvGRU parameters are fixed during online training, as the spatio-temporal information is independent of the object's appearance.

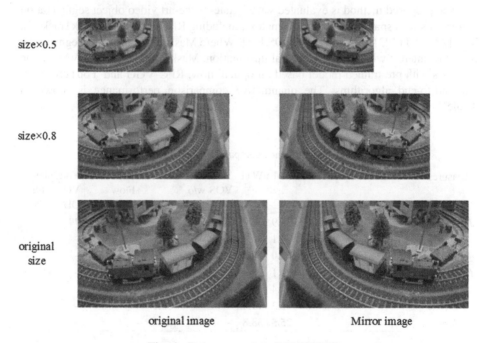

Fig. 4. Data augment on DAVIS2016.

The DAVIS2016 training set is used for offline training, and the initial learning rate is set at 0.01 and will decay by 0.02 per 500 steps. Adam optimizer is used, and each video sequence in the training set is iterated for 500 times. During online training, the data of the first frame in the test set is used to fine-tune the convolutional neural network layers of the initialization, encoder and decoder to focus on the object category of the current video sequence. The first frame data will be iterated for 100 times and ConvGRU parameters are not updated during online training.

4 Experiment

Our experiment is conducted on the most popular video object segmentation dataset DAVIS2016 [3]. The DAVIS dataset is a special dataset for video object segmentation. Its design takes into account the data amount and quality, experimental validation, object presence, unconstrained video challenges and many other factors. There are 50 sequences (30 train sequences and 20 test sequences) and 3,455 annotated frames in total, all of which were obtained at 24fps and full HD 1080p resolution. Considering the problem of computational resources, video is compressed to 480p in experiment.

As for the evaluation protocol, we adopt the three measurements suggested in [3] to evaluate the pixel-wise object segmentation algorithm. Metrics are (i) region similarity J, which is suggested to measure similarity in region between segmentation mask M and the ground-truth G; (ii) contour precision F is used to calculate accuracy based on contour; (iii) temporal stability T is utilized to evaluate the turbulence and inaccuracy of the contours.

The proposed method is evaluated with 5 state-of-the-art video object segmentation algorithms with spatio-temporal information, including RFCVGG [21], MaskTrack [7], VM [22], WTI [23] and YouTube-VOS [13]. Where MaskTrack and WTI segment the object of interest with weakly temporal information. MaskTrack+Flow and VM are the methods with pre-trained model based on optical flow. RFC-VGG and YouTube-VOS are end-to-end algorithms. The quantitative comparison performance is shown in Table 1.

Table 1. Performance comparison on DAVIS2016.

Measures		RFCVGG	MaskTrack	VM	WTI	YouTube-VOS w/o OL	Ours	MaskTrack +Flow	YouTube-VOS with OL
J	Mean ↑	69.84	74.8	75.9	76.0	76.5	77.8	78.4	**79.1**
	Recall ↑	–	–	89.1	89.2	–	**93.7**	–	–
	Decay ↓	–	–	**0.0**	14.8	–	11.6	–	–
F	Mean ↑	–	–	72.1	**78.7**	–	**78.7**	–	–
	Recall ↑	–	–	83.4	**92.5**	–	89.5	–	–
	Decay ↓	–	–	1.3	17.4	–	13.7	–	–
T	Mean ↓	–	–	**25.5**	38.8	–	29.0	–	–

The proposed method is superior to most of the above algorithms and slightly inferior to MaskTrack+Flow and YouTube-VOS with online learning. Due to the limitation of hardware resources, RFCVGG compressed video frame to 240×360 during training, resulting in the decline of segmentation accuracy. VM is a two-stream video object segmentation algorithm, in which the motion prediction network still uses optical flow technology, but due to the lack of large-scale dataset, the segmentation performance is not satisfactory despite huge computational resource consumption. MaskTrack and WTI both the method employing weakly temporal features between successive video frames. The weakly temporal information is not enough to achieve high precision segmentation. However, after introducing the optical flow, the variant of MaskTrack gain a higher score. YouTube-VOS is the best end-to-end video object segmentation method, which benefits from large-scale sparse annotated VOS dataset YouTube-VOS and huge neural network parameters. Our method achieves end-to-end video object segmentation in a lightweight way and gets competitive performance. Theoretically, the presented method can also gain higher scores through pre-trained models such as optical flow and more complex networks.

The visual comparison performance of the available methods is shown in Fig. 5. Compared with RFCVGG, VM and YouTube-VOS w/o OL, the method presented is more accurate in the region, especially when RFCVGG and VM method has a large area of missing and noise, our method can still accurately locate the object at pixel-level. Compared with YouTube-VOS with OL, our method can accurately locate the region, while its performance in details is not robust.

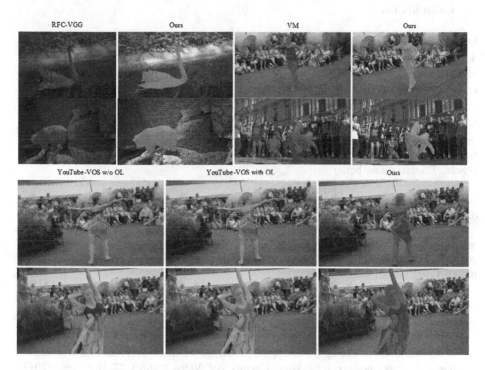

Fig. 5. Visualization comparison of different algorithms.

The proposed method can obviously improve the region similarity and temporal stability but has little effect on contour precision. In order to explore the deeper factor, we carefully observe the segmentation masks of each test sequence. Partial visualization performance is shown in Fig. 6. It can be found that with the introduction of spatio-temporal context information, our method can accurately locate object in region. In addition, the segmentation in consecutive frames is more coherently. However, our approach cannot deal with occlusion and handle details well.

Fig. 6. Typical performance on test sequences.

5 Conclusion

In this paper, we propose a video object segmentation method that combines the advantages of convolutional neural network and recursive neural network. The end-to-end segmentation model based on ConvGRU can deeply fuse the visual features and spatio-temporal context information from the whole video. Depthwise separable convolution from MobileNet is suggested to reduce the computation and model parameters. Experiments on benchmark dataset DAVIS2016 demonstrate the competitiveness of our algorithm. With the popularity of intelligent hardware, more visual applications will be activated on mobile terminals, and the lightweight model can meet the needs of practical applications better.

Acknowledgements. This work was supported in part by the National Natural Science Foundation of China under Grant 61772530, 61572505, U1610124, and 61806206, in part by the State's Key Project of Research and Development Plan of China under Grant 2016YFC0600900, in part by the Six Talent Peaks Project in Jiangsu Province under Grant 2018-XYDXX-044 and 2015-DZXX-010, in part by the Natural Science Foundation of Jiangsu Province under Grant BK20171192, BK20180639.

References

1. Wang, Z., Liu, S., Zhang, J., Chen, S., Guan, Q.: A spatio-temporal CRF for human interaction understanding. IEEE Trans. Circuits Syst. Video Technol. **27**, 1647–1660 (2017)
2. Wang, Z., et al.: Understanding human activities in videos: a joint action and interaction learning approach. Neurocomputing **321**, 216–226 (2018)
3. Perazzi, F., Pont-Tuset, J., McWilliams, B., Van Gool, L., Gross, M., Sorkine-Hornung, A.: A benchmark dataset and evaluation methodology for video object segmentation. In: 2016 IEEE Conference on Computer Vision and Pattern Recognition (CVPR), pp. 724–732 (2016)

4. Caelles, S., Maninis, K.K., Pont-Tuset, J., Leal-Taixe, L., Cremers, D., Van Gool, L.: One-shot video object segmentation. In: 30th IEEE Conference on Computer Vision and Pattern Recognition, pp. 5320–5329 (2017)
5. Caelles, S., Chen, Y., Pont-Tuset, J., Van Gool, L.: Semantically-guided video object segmentation. arXiv preprint arXiv:1704.01926 (2017)
6. Yang, L., Wang, Y., Xiong, X., Yang, J., Katsaggelos, A.K.: Efficient video object segmentation via network modulation. In: 31st IEEE/CVF Conference on Computer Vision and Pattern Recognition (CVPR), pp. 6499–6507 (2018)
7. Perazzi, F., Khoreva, A., Benenson, R., Schiele, B., Sorkine-Hornung, A.: Learning video object segmentation from static images. In: 30th IEEE/CVF Conference on Computer Vision and Pattern Recognition (CVPR), pp. 3491–3500 (2016)
8. Li, X., et al.: Video object segmentation with re-identification. arXiv preprint arXiv:1708.00197 (2017)
9. Wang, W., Shen, J., Porikli, F., Yang, R.: Semi-supervised video object segmentation with super-trajectories. IEEE Trans. Pattern Anal. Mach. Intell. **41**, 985–998 (2019)
10. Hopfield, J.J.: Neural networks and physical systems with emergent collective computational abilitieS. Proc. Natl. Acad. Sci. U.S.A. Biol. Sci. **79**, 2554–2558 (1982)
11. Shi, X., Chen, Z., Wang, H., Yeung, D.-Y., Wong, W., Woo, W.: Convolutional LSTM network: a machine learning approach for precipitation nowcasting. In: Advances in Neural Information Processing Systems 28 (Nips 2015) 28 (2015)
12. Howard, A.G., et al.: Mobilenets: efficient convolutional neural networks for mobile vision applications. arXiv preprint arXiv:1704.04861 (2017)
13. Xu, N., et al.: YouTube-VOS: sequence-to-sequence video object segmentation. In: Ferrari, V., Hebert, M., Sminchisescu, C., Weiss, Y. (eds.) ECCV 2018. LNCS, vol. 11209, pp. 603–619. Springer, Cham (2018). https://doi.org/10.1007/978-3-030-01228-1_36
14. Simonyan, K., Zisserman, A.: Very deep convolutional networks for large-scale image recognition. arXiv preprint arXiv:1409.1556 (2014)
15. Sandler, M., Howard, A., Zhu, M., Zhmoginov, A., Chen, L.-C.: MobileNetV2: inverted residuals and linear bottlenecks. In: 31st IEEE/CVF Conference on Computer Vision and Pattern Recognition (CVPR), pp. 4510–4520 (2018)
16. Iandola, F.N., Han, S., Moskewicz, M.W., Ashraf, K., Dally, W.J., Keutzer, K.: SqueezeNet: AlexNet-level accuracy with 50x fewer parameters and <0.5 MB model size. arXiv preprint arXiv:1602.07360 (2016)
17. Huang, G., Liu, S., van der Maaten, L., Weinberger, K.Q.: CondenseNet: an efficient DenseNet using learned group convolutions. In: 31st IEEE/CVF Conference on Computer Vision and Pattern Recognition (CVPR), pp. 2752–2761 (2018)
18. Ma, N., Zhang, X., Zheng, H.T., Sun, J.: ShuffleNet V2: practical guidelines for efficient CNN architecture design. In: Ferrari, V., Hebert, M., Sminchisescu, C., Weiss, Y. (eds.) ECCV 2018. LNCS, vol. 11218, pp. 122–138. Springer, Cham (2018). https://doi.org/10.1007/978-3-030-01264-9_8
19. Zhang, X., Zhou, X., Lin, M., Sun, J.: ShuffleNet: an extremely efficient convolutional neural network for mobile devices. In: Proceedings of the IEEE Conference on Computer Vision and Pattern Recognition, pp. 6848–6856 (2018)
20. Xie, G., Wang, J., Zhang, T., Lai, J., Hong, R., Qi, G.-J.: Interleaved structured sparse convolutional neural networks. In: Proceedings of the IEEE Conference on Computer Vision and Pattern Recognition, pp. 8847–8856 (2018)

21. Valipour, S., Siam, M., Jagersand, M., Ray, N.: Recurrent fully convolutional networks for video segmentation. In: 17th IEEE Winter Conference on Applications of Computer Vision (WACV), pp. 29–36 (2016)
22. Tokmakov, P., Inria, K.A., Schmid, C.: Learning video object segmentation with visual memory. In: 16th IEEE International Conference on Computer Vision (ICCV), pp. 4491–4500. (2017)
23. Zhang, Y., Yao, R., Jiang, Q., Zhang, C., Wang, S.: Video object segmentation with weakly temporal information. KSII Trans. Internet Inf. Syst. 13, 1434–1449 (2019)

Crowd Counting via Conditional Generative Adversarial Networks

Tao Xu[1,2], Yinong Duan[1,2], Jiahao Du[1,2], and Caihua Liu[1,2(✉)]

[1] Information Technology Base of Civil Aviation Administration of China,
Civil Aviation University of China, Tianjin, China
chliu@cauc.edu.cn
[2] College of Computer Science and Technology,
Civil Aviation University of China, Tianjin, China

Abstract. Most of current crowd counting algorithms use Euclidean loss to narrow the gap between density map and ground-truth, which leads to the low quality of density maps. In order to alleviate the above problems, we propose a crowd counting method based on conditional generative adversarial framework, which utilizes the game between generator and discriminator to achieve high quality conversion of crowd images to density maps. Specifically, CSRNet is designed as a generator, which uses the method of dilated convolution to extract the detailed information of images under the condition of adapting the scale variation. PatchGAN is designed as a discriminator to simulate high-frequency structures to further improve the quality of density maps. Benefiting from the joint optimization of adversarial loss and L2 loss, our framework can not only accurately capture the low-frequency informations, but also better model the high-frequency informations. We tested on two challenging public datasets (ShanghaiTech, UCF_CC_50) and achieved better performance, which demonstrates the effectiveness of the proposed method.

Keywords: Crowd counting · Conditional generative adversarial framework · High frequency structures

1 Introduction

With the widespread use of cameras and the growing demand for public safety, crowd analysis based on video content has become a hot research issue in the field of computer vision. It has broad application prospects in public security monitoring and early warning. As one of the most fundamental and important contents in crowd analysis research, crowd counting aims to estimate the total number of pedestrians in video or image scenes. Methods developed for crowd counting are also widely applicable in other fields, such as cell counting [1],

Supported by the Fundamental Research Funds for the Central Universities (No. 3122018C024), the Starting Research Fund from the Civil Aviation University of China (No. 2017QD16X), the Natural Science Foundation of Tianjin (No. 18JCYBJC85100).

vehicle counting [2], animal migration surveillance [3] and so on. However, due to the influence of illumination, heavy occlusions, perspective variations, human scale variations and other factors, crowd counting is still a challenging research topic.

Researchers have proposed a number of solutions to the problem of crowd counting. Benefiting from the success of deep learning in the field of computer vision, recent literatures are mostly based on deep learning methods. Some researchers [2,13,14] have achieved significant progress by overcoming crowd scale variations with multi-column architecture. Each column is designed to extract features at different scales in crowd images. More recently, dilated convolution based architecture [15] or growing CNN architecture [22] are proposed to improve the counting accuracy.

However, these CNN-based methods all have one drawback. Only pixel-wise Euclidean loss is used to optimize these models, which assumes each pixel is independent and result in image blur. In other words, the Euclidean loss may have defects in the high-frequency detail processing of the image, thus causing a decrease in the counting accuracy and a decrease in the quality of the generated density map. Each pixel value in the density map represents the crowd density at the corresponding location in the image, while also reflects the crowd distribution relationship. Therefore, it is helpful for crowd density estimation to generate the high-quality of density maps.

To address these issues, we propose a crowd density map generation method based on the conditional generative adversarial network, which contains an adversarial loss to alleviate the blurring effect caused by Euclidean losses. CSR-Net [15] as a generator to aggregate multi-scale contextual information and perform high quality translation from images to density maps. Motived by the achievement of image conversion work [16], we employ the PatchGAN to simulate high-frequency features, which further promotes image quality. The proposed framework can combine the advantages of the above two models. Besides, the joint optimization of the adversarial loss and the L2 loss enables our method to better model the high frequency information while accurately capturing the low frequency information. We conducted experiments on two challenging crowd datasets (ShanghaiTech [13], UCF_CC_50 [20]) and compared them with the most advanced work to verify the effectiveness of the proposed method. The rest of the paper is structured as follows. The second section reviews the work related to crowd counting. The third section introduces our model architecture while the fourth section conducts experiments and comparisons. In the fifth section, we conclude the article.

2   Related Work

Researchers have proposed a number of methods to solve the crowd counting problem. These methods can be divided into early traditional methods and CNN-based methods.

2.1   Early Traditional Methods

Early researches [4–6] considered crowd counting as detection problems. These methods used body and component detectors to lock pedestrians in the image for counting purposes. However, it is difficult for the detection method to play its role due to the serious occlusion and background clutter in the highly crowded scenes.

In order to adapt to high density crowd images, the researchers proposed regression-based approaches. The main idea is to learn the mapping relationship from the features of local image patches to the number of people in the region [7–9]. These methods can predict the number of people, but ignore the spatial information contained in the crowd image. Lempitsky et al. [1] proposed a method to learn the linear mapping between local image features and its object density maps. Pham et al. [10] observed the difficulty of learning ideal linear mapping, and used random forest regression to learn the nonlinear mapping instead of the linear one. However, the quality of low-level features extracted by manual is still a major limitation of regression-based methods.

2.2   CNN-Based Methods

In recent years, convolutional neural networks (CNN) becomes popular in the field of computer vision and shows good performance. Wang et al. [11] trained a classic Alexnet style CNN model to predict the number of people, but the model could not show the spatial distribution of the crowd. Zhang et al. [12] proposed a convolutional neural network alternately trained by the crowd density and the crowd count. Such switchable objective-learning helps improve the performance of both tasks. However, this method requires unobtainable perspective map during training and testing, which makes it limited in practical applications. To overcome the scale variations of the crowd image, Zhang et al. [13] proposed a multi-column architecture (MCNN), which contains three columns of convolution networks with different filter sizes to process crowd images of different scales, and then features from these columns are fused together by a 1×1 convolutional layer to regress density map. Inspired by MCNN, a Switching-CNN model is employed in [14], which firstly trains a classifier to intelligently select the most suitable feature extraction network for input images. The performance of this classifier directly affected the prediction effect of the model. To improve the quality of the density map, Li et al. [15] proposed CSRNet that combines a pre-trained VGG-16 [18] with dilated convolutional layers to extract more detailed image features. These CNN-based methods achieved significant results in crowd counting studies.

The above methods generally use L2 loss as a model optimization basis. They pay more attention to the universality of the network structure, but ignore the quality of the generated density map. It is well known that L2 loss tends to average multiple possible outcomes from the model, thus results in low quality and even blurred density maps. Actually, low quality density maps directly affect the accuracy of the counting task, and may adversely affect the deeper cognitive tasks that depend on them. Therefore, we propose a method based on the conditional generative adversarial framework, which focuses on optimizing the detailed information of the image and generating high quality density map.

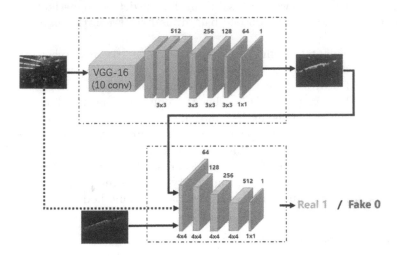

Fig. 1. The architecture of the proposed Conditional Generative Adversarial Networks.

3   Method

Figure 1 shows the architecture of our proposed conditional generative adversarial network, which is partly motivated by the recent success of image conversion task [16,17]. The current crowd counting works often extract image features and generate crowd density maps through the CNN model. To a certain extent, the crowd counting work can be understood as having similar goals to the image conversion task. Therefore, we realize the counting task by constructing conditional generative adversarial network. The game process between the generator and the discriminator causes the network to generate higher quality density maps.

3.1   Network Architecture

Following the similar idea in [14], VGG-16 is employed as the backbone of the generator because of its powerful feature extraction capabilities. More specific, we choose the first ten convolutional layers of VGG-16 (retaining three max pooling layers). The parameters of the corresponding layers are pre-trained by the ImageNet dataset [19].

Referring to the successful experience of the CSRNet [15], we added six dilated convolutional layers (dilation rate = 2) after the backbone of the generator. Each layer uses ReLU as activation function. Then a 1×1 convolutional layer is used to fuse the features and output the density maps. Dilated convolution expands the perceptual domain without increasing the number of parameters, allowing more rich context information to be integrated from a wider input view. Compared to schemes such as deconvolution, dilated convolution can extract more detailed features of the image and have a positive effect on our goal of generating high quality density maps.

Since the L2 loss encourages the averaging effect, which causes the blurring of the generated image. To improve the quality of density map by mitigating this phenomenon, we add a discriminator to train the network in an adversarial way. Inspired by the recent successful conditional generative adversarial network [16], we implement with PatchGAN as the discriminator of the framework. The discriminator contains five convolution layers while each layer (except for the last one) uses batch normalization and LeakyReLU as activation function. Its architecture and parameters are described as follows: C(64,4,2)-C(128,4,2)-C(256,4,2)-C(512,4,1)-C(1,4,1), where C represents the convolutional layer and the numbers in each bracket respectively represent the number of filters, filter size and stride. The discriminator's attention is limited to local areas, which makes it more focused on high-frequency information. Specifically, the input of discriminator is concatenated pairs of original images and (generated/ground-truth) density maps. After that, the discriminator will judge the authenticity of each $N \times N$ image block and provide the final output after averaging all results. The discriminator's judgment will encourage the generator to match the real distribution, which can mitigate blurring and generate high quality density maps.

3.2 Loss Function

The adversarial loss of our framework is defined as follows:

$$L_{cGAN} = E_{x,y \sim P_{data}(x,y)}[log D(x,y)] + E_{x \sim P_{data}(x)}[log(1 - D(x, G(x)))] \quad (1)$$

Where x represents the input image and y represents the generated density map. Generator G tries to minimize the function, while discriminator D tries to maximize the function, and the game relationship of the adversarial loss is reflected here. Note that our discriminator needs to observe the original image x for true and false judgment.

Due to the lack of direct punishment for the spatial structure of the image, the generator may ignore the difference of the input images and lead to a single output mode. Therefore, L2 loss is employed to limit the low frequency structure of the image. In this way, the generator's task is not only to trick the discriminator, but also to generate an output near the ground-truth at L2 level. The L2 loss is defined as follows:

$$L_2(G) = \frac{1}{n} \sum_{i=1}^{n} ||G(x_i) - y_i||_2^2 \quad (2)$$

Where n represents the number of training samples, x_i represents the input image, $G(x_i)$ represents the generated density map, and y_i represents the ground-truth corresponding to x_i.

Finally, the weighted combination of adversarial loss and L2 loss is used as the integrated loss. It is defined as follows:

$$L = \arg \min_{G} \max_{D} L_{cGAN}(G, D) + \lambda L_2(G) \tag{3}$$

Where λ is a hyper parameter to balance L_{cGAN} and L_2.

4   Experiments

4.1   Crowd Counting Datasets

We conducted experiments on two major crowd counting datasets, the Shang-haiTech dataset [13] and the UCF_CC_50 dataset [20].

ShanghaiTech. The ShanghaiTech dataset contains a total of 1198 annotated crowd images, which are divided into Part_A and Part_B. The Part_A section contains a total of 482 high-density crowd images from the Internet, which are divided into 300 training images and 182 test images. The Part_B section includes 716 streetscape images with low crowd density, which are divided into 400 train-ing images and 316 test images.

UCF_CC_50. The UCF_CC_50 dataset contains a total of 50 annotated crowd images, with a large number of people and scenes, ranging from 94 to 4543. Due to the small number of UCF_CC_50 dataset samples, we followed the criteria set out in [20] and evaluated our approach using the five-fold cross-validation approach.

4.2   Density Map for Training

The label given by the crowd datasets is the position of the center point of each person's head, so the position to density map conversion is required. We follow the method proposed in [13] to generate the ground-truth density map using the geometry-adaptive kernel. The method is well adapted to perspective distortion and head size variation.

4.3   Training Details

The output of the generated network is 1/8 of the input. Thus we choose bilinear interpolation with the factor of 8 for scaling so that the input and output have the same size. To augment training data, we crop several patches randomly from each image at different locations with 1/4 size of the original image.

We jointly train the overall network with a fixed learning rate of 1e−7, and optimized network parameters with the SGD (stochastic gradient descent) opti-mizer. Except for the pre-trained VGG-16 network layers, the other network layer parameters are Gaussian initialization with a standard deviation of 0.01. The implementation of our model is based on the Pytorch framework [21].

4.4 Evaluation Metrics

MAE (mean absolute error) and MSE (mean square error) are used as the evaluation of crowd counting. In contrast, MAE is used to measure model prediction accuracy, and MSE is used to evaluate model prediction robustness. MAE and MSE are specifically defined as follows:

$$\text{MAE} = \frac{1}{n} \sum_{i=1}^{n} |S_i - S_i^{GT}| \tag{4}$$

$$\text{MSE} = \sqrt{\frac{1}{n} \sum_{i=1}^{n} |S_i - S_i^{GT}|^2} \tag{5}$$

Where n is the number of training samples, S_i is the number of people calculated by the model prediction density map, and S_i^{GT} is the actual number of people in the image.

4.5 Results and Analysis

The proposed method is compared with several advanced works. Tables 1 and 2 show the comparison of ShanghaiTech Part_A and UCF_CC_50 datasets. We obtain the best MAE and comparable MSE among the other six recent works, which indicates that the proposed conditional generative adversarial framework can better model the details of high-density crowd images. Table 1 also shows that in ShanghaiTech Part_B, we get 2.1 lower MAE and 1.3 lower MSE than the state-of-the-art called CSRNet. Samples of the test cases can be found in Figs. 2 and 3. It is worth noting that our predicted density maps are closer to ground-truth in detail than CSRNet's with less blur and result in much lower errors.

Table 1. Comparisons on ShanghaiTech dataset [13].

Methods	Part_A		Part_B	
	MAE	MSE	MAE	MSE
Zhang et al. [12]	181.8	277.7	32.0	49.8
MCNN [13]	110.2	173.2	26.4	41.3
Switch-CNN [14]	90.4	135.0	21.6	33.4
IG-CNN [22]	72.5	118.2	13.6	21.1
ACSCP [23]	75.7	**102.7**	17.2	27.4
CSRNet [15]	68.2	115.0	10.6	16.0
Ours	**65.6**	103.7	**8.5**	**14.7**

Table 2. Comparisons on UCF_CC_50 dataset [20].

Methods	MAE	MSE
Zhang et al. [12]	467.0	498.5
MCNN [13]	377.6	509.1
Switch-CNN [14]	318.1	439.2
IG-CNN [22]	291.4	349.4
ACSCP [23]	291.0	404.6
CSRNet [15]	266.1	397.5
Ours	**214.1**	**308.8**

Fig. 2. Comparison of estimated density maps on ShanghaiTech. First column: input image; Second column: ground-truth density maps; Third column: estimated density maps by our method; Forth column: estimated density maps by CSRNet [15].

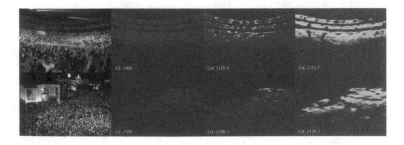

Fig. 3. Comparison of estimated density maps on UCF_CC_50. First column: input image; Second column: ground-truth density maps; Third column: estimated density maps by our method; Forth column: estimated density maps by CSRNet [15].

5   Conclusion

In this paper, we proposed a cGAN-based crowd counting method to perform high-quality translation of crowd images to density maps. We make full use of the game relationship between the generator and discriminator of GAN. Then the joint optimization of the adversarial loss and the L2 loss enables the proposed method to better model the low frequency and high frequency information of the image. We conduct evaluations on two challenging crowd public datasets. The results show that our proposed method performs better than or comparable to state-of-the-arts in terms of accuracy and robustness. We hope to further study the model construction and loss function settings in the future.

References

1. Lempitsky, V., Zisserman, A.: Learning to count objects in images. In: Advances in Neural Information Processing Systems, pp. 1324–1332 (2010)
2. Oñoro-Rubio, D., López-Sastre, R.J.: Towards perspective-free object counting with deep learning. In: Leibe, B., Matas, J., Sebe, N., Welling, M. (eds.) ECCV 2016. LNCS, vol. 9911, pp. 615–629. Springer, Cham (2016). https://doi.org/10.1007/978-3-319-46478-7_38
3. Arteta, C., Lempitsky, V., Zisserman, A.: Counting in the wild. In: Leibe, B., Matas, J., Sebe, N., Welling, M. (eds.) ECCV 2016. LNCS, vol. 9911, pp. 483–498. Springer, Cham (2016). https://doi.org/10.1007/978-3-319-46478-7_30
4. Topkaya, I.S., Erdogan, H., Porikli, F.: Counting people by clustering person detector outputs. In: Proceedings of the Advanced Video and Signal Based Surveillance, pp. 313–318 (2014)
5. Lin, Z., Davis, L.S.: Shape-based human detection and segmentation via hierarchical part-template matching. IEEE Trans. Pattern Anal. Mach. Intell. **32**(4), 604–618 (2010)
6. Wu, B., Nevatia, R.: Detection of multiple, partially occluded humans in a single image by Bayesian combination of edgelet part detectors. In: Proceedings of the International Conference on Computer Vision, vol. 1, pp. 90–97 (2005)
7. Chan, A.B., Vasconcelos, N.: Bayesian Poisson regression for crowd counting. In: Proceedings of the International Conference on Computer Vision, pp. 545–551 (2009)
8. Chen, K., Loy, C.C., Gong, S., Xiang, T.: Feature mining for localised crowd counting. In: British Machine Vision Conference, vol. 1, p. 3 (2012)
9. Ryan, D., Denman, S., Fookes, C., Sridharan, S.: Crowd counting using multiple local features. In: Digital Image Computing: Techniques and Applications, pp. 81–88 (2009)
10. Pham, V.Q., Kozakaya, T., Yamaguchi, O., Okada, R.: Count forest: co-voting uncertain number of targets using random forest for crowd density estimation. In: Proceedings of the International Conference on Computer Vision, pp. 3253–3261 (2015)
11. Wang, C., Zhang, H., Yang, L., Liu, S., Gao, X.: Deep people counting in extremely dense crowds. In: Proceedings of the ACM International Conference on Multimedia, pp. 1299–1302 (2015)

12. Zhang, C., Li, H., Wang, X., Yang, X.: Cross-scene crowd counting via deep convolutional neural networks. In: Proceedings of the Computer Vision and Pattern Recognition, pp. 833–841 (2015)
13. Zhang, Y., Zhou, D., Chen, S., Gao, S., Ma, Y.: Single-image crowd counting via multi-column convolutional neural network. In: Proceedings of the Computer Vision and Pattern Recognition, pp. 589–597 (2016)
14. Sam, D.B., Surya, S., Babu, R.V.: Switching convolutional neural network for crowd counting. In: Proceedings of the Computer Vision and Pattern Recognition, vol. 1, p. 6 (2017)
15. Li, Y., Zhang, X., Chen, D.: CSRNet: dilated convolutional neural networks for understanding the highly congested scenes. In: Proceedings of the Computer Vision and Pattern Recognition, pp. 1091–1100 (2018)
16. Isola, P., Zhu, J.Y., Zhou, T., Efros, A.A.: Image-to-image translation with conditional adversarial networks. In: Proceedings of the Computer Vision and Pattern Recognition, pp. 1125–1134 (2017)
17. Zhu, J.Y., Park, T., Isola, P., Efros, A.A.: Unpaired image-to-image translation using cycle-consistent adversarial networks. In: Proceedings of the International Conference on Computer Vision, pp. 2223–2232 (2017)
18. Simonyan, K., Zisserman, A.: Very deep convolutional networks for large-scale image recognition. arXiv preprint arXiv:1409.1556 (2014)
19. Deng, J., Dong, W., Socher, R., Li, L.J., Li, K., Li, F.F.: ImageNet: a large-scale hierarchical image database. In: Proceedings of the Computer Vision and Pattern Recognition, pp. 248–255 (2009)
20. Idrees, H., Saleemi, I., Seibert, C., Shah, M.: Multi-source multi-scale counting in extremely dense crowd images. In: Proceedings of the Computer Vision and Pattern Recognition, pp. 2547–2554 (2013)
21. Paszke, A., et al.: Automatic differentiation in pytorch. In: Neural Information Processing Systems Workshop (2017)
22. Sam, D.B., Sajjan, N.N., Babu, R.V.: Divide and grow: capturing huge diversity in crowd images with incrementally growing CNN. In: Proceedings of the Computer Vision and Pattern Recognition, pp. 3618–3626 (2018)
23. Shen, Z., Xu, Y., Ni, B., Wang, M., Hu, J., Yang, X.: Crowd counting via adversarial cross-scale consistency pursuit. In: Proceedings of the Computer Vision and Pattern Recognition, pp. 5245–5254 (2018)

Gemini Network for Temporal Action Localization

Hongru Li[1], Ying Wang[2], and Yuan Zhou[1]([✉])

[1] Tianjin University, Tianjin 300072, China
zhouyuan@tju.edu.cn
[2] Unit 61660 of PLA, Beijing 100020, China

Abstract. Temporal Action Localization in untrimmed videos is an important yet difficult task. It's important for accurate temporal action localization to model temporal structure. In this work, we propose a novel model, Gemini CNN, which can effectively model temporal structure via several separated CNNs. Our first contribution is the idea of modular design of temporal structure modeling. Temporal structure is divided into long-range temporal structure and short-range temporal structure. Two types of temporal structures are respectively modeled in two subnets. The other contribution is the idea of auxiliary supervision. We add classifiers at not only the end of our framework, but also intermediate layers. The loss of auxiliary classifiers increases the gradient signal that gets propagated back, and boosts our framework's performance. We achieve state-of-the-art performance for temporal action localization on two challenging temporal action localization datasets, THUMOS14 and ActivityNet.

Keywords: Action localization · Spatial-temporal feature · Video content analysis · Supervised learning

1 Introduction

Owing to the explosive growth of video data, video content analysis has attracted significant attention in both industry and academia in recent years. An important aspect of video content analysis is temporal action localization [6,10,14], which requires not only the determination of the category of video clips, but also identification of the temporal boundaries of the action instances in the untrimmed videos.

Temporal action localization can be regarded as a temporal version of object detection in an image, because the aim of both tasks is to determine the boundaries and categories of multiple instances, in time and space, respectively. Compared with object detection [2,11,20], temporal action localization requires modeling of not only spatial structures, but also temporal structures. To model temporal structure better, we develop several innovative techniques to achieve accurate temporal action localization. First, we propose three parallel long-range

© Springer Nature Switzerland AG 2019
Z. Lin et al. (Eds.): PRCV 2019, LNCS 11858, pp. 463–474, 2019.
https://doi.org/10.1007/978-3-030-31723-2_39

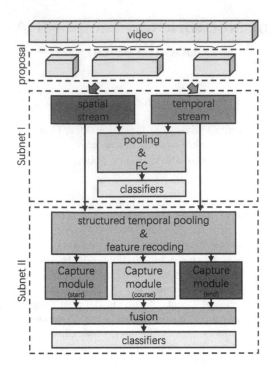

Fig. 1. Gemini Network architecture. The network contains two subnets, which separately model the short-range and long-range temporal structures of video data.

temporal structure modeling pipelines that extract features from three stages of action instance, namely, start, course and end. Three parallel modules are isolated from each other to prevent interference between the extraction of different stage features. Second, we propose a feature recoding module and a structured temporal pooling module to strengthen our framework's capacity to model long-range temporal structure. Feature recoding module embeds sparse feature vectors extracted by Subnet I into dense feature vectors, and makes temporal feature extraction of Subnet II easier. Structured temporal pooling module removes redundant temporal information and explicitly model temporal structures, achieving improved performance. Third, we propose a multiple supervisory strategy for temporal action localization. Specifically, we add several auxiliary classifiers connected to the Subnet I. These classifiers offer Subnet I additional constraint to model short-range temporal structure and increase the gradient signal that gets propagated back.

The proposed Gemini network was extensively investigated by applying it to a publicly available benchmark datasets, namely, THUMOS14 [12], with the state-of-the-art result obtained. The main contributions of this study are threefold:

(1) We provide an effective framework to model temporal structure in arbitrary length videos and thus achieve more accurate temporal action localization.

(2) Our proposed method achieves fast training speeds (4 to 6 h over a large dataset, e.g. THUMOS14, on four TITAN XP GPU). Once trained, it can perform fast inference of temporal action localization.

(3) We show state-of-the-art generalization performance of Gemini Network across different action datasets without dataset specific fine-tuning.

2   Related Work

In early works in this area, sliding windows were used to generate proposals, with a focus on the design of hand-crafted feature representations for category classification [17,25]. Recently, deep networks were applied to action localization to achieve improved performance [1,5,9,15,22,29,32]. Inspired by Faster R-CNN [20], researchers [29] developed an R-C3D architecture that uses C3D [26] to extract features, and pooling of the 3D region of interest (RoI) to fix the size of the feature maps. However, the 3D convolutional feature extractor limits the capability of this method for modeling temporal dependencies. The pooling of the 3D region of interest (RoI) causes the classifiers to lose some important features, resulting in unsatisfactory performance.

Just as image classification network can be used in image object detection, action recognition models can be used in temporal action detection for feature extraction. In addition, the two-stream ConvNet architecture [23] has been proved to be effective for action recognition [27]. It is used in SSN [32] to extract spatio-temporal features for proposal classification. However, the spatio-temporal features, which are extracted from each short temporal segment, are simply fused to represent the entire proposal in a fully connected (FC) layer. This results in the long-range temporal dependencies not being properly captured.

Some new methods were recently developed [3,4,6,24] for modeling the temporal evolution of activities using long-short-term memory (LSTM) networks, with the prediction of an activity label performed at each time step. However, [13] found that LSTM has limited capability for capturing long-term dependencies. Hence, CNN was preferentially used in this study to model the temporal dependencies of an arbitrary proposal granularity, with significantly higher accuracy achieved.

3   Method

The proposed Gemini Network is intended for action localization in continuous video streams. As illustrated in Fig. 1, the network consists of two components, namely, Subnet I and Subnet II. Subnet I is used for the extraction of spatial features and to capture the short-range temporal dependencies, while Subnet II is used to capture long-range temporal dependencies. The proposal generation, Subnet I, and Subnet II are described in Sects. 3.1–3.3, respectively. Section 3.4 presents the proposal type and the multi-task loss.

3.1   Proposal Generation

Let T denote the number of frames in a video. A video is divided into T/n_u consecutive video units, where n_u is the frame number of a unit. The video unit is set as the basic processing unit; that is, the proposed framework considers the units as the inputs. Let I_k denote the k-th frame. If n_u is set to 5, the i-th unit of the video can be denoted by $u_i = \{I_k\}_{k=5(i-1)+1}^{5i}$, where $5(i-1) + 1$ is the starting frame and $5i$ is the ending frame. In existing methods, the proposal generation is implemented by sliding windows, which involves an extremely high computational cost [22,30]. To avoid this disadvantage, we used temporal actionness grouping (TAG) [28] to generate a set of proposals. TAG is an effective proposal method that enables filtering of background proposals, ensuring a certain level of performance for a small number of proposals.

Consider a given set of N proposals $P = \{p_i = [s_i, e_i]\}_{i=1}^N$. Each proposal is composed by a starting point s_i and ending point e_i. The duration of the proposal p_i is given by $d_i = e_i - s_i + 1$. In order to capture more context information, we tripled the span of p_i by extending it beyond the starting and ending points, thereby obtaining the augmented proposal $p_i' = [s_i', e_i']$, where $s_i - s_i' + 1 = e_i' - e_i + 1 = d_i$. Consider a given augmented proposal p_i' containing M video units, we have $p_i' = \{u_j\}_{j=1}^M$.

3.2   Subnet I

The input to the spatial stream ConvNet is a single RGB image randomly picked from a unit, and the output is a vector $v_j^s \in R^{2048}$ (here, s indicates spatial). The output v_j^s can be considered as the spatial feature of unit u_j. For each proposal, we concatenate the v_j^s of each unit u_j to form a feature map of augmented proposal p_i'. The spatial feature map of augmented proposal p_i' can be represented by $V_i^s = [v_1^s, v_2^s, v_3^s, \ldots, v_M^s]$.

On the other side, the temporal stream ConvNet takes a stack of consecutive optical flow fields as input. An optical flow can be considered as a set of displacement vector fields between consecutive frames k and $k+1$. Let O_m^x and O_m^y represent the horizontal and vertical channels of the optical flow field, respectively. The stack of the consecutive optical flow fields in unit u_j can be denoted by $S_j = \{O_m^x, O_m^y | m \in [1,5]\}$. The input $S_j \in \mathbb{R}^{10 \times H \times W}$ is mapped to a feature vector $v_j^t \in R^{2048}$ (here, t indicates temporal). The temporal feature map of the augmented proposal p_i' can be denoted as $V_i^t = [v_1^t, v_2^t, v_3^t, \ldots, v_M^t]$.

So far, each proposal has been represented by a spatial feature map $V_i^s = [v_1^s, v_2^s, v_3^s, \ldots, v_M^s]$ and a temporal feature map $V_i^t = [v_1^t, v_2^t, v_3^t, \ldots, v_M^t]$.

3.3   Subnet II

Subnet II is designed to capture long-range temporal dependencies. Subnet II has three components: (1) Structured temporal pooling, which is used to extract fixed-size feature maps for variable-length proposals. (2) Feature recoding, which is used to create a new representation of the fixed-size feature maps. (3) Capture module, which is used to capture long-range temporal dependencies of augmented proposals.

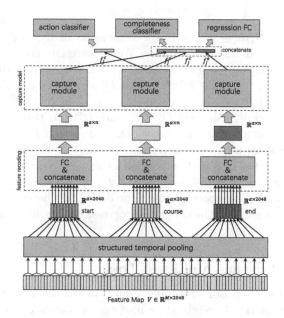

Fig. 2. Details of Subnet II. A temporal or spatial feature map is divided into 3α segments. Here, α is set to 9. The green, yellow, and red parts respectively represent the start, course, and end stages. FCs are used for feature recoding. (Color figure online)

The spatial feature map $V_i^s = [v_1^s, v_2^s, v_3^s, \ldots, v_M^s]$ and temporal feature map $V_i^t = [v_1^t, v_2^t, v_3^t, \ldots, v_M^t]$, which are obtained by Subnet I, are considered as the inputs to Subnet II, which is illustrated in Fig. 2. The operations performed on the spatial and temporal feature maps are entirely the same. The spatial feature map is considered here as an example.

(1) Structured temporal pooling. Spatial feature map $V_i^s = [v_1^s, v_2^s, v_3^s, \ldots, v_M^s]$ of augmented proposal p_i' is first divided into 3α segments. The spatial feature map is rewritten as $p_i' = [seg_1, seg_2, seg_3, \ldots, seg_{3\alpha}]$, where $seg_j = \{u_j | s \leqslant j \leqslant e, s = 1 + \frac{(j-1)M}{3\alpha}, e = \frac{jM}{3\alpha}\}$ (here, seg indicates segment). The spatial feature map is then fed into the structured temporal pooling, which pools each segment of the vectors into one vector. For seg_j, the following vector can be obtained:

$$r_j = \frac{1}{|e - s + 1|} \sum_{j=s}^{e} v_j. \tag{1}$$

The structured temporal pooling subsequently separates the vectors into three groups: start $R_i^s = [r_1, r_2, r_3, \ldots, r_\alpha]$, course $R_i^c = [r_{\alpha+1}, r_{\alpha+2}, r_{\alpha+3}, \ldots, r_{2\alpha}]$, end $R_i^e = [r_{2\alpha+1}, r_{2\alpha+2}, r_{2\alpha+3}, \ldots, r_{3\alpha}]$.

(2) Feature recoding. The three vector groups are separately fed into three fully connected (FC) layers to recode the features. Through the FC layers, vector r_j can be mapped to a new vector as follows:

$$d_j = W r_j + b, \tag{2}$$

where $W \in \mathbb{R}^{n \times 2048}$, $b \in \mathbb{R}^n$, n is the dimension of d_j, and W_i and b_i are respectively a weight matrix and its bias. We concatenate the new vectors d_j in each of the three groups to form three fixed-size feature maps for the three stages: start $D_i^s = [d_1, d_2, d_3, \ldots, d_\alpha] \in \mathbb{R}^{\alpha \times n}$, course $D_i^c = [d_{\alpha+1}, d_{\alpha+2}, d_{\alpha+3}, \ldots, d_{2\alpha}] \in \mathbb{R}^{\alpha \times n}$ and end $D_i^e = [d_{2\alpha+1}, d_{2\alpha+2}, d_{2\alpha+3}, \ldots, d_{3\alpha}] \in \mathbb{R}^{\alpha \times n}$.

(3) Capture Module. We feed D_j^s, D_j^c and D_j^e into three capture models respectively, and computed the stage-level feature vectors f_j^s, f_j^c, f_j^e. The architecture of the capture module is a redesign of that of ResNet-18. The course feature vector f_j^c is fed into a classification layer for predicting the confidence score of each category. In addition, $f_j = [f_j^s, f_j^c, f_j^e]$ is fed into two FCs, one of which served as a completeness classifier for detecting the completeness of the corresponding proposal, and the other as a regression layer for generating refined start-end times.

3.4 Proposal Type and Multi-task Loss

We train the Gemini Network by solving a multi-task optimization problem. The overall loss function is the weighted sum of the action category loss (als), the completeness loss (comp), and the regression loss (reg):

$$L = L_{als} + \alpha \cdot L_{comp} + \beta \cdot L_{reg}, \tag{3}$$

where α and β are the weight terms balancing the contribution of each part.

The action category loss L_{als} is used to train an action classifier. We specifically employ the **softmax loss** over multiple categories.

The completeness loss L_{comp} is used to train the completeness classifier, which contains k binary classifiers, each for one activity class. The completeness loss is given by:

$$L_{comp} = \frac{1}{N_{pos} + N_{inc}} \sum_{i=1}^{N_{pos}+N_{inc}} (-log(P_i^{(c^i)})), \tag{4}$$

where $P_i^{(c_i)} = \frac{exp(p_{comp}^i) \cdot c^i}{\sum_j exp(p_{comp,j}^i) \cdot c_j^i}$ (p_{comp}^i is the completeness score vector of length k of the i-th proposal, and c^i is the completeness label vector of the i-th proposal), and N_{pos} and N_{inc} are respectively the number of positive and incomplete proposals in each mini-batch.

The regression loss L_{reg} is a smooth L1 loss function used for regression. The regression loss is given by:

$$L_{reg} = \frac{1}{N_{pos}} \sum_{i=1}^{N_{pos}} SL_1(\Delta loc_i, \Delta len_i), \tag{5}$$

where $SL_1(\cdot)$ is the smooth L1 loss [20], and Δloc_i and Δlen_i are respectively the relative offsets of location and length.

4   Experiments

The proposed framework was evaluated on a large-scale action detection benchmark datasets, namely,THUMOS14 [12]. The datasets, the experimental settings, and the evaluation metrics are introduced in Sect. 4.1. Section 4.2 presents analysis of the different modules of the Gemini Network, and Sect. 4.3 compares its performance with those of other state-of-the-art approaches.

4.1   Experimental Settings

Dataset. THUMOS14 [12] contains 1010 videos for validation and 1574 videos for testing. This dataset does not contain untrimmed videos for training. In practice, the validation and testing video sets are usually used for training and evaluation, respectively. On these two sets, 220 of the validation videos and 212 of the testing videos have temporal annotations.

Implementation Details. The parameters of the proposed framework were learned using SGD, with batch size 128 and momentum 0.9. In each mini-batch, we maintained the ratio of the three types of proposals, namely, positive, incomplete, and background proposals, at 1:6:1. For the completeness classifiers, only the samples, the loss values of which were ranked in the first 1/6 of a mini-batch, were used to calculate the gradients. To augment the dataset, location jittering, horizontal flipping, corner cropping, and scale jittering techniques were employed. For optical flow extraction, we applied the TVL1 [19] optical flow algorithm, which was implemented in OpenCV using CUDA.

Evaluation Metrics. For both datasets, conventional metrics were used to evaluate the average precision (AP) for each action category and calculate the mean average precision (mAP). A proposal prediction was judged to be correct if it was determined to be in the same category as the ground truth instance and its temporal Intersection-over-Union (tIoU) with this ground truth instance was greater than the tIoU threshold θ. The tIoU thresholds for the THUMOS14 database were $\{0.1, 0.2, 0.3, 0.4, 0.5, 0.6, 0.7\}$.

4.2   Model Analysis

Here we study the influence of different temporal pooling strategies in structured temporal pooling. In addition, we attempt to find appropriate values for different pooing strategies. The number of segments α chosen for THUMOS14 are 1, 3, 5, 9, 17, and 33. We configured the dimension n of d_j to 129 for the comparison of two temporal pooling methods, namely, average pooling and max pooling. The results are summarized in Table 1. We observe that increasing the number of divided segments, α, can give dramatical performance gain. However, when α

surpasses some threshold, the performance no longer increases, or even decreases. In addition, it can be observed from the results in Table 1 that max pooling is more suitable for Structured Temporal Pooling when the number of segments is small.

Table 1. Comparison between different α and pooling methods. Results are measured by mAP at tIoU threshold 0.5. α indicates the number of segments.

mAP(%) @0.5tIoU	α					
	1	3	5	9	17	33
Max pool	32.6	39.8	41.8	42.6	37.6	35.3
Avg pool	33.2	36.6	37.7	39.9	39.3	39.4

Feature Recoding. We also investigated the influence of the dimension n of the feature vector during feature recoding. For this purpose, to control the computational complexity and performance, the number of segments, α, was set to 9 and the feature vector dimension n was varied as 9, 17, 33, 65, and 129. We attempt to find an appropriate value from these values. In addition, we verify the importance of this recoding function by comparing with the model that ablates it. The results are all summarized in Table 2. We observe that the case removed feature recoding has inferior performance whatever pooling method is. This result shows that the feature recoding is important for accurate localization. We also notice that the performance is unsatisfactory when the dimension n is less than 65. We suspect the reason for this is that the recoded feature vector loses some useful information for temporal action localization when the dimension n is small.

Table 2. Comparison between different n and pooling methods. Results are measured by mAP at tIoU threshold 0.5. n indicates the dimension of unit-level feature vector.

mAP(%) @0.5tIoU	n					
	9	17	33	65	129	–
Max pool	40.1	41.5	41.8	42.3	42.6	39.4
Avg pool	36.3	38.0	37.9	38.2	39.9	37.6

Long-Range Temporal Structure Modeling. Here we compare different methods of long-range temporal structure modeling, including temporal average pooling, temporal convolution and 2D convolution. In addition, we attempt different convolutional filters to find a suitable architecture. The results are summarized in Table 3. From the results we can see that 2D convolution is better at modeling long-range temporal structure than temporal average pooling and temporal convolution. We also compare the performance of the network which remove Subnet II and the network which contains both subnets in Table 3. We observe that using only one subnet to model temporal structure would lead to worse result. This result proves that the subnet II is important to long-range temporal structure modeling.

Table 3. Comparison between different methods for long-range temporal structure modeling. Results are measured by mAP at tIoU threshold 0.5

Temporal avg	30.6	
Kernel size	3	5
Temporal conv	35.9	35.6
Kernel size	1×3 & 3×1	1×5 & 5×1
1-D Conv+1-D conv	39.2	39.4
Kernel size	3×3	5×5
2-D conv	39.9	39.3

4.3 Comparison with State-of-the-Art Methods

We compared the proposed method with other state-of-the-art temporal action localization methods using the THUMOS14 [12], based on the above-mentioned performance metrics. The average action duration and the average video duration in THUMOS14 were observed to be 4 and 233 s, respectively.

Table 4. Temporal action localization result on THUMOS14, measured by mAP at different tIoU thresholds θ.

THUMOS14, mAP@θ							
tIoU	0.1	0.2	0.3	0.4	0.5	0.6	0.7
Shou et al. [21]	–	–	40.1	29.4	23.3	13.1	7.9
Yuan et al. [31]	51.0	45.2	36.5	27.8	17.8	–	–
Gao et al. [7]	60.1	56.7	50.1	41.3	31.0	19.1	9.9
Gao et al. [8]	54.0	50.9	44.1	34.9	25.6	–	–
Xu et al. [29]	54.5	51.5	44.8	35.6	28.9	–	–
Zhao et al. [32]	60.3	56.2	50.6	40.8	29.1	–	–
Nguyen et al. [16]	52.0	44.7	35.5	25.8	16.9	9.9	4.3
Paul et al. [18]	55.2	49.6	40.1	31.1	22.8	–	7.6
Alwassel et al. [1]	–	–	51.8	42.4	30.8	20.2	11.1
Chao et al. [5]	59.8	57.1	53.2	48.5	**42.8**	**33.8**	20.8
Ours	**63.5**	**61.0**	**56.7**	**50.6**	42.6	32.5	**21.4**

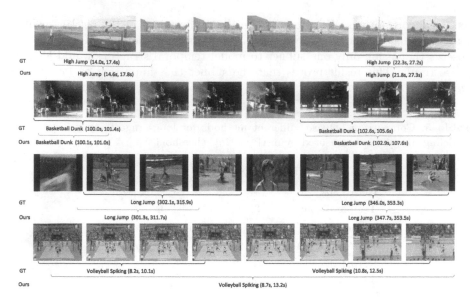

Fig. 3. Qualitative visualization of activities predicted by the gemini network on the THUMOS14 and ActivityNet datasets. The videos are shown as sequences of frames, where GT indicates ground truth. The ground truth activity segments are marked in black, while the predicted activity segments are marked in green for correct prediction on the condition tIoU $\geqslant$ 0.5. The segments marked in red are the wrong ones for the condition tIoU $\leqslant$ 0.5. (Color figure online)

The results of the comparison of the present model with existing state-of-the-art methods on THUMOS14 are shown in Table 4. It can be seen that, in most cases, the proposed method outperforms the existing methods. Figure 3 shows some representative qualitative results for two videos in THUMOS14.

5   Conclusion

In this paper, we attempted a new method to model spatial-temporal structure of videos and presented a generic framework for temporal action localization, which consists of a unit-level feature extraction subnet and a global feature extraction subnet, respectively for modeling short-time spatial-temporal structure and long-time spatial-temporal structure. As demonstrated on two challenging datasets, this work established new state-of-the-art, while maintaining a reasonable computational cost. Moreover, this work is generic working on dataset with different temporal structure of activities.

References

1. Alwassel, H., Caba Heilbron, F., Ghanem, B.: Action search: spotting actions in videos and its application to temporal action localization. In: Ferrari, V., Hebert, M., Sminchisescu, C., Weiss, Y. (eds.) ECCV 2018. LNCS, vol. 11213, pp. 253–269. Springer, Cham (2018). https://doi.org/10.1007/978-3-030-01240-3_16
2. Ning, C., Zhou, H., Song, Y., Tang, J.: Inception single shot multibox detector for object detection. In: 2017 IEEE International Conference on Multimedia Expo Workshops (ICMEW), pp. 549–554, July 2017. https://doi.org/10.1109/ICMEW. 2017.8026312
3. Buch, S., Escorcia, V., Ghanem, B., Fei-Fei, L., Niebles, J.: End-to-end, single-stream temporal action detection in untrimmed videos. In: Proceedings of the British Machine Vision Conference (BMVC) (2017)
4. Buch, S., Escorcia, V., Shen, C., Ghanem, B., Niebles, J.C.: SST: single-stream temporal action proposals. In: 2017 IEEE Conference on Computer Vision and Pattern Recognition (CVPR), pp. 6373–6382. IEEE (2017)
5. Chao, Y.W., Vijayanarasimhan, S., Seybold, B., Ross, D.A., Deng, J., Sukthankar, R.: Rethinking the faster R-CNN architecture for temporal action localization. In: CVPR, pp. 1130–1139 (2018)
6. Dave, A., Russakovsky, O., Ramanan, D.: Predictive-corrective networks for action detection. In: Proceedings of the Computer Vision and Pattern Recognition (2017)
7. Gao, J., Yang, Z., Nevatia, R.: Cascaded boundary regression for temporal action detection (2017)
8. Gao, J., Yang, Z., Sun, C., Chen, K., Nevatia, R.: Turn tap: temporal unit regression network for temporal action proposals (2017)
9. Heilbron, F.C., Lee, J.-Y., Jin, H., Ghanem, B.: What do I annotate next? An empirical study of active learning for action localization. In: Ferrari, V., Hebert, M., Sminchisescu, C., Weiss, Y. (eds.) ECCV 2018. LNCS, vol. 11215, pp. 212–229. Springer, Cham (2018). https://doi.org/10.1007/978-3-030-01252-6_13
10. Hu, Q., Jiang, F., Mei, C., Shen, R.: CCT: a cross-concat and temporal neural network for multi-label action unit detection. In: 2018 IEEE International Conference on Multimedia and Expo (ICME), pp. 1–6, July 2018. https://doi.org/10. 1109/ICME.2018.8486516
11. Huang, S., Li, X., Jiang, Z., Guo, X., Men, A.: Hyper feature fusion pyramid network for object detection. In: 2018 IEEE International Conference on Multimedia Expo Workshops (ICMEW), pp. 1–6, July 2018. https://doi.org/10.1109/ICMEW. 2018.8551547
12. Jiang, Y.G., et al.: THUMOS challenge: action recognition with a large number of classes (2014)
13. Khandelwal, U., He, H., Qi, P., Jurafsky, D.: Sharp nearby, fuzzy far away: how neural language models use context. arXiv preprint arXiv:1805.04623 (2018)
14. Li, W., Wang, W., Chen, X., Wang, J., Li, G.: A joint model for action localization and classification in untrimmed video with visual attention. In: 2017 IEEE International Conference on Multimedia and Expo (ICME), pp. 619–624, July 2017. https://doi.org/10.1109/ICME.2017.8019335
15. Lin, T., Zhao, X., Su, H., Wang, C., Yang, M.: BSN: boundary sensitive network for temporal action proposal generation. arXiv preprint arXiv:1806.02964 (2018)
16. Nguyen, P., Liu, T., Prasad, G., Han, B.: Weakly supervised action localization by sparse temporal pooling network. In: CVPR, pp. 6752–6761 (2018)

17. Oneata, D., Verbeek, J., Schmid, C.: Action and event recognition with fisher vectors on a compact feature set. In: Proceedings of the IEEE International Conference on Computer Vision, pp. 1817–1824 (2013)
18. Paul, S., Roy, S., Roy-Chowdhury, A.K.: W-TALC: weakly-supervised temporal activity localization and classification. arXiv preprint arXiv:1807.10418 (2018)
19. Pérez, J.S., Meinhardt-Llopis, E., Facciolo, G.: TV-L1 optical flow estimation. Image Process. On Line **2013**, 137–150 (2013)
20. Ren, S., He, K., Girshick, R., Sun, J.: Faster R-CNN: towards real-time object detection with region proposal networks. In: Advances in Neural Information Processing Systems, pp. 91–99 (2015)
21. Shou, Z., Chan, J., Zareian, A., Miyazawa, K., Chang, S.F.: CDC: convolutional-de-convolutional networks for precise temporal action localization in untrimmed videos. In: 2017 IEEE Conference on Computer Vision and Pattern Recognition (CVPR), pp. 1417–1426. IEEE (2017)
22. Shou, Z., Wang, D., Chang, S.F.: Temporal action localization in untrimmed videos via multi-stage CNNs. In: Proceedings of the IEEE Conference on Computer Vision and Pattern Recognition, pp. 1049–1058 (2016)
23. Simonyan, K., Zisserman, A.: Two-stream convolutional networks for action recognition in videos. In: Advances in Neural Information Processing Systems, pp. 568–576 (2014)
24. Singh, B., Marks, T.K., Jones, M., Tuzel, O., Shao, M.: A multi-stream bi-directional recurrent neural network for fine-grained action detection. In: Computer Vision and Pattern Recognition, pp. 1961–1970 (2016)
25. Tang, K., Yao, B., Fei-Fei, L., Koller, D.: Combining the right features for complex event recognition. In: Proceedings of the IEEE International Conference on Computer Vision, pp. 2696–2703 (2013)
26. Tran, D., Bourdev, L., Fergus, R., Torresani, L., Paluri, M.: Learning spatiotemporal features with 3D convolutional networks. In: Proceedings of the IEEE International Conference on Computer Vision, pp. 4489–4497 (2015)
27. Wang, L., et al.: Temporal segment networks: towards good practices for deep action recognition. In: Leibe, B., Matas, J., Sebe, N., Welling, M. (eds.) ECCV 2016. LNCS, vol. 9912, pp. 20–36. Springer, Cham (2016). https://doi.org/10.1007/978-3-319-46484-8_2
28. Xiong, Y., Zhao, Y., Wang, L., Lin, D., Tang, X.: A pursuit of temporal accuracy in general activity detection. arXiv preprint arXiv:1703.02716 (2017)
29. Xu, H., Das, A., Saenko, K.: R-C3D: region convolutional 3D network for temporal activity detection. In: IEEE International Conference on Computer Vision (ICCV), pp. 5794–5803 (2017)
30. Yuan, J., Ni, B., Yang, X., Kassim, A.A.: Temporal action localization with pyramid of score distribution features. In: Proceedings of the IEEE Conference on Computer Vision and Pattern Recognition, pp. 3093–3102 (2016)
31. Yuan, Z.H., Stroud, J.C., Lu, T., Deng, J.: Temporal action localization by structured maximal sums. In: CVPR, vol. 2, p. 7 (2017)
32. Zhao, Y., Xiong, Y., Wang, L., Wu, Z., Tang, X., Lin, D.: Temporal action detection with structured segment networks. In: ICCV, vol. 2 (2017)

SS-GANs: Text-to-Image via Stage by Stage Generative Adversarial Networks

Ming Tian[1], Yuting Xue[1], Chunna Tian[1(✉)], Lei Wang[1], Donghu Deng[2],
and Wei Wei[3]

[1] VIPS Lab, School of Electronic Engineering, Xidian University, Xian, China
chnatian@xidian.edu.cn
[2] Troops 95841 of PLA, Jiuquan, China
[3] School of Computer Science, Northwestern Polytechnical University, Xian, China

Abstract. Realistic text-to-image synthesis has achieved great improvements in recent years. However, most work ignores the relationship between low and high resolution and prefers to adopt identical module in different stages. It is obviously inappropriate because the differences in various generation stages are huge. Therefore, we propose a novel structure of network named SS-GANs, in which specific modules are added in different stages to satisfy the unique requirements. In addition, we also explore an effective training way named coordinated train and a simple negative sample selection mechanism. Lastly, we train our model on Oxford-102 dataset, which outperforms the state-of-the-art models.

Keywords: Text-to-image · Negative samples · Coordinated train ·
Different stages

1 Introduction

Since Goodfellow et al. proposed Generative Adversarial Networks (GANs) [6], image generation has achieved rapid development. Many outstanding methods [1,8,18,21] were proposed to improve the quality and diversity of synthetic images from different aspects. Text-to-image goes a further step which is regarded as conditional GANs, i.e., giving a refined description to generate related images. Recent works have changed from one-step generation [14] to multi-step [4] or stacked structure [23]. While the resolution of image has changed from low resolution (64×64) to high resolution (at least 256×256). Lately, Xu et al. [19] propose Deep Attentional Multimodal Similarity Model (DAMSM) to increase the interpretability of image generation and improve the relevance between description and image content. Yuan et al. [20] explore to align from low-level to high-level features using perceptual loss and a completely symmetrical structure to synthesize realistic images.

The first author Ming Tian is master candidate.

© Springer Nature Switzerland AG 2019
Z. Lin et al. (Eds.): PRCV 2019, LNCS 11858, pp. 475–486, 2019.
https://doi.org/10.1007/978-3-030-31723-2_40

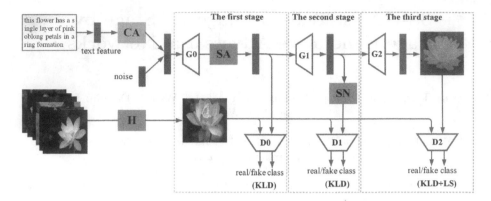

Fig. 1. The overall framework of our model SS-GANs. In the diagram, **CA** represents condition augmentation, **SA** means self-attention, **SN** indicates spectral normalization and **H** denotes hard samples selection. **KLD** implies that the format of loss function is KL divergence while **KLD+LS** represents that adding extra least squares loss based on KLD.

However, there are still some problems that have not been solved. Specifically, for fine-grained datasets such as Oxford-102 [12] and CUB-200 [17], the generated images lack more fine texture. We believe that the main reason is that most work fails to recognize the characteristics of generation with different resolution and blindly adopts the same or similar structure at each stage. Undoubtedly, the features of diverse resolutions are different. For example, when the image resolution is low, we should pay attention to the general outline of the object and the layout of image. While for the high resolution, the details, texture and color information of the image become more important and the spatial position is secondary.

In summary, we propose a novel network and training strategy named Stage by Stage GANs (SS-GANs). Our main attributes are as follows:

- For training way, we explore an effective method called coordinated train, which can make full use of every stage to generate high resolution images.
- In different stage, we introduce specific modules to satisfy the special requirement such as self-attention [21], spectral normalization [11], least squares loss [10] and classification loss [3].
- We also propose a simple hard negative samples selection mechanism, which further promotes the discriminator ability.

2   SS-GANs for Text-to-Image Generation

As shown in Fig. 1, SS-GANs adopt the hierarchical structure of coarse-to-fine to generate high resolution images. According to different concerns, SS-GANs can be divided into three stages. The first stage focuses on the outline of generated images, the third stage pays attention to the supplement of fine texture, and the middle stage carries out the transition.

2.1   The First Stage: Coarse-Grained Generation

As the lowest resolution of image, the task is to complete the basic composition of the image: Grasp the overall layout and the generation of object edge contour. Therefore, we add self-attention [21] module to the high-level feature map, i.e., the feature map is passed through three different paths and the first two paths learn an attention map which is applied to the third path to get the final feature map with visual attention. Self-attention mechanism can make the generator respond to the shape of the object with its surrounding environment, instead of directly using the local area of fixed shape. Thus, this module ensures the reasonability and global consistency of the generated image.

In addition, inspired by TAC-GAN [3] and the characteristics of fine-grained dataset, we believe it is not enough to judge the generated images are fake or real. It needs more fine-grained discrimination. So we introduce classifiers on the basis conditional and unconditional loss to judge the categories of the generated images. Meantime, we adopt condition augmentation in generator which is applied in many works [23,23] and our hard negative sample selection method further improves the ability of discriminator.

2.2   The Second Stage: Transitional Stage

Based on the results of the initial stage, the middle stage handles the transition between coarse-grained and fine-grained image generation. It is necessary to further improve the outline of salient object and to generate a small number of details. Therefore, in the second phase, we prefer to adopt spectral normalization [11] in the convolutional layer and remove self-attention module. There are two reasons: Firstly, in the second stage, the image resolution is higher and the more powerful generation ability is expected, which lead to unstable training, poor quality of image and difficult converge. Thus, we adopt spectral normalization to make the parameter matrix meet the Lipschitz constraint, accelerate the convergence, learn a better network, and improve the quality of generated images. Secondly, self-attention occupies too much GPU memory, for instance, 64×64 self-attention module needs extra 5G memory for storage and computation. To save the computing resources, we chose to abandon self-attention mechanism in the following stage.

2.3   The Third Stage: Fine-Grained Generation

In this stage, we emphasis on the generation of finer texture and more details of images. Therefore, we introduce least squares loss [10] on the basis of previous stages. In the first and second stages, the format of generator and discriminator loss is KL (Kullback-Leibler) divergence. However, the loss of KL divergence has the disadvantages of unstable training and gradient dispersion, especially in the high resolution stage. So, we chose to add extra other types of loss to mitigate these problems and explore two mainstream losses: Least squares loss and WGAN-GP [7] loss. In theory, both of them are superior to KL divergence, which can solve the problem of gradient disappearance. But in fact, the least squares loss is significantly reduced by the Adam [9] optimizer. The generated and real distribution is more consistent. Consequently, we take least squares loss as the extra constraint to further stabilize the training process and provide a reliable index which is highly related to the quality of the generated samples.

2.4 Objective Function

We give the loss functions of generator and discriminator in three stages as follows. It should be noted that since the loss function of each part is only slightly different with the related works listed below, we do not expand it in details. The details of the formula can be referred to the relevant research.
64×64 Loss Function:

$$
\begin{aligned}
L_{D_{64}} &= L_{D_{S\_64}} + L_{D_{CF\_64}} \\
L_{G_{64}} &= L_{G_{S\_64}} + L_{G_{CF\_64}}
\end{aligned}
\tag{1}
$$

128×128 Loss Function:

$$
\begin{aligned}
L_{D_{128}} &= L_{D_{S\_128}} + L_{D_{CF\_128}} + L_{D_{64}} \\
L_{G_{128}} &= L_{G_{S\_128}} + L_{G_{CF\_128}} + L_{G_{64}}
\end{aligned}
\tag{2}
$$

256×256 Loss Function:

$$
\begin{aligned}
L_{D_{256}} &= L_{D_{S\_256}} + L_{D_{CF\_256}} + L_{D_{LS}} + L_{D_{128}} \\
L_{G_{256}} &= L_{G_{S\_256}} + L_{G_{CF\_256}} + L_{G_{LS}} + L_{G_{128}}
\end{aligned}
\tag{3}
$$

where $\{L_{D_S}, L_{G_S}\}, \{L_{D_{CF}}, L_{G_{CF}}\}, \{L_{D_{LS}}, L_{G_{LS}}\}$ are inspired from StackGAN++ [22], TAC-GAN [3], LS-GAN [10], respectively. The forms of these three loss functions are in turn that binary cross entropy, cross entropy and mean square error.

3 Hard Sample Selection and Coordinated Training

3.1 Hard Sample Selection

In order to further improve the ability of discriminator, we propose a hard sample selection mechanism. Compared with previous works, random negative samples search strategy are adopted in [14, 22, 23], which simply select a random sample from the dataset. Because most of the randomly selected images are quite different from the ground truth, it is obviously less helpful to discriminator. Cha et al. [2] design a progressive negative sample selection method. They find the description which is closest to the given sentence according to cosine similarity. The image corresponding to the found description is treated as a negative sample. Although their method is much better than the previous one, they have two main drawbacks: Firstly, due to language is really abstract and there may be

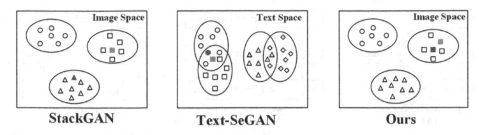

StackGAN   **Text-SeGAN**   **Ours**

Fig. 2. Three forms of negative samples selection and each ellipse is of the same class. Image space indicates real image dataset and there is no overlap between different categories. Text space is certain language embedding space and there is overlap between different categories.

great differences between images with similar description. Secondly, it is unnecessary to train a separate negative samples selection network because it needs additional computation.

Based on the above analysis, we propose a simple and effective negative sample selection method. Inspired by VSE++ [5], we explore randomly selected image which is in the same category with ground truth as the negative sample. As we all know, the images belong to the common category are roughly same, especially for the fine-grained dataset. But there exists some differences such as the spatial location, target size and background, these subtle differences are more difficult to capture for the discriminator. Thus, they are better negative samples for training phase. The subsequent experiments also prove the validity of our selection mechanism.

3.2 Coordinated Training

For high resolution image generation, the structure of network can be divided into two types: Dynamic network and static network. For example, PG-GAN [8] is a classical dynamic network: Different resolution image generation adapts to different depth network structure and the network is flexible. However, this strategy occupies a large amount of memory and need too much time to train network parameters (PG-GAN need 8 Tesla V100 GPUs to train 4 days). [14,19, 22] are typical static network: The network structure is pre-designed and does not change with the resolution, as shown in Fig. 2(a). This structure puts all loss functions together to optimize. Thus, it is hard for us to analyze which part of the loss is at work and which stage of the training is functioning. To address these problems, we chose to separate each stage for training.

Here we explore two different ways as shown in Fig. 2(b) and (c). The first one named independent train is that training its own loss in each stage and next stage don not optimize previous stage. The second one named coordinated train not only optimizes present loss function but also optimizes the network parameters of all previous stages. It is obvious that coordinated train is more proper because different resolution image has certain relationship and are interrelated. Although

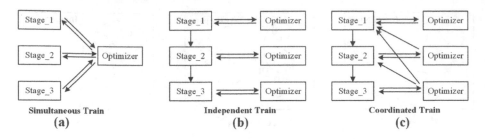

Fig. 3. Three types of training strategies.

these two methods all utilize previous parameters as the initialization parameters in present stage, coordinated train is better to take advantage of modules in different stages than independent train. Therefore, we prefer coordinated train in our method (Fig. 3).

4 Experiments

4.1 Datasets

We mainly train our model on Oxford-102 and CUB-200 which are famous fine-grained datasets. The former is divided in 102 categories and includes 7034 images for training and 1155 images for testing. While the latter is divided in 200 categories and contains 8855 images for training and 2933 images for testing. Every image in these datasets has 10 corresponding descriptions. In addition, we also chose Character-level Convolution Recurrent Network [13] (Char-CNN-RNN) as our text feature extractor and encode every sentence into a 1024-D feature vector.

4.2 Evaluation Metric

Inception Score. Like most of previous works, we use Inception Score (IS) [15] as the measure of image quality and diversity. Specifically, we input the generated image to the classification network inception_V3 [16]. On the one hand, the better the quality of the generated images is, the more accurate the classification results will be. On the other hand, the more diverse the generated images are, the more average the edge distribution of the categories will be. Inception score measures the performance of the model through calculating the divergence of these two probability distributions and the higher the better.

4.3 Experimental Comparison

Training Way Comparison. As shown in Table 1, we compare inception scores with diverse training strategies: Simultaneous train, independent train and coordinated train. To be fair, the modules of each stage of the three training methods are the same. As we analyzed in Sect. 3.2, coordinated training way is better than the other two at all stages (the initial stages are the same) and the inception score is much higher than others. Although independent train outperforms simultaneous train at middle stage, the performance of this model declines sharply at the final high-resolution stage and our training way is more stable.

Table 1. The inception score of three training strategies on Oxford-102 dataset.

Resolution	Simultaneous	Independent	Coordinated (Ours)
64×64	2.70 ± 0.03	2.70 ± 0.03	$\mathbf{2.70 \pm 0.03}$
128×128	3.08 ± 0.06	3.20 ± 0.05	$\mathbf{3.31 \pm 0.05}$
256×256	2.78 ± 0.05	2.58 ± 0.05	$\mathbf{3.32 \pm 0.04}$

Quantitative Comparisons. As shown in Table 2, we compare inception scores with the state-of-art methods: GAN-INT-CLS [14], StackGAN [23], StackGAN++ [22] and TAC-GAN [3]. We select the best results among all resolutions such as for StackGAN++, we prefer to the score of 128×128 resolution. In addition, because of the inception score of StackGAN++ on Oxford-102 dataset is not released, the corresponding results in the table are obtained directly from the open source code.

Table 2. Compared with the state-of-art models on Oxford-102 and CUB-200.

Methods	Resolution	IS(Oxford-102)	IS(CUB-200)
GAN-INT-CLS [14]	64×64	2.66 ± 0.03	2.88 ± 0.04
StackGAN [23]	256×256	3.20 ± 0.01	3.70 ± 0.04
StackGAN++ [22]	256×256	$3.08 \pm 0.06(128)$	$\mathbf{4.04 \pm 0.05}$
TAC-GAN [3]	128×128	3.45 ± 0.05	\
Our work	$\mathbf{256 \times 256}$	$\mathbf{3.65 \pm 0.06}$	3.75 ± 0.05

The experimental results show that our method achieved the highest inception score on Oxford-102. In particular, it is about 14% higher than StackGAN and 37% higher than GAN-INT-CLS, which obviously indicates that our method generates the higher quality of images. Meanwhile, the variance value in inception score (0.06) also shows that our method can produce the richer diversity of images. While on CUB-200, our model is only lower than StackGAN++ and the diversity of images (0.05) is still very high.

Fig. 4. The images generated via our model under three resolutions (red words), our baseline StackGAN++ in 256 × 256 resolution and GAN-INT-CLS in 64 × 64 resolution. (Color figure online)

Fig. 5. The results of three negative sample selection methods. Anchor denotes ground truth and images in each row are selected negative samples. (Color figure online)

Qualitative Comparisons

Subjective Visual Comparisons. We show the generated images of different resolution from 64 to 256 and compare them with the baseline StackGAN++ and GAN-INT-CLS (see Fig. 4). It is easy to see that the image synthesized through our model is more realistic and consistent with given description than

64x64   128x128   256x256   64x64   128x128   256x256

Independent Train

Simultaneous Train

Coordinated Train

Fig. 6. The synthetic images of different resolutions (64×64, 128×128 and 256×256) through three training methods. (Color figure online)

StackGAN++ and GAN-INT-CLS. For instance, **folded together** (the first line), **pale pink petals** (the second line) and **thick yellow petals** (the third line), it is obvious that the content of our generated images fits the given description better. What's more, our three generative stages are closely connected and final image is especially smooth, which is undoubtedly the role of our superior training methods and least squares loss.

Hard Sample. As the negative samples of the numerous works are selected randomly, we can see that most of the selected images are quite different from the real ones (see Fig. 5). So it is easy for the discriminator to classify the images is real or wrong and cannot improve the performance of discriminator very well. For text-SeGAN, the negative samples selected via cosine distance between the related description. Although the negative samples selected have similar descriptions, the shapes of the flowers are still different somehow. For our method, due to negative samples are selected in the same category, whether the related description or the feature of shape are more similar and it can be regarded as the better negative samples.

Train Way. Figure 6 shows some images of different stages produced through three training methods. Among these training ways, the result of coordinated training is the best, followed by simultaneous train and the independent train is the worst. The color and shape of the generated flowers through independent train are fuzzy and unnatural at high-resolution level. Overall, simultaneous train is little better than independent train methods and the synthetic images are smoother and the objects are more realistic. While the images generated via our training method has more details and textures on petals and stamens, it is viewed as the great advantage of joint training.

Table 3. The result of ablation studies on Oxford-102. WGAN-GP, LS, Base, CF, H, SA and SN are WGAN-GP loss, Least Squares loss, StackGAN++ loss, Classification loss, Hard sample, Self-attention and Spectral normalization, respectively. Moreover, due to the inception score of WGAN-GP is too low (About 1.1), we use <2.0 instead. The bold part of the table is the final model of our each stage and the result of corresponding stages on CUB-200 are 3.28 ± 0.02, 3.56 ± 0.04, 3.75 ± 0.05.

Methods	Batch size	Inception score
Baseline(64) [22]	12	2.62 ± 0.05
WGAN-GP	12	<2.0
LS	12	2.56 ± 0.04
Base+WGAN-GP	12	2.65 ± 0.04
Base+LS	12	2.74 ± 0.04
H(only)	12	2.67 ± 0.05
CF+H	12	2.79 ± 0.04
SA+CF+H	12	**2.81 ± 0.04**
Baseline(128)	12	3.08 ± 0.06
CF+H	12	3.24 ± 0.04
SN+CF+H	**12**	**3.27 ± 0.08**
Baseline(256)	12	2.78 ± 0.05
CF+H	12	3.51 ± 0.05
SN+CF+H	12	3.34 ± 0.08
LS+SN+CF+H	12	3.42 ± 0.06
LS+CF+H	**12**	**3.65 ± 0.06**

4.4   Ablation Studies

In order to verify the effectiveness of our method, relevant ablation experiments are conducted for the strategy we introduced, that is, the effect of adding or not adding the module on the experimental results.

As shown in Table 3, the first part is the results of each module at 64×64 resolution. Baseline is the original StackGAN++ method. We introduce SA, H and CF modules (SA+CF+H in Table 3) one by one to form our final model at this stage. According to the experimental results, the performance of H and CF modules added separately can be improved correspondingly. The inception score is the highest when all three modules are added, which also proves the validity of our model in the first stage. It is noticed that the performance of SA module is degraded because SA module is added to the generator, which guarantees the global consistency of the generated image. However, the original discriminator is difficult to judge the global image and needs extra loss to improve. Therefore, when CF and SA are used together, SA can give full play to its role and improve the performance of GAN. The second part is testing the module introduced in 128×128. In the model of the first stage, SN is used to replace SA to constitute the model of the second stage (SN+CF+H in Table 3). The experimental results show that the performance of SN is about 10% higher than that of baseline, which proves the validity of SN. The third part is about the different GAN losses at 256×256 resolution. As mentioned in the third section, we introduce two improved GAN losses: LS-GAN and WGAN-GP. Of course, in order to save time, we test on 64×64 resolution. Obviously, the results of LS-GAN or WGAN-GP are not very ideal, especially WGAN-GP. It is reasonable for us to consider this situation. First of all, these two methods are worse than the original GAN, because in fact, at 64×64 resolution, the ability of generator and discriminator does not differ greatly. GAN training is relatively easy. At this time, the use of improved GAN loss will affect the effect. Therefore, we consider combining them with the loss of the original GAN and find that the effect is much better than that of directly use of the original GAN, especially LS-GAN. But we do not recommend doing so at the low resolution stage because it will introduce unnecessary parameters. From the final result, we can see that LS has the highest score. Meanwhile, because the second stage of SN also has the effect of stable training, so we further test the effect of using LS-GAN and SN together. We find that the effect of SN is about 3% higher than that of SN alone and 7% lower than that of LS alone. This also shows that SN and LS are effective for stable training, but the sharing of multiple strategies does not necessarily play an overlapping role (so we chose LS+CF+H as our final model). It also shows that LS is more suitable for the generation of higher resolution images.

5   Conclusion and Future Work

In this paper, we propose a special stage by stage text-to-image generation method. In this method, the process of image generation is divided into different stages and every stage has specific modules. In addition, we also introduce an effective hard negative sample selection mechanism, which greatly promotes the ability of discriminator. According to our extended experimental results on Oxford-102 dataset, our method surpasses the performance of the state-of-the-art models. Although our method makes great progress, there is still something to be improved. In the future, we will further focus on the consistency of image and text to ensure that the generated image is not only of higher quality and richer diversity but also matches the description better.

Acknowledgement. This work was supported in part by the National Natural Science Foundation of China under Grants 61571354 and 61671385. In part by China Post doctoral Science Foundation under Grant 158201.

References

1. Brock, A., Donahue, J., Simonyan, K.: Large scale GAN training for high fidelity natural image synthesis. arXiv preprint arXiv:1809.11096 (2018)
2. Cha, M., Gwon, Y.L., Kung, H.T.: Adversarial learning of semantic relevance in text to image synthesis. In: The Thirty-Third Conference on Artificial Intelligence, pp. 3272–3279 (2019)

3. Dash, A., Gamboa, J.C.B., Ahmed, S., Liwicki, M., Afzal, M.Z.: TAC-GAN-text conditioned auxiliary classifier generative adversarial network. arXiv preprint arXiv:1703.06412 (2017)
4. Denton, E.L., Chintala, S., Fergus, R., et al.: Deep generative image models using a Laplacian pyramid of adversarial networks. In: Advances in Neural Information Processing Systems, pp. 1486–1494 (2015)
5. Faghri, F., Fleet, D.J., Kiros, J.R., Fidler, S.: VSE++: improving visual-semantic embeddings with hard negatives. In: British Machine Vision Conference, p. 12 (2018)
6. Goodfellow, I., et al.: Generative adversarial nets. In: Advances in Neural Information Processing Systems, pp. 2672–2680 (2014)
7. Gulrajani, I., Ahmed, F., Arjovsky, M., Dumoulin, V., Courville, A.C.: Improved training of Wasserstein GANs. In: Advances in Neural Information Processing Systems, pp. 5767–5777 (2017)
8. Karras, T., Aila, T., Laine, S., Lehtinen, J.: Progressive growing of gans for improved quality, stability, and variation. arXiv preprint arXiv:1710.10196 (2017)
9. Kingma, D.P., Ba, J.: Adam: a method for stochastic optimization. arXiv preprint arXiv:1412.6980 (2014)
10. Mao, X., Li, Q., Xie, H., Lau, R.Y.K., Wang, Z., Smolley, S.P.: Least squares generative adversarial networks. In: IEEE International Conference on Computer Vision, pp. 2813–2821 (2017)
11. Miyato, T., Kataoka, T., Koyama, M., Yoshida, Y.: Spectral normalization for generative adversarial networks. arXiv preprint arXiv:1802.05957 (2018)
12. Nilsback, M.E., Zisserman, A.: Automated flower classification over a large number of classes. In: 2008 Sixth Indian Conference on Computer Vision, Graphics and Image Processing, pp. 722–729. IEEE (2008)
13. Reed, S., Akata, Z., Lee, H., Schiele, B.: Learning deep representations of fine-grained visual descriptions. In: Proceedings of the IEEE Conference on Computer Vision and Pattern Recognition, pp. 49–58 (2016)
14. Reed, S., Akata, Z., Yan, X., Logeswaran, L., Schiele, B., Lee, H.: Generative adversarial text to image synthesis. arXiv preprint arXiv:1605.05396 (2016)
15. Salimans, T., Goodfellow, I., Zaremba, W., Cheung, V., Radford, A., Chen, X.: Improved techniques for training GANs. In: Advances in Neural Information Processing Systems, pp. 2234–2242 (2016)
16. Szegedy, C., Vanhoucke, V., Ioffe, S., Shlens, J., Wojna, Z.: Rethinking the inception architecture for computer vision. In: Proceedings of the IEEE Conference on Computer Vision and Pattern Recognition, pp. 2818–2826 (2016)
17. Wah, C., Branson, S., Welinder, P., Perona, P., Belongie, S.: The Caltech-UCSD birds-200-2011 dataset. California Institute of Technology (2011)
18. Wang, C., Chang, X., Xin, Y., Tao, D.: Evolutionary generative adversarial networks. IEEE Trans. Evol. Comput. (99), 1 (2018)
19. Xu, T., et al.: AttnGAN: fine-grained text to image generation with attentional generative adversarial networks. In: Proceedings of the IEEE Conference on Computer Vision and Pattern Recognition, pp. 1316–1324 (2018)
20. Yuan, M., Peng, Y.: Text-to-image synthesis via symmetrical distillation networks. arXiv preprint arXiv:1808.06801 (2018)
21. Zhang, H., Goodfellow, I., Metaxas, D., Odena, A.: Self-attention generative adversarial networks. arXiv preprint arXiv:1805.08318 (2018)
22. Zhang, H., et al.: StackGAN++: realistic image synthesis with stacked generative adversarial networks. arXiv preprint arXiv:1710.10916 (2017)
23. Zhang, H., et al.: StackGAN: text to photo-realistic image synthesis with stacked generative adversarial networks. In: Proceedings of the IEEE International Conference on Computer Vision, pp. 5907–5915 (2017)

Face Super-Resolution via Discriminative-Attributes

Ning Dong[1,2], Xiaoguang Li[1,2]([⊠]) [iD], Jiafeng Li[1,2], and Li Zhuo[1,2]

[1] Beijing Key Laboratory of Computational Intelligence and Intelligent System,
Beijing University of Technology, Beijing 100124, China
S201739020@emails.bjut.edu.cn,
{lxg,lijiafeng,zhuoli}@bjut.edu.cn
[2] Faculty of Information Technology, Beijing University of Technology,
Beijing 100124, China

Abstract. The limited resolution of cameras and the wide field of the video surveillance systems lead to low quality captured facial images and difficult to identify. Face super-resolution methods are proposed to enhance the resolution of facial images. However, it remains a challenging issue to restore discriminative features to identify a specific person in surveillance videos. An algorithm that helps face super-resolution and recognition with the aid of discriminative-attributes is proposed in this paper. We introduce discriminative-attributes for face recognition to recover discriminative features in the reconstructed facial images. Attributes with more discriminative power are selected to input the network together with the low-resolution face image. The experimental results of the LFW-a benchmark test show that our method achieves promising results in both subjective visual quality and face recognition accuracy.

Keywords: Super-resolution · Discriminative-attributes · Face recognition

1 Introduction

Intelligent video surveillance systems have a wide range of demands for high-quality face images. However, due to the complex capturing factors such as distance, view, compression distortion and noise of the acquisition devices, the faces in the surveillance video tend to be of low resolution and low quality. Not only do low-quality face images seriously affect the perceptual experience, but also they seriously affect the efficiency of the intelligent analysis applications, such as face recognition. Therefore, how to improve the quality of face images for surveillance video is one of the issues that need to solve urgently.

Most of the existing Super-Resolution (SR) technologies are aiming to improve the visual quality of face images in surveillance videos, but they pay less attention to further face analysis. The reconstructed image is close to the "mean face". Although the objective PSNR and the visual quality may be improved, in the super-resolved face images, it is difficult to preserve the face personal information. Therefore, there are still deficiencies in image detail reconstruction, which is not conducive to the intelligent processing of subsequent face recognition.

© Springer Nature Switzerland AG 2019
Z. Lin et al. (Eds.): PRCV 2019, LNCS 11858, pp. 487–497, 2019.
https://doi.org/10.1007/978-3-030-31723-2_41

Deep learning networks have been widely employed in image super-resolution recently. A convolutional neural network (CNN) was first introduced to image super-resolution in SRCNN [1]. It mapped the traditional image super-resolution steps to a simple network architecture and achieved a good restoration quality with a feasible runtime. Zhang et al. [2] proposed a denoising convolutional neural network (DnCNN). The method learns the noise image through the residual network, and improves the visual quality as well as remove noise.

The framework of Generative Adversarial Neural Network (GAN) [3] is successfully applied to many image generation tasks, such as super-resolution. There are a generator and a discriminator network in the GAN framework. A super-resolution generative adversarial network (SRGAN) [4] was proposed to make the reconstructed images to be more photo-realistic, which employs a deep residual network (ResNet) and perceptual loss function. Compared with the supervised SR methods with the Mean Squared Error (MSE) as the optimization function, SRGAN minimizes the perceptual difference of the ground truth (GT) and the reconstructed HR images to improve the visual quality of the super-resolved images. These GAN-based algorithms have shown excellent performance for generic SR tasks, as well as facial images.

To recover the details of the image, StackGAN [5] was proposed by Zhang et al. In which text description information was sequentially added to the two-stage Generative Adversarial Networks to help restore more detailed high-resolution images with text description features. Chen et al. [6] proposed a Face Super-Resolution method with Facial Priors (FSRNet), which used a prior estimation network to extract facial geometric prior information to help the reconstruction the discriminative details. In [7], Yu et al. proposed a Super-Resolving method with Supplementary Attributes, which fused the attribute information with the residual features after encoding to further restore the high-frequency information. However, the randomly selected attributes maybe not conducive to face recognition. Attribute Augmented Convolutional Neural Network (AACNN) was proposed in [8], which complete the attribute addition through the direct concatenation of images and attributes, and it's easy to cause interference to use 38 kinds of attributes.

The above-mentioned deep-learning-based image super-resolution methods aim to produce either High Resolution (HR) images with high subjective visual quality or higher PSNR evaluations. However, in the super-resolved HR facial images, the discriminative features, which will be helpful to identify a specific subject from others, may fail to be recovered. Therefore, the super-resolved face images are not necessarily beneficial to face recognition. For surveillance image reconstruction of the suspect, if there is some descriptive attribute information, it can help the reconstruction algorithm to reconstruct more reliable facial details. In this paper, we propose a discriminative-attributes aided face super-resolution algorithm for both visual quality and face recognition. Our framework can handle the problem of face hallucination, as well as LR face recognition. The main contributions of this paper are as follows:

(1) We proposed a discriminative-attributes aided face super-resolution algorithm with Generative Adversarial Network framework, in which the discriminative-attributes are selected based on their contributions on face recognition as the input of face hallucination network.

(2) In the generator network, feature fusion of face image and attribute is implemented using a shared feature extractor-decoder network with residual blocks to enhance the details of the discriminative features and super-resolution facial images with 8 times scaling factor.

(3) Experimental results demonstrate that the proposed algorithm can achieve better results in terms of subjective performances, as well as high recognition rates for face recognition.

2 The Proposed Algorithm

The main idea of the proposed algorithm is that several specific facial attributes or descriptions may be helpful to identify a specific human subject, and it will be useful to identify one person from another. The previous methods of attribute selection are random without considering face recognition. In the real world scenarios, some attributes such as Eyeglasses and Wearing-hat may be irrelative to face recognition. We made a fine screen of the attributes to find out those more discriminative to face recognition. We applied only one of the attributes of forty attributes to the Discriminator network as constraints, and the generated face will be used the current effective recognition algorithm named Sphereface [9] as face recognition verification. The contributions of different attributes are ranked from high to low. We arrange the attributes which have higher recognition rates than those without attribute constraints, as shown in Fig. 1.

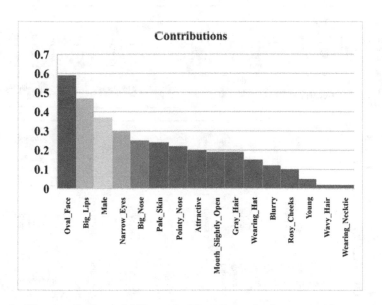

Fig. 1. The contributions of different facial attributes for face recognition accuracy.

However, if all of the 16 attributes are used as attribute description, face recognition rate will decrease. Some attributes such as (Wearing-Hat) and (Wearing-Necktie) may become noise. Therefore, the top five more representative attributes covered facial features are selected. Finally, the five attributes, eyes (Narrow-Eyes), nose (Big-Nose), mouth (Big-Lips), face (Oval-Face) and gender (Male/Female), which have more discriminative power to face recognition, are selected as discriminative-attributes to our Generator network. The facial attribute label is incorporated into the GAN framework in a fusion method of image and attribute to help the reconstruction of the facial images so that more discriminative features can be recovered.

A discriminative-attributes aided face super-resolution algorithm with GAN framework is proposed in this paper. The framework of our proposed algorithm is shown in Fig. 2. In our GAN framework, there are three subnets, a Generator network, a Classifier network and a Discriminator network. The Generator is composed of a shared feature extractor-decoder network with residual blocks [10] to fuse face attribute description into an image and perform an 8 times up-sampling of the face images. The output of the Generator network is connected to the Classifier and the Discriminator, respectively. The Classifier is used to determine the correctness of the face attribute. In the Discriminator, the adversarial network can be used as another classifier, which is used to determine whether the two sets of input images are real or fake. The perception network is a pre-trained neural network VGG19 [11] for image classification, and uses a perceptual loss function to ensure similarity between high resolution and ground-truth (GT) images.

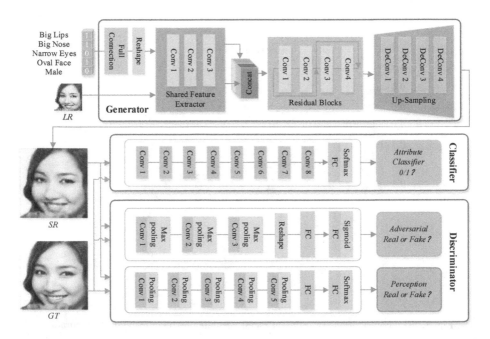

Fig. 2. The architecture of our proposed a discriminative-attributes aided face super-resolution algorithm with Generative Adversarial Network framework.

2.1 Generator Network

For the Generator, LR face images are fed into shared feature extractor with three convolution layers to extract fine-grained features before up-sampling. Simultaneously, we take attribute as input, expand its dimension by fully connection layer, and then reshape it to the same size of LR image. The image features and the attribute features are concatenated along the channel dimension. The encoded image features coupled with attribute features are fed into residual blocks, which are designed to learn features across image and attribute. Finally, a series of up-sampling layers (i.e., decoder) are used to generate a high-resolution image. Such a generator is able to help add more details to generate the realistic high-resolution image. The convolutional layer is used a 3×3 kernel size in each layer and set the stride to 1. The deconvolution layer is used a 5×5 kernel size in each layer and set the stride to 2. We use PReLU [12] activation function after each layer convolution and deconvolution stage except for image reconstruction without activation.

In the generator network, the input layer is a LR face image, with an image size of 12×12 pixels. The output layer is a reconstructed HR face image, with an image size of 96×96 pixels. The generator contains 11 convolution layers. Residual blocks are formed by the convolution layers, where residual blocks are composed of four convolution layers. To hallucinate low-resolution face images with 8 times scaling factor, we use three deconvolution layers, each can achieve image 2 times up-sampling. The last deconvolution layer is used to complete the final image generation. If it needs to hallucinate low-resolution face images with 4 times scaling factor, two deconvolution layers should be used.

2.2 Classifier Network

The Classifier network connected to the Generator network output is used to constrain the reconstructed image to contain the target attribute correctly. The super-resolved image from the output of the Generator network and the corresponding ground-truth (GT) image are input to the Classifier network. And our attribute classifier mainly refers to the Multi-Net Learning network (MNL) [13]. The convolutional layer is used a 3×3 kernel size in each layer and set the stride to 2, followed by the batch normalization (BN) and Leaky-ReLU (LReLU) [14] activation layers. In the final classification stage, the output of the network node is the same as the number of attribute categories.

2.3 Discriminator Network

The Discriminator network also connected to the Generator network output contains two branches, each with different functions. As shown in Fig. 2, the super-resolution SR image from the output of the Generator network and the corresponding ground-truth (GT) image are input to the discriminator network.

The adversarial network is used to determine whether the two sets of input images are real or fake. The convolution layer is used a 5×5 kernel size in each layer and set the stride to 1. We follow the setting of DCGAN [15] which uses Leaky-ReLU as activation function except for the last layer which uses a sigmoid function, and batch normalization added to all convolution layers.

The perception network can ensure the similarity between the perceptual features [16] of the SR image and the corresponding GT image. The pre-trained VGG 19 was modified in which the convolutional layer used a 3×3 kernel size in each layer and set the stride to 1, followed by the batch normalization (BN) and Leaky-ReLU (LReLu) activation layers.

2.4   Loss Function

The proposed discriminative-attributes aided face super-resolution algorithm with Generative Adversarial Network framework is shown in Fig. 2, which contains three sub-nets. One is for image reconstruction with attribute aided, and the others are one is for attribute classification and image discrimination with three branches. These branches are then used to update the Generator network. The LR image I^{LR} is obtained by down-sampling the ground-truth image I^{HR}. I^{LR} and I^{A} are taken as the input to the Generator network, to generate a SR image I^{SR} at the output. Three branches in the Classifier and Discriminator correspond to three loss functions. During training, G, C and D are optimized in the opposite direction, with the aim of achieving Nash equilibrium. The optimization is listed as follows:

$$\min_G \max_{C,D} f(G, C, D) \tag{1}$$

The attribute classifier C is trained to constrain the generated image I^{SR} to own the target attribute. For a LR face input is I_i^{LR}, its corresponding attribute input is $I_i^A = \{I_1^A, I_2^A, \cdots, I_5^A\}$ and $I_i^A \in \{0, +1\}$, $i = 1, 2, \ldots, 5$. Where $\{+1\}$ means that the face contains the target attribute and $\{0\}$ means that the face doesn't contain target attribute. The loss of the attribute Classifier is L_{attr}, formulated as follows:

$$L_{attr} = \frac{min}{C} E\left(I_i^{SR}, I_i^A\right) \tag{2}$$

$$E\left(I_i^{SR}, I_i^A\right) = \sum_{i=1}^{5} -I_i^A \log C\left(I_i^{SR}\right) - \left(1 - I_i^A\right) \log\left(1 - C\left(I_i^{SR}\right)\right) \tag{3}$$

$E\left(I_i^{SR}, I_i^A\right)$ is the binary cross entropy loss of the attributes. The loss function of the Generator is given as follows:

$$L_G = L_{per} + \alpha L_{fake} \tag{4}$$

where, L_{per} is the content loss function of the perception branch, L_{fake} is the loss function of detecting fake images in the adversarial network, and α is a weight for L_{fake}.

$$L_{per} = \frac{1}{2} \sum_{i=1}^{5} \left(P_i\left(I^{SR}\right) - P_i\left(I^{HR}\right)\right) \tag{5}$$

The ground-truth image I^{HR} and the SR image I^{SR} are input to the perception network. $P_i(I^{HR})$ is the activation of the i-th layer in the perception network. The error between I^{SR}

and I^{HR} is represented by the squared error loss. In the adversarial network, the label is "0" if the SR image is a generated image, and if the ground-truth image is set at 1.

$$L_{fake} = -\log\left(D\left(G_j\left(I_j^{LR}, I_j^A\right)\right)\right), \ j = 0 \tag{6}$$

$$L_{real} = \log\left(\left(D\left(I_j^{HR}\right)\right)\right), \ j = 1 \tag{7}$$

The Discriminator loss function is given as follows:

$$L_D = L_{adv} \tag{8}$$

where, L_{adv} is the weighted average of all the objectives.

$$L_{adv} = M - \beta L_{fake} + \beta L_{real} \tag{9}$$

where, M is the margin between L_{fake} and L_{real}, and β is usually set at 1. The total loss function is given as follows:

$$L_{total} = L_G + L_{attr} + L_D \tag{10}$$

3 Experimental Results and Discussions

3.1 Experiment Settings

Datasets. The CelebA dataset [17] and Labeled Faces in the Wild-a (LFW-a) [18] were employed in our experiments. The CelebA dataset, which contains a total of 202,599 images, each with 40 binary attributes, was employed in the training stage. The five attributes, eyes (Narrow-Eyes), nose (Big-Nose), mouth (Big-Lips), face (Oval-Face) and gender (Male/Female), which are important and have a great influence on face recognition, are selected and added as attribute description to our Generator network. There are 80% of the images in the CelebA dataset were selected to compose the training set, and the remaining images compose the validation set. Images in LFW-a, which contains 13,300 images, were used for testing and face recognition.

Implementation Details. In order to clean the dataset, the training images from CelebA and the testing images from LFW-a were all preprocessed by MTCNN [19], which performs joint face detection and alignment. All the face images are scaled to the size of 96 × 96 pixels. We have conducted 4 times and 8 times zooming factors. Then, HR images are 8× downscaled and 4× downscaled respectively to generate 12 × 12 and 24 × 24 LR images. Finally, the five face attributes were picked out from the forty face attributes, and the samples are labeled for classification, where 1 and 0 represent it has the current attribute and it has no the attribute, respectively. In the Generator, the Classifier and the Discriminator, the proposed model is trained with a batch size of 32, and a fixed learning rate of 0.0001.

Evaluation Metric and Methods Compared. To evaluate the performance of the proposed method, we have compared it with several state-of-the-art methods, including DnCNN [2], SRGAN [4], AACNN [8] and AAGAN [8]. In all the experiments, the original source codes with default parameters were utilized. In the training and testing stages, we implement our methods using the TensorFlow platform, with GeForce GTX1080. The training time required is about one day. We use subjective visual effects and objective indicators to evaluate our experimental results. The objective evaluation indexes are PSNR, SSIM and face recognition accuracy in Sphereface [9].

3.2   Experimental Results and Discussions

Some input 8 times down-sampling LR facial images based on different image restoration algorithms and their corresponding subjective representations are shown in Fig. 3. From left to right shows the LR images, the original HR images, the Bicubic, the results of the AACNN [8], AAGAN [8], our method without attribute description (Our-Attr0), and our method with five attributes description(Our-Attr5). In the case of 8 times up-sampling, our method with attribute description outperforms that without attribute and the three other methods in terms of subjective quality. Some methods exhibit blurring near edges, but we can perceive sharp edges in the results generated by our method.

(a) LR   (b) HR   (c) Bicubic   (d) AACNN (e) AAGAN (f) Our-Attr0 (g) Our-Attr5

Fig. 3. The SR results of different methods for face images with 8 times scaling factor.

Table 1. Average PSNR, SSIM and Accuracy of different methods on LFW-a, with 8 times scaling factor.

	PSNR	SSIM	Accuracy
LR	22.3274	0.4931	69.10%
HR	–	1	99.27%
Bicubic	23.7142	0.6261	74.17%
AACNN	**26.8197**	**0.7653**	86.83%
AAGAN	24.9357	0.6818	81.40%
Our-Attr0	26.1227	0.7471	88.22%
Our-Attr5	26.5127	0.7652	**91.37%**

To show the objective performances under 8 times upscaling, the PSNRs, SSIMs and face recognition accuracy on the LFW-a dataset are tabulated in Table 1. With the LFW-a dataset, the best results are highlighted. Although PSNR and SSIM are no better than AACNN, our method can better restore the details of the face from the subjective visual quality, and the recognition accuracy is also significantly improved. Objective results show that our method with attribute description is more helpful for face recognition. We have also tested on different number of the selected attributes. When only the top three representative attributes are added to the Super-Resolution framework, the PSNR, SSIM and Accuracy are decreased by 0.3681, 0.0147 and 1.35% respectively than five attributes. When the top seven representative attributes are added to the framework, the PSNR, SSIM and Accuracy are decreased by 0.3005, 0.0124 and 1.47% respectively than five attributes. So we can understand that adding the first five attributes is a better decision. We have not compared our method with the latest face recognition or identity-based SR methods, such as Super-Identity Convolutional Neural Network (SICNN) [20], due to their source code is unavailable. Although we can't show its subjective images, from the same LFW-a results with 8 times up-sampling factor from 12 × 14 given in its paper, we can give a comparison. The PSNR, SSIM and Accuracy are 26.8945, 0.7689 and 98.25%, respectively. Although our recognition rate may be a little inferior to their reported results, while, our PSNR and SSIM may be comparable. And we made a contribution to the attribute-assisted reconstruction.

In the case of 4 times up-sampling, we can see that our method with attribute description preserves the original structure with sharper edges in the reconstructed image. From the results, compared with three different methods, the Bicubic, the results of the DnCNN [2], SRGAN [4], as shown in Fig. 4. As shown in Fig. 4(d), and (e), we can see that not only the facial structure in the image is destroyed, but also the flat or smooth regions are also distorted. The reconstruction results without attribute description (Our-Attr0) and with five attributes description (Our-Attr5) are shown respectively in the Fig. 4(f) and (g), which are significantly better than the comparison method. To show the objective performances under 4 times scaling factor, the PSNR, SSIMs and recognition accuracy on the LFW-a dataset are tabulated in Table 2. With the LFW-a dataset, the best results are highlighted. The method of this paper is based on the alignment and attribute classification algorithms. The performance of these two

(a) LR   (b) HR   (c) Bicubic (d) DnCNN (e) SRGAN (f) Our-Attr0 (g) Our-Attr5

Fig. 4. The SR results of different methods for face images with 4 times scaling factor.

algorithms may have an impact on the performance of our method. This issue is beyond the scope of the consideration of this paper.

Table 2. Average PSNR, SSIM and Accuracy of different methods on LFW-a, with 4 times scaling factor.

	PSNR	SSIM	Accuracy
LR	23.8700	0.6609	83.65%
HR	–	1	99.27%
Bicubic	26.8257	0.7629	88.17%
DnCNN	30.9374	0.8726	96.75%
SRGAN	26.0387	0.8210	96.12%
Our-Attr0	30.3406	0.8754	97.02%
Our-Attr5	**31.1223**	**0.8858**	**97.42%**

4   Conclusion

We have proposed a Discriminative-Attributes aided face super-resolution algorithm. Face attributes that work as aided information are selected based on their contributions on face recognition. The proposed framework is implemented with GAN. In the Generator network, we used the residual blocks to learn the common features of the face and attributes extracted by the shared feature extractor. In addition, we added an attribute Classifier to constrain the correctness of the generated attributes. With the proposed algorithm, the facial details can be restored according to the attribute description, and the fine visual effect is obtained subjectively. At the same time, the discriminative features are also preserved to improve the accuracy of face recognition.

Acknowledgments. The work in this paper is supported by the National Natural Science Foundation of China (No. 61471013 and No. 61701011), the Beijing Municipal Natural Science Foundation Cooperation Beijing Education Committee (KZ201810005002, KZ201910005007).

References

1. Dong, C., Loy, C.C., He, K., et al.: Image super-resolution using deep convolutional networks. IEEE Trans. Pattern Anal. Mach. Intell. **38**(2), 259–307 (2016)
2. Zhang, K., Zuo, W., Chen, Y., et al.: Beyond a Gaussian denoiser: residual learning of deep CNN for image denoising. IEEE Trans. Image Process. **26**(7), 3142–3155 (2017)
3. Goodfellow, I.J., Pouget-Abadie, J., Mirza, M., et al.: Generative adversarial nets. In: International Conference on Neural Information Processing Systems, pp. 2672–2680 (2014)
4. Ledig, C., Theis, L., Huszar, F., et al.: Photo-realistic single image super-resolution using a generative adversarial network. In: Computer Vision and Pattern Recognition, pp. 105–114 (2017)

5. Zhang, H., Xu, T., Li, H., et al.: StackGAN: text to photo-realistic image synthesis with stacked generative adversarial networks. In: Proceedings of the IEEE International Conference on Computer Vision, pp. 5908–5916 (2016)
6. Chen, Y., Tai, Y., Liu, X., et al.: FSRNet: end-to-end learning face super-resolution with facial priors. In: Proceedings of the IEEE Conference on Computer Vision and Pattern Recognition, pp. 2492–2501 (2018)
7. Yu, X., Fernando, B., Hartley, R., et al.: Super-resolving very low-resolution face images with supplementary attributes. In: Proceedings of the IEEE Conference on Computer Vision and Pattern Recognition, pp. 908–917 (2018)
8. Lee, C.H., Zhang, K., Lee, H.C., et al.: Attribute augmented convolutional neural network for face hallucination. In: IEEE Proceedings of International Conference on Computer Vision and Pattern Recognition workshops, pp. 721–729 (2018)
9. Liu, W., Wen, Y., Yu, Z., et al.: SphereFace: deep hypersphere embedding for face recognition. In: IEEE Conference on Computer Vision and Pattern Recognition, pp. 6738–6746 (2017)
10. He, K., Zhang, X., Ren, S., et al.: Deep residual learning for image recognition. In: The IEEE Conference on Computer Vision and Pattern Recognition (2016)
11. Simonyan, K., Zisserman, A.: Very deep convolutional networks for large-scale image recognition. Computer Science (2014)
12. He, K., Zhang, X., Ren, S., et al.: Delving deep into rectifiers: surpassing human-level performance on imagenet classification. In: Proceedings of the IEEE International Conference on Computer Vision, pp. 1026–1034 (2015)
13. Ding, H., Zhou, H., Zhou, S.K., et al.: A deep cascade network for unaligned face attribute classification (2017)
14. Bing, X., Naiyan, W., Tianqi, C., Mu, L.: Empirical evaluation of rectified activations in convolutional network. arXiv:1505.00853 (2015)
15. Radford, A., Metz, L., Chintala, S.: Unsupervised representation learning with deep convolutional generative adversarial networks. arXiv:1511.06434 (2015)
16. Johnson, J., Alahi, A., Fei-Fei, L.: Perceptual losses for real-time style transfer and super-resolution. In: Leibe, B., Matas, J., Sebe, N., Welling, M. (eds.) ECCV 2016. LNCS, vol. 9906, pp. 694–711. Springer, Cham (2016). https://doi.org/10.1007/978-3-319-46475-6_43
17. Liu, Z., Luo, P., Wang, X., et al.: Deep learning face attributes in the wild. In: IEEE International Conference on Computer Vision, pp. 3730–3738 (2016)
18. Wolf, L., Hassner, T., Taigman, Y.: Effective unconstrained face recognition by combining multiple descriptors and learned background statistics. IEEE Trans. Pattern Anal. Mach. Intell. 33(10), 1978–1990 (2011)
19. Zhang, K., Zhang, Z., Li, Z., et al.: Joint face detection and alignment using multitask cascaded convolutional networks. IEEE Signal Process. Lett. 23(10), 1499–1503 (2016)
20. Zhang, K., et al.: Super-identity convolutional neural network for face hallucination. In: Ferrari, V., Hebert, M., Sminchisescu, C., Weiss, Y. (eds.) ECCV 2018. LNCS, vol. 11215, pp. 196–211. Springer, Cham (2018). https://doi.org/10.1007/978-3-030-01252-6_12

RefineNet4Dehaze: Single Image Dehazing Network Based on RefineNet

Kuan Ma, Hongwei Feng, Jie Luo, and Qirong Bo$^{(\boxtimes)}$

Northwestern University, Xi'an, Shaanxi, China
boqirong@nwu.edu.cn

Abstract. In recent years, the image dehazing technology with deep learning has been updated rapidly. These deep learning method shows more potential compared with traditional methods which need to estimate the atmospheric scattering model and prior information. In this paper, we proposed an end-to-end multi-scale single image dehazing method, and the method does not rely on the parameter estimation of atmospheric scattering model. We use the residual network (ResNet) to extract the residual features of hazy images at different scales, and then we use a kind of enhanced RefineNet to fuse these features. Finally we use recursively network to directly learn the nonlinear mapping from hazy images to haze-free images. We assessed our method on two datasets, and compared with two representative and effective methods. The results demonstrated that the proposed method has better performance on image dehazing.

Keywords: Single image dehazing · RefineNet · Image denoising · Multi-scale

1 Introduction

Fog and haze are the main factor affecting the performance of some outdoor computer vision systems, because the haze will cause a significant decline in the color and contrast of the acquired images, which will affect image features extraction result, and this will affect the normal operation of visual systems such as navigation and guidance, remote sensing and unmanned aerial vehicle. This has become an important factor hindering the wider application of the visual system [1].

The studies of image dehazing can be divided into two categories: prior-based approaches and non-prior-based approaches.

Prior-based methods estimate the parameters of the atmospheric scattering model [2] with prior information. Such as dark channel prior (DCP) [3], color attenuation prior (CAP) [4] and multi-scale convolutional neural networks (MSCNN) [5]. Transmission map lie on the estimation of the varying scene depth, it is hard to obtain the correct estimate of transmission map without accurate depth information. In addition, the estimation accuracy of global atmosphere light called airlight [3, 6] also effect the imaging dehazing result, and the variable airlight makes single image dehazing more complicated. As mentioned in the previous works [3–5], researchers assumed a model

---

K. Ma—Student as the first author.

© Springer Nature Switzerland AG 2019
Z. Lin et al. (Eds.): PRCV 2019, LNCS 11858, pp. 498–507, 2019.
https://doi.org/10.1007/978-3-030-31723-2_42

to describe the image dehazing process instead of using atmospheric scattering model, thist make the image dehazing more mathematically tractable.

In non-prior-based methods, which simplify the model and implement it in end-to-end network. Such as All-in-one Dehazing (AOD) [7], and deep residual learning (DRL) [8]. These methods directly output the clear image with the input of hazy image.

Inspired by the similarity of dehazing and denoising, we proposed a method that learn the multi-scale residual by deep ResNet [9], then we fuse the residual by enhanced RefineNet [10] to learn the integral residual from hazy image to clear image. Through make the output into the input recursively, we can get the nonlinear map between the hazy image and haze-free image. In this procedure we need to estimation of the transmission map.

In this paper, our method has the following contribution: (1) We propose an end-to-end multi-scale single image dehazing method by combining the ResNet and Refine-Net. (2) An enhanced combination is proposed, providing a more suitable loss function for our network. (3) The proposed method achieves a good performance on two typical datasets [11, 12].

2 Related Work

The prior-based methods can be divided into traditional methods and learning-based methods. Traditional methods mainly base on the parameter estimation of the atmosphere scattering model with prior information. This model can be expressed as following:

$$I(x) = J(x) + (A - J(x))(1 - t(x)) \qquad (1)$$

where $I(x)$ is the hazy image (source), $J(x)$ is the clear image without fog (target), A is the global atmospheric light, and $t(x)$ is the refractive index (atmospheric transfer coefficient). $J(x)t(x)$ is a direct decay term called *direct attenuation* in [3, 6], It represents the extent to which the scene light is attenuated in the transmission medium by scattering of atmospheric particles. And $A(1-t(x))$ is *airlight* [3, 6], it's the main cause of the brightness and color deviation of the scene. The relation between $t(x)$ and scene depth is:

$$t(x) = e^{-\beta d(x)} \qquad (2)$$

where β represents the scattering coefficient of the atmosphere and $d(x)$ is scene depth at location x.

He *et al.* [3] proposed a dark channel prior (DCP) based on statistics is proposed, the prior is that, in a haze-free image, all local patches will contain some low-intensity pixels in at least one color channel. He *et al.* [3] calculate $t(x)$ according to the existing formula and prior information, then obtain the clear image with the transmittance and airlight. Kratz [13] converts the regularization of atmospheric scattering model into the maximum posterior probability problem, and then regularizes the probability model to obtain depth images and transmission graphs. In addition, Zhu *et al.* [4] proposed a color attenuation prior (CAP) using local priors, this model is created to model the scene depth of hazy images, and then parameters in the model are trained in the mode of supervised learning to obtain a depth map, which is then recovered through the atmospheric model. Contrary to local priors, Berman et al. proposed to recover depth information with non-local color prior (NCP) [14], which is based on the approximation of the entire haze-free image including hundreds of different colors. These methods all obtain the clear image by estimating the transmission map and scene depth, they get pretty results because of effective prior information, but these types of methods need more time to process the image than other approaches.

Due to the success of deep learning, many researchers start to use CNNs to learn to estimate the transmission map and/or atmosphere light (*airlight*) for recovering the clean image via atmosphere scattering model. A multi-scale CNN (MSCNN) that consists of coarse-scale and fine-scale network was suggested by Ren et al. [5]. Cai et al. [15] proposed an end-to-end system for single image haze removal (DehazeNet), which is deformation from classical CNNs by adding the feature extraction and non-linear regression layers. Zhang et al. [16] pointed out that the previous methods focus more on the estimation of the transmission map t(x) in Eq. 1. They only used empirical formulas to estimate atmospheric scattering A in Eq. 1, and paid insufficient attention to A. Therefore, Zhang et al. Proposed Densely Connected Pyramid Dehazing Network (DCPDN). These methods take less time than previous works, and they still recover clean image by estimating the transmission map and/or airlight with prior information.

Recently, more researchers start to use neural network to recover clear image directly without estimation. Li et al. [7] proposed an All-In-One Dehazing Network (AOD-net) to get the clear image, and he proposed new objective criteria for comparing fog removal effects and quantitatively studied how fog removal quality affected subsequent high-level visual tasks. Du et al. [8] proposed a recursive deep residual network (DRL) to learn nonlinear mapping from hazy image to haze-free image. Nah et al. [17] proposes Gated Fusion Network (GFN), which is consists of a coding and decoding network. The coding network is used to encode the haze image itself and its various transformed images, and the decoding network is used to estimate the corresponding weights of these transformed images. These learning-based without prior information works only extracts image features at a single scale, and they neglect the high-level semantic information of the image that can be obtained from the deep ResNet and inevitably cause information loss in the process of image restoration. Hence, we combine the multi-scale method and learning-based technique to propose a network for single image dehazing without prior information.

3   RefineNet4Dehaze

RefineNet is a network architecture for realizing high-precision semantic segmentation task. It provides a multi-scale fusion method to solve the information loss in the network downsampling process, collect the available information in the sampling process, and make high-resolution prediction by using long-distance residual connection.

RefineNet4Dehaze is an enhanced version of RefineNet [10] architecture for single image dehazing. The construction of our network is shown in the Fig. 1. Firstly, we combined RefineNet and ResNet to form our RefineNet. In addition, we introduce perceptual loss inspired by VGG16 in order to increase visual quality index, *PSNR* and *SSIM*. This loss provide us a way to compare images (hazy image and haze-free image) in the feature space rather than in a pixel space. Therefore we combine the MSE loss and VGG perceptual loss to compare the images both in feature space and pixel space.

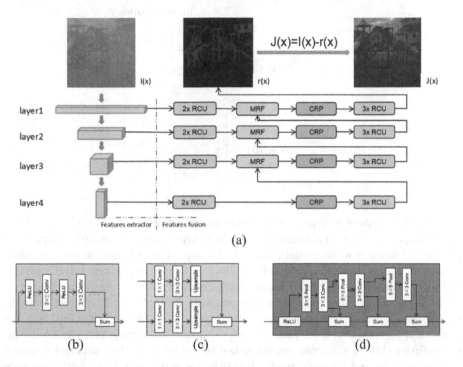

Fig. 1. The network structure of RefineNet4Dehaze. (a) our network for image dehazing, (b) residual Conv Units block, (b) new multi-resolution fusion block, (d) chained residual pooling block.

3.1 RefineNet4Dehaze

Equation 1 can be reformulated as following:

$$I(x) = J(x) + (A - J(x))(1 - t(x))$$
$$= J(x) + r(x) \tag{3}$$

Where $r(x) = (A-j(x))(1-t(x))$ can be described as an error term. Similarly inspired by [18], we propose to use deep ResNet to extract features at different scales, then we fuse these features to obtain the error term. After that we can get the clear J(x) by elementary subtract.

The network architecture is shown in Fig. 1. It contains two parts: features extractor and feature fusion. In the part of feature extractor, it contains 4 layers, and its architecture is shown in Table 1.

Table 1. Architectures for the part features extractor

Layer name	Output size	Architecture
Layer 1	80 × 80	3 × 3, 64, stride 2 3 × 3,, maxpool, stride 2 $\begin{bmatrix} 3 \times 3, 64 \\ 3 \times 3, 64 \end{bmatrix} \times 3$
Layer 2	40 × 40	$\begin{bmatrix} 3 \times 3, 128 \\ 3 \times 3, 128 \end{bmatrix} \times 4$
Layer 3	20 × 20	$\begin{bmatrix} 3 \times 3, 256 \\ 3 \times 3, 256 \end{bmatrix} \times 6$
Layer 4	10 × 10	$\begin{bmatrix} 3 \times 3, 512 \\ 3 \times 3, 512 \end{bmatrix} \times 3$

Layer1 consists of 64 feature maps generated by 64 filters sized by $3 \times 3 \times 3$ (an input image has 3 color channels) and the Relu layer (performs *max(0, x)* operation adding non-linearity to the model), then add a maxpool layer before adding 3 residual blocks, the blocks are as the same as basic block in ResNet18 [9] seen. Layer2, layer3, and layer4 consist of 4, 6, and 3 blocks respectively.

In the part of feature fusion, we use enhanced RefineNet to fuse these features. RefineNet has been proposed as a target for detection. As shown in the Fig. 1(a), the network is composed of three parts, namely, residual convolution unit (RCU), multi-scales fusion (MRF), and chain-based residual pooling (CRP). Their structure is shown in Fig. 1(a), (b) and (c) respectively. In MRF, we add 1×1 Conv before original 3×3 Conv to in order to add nonlinear excitation to the previous layer of learning representation to improve the expression ability of network.

After the part of feature fusion, we obtain a residual image that is a quarter of the size of the original image. Then we take 2 upsample convolution layer to recover the sizc of original image. We can get the clear image J(x) by elementary subtract.

At last, we recursively feed the J(x) back to our RefineNet4Dehaze when we train the network to obtain the nonlinear mapping relationship between the haze-free image and the hazy image. This idea was first proposed for image recognition [3], and then applied to image super-resolution [19, 20] and denoising [18]. Especially compare with DRL [8] that use the recursive structure to dehaze as well, and it just make the ResNet to recursively to learn the nonlinear mapping, but we recursively call the whole

RifineNet4Dehaze, which enables the feature extraction part and the feature fusion part to learn nonlinear mapping together, making the whole network more robust.

3.2 Ablation Analysis for RefineNet

3.3 MSE and Perceptual Combined Loss

Most of previous works uses MSE loss only, it calculate the distance between pixels and pixels. These methods ignore the semantic information of the image background in the process of image restoration, which leads to the incomplete details of the haze-free image.

RefineNet4Dehaze uses the perceptual loss, due to the MSE loss is not sufficient to recover all the texture information between the original image and the restored image, we combine the MSE loss and perceptual loss as our criterion loss:

$$L_{cri} = L_{MSE} + \gamma * L_{perceptual} \tag{4}$$

where γ controls the weight of the perceptual loss, and we set $\gamma = 0.001$ in our experiments which is $1e + 3$ times lower than the weight of the MSE loss. Ours purpose of using perceptual loss is to maintain the original image structure and background information by looking at the combination of high and low level features extracted:

$$L_{perceptual} = \| \phi(J(x)) - \phi(J_G(x)) \|_i^2 \tag{5}$$

where $J(x)$ and $J_G(x)$ represent the haze-free image that restored from RefineNet4Dehaze and ground truth paired image set, and ϕ is a VGG16 [20] feature extractor from i^{th} layer, the value of i are 2 and 5. MSE loss can calculate the mean square error of the recovered image and ground truth, so that they can be compared pixel by pixel. The formula is:

$$L_{MSE} = \frac{1}{WH} \| J(x) - J_G(x) \|^2 \tag{6}$$

where W and H represent the width and height of the image, respectively. By combining MSE loss and perceptual loss, we can get the haze-free image with higher PSNR and keep more detail information at same time.

4 Experiments and Results

In this section, we present our experimental results and compare it with the other two algorithms. The two methods are DCP and DRL. Among them, DCP is the traditional model-based method and DRL is the learning-based method. The comparison method uses two objective image quality evaluation indexes: PSNR and SSIM.

During the progress of the training, we set 500 epochs in all, the learning rates of the first 300 and the remaining 200 are set as 0.0001 and 0.00001, respectively. The solver was stochastic gradient descent (SDG), and the momentum parameter was 0.9. The network uses an i7-4900 processor and nvidia 1080Ti to train on a PC for a total of 40 h.

4.1   Datasets

We used Nyu-depth v2 dataset [20] to create the composite training image. Nyu-depth v2 dataset is composed of 1449 indoor color images with dense marks of real depth information. The original depth map has been projected and colored as [20] to fill in the missing depth labels. These images are all 640 by 480 dimensions.

By simulating and synthesizing hazy images, 1288 pairs of images from 1449 pairs were randomly selected as the training data set, and the remaining 161 pairs were used as ImageSet a. And then we use all the images in O-HAZE and I-HAZE as ImageSet b. For each image in the training set, we resize it to 320*320 before input into the network.

4.2   Evaluation Metrics

We use two metrics for quantitative performance comparison and analysis, including Peak Signal to Noise Ratio (PSNR) and Structural Similarity Index Metric (SSIM). PSNR is the most widely used objective measure of picture quality. It is based on the error between the corresponding pixels, that is, the image quality evaluation based on error sensitivity:

$$PSNR = 10 \times \log_{10}\left(\frac{(2^n - 1)^2}{MSE}\right) \tag{7}$$

where MSE represents mean square error between the restore image and groundtruth. The larger the PSNR value, the less distortion it represents. SSIM is an index to measure the similarity of two images, and it measures image similarity from three aspects: brightness, contrast and structure. Its calculation formula is as follows:

$$SSIM(x, y) = \frac{\left(2\mu_x\mu_y + c_1\right)\left(2\sigma_{xy} + c_2\right)}{\left(\mu_x^2 + \mu_y^2 + c_1\right)\left(\sigma_x^2 + \sigma_y^2 + c_2\right)} \tag{8}$$

where x and y represents the restore image and groundtruth, μ_x and μ_y are the average of x and y, σ_x^2 and σ_y^2 are the variance of x and y, and σ_{xy} is the covariance of x and y. $c_1 = (k_1 L)^2$ and $c_2 = (k_2 L)^2$ are the constant used to maintain stability. L is the dynamic range of pixel values. $k_1 = 0.01$ and $k_2 = 0.03$. SSIM ranges from 0 to 1. When two images are identical, the value of SSIM equals 1.

4.3 Results

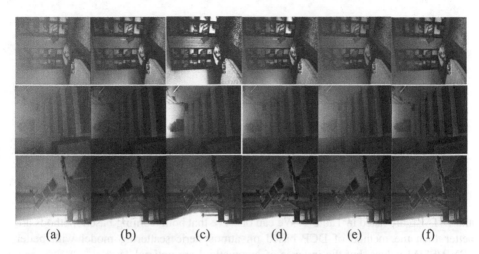

Fig. 2. Dehazing results on I-HAZE datasets. (a) are the inputs of the hazy images, (b), (c), (d), (e) and (f) are the dehazing results of DCP, BCCR, DRL, DehazeNet and ours methods respectively.

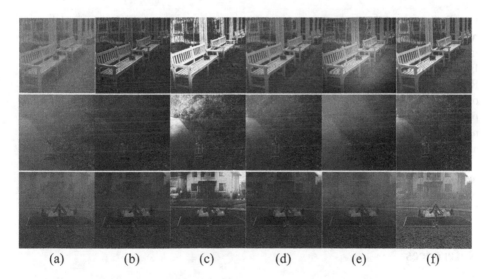

Fig. 3. Dehazing results on O-HAZE datasets. (a) are the inputs of the hazy images, (b), (c), (d), (e) and (f) are the dehazing results of DCP, BCCR, DRL, DehazeNet and ours methods respectively.

We show the results of comparison with other methods in Figs. 2 and 3, and we can see our results are more complete in the background information and clearer in some edge details. The combination of perceptual loss and MSE loss makes the background information more complete in the process of recovering haze-free images. The fusion of depth residual network and multi-scale leads to clearer edges.

Table 2. Average PSNR and SSIM results on ImageSet a and ImageSet b.

	DCP [5]	BCCR [21]	DRL [8]	DehazeNet [15]	Ours
ImageSet a: I-HAZE [11]					
PSNR	14.24	18.43	17.35	16.70	**19.29**
SSIM	0.76	0.82	0.83	0.78	**0.85**
ImageSet b: O-HAZE [12]					
PSNR	13.53	15.94	15.37	16.93	**17.28**
SSIM	0.76	0.73	0.78	0.80	**0.81**

The average PSNR and SSIM values of the three methods on the datasets O-HAZE and I-HAZE are listed in Table 2. We can observe that both learning based methods are better than the method of DCP based on atmospheric scattering model with better PSNR/SSIM values, but the indexes of our method are optimal.

5 Conclusion

Use Refinenet as the basic framework, this paper proposes a single image dehazing network called RefineNet4Dehaze, which uses paired hazy images and groundtruth for training, and finally directly generates haze-free image output from hazy image input. In order to make the haze-free image have high visual quality, we changed the original Refinenet cross entropy loss function to the perceptual loss. When the final size of the original image is large, we use upsampling twice, and try to let the network learn more parameters to obtain higher quality image. The experimental results showed that the recovered haze-free image with improved RefineNet4Dehaze had better visual effect and higher PSNR and SSIM values in the dehazing experiment.

Acknowledgement. This work is supported by Shaanxi international science and technology cooperation and exchange program of china (2017KW-010), Scientific Research Project of Shaanxi Education Department of China (15JK1689).

References

1. Fattal, R.: Single image dehazing. ACM Trans. Graphics **27**(3), 1–9 (2008)
2. Bruneton, E., Neyret, F.: Precomputed atmospheric scattering. In: Computer Graphics Forum, vol. 27, no. 4, pp. 1079–1086 (2010)
3. He, K., Sun, J., et al.: Single image haze removal using dark channel prior. IEEE Trans. Pattern Anal. Mach. Intell. **33**(12), 2341–2353 (2011)
4. Zhu, Q., Mai, J., Shao, L.: A fast single image haze removal algorithm using color attenuation prior. IEEE Trans. Image Process. **24**(11), 3522–3533 (2015)

5. Ren, W., Liu, S., Zhang, H., et al.: Single image dehazing via multi-scale convolutional neural networks. In: Leibe, B., Matas, J., Sebe, N., Welling, M. (eds.) ECCV 2016. LNCS, vol. 9906, pp. 154–169. Springer, Cham (2016). https://doi.org/10.1007/978-3-319-46475-6_10

6. Narasimhan, S.G., Nayar, S.K.: Vision and the atmosphere. Int. J. Comput. Vis. **48**(3), 233–254 (2002)

7. Li, B., Peng, X., Wang, Z., et al.: AOD-Net: all-in-one dehazing network. In: IEEE International Conference on Computer Vision (2017)

8. Du, Y., Li, X.: Recursive deep residual learning for single image dehazing. In: 2018 IEEE/CVF Conference on Computer Vision and Pattern Recognition Workshops (CVPRW). IEEE Computer Society (2018)

9. He, K., Zhang, X., Ren, S., et al.: Deep residual learning for image recognition (2015)

10. Lin, G., Milan, A., Shen, C., et al.: RefineNet: multi-path refinement networks for high-resolution semantic segmentation (2016)

11. Ancuti, C.O., Ancuti, C., Timofte, R., et al.: I-HAZE: a dehazing benchmark with real hazy and haze-free indoor images. In: Blanc-Talon, J., Helbert, D., Philips, W., Popescu, D., Scheunders, P. (eds.) ACIVS 2018. LNCS, vol. 11182, pp. 620–631. Springer, Cham (2018). https://doi.org/10.1007/978-3-030-01449-0_52

12. Ancuti, C.O., Ancuti, C., Timofte, R., et al.: O-HAZE: a dehazing benchmark with real hazy and haze-free outdoor images (2018)

13. Nishino, K., Kratz, L., Lombardi, S.: Bayesian defogging. Int. J. Comput. Vis. **98**(3), 263–278 (2012)

14. Berman, D., Treibitz, T., Avidan, S.: Non-local Image dehazing. In: IEEE Conference on Computer Vision & Pattern Recognition (2016)

15. Cai, B., Xu, X., Jia, K., et al.: DehazeNet: an end-to-end system for single image haze removal. IEEE Trans. Image Process. **25**(11), 5187–5198 (2016)

16. Zhang, H., Patel, V.M.: Densely connected pyramid dehazing network (2018)

17. Ren, W., Ma, L., Zhang, J., et al.: Gated fusion network for single image dehazing (2018)

18. Zhang, K., Chen, Y., Chen, Y., et al.: Beyond a gaussian denoiser: residual learning of deep cnn for image denoising. IEEE Trans. Image Process. **26**(7), 3142–3155 (2016)

19. Simonyan, K., Zisserman, A.: Very deep convolutional networks for large-scale image recognition. Computer Science (2014)

20. Silberman, N., Hoiem, D., Kohli, P., Fergus, R.: Indoor segmentation and support inference from RGBD images. In: Fitzgibbon, A., Lazebnik, S., Perona, P., Sato, Y., Schmid, C. (eds.) ECCV 2012. LNCS, vol. 7576, pp. 746–760. Springer, Berlin (2012). https://doi.org/10.1007/978-3-642-33715-4_54

21. Meng, G., Wang, Y., Duan, J., Xiang, S., Pan, C.: Efficient image dehazing with boundary constraint and contextual regularization. In: Proceedings of the IEEE ICCV, pp. 617–624 (2013)

Level Set Image Segmentation Based on Non-independent and Identically Distributed

Yaxin Wang[1], Yuanfeng Lian[1(✉)], Dianzhong Wang[2],
and Jianbin Zhang[1]

[1] China University of Petroleum Beijing, Beijing 102249, China
lianyuanfeng@cup.edu.cn
[2] Beijing Institute of Space Mechanics and Electricity, Beijing 100094, China

Abstract. Aiming at the problems of traditional image segmentation methods such as single image type and falling into false boundary, a level set image segmentation algorithm based on non-independent and identically distributed (non-IID) is proposed. The traditional image segmentation method basically assumes that all samples are independent and have the same distribution. However, this assumption does not hold. In this paper, the image is segmented into several pixel blocks by super-pixel segmentation method. The feature vectors are extracted from the pixel blocks by non-IID method. We combine the obtained feature vectors with the CV model to change the energy function of the level set method and apply the new energy function to image segmentation. The experimental results show that the proposed algorithm can segment all kinds of images and has a good segmentation effect for weak edge images.

Keywords: Non-independent and identically distributed · Image segmentation · Level set · SLIC · CV model

1   Introduction

Level set method is an image segmentation algorithm developed on the basis of active contour model. The main idea of the level set method is to embed the continuously deformed dimension curve (surface) as a zero-level set into the higher dimension function. Osher and Steiner [1] proposed the horizontal setting method in the field of fluid mechanics, and then widely used in various scientific research and engineering fields related to curve evolution. Vicent et al. [2] took the lead in applying this theory to the field of image science, and began the research of image processing technology based on level set method. CV (Chan-Vese) model [3] is a level set model based on region segmentation. The model uses the minimum of energy function to evolve the curve and get the segmentation result. Bernard algorithm uses two-dimensional third-order B-spline basis function to represent the level set function as a discrete form [4], which can effectively suppress noise. Li et al. [5] proposed a new level set image

---

Student as first author.

© Springer Nature Switzerland AG 2019
Z. Lin et al. (Eds.): PRCV 2019, LNCS 11858, pp. 508–518, 2019.
https://doi.org/10.1007/978-3-030-31723-2_43

segmentation method based on region, which can achieve segmentation in the case of uneven distribution of image intensity. Zhang et al. [6] introduced the dislocation theory in material science into the level set method, and proposed a distance regularization level set image segmentation algorithm based on the dislocation theory, which has a good segmentation effect for weak edge images. In order to improve the quality of level set image segmentation and reduce the number of iterations of level set, Zhang et al. [7] presented a level set image segmentation method based on rough set and new energy formula. In order to solve the unstable problems of DRLSE model [20], such as easy to fall into false boundary, sensitive to noise, slow convergence speed and easy to leak from weak edge, Zhu et al. [8] proposed the level set evolution function of area term energy enhancement to improve the level set method.

In recent years, the methods with non-IID for image segmentation have been explored to overcome the difficulties that the gray level distribution of the image is not uniform and the boundary of the target is blurred. Cao [9] presented a method of combining non-IID method with image segmentation. Teney et al. [10] proposed non-IID features to capture spatial/temporal information. In [11], the principle of non-IID was introduced to explain the inherent nature of traditional recommendation system from the perspective of coupling and heterogeneity. The traditional image segmentation method basically assumes that all samples are independent and have the same distribution. However, this assumption does not hold. In fact, they are non-independent and identically distributed. Based on previous research on non-IID, we apply this theory to image segmentation and propose a new non-IID level set image segmentation method.

2 The Proposed Approach

2.1 Level Set Method

Mumford-Shah model is an image segmentation algorithm by solving the minimum value of energy function. The purpose is to solve the piecewise smooth image and contour curve similar to the original image by minimizing the energy function. In order to reduce the complexity of the model in solving process, the CV model was presented to use piecewise constant function to approximate the original image and obtain the evolution of the advancing curve. The energy equation is

$$E(C_1, C_2, C) = \alpha L(C) + \beta A(C) + \lambda_1 \int_C |I - C_1|^2 dxdy + \lambda_2 \int_C |I - C_2|^2 dxdy \quad (1)$$

where α and β are non-negative parameters. Generally, $\beta = 0$, λ_1 and λ_2 are positive numbers. The image to be segmented is represented by symbol I. C_1 and C_2 are the internal and external gray average values of evolutionary curve C on the image to be segmented, respectively. The first term of the energy function is the constraint term, which is used to constrain the minimum length of the evolutionary curve, and the last two terms are the fidelity term, which is used to express the similarity between the segmentation result and the original image.

The zero-level set of Lipschitz function is used to implicitly represent the curve C in the plane. In order to describe the interior and exterior of evolution curve mathematically, Heaviside function and Dirac function are introduced into the energy function of Eq. (1). Then the function of Eq. (1) can be rewritten as follows:

$$E(C_1, C_2, C) = \alpha \int_\Omega \delta(\varphi)|\nabla_\varphi|dxdy + \beta \int_\Omega H(\varphi)dxdy +$$
$$\lambda_1 \int_\Omega |I - C_1|^2 H(\varphi)dxdy + \lambda_2 \int_\Omega |I - C_2|^2(1 - H(\varphi))dxdy \quad (2)$$

where $H(\varphi) = \frac{1}{2} + \frac{1}{\pi}arc\,tan(\frac{\varphi}{\epsilon})$, $\delta(\varphi) = \frac{1}{\pi}\frac{1}{1+(\varphi/\epsilon)^2}$, ε is constant, and $\varepsilon \to 0$, the symbol Ω represents the image domain.

2.2 Non-independent and Identically Distributed

The basic idea of Non-IID is to respect the original characteristics and complexity of a learning problem, to maintain the original heterogeneity, and to fully learn and express the original relationship. For example, when judging which mode, group, class or anomaly O_3 is in Fig. 1, we should consider whether O_3 is affected by O_1 or O_2, so we should consider r_{13} and r_{23} when calculating d_3. When looking for O-point (benchmark), we should also consider that it will be affected by d_1 and d_2. Combining these two aspects, the objective function is very complex. This is a highly abstract expression of Non-IID learning.

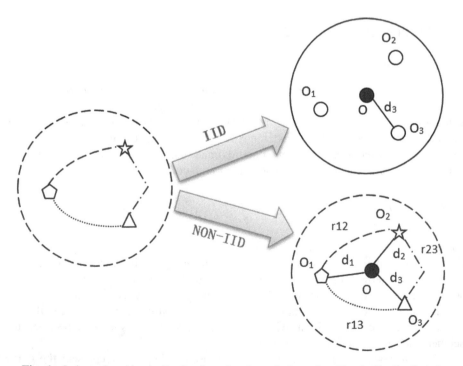

Fig. 1. Independent identically distributed and non-independent identically distributed

In order to represent the relationship of independent and identically distributed, we introduce the form of undirected graph, which uses different nodes to represent different samples. The samples currently being compared are the central nodes, and the nodes around the central nodes represent their adjacent samples.

The graph kernel functions are defined by representing and measuring undirected graphs constructed by different samples. The simplest way to calculate the similarity between two undirected graphs is to calculate the distance between two central nodes, and then calculate the average distance between two groups of peripheral nodes that contribute to the direct product kernel.

Given two samples y_m and y_n whose h_m and h_n neighbors are $y_{m, p}$ $(p = 1, ..., h_m)$ and $y_{n, q}$ $(q = 1, ..., h_n)$, the direct product kernel is defined as follows:

$$K_{DP}(m, n) = f(y_m, y_n) + \frac{1}{h_m \cdot h_n} \sum_{p=1}^{h_m} \sum_{q=1}^{h_n} f(y_{m,p}, y_{n,q}) \tag{3}$$

where f is a positive and semi-definite core. In this paper, Gauss radial basis function is chosen as $f(y_m, y_n) = exp\left(-\alpha_1 ||y_m - y_n||^2\right)$, where α_1 is a parameter.

2.3 Combination of CV Model and Non-IID

According to the following lemma, the original representation is equivalent to the kernel-based representation [12].

Lemma 1. Given M (learning measure in original feature space) and non-linear mapping Φ, the projection of eigenvector transformation is equivalent to that of eigenvector transformation.

$$M\Phi = \Psi K \tag{4}$$

where Ψ represents the approximate combination of eigenvectors, and K is the corresponding core matrix corresponding to the non-linear mapping Φ. Therefore, in the kernel space, the original optimization of solving metric M in the original feature space (using the non-linear mapping Φ) is converted to the equivalent form by solving Ψ (using the kernel matrix K).

Inspired by Torresani and Lee [12], given K calculated on all training samples of known labels, the task of learning metric Ψ and single non-IID representation can be defined as the following objective functions:

$$\varepsilon(\Psi; K) = \sum_{m,n} \eta_{mn} ||\Psi(k_m - k_n)||^2 + \lambda \sum_{m,n,l} \eta_{mn}(1 - y_{ml})$$
$$h\left(||\Psi(k_m - k_n)||^2 - ||\Psi(k_m - k_n)||^2 + 1\right) \tag{5}$$

where $\eta_{mn} \in \{0,1\}$ denotes that if the j-th training sample is one of the k nearest neighbors of the m-th training sample with the same label y_m. $y_{ml} \in \{0,1\}$ denotes whether the m-th training sample and the l-th training sample have the same label. $h(g) = max(g, 0)$ is the hinge loss function. λ is the weight parameter of the second term. K_m is column m of K. Gradient descent method is used to get Ψ, and learning metric Ψ is used to map from the kernel space to the transformation space, thus the mapping eigenvector is obtained.

The proposed level set segmentation method is based on the region-based CV model. After SLIC algorithm [13] processing, the K pixels are selected. The region composed of these pixels is defined as Ω', and the energy function of the proposed method:

$$E_{CV} = \mu \int_{\Omega} \delta(\varphi) |\nabla_\varphi| dxdy +$$
$$\lambda_1 \int_{\Omega} |I - C_1|^2 H(\varphi) dxdy + \lambda_2 \int_{\Omega} |I - C_2|^2 (1 - H(\varphi)) dxdy \tag{6}$$

where I represent the information of K pixels, C_1 represents the information of the pixels marked as the target in the evolution process, and C_2 represents the information of the pixels marked as the background in the evolution process. In the existing theory, the pixel information represented by C_1 and C_2 is gray mean, which is better applied in images with obvious gray change and clear boundary. But for images with little gray change and blurred boundary, the segmentation effect of using gray mean to segment information is poor. In this paper, a single gray level information is replaced by multi-dimensional information to improve the segmentation accuracy.

For the experimental settings, each super-pixel block in the image is selected as its neighborhood, and the method of non-IID is introduced. We use SLIC [13] to segment super-pixels and extract 148-dimension features. The gray information in C_1 and C_2 is replaced by the image information in the feature matrix, which makes the level set method more accurate.

The implementation steps of image segmentation algorithm based on non-IID and level set are summarized as follows:

(1) The image is segmented into super-pixels using SLIC algorithm, and then 148-dimensional feature vectors are extracted from each image block to represent the super-pixel block.
(2) The seed points are given by the user, and each super-pixel containing the color points is assigned a corresponding label (i.e. background or foreground).
(3) Each super-pixel and its adjacent super-pixels are modeled by the non-IID representation. The kernel function K and learning metric Ψ are calculated by the non-IID method. After the transformation of feature space, new high-dimensional feature vectors are obtained.
(4) The obtained eigenvectors are introduced into the energy function to represent C_1 and C_2, and the updated energy function is continuously calculated. When the energy function reaches the minimum, the iteration is stopped and the segmentation results are obtained.

3 Experimental Results and Analysis

In order to verify the validity of the level set method based on non-IID, this paper carries out image segmentation experiments, and compares the results with those of other classical image segmentation algorithms, and makes a lot of comparative experiments. The algorithms of our proposed model are implemented by MATLAB R2016b on a 2.70-GHz PC.

Error rate is the most common, simple and rough classification index. The calculation method is as follows: Let the test sample set $T = \{(X_1, Y_1), ..., (X_n, Y_n)\}$, in which X_i is the input feature of the sample I and Y_i is the real label of the sample. The predicted results of T: $PY = \{PY_1, PY_2, ..., PY_n\}$, in which PY represents the predicted results of the model for the first sample in T. In fact, the error rate is the proportion of all the wrong samples to all the samples.

$$Error\ rate = \frac{\sum\{1|Y_i \neq PY_i\}}{\sum\{1|Y_i = Y_i\}} \tag{7}$$

3.1 Simple Image Segmentation

For the problem of image segmentation with clear and simple boundary, the general level set method can get the desired segmentation results. Figure 2 shows the results of eight simple image segmentation methods. However, MSRM [15] and Grab Cut [18] methods cannot process such images. Moreover, our method greatly improves the operation speed and reduces the number of iterations. For the image segmentation of Fig. 2, our method has 10 iterations and 0.68 s iteration time.

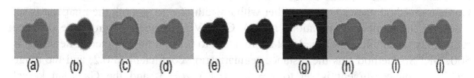

Fig. 2. Simple image segmentation results (a) original image (b) active contours [14] (c) Chan-Vese (d) DRLSE [20] (e) GAC [2] (f) bias correction (g) one cut [17] (h) random walks [19] (i) RSF [16] (j) our method

3.2 Image Segmentation with Weak Edges

The segmentation results of complex images are shown in Fig. 3. The experimental results show that only our method can successfully segment all kinds of complex images, eliminate the interference of complex lines in foreground background, solve the unstable problems such as weak edge leakage, and have strong robustness.

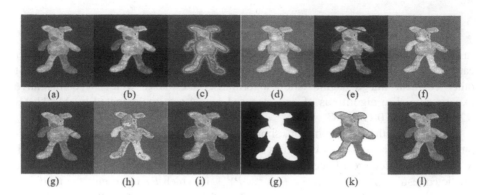

Fig. 3. Image segmentation results with weak edges (a) original image (b) active contours (c) Chan-Vese (d) DRLSE (e) GAC (f) bias correction (g) random walks (h) RSF (i) MSRM (j) one cut (k) grab cut (l) our method.

As shown in Fig. 3, we chose a weak edge image, whose partial foreground and background color are similar. We analyze the processing results of various segmentation methods. Our method obviously solves the problem of weak edge leakage. Compared with other classical methods, we have achieved better segmentation results. The error rate of our method is only 0.0099.

3.3   Segmentation of Complex Images

When the image is relatively complex, our method can get good segmentation results compared with the traditional image segmentation methods. In this part of the experiment, the data set we used is MSRA Salient Object Database [21]. As shown in Fig. 4, the parameters for various image segmentation methods are set as follows: Active Contours method uses a Gaussian filter with a width of σ to smooth the image, σ is set to 1 and the number of iterations is 200; Chan-Vese method controls the distance regularization coefficient of the level set function to 0.2 and the number of iterations is 500; DRLSE method sets the distance regularization coefficient to 0.2, and the range regularization coefficient is set to $\lambda = 5$, $e = 1.5$, $a = 3$, and the Gaussian kernel function. The number variance σ is set to 8 and the number of iterations is 110; RSF method, $\varepsilon = 1$, $\mu = 1$, $\sigma = 3$, the number of iterations is 300.

As can be seen from Fig. 4, our method can deal with various complex images effectively, but other methods cannot deal with these images successfully because of the influence of texture changes, shading changes and so on. Our method not only has high accuracy, but also has short iteration time. To quantitatively evaluate the performance of the proposed method, the comparisons of the processing performance of our method for different pictures are shown in Table 1.

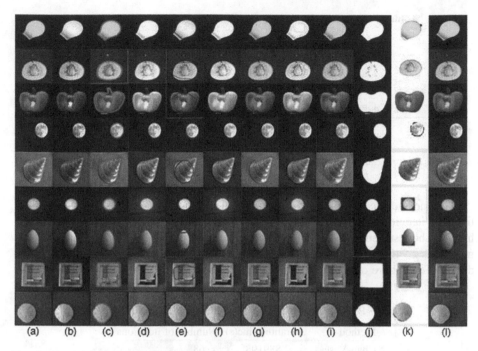

Fig. 4. Foreground complex image segmentation results (a) original image (b) active contours (c) Chan-Vese (d) DRLSE (e) GAC (f) bias correction (g) random walks (h) RSF (i) MSRM (j) one cut (k) grab cut (l) our method.

Table 1. Comparisons of the processing performance of our method for different pictures

Image	Iteration time(s)	Number of iterations	Error rate
A	4.833563	20	0.0140
B	8.498210	30	0.0052
C	3.059185	10	0.0015
D	6.279207	20	0.0052
R	2.222496	10	0.0083
F	2.647067	10	0.0018
G	6.250935	20	0.0014
H	2.945341	10	0.0016

From Table 1, we can see that for the different pictures in Fig. 4, our method shows good performance, low iteration times, short running time, low error rate, and the highest error rate is only 0.014.

Table 2. Performance comparison of different methods for shell image

Method	Iteration time(s)	Number of iterations
Chan-Vese	3.101399	85
DRLSE	7.397219	110
GAC	23.504559	1050
Grab cut	114.668891	12
Bias correctio	15.814876	20
RSF	19.005226	300
Ours	2.945341	10

Our method is compared with other classical methods horizontally, and the iteration time and iteration times of each method are also compared. We can see that our method has the shortest iteration time and the least iteration times. The iteration time of our method is 2.945 s, and the number of iterations is 10, and the error rate is 0.0016. The data in Table 2 are obtained by processing the ninth picture in Fig. 4.

Table 3. Performance comparison of different methods for egg image

Method	Iteration time(s)	Number of iterations
Chan-Vese	2.889198	68
DRLSE	7.794251	110
GAC	26.259603	1050
Grab cut	193.291041	28
Bias correctio	18.784614	34
RSF	17.399456	300
Ours	2.647067	10

The data in Table 3 are obtained by processing the seventh picture in Fig. 4. As you can see, our iteration time is 2.647 s, the iteration times are only 10 times, and for this picture, our error rate is 0.0018. Our method is not only fast but also accurate, so our performance is the best compared with other methods.

4   Conclusion

In this paper, a level set image segmentation method based on the non-IID method is proposed. The idea of non-IID is introduced into the level set method. The new eigenvectors are obtained by non-IID methods and new energy functions are constructed by using the new eigenvectors. It solves the unstable problems of the traditional level set method, such as single image type, sensitive to noise, easy to fall into false boundary, slow convergence speed and easy to leak from weak edge, and has strong robustness. At the same time, the model also has some areas to be improved, for example, it is sensitive to the initial boundary. If the foreground and background are not given well, it cannot be effectively segmented. This is also the direction of further improvement based on the model in the future.

Acknowledgments. This work was supported by National Key R&D Program of China (2016YFC0303707).

References

1. Osher, S., Sethian, J.A.: Fronts propagating with curvature dependent speed algorithms based on Hamilton-Jacobi formulations. J. Comput. Phys. **79**(1), 12–49 (1988)
2. Vicent, C., Ron, K., Guillermo, S.: Geodesic active contours. Int. J. Comput. Vis. **22**(1), 61–79 (1997)
3. Tony, F., Luminita, A.: Active contours without edges. IEEE Trans. Image Process. **10**(2), 266–277 (2001)
4. Olivier, B., Denis, F., Philippe, T., et al.: Variational b-spline level-set: a linear filtering approach for fast deformable model evolution. IEEE Trans. Image Process. **18**(6), 1179–1191 (2009)
5. Li, C., Huang, R., Ding, Z., et al.: A level set method for image segmentation in the presence of intensity inhomogeneities with application to MRI. IEEE Trans. Image Process. **20**(7), 2007–2016 (2011)
6. Zhang, F., Zhang, X.: Distance regularized level set image segmentation based on dislocation theory. J. Autom. **44**(5), 943–952 (2017)
7. Zhang, Y., Guo, H.: Level set image segmentation based on rough set and new energy formula. J. Autom. **41**(11), 1913–1925 (2015)
8. Zhu, Y., Weng, G.: Evolution model of distance rule level set with energy enhancement of area term. Cartography J. **39**(1), 12–20 (2018)
9. Shi, Y., Li, W., Gao, Y., Cao, L., et al.: Beyond IID: learning to combine non-IID metrics for vision tasks. In: AAAI-17 (2017)
10. Teney, D., Brown, M., Kit, D., Hall, P.: Learning similarity metrics for dynamic scene segmentation. In: CVPR 2015 (2015)
11. Cao, L.: Independent and distributed recommendation system: summary and framework of recommendation paradigm conversion. Engineering **2**(02), 138–165 (2016)
12. Torresani, L., Lee, K.: Large margin component analysis. In: NIPS, pp. 1385–1392(2007)
13. Achanta, R., Shaji, A., Smith, K., et al.: SLIC superpixels compared to state-of-the-art superpixel methods. TPAMI **34**(11), 2274–2282 (2012)
14. Zhang, K., Xu, S., Zhou, W., et al.: Active contours based on image laplacian fitting energy. Chin. J. Electron. **18**(2), 281–284 (2009)
15. Ning, J., Zhang, L., Zhang, D., et al.: Interactive image segmentation by maximal similarity-based region merging. Pattern Recogn. **43**(2), 445–456 (2010)
16. Li, C., Kao, C., et al.: Minimization of region-scalable fitting energy for image segmentation. IEEE Trans. Image Process. **17**(10), 1940–1949 (2008)
17. Tang, M., Gorelick, L., Olga, V., et al.: GrabCut in one cut. In: ICCV 2013 (2013)
18. Carsten, R., Vladimir, K., Andrew, B.: Grab cut: interactive foreground extraction using iterated graph cuts. ACM Trans. Graph. **23**(3), 309–314 (2004)

19. Leo, G.: Random walks for image segmentation. IEEE Trans. Pattern Anal. Mach. Intell. **28**(11), 1768–1783 (2006)
20. Li, C., Xu, C., et al.: Distance regularized level set evolution and its application to image segmentation. IEEE Trans. Image Process. **19**(12), 3243–3254 (2010)
21. Cheng, M., Mitra, N., et al.: Global contrast based salient region detection. IEEE Trans. Pattern Anal. Mach. Intell. **37**, 569–582 (2015)

KSLIC: K-mediods Clustering Based Simple Linear Iterative Clustering

Houwang Zhang[1,2](✉) and Yuan Zhu[1,2]

[1] School of Automation, China University of Geosciences,
Wuhan 430074, China
{zhanghw,zhuyuan}@cug.edu.cn
[2] Hubei Key Laboratory of Advanced Control and Intelligent Automation
for Complex Systems, Wuhan 430074, China

Abstract. Simple Linear Iterative Clustering (SLIC) is one of the most excellent superpixel segmentation algorithms with the most comprehensive performance and is widely used in various scenes of production and living. As a preprocessing step in image processing, superpixel segmentation should meet various demands in real life as much as possible, but SLIC is highly sensitive to noise. In this paper, a K-mediods clustering based simple linear iterative clustering (KSLIC) is proposed, which replaces the K-means clustering in SLIC with a modified local K-mediods clustering. To evaluate the performance of KSLIC, we test it on BSD500 benchmark dataset. The results show that it outperforms SLIC in terms of different noise environments including Gaussian noise, multiplicative noise and salt and pepper noise.

Keywords: Superpixel segmentation · SLIC · K-mediods clustering method · Noise-insensitive

1 Introduction

Image segmentation is to subdivide an image into sub regions based on similarities in features such as grayscale, color, and texture, and exhibit differences among different regions. Image segmentation, as a basic problem in the field of computer vision, is an important part of image processing. The traditional segmentation methods use pixels as the basic processing unit, and the computational efficiency is often low when processing a large scale of images [17]. In 2003, Ren *et al.* [11] proposed the concept of superpixel, which refers to sub regions these are local and continuous in the image, can maintain the local structural features of the image. Superpixel segmentation technology is often used in the image preprocessing stage, replacing the original pixels of the image with

This work was jointly supported by the Natural Science Foundation of Hubei Province with Grant No. 2016CFB481, the National Natural Science Foundation of China with Grant No. 61703375, and the 111 project with Grant No. B17040.

© Springer Nature Switzerland AG 2019
Z. Lin et al. (Eds.): PRCV 2019, LNCS 11858, pp. 519–529, 2019.
https://doi.org/10.1007/978-3-030-31723-2_44

superpixels, which can reduce redundant information and complexity, and avoid under-segmentation. There are many applications in the fields of image quality assessment [14], color image segmentation [5,17], object tracking [13], object localization [4], hand gesture recognition [16], body model estimation [8] and more.

Generally, a good superpixel segmentation algorithm takes into consideration the properties of compactness, partition, connectivity, boundary adherence, computational complexity, memory efficiency, and controllable number superpixels [10,18]. Simple Linear Iterative Clustering algorithm (SLIC) meets most of these properties and has good performance at the same time [2,10]. The main idea of SLIC is that the image is transformed from RGB space to CIELAB space, each pixel can be represented as a five-dimensional vector $V = [l, a, b, x, y]^T$, where $[l, a, b]^T$ is the pixel color vector in CIELAB color space, and $[x, y]^T$ is the pixel position. The SLIC uses the Euclidean distance as a similarity measurement to cluster pixels into superpixels. Therefore, SLIC can segment the image into sub regions with good boundary adherence and regular size.

However, SLIC is very sensitive to noise [7,18], when the image is contaminated by noise, SLIC tends to perform poorly. And the number of superpixels generated by SLIC will also fall sharply [18]. To solve this problem, some researchers proposed local spatial constrained fuzzy C-means clustering and dynamic fuzzy superpixels, and their method achieves quite good results against noise [18]. Inspired by that, in this paper, we propose K-mediods clustering based simple linear iterative clustering (KSLIC) which is based on a modified local K-mediods clustering method.

The rest of paper is organized as follows. In Sect. 2, we introduce the details of our new proposed method KSLIC. The comparison experiments and the results are demonstrated in Sect. 3. Section 4 concludes the paper.

2   KSLIC Algorithm

Like SLIC, first we initialize the cluster centers in the image plane, which is done in the five-dimensional space. According to the number of superpixels k, seed points are evenly distributed in the image with size $M \times N$. Then the image is pre-segmented into k superpixels of the same size, i.e. each superpixel consists of $\frac{M*N}{k}$ pixels, and the distance s of the adjacent seed points is $\sqrt{\frac{M*N}{k}}$.

2.1   Distance Measure

In the clustering process, the affinity of a pixel to a center is measured using a distance in the space of CIELAB color and spatial coordinates. Here KSLIC uses the same distance measure as SLIC. The distance between the ith superpixel center $[l_i, a_i, b_i, x_i, y_i]^T$ and the jth candidate pixel $[l_j, a_j, b_j, x_j, y_j]^T$ in the image with size of $M \times N$ is defined as follows:

$$d_{i,j} = d_{lab} + \frac{m}{s}d_{xy}$$

$$d_{lab} = \sqrt{(l_i - l_j)^2 + (a_i - a_j)^2 + (b_i - b_j)^2}$$

$$d_{xy} = \sqrt{(x_i - x_j)^2 + (y_i - y_j)^2} \tag{1}$$

where s and m are used to normalize the spatial distances d_{xy} and color distances d_{lab}, respectively. s is the maximum spatial distance within a class, defined as $s = \sqrt{\frac{M*N}{k}}$, which is suitable for each cluster. The maximum color distance m, also called compactness factor, its value is user-provided and can be set in the range $[1, 40]$.

2.2 Calculation of Centers

In each iteration, SLIC sets the ith center $C_i = [l_i, a_i, b_i, x_i, y_i]^T$ by computing the mean values of pixels belonging to ith superpixel in five-dimensional space. But when the image is contaminated by noise, the information of pixels will deviate from original values, so using the mean values of pixels in the superpixel as the cluster center is not a suitable choice. And we know that for clustering algorithms, the selection and distribution of cluster centers play an important role, while K-means clustering is sensitive to noise. In order to reduce the influence of noise and ensure the clustering effect, we consider using the K-mediods clustering method to choose centers rather than just using mean values as a cluster center for expecting the algorithm with better robustness and stability.

Considering that K-mediods method is much more expensive to implement than K-means method and the center of surperpixel has a certain similarity with the mean values of pixels in currant superpixel. In KSLIC, we suppose that the center is generally distributed around the mean values, we firstly calculate the mean values, then set a search range nearby the mean values, after that, search for the elements with the smallest distance from all the pixels of the current superpixel, and finally use these elements as the center of the superpixel.

Suppose that the ith superpixel contains n pixels, $\bar{l}, \bar{a}, \bar{b}, \bar{x}$ and $\bar{y}$ are the mean of correspond elements during the ith superpixel. Then, we take the element L within dimension l for example to illustrate the KSLIC for calculating the cluster center. Elements of other dimensions are handled in the same way. We give a definition before giving the flowchart of the calculation.

Definition: The distance between an element L and the ith superpixel S_i of the image is denoted by $D(L, S_i)$ and defined by Eq. (2).

$$D(L, S_i) = \sum_{j=1}^{n} |L - l_{ij}| \tag{2}$$

where n is the pixel number of S_i, $\{l_{ij}, j = 1, 2, ..., n\}$ are the n elements of n pixels in S_i within dimension l.

The specific calculation process is as follows:

- **Step 1.** Fix element $\bar{l}$ as the center.
- **Step 2.** Set the search range. Specifically, the search set is $F_l \triangleq [\bar{l} - \frac{n}{20}, \bar{l} + \frac{n}{20}]$ with the range of $n/10$ and the step width of 1. For different element in five-dimensional space, we can also get the corresponding search sets F_a, F_b, F_x and F_y, respectively.
- **Step 3.** Calculate the distance $D(l_p, S_i)$ between every element l_p and S_i, where $l_p \in F_l$, $p = 1, 2, ..., n/10$.
- **Step 4.** Compare the distance and gain the smallest one, namely, $D_{min} = \min\limits_{p} D(l_p, S_i)$, and get the cluster element of $\hat{l} = \arg\min\limits_{l_p \in F_l} D(l_p, S_i)$.

According to this process, we can finally get $\hat{a}$, $\hat{b}$, $\hat{x}$ and $\hat{y}$. The cluster center is $[\hat{l}, \hat{a}, \hat{b}, \hat{x}, \hat{y}]^{\mathrm{T}}$ for S_i, and our method for calculation of the center of the super-pixel is illustrated in Fig. 1.

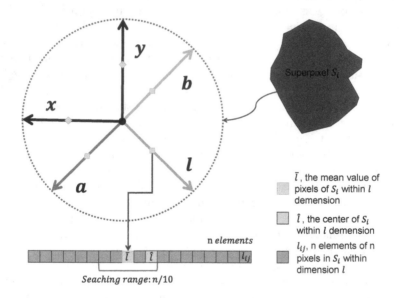

Fig. 1. Calculation of center: firstly, calculate the mean values of pixels within the current superpixel in the five dimensions, respectively. And then the center element is selected based on the principle of minimizing the distance between all pixels in the current superpixel in a range of $n/10$.

Other processes of the algorithm are consistent with SLIC. Referring to the specific algorithm flow of SLIC, here we give the algorithm pseudo code of KSLIC in Algorithm 1.

Algorithm 1. KSLIC

Input: Image, number of superpixels k, compactness factor m;
Output: Label matrix l;

/* Initialization */
Initialize cluster centers C_k by sampling pixels at regular grid steps $S = \sqrt{\frac{M*N}{k}}$.
Move cluster centers to the lowest gradient position in a $3*3$ neighborhood.
Set label $l(i) = -1$ for each pixel i.
Set distance $d(i) = \infty$ for each pixel i.

repeat

    /*Assignment*/
    for each cluster center C_k **do**
        for each pixel i in a $2S*2S$ region around C_k **do**
            Compute the distance d between C_k and i.
                if $d < d(i)$
                    Set $d(i) = d$.
                    Set $l(i) = k$.
                endif
        endfor
    endfor

    /*update*/
    for each superpixel S_i with n pixels **do**
        compute its mean values $[\hat{\mathbf{l}}, \hat{\mathbf{a}}, \hat{\mathbf{b}}, \hat{\mathbf{x}}, \hat{\mathbf{y}}]^{\mathrm{T}}$.
        for each dimension j in the five-dimensional space
            Set distance $D(j) = \infty$.
            for each element f_p in searching range $n/10$ **do**
                if $D(f_p, S_i) \leq D(j)$
                    Set $D(j) = D(f_p, S_i)$.
                    Set $f_j = f_p$.
                endif
            endfor
        endfor
        Set cluster center $[\mathbf{l_i}, \mathbf{a_i}, \mathbf{b_i}, \mathbf{x_i}, \mathbf{y_i}]^{\mathrm{T}} = [\mathbf{f_1}, \mathbf{f_2}, \mathbf{f_3}, \mathbf{f_4}, \mathbf{f_5}]^{\mathrm{T}}$.
    endfor

    Computer new residual error E.

until $E \leq threshold$

Enforce connectivity.

3   Experiments and Results

In this section, we compare KSLIC with SLIC. And for the fairness, we use the published source code of SLIC [1].

In the experiments, we compare the performance of SLIC and KSILC on the Berkeley benchmark (BSD500) [3] under four kinds of environments, which contain non-noise environment, Gaussian noise environment, multiplicative noise environment, and salt and pepper noise environment.

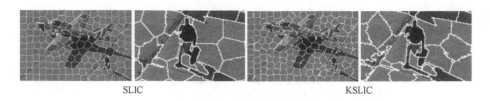

SLIC   KSLIC

Fig. 2. Image segmentation results of SLIC and KSLIC in non-noise environment. Note: the number of desired superpixels and compactness factor of SLIC and KSLIC are set to 200 and 20, respectively.

3.1   Evaluation Metrics

Three standard evaluation metrics are chosen to compare the performance between SLIC and KSLIC: boundary recall rate [6], under segmentation error [15] and compactness metric [12].

Boundary recall (BR) is used to measure the hitting rate between the super-pixels boundary and the image boundary. The larger BR rate is, the better preservation effect of the generated superpixels on the image boundary is.

Under segmentation error (UE) means the proportion of the area in the image that cannot be completely covered by superpixels. The lower UE is, the more accurate the algorithm is.

Compactness refers to the degree to which the shape of a superpixel is closer to a circle. Compactness metric (CO) can measure the compactness of super-pixels based on the isoperimetric quotient [9], and higher CO rate means better compactness.

3.2   Parameter Settings of Algorithms

In the experiments, the parameters settings between SLIC and KSLIC are the same with the max iterations 10 and compactness coefficient 20.

3.3   Results and Analysis

Figures 2, 3 show the image segmentation results of SLIC and KSLIC in non-noise environment and noise environments, respectively. Figure 2 shows that KSLIC

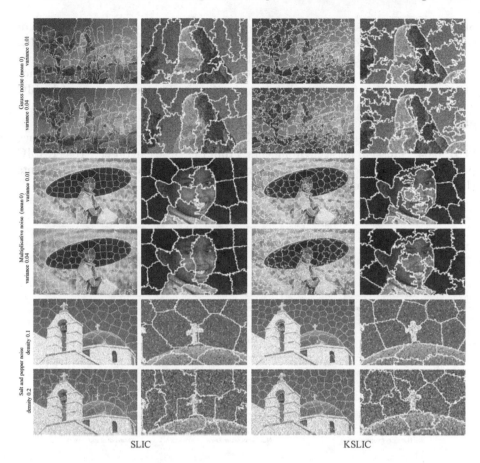

Fig. 3. Image segmentation results of SLIC and KSLIC in noise environments, which consists of Gaussian noise environment, multiplicative noise environment, salt and pepper noise environment. Note: the number of desired superpixels and compactness factor of SLIC and KSLIC are set to 200 and 20, respectively.

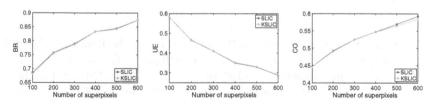

Fig. 4. Results from the non-noise experiment group.

can segment more image details than SLIC. From Fig. 3, we can see that SLIC and KSLIC both perform poorly in the case of Gaussian noise and multiplicative noise, but KSLIC can still maintain the number of superpixels while the number of superpixels generated by SLIC reduces much more severely, and in the case of salt and pepper noise, the performance KSLIC is significantly better than SLIC.

Figure 4 shows the performance of KSLIC and SLIC in the non-noise environment. We can see that although SLIC has better compactness, the difference of CO among these two methods is not significant. The performance of KSLIC and SLIC in BR rate and UE is almost the same. Some visual comparison results are shown in Fig. 2.

Figure 5 shows the performance of KSLIC and SLIC in the mean 0, variance [0.01, 0.04] Gaussian noise environments. From Fig. 5 we can observe that KSLIC performs better under both high and low variance Gaussian noise environments (KSLIC obtain higher BR rate, CO and lower UE).

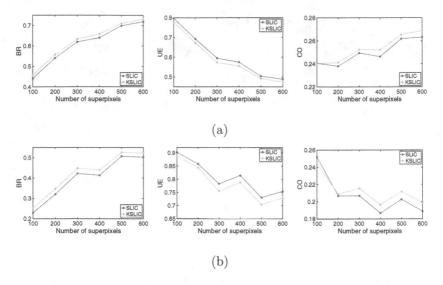

Fig. 5. Results from the experiment group with different Gaussian noise. (a) The Gaussian noise with mean 0 and variance 0.01. (b) The Gaussian noise with mean 0 and variance 0.04.

Figure 6 shows performance of SLIC and KSLIC in the multiplicative noise environments (multiplied by mean 0, variance [0.01, 0.04] Gaussian noise). From Fig. 6 we can see that although the BR rate and UE of SLIC is slightly better than that of KSLIC at the case of variance of 0.01, but the CO of KSLIC is obviously higher than that of SLIC, and KSLIC performs significantly better than SLIC at the case of variance of 0.04.

Figure 7 shows performance of SLIC and KSLIC in the salt and pepper noise environments (noise density [0.1, 0.2]). From Fig. 7 we can see that KSLIC achieves higher BR rate, CO and lower UE under both high and low level salt and pepper noise environments, which further proves the robustness of KSLIC. Some visual comparison results under noise environments are shown in Fig. 3.

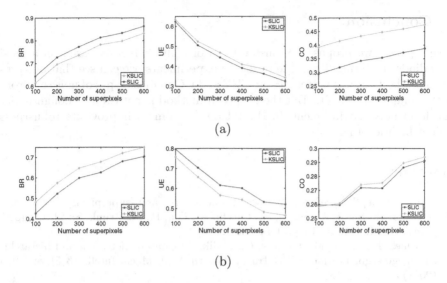

(a)

(b)

Fig. 6. Results from the experiment group with different multiplicative noise. (a) Multiplied by mean 0 and variance 0.01 Gaussian noise. (b) Multiplied by mean 0 and variance 0.04 Gaussian noise.

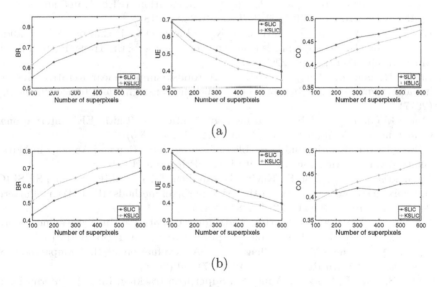

(a)

(b)

Fig. 7. Results from the experiment group with different noise density. (a) The salt and pepper noise with density 0.1. (b) The salt and pepper noise with density 0.2.

4   Conclusion

In this paper, we propose a robust version of SLIC, which is based on a local K-mediods clustering. From the results of experiments, we can see that our proposed method obtains better BR rate, UE and CO in most types of noise environments compared to SLIC. But the proposed method is not robust enough under high-level noise environment, in the future, we aim to improve its robustness against high-level noise.

References

1. https://ivrl.epfl.ch/research-2/research-current/research-superpixels/
2. Achanta, R., Shaji, A., Smith, K., Lucchi, A., Fua, P., Süsstrunk, S.: SLIC superpixels. EPFL Technical report 149300 (2010)
3. Arbelaez, P., Maire, M., Fowlkes, C., Malik, J.: Contour detection and hierarchical image segmentation. IEEE Trans. Pattern Anal. Mach. Intell. **33**(5), 898–916 (2011)
4. Fulkerson, B., Vedaldi, A., Soatto, S.: Class segmentation and object localization with superpixel neighborhoods. In: 2009 IEEE 12th International Conference on Computer Vision, pp. 670–677 (2009)
5. Lei, T., Jia, X., Zhang, Y., Liu, S., Meng, H., Nandi, A.K.: Superpixel-based fast fuzzy C-means clustering for color image segmentation. IEEE Trans. Fuzzy Syst. (2018). https://doi.org/10.1109/TFUZZ.2018.2889018
6. Levinshtein, A., Stere, A., Kutulakos, K.N., Fleet, D.J., Dickinson, S.J., Siddiqi, K.: Turbopixels: fast superpixels using geometric flows. IEEE Trans. Pattern Anal. Mach. Intell. **31**(12), 2290–2297 (2009)
7. Li, S., Huang, J., Shang, J., Wei, X.: A robust simple linear iterative clustering algorithm. In: IEEE International Conference on Signal and Image Processing (2017)
8. Mori, G.: Guiding model search using segmentation. In: Tenth IEEE International Conference on Computer Vision, 2, pp. 1417–1423 (2005)
9. Pólya, G.: Mathematics and Plausible Reasoning: Induction and Analogy in Mathematics, vol. 1. Princeton University Press, Princeton (1990)
10. Radhakrishna, A., Appu, S., Kevin, S., Aurelien, L., Pascal, F., Sabine, S.: SLIC superpixels compared to state-of-the-art superpixel methods. IEEE Trans. Pattern Anal. Mach. Intell. **34**(11), 2274–2282 (2012)
11. Ren, M.: Learning a classification model for segmentation. In: Proceedings Ninth IEEE International Conference on Computer Vision, vol. 1, pp. 10–17 (2003)
12. Schick, A., Fischer, M., Stiefelhagen, R.: An evaluation of the compactness of superpixels. Pattern Recogn. Lett. **43**(1), 71–80 (2014)
13. Wang, S., Lu, H., Yang, F., Yang, M.: Superpixel tracking. In: 2011 International Conference on Computer Vision, pp. 1323–1330 (2011)
14. Sun, W., Liao, Q., Xue, J.H., Zhou, F.: SPSIM: a superpixel-based similarity index for full-reference image quality assessment. IEEE Trans. Image Process. **27**(9), 4232–4244 (2018)
15. Veksler, O., Boykov, Y., Mehrani, P.: Superpixels and supervoxels in an energy optimization framework. In: Daniilidis, K., Maragos, P., Paragios, N. (eds.) ECCV 2010. LNCS, vol. 6315, pp. 211–224. Springer, Heidelberg (2010). https://doi.org/10.1007/978-3-642-15555-0_16

16. Wang, C., Liu, Z., Chan, S.C.: Superpixel-based hand gesture recognition with kinect depth camera. IEEE Trans. Multimed. **17**(1), 29–39 (2014)
17. Wu, C., Zhang, L., Zhang, H., Yan, H.: Improved superpixel-based fast fuzzy C-means clustering for image segmentation. In: IEEE International Conference on Image Processing (ICIP) (2019)
18. Wu, C., Zhang, L., Zhang, H., Yan, H.: Fuzzy SLIC: fuzzy simple linear iterative clustering. arXiv preprint arXiv:1812.10932 (2018)

Social Behavior Recognition in Mouse Video Using Agent Embedding and LSTM Modelling

Zhenchuan Zhang, Yingchun Yang[(⊠)], and Zhaohui Wu

College of Computer Science and Technology,
Zhejiang University, Hangzhou 310027, Zhejiang, China
{11221052,yyc,wzh}@zju.edu.cn

Abstract. Growing demands for automated analysis of animal behavior in areas such as neuroscience, psychology, genetics and pharmacology have been witnessed in recent decades. Some progresses have been made, but studies on social behavior analysis, which is more challenging, are rarely seen and almost all of them rely on hand-crafted features. Motivated by the concept of word embedding in NLP and the success of deep learning, we present a method that extracts features for both of the mouse agents involved in social behavior events and the scenario context using embedding networks, then uses an LSTM network to model the behaviors based on the agent and context embeddings. Our method is tested on a novel dataset, RatSI [8]. We find our mouse state embedding method outperforms traditional hand-crafted feature based methods.

Keywords: Behavior recognition · Social behavior recognition · Mouse social behavior recognition · Rat social interaction recognition

1 Introduction

Rats and mice are widely used in the scientific and preclinical research experiments in neuroscience, psychology, genetics and pharmacology. These experiments demand for massive behavior analysis work. The most common way of measuring the animal behaviors from the video is to resort to human experts to watch the video carefully and manually annotate. This process is dull, labor-intensive, low throughput, subjective and difficult to reproduce.

Having seen these defects, researchers have turned to automated analysis methods for help, which are developing fast with advancements in computer vision, computing power and machine learning techniques. These works could be roughly divided into two types: 1. using hand-crafted geometric or motion features and a powerful classifier backend such as SVM or AdaBoost, these works

---

Student paper.

© Springer Nature Switzerland AG 2019
Z. Lin et al. (Eds.): PRCV 2019, LNCS 11858, pp. 530–541, 2019.
https://doi.org/10.1007/978-3-030-31723-2_45

include [1,4,5,8,11,12,16,17]; 2. using automatically learned spatio-temporal features or end-to-end classifier inspired by recent progresses in deep learning and computer vision, such as works in [1,2,10].

On the other hand, these works mainly focus on the behavior analysis for a single mouse, while mouse social interactions are gradually getting more attention in experiments on several diseases and drug effects on emotion [3,7,9,15], yet few works have been done on this topic. The only works on this topic include [1,4,8]. They share similarities to traditional single mouse behavior recognition: they use hand-crafted features and encode temporal information by stacking these features in a relative naive way.

In our opinion, although the hand-crafted features and methods provide acceptable performance in their original work, they are too compact and not so informative that they restrict the possibility of a powerful backend to distinguish among the temporal behaviors. Moreover, they are specified to their own task, hard to design and difficult to transfer to new tasks. And most of these works lack elaborate treatment of temporal information.

Inspired by methods in NLP and caption tasks, we reckon that embeddings for the agents are necessary, and based on these embeddings, powerful temporal backend models could be used.

In this work, we propose a method for mouse or rat social behavior recognition and test it on RatSI dataset [8]. Our main contributions are:

1. The introduction of agent embedding networks on mouse foreground images. The benefits are two-folds. First, the foreground images of mice are of high consistency within the target dataset and even across different datasets, thus embedding networks are supposed to be robust and have great generalization ability. Second, the embedding networks save researchers from the labor of developing powerful hand-crafted features, meanwhile provide even more powerful representation of the agent state.
2. The usage of an LSTM to recognize social interactions based on agent embeddings. This LSTM greatly mitigates the side-effect of the large variance of interaction durations, which is a key obstacle that restricts the application of human behavior analysis methods into the field of mouse behavior analysis.

Our method outperforms several traditional recognition methods for mouse social behaviors. The results are shown in Sect. 4.

2   Proposed Method

The diagram of our method is shown in Fig. 1, which consists of 3 stages.

In the preprocessing stage, the rat body foreground is extracted from the frame. Different background subtraction methods could be used. We use a median image as the background, and after simple subtraction and thresholding we get the rat foreground image. The mouse foreground image is resized to a fixed size of 112×112. To do social interaction recognition, identity tracking is

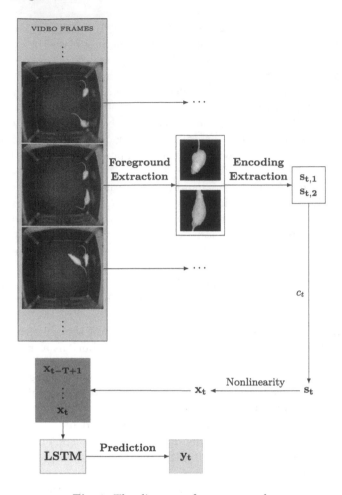

Fig. 1. The diagram of our approach.

necessary. The datasets provides tracking information for each rat so this topic is not discussed here.

In the feature extracting stage, the agent embedding is extracted from the mouse foreground image using a CNN based embedding network, which is first trained on individual mouse agent annotations provided by the dataset. The embeddings $s_{t,i}$ of the two mouses are connected together along with a set of scene context features d_t as s_t, and s_t go through a nonlinear transformation into x_t.

In the final social interaction recognition stage, the time series of x_t is fed into an LSTM network, the hidden state of which go through another nonlinear transformation and then is used to make predictions about the interaction possibility.

2.1   Agent Embedding

We use a modified VGG11 [14] architecture as the agent embedding network, the details are given in Table 1. The dimension for the input and output of the network is given by $\#channels \times height \times width$.

Table 1. The rat agent embedding network architecture. The input image is a monochrome foreground, whose size is $1 \times 112 \times 112$. The input to each layer is the output of the last layer. Embeddings are extracted at layer conv5, after squeezing and before nonlinearity. The N in the softmax layer corresponds to the number of behaviors.

Layer	Output size
conv1_1	$64 \times 112 \times 112$
maxpooling	$64 \times 56 \times 56$
conv2_1	$128 \times 56 \times 56$
maxpooling	$128 \times 28 \times 28$
conv3_1	$256 \times 28 \times 28$
conv3_2	$256 \times 28 \times 28$
maxpooling	$256 \times 14 \times 14$
conv4_1	$512 \times 14 \times 14$
conv4_2	$512 \times 14 \times 14$
maxpooling	$512 \times 7 \times 7$
conv5	$1024 \times 1 \times 1$
fc1	1024
fc2	softmax	N

The main modification is in the conv5 layers. The two consecutive convolutional layers kernel size of 3 in the original VGG11 are replaced with one new convolutional layer kernel size of 7, and the maxpooling layer is discarded. The main reason to this modification is that our input to this embedding network is very pure and compact, containing only the rat foreground and ideally nothing else, thus we are more interested in a global representation. So the new convolutional layer with a 7×7 kernel size is used to fuse the $512 \times 7 \times 7$ output of last layer. The resulting $1024d$ output of conv5 is used as agent embedding.

To train the embedding network, two fully connected layers are added following the conv5 layer to enable the network to classify the individual rat behavior. The training data are the individual agent behavior annotations.

The notation is as follows. The state embedding for each rat at frame t is given by

$$s_{t,i} = Embedding(fgd_{t,i}) \tag{1}$$

where $i = [1, 2]$ is the index of the rat, $fgd_{t,i}$ is the foreground image of each rat, $Embedding$ function is the embedding network up to conv5.

2.2   Interaction Modelling

We make an assumption that the social interaction could be fully told if the two states of both agents in recent moments are given along with scene context. This is reasonable since all the factors contributing to the occurrence of social interaction are considered.

Back in this rat social behavior scenario, we use an LSTM to model the interactions based on time series of state embeddings of both rats and the scene context. The states of each agent rat are given by their foreground embeddings $s_{t,i}$ described in previous Sect. 2.1. We use an additional CNN to extraction context information from the whole frame frm_t. For simplicity and convenience, this context network uses the same VGG11 architecture as the agent embedding networks. The input to this network is the resized video frame frm_t, and the $1024d$ output of conv5 is treated as context embedding c_t.

The recognition process is shown in Fig. 2.

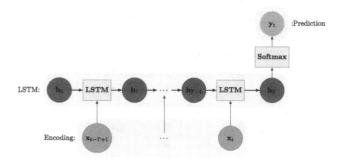

Fig. 2. The LSTM system for social behavior recognition.

The two state embeddings $s_{t,i}$ for each rat and the context feature c_t are connected as a single state embedding vector s_t:

$$s_t = [s_{t,1}, s_{t,2}, c_t].$$
(2)

To model the interaction within the embedding s_t, this vector is first fed into one non-linear transform layer:

$$x_t = ReLU(W_{is} * s_t),$$
(3)

the resulting vector x_t is then fed into the LSTM.

Based on the hidden state h_t of the LSTM, the behavior recognition result is obtained from one more non-linear layer:

$$y_t = Softmax(ReLU(W_{hp} * h_t)),$$
(4)

where y_t gives the probabilities of all social interactions at current frame t.

The LSTM we used has two layers, and the hidden state size is 1024. The length of the x_t series is described in Sect. 3.4. The loss function is the traditional cross-entropy between the predication y_t and ground truth gt_t:

$$loss_t = cross\_entropy(y_t, gt_t) \tag{5}$$

3 Experiment Setup

In this section, we detail our choice, preprocessing and postprocessing of the data for different modules.

3.1 Datasets

Currently, there are only three rodent social interaction behavior datasets publicly available for researchers, namely CRIM13 [1], MBADA [4] and RatSI [8]. We choose RatSI because it is the only one that provides individual rat behavior annotations which is necessary for embedding training.

The Rat Social Interaction (RatSI) [8] dataset comprises 9 fully annotated videos of two rats interacting socially in a 90 cm × 90 cm cage without bedding and accessories. The recordings are made from top-view perspective and each is about 15 min long. The tracking data of three points of rat body (head, body center and tail) and the social interaction type are provided frame-by-frame. For most frames, the individual behavior type is also provided.

The video resolution is of 576 × 576, and the frame rate is 25 fps. The video frame is 8-bit, monochrome.

The social and individual behavior annotations are one from the following nine: *allogrooming, approaching, following, moving away, nape attacking, pinning, social nose contact, solitary, other*. Example video frames for these behaviors are shown in Fig. 3.

Like all other rat behavior datasets, the occurrence frequencies of different behaviors have an extremely imbalanced distribution, where the most frequent type comprises 58.6% of the dataset while the least frequent type only accounts for 0.6%. The distribution of the 9 behavior annotation types is shown in Fig. 4.

3.2 Data Preparation

Here we detail how to prepare data for agent embedding network, context embedding network and the LSTM.

To train the agent embedding network, the foreground images of each of the agents should be first extracted from all video frames and resized to 112 × 112. This process is described in the beginning of Sect. 2. The ground truth is the corresponding annotation for that frame.

To train the context embedding network, the video frames should be resized to 112 × 112. The ground truth is the corresponding annotation for that frame.

As for LSTM, to give frame-by-frame predictions utilizing history frames, we split the videos into sequences of T-frame clips with $T - 1$ frames overlapped

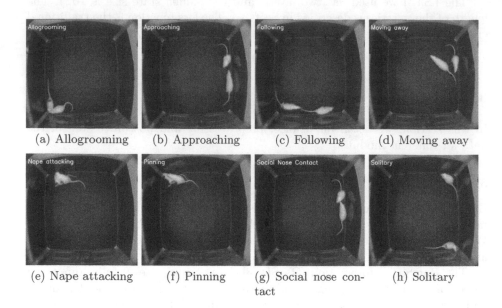

(a) Allogrooming   (b) Approaching   (c) Following   (d) Moving away

(e) Nape attacking   (f) Pinning   (g) Social nose con-   (h) Solitary
                                           tact

Fig. 3. RatSI dataset examples: video frames for each type of social interactions.

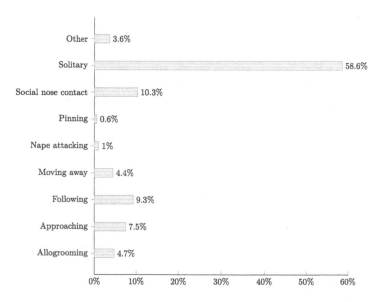

Fig. 4. The distribution of the 9 types of behavior annotations for RatSI.

between two consecutive clips. To enhance the generalization ability of LSTM, 5 settings of T are chosen: 5, 15, 25, 35 and 50. So each video is split into 5 sets of clip sequences. For each clip, all the three embeddings for each of the frames are first extracted. The ground truth for each clip is the manual label for the last frame within the clip. This process is also shown in Sect. 3.4.

As shown in last subsection, the distribution of behavior types is extremely imbalanced. We augment the less frequent behaviors by several forms of data augmentation. The clips for less frequent behaviors are randomly adjusted in brightness and contrast for context embedding training data. As for agent embeddings training data, the foreground masks are augmented with a random choice among 2 types of dilations and 1 type of erosion. The dilations and erosion are all of 3×3 kernels, one of the dilations and the erosion are of 1 iteration while the other dilation are of 2 iterations. Then, the masked frame, i.e. the foreground image is augmented with random noise. After these steps, the training become balanced.

Of the nine videos of RatSI, 6 of them are used as training data for all systems, and the other 3 of them are only used as test data. Data augmentation is only done for the training data.

3.3   Embedding Training

The three embedding networks are all trained from scratch with a batch size of 64 and an initial learning rate of 0.001. The training method is SGD with a momentum of 0.9. The learning rate was divided by 10 after every 4 epochs. The training was terminated after 20 epochs. The data used are described in last subsection.

After this training process, the embedding networks are frozen and not modified afterwards in LSTM training stage. The network up to conv5 are used to extract embeddings (the output of conv5).

3.4   LSTM Training and Evaluation

As described in Sect. 3.2, the training videos are split into overlapped clips of different durations: 5, 15, 25, 35, 50 frames. That is, for duration T, the training sample at frame t is,

$$
\begin{aligned}
input &= [s_{t-T+1}, s_{t-T+2}, ..., s_{t-1}, s_t] \\
output &= gt_t.
\end{aligned}
\tag{6}
$$

During training, the duration is first randomly determined for a mini-batch, then the mini-batch is sampled from the corresponding duration split.

This split process is done to enhance the generalization ability of LSTM to different time span.

In evaluation stage, the beginning 4 frames of a video are discarded and not for test. For the frames afterwards, the input is

$$
input = [s_{t-T'+1}, ..., s_t]
\tag{7}
$$

where $T' = max(25, t)$. That is, the recognition is mostly done based on a history of 25 frames.

3.5   Two Stream System

The two stream [13] is the baseline system for human behavior recognition and usually outperforms C3D. We have set up an 2 stream system as a comparison. The architecture is basically the same as the original work [13], the optical flows for each frame are stacked into an optical flow block for 10 frames, that is, nearly half a second. The only modification is that the spatial stream accepts monochrome images instead of rgb images.

The videos are split into clip sequences of equal length, each consists of 10 frames. For each time t, the resized frame frm_t is fed into the spatial stream, and 10 frames of optical flow prior time t, i.e., $[opfH_{t-9}, opfV_{t-9}, \dots, opfH_t, opfV_t]$, are fed into the temporal stream as in [13], where $opfH$ is the optical flow image in horizontal direction and $opfV$ is the optical flow image in vertical direction. The ground truth is the annotation for frame t.

4   Results

In this section, we provide our results.

In their original work [8], the evaluation is done on a simplified ethogram where *Allogrooming, Nape attacking, Pinning and Social nose contact* are merged into one common *Contact* class. Thus the 9 interaction types are now 5 where the results for *Other* are ignored.

We first report our results on this original setting shown in Table 2, and then give our results on the full ethogram in Table 3.

Table 2. Results on 5 interaction type settings. Matle *et al.* is the results of the original work in [8].

Class	Malte *et al.*	2-stream	Ours
Approaching	0.43	0.44	0.46
Contact	0.58	0.50	0.60
Following	0.53	0.48	0.55
Moving away	0.26	0.22	0.31
Solitary	0.80	0.93	0.85

Here we can see our method outperforms the traditional method based on trajectory features (Matle *et al.*) and 2-stream. The main reasons for the poor performance of 2-stream may be the lack of a mechanism to identify between the two subjects involved and the data imbalance. In contrast, although the

Table 3. Results on 9 interaction type settings.

Class	2-Stream	Ours
Allogrooming	0.49	0.56
Approaching	0.44	0.46
Following	0.48	0.55
Moving away	0.22	0.31
Nape attacking	0.11	0.13
Pinning	0.09	0.09
Social nose contact	0.57	0.68
Solitary	0.93	0.85
Other	0.33	0.29
Overall	0.73	0.71
Average	0.41	0.44

feature number is limited, the traditional trajectory feature method gives quite acceptable results. And our agent embedding method seems to benefit from explicit modelling of the two agents and context, and gives the best performance.

In Table 3, we show the recognition results of two methods on all the 9 inter- action types. The results demonstrate the influence of the data imbalance. The less occurring annotations get very low correctness. Our method outperforms 2-Stream in most of the behavior types except *Solitary*, and gives a higher mean recognition rate and a lower overall recognition rate.

5   Conclusions

In this paper, we propose a method to extract agent embedding from rat fore- ground image of video frame and use the embeddings to recognize the social interactions between two rats with the help of an LSTM. The embedding from foreground image is supposed to be easier to learn than features on whole image, and has better generalization ability. The additional cost is a pre-computing of rat foreground mask, which is easy for most of the rat experiments done in con- stant experiment settings. And the choice of LSTM mitigates the side-effect of the large variance in interaction durations.

We test our method on RatSI dataset, which outperforms 2-stream and the original hand-crafted feature based method in [8]. Like the performance of C3D [6] system in [10], straight forward adoptions of traditional neural networks based human behavior recognition methods struggle in rat behavior recognition tasks. The authors of [10] ascribe the less-than-ideal performance of C3D to the fixed temporal depth of the network, since the length of a rodent's behavior considered in their scenario can vary from as short as 3 frames (0.1 s) to as long as 45 frames (1.5 s), longer temporal depth may fail to capture short behaviors. Which is quite true for our experiment.

To our knowledge, this is the first work to extract agent embedding and use these embeddings along with context feature to recognize social interactions. We hope this work would be helpful to researchers interested in social interaction recognition.

References

1. Burgos-Artizzu, X.P., Dollár, P., Lin, D., Anderson, D.J., Perona, P.: Social behavior recognition in continuous video. In: 2012 IEEE Conference on Computer Vision and Pattern Recognition (CVPR), pp. 1322–1329. IEEE (2012)
2. Dollár, P., Rabaud, V., Cottrell, G., Belongie, S.: Behavior recognition via sparse spatio-temporal features. In: 2nd Joint IEEE International Workshop on Visual Surveillance and Performance Evaluation of Tracking and Surveillance, pp. 65–72. IEEE (2005)
3. File, S.E., Seth, P.: A review of 25 years of the social interaction test. Eur. J. Pharmacol. **463**(1–3), 35–53 (2003)
4. Giancardo, L., et al.: Automatic visual tracking and social behaviour analysis with multiple mice. PLoS ONE **8**(9), e74557 (2013)
5. Jhuang, H., et al.: Automated home-cage behavioural phenotyping of mice. Nat. Commun. **1**, 68 (2010)
6. Ji, S., Xu, W., Yang, M., Yu, K.: 3D convolutional neural networks for human action recognition. IEEE Trans. Pattern Anal. Mach. Intell. **35**(1), 221–231 (2013)
7. Lewejohann, L., Hoppmann, A.M., Kegel, P., Kritzler, M., Krüger, A., Sachser, N.: Behavioral phenotyping of a murine model of alzheimer's disease in a seminaturalistic environment using RFID tracking. Behav. Res. Methods **41**(3), 850–856 (2009)
8. Lorbach, M., Kyriakou, E.I., Poppe, R., van Dam, E.A., Noldus, L.P., Veltkamp, R.C.: Learning to recognize rat social behavior: Novel dataset and cross-dataset application. J. Neurosci. Methods **300**, 166–172 (2017)
9. Peters, S.M., Pothuizen, H.H., Spruijt, B.M.: Ethological concepts enhance the translational value of animal models. Eur. J. Pharmacol. **759**, 42–50 (2015)
10. Ren, Z., Annie, A.N., Ciernia, V., Lee, Y.J.: Who moved my cheese? Automatic annotation of rodent behaviors with convolutional neural networks. In: 2017 IEEE Winter Conference on Applications of Computer Vision (WACV), pp. 1277–1286. IEEE (2017)
11. Rousseau, J., Van Lochem, P., Gispen, W., Spruijt, B.: Classification of rat behavior with an image-processing method and a neural network. Behav. Res. Methods Instrum. Comput. **32**(1), 63–71 (2000)
12. Salem, G.H., et al.: SCORHE: a novel and practical approach to video monitoring of laboratory mice housed in vivarium cage racks. Behav. Res. Methods **47**(1), 235–250 (2015)
13. Simonyan, K., Zisserman, A.: Two-stream convolutional networks for action recognition in videos. In: Advances in Neural Information Processing Systems, pp. 568–576 (2014)
14. Simonyan, K., Zisserman, A.: Very deep convolutional networks for large-scale image recognition. arXiv preprint arXiv:1409.1556 (2014)

15. Urbach, Y.K., Bode, F.J., Nguyen, H.P., Riess, O., von Hörsten, S.: Neurobehavioral tests in rat models of degenerative brain diseases. In: Anegon, I. (ed.) Rat Genomics. MIMB, vol. 597, pp. 333–356. Humana Press, Totowa (2010). https://doi.org/10.1007/978-1-60327-389-3_24
16. Wang, Z., Mirbozorgi, S.A., Ghovanloo, M.: An automated behavior analysis system for freely moving rodents using depth image. Med. Biol. Eng. Comput. **56**, 1–15 (2018)
17. Zhang, Z., Yingchun, Y., Zhaohui, W., Qian, M.: A posture recognition system for rat cyborg automated navigation. Chin. J. Electron. **27**(4), 687–693 (2018)

Unsupervised Global Manifold Alignment for Cross-Scene Hyperspectral Image Classification

Wei Feng[1], Yuan Zhou[2], and Dou Jin[2(⊠)]

[1] Systems Engineering Research Institute of China State Shipbuilding Corporation,
Beijing 100036, China
[2] Tianjin University, Tianjin 300072, China
zhouyuan@tju.edu.cn,1577251747@qq.com

Abstract. Cross-scene hyperspectral image (HSI) classification has recently become increasingly popular due to its crucial use in various applications. It poses great challenges to existing domain adaptation methods because of the data set shift, that is, two scenes exhibit huge distribution discrepancy. To tackle this problem, we propose a new domain adaptation method called Unsupervised Global Manifold Alignment (UGMA) for cross-scene HSI classification. The proposed UGMA method learns a common subspace by introducing two different projection matrices to extract the transferable knowledge from the source domain to the target domain. Specifically, UGMA takes the advantages of manifold learning that reduces the dimensionality and preserves the geometry structure. What's more, in UGMA, we define a global geometry preserving term to deal with the situation where the global manifold geometry needs to be respected.

Keywords: Hyperspectral image classification · Cross-scene · Manifold alignment

1 Introduction

Pixel classification of hyperspectral images (HSIs) is of great importance for many applications [3–5,8,10,16]. However, the lack of well-labeled training sample is a big problem in such tasks, which makes the classification accuracy remains low [15]. In real-world applications, we often encounter the situation that an HSI scene has only very few labeled samples in that it is expensive and time consuming to collect labeled samples [14]. But there may be sufficient labeled hyperspectral samples in different but similar scenes. In this case, it is a natural idea to use the labeled training images collected from one scene to help to classify the images collected in the other. This problem is called cross-scene HSI classification.

The most straightforward method for cross-scene classification is to use the source domain samples directly, i.e., when no labeled samples are available in

© Springer Nature Switzerland AG 2019
Z. Lin et al. (Eds.): PRCV 2019, LNCS 11858, pp. 542–550, 2019.
https://doi.org/10.1007/978-3-030-31723-2_46

the target scene, the source domain samples are directly employed to train a classifier; when a few labeled samples are available in the target scene, we can merge the labeled samples in both scenes for training. However, this simple way suffers from spectral shift, i.e., pixels belonging to the same land cover class may vary in spectral distribution from two different HSI scenes. This phenomenon is also called spectral drift, covariate shift, population drift, or data set shift [9,11,12], which occurs when the training and test scenes are spatially or temporally different. The spectral shift is caused by many factors, including different atmospheric and light conditions at the image acquisition stage, different sensor nonlinearities, the different substance compositions of the same land cover class in different sizes and times, and so on [2]. Therefore, even though a large number of training data are available in the source scenes, the classifiers trained from those data or the combined data from both the source and target scenes may perform poorly on the test samples from the target scene [1,7]. Therefore, a more complex strategy is necessary to better solve the cross-scene classification problem.

Based on the assumption that datasets of the same theme usually have similar manifold structures, in this paper, we propose an unsupervised global manifold alignment (UGMA) method, which projects the high dimensional feature spaces of the source and target domains into a shared low dimensional subspace. Our UGMA method takes advantage of manifold learning that explores intrinsic information concealed in high-dimensional data and to capture nonlinearity within hyperspectral data, whereby data are projected onto a lower dimensional feature space that retains global geometric structures of the data. What's more, our unsupervised method allows us to align the target images when we can not get any groundtruth of them.

The major contributions of this paper are three fold:

(1) Our first contribution is that this paper extends and develops the conception of unsupervised manifold alignment to the field of cross scene domain adaptive hyperspectral image classification for the first time, which can reduce the pressure of human annotation.

(2) Our second contribution lies in the design of a new model, unsupervised global manifold alignment(UGMA). In contrast to other supervised or semisupervised methods that rely on the prior known label [13,17], we just take advantage of data intrinsic information. And it is amazing that our method can be compared with some semi-supervised learning methods or even supervised learning methods, and our accuracies are even not lower than them at all.

(3) Another contribution is the proposition of a global geometry preserving term using in manifold alignment. As we all know that the basic idea of manifold alignment is to map all input data sets to a new space preserving the local geometry of each data set, but this could lead to poor performance in some tasks. We describe a novel geometry preserving term that matchs the instances in correspondence and preserving geodesic distances (global geometry).

Based on experiments on KSC dataset, Indian Pines dataset and Pavia dataset, experimental results demonstrate the effectiveness of our proposed algorithms over several state-of-the-art methods. The remainder of this paper is arranged as follows: Sect. 2 describes the formulation of the observed model and the solving algorithm. The experiments on three hyperspectral data sets are reported in Sect. 3 to show the benefits of UGMA. Finally, the conclusions are drawn in Sect. 4.

2   Method

2.1   Notation

We first define the notations used in this paper. $X_{i.}(X_{.j})$ indicates the ith row (j^{th} column) of matrix X. $[X]_{ij}$ denotes the element at the ith row and j^{th} column of matrix X. $\mathbf{1}^{m \times n}, \mathbf{0}^{m \times n} \in \mathbb{R}^{m \times n}$ are matrices only have ones and zeros. $I_n \in \mathbb{R}^{n \times n}$ means an identity matrix. $tr(.)$ means the trace norm and the superscript ^{T} represents the transpose of a vector or matrix. $\|X\|_F^2 = tr(X^T X)$ shows the Frobenius norm. diag(X) means the diagonalization on matrix X, and diag(X) returns a diagonal matrix of the diagonal elements. $vec(x)$ is the vectorization of matrix X in columns. $X \otimes Z$ and $X \odot Z$ represent the Kronecker and Hadamard mathematical operation, respectively.

Let $X \in \mathbb{R}^{d_x \times n_x}$ and $Z \in \mathbb{R}^{d_z \times n_z}$ represent two datasets, residing in two different manifolds μ_x and μ_z. Where $n_x(n_z)$ and $d_x(d_z)$ respectively denote the cardinalities and dimensionalities of the datasets. In particular but without loss of generality, we suppose that $n_x \leq n_z$. The goal of unsupervised manifold alignment is to build connections between two data manifold, X and Z, without any prior knowledge in label matching. In result of this, we design a 0–1 integer matrix $F \in \{0,1\}^{n_x \times n_z}$ to indicates the matching relationship between X and Z. $[F]_{ij} = 1$ means that the ith point of X and the jth point of Z are likely to be the same class, we define them as matching counterparts. If all counterparts are limited to one-to-one, this means that $n_x = n_z$, then the set of integer matrices F can be defined as

$$\prod = \{F | F \in \{0,1\}^{n_x \times n_z}, 1_{n_x} = 1_{n_z}, 1_{n_x}^T F \leqslant 1_{n_x}^T, n_x \leq n_z\} \qquad (1)$$

2.2   Overall Objective Function

We expect to project two data manifolds into a lower-dimensional space to learn their low-dimensional features and representations. $P_x \in \mathbb{R}^{d \times d_x}$ and $P_z \in \mathbb{R}^{d \times d_z}$ are mapping functions from the two datasets to the latent embedding space. To this end, the matching matrix F as well as the mapping function P_x and P_z are what we need to learn to achieve the goal of UGMA.

Aligning two manifolds is not a trivial work, especially when they share different dimensions. Even so, we can still find the relationship between data manifolds and its intrinsic representation to build the alignment. In general, we propose an optimization objective for UGMA, we transfer UGMA into an optimization problem with 0–1 integer constraints:

$$\min_{P_x, P_z, F} \gamma_s E_s + \gamma_f E_f / E_p$$

$$s.t. F \in \prod, P_x.P_z \in \theta \tag{2}$$

where γ and γ_s are the balance parameters, θ is a constraint to avoid trivial solutions. E_s, E_f and E_p are three terms respectively representing the evaluation of geometry matching, feature matching and global geometry preserving, the specific content will be introduced in turn.

E_s is named as geometry matching term. To discover the relationship between the two data manifolds, the first thing to do is geometric matching. However, in many cases, the two data manifolds cannot be completely aligned, as $n_x \neq n_z$, this means that there are some points from one data manifold might not have any matching point on the other data manifold. To solve this problem, we establish the distance matrice K of the entire data sample, $[K]_{ij} = d(X_i, X_j)$ means the geodesic distance between data points X_i and X_j. It should be noted that both source and target data should be standardized to reduce the impact of inconsistent data scales. Geometry matching term in UGMA can be defined as follows:

$$E_s = \|S \cdot K_x \cdot S^T - F \cdot K_z \cdot F^T\|_F^2 \tag{3}$$

where $F \in \prod$ is the (partial) matching matrix defined in Eq. (1). $S \in \mathbb{R}^{n_x \times n_x}$ is the selective matrix which is a diagonal matrix which is used to filter out data points that have been given label.

E_f is called feature matching term. For two data manifolds, the distance between the aligned data points should be small in the mutual embedding space, as they have similar intrinsic representation. Thus we can characterize the feature matching term as follows:

$$E_f = \|P_x^T \cdot X \cdot S - P_z^T \cdot Z \cdot F^T\|_F^2 \tag{4}$$

where P_x, P_z are the projecting function respectively for X and Z. This term penalizes the divergence of intrinsic features of current alignment points in the public latent space μ.

E_p is defined as global geometry preserving term. As discussed before, only preserving neighborhood relationship may not be sufficient for many applications. The loss of information can be effectively reduced by protecting global geometry. The global geometry preserving term can be denoted as:

$$E_p = tr[f^T \cdot G \cdot \tau(D) \cdot G^T \cdot f] \tag{5}$$

where $f = \begin{bmatrix} P_x & 0 \\ 0 & P_z \end{bmatrix}$ is the matrix of projecting functions, $G = \begin{bmatrix} X & 0 \\ 0 & Z \end{bmatrix}$ is the matrix of data, $D = \begin{bmatrix} D_{x,x} & D_{x,z} \\ D_{z,x} & D_{z,z} \end{bmatrix}$ is matrix of distance, where $D_{x,x}$ and $D_{z,z}$ are easily computed using the shortest path distance measure. To measure $D_{x,z}$, the corresponding pairs according to F can then be treated as bridges to connect the two data manifolds. For any pair $(x_i$ and $z_j)$, we compute the distance between them through all possible bridges $(x_{a_\mu}$ and $z_{b_\mu})$, and set $D_{x,z}(i,j)$ to be the minimum of them. For instance, $D_{x,z}(i,j) = \min_{\mu \in [1,l]} [D_{x,x}(x_i, x_{a_\mu}) + D_{z,z}(z_j, z_{b_\mu})]$. The τ operator converts the Euclidean distance matrix D into an appropriate inner product (Gram matrix, $\tau(D) = -HSH/2$, here, $S_{i,j} = A_{i,j}^2, H_{i,j} = \delta_{i,j} - 1/m$, $\delta_{i,j} = 1$ when $i = j$; 0, otherwise.

2.3   Optimized Iterative Method

The solution to the objective function is difficult, we propose an optimized solution by using alternating iterations. Specifically, the objective function is divided into two subfunctions, the one is to optimize the matching matrix F and the other is to get the projection function P_x and P_z, respectively. With P_x and P_z fixed, the proposed method for the subfunction is solving non-convex quadratic integer programming, whose approximate solution is computed along the gradient-descent path of a relaxed convex model by extending the Frank-Wolfe algorithm. When fixing F, another subfunction is used to obtain P_x and P_z. The two subfunctions reach their optimum when the alternate iteration converges.

When fixing P_x, P_z, the original problem evolves to minimize the function as follows:

$$\min_F E_s + \gamma E_f \tag{6}$$

Let $X' = P_x^T X$ and $Z' = P_z^T Z$ denote the data in the latent space. After a series of calculations and derivation, the current objective function can be rewritten as:

$$\min_{F \in \Pi} \|K_x F - F K_z\|_F^2 + tr(F^T 11^T F K_{zz}) + tr(F^T B) \tag{7}$$

Where $K_{zz} = K_z \odot K_z$ and $B = \gamma_f [11^T(Z' \odot Z' - 2X'^T Z')] - 11^T K_{zz}$. This problem is NP-hard with $n!$ enumerations under an exhaustive search strategy. For a reliable solution, we relax this optimization problem under the framework of Frank-Wolfe (FW) algorithm [6], which is designed for convex models over a compact convex set.

We use Algorithm 1 to get the matching matrix F. In step (5), the optimized solution is obtained according to the KuhnCMunkres (KM) algorithm in the 0–1 integer space. Meanwhile, each iteration results in a gradual decrease from step (6) to step (13) due to the convexity of function ψ, thus avoid falling into a local optimal solution. Furthermore, it can be proved that the objective value $\psi(F_k)$ is non-increasing at each iteration and $\{F_1, F_2, ...\}$ will converge into a fixed point.

When fixing F, the embedding transforms can be obtained by minimizing the following function,

$$\min_{P_x, P_z} \frac{E_s}{E_f} = \frac{\|P_x^T \cdot X \cdot S - P_z^T \cdot Z \cdot F^T\|_F^2}{tr[f^T \cdot G \cdot \tau(D) \cdot G^T \cdot f]}$$

$$= \frac{tr[(P_x^T \cdot X \cdot S - P_z^T \cdot Z \cdot F^T) \cdot (P_x^T \cdot X \cdot S - P_z^T \cdot Z \cdot F^T)]}{tr[f^T \cdot G \cdot \tau(D) \cdot G^T \cdot f]} \qquad (8)$$

To this end, the Rayleigh Quotient method is used to solve the problem of generalized eigenvalue decomposition. That is, finding the following minimum eigenvector for f:

$$G \cdot \begin{bmatrix} S \cdot S^T & -S \cdot F \\ -F^T \cdot S^T & F \cdot F^T \end{bmatrix} \cdot G^T \cdot f = \lambda G \cdot \tau(D) \cdot G^T \cdot f \qquad (9)$$

3   Experiments and Results

In the experiments, three hyperspectral data sets are used and the details of them are presented as follows. It needs to be declared that what we are exploring is the domain adaptation under the condition of disjoint space. Therefore, we select part of the hyperspectral image as the source domain and another part as the target domain. We only select the data categories shared by both source domain and target domain for training and testing. Experimental setting and evaluations are as follows. We explore the classification accuracy with the sensitivity of dimensionality. Then, we use feature space visualizations of UGMA to illustrate how we use unsupervised learning.

3.1   Dataset

KSC data set: The NASA AVIRIS satellite collected data at 18-m spatial resolution over the Kennedy Space Center (KSC), Florida, area on March 23, 1996. The reflectance data consist of 224 bands of 10-nm width from 400 to 2500 nm. Two hyperspectral images, KSC1 and KSC2, are composed of water, woodland, marsh and scrub classes. Many categories in this environment are mixed together, making it difficult to classify. The class information of KSC data is listed in Table 1. RGB composite images and class maps are displayed in Fig. 1. Some objects in the images of this dataset are challenging to be classified without any prior knowledge because the features of them are quite similar.

Indian Pines data set: The dataset was collected by Airborne Visible Infrared Imaging Spectrometer (AVIRIS) over the Indian Pines test site in North-western Indiana, which is consisted of 145145 pixels and 224 spectral reflectance bands. The Indian Pines scene contains two-thirds agriculture, and onethird forest or other natural perennial vegetation. Several spectral bands with noise and water absorption phenomena are removed from the data set, leaving a total of 200 radiance channels to be used in the experiments (Fig. 2).

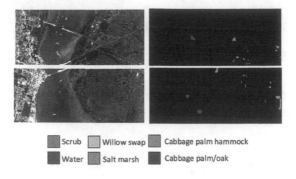

Fig. 1. KSC hyperspectral image.

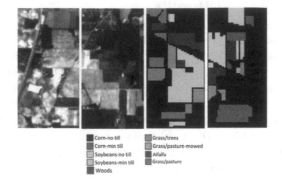

Fig. 2. Indian Pines hyperspectral image.

Table 1. Outperform all the DA methods

Dimensions after DA methods			30	40	50	60	70	80	90	100
KSC	TCA	OA	54.08	67.67	75.68	72.66	76.74	78.85	77.64	77.49
		Kappa	0.6081	0.6187	0.7120	0.6289	0.7124	0.7363	0.7284	0.7269
	JDA	OA	54.08	64.05	67.37	68.73	71.75	72.36	73.56	71.00
		Kappa	0.5974	0.6011	0.6154	0.0.6209	0.6628	0.6716	0.6831	0.6453
	BDA	OA	68.73	73.87	72.21	73.87	71.30	72.21	70.54	72.36
		Kappa	0.6222	0.6845	0.6682	0.6744	0.6519	0.6616	0.6487	0.6689
	GFK	OA	62.24	68.43	70.85	64.80	72.41	71.30	69.54	68.67
		Kappa	0.5725	0.6267	0.6379	0.5997	0.6498	0.6416	0.6329	0.6301
	Ours	OA	69.73	71.87	74.21	75.70	75.21	76.14	77.64	75.67
		Kappa	0.6418	0.6791	0.6898	0.7131	0.7129	0.7261	0.7287	0.7169
Indiana	TCA	OA	35.21	33.89	40.17	57.75	67.22	73.56	57.95	42.05
		Kappa	0.2743	0.2659	0.3086	0.4931	0.5668	0.6404	0.4987	0.3473
	JDA	OA	45.80	40.22	56.38	58.87	63.58	70.52	74.47	62.51
		Kappa	0.3489	0.3170	0.4914	0.5011	0.5104	0.5809	0.6451	0.5074
	BDA	OA	40.48	46.45	58.16	67.02	72.14	54.91	39.11	38.91
		Kappa	0.3231	0.3497	0.5001	0.5664	0.6394	0.4987	0.3099	0.3067
	GFK	OA	36.88	34.50	39.21	37.69	40.32	42.00	53.75	57.22
		Kappa	0.3017	0.2734	0.3109	0.3059	0.3220	0.3291	0.4870	0.4929
	Ours	OA	43.80	45.22	60.68	64.87	70.58	72.52	78.47	74.51
		Kappa	0.3581	0.3521	0.5087	0.5274	0.5768	0.5969	0.6844	0.6321

3.2 Illustrate How We Use Unsupervised Learning

Here, we explain how our proposed method takes an unsupervised way by visualizing the feature space. Simply take the KSC for example, as we can see in the Fig. 3, samples from both source and target domains were projected to a public feature space. And in this space, the manifold alignment can be seen as a clustering problem, which data of same categories get clustered. Note that the data from the source image was used as training data, but the labels from both source image and the target image were only used to validate the predicted results and provide classification accuracies. That is, unsupervised classification was performed on the target image, and the overall accuracies were reported.

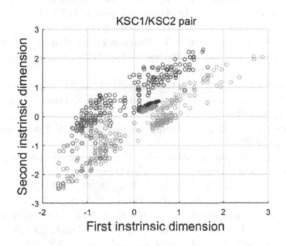

Fig. 3. Feature space visualizations of UGMA for the KSC1/KSC2 data pair.

4 Conclusions

As the characteristics of remote sensing imagery itself, the lack of training samples has made data mining tasks challenging. In this paper, we propose a new approach that simultaneously protects of both local and global geometric features of data manifolds for cross scene hyperspectral image classification. Our proposed method UGMA has good performance in domain adaptive circumstance, especially in crocss scene domain adaptation. We formulate unsupervised manifold alignment by considering geometric structure, intrinsic feature, and global geometry. An efficient optimization algorithm is further proposed by alternately solving two subfunctions, one is to find matching pairs between source and target domains, the other is to get the mutual embedding subspace. Further, unlike previous approaches based on local geometry preservation, the proposed method is better suited to applications where the global geometry of manifold needs to be respected.

References

1. Ben-David, S., Blitzer, J., Crammer, K., Pereira, F.: Analysis of representations for domain adaptation. In: Advances in Neural Information Processing Systems, pp. 137–144 (2007)
2. Bruzzone, L., Prieto, D.F.: Unsupervised retraining of a maximum likelihood classifier for the analysis of multitemporal remote sensing images. IEEE Trans. Geosci. Remote Sens. **39**(2), 456–460 (2001)
3. Chen, C., Li, W., Tramel, E.W., Cui, M., Prasad, S., Fowler, J.E.: Spectral-spatial preprocessing using multihypothesis prediction for noise-robust hyperspectral image classification. IEEE J. Sel. Topics Appl. Earth Observations Remote Sens. **7**(4), 1047–1059 (2014)
4. Damodaran, B.B., Nidamanuri, R.R.: Dynamic linear classifier system for hyperspectral image classification for land cover mapping. IEEE J. Selected Topics Appl. Earth Observations Remote Sens. **7**(6), 2080–2093 (2014)
5. Kang, X., Li, S., Benediktsson, J.A.: Feature extraction of hyperspectral images with image fusion and recursive filtering. IEEE Trans. Geosci. Remote Sens. **52**(6), 3742–3752 (2014)
6. Kim, W., Crawford, M.M.: Adaptive classification for hyperspectral image data using manifold regularization kernel machines. IEEE Trans. Geosci. Remote Sens. **48**(11), 4110–4121 (2010)
7. Pan, S.J., Yang, Q.: A survey on transfer learning. IEEE Trans. Knowl. Data Eng. **22**(10), 1345–1359 (2010)
8. Ramzi, P., Samadzadegan, F., Reinartz, P.: Classification of hyperspectral data using an adaboostsvm technique applied on band clusters. IEEE J. Selected Topics Appl. Earth Observations Remote Sens. **7**(6), 2066–2079 (2014)
9. Sun, Z., Wang, C., Li, P., Wang, H., Li, J.: Hyperspectral image classification with SVM-based domain adaption classifiers. In: 2012 International Conference on Computer Vision in Remote Sensing, pp. 268–272. IEEE (2012)
10. Tarabalka, Y., Chanussot, J., Benediktsson, J.A.: Segmentation and classification of hyperspectral images using minimum spanning forest grown from automatically selected markers. IEEE Trans. Syst. Man Cybern. Part B (Cybern.) **40**(5), 1267–1279 (2010)
11. Tuia, D., Pasolli, E., Emery, W.J.: Using active learning to adapt remote sensing image classifiers. Remote Sens. Environ. **115**(9), 2232–2242 (2011)
12. Tuia, D., Pasolli, E., Emery, W.J.: Dataset shift adaptation with active queries. In: 2011 Joint Urban Remote Sensing Event, pp. 121–124. IEEE (2011)
13. Voisin, A., Krylov, V.A., Moser, G., Serpico, S.B., Zerubia, J.: Supervised classification of multisensor and multiresolution remote sensing images with a hierarchical copula-based approach. IEEE Trans. Geosci. Remote Sens. **52**(6), 3346–3358 (2014)
14. Yang, J., Zhou, Y., Cao, Y., Feng, L.: Heterogeneous image change detection using deep canonical correlation analysis. In: 2018 24th International Conference on Pattern Recognition (ICPR), pp. 2917–2922. IEEE (2018)
15. Yang, L., Yang, S., Jin, P., Zhang, R.: Semi-supervised hyperspectral image classification using spatio-spectral laplacian support vector machine. IEEE Geosci. Remote Sens. Lett. **11**(3), 651–655 (2014)
16. Yuan, Z., Feng, L., Hou, C., Kung, S.Y.: Hyperspectral and multispectral image fusion based on local low rank and coupled spectral unmixing. IEEE Trans. Geosci. Remote Sens. **55**(10), 5997–6009 (2017)
17. Zhong, Y., Zhang, L.: An adaptive artificial immune network for supervised classification of multi-/hyperspectral remote sensing imagery. IEEE Trans. Geosci. Remote Sens. **50**(3), 894–909 (2012)

Poleward Moving Aurora Recognition with Deep Convolutional Networks

Yiping Tang, Chuang Niu, Minghao Dong, Shenghan Ren, and Jimin Liang[✉]

Engineering Research Center of Molecular and Neuro Imaging of Ministry of
Education, School of Life Science and Technology,
Xidian University, Xi'an, China
jimleung@mail.xidian.edu.cn

Abstract. Deep learning has become the most powerful tool for action
recognition in recent years. The aim of this paper is to investigate the
proper convolutional network architecture to classify poleward moving
auroras (PMAs). The first challenge is that the auroral images have
complex morphological and motion characteristics, so it is difficult to
get the discriminative motion information to recognize the PMA events.
Second, the imbalanced dataset will cause the serious problems, such as
the network tends to identify a given sequence as the majority of events
(non-PMAs). To address these issues, we use 3D ResNet-18 to get the
motion information of auroral image sequence based on optical flow and
also use the spatial attention mechanism to make the network pay more
attention to PMA events. The empirical results demonstrate that our
method achieves significant performance improvement compared with
the previous method.

Keywords: Poleward moving auroras · Spatial attention · Auroral
event recognition

1 Introduction

Poleward moving auroral forms (PMAFs) are one of the most important auroral
phenomena and have attracted wide research attention [1–3]. The PMAFs usually appear at the equatorward boundary of the dayside auroral oval and move
to the polar cap where they fade [4,5]. However, PMAFs are usually defined
in keograms [6], so it is complicated to identify and the all-sky camera/imager
(ASC/ASI) images are only used to assist in recognizing PMAFs. Many auroras
with poleward moving characteristics are not defined as PMAFs. These auroras
also have the research significance in aurora physical mechanism study. In this
study, we hope to find a way to recognize poleward moving auroras (PMAs)
automatically by making full use of the all-sky auroral images. The concept of

This work was supported by the National Natural Science Foundation of China under
Grant No. 61571353. Student paper.

Z. Lin et al. (Eds.): PRCV 2019, LNCS 11858, pp. 551–560, 2019.
https://doi.org/10.1007/978-3-030-31723-2_47

PMAs was first defined in [7] for all-sky auroral image sequences. It contains three types of auroral events: (1) PMAFs; (2) poleward moving motion shown in keograms but not classified as PMAFs; and (3) poleward moving motion not shown in keograms but can be found from all-sky images. In this paper, deep convolutional network is used to classify PMA events. We investigate multiple designs. The empirical results show that our network can significantly improve the performance on PMA events recognition compared with the performance proposed in [7].

1.1 Related Work

The great success of deep learning in image classification makes researchers transfer the same idea on video classification. The image-based video classification methods usually use the pre-trained convolutional neural network (CNN) models to extract the feature of each frame. And then the averaged frame-level feature, which is called video-level feature, is sent to a classifier such as SVMs. The image-based methods have proved to be effective when combined with kernel SVMs [8]. However, in PMAs classification, there is not much useful information for classification from each single frame. This is because PMA events are recognized by the direction of auroral motion in video clips. Using the spatial information alone can't classify PMA events effectively. To get more robust spatio-temporal information, [9] proposed a 3D CNN architecture to classify video clips directly. The 3D CNN accepts the frames of a given clip as input and can learn the spatio-temporal feature well. Furthermore, more architectures have emerged, such as C3D [10], P3D [11], R(2+1)D [12], and SlowFast networks [13]. These architectures, by learning the spatio-temporal feature directly, have shown great performance on video recognition task. In addition, the two-stream network [14] learns the spatial and temporal feature separately. It models the spatial feature with image frames and models the temporal feature with dense optical flow which is generated from adjacent frames. At the test time, the output is the weighted sum of the two streams' scores.

Obviously, many frames in a video clip are similar, which means that there is a lot of redundant information. [15] introduced a LSTM model with soft-attention mechanism for action recognition. Their model can catch the important information to learn the more relevant parts in video frames. VideoLSTM [16] introduced a motion-based attention mechanism derived from optical flow to get better spatio-temporal features. Unlike the action recognition videos, the interval between adjacent frames in auroral image sequences is 10 s. So each frame in a video clip is important and there is not much redundant frames. This requires us to make full use of all the frames in auroral sequences.

Automatic methods for all-sky auroral image analysis have been studied for years. [17] used a shape-constrained sparse and low-rank decomposition (SCSLD) framework to automatically detect auroral substorm. [7] recognized the PMA events by combining the hidden markov models (HMMs) with SVMs. In this paper, we focus on the extraction of discriminative motion features which can represent the PMA events and address the problem of imbalanced dataset. We will show more details of our method in Sect. 2.

2 Our Approach

In this section, we describe our approach for PMA event classification. An example of PMA event is shown in Fig. 1. The auroral image data used in this study were observed by the ASIs installed at the Chinese Arctic Yellow River Station (YRS), Ny-Ålesund, Svalbard. More information about the data and the preprocessing method can be found in [18].

Optical Flow. The evidence for recognizing PMA events is whether there is upward moving auroras in a sequence. However, auroras are very complex. Their shape, duration, brightness and the motion mode can be very different. It is difficult to get the information we expect from the ASI images directly. Considering that the motion information is the most direct basis for recognizing PMA events, we can naturally associate it with the optical flow. Four consecutive ASI images from a sequence and the optical flows of them are shown in Fig. 1. We can see that there is much less interference in the optical flow and it makes the motion information among these images more visible.

Network Architecture. The two-stream network has shown great results on action recognition benchmarks, such as UCF-101 [19] and HMDB-51 [20]. Nevertheless, it is not competent to obtain the spatial information of auroral images (see Sect. 3). Compared with the traditional 2D CNN, 3D CNN can capture more robust spatio-temporal features, which is important for the recognition task. By inputting the optical flow of an auroral sequence to the network, we can get the idea about where and how the auroras moves. Considering the computation cost and accuracy, we use 3D ResNet-18 [21] to extract the motion features. The architecture of our model is shown in Fig. 2. Figure 2(a) shows our motion-sensitive network that is based on 3D ResNet-18 with attention blocks which are shown in Fig. 2(b).

The Conv1 and Conv2 in Fig. 2(b) are convolutional layers of the same structure with the blocks in 3D ResNet-18, while Conv2 is followed by a max pooling operation to generate the attention map which focuses on the spatial information. For convenience, we use x to represent the input of the attention block and its output y can be denoted as:

$$y = \mathrm{Conv1}(x) + \mathrm{Conv1}(x) \times \sigma(\mathrm{MaxPool}(\mathrm{Conv2}(x))). \qquad (1)$$

The sigmoid function is denoted by σ. The size of x is (C, L, H, W) where C represents the number of channels, L is the number of frames, H and W are the height and width. $\mathrm{Conv1}(x)$, $\mathrm{Conv2}(x)$ and y are of the same size of (C', L', H', W').

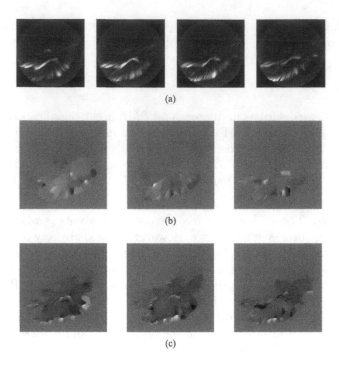

Fig. 1. Example of PMA events. (a) consecutive video frames of a PMA event. (b) horizontal component of optical flow filed. (c) vertical component of optical flow filed.

3   Experiments

Dataset. We use the same auroral event dataset built in [7]. Auroras of 5 days in December 2003 were selected for labeling, and 137 PMA sequences and 411 non-PMA sequences were finally labeled. The duration of PMA events varies from 2 min to 18 min. Non-PMA events are selected from the remaining auroral sequences, and their morphology, brightness and duration vary greatly.

Evaluation Metrics. The proportion of positive and negative samples in the dataset is one to three, so the accuracy is even acceptable if methods predict all the samples to be non-PMAs. Some evaluation metrics about imbalanced dataset were used in [7]. In order to facilitate comparison with their method and prove the superiority of our method, we also use the metrics. We use TP, FP, TN and FN to represent the number of true positive samples, false positive samples, true negative samples and false negative samples, respectively.

The balanced accuracy (BAC) is shown in Eq. 2, which is usually used instead of regular accuracy when the dataset is imbalanced. It simply computes the mean of true positive rate and true negative rate. The true positive rate and the true negative rate are also considered in GMean, which is calculated according to Eq. 3. F-measure (FM) takes into account both the accuracy and recall of

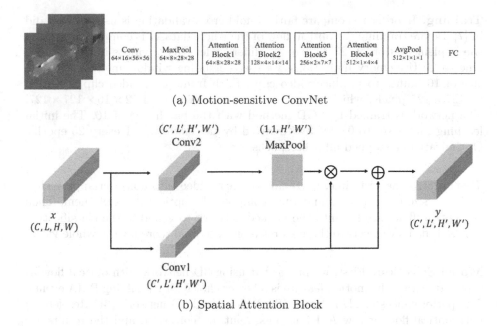

(a) Motion-sensitive ConvNet

(b) Spatial Attention Block

Fig. 2. 3D ResNet-18 with attention blocks.

the model and the formula is shown in Eq. 4. Mean F-measure (MFM) [22] is obtained by averaging F-measures of positive and negative samples. In Eq. 5, F-measure of positive and negative samples are represented by FM(1) and FM(0) respectively. Receiver operating characteristic (ROC) curve can also represent the performance of classifier when the samples are imbalanced. However sometimes the ROC curve can't indicate which classifier works better clearly. Hence, we use the area under curve (AUC) which represents the area of under the ROC curve to denote the performance of classifier.

$$BAC = \frac{(TP/(TP+FN) + TN/(TN+FP))}{2}, \tag{2}$$

$$GMean = \sqrt{\frac{TP}{TP+FN} \times \frac{TN}{TN+FP}}, \tag{3}$$

$$FM = 2 \times \frac{TP/(TP+FP) \times TP/(TP+FN)}{TP/(TP+FP) + TP/(TP+FN)}, \tag{4}$$

$$MFM = \frac{1}{2} \times (FM(0) + FM(1)). \tag{5}$$

Training. In order to compare fairly, 5-fold cross-validation is used as that did in [7]. Before training, the optical flow of the whole dataset is computed by using the implementation of [23]. There are different lengths of videos in the dataset. Due to GPU memory limitations, we use the sliding window method with the size of 16 frames to produce video clips. Each frame in a video clip is resized to 127×127 pixels, which means that the size of input is $2 \times 16 \times 127 \times 127$. The network is trained by SGD method with the batch size of 16. The initial learning rate is set to 0.0001 and decayed by the factor of 0.1 every 25 epochs. Optimization is stopped after 60 epochs.

Testing. At the test time, we divide the test video into non-overlapping clips with the size of 16 frames and then compute the optical flows of them. Then the optical flows are fed into the trained network to generate the classification scores. Finally, we average these scores to get the final score for the whole video.

Model Selection. First, we prove that using 3D network with optical flow as input to extract the motion feature is a better choice for classifying PMA events. The performances of 2D network (ResNet-18) and 3D network (3D ResNet-18) with optical flow or raw ASI image as input are compared and the results are shown in Fig. 3. It can be seen that the 3D network always performs better than the 2D network for all the evaluation metrics. The results indicate that the 3D network is more capable to access the spatio-temporal information of the auroral video.

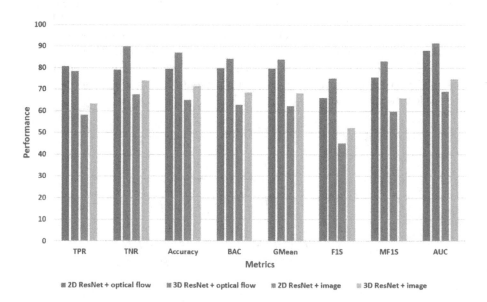

Fig. 3. Performance of 3D and 2D networks with optical flow or ASI images as input.

Attention Blocks. However, as shown in Fig. 3, there is a big gap between true positive rate and true negative rate of 3D ResNet-18 method, which is caused by the imbalance of data. Even in the case of low true positive rate and high true negative rate, we can still get the acceptable accuracy. Therefore, it is obviously inappropriate if we measure the performance of the model only by the accuracy metric. This is why we adopt several other metrics to evaluate the performance. We also introduce the attention mechanism to make the network focus on the moving parts in the video, so as to balance the performance between positive samples and negative samples.

There are many methods based on the attention mechanism are proposed for action recognition task. However, not all these methods are well adapted to auroral data. We investigate three attention methods to find the most suitable way for PMA events recognition, including spatial attention, channel attention, and frame attention generated by 3D network directly. Assume that the input size of the attention block is (C, L, H, W), then the spatial attention will generate the attention map with the size of $(1, 1, H', W')$ and channel attention will generate the attention map with size of $(C', 1, 1, 1)$. The size of frame attention map will be $(1, L', 1, 1)$. Where (C', L', H', W') indicates the output of the attention block in Fig. 2(a).

The empirical results are shown in Table 1. All three kinds of attention methods can improve the network performance and satisfy the expectation to balance the true positive rate and true negative rate to some extent. The three methods perform comparatively, while the spatial attention method is slightly better than the other two. The result attributes to that the spatial attention puts more attention on the motion regions in auroral sequences, which is also the basis for human to recognize PMA events.

Table 1. Results of three attention methods

Attention	TPR	TNR	Accuracy	BAC	GMean	F1S	MF1S	AUC
Spatial	**85.70**	88.23	**87.60**	**86.96**	**86.88**	**77.41**	**84.43**	**91.77**
Channel	84.96	87.99	87.24	86.48	86.42	76.85	84.01	90.44
Frame	83.48	**88.59**	87.32	86.03	85.82	76.32	83.82	90.93

Figure 4 gives the PMA event recognition performance of different methods. [7] uses HMM to model the auroral sequences and GMean metric-driven biased SVM for classification (denoted as GMean-SVM). The 3D ResNet-18 with optical flow as input performs better than the GMean-SVM method. The true positive rate of 3D ResNet-18 method is slightly lower than that of GMean-SVM method, while other metrics are better. Regarding all the evaluation metrics, our method is the best among all the three methods, which further demonstrates that the spatial attention mechanism benefits the recognition of PMA events.

Figure 5 shows the attention map of three PMA sequences. The first frame in a sequence is shown in the first column, the intermediate frame of the sequence

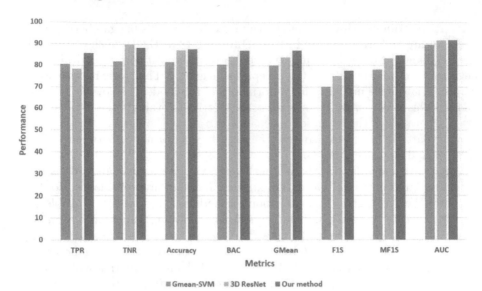

Fig. 4. Methods comparison. Blue denotes [7]'s method, green for 3D ResNet-18, and red for our method. (Color figure online)

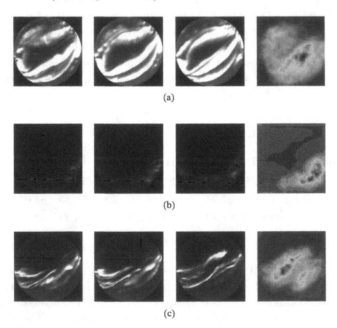

Fig. 5. Three PMA sequences and the corresponding attention maps. The start, intermediate, and end frame of each event are shown from left to right. The last image is the attention map.

is the second column, and the last frame of the sequence is the third column. The brighter areas represent regions with larger weights in the attention maps, which means that the network will pay more attention to these areas. It can be seen that the motion area of a sequence from the first frame to the last frame is enhanced on the attention map.

4 Conclusions

In this study, we adopt the 3D ResNet-18 network with spatial attention block to tackle the problem of PMA event recognition. We show that using optical flow as input and 3D network to extract features is an effective way to model the auroral events. Although using the 3D network only to classify PMAs can get good accuracy, it can't balance the true positive rate and true negative rate well. Further, we propose a spatial attention mechanism to alleviate the imbalanced performance problem. Empirical results demonstrate that our proposed method is much better than the traditional machine learning method. Our work provides a new method for automatic classification of massive auroral data.

References

1. Vorobjev, V.G., Gustafsson, G., Starkov, G.V., Feldstein, Y.I., Shevnina, N.F.: Dynamics of day and night aurora during substorms. Planet. Space Sci. **23**(2), 269–278 (1975)
2. Milan, S.E., Yeoman, T.K., Lester, M., Moen, J., Sandholt, P.E.: Post-noon two-minute period pulsating aurora and their relationship to the dayside convection pattern. Ann. Geophys. **17**, 877–891 (1999)
3. Kozlovsky, A., Kangas, J.: Motion and origin of noon high-latitude poleward moving auroral arcs on closed magnetic field lines. J. Geophys. Res.: Space Phys. **107**(A2), 1017 (2002)
4. Wang, B.: Investigation of triggering of poleward moving auroral forms using satellite-imager coordinated observations. J. Geophys. Res.: Space Phys. **121**(11), 10–929 (2016)
5. Xing, Z.Y., et al.: Poleward moving auroral forms (PMAFs) observed at the yellow river station: a statistical study of its dependence on the solar wind conditions. J. Atmos. Solar Terr. Phys. **86**, 25–33 (2012)
6. Fasel, G.J.: Dayside poleward moving auroral forms: a statistical study. J. Geophys. Res.: Space Phys. **100**(AZ), 11891–11905 (1995)
7. Yang, Q., Liang, J., Zejun, H., Xing, Z., Zhao, H.: Automatic recognition of poleward moving auroras from all-sky image sequences based on HMM and SVM. Planet. Space Sci. **69**(1), 40–48 (2012)
8. Zha, S., Luisier, F., Andrews, W., Srivastava, N., Salakhutdinov, R.: Exploiting image-trained CNN architectures for unconstrained video classification. arXiv preprint arXiv:1503.04144 (2015)
9. Ji, S., Wei, X., Yang, M., Kai, Y.: 3D convolutional neural networks for human action recognition. IEEE Trans. Pattern Anal. Mach. Intell. **35**(1), 221–231 (2013)
10. Tran, D., Bourdev, L., Fergus, R., Torresani, L., Paluri, M.: Learning spatiotemporal features with 3D convolutional networks. In: Proceedings of the IEEE International Conference on Computer Vision, pp. 4489–4497 (2015)

11. Qiu, Z., Yao, T., Mei, T.: Learning spatio-temporal representation with pseudo-3D residual networks. In: proceedings of the IEEE International Conference on Computer Vision, pp. 5533–5541 (2017)
12. Tran, D., Wang, H., Torresani, L., Ray, J., LeCun, Y., Paluri, M.: A closer look at spatiotemporal convolutions for action recognition. In: Proceedings of the IEEE conference on Computer Vision and Pattern Recognition, pp. 6450–6459 (2018)
13. Feichtenhofer, C., Fan, H., Malik, J., He, K.: Slowfast networks for video recognition. arXiv preprint arXiv:1812.03982 (2018)
14. Simonyan, K., Zisserman, A.: Two-stream convolutional networks for action recognition in videos. In: Advances in Neural Information Processing Systems, pp. 568–576 (2014)
15. Sharma, S., Kiros, R., Salakhutdinov, R.: Action recognition using visual attention. arXiv preprint arXiv:1511.04119 (2015)
16. Li, Z., Gavrilyuk, K., Gavves, E., Jain, M., Snoek, C.G.M.: VideoLSTM convolves, attends and flows for action recognition. Comput. Vis. Image Underst. **166**, 41–50 (2018)
17. Yang, X., Gao, X., Tao, D., Li, X., Han, B., Li, J.: Shape-constrained sparse and low-rank decomposition for auroral substorm detection. IEEE Trans. Neural Netw. Learn. Syst. **27**(1), 32–46 (2016)
18. Wang, Q., et al.: Spatial texture based automatic classification of dayside aurora in all-sky images. J. Atmos. Solar Terr. Phys. **72**(5–6), 498–508 (2010)
19. Soomro, K., Zamir, A.R., Shah, M.: UCF101: a dataset of 101 human actions classes from videos in the wild. arXiv preprint arXiv:1212.0402 (2012)
20. Kuehne, H., Jhuang, H., Garrote, E., Poggio, T., Serre, T.: HMDB: a large video database for human motion recognition. In: 2011 International Conference on Computer Vision, pp. 2556–2563. IEEE (2011)
21. Hara, K., Kataoka, H., Satoh, Y.: Learning spatio-temporal features with 3D residual networks for action recognition. In: Proceedings of the IEEE International Conference on Computer Vision, pp. 3154–3160 (2017)
22. Ferri, C., Hernández-Orallo, J., Modroiu, R.: An experimental comparison of performance measures for classification. Pattern Recogn. Lett. **30**(1), 27–38 (2009)
23. Brox, T., Bruhn, A., Papenberg, N., Weickert, J.: High accuracy optical flow estimation based on a theory for warping. In: Pajdla, T., Matas, J. (eds.) ECCV 2004. LNCS, vol. 3024, pp. 25–36. Springer, Heidelberg (2004). https://doi.org/10.1007/978-3-540-24673-2_3

Robust Hyperspectral Image Pan-Sharpening via Channel-Constrained Spatial Spectral Network

Na Li[1,2] and Licheng Liu[1,2(✉)]

[1] Department of Electrical and Information Engineering,
Hunan University, Changsha 410082, China
`Lichenghnu@gmail.com`
[2] Key Laboratory of Visual Perception and Artificial Intelligence of Hunan Province,
Hunan University, Changsha 410082, China

Abstract. Hyperspectral image (HSI) pan-sharpening, in which high-resolution (HR) spatial details from multispectral image (MSI) are employed to enhance the spatial resolution of HSI, has recently attracted much attention. Convolutional neural network (CNN) extracts more comprehensive features and is proved to be effective in pan-sharpening. However, the conventional CNN model becomes less efficient in handling noisy LR-HSI. Especially, most of the existing CNN based methods treat low-resolution (LR) HSI with abundant low-frequency information equally across channels, hence hindering the representation ability of CNN. To address this problem, we propose a robust channel-constrained spatial spectral network (RCSSN). Specifically, it is formed by two robust channel-constrained blocks (RCB) with short skip connections. Furthermore, we conjoin the traditional mean square error (MSE) loss and the first-order derivative feature error (FODFE) loss together to learn network parameters, which enables the network to suppress the effect of noise on image edge and texture. Both the quantitative assessment and the visual assessment results confirm that the proposed network yields HR-HSI that are superior to the images obtained by the compared state-of-the-art methods.

Keywords: Convolutional neural network (CNN) · Pan-sharpening · Hyperspectral imaging · Channel constraint · Feature error

This work was supported in part by the National Natural Science Foundation of China under grant 61702169, the Natural Science Foundation of Hunan Province under Grant 2018JJ3070, the National Natural Science Fund of China for International Cooperation and Exchanges under Grant 61520106001, and the Fundamental Research Funds for the Central Universities under Grant 531107050878. The authors would like to thank Prof. Shutao Li and Hui Lin in the Hunan University for their consistent and illuminating encouragement and guidance to this work.

Z. Lin et al. (Eds.): PRCV 2019, LNCS 11858, pp. 561–571, 2019.
https://doi.org/10.1007/978-3-030-31723-2_48

1   Introduction

Hyperspectral imaging is a promising imaging mode that simultaneously captures images of the same scene at multiple different wavelengths. HSIs have been widely used in many computer vision tasks, including tracking [1], face recognition [2], and segmentation [3], owe to its hundreds of spectral bands that provide abundant spectral features. The application potential of HSI is closely related to its high spatial resolution, but there is a trade-off between spatial resolution and spectral resolution due to the limitations of existing imaging sensors. Hyperspectral imaging systems require a large amount of exposure to achieve many bands simultaneously in a narrow spectral window. To ensure adequate signal-to-noise ratio, photon collection in hyperspectral sensors is typically performed in a larger spatial region, resulting in low spatial resolution existing in high spectral resolution image acquired by hyperspectral imaging sensors. Considering that images provided by multispectral imaging systems have lower spectral resolution but higher spatial resolution than HSIs, HR-HSIs are typically obtained by fusing LR-HSIs with HR-MSIs of the same scene. This process is called HSI sharpening or HSI super resolution.

Most current HSI pan-sharpening methods are based on optimization. The spectral representation reconstruction errors are minimized by spectral decomposition with different prior constraints (e.g., sparse representation [4], spectral physical properties [5], spatial background similarity [6]) to obtain desired performance. Generally, the reconstruction accuracy of optimization-based methods is highly dependent on the predefined prior. And choosing priors may be difficult since different types of priors are applicable to different types of HSIs. Furthermore, the optimization process usually costs high computation due to the large number of constraints.

Recently, deep convolutional networks have been widely used because of their powerful learning ability. Experiments have shown that they have significant effects on the learning and expressing image features [7–9]. However, most existing CNN-based methods are fragile in noise environment, and unable to effectively recover edge and texture information that is severely corrupted by noise. In addition, most networks treat channel-wise features equally ignoring difference between channels, thus hindering better discrimination of different types of features.

In this paper, we propose a robust channel-constrained spatial spectral network (RCSSN) for fusing noisy LR-HSI and HR-MSI of the same scene. RCSSN has the capacity of protecting noise-corrupted edge and texture information while adaptively learning different types of channel-wise features during the pan-sharpening process. We use two robust channel-constrained blocks (RCB) to learn the high-level features of HSI and the interdependencies between HSI channels. Since the information in the LR-HSI is contaminated by noise, we cascade the HR-MSI to the input of each RCB in order to make full use of the clean HR spatial information existing in the HR-MSI. Besides, most recent CNN-based methods treat channel-wise features equally, which lacks exibility in dealing with different types of information (e.g., low- and high-frequency information). Considering the channel difference, we introduce a channel constraint mechanism to adaptively rescale channel-wise features to enhance the network's discriminative learning ability. In addition, in order to protect the edge and texture information which is severely corrupted by noise, we propose a loss function based on the first-order derivative feature to ensure the high-frequency features of the reconstructed HR-HSI in the spatial and spectral domains.

Overall, our contributions are four-fold: (1) We propose RCSSN for robust fusion of noisy LR-HSI and HR-MSI with better super-resolution performance. (2) We propose the RCB to learn the high-level features of the network, which contains short connections between the HR-MSI and its input to make full use of HR spatial information to compensate for the serious information loss caused by noise and low spatial resolution. (3) We propose a channel constraint mechanism to treat various types of feature channels differently, and further learn the interdependencies between channels and improve the discriminative learning ability of the network. (4) We propose a loss function based on the first-order derivative feature to protect the edge and texture information which is heavily corrupted by noise, and further improve the robustness of the network.

2   Robust Channel-Constrained Spatial Spectral Network

In this section, we describe the proposed robust channel-constrained spatial spectral network (RCSSN) and the first-order derivative feature error (FODFE) loss function.

Assuming that the LR-HSI is considered as a degraded observation $x \in R^{(w \times h \times B)}$, where w and h denote the spatial dimensions and B denotes the number of spectral bands. And the HR-MSI $y \in R^{(W \times H \times h)}$ ($W \gg w, H \gg h, b \ll D$) is included to estimate the HR-HSI $z \in R^{(W \times H \times B)}$ which is an estimation of the groundtruth $s \in R^{(W \times H \times B)}$. In our experiments, the available HR-MSIs are RGB images with three spectral bands. Both x and y can be expressed as linear combinations of the desired hyperspectral image s:

$$x = sD + N, \quad y = Ps \tag{1}$$

where D denotes the blurring and down-sampling degradation operator acting on the spatial domain. N denotes the zero mean noise following a Gaussian distribution. And P, which is decided by camera design, is the transformation matrix acting on the spectral domain to map the HR-HSI s to its RGB observation y.

2.1   Network Architecture

In order to better learn the residuals of the network, before inputting the image to the network, we use bicubic interpolation to upsample LR-HSI to the same size as the HR-MSI in spatial domain and name the upsampled image bic-HSI. As shown in Fig. 1, our input is obtained by cascading the bic-HSI and HR-MSI and the proposed RCSSN consists two parts: robust deep feature extraction and reconstruction.

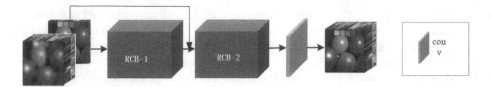

Fig. 1. Network architecture of our robust channel-constrained special spectral network (RCSSN).

We use only one convolutional layer with size 5×5 to reconstruct HR-HSI from the deep feature which is learned from the deep feature extraction model. And the RCSSN is optimized with the loss function linear weighted by mean squared error (MSE) and the first-order derivative feature error (FODFE). Since the reconstruction process is similar to the existing methods (e.g., GDRRN [20]), we focus on the robust deep feature extraction and FODFE proposed in this paper.

2.2 Robust Deep Feature Extraction

As shown in Fig. 1, our proposed robust deep feature extraction consists two robust channel-constrained blocks (RCB) whose structure is shown in Fig. 2.

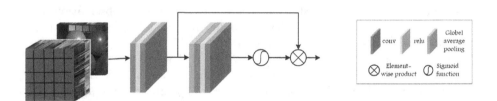

Fig. 2. Robust channel-constrained block (RCB).

Considering that original image information has been seriously destroyed by noise, in order to make full use of HR spatial information existing in HR-MSI to compensate for the information missing and information pollution due to downsampling, blurring, and noise, we cascade HR-MSI with the input of each RCB and then serve as the input of the next RCB. By cascading HR-MSI within the network multiple times, the network can make full use of HR spatial information to enhance learning capability of the network.

Moreover, the existing CNN-based pan-sharpening methods treat each channel of the HSI equally, ignoring the interdependence between feature channels. This hinders the ability of the network to distinguish and express different types of feature channels. In addition, the global information cannot be utilized since the filters in the convolutional layer can only operate with the local receptive field, and this brings difficulties for information mining and network optimization. To address this problem, we propose a channel constraint mechanism based on global pooling to exploit the difference between spectra, and at the same time share the global information with the local filtering operation. In order to show the structure of channel constraint mechanism more clearly, we give more details in Fig. 3.

We use the global average pooling to convert global spatial information into channel descriptor. As shown in Fig. 3, let the input has C feature maps and GP denotes the global pooling function. The channel descriptor with C feature maps after global pooling can describe the correlation between the channels. To further capture the relationship between the channels, we use upsampling and downsampling operation, W_d and W_u, to adjust the channel descriptor. In addition, we use the sigmoid function as a gating mechanism to learn the nonlinear interactions between channels and the non-mututally-exclusive relationship that can emphasize channel-wise features. Through channel constraint, the learning capabilities of network can be enhanced based on the correlation between channels and the fusion of global information with local information.

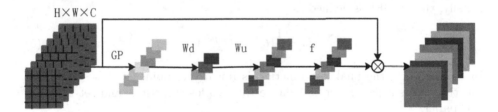

Fig. 3. Channel-constrained (Cc). $\otimes$ denotes the element-wise product.

2.3 Loss Function

In this section, we describe the loss function of the network. Suppose there is a training dataset $\{x^i, s^i\}_{i=1}^N$, where x^i or s^i represents the ith image in the dataset, where x is LR-HSI and s is the corresponding HR-HSI, N is the number of images. Our goal is to obtain the estimated image z of s.

MSE is widely used in least-squares regression setting to optimize the network parameters. We increase the Peak Signal-to-Noise Ratio (PSNR) by minimizing the first loss function.

$$l_1 = \frac{1}{2N} \sum_{i=1}^N \left\| s^i - z^i \right\|_2^2 \tag{2}$$

Since noise can have a severe impact on image edge and texture information, we propose a feature error loss based on the first-order derivative features to protect the edge and texture of the image. We define l_2^{spat} as FODFE in spatial domain where filtering is performed for each band.

$$l_2^{spat} = \frac{1}{2N}\sum_{i=1}^{N}\frac{1}{2}(\left\|\nabla_h s^i - \nabla_h z^i\right\|_2^2 + \left\|\nabla_w s^i - \nabla_w z^i\right\|_2^2) \qquad (3)$$

where ∇_h and ∇_w are the first-order difference operators in the h and w directions of the image.

Although spatial denoising has a strong influence on HSIs, it has been proven to be insufficient to suppress noise existing in the spectral domain. In this case, spectral denoising is also required. When analyzing spectral domain, an HSI can be viewed as a set of spectral signatures or as a multivalued 1D signal. Therefore, we use the first-order difference operator in the spectral domain as ∇_d, and the FODFE in spectral domain is defined as l_2^{spec}.

$$l_2^{spec} = \frac{1}{2N}\sum_{i=1}^{N}\left\|\nabla_d s^i - \nabla_d z^i\right\|_2^2 \qquad (4)$$

Finally, the FODFE is defined as

$$l_2 = \frac{1}{2}(l_2^{spat} + l_2^{spec}) \qquad (5)$$

In our network, the final loss function is linearly combined by these two loss functions. α is a parameter to balance the two loss functions and set to 0.5 in this paper.

$$l_{loss} = l_1 + \alpha l_2 \qquad (6)$$

2.4   Implementation Details

In this section, we describe the parameter settings of the RCSSN network. In each RCB, we set the size of all conv layers to 3×3, except for the channel-downsampling and channel-upsampling whose filter size is 1×1 and the conv layer in the channel-downsampling has 4 filters. In addition, the filter size of the conv layer in the reconstruction process is set to 5×5. The last conv layer has 31 filters as the spectral resolution of the output HSI is the same as the groundtruth.

3   Experiments

3.1   Database Description and Parameter Setting

In this section, we evaluate the effectiveness of the proposed method using the CAVE database [12] including 32 indoor images. In the CAVE database, the HSIs have 31 spectral bands of 10 nm wide, covering the visible spectrum from

400 to 700 nm, and the size of each band is 512×512. The CAVE database has been widely used in the literature of HSI pan-sharpening [5, 6, 14].

We consider the original images in the database as the groundtruths. The LR-HSI is created by downsampling by a factor of 32 and applying a Gaussian filter (with a mean of 0 and a standard deviation of 2). The corresponding HR-MSI image y is simulated by integrating the groundtruth over the spectral channels using the spectral response P of a Nikon D700 camera. We use the first 20 (about 60%) HSIs of the CAVE database for training, and the last 12 HSIs for testing. In the training process, both x and s are divided into several 32×32 patches.

3.2 Experimental Results

We have compared the proposed RCSSN method with four recent state-of-the-art HSI sharpening methods: the nonnegative-structured sparse representation (NSSR) [6], NLSTF method [13], Deep HSI sharpening (DHSIS) [18] and Partial Dense Connected spatial and spectral fusion architectures of CNN (PDCon-SSF) [19]. The NSSR is based on matrix factorization, the NLSTF is based on tensor factorization, the DHSIS and the PDCon-SSF are based on deep learning. In order to make all the methods get the best pan-sharpening results, we changed the number of optimization iteration in NSSR to 60.

In order to assess quantitatively the methods, four objective evaluation metrics including peak-signal-to-noise ratio (PSNR), the Structure Similarity (SSIM), the universal image quality metric (UIQI) [15], and spectral angle mapper (SAM) [16] are used to evaluate the quantitative accuracy of the estimated HSIs.

Table 1 lists the average objective results of the CAVE dataset for all test methods and the best results are marked in bold for clarity. As can be seen from the Table 1, RCSSN has lower SAM and higher PSNR, SSIM and UIQI, which means the proposed RCSSN has better robust pan-sharpening performance than other methods. Since DHSIS, NLSTF and NSSR do not have clean HR-HSIs as reference but deal directly with noisy LR-HSIs, it is inevitable to avoid the influence of noise and lead to unexpected results.

Table 1. Average quantitative results (PSNR, SSIM, SAM, UIQI) of the methods on the CAVE database.

Method	NLSTF	DHSIS	NSSR	PDCon-SSF	RCSSN
PSNR	20.5578	29.118	29.5792	36.1967	**36.3936**
SSIM	0.6378	0.7361	0.8613	0.9783	**0.9795**
SAM	29.1713	28.3035	20.758	8.4262	**7.7158**
UIQI	0.3879	0.6017	0.6367	0.9063	**0.9343**

For visual comparison, we show the 14th and 22st bands of the estimated HR-HSI Peppers in Fig. 4. In addition, Fig. 4 also shows the error image between the selected bands of estimated image and corresponding groundtruth. It can be seen that the estimated HR-HSIs reconstructed by NLSTF, DHSIS and NSSR have stripe artifacts, grid artifacts and fuzzy details, respectively, which cannot well eliminate noise exiting in the original image. In order to further compare the visual effects of PDCon-SSF and RCSSN, we mark two meaningful regions in the image to facilitate visual comparison. From the two meaningful regions, it can be seen that PDCon-SSF produces artifacts in smooth regions and worse effect at the edge of image texture due to the influence of noise.

To further demonstrate the effectiveness of the channel constraint strategy proposed in RCSSN, Fig. 5 shows the average PSNR curves for all spectral bands of experimental results for all test methods on the CAVE database. It can be seen that RCSSN performs best in most spectral bands in all comparison methods. In addition, since there is blur existing in the first and second frequency bands [17], all the test methods perform well in the middle spectral band and perform relatively poorly in these two bands.

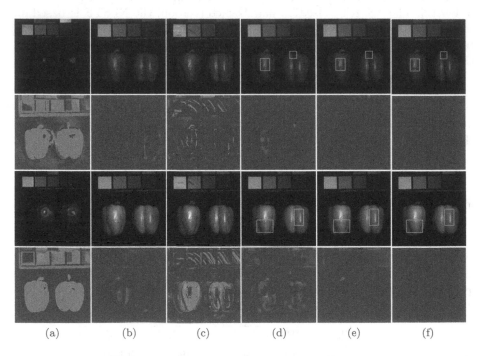

(a)   (b)   (c)   (d)   (e)   (f)

Fig. 4. First row: reconstructed images of Peppers (an HSI in the CAVE database) at 14th band. Second row: corresponding error images of the competing approaches for the image Peppers at 14th band. Third row: reconstructed images of Peppers at 22st band. Fourth row: corresponding error images of the competing approaches for the image Peppers at 22st band. (a) NLSTF (b) DHSIS (c) NSSR (d) PDCon-SSF (e) RCSSN (f) Groundtruth.

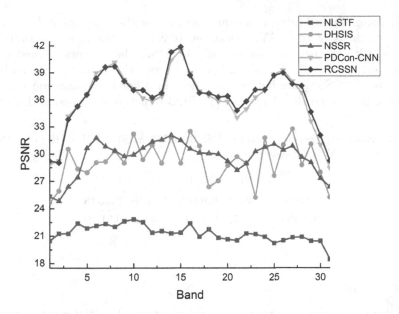

Fig. 5. Average PSNR curves as functions of the spectral bands for the test method.

3.3   Running Time

In this section, taking a HSI randomly selected from the CAVE database as an example, we compare the running time of all testing methods. All experiments are performed using a computer equipped with an Intel i7-9700-GHz CPU and 16-GB random access memory. As can be seen from Table 2, PDCon-SSF and RCSSN run fast when trained well due to their end-to-end network structures. PDCon-SSF has less network layers and therefore has the highest running speed. Since DHSIS requires three steps and the network contained is not end-to-end, it is not as fast as the other two CNN-based methods. However, NSSR and NLSTF need to solve complex optimization problems and therefore need more running time.

Table 2. Comparison of running time on one randomly selected testing HSI in CAVE database.

Method	NLSTF	DHSIS	NSSR	PDCon-SSF	RCSSN
Time	131	3.1971	144.8253	**0.4683**	0.9602

3.4   Effectiveness of FODFE in RCSSN

In order to prove the validity of the proposed FODFE, we use the estimated results reconstructed by the network RCSSN- which is trained only by MSE as a comparison. Table 3 lists the average metrics for the experimental results for the two methods of the CAVE database. It can be seen from the table that compared with the network trained only by MSE, the network trained by the weighted errors of FODFE and MSE can improve the indicators. In addition, the results of RCSSN- are better than those of other four compared methods, which also proves the effectiveness of the RCB structure proposed in this paper.

Table 3. Average quantitative results (PSNR, SSIM, SAM, UIQI) of the RCSSN and RCSSN- on the CAVE database.

	PSNR	SSIM	SAM	UIQI
RCSSN	**36.3936**	**0.9795**	**7.7158**	**0.9343**
RCSSN-	36.2057	0.9791	7.8885	0.9152

3.5 Conclusion

In this study, we propose a robust channel-constrained spatial spectral network (RCSSN) for HSI pan-sharpening. The multi-secondary connection of the HR-MSI in the RCB can compensate for information pollution and information loss caused by noise and low resolution. And the channel constraint mechanism allows the network to learn the difference between channels to improve the ability of the network to distinguish and express different types of features. In addition, we develop a joint loss of the training network, which combines the traditional MSE loss with the first-order derivative feature loss, to recover the edge and texture information severely corrupted by noise. Sufficient experimental results on publicly available dataset demonstrate that the promising potential of the proposed method in terms of LR-HSI pan-sharpening.

References

1. Nguyen, H.V., Banerjee, A., Chellappa, R.: Tracking via object reflectance using a hyperspectral video camera. In: IEEE Computer Society Conference on Computer Vision and Pattern Recognition Workshops (CVPRW), pp. 44–51 (2010)
2. Pan, Z., Healey, G., Prasad, M., Tromberg, B.: Face recognition in hyperspectral images. IEEE Trans. Pattern Anal. Mach. Intell. **25**(12), 1552–1560 (2003)
3. Tarabalka, Y., Chanussot, J., Benediktsson, J.A.: Segmentation and classification of hyperspectral images using watershed transformation. Pattern Recogn. **43**(7), 2367–2379 (2010)
4. Wei, Q., Bioucas-Dias, J., Dobigeon, N., Tourneret, J.Y.: Hyperspectral and multispectral image fusion based on a sparse representation. IEEE Trans. Geosci. Remote Sens. (TGRS) **53**(7), 3658–3668 (2015)
5. Akhtar, N., Shafait, F., Mian, A.: Sparse spatio-spectral representation for hyperspectral image super-resolution. In: Fleet, D., Pajdla, T., Schiele, B., Tuytelaars, T. (eds.) ECCV 2014. LNCS, vol. 8695, pp. 63–78. Springer, Cham (2014). https://doi.org/10.1007/978-3-319-10584-0_5

6. Dong, W., et al.: Hyperspectral image super-resolution via non-negative structured sparse representation. IEEE Trans. Image Process. **25**, 2337–2352 (2016)

7. Yan, C., Xie, H., Yang, D., Yin, J., Zhang, Y., Dai, Q.: Supervised hash coding with deep neural network for environment perception of intelligent vehicles. IEEE Trans. Intell. Transp. Syst. **19**(1), 284–295 (2017)

8. Dong, C., Loy, C.C., He, K., Tang, X.: Image super-resolution using deep convolutional networks. IEEE Trans. Pattern Anal. Mach. Intell. **38**(2), 295–307 (2014)

9. Samek, W., Binder, A., Montavon, G., Lapuschkin, S., Mller, K.-R.: Evaluating the visualization of what a deep neural network has learned. IEEE Trans. Neural Netw. Learn. Syst. **28**(11), 2660–2673 (2015)

10. Dundar, A., Jin, J., Martini, B., Culurciello, E.: Embedded streaming deep neural networks accelerator with applications. IEEE Trans. Neural Netw. Learn. Syst. **28**(7), 1572–1583 (2017)

11. Li, J., Mei, X., Prokhorov, D., Tao, D.: Deep neural network for structural prediction and lane detection in traffic scene. IEEE Trans. Neural Netw. Learn. Syst. **28**(3), 690–703 (2016)

12. Yasuma, F., Mitsunaga, T., Iso, D., Nayar, S.K.: Generalized assorted pixel camera: postcapture control of resolution, dynamic range, and spectrum. IEEE Trans. Image Process. **19**(9), 2241–2253 (2010)

13. Dian, R., Fang, L., Li, S.: Hyperspectral image super-resolution via non-local sparse tensor factorization. In: IEEE Conference on Computer Vision and Pattern Recognition (CVPR), pp. 3862–3871, July 2017

14. Lanaras, C., Baltsavias, E., Schindler, K.: Hyperspectral superresolution by coupled spectral unmixing. In: Proceedings of IEEE Conference on Computer Vision and Pattern Recognition (CVPR), pp. 3586–3594, December 2015

15. Wang, Z., Bovik, A.C.: A universal image quality index. IEEE Signal Process. Lett. **9**(3), 81–84 (2002)

16. Yuhas, R.H., Boardman, J.W., Goetz, A.F.H.: Determination of semi-arid landscape endmembers and seasonal trends using convex geometry spectral unmixing techniques. In: Summaries of the 4th Annual JPL Airborne Geoscience Workshop, vol. 1, 205–208, October 1993

17. Akhtar, N., Shafait, F., Mian, A.: Hierarchical beta process with gaussian process prior for hyperspectral image super resolution. In: Leibe, B., Matas, J., Sebe, N., Welling, M. (eds.) ECCV 2016. LNCS, vol. 9907, pp. 103–120. Springer, Cham (2016). https://doi.org/10.1007/978-3-319-46487-9_7

18. Dian, R., Li, S., Guo, A., Fang, L.: Deep hyperspectral image sharpening. IEEE Trans. Neural Netw. Learn. Syst. 1–11 (2018)

19. Han, X., Shi, B., Zheng, Y.: SSF-CNN: spatial and spectral fusion with CNN for hyperspectral image super-resolution. In: IEEE International Conference on Image Processing (ICIP), pp. 2506–2510, October 2018

20. Li, Y., Zhang, L., Dingl, C., Wei, W., Zhang, Y.: Single hyperspectral image super-resolution with grouped deep recursive residual network. In: IEEE Fourth International Conference on Multimedia Big Data (BigMM), pp. 1–4, September 2018

Ensemble Transductive Learning for Skin Lesion Segmentation

Zhiying Cui[1,2], Longshi Wu[1,2], Ruixuan Wang[1,2(✉)], and Wei-Shi Zheng[1,2]

[1] School of Data and Computer Science, Sun Yat-sen University, Guangzhou, China
wangruix5@mail.sysu.edu.cn
[2] Key Laboratory of Machine Intelligence and Advanced Computing, MOE,
Guangzhou, China

Abstract. Automated segmentation of skin lesions from dermoscopy images is helpful for the diagnosis and treatment of skin cancers. However, due to small annotated training set and the large visual difference in skins and lesions between subjects, the generalization performance of segmentation models are often limited. Inspired by the transductive learning for image classification, we propose a transductive segmentation approach for skin lesion segmentation, by choosing some of the pixels in test images to participate the training of any segmentation model together with the training set. In this way, visual features in the test images can be effectively learned during model training. Comprehensive evaluations with different model structures and transductive learning strategies showed that the proposed transductive segmentation approach always improve the performance of the corresponding state-of-the-art segmentation models in skin lesion segmentation.

Keywords: Transductive learning · Medical image segmentation · Skin lesions

1 Introduction

Skin cancer is one of the most common cancers, with over 5,000,000 new patients every year in the United States [5]. To effectively diagnose skin cancers and evaluate the effect of various treatments, it is necessary to record and measure the progression of skin lesion regions over time. However, it is time consuming for dermatologists to accurately delineate skin lesion regions. In this case, the state-of-the-art automated image segmentation techniques could potentially help clinicians to efficiently segment skin lesion regions from healthy parts.

Multiple deep learning models have recently been developed for image segmentation, including the first fully convolutional network (FCN) [8], the well-known U-Net [9] which was initially proposed for medical image segmentation

---

Z. Cui and L. Wu—The authors contribute equally to this paper.

© Springer Nature Switzerland AG 2019
Z. Lin et al. (Eds.): PRCV 2019, LNCS 11858, pp. 572–581, 2019.
https://doi.org/10.1007/978-3-030-31723-2_49

by extending the original FCN model with skip-connections between the down-sample and the corresponding up-sample layers, and the state-of-the-art segmentation model DeepLab [2,3]. For the segmentation task of skin lesions, the method with top accuracy applied target detection on the skin lesion to reduce reverse effect from different size of skin lesion [4]. This approach is cumbersome in training and requires a large number of pre-trained models, so we did not perform detection on our segmentation pipeline. But it should be noted that the baseline models we used is as same as baseline models in previous work. Due to the difficulty in annotating medical images for segmentation, deep learning models are often over-trained with limited annotated medical images. The over-training becomes exacerbated when there is large difference in images between subjects. In this case, images of certain subjects from the test set cannot be typically represented by any image from the training set, and therefore even more training data would not fundamentally solve the problem of limited generalization performance on the test data from new subjects. Unfortunately, such subject-level difference frequently appears in skin image analysis, where each subject may demonstrate distinctive visual features.

To reduce the effect of the subject-level difference, transfer learning is often applied in image classification and segmentation tasks [12,13], by pretraining a model on another large (either natural or medical) dataset and then fine-tuning the pre-trained model on the task data. However, transfer learning based on a large set of natural images may be limited in improving the performance on medical images, while it is often difficult or infeasible to obtain a large set of medical images to pre-train a segmentation model for later-on use. Another solution is to employ ensemble models by combining multiple individual ones, including the well-known Bagging [1] and Boosting [6] methods. However, these learning strategies cannot fundamentally solve the issue caused by the subject difference.

Instead of exploring novel model architectures or knowledge from additional dataset to help improve segmentation performance on medical images, we propose to directly learn to extract knowledge from the test data during model training. Inspired by transductive learning for classification tasks [11], which tries to use both the annotated training data and the un-annotated test data during model training, we hypothesize that extraction of information from test data and then embedding to the process of model training would largely help the final model to effectively segment the test images. In transductive learning for classification tasks, considering that there are always incorrect prediction on test data by the (initially trained) model, often only those of the test data with high prediction confidence are selected to join the model training, where the predicted label for the selected test data were considered as the ground truth.

While transductive learning has been applied for image classification tasks [10], there is little work particularly for medical image segmentation tasks. In this paper, we propose a transductive learning approach to the segmentation of skin lesion regions, aiming to improve the segmentation performance on the test images by directly learning subject-level visual features from test images during model training. Different from image classification tasks in which each image has a class label, image segmentation can be considered as a pixel-level classification task, in which different pixels in one image may have different class labels and prediction confidence levels. Therefore, we propose choosing high-confidence pixels from test images during transductive learning rather than using all pixels of each image. Experiments showed the superior performance of the pixel-level test data selection for transductive learning. To further improve the segmentation performance, an ensemble strategy was combined with the transductive learning, in which multiple individual segmentation models are trained with transductive learning and then combined together to segment test images. Experiments with various deep learning models showed that the transductive learning with the ensemble strategy always performs better than corresponding baseline models in skin lesion segmentation.

2   Transductive Skin Lesion Segmentation

The objective of the study is to alleviate the influence of subject-level difference between training and test set, such that the trained segmentation model can have better generalization ability. Instead of focusing on exploring information from training set or other seemingly irrelevant large dataset, here we focus on directly exploring information from the test set during model training, inspired by the transductive learning strategy.

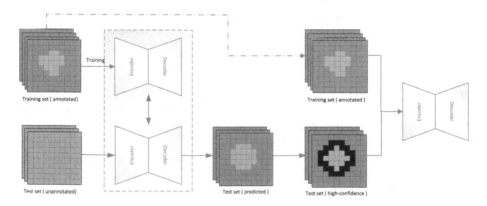

Fig. 1. The framework for transductive skin lesion segmentation. The line with double arrows indicates that the two segmentation models pointed by the arrows are identical.

2.1   Transductive Learning

To use transductive learning strategy, an initial segmentation model based only on the training images need to be trained (Fig. 1, upper left) and then used to

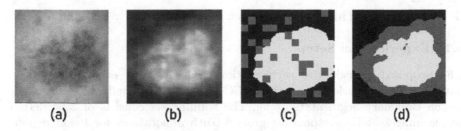

Fig. 2. Example of generating annotation of a test image for transductive learning. (a) a test skin image. (b) the probability output of the initial segmentation model for the test image, with brighter pixels indicating higher probability of belonging to lesion. (c) an example of random selection of pixels for transductive learning. Pixels within randomly generated purple regions are discarded and the other pixels are selected. Each selected pixel was assigned to either 'lesion' (yellow) or 'healthy' (black) class label by thresholding the probability output with 0.5. (d) High-confidence pixel selection for transductive learning. A pixel was considered high-confidence when the probability output is either close to 1.0 (highly likely being lesion) or to 0.0 (likely being healthy), therefore the pixels whose output probability is around 0.5 (purple regions) are discarded and all the other pixels are selected for tranductive learning. (Color figure online)

predict the initial segmentation result for each test image (Fig. 1, lower left). The initial predictions would be used as ground-truth annotations for the test images, and finally such 'annotated' test images are used together with the training set to train a new segmentation model (Fig. 1, right half), finishing the process of transductive learning. Considering the initial segmentation of test images are often noisy, for each *test* image, only the pixels with high-confidence predictions were selected for model training, where the confidence for each pixel can be directly obtained from the prediction (probability) output from the initial segmentation model. As supported by experiments (Sect. 3.2), such confidence-based pixel selection strategy is more effective than other candidate selections, including selecting pixels randomly from each test image or using all pixels from a subset of test images. This is also consistent with the strategy of selecting high-confidence test images for transductive image classification [10].

2.2   Ensemble Transductive Learning

To further improve the generalization of segmentation, we propose combining the ensemble strategy with the transductive learning, i.e., multiple segmentation models were respectively trained by transductive learning and then combined together when predicting the segmentation result for any new image. The variations between these models can be obtained by either training from differential initialized model parameters or by randomly selecting a subset of test images for tranductive learning. To make full use of test images, the former option was selected here, i.e., using high-confidence pixels of all test images, but training models from different initialized parameters.

3   Experimental Evaluations

3.1   Experimental Setup

The proposed transductive segmentation approach was evaluated on ISIC dataset which was released for the MICCAI'2018 grand challenge "ISIC task1: Lesion Boundary Segmentation" [5]. The training set consists of 2594 dermoscopic images and corresponding ground-truth annotations for lesion regions. The validation set and test set contain 100 images and 1000 images respectively, with ground-truth annotations kept by the organizer. The predicted segmentation result by any model was submitted online to obtain the prediction result via the live leaderboard.

During training of a segmentation model, unless mentioned otherwise, SGD optimizer was used with initial learning rate 0.007 and the momentum value 0.9. Learning rate was updated with a poly scheduler. For the evaluation metric, besides the general measurements (accuracy, dice score, Jaccard index or intersection over union, sensitivity, specificity), the organizer particularly chose the Threshold Jaccard Index (TJI) as the essential metric. In this metric, Jaccard index for the predicted segmentation of any test image was set to zero when the index is lower than a pre-defined threshold (0.65 here), while the index was kept unchanged when it is higher than the threshold. TJI was calculated by averaging the thresholded index values over all test images. TJI can more accurately reflect the number of images in which automated segmentation fails or falls outside expert inter-observer variability. Note that the number of images in which automated segmentation fails is a direct measure of the amount of labor required to correct an algorithm.

In all the subsequent experimental results, if there is no special explanation, we use the same settings to train three identical models at the same time, and then simply use voting strategy and average strategy for ensemble learning. The three models differ only in the random process of parameter initialization and the randomness of the selected samples during the training process. The purpose of the integration is to make the experimental results more reliable and stable.

3.2   Effectiveness of Transductive Segmentation

To evaluate the effectiveness of transductive segmentation, we first compared the proposed ensemble transductive model with several alternative strategies. One baseline is the traditional ensemble of three segmentation models without using transductive learning ('No transductive' in Table 1). Another strategy is the ensemble of three transductive segmentaion models, with each model trained with all pixels of randomly selected 80% test images ('Random test images' in Table 1). The third strategy is the ensemble of three transductive segmentaion models, with each model trained with all pixels of all test images ('All test images' in Table 1), the fourth strategy is the ensemble of three transductive segmentaion models, with each model trained with randomly selected 80% pixels from each test images ('Random pixels' in Table 1). The last row

('High-confidence pixels' in Table 1) shows the segmentation performance of the proposed semble of three transductive segmentaion models, with each model trained with high-confidence pixels from each test images. High-confidence pixels were selected by discarding those pixels whose prediction probability values is within the range [0.25, 0.75]. Table 1 clearly shows that the proposed ensemble transductive segmentation model outperforms all the other strategies, with 3.5% improvement in TJI compared to the traditional ensemble model (78.1% vs. 74.6%), and more than 1% improvement compared to the ensemble transductive model based on all test images (78.1% vs. 76.8%). Another observation is that the all the ensemble transductive segmentations (the last four rows in Table 1) outperform the ensmble model without using transductive learning, supporting that transductive learning is effective in improving the segmentation of skin lesions, no matter which strategy was used to select pixels or images from the test set.

Table 1. Comparison of transductive segmentations with different strategies. DeepLab v3+ was used as the backbone segmentation model.

Transductive strategy	Accuracy	Dice	Jaccard	Sensitivity	Specificity	TJI
No transductive	0.935	0.883	0.808	0.95	0.928	0.746
Random test images	0.934	0.887	0.816	0.935	0.936	0.756
All test images	0.933	0.888	0.82	0.921	0.938	0.768
Random pixels	0.933	0.889	0.82	0.929	0.933	0.765
High-confidence pixels	**0.941**	**0.896**	**0.83**	0.919	**0.957**	**0.781**

3.3 Robustness of Transductive Segmentation over Model Structures

To evaluate the robustness of the ensemble transductive segmentation, we compared its performance with the 'No transductive' ensemble model and the ensemble tranductive segmentation with 'All test images' under three different segmentation model structures, the well-known U-Net, the DeepLab V3+, and the recently proposed Dual Attention Network (DAN) [7]. Table 2 shows that, while different backbone segmentation models performed differently, all the three models with the proposed high-confidence pixel transductive learning (last row) performed better than the two strong baselines (first and second rows) in skin lesion segmentation. This confirms that the transductive segmentation is independent of segmentation model structures.

3.4 Effectiveness of Single Transductive Segmentation

So far, the evaluation was based on ensemble of multiple single segmentation models. To show that the proposed transductive segmentation approach works

Table 2. Performance of ensemble transductive learning with different segmentation model structures. Threshold Jaccard Index (TJI) was used as the metric.

Method	UNet	DAN	DeepLab
No transductive	0.702	0.756	0.746
All test images	0.728	0.762	0.768
High-confidence pixels	**0.730**	**0.779**	**0.781**

not just on ensemble models, here we compared single transductive segmentation model ('High-confidence' in Fig. 3) with the baseline single segmentation without using transductive learning ('Baseline' in Fig. 3). In each case, three single models were trained and averaged. Consistent with the previous results with ensemble models, transductive segmentation works better than the one without transductive learning on single models as well, no matter which model structure is used.

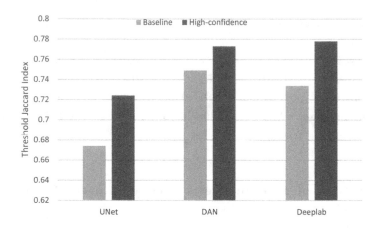

Fig. 3. Comparison between single transductive segmentation and the traditional segmentation without transductive learning on three different model structures.

3.5   Influence of Hyper-parameters

One key hyper-parameter in the proposed approach is the threshold value to select high-confidence pixels. All the reported performance above was based on the threshold 0.75, i.e., selecting pixels in each test image whose prediction probability is either larger than 0.75 (likely 'lesion') or less than 0.25 (likely 'healthy'). Here we evaluated the performance of the proposed transductive segmentation with different threshold values 0.65 (i.e., selecting pixels whose prediction probability is either larger than 0.65 or less than 0.35), 0.75, 0.85, and 0.90 (i.e., selecting pixels whose prediction probability is either larger than 0.90 or less than 0.10). Figure 4 demonstrates the selected pixels at different thresholds, with higher threshold leading to fewer selected pixels, and lower threshold leading to more selected pixels. It is not surprising that higher (e.g., 0.85 or 0.90) or lower threshold value (0.65) would cause relatively worse performance compared to the threshold 0.75 (Table 3), because higher threshold values would make the transductive learning discard too many pixels from test images and therefore cannot extract enough information from test images, while lower threshold value would make the transductive learning select too many pixels from test images which would increase the likelihood of incorrect prediction labels for model training.

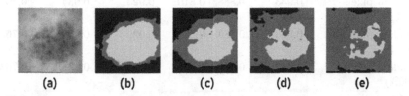

Fig. 4. High-confidence pixel selection from each test image with a different threshold. (a) a test image, (b–e) selected pixels (black and yellow) when threshold is 0.65, 0.75, 0.85, and 0.90 respectively. Yellow regions correspond to high-confidence lesions and black regions correspond to high-confidence healthy regions, while purple regions correspond to excluded pixels. (Color figure online)

Table 3. The performance of transductive segmentation with different threshold to select high-confidence pixels from each test image.

Threshold	Accuracy	Dice	Jaccard	Sensitivity	Specificity	TJI
0.65	0.935	0.889	0.818	**0.943**	0.933	0.767
0.75	**0.941**	**0.896**	**0.83**	0.919	**0.957**	**0.781**
0.85	0.937	0.89	0.819	0.936	0.945	0.767
0.90	0.937	0.887	0.813	0.942	0.943	0.757

One may doubt that the reported comparison results above is based on the optimal selection of the hyperparameter for the proposed model, but not for the baseline models. Here we also performed experiments by varying relevant hyperparameters within the baseline models. Specifically, we varied the percent of test images under the 'Random test images' condition (see Table 1 and Sect. 3.2) for transductive learning, and also varied the percent of randomly selected pixels under the 'Random pixels'. Table 4 showed that even with the optimal hyperparameters, the transductive segmentations under these two conditions were outperformed by the proposed transductive segmentation with high-confidence pixel selection.

Table 4. The performance of transductive models with varying relevant hyperparameters for alternative pixel/image selection. Note that the 'Random test images' with 100% image selection is equivalent to the 'Random pixels' with 100% pixel selection.

Method	Accuracy	Dice	Jaccard	Sensitivity	Specificity	TJI
Random test images (60%)	0.934	0.887	0.815	**0.939**	0.936	0.759
Random test images (80%)	0.934	0.887	0.816	0.935	0.936	0.756
Random test images (100%)	0.933	0.888	0.82	0.921	0.938	0.768
Random pixels (60%)	0.933	0.888	0.819	0.923	0.934	0.767
Random pixels (80%)	0.933	0.889	0.82	0.929	0.933	0.765
Random pixels (100%)	0.933	0.888	0.82	0.921	0.938	0.768
High-confidence pixels (0.75)	**0.941**	**0.896**	**0.83**	0.919	**0.957**	**0.781**

4   Conclusion

This paper proposed an ensemble transductive learning strategy for automatically segmenting lesion regions from skin images. By learning directly from both training and test set, the proposed approach can effectively reduce the subject-level difference between training and test set, thus improving the generalization performance of segmentation models. The superior performance of transductive segmentation has been consistently confirmed with varying model structures and strategies to select pixels from test images. Considering that the number of annotated training images are often very limited in medical image segmentation tasks, the transductive segmentation approach may provides an alternative effective way to improve the performance of any segmenatation model, besides the widely adopted transfer learning and ensemble modeling.

References

1. Breiman, L.: Bagging predictors. Mach. Learn. **24**, 123–140 (1996)
2. Chen, L.C., Papandreou, G., Kokkinos, I., Murphy, K., Yuille, A.L.: Semantic image segmentation with deep convolutional nets and fully connected CRFs. arXiv preprint arXiv:1412.7062 (2014)
3. Chen, L.C., Papandreou, G., Schroff, F., Adam, H.: Rethinking atrous convolution for semantic image segmentation. arXiv preprint arXiv:1706.05587 (2017)
4. Qian, C., et al.: A detection and segmentation architecture for skin lesion segmentation on dermoscopy images. arXiv preprint arXiv:1809.03917 (2018)

5. Codella, N.C., et al.: Skin lesion analysis toward melanoma detection. In: IEEE International Symposium on Biomedical Imaging, pp. 168–172 (2018)
6. Freund, Y., Schapire, R.E., et al.: Experiments with a new boosting algorithm. In: International Conference on Machine Learning, pp. 148–156 (1996)
7. Fu, J., Liu, J., Tian, H., Fang, Z., Lu, H.: Dual attention network for scene segmentation. arXiv preprint arXiv:1809.02983 (2018)
8. Long, J., Shelhamer, E., Darrell, T.: Fully convolutional networks for semantic segmentation. In: Proceedings of the IEEE Conference on Computer Vision And Pattern Recognition, pp. 3431–3440 (2015)
9. Ronneberger, O., Fischer, P., Brox, T.: U-net: convolutional networks for biomedical image segmentation. In: International Conference on Medical Image Computing and Computer-assisted Intervention, pp. 234–241 (2015)
10. Song, J., Shen, C., Yang, Y., Liu, Y., Song, M.: Transductive unbiased embedding for zero-shot learning. In: Proceedings of the IEEE Conference on Computer Vision and Pattern Recognition, pp. 1024–1033 (2018)
11. Vapnik, V.: The Nature of Statistical Learning Theory. Springer, Heidelberg (2013). https://doi.org/10.1007/978-1-4757-3264-1
12. Zamir, A.R., Sax, A., Shen, W., Guibas, L.J., Malik, J., Savarese, S.: Taskonomy: disentangling task transfer learning. In: Proceedings of the IEEE Conference on Computer Vision and Pattern Recognition, pp. 3712–3722 (2018)
13. Zhuang, N., Yan, Y., Chen, S., Wang, H., Shen, C.: Multi-label learning based deep transfer neural network for facial attribute classification. Pattern Recogn. **80**, 225–240 (2018)

MobileCount: An Efficient Encoder-Decoder Framework for Real-Time Crowd Counting

Chenyu Gao[1(✉)], Peng Wang[1], and Ye Gao[2]

[1] School of Computer Science, Northwestern Polytechnical University, Xi'an, China
{chenyugao,gaoye}@mail.nwpu.edu.cn
peng.wang@nwpu.edu.cn
[2] National Engineering Laboratory for Integrated Aero-Space-Ground-Ocean Big Data Application Technology, Beijing, China

Abstract. In this work, we propose a computation-efficient encoder-decoder architecture, named MobileCount, which is specifically designed for high-accuracy real-time crowd counting on mobile or embedded devices with limited computation resources. For the encoder part, MobileNetV2 is tailored in order to significantly reduce FLOPs at a little cost of performance drop, which has 4 bottleneck blocks preceded by a max pooling layer of stride 2. The design of decoder is motivated by Light-weight RefineNet, which further boosts counting performance with only a 10% increase of FLOPs. In comparison with state-of-the-arts, our proposed network is able to achieve comparable counting performance with 1/10 FLOPs on a number of benchmarks.

Keywords: Crowd counting · Light-weight neural networks · Fully convolutional networks

1 Introduction

Crowd counting is a task to estimate the number of people in congested scenes. It has gained a lot of interests in recent years due to its significant importance in surveillance and security applications. As in many computer vision tasks, such as object detection [2,7], image classification [9,15,32] and semantic segmentation [5,18,20], state-of-the-art approaches for crowd counting are also based on deep neural networks. The approaches to tackle this problem could be classified into detection-based [36], regression-based [4] and density map estimation-based methods [1,14,16,28,29,37,39]. Instead of regress the overall count of the entire image, density map estimation-based methods predict the density at each pixel and obtain the crowd count by summing over all pixels. This method

The first author is a student. This work is supported in part by the National Natural Science Foundation of China (No. 61876152).

is trained with pixel-level supervision information and more suitable for high-density scenes. Our proposed model is also based on density map estimation.

In real applications with mobile or embedded systems, it is almost equivalently important to obtain an acceptable accuracy and to achieve fast inference speed with a limited computation budget. A variety of light-weight neural networks have been proposed for image classification [10,30,38], segmentation [23,24,27] and object detection [25,26,34]. However, light-weight crowd counting models have been rarely studied, despite its importance in surveillance.

In our work, we propose a light-weight encoder-decoder structure for crowd counting. We carefully design the encoder-decoder structure to achieve an optimized trade-off between model accuracy and computation speed. For the encoder part, we further simplify the original MobileNetV2 [30] by using few convolution layers (4 bottlenecks instead of 7 bottlenecks) and smaller feature map resolution (a 3 × 3 max pooling layer of stride 2 is inserted before bottlenecks), with a small performance drop. On the other hand, we adopt the decoder design of Light-Weight RefineNet [23] that is originally designed for semantic segmentation. Compared with the FPN decoder, our decoder is approximately 29 times faster, and also achieves better counting performance. In the experiments, we show that our design dramatically reduce the number of floating point operations (FLOPs) without a significant drop in accuracy. The proposed MobileCount model is able to achieve comparable performance with state-of-the-arts, with a much smaller computation cost.

Our main contributions are summarized as follows:

(1) An efficient encoder-decoder framework is specifically designed for real-time crowd counting. The MobileNetV2-based encoder and RefineNet-based decoder are carefully tailored to achieve a good balance between accuracy and speed.

(2) The experimental study demonstrates that our proposed MobileCount can reduce both the number of parameters and floating point operations without a significant drop in accuracy.

2 Related Work

We categorize our discussion of related work into three main groups: crowd counting, Fully Convolutional Network (FCN) decoder architectures, and light-weight model designs.

2.1 Crowd Counting

The earliest approaches to address crowd counting problem based on detection [36], these methods attempt to detect the head or full body of each individual with the number of detected bounding boxes being the estimated crowd count. Unfortunately, detection-based methods suffer from the person size is too small or the crowd is extremely dense.

Fig. 1. Illustration of density maps generated by MobileCount on ShanghaiTech Part_A and Part_B and UCF-QNRF dataset. The first row shows test images from different datasets are chosen randomly. The second row shows the ground truth of each images. The last row shows the predicted density map of corresponding image.

Regression-based method [4] directly computing the number of objects based on features extracted from cropped image patches. Since these methods only produce counts, they cannot be used for density map estimation or provide more valuable information about the input.

Due to density map estimation-based methods [1,14,16,28,29,37,39] can offer stronger supervision and preserve more fine-grained information, the mainstream methods are based on it. Zhang *et al.* [39] proposed MCNN based on density map estimation. The input of MCNN is an image and the output is a crowd density map whose integral gives the overall crowd count. Similarly, Switch-CNN [28] using a switching mechanism multi-column architecture to utilize features at different scales all together in order to accurately estimate crowd counts for images of multi-scale. Finding Multi-column CNNs are hard to train and the granularity of density level is hard to define in real-time congested scene analysis, Li *et al.* [16] proposed CSRNet, which is a single column Fully Convolutional Network (FCN) [20] architecture with cascaded dilated convolutional layers, and the simple architecture achieve exciting performance. Besides, many other architectures are designed to improve accuracy. Sindagi *et al.* [33] designed a multi-task architecture, Sam *et al.* [29] trained a recursively growing CNN tree for routing input image patches to appropriate expert regressors, Shi *et al.* [31] proposed a pool of decorrelated regressors based on deep negative correlation learning and so on.

2.2   FCN Decoder Architectures

Decoder network in FCN learns to upsample the input feature map(s) and generate high-resolution output. The decoder architectures are widely used in semantic segmentation [5,17,23] on account of the encoder network always produce's

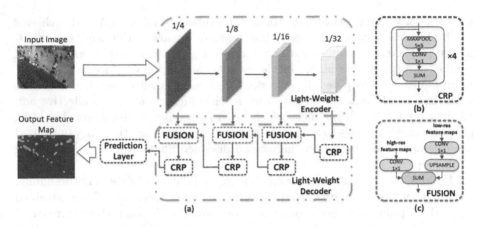

Fig. 2. Overview of the proposed MobileCount architecture for crowd counting. (a) General network architecture consisting of encoder, decoder and prediction layer. (b)–(c) CRP and FUSION blocks in our decoder architecture.

low-resolution representations which need to be restored to high-resolution image representations in order to do pixel-wise predictions. Convolutional layers before the full connected layers of classification networks (*i.e.*, VGG16 [32], and ResNet50 [9]) can be directly employed as encoder networks in all of these architectures. In other words, the performance of the decoder architecture determines the performance of the aforementioned semantic segmentation architectures.

In addition to manually designing decoders, researchers also designed decoder architecture based on Neural architecture search (NAS). For instance, Nekrasov *et al.* [22] are interested in searching for high-performance compact segmentation architectures being able to run in real-time using limited resources. They rely on a recurrent neural network to recover such encoder-decoder architectures as FCN [20], or RefineNet [17].

As a kind of pixel-wise task, density map estimation-based crowd counting also needs decoder architectures to generate high-quality density map of the same size as the original input. Researchers design the decoder from simply use several layers of upsampling convolutions [33] to deploy dilated convolutional layers as the back-end [16] to boost architectures' performance in crowd counting and so on.

2.3 Light-Weight Networks

It has been an area of active research that how to tune deep neural architectures to strike an optimal balance between accuracy and performance for the last several years.

Most state-of-the-art efficient networks based on efficient CNN architectures designing. SqueezeNet [12] can be trained from scratch, it can achieve AlexNet-level [15] accuracy by using a bottleneck approach to design the very small network. Based on depthwise separable convolutions, MobileNetV1 [10] achieves 4% better accuracy on ImageNet than SqueezeNet about the same size. Shuf-fleNet [38] reduce computation cost based on group convolution and channel shuffle, and it achieves higher efficiency than MobileNetV1. MobileNetV2 [30] build lightweight deep neural networks based on an inverted residual structure with liner bottleneck, this architecture reaches high performance effective and efficient, and it is still the most widely used lightweight architecture. Ma *et al.* proposes four principles to reduce the amount of calculation, then they optimized the calculation amount of ShuffleNet and designed ShuffleNetV2 [21] according to those principles.

Besides, there are many other approaches for light-weight networks designing. Network compression approaches [8,35] improve the inference of a pre-trained network by pruning network connections or channels; Neural architecture search (NAS) [34] search over a huge network to get an architecture with the best speed and performance; Low-bit representation of network weights using quantization [11] to improve inference of a pre-trained network, and so on.

Benefit from previous researches, we present a clear and simple end-to-end FCN architecture for crowd counting task. In our work, we use a variant of fast but low-resolution MobileNetV2 [30] as our backbone and boldly adding a Light-Weight RefineNet decoder [23].

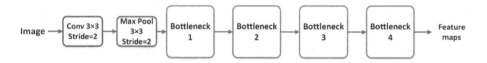

Fig. 3. The detail architecture of the proposed light-weight encoder (Fig. 2(a)). As for MobileCount, the specific settings of each bottleneck can be referred to Table 1.

3   Method

In this section, we will describe the proposed MobileCount model for efficient crowd counting, including its overall architecture, loss functions and the ground truth generation procedure.

3.1   Network Architecture

As shown in Fig. 2, our model architecture is based on FCNs with encoder and decoder, which can be trained end-to-end.

Encoder. MobilenetV2 [30] is specifically designed for mobile applications, with significantly reduced memory footprint and improved classification accuracy. MobilenetV2 architecture is based on an inverted residual structure with linear bottlenecks. The structure of bottleneck is mainly composed of these two kinds convolution operations: 1×1 Point-wise convolution and 3×3 Depth-wise convolution. In this work, to reduce both the number of parameters and floating point operations without a significant drop in accuracy, we choose MobileNetV2 [30] as the backbone network and tailor it specifically for crowd counting. Through experimental study, we find that using 4 bottlenecks instead of 7 can obtain better performance with lower FLOPs, we remove the last three bottlenecks to both save computation and improve accuracy. Inspired from ShuffleNetV2 [21], to make our model even lighter, we reduce the input resolution at the beginning of the encoder by adding a 3×3 max pooling layer of stride 2 before bottleneck operators. Experimental results (see Table 2) also shows that adding this pooling layer reduce over 70% FLOPs with a tolerable drop of accuracy. As shown in Table 1, we also experiment with different model sizes by changing the number of feature channels, in order to find an optimal balance between accuracy and performance. The detail of our encoder architecture is shown in Fig. 3.

Decoder. Correctly estimating the crowd density of a particular pixel cannot only rely on the information of the pixel itself: we should incorporate the context information of multiple scales to tackle different person sizes. In this work, we choose the Light-Weight RefineNet [23] decoder that is originally designed for semantic segmentation. This decoder has been sepcifically simplied from RefineNet [17] to achieve real-time performance, which can be combined with any encoder of multi-scale feature maps.

The decoding process of the Light-Weight RefineNet starts with the propagation of the last output from the backbone (with the lowest resolution) through chained residual pooling (CRP) block (Fig. 2(b)) before being fed into a FUSION block (Fig. 2(c)) along with the second to last feature map. Inside the FUSION block, each path is convolved with 1×1 convolution and the low-resolution feature maps are upsampled to the high-resolution among the paths. Two paths are then summed up, and analogously further propagated through several CRP and FUSION blocks until the desired resolution is reached. After that, the generated feature maps are fed into the prediction layer to produce the final density map.

Prediction Layer. The regression-based prediction layer applies a 1×1 convolution, embedding the d-dimensional feature vector at each pixel of an input feature map to a density value firstly. Then the resulting density map is upsampled to the original image size by bilinear interpolation.

Table 1. Different settings of our proposed encoder. The Bottleneck is residual bottlenecks proposed in MobileNetV2. The intermediate expansion layer uses lightweight depthwise convolutions to filter features and t represent expansion factor. Conv2d represents a 3×3 convolution layer. MaxPool represents a 3×3 max pooling layer. Each row describes an operation with n repeats, stride s, expansion factor t and output channels c. We present three different settings by changing the output channels c for individual operations.

Operator	Output size	t	n	s	Output channels (c)		
					MobileCount	MobileCount ($\times 1.25$)	MobileCount ($\times 2$)
Image	1				3	3	3
Conv2d	1/2	-	1	2	32	64	64
MaxPool	1/4	-	1	2			
Bottleneck	1/4	1	1	1	32	64	64
Bottleneck	1/8	6	2	2	64	96	128
Bottleneck	1/16	6	3	2	128	160	256
Bottleneck	1/32	6	4	2	256	320	512

3.2   Loss Functions

Our end-to-end architecture directly transforms the input image to a real-valued density map. The mean squared error loss is adopted in this work:

$$L_{den} = \frac{1}{N} \sum_{i=1}^{N} \|D^{PM}(i) - D^{GT}(i)\|_2^2 \, , \tag{1}$$

where N is the number of training samples; $D^{PM}(i)$ represents the predicted density map and $D^{GT}(i)$ represents the ground truth density map; i denotes the i-th training sample; $\|\cdot\|_2$ represents the Euclidean distance.

3.3   Ground Truth Generation

Our ground truth density map is generated by applying a Gaussian blur kernel at each annotated head position:

$$D(x) = \sum_{i=1}^{M} \delta(x - x_i) * G_{\sigma_i}(x), \tag{2}$$

where $\delta(\cdot)$ represents a delta function and x_i, $i = 1, \ldots, M$ denote the positions of the i-th annotated head; σ_i denotes the variance of the Gaussian kernel applied at position i. For ShanghaiTech Part_A, the variance is geometry-adaptive as in [39]. More specifically, $\sigma_i = 0.3\bar{d}_i$ where $\bar{d}_i$ is the average distance to k nearest neighbors. We simply fixed the value of variance σ_i to 4 for other datasets.

4 Experiments

In this section, we will firstly present the implementation details, and introduce the evaluated datasets and adopted evaluation metrics. Secondly, we evaluate the performance of different encoders without any decoder. Experimental results prove that using 4 bottlenecks preceded with a stride-2 max pooling can obtain better performance and lower FLOPs. Third, we experiment with different types of decoders, including the FPN decoder, the Light-weight RefineNet decoder (LWRN) and its another version with more feature channels (refered to as LWRN+). The results show that LWRN achieves the best balance between accuracy and speed. Finally, we compare three settings of our full models with state-of-the-art crowd counting approaches. Our models achieve comparable counting performance and real-time processing speed.

4.1 Implementation Details

The training and testing are performed on an NVIDIA GeForce GTX 1080Ti GPU using PyTorch framework. In our experiment, we use Adam optimization with a batch size of 6 and a weight decay rate of 1×10^{-4}. The initial learning rate is set to 1×10^{-4}.

Different from [39] using datasets processed offline, we follow [6] randomly crop 80%-sized patches from each image for each training epoch online.

4.2 Datasets

ShanghaiTech [39]. The ShanghaiTech dataset contains $1,198$ images with total $330,165$ heads. It consists of two parts, Part_A with 482 images (300 images for training and 182 images for testing) obtained from the Internet, and Part_B with 716 images (400 images for training and 316 images for testing) taken from the shopping street.

WorldExpo10 [37]. The WorldExpo'10 dataset consists of $3,380$ frames in 103 scenes in training set and 600 labeled frames from the remaining 5 scenes in the testing set. All of these images were taken by 108 surveillance cameras during the 2010 Shanghai World Expo. We only consider the number of people in these ROIs provides by this dataset.

UCF_CC_50 [13]. The UCF_CC_50 dataset includes 50 images from different scenes with different size of the Internet. In UCF_CC_50 dataset, the crowd counts ranging from 94 to 4543. We divide the dataset into 5 splits and use five-fold cross-validation as the setting in [13].

UCF_QNRF [14]. The UCF_QNRF dataset is a new and the largest crowd dataset for both crowd counting and localization tasks. This dataset has the most number of high-count crowd images and annotations with a wider variety of scenes containing the most diverse set of viewpoints, densities and lighting variations, which makes this dataset more realistic as well as difficult. It contains 1535 dense crowd images (1201 images for training and 334 images for testing).

4.3 Evaluation Metrics

Following [16,33,37], we use Mean Absolute Error (MAE) and Mean Square Error (MSE) to evaluate our model. They are defined as:

$$\text{MAE} = \frac{1}{N} \sum_{i=1}^{N} \left| C_i^{PM} - C_i^{GT} \right| \tag{3}$$

$$\text{MSE} = \sqrt{\frac{1}{N} \sum_{i=1}^{N} \left(C_i^{PM} - C_i^{GT} \right)^2} \tag{4}$$

where N is the image number for test; C_i^{PM} is the predicted crowd count of each image by summing over all pixels of the density map; and C_i^{GT} is the real count.

Table 2. The comparison of the different encoders without using any decoder. The result shows that adding a max pooling layer (stride 2) before bottleneck operators can directly reduce over 70% FLOPs with a tolerable reduction of accuracy. (BN = Bottleneck, w/o = without, MNV2 = MobileNetV2.)

Encoder	GFLOPs	Params (MB)	Part_A		Part_B		UCF-QNRF		UCF_CC_50		WorldExpo'10
			MAE	MSE	MAE	MSE	MAE	MSE	MAE	MSE	MAE
Vanilla MNV2 7BN	13.58	1.89	99.2	170.8	11.6	18.1	146.3	250.0	340.6	468.1	12.9
Vanilla MNV2 7BN Pool	3.79	1.89	113.5	173.9	11.2	17.5	180.5	293.7	378.3	510.0	15.4
Vanilla MNV2 4BN	7.93	0.25	88.3	143.0	8.8	14.8	125.8	198.8	283.4	402.1	10.6
Vanilla MNV2 4BN Pool	2.37	0.25	96.1	161.4	10.6	16.1	143.6	241.8	333.0	486.8	13.8
MobileCount w/o Pool	59.19	3.34	84.6	144.4	7.9	12.5	112.8	188.7	253.6	361.5	10.8
MobileCount	15.22	3.34	98.6	162.9	9.1	15.1	137.8	238.2	321.7	437.1	12.2

4.4 Results and Analysis

Comparison of Different Encoders. Firstly, we make a comparison of different standalone encoders, with no decoder adopted. The tested encoder architectures include the vanilla MobileNetV2 [30] with 7 bottlenecks (denoted as Vanilla-MNV2-7BN) and 4 bottlenecks (denoted as Vanilla-MNV2-4BN), and their counterparts with the inserted stride-2 max pooling layer (Vanilla-MNV2-4BN-Pool and Vanilla-MNV2-7BN-Pool). Our proposed MobileCount encoder is also evaluated with or without the inserted max pooling layer (denoted as MobileCount and MobileCount w/o Pool respectively). From Table 2, we can see that adding a max pooling layer can directly reduce over 70% FLOPs with a roughly 10% reduction of accuracy. On the other hand, removing the last three bottleneck blocks does not have significant impact on the counting metrics.

Table 3. The comparison of different decoders, with the MobileCount encoder. FPN has a much larger FLOPs, while does not significantly improve performance. Meanwhile, LWRN+ slightly increases the computation complexity and memory footprint over LWRN, but its performance is still close to that of LWRN.

Decoder	GFLOPs	Params (MB)	Part_A		Part_B		UCF-QNRF		UCF_CC_50		WorldExpo'10
			MAE	MSE	MAE	MSE	MAE	MSE	MAE	MSE	MAE
LWRN decoder	16.49	3.40	89.4	146.0	9.0	15.4	131.1	222.6	284.8	392.8	11.1
FPN decoder	474.81	5.83	90.5	147.6	9.5	17.0	134.4	230.4	390.2	570.4	11.7
LWRN+ Decoder	18.55	3.84	87.6	146.0	8.8	14.6	131.8	228.9	278.7	421.2	11.6

Comparison of Different Decoders. We compare three decoders for fusing multi-scale feature maps, which are LWRN, LWRN+ and FPN, with the MobileCount encoder. The LWRN decoder is originally used in the Light-Weight RefineNet for real-time semantic segmentation. The LWRN+ decoder is constructed by increasing the feature channels of LWRN. We also compare with the decoder used in the Feature Pyramid Networks (FPN) [19]. Through Table 3, we can see that the computation complexity of the FPN decoder is more than 25 times larger than LWRN and LWRN+, but its counting performance is slightly worse. On the other hand, the counting performance of LWRN and LWRN+ are close, while LWRN has a smaller memory footprint and fewer FLOPs. Therefore, we adopt LWRN as our decoder in the following experiments.

Comparison with State-of-the-arts. We compare state-of-the-art counting approaches with our proposed MobileCount model of three different sizes ($\times 1$, $\times 1.25$ and $\times 2$). Compared to the evaluated 4 methods in Table 4, our MobileCount ($\times 1.25$) and MobileCount ($\times 2$) models achieve higher accuracy with fewer floating point operations on the ShanghaiTech Part_B [39] and UCF-QNRF [14] datasets. On ShanghaiTech [39] Part_A and WorldExpo10 [37], our results are worse than the best performing method but still comparable. Note that our architecture uses one column of FCN with lowest FLOPs and a single objective function, while previous approaches usually rely on multiple columns or more than one objective function. Density maps obtained using MobileCount are shown in Fig. 1, which indicate that even the smallest configuration of our architecture can generate density maps of good quality. Quantitatively, we are able to closely match the performance of the original network while significantly accelerate its computation. As shown in Table 5, we also compare the inference time and FPS of different models, for 1920 × 1080 input images, on two GPU platforms (GTX 1080Ti and GTX 1080), and with two batch sizes (2 and 4). In accordance to the theory GFLOPs, our MobileCount model is significantly faster than all the compared existing approaches. It arrive at 37 FPS on GTX 1080Ti with batch size equals 2, while SANet, CSRNet and CMTL are 4 to 8 times slower. MCNN is much faster than SANet, CSRNet and CMTL, but its performance is worse than them and our models.

Table 4. The comparison of our proposed method of different backbone settings with state-of-the-arts in terms of MAE and MSE, on five public crowd counting datasets. MAE, MSE and the number of FLOPs on 1920 × 1080 inputs are reported.

Net	GFLOPs	Params(MB)	Part_A		Part_B		UCF-QNRF		UCF_CC_50		WorldExpo'10
			MAE	MSE	MAE	MSE	MAE	MSE	MAE	MSE	MAE
MCNN [39]	56.21	0.13	110.2	173.2	26.4	41.4	277.0	426.0	377.6	509.1	11.6
CMTL [33]	243.80	2.46	101.3	152.4	20.0	31.1	252.0	514.0	322.8	397.9	–
CSRNet [16]	857.84	16.26	68.2	115.0	10.6	16.0	–	–	266.1	397.5	8.6
SANet [3]	182.26	1.39	67.0	104.5	8.4	13.6	–	–	258.4	334.9	8.2
MobileCount	16.49	3.40	89.4	146.0	9.0	15.4	131.1	222.6	284.8	392.8	11.1
MobileCount (×1.25)	34.07	5.47	82.9	137.9	8.2	13.2	124.5	207.6	283.1	382.6	11.1
MobileCount (×2)	63.03	13.39	81.4	133.3	8.1	12.7	117.9	207.5	284.5	421.2	11.5

Table 5. The comparison of our proposed method with state-of-the-arts in terms of inference Time and FPS. inference Time and FPS on 1920 × 1080 inputs are reported.

Net	GTX 1080Ti				GTX 1080			
	Batch size = 2		Batch size = 4		Batch size = 2		Batch size = 4	
	Time (ms)	FPS	Time (ms)	FPS	Time (ms)	FPS	Time (ms)	FPS
MCNN	36.3	27.5	36.5	27.4	50.1	20.0	51.6	19.4
CMTL	124.9	8.0	125.9	7.9	167.2	6.0	183.1	5.5
CSRNet	193.0	5.2	200.4	5.0	278.9	3.6	286.0	3.5
SANet	136.9	7.3	112.8	8.9	191.0	5.2	167.2	6.0
MobileCount	26.7	37.5	26.3	38.0	33.7	29.7	33.5	29.9
MobileCount (×1.25)	45.7	21.9	44.7	22.4	58.0	17.2	58.1	17.2
MobileCount (×2)	56.5	17.7	55.8	17.9	73.8	13.6	73.5	13.6

5   Conclusion

In this work, we proposed an end-to-end trainable light-weight architecture of crowd counting, named MobileCount. The encoder and decoder of our proposed model are carefully designed to strike an optimal balance between accuracy and speed. Extensive experiments performed on challenging datasets and comparison with state-of-the-art approaches demonstrated that our method achieves comparable counting performance using a significantly reduced computation resources.

References

1. Boominathan, L., Kruthiventi, S.S., Babu, R.V.: CrowdNet: a deep convolutional network for dense crowd counting. In: Proceedings Conference of ACM Multimedia (2016)
2. Cai, Z., Vasconcelos, N.: Cascade R-CNN: delving into high quality object detection. In: Proceedings of the IEEE Conference on Computer Vision and Pattern Recognition, pp. 6154–6162 (2018)

3. Cao, X., Wang, Z., Zhao, Y., Su, F.: Scale aggregation network for accurate and efficient crowd counting. In: Ferrari, V., Hebert, M., Sminchisescu, C., Weiss, Y. (eds.) ECCV 2018. LNCS, vol. 11209, pp. 757–773. Springer, Cham (2018). https://doi.org/10.1007/978-3-030-01228-1_45

4. Chan, A.B., Vasconcelos, N.: Bayesian poisson regression for crowd counting. In: Proceedings of IEEE International Conference Computer Vision (2009)

5. Chen, L.C., Papandreou, G., Kokkinos, I., Murphy, K., Yuille, A.L.: DeepLab: semantic image segmentation with deep convolutional nets, atrous convolution, and fully connected CRFs. IEEE Trans. Pattern Anal. Mach. Intell. **40**, 834–848 (2018)

6. Gao, J., Lin, W., Zhao, B., Wang, D., Gao, C., Wen, J.: C-3-framework: an opensource PyTorch code for crowd counting. arXiv preprint arXiv:1907.02724 (2019)

7. Girshick, R., Donahue, J., Darrell, T., Malik, J.: Rich feature hierarchies for accurate object detection and semantic segmentation. In: Proceedings of IEEE Conference Computing Vision Pattern Recognition, pp. 580–587 (2014)

8. Han, S., Pool, J., Tran, J., Dally, W.: Learning both weights and connections for efficient neural network. In: Proceedings of Advances in Neural Information Processing Systems, pp. 1135–1143 (2015)

9. He, K., Zhang, X., Ren, S., Sun, J.: Deep residual learning for image recognition. In: Proceedings of IEEE Conference Computing Vision Pattern Recognition, pp. 770–778 (2016)

10. Howard, A.G., et al.: MobileNets: Efficient convolutional neural networks for mobile vision applications. arXiv preprint arXiv:1704.04861 (2017)

11. Hubara, I., Courbariaux, M., Soudry, D., El-Yaniv, R., Bengio, Y.: Quantized neural networks: training neural networks with low precision weights and activations. J. Mach. Learn. Res. **18**(1), 6869–6898 (2017)

12. Iandola, F.N., Han, S., Moskewicz, M.W., Ashraf, K., Dally, W.J., Keutzer, K.: SqueezeNet: AlexNet-level accuracy with 50x fewer parameters and <0.5 MB model size. arXiv preprint arXiv:1602.07360 (2016)

13. Idrees, H., Saleemi, I., Seibert, C., Shah, M.: Multi-source multi-scale counting in extremely dense crowd images. In: Proceedings of the IEEE Conference on Computer Vision and Pattern Recognition (2013)

14. Idrees, H., et al.: Composition loss for counting, density map estimation and localization in dense crowds. In: Ferrari, V., Hebert, M., Sminchisescu, C., Weiss, Y. (eds.) ECCV 2018. LNCS, vol. 11206, pp. 544–559. Springer, Cham (2018). https://doi.org/10.1007/978-3-030-01216-8_33

15. Krizhevsky, A., Sutskever, I., Hinton, G.E.: ImageNet classification with deep convolutional neural networks. In: Advances in Neural Information Processing Systems (2012)

16. Li, Y., Zhang, X., Chen, D.: CSRNet: dilated convolutional neural networks for understanding the highly congested scenes. In: Proceedings of the IEEE Conference on Computer Vision and Pattern Recognition (2018)

17. Lin, G., Milan, A., Shen, C., Reid, I.: RefineNet: multi-path refinement networks for high-resolution semantic segmentation. In: Proceedings of the IEEE Conference on Computer Vision and Pattern Recognition, pp. 1925–1934 (2017)

18. Lin, G., Shen, C., Van Den Hengel, A., Reid, I.: Efficient piecewise training of deep structured models for semantic segmentation. In: Proceedings of the IEEE Conference on Computer Vision and Pattern Recognition (2016)

19. Lin, T.Y., Dollár, P., Girshick, R., He, K., Hariharan, B., Belongie, S.: Feature pyramid networks for object detection. In: Proceedings of the IEEE Conference on Computer Vision and Pattern Recognition, pp. 2117–2125 (2017)

20. Long, J., Shelhamer, E., Darrell, T.: Fully convolutional networks for semantic segmentation. In: Proceedings of the IEEE Conference on Computer Vision and Pattern Recognition (2015)
21. Ma, N., Zhang, X., Zheng, H.-T., Sun, J.: ShuffleNet V2: practical guidelines for efficient CNN architecture design. In: Ferrari, V., Hebert, M., Sminchisescu, C., Weiss, Y. (eds.) Computer Vision – ECCV 2018. LNCS, vol. 11218, pp. 122–138. Springer, Cham (2018). https://doi.org/10.1007/978-3-030-01264-9_8
22. Nekrasov, V., Chen, H., Shen, C., Reid, I.: Fast neural architecture search of compact semantic segmentation models via auxiliary cells. arXiv preprint arXiv:1810.10804 (2018)
23. Nekrasov, V., Shen, C., Reid, I.: Light-weight refineNet for real-time semantic segmentations. arXiv preprint arXiv:1810.03272 (2018)
24. Paszke, A., Chaurasia, A., Kim, S., Culurciello, E.: ENet: a deep neural network architecture for real-time semantic segmentation. arXiv preprint arXiv:1606.02147 (2016)
25. Redmon, J., Divvala, S., Girshick, R., Farhadi, A.: You only look once: unified, real-time object detection. In: Proceedings of the IEEE Conference on Computer Vision and Pattern Recognition, pp. 779–788 (2016)
26. Ren, S., He, K., Girshick, R., Sun, J.: Faster R-CNN: towards real-time object detection with region proposal networks. In: Advances in Neural Information Processing Systems, pp. 91–99 (2015)
27. Romera, E., Alvarez, J.M., Bergasa, L.M., Arroyo, R.: ERFNet: efficient residual factorized convnet for real-time semantic segmentation. IEEE Trans. Intell. Transp. Syst. 19(1), 263–272 (2018)
28. Sam, D.B., Surya, S., Babu, R.V.: Switching convolutional neural network for crowd counting. In: Proceedings of IEEE Conference on Computer Vision and Pattern Recognition (2017)
29. Sam, D.B., Sajjan, N.N., Babu, R.V., Srinivasan, M.: Divide and grow: capturing huge diversity in crowd images with incrementally growing CNN. In: Proceedings of the IEEE Conference on Computer Vision and Pattern Recognition (2018)
30. Sandler, M., Howard, A., Zhu, M., Zhmoginov, A., Chen, L.C.: MobileNetV 2: inverted residuals and linear bottlenecks. In: Proceedings of the IEEE Conference on Computer Vision and Pattern Recognition (2018)
31. Shi, Z., et al.: Crowd counting with deep negative correlation learning. In: Proceedings of the IEEE Conference on Computer Vision and Pattern Recognition (2018)
32. Simonyan, K., Zisserman, A.: Very deep convolutional networks for large-scale image recognition. In: Proceedings of International Conference Learning Representations (2015)
33. Sindagi, V.A., Patel, V.M.: CNN-based cascaded multi-task learning of high-level prior and density estimation for crowd counting. In: IEEE International Conference on Advanced Video and Signal Based Surveillance (2017)
34. Tan, M., Chen, B., Pang, R., Vasudevan, V., Le, Q.V.: MnasNet: platform-aware neural architecture search for mobile. arXiv preprint arXiv:1807.11626 (2018)
35. Veit, A., Belongie, S.: Convolutional networks with adaptive inference graphs. In: Proceedings of the European Conference on Computer Vision, pp. 3–18 (2018)
36. Viola, P., Jones, M.J., Snow, D.: Detecting pedestrians using patterns of motion and appearance. Int. J. Comput. Vis. 63, 153–161 (2005)
37. Zhang, C., Li, H., Wang, X., Yang, X.: Cross-scene crowd counting via deep convolutional neural networks. In: Proceedings of the IEEE Conference on Computer Vision and Pattern Recognition (2015)

38. Zhang, X., Zhou, X., Lin, M., Sun, J.: ShuffleNet: an extremely efficient convolutional neural network for mobile devices. In: Proceedings of the IEEE Conference on Computer Vision and Pattern Recognition, pp. 6848–6856 (2018)
39. Zhang, Y., Zhou, D., Chen, S., Gao, S., Ma, Y.: Single-image crowd counting via multi-column convolutional neural network. In: Proceedings of the IEEE Conference on Computer Vision and Pattern Recognition (2016)

Multi-scale Densely 3D CNN for Hyperspectral Image Classification

Yong Xiao, Qin Xu$^{(\boxtimes)}$, Dongyue Wang, Jin Tang, and Bin Luo

School of Computer Science and Technology, Anhui University,
Hefei 230601, China
e11414110@stu.ahu.edu.cn, {xuqin,tj,luobin}@ahu.edu.cn,
m18192496362@163.com

Abstract. Convolutional neural networks (CNNs) have shown good performance in hyperspectral image classification. However, there are still several
problems unsolved. To address the existing problems, in this paper, we develop
a multi-scale densely 3D convolutional neural network (CNN) for hyperspectral
image classification. To characterize the hierarchical spatial-spectra feature, we
design several branches with 3D convolutional kernels of different size. To
overcome the gradient vanishing, we explore the dense connection where the
input of each layer includes all the feature map produced in the previous layer.
The proposed network that has five convolutional layers in total is shallow and
short. The experimental results on Indian Pines and University of Pavia datasets
have demonstrate the proposed method can acquire significant improvements
over the state-of the-arts and require less computation and implementation time.

Keywords: Hyperspectral image classification · Convolutional neural network ·
3D convolution · Multi-scale · Dense connection

1 Introduction

The rapid development of hyperspectral remote sensing technology makes the narrow
and contiguous bands available [1]. Classifying a hyperspectral image (HSI) that is
composed of hundreds of narrow contiguous wavelength bands for the same object on
the surface of Earth is to label every pixel with a certain land-cover type [2]. It has
attracted more attention in a broad applications, including military, agricultural and
earth observation [3, 4]. However, hyperspectral image classification faces two major
challenges. One is the famous Hughes phenomenon, which is caused by the limited
training sample and the high dimensional spectra, leads to the accuracy of classification
decreases sharply as the dimension increases [5]. Another is, the spectra variabilities
which is brought by many factors such as incident illumination, atmospheric effects,
unwanted shade and shadow, natural spectrum variation, and instrument noises [6].

There are an amount of approaches for hyperspectral image classification in the
literature. The earlier and simpler method is K-nearest neighbor method [7], which
employs the Euclidean distance for calculating the distance between the training
samples and an unlabeled sample. To solve the Hughes phenomenon, the support
vector machine (SVM) [8] method which utilizes the kernel to classify has become a

© Springer Nature Switzerland AG 2019
Z. Lin et al. (Eds.): PRCV 2019, LNCS 11858, pp. 596–606, 2019.
https://doi.org/10.1007/978-3-030-31723-2_51

benchmark. On the observation that a hyperspectral pixel can be sparsely represented by a linear combination of a few training samples through a structured dictionary, Chen et al. proposed to incorporated the contextual information into the sparse recovery optimization problem to improve the accuracy [9]. Based on the same perspective, Shao et al. proposed a spatial and class structure regularized sparse representation (SCSSR) graph for semi-supervised HSI classification [10].

The features extraction mentioned above are all hand-craft features which involve expert's experience. Recently, the deep learning techniques, a kind of more complex hierarchical architecture simulating human brains, have been explored and applied to the hyperspectral image classification. In deep learning, the convolutional neural networks (CNNs) play an important role and have achieved success in HSI classification [11–15]. In literature [13], the authors proposed a network, named as C-CNN, using recent multiple advances in deep learning area, such as batch normalization, dropout, and parametric rectified linear unit (PReLU) activation function. Li et al. constructed pixel-pairs by combining the test pixel and each of the surrounding pixels and classified the HSI by the deep CNN so that the similarity between pixels are mined and a sufficient amount of input data to learn a large number of parameters in the CNN is ensured, including ten learnable convolutional layers and three max-pooling layers [14]. To address the problems that some important information is neglected by CNNs, Ma et al. designed an end-to-end deconvolution network with two branches which is the spatial branch and spectral branch to learn the spectral–spatial features. The network is reported can recover the erased information of the pooling layers and learn pixelwise spatial representation hierarchically [15]. To solve the problem of the limited samples, Zhu et al. proposed to utilize the generative adversarial network (GAN) for HSI classification, where a convolutional neural network (CNN) is designed to discriminate the inputs and another CNN is used to generate the fake inputs [16]. In order to extract the spatial-spectral features simultaneously, a 3D convolutional neural network (3D-CNN) framework [17] and a multi-scale 3D deep convolutional neural network (M3D-CNN) framework [18] are proposed for HSI classification.

The CNN-based approaches have provided better performance than the traditional methods. But there are still several problems unresolved: (1) The gradient is vanishing as the network becoming deep which results in a decrease in the classification accuracy. (2) It requires a large number of samples to train to get good results avoiding over fitting, and in some methods some categories of small sample are removed directly. (3) The deep learning techniques are time-consuming. To address these problems, inspired by the Densenet [19], we propose a multi-scale densely 3D convolutional neural network for hyperspectral image classification. The proposed network model consists of three different scale dense blocks, where each block has three convolution kernels, two convolutional layers, a pooling layer and a full connected layer. Therefore, there are only five convolution layers in total, which can be quickly trained and tested. Meanwhile, in order to learn the spatial-spectral information, we adopt three-dimensional convolution operation, which is originally used for video analysis [20].

The main contributions of this paper are as follows. (1) Multi-scale and densely three-dimensional convolutional connections are effectively combined. The sample and feature maps are fully utilized, which can alleviate the phenomenon of gradient disappearance, and obtains better results compared with some advanced methods. The proposed method can provide a good classification accuracy for the small-sample categories in the HSI dataset, which are discarded directly in several CNN-based methods. (2) The network is compact and does not introduce any data pre-processing operations such as data enhancement and PCA dimensionality reduction. The network is short and succinct and therefore observably reduces the experiment time.

The remainder of this paper is organized as follows. The proposed classification framework is described in Sect. 2. The experiments and analysis are discussed in Sect. 3. The conclusion is drawn in Sect. 4.

2 Multi-scale Densely 3D CNN

To improve the feature representational ability and alleviate the vanishing gradient, we propose a multi-scale densely 3D CNN for HSI classification. In our network, there are three 3D dense blocks of different scales, two convolutional layers, a pooling layer and a fully connected layer. The proposed network has a compact and brief architecture and can provide a desired classification accuracy.

2.1 3D Dense Block

Although the HSI classification via CNN has achieved state-of-the-art results, the classification accuracy decreases as the convolutional layers increase because the input or gradient vanishes when it reaches the end of the network. To this end, we design 3D dense block where each convolutional layer connects with the input and the feature maps produced in all previous layers.

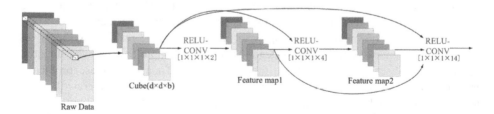

Fig. 1. 3D dense block structure

To explore the spatial-spectral information, we employ 3D convolutional kernels and take raw 3D HSI cubes as the input of our network, as shown in Fig. 1. The 3D cubes are size of $d \times d \times b$, where $d \times d$ represents the length and width, and b

represents the number of spectral bands, which can also be understood as depth. The 3D cube input characterizes the spatial relation between the center pixel and its neighboring pixels. The common way is to use a size-fixed window, such as 3×3, 5×5. To concatenate the feature maps and the input data, we set the size of the feature map equals to the size of the raw cube.

Let P^i denote the input of the i th layer, X^i represent the output of the i th layer, $G[,]$ be the concatenation operation, the input and output of i th layer are defined as

$$P^i = G[P^{i-1}, X^{i-1}] \tag{1}$$

$$X^i = F(R(P^i)) + b^i \tag{2}$$

where $R(.)$ is the RELU function, $F(.)$ means 3D convolution and b^i is the corresponding bias in i th layers. The operations on the original data and the feature map include rectified linear units (RELU) and 3D convolution.

2.2 MSD 3D-CNN Architecture

The CNNs with multi-scale can improve the representational ability for the hyperspectral image. Based on this, we develop multiple branches of dense block to extract multi-level features to improve the performance of HSI classification. The overall network framework is illustrated in Fig. 2. In our approach, there are three branches of the dense block, one block has a 3D convolution kernel of a different size. The size of the 3D convolution kernels in each dense block is the same, i.e. $w_1 \times w_2 \times w_3 \times m$, where w_1, w_2, w_3, m represents the length, width, depth and channel of the 3D convolution kernel, respectively.

Let Q^1, Q^2, Q^3 denotes the output of the dense block 1, the dense block 2 and the dense block 3 respectively, and Q denotes the fusion result of the outputs of the multiscale dense block, which is defined as

$$Q = G[Q^1, Q^2, Q^3] \tag{3}$$

where $G[,]$ is the concatenation operation. After two convolutional layers, an average pooling layer is used to reduce the parameters and remove the noise. In the end of the network, a fully connected layer is used to generate a vector whose dimension is equal to the number of label classes. The cross entropy E is used as the loss function for training and defined as

$$E = -\sum_k t_k \log y_k \tag{4}$$

where the t_k is a label, y_k is the output of the network. Moreover, the dropout is adopted in the fully connected layer to overcome over fitting.

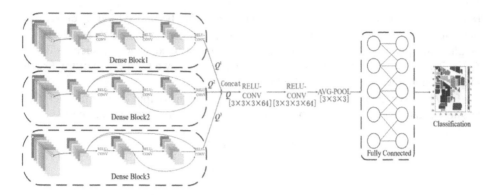

Fig. 2. The overall flowchart of the proposed MSD 3D-CNN

3 Experimental Results and Discussion

To verify the proposed MSD 3D-CNN for HSI classification, we conduct it on two benchmark datasets, i.e. Indian Pines and University of Pavia, and compare the results with five state-of-the-arts methods, including CNN [11], R-PCA-CNN [12], C-CNN [13], CNN-PPF [14], 3D-GAN [16], 3D-CNN [17] and M3D-CNN [18]. All the experiments are implemented in TensorFlow with the GPU gtx1060.

3.1 Datasets

Indian Pines dataset is Airborne Visible/Infrared Imaging Spectrometer (AVIRIS) Indian Pines image, which consists of 145×145 pixels and has 16 different ground-truth classes [21]. There are 220 spectral bands covering the range from 0.2 to 2.4 μm with spatial resolution of 20 m. The spectral bands are reduced to 200 by removing 20 water absorption bands [22]. As shown in Table 1, we randomly select 200 samples for training for the classes having more than 400 samples and the rest as the test set. For the other classes, we randomly select the half for training and the rest as the test set too.

University of Pavia dataset is urban image acquired by the Reflective Optics System Imaging Spectrometer (ROSIS), which generates 115 wavelength bands ranging from 0.43 to 0.86 μm and has a spatial resolution of 1.3 m per class [23]. The University of Pavia contains 610×340 pixels with 103 wavelength bands, which 13 noisy bands have been removed. We randomly select the training and testing samples, and the numbers of training and testing samples are listed in Table 2.

Table 1. The number of training and testing samples for the Indian Pines dataset

#	Class	Train	Test
1	Alfalfa	23	23
2	Corn-notill	200	1228
3	Corn-min	200	630
4	Corn	118	119
5	Grass/Pasture	200	283
6	Grass/Trees	200	530
7	Grass/Pasture-mowed	14	14
8	Hay-windrowed	200	278
9	Oats	10	10
10	Soybeans-notill	200	772
11	Soybeans-min	200	2255
12	Soybeans-clean	200	393
13	Wheat	102	103
14	Woods	200	1065
15	Building-Grass-Trees-Drives	193	193
16	Stone-steel Towers	46	47
–	Total	2309	7940

Table 2. The number of training and testing samples for the University of Pavia dataset

#	Class	Train	Test
1	Asphalt	200	6431
2	Meadows	200	18449
3	Gravel	200	1899
4	Trees	200	2864
5	Sheets	200	1145
6	Baresoil	200	4829
7	Bitumen	200	1130
8	Bricks	200	3482
9	Shadows	200	747
–	Total	1800	40976

3.2 Results and Analysis

In order to minimize the training time and speed up the convergence, we set the initial learning rate, a crucial parameter, to $1e - 4$, which will increase sequentially as the number of iterations increases. The sizes of the 3D convolution kernels in the three dense blocks are of $1 \times 1 \times 1, 3 \times 3 \times 3$ and $5 \times 5 \times 5$ respectively. The class-specific accuracy, overall accuracy (OA) and average accuracy (AA) are shown in Tables 3 and 4.

Table 3. Classification accuracy (%) for the Indian Pines dataset

Class	CNN [11]	R-PCA-CNN [12]	C-CNN [13]	CNN-PPF [14]	3D-GAN [16]	Proposed
1	-	82.39	-	-	30.21	95.65
2	78.58	85.41	96.28	92.99	81.79	**97.80**
3	85.24	-	92.26	96.66	75.93	**99.52**
4	-	95.24	-	-	90.08	100
5	96.10	-	99.30	98.58	86.39	**100**
6	-	-	-	-	93.28	100
7	-	**100**	-	-	40.71	100
8	99.64	-	**100**	**100**	98.11	**100**
9	-	82.76	-	-	20.00	100
10	89.64	96.20	92.84	96.24	74.28	**98.96**
11	81.55	82.14	98.21	87.80	91.12	**98.67**
12	95.42	-	92.45	98.98	84.99	**99.49**
13	-	**99.81**	-	-	49.75	100
14	98.59	-	98.98	**99.81**	94.38	99.72
15	-	-	-	-	94.47	100
16	-	-	-	-	88.22	100
OA	87.01	91.13	96.63	93.9	89.09	**99.07**
AA	90.60	90.49	96.29	96.38	83.14	**99.17**

Table 4. Classification accuracy (%) for the University of Pavia dataset

Class	CNN [11]	R-PCA-CNN [12]	C-CNN [13]	CNN-PPF [14]	Proposed
1	88.38	92.43	97.4	97.42	**98.82**
2	91.27	94.84	99.4	95.76	**99.63**
3	85.88	90.89	94.84	94.05	**98.84**
4	97.25	93.99	99.16	97.52	**99.67**
5	99.91	**100**	**100**	**100**	**100**
6	96.41	92.86	98.7	99.13	**99.21**
7	93.62	93.89	**100**	96.19	99.91
8	87.45	91.18	94.57	93.62	**97.50**
9	99.57	99.33	99.87	99.60	**99.87**
OA	92.27	93.87	98.41	96.48	**99.26**
AA	93.36	94.38	98.22	97.03	**98.98**

To compare with other methods, the numbers of training samples are selected equally for all methods in our experiments, except the classes that have been directly discarded in some other experiments. From Tables 3 and 4, we can see that our proposed method obviously outperforms to all other methods. For Indian Pines dataset, we can not only provide better classification accuracy than other methods, but also classify small categories very well. The classification OA is 99.07%, nearly 5% higher than CNN-PPF [14] (i.e., 93.9%). Furthermore, for University of Pavia dataset, the class-specific accuracy obtained by proposed method is more outstanding than others. The classification performance of the proposed method is better than the best baseline classification performance by approximately 3% and 1% for the Indian Pines dataset and the University of Pavia dataset, respectively.

To evaluate the effectiveness of proposed MSD 3D-CNN, we compare it to the 3D-CNN [17] and M3D-CNN [18], which are 3D-CNN method and multiscale 3D-CNN method without densely connected design. For the three methods, the same number of training samples is selected. The results of OA for two datasets are presented in Table 5. As we can see, the densely connected design improves the performance significantly. For example, for Indian Pines dataset, the OA obtained by us improves about 3.6% and 1.5%, compared to other two methods.

Table 5. Accuracy comparisons (%) with 3D-CNN, M3D-CNN

Dataset	3D-CNN	M3D-CNN	Proposed
Indian Pines	95.45	97.61	99.07
University of Pavia	98.04	98.49	99.26

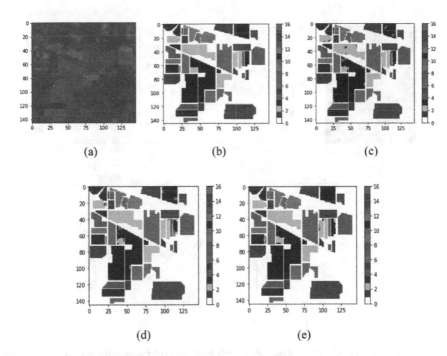

Fig. 3. The Indian Pines dataset (From left to right): (a) False color image, (b) Ground-truth map, (c) 3D-CNN, (d) M3D-CNN, (e) Proposed

Figures 3 and 4 illustrate the false color images, ground-truth maps (labels) and classification maps of 3D-CNN, M3D-CNN and ours for two datasets. By comparing labels and classification maps, there are still a few points of mis-existence in our method. But the classification maps of ours are smoother than others.

Table 6. Time spent (h: hours, s: seconds) of training and testing on two datasets

Methods / Time / Dataset		CNN [11]	CNN-PPF [14]	Proposed
Indian Pines	Training(h)	0.50	6	0.2
	Testing(s)	0.21	4.76	16.2
University Of Pavia	Training(h)	0.60	1	0.17
	Testing(s)	0.37	16.92	16.2

The time spent on training and testing by different methods has been summarized in Table 6. It is obviously that our training time is far less than CNN [10] and CNN-PPF [14]. This mainly because our network is compact and brief, and it does not contain any pre-processing operation. While in the testing phase, it is time-consuming, since the size of test batch is 5 we set, with the limited GPU memory.

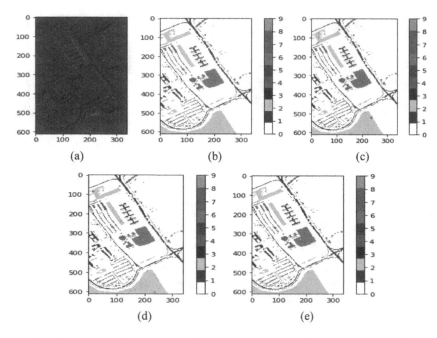

Fig. 4. The University of Pavia dataset (From left to right): (a) False color image, (b) Ground-truth map, (c) 3D-CNN, (d) M3D-CNN, (e) Proposed

4 Conclusion

In this paper, we propose a novel, shallow and efficient network for hyperspectral image classification with 3D-CNN. The proposed method effectively extracts spatial and spectral information through multi-scale dense connection, which also overcomes the gradient vanishing. Without excessively increasing network complexity, a lot of time is saved. Experimental results show that the method can provide better performance on HSI classification and require less computation and implementation time than some state-of-the-art methods.

Acknowledgment. The authors would like to thank the anonymous referees for their constructive comments which have helped improve the paper. The research is supported by the National Natural Science Foundation of China (Nos. 61502003, 61472002, 61671018 and 61860206004), Natural Science Foundation of Anhui Province (Nos. 1608085QF133).

References

1. Tu, B., et al.: KNN-based representation of superpixels for hyperspectral image classification. IEEE J. Sel. Topics Appl. Earth Obs. Remote Sens. **11**(11), 4032–4047 (2018)
2. Zhou, S., Xue, Z., Du, P.: Semisupervised stacked autoencoder with cotraining for hyperspectral image classification. IEEE Trans. Geosci. Remote Sens. **57**, 1–14 (2019) https://doi.org/10.1109/tgrs.2018.2888485
3. Yuan, Y., Feng, Y., Lu, X.: Projection-based NMF for hyperspectral unmixing. IEEE J. Sel. Topics Appl. Earth Obs. Remote Sens. **8**(6), 2632–2643 (2015)
4. Li, W., Du, Q., Zhang, B.: Combined sparse and collaborative representation for hyperspectral target detection. Pattern Recogn. **48**(12), 3904–3916 (2015)
5. Zhang, L., Zhong, Y., Huang, B., et al.: Dimensionality reduction based on clonal selection for hyperspectral imagery. IEEE Trans. Geosci. Remote Sens. **45**(12), 4172–4186 (2007)
6. He, L., Li, J., Liu, C., et al.: Recent advances on spectral–spatial hyperspectral image classification: an overview and new guidelines. IEEE Trans. Geosci. Remote Sens. **56**(3), 1579–1597 (2018)
7. Blanzieri, E., Melgani, F.: Nearest neighbor classification of remote sensing images with the maximal margin principle. IEEE Trans. Geosci. Remote Sens. **46**(6), 1804–1811 (2008)
8. Melgani, F., Bruzzone, L.: Classification of hyperspectral remote sensing images with support vector machines. IEEE Trans. Geosci. Remote Sens. **42**(8), 1778–1790 (2004)
9. Chen, Y., Nasrabadi, N.M., Tran, T.D.: Hyperspectral image classification using dictionary-based sparse representation. IEEE Trans. Geosci. Remote Sens. **49**(10), 3973–3985 (2011)
10. Shao, Y., Sang, N., Gao, C., et al.: Spatial and class structure regularized sparse representation graph for semi-supervised hyperspectral image classification. Pattern Recogn. **81**, 81–94 (2018)
11. Hu, W., Huang, Y., Wei, L., et al.: Deep convolutional neural networks for hyperspectral image classification. J. Sens. **2015**, 12 (2015)
12. Makantasis, K., Karantzalos, K., Doulamis, A., et al.: Deep supervised learning for hyperspectral data classification through convolutional neural networks. In: 2015 IEEE International Geoscience and Remote Sensing Symposium (IGARSS), pp. 4959–4962 (2015)
13. Mei, S., Ji, J., Hou, J., et al.: Learning sensor-specific spatial-spectral features of hyperspectral images via convolutional neural networks. IEEE Trans. Geosci. Remote Sens. **55**(8), 4520–4533 (2017)
14. Li, W., Wu, G., Zhang, F., et al.: Hyperspectral image classification using deep pixel-pair features. IEEE Trans. Geosci. Remote Sens. **55**(2), 844–853 (2017)

15. Ma, X., Fu, A., Wang, J., Wang, H., Yin, B.: Hyperspectral image classification based on deep deconvolution network with skip architecture. IEEE Trans. Geosci. Remote Sens. **56** (8), 4781–4791 (2018)
16. Zhu, L., Chen, Y., Ghamisi, P., et al.: Generative adversarial networks for hyperspectral image classification. IEEE Trans. Geosci. Remote Sens. **56**(9), 5046–5063 (2018)
17. Chen, Y., Jiang, H., Li, C., et al.: Deep feature extraction and classification of hyperspectral images based on convolutional neural networks. IEEE Trans. Geosci. Remote Sens. **54**(10), 6232–6251 (2016)
18. He, M., Li, B., Chen, H.: Multi-scale 3D deep convolutional neural network for hyperspectral image classification. In: 2017 IEEE International Conference on Image Processing (ICIP) (2017)
19. Huang, G., Liu, Z., Van Der Maaten, L., et al.: Densely connected convolutional networks In: Proceedings of the IEEE Conference on Computer Vision and Pattern Recognition, pp. 4700–4708 (2017)
20. Tran, D., Bourdev, L., Fergus, R., et al.: Learning spatiotemporal features with 3D convolutional networks. In: Proceedings of the IEEE International Conference on Computer Vision, pp. 4489–4497 (2015)
21. AVIRIS NW Indiana's Indian Pines 1992 Data Set. http://cobweb.ecn.purdue.edu/biehl/ MultiSpec/documentation.html. Accessed 21 Mar 2019
22. Gualtieri, J.A., Cromp, R.F.: Support vector machines for hyperspectral remote sensing classification. In: 27th AIPR Workshop: Advances in Computer-Assisted Recognition. International Society for Optics and Photonics, vol. 3584, pp. 221–233 (1999)
23. Plaza, A., Benediktsson, J.A., Boardman, J.W., et al.: Recent advances in techniques for hyperspectral image processing. Remote Sens. Environ. **113**, S110–S122 (2009)

No-Reference Image Quality Assessment via Multi-order Perception Similarity

Ziheng Zhou[1,2](✉), Wen Lu[1], Jiachen Yang[3], and Shishuai Han[1]

[1] School of Electronic Engineering, Xidian University, Xi'an, China
Zhzhou_1@stu.xidian.edu.cn
[2] Science and Technology on Communication Networks Laboratory, Xi'an, China
[3] School of Electronic Information Engineering, Tianjin University, Tianjin, China
yangjiachen@tju.edu.cn

Abstract. No-reference image quality assessment (NR-IQA) aims to develop models that can predict the quality of distorted image automatically and accurately without the reference. Lack of reference makes NR-IQA based on feature learning difficult to avoid the impact of image contents on features. In this paper, we follow an innovative strategy and present a novel NR-IQA approach based on multi-order perception similarity to overcome the difficulty. The key to our strategy is that the high and low order feature maps can be the reference to each other to reduce the dependence of features on image content. In our framework, the similarity relies on describing the retention of fine structures that is extremely sensitive to distortion in distorted image to predict quality degradation, which is monotonic with respect to the distortion level. The similarities of features from structure to texture between high and low order feature maps are utilized to predict image quality. Finally, a regression model is trained to learn the mapping from feature similarities to perceptual quality. Extensive experiments demonstrate the effectiveness and superiority of our approach against compared methods.

Keywords: No-reference image quality assessment · Multi-order perception · Feature similarity · Fine structure statistics

1 Introduction

The explosive growth of visual media in recent years, owing to popularity of imaging equipment and advances of internet technology, is driving a critical need for image qality assessment (IQA) [10]. Designing reliable IQA models that

The first author is a postgraduate with email addresses: zhzhou_1@stu.xidian.edu.cn. This research was supported in part by the National Natural Science Foundation of China (Grant Nos. 61432014, 61871311, 61876146), the National Key Research and Development Program of China (Grant No. 2016QY01W0200) and the Key Industrial Innovation Chain Project in Industrial Domain (Grant No. 2016KTZDGY04-02).

Z. Lin et al. (Eds.): PRCV 2019, LNCS 11858, pp. 607–619, 2019.
https://doi.org/10.1007/978-3-030-31723-2_52

can be consistent with evaluation of human visual system (HVS) has captured substantial attention.

In previous literature, some full-reference (FR) IQA metrics [5, 23, 26, 28, 30] achieve good performance, in which quality is calculated based on the perceptual discrepancy between the distorted and reference image. The conventional similarity framework that utilizes similarity function to describe perceptual discrepancy of feature maps of the distorted and pristine image for quality prediction, has been followed by most FR metrics, *e.g.*, structural similarity index (SSIM) [23] and feature similarity index (FSIM) [30]. The way in these FR metrics that IQA is carried out by comparision is in line with the detailed process in which human beings perceive and assess distorted image.

In contrast, no-reference (NR) IQA takes only the distorted image as input and thus is more practical yet challenging. In this case, lack of reference makes it unfeasible to extended the HVS-related FR framework to NR-IQA. NR-IQA always follows the routine principle that properties sensitive to distortions are extracted to monitor quality degradation, and then a regression model is trained to learn the mapping from quality-aware features to quality scores. Most NR-IQA models based on statistic learning [4, 15, 16, 21, 29] are designed to evaluate the unnaturalness extent to quantify possible quality degradation of image, in which statistics features only extracted from distorted image always have significantly correlation of the image content. In addition, the codebook-based framework are introduced into NR-IQA [24, 25, 27], but the limited codebook size cannot represent perceptual quality of various content of images.

Since HVS needs a reference for comparsion to quantify the perceptual discrepancy [6, 12], it is counter-intuitive to employ statistical features that is directly extracted from distorted image and significantly dependent on image content to assess perceptual quality. According to our analysis, the lack of reference information leading to the dependence of features on image content has become a major problem limiting the generalization capability of NR-IQA. In order to ease the aforementioned problem, we propose a novel approach based on Feature Similarity of Multi-order Perception (FSMP) for NR-IQA. The FSMP approach investigates to utilize the similarity to measure the differences of structures between high and low order feature maps of the distorted image to form an efficient NR-IQA model to overcome the problem.

Our key insight is that high and low order feature maps of an image can be reference to each other to reduce the dependence of features on image content. As Fig. 1 illustrates, our inspiration originates from a simple phenomenon that fine structures such as texture and other details are more sensitive to distortion and easier to be obliterated than coarse structures such as thick contours. Besides, containing richer fine features is the main difference of high to low order feature maps. Hence, the feature similarity of multi-order perception is able to describe the retention of fine structures in distorted image, which is monotonic with respect to distortion level and can be utilized for quality prediction.

The main contributions of this work are summarized into two folds: (1) An innovative strategy that multi-order views of the same image can be the refer-

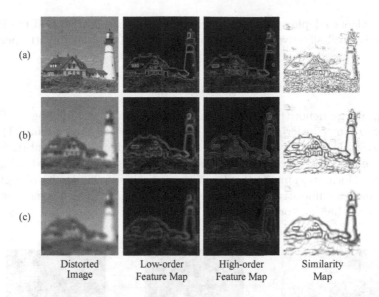

Fig. 1. An illustration of our strategy. The first column is image patches with rising distortion. The second and third columns present examples of low and high order feature maps via gradient operators. The fourth column is the similarity map of low and high order feature maps which describes the fine-structure retention that can be utilized for quality prediction.

ence to each other is introduced to reduce the dependence of features on image content for quality prediction. (2) A novel approach based on feature similarity of multi-order perception is proposed to inherit the advantage of HVS-related FR framework to further improve the performance of handcrafted NR-IQA.

2 Methodology

In this section, we present how to form the proposed NR-IQA approach based on feature similarities of HM and LM in detail. The framework of the proposed FSMP method is illustrated as Fig. 2. The key components of our framework including the construction of high and low order feature maps, the extraction of feature similarity and the application of multiple scales and channels are introduced as following.

2.1 High and Low Order Maps Construction

The key to our strategy is that the high and low order feature maps of an image can be reference to each other to reduce the dependence of features on image contents. Hence, we need to construct high and low order feature maps at first.

As is shown in Fig. 2, the natural image is viewed as 0-order map, and we employ a simple gradient operator to obtain two higher order feature maps with

1 and 2 orders to deploy our strategy. Since it is indicated in [5] that the Prewitt operator is more effective than other operators for IQA, the Prewitt operator is applied to 1-order gradient map $\dot{\mathbf{g}}$ as defined below:

$$\dot{\mathbf{g}} = \sqrt{\mathbf{g}_h^2 + \mathbf{g}_v^2}, \tag{1}$$

where $\mathbf{g}_v$ and $\mathbf{g}_h$ denote the vertical and horizontal gradient applying the Prewitt operator. Then, 2-order gradient map $\ddot{\mathbf{g}}$ can be obtained by applying (1) on $\dot{\mathbf{g}}$.

It is suitable to deploy our strategy on low and high order gradient maps. Natural image is highly structured, and image gradient is widely adopted to highlight structural information in perceived quality prediction [5,26]. High-order gradient can well describe fine structures and details in the image, which is more sensitive to distortion than low-order gradient.

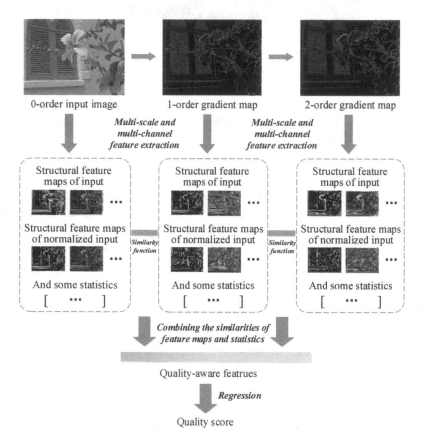

Fig. 2. Pipeline of the we proposed FSMP model.

2.2   Feature Similarity Extraction

In this part, we take the gray-scale channel as an example to describe how to extract feature similarities in one channel. For an $m \times n$ gray-level image I, some feature maps and statistics from structure to texture are extracted from its 0-order gray-level image I, 1-order gradient $\dot{g}$ and 2-order gradient $\ddot{g}$ respectively. The similarity between each kind of feature pairs of low-order map (LM) and high-order map (HM) (*e.g.*, I and $\dot{g}$ or $\dot{g}$ and $\ddot{g}$) is a single metric. In this work, six kinds of feature similarities are utilized to predict image quality, which are summaried in Table 1.

Firstly, two advanced FR-IQA metrics are used to measure the structure similarity of LM and HM. GMSD [26] captures structural information by combining gradient and luminance information, and FSIM [30] uses gradient magnitude (GM) and phase congruency (PC) features as complementary aspects, which is the first two similarities S_{1-2} used in the work.

Then, the highly discriminative texture operator, local binary pattern (LBP) is adopted to represent local image texture, which is frequencely used in IQA because the changing of fine structures caused by distortion can be modeled by LBP [2,13,14,31]. For a specific operator $LBP_{P,R}$, P, R indicate the neighbour number and radius of the LBP structure. Min *et al.* [14] introduce a new non-uniform LBP as defined:

$$LBP_{P,R} = \sum_{p=0}^{P-1} s\left(g_p - g_c\right),\qquad(2)$$

where g_c and g_p denote the luminance values of a center pixel and its circularly symmetric neighborhoods, and

Table 1. A summary of six kinds of metrics employed to compute feature similarities

Statistics metrics	Feature types	Computation of similarity
S_1	Map	$FSIM\left(LM, HM\right)$
S_2	Map	$GMSD\left(LM, HM\right)$
S_3	Map	$Sim\left(f_{LBP1,LM}, f_{LBP1,HM}\right)$
S_4	Statistics	$Sim\left(f_{LBP2,LM}, f_{LBP2,HM}\right)$
S_5	Map	$Sim\left(f_{NCM1,LM}, f_{NCM1,HM}\right)$
S_6	Statistics	$Sim\left(f_{NCM2,LM}, f_{NCM2,HM}\right)$

$$s\left(x\right) = \begin{cases} 1 & x \geq 0 \\ 0 & x < 0. \end{cases}\qquad(3)$$

Following [14], the $LBP_{4,1}$ that is sensitive to several distortions easy to happen can be adopted, and the $LBP_{4,1}$ operator outputs accumulated over the input image can be written as:

$$f_{LBP1} = Map\,(LBP_{4,1})\,. \tag{4}$$

Furthermore, the improved rotation-invariant and uniform LBP that highlights spatial transitions in local image is also used to describe texture [13,17], which is in the form of:

$$LBP_{P,R}^{riu2} = \begin{cases} \sum_{p=0}^{P-1} s\,(g_p - g_c) & \text{if } U(LBP_{P,R} \leq 2) \\ P+1 & \text{otherwise,} \end{cases} \tag{5}$$

where the ^{riu2} denotes the use of rotation-invariant uniform patterns with a uniformity measure U value of at most 2, and

$$U\,(LBP_{P,R}) = |s\,(g_{P-1} - g_c) - s\,(g_0 - g_c)| + \sum_{p=0}^{P-1} |s\,(g_p - g_c) - s\,(g_{p-1} - g_c)|. \tag{6}$$

We choose $P = 8$ and $R = 1$, and the histogram of $LBP_{8,1}^{riu2}$ operator outputs accumulated over the input image can be written as:

$$f_{LBP2} = Hist\,(LBP_{8,1}^{riu2})\,. \tag{7}$$

The feature map f_{LBP1} and statistics f_{LBP2} are texture features based on LBP in this work. Similarities between these two feature pairs of LM and HM are labeled as S_{3-4}.

In addition, the neighborhood co-occurrence matrix (NCM) introduced in [32] is employed as another structure descriptor to reflect spatial correlation of pixels, which is constructed through a mapping and can highlight changes of detail in local image. For an $m \times n$ gray-level image I with N gray scales, a $N \times N$ NCM is defined as:

$$NCM(l,m) = -\sum_{i=2}^{m-1}\sum_{j=2}^{n-1} \begin{cases} 1 & I(i,j) = l \,\&\, u(i,j) = m \\ 0 & \text{otherwise,} \end{cases} \tag{8}$$

$$u(i,j) = \frac{1}{3}\,(I\,(i,j+1) + I\,(i+1,j+1) + I\,(i-1,j+1))\,, \tag{9}$$

where $u(i,j)$ is a integer approximated by the mean of intensity values of partial pixels in neighborhood. The entire NCM distribution is another feature map denoted as f_{NCM1}.

The distribution of NCM tends to be more chaotic and away from the natural shape in presence of distortions, and several related statistics metrics are used to measure the unnaturalness of distribution. The entropy of NCM is defined as:

$$E = -\sum_{l=1}^{N}\sum_{m=1}^{N} P\,(l,m)\ln P\,(l,m) \tag{10}$$

where $P(l, m)$ is the probability for occurrence of $NCM(l, m)$ in NCM of the image and can be written as:

$$P(l, m) = \frac{NCM(l, m)}{\sum\limits_{i=1}^{N} \sum\limits_{j=1}^{N} NCM(i, j)}. \tag{11}$$

The contrast gives a measure of the local variations of NCM, and the homogeneity characterizes the closeness of the distribution of elements to the NCM diagonal. They are defined as:

$$C = \sum_{l=1}^{N} \sum_{m=1}^{N} |l - m|^2 P(l, m), \tag{12}$$

$$H = \sum_{l=1}^{N} \sum_{m=1}^{N} \frac{P(l, m)}{|l - m| + 1}. \tag{13}$$

These three metrics are the last kind of structural statistics in this work, which can be written as:

$$f_{NCM2} = [E, C, H]. \tag{14}$$

Similarities between these two feature pairs of LM and HM are S_{5-6} as presented in Table 1.

All features are extracted on each LM and HM pairs respectively to represent structural information. Obviously, HM contains richer fine structures than LM. As distortion level rises, the structural differences between LM and HM, *i.e.*, the part of the high-order fine structures that HM contains richer than LM, are gradually obliterated. The similarity function always adopted in FR-IQA is utilized to measure the differences of these structural features between LM and HM, which can describe the retention of fine structures in distorted image for quality prediction. For feature f_i, the similarity is defined as:

$$Sim(f_{i,LM}, f_{i,HM}) = \frac{2 f_{i,LM} \cdot f_{i,HM} + t}{f_{i,LM}^2 + f_{i,HM}^2 + t}, \tag{15}$$

where t is a positive constant for numerical stability, and all operations in Eq. 15 are element-wise. Finally, the standard deviation (STD) of output is used for quality prediction.

At last, the entire process including feature extraction and similarity calculation is also performed once in the normalied input of each channel. The normalization process has been widely used in NR-IQA [8, 9, 15, 29], which can be described as:

$$\bar{I}(i, j) = \frac{I(i, j) - \mu}{\sigma + 1}, \tag{16}$$

where μ and σ are the local mean and standard deviation of patch $I(i; j)$. The similarities calculated from the normalied input is used as a supplement to the similarities calculated from on the channel input, and they are used together for quality prediction. In the end, we extracted a 24-dimension similarities features from 2 pairs of LM and HM (*i.e.* I and $\dot{g}$, $\dot{g}$ and $\ddot{g}$) in each channel.

2.3 Multi-scale and Multi-channel Application

Some color distortions are easy to happen, which is inherently difficult to be perceived only from gray scale. Hence, We also deploy feature similarities on the LMS color space. The LMS color space mimics the responses of the three types of cones in the human retina that selectively sensitive to different color mixtures of Long, Medium, and Short wavelengths [4]. Ruderman *et al.* [20] indicates that there is a strong correlation between the three channels of the LMS color space, especially L and M. After transforming the image into LMS color space, the M and S components are processed as above.

For each channel, feature similarities are extracted at two scales to capture multiscale behavior, by down sampling via a factor of 2. In a word, all feature similarities of an image used to predict image quality are extracted at two scales from three channels including gray-scale, M and S components.

2.4 Regression

Finally, The quality-aware features for quality prediction are acquired after combining feature similarities extracted from all channels. Given a distorted images database with subjective quality scores, a regression model is learned to predict quality scores from normalized quality-aware features consisting of all feature similarities by support vector regression (SVR).

3 Experimental Results and Analyses

In this part, extensive experiments are constructed on five popular benchmarks and thorough analyses are presented. Five databases used to evaluate the proposed approach are: LIVE [22], CSIQ [11], TID2013 [19], LIVE Multiple Distorted (MD) [7] and LIVE Challenge (CLIVE) [3]. LIVE, CSIQ and TID2013 databases are images with artificially single distortions. LIVEMD database consists of images with multiple types of distortion. CLIVE database covers variety of unique authentically distorted images taken by mobile cameras, without any reference. Important information about five databases is summarized in Table 2. By comparing the experimental results on these five databases with other NR-IQA methods, the approach we proposed can be evaluate fairly.

Following most previous works (*e.g.* [14,18,24]), two mainstream metrics as the evaluation criteria are adopted in this paper: Spearman's rank order correlation coefficient (SRCC) and Pearson's linear correlation coefficient (PLCC) between the objective scores predicted by the models and the subjective mean opinion scores (MOS) provided by the dataset. SRCC operates only on the rank of the data points and ignores the relative distances between data points, hence

Table 2. A comparison of five popular IQA databases.

Database	Ref. images	Dist. images	Dist. types	Mixtures of dis.	Published date
LIVE [22]	29	779	5	N/A	2003
CSIQ [11]	30	866	6	N/A	2010
TID2013 [19]	25	3000	24	N/A	2015
LIVEMD [7]	15	450	2	√	2012
CLIVE [3]	N/A	1169	N/A	√	2016

Table 3. The SRCC and PLCC comparison on five public-domain distorted image databases.

	LIVE		CSIQ		TID2013		LIVEMD		CLIVE	
	SRCC	PLCC	SRCC	PLCC	SRCC	PLCC	SRCC	PLCC	SRCC	PLCC
BRISQUE [15]	0.928	0.930	0.695	0.708	0.572	0.651	0.888	0.897	0.607	0.585
CORNIA [27]	0.892	0.880	0.714	0.781	0.549	0.613	0.900	0.915	0.618	0.662
IL-NIQE [29]	0.902	0.908	0.814	0.835	0.521	0.648	0.902	0.914	0.498	0.524
HOSA [24]	**0.941**	**0.942**	0.781	0.841	0.688	0.764	0.902	0.926	0.659	0.678
BPRI [14]	0.883	0.881	0.568	0.725	0.222	0.466	0.104	0.464	0.222	0.466
BQEMSS [1]	0.921	0.931	0.823	**0.846**	0.667	0.697	-	-	0.621	0.634
FSMP	0.928	0.930	**0.831**	0.839	**0.724**	0.763	**0.919**	**0.935**	**0.675**	**0.706**

measures the prediction monotonicity of an IQA index. PLCC measures the prediction linearity of IQA methods. Higher values of both SRCC and PLCC indicate better performance both in terms of correlation with human opinion as well as the performance of the learner.

In all experiments, we follow the experimental protocols in some recently introduced methods (e.g. [1,24,29]), where each database is randomly divided into 80% for training and 20% for testing by reference images, by which the test datasets have no overlap on image content with train datasets. All the experiments are under 100 times random train-test splitting operation to eliminate the bias caused by data division, and the median SRCC and PLCC are reported.

Single Database Evaluations. The proposed FSMP approach is comapred with several NR-IQA methods, including BRISQUE [15], CORNIA [27], IL-NIQE [29], HOSA [24], BPRI [14] and BQEMSS [1]. BQEMSS is the most recent NR-IQA model in these method. Since IL-NIQE do not need training on the databases, we report their results on the partitioned test subsets for the comparison consistency. The results on five popular database are shown in Table 3, in which the best result of each column is highlighted.

Combining the experimental results in Table 3, our FSMP outperforms all compared NR-IQA methods. Firstly, The FSMP outperforms all of compared methods for both SROCC and PLCC evaluations on the most challenged database CLIVE and the multiple distorted image databases LIVEMD. In addition, our method performs similar to BQEMSS on CSIQ. Although the FSMP dose not achieve the best evaluation results on LIVE database, our model is also effective. After observing many mismatch samples, we analyze the reason is that our model is not efficient enough to further distinguish between samples with high distortion levels. The similarities we extracted rely on describing the retention of fine features to predict image quality. When the global distortion is severe to a certain extent, the fine structure has been almost destroyed completely. Since the LIVE database contains many severely distorted images with low perceptual quality, our model does not achieve enough discrimination.

Single Distortion Evaluations. In order to evaluate the performance of the proposed IQA model adequately, we evaluate FSMP on TID2013 database taking into account each individual distortions. The reason why we choose the database is that TID2013 is the largest among these databases and consists of 25 reference images and 24 different distortion types. The performance of each type of distortion are summarized in Table 4 in term of SRCC, in which the best result of each distortion is highlighted.

From the results presented in Table 4, we make the following observations. Our method significantly outperforms compared NR-IQA methods on more than a half of 24 types of distortion. Moreover, it is evident that the FSMP exhibits significant improvement across some difficult distortions clearly outperforming compared NR methods, e.g., distortion types # 14, # 15, # 16, # 17, # 18 and # 20. These distortions are almost associated with color change. As to entire TID2013, our method achieves over 5% improvements than BQEMSS. The significant improvement of our results obtained by FSMP is encouraging and justifies our innovative strategy.

Table 4. Performance evaluation (SROCC) on the entire TID2013 database.

	# 1	# 2	# 3	# 4	# 5	# 6	# 7	# 8	# 9	# 10	# 11	# 12
BRISQUE [15]	0.630	0.424	0.727	0.321	0.775	0.669	0.592	0.845	0.553	0.742	0.799	0.301
CORNIA [27]	0.341	0.196	0.689	0.184	0.607	0.014	0.673	**0.896**	0.787	0.875	0.911	0.310
IL-NIQE [29]	0.890	0.823	0.929	0.649	0.881	0.802	0.881	0.845	0.778	0.875	0.911	0.310
HOSA [24]	0.853	0.625	0.782	0.368	0.905	0.775	0.810	0.892	**0.870**	0.893	**0.932**	0.747
BPRI [14]	**0.918**	0.859	0.529	0.748	**0.926**	0.458	0.489	0.859	0.421	0.911	0.868	0.789
BQEMSS [1]	0.864	0.727	**0.846**	0.605	0.839	0.711	0.887	0.822	0.795	**0.914**	0.908	0.349
FSMP	0.909	**0.888**	0.816	**0.789**	0.804	**0.875**	**0.944**	0.842	0.865	**0.914**	0.905	**0.826**

	# 13	# 14	# 15	# 16	# 17	# 18	# 19	# 20	# 21	# 22	# 23	# 24
BRISQUE [15]	0.672	0.175	0.184	0.155	0.125	0.032	0.560	0.282	0.680	0.804	0.715	0.800
CORNIA [27]	0.625	0.161	0.096	0.008	0.423	0.055	0.259	0.606	0.555	0.592	0.759	0.903
IL-NIQE [29]	0.627	0.117	0.051	0.222	0.026	0.101	0.736	0.388	**0.869**	0.793	0.789	0.893
HOSA [24]	0.701	0.199	0.327	0.233	0.294	0.119	0.782	0.532	0.835	0.855	**0.801**	0.905
BPRI [14]	0.488	0.009	0.233	0.111	0.185	0.379	**0.861**	0.069	0.598	0.675	0.725	0.787
BQEMSS [1]	0.317	0.202	0.188	0.176	0.653	0.383	0.789	0.418	0.780	0.707	0.621	0.858
FSMP	**0.870**	**0.533**	**0.883**	**0.873**	**0.891**	**0.891**	0.669	**0.834**	0.848	**0.935**	0.592	**0.945**

4   Conclusion

In this paper, we present a novel approach based on feature similarity of multi-order perception for NR-IQA. Our approach follows an innovative strategy that high and low order feature maps can be the reference to each other to overcome the difficulty that quality-aware features are affected by image contents. The similarity of feature from structure to texture between HM and LM relies on describing the retention of fine structures in distorted image to predict image quality, which is monotonic with respect to distortion level. The significant improvement of our results obtained by HLFSIM relative to compared NR-IQA methods is encouraging and justifies the effectiveness of our approach and strategy for the difficulty coming with handcrafted features.

References

1. Cai, H., Li, L., Yi, Z., Gong, M.: Towards a blind image quality evaluator using multi-scale second-order statistics. Sig. Process. Image Commun. **71**, 88–99 (2019)
2. Freitas, P., Akamine, W., Farias, M.: No-reference image quality assessment using orthogonal color planes patterns. IEEE Trans. Multimedia **20**(12), 3353–3360 (2018)
3. Ghadiyaram, D., Bovik, A.C.: Massive online crowdsourced study of subjective and objective picture quality. IEEE Trans. Image Process. **25**(1), 372–387 (2015)
4. Ghadiyaram, D., Bovik, A.C.: Perceptual quality prediction on authentically distorted images using a bag of features approach. J. Vis. **17**(1), 1–29 (2017)
5. Gu, K., Li, L., Lu, H., Min, X., Lin, W.: A fast reliable image quality predictor by fusing micro- and macro-structures. IEEE Trans. Ind. Electron. **64**(5), 3903–3912 (2017)
6. Ren, H., Wang, D.C.Y.: RAN4IQA: restorative adversarial nets for no-reference image quality assessment. In: Thirty-Second AAAI Conference on Artificial Intelligence (2018)
7. Jayaraman, D., Mittal, A., Moorthy, A.K., Bovik, A.C.: Objective quality assessment of multiply distorted images. In: 2012 Conference Record of the Forty Sixth Asilomar Conference on Signals, Systems and Computers (ASILOMAR), pp. 1693–1697 (2012)
8. Kang, L., Ye, P., Li, Y., Doermann, D.: Convolutional neural networks for no-reference image quality assessment. In: 2014 IEEE Conference on Computer Vision and Pattern Recognition, pp. 1733–1740 (2014)
9. Kim, J., Lee, S.: Fully deep blind image quality predictor. IEEE J. Sel. Top. Sign. Process. **11**(1), 206–220 (2017)
10. Kim, J., Zeng, H., Ghadiyaram, D., Lee, S., Zhang, L., Bovik, A.C.: Deep convolutional neural models for picture-quality prediction: challenges and solutions to data-driven image quality assessment. IEEE Sig. Process. Mag. **34**(6), 130–141 (2017)
11. Larson, E., Cooper, E., Chandler, D.M.: Most apparent distortion: full-reference image quality assessment and the role of strategy. J. Electron. Imaging **19**(1), 011006 (2010)

12. Lin, K., Wang, G.: Hallucinated-IQA: no-reference image quality assessment via adversarial learning. In: 2018 IEEE/CVF Conference on Computer Vision and Pattern Recognition, pp. 732–741 (2018)
13. Liu, T., Liu, K.: No-reference image quality assessment by wide-perceptual-domain scorer ensemble method. IEEE Trans. Image Process. **27**(3), 1138–1151 (2018)
14. Min, X., Gu, K., Zhai, G., Liu, J., Yang, X., Chen, C.W.: Blind quality assessment based on pseudo-reference image. IEEE Trans. Multimedia **20**(8), 2049–2062 (2018)
15. Mittal, A., Moorthy, A.K., Bovik, A.C.: No-reference image quality assessment in the spatial domain. IEEE Trans. Image Process. **21**(12), 4695–4708 (2012)
16. Mittal, A., Soundararajan, R., Bovik, A.C.: Making a "completely blind" image quality analyzer. IEEE Sig. Process. Lett. **20**(3), 209–212 (2013)
17. Ojala, T., Pietikainen, M., Maenpaa, T.: Multiresolution gray-scale and rotation invariant texture classification with local binary patterns. IEEE Trans. Pattern Anal. Mach. Intell. **24**(7), 971–987 (2002)
18. Oszust, M.: Local feature descriptor and derivative filters for blind image quality assessment. IEEE Sig. Process. Lett. **26**(2), 322–326 (2019)
19. Ponomarenko, N., et al.: Color image database TID2013: Peculiarities and preliminary results. In: European Workshop on Visual Information Processing (EUVIP), pp. 106–111 (2013)
20. Ruderman, D.L., Cronin, T.W., Chiao, C.C.: Statistics of cone responses to natural images: implications for visual coding. J. Opt. Soc. Am. A **15**(15), 2036–2045 (1998)
21. Saad, M.A., Bovik, A.C., Charrier, C.: Blind image quality assessment: a natural scene statistics approach in the DCT domain. IEEE Trans. Image Process. **21**(8), 3339–3352 (2012)
22. Sheikh, H.R., Sabir, M.F., Bovik, A.C.: A statistical evaluation of recent full reference image quality assessment algorithms. IEEE Trans. Image Process. **15**(11), 3440–3451 (2006)
23. Wang, Z., Bovik, A.C., Sheikh, H.R., Simoncelli, E.P.: Image quality assessment: from error visibility to structural similarity. IEEE Trans. Image Process. **13**(4), 600–612 (2004)
24. Xu, J., Ye, P., Li, Q., Du, H., Liu, Y., Doermann, D.: Blind image quality assessment based on high order statistics aggregation. IEEE Trans. Image Process. **25**(9), 4444–4457 (2016)
25. Xue, W., Zhang, L., Mou, X.: Learning without human scores for blind image quality assessment. In: 2013 IEEE Conference on Computer Vision and Pattern Recognition, pp. 995–1002 (2013)
26. Xue, W., Zhang, L., Mou, X., Bovik, A.C.: Gradient magnitude similarity deviation: a highly efficient perceptual image quality index. IEEE Trans. Image Process. **23**(2), 684–695 (2014)
27. Ye, P., Kumar, J., Kang, L., Doermann, D.: Unsupervised feature learning framework for no-reference image quality assessment. In: 2012 IEEE Conference on Computer Vision and Pattern Recognition, pp. 1098–1105 (2012)
28. Zhang, L., Shen, Y., Li, H.: VSI: a visual saliency-induced index for perceptual image quality assessment. IEEE Trans. Image Process. **23**(10), 4270–4281 (2014)
29. Zhang, L., Zhang, L., Bovik, A.C.: A feature-enriched completely blind image quality evaluator. IEEE Trans. Image Process. **24**(8), 2579–2591 (2015)
30. Zhang, L., Zhang, L., Mou, X., Zhang, D.: FSIM: a feature similarity index for image quality assessment. IEEE Trans. Image Process. **20**(8), 2378–2386 (2011)

31. Zhang, M., Muramatsu, C., Zhou, X., Hara, T., Fujita, H.: Blind image quality assessment using the joint statistics of generalized local binary pattern. IEEE Trans. Image Process. **22**(2), 207–210 (2015)
32. Zhou, Z., Lu, W., Yang, J., He, L., Gao, X.: Blind image quality assessment based on visuo-spatial series statistics. In: 2018 IEEE International Conference on Acoustics, Speech and Signal Processing (ICASSP), pp. 3161–3165 (2018)

Blind Quality Assessment for DIBR-Synthesized Images Based on Chromatic and Disoccluded Information

Mengna Ding, Yuming Fang$^{(\boxtimes)}$, Yifan Zuo, and Zuowen Tan

School of Information Management, Jiangxi University of Finance and Economics,
Nanchang 330032, China
fa0001ng@e.ntu.edu.sg

Abstract. In this paper, we propose a novel method for no reference image quality assessment. It evaluates the visual quality of the synthesized images by considering chromatic and disoccluded information. Since human is sensitive to chromatic information, the chromatic information is extracted which is represented by the features of saturation and hue. Specially, we calculate the first derivative of saturation and hue maps by using local binary pattern (LBP) algorithm and extract features from LBP maps. In addition, inspired by the characteristic of the human visual system (HVS) and the synthesized image-specific distortion type, the proposed method extracts disoccluded maps as weighting maps for LBP maps. The support vector regression (SVR) model is used to predict the visual quality of images by using the extracted features. Compared with 8 state-of-the-art no-reference methods for natural or synthesized images, the proposed method shows improved performance on IRCCyN/IVC DIBR and MCL-3D databases.

Keywords: Blind quality assessment · Depth-image-based rending (DIBR) · Chromatic feature

1 Introduction

With the rapid development of imaging techniques, the demand for high quality images/videos has been significantly increased. To improve the visual experiences of 2D images and videos, various free-viewpoint TV (FTV) [1] techniques are designed to obtain 3D images/videos. However, it is difficult to capture and transfer the multi-view data in FTV [1]. To address the challenge, depth-image-based-rendering (DIBR) method is proposed to generate images of virtual viewpoints [2], it only needs a small number of texture images and their corresponding depth maps. Although some works have investigated the visual quality of DIBR images, this problem is still open. Some more fine-grained models are required.

Image quality assessment (IQA) methods are divided into three categories: full-reference IQA (FR-IQA), reduced-reference IQA (RR-IQA) and no-reference

© Springer Nature Switzerland AG 2019
Z. Lin et al. (Eds.): PRCV 2019, LNCS 11858, pp. 620–631, 2019.
https://doi.org/10.1007/978-3-030-31723-2_53

IQA (NR-IQA). So far, the FR-IQA method has been widely studied for natural images with the distortions of blur, blockiness, noise and etc., the corresponding research on synthesized images is less activate. Actually, the distorted types of synthesized images mainly include object shifting, incorrect rendering of textured areas, flickering, stretching and crumbling which are significantly different from distortions of natural images. Dragana et al. [3] propose the morphological wavelet peak signal-to-noise ratio (MW-PSNR) which divides the synthesized image into multiple scales by the morphological wavelet and predicts the visual quality for each scale based on the peak signal-to-noise ratio (PSNR). Sandic et al. [4] propose a method replacing morphological wavelets with morphological pyramids to divide image into multiple scales. Battisti et al. [5] design a 3D synthesized view image quality metric (3DSwIM) based on block similarity. It adopts Exhaustive Search (ES) like algorithm to search the most similar blocks from the synthesized image and the reference image. And the Kolmogorov-Smirnov distance is calculated by the histogram of discrete wavelet coefficients between the similar blocks. Li et al. [6] evaluate the visual quality of synthesized images by computing local geometric distortions in disoccluded regions and global sharpness. The SIFT-flow-based warping technology is used to attain the disoccluded regions in synthesized images.

In addition to the research on FR-IQA methods, there are also some NR-IQA methods for synthesized images. Gu et al. [7] propose a autoregression plus thresholding (APT) method for visual quality assessment of synthesized images. It predicts a new synthesized image by using the autoregression method. Finally, the quality of image is judged by comparing the similarity between the predicted image and the original synthesized image. The APT algorithm has better performance in predicting the quality of images with disoccluded regions than the existing NR-IQA methods at the cost of high computation complexity, it does not work for images with other types of distortion. Tian et al. [8] design a no-reference image quality assessment for synthesized views which uses a set of morphological operations. Following the study [8], Tian et al. [9] introduce a method for 3D synthesized views (NIQSV+) to improve the performance of NIQSV [8]. It further considers the hole and the stretch of the edge in the synthesized image. Compared to APT [7], it not only has better performance, but also less computation complexity. Yue et al. [10] detect the hole and the stretching region of image using uniform local binary pattern (LBP) and calculate global sharpness by self-similarity. These methods have a common drawback which do not take the chromatic distortion of synthesized images into account.

In this paper, we propose a novel NR-IQA method for DIBR-synthesized images. We firstly calculate saturation and hue maps to capture the chromatic distortions of synthesized images. Different from the previous IQA algorithms [11] for natural images, we use the number of each bin in the histograms of the saturation and hue maps as 20-dimensional features. Since the relationship between adjacent pixels is changed in the distorted image, the LBP algorithm is used to obtain the relationship between adjacent pixels from saturation and hue

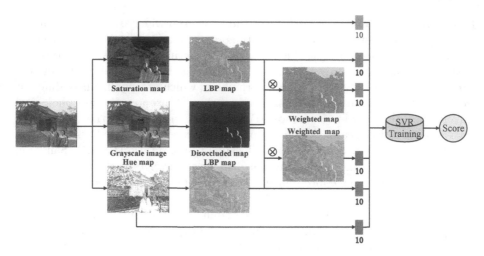

Fig. 1. The framework of proposed method. The symbol ⊗ represents the operation of multiplying corresponding pixels.

(a) Blurring   (b) Stretching   (c) Crumbling   (d) Deforming

Fig. 2. Visual samples of different distortions of synthesized images.

maps. Some algorithms calculate the difference between horizontal pixels and vertical pixels to obtain the relationship of adjacent pixels. However, the LBP algorithm considers the difference between the center pixel and surrounding pixels within the radius R, more detailed information can be obtained. In addition, we also extract the texture and structure information from LBP maps. After the LBP operator, the corresponding saturation and hue maps called as S_l, H_l consist of 20-dimensional features. Inspired by the unique disoccluded areas in synthesized images [9,10], we design a simple and effective operation to extract the disoccluded regions in synthesized images. It is based on a assumption that only pixel values of disoccluded areas are 0. Whether it is a disoccluded region depending on the number of pixels in a window whose value is 0. The extracted disoccluded map W_{map} which is used to weight S_l and H_l. This idea is inspired by generally distortions in regions that attract viewers attention. The distorted regions are assumed to be more disturbing than other regions. The weighted S_l and H_l is called as S_{final} and H_{final}, and the last 20-dimensional features are obtained from the histograms of S_{final} and H_{final}. In this paper, we extract three sets of features to assess the visual quality of synthesized images. SVR is used to learn the mapping function from all features to predict perceptual quality scores of synthesized images.

The key contributions of our method have three aspects: (1) It is the first work which considers saturation and hue of synthesized images. Most existing NR-IQA methods for synthesized images are designed based on grayscale image or luminance channel of color image. (2) We use LBP operator to explore the relationship between the center pixel and surrounding pixels in saturation and hue maps, it extracts the texture information and structure information in maps. (3) We design a new method to extract disoccluded areas from synthesized images which is used as a weighting map. (4) The proposed method is compared with the current related state-of-the-art methods and the experimental results show improved performance.

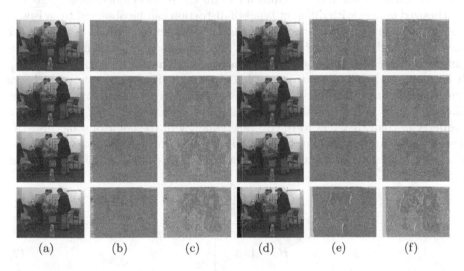

(a)	(b)	(c)	(d)	(e)	(f)

Fig. 3. Visual samples of synthesized images and extracted saturation and hue maps. Columns (a) and (d) are a original image and its seven corresponding synthesized images obtained using different synthetic algorithms. From top to bottom, the (a) column images are: a original image, a synthesized image is obtained using Fehn cropped algorithm [12], Fehn interpolated algorithm [12], MPEG_VSRS algorithm [13]. From top to bottom, the (d) column images are: a synthesized image is obtained using Mueller algorithm [14], Ndjiki algorithm [15], Kppel algorithm [16], a unfilled synthesized image. Column (b) and column (e) are corresponding saturation maps extracted from the columns (a) and (d), and column (c) and (f) are corresponding hue maps.

2 Proposed Method

In this section, we introduce the details of our method. We mainly evaluate synthesized images from three aspects. Firstly, it is considered that there is a loss of chromatic information in synthesized images, and the previous synthesized image quality algorithms ignore this. Secondly, we consider the texture and structure information based on chromatic maps. Finally, we consider the disoccluded regions in synthesized images. The framework of our proposed metric is shown in Fig. 1.

2.1   Chromatic Maps

The main distortion areas of synthesized image are shown in the Fig. 4. The existing synthesized algorithms generally fill the disoccluded point using pixels around it. From Fig. 4, we can observe that most of the disoccluded areas are in the edge areas, the edge areas are the boundary between the foreground and the background. Therefore, it is difficult to fill these disoccluded areas. The four synthesized images with different types of distortion can be observed from Fig. 2. To better observe the distortions of image, the upper left corner of the images show the details of distortions in Fig. 2. There are some algorithms in natural images indicate that the distorted images have chromatic distortions [11,17,18]. It is introduced that saturation and hue are the attributes of color, which are sensitive to chromatic distortions. If the saturated color which represents the purity of color is diluted, the saturation will be decreased [19]. Hue is also a property of color, it refers to the overall tendency of the color of a picture [19]. Therefore, saturation and hue are used to represent image chromatic characteristics in our method. Saturation S_d and hue H_d can be calculated by the following formula [20].

$$S_d = 1 - \left[\frac{3 \times \mu_1}{\nu_1} \right] \tag{1}$$

$$H_d = \tan^{-1} \left[\frac{\mu_2}{\nu_2} \right] \tag{2}$$

where $\mu_1 = min(R, G, B)$; $\nu_1 = R + G + B$; $\mu_2 = \sqrt{3}(R - G)$; $\nu_2 = R + G - 2B$. R, G, B represent the pixel values of the three channels of the color images. According to Eqs. (1) and (2), the saturation maps and the hue maps are attained which are shown in Fig. 3. The saturation maps of synthesized images have more obvious structure related to the original image. In Fig. 3, images are obtained by Fehn interpolated algorithm [12], MPEG_VSRS algorithm [13] and Mueller algorithm [14], these images have partial stretch on the left side, the saturation and hue maps can capture this type of distortion. The last line of (e) and (f) can roughly capture disoccluded regions in the unfilled synthesized image. Since the images are obtained by Ndjiki [15], Kppel [16] algorithms are similar, the differences of the extracted maps are small. From the Fig. 3, we observe that hue maps are more sensitive to changes in synthesized images. We extract the 10-dimensional features from the histogram of saturation map and hue map separately. Inspired by that center-surround receptive fields are highly selective in spatial frequency and orientation [17], we use LBP [21] algorithm to extract features. In our method, LBP can be regarded as a first derivative operation [22]. The traditional LBP algorithm can be expressed by the following formula.

$$LBP_{N,R} = \sum_{i=0}^{N-1} D(I(i) - I(c)) \times 2^i \tag{3}$$

where R denotes the radius and N denotes the number of pixels in a circular field of radius R. $I(c)$ is the center pixel and $I(i)$ is its neighbor pixel. $D(*)$ is the thresholding function, expressed as the following formula.

$$D(x) = \begin{cases} 1, & x \geq 0 \\ 0, & others \end{cases} \tag{4}$$

The derivation of LBP is designed [21] to satisfy the rotation invariance, which is expressed as follows.

$$\Psi_{N,R} = \begin{cases} \sum_{i=0}^{N-1} D(I(i) - I(c)), & \Phi(LBP_{N,R}) \leq 2 \\ N+1, & others \end{cases} \tag{5}$$

where Φ is calculated as the number of bitwise transitions, which is expressed as follows.

$$\Phi(LBP_{N,R}) = \| D(I(N-1) - I(c)) - D(I(0) - I(c)) \|$$
$$+ \sum_{i=0}^{N-1} \| D(I(i) - I(c) - D(I(i-1) - I(c))) \| \tag{6}$$

Through Eqs. (3)–(6), we get $N+2$ different patterns from one uniform LBP map. In this metric, we set $N = 8$, and 10 bins for one LBP map are obtained. The number of each bin is used as a one-dimensional feature. 20-dimensional features are obtained based on S_l and H_l.

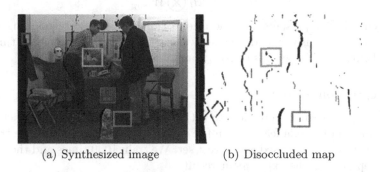

(a) Synthesized image   (b) Disoccluded map

Fig. 4. Samples of synthesized images and disoccluded maps. The blue, green, and red boxes in (a) and (b) are for better observation of the similarity of the disoccluded regions in the two images. (Color figure online)

2.2   Disoccluded Regions

DIBR technique is a typical synthetic algorithm. In the process of converting from 2D space to 3D world space and 3D space mapping back to 2D space, some areas that are not visible are changed into visible areas. These areas are called disoccluded areas. In Fig. 4, the black areas of the synthesized image are the so-called disoccluded areas, they cause great discomfort for observers. Therefore, for synthesized images, we design a new method to detect disoccluded regions. The idea is based on a assumption that only pixel values of disoccluded areas are 0. The following formula is used to extract disoccluded areas.

$$W_{map} = \begin{cases} 0.9, \ count(x == 0) \geq 4 \\ 0.1, \qquad others \end{cases} \tag{7}$$

where $count(*)$ is used to calculate the numbers of pixel whose value is 0 in a local window. To better conform to the theory that human eyes are more sensitive to the distortion region, the disoccluded region is set as 0.9 which represents a greater weight. In the Sect. 3, we prove the feasibility of this idea. Since most disoccluded areas are small, the small window is enough to extract disoccluded areas. In blue boxes of Figs. 4(a) and (b), we observe that there are similar disoccluded area. In the green and red boxes, we also can extract small disoccluded areas shown in (b). In the experiment, we set $W = 3$. The disoccluded areas extracted by our technique are shown in Fig. 4.

2.3   Weighted Maps

In this section, we introduce the fusion method of maps and get the third type of features. We combine the disoccluded maps with S_l and H_l respectively to get final maps. The final maps are obtained by the following fusion operation.

$$S_{final} = S_l \bigotimes W_{map} \tag{8}$$

$$H_{final} = H_l \bigotimes W_{map} \tag{9}$$

where symbol $\bigotimes$ represents the operation of multiplying corresponding pixels. W_{map} denotes the disoccluded map shown in Fig. 4. 20-dimensional features are obtained from the histograms of S_{final} and H_{final}.

2.4   Regression Model

We use support vector regression (SVR) implemented by LibSVM package to train extracted two scale features. In the experiment, we use 80% as the training set and the rest 20% are used as the test set. We train 1000 times and the median value is reported as the experiment result.

3   Experimental Results

In the experiment, we evaluate the proposed method on different datasets including IRCCyN/IVC DIBR [23] and MCL-3D [24].

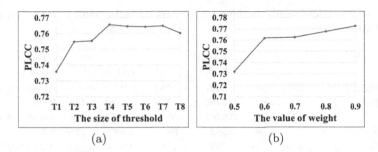

Fig. 5. Impact of different parameter settings on performance. (a) is the comparison results with different sizes of threshold in terms of PLCC. (b) is the comparison results with different sizes of weight in terms of PLCC.

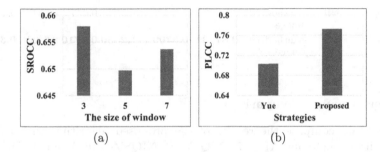

Fig. 6. The results of different size of window and different methods for extracting disoccluded regions. (a) is the comparison results with different sizes of window in terms of SROCC. (b) is the comparison results with different methods in terms of PLCC.

3.1 Databases

– IRCCyN/IVC DIBR [23]: this database includes 84 synthesized images from 3 scene. Images are synthesized using seven image synthesized algorithms. Therefore, there are seven distorted types in this database.
– MCL-3D [24]: this database contains 684 pairs of synthesized images from 9 scene. These virtual images are synthesized by a virtual video synthesis reference software (VSRS).

3.2 Evaluation Indicators

In order to judge the performance of the proposed method. We use the following three metrics for performance evaluation: Pearson Linear Correlation Coefficient (PLCC), Root Mean Squared Error (RMSE) and Spearman Rank-order Correlation Coefficient (SROCC).

Table 1. Performance results on different datasets including IRCCyN/IVC DIBR [23] and MCL-3D [24].

Metrics	Type	Category	MCL-3D			IRCCyN/IVC		
			PLCC	SROCC	RMSE	PLCC	SROCC	RMSE
DIIVINE [25]	NR	2D image	0.6507	0.6482	1.9755	0.6681	0.6201	0.4445
NIQE [26]	NR	2D image	0.6756	0.6375	1.9181	0.4363	0.3974	0.5704
QAC [27]	NR	2D image	0.6361	0.6531	2.0075	0.5094	0.5099	0.5455
BRISQUE [28]	NR	2D image	0.6624	0.6253	1.9490	0.4235	0.4287	0.5742
APT [7]	NR	synthesized image	0.2534	0.1733	2.5167	0.7307	**0.7157**	0.4546
NIQSV [8]	NR	synthesized image	0.6808	0.6236	1.9057	0.6346	0.6167	0.5146
NIQSV+ [9]	NR	synthesized image	-	-	-	0.7114	0.6668	0.4679
Yue [10]	NR	synthesized image	-	-	-	0.675	0.652	0.462
Proposed	NR	synthesized image	**0.8746**	**0.8709**	**1.2550**	**0.7710**	0.6826	**0.3864**

3.3 Performance Comparison

In Table 1, we compare the results of the proposed algorithm with existing NR algorithms including APT [7], NIQSV [8], NIQSV+ [9], Yue [10], DIIVINE [25], NIQE [26], quality-aware clustering (QAC) [27], BRISQUE [28]. The optimal performance values are marked in boldface and sub-optimal performance is underline. The codes for these algorithms are provided by the authors. Among these existing algorithms, DIIVINE [25], NIQE [26], QAC [27] and BRISQUE [28] are no-reference IQA algorithms designed for natural images. APT [7], NIQSV [8], NIQSV+ [9], Yue [10], and our method are no-reference IQA algorithms for synthesized images. In APT [7], authors prove that the statistics of mean subtracted contrast normalized (MSCN) coefficients are insensitive to the geometric distortion of synthesized images. Therefore, NIQE [26] and BRISQUE [28] get poor performance on IRCCyN/IVC [23] database. QAC [27] is a model learned by database [29] that only includes naturally distorted images without the distortion of synthesized images, so the corresponding PLCC are low which are 0.6361 and 0.5094. Our algorithm can get the highest PLCC value of 0.7710 on the IRCCyN/IVC database. In Table 1, the experimental results on the MCL-3D [24] dataset are not ideal for the algorithms of synthesized IQA. The reason is that the MCL-3D [24] dataset contains natural image distortions. Because some artificial noises are added in this dataset, previous methods of synthesized IQA ignore it. However, our algorithm can get 0.8746 for PLCC on the MCL-3D dataset, indicating that our algorithm can also be applied to synthesized images which have natural distortions. Although APT [7] algorithm can obtain promising results, its computational complexity is high as shown in Table 2. Although the performance of our method, NIQSV [8], NIQSV+ [9] and Yue [10] worse than APT [7], they reach the balance of performance and complexity, especially for our method.

3.4 Parameters Sensitivity

In this subsection, we discuss the choice of three parameters on IRCCyN/IVC DIBR [23] database. These are the window size W, the threshold size T and the weight size W_e. When one parameter's effect is explored, it is necessary to fix other parameters. In Fig. 5, the influence of weight and threshold on the PLCC are shown. The threshold is choosed from $\{1, 2, 3, 4, 5, 6, 7, 8\}$ based on $W = 3$, $W_e = 0.9$. In Fig. 5(a), when $T \leq 3$, the algorithm performances are poor, PLCC is the maximum value when $T = 4$. But as T increases, the performances show slight decrease. This phenomenon indicates that the lager threshold shrinks disoccluded areas, and vice versa. In our experiment, we set $T = 4$. In Fig. 5(b), as the weight of disocclusion area increases, the value of PLCC also increases. The reason is that human eyes are more sensitive to distorted areas, a larger weight should be set for distorted area, we empirically set $W_e = 0.9$. The window size W does not have a significant impact on the performance of our algorithm from Fig. 6(a). We choose $W = 3$ which contributes to the best performance.

Table 2. Algorithms for running time (in seconds) an image on IRCCyN/IVC DIBR [23] dataset.

Metrics	Proposed	APT [7]	NIQSV [8]	NIQSV+ [9]	Yue [10]
time	8.5018	90.454	0.097	0.113	0.196

3.5 Comparison of Different Disoccluded Regions Extraction Strategies

Yue *et al.* [10] extract disoccluded regions using LBP [21] algorithm. Authors indicate that it is the disoccluded area whose pixel value in LBP map is 8. In order to compare with disoccluded regions we extracted, we extract disoccluded map using LBP as weighting map. The final result comparison chart is shown in Fig. 6(b), the value of PLCC we get is 0.07 higher than Yue. Therefore, our method is better way to extract disoccluded maps.

4 Conclusion

In this paper, we design a NR-IQA algorithm for synthesized images. The histograms of saturation and hue maps are calculated as the first type of features based on human eyes' sensitivity to color. The LBP algorithm is used as the first derivative to extract texture and structure information from saturation and hue maps, the second type of features are extracted from LBP maps. We design a method extracting disoccluded region to conform to the theory that human eyes are more sensitive to distortion areas. The disoccluded map is used to weight LBP maps. Finally, the histograms of the weighted LBP maps are taken as third type of features, and the SVR is used to learn the mapping from extracted features to the quality score of the images. Experimental results show that the proposed model obtain better performance than existing state-of-the-art methods.

References

1. Tanimoto, M., Tehrani, M.P., Fujii, T., Yendo, T.: Free-viewpoint TV. IEEE Sig. Process. Mag. **28**(1), 67–76 (2011)
2. Fehn, C.: Depth-image-based rendering (DIBR), compression, and transmission for a new approach on 3D-TV. Proc. SPIE **5291**, 93–104 (2004)
3. Sandićstanković, D., Kukolj, D., Le Callet, P.: Multi-scale synthesized view assessment based on morphological pyramids. J. Electr. Eng. **67**(1), 3–11 (2016)
4. Sandic-Stankovic, D., Kukolj, D., Le Callet, P.: DIBR synthesized image quality assessment based on morphological pyramids. In: 3DTV-Conference: the True Vision - Capture, Transmission and Display of 3D Video, pp. 1–4, October 2015
5. Battisti, F., Bosc, E., Carli, M., Le Callet, P., Perugia, S.: Objective image quality assessment of 3D synthesized views. Sig. Process. Image Commun. **30**(C), 78–88 (2015)
6. Li, L., Zhou, Y., Gu, K., Lin, W., Wang, S.: Quality assessment of DIBR-synthesized images by measuring local geometric distortions and global sharpness. IEEE Trans. Multimedia **20**(99), 1 (2017)
7. Gu, K., Jakhetiya, V., Qiao, J.F., Li, X., Lin, W., Thalmann, D.: Model-based referenceless quality metric of 3D synthesized images using local image description. IEEE Trans. Image Process. **27**(1), 394–405 (2017)
8. Tian, S., Zhang, L., Morin, L., Deforges, O.: NIQSV: a no reference image quality assessment metric for 3D synthesized views. In: IEEE International Conference on Acoustics, Speech and Signal Processing, June 2017
9. Shishun Tian, L., Zhang, L.M., Deforges, O.: NIQSV+: a no-reference synthesized view quality assessment metric. IEEE Trans. Image Process. **27**(4), 1652–1664 (2017)
10. Yue, G., Zhou, T., Zhai, G., Hou, C., Gu, K.: Combining local and global measures for DIBR-synthesized image quality evaluation. IEEE Trans. Image Process. **28**(3), 1 (2018)
11. Lee, D., Plataniotis, K.N.: Towards a no-reference image quality assessment using statistics of perceptual color descriptors. IEEE Trans. Image Process. **25**(8), 3875–3889 (2016)
12. Telea, A.: An image inpainting technique based on the fast marching method. J. Graph. Tools **9**(1), 23–34 (2004)
13. Mori, Y., Fukushima, N., Yendo, T., Fujii, T., Tanimoto, M.: View generation with 3D warping using depth information for FTV. Sig. Process. Image Commun. **24**(1–2), 65–72 (2009)
14. Moller, K., Smolic, A., Dix, K., Merkle, P., Kauff, P., Wiegand, T.: View synthesis for advanced 3D video systems. Eurasip J. Image Video Process. **2008**(1), 1–11 (2009)

15. Ndjiki-Nya, P., et al.: Depth image based rendering with advanced texture synthesis. In: IEEE International Conference on Multimedia and Expo, pp. 424–429, July 2010
16. Koppel, M., et al.: Temporally consistent handling of disocclusions with texture synthesis for depth-image-based rendering. In: IEEE International Conference on Image Processing, pp. 1809–1812, September 2010
17. Che-Chun, S., Cormack, L.K., Bovik, A.C.: Color and depth priors in natural images. IEEE Trans. Image Process. A Publ. IEEE Sig. Process. Soc. 22(6), 2259–2274 (2013)
18. Ruderman, D.L., Cronin, T.W., Chiao, C.C.: Statistics of cone responses to natural images: implications for visual coding. J. Opt. Soc. Am. A: 15(15), 2036–2045 (1998)
19. Naik, S.K., Murthy, C.A.: Hue-preserving color image enhancement without gamut problem. IEEE Trans. Image Process. 12(12), 1591–1598 (2003)
20. Preucil, F.: Color hue and ink transfer—their relation to perfect reproduction. In: TAGA Proceedings, pp. 102–110 (1953)
21. Ojala, T., Pietikäinen, M., Mäenpää, T.: Gray scale and rotation invariant texture classification with local binary patterns. IEEE Trans. Pattern Anal. Mach. Intell. 24(7), 971–987 (2002)
22. Fang, Y., Yan, J., Li, L., Wu, J., Lin, W.: No reference quality assessment for screen content images with both local and global feature representation. IEEE Trans. Image Process. A Publ. IEEE Sig. Process. Soc. 27(4), 1600–1610 (2018)
23. Bosc, E., et al.: Towards a new quality metric for 3-D synthesized view assessment. IEEE J. Sel. Top. Sig. Process. 5(7), 1332–1343 (2011)
24. Song, R., Ko, H., Kuo, C.C.J.: MCL-3D: a database for stereoscopic image quality assessment using 2D-image-plus-depth source. J. Inf. Sci. Eng., 31(5) (2014)
25. Moorthy, A.K., Bovik, A.C.: Blind image quality assessment: from natural scene statistics to perceptual quality. IEEE Trans. Image Process. 20(12), 3350–3364 (2011)
26. Mittal, A., Soundararajan, R., Bovik, A.C.: Making a "completely blind" image quality analyzer. IEEE Sig. Process. Lett. 20(3), 209–212 (2013)
27. Xue, W., Zhang, L., Mou, X.: Learning without human scores for blind image quality assessment. In: Computer Vision and Pattern Recognition, pp. 995–1002, October 2013
28. Mittal, A., Moorthy, A.K., Bovik, A.C.: No-reference image quality assessment in the spatial domain. IEEE Trans. Image Process. 21(12), 4695 (2012)
29. Martin, D.R., Fowlkes, C., Tal, D., Malik, J.: A database of human segmented natural images and its application to evaluating segmentation algorithms and measuring ecological statistics. Int. Conf. Comput. Vis. 2(11), 416–423 (2001)

Gait Recognition with Clothing and Carrying Variations Based on GEI and CAPDS Features

Fengjia Yang, Xinghao Jiang$^{(\boxtimes)}$, Tanfeng Sun, and Ke Xu

School of Electronic Information and Electrical Engineering,
Shanghai Jiao Tong University, Shanghai, People's Republic of China
xhjiang@sjtu.edu.cn

Abstract. Gait recognition is a promising technology in biometrics. The accuracy of gait recognition can be decreased by many interference variations, such as view angle, clothing and carrying. A novel method is proposed based on the Gait Energy Image (GEI) feature and Coordinate-Angle-Position-Distance Skeleton (CAPDS) feature to eliminate the interference of clothing and carrying variations. GEI is a common feature widely used in gait recognition, but it is sensitive to the change of clothing and carrying. The CAPDS proposed in this paper is robust to the clothing and carrying variations. They are fused in backward to complement each other for recognition. Two novel networks, the Paird ResNet (PRN) and the Temporal-Spatial Paired Network (TSPN), are designed to extract the deep features of GEI and CAPDS. The experiments evaluated on the dataset CASIA-B show that the proposed method based on the backward fusion strategy of GEI and CAPDS features can achieve better performance than most methods in gait recognition with clothing and carrying variations.

Keywords: Gait recognition · GEI · CAPDS · PRN · TSPN

1 Introduction

Gait recognition is an emerging biometric technology suitable for long-distance identification. Comparing with other biometrics in application, such as face, iris, palmprint and fingerprint, gait has significant advantages of non-contact, non-invasive, far effective range. Therefore, it has great promising application values in video surveillance and public security. For these reasons, gait recognition has become a popular trend in computer vision community.

Unfortunately, there remains serious challenges before automatic and intelligent gait recognition. The main problem is that many potential variations enable to alert the appearance of one's gait drastically, which can deteriorate the recognition greatly. View, clothing, carrying are the trickiest three of them. The view transform models [1–3] and the view invariant features [4] have been proposed to achieve cross-view gait recognition. Liao et al. [5] firstly propose a novel method based on the features of pose

---

The first author of this paper is a student.

© Springer Nature Switzerland AG 2019
Z. Lin et al. (Eds.): PRCV 2019, LNCS 11858, pp. 632–643, 2019.
https://doi.org/10.1007/978-3-030-31723-2_54

coordinates robust to clothing and carrying variations than appearance-based features. Aggarwal et al. [6] design a covariate cognizant framework using average Energy Silhouette Image (AESI) to deal with the variations of clothing and carrying. Li et at. [7] propose the Gait Energy Response Function (GERF) to make the gait energy image (GEI) more suitable for handling conditions with clothing and carrying variations.

In this paper, a novel approach is proposed based on the backward fusion strategy of GEI and CAPDS features. The GEI feature including both the spatial and temporal information of gait, which prove to be efficient to gait recognition [1–4]. However, it's easily to be changed by clothing and carrying variations. Different from GEI, the skeleton-based feature CAPDS maintain constant whatever the person wears or carries, and skeleton features is widely be applied in action recognition [8]. Therefore, they are merged in backward in this paper to eliminate the interference of clothing and carrying variations in gait recognition. Two architectures of networks named Paired ResNet (PRN) and Temporal-Spatial Paired Network (TSPN) are also well designed to extract the deep features of GEI and CAPDS respectively.

The main contributions of this paper are the application of the backward fusion strategy of GEI and CAPDS features in gait recognition and the design of two novel architectures of networks to extract deep features. The proposed method has out-standing performance in gait recognition with clothing and carrying variations.

2   Feature Modeling

The raw video sequences are full of background noise, and they will cause the network failing to converge or over-fitting if they are put into network directly. Therefore, it is necessary to separate pedestrians from the raw videos and further model the handcraft features. The feature applied in this paper are GEI and CAPDS feature.

2.1   GEI Feature Modeling

The GEI [9] is one of the most popular features in gait recognition for its simplicity, effectiveness and robustness over other features. GEI can be computed by averaging the silhouettes in one gait sequence as illustrated in Fig. 1. Given a preprocessed binary gait silhouette sequences, the pixel value in GEI can be computed as follows:

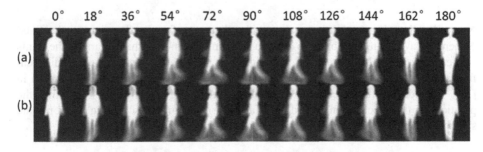

Fig. 1. Two examples of GEIs from CASIA-B datasets, with 11 views.

$$G(x,y) = \frac{1}{N} \sum_{t=1}^{N} B_t(x,y) \qquad (1)$$

where x and y are the pixel's coordinates in a 2D image, N is the number of frames in a gait sequence, $B_t(x,y)$ is the prime pixel value in moment t. The pixel values in GEIs can indicate the occurrence probability of the pixel in one gait cycle, including both the temporal and spatial information of the gait. Those GEIs will be paired as the input in the network designed in this paper.

2.2   CAPDS Feature Modeling

Clothing and carrying variations can greatly change the GEI of the same person. This will seriously decrease the accuracy of cross-condition recognition. Therefore, the skeleton-based features are introduced to assist gait recognition. Gait is one of the common actions of human, so the skeleton-based features for action recognition can be transferred to gait recognition for better characterizing the diversities of human's gaits. Liao et al. [5] propose to utilize the pose coordinates of the pedestrians for gait recognition. Inspired by [5], this paper constructs several skeleton features by Lie group and Lie algebra [8], which is as described below. The human skeleton obtained by the pose estimate algorithm in [10] can be considered as a connected set of body parts and each part consist two adjacent joints. Suppose $S = (J, E)$ is a skeleton, where $J = \{j_1, \ldots, j_N\}$ is the set of joints and $E = \{e_1, \ldots, e_M\}$ is the set of body parts represented by vectors.

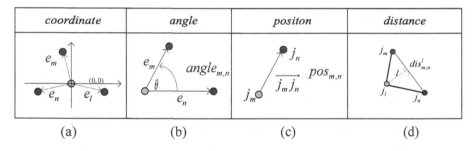

coordinate	angle	positon	distance
(a)	(b)	(c)	(d)

Fig. 2. The composition of CAPDS feature

Normalization Joints. During walking, the distances from pedestrians to the fixed camera always change. In order to eliminate the interference of this covariate, the joints sequences need to be normalized, ensuring that the size of human body in different frames are always be the same. There are 14 limb joints obtained by the algorithm in [10]. Considering the Neck is most stable joints during walking. Firstly, fixing the position of the Neck, then regarding it as the origin and establishing a coordinate system to represent other joints. The equation of normalization is as follows:

$$F_{J_i} = (J_i - J_{neck})/(\frac{L}{y_{max} - y_{min}}) \tag{2}$$

where L is a preset constant representing the normalized size of silhouettes, y_{max} and y_{min} are the maximum and minimum of the joints ordinate, respectively, $J_i \in \mathbb{R}^2$ is the coordinate of the joint i, F_{J_i} is the normalized coordinate of J_i, J_{neck} is the fixed coordinate of the Neck.

Modeling CAPDS. The feature proposed is named CAPDS (Coordinate-Angle-Position-Distance Skeleton) based on joints and body parts as illustrated in Fig. 2. It can be denoted as follows:

$$F_{CAPDS} = \{F_{coordinate}, F_{angle}, F_{position}, F_{distance}\} \tag{3}$$

which is composed by four skeleton features.

The first feature recorded as *coordinate* is the concatenation of normalized coordinates of joints mentioned above as illustrated in Fig. 2(a). It can be denoted as follows:

$$F_{coordinate} = \{F_{J_1}, F_{J_2}, \ldots, F_{J_N}\} \tag{4}$$

where N is the number of joints.

The second feature recorded as *angle* illustrated in Fig. 2(b), is the concatenation of all the angles, represented as cosine and sine, between pairs of adjacent body parts. It can be denoted as $F_{angle} = \{\ldots, F_{angle_{m,n}}, \ldots\}$., where m and n are indexes of the pairs of adjacent body parts. The $F_{angle_{m,n}}$ is calculated as follows:

$$F_{angle_{m,n}} = \left[\frac{e_n \cdot e_m}{|e_n| \cdot |e_m|}, \frac{e_n \times e_m}{|e_n| \cdot |e_m|}\right] \tag{5}$$

where $e_n \cdot e_m$ and $e_n \times e_m$ are inner product and outer product of e_n and e_m, respectively. The $angle_{m,n}$ indicates that e_n can reach the position and direction of e_m by rotating θ. This feature can well characterize the amplitude of swing arm and strides.

The third feature recorded as *position* illustrated in Fig. 2(c), is the concatenation of vectors formed by all the pairs of joints. It can be shown as follows:

$$F_{position} = \{\overrightarrow{j_1j_2}, \overrightarrow{j_1j_3}, \ldots, \overrightarrow{j_mj_n}, \ldots\} \tag{6}$$

where $J = \{j_1, \ldots, j_N\}$ is the set of joints. The interval between m and n is $[1, N]$ and N is the number of joints. The *position* can be selected for gait recognition due to its good performance on describing static information of all the joints in skeleton.

The last feature recorded as *distance* illustrated in Fig. 2(d), is the concatenation of distances represented by one height of the triangle formed by three adjacent joints. It can be denoted as $F_{distance} = \left[\ldots, F_{dis_{m,n}^l}, \ldots\right]$, where m, n and l are indexes of the three adjacent joints. The $F_{dis_{m,n}^l}$ can be computed by Helen formula as follows:

$$F_{distance} = \frac{2 \cdot \sqrt{p(p - l_{mn})(p - l_{nl})(p - l_{ml})}}{l_{mn}} \tag{7}$$

where l_{mn}, l_{nl} and l_{ml} are distances between three adjacent joints, $p = (l_{mn} + l_{ml} + l_{nl})/2$, denoting the half of the perimeter of Δ_{mnl}. This feature is adopted because Zhang et al. in [11] have proved its efficiency and robustness in action recognition and it works well on the actions of hand and foot, such as waving, swing arm, running and so on. Based on this, it can be introduced to gait recognition. After extracting the CAPDS feature of each frame, sequencing the features of all the frames in one video in chronological order to get the CAPDS feature of the video.

3 Network Architecture

In this section, two architectures of networks are well designed to extract the deep feature of GEI and CAPDS separately. Inspired by the LBNet in [4], PRN are proposed to transform ResNet into a two-channel input and two-classification network. Meanwhile, TSPN, which is the connection of the PRN and the Paired LSTM in parallel, is proposed to train the CAPDS sequences.

3.1 The Architecture of PRN

ResNet was proposed by He et al. in [12], which have been widely used in tasks of image recognition such as classification, detection, and semantic segmentation. The mechanism of the "shortcut connections" is the most prominent contribution. Shortcut connections are those skipping one or more layers, which has avoided the gradient disappearance and gradient explosion in deeper layers of network during training. It makes deeper and more sophisticated architecture of network possible.

The original ResNet is a multiple classification network with single-channel input. As far as the gait recognition is concerned, the difference of gaits between individuals is so tiny that the multi-class classifier, such as softmax, do worse in identification like the approach in [1]. The LBNet proposed in [4] has applied a binary classifier to constrain the network. Inspired by LBNet, the Paird ResNet (PRN) is proposed as illustrated in Fig. 3.

Firstly, pairwise GEIs are formed by one GEI from galleries and the other form probes. Then those pairs are concatenated as the input of PRN. The output is binary, classified by sigmoid. The output indicates whether the identities of this pairwise GEIs are the same. Just like LBNet, the pairwise GEIs are compared within local regions and the difference between pairwise GEIs is projected into a high dimensional linear space for comparing by convolution layers. Unlike LBNet, there are more convolution kernels and layers with sophisticated architecture in PRN. The experiments have shown that ResNet18 performs best and the ResNets with more layers are over-fitting, so the ResNet18 has been selected as the basic architecture of the PRN.

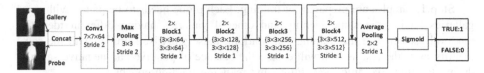

Fig. 3. The architecture of PRN

3.2 The Architecture of TSPN

As the CAPDS feature of gait videos are sequences, they need to be input into the RNN-based network to extract dynamic information between frames. Zhang et al. [11] have proposed a multi-stream LSTM architecture with multiple skeleton features input for action recognition. And Liao et al. [5] design PSTN formed by the connection of CNN and LSTM in parallel. Inspired by them, the Temporal-spatial Paired Network (TSPN) proposed in this paper concatenate the Paired ResNet and Paired LSTM in the top by fully convolutional layer and merge the multi-stream skeleton features by backward fusion as illustrated in Fig. 4.

In TSPN, the pairwise skeleton features in CAPDS are input into the architectures of ResNet and LSTM simultaneously as illustrated in Fig. 4. The part of Resnet has the outstanding performance in extracting spatial information of each frame and the part of LSTM does well in extracting temporal information between frames, so that the fusion of two kinds of information via full convolution network can boost the performance of skeleton features. Since the four skeleton features in CAPDS contribute differently to gait recognition and hard to be unified normalized, pre-experiment has verified that the effect of forward fusion performed bad. Therefore, the weighted backward fusion is applied in this paper. The multiple skeleton features in CAPDS are input into TSPN separately and merged by weights before the sigmoid layer, whose weights are initially random and further updated by training.

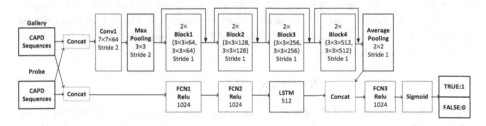

Fig. 4. The architecture of TSPN

4   Framework of the Proposed Method

In this paper, the proposed method using the backward fusion strategy of GEI and CAPDS features for gait recognition, which makes them complementary. At the same time, PRN and TSPN are designed to extract deep features in GEI and CAPDS, respectively. The framework of the proposed method is as illustrated in Fig. 5.

Step 1, samples are prepared for training. Each probe needs to be paired with the 4 galleries having the same identity and other 4 galleries having different identities randomly selected in the training set. Marking these pairwise samples with the same identity as 1, the rest as 0. It will ensure the balance of positive and negative samples during training, avoiding over- fitting and reducing training epochs.

Step 2, the two proposed networks are trained. Extracting both the GEI and CAPDS features from the pairwise samples and training the PRN with pairwise GEIs input and TSPN with pairwise CAPDSs input separately.

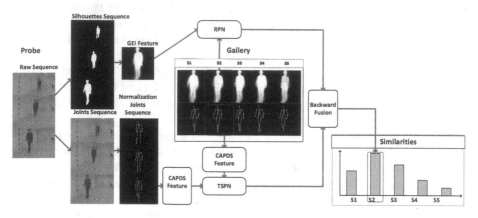

Fig. 5. The framework of the proposed method

Step 3, samples are prepared for testing. Each probe should be paired with all the galleries in the test set in order to seek the gallery which is the most similar to the probe.

Step 4, similarities of the samples in test set are computed. Extracting the features from pairwise samples and inputting them into the two pre-trained networks to compute the similarity of the two individuals in every pairwise samples. The output probabilities of the sigmoid layers from both RPN and TSPN, are combined by the strategy of backward fusion as follows:

$$R = \alpha R_{RPN} + (1 - \alpha) R_{TSPN} \qquad (8)$$

where R is the fusion probability, R_{RPN} and R_{TSPN} are the output probabilities of the PRN and TSPN, $\alpha(\alpha < 1)$ is a hyperparameter obtained by the verifications of multiple experiments. This paper has evaluated several experimental result of different hyperparameters α, as shown in Fig. 6. The best performance can be achieved when α is 0.75. It proves that RPN contributes more for the comparison of similarities.

Step 5, identity matching is processed. The identity matching is according to the principle of the nearest neighbor classification. After testing all the galleries from test set paired with the input probe, the gallery with the highest fusion probability is the most similar to the probe, which is the result of identity matching.

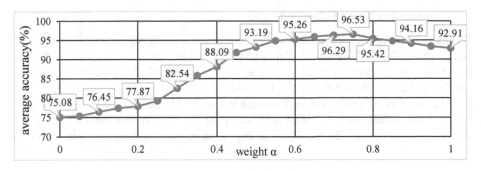

Fig. 6. The average accuracy with different values of α

5 Experiments and Analysis

5.1 Setups

The experiments are evaluated on the challenging datasets CASIA-B. CASIA-B is one of the largest public gait datasets, created by the Institute of Automation, Chinese Academy of Sciences. It consists of 124 subjects in total, and each subject has 110 sequences. Among the 110 sequences of each subject, there are 11 views ranging from 0° to 180° (0°, 18°, 36°,... 180°), and 10 sequences for each view including 6 sequences of normal walking ("nm"), 2 sequences of walking with bag ("bg") and 2 sequences of walking with coat ("cl").

The experiments settings adopted are the same as those of PSTN [5] and Gait-GANv2 [3], setting the sequences of the first 62 subjects for training and the rest for testing. For each subject, the first 4 normal walking sequences are put into the gallery set and the others are put into the probe set both in training and test set, as illustrated in Table 1.

Table 1. Experimental setting I

Training		Test	
Gallery set	Probe set	Gallery set	Probe set
ID: 001-062	ID: 001-062	ID: 063-124	ID: 063-124
Seqs: nm-01–nm-04	Seqs: nm-05–06, bg-01–02, cl-01–02	Seqs: nm-01–nm-04	Seqs: nm-05–06, bg-01–02, cl-01–02

The two networks proposed are trained with the binary cross-entropy loss which is suitable for two-class classification. The optimizer selected is Adam. The weights of layers are initialized as the same as the prime ResNet does. The initial learning rate is 0.0001 and updating the weights with a batch of size 128. The experiment was done on the computer with 8 cores at 2.1 GHz, 32 GB of RAM and a GPU NVidia GeForce GTX 1080 Ti. It has cost 2000 and 5000 epochs to train PRN and TSPN, separately.

5.2   Comparison with Other Networks

The experiment results of the proposed method are compared with those of SPAE [13], GaitGANv1 [2], PSTN [5] and GaitGANv2 [3] under the settings in Table 1. The probe sets are divided into three subsets as nm-05–06, bg-01–02 and cl-01–02, which are denoted as Set-A, Set-B and Set-C, respectively.

The result of comparison is as illustrated in Fig. 7. All the average recognition rates in Fig. 7 are without view variation represented by the mean of recognition rates on 11 single views in CASIA-B. As shown in Fig. 7, in normal walking condition with no

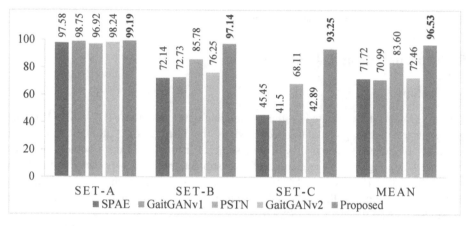

Fig. 7. The average recognition rates of the proposed method compared with other networks

variations (Set-A), the proposed method have a slight improvement than others, which is 99.19% compared with the best of others, 98.75% in GaitGANv1 [3]. In walking condition with carrying variation (Set-B), the proposed method is much superior than others, which is higher than the best result of others by 11%. In walking condition with clothing variation (Set-C), the average recognition rate of the proposed method is over 90%, exceeding the best of others more than 25%. The average recognition on total probe of the proposed method is more than 95%, nearly 13% higher than the best of others, 83.60% in PSTN [5] which applies only the pose coordinates in gait recognition. The comparison shows the proposed method based on backward fusion strategy of GEI and CAPDS features has an extraordinary performance in gait recognition with clothing and carrying variations.

5.3   Generalization Experiment with a Small Training Set

To further verify the effectiveness of the proposed method, the proposed method is further compared with some state-of-art methods, which are GEINet [1], DCNN [14], AESI + ZNK [6], L-CRF [15], Gabor + Global GERF [16], Gabor + SD-GERF [7]. The experiments settings adopted are as the same as those in [7, 15] and [16] as illustrated in Table 2, which is specially designed for methods without deep learning.

The size of training set is only 24, less than a quarter of the test set, which is a tough challenge for methods based on the deep learning.

Table 2. Experimental setting II

Training		Test	
Gallery set	Probe set	Gallery set	Probe set
ID: 001-024	ID: 001-024	ID: 025-125	ID: 025-125
Seqs: nm-01–nm-04	Seqs: nm-05–06, bg-01–02, cl-01–02	Seqs: nm-01–nm-04	Seqs: nm-05–06, bg-01–02, cl-01–02

All the methods mentioned above are tested under the settings of experimental setting II. The results are illustrated in Table 3. The composition of Set-A, Set-B and Set-C are as the same as those in 5.2. All the average recognition rates in Table 3 are also without view variation.

As is shown in Table 3, although the proposed method fails to achieve the first place, it still maintains high accuracies even the training set is small, which are the 2nd in Set-A, the 2nd in Set-B and the 3rd in Set-C. While, the average recognition of the other two CNN-based methods with only appearance features, GEINet [1] and DCNN [14], decrease dramatically due to the tiny size of training sets, which are 84.6% and 86.7%. Benefit from the fusion feature, the proposed method deteriorates little which still exceeds some approaches without deep learning, such as AESI + ZNK [6] and L-CRF [15].

The methods Gabor + Global GERF [16] and Gabor + SD-GERF [7] has achieve better performance than the proposed method. Especially, the accuracy of [7] in Set-C is 10% higher than the proposed method as illustrated in Table 3. The reasons maybe as follows, in walking condition with clothing variation (Set-C), the clothing has a wide variety and its influence on silhouettes is more global and significant compared to the carrying, so the networks in the proposed method maybe slightly under-fitting due to too little training data. While, the methods in [7] and [16] aims to refine the feature of GEI itself, they perform better than the proposed method without data capacity constraints. Nonetheless, the proposed method is an end-to-end approach, having less procedures compared to [7] and [16] which require complex mathematical calculations and processing.

Table 3. Generalization experiment on CASISA-B dataset

Methods	Set-A	Set-B	Set-C	Mean
GEINet [1]	97.5	84.5	71.8	84.6
DCNN [14]	95.6	88.3	76.2	86.7
AESI + ZNK [6]	**100.0**	93.1	81.3	91.5
L-CRF [15]	98.6	90.2	85.8	91.5
Gabor + Global GERF [16]	99.0	91.0	92.0	94.0
Gabor + SD-GERF [7]	99.0	**100.0**	**96.0**	**98.3**
Proposed	99.5	93.6	85.9	93.0

5.4 Contribution of the Features

In order to evaluate the independent contribution of GEI and CAPDS features on recognition, the method of GEI with PRN and CAPDS with TSPN are tested separately under the settings in Table 1 and compared with the method of fusion feature. The results are as shown in Table 4.

From Table 4, the results put that the method of GEI + PRN has achieved good accuracy in gait recognition with the clothing and carrying variations, which are 98.97% (Set-A), 91.13% (Set-B), and 88.64% (Set-C), having proved its efficiency on

Table 4. Contribution of the GEI and CAPDS features

Methods	Set-A	Set-B	Set-C	Mean
GEI + PRN	98.97	91.13	88.64	92.91
CAPDS + TSPN	89.95	77.70	57.59	75.08
Backward fusion	**99.19**	**97.14**	**93.26**	**96.53**

recognition and robustness to variations. While, the method of CAPDS + TSPN, do not perform as well as the former on gait recognition with a mean recognition of 75.08%. However, after GEI and CAPDS features are fused in backward, the CAPDS feature plays its part. With the help of CAPDS, the accuracies of Set-B and Set-C reach 97.14% and 93.26%, increased by 6% and 4.6%, respectively. In Set-A, the recognition of GEI + PRN is already high enough that the contribution of CAPDS features is not significant in the proposed method.

The experimental results show that the method of GEI + PRN can perform well in gait recognition with the clothing and carrying variations, and the fusion of it with CAPDS + TSPN can improve the results to be better. The CAPDS feature still have some limitations in recognition accuracy. The skeleton features in CAPDS will be refined and extended to be more robust to clothing and carrying variations in future.

6 Conclusions

In this paper, a novel approach is proposed based on backward fusion strategy of GEI and CAPDS features for the gait recognition with clothing and carrying variations. The skeleton-based feature CAPDS is firstly be introduced into the gait recognition and two architectures of networks are designed to extract the spatial-temporal information of the handcraft features. The experiment results show that the proposed method has substantially improved the gait recognition rate with clothing and carrying variations and achieve better performance than most methods.

Acknowledgement. This work is funded by National Natural Science Foundation of China (Grant No. 61572321 & 61572320). It is supported by the National Key Research and Development Projects of China (2018YFC0830703). It is also supported by the Foundation of Shanghai Fusion and Innovative Research Laboratory for Procuratorial Big Data.

References

1. Shiraga, K., Makihara, Y., Muramatsu, D., Echigo, T., Yagi, Y.: GEINet: view-invariant gait recognition using a convolutional neural network. In: 2016 International Conference on Biometrics (ICB), pp. 1–8, June 2016
2. Yu, S., Chen, H., Reyes, E.B.G., Poh, N.: GaitGan: invariant gait feature extraction using generative adversarial networks. In: 2017 IEEE Conference on Computer Vision and Pattern Recognition Workshops (CVPRW), pp. 532–539, July 2017
3. Yu, S., et al.: GaitGanv2: invariant gait feature extraction using generative adversarial networks. Pattern Recogn. **87**, 179–189 (2019)
4. Wu, Z., Huang, Y., Wang, L., Wang, X., Tan, T.: A comprehensive study on cross-view gait based human identification with deep cnns. IEEE Trans. Pattern Anal. Mach. Intell. **39**(2), 209–226 (2017)
5. Liao, Rijun, Cao, Chunshui, Garcia, Edel B., Yu, Shiqi, Huang, Yongzhen: Pose-based temporal-spatial network (PTSN) for gait recognition with carrying and clothing variations. In: Zhou, Jie, et al. (eds.) CCBR 2017. LNCS, vol. 10568, pp. 474–483. Springer, Cham (2017). https://doi.org/10.1007/978-3-319-69923-3_51
6. Aggarwal, H., Vishwakarma, D.K.: Covariate conscious approach for gait recognition based upon zernike moment invariants. IEEE Trans. Cogn. Dev. Syst. **10**(2), 397–407 (2018)
7. Li, X., Makihara, Y., Xu, C., Muramatsu, D., Yagi, Y., Ren, M.: Gait energy response functions for gait recognition against various clothing and carrying status. Appl. Sci. **8**(8), 1380 (2018)
8. Yao, H., Jiang, X., Sun, T., Wang, S.: 3D human action recognition based on the spatial-temporal moving skeleton descriptor. In: 2017 IEEE International Conference on Multimedia and Expo (ICME), pp. 937–942, July 2017
9. Han, J., Bhanu, B.: Individual recognition using gait energy image. IEEE Trans. Pattern Anal. Mach. Intell. **28**(2), 316–322 (2006)
10. Cao, Z., Simon, T., Wei, S.E., Sheikh, Y.: Realtime multi-person 2D pose estimation using part affinity fields. In: Proceedings of the IEEE Conference on Computer Vision and Pattern Recognition, pp. 7291–7299 (2017)
11. Zhang, S., et al.: Fusing geometric features for skeleton-based action recognition using multilayer lstm networks. IEEE Trans. Multimedia **20**(9), 2330–2343 (2018)
12. He, K., Zhang, X., Ren, S., Sun, J.: Deep residual learning for image recognition. In: 2016 IEEE Conference on Computer Vision and Pattern Recognition (CVPR), pp. 770–778, June 2016
13. Yu, S., Chen, H., Wang, Q., Shen, L., Huang, Y.: Invariant feature extraction for gait recognition using only one uniform model. Neurocomputing **239**, 81–93 (2017)
14. Alotaibi, M., Mahmood, A.: Improved gait recognition based on specialized deep convolutional neural networks. In: 2015 IEEE Applied Imagery Pattern Recognition Workshop (AIPR), pp. 1–7, October 2015
15. Chen, X., Weng, J., Lu, W., Xu, J.: Multi-gait recognition based on attribute discovery. IEEE Trans. Pattern Anal. Mach. Intell. **40**(7), 1697–1710 (2018)
16. Li, Xiang, Makihara, Yasushi, Xu, Chi, Muramatsu, Daigo, Yagi, Yasushi, Ren, Mingwu: Gait energy response function for clothing-invariant gait recognition. In: Lai, Shang-Hong, Lepetit, Vincent, Nishino, Ko, Sato, Yoichi (eds.) ACCV 2016. LNCS, vol. 10112, pp. 257–272. Springer, Cham (2017). https://doi.org/10.1007/978-3-319-54184-6_16

Stage-by-Stage Based Design Paradigm of Two-Pathway Model for Gaze Following

Zhongping Cao[1,2], Guoli Wang[1,2(✉)], and Xuemei Guo[1,2]

[1] School of Data and Computer Science, Sun Yat-sen University,
Guangzhou 510006, People's Republic of China
caozhp3@mail2.sysu.edu.cn,
{isswgl,guoxuem}@mail.sysu.edu.cn
[2] Key Laboratory of Machine Intelligence and Advanced Computing,
Ministry of Education, Beijing, People's Republic of China

Abstract. Gaze, which is an important non-verbal cue of interactions between human beings, can be used to estimate a person's point of regard as well as deduce his intention. And gaze following is an task to estimate the visual attention of people in a single image. To tackle this challenging problem, earlier state-of-the-art work try to combine the information from image saliency as well as the gaze directions of people, thus demonstrate a deep-learning based two-pathway model. However, previous work do not focus much on why such a two-pathway model works well. Thus, in this paper, we divide the two-pathway model into three stages, compare different mechanisms in those stages to better understand how each stage may influence the model performance. Finally, we find out the best combinations of the mechanism in three stages and evaluate the model on the benchmark GazeFollow.

Keywords: Gaze following · Two-pathway model · Deep learning

1 Introduction

Gaze, an important non-verbal signal of a person, can tell other people what the person is paying attention to in a scene. That is, humans have the remarkable ability to precisely follow the gaze direction of another person, a task commonly referred to as gaze following [1]. Similarly, if a computer vision system can have such an ability, it can understand people object of interest or their attention state in a scene and further deduce what they intend to do next, which is helpful in many fields such as salient region detection [19], assisted driving [18], human-robot interaction [20] and so on. There are two research fields related to the gaze following task. One is called image saliency model, which attempts to predict an observer's fixation location when given a picture. The other is called gaze estimation, which usually takes a person's face image as input and outputs his

---

The first author is a student.

© Springer Nature Switzerland AG 2019
Z. Lin et al. (Eds.): PRCV 2019, LNCS 11858, pp. 644–656, 2019.
https://doi.org/10.1007/978-3-030-31723-2_55

gaze direction or point of regard (PoR). Some data samples of three datasets called Salicon [2], GazeFollow [1], GazeCapture [3] of these three tasks can be seen in Fig. 1.

Intuitively, When we try to follow where another person is looking at, firstly we will look at the person's head and eyes to estimate their gaze direction to attain the possible field of view in a scene. Next, we may find out the salient objects in that field by standing in their shoes to predict what they are focusing on. Based on such a motivation, Recasens [1] firstly proposed a deep-learning based two-pathway model, in which they build a saliency pathway to model the importance of object in an image and build a gaze pathway to predict a person's field of view in the image. By combining the information from two pathways through an element-wise product operation, they can obtain the fixation probabilistic heatmap and finally get the gaze point by taking the maximum response location in that heatmap. Following such a two-pathway model architecture, [4] predicts the focus of a person's gaze across views in commercial movies which include a series of frames that follow the actor's attention. [5] proposes a similar two-pathway architecture by using stronger backbone network Resnet50 [6] to design a generalized model to predict a person's visual attention in unconstrained scenarios.

Although these two-pathway models achieve considerable accuracy, few of work pay attention to the design of the two-pathway model architecture. To address this, in this paper we divide the common two-pathway model for gaze following into three important stages, and then we design different mechanisms in those stages to find out which can benefit more to the model performance. From the experimental results, we obtain the best combinations of the mechanism in three stages.

The main contributions of our work are as follows:

- We use a stage-by-stage paradigm to divide the common two-pathway model for gaze following into three important stages, that is, the backbone network for feature extraction in both two pathways, the fusion mechanism to merge the information from the two pathways and the post-processing operation of the heatmap to obtain final fixation point.
- As for the first stage, we use three advanced image classification networks called AlexNet, VGG and ResNet as our backbone network. And the result shows that stronger backbone network leads to higher performance.
- As for the second stage, we compare two kinds of mechanism to better fuse the information from the two pathways. One is explicit-specified way using element-wise product. The other acts as an implicit way to learn automatically by means of a small convolution neural network.
- As for the third stage, to directly use ground truth coordinate as supervision, we introduce a post-processing operation called integral regression to regress 2D coordinate of the fixation point from heatmap produced by the second stage.

The rest of this paper is organized as follows. In Sect. 2, we explore related work. Section 3 presents our model for gaze following. In Sect. 4, we show the experimental results and provide sample visualization. At last, Sect. 5 makes a brief conclusion for this paper.

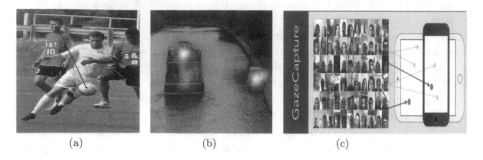

(a)   (b)   (c)

Fig. 1. Data samples of different tasks. (a) is an sample of gaze following task, where the blue line comes from the eye position(white dot) to the fixation point(black dot). (b) is an sample of image saliency task, where the heatmap is the ground truth salient region. (c) is an sample of gaze estimation task, where head image are used to estimate the fixation point on the small phone screen.

2   Related Works

Gaze Estimation. Gaze estimation aims to predict the gaze of a human subject. In general, it often takes a person's eye or face image as input such as the image captured by a laptop camera, then outputs the gaze direction or the fixation of the gaze on a screen. Recent years deep-learning based methods have achieved better performance to traditional methods using hand-crafted feature in such a field. They often use CNN to directly estimate the gaze direction from input image. Krafka et al. [3] propose an end-to-end CNN called iTracker, which takes face image and eye image as input to infer user's gaze location on the smart phone. Vora et al. [18] focus on the generalized driver gaze zone estimation system, in which they do a systematic analysis of different CNN architectures and input strategies for driver's head image. Similarly, We also compare multiple CNN architectures in the first stage in our proposed method to extract meaningful information from the two pathways.

Saliency Detection. For saliency detection task, it usually gives an image, and the model should be able to estimate the salient region in that image, such as the region that attracts the attention of an observer who is looking at that image. Early work were proposed by Itti et al. [7], and recently deep-learning based methods show superior performance on this task. For example, [9,10] deal with salient region detection(SOD) in RGB image, using CNN architecture like AlexNet [11], VGG network [12]. For RGBD based SOD, Zhao et al. [21] propose an effective fuse strategy to fuse RGB and depth features, which help improve the performance. In our proposed stage-by-stage design paradigm, we also pay great attention to design the fusion mechanism for the two pathways.

Third-Person Gaze Following. Recasens et al. [1] do a pioneering work of third-person gaze following. They formulate the gaze problem as: given a single image containing one or more people, predict the location that each person in the scene is looking at. Our work is based on the two-pathway architecture proposed by Recasens [1] but we go further by dividing the model into three stages and try to find out the best mechanisms in those stages, thus being helpful in better designing the two-pathway model architecture.

3 Method

Figure 2 is an overview of our proposed two-pathway model as well as its input and output. The model takes three inputs: the whole image, a crop of the subject's head, and the location of the subject's head. Given the inputs, the model estimates the 2D coordinate of fixation point of the subject in the image.

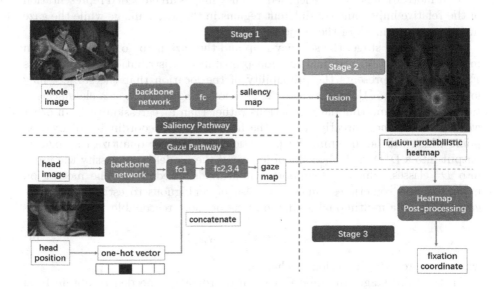

Fig. 2. Overview of the three stages in the two-pathway model

We illustrate the gaze following problem in Subsect. 3.1 and then describe the model architecture in more detail in Subsect. 3.2. Loss function is discussed in Subsect. 3.3.

3.1 Problem Statement

Given the image I and the head position P of a person for whom we want to estimate his gaze, and then we can crop a head image H based on the head position.

Assume that the estimated gaze point coordinate is Y, we can parameterize the gaze following problem as:

$$Y = f(H, I, P) \tag{1}$$

As is shown in Fig. 2, we can see how the model works. In the first stage, both saliency pathway and gaze pathway receive a subset of inputs to solve a sub-problem. Saliency pathway takes the whole image I as input, and outputs a D*D saliency map(noted as S_{map}) through the backbone network. Similarly, gaze pathway receives the head position P and head image H as input, then it outputs an D*D gaze map(noted as G_{map}) through backbone network and several fully connected layers.

$$G_{map} = F_1(H, P) \tag{2}$$

$$S_{map} = F_2(I) \tag{3}$$

where F_1, F_2 are the mapping function of the two pathways.

Our motivation is that the learned saliency map is an embeded representation of the relative importance of different regions in the whole image while the gaze map serves as a mask of the subject's gaze field.

In the second stage, the saliency map and the gaze map go through a fusion mechanism to attain the final fixation probabilistic distribution map(noted as F_{map}), which represents the probability of the location that the subject may look at. Similar to [1], we consider the gaze following problem as a classification task to support multimodal estimations rather than a regression task. In other words, we does not directly regress the final Cartesian coordinates of fixation point which will be an unimodal prediction. Instead, we quantize the fixation output into a D*D grid, then the objective of the model is to classify the input into D^2 classes, which can support a multimodal prediction. The motivation behind is that sometimes human can also be ambiguous to estimate the true gaze object so a multimodal prediction may be more reasonable.

$$F_{map} = \phi(G_{map}, S_{map}) \tag{4}$$

where ϕ represents the fusion mechanism.

In the third stage, the final Cartesian coordinate is needed to obtain from the output F_{map} of the second stage. Thus we need a heatmap post-processing operation to finish the transformation. Intuitively, a simple take-maximum operation can be used to get the maximum response point as final output. But such a non-differentiable operation will bring drawbacks during training. In this paper, we introduce a novel differentiable operation called integral regression, which works better in the model. More details will be discussed in Subsect. 3.2.

$$Y \doteq \varphi(F_{map}) \tag{5}$$

where φ represents the heatmap post-processing operation.

3.2   Stage-by-Stage Based Design Paradigm of Two-Pathway Model

In this section, we introduce the details of the different mechanisms in three stages mentioned above.

Backbone Network: The backbone network in both saliency pathway and gaze pathway can serve as a feature extractor which embeds the inputs into a high-level representation, thus the power of its abstract ability is essential in the model to solve the classification task of gaze following. In recent years, many advanced models have been proposed for the ImageNet classification task and have shown their strong representative power to process image data. In this paper, we also take advantage of these state-of-the-art classification models and we adopt AlexNet [11], VGG network [12] and ResNet [6] as the backbone network in two pathways.

Fusion: After the first stage, we obtain the saliency map as well as the gaze map. From our viewpoint, both these two maps provide a certain degree of but incomplete cues for the gaze following tasks. For example, the saliency map can provide the saliency of the image which may attract an observer's attention but the subject may not look at such a salient region. Also, the gaze map can give an coarse estimation where the subject look at but it needs to be refined by other cues. So a proper fusion mechanism is important to combine these two maps to attain the final fixation probabilistic map. In this paper, we consider two kinds of fusion mechanism. One is an explicit way to fusion the maps through a element-wise product. In the other fusion mechanism called "concatenate and convolution", we firstly concatenate the saliency map and gaze map and then take it into several convolution layers to get the final fixation map. Such a mechanism acts as an implicit way to automatically learn to fuse the maps rather than explicitly specified.

Heatmap Post-processing Operation: As is mentioned above, what we attain after the second stage is a D*D grid map but our goal is to obtain the 2D Cartesian coordinates of the estimated fixation point. One simple post-processing operation is to take the maximum response point in the fixation heatmap. But such a non-differentiable operation cannot be used in training the model through the backward propagation algorithm. Consequently, we need to transform the ground truth 2D coordinate to a heatmap which has the same size as the estimated map to calculate the loss. Such a transformation bring two drawbacks. Firstly, we cannot directly use the ground truth 2D coordinate as supervision to train the model but instead use the transformed heatmap. Secondly, the resolution of the heatmap is hard to decide because low resolution may lead to information loss while high resolution increases the computation cost. In this paper, inspired by the work [13] in the research field of human pose estimation, we introduce a novel post-processing operation called integral regression to regress the coordinate from the fixation map F_{map}, which is differentiable and can be used in both training and testing procedure. The integral regression, similar to the soft argmax, works as the follow steps [13]:

$$Y = \int_{p \in \Omega} p \cdot \tilde{H}(p) \tag{6}$$

where $\tilde{H}$ is the normalized heatmap and Ω is its domain, p is the location in heatmap, Y is the output point.

For the normalization, use softmax:

$$\tilde{H}(p) = \frac{e^{H(p)}}{\int_{q \in \Omega} e^{H(q)}} \tag{7}$$

and the discrete form of Eq. (6) is

$$Y = \sum_{p_y=1}^{H} \sum_{p_x=1}^{W} p \cdot \tilde{H}(p) \tag{8}$$

3.3   Loss Function

In the scenario that we adopt take-maximum as the heatmap post-processing operation in the third stage, we can only calculate the loss between the estimated fixation map and the ground truth map. As for this, we adopt L2 loss as the heatmap loss $L_{heatmap}$. In contrast, while we use the integral regression as post-processing operations, we can obtain the estimated coordinates in the training procedure in a differentiable way, thus we can calculate the loss between the estimated coordinate and the ground truth coordinate. As for this, we adopt L1 loss as the regression loss L_{reg}. Moreover, experimental results shows that training with the joint of heatmap loss and regression loss works better. So our loss in the experiment is like the following formula:

$$L = L_{heatmap} + \lambda * L_{reg} \tag{9}$$

where $\lambda = 0$ while adopt argmax as the post-processing operation and $\lambda = 2$ while adopt integral regression.

4   Experiments

4.1   Experiments on GazeFollow

We evaluate the performance of our model while adopting different mechanisms in the three stages mentioned above, using the suggested test split of the Gaze-Follow dataset.

Datasets. GazeFollow dataset [1] is an image dataset with manual annotations of the locations where people are looking. The images are taken from other datasets such as MS COCO [14] and PASCAL [15]. As a result, the images cover a wide range of scenarios where people performing diverse activities.

The training set contains 130339 people in 125,557 images while the test set contains 4782 images. All the images are provided the annotations of the head position and fixation position of a subject. Moreover, to evaluate human consistency on gaze-following, 10 gaze annotations per person were collected for the test set.

Implementation Details. All of our implementation and experiments are done in PyTorch [16]. The input whole image as well as the cropped head image is normalized to 224*224 while the 2-D head position coordinate is transform to an 169-D one-hot vector. For the backbone network, we use the pre-trained model of AlexNet,VGG16 and ResNet50 on the ImageNet [8]. As for the fully connected layers in the gaze pathway, their size are 100,400,200 and 169. And the size of fully connected layer in the saliency pathway is 169. Thus, the size of S_{map}, G_{map} and F_{map} is 13*13. Moreover, the parameter of the convolution layers in the second fusion mechanism is summarized in Table 1. Note that a batch normalization and a ReLU activation follows every convolution layer, successively.

Table 1. The parameters of the "concatenate and convolution" fusion mechanism

Parameter	Conv1	Conv2	Conv3
Kernel size	5*5	3*3	1*1
Input channels, output channels	(2, 64)	(64, 32)	(32, 1)
Stride	1	1	1
Padding	1	1	1

As for the training procedures, we use the Adam optimization algorithm with a learning rate of 1e4 and a weight decay of 1e-4. In all experiments, the base learning rate is 1e-4 and it drops to one-tenth of the origin learning rate after 15 epochs. Mini-batch size is 80. Training usually converges within 30 epochs.

Evaluation Metrics. We adopt two evaluation metrics. ***Normalized L2 distance:*** We evaluate the Euclidean distance between our estimated fixation point and the average of 10 ground truth fixations in the test set. ***Angular Error:*** Using the ground truth head position from the annotation, we compute the gaze vectors for the average ground truth fixations and our estimation and then calculate the angular difference between these two gaze vectors.

Effect of the First Stage. Table 2 shows results using different backbone network in the two pathways. We can see that the model performance is better while both saliency pathway and gaze pathway adopt ResNet50 as backbone network compared with adopting AlexNet and VGG16, which shows a stronger backbone can help improve the model accuracy. Therefore, in the following experiments where we compare different mechanisms in the second and third stage, we use ResNet50 as the backbone network by default.

Table 2. Comparision among using different backbone network in two pathways

Saliency pathway	Gaze pathway	Normalized L2 distance	Angular error
AlexNet	AlexNet	0.270	42.7°
	VGG16	0.313	48.8°
	ResNet50	0.244	38.1°
VGG16	AlexNet	0.279	41.4°
	VGG16	0.282	42.8°
	ResNet50	0.257	38.9°
ResNet50	AlexNet	0.281	41.9°
	VGG16	0.283	41.7°
	ResNet50	**0.234**	**35.3°**

Effect of the Second Stage. Table 3 shows results using different fusion mechanisms. The element-wise product way works better than that of implicitly learning through convolution layers. We think there may be two reasons. The first one is that the concatenate-and-convolution way introduces extra parameters which may not be learned well during the training. And the second reason is that though element-wise product is simple and explicit, it forces that the fixation map has a high response only if both the gaze map and the saliency map have a high response. In other words, it can remove some noises or biases produced by the single pathway which is benefitial to improving the model performance.

Table 3. Comparision among using different fusion mechanisms

Fusion mechanism	Normalized L2 distance	Angular error
Element-wise product	**0.234**	**35.3°**
Concatenate and convolution	0.246	38.7°

Effect of the Third Stage. Table 4 shows results using two kinds of heatmap post-processing operations in the third stage. And we can see that by introducing the integral regression, the model performance improve a large margin compared with taking maximum as the post-processing operation. We believe that such an improvement results from the differentiable integral regression operation. By using it, the estimated fixation coordinate can be regressed in the training procedure and thus we can use the ground truth coordinate directly as supervision without transforming it to the intermediate form like heatmap. Due to such a direct supervision, the model can learn to attain a more accurate estimation and then benefits the model performance.

Discussions. Here we want to summary some insights on designing or improving the two-pathway architecture for gaze following. Firstly, the first stage, which

Table 4. Comparision among using different heatmap post-processing operations

Heatmap post-processing operation	Normalized L2 distance	Angular error
Argmax	0.234	35.3°
Integral regression	**0.214**	**33.0°**

acts as a feature extractor, needs strong representation power such as utilizing stronger CNN backbone to extract the information of the scene image and the face image. Secondly, a proper fusion strategy is of great importance to produce the heatmap, which should be able to help remove the noises produced by single pathway. Lastly, we need a post-processing step from the estimated heatmap to the 2D Cartesian coordinates. And the heuristic insight about post-processing step consists two aspects. One is that the "coarse-to-fine" idea to refine the result, like the introduced integral regression. Secondly, both coarse and fine-grained ground truth can be used as supervision in learning process, such as the Gaussian heatmap and 2D coordinate ground truth.

Compared with Baseline and State-of-the-art Algorithms. To further demonstrate our model's superior performance, we also compare our model with several baseline algorithms as well as the origin two-pathway model proposed in [1]. In the origin two-pathway model, they adopt AlexNet as the pathway's backbone network in the first stage, element-wise product as fusion mechanism and take-maximum operation in the third stage. Note that the performance of the baseline algorithms summarized in Table 5 are reported in [1]. More details please refer to that paper. Moreover, while reimplementing the two-pathway model in that paper, we do not use the shift-grid strategy proposed by [1] in all experiments for a fair comparison, so that the performance of the reimplemented model is lower than that reported in the origin paper.

Table 5. Comparision with baselines and state-of-the-art

Model	Normalized L2 distance	Angular error
Random	0.484	69°
Center	0.313	49°
Fixed bias	0.306	48°
Judd [17]	0.337	54°
Recasens [1]	0.270	42°
Ours	**0.214**	**33°**

Ablation Study. Also, we want to see whether both two pathways can provide some cues to benefit the task of gaze following. So we conduct an ablation study by removing one pathway to see how the performance changes. Results are shown in Table 6. It shows that while removing the saliency or gaze pathway, the model's performance drops, which shows both two pathway is both essential in the model.

Table 6. Ablation study

Model	Normalized L2 distance	Angular error
Only preserve gaze pathway	0.232	35°
Only preserve saliency pathway	0.260	40°
Two-pathway	**0.214**	**33°**

Qualitative Results. In Fig. 3, some qualitative results on GazeFollow dataset are shown, from which we can see the proposed method can estimate the subject's fixation under various scenarios.

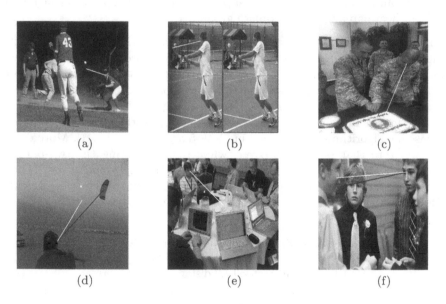

(a)   (b)   (c)

(d)   (e)   (f)

Fig. 3. Qualitative results. The blue line is the ground truth gaze vector and the white line is the estimated gaze vector (Color figure onlline)

5   Conclusion

In this paper, we divide the common two-pathway model for gaze following into three stages and find out the best mechanisms through extensive experiments on benchmark dataset, which can provide some insights on better designing or improving the two-pathway model architecture for gaze following.

Acknowledgements. This work was supported by the National Natural Science Foundation of P.R. China Under Grant Nos. 61772574 and 61375080.

References

1. Recasens, A., Khosla, A., Vondrick, C., Torralba, A.: Where are they looking? In: Advances in Neural Information Processing Systems (NIPS) (2015)
2. Jiang, M., Huang, S., Duan, J., et al.: Salicon: saliency in context. In: Proceedings of the IEEE Conference on Computer Vision and Pattern Recognition, pp. 1072–1080 (2015)
3. Krafka, K., Khosla, A., Kellnhofer, P., et al.: Eye tracking for everyone. In: Proceedings of the IEEE Conference on Computer Vision and Pattern Recognition, pp. 2176–2184 (2016)
4. Recasens, A., Vondrick, C., Khosla, A., Torralba, A.: Following gaze in video. In: IEEE International Conference on Computer Vision (2017)
5. Chong, E., Ruiz, N., et al.: Connecting gaze, scene, and attention: generalized attention estimation via joint modeling of gaze and scene saliency. In: The European Conference on Computer Vision (2018)
6. He K, Zhang X, Ren S, et al.: Deep residual learning for image recognition. In: Proceedings of the IEEE Conference on Computer Vision and Pattern Recognition, pp. 770–778 (2016)
7. Itti, L., Koch, C., Niebur, E.: A model of saliency-based visual attention for rapid scene analysis. IEEE Trans. Pattern Anal. Mach. Intell. **20**(11), 1254–1259 (1998)
8. Deng, J., Dong, W., Socher, R., et al.: ImageNet: a large-scale hierarchical image database. In: IEEE Conference on Computer Vision and Pattern Recognition, pp. 248–255 (2009)
9. Matthias, K., Lucas, T., Matthias, B.: Deep gaze I: boosting saliency prediction with feature maps trained on imagenet. CoRR, vol.abs/1411.1045 (2014)
10. Kruthiventi, S.S., Ayush, K., et al.: DeepFix: a fully convolutional neural network for predicting human eye fixations. IEEE Trans. Image Process. **26**(9), 4446–4455 (2017)
11. Krizhevsky, A., Sutskever, I., Hinton, G.: ImageNet classification with deep convolutional neural networks. Adv. Neural Inf. Process. Syst. **25**(2), 1097–1105 (2012)
12. Simonyan, K., Zisserman, A.: Very deep convolutional networks for large-scale image recognition. CoRR, vol.abs/1409.1556 (2014)
13. Sun, X., Xiao, B., Liang, S., et al.: Integral human pose regression. CoRR, vol. abs/1711.08229 (2017)
14. Lin, T.Y., et al.: Microsoft COCO: common objects in context. In: Fleet, D., Pajdla, T., Schiele, B., Tuytelaars, T. (eds.) ECCV 2014. LNCS, vol. 8693, pp. 740–755. Springer, Cham (2014). https://doi.org/10.1007/978-3-319-10602-1_48
15. Everingham, M., Van Gool, L., Williams, C.K., Winn, J., Zisserman, A.: The pascal visual object classes (VOC) challenge. Int. J. Comput. Vis. **88**(2), 303–338 (2010)
16. Pytorch: tensors and dynamic neural networks in python with strong GPU acceleration. https://github.com/pytorch/pytorch. Accessed 03 Nov 2017
17. Judd, T., Ehinger, K., Durand, F., et al.: Learning to predict where humans look. In: Proceedings of the 2009 IEEE International Conference on Computer Vision (2009)
18. Sourabh, V., Akshay, R., Trivedi, M.M.: Gaze zone estimation using convolutional neural networks: a general framework and ablative analysis. IEEE Trans. Intell. Veh. **3**(3), 254–265 (2018)

19. Cheng, M.M., Mitra, N.J., Huang, X., et al.: Global contrast based salient region detection. IEEE Trans. Pattern Anal. Mach. Intell. **37**(3), 569–582 (2018)
20. Saran, A., Majumdar, S., Shor, E.S., et al.: Human gaze following for human-robot interaction. In: IEEE/RSJ International Conference on Intelligent Robots and Systems (IROS), pp. 8615–8621 (2018)
21. Zhao, J.X., Cao, Y., Cheng, M.M., et al.: Contrast prior and fluid pyramid integration for RGBD salient object detection. In: Proceedings of the IEEE International Conference on Computer Vision (2019)

Multi-modal Feature Fusion Based on Variational Autoencoder for Visual Question Answering

Liqing Chen, Yifan Zhuo, Yingjie Wu, Yilei Wang[(⊠)], and Xianghan Zheng

College of Mathematics and Computer Science, Fuzhou University,
Fuzhou, Fujian Province, China
yilei@fzu.edu.cn

Abstract. Visual Question Answering (VQA) tasks must provide correct answers to the questions posed by given images. Such requirement has been a wide concern since this task was presented. VQA consists of four steps: image feature extraction, question text feature extraction, multi-modal feature fusion and answer reasoning. During multi-modal feature fusion, outer product calculation is used in existing models, which leads to excessive model parameters, high training overhead, and slow convergence. To avoid these problems, we applied the Variational Autoencoder (VAE) method to calculate the probability distribution of the hidden variables of image and question text. Furthermore, we designed a question feature hierarchy method based on the traditional attention mechanism model and VAE. The objective is to investigate deep questions and image correlation features to improve the accuracy of VQA tasks.

Keywords: Visual Question Answering · Multi-modal feature fusion · Variational Auroencoder · Attention mechanism

1 Introduction

Visual Question Answering (VQA) [1] tasks must provide correct answers to the questions posed by given images. In comparison with the traditional Question Answering system, the search and reasoning parts must be based on the image content. This system contains the knowledge of target location detection, scene classification and knowledge reasoning. VQA tasks can be easily expanded to other tasks and play a significant role in various practical scenarios such as automobile navigation, medical system and education system.

In this paper, we propose a multi-modal feature fusion method for combining image and question features. The central idea is to use Variational Autoencoder

Student Paper. This work is supported by the Natural Science Foundation of Fujian Province of China (2017J01754). This work is supported by the Natural Science Foundation of Fujian Province of China (2018J01799).

Z. Lin et al. (Eds.): PRCV 2019, LNCS 11858, pp. 657–669, 2019.
https://doi.org/10.1007/978-3-030-31723-2_56

(VAE) [2] to calculate the hidden coding of image and question features and then fuse them in the hidden layer to obtain the associated image and question representations for improved answer reasoning. We use the fusion method to the basic model and verify its validity on the VQA 2.0 dataset. Subsequently, in decoding the attention weight, the sampling method is added to the attention mechanism of VQA tasks to increase randomness and the hierarchical attention mechanism model is designed by using hidden variables, and a further generalized attention mechanism weighting matrix, which can weight image and question features, is generated. Experimental results show that our model further improves the accuracy of VQA tasks.

The remainder of this paper is presented as follows: In Sect. 2, we introduce the relevant work in recent years. In Sect. 3, we present the implementation details of the model. In Sect. 4, we compare basic models and our model on VQA 2.0 dataset. In Sect. 5, we conclude this paper.

2   Related Work

2.1   Visual Question Answering

VQA tasks have been proposed in 2015. In recent studies, majority of the methods in VQA are based on neural networks. Convolution Neural Networks (CNNs) [3] are generally used to extract image features, whereas Recurrent Neural Networks (RNNs) [4] are utilized to extract question features. Then, the two features are fused to form a new feature, which is used for answer reasoning (see Fig. 1).

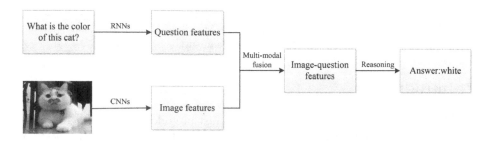

Fig. 1. Simple model of the VQA task.

Recently, most VQA tasks use VGGNet [5] and ResNet [6] to extract image features. Girshick et al. [7] proposed the use of Fast Region-based Convolutional Network (Fast-R-CNN)to extract image features consisting of multiple objects and obtained new state-of-the-art results. By contrast, almost all VQA models use GRU [8] and LSTM [9] to extract question features. These two models can efficiently obtain the question contextual information. Multi-model feature fusion is a method for associate images with question textual information.

Fukui et al. [10] first introduced the bilinear model into multi-modal feature fusion in VQA. They proposed the Multi-modal Compact Bilinear (MCB) pooling method and achieved good results. Then Yu et al. [11] designed a Multi-modal Factorized High-order (MFH) pooling method to improve the result further.

VQA reasoning method is simple. We must develop a limited quantity answer set in accordance with the frequency of the answers and perform classification tasks on it.

2.2   Attention Mechanism

Recently, attention mechanism, which finds the most deserving word or phrase in the text, has been successfully applied in the field of natural language processing. In the VQA task, researchers use the attention mechanism to discover picture areas that are most related to the semantic information of the question (see Fig. 2).

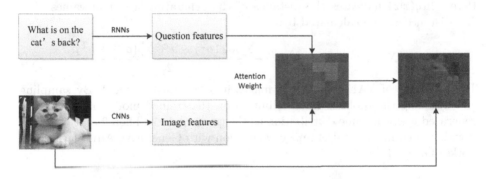

Fig. 2. Simple attention mechanism model for VQA.

[12] proposed a question-oriented image attention mechanism. This method assigns attention weights to image features based on the question features. [13] introduced a collaborative attention mechanism to associated images and questions that became the baseline method at that time. [14] firstly introduced the multi-objective feature extraction method in the field of target detection into the VQA model and named it as bottom-up attention. Compared with the method of weighting the attention of the whole image, this model can directly focus on the image target itself by weighting the entire object's attention, which has been significantly improved and has become one of the best models in the field of VQA.

2.3   Variational Autoencoder

VAE is a probabilistic approximation model based on variational inference and autoencoder structure. Suppose two variables x and z, the variational inference uses simple distribution $q(z)$ to approximate complex posterior distribution

$p(z|x)$ and Kullback-Leibler (KL) distance for measuring the distance between probability distributions:

$$KL(q(z)\|\mathrm{p}(z|x)) = \int q(z)\ln\frac{q(z)}{p(z|x)}dz \qquad (1)$$

The smaller the KL distance, the closer the two probability distributions are. The goal is to minimize the KL distance. Further derivation form is as follows:

$$\ln p(x) - KL(q(z)\|p(z|x)) = \int q(z)\ln p(x|z)dz - KL(q(z)\|p(z)) \qquad (2)$$

VAE assumes that $q(z)$ obeys a normal distribution $N\left(\mu,\sigma^2\right)$, and $p(z)$ obeys a normal distribution $N(0, I)$. The optimization objectives of the model can be expressed as:

$$L = E_{x\sim p(x)}[-\ln q(x|z) + KL(p(z|x)\|q(z))], z \sim p(z|x) \qquad (3)$$

Here,$-\ln q(x|z)$ indicates the distance of the generating and real values. The KL distance can be calculated by:

$$KL\left(N\left(\mu,\sigma^2\right)\|N(0, I)\right) = \frac{-\sum\log\left(\sigma^2\right) - d + \sum\left(\sigma^3\right) + \mu^T\mu}{2} \qquad (4)$$

The structure of VAE (see Fig. 3) makes it a generating model. By sampling and decoding the probability distribution on the trained model, new data are generated with the same distribution as the training data. Therefore, this model is widely used in the field of image generation with Generative Adversarial Networks (GAN) [15].

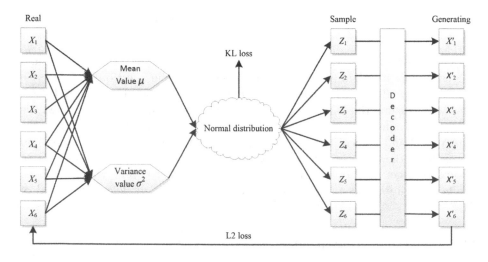

Fig. 3. Model of the Variational Autoencoder.

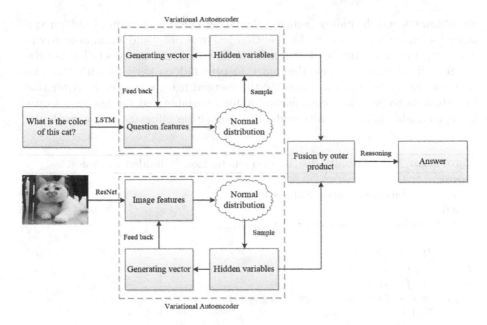

Fig. 4. Structure of multi-modal feature fusion model.

3 Proposed Method

3.1 Multi-modal Feature Fusion

Traditional VQA fusion methods only consider the external representation of features instead of the important hidden links between images and questions, thereby losing information during fusion.

Currently, multi-modal feature fusion methods are based on the calculation of the outer product or approximate outer product of the features. This case limits the scope of application because numerous parameters and computational loads are required during calculation, and the dimension reduction methods of the optimization calculation process are sensitive to the super-parameters and slow convergence speed of the model.

Our first work is to attempt to use VAE to solve the above-mentioned problem (see Fig. 4). In this model, we use ResNet to extract image features and LSTM to extract question features. Then we apply the VAE model mentioned in Sect. 2.3 to calculate the hidden vector probability distribution of the features. Finally, the hidden variables of features are sampled and fused.

The algorithm for calculating the probability distribution of hidden variables is shown as Algorithm 1. The extracted image hidden variables are multiplied by the question hidden variables and the results are input into the full connection layer. By locally adjusting the model structure, several different models are obtained, which mainly include calculating the distribution of hidden variables for image features only, for question features only, and simultaneously for image features and question features. In order to ensure the association between image and question, we fuse the image feature hidden variable with the question feature hidden variable, then use the merged feature to decode. After that, we attempts to fuse the image feature hidden variable and the question feature hidden variable into the multi-modal decomposition bilinear pooling method.

Algorithm 1. Probability distribution calculation of hidden variables.

Input:
image features or question features, F
Output:
Distribution parameters of latent variables, (μ, σ);
loss value, $loss$;
1: $f \leftarrow \text{Relu}(W_I F + b_I)$;
2: $\mu \leftarrow W_\mu f + b_\mu$;
3: $\sigma \leftarrow W_\sigma f + b_\sigma$;
4: $kld\_loss \leftarrow \frac{1}{2}\left(1 - \|\mu\|^2 - \|\sigma\|^2 - \log\left(\sigma^2\right)\right)$;
5: $z \sim N(0, I)$;
6: $z' \leftarrow \mu + \sigma z$;
7: $F' \leftarrow W_{F2}(W_{FI} z' + b_{FI}) + b_{F2}$;
8: $l2\_loss \leftarrow \|F - F'\|^2$
9: $loss \leftarrow kld\_loss + l2\_loss$
10: **return** (μ, σ), $loss$;

3.2 Variational Attention Mechanism

Our second work is to introduce a variational attention mechanism in the process of multi-modal feature fusion to reduce the complexity of the parameters.

We use Faster-R-CNN to extract multi-target features from images. Then, an implicit variable model of attention is established on the basis of bottom-up attention mechanism model and variational inference. Finally, a method for the multi-sample fusion of attention weighted features is designed (see Fig. 5).

For a further a generalized expression of attention weight of the feature of local question, the feature of the question text need to be generated hierarchically. However, the above model still directly calculates the attention weight for the image many times, and the number of parameters required for the untreated image will lead to inefficiency, then we sampled the hidden variables of the image several times. Therefore, we sampled the hidden variables of the image several times, and calculated the attention weight of the image features by combining with the previous features of each layer. The number of parameters can be greatly reduced and the training speed of the model can be improved due to the low dimension of the problem text features after hidden variable coding and layering (see Fig. 6). Algorithm 2 shows the algorithm for question feature hierarchy.

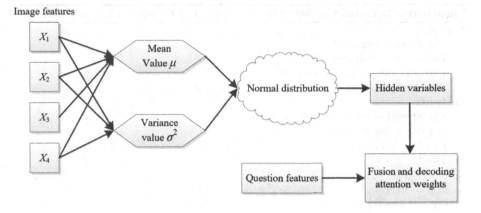

Fig. 5. Calculation of attention weight with VAE.

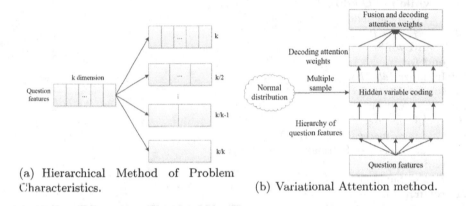

(a) Hierarchical Method of Problem Characteristics.

(b) Variational Attention method.

Fig. 6. Variational attention mechanism model.

4 Experiment

4.1 Datasets

The dataset used in the experiment is test-dev of VQA 2.0. The images are obtained from MS-COCO dataset, including 123,287 images, of which 72,738 are used for training and 38,948 for testing. Each image has a corresponding question and answer. The evaluation of answers can be divided into three types: yes/no, number and others. The three types correspond to judgment, counting and open questions respectively. On the VQA2.0 dataset, the calculation of accuracy rate does not directly measure the proportion of the correct answered samples. The calculation formula is as follows:

$$Acc = \frac{1}{M} \sum_{i=1}^{M} \min \left\{ \frac{\text{human that provided that answer}}{3}, 1 \right\} \qquad (5)$$

Algorithm 2. Variational attention mechanism for question feature hierarchy.

Input:

    The image features, I;

    The question features, F;

    The question features length, k;

    The threshold of KL, r;

Output:

    The attention weight matrix, $Iatt$;

    loss value, $loss$;

1: $f \leftarrow \text{Relu}\,(W_1 I + b_1)$;

2: $\mu \leftarrow W_\mu f + b_\mu$;

3: $\sigma \leftarrow W_\sigma f + b_\sigma$;

4: $loss \leftarrow \max\left(r, \frac{1}{2}\left(1 - \|\mu\|^2 - \|\sigma\|^2 - \log\left(\sigma^2\right)\right)\right)$;

5: **for** $i = 1$ to k **do**

6:     Initialize $Q\_$ Level $_i$;

7:     $j = 0$;

8:     **while** $j < |Q_i|$ **do**

9:         $Q\_\text{Level}_i.\text{add}\,(Q_{i,j})$;

10:       $j = j + i$;

11:     **end while**

12: **end for**

13: Initialize $Iatt\_Level$

14: **for** $i = 1$ to k **do**

15:    $z \sim N(0, I)$;

16:    $z' \leftarrow \mu + \sigma z$;

17:    $Q\_z \leftarrow \text{merge}\,(Q\_Level_i, z')$

18:    $Iatt\_Level_i \leftarrow \text{Softmax}\,(\text{Conv}\,(Q\_z))$

19: **end for**

20: $Iatt \leftarrow \text{Sumpooing}(\frac{Iatt\_Level}{k})$

21: **return** $Iatt, loss$;

where M represents the total number of tested samples, and "humans that provided that answer" indicates the number of answers predicted by the model consistent with those manually collected by VQA 2.0.

4.2 Configurations

In the training process of this study, the neural networks built by different models use uniform hyperparameters. Table 1 shows the key parameters, in which Weight_VQAVae denotes the weights used in the multi-modal feature fusion method. Weight_VQAVaeAtt indicates the weights used in variational attention mechanism.

4.3 Results

Multi-modal Feature Fusion Results. The different structures of the local model are as follows, and Table 2 shows the experimental results.

Table 1. Key parameters of our methods.

Parameters	Weight_VQAVae	Weight_VQAVae Att
Batch Size	128	64
Loss	KLDivloss	KLDivloss
Learning rate	0.001	0.007
Learning rate decay	0.5	0.5
Decay step	20000	20000
Training interval	60000	100000
Drop	0.5	0.5
Hidden code size	128	128
Variational weight	-	0.000005
Image number	-	36
Optimizer	Momentum	Momentum

Table 2. Experimental results of multi-modality feature fusion method.

I_h	Q_h	Concat	OP	Merge	Yes/No	Number	Others	All
		✓			74.14	36.18	45.45	55.02
✓		✓			75.32	35.84	45.12	55.25
	✓	✓			75.45	35.85	44.21	54.74
✓	✓	✓			74.85	36.13	45.09	55.09
✓			✓		76.55	37.24	47.06	56.85
	✓		✓		76.39	36.56	45.28	56.02
✓	✓		✓		77.09	36.66	45.33	56.24
✓	✓			✓	77.73	36.74	48.36	57.87
✓			✓	✓	**77.68**	**37.56**	**48.37**	**58.01**

* I_h: Image feature hidden variable
* Q_h: Problem feature hidden variable
* Concat: Fusion feature using stitching method
* $OuterProduct(OP)$: Fusion feature using outer product method
* Merge: Binding of hidden variables based on bilinear pooling

Experimental results show that implicit vector coding using image features, encoding without question features, and multi-modal feature fusion using outer products are significant improvements in the accuracy of the VQA model. We rename $I\_h + Q + OP + Merge$ with the best experimental results on the model as VQAVae, jointly use the training and verification sets to train the model, and evaluate the model accuracy on the test set. Table 3 shows the results compared with the existing basic VQA model.

Table 3. VQAVae compared with existing base models.

Method	Yes/No	Number	Others	All
IBOWING [16]	76.5	35.0	42.6	55.7
DPPnet [17]	80.7	37.2	41.7	57.2
Norm LSTM I+Q [1]	80.5	36.8	43.1	57.8
AYN [18]	78.4	36.4	46.3	58.4
AMA [19]	81.0	38.4	45.2	59.2
MCB [10]	81.2	35.1	49.3	60.8
MFB [11]	79.02	39.21	50.57	61.0
VQAVae	**80.92**	**39.69**	**50.92**	**61.48**

Results show that the proposed multi-modal feature fusion method based on variational inference outperforms most of the existing basic VQA models. The possible original meaning is that the question text is a discrete word sequence, and the image features are further continuous. In decoding the new features and calculating the error with the original features, the image features can be efficiently restored to the original features. During training, the difference value can be easily optimized as part of the loss value, so that the coding probability of the hidden variable coding can be calculated further accurately.

Variational Attention Mechanism Results. We name the used methods as follow:

* ResNet (Res): Extracting image features using a residual network
* Fast-R-CNN (FRC): Extracting multi-target image features using Fast-R-CNN
* Qatt: Problem-oriented self-attention mechanism
* Iatt: Problem-oriented attention mechanism for images
* Concat: Splicing combines multiple sampling features
* Average (Ave): Weighted average blends multiple sampling features.

Table 4 presents the compared experimental results. Then we rename VQAVaeAtt as the model with the best experimental results on the verification, jointly use the training and verification sets to train the model, and calculate the model accuracy on the test set. Table 5 shows the results compared with the existing basic VQA model.

The proposed attention mechanism method based on VAE outperforms most existing VQA models. Because (1) the attention mechanism is modeled as an implicit variable model and the probability distribution of attention weight is calculated through VAE; (2) multiple attention weight sampling is added to the model and (3) the attention weight of image is calculated combined with the feature information of subsection questions, which is helpful for obtaining additional information. To sum up, modeling the effective method to model the attention mechanism as an implicit variable model based on the complete image attention weighted feature is a novel and effective method.

Table 4. Experimental results of the variational attention method

Res	FRC	Iatt	Qatt	Concat	Ave	Yes/No	Number	Others	All
✓						77.68	37.56	48.37	58.01
✓		✓				78.64	38.37	49.9	60.43
	✓	✓				80.11	40.28	52.7	61.35
	✓	✓	✓			80.05	41.77	52.64	61.53
	✓	✓	✓	✓		80.42	41.04	53.68	52.15
	✓	✓	✓		✓	**80.4**	**40.67**	**54.13**	**62.23**

Table 5. VQAVaeAtt compared with existing base models.

Method	Yes/No	Number	Others	All
DPPnet [18]	80.7	37.2	41.7	57.2
SMem [12]	80.9	37.3	43.1	58.0
NMN [20]	81.2	38.0	44.0	58.6
SAN [13]	81.1	36.6	46.1	58.7
HieCoAtt [21]	79.7	38.7	51.7	61.8
MRN [22]	81.9	39.0	53.0	63.18
MCB [10]	82.2	37.7	54.8	64.2
VQAVaeAtt	**81.79**	**42.76**	**55.5**	**64.89**

5   Conclusion

This study investigates the feature fusion of VQA, including multi-modal feature fusion and attention mechanism. VAE is introduced to overcome the limitations of existing methods, and greatly improves the accuracy of the VQA model. The main contribution of this work includes two parts:

The VAE is introduced to calculate the probability distribution of hidden variables of image and question text features, and a multi-modal feature fusion method based on hidden variables is designed to reduce the computational complexity of the model effectively. Furthermore, the random sampling increases the anti-over-fitting of the model. Comparative experiments show that the model effectively improves the accuracy of VQA tasks.

We attempted to introduce a variational attention mechanism in the process of multi-modal feature fusion. Based on the VAE model, the question text information is used to guide the autoencoding of image features in accordance with their attention weights. As such, a hierarchical attention mechanism, which effectively reduces the number of parameters required by the model, is established. The comparative experiments show that the variational attention mechanism can further improve the model accuracy in VQA tasks.

References

1. Agrawal, A., et al.: AQA: visual question answering. Int. J. Comput. Vis. **123**, 4–31 (2017)
2. Kingma, D.P., Welling, M.: Auto-encoding variational bayes. arXiv preprint arXiv:1312.6114 (2013)
3. Krizhevsky, A., Sutskever, I., Hinton, G.E.: ImageNet classification with deep convolutional neural networks. In: Advances in Neural Information Processing Systems, pp. 1097–1105 (2012)
4. Elman, J.L.: Finding structure in time. Cogn. Sci. **14**, 179–211 (1990)
5. Simonyan, K., Zisserman, A.: Very deep convolutional networks for large-scale image recognition. arXiv preprint arXiv:1409.1556 (2014)
6. He, K., Zhang, X., Ren, S., Sun, J.: Deep residual learning for image recognition. In: Proceedings of the IEEE Conference on Computer Vision and Pattern Recognition, pp. 770–778 (2016)
7. Girshick, R.: Fast R-CNN. In: Proceedings of the IEEE International Conference on Computer Vision, pp. 1440–1448 (2015)
8. Cho, K., et al.: Learning phrase representations using RNN encoder-decoder for statistical machine translation. arXiv preprint arXiv:1406.1078 (2014)
9. Donahue, J., et al.: Long-term recurrent convolutional networks for visual recognition and description. In: Proceedings of the IEEE Conference on Computer Vision and Pattern Recognition, pp. 2625–2634 (2015)
10. Fukui, A., Park, D.H., Yang, D., Rohrbach, A., Darrell, T., Rohrbach, M.: Multimodal compact bilinear pooling for visual question answering and visual grounding. arXiv preprint arXiv:1606.01847 (2016)
11. Yu, Z., Yu, J., Xiang, C., Fan, J., Tao, D.: Beyond bilinear: generalized multimodal factorized high-order pooling for visual question answering. IEEE Trans. Neural Netw. Learn. Syst. **14**, 1–13 (2018)
12. Xu, H., Saenko, K.: Ask, attend and answer: exploring question-guided spatial attention for visual question answering. In: Leibe, B., Matas, J., Sebe, N., Welling, M. (eds.) ECCV 2016. LNCS, vol. 9911, pp. 451–466. Springer, Cham (2016). https://doi.org/10.1007/978-3-319-46478-7_28
13. Yang, Z., He, X., Gao, J., Deng, L., Smola, A.: Stacked attention networks for image question answering. In: Proceedings of the IEEE conference on computer vision and pattern recognition, pp. 21–29 (2016)
14. Anderson, P., et al.: Bottom-up and top-down attention for image captioning and visual question answering. In: Proceedings of the IEEE Conference on Computer Vision and Pattern Recognition, pp. 6077–6086 (2018)
15. Goodfellow, I., et al.: Generative adversarial nets. In: Advances in Neural Information Processing Systems, pp. 2672–2680 (2014)

16. Zhou, B., Tian, Y., Sukhbaatar, S., Szlam, A., Fergus, R.: Simple baseline for visual question answering. arXiv preprint arXiv:1512.02167 (2015)
17. Noh, H., Hongsuck Seo, P., Han, B.: Image question answering using convolutional neural network with dynamic parameter prediction. In: Proceedings of the IEEE conference on computer vision and pattern recognition, pp. 30–38 (2016)
18. Malinowski, M., Rohrbach, M., Fritz, M.: Ask your neurons: a neural-based approach to answering questions about images. In: Proceedings of the IEEE international conference on computer vision, pp. 1–9 (2015)
19. Wu, Q., Wang, P., Shen, C., Dick, A., van den Hengel, A.: Ask me anything: free-form visual question answering based on knowledge from external sources. In: Proceedings of the IEEE Conference on Computer Vision and Pattern Recognition, pp. 4622–4630 (2016)
20. Andreas, J., Rohrbach, M., Darrell, T., Klein, D.: Neural module networks. In: Proceedings of the IEEE Conference on Computer Vision and Pattern Recognition, pp. 39–48 (2015)
21. Lu, J., Yang, J., Batra, D., Parikh, D.: Hierarchical question-image co-attention for visual question answering. In: Advances In Neural Information Processing Systems, pp. 289–297 (2016)
22. Noh, H., Han, B.: Training recurrent answering units with joint loss minimization for VQA. arXiv preprint arXiv:1606.03647 (2016)

Local and Global Feature Learning for Subtle Facial Expression Recognition from Attention Perspective

Shaocong Wang[1,2], Yuan Yuan[3], and Yachuang Feng[1(✉)]

[1] Key Laboratory of Spectral Imaging Technology CAS, Xi'an Institute of Optics and Precision Mechanics, Chinese Academy of Sciences, Xi'an 710119, China
yachuang.feng@gmail.com
[2] University of Chinese Academy of Sciences, Beijing 100049, China
wangshaocong17@mails.ucas.ac.cn
[3] Center for Optical Imagery Analysis and Learning,
Northwestern Polytechnical University, Xi'an, China
y.yuan1.ieee@gmail.com

Abstract. Subtle facial expression recognition is important for emotion analysis. In the field of subtle facial expression recognition, there are two intrinsic characters. Firstly, subtle facial expression usually exhibits very small variations in different facial areas. Secondly, those small variations are closely correlated, and they together form an expression. Inspired by these two characteristics of facial expression, a model focus on local variations and their correlations is proposed in this paper. We utilize several attention maps to automatically attend to distinct local regions and extract local features. And then, a self-attention operation is ensembled to extract global correlation feature over the whole image. The global and local features are further fused in an efficient way to classify the facial expression. Extensive experiments have been carried out on LSEMSW and CK+ datasets.

Keywords: Subtle facial expression recognition · Attention

1 Introduction

Facial expression is a kind of nonverbal communication, which plays a vital role in revealing human inner thoughts and emotions. Therefore, facial expression recognition (FER) can benefit a wide range of applications such as human computer interaction [22], pain detection [13], and detection of drowsy driver [6]. Traditional macro facial expression recognition is to handle posed, exaggerated expressions in lab conditions, which has already been well studied. Subtle expression refers to expressions with low intensity, which can be considered as hard

---

The first author is a Master's student.

© Springer Nature Switzerland AG 2019
Z. Lin et al. (Eds.): PRCV 2019, LNCS 11858, pp. 670–681, 2019.
https://doi.org/10.1007/978-3-030-31723-2_57

examples of traditional facial expression. It has smaller inter-class distance and large intra-class distance, making recognition process much more difficult. In this paper we mainly deal with subtle expressions, and also transfer our model to traditional macro facial expression recognition.

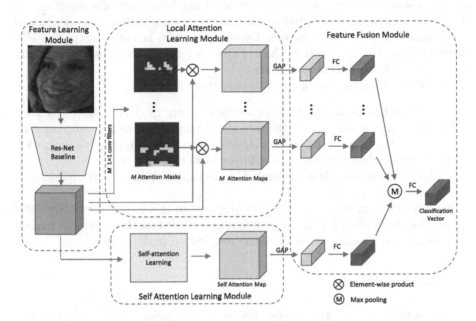

Fig. 1. The over-all framework of our model. An aligned image is first feed into feature learning module to extract basic feature map. In local attention learning module, M 1×1 conv filters are implemented to get M local attention maps, which is to extract M attention maps through element-wise product. The self attention learning module is to get correlations between local facial parts. In the feature fusion module, the M attention maps and self attention map are first pooled into $M + 1$ vectors through global average pooling (GAP). Then each vector is feed into a distinct fully connected (FC) layer. Subsequently, the resulting $M + 1$ vectors are max-pooled to a single vector, which is used to recognize subtle expressions.

Although many methods based on hand-crafted features have been developed for traditional FER, they are not suitable for real-world subtle expression recognition tasks, due to their limited discriminative power. With the rapid development of artificial intelligence and machine learning, approaches based on deep learning have become dominating and achieved huge progress in the field of FER. However, most of them failed to exploit the local facial variations and their correlation, which are crucial for subtle expression recognition. Li et al. [9] ensembled an edge filter in their CNN to capture detail informations like wrinkles and muscle contours. However, edge can be very noisy, and is a low level feature containing little semantic informations. Chen et al. [3] directly clipped the face and only extracted three regions of interest, *i.e.*, eyebrows, eyes and mouth, which could be very lossy.

In contrast with the previous methods, we make use of local variations and their strong correlation. In this paper, attention mechanism is utilized to focus on the salient local parts, which is widely used in communities of natural language processing and computer vision. Moreover, in contrast to the basic convolutional operation which only takes into account local neighborhood of a position, self attention mechanism is adopted to efficiently compute global dependency and correlation of different local regions. By utilizing multi attention maps and self-attention map, the proposed method is able to leverage the local features and global correlation of an expressed face.

The main contributions of this work are three fold:

- A novel multi-attention module is introduced in our model to retrieve the local features automatically. To make sure the attention masks not concentrating on an identical local area, we implemented a non-overlapping regularization to encourage them attending to different local regions.
- A self-attention module is ensembled in the model to discover the correlation of different local parts.
- An efficient feature fusion method is proposed in this paper to combine local and global attention features. It can significantly reduce the amount of parameters and simultaneously enhance the recognition performance.

2   Related Work

In this section, we will give a brief review on the prior works related to our model, covering the ideas of feature merging in face-related tasks, and attention mechanism.

2.1   Feature Merging in Face-Related Tasks

The thought of combining local and global features of face existed in the literature since hand-crafted era. Liao et al. [11] used extended LBP and Tsallis entropy to extract texture local features and null-space based LDA to acquire discriminating global appearance features. Kakumanu et al. [8] embedded both local and global information in a graph perspective with each node in graph as a facial region and the whole graph as a face. Su et al. [20] exploited Fourier transform to encode the holistic facial information, and Gabor wavelets to encode the local features. Then, Fisher's linear discriminant is applied separately to the global and each local feature. Finally, all the classifiers are combined to form the ensemble classifier.

2.2   Attention Mechanism

Attention mechanism is a prevailing bio-inspired method to focus more detail on certain regions of the input and filter out irrelevant information. Recently attention mechanism has been successfully used in image caption [2], fine-grained image recognition [26], and multiple object recognition [1]. In [18], a face is partitioned into blocks, and reinforcement learning is exploited to learn an attention control strategy. Juefei-Xu et al. [7] used training samples of multiple blur levels to enforce the attention shift.

As for self attention, for a position in the image or sequence, it attends to all positions and takes their weighted average as the response of the certain position. Wang et al. [23] proposed nonlocal operation to grasp the global correlation in video sequences by computing the long distance spatial-temporal dependency of each position. This insight is further utilized in Self-Attention GAN [24], which significantly boosted the performance of Generative Adversarial Networks. In spite of those improvements, self-attention remains unexplored in the context of FER or subtle facial expression recognition.

3   Method

The framework of our proposed model is illustrated in Fig. 1, which is composed of four modules, *i.e.*, feature learning module, local attentions learning module, self attention learning module, and feature fusion module. First of all, the feature learning module is implemented to extract a basic feature map from the input image $I \in \mathbb{R}^{H_{in} \times W_{in} \times 3}$, which would be shared as the input of the next two modules. Therefore this module could be regarded as the foundation of our proposed model. We directly implemented the standard Resnet 50 and used the feature map $F \in \mathbb{R}^{H \times W \times C}$ of *conv 4_1* as output representation of this module for its proper receptive field. H and W is $1/8$ of H_{in} and W_{in}, respectively. Then, a local attention learning module is devised as a multi-branch network to automatically focus on the small variations of different facial parts. Meanwhile, a self attention learning module is designed in parallel with the local attention learning module. It extracts the correlation of variations in different facial parts as the global correlation feature. Finally, a feature fusion module is ensembled to merge the local features and global feature in a proper and efficient way. The details of local attention learning module, self attention learning module and feature fusion module are introduced as follows.

3.1   Local Attention Learning

Different facial parts usually have different patterns, thus we implement M attention filters, each focuses on a certain expression and facial part. For example, one attention filter could be sensitive to frowned brows, and another filter would be aware of narrowed eyes. The local attention learning module is illustrated in Fig. 2. We take the basic feature map from feature learning modules as input. The input feature map is of size $F \in \mathbb{R}^{H \times W \times C}$, where H, W, C refer to height, width, and channel, respectively. We implemented a set of attention masks, each of which attend to a certain region of interest. The attention masks $A \in \mathbb{R}^{H \times W \times M}$ are extracted by 1×1 convolution operation, where M is the number of attention masks, which is also the number of local features.

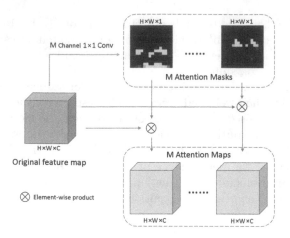

Fig. 2. Local attention learning module. An M channel 1×1 convolution filter takes the origin feature map as input, obtaining M attention masks as output. Each attention mask is then element-wise multiplied with origin feature map, resulting in M attention maps.

The masks are expected to focus on different facial regions that contribute to facial expression recognition. However, those masks may attend to facial regions seriously overlapped, or even attend to an identical region. In order to encourage the masks to focus on distinct facial parts, we implement a regularizer on the masks inspired by diversity loss [21]. Firstly, each mask $\boldsymbol{A}^m$ is normalized so that all its elements sum to 1 as Eq. 1,

$$\bar{A}_{ij}^m = \frac{A_{ij}^m}{\sum_{i,j} A_{ij}^m}. \tag{1}$$

Then, we take the max value along the masks via channel-wise max pooling. Ideally, if all the masks do not overlap with each other, the max projection of M masks should exactly sum to M. Therefore, we formulate the regularization loss as Eq. 2,

$$\mathcal{L}_{reg} = M - \sum_{i,j} \max_{m=1,\dots,M} \bar{A}_{ij}^m. \tag{2}$$

Given M mutual exclusive attention masks, we apply element-wise product between each mask and the input feature map, which results in M attention maps $\boldsymbol{F}_A \in \mathbb{R}^{H \times W \times C}$.

3.2   Self Attention Learning

Convolutional operation only takes into account informations of a local neighborhood. Therefore, we use self attention module to efficiently compute the long-dependency or correlation of local facial regions in subtle facial expression scenario.

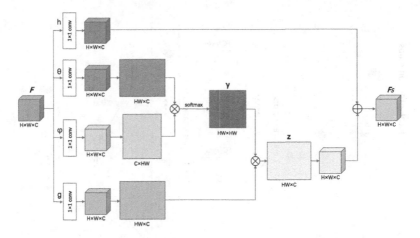

Fig. 3. The self attention learning module is to learn the correlation of different local facial parts. $\otimes$ refers to element-wise product, and $\oplus$ refers to addition.

The self attention learning module is shown in Fig. 3. This module also takes basic feature map $\boldsymbol{F}$ from feature learning module as input. The input feature map $\boldsymbol{F}$ is first flattened as $\bar{\boldsymbol{F}} \in \mathbb{R}^{C \times HW}$, and mapped into two embedded spaces θ and ϕ to extract two global attention masks, where $\theta(\boldsymbol{x}) = \boldsymbol{W}_\theta \boldsymbol{x}$ and $\phi(\boldsymbol{x}) = \boldsymbol{W}_\phi \boldsymbol{x}$ are linear functions. Then dot-product of $\theta(\boldsymbol{x})$ and $\phi(\boldsymbol{x})$ is calculated and further fed into softmax to extract correlations. This process is formulated as Eq. 3,

$$\gamma_{i,j} = \frac{e^{\theta(\boldsymbol{x}_i)^T \phi(\boldsymbol{x}_j)}}{\sum_{j=1,\dots,n} e^{\theta(\boldsymbol{x}_i)^T \phi(\boldsymbol{x}_j)}}, \tag{3}$$

where $\gamma_{i,j}$ implies the effect of j_{th} position to i_{th} position. It can be regarded as the correlation of j_{th} position to i_{th} position. We further calculate $\boldsymbol{z}$ as shown in Eq. 4,

$$\boldsymbol{z}_i = \sum_{j=1}^{n} \gamma_{i,j} g(\boldsymbol{x}_j), \tag{4}$$

where $g(\boldsymbol{x}_j) = \boldsymbol{W}_g \boldsymbol{x}_j$. In practice, the above linear functions $\boldsymbol{W}_\theta \in \mathbb{R}^{\bar{C} \times C}$, $\boldsymbol{W}_\phi \in \mathbb{R}^{\bar{C} \times C}$, and $\boldsymbol{W}_g \in \mathbb{R}^{C \times \bar{C}}$ are implemented by feeding a feature map into 1×1 conv layer, and flattening the output as a representation with size $\mathbb{R}^{HW \times \bar{C}}$ as shown in Fig. 3. We choose $\bar{C} = C/2$ in our experiment. Next, a skip connection is implemented to pass the original feature map,

$$\boldsymbol{s}_i = \boldsymbol{W}_h \boldsymbol{z}_i + \boldsymbol{x}_i, \tag{5}$$

where $\boldsymbol{W}_h \in \mathbb{R}^{\bar{C} \times C}$ is also implemented with 1×1 conv layer. Finally, we get the self attention feature map $\boldsymbol{F}_S \in \mathbb{R}^{H \times W \times C}$ as the global correlation feature.

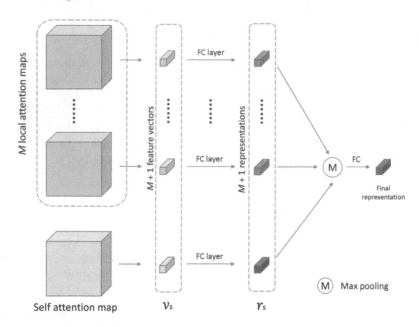

Fig. 4. Our feature fusion module is to efficiently combine the knowledge of local attention maps and self attention map. Firstly, the M attention maps and self attention map are first projected into $M+1$ vectors through global average pooling (GAP). Then, each vector is fed into a distinct fully connected (FC) layer. Moreover, the resulting $M+1$ vectors are max-pooled to a single vector, which is used to recognize subtle expressions.

3.3   Feature Fusion

The input of this module is the concatenation of M local attention maps and a self attention map, which is of size $\mathbb{R}^{H \times W \times C(M+1)}$. Directly feeding this representation into a fully connected layer would significantly boost the magnitude of parameters, and computational load. Therefore, we fuse the knowledge of local attention learning module and self attention learning module in a more efficient way. The proposed feature fusion module is presented in Fig. 4. We first apply Global Average Pooling (GAP) to all the feature maps, which result in $M+1$ feature vectors $v \in \mathbb{R}^{C}$. We then utilize $M+1$ fully connected (FC) layers. Each of them takes a feature vector v as input and outputs a feature representation $r \in \mathbb{R}^{K}$. Those $M+1$ fully connected layers do not connect with each other. We don't directly concatenate the $M+1$ feature vectors as a single vector $u \in \mathbb{R}^{C(M+1)}$ and feed it into a single FC layer, which would increase the quantity of parameter drastically. Those $M+1$ representations r are then max projected into a single feature representation $w \in \mathbb{R}^{K}$, which would further processed to a classification vector through a fully connected layer and softmax.

3.4   Loss Function

In addition to the model design, a proper loss function is also important for the subtle expression recognition. In this paper, our network is trained by simultaneously optimizing two losses:

$$\mathcal{L} = \mathcal{L}_{cls} + \alpha\mathcal{L}_{reg}, \tag{6}$$

where $\mathcal{L}_{cls}$ is a standard cross-entropy loss for classification, and $\mathcal{L}_{reg}$ (discussed in Sect. 3.1) is a regularization loss from local attention learning part to encourage the local attention maps to attend to different facial parts.

4   Experiments

We evaluate the performance of the proposed model on two datasets, namely CK+ [14], and LSEMSW [5]. In this section, we first give a brief description of the datasets and corresponding protocols used in our experiments, and then present the detailed network implementation and evaluation.

4.1   Datasets and Protocols

LSEMSW [5]. It is a newly released subtle expression dataset. Other than traditional Facial Expression Dataset which contains only exaggerated emotions of six basic emotions, LSEMSW consists of 176,000 subtle expression images with 13 emotion classes, *i.e.*, angry, scared, happy, sad, surprised, helpless, indifferent, questioning, anxious, arrogant, hesitant, suspicious, and thinking (Fig. 5). This dataset is much more challenging with huge intraclass distances and small interclass distances. The proposed method mainly tackles this dataset. In our experiment, the dataset is divided into training, validation and test sets by 80%, 10%, 10%, respectively. We report top 1 recognition rate (accuracy) on the test set.

Fig. 5. LSEMSW dataset and its 13 classes of subtle facial expression

CK+ [14]. We also fine-tuned our model on CK+ to demonstrate that it could be generalized to traditional facial expression recognition. CK+ is a widely used classic macro facial expression dataset for evaluation. It contains 327 video sequences of 118 subjects. Each sequence captured a gradual expression evolvement from neutral to peak, where only the last frame is labeled with one of the seven expression, namely angry, happy, surprise, sad, disgust, fear and contempt. In our experiment, only the last frame (apex frame) of each image sequence is used. We follow [5,10] to conduct 5-fold validation on this dataset. As to data augmentation, random horizontal flip in the fly is implemented.

4.2   Implementation Details

Our end-to-end model is implemented with PyTorch. In our experiment, only standard preprocessing is conducted. We first apply the MTCNN [25] to detect face region and the landmarks. The aligned images are then resized and cropped to 128×128 pixels to feed into the proposed network. We choose $M = 5$ and $\alpha = 0.03$ experimentally. During training, Adam optimizer is utilized, the initial learning rate is 0.001, which would be reduced by 10 times if the accuracy does not increase.

Table 1. Accuracy (%) of subtle expression recognition on LSEMSW

Methods		Accuracy
Hand-crafted features	LBP [19]	10.53
	LPQ [4]	10.86
	EOH [16]	13.44
Deep learning methods	Hu et al. [5]	36.72
	Ours (RB)	33.3
	Ours (RB+SA)	36.68
	Ours (RB+LA+FF)	37.27
	Ours (RB+SA+LA+FF)	**37.97**

4.3   Results

Table 1 shows the recognition accuracy on LSEMSW. First, we directly use the basic feature map of resnet backbone (RB) for classification, the accuracy is only 33.30%. And then, we add self attention (SA) module to RB and the performance boosts to 36.68%. Next, we implement local attention (LA) module and feature fusion (FF) module upon RB, the accuracy reaches 37.27%. Finally, we combine all four modules together, the result is 37.97%, which is the best performance on LSEMSW.

From the confusion matrix (Fig. 6), we can observe that the recognition rate on "hesitant" expression is worst because of its amount of samples is least in the dataset. Some of expressions such as "hesitant", "helpless" and "indifferent" are classified as "thinking" because these classes are much more similar, some of those samples are difficult to distinguish even by humans. The relationships between these close classes will be considered in our future work.

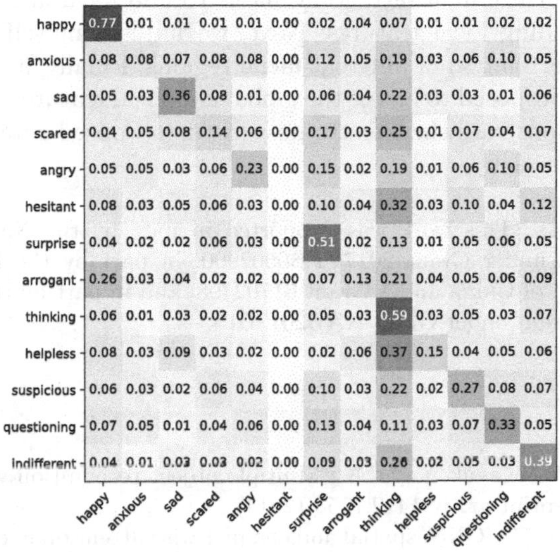

Fig. 6. Confusion matrix in LSEMSW

The experiment result on CK+ dataset is reported in Table 2. Our model pretrained on LSEMSW dataset achieves the best performance among the compared methods. That is because our network could extract discriminative local features and their correlation, which are also important on traditional expression dataset. What's more, it learned knowledge from LSEMSW data, which can be considered as hard examples of traditional facial expression recognition. Therefore, the model can easily recognize the conditioned and exaggerated facial expressions in CK+.

Table 2. Accuracy (%) of traditional FER on CK+

Methods	Accuracy (%)
AUDN [12]	93.7
FP+SAE [15]	91.1
Mollahosseini [17]	93.2
DLP-CNN [10]	95.8
Hu [5]	96.4
Ours (from scratch)	68.0
Ours	**96.9**

5 Conclusion

In this paper, we designed a novel network for subtle facial expression recognition. Our model automatically concentrates on small variations in local facial regions. We first utilize multi-attention masks to find local facial variations and extract corresponding local features. Next, we implement self attention module to learn the correlation of different facial regions. Finally, an efficient feature fusion method is proposed to merge the global and local features. Experiments on two datasets demonstrate the effectiveness of our proposed subtle facial expression recognition model.

Acknowledgments. This work was supported in part by the National Key R&D Program of China under Grant 2017YFB0502900, in part by the National Natural Science Foundation of China under Grant 61702498, and in part by the CAS "Light of West China" Program under Grant XAB2017B15.

References

1. Ba, J., Mnih, V., Kavukcuoglu, K.: Multiple object recognition with visual attention. arXiv preprint arXiv:1412.7755 (2014)
2. Chen, L., et al.: SCA-CNN: spatial and channel-wise attention in convolutional networks for image captioning. In: Proceedings of the IEEE Conference on Computer Vision and Pattern Recognition, pp. 5659–5667 (2017)
3. Chen, L., Zhou, M., Su, W., Wu, M., She, J., Hirota, K.: Softmax regression based deep sparse autoencoder network for facial emotion recognition in human-robot interaction. Inf. Sci. **428**, 49–61 (2018)
4. Dhall, A., Asthana, A., Goecke, R., Gedeon, T.: Emotion recognition using PHOG and LPG features. In: Face and Gesture 2011, pp. 878–883. IEEE (2011)
5. Hu, G., et al.: Deep multi-task learning to recognise subtle facial expressions of mental states. In: Proceedings of the European Conference on Computer Vision (ECCV), pp. 103–119 (2018)
6. Jie, Z., Mahmoud, M., Stafford-Fraser, Q., Robinson, P., Dias, E., Skrypchuk, L.: Analysis of yawning behaviour in spontaneous expressions of drowsy drivers. In: 2018 13th IEEE International Conference on Automatic Face & Gesture Recognition (FG 2018), pp. 571–576. IEEE (2018)
7. Juefei-Xu, F., Verma, E., Goel, P., Cherodian, A., Savvides, M.: Deepgender: occlusion and low resolution robust facial gender classification via progressively trained convolutional neural networks with attention. In: Proceedings of the IEEE conference on computer vision and pattern recognition workshops, pp. 68–77 (2016)
8. Kakumanu, P., Bourbakis, N.: A local-global graph approach for facial expression recognition. In: 2006 18th IEEE International Conference on Tools with Artificial Intelligence (ICTAI 2006), pp. 685–692. IEEE (2006)
9. Li, L., Baltrusaitis, T., Sun, B., Morency, L.P.: Edge convolutional network for facial action intensity estimation. In: 2018 13th IEEE International Conference on Automatic Face & Gesture Recognition (FG 2018), pp. 171–178. IEEE (2018)
10. Li, S., Deng, W., Du, J.: Reliable crowdsourcing and deep locality-preserving learning for expression recognition in the wild. In: Proceedings of the IEEE Conference on Computer Vision and Pattern Recognition. pp. 2852–2861 (2017)

11. Liao, S., Fan, W., Chung, A.C., Yeung, D.Y.: Facial expression recognition using advanced local binary patterns, tsallis entropies and global appearance features. In: 2006 International Conference on Image Processing, pp. 665–668. IEEE (2006)
12. Liu, M., Li, S., Shan, S., Chen, X.: Au-inspired deep networks for facial expression feature learning. Neurocomputing **159**, 126–136 (2015)
13. Lucey, P., Cohn, J., Lucey, S., Matthews, I., Sridharan, S., Prkachin, K.M.: Automatically detecting pain using facial actions. In: 2009 3rd International Conference on Affective Computing and Intelligent Interaction and Workshops, pp. 1–8. IEEE (2009)
14. Lucey, P., Cohn, J.F., Kanade, T., Saragih, J., Ambadar, Z., Matthews, I.: The Extended Cohn-Kanade dataset (CK+): a complete dataset for action unit and emotion-specified expression. In: 2010 IEEE Computer Society Conference on Computer Vision and Pattern Recognition-Workshops, pp. 94–101. IEEE (2010)
15. Lv, Y., Feng, Z., Xu, C.: Facial expression recognition via deep learning. In: 2014 International Conference on Smart Computing, pp. 303–308, November 2014. https://doi.org/10.1109/SMARTCOMP.2014.7043872
16. Meng, H., Romera-Paredes, B., Bianchi-Berthouze, N.: Emotion recognition by two view SVM_2K classifier on dynamic facial expression features. In: Face and Gesture 2011, pp. 854–859. IEEE (2011)
17. Mollahosseini, A., Chan, D., Mahoor, M.H.: Going deeper in facial expression recognition using deep neural networks. In: 2016 IEEE Winter Conference on Applications of Computer Vision (WACV), pp. 1–10. IEEE (2016)
18. Norouzi, E., Ahmadabadi, M.N., Araabi, B.N.: Attention control with reinforcement learning for face recognition under partial occlusion. Mach. Vis. Appl. **22**(2), 337–348 (2011)
19. Shan, C., Gong, S., McOwan, P.W.: Facial expression recognition based on local binary patterns: a comprehensive study. Image vis. Comput. **27**(6), 803–816 (2009)
20. Su, Y., Shan, S., Chen, X., Gao, W.: Hierarchical ensemble of global and local classifiers for face recognition. IEEE Trans. Image Process. **18**(8), 1885–1896 (2009)
21. Thewlis, J., Bilen, H., Vedaldi, A.: Unsupervised learning of object landmarks by factorized spatial embeddings. In: Proceedings of the IEEE International Conference on Computer Vision, pp. 5916–5925 (2017)
22. Vinciarelli, A., Pantic, M., Bourlard, H.: Social signal processing: Survey of an emerging domain. Image Vis. Comput. **27**(12), 1743–1759 (2009)
23. Wang, X., Girshick, R., Gupta, A., He, K.: Non-local neural networks. In: Proceedings of the IEEE Conference on Computer Vision and Pattern Recognition, pp. 7794–7803 (2018)
24. Zhang, H., Goodfellow, I., Metaxas, D., Odena, A.: Self-attention generative adversarial networks. arXiv preprint arXiv:1805.08318 (2018)
25. Zhang, K., Zhang, Z., Li, Z., Qiao, Y.: Joint face detection and alignment using multitask cascaded convolutional networks. IEEE Signal Process. Lett. **23**(10), 1499–1503 (2016)
26. Zheng, H., Fu, J., Mei, T., Luo, J.: Learning multi-attention convolutional neural network for fine-grained image recognition. In: Proceedings of the IEEE International Conference on Computer Vision, pp. 5209–5217 (2017)

Multi-label Chest X-Ray Image Classification via Label Co-occurrence Learning

Bingzhi Chen⬦, Yao Lu⬦, and Guangming Lu$^{(\boxtimes)}$⬦

Harbin Institute of Technology, Shenzhen, China
chenbingzhi@stu.hit.edu.cn, yaolu_1992@126.com, luguangm@hit.edu.cn

Abstract. Existing multi-label medical image datasets generally exist a large number of co-occurring label pairs. This phenomenon is interpreted as label co-occurrence. Obviously, label co-occurrence is available and its effect should be taken into account for automated medical diagnosis. In this paper, we propose a novel label co-occurrence learning (LCL) method for multi-label chest X-ray (CXR) image classification. By taking advantage of the dependencies between pathologies, the proposed LCL module in our model is designed to generate a set of inter-dependent weighting adapters for exploring the potential pathologies. Specifically, these classifiers are initialized with the weight coefficients extracted from the co-occurrence matrix of training data. In the training phase, the LCL module can accurately tweak the multi-label outputs with their corresponding object weights, and further predict additional abnormal findings. Moreover, the LCL module can be directly integrated into any Convolutional Neural Networks (CNNs) with end-to-end training. Extensive experiments on the ChestX-ray14 dataset substantiate the effectiveness of the proposed method as compared with the state-of-the-art baselines.

Keywords: Label co-occurrence learning · Multi-label CXR image classification · Weight coefficients

1 Introduction

With the increased availability of large-scale annotated medical image archives, many state-of the-art approaches [8,10–12] have achieved tremendous progress in the field of automated medical diagnosis, e.g. skin cancer classification [6], pulmonary tuberculosis classification [9] and musculoskeletal abnormality classification [14], etc. In contrast to CNNs [7,21] which only exploit the technique of binary relevance, the evaluation of pathology in clinical practice do not depend only on image interpretation and clinical pathology features [10,11], but also always utilize varieties of relationship information among pathologies, especially for the multi-label pathologies tasks.

(Student First Author).

© Springer Nature Switzerland AG 2019
Z. Lin et al. (Eds.): PRCV 2019, LNCS 11858, pp. 682–693, 2019.
https://doi.org/10.1007/978-3-030-31723-2_58

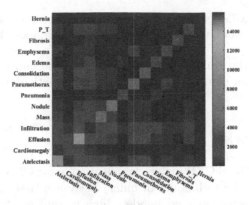

Fig. 1. Illustration of labels' co-occurrence statistics extracted from training data in the ChestX-ray14 dataset

In general, many real-world medical images such as CXR images might be associated with multiple pathological labels and they normally abound with a large number of co-occurring label pairs, as shown in Fig. 1. For example, Atelectasis often occurs with Effusion and Infiltration. As the accumulating of annotated images, the label co-occurrence phenomenon has become more prominent and perceptible, which implies that the label co-occurrence information is of great importance for the clinical diagnosis. Furthermore, it is a great challenge for radiologists to completely annotate each instance with all of the relevant labels. Thus, there are some shortages for automated multi-label CXR classification [1,4,15,18] in deep learning, resulting in a certain misdiagnosis. To curb these negative impacts, researchers have expended considerable effort to design much deeper and wider networks. However, most previous works have overlooked label co-occurrence information between pathologies.

In this paper, we propose a novel label co-occurrence learning (LCL) network called LCL-Net to explore the potential co-occurring labels in CXR images by leveraging label co-occurrence and dependencies information. Specifically, our model consists of two modules, i.e., the image module and the LCL module. Specifically, the key of the proposed LCL module is to map the dependencies between each pair of the co-occurring labels into the corresponding weight coefficients based on the label co-occurrence matrix of the ChestX-ray14 dataset, as described Sect. 3.2. With these weight coefficients, the LCL module can be considered as a set of inter-dependent weighting adapters. Then, these classifiers are integrated with the image-level features provided by the image module to fine-tune the multi-label output and explore the potential abnormal findings. The main contributions of this work are summarized as follows:

(1) The major contribution of this work is to improve the performance of multi-label CXR classification by leveraging label co-occurrence dependencies based on the label co-occurrence matrix of the dataset.

(2) The proposed LCL-Net is an adaptive optimization framework since the co-occurring labels can be captured by a learnable LCL module with end-to-end training.
(3) The LCL modules can be easily inserted into the end of any CNN-based model, which can demonstrate the flexibility effectiveness of the proposed method.

2   Related Works

In the field of multi-label CXR image classification, most CNN-based approaches have only exploited the techniques of binary relevance that consider the multi-label classification as multiple independent binary problems. For instance, Wang et al. [23] first announced the ChestX-ray14 dataset with their corresponding label annotations. They also investigated the ImageNet [16] pre-trained CNN models to perform weakly supervised disease classification and localization on the ChestX-ray14 dataset. Though they had noticed the signs of label co-occurrence in ChestX-ray14, they didn't take the label co-occurrence into account. Rajpurkar et al. [15] proposed a modified 121-layer DenseNet called CheXNet to detect all 14 pathologies in the ChestX-ray14 dataset, especially for "Pneumonia". Tang et al. [22] presented an attention-guided curriculum learning framework that focused on the heatmaps via weakly supervised localization. And Shen et al. [18] addressed the multi-label thoracic disease classification task by introducing the routing-by agreement mechanism into their architecture and extending the routing to layer connections.

Furthermore, some approaches have also considered the clinical data and tried to utilize such available information to further improve the performance on the multi-label CXR image classification task. For example, Shin et al. [19] and Wang et al. [24] used a CNN-RNN architecture to model the dependencies between text words and image regions, and sequentially predict the chest X-rays' labels. Yao et al. [25] focused on interdependencies among target labels, and they utilized Long short-term memory (LSTM) [17] to explore the potential labels. By taking advantage of non-image data such as view position, patient age and gender, Baltruschat et al. [18] incorporate the prior knowledge to fine-tune the pre-trained ResNet-50 model and achieved a better performance than the previous techniques. Inspired by the aforementioned works, we focus on the label co-occurrence and dependencies information based on the label co-occurrence matrix of the dataset, which would be beneficial for improving the performance of multi-label CXR image classification.

3   Method

3.1   Notations and Problem Definition

The following notations are used throughout the paper. Denote $I \in M^{w \times h \times c}$ as an input image. Denote N_i as the total number of abnormalities for each label.

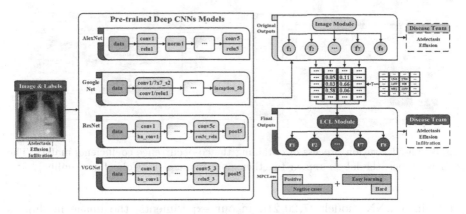

Fig. 2. Illustration of the proposed LCL-Net: (a) Image module: the image module is built on the pre-trained DCNNs. It is required to extract the image representation and provide the original output for the LCL module; (b) LCL module: the LCL module is designed to map the dependencies between each pair of the co-occurring labels into the corresponding weight coefficients and adaptively regularize the multi-label outputs in the training phase.

Labels in each chest X-ray image are expressed as a multi-dimensional label vector $x = [x_1, \ldots, x_i, \ldots, x_n]$, where $x_i \in \{0,1\}$ represents the ground truth of the ith label. The superscripts and subscripts indicate the specific dimensionality and label number, respectively. For instance, (x_i, x_j) is a pair of co-occurring labels. The label-label co-occurring coefficient matrix of chest X-ray14 dataset is $\mathbb{R}_\alpha^{n \times n}$. The first transformational result is label-label frequency matrix $\mathbb{R}_\delta^{n \times n}$, and the final transformational result is the proposed weigh coefficient matrix $\mathbb{R}_\beta^{n \times n}$. The total number of label co-occurrence is denoted as $\alpha_{i,j}$ ($\alpha_{i,j} \in \mathbb{R}_\alpha^{n \times n}$), and the co-occurrence frequency is denoted as $\delta_{i,j}$ ($\delta_{i,j} \in \mathbb{R}_\delta^{n \times n}$). Moreover, the co-occurrence coefficients is denoted by $\beta_{i,j}$ ($\beta_{i,j} \in \mathbb{R}_\beta^{n \times n}$). The entire transformation can be denoted as below:

$$\beta = T_2(\delta) = T_2(T_1(\alpha)) \tag{1}$$

Besides, $F_n(x) = [f_1(x), \ldots, f_i(x), \ldots, f_n(x)]$ and $R_n(x) = [r_1(x), \ldots, r_i(x), \ldots, r_n(x)]$ are the outputs of image module (Initial outputs) and the LCL module (Final outputs) respectively. And p_t is the probability that the network assigns to the label and ω is the weight parameter of neuron in the LCL module. In addition, we assume that the relationship between the training sample and the original output is represented as a mapping $\Gamma : x \rightarrow F_n(x)$, and the relationship between the underlying classification and the final outputs is represented as a mapping $\Theta : F_n(x) \rightarrow R_n(x)$.

3.2   Achitecture of LCL-Net

The architecture of the proposed LCL-Net for multi-label pathology classification in chest X-rays is shown in Fig. 2. Specifically, the image module is built on the

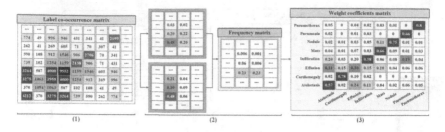

Fig. 3. The derivation process of obtaining the co-occurrence coefficients matrix. The color is deeper, the labels appear together more frequently. (Color figure online)

pre-trained CNN models [7,20,21]. In our experiments, the image module is initialized with the ResNet-50 [7] pre-trained model, while the LCL module is initialized with the weight coefficients extracted from the co-occurrence matrix of the ChestX-ray14 dataset. Moreover, the LCL module is then incorporated with the image module with an end-to-end training and adaptively recalibrate the prediction output for each pathology. Details of the LCL module are given in the following subsections.

Weight Coefficient Mining. In this paper, when the pathologies tend to occur together, they will share a larger weight coefficient. By contrast, when two pathologies are irrelevant and independent, it means their corresponding weighting adapter will be initialized with a small weight coefficient. Thus, how to conduct the weight coefficient mining is the key to the proposed LCL-Net.

As mentioned, in the multi-label CXR image classification task, the label co-occurrence has become the focus as the number of CXR images increases. In our experiments, we focus on the label co-occurrence matrix of the dataset since it is a collection of label co-occurrence. Based on the label co-occurrence matrix of the ChestX-ray14 dataset, the weight coefficient mining operation is conducted to explore a set of the weight coefficients. In this way, we can map the dependencies between each pair of the co-occurring pathologies into the corresponding weight coefficients. The process of implementation is described Fig. 3:

(1) Initially, the label co-occurrence matrix $\mathbb{R}_\alpha^{n \times n}$ be counted from the ChestX-ray14 dataset.
(2) Next, we count the label frequency matrix for the first transformational T_1, as defined in Eq. 2:
$$T_1 : \quad \delta_{i,j} = \alpha_{i,j}^2 / N_i / N_j \tag{2}$$
(3) Finally, based on the frequency matrix $\mathbb{R}_\delta^{n \times n}$), we can achieve the second transformational T_2 (as defined in Eq. 3) and finally get the proposed weight coefficients matrix $\mathbb{R}_\beta^{n \times n}$, which is a collection of a set weight coefficients for each pair of label co-occurrence.

$$T_2 : \quad \beta_{i,j} = \delta_{i,j} / \sum_{k=1}^{n} \delta_{i,k} \tag{3}$$

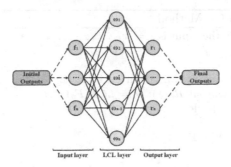

Fig. 4. Illustration of the proposed multilayer perceptron in the LCL module

Label Co-occurrence Learning. To model the dependencies between pathologies in the ChestX-ray14 dataset, we introduce a multilayer perceptron [3] into the LCL module, since it is compatible with the structure of the image module. The multi-layer perceptron is a universal function approximator that can adaptively recalibrate the multi-label outputs in the training phase and improve the performance of the LCL-Net. As shown in Fig. 4, the proposed multilayer perceptron consists of three layers, i.e., the input layer, the LCL layer, and the output layer. Importantly, the LCL layer is initialized with the obtained weight coefficients to generate a set of inter-dependent weighting adapters. Finally, these adapters are integrated with the Initial outputs extracted from the image module to adaptively modify the prediction output for each pathology, as defined in Eq. 4.

$$r_i(x) = \sigma(\mu * (f_i(x) + \sum_{j=1}^{n} \beta_{i,j} f_j(x))) \tag{4}$$

where σ is the sigmoid function and μ is the modulating factor. In our experiments, the proposed LCL-Net achieves the best performance when the value of μ is set to be 0.85. Moreover, the calculation performed by the LCL method is summarized in Algorithm 1.

The Proposed MPCLoss. In our experiments, we are subject to the class imbalance problem of the positives and negatives in the ChestX-ray14 dataset. Moreover, we noticed that the ChestX-ray14 dataset also suffers a huge imbalance between the easily-classified samples and hard-classified samples. A large number of easy-learning samples can comprise the majority of the loss and dominate the gradient in the training phase. To tackle the class imbalance problem, a common method is to introduce a weighted Cross Entropy Loss (W-CELoss). By contrast, we introduce a novel multi-label pathology classification function

---

Algorithm 1. The LCL Method

Require: set $\mu = 0.85$, the input is $x = [x_1, \ldots, x_i, \ldots, x_n]$, and the weight coefficient is $\beta_{i,j}$.

Ensure:

1: Select f:=Nets(x,I), and the initial output is: $F_n(x) = [f_1(x), \ldots, f_i(x), \ldots, f_n(x)]$
2: Compute the final Output $R_n(x)$: $\Theta := LCL(F_n(x), \beta_{i,j})$
3: **for** $i = 1; i \leq n; i++$ **do**
4:     **if** $i \neq j$ **then**
5:         Estimate $R_n(x)$ by **Eq. 4**;
6:     **end if**
7: **end for**
8: The final output is: $R_n(x) = [r_1(x), \ldots, r_i(x), \ldots, r_n(x)]$.

(MPCLoss) with an extra factor $(1 - p_t)^\gamma$ for the proposed LCL-Net, as defined in Eq. 5.

$$L(p_t, x_i) = -\frac{1}{|p|}(1 - p_t)^\gamma \sum_{x_i=1} \ln(p_t) - \frac{1}{|N|}(p_t)^\gamma \sum_{x_i=0} \ln(1 - p_t) \qquad (5)$$

where p_t is the obtained probability score for the label t, $|P|$ and $|N|$ are the total numbers of positive labels and negatives labels in a batch of the training set, and γ ($\gamma \in [0, 2]$) is consider to focus on hard-learning samples. When an existing sample is difficult to classify, the corresponding probability score $(p(i|I))$ tends to be 0, and the $(1 - p(i|I))^\lambda$ is near 1, it means that the loss contribution would be enlarged, and vice versa. In our experiments, the LCL-Net achieves the best performance when γ is set to be 0.5.

4   Experiments

In this section, the proposed LCL-Net is evaluated on the ChestX-ray14 dataset. We first give descriptions of the dataset. Next, we go into details of implementation details. Then we give detailed parameter. Finally, we evaluate the effectiveness of LCL-Net and make a comparison with state-of-the-art methods.

4.1   Dataset

In this paper, we focus on the ChestX-ray14 dataset which is provided by the NIH Clinical Center. It is a large-scale CXR dataset contains 112,120 frontal-view X-ray images from 32,717 patients with 14 common thoracic disease categories. As shown in Table 1, the ChestX-ray14 dataset suffers the problem of class imbalance. For example, 60,412 samples are normal that are marked with "No Finding", while only 227 samples are marked with "Hernia".

Table 1. The total number of images across all abnormalities in the ChestX-ray14 dataset.

Items	Labels	Items	Labels
Atelectasis	11559	Consolidation	4667
Cardiomegaly	2776	Edema	2303
Effusion	13317	Emphysema	2516
Infiltration	19894	Fibrosis	1686
Mass	5782	P_T	3385
Nodule	6331	Hernia	227
Pneumonia	1431	**No Finding**	60412
Pneumothorax	5302		

4.2   Implementation Details

In our experiments, we first randomly split the entire dataset into training (70%), validation (10%), and test (20%) sets. Moreover, we also randomly scramble the input order of training data after each training epoch and augment the training data with random horizontal flipping. To compare with previous works on the ChestX-ray14 dataset, we consider the AUC score [13] (the area under the ROC curve [5]) as the evaluation metric to evaluate the proposed LCL-Net. Moreover, we use stochastic gradient descent (SGD) [2] with 0.9 momentum. Moreover, the images are rescaled from 1024×1024 to 224×224 to fit the input size of the network. The learning rate in training is $lr = 0.01$, it will be reduced to one fifth when the validation loss reaches a plateau.

4.3   Parameter Analysis

In this part, we mainly evaluate the proposed LCL-Net with different parameters μ in Eq. 4 and γ in Eq. 5 to explore the optimum parameter setting.

Evaluation on Modulating Factor μ. The modulating factor μ in Eq. 4 is one of the key parameters to obtain a better evaluating adjustment of the LCL method. By fixing other parameters, we conduct LCL-Net with a range of different values μ, i.e., $\mu \in \{0.50, 0.55, 0.60, \cdots, 0.90, 0.95, 1.0\}$. As shown in Fig. 5(a), the proposed LCL-Net achieves the best performance when the value of μ is set to be 0.85.

Evaluation on Parameter γ. The parameter γ in Eq. 5 is concerned with the hard-learning samples. Similarly, by fixing other parameters, we also evaluate a range of different values of parameter γ, i.e., $\gamma \in \{0, 0.5, 0.10, 0.15, 0.20\}$. As shown in Fig. 5(b), when the value of γ is set to be 0.5, the proposed LCL-Net achieves the best performance and outperforms the classification results of γ is 0 (0.8142 vs. 0.8113). Thus, the experiment result proves the validity of the proposed MPCLoss.

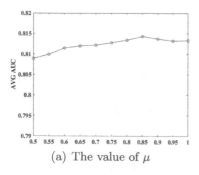

(a) The value of μ

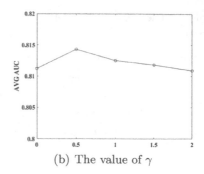

(b) The value of γ

Fig. 5. Comparison of average AUC scores for different values of μ and γ, respectively.

Table 2. Comparison of the AUC scores between LCL-Net and other published baselines using the ChestX-Ray14 test set. Note that '$*$' represents the combination of the LSTM and DenseNet used in [25] and '$\natural$' represents the network used in the corresponding reference is not illustrated. For each row, the best results are highlighted in **bold**.

Baselines	U-CNN [23]	L-DNet [25]	D_CNN [18]	AGCL [22]	CheXNet [15]	ResNet50	LCL-Net
CNN	R-50	$*$	$\natural$	$\natural$	D-121	R-50	R-50
Atelectasis	0.700	0.733	0.766	0.848	0.769	0.767	**0.773**
Cardiomegaly	0.810	0.856	0.801	**0.887**	0.885	0.866	0.880
Effusion	0.759	0.806	0.797	0.819	**0.825**	0.818	0.823
Infiltration	0.661	0.673	**0.751**	0.689	0.694	0.692	0.697
Mass	0.693	0.718	0.760	0.814	0.824	0.803	**0.826**
Nodule	0.669	0.777	0.741	0.755	0.759	0.754	**0.786**
Pneumonia	0.658	0.684	**0.778**	0.729	0.715	0.695	0.720
Pneumothorax	0.799	0.805	0.800	0.850	0.852	0.855	**0.871**
Consolidation	0.703	0.711	**0.787**	0.728	0.745	0.728	0.736
Edema	0.805	0.806	0.820	0.848	0.842	0.836	**0.845**
Emphysema	0.833	0.842	0.773	0.906	0.906	0.919	**0.938**
Fibrosis	0.786	0.743	0.765	0.818	0.821	0.821	**0.823**
P_T	0.684	0.724	0.759	0.765	0.766	0.765	**0.782**
Hernia	0.872	0.775	0.748	0.875	**0.901**	0.890	0.899
AVG AUC	0.745	0.761	0.775	0.803	0.807	0.801	**0.814**

4.4   Comparison to State-of-the-Art Methods

To evaluate the quality of the proposed LCL-Net, some state-of-the-art baselines for multi-label CXR image classification are applied to the comparative experiments. In this section, we compare to a variety of methods based on the ChestX-ray14 dataset, including U-CNN (Wang et al. [23]), LSTM-Net (Yao

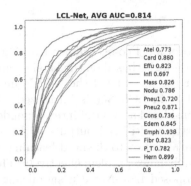

Fig. 6. ROC curves of LCL-Net on all 14 pathologies of the ChestX-ray14 dataset.

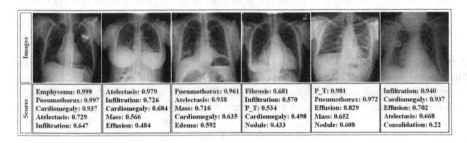

Fig. 7. Test results of the multi-label CXR image classification with LCL-Net on the ChestX-ray14 dataset. In this figure, the ground truth pathologies are highlighted in red. (Color figure online)

et al. [25]), D_CNN (Shen et al. [18])AGCL (Tang et al. [22]), as shown in Table 2. Clearly, the proposed LCL-Net achieves superior performance on multi-label CXR classification in chest X-rays and the average AUC score for 14 pathologies is 0.814. Moreover, LCL-Net achieves the top performance for 8 pathologies, i.e., "Atelectasis", "Pneumothorax" and "Emphysema". Meanwhile, LCL-Net outperforms these baselines, especially U-DCNN (0.745) and LSTM-DNet (0.761) with improvements of 6.9% and 5.3%. Furthermore, LCL-Net also achieves better performance over the corresponding original networks (0.801 vs. 0.814), especially for the "Cardiomegaly" (0.866 vs. 0.880), "Mass" (0.803vs. 0.826), "Pneumothorax" (0.855 vs. 0.871) and "P_T" (0.765 vs. 0.782). Thus, we can further demonstrate the effectiveness of the proposed method.

4.5 Qualitative Results

As presented in Fig. 6, we reach the state-of-the-art performance: the average AUC score for 14 pathologies of the ChestXray14 dataset is 0.814. Furthermore, Fig. 7 gives intuitive presentations of the classification results and the top-5 probability scores of the test CXR image are presented.

5 Conclusion

This paper proposes a novel label co-occurrence learning method to leveraging dependencies between pathologies based on the label co-occurrence matrix of the ChestX-ray14 dataset for the multi-label chest CXR image classification task. The proposed LCL module in LCL-Net is initialized with the corresponding weight coefficients and considered as a set of inter-dependent weighting adapters to adaptively regularize the multi-label outputs with an end-to-end training. Furthermore, we pay more attention to the hard-learning and misdiagnosed samples to address the class imbalance problem effectively. The experimental results demonstrate that the proposed LCL-Net can significantly improve the performance of the multi-label CXR classification on the ChestX-ray14 dataset. Our research shows that label co-occurrence is beneficial to multi-label medical image classification, yet more sophisticated techniques remain unexplored, it is worth discussing in the future.

Acknowledgement. The work is supported by the NSFC fund (61332011), Shenzhen Fundamental Research fund (JCYJ20170811155442454, JCYJ20180306172023949), China Postdoctoral Science Foundation (2019TQ0316), and Medical Biometrics Perception and Analysis Engineering Laboratory, Shenzhen, China.

References

1. Baltruschat, I.M., Nickisch, H., Grass, M., Knopp, T., Saalbach, A.: Comparison of deep learning approaches for multi-label chest x-ray classification. Sci. Rep. **9**(1), 6381 (2019)
2. Bottou, L.: Large-scale machine learning with stochastic gradient descent. In: Lechevallier Y., Saporta G. (eds): Proceedings of COMPSTAT'2010, pp. 177–186. Springer, Heidelberg (2010) https://doi.org/10.1007/978-3-7908-2604-3_16
3. Bourlard, H., Kamp, Y.: Auto-association by multilayer perceptrons and singular value decomposition. Biol. Cybern. **59**(4–5), 291–294 (1988)
4. Cai, J., Lu, L., Harrison, A.P., Shi, X., Chen, P., Yang, L.: Iterative attention mining for weakly supervised thoracic disease pattern localization in chest x-rays. In: Frangi, A.F., Schnabel, J.A., Davatzikos, C., Alberola-López, C., Fichtinger, G. (eds.) MICCAI 2018. LNCS, vol. 11071, pp. 589–598. Springer, Cham (2018). https://doi.org/10.1007/978-3-030-00934-2_66
5. Davis, J., Goadrich, M.: The relationship between precision-recall and ROC curves. In: Proceedings of the 23rd International Conference on Machine Learning, pp. 233–240. ACM (2006)
6. Esteva, A., et al.: Corrigendum: dermatologist-level classification of skin cancer with deep neural networks. Nature **546**(7660), 686 (2017)
7. He, K., Zhang, X., Ren, S., Sun, J.: Deep residual learning for image recognition. In: Proceedings of the IEEE Conference on Computer Vision and Pattern Recognition, pp. 770–778 (2016)
8. Huang, G., Liu, Z., Van Der Maaten, L., Weinberger, K.Q.: Densely connected convolutional networks. In: Proceedings of the IEEE Conference on Computer Vision and Pattern Recognition, pp. 4700–4708 (2017)

9. Lakhani, P., Sundaram, B.: Deep learning at chest radiography: automated classification of pulmonary tuberculosis by using convolutional neural networks. Radiology **284**(2), 574–582 (2017)

10. Li, J., Yong, H., Zhang, B., Li, M., Zhang, L., Zhang, D.: A probabilistic hierarchical model for multi-view and multi-feature classification. In: Thirty-Second AAAI Conference on Artificial Intelligence (2018)

11. Li, J., Zhang, B., Lu, G., Zhang, D.: Generative multi-view and multi-feature learning for classification. Inf. Fusion **45**, 215–226 (2019)

12. Li, J., Zhang, D., Li, Y., Wu, J., Zhang, B.: Joint similar and specific learning for diabetes mellitus and impaired glucose regulation detection. Inf. Sci. **384**, 191–204 (2017)

13. Lobo, J.M., Jiménez-Valverde, A., Real, R.: AUC: a misleading measure of the performance of predictive distribution models. Global Ecol. Biogeogr. **17**(2), 145–151 (2008)

14. Rajpurkar, P., et al.: Mura: Large dataset for abnormality detection in musculoskeletal radiographs. arXiv preprint arXiv:1712.06957 (2017)

15. Rajpurkar, P., et al.: Chexnet: Radiologist-level pneumonia detection on chest x-rays with deep learning. arXiv preprint arXiv:1711.05225 (2017)

16. Russakovsky, O., et al.: Imagenet large scale visual recognition challenge. Int. J. Comput. Vis. **115**(3), 211–252 (2015)

17. Sak, H., Senior, A., Beaufays, F.: Long short-term memory based recurrent neural network architectures for large vocabulary speech recognition (2014). CoRR abs/1402.1128

18. Shen, Y., Gao, M.: Dynamic routing on deep neural network for thoracic disease classification and sensitive area localization. In: Shi, Y., Suk, H.-I., Liu, M. (eds.) MLMI 2018. LNCS, vol. 11046, pp. 389–397. Springer, Cham (2018). https://doi. org/10.1007/978-3-030-00919-9_45

19. Shin, H.C., Roberts, K., Lu, L., Demner-Fushman, D., Yao, J., Summers, R.M.: Learning to read chest x-rays: recurrent neural cascade model for automated image annotation. In: Proceedings of the IEEE Conference on Computer Vision and Pattern Recognition, pp. 2497–2506 (2016)

20. Simonyan, K., Zisserman, A.: Very deep convolutional networks for large-scale image recognition. arXiv preprint arXiv:1409.1556 (2014)

21. Szegedy, C., et al.: Going deeper with convolutions. In: Proceedings of the IEEE Conference on Computer Vision and Pattern Recognition, pp. 1–9 (2015)

22. Tang, Y., Wang, X., Harrison, A.P., Lu, L., Xiao, J., Summers, R.M.: Attention-guided curriculum learning for weakly supervised classification and localization of thoracic diseases on chest radiographs. In: Shi, Y., Suk, H.-I., Liu, M. (eds.) MLMI 2018. LNCS, vol. 11046, pp. 249–258. Springer, Cham (2018). https://doi.org/10. 1007/978-3-030-00919-9_29

23. Wang, X., Peng, Y., Lu, L., Lu, Z., Bagheri, M., Summers, R.M.: Chestx-ray8: hospital-scale chest x-ray database and benchmarks on weakly-supervised classification and localization of common thorax diseases. In: Proceedings of the IEEE Conference on Computer Vision and Pattern Recognition, pp. 2097–2106 (2017)

24. Wang, X., Peng, Y., Lu, L., Lu, Z., Summers, R.M.: Tienet: text-image embedding network for common thorax disease classification and reporting in chest x-rays. In: Proceedings of the IEEE Conference on Computer Vision and Pattern Recognition, pp. 9049–9058 (2018)

25. Yao, L., Poblenz, E., Dagunts, D., Covington, B., Bernard, D., Lyman, K.: Learning to diagnose from scratch by exploiting dependencies among labels. arXiv preprint arXiv:1710.10501 (2017)

Asymmetric Pyramid Based Super Resolution from Very Low Resolution Face Image

Xuebo Wang[1], Yao Lu[1(✉)], Xiaozhen Chen[1], Weiqi Li[1], and Zijian Wang[1,2]

[1] Beijing Laboratory of Intelligent Information Technology,
Beijing Institute of Technology, Beijing, China
vis_yl@bit.edu.cn
[2] China Central Television, Beijing, China

Abstract. Most of the existing one-step upsampling super-resolution (SR) methods could not clearly reconstruct a higher resolution image from a very low-resolution image because there is not enough supervision information to be available. Inspired by the laplacian pyramid, we propose a novel Asymmetric and Progressive Face Super-Resolution Network (APFSRNet) to progressively reconstruct a super-resolution face image from a very low-resolution face image. To further improve the accuracy of the reconstruction, we use the densely connected layers to deepen our network which also alleviate the vanishing-gradient problem. We use the entire face image to train our network instead of using face image patches to maintain the global structure of the face image. Furthermore, we employ structural similarity index (SSIM) as a part of loss function to satisfy human observation. Our extensive experiments demonstrate the effectiveness of the proposed model qualitatively and quantitatively.

Keywords: Super resolution · Very low resolution · Face image · Cascading neural network · Laplacian pyramid

1 Introduction

Single Image Super-Resolution (SISR) aims to reconstruct a visually pleasing high-resolution (HR) image from a low-resolution (LR) image. In recent years, many learning algorithms [1,5,7,9,11] have been proposed to solve this ill-posed inverse problem. Specially face image super-resolution is paid more attentions and widely used in applications such as face recognition, security and surveillance system.

This paper focuses on reconstructing a super-resolution face image from a very low-resolution face image, for example, super-resolving a very low-resolution face image of 16×16 pixels to its $8\times$ high-resolution face image of 128×128 pixels. Although there have been some recent works focusing on face super-resolution and achieving promising results, there are still some problems. First,

© Springer Nature Switzerland AG 2019
Z. Lin et al. (Eds.): PRCV 2019, LNCS 11858, pp. 694–702, 2019.
https://doi.org/10.1007/978-3-030-31723-2_59

most of the current face super-resolution methods only work well when the input is of a middle-level resolution (64 × 64, 32 × 32) and super-resolution magnification is not larger i.e. 4. Second, most end-to-end networks learn the mapping from LR to HR image patches through just one step, which will make the network more difficult to converge. Although Lai et al. [7] proposes Deep Laplacian Pyramid Networks (Lapsrn) to progressively reconstruct a high-resolution image, directly fine-tuning Lapsrn with face image dataset will lead it to generate heavily blurred images due to it's ignorance of the characteristics of very low-resolution face images, as shown in Fig. 2.

To overcome these drawbacks, we propose a novel Asymmetric and Progressive Face Super-Resolution Network (APFSRNet) based on dense blocks to super-resolve a very low-resolution face image of less pixels (for example, 16 × 16 pixels) to a larger version of high-resolution image (for example, 128 × 128 pixels). This is a challenging work because the input face image of our network have only 16 × 16 pixels, which is heavily blur and contains much less facial details. Main contributions of our work are summarized as follows:

(1) We use laplacian pyramid to progressively reconstruct a larger version of face image from a very low-resolution face image, which will make the network easier to converge, because we use more supervision information. In addition, in order to further improve the accuracy of reconstruction, we add densely connected layers in our network to acquire deep features.
(2) We modify the loss function by appending SSIM to satisfy Human Vision System (HVS) better. We demonstrate the validity of our method qualitatively and quantitatively.

2   Related Work

Generic Single Image Super-Resolution (SISR) Based on Neural Network: With the improvement of computing performance, many neural network based super-resolution methods have emerged and demonstrated better performance than traditional methods. SRCNN [1] is the pioneering work of the deep learning based super-resolution reconstruction. It first upsamples the low-resolution image to the desired size by bicubic interpolation, and then learns the mapping of the low-resolution and high-resolution image patches through only three convolution layers. ESPCN [9] proposes a sub-pixel convolution layer to improve the computational efficiency of the network. Lapsrn [7] uses a cascading network to learn high-frequency residual details progressively, enabling 8× super-resolution. One of the most straightforward methods to solve our problem is to retrain these generic patch-based super-resolution methods using face dataset. But they [7,9] cannot capture the global structure of face, which fail to produce realistic face image as shown in Fig. 2.

CNN-Based Super-Resolution for Face Image: Deep neural network, especially convolution neural network (CNN), is capable for exploring the information available in face image by learning large-scale face datasets, to infer a larger face image from smaller resolution face image [4,14]. URDGN [14] uses Generative Adversarial Network (GAN) to generate a face image with much sharper detail. Although the image generated by URDGN is more realistic, the image has a relatively lower Peak Signal to Noise Ratio (PSNR). Wavelet-SRNet [4] reconstructs a high-resolution face image by predicting wavelet coefficients and can super-resolve a very low-resolution face image of 16 × 16 pixels to its larger version. But the author uses more than 200 parallel convolution layers to enlarge the face image of 16 × 16 resolution by 8×, which takes more time to train and consumes more memory.

In order to solve the problem of reconstruction of very low-resolution face image using simpler model to achieve better results, we borrow the idea of laplacian pyramid used in Lapsrn [7] to reconstruct face image progressively.

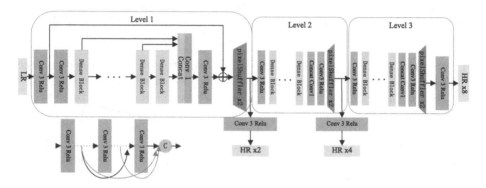

Fig. 1. Network structure of our method. Each level of the pyramid has a similar structure. The only difference is that each level contains a different number of dense blocks n. $n_1 = 4, n_2 = n_3 = 8$ is the best parameter that has been experimentally verified.

3   Proposed Method

The architecture of our APFSRNet is shown in Fig. 1.

3.1   Pyramidal Network for Large Upscale Factor

In order to enlarge the low-resolution face image by 8×, we divide the network into three levels, each of which enlarges the low-resolution image by 2×, as shown in Fig. 1. At each level of the pyramid, we use one convolution layer to extract the shallow feature of the low-resolution face image, followed by a different number of dense blocks to extract the deep feature of the image, and finally use sub-pixel convolution layer to enlarge the image.

Let's denote I_{LR} and I_{HR} as the input and output of our network respectively. Our goal is to find the mapping u from I_{LR} to I_{HR}:

$$I_{HR} = u(I_{LR}; \theta) \tag{1}$$

θ is a collection of all parameters in our network. We decompose u into a series of simple functions and learn it gradually:

$$I_{16 \times 16} \xrightarrow{u_1} I_{32 \times 32} \xrightarrow{u_2} I_{64 \times 64} \xrightarrow{u_3} I_{128 \times 128} \tag{2}$$

u_i is a mapping function of the i_{th} level of the pyramid and u is composite of u_1, u_2, u_3. At each level of the pyramid, we use one convolution layer to extract the shallow feature of the low-resolution face image and preserve it as residual information of the face image, which we consider as residual learning. This approach also prevents the problem of gradient disappearance caused by deep network. As shown in Fig. 1, in the i_{th} level of pyramid, shallow feature $F_{shallow}$ is extracted by one convolution layer:

$$F_{shallow} = f_{shallow}(I_{fm}) \tag{3}$$

Where I_{fm} indicates the input low-resolution face image in level 1, and the enlarged feature map in level 2 and level 3. And Next, we use dense blocks to extract deep feature F_{deep} of face image, followed by one sub-pixel convolution layer and one reconstruction layer including one 3×3 convolution.

$$F_{deep} = f_{deep}(F_{shallow}) \tag{4}$$

$$I_{SR} = f_{up}(F_{deep} + F_{shallow}) \tag{5}$$

where f_{up} denotes the collection of sub-pixel convolution layer and reconstruction layer. I_{SR} denotes the reconstructed high-resolution face image.

3.2 Dense Block Unit

DenseNet structure [3] is used to extract deep feature in our method. Lapsrn [7] simply stacks 5 or 10 convolution layers to extract feature of low-resolution image, which is not suitable for our very low-resolution face image (16×16 pixels), because 10 convolution layers with 3×3 kernels have a 21×21 effective receptive field [10], which is out of the size of the low-resolution face image (16×16 pixels). This is why Lapsrn doesn't choose more convolution layers to extract feature for $8\times$ model. However, deeper networks will take more contextual information from input image to predict high-frequency detail in high-resolution images [5,6], so we use dense blocks to deepen our network and improve gradient flow to alleviate the vanishing-gradient problem [3].

In each dense block, i_{th} layer receives the feature maps of all of the preceding layers as input:

$$X_i = active(w_i * [x_1, x_2, ..., x_{i-1}] + b_i) \tag{6}$$

Where $[x_1, x_2, ..., x_{i-1}]$ represents the concatenation of feature maps generated in the preceding convolution layers $1, 2, ..., i-1$. The original dense block composed of BN-ReLU-Conv (3×3). We remove batch normalization following recent research in super-resolution [2]. There are 4 convolution layers in each dense block in our network. Meanwhile, we set growth rate to 16 to prevent the network from growing too wide. In addition, We concatenate all the output of the dense blocks through a bottleneck layer to better reconstruct the edge details, which has been proved in [12]. Finally, the deep information is merged with the shallow information and inputed into the sub-pixel convolution layer to predict the HR face image of i_{th} level in pyramid.

3.3   Asymmetric Structure

At each level of the pyramid, the size of the input feature map is different (in the level 1 of the pyramid, the input feature map is a low-resolution face image), resulting in different effective receptive field. We use different numbers of dense blocks to extract deep feature in different levels so APFSRNet is an asymmetric structure. We set $n_1 = 4, n_2 = 8, n_3 = 8$ for three levels respectively.

3.4   Optimization and Implementation Details

Optimization: We design a new loss function for our problem. Most of the existing methods [1,5,6,9] employ l_2 norm as loss function and achieve good results in PSNR. But l_2 correlates poorly with image quality as perceived by a human observation [15]. On the contrary, the sensitivity of the Human Visual System (HVS) to noise depends on local luminance, contrast, and structure-SSIM [13]. So we propose to weight sum of l_1 norm and SSIM as our new loss function. Meanwhile, we have found by experiments that SSIM has different weights at different levels of the pyramid, which will improve the performance of the network. Our model is implemented on a single channel. The loss function L is below:

$$L(\theta) = L_1 + \alpha \cdot (1 - SSIM)$$
$$= \sum_{s' <= s} (l_1(f_{down}^{s'}(y_i), \hat{y}_i^{s'}) + \alpha^s \cdot (1 - SSIM)) \tag{7}$$

Where s indicates the level number in pyramid. $f_{down}^{s'}$ indicates the down-sampling operation that we use the bicubic to downsample the original 128 pixels face image as ground truth for each level of the pyramid (No downsampling in level 3). α^s is a weight of SSIM of s level in pyramid. We take different values $\alpha^1 = 0.08, \alpha^2 = 0.04, \alpha^3 = 0.01$ to acquire best results in our experiment. SSIM is defined as:

$$SSIM(x, y) = \frac{2\mu_x\mu_y + C_1}{\mu_x^2 + \mu_y^2 + C_1} \cdot \frac{2\sigma_{xy} + C_2}{\sigma_x^2 + \sigma_y^2 + C_2} \tag{8}$$

Where x, y represent image x and image y respectively. μ and σ represent the mean and variance of the image, σ_{xy} represents the covariance of image x and image y, C_1 and C_2 are constant set to 0.01.

Implementation Details: In order to keep the size of the feature map unchanged, we set all the convolution kernel size to 3 × 3 and padding to 1 (except that the bottleneck layer convolution kernel size is set to 1 × 1 and padding is 0). At the same time, the growth rate of the dense block is set to $k = 16$, and each of the dense blocks contains 4 convolution layers. The number of input channels of the sub-pixel convolution layer is $r × r × 64$, r indicates up-scaling factor in each level of pyramid. The channels of remaining convolution layers are 64. All convolution layers are followed by ReLU activation functions (except sub-pixel layers). Our loss function is minimized using Adam with a batch size of 64. The weight of each level of our pyramid network is randomly initialized based on a Gaussian distribution. We use an end-to-end approach to train our network. Our model is implemented using Pytorch. For the hyper-parameters, we set learning rate to 0.0001 initially and reduced by a factor of 10 each 30 epoch. The experiment is iterated 100 times in total.

Table 1. Ablation study

Ablation study	Method	PSNR
Baseline	One-step upsampling	23.0805
Pyramid structure	Three level pyramid structure	23.6561
Dense blocks	4 dense blocks in each level	**24.4326**

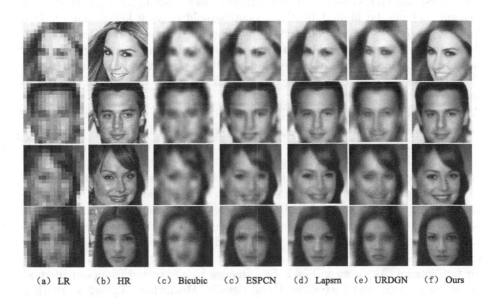

(a) LR   (b) HR   (c) Bicubic   (c) ESPCN   (d) Lapsrn   (e) URDGN   (f) Ours

Fig. 2. Visual comparison for 8× face SR on celebA test sets

Table 2. Comparison of SR results in terms of PSNR/SSIM using different methods

Methods	Bicubic	ESPCN	Lapsrn	URDGN	APFSRNet_A	APFSRNet_B	APFSRNet_F
PSNR	22.2025	23.1868	23.7084	24.1000	24.4326	23.8004	**24.8046**
SSIM	0.5653	0.6218	0.6633	0.6710	0.6952	0.6723	**0.7117**

4   Experiment Result

Our experiments are performed on CelebA [8] dataset, which is a large-scale face attributes dataset with 202,599 number of face images. We randomly sample 5,000 images as verification set images, 1,000 images as test set images, and other images as training set images. Cropping all the images to 128×128 pixels around the face with eyes aligned horizontally as the only preprocessing step.

In order to verify the validity of our proposed network structure, we design an ablation study. We use one convolution layer to extract the shallow feature of the face image, and use 15 consecutive convolution layers to extract the deep feature of the face image, then merge with the shallow feature and use three consecutive sub-pixel convolution layer to enlarge the face image. Above as our base model.

Pyramid Structure: We enlarge the feature map by $2 \times$ after each 5 convolution layers, and use the supervision to optimize our model. As shown in Table 1, pyramidal structure improves the reconstruction accuracy compared with one-step upsampling.

Dense Block with Concatenation: In order to extract more contextual information and not be limited by the receptive field of very low-resolution face images, we replace the 5 consecutive convolution layers in each level with 4 dense blocks in each level. The internal structure of each dense block is shown in the Fig. 1. Finally concatenate each dense block as deep information. Table 1 show that deeper model with dense block can improve the accuracy of face image reconstruction.

Asymmetric Structure: We train the proposed model with different number of dense block in each level of pyramid. We set $n_1 = n_2 = n_3 = 4$ called APFSRNet_A, set $n_1 = n_2 = n_3 = 8$ called APFSRNet_B and set $n_1 = 4, n_2 = 8, n_3 = 8$ called APFSRNet_F. As shown in Table 1, simply increasing the depth of the network will reduce the performance of the restoration. Experiments prove that asymmetric structure is more suitable for our problem.

Comparing with Other Methods: We evaluate the performance of our method on 16×16 input resolutions, comparing with bicubic interpolation, Lapsrn [7], ESPCN [9], URDGN [14]. Lapsrn and ESPCN were trained for generic image super-resolution, so we retrain them on celebA training set to suit better for face images. As shown in Fig. 2, face images reconstructed using our method are more realistic and have more facial details. Meanwhile, Table 2 show that we have achieved the best results than the other methods on both PSNR and SSIM.

5   Conclusion

In this paper, we propose a novel framework based on cascade neural network to super-resolve a face image of very low quality to its $8\times$ version progressively. For very low-resolution face images, we use dense block to fully extract feature and ignore the limitations of the receptive field. Meanwhile, we divide the one-step upsampling into multiple steps to reduce the difficulty of reconstruction. Moreover, we add SSIM as a part of loss function to predict high-resolution face image accurately. The effectiveness of our proposed method is verified both quantitatively and qualitatively.

References

1. Dong, C., Loy, C.C., He, K., Tang, X.: Image super-resolution using deep convolutional networks. In: IEEE Transactions on Pattern Analysis and Machine Intelligence, vol. 38, pp. 295–307. IEEE (2016)
2. Fan, Y., et al.: Balanced two-stage residual networks for image super-resolution. In: CVPR Workshops 2017, pp. 1157–1164. IEEE (2017)
3. Huang, G., Liu, Z., Maaten, L.V.D., Weinberger, K.Q.: Densely connected convolutional networks. In: 2017 IEEE Conference on Computer Vision and Pattern Recognition (CVPR), pp. 2261–2269. IEEE (2017)
4. Huang, H., He, R., Sun, Z., Tan, T.: Wavelet-SRNET: a wavelet-based cnn for multi-scale face super resolution. In: 2017 IEEE International Conference on Computer Vision (ICCV), pp. 1698–1706. IEEE (2017)
5. Kim, J., Lee, J.K., Lee, K.M.: Accurate image super-resolution using very deep convolutional networks. In: 2016 IEEE Conference on Computer Vision and Pattern Recognition (CVPR), pp. 1646–1654. IEEE (2016)
6. Kim, J., Lee, J.K., Lee, K.M.: Deeply-recursive convolutional network for image super-resolution. In: 2016 IEEE Conference on Computer Vision and Pattern Recognition (CVPR), pp. 1637–1645 (2016)
7. Lai, W., Huang, J., Ahuja, N., Yang, M.: Deep Laplacian pyramid networks for fast and accurate super-resolution. In: 2017 IEEE Conference on Computer Vision and Pattern Recognition, CVPR 2017, Honolulu, HI, USA, July 21–26, 2017, pp. 5835–5843 (2017). https://doi.org/10.1109/CVPR.2017.618
8. Liu, Z., Luo, P., Wang, X., Tang, X.: Deep learning face attributes in the wild. In: 2015 IEEE International Conference on Computer Vision (ICCV), pp. 3730–3738. IEEE (2015)
9. Shi, W., et al.: Real-time single image and video super-resolution using an efficient sub-pixel convolutional neural network. In: 2016 IEEE Conference on Computer Vision and Pattern Recognition (CVPR), pp. 1874–1883. IEEE (2016)
10. Simonyan, K., Zisserman, A.: Very deep convolutional networks for large-scale image recognition. In: ICLR (2015)
11. Tai, Y., Yang, J., Liu, X.: Image super-resolution via deep recursive residual network. In: 2017 IEEE Conference on Computer Vision and Pattern Recognition (CVPR), pp. 2790–2798. IEEE (2017)
12. Tai, Y., Yang, J., Liu, X., Xu, C.: MemNet: a persistent memory network for image restoration. In: 2017 IEEE International Conference on Computer Vision (ICCV), pp. 4549–4557. IEEE (2017)

13. Wang, Z., Bovik, A.C., Sheikh, H.R., Simoncelli, E.P.: Image quality assessment: from error visibility to structural similarity. IEEE Trans. Image Process. **13**(4), 600–612 (2004)
14. Yu, X., Porikli, F.: Ultra-resolving face images by discriminative generative networks. In: 2016 European Conference on Computer Vision (ECCV), pp. 318–333 (2016)
15. Zhang, L., Zhang, L., Mou, X., Zhang, D.: A comprehensive evaluation of full reference image quality assessment algorithms. In: 2012 19th IEEE International Conference on Image Processing, pp. 1477–1480. IEEE (2012)

A Hybrid Pan-Sharpening Approach Using Nonnegative Matrix Factorization for WorldView Imageries

Guiqing He[✉][iD], Jiaqi Ji[iD], Qiqi Zhang, and Zhaoqiang Xia[iD]

School of Electronics and Information, Northwestern Polytechnical University,
Shaanxi 710072, China
guiqing_he@nwpu.edu.cn

Abstract. With the advent of WorldView series imageries (WorldView-2/3/4), it is necessary to develop new fusion approaches for remote sensing images with higher spatial and spectral resolutions. Since most existing fusion approaches are not well capable of merging multi-spectral images with eight bands, a new hybrid pan-sharpening approach is proposed in this paper. The hybrid framework integrates the multiplicative model and additive model to improve the quality of multi-spectral images. In the additive procedure, the nonnegative matrix factorization (NMF) algorithm is utilized to synthesize the intensity component for obtaining the mutual information from multi-spectral images. Then the difference information between the panchromatic image and synthetic component is injected into multi-spectral images by the spectral-adjustable weights. In the multiplicative procedure, the smoothing filter-based intensity modulation (SFIM) is used to modulate the preliminary fusion. The nonlinear fitting method is utilized to calculate the optimal parameters of the hybrid model. Visual and quantitative assessments of fused images show that the proposed approach clearly improves the fusion quality compared to the state-of-the-art algorithms.

Keywords: Image fusion · Smoothing filter-based intensity modulation · Nonnegative matrix factorization · Spectral-adjustable weight · Nonlinear fitting

1 Introduction

The fusion between the panchromatic (PAN) image and multi-spectral (MS) images aims to synthesize images with the high spatial resolution and the appropriate spectral content. So far, an amount of fusion approaches have been proposed and applied to many fields, such as remote sensing image segmentation and

Supported by the National Nature Science Foundation of China (NO.61402368 and NO.61702419), Aerospace Support Fund (2017-HT-XGD), Aerospace Science and Technology Innovation Foundation (2017 ZD 53047).

Z. Lin et al. (Eds.): PRCV 2019, LNCS 11858, pp. 703–713, 2019.
https://doi.org/10.1007/978-3-030-31723-2_60

classification [1–3]. Recently, remote sensing images with more spectral bands and higher spatial resolutions can be achieved with the development of senor imageries [4]. Especially, the satellites of WorldView series (i.e., WorldView-2, WorldView-3 and WorldView-4) can collect high-resolution data in at least eight spectral bands. These WorldView-series imageries with higher spatial and spectral resolutions can be used to overcome the camouflage techniques and adversarial strategies in remote sensing.

Several (but not all) existing fusion approaches can be used to fuse images with higher resolutions and more bands. These approaches can generally be categorized into three classes: *multiplicative model, additive model* and *substitutive model*. The multiplicative models include the smoothing filter-based intensity modulation (SFIM) algorithm, Brovey transform (BT) algorithm and their extensions [5,6]. The multiplicative models have limited the ability of extracting spatial details while the spectral distortions are not apparent. The additive models contain the Gram-Schmidt (GS) based algorithms [7–9] and filter based algorithms [10–12]. These approaches can obviously improve the spatial details but suffer from spectral distortions. The substitutive models include the generalized intensity-hue-saturation (GIHS) [13], principal component analysis (PCA) [14], multi-resolution analysis (MRA) [15,16] and hyper-spherical color sharpening (HCS) [17]. These algorithms would suffer from the spatial distortions. Among these techniques, the hybrid approaches combined different models are attractive as they can leverage the advantages of two types of models. For instance, the BT-SFIM [6] can enhance the spatial resolution when the spectral distortions are limited; the adaptive GS and generalized Laplacian pyramid (GLP) are combined to inject the global counterparts [18]. However, these hybrid approaches are more concerned with the lower-resolution and less-band imageries, especially for the four-band imageries, such as IKONOS and Quickbird, while these approaches are not well capable of images with higher spatial and spectral resolutions. Thus, it is necessary to develop new fusion approaches for such remote sensing images (i.e. WorldView imageries).

In this paper, a novel hybrid approach combined the multiplicative model (i.e. SFIM [5]) with additive model (i.e. GS based approach) is presented to fuse eight-band multi-spectral images from a series of WorldView satellites. In the hybrid framework, the nonnegative matrix factorization (NMF) algorithm is proposed to synthesize the intensity component for additive GS procedure. The spectral-weighted fusion is utilized to inject the information of the PAN image into MS images and then modulated by the multiplicative SFIM algorithm. The nonlinear fitting method is used to calculate the optimal parameters of hybrid model.

The hybrid framework is introduced briefly in Sect. 2. In Sect. 3, the NMF algorithm as well as the nonlinear fitting method are described for fusing the PAN and MS images. To verify the efficiency of our proposed method, visual and quantitative assessments are performed on PAN and MS images in Sect. 4. Finally, the conclusion is presented in Sect. 5.

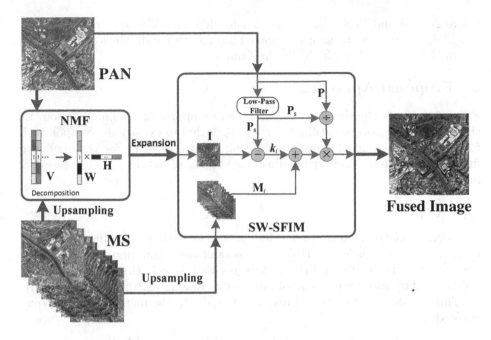

Fig. 1. Illustration of our proposed approach for image fusion.

2   Hybrid Framework

The general hybrid framework combined the multiplicative model with additive model, which has been presented in some works [6,19], can be expressed as

$$\mathbf{M}_i^F = \frac{\mathbf{P}}{\mathbf{P}_L}\Big(\mathbf{M}_i + k(\mathbf{P}_s - \mathbf{P}')\Big),\ 1 \leq i \leq N \tag{1}$$

where N is the number of bands and $N = 4$ in [19] and [6]. The PAN image, ith-band MS image and the fused MS image are denoted as $\mathbf{P}$, $\mathbf{M}_i$ and $\mathbf{M}_i^F$, respectively. $\mathbf{P}_s$ is the smoothed version of $\mathbf{P}$ and can be achieved by the filtering methods. $\mathbf{P}_L$ preserves the most spatial information of $\mathbf{P}$ and can be $\mathbf{P}_s$ or other alternatives. $\mathbf{P}'$ represents the synthetic component, which can be achieved by averaging MS images [6] or low-pass filtering [18].

It is required that the synthetic component represents the mutual information among the remote sensing images in the hybrid model. However, the mutual information for each band cannot be obtained by merely averaging. Thus, in this paper, we propose to utilize the NMF algorithm to extract the component and inject it into MS images with adjustable spectral weights. To distinguish from Eq. 1, our proposed model can be rewritten as

$$\mathbf{M}_i^F = \frac{\mathbf{P}}{\mathbf{P}_s}\Big(\mathbf{M}_i + k_i(\mathbf{P}_s - \mathbf{I})\Big),\ 1 \leq i \leq N \tag{2}$$

where $N = 8$ and $k_1, k_2, \ldots, k_n$ are usually different. The spectral-adjustable weight k_i determines the supplementary ratio for ith band. The synthetic component $\mathbf{I}$ is extracted by the NMF algorithm.

3   Proposed Approach

Figure 1 presents the flowchart of our proposed approach for image fusion. In the proposed method, we utilize the NMF algorithm to extract the component $\mathbf{I}$ for obtaining the mutual information among images. Then we use the nonlinear fitting method to learn spectral-adjustable weights of hybrid model to fuse MS images.

3.1   NMF

Nonnegative matrix factorization techniques can be viewed as casting the original matrix to the subspace and finding a low-rank approximation to the original matrix, which the matrix values are kept positive. Hence, the NMF techniques can be used to discover the mutual information among multiple images [20, 21].

Through the vectorization of matrices $\mathbf{P}$ and $\mathbf{M}_i$, the matrix $\mathbf{V}$ can be constituted as

$$\mathbf{V} = [vec(\mathbf{P}), vec(\mathbf{M}_1), \ldots, vec(\mathbf{M}_i), \ldots, vec(\mathbf{M}_N)].$$

where the $vec(\cdot)$ operation represents a column vector concentrated by the elements of one matrix. Since the MS images have lower resolutions than the PAN image, the size of matrix $\mathbf{P}$ is usually larger than $\mathbf{M}_i$. To compose the matrix $\mathbf{V}$, it is mandatory to perform the interpolation operation on the MS images and make the size of matrix $\mathbf{M}_i$ equal to the matrix $\mathbf{P}$.

The objective of the NMF algorithm is to minimize the cost of reconstructing the matrix $\mathbf{V}$ and it can be derived by solving the problem as follows

$$\min_{W, H} \ \frac{1}{2} \sum_{i=1}^{M} \sum_{j=1}^{N} \left(\mathbf{V}_{ij} - (\mathbf{WH})_{ij} \right)^2 \tag{3}$$

$$s.t. \quad \mathbf{W}_{ia} \geq 0, \ \mathbf{H}_{bj} \geq 0, \ \forall i, a, b, j$$

where M is the amount of pixels of PAN image and upsampled MS images. $\mathbf{V} \approx \hat{\mathbf{V}} = \mathbf{WH}$ and i, j, a, b are the indices of matrix. Here, $\mathbf{W}$ and $\mathbf{H}$ are the decomposing factors of the matrix $\mathbf{V}$, where $\mathbf{W} \in R^{M \times 1}$ and $\mathbf{H} \in R^{1 \times N}$. Furthermore, $\mathbf{WH}$ can be interpreted as the product of coefficient matrix $\mathbf{H}$ and basis matrix $\mathbf{W}$. From this point of view, the basis matrix $\mathbf{W}$ describes the latent low-rank subspace, in which the mutual information of images can be discovered.

To fast solve the aforementioned optimization problem, we use the projected gradient method to decompose the matrix $\mathbf{V}$ [22]. The updated rules for two decomposing factors $\mathbf{W}$ and $\mathbf{H}$ are directly given by

$$\mathbf{W}^{t+1} = max\left(0, \mathbf{W}^t - \alpha(\mathbf{WH} - \mathbf{V})\mathbf{H}^T\right)$$

$$\mathbf{H}^{t+1} = max\left(0, \mathbf{H}^t - \alpha\mathbf{W}^T(\mathbf{WH} - \mathbf{V})\right) \tag{4}$$

where α represents the learning rate and the superscript t denotes the iterative state. Through the matrix decomposition, the matrix $\mathbf{W}$ can exclude the variation and obtain the mutual information among images. So, in this context, the estimated intensity component $\mathbf{I}$ can be achieved by expanding decomposed matrix $\mathbf{W}$ in columns.

3.2 Nonlinear Fitting

Since the component $\mathbf{I}$ represents the mutual information between PAN image and MS images, we utilize their correlation coefficients to learn the spectral-adjustable weights. For ith band, the correlation coefficient c_i can be calculated as

$$c_i = \frac{Cov(\mathbf{M}_i, \mathbf{P})}{\sigma(\mathbf{M}_i)\sigma(\mathbf{P})} \tag{5}$$

where the covariance of two images is denoted as $Cov(\mathbf{M}_i, \mathbf{P})$. $\sigma(\mathbf{M}_i)$ and $\sigma(\mathbf{P})$ represent the standard deviations of images $\mathbf{M}_i$ and $\mathbf{P}$ respectively.

To discover the nonlinear relation between the correlation coefficient and best spectral-adjustable weight, we utilize a five-parameter logistic function for mapping their relevance, which is usually applied in the field of image quality assessment [23].

$$k_i = \beta_1 \left(\frac{1}{2} - \frac{1}{1 + e^{\left(\beta_2(c_i - \beta_3)\right)}} \right) + \beta_4 c_i + \beta_5 \tag{6}$$

where $\beta_1, \ldots, \beta_5$ are the fitting parameters. We use the best experimental weights to learn these parameters, which will be introduced in Sect. 4.1.

3.3 Fusion

Based on the NMF and SFIM algorithms, the steps of image fusion are summarized as follows, which is also shown in Fig. 1.

Step 1. Upsample MS images to the same size of the PAN image and obtain $\mathbf{M}_1, \ldots, \mathbf{M}_i, \ldots, \mathbf{M}_N$; Smooth the PAN image with average filtering to obtain $\mathbf{P}_s$.

Step 2. Concentrate all the upsampled MS images and PAN image to the matrix $\mathbf{V}$; Calculate the optimized basis matrix $\hat{\mathbf{W}}$ by minimizing

$$\hat{\mathbf{W}} = arg \min_{W,H} \quad \frac{1}{2} \|\mathbf{V} - \mathbf{WH}\|_F^2$$

Expand the matrix $\hat{\mathbf{W}}$ to obtain the estimated intensity component $\mathbf{I}$.

Step 3. Calculate the correlation coefficients for MS images; Estimate the spectral-adjustable weight k_i by

$$\hat{k}_i = \beta_1 \left(\frac{1}{2} - \frac{1}{1 + e^{\left(\beta_2(c_i - \beta_3)\right)}} \right) + \beta_4 c_i + \beta_5$$

Step 4. Fuse the images for ith band according to the estimated coefficients $\hat{k}_i$ as

$$\mathbf{M}_i^F = \frac{\mathbf{P}}{\mathbf{P}_s}\Big(\mathbf{M}_i + \hat{k}_i(\mathbf{P}_s - \mathbf{I})\Big).$$

4   Experiment Result and Analysis

In the experiments, two types of satellite images from WorldView imageries are used to evaluate our proposed algorithm. As the images from WorldView-4 have the same spatial resolution and geometry precision with the images from WorldView-3. So we choose two sets of images from the WorldView-2 and WorldView-3 imageries. The first images are of size 2048 × 2048 pixels for MS images and 8192 × 8192 pixels for PAN images (over San Clementa, California, USA, taken in March 2012 by WorldView-2). The second ones are of size 3778 × 2709 pixels for MS images and 15112 × 10836 pixels for PAN images (over Sydney, Australia, taken in October 2014 by WorldView-3). These images are very large and not appropriate for visualization, so we randomly choose some detailed sub-regions from source images for fast evaluation and visualization.

Total five approaches are used to compare the performance of our proposed algorithm (denoted as NMF-SW-SFIM): CS-PR [8], CS-PSO [9], BT-SFIM [6], OF [12] and SFIM [5]. Among these approaches, the CS-PR and CS-PSO (using the correlation coefficients as the similarity criteria) approaches are the additive models using different methods of extracting components while the SFIM approach is the multiplicative model. The optimal filter (OF) approach is on behalf of filter based fusion while the BT-SFIM approach combines the multiplicative and additive models.

To investigate the fused images, the visual analysis and quantitative assessment are jointly used to evaluate the spatial and spectral performance of our proposed algorithm. To inspect the visual content of fused images, we choose the R, G and B bands to synthesize the color images. For quantitative assessment, the conventional evaluation metrics are used [24], including the mean of spatial correlation coefficients and spectral correlation coefficients (mCC), ERGAS, spectral angle mapper (SAM) and quality with no reference (QNR) [25].

4.1   Parameter Learning

To fit the parameters in Eq. 6, we generate best experimental weights by twenty experiments (i.e. fusing twenty sub-region images) for each imagery. In the experiments, twenty sub-regions of each source image are chosen randomly as the training samples and will not be used for testing. For the MS images of each sub-region, the proposed algorithm is used by replacing the values k_i in Eq. 6 with best experimental weights, which are achieved by grid search. In other words, the values of weight k_i would increase from 0.1 to 1.5 with the step 0.1. The weights that obtain the highest metrical value (i.e. the mCC) will be chosen as best experimental weights k_i.

With the values of c_i and k_i, the parameters of nonlinear fitting can be obtained by iterative least squares estimation. Table 1 shows the values of parameter fitting for WorldView-2 (WV-2) and WorldView-3 (WV-3) imageries.

Table 1. The values of fitting parameters for WorldView-2 and WorldView-3 data.

The fitting parameters					
Imagery	β_1	β_2	β_3	β_4	β_5
WV-2	−1.273	−150.168	0.694	−2.775	2.764
WV-3	0.380	−534.236	0.891	0.299	0.221

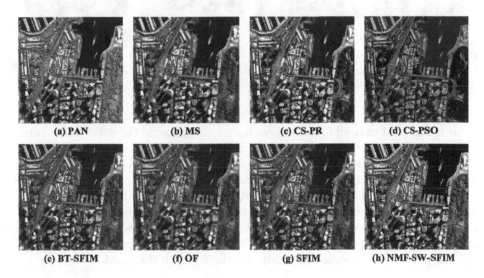

Fig. 2. Exemplar WorldView-2 data (512×512 sub-region image). (a) PAN image; (b) MS image; (c) CS-PR; (d) CS-PSO;(e) BT-SFIM; (f) OF; (g) SFIM; (h) NMF-SW-SFIM (Our proposed approach).

4.2 Visual Analysis

The visual inspection of three bands (Bands 2–3, 5, i.e., R, G, and B bands) with all comparison approaches from WV-2 and WV-3 imageries are shown in Figs. 2 and 3. The fusion results of other five bands (Bands 1, 4, 6–8) with our proposed approach are visually shown in Fig. 4.

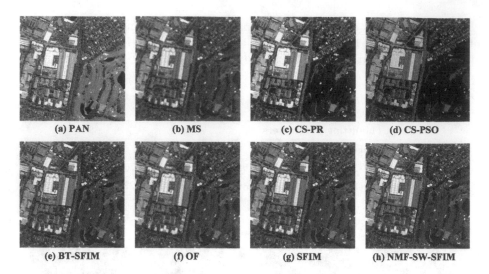

Fig. 3. Exemplar WorldView-3 data (512 × 512 sub-region image). (a) PAN image; (b) MS image; (c) CS-PR; (d) CS-PSO;(e) BT-SFIM; (f) OF; (g) SFIM; (h) NMF-SW-SFIM (Our proposed approach).

It is observed that all fusion images have well enhanced the details of colored MS images. However, the CS-PR and CS-PSO algorithms lead to the spectral distortions as the colors of fused images have been changed compared to source images. It might be induced that the intensity component is directly generated by all MS images. The OF and SFIM algorithms cannot sharpen the edges of MS images as both of them merely utilize the low-pass filters, where the SFIM algorithm uses the average filter and the OF algorithm uses the Gaussian-like optimal filter. Compared to the BT-SFIM algorithm, our proposed algorithm obtains more spatial details, especially for the edges in the fused images.

4.3   Quantitative Assessment

Tables 2 and 3 show the quantitative comparison results of the state-of-the-art approaches on all sub-region images from WorldView-2 and WorldView-3 imageries. The QNR metric evaluates the fused images without references while other three metrics evaluate the fusion by degrading the MS and PAN images to use the original MS images as the references. According to the results, it is noticed that the fused images by our proposed approach can provide the richest information including the spatial and spectral details. The most important merit of the proposed approach is that it can be more capable of higher spectral resolutions than other algorithms.

Table 2. The quantitative metric values of all approaches for WorldView-2 imagery.

Approach	Reduced resolution		Full resolution	
	mCC	ERGAS	SAM	QNR
CS-PR	0.8713	5.6037	5.2975	0.8134
CS-PSO	0.8641	5.8014	5.1225	0.8089
BT-SFIM	0.8953	5.0785	4.5137	0.8396
OF	0.8714	5.3241	4.9036	0.8217
SFIM	0.8601	6.7033	6.4061	0.8045
NMF-SW-SFIM	**0.9080**	**4.2517**	**3.9028**	**0.8573**

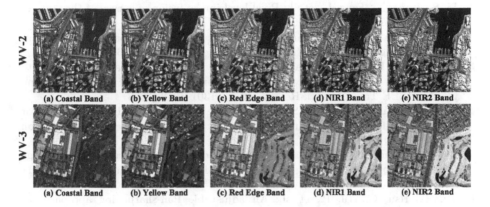

Fig. 4. The fusion results of multiple bands from WV-2 and WV-3 data (512 × 512 sub-region image) using our proposed approach. (a) Coastal Band; (b) Yellow Band; (c) Red Edge Band; (d) NIR1 Band; (e) NIR2 Band.

Table 3. The quantitative metric values of all approaches for WorldView-3 imagery.

Approach	Reduced resolution		Full resolution	
	mCC	ERGAS	SAM	QNR
CS-PR	0.8834	5.4302	5.0595	0.8673
CS-PSO	0.8791	5.5143	4.9867	0.8550
BT-SFIM	0.9079	4.9506	4.4637	0.8803
OF	0.8902	5.1601	4.6830	0.8692
SFIM	0.8698	6.5230	6.1476	0.8203
NMF-SW-SFIM	**0.9183**	**4.1342**	**3.6584**	**0.8914**

5   Conclusion

A novel hybrid approach combined the multiplicative model and additive model was presented to fuse the satellite images with higher spatial and spectral resolutions. In additive procedure, the NMF algorithm was proposed to extract the mutual component among images, which was injected into MS images with the adjustable weights. These weights were spectrally valued and calculated by nonlinear fitting. The preliminary fusion by the additive model was then modulated by SFIM algorithm for achieving the final fusion. Through the visual inspection and quantitative analysis on the imageries of WorldView series, it is demonstrated that our proposed approach improved the spatial details with less spectral distortions compared to the state-of-the-art approaches.

References

1. Li, S., Kang, X., Fang, L., et al.: Pixel-level image fusion: a survey of the state of the art. Inform. Fusion **33**, 100–112 (2017)
2. Vivone, G., Alparone, L., Chanussot, J., et al.: A critical comparison among pansharpening algorithms. IEEE Trans. Geosci. Remote **53**(5), 2565–2586 (2014)
3. Thomas, C., Ranchin, T., Wald, L., et al.: Synthesis of multispectral images to high spatial resolution: a critical review of fusion methods based on remote sensing physics. IEEE Trans. Geosci. Remote **46**(5), 1301–1312 (2008)
4. Zhang, Q., Liu, Y., Blum, R.S., et al.: Sparse representation based multi-sensor image fusion for multi-focus and multi-modality images: a review. Inform. Fusion **40**, 57–75 (2018)
5. Liu, J.G.: Smoothing filter-based intensity modulation: a spectral preserve image fusion technique for improving spatial details. Int. J. Remote Sens. **21**(18), 3461–3472 (2000)
6. Tu, T., Hsu, C., Tu, P., et al.: An adjustable Pan-sharpening approach for IKONOS/QuickBird/GeoEye-1/WorldView-2 imagery. IEEE J.-STARS **5**, 125–134 (2012)
7. Aiazzi, B., Baronti, S., Selva, M.: Improving component substitution pansharpening through multivariate regression of ms +pan data. IEEE Trans. Geosci. Remote **45**(10), 3230–3239 (2007)
8. Choi, J., Yu, K., Kim, Y.: A new adaptive component-substitution-based satellite image fusion by using partial replacement. IEEE Trans. Geosci. Remote **49**(1), 295–309 (2011)
9. Wang, W., Jiao, L., Yang, S.: Novel adaptive component-substitution-based pansharpening using particle swarm optimization. IEEE GRSL **12**(4), 781–785 (2015)
10. Garzelli, A., Nencini, F.: Panchromatic sharpening of remote sensing images using a multiscale kalman filter. Pattern Recogn. **40**(12), 3568–3577 (2007)
11. Mahyari, A.G., Yazdi, M.: Panchromatic and multispectral image fusion based on maximization of both spectral and spatial similarities. IEEE Trans. Geosci. Remote **49**(6), 1976–1985 (2011)
12. Shahdoosti, H., Ghassemian, H.: Fusion of MS and PAN images preserving spectral quality. IEEE GRSL **12**(3), 611–615 (2015)
13. Tu, T., Huang, P.S., Hung, C., et al.: A fast intensity-hue-saturation fusion technique with spectral adjustment for IKONOS imagery. IEEE GRSL **1**(4), 309–312 (2004)
14. Wang, Z., Ziou, D., Armenakis, C., et al.: A comparative analysis of image fusion methods. IEEE Trans. Geosci. Remote **43**(6), 1391–1402 (2005)

15. Gonzalez-Audicana, M., Saleta, J.L., Catalan, R.G., et al.: Fusion of multispectral and panchromatic images using improved IHS and PCA mergers based on wavelet decomposition. IEEE Trans. Geosci. Remote **42**(6), 1291–1299 (2004)
16. Alparone, L., Aiazzi, B.: MTF-tailored multiscale fusion of high-resolution MS and PAN imagery. Photogramm. Eng. Remote Sens. **72**(5), 591–596 (2006)
17. Guo, Q., Ehlers, M., Wang, Q., et al.: Ehlers pan-sharpening performance enhancement using HCS transform for n-band data sets. Int. J. Remote Sens. **38**(17), 4974–5002 (2017)
18. Aiazzi, B., Baronti, S., Lotti, F., et al.: A comparison between global andcontext-adaptive pansharpening of multispectral images. IEEE GRSL **6**(2), 302–306 (2009)
19. Tu, T., Lee, Y., Huang, P., et al.: Modified smoothing-filter-based technique for IKONOS-quickbird image fusion. Opt. Eng. **45**(6), 711–725 (2006)
20. Xia, Z., Feng, X., Peng, J., et al.: A regularized optimization framework for tag completion and image retrieval. Neurocomputing **147**, 500–508 (2015)
21. Xia, Z., Peng, X., Feng, X., et al.: Scarce face recognition via two-layer collaborative representation. IET Biom. **7**(1), 56–62 (2018)
22. Lin, C.: Projected gradient methods for nonnegative matrix factorization. Neural Comput. **19**(10), 2756–2779 (2007)
23. Chang, H.W., Yang, H., Gan, Y., et al.: Sparse feature fidelity for perceptual image quality assessment. IEEE Trans. Image Process. **22**(10), 4007–4018 (2013)
24. Alparone, L., Wald, L., Chanussot, J., et al.: Comparison of pansharpening algorithms: Outcome of the 2006 GRS-S data-fusion contest. IEEE Trans. Geosci. Remote **45**(10), 3012–3021 (2007)
25. Alparone, L., Aiazzi, B., Baronti, S., et al.: Multispectral and panchromatic data fusion assessment without reference. Photogramm. Eng. Remote Sens. **74**(2), 193–200 (2008)

Distinguishing Individual Red Pandas from Their Faces

Qi He[1], Qijun Zhao[1(✉)], Ning Liu[1], Peng Chen[2], Zhihe Zhang[2], and Rong Hou[2(✉)]

[1] College of Computer Science, Sichuan University, Chengdu 610065, Sichuan, China
qjzhao@scu.edu.cn
[2] Sichuan Key Laboratory of Conservation Biology for Endangered Wildlife, Chengdu Research Base of Giant Panda Breeding, Chengdu 610086, Sichuan, China
405536517@qq.com

Abstract. Individual identification is essential to animal behavior and ecology research and is of significant importance for protecting endangered species. Red pandas, among the world's rarest animals, are currently identified mainly by visual inspection and microelectronic chips, which are costly and inefficient. Motivated by recent advancement in computer-vision-based animal identification, in this paper, we propose an automatic framework for identifying individual red pandas based on their face images. We implement the framework by exploring well-established deep learning models with necessary adaptation for effectively dealing with red panda images. Based on a database of red panda images constructed by ourselves, we evaluate the effectiveness of the proposed automatic individual red panda identification method. The evaluation results show the promising potential of automatically recognizing individual red pandas from their faces. We are going to release our database and model in the public domain to promote the research on automatic animal identification and particularly on the technique for protecting red pandas.

Keywords: Red panda · Animal identification · Face recognition

1 Introduction

Ailurus fulgens, also known as lesser panda and red panda (see Fig. 1), is endemic to the Himalayan - hengduan mountains. They are mainly distributed in China, Nepal, India, Bhutan and Myanmar. It is estimated that there are only 16,000 to 20,000 red pandas in the world while 6400 to 7600 of them are in China. According to [1], over the past 50 years, the number of wild red pandas has decreased by about 40% in China due to habitat loss, human activities and hunting. The population of wild red pandas in the world is also decreasing year by year [2].

The first author Qi He is a graduate student.

© Springer Nature Switzerland AG 2019
Z. Lin et al. (Eds.): PRCV 2019, LNCS 11858, pp. 714–724, 2019.
https://doi.org/10.1007/978-3-030-31723-2_61

Existing red pandas were listed as endangered species by IUCN in 2000, and they were classified as a Category II species under the Wild Animal Protection Law in China. In order to protect red pandas, it is important to maintain precise and up-to-date information of the population and distribution of red pandas, which requires the technique of distinguishing individual red pandas.

Traditionally, people have to spend many months to collect the excreta and biology samples of wild red pandas, based on which different red pandas are identified. This method is obviously labour-intensive and has long identification cycles. As more and more surveillance cameras are deployed for monitoring animals, people manually identify individual red pandas on the camera-trap images based on their appearance. For captive breeding red pandas, people distinguish individual red pandas either via visual inspection or by scanning the microelectronic microchips implanted in the body of red pandas. However, manual identification and visual inspection are tedious and error-prone, especially for people without training. Identification using microchips is generally more accurate, but as an invasive approach, it is hurtful to red pandas and unfriendly to operate.

Fig. 1. Examples of red panda images of the same (top row) and different individuals (bottom row).

With the rapid development of computer vision technology in the past decade, some researchers attempt to automatically identify individuals of specific species based on images of the animals [3–12]. Following the pipeline of typical pattern recognition systems, they extract discriminative features from certain body parts of the animals, compute the similarity scores between images of the animals based on the extracted features, and finally determine the identities of the individual animals in the images according to their similarity scores with the reference images. Table 1 summarizes existing research on image-based automatic individual identification of animals. Compared with traditional methods, these automatic methods are not only more friendly but also more efficient. Some of them achieve very promising identification accuracy, which demonstrates the potential of image-based automatic identification of individual animals.

Motivated by these studies, we aim to investigate in this paper the feasibility of automatically distinguishing individual red pandas based on their face images. To this end, we construct an image database of red pandas with labeled identities, which is going to be released for research purpose. By exploring latest deep learning techniques, we develop methods for automatically detecting red panda faces, locating their eyes and noses, and extracting features from the aligned red panda faces. We finally build a framework for automatic identification of individual red pandas, and evaluate its effectiveness on the constructed database. In the rest of this paper, we first review related work on automatic individual identification of animals in Sect. 2, then introduce in detail our framework for red panda identification in Sect. 3, followed by evaluation results in Sect. 4, and finally conclude the paper in Sect. 5.

2   Related Work

As summarized in Table 1, automatic individual identification methods have been studied for a number of species, including African penguins [3], northeast tigers [4], cattle [5], lemurs [6], dairy cows [7], great white sharks [8], pandas [9], primates [10], pigs [11], and ringed seals [12]. Different species usually have largely different appearance; however, different individual animals of the same species may differ quite slightly in their appearance, and can be distinguished only by fine-grained detail. Almost all of the related studies are based on specific body parts of an animal to determine its identity. For those species that have salient characteristics in their appearance (e.g., the spots on the breast of penguins [3], and the rings on the body of ringed seals [12]), individual identification can be done by extracting and comparing their salient features. For those species that have subtle appearance differences between different individuals, such as pigs [11], lemurs [6], and pandas [9], the most common solution to individual identification is to focus on the body parts with relatively rich textures and extract discriminative features from the parts.

Red pandas obviously belong to those species that have subtle appearance differences between different individuals. Fortunately, their faces have relatively salient textures. According to Table 1, most methods for the species that do not have salient appearance differences are based on learned features. With learning based models, researchers do not have to manually find out the exact parts that are helpful to identification. Inspired by these works, we build a deep neural network model for identifying individual red pandas based on their face images. Compared with existing animal identification methods, ours is fully automatic. Almost all existing methods are based on pre-cropped pictures of specific body parts, such as the tailhead images of dairy cows [7] and face images of pig [11]. In contrast, our method takes the image of a red panda as input and automatically detect its face, extracts features and matches the features to the ones enrolled in

Table 1. A summary of existing image-based individual identification of animals.

Species	Discriminative body parts	Database		Features		Accuracy
		#subjects	#images	Hand-crafted	Learned	
African penguins [3]	Spots on breast	N/A		✓		75.5%
Northeast tigers [4]	Texture on body	103	10300		✓	N/A
Cattle [5]	Muzzle print	N/A		✓		N/A
Lemurs [6]	Face	80	462	✓		98.7% ± 1.81%
Dairy cows [7]	Tailhead	10	1965	✓		99.7%
Great white sharks [8]	Fin shape	N/A	240	✓		N/A
Pandas [9]	Face	18	131		✓	58.82%
Primates [10]	Face	280	11637		✓	N/A
Pigs [11]	Face	10	1553		✓	96.7%
Ringed seals [12]	Rings on body	131	591	✓		N/A

the gallery to determine its identity. In addition, to the best of our knowledge, the research in this paper is the first attempt to image-based automatic individual identification of red pandas.

3 Method

3.1 Overview

The proposed automatic individual red panda recognition framework mainly includes three modules: face detection, face alignment and identification. See Fig. 2. Given an image of red panda, the first step is to detect whether there is a red panda face in the image or not. If there is a red panda face, its eyes are located, according to which the red panda face image is aligned such that the line connecting the two eyes is horizontal. Finally, features are extracted from the cropped and aligned face image and compared to obtain the red panda's identity. In the remainder of this section, we introduce the detail of each module.

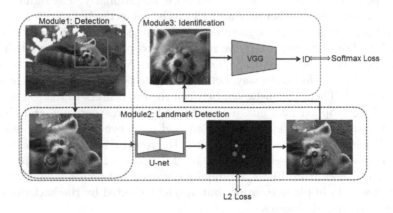

Fig. 2. The flowchart of proposed method.

3.2   Red Panda Face Detection

In this paper, we use the well-known object detection model YOLOv2 [19] to detect red panda faces because of its balance between efficiency and accuracy. We fine-tune the pre-trained YOLOv2 model in [20] by using our collected red panda images. Using the fine-tuned detection model, the bounding boxes of the red panda faces in the images are obtained. If more than one red panda faces are detected in one image, only the largest one is identified. Red panda face images are then cropped according to the bounding boxes. In these images, the red panda faces could be rotated (see Fig. 2), and the resulting face images would contain much background that may distract the identification process. Therefore, in the next module, we align and further crop the red panda face images to minimize the influence of posture on the identification of the red pandas.

3.3   Red Panda Face Alignment

Like in human face recognition, we align red panda face images based on the centers of the two eyes such that the line connecting the eye centers is horizontal. For this sake, we have first to locate the eye centers on red panda faces. Looking closely at the red panda faces, it is easy to notice that the eyes and nose of red pandas have obvious distinct characteristics compared with other regions on the face; that is, they appear as round and black spots. Inspired by this observation, we locate the centers of eyes and nose on red panda face by segmenting the eye and nose regions rather than directly estimating their coordinates.

Specifically, given a red panda face image, we employ U-Net [16] to segment two eye regions and one nose region. The output of this U-Net is a three-channel image that has the same size as the input image, and each of its three channels represents one of the three regions (see Fig. 2). Take one of the eye regions as an example. Its corresponding channel is a binary mask, on which the values of pixels in the eye region equal to 255 and the values of the rest pixels are set to 0. The eye region is defined as a circular region centered at the eye center and of a pre-specified radius. The nose region is defined similarly. The radius of eye regions and nose region is set as 7 and 13 pixels, respectively.

Once the eye regions are segmented, we compute their centroids as the eye centers. Based on the eye centers, we rotate the red panda face image such that the two eye centers are on the same horizontal line. Afterwards, we further crop the face image in the following way. Let the distance between the two eye centers be denoted as d. Then, the distances between the eye centers to the top and the bottom of the cropped face image are a*d and b*d, respectively, and the left and right margins with respect to the left and right eye centers are both c*d. Here, a, b, and c are chosen by experience. To crop the red panda face images, the ratio parameters are set as a = 1.3, b = 1.7 and c = 1.2 in this paper. This way, as can be seen from Fig. 2, the finally obtained red panda face images are not only free from in-plane rotation, but also less affected by the background in the original red panda images.

Note that the nose center is not utilized when cropping the red panda face images. But we include the nose region during segmentation. This is because nose regions have similar appearance as eye regions and they, if not segmented together with the eye regions, could lead to false detection of eye regions. Besides, they can effectively constrain eye regions from irregular positions because of the relative spatial distribution of eyes and nose on red panda faces.

3.4   Red Panda Identification

Given an aligned and cropped red panda face image, we use the VGG-16 network [17] to extract features for identification. VGG-16 is widely used in human face recognition. Here, we take the VGG-16 model in [21] as a pre-trained model, and use our collected red panda face images to fine-tune it. The obtained VGG-16 model is applied to extract features from the input red panda face images, and the similarity between two red panda face images is calculated based on the cosine distance between their features.

To determine the identity of an input probe red panda image, its facial feature is first extracted as mentioned above, and then compared with the features of all the red pandas enrolled in the gallery. Its identity is finally determined as the one that has the highest similarity with it. Note that if a similarity threshold is specified and the highest similarity is below the threshold, then the probe red panda image is not from any of the red pandas in the gallery; in other words, it is an unknown new individual red panda.

4   Experiments

4.1   Database

In order to evaluate the effectiveness of the proposed method, we construct a database of red panda images by ourselves because no such database is available in the public domain. All our data are collected at the Chengdu Research Base of Giant Panda Breeding from three sources: (i) high resolution pictures taken by a professional photographer, (ii) images extracted from videos (one image every ten frames), and (iii) lower resolution pictures taken with mobile phones. Totally, 51 individual red pandas are imaged, whose identity information is obtained by scanning the microchips implanted in their bodies. The total number of acquired red panda images is 7,091. Note that in this paper we require that both eyes of the red pandas should be visible in the images. For each image, we manually mark the bounding box of the red panda face together with three landmarks in it (i.e., nose center, left and right eye centers). See Fig. 1 for example images of individual red pandas in our database.

It is worthy mentioning that the images extracted from the same video might be highly correlated. Consequently, using such images for training, the generalization ability of the obtained model would be poor, while using them for testing, the resulted recognition accuracy could be misleadingly high. Being aware of this problem, we use SSIM [18] to measure the image-level similarity among the video images of each individual. Starting from a randomly chosen image of an individual, we establish the image set of the individual by gradually adding other images of it if the similarity between the images and the already retained images is smaller than a pre-specified threshold. After processing the images of all the individuals, we finally get a database of 2,877 images of 51 red pandas.

In the following experiments, we randomly choose the images of 34 individual red pandas as training data, while the images of the rest 17 individuals are used for test. In the identification experiments, the gallery consists of all the images of the 34 training individuals and 50% of the images of the 17 test individuals, and the probe consists of the other 50% of the images of the 17 test individuals.

4.2   Identification Accuracy by Different Features

In this experiment, we compare the identification accuracy of our learned features (denoted by VGG) with that of some representative hand-crafted features, including local binary patterns (LBP) [14], histograms of orientation of gradients (HOG) [15], and the feature extracted by applying principal component analysis to the red panda face images (PCA) [13]. These hand-crafted features have been explored by other researchers for identifying individuals of other species. Figure 3 plots the obtained Cumulative Match Characteristic (CMC) curves. Obviously, our learned features achieve the highest accuracy among the four different feature representations. In all the following experiments, we use the learned VGG features.

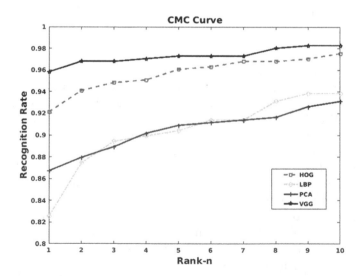

Fig. 3. Cumulative Match Characteristic (CMC) curves by different feature extraction algorithms.

4.3   Performance Before and After Discarding Correlated Images

In this experiment, we consider the following three cases: (i) training VGG-16 with the original image set, and testing it on the cleaned image set (i.e., correlated images are discarded), (ii) training and testing VGG-16 both with cleaned image set, (iii) training VGG-16 with the cleaned image set, while testing it on the original image set. To compute the recognition accuracy, we randomly construct 1,000 genuine pairs and 1,000 imposter pairs. The obtained Receiver Operating Characteristic (ROC) curves are shown in Fig. 4. These results prove the necessity of discarding correlated images in the database to improve the generalization ability of the trained model as well as to make the evaluation more reliable.

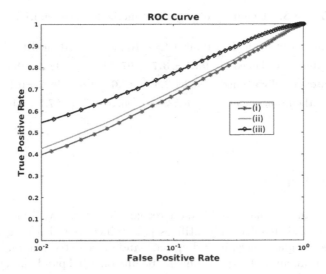

Fig. 4. The Receiver Operating Characteristic (ROC) curves of the models trained and evaluated on different data sets. (i) training with the original image set, and testing on the cleaned image set, (ii) training and testing both with cleaned image set, (iii) training with the cleaned image set, while testing on the original image set.

4.4   Impact of Face Alignment

We first evaluate the precision of our proposed method in localizing the nose and eye centers. We measure the landmark localization precision by the mean squared errors (MSE) between the predicted and the ground truth coordinates of the landmarks on all the images of the 17 test individuals. The results are reported in Table 2. On average, our proposed method achieves a landmark localization error of about 3 pixels on 224*224 images.

To assess the impact of alignment on the identification accuracy, we compare the performance of VGG-16 on manually aligned images, automatically aligned

Table 2. Error of landmarks predicted by our model.

Landmarks	Left eye center	Right eye center	Nose center	Average error
MSE (pixels)	3.09	2.98	3.32	3.13

images by our method, and original unaligned images. Table 3 presents the three-fold cross validation identification results in terms of rank-1, rank-5 and rank-10 identification rates. As can be seen from the results, alignment is helpful for more accurate identification, and the automatic face alignment method can work well for individual identification of red pandas.

Table 3. The impact of alignment methods on recognition.

Alignment methods	Rank-1 (%)	Rank-5 (%)	Rank-10 (%)
Manually aligned	**93.5 ± 3.7**	97.6 ± 0.6	**98.3 ± 0.4**
Automatically aligned	93.3 ± 2.5	**97.6 ± 0.8**	98.2 ± 0.4
Without alignment	91.6 ± 2.4	95.1 ± 0.7	97.2 ± 0.9

5 Conclusion

In this paper, an automatic red panda recognition framework based on facial images is proposed. It effectively utilizes pre-trained deep learning models for processing red panda images, including red panda face detection, alignment and feature extraction, and achieves promising results on a red panda image database constructed by ourselves. However, this paper still has the following limitations. (i) The red panda images are captured in relatively constrained conditions rather than in-the-wild conditions. It is much more challenging but of even more importance to deal with in-the-wild red panda images. (ii) The size of the database is small. The effectiveness of automatic individual identification still needs to be further evaluated on larger scale datasets of more challenging images (e.g., with large variations in pose and illumination). Nevertheless, as the first attempt to automatically identify individual red pandas, this paper presents a promising effort along this direction, and we expect more significant advance as more data become available.

Acknowledgements. This research is supported by the National Natural Science Foundation of China (31300306), the Sichuan Science and Technology Program (2018JY0096), Chengdu Research Base of Giant Panda Breeding (CPB2018-02, CPB2018-01), the Chengdu Research Base of Giant Panda Breeding Research Foundation (CPF Research 2014-02, 2014-05), and the Panda International Foundation of the National Forestry Administration, China (CM1422, AD1417). The authors would like to thank Huan Tu for her constructive suggestions on paper writing, thank Zhicong Feng and Chengdong Wang from Sichuan University for their helpful discussion and assistance in data collection, as well as Kongju Wu, Kai Cui and other colleagues from Chengdu Research Base of Giant Panda Breeding for their help with acquiring data of red pandas.

References

1. Xiu, Y.: Genetic Diversity of the Captive Red Panda in China and Paternity. Yangzhou University, Doctor (2015)
2. The IUCN red List of threatened species. https://doi.org/10.2305/IUCN.UK.2015-4.RLTS.T714A45195924.en. Accessed 18 Apr 2018
3. Burghardt, T., Thomas, B., Barham, P., et al.: Automated visual recognition of individual African penguins. In: Fifth International Penguin Conference, Ushuaia (2004)
4. Zhang, P.: Study on Northeast Tiger Skin Texture Extraction and Recognition Based on BP Network. Northeast Forestry University, Doctor (2008)
5. Tharwat, A., Gaber, T., Hassanien, A.E., Hassanien, H.A., Tolba, M.F.: Cattle identification using muzzle print images based on texture features approach. In: Körner, P., Abraham, A., Snášel, V. (eds.) Proceedings of the Fifth International Conference on Innovations in Bio-Inspired Computing and Applications IBICA 2014. AISC, vol. 303, pp. 217–227. Springer, Cham (2014). https://doi.org/10.1007/978-3-319-08156-4_22
6. Crouse, D., Jacobs, R.L., Richardson, Z., et al.: LemurFaceID: a face recognition system to facilitate individual identification of lemurs. Bmc Zool. 2(1), 2 (2017)
7. Li, W., Ji, Z., Wang, L., et al.: Automatic individual identification of Holstein dairy cows using tailhead images. Comput. Electron. Agric. 142, 622–631 (2017)
8. Hughes, B., Burghardt, T.: Automated visual fin identification of individual great white shark. Int. J. Comput. Vis. 122(3), 542 557 (2017)
9. Hou, J., Zheng, B., et al.: Facial recognition of giant pandas based on developmental network recognition. ACTA Theriol. Sin. 39(1), 43–51 (2019)
10. Deb, D., et al.: Face recognition: primates in the wild. In: IEEE 9th International Conference on Biometrics Theory, Applications and Systems (BTAS), pp. 1–10. IEEE (2019)
11. Hansen, M.F., Smith, M.L., Smith, L.N., et al.: Towards on-farm pig face recognition using convolutional neural networks. Comput. Ind. 98, 145–152 (2018)
12. Chehrsimin, T., Eerola, T., Koivuniemi, M., et al.: Automatic individual identification of Saimaa ringed seals. IET Comput. Vis. 12(2), 146–152 (2018)
13. Jolliffe, I.T.: Pincipal component analysis. J. Mark. Res. 25(4), 513 (2002)
14. Liao, S., Zhu, X., Lei, Z., Zhang, L., Li, S.Z.: Learning multi-scale block local binary patterns for face recognition. In: Lee, S.-W., Li, S.Z. (eds.) ICB 2007. LNCS, vol. 4642, pp. 828–837. Springer, Heidelberg (2007). https://doi.org/10.1007/978-3-540-74549-5_87
15. Dalal, N., Triggs, B.: Histograms of oriented gradients for human detection. In: International Conference on Computer Vision and Pattern Recognition, pp. 886–893. IEEE Computer Society (2005)
16. Ronneberger, O., Fischer, P., Brox, T.: U-Net: convolutional networks for biomedical image segmentation. In: Navab, N., Hornegger, J., Wells, W.M., Frangi, A.F. (eds.) MICCAI 2015. LNCS, vol. 9351, pp. 234–241. Springer, Cham (2015). https://doi.org/10.1007/978-3-319-24574-4_28

17. Simonyan, K., Zisserman, A.: Very deep convolutional networks for large-scale image recognition. In: CoRR abs/1409.1556 (2015)
18. Wang, Z., Bovik, A.C., Sheikh, H.R., et al.: Image quality assessment: from error visibility to structural similarity. IEEE Trans. Image Process. **13**(4), 600–612 (2004)
19. Redmon, J., Farhadi, A.: YOLO9000: better, faster, stronger. In: 2017 IEEE Conference on Computer Vision and Pattern Recognition (CVPR2017), pp. 6517–6525. IEEE Computer Society (2017)
20. The pretrained YOLOv2 Model. https://pjreddie.com/darknet/yolov2/. Accessed 30 Jan 2019
21. The pretrained VGG_FACE.caffemodel. http://www.robots.ox.ac.uk/~vgg/software/vgg_face/. Accessed 30 Jan 2019

Facial Expression Recognition: Disentangling Expression Based on Self-attention Conditional Generative Adversarial Nets

Haohao Li[1(✉)], Qiong Liu[1], Xiaoming Wei[2], Zhenhua Chai[2], and Wenbai Chen[1]

[1] Beijing Information Science and Technology University,
Beijing 100192, China
lihaohao@mail.bistu.edu.cn
[2] Meituan Corporation, Beijing 100192, China

Abstract. The accuracy of facial expression recognition is greatly impacted by individual attributes. To address this problem, we propose a Disentangle Expressions based on Self-Attention Conditional Generative Adversarial Nets method, where facial expression recognition takes by two steps. The first step constructed a generative model to generate the corresponding neutral face image and disentangle expression features. The second step trained the classifier with preserved disentangled expression features. A self-attention layer is used to learn correlations among different facial motion units. Inspired by the relativistic GAN [1], we use the discriminator to predict the relative realness of the generated images and provide strong supervision for more details recovery. The results from extensive experiments on three public facial expression datasets (CK+ , MMI, Oulu-CASIA) proved that our method is more effective than the known state-of-the-art methods in recognition accuracy.

Keywords: Facial expression recognition · Self-attention · CGAN · Expressive image · Neutral image

1 Introduction

Face expression, as one of the most important biometric features, is an indispensable part for human-computer interactions. The research on facial expression recognition has been transformed from lab-controlled settings to complex and rapidly changeable realistic environment. However, there are many interference factors [2–5], such as illumination brightness, head postures, identity characteristics, human races and individual ages, etc., which can significantly impact the effectiveness of recognition. Recently, the study of facial expression recognition has helped to improve the effectiveness in the changes of light and head postures [6]. However, the other influencing factors that are closely related to individual attributes: age, race and gender, still remain

---

Haohao Li is a student at Beijing Information Science and Technology University.

© Springer Nature Switzerland AG 2019
Z. Lin et al. (Eds.): PRCV 2019, LNCS 11858, pp. 725–735, 2019.
https://doi.org/10.1007/978-3-030-31723-2_62

challenging and attract many research activities. For example, some researchers began to focus on the impact of individual identity differences [7, 8].

Some researchers compared the expression image with its neutral image to calculate the differences for further distinguishing, conceiving that the expression image was the addition of expression features and the neutral face image [9, 10]. Some researchers have combined the image-differences with feature-differences for facial expression recognition [8, 11, 12]. However, these methods limited to the neutral image are not always available. So many researchers resort to deep learning method to generate the corresponding neutral images based on expression images. As we known, the Generative Adversarial Network (GAN) is good at generating data in various forms (images, sounds, languages, etc.) [13]. It contains two models, one is the generative model (Generator), and the other is the discrimination model (Discriminator). During the training period, the goal of generator is to generate more realistic pictures for deceiving discriminator, and the objective of discriminator is to distinguish the sample is true or false. Therefore, the training of generator and discriminator is a dynamic "game process". In order to solve the problem that GAN cannot generate pictures with specific attributes, some research puts forward Conditional Generative Adversarial Nets (CGAN) [14]. The condition variable y is introduced into discriminator and generator and used for generating specific results. It has been proved to be effective and widely used in subsequent works, including face attributes editing [15], architectural reconstruction from edge maps [16] and image de-raining [17].

In this paper, we focus on how to extract expression features and commit to disentangle expressions based on self-attention CGAN (DESA-CGAN) method. Different from the previous works [8, 11, 12], that utilize pixel-level differences and feature-level differences between expression images and neutral images to recognize the expressive image, while our approach tries to disentangle face expression features directly through training the DESA-CGAN model and implement the classifier training process by expression features. It is remarkable that the expression features are preserved in the network to train the classifier after generating the corresponding neutral image of any input expressive image. Meanwhile, the attention mechanism is introduced into our model. We specially take the correlation among face motion units and texture details into account for facial expression recognition. In this way, our proposed method can overcome the influences of individual attributes and improve the accuracy of facial expression recognition. The framework of our work is shown in Fig. 1. The main contributions of this paper are as follows:

1. We propose the DESA-CGAN model to generate neutral facial images for disentangling their corresponding expression features, which enhances the validity of feature representations and alleviates the issues of individual attributes.
2. The attention mechanism is introduced to learn the relationship between expression-related motion units. It obviously improves the recognition accuracy by modeling the dependencies of motion units.
3. We pay more attention to the detail features and the high frequency information by using relativistic discriminator. It achieves a better performance on generating the neutral expression images.

2   Related Works

In the past few decades, facial expression recognition has made great progress. The human-designed features were widely used in researches, including Gabor filter, histograms of Local Binary Patterns (LBP) [18], Histograms of Oriented Gradients (HOG) [19], Scale Invariant Feature Transform (SIFT) [20], Spatiotemporal Manifold (STM-ExpLet) [5] and temporal modeling of shapes (TMS) [21]. However, these human-designed features cannot adapt to the changes well and just achieve good performance on the specific dataset. Recently, Deep Learning as the hierarchical structure learning attempts to model high-level abstractions in data by using a group of processing layers and it has been proved to be more practical in real-world scenarios.

Some previous work [8, 11, 12, 22] has shown that facial expression recognition can be improved by calculating the differences between the expression images and the neutral images. In this way, the facial expression image was subtracted by the corresponding neutral image to obtain its expression features, emphasizing the expression features while weakening the influence of the individual's attributes. Zafeiriou et al. [10] formulated the feature extraction process as an L1 optimization problem and utilized different images for sparse facial expression representations. Kim et al. [8] proposed to utilize contrastive representation features for recognition, that were calculated at the embedding layer of a deep network by comparing the given image with its generated neutral image from a deep encoder-decoder network. Yang et al. [22] proposed a De-expression Residual Learning method (De-RL) to extract the expressive component for recognition. However, the correlation of the motion units wasn't taken into account in previous researches.

In this paper, we propose the DESA-CGAN method to learn facial expression features. Through the comparison of differences between expression images and neutral images, its features are disentangled by network and attention layer is embedded to learn the relationship among motion units. Meanwhile, features are used to train classifiers in the en-coding network. The proposed method pays more attention to learning the relationship between the expression motion units and the detail features for capturing more effective information and improving the robustness of expression recognition.

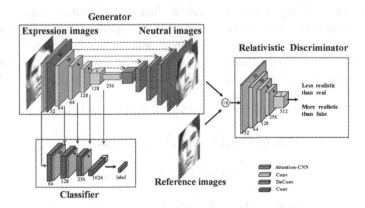

Fig. 1. The framework of DESA-CGAN model.

3 The Proposed Method: DESA-CGAN

Feature-differences obtained by comparing expression images with its neutral images are more effective. For example, an expression image has tiny variations. We have acquired reliable results by analyzing feature-differences. Neutral expressions have no facial expression features, so we use the neutral image as a reference image. Differences in facial expressions are influenced by the changes of individual attributes. The method uses the network to learn the feature-differences that are the potential factors of expression. In this way, the influences of identity, posture changes and other factors on facial expressions accuracy will be eliminated, and the recognition accuracy will be improved further.

We define β as the feature-differences hiding factor, assuming a pair of images $<I_{exr}, I_{refer}>$, where I_{exr} is the expression image and I_{refer} is the reference image, so

$$I_{exr} = I_{refer} + \beta \tag{1}$$

The proposed DESA-CGAN (Fig. 1) method contains two steps. First, the reference images are generated by the DESA-CGAN, which is the disentangling expressions process. Expression features (β) remain in the network layers. As shown in formula (1), I_{exr} represents the input of any expression images, and I_{refer} is the reference images generated by the network. Second, expression features are extracted from the encoding layer in DESA-CGAN network to further train the classifier.

3.1 Neutral Face Regeneration

We use DESA-CGAN model to generate the corresponding reference images for the input of any expression images. The GAN contains two models, one is the generator (G), and the other is the discriminator (D). In the training process, G is to capture the data distribution, and D is to distinguish the sample from real data or generate data. A pair of image $<I_{input}, I_{reference}>$ is used as the input data of the network. Generator uses I_{input} to reconstruct the reference image I_{output}. Then $<I_{input}, I_{reference}, yes>$ and $<I_{input}, I_{output}, no>$ are used as the input of discriminator. Discriminator predicts the probability that real images are more realistic than the generated images relatively, which is different from the previous discriminator. In formula (3), the value of $D(I_r, I_f)$ is close to 1, it means that the input image is more realistic than the generated image. At the same time, we add L_{per} loss into discriminator so that the generated image is sufficiently sharp. Therefore, the objective of the discriminator is expressed as follows:

$$L_{DESA-CGAN}(D) = [logD(I_r, I_f) + \log(1 - D(I_f, I_r))] \tag{2}$$

$$D(I_r, I_f) = \sigma(C(I_{reference}) - C(G(I_{input}))) \tag{3}$$

$$D(I_f, I_r) = \sigma(C(G(I_{input})) - C(I_{reference})) \tag{4}$$

where σ is sigmoid function, $C(x)$ is the output of non-transform discriminator.

The objective for the generator is expressed as:

$$L_{DESA-CGAN}(G) = log\big(1 - D(I_r, I_f)\big) + log\big(D(I_f, I_r)\big) + \theta_1 L_s \qquad (5)$$

$$L_s = ||I_{reference} - G(I_{input})||_1 \qquad (6)$$

where L1 is to evaluate the content loss of 1-norm distance between the generated images and the real images, θ_1 is the coefficient that balances the different loss terms.

3.2 The Self-attention Layer

The method adopted by Kim and Yang [8, 22] is to generate neutral images for the input expression images based on CGAN model that is constructed by the convolution layer. Because the convolution layer can deal with the information in a local neighborhood, but cannot effectively learn the dependencies among the long-distance parts. In the process of expression, there is a strong correlation between different motor units. In this section, we introduce the self-attention mechanism (Fig. 2) into the CGAN model so that the generator can learn the correlation of different parts.

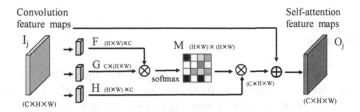

Fig. 2. The details of the self-attention layer. The softmax operation is performed on each row. The ⊗ denotes matrix multiplication. The ⊕ denotes element-wise sum operation. Best viewed in color.

The features $I_j \in R^{C \times H \times W}$ from the previous network layer are first converted into two features $(F, G) \in R^{C \times H \times W}$ for further studying the correlation of different parts. Then, we reshape them into $R^{C \times (H \times W)}$ shape and transpose F into $R^{(H \times W) \times C}$ shape. After that, we perform a matric multiplication between F and G and apply softmax layer to calculate the attention map $M \in R^{(H \times W) \times (H \times W)}$. Meanwhile, the feature I_j convert into $H \in R^{C \times H \times W}$ and H is reshaped into $R^{C \times (H \times W)} R^{(H \times W) \times C}$. Then we perform a matric multiplication between M and H. Finally, we reshape the result into $R^{C \times H \times W}$ and multiply it by a scale parameter α and perform element-wise sum operation with the features I_j.

$$M_{j,i} = \frac{exp\left(F_i \times G_j\right)}{\sum_{i=1}^{N} exp\left(F_i \times G_j\right)} \tag{7}$$

$$O_j = \alpha \sum_{i=1}^{N} \left(M_{j,i} \ H\right) + I_j \tag{8}$$

where $N = H \times W$, $\beta_{j,i}$ represents the ith location impact on the jth region, α is initialized as 0 and gradually learns to assign more weight [23], and $O_j \in R^{C \times H \times W}$ is the output of the self-attention layer.

3.3   The Classification of Facial Expression

In this experiment, we extract expression features from the generator and find that the features in encoding layer are more representative. So we only select the features in the encoding layer. As shown in Fig. 1, we get the output of the generator in the previous layer, during the process of constructing classifier, then extract the features through the local convolution network and merge them with the same size generator features. We adopt the cross entropy loss function for classification. In order to utilize the feature effectively, the number of local CNN channels is greater than that of feature channels of generator.

4   Experiments

Compared with the state-of-the-arts methods, our proposed method has been evaluated on three public facial expression databases, including CK+ [24], Oulu-CASIA [25] and MMI [26]. We apply the Viola Jones [27] face detector for face detection and landmark detection. The face region is cropped and resized to the size of 70×70. To avoid over-fitting, we use data augmentation method to generate more training data. Five patches of 64×64 are cropped out from five locations of each image (center and four corners, respectively), and then each image is rotated respectively by [−10, −8, −6, −4, −2, 0, 2, 4, 6, 8, 10]. All of images are flipped horizontally and vertically. Regard with the different databases, we adopt the same network architecture to train all parameters in the same database shared. The generator model is not pre-trained on the relevant database. We use Adam optimizer with a base learning rate of 0.0002, momentum of 0.9, batch size of 64 and dropout of 0.3 for fully connected layers during training. We use 150 epochs for training generative model and 80 epochs for the classification model. We set $\theta_1 = 100$. All the experiments are implemented on Python and deep learning framework TensorFlow and are trained on the NVIDIA 1080ti GPU.

CK+ Database. The Extended Cohn-Kanade database (CK+) [24] is widely used by researchers and served as the benchmark database for recognition tasks. It is composed of 123 individuals and 593 image sequences. Each image sequence starts from a neutral face and ends with peak facial expression. The 327 valid image sequences of 118 individuals are labeled with one of seven expressions, i.e. sadness, surprise, disgust, fear, happiness, contempt and anger. This database is relatively small, so we select the last three images reasonably, which results in 981 images. We divide the database into

10 independent individual subsets according to the identity information. Therefore, the image of one individual will not appear in two independent subsets. This 10-fold cross-validation follows the previous works.

Oulu-CASIA Database. The Oulu-CASIA database [25] images are captured from two types of cameras under three illumination conditions. We chose image sequences under strong illumination condition with the VIS camera as the experimental data. The database contains 480 image sequences that are made up of 80 individuals. Each of them is labeled as one of six basic expressions (excluding the contempt of CK + database). Each image sequence is transited from neutral expression to peak expression. We select the last three images for getting more data. Similar to CK + database, we adopt 10-fold cross-validation method to divide the database into 10 subsets in terms of individual identity.

MMI Database. MMI [25] database contains 236 image sequences composed of 31 individuals. Each image sequence is marked as one of six basic expressions (excluding the contempt of CK+ database). This database has profile facial expression, even beyond six basic expressions. So we select 208 image sequences from the database. Each image sequence starts with neutral expression, reaches the peak in the intermediate point video and ends with neutral expression. We select the middle three images and get 624 images for the experiment. Similar to the CK+ database, we adopt the 10-fold cross-validation method to divide the database into 10 subsets with independent individuals in term of individual identity.

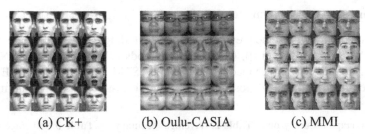

(a) CK+   (b) Oulu-CASIA   (c) MMI

Fig. 3. The illustration of the generated neutral faces on three databases. On each group, from the left column to the right column are the generated images by CGAN, DESA-CGAN (ours), the ground-truth and the input expression image respectively.

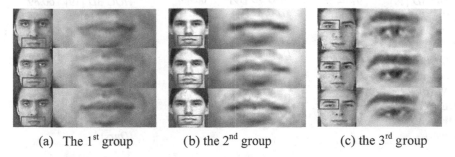

(a) The 1st group   (b) the 2nd group   (c) the 3rd group

Fig. 4. The details of the generated neutral face images. On each group, from top to bottom are the results of CGAN, DESA-CGAN (ours), and the ground-truth respectively

4.1 Visualization of Regenerated Neutral Faces

In this section, we observe the neutral face images by different generation model to understand the reconstruction of the details. Figure 3 illustrates several samples of the generated neutral face images on CK+ , Oulu-CASIA and MMI databases respectively. Figure 4 illustrates the details of several generated neutral face images. As shown in Figs. 3 and 4, the image generated by our method is more clearly than that of CGAN method, especially around the mouth and eyes, which means that our approach is more effective on the face details recovery.

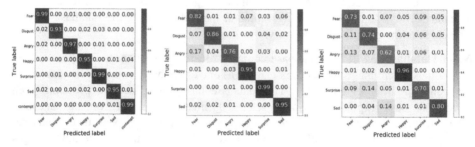

Fig. 5. The confusion matrix on CK+   **Fig. 6.** The confusion matrix on Oulu-CASIA   **Fig. 7.** The confusion matrix on MMI.

4.2 Expression Recognition Results

Through comparing with some previous methods, including hand-craft feature methods (LBP-TOP [18] and HOG [19]), CNN-based methods (3D-CNN [4], 3D-CNN-DAP [4], IACNN [7], DeRL [22]), video-based methods (STM-ExpLet [5]) and DE-CGAN (without self-attention), our proposed method outperforms the state-of-the-art methods.

Table 1. Average accuracy on the CK+ database

Methods	Accuracy
BP-TOP [18]	*88.99*
HOG 3D [19]	*91.44*
3D-CNN [4]	*85.90*
3D-CNN-DAP [4]	*92.40*
IACNN [7]	*95.37*
STM-ExpLet [5]	*94.19*
DeRL [22]	*97.30*
CNN (baseline)	*88.20*
DE-CGAN	*96.80*
DESA-CGAN (Ours)	*98.00*

Table 2. Average accuracy on the Oulu-CASIA database

Method	Accuracy
LBP-TOP [18]	*59.51*
HOG 3D [19]	*60.89*
3D-CNN [4]	*53.20*
3D-CNN-DAP [4]	*63.40*
STM-ExpLet [5]	*75.12*
DeRL [22]	*88.00*
CNN (baseline)	*71.80*
DE-CGAN	*86.31*
DESA-CGAN (Ours)	*88.80*

Table 3. Average accuracy on the MMI database

Method	Accuracy
LBP-TOP [18]	*59.51*
HOG 3D [19]	*60.89*
IACNN [4]	*71.55*
DeRL [22]	*73.23*
STM-ExpLet [5]	*75.12*
CNN (baseline)	*56.40*
DE-CGAN	*74.50*
DESA-CGAN (Ours)	*75.80*

In the CK+ database, we use static images for training and testing. As shown in Table 1, our method DE-CGAN and DESA-CGAN gets the high recognition accuracy value up to 96.8% and 98.0% respectively. Figure 5 illustrates the confusion matrix of our method conducted in the CK+ database. It can be concluded that our method is superior to other methods and the attention mechanism is critical for facial expression recognition.

In the Oulu-CASIA VIS database, similar to the CK+ case, our method DESA-CGAN (Table 2) achieves the highest accuracy value of 88.8% for facial expression recognition. By adding self-attention mechanism, the accuracy of expression recognition increases by 2.49% (from 86.31% to 88.0%). Comparing with other methods, only our method and DeRL [22] method use static images for facial expression recognition. Figure 6 illustrates the confusion matrix of our method conducted in the Oulu-CASIA database and our method achieves a high accuracy rate in happy, surprise and sad.

In the MMI database, similar to the CK+ case, our method DESA-CGAN (Table 3) achieves the highest recognition accuracy value of 75.8% compared with others. Figure 7 is the corresponding confusion matrix on the MMI database. It can be seen that our proposed method is 2.57% and 1.3% higher than DeRL [22] DE-CGAN. The recognition accuracy is relatively lower comparing to that on CK+ and Oulu-CASIA since variable wearing appearance or other factors are included in the MMI database, such as the person wears a hat, the expression peak is in the intermediate point of a video. However, our method is still superior to other methods as shown in Table 3.

5 Conclusion

In this paper, we propose a new method, named Disentangle Expressions based on Self-Attention CGAN (DESA-CGAN), to effectively learn facial expression features by reducing the impact of personal attributes for facial expression recognition. In the first step of this algorithm, the self-attention CGAN network is trained to generate the corresponding neutral facial images for any input expression images. This training step aims at disentangling expression features so that the extracted expression features are more efficient for further classification. Secondly, the disentangled facial expression features are used to train the classifier. In order to learn more effective features, we introduce the attention layer to study the correlations between different facial motion units. According to the extensive experiment on three widely used databases, our proposed method is superior to the baseline CNN method and the most of state-of-the-art methods that extract features from image sequences. Moreover, it specifically highlights that our method can learn more effective expression information for classification tasks in facial expression recognitions.

Acknowledgement. This work is supported by the Program for the Outstanding Young Talents of Municipal Colleges and Universities of Beijing under contract No.CIT&TCD201804054.

References

1. Jolicoeur-Martineau, A.: The relativistic discriminator: a key element missing from standard GAN. arXiv preprint arXiv:1807.00734 (2018)
2. Zhao, X., Lin, Y., Heikkila, J.: Dynamic texture recognition using volume local binary count patterns with an application to 2D face spoofing detection. IEEE Trans. Multimedia **20**(3), 552–566 (2018)
3. Klaser, A., Marszałek, M., Schmid, C.: A spatio-temporal descriptor based on 3D-gradients. In: British Machine Vision Conference, pp. 1–10 (2008)
4. Liu, M., Li, S., Shan, S.: Deeply learning deformable facial action parts model for dynamic expression analysis. In: Asian Conference on Computer Vision, pp. 143–157 (2014)
5. Liu, M., Shan, S., Wang, R.: Learning expression lets on spatio-temporal manifold for dynamic facial expression recognition. In: IEEE Conference on Computer Vision and Pattern Recognition, pp. 1749–1756 (2014)
6. Zhang, F., Zhang, T., Mao, Q.: Joint pose and expression modeling for facial expression recognition. In: IEEE Conference on Computer Vision and Pattern Recognition, pp. 3359–3368 (2018)
7. Meng, Z., Liu, P., Cai, J.: Identity-aware convolutional neural network for facial expression recognition. In: IEEE International Conference on Automatic Face & Gesture Recognition, pp. 558–565 (2017)
8. Kim, Y., Yoo, B.I., Kwak, Y.: Deep generative-contrastive networks for facial expression recognition. arXiv preprint arXiv:1703.07140 (2017)
9. Lee, S.H., Plataniotis, K.N.K., Ro, Y.M.: Intra-class variation reduction using training expression images for sparse representation based facial expression recognition. IEEE Trans. Affect. Comput. **5**(3), 340–351 (2014)
10. Zafeiriou, S., Petrou, M.: Sparse representations for facial expressions recognition via l1 optimization. In: IEEE Conference on Computer Vision and Pattern Recognition, pp. 32–39 (2010)
11. Zeng, Z., Pantic, M., Roisman, G.I.: A survey of affect recognition methods: audio, visual, and spon-taneous expressions. IEEE Trans. Pattern Anal. Mach. Intell. **31**(1), 39–58 (2009)
12. Sariyanidi, E., Gunes, H., Cavallaro, A.: Automatic analysis of facial affect: a survey of registration, representation, and recognition. IEEE Trans. Pattern Anal. Mach. Intell. **37**(6), 1113–1133 (2015)
13. Pantic, M., Pentland, A., Nijholt, A., Huang, T.S.: Human computing and machine understanding of human behavior: a survey. In: Huang, T.S., Nijholt, A., Pantic, M., Pentland, A. (eds.) Artifical Intelligence for Human Computing. LNCS (LNAI), vol. 4451, pp. 47–71. Springer, Heidelberg (2007). https://doi.org/10.1007/978-3-540-72348-6_3
14. Valstar, M.F., Mehu, M., Jiang, B.: Meta-analysis of the first facial expression recognition challenge. IEEE Trans. Syst. Man, Cybern. **42**(4), 966–979 (2012)
15. Lu, Y., Tai, Y.W., Tang, C.K.: Attribute-guided face generation using conditional cycleGAN. In: European Conference on Computer Vision, pp. 282–297 (2018)
16. Isola, P., Zhu, J.Y., Zhou, T.: Image-to-image translation with conditional adversarial networks. In: IEEE Conference on Computer Vision and Pattern Recognition, pp. 1125–1134 (2017)
17. Zhang, H., Sindagi, V., Patel, V.M.: Image de-raining using a conditional generative adversarial network. IEEE Trans. Circ. Syst. Video Technol. (2019)
18. Zhao, G., Pietikainen, M.: Dynamic texture recognition using local binary patterns with an application to facial expressions. IEEE Trans. Pattern Anal. Mach. Intell. **6**, 915–928 (2007)

19. Klaser, A., Marszalek, M., Schmid, C.: A spatio-temporal descriptor based on 3D-gradients. In: British Machine Vision Conference, pp. 1–10 (2008)
20. Yuce, A., Gao, H., Thiran, J.P.: Discriminant multi-label manifold embedding for facial action unit detection. In: IEEE International Conference and Workshops on Automatic Face and Gesture Recognition, pp. 1–6 (2015)
21. Jain, S., Hu, C., Aggarwal, J.K.: Facial expression recognition with temporal modeling of shapes. In: IEEE International Conference on Computer Vision Workshops, pp. 1642–1649 (2011)
22. Yang, H., Ciftci, U., Yin, L.: Facial expression recognition by de-expression residue learning. In: IEEE Conference on Computer Vision and Pattern Recognition, pp. 2168–2177 (2018)
23. Zhang, H., Goodfellow, I., Metaxas, D.: Self-attention generative adversarial networks. arXiv preprint arXiv:1805.08318 (2018)
24. Lucey, P., Cohn, J.F., Kanade, T.: The extended Cohn-Kanade dataset (CK+): a complete dataset for action unit and emotion-specified expression. In: IEEE Conference on Computer Vision and Pattern Recognition-Workshops, pp. 94–101 (2010)
25. Zhao, G., Huang, X., Taini, M.: Facial expression recognition from near-infrared videos. Image Vis. Comput. 29(9), 607–619 (2011)
26. Pantic, M., Valstar, M., Rademaker, R.: Web-based database for facial expression analysis. In: IEEE International Conference on Multimedia and Expo (2005)
27. Viola, P., Jones, M.J.: Robust real-time face detection. Int. J. Comput. Vis. 57(2), 137–154 (2004)

Image Enhancement of Shadow Region Based on Polarization Imaging

Mohamed Reda[1], Linghao Shen[1,2], and Yongqiang Zhao[1,2(✉)]

[1] School of Automation, Northwestern Polytechnical University,
Xi'an, China
{mohamedredaismail, shenly}@mail.nwpu.edu.cn,
zhaoyq@nwpu.edu.cn
[2] Research & Development Institute of Northwestern Polytechnical University
in Shenzhen, Shenzhen, China

Abstract. Object of shadow area suffers from low contrast and noise, causing difficulties for object detection and recognition. However, conventional image enhancement methods perform inefficiently in severer shadow conditions, where the contrast enhancement is not obvious, or the noise amplification is huge. In fact, Polarization information can be preserved even in very heavy shadows. Combining the polarization information with the intensity and chromaticity information of the original image can overcome the above problems. This paper proposes a method of object enhancement in shadow based on polarization imaging. Firstly, this paper puts forward degree of polarization (*DOP*) Invariance Prior and *DOP*-Chromatic Consistency Prior. Then, based on these two priors, a feedback image enhancement method based on polarization imaging is proposed. Experiments show that the proposed method is superior to the other conventional image enhancement methods.

Keywords: Shadow enhancement · Polarized imaging · DOP Invariance Prior · DOP-Chromatic Consistency Prior

1 Introduction

The existence of shadow will annihilate the object in the background, so that the performance of the algorithms, such as image segmentation, object detection, tracking, and 3D structure reconstruction, can be affected or even be failed [1–3]. The shadow area has the following characteristics with respect to the non-shadow area around it [4]: the light is partially occluded, and the shadow area has a lower brightness. In general, the shadow and the non-shadow region have different chromaticity, and the shadow does not change the texture features of the original surface.

According to the characteristics of the shadow above, the researches of image enhancement technology are achieved for object detection and recognition [5, 6]. Recently, there are several ways to enhance the visible light images: by using a relational graph of paired regions, Hoiem realized the removal of the shadow area effectively [7, 8]. In the framework of deep learning, Li proposed an effective shadow removal method based on CNN [9]. These methods depend on the single image and

© Springer Nature Switzerland AG 2019
Z. Lin et al. (Eds.): PRCV 2019, LNCS 11858, pp. 736–748, 2019.
https://doi.org/10.1007/978-3-030-31723-2_63

enhance the existing image information. Existing methods of objects enhancement in shadow are mostly based on intensity and chromaticity attributes. If chrominance and intensity are similar, the objects and background in shadow cannot be distinguished without prior condition. In addition to the method of using panchromatic images only, Rüfenacht fused the near-infrared image and the panchromatic image to distinguish between dark objects and shadow [10]. The shortcoming of the image enhancement in the shadow area can be overcome by using effective contrast stretching. A generalized ambiguity masking algorithm is proposed by Deng, which significantly improved the contrast and clarity of the image [2]. Wang proposed an image enhancement algorithm based on non-uniform illumination [1], which enhances the image details and preserves the naturalness of the image. Fu proposed a new image enhancement probability method based on the simultaneous estimation of illumination and reflectivity [4]. Ying designed a low-light image enhancement framework based on multi-exposure fusion [11]. On the other hand, these methods perform inefficiently in severer shadow conditions [12, 13]. Moreover, the image cannot be recovered efficiently based on the intensity and chromaticity information especially in severer shadow condition.

Polarization is one of the main characteristics of light. The polarization state of the electromagnetic wave will varies according to the material surface characteristics [14, 15]. The change of illumination does not change polarization characteristics [16]. Through theoretical derivation and statistical analysis, meanwhile it is found that the polarization information and color images are locally consistent in the clear image. With these two priors, an Image Enhancement method based on the joint constraint of degree of polarization (DOP) and chromatic is proposed. According to the invariance of polarization and the consistence between polarization information and panchromatic images, the irradiance of the object is estimated.

In this paper, our contribution can be summarized as follows:

1. Based on theories and experiments, we sum the close relationships between polarization information and panchromatic image up into two priors: *DOP* Invariance Prior and *DOP*-Chromatic Consistency Prior.
2. Based on the two priors, an Image Enhancement method based on the joint constraint of *DOP* and chromatic is proposed. Experiments show that our method is superior to other conventional methods.

2 *DOP* Invariance and *DOP*-Chromatic Consistency Priors

2.1 Polarization Imaging Model in Shadow Region

Shadow will reduce the visibility of the image due to the existence of the veil, which keeps out the straight light on the object. The incident light on the object is mainly from the scattering of the air particles, as shown in Fig. 1 [17, 18]. So, the image becomes dimmed and distinguishing the object from the shadow will be difficult [19]. In addition, as the exposure is low in the shadow, so more current noise can be generated [20]. The features of the shadow region will be blurred by the noise effect caused by shadow, which affects the analysis of the image [21]. Considering the shadow's degradation effects of two images, we propose a new imaging model:

$$I(x) = f(x)L(x) + n \qquad (1)$$

where x represents the coordinate of a pixel point. I represents the irradiance observed by imager. L represents the original irradiance of the image, f means the degradation caused by shadow: image intensity reduction and contrast reduction, and n represents the random noise generated in the camera.

Then, the ordinary irradiance L can be obtained from (1) as follows:

$$L(x, y) = f^{-1}(x, y)I(x, y) - f^{-1}(x, y)n \qquad (2)$$

where f^{-1} is the inverse of f process in (1) which means the progress of enhancing the brightness and contrast of the image, but it also amplifies the noise.

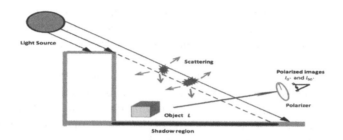

Fig. 1. Imaging model of objects in shadow.

The polarization characteristics of objects in the shadow region can be calculated from polarized images. However, conventional imaging cannot obtain polarized images. The polarizer places in front of the camera rotates at different angles to obtain the polarized images with its two different polarization angles ($I_{0°}$ and $I_{90°}$). Then the irradiance observed I of the polarized color images can be written as:

$$I(x) = I_{0°}(x) + I_{90°}(x) \qquad (3)$$

2.2 *DOP* Invariance of Different Light Intensities

The polarization state of objects in shadow can be measured by *DOP*. *DOP* is defined as the proportion of polarized light to the total incident light. And it can be written as:

$$DOP(x) = \frac{I_{0°}(x) - I_{90°}(x)}{I_{0°}(x) + I_{90°}(x)} \approx \frac{f(x)L_{0°}(x) - f(x)L_{90°}(x)}{f(x)L_{0°}(x) + f(x)L_{90°}(x)} = \frac{L_{0°}(x) - L_{90°}(x)}{L_{0°}(x) + L_{90°}(x)} \qquad (4)$$

where $L_{0°}$ and $L_{90°}$ are the ordinary irradiances of $I_{0°}$ and $I_{90°}$, respectively. It is noticed from (4) that the approximately equal ($\approx$) is used due to the presence of noise. As can be seen from (4) and Fig. 1, when the intensity of light changed, the light path does not change. The polarization state depends only on the incident Angle of light and the target material properties.

By keeping the light source direction unchanged and by changing the degree of the shadow, the polarization images of the 0° and 90° angles are collected and the degree of polarization is calculated. Where the light source intensity is increased gradually from left to right column, as shown in Fig. 2. The first row represents the original image under different light intensities and the second row represents its *DOP* images. Experiments show that the polarization image can maintain consistency under different light intensities, and the edge features of the image can be obviously preserved.

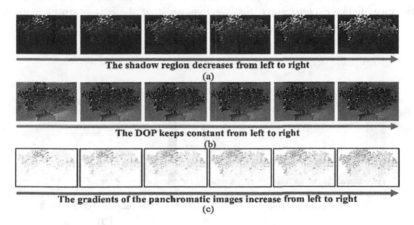

Fig. 2. The implementation of different degree of shadow for (a) Panchromatic images, (b) *DOP* images, and (c) the gradient of the panchromatic images.

2.3 *DOP*-Chromatic Consistency in Local Region

The color image and polarization image both have a large gradient value at the edge and a small gradient value for the smooth region. This suggests the correlation between them. To measure this correlation, we define the *DOP* distance and the chrominance distance to analyze this. For the *DOP* intensity image, the distance of two pixels' *DOP* is defined as:

$$D_1(x,y) = |DOP(x) - DOP(y)| \tag{5}$$

where x, y represent two different pixel points. The values of distances are normalized to have values between 0 and 1.

The chrominance distance between two pixels is defined as follows:

$$D_2(x,y) = |C(x) - C(y)| \tag{6}$$

where $C(.)$ represents the intensity values of different color channels at different coordinate points (for the color image, it is the intensity value of RGB three channels) and normalized to be between 0 and 1. For further analyze, the correlation between *DOP* image and original light intensity image are collected. Where 100 shadow-free images and their corresponding *DOP* images, and a 3 × 3 sliding window is used. The distance between *DOP* and chrominance of the center pixel and its surrounding pixels is calculated. In order to analyze the correlation between D_1 and D_2, the distance obtained above is used to calculate the distribution.

It can be noticed from the original histogram of chrominance distance, shown in Fig. 3(a), that about 65% of pixel pairs have polarization distances less than 0.05, but when we limit the chrominance distance less than 0.05, The *DOP* distance is more than 80% of the pixel pairs when chrominance distance is less than 0.05. It can be seen from this that the local consistency of polarization distance is greatly enhanced by adding chrominance distance constraints. So, we can see that there is a strong correlation between local polarization and chromatic.

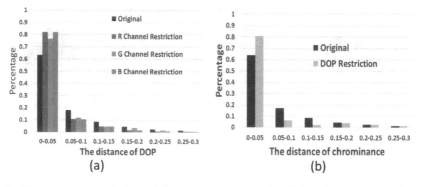

Fig. 3. The histogram of the original images versus (a) *DOP* distance constrained by chrominance distance, and (b) the chrominance distance constrained by *DOP* distance.

Accordingly to Fig. 3(b) which represents the statistics of 100 clear natural images, that the original statistical histogram of polarization distance is only about 62% of the pixel pairs with a polarization distance of less than 0.05; but when we limit chrominance distance less than 0.05, the polarization distance is more than 80% of the pixel pairs in the R and B channels with less than 0.05. While in the G channel, the polarization distance is about 78% of pixel pairs with polarization distance also less than 0.05. The local consistency of polarization distance is greatly enhanced with the addition of chrominance distance constraints. Therefore, we can see that there is a high correlation between local polarization and chromaticity.

Therefore, in the shadow image restoration enhancement, we should ensure the consistent correlation between local chroma and polarization degree. Based on this prior, a shadow image restoration method based on feedback is proposed in this paper.

3   Image Enhancement Method Based on Polarizing Imaging

Based on the two priors we mentioned previously, this paper proposes a new image enhancement method based on polarization imaging. The proposed method contained two parts: enhancement method and noise suppression method. The flow chart of the proposed method is illustrated in Fig. 4. Starting from the fusion of the polarized images and the *DOP* image, going through the joint optimization, then obtain the output enhanced image.

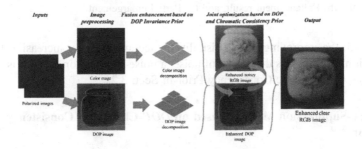

Fig. 4. Flow chart of the proposed method.

3.1   Image Enhancement Method Based on *DOP* Invariance Prior

In Fig. 2, it can be seen the image getting blurry as the shadows increase. As the shadows increase, the gradients decreased sharply as shown in Fig. 2(c). Inspired by *DOP* Invariance Prior, polarization images contain a lot of detailed information about edges and textures, which kept constant for different degrees of shadow. In order to enhance the image effectively, it is required to retaining its color features and its detail texture features at the same time.

It is known that local color information has low frequency, and local texture edge information has high frequency. So, the fusion of panchromatic image and polarized image at different scales is needed. For low frequency scale, the main operation is to stretch the color image. While for high frequency scale, the main operation is to strengthen the outline. Then after the ordinary scene image is decomposed into N layers according to the frequency, the fusion process can be described as:

$$L^k(x) = \begin{cases} W_1^k S(I^k(x)) + W_2^k DOP^k(x), & W_1^k \propto k \quad and \quad W_2^k \propto 1/k, \quad k \in low \quad frequency \\ W_1^k I^k(x) + W_2^k DOP^k(x), & W_1^k \propto 1/k \quad and \quad W_2^k \propto k, \quad k \in high \quad frequency \end{cases}$$

$$(7)$$

where k is the scale of the layer. W_1 and W_2 are representing the weights of fusion process. S represents the contrast stretching operation. The existing methods such as wavelet decomposition and Laplace pyramid decomposition can fuse images at different scales. This retains the chromaticity information in the low frequency part and more detailed information in the high frequency part are retained. This is done by using the *DOP* image.

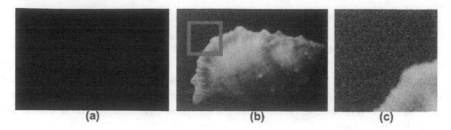

Fig. 5. Enhancing result of image enhancement method with *DOP* Invariance Prior (a) The ordinary scene, (b) Enhancement result, and (c) Partial enlargement.

In Fig. 5, the improving in the visibility is accompanied by increasing the noise amplification. To suppress the effects of noise, a noise-suppression method is proposed based on *DOP*-Chromatic Consistency Prior in Sect. 3.2.

3.2   Noise-Suppression Method Based on *DOP*-Chromatic Consistency Prior

According to the *DOP* and chromatic consistency prior, the estimated *DOP* must maintain a high correlation in the chrominance corresponding region. In order to ensure the consistency between enhancement results and *DOP*, the joint *DOP* chromaticity compensation regularization is defined as:

$$E_1(DOP, L) = \sum_x \sum_{y \in \Omega(x)} W_3(x, y) \|DOP(x) - DOP(y)\|_2 \tag{8}$$

$$W_3(x, y) = \frac{1}{2\sigma^2} \exp\left(-\sum_{k \in R,G,B} \|L(x) - L(y)\|_2^2\right) \tag{9}$$

where x, y represent the spatial coordinates of two pixels points and $\Omega(x)$ repents their adjacent area. $W_3(x, y)$ is the leading weight function, k is the color channel, and σ represents the standard deviation of the local neighborhood.

In the adjacent area of the polarization degree image, the values of adjacent pixels differ obviously because the pixels are distributed in the edge region of the image. While the difference in the intensity of the color channels in this region is usually quite different. Therefore, the proposed guided weighted canonical term constraint can effectively suppress the noise amplification and distortion of the image edge. It also effectively retains the edge detail information of the image. The calculation of *DOP* image after de-noising can be expressed as:

$$DOP(x) = \arg\min_{Dop} \|DOP(x) - DOP_0(x)\|_2^2 + \lambda E_1(DOP, L) \tag{10}$$

where DOP_0 is the initial degree of polarization and λ is standard Lagrange multiplier, the expression of the *DOP* in (10) can be calculated by using the standard gradient descent method. A better intensity image L can be obtained by using the optimized polarization degree or polarization angle image.

Similarly, intensity images can be optimized by using the local consistency between them and the *DOP* images. Thus, in this paper, the results of the *DOP* image are used as feedback to guide the weighted regularization, and a guided weighted regularization strategy of feedback mechanism is proposed to optimize the intensity image. The regular term expression is expressed as follows:

$$E_2(L, DOP) = \sum_x \sum_{y \in \Omega(x)} W_4(x, y) \|L(x) - L(y)\|_2 \tag{11}$$

$$W_4(x, y) = \frac{1}{2\sigma^2} \exp\left(- \sum_{k \in R, G, B} \|DOP(x) - DOP(y)\|_2^2 \right) \tag{12}$$

where $W_4(x, y)$ represents the weight function. If the value of the adjacent pixel points varies obviously, that's because the pixel points are distributed in the edge region of the image, the difference of *DOP* of the region is probly quite different. Therefore, the guided weighted regular term constraint proposed in this paper can effectively suppress the noise amplification and distortion of the image edge, and effectively retain the edge details of the image. The intensity image after de-noising is expressed as follows:

$$L(x) = \arg \min_L \|L(x) - L_0(x)\|_2^2 + \beta E_2(L, DOP) \tag{13}$$

where L_0 is the initial image strength and β is the standard Lagrange multiplier. L in (13) can be solved by the standard gradient descent method.

By using the above joint optimization method, the noise caused by the imaging can be effectively reduced. The optimized *DOP* image can be used to further optimize the intensity image, and the optimized intensity image can be used to reduce the noise in the polarization image. This paper proposes an image restoration method based on feedback, so that intensity image and degree of polarization image can be optimized at the same time.

By obtaining a set of images with $0°$ and $90°$ polarization angles, the initial degree of polarization can be calculated using (4). The initial value (L_0) is calculated by using the proposed enhancement method in discussed in Sect. 3.2. Therefore, the iteration process is performed according to the following equations:

$$DOP_{i+1}(x) = \arg \min_{Dop_{i+1}} \|DOP_{i+1}(x) - DOP_i(x)\|_2^2 + \lambda E_1(DOP_{i+1}, L_i) \tag{14}$$

$$L_i'(x) = \frac{1}{M} \sum_{y \in \omega(x)} m(x, y, DOP) \cdot L_{i+1}(x) \tag{15}$$

$$L_{i+1}(x) = \arg \min_{L_{i+1}} \|L_{i+1}(x) - L_i'(x)\|_2^2 + \beta E_2(L_{i+1}) \tag{16}$$

where L_i' is the intermediate result of the iterative intensity image. The termination condition for this iteration set in this paper is $\|DOP_i(x)-DOP_{i-1}(x)\| < \varepsilon$, which usually terminates after three to four iterations. In each period of iteration, the noise of intensity image and DOP image is reduced, and the accuracy is improved.

4   Experiments

An object polarization image database, captured in the shadow area, is established in this paper. For each scene, two images are captured with the linear polarizer at angles of 0° and 90° at the same time, respectively. For each kind of objects (metal, non-metal), the polarization images under different shadow conditions are collected for more than 1000 groups. This database provides enough data for supporting our experiments.

By using the constructed polarization shadow image database, the proposed method of polarization objects image enhancement in the shadow is compared with the recent methods: Wang [1], Deng [2], Fu [4], and Ying [11]. Each method shows its result respectively.

The shadow recovery results of the proposed method and the other conventional methods are illustrated in Fig. 6. The red marked region is magnified to evaluate our experimental results clearly. It is obviously noticed from the selective images chosen from the captured image database that the object shadows are heavy, and the quality of the images drops substantially. According, it shows that the polarization method out-performs panchromatic image-based methods in extreme conditions. The proposed method can effectively improve the contrast without sacrificing much information on texture and edge. There is no obvious color distortion in the image, and noise is not significantly amplified in this process.

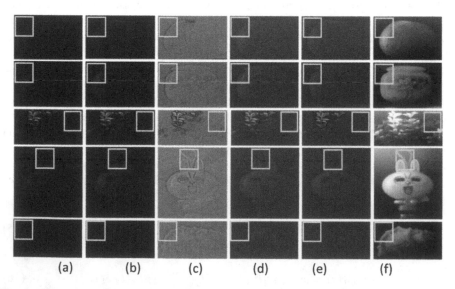

Fig. 6. Enhancing results of different objects. (a) Original scene, (b) Deng [2], (c) Wang [1], (d) Ying [11], (e) Fu [4], and (f) Proposed method. (Color figure online)

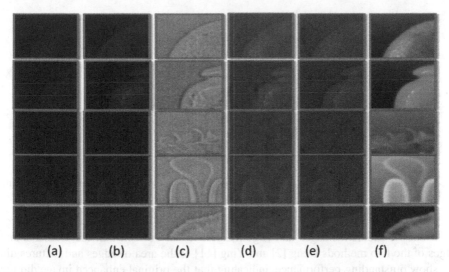

Fig. 7. The magnified red marked region of Fig. 5. (a) Original scene, (b) Deng [2], (c) Wang [1], (d) Ying [11], (e) Fu [4], and (f) Proposed method. (Color figure online)

The experimental results in Fig. 7 (b) show that Wang [1] method has no significant improvement in contrast. In Fig. 7, methods of Deng [2], Fu [4], and Ying [11] increase image contrast. However, methods of Wang [1] and Fu [4] show obvious color distortion and results of Ying [11] and Fu [4] are blurred because of the existence of noise. Comparatively, our method gives a superior result and preserves the sharpness of the object edges. The shortcomings of these methods will be more prominent in the evaluation section below.

5 Evaluation

It is known that the clearer the image, the sharper the edge, and the larger the gradient. So, the edge or gradient of the image can be used to represent the performance of the enhancement algorithm. To analyze the experimental results, two sets of images in Fig. 6 are chosen to calculate the image gradients of the enhancement. The results of their image gradients of different methods. (a) Original scene, (b) Deng [2], (c) Wang [1] (d) Ying [11] (e) Fu [4] (f) Proposed method, are shown in Fig. 8. The visible edges of the images by using the Canny operator applied on the mentioned conventional methods and the proposed method, are shown in Fig. 9. In order to display these images clearly, the color reversal processing is carried out.

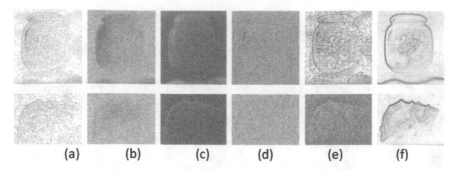

Fig. 8. Gradients of original image and results of different methods. (a) Original scene, (b) Deng [2], (c) Wang [1], (d) Ying [11], (e) Fu [4], and (f) Proposed method.

From the gradient images and edge images, it can be seen that the gradients and edges of the two methods Deng [2] and Ying [11] at the area of edges and textures did not show outstanding performance, indicating that the original enhanced image did not significantly improve the image clarity. While the other two methods: Wang [1] and Fu [4] show many false gradients and edges caused by noise, which indicates that the processes of image enhancement enlarge the noise obviously. It is shown that the proposed method generates the clearest edges and reduces noise. This shows that the proposed algorithm is superior to the other four conventional image enhancement methods. Also, the experiments show that proposed method improves image quality obviously.

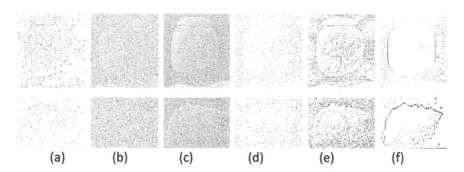

Fig. 9. Visible edges of original image and results of different methods. (a) Original scene, (b) Deng [2], (c) Wang [1], (d) Ying [11], (e) Fu [4], and (f) Proposed method.

6   Conclusion

This paper proposed an Image Enhancement method based on the joint constraint of *DOP* and chromatic. Combining the polarization information with the intensity and chromaticity information of the original image can overcome the contrast enhancement and the noise amplification shortcoming.

The main contribution in this paper is based on the *DOP* Invariance Prior and the *DOP*-Chromatic Consistency Prior. Based on these two priors, a feedback polarization image enhancement method is proposed. Experiments show that the edge texture and other details of the proposed method are more obvious than the existing methods with less noise meanwhile. This shows that the proposed algorithm in this paper is superior to the other four conventional image enhancement methods.

Acknowledgements. This work was supported in part by the Shenzhen Municipal Science and Technology Innovation Committee under Grant JCYJ20170815162956949 and JCYJ20180 306171146740, in part by the National Natural Science Foundation of China under Grant 61371152 and Grant 61771391.

References

1. Wang, S., et al.: Naturalness preserved enhancement algorithm for non-uniform illumination images. IEEE Trans. Image Process. **22**(9), 3538–3548 (2013)
2. Deng, G.: A generalized unsharp masking algorithm. IEEE Trans. Image Process. **20**(5), 1249–1261 (2011)
3. Coifman, R.R., Wickerhauser, M.V.: Entropy-based algorithms for best basis selection. IEEE Trans. Inf. Theory **38**(2), 713–718 (1992)
4. Fu, X., et al.: A probabilistic method for image enhancement with simultaneous illumination and reflectance estimation. IEEE Trans. Image Process. **24**(12), 4965–4977 (2015)
5. Naik, S.K., Murthy, C.A.: Hue-preserving color image enhancement without gamut problem. IEEE Trans. Image Process. **12**(12), 1591–1598 (2003)
6. Lecun, Y., et al.: Gradient-based learning applied to document recognition. Proc. IEEE **86** (11), 2278–2324 (1998)
7. Prati, A., et al.: Detecting moving shadows: algorithms and evaluation. IEEE Trans. Pattern Anal. Mach. Intell. **25**(7), 918–923 (2003)
8. Guo, R., Dai, Q., Hoiem, D.: Single-image shadow detection and removal using paired regions. In: CVPR 2011. IEEE (2011)
9. Shahtahmassebi, A., et al.: Review of shadow detection and de-shadowing methods in remote sensing. Chin. Geogra. Sci. **23**(4), 403–420 (2013). https://doi.org/10.1007/s11769-013-0613-x
10. Surkutlawar, S., Kulkarni, R.K.: Shadow suppression using RGB and HSV color space in moving object detection. Int. J. Adv. Comput. Sci. Appl. **4**(1) (2013)
11. Ying, Z., Li, G., Gao, W.: A bio-inspired multi-exposure fusion frame-work for low-light image enhancement. In: Computer Science - Computer Vision and Pattern Recognition (2017)
12. Rüfenacht, D., Fredembach, C., Süsstrunk, S.: Automatic and accurate shadow detection using near-infrared information. IEEE Trans. Pattern Anal. Mach. Intell. **36**(8), 1672–1678 (2014)
13. Prati, A., et al.: Comparative evaluation of moving shadow detection algorithms. In: IEEE CVPR Workshop on Empirical Evaluation Methods in Computer Vision (2001)
14. Wu, Y., Fang, T., Li, C.: An approach for image enhancement based on wavelet analysis and properties of human visual system. J. Data Acquis. Process. **18** (2003)
15. Zhao, Y., Yi, C., Kong, S.G., Pan, Q., Cheng, Y.: Multi-band Polarization Imaging and Applications. ACVPR. Springer, Heidelberg (2016). https://doi.org/10.1007/978-3-662-49373-1

16. Li, X., et al.: Optimal distribution of integration time for intensity measurements in degree of linear polarization polarimetry. Opt. Express **24**(7), 7191–7200 (2016)
17. Pinnick, R., Carroll, D., Hofmann, D.: Polarized light scattered from monodisperse randomly oriented nonspherical aerosol particles: measurements. Appl. Opt. **15**(2), 384–393 (1976)
18. Fang, S., et al.: Image dehazing using polarization effects of objects and airlight. Opt. Express **22**(16), 19523–19537 (2014)
19. He, K., Sun, J., Tang, X.: Guided image filtering. IEEE Trans. Pattern Anal. Mach. Intell. **35**(6), 1397–1409 (2013)
20. Wang, B., Lu, T., Xiong, Z.: Adaptive boosting for image denoising: beyond low-rank representation and sparse coding. In: 2016 23rd International Conference on Pattern Recognition (ICPR). IEEE (2016)
21. Shen, L., Wee Chua, T., Leman, K.: Shadow optimization from structured deep edge detection. In: Proceedings of the IEEE Conference on Computer Vision and Pattern Recognition (2015)

Multi-scale Convolutional Capsule Network for Hyperspectral Image Classification

Dongyue Wang, Qin Xu$^{(\boxtimes)}$, Yong Xiao, Jin Tang, and Bin Luo

School of Computer Science and Technology, Anhui University,
Hefei 230601, China
dongyuewangahu@163.com, {xuqin,tj,luobin}@ahu.edu.cn,
e11414110@stu.ahu.edu.cn

Abstract. The conventional CNNs-based hyperspectral image classification faces the challenges of quite limited training samples which lead to over fitting and dissatisfied ability to describe the correlation between features. Recent Capsules network can deal with the data of limited training samples and capture the correlation between the features, but the low-level features extraction is used by a single-scale CNN whose feature representation capability is limited. In this paper, we propose a multi-scale convolutional capsule network for hyperspectral image classification, which is composed of a multi-scale convolutional layer, a single-scale convolutional layer, a PrimaryCaps layer, a DigitCaps layer and a fully connected layer. The proposed network can learn high-level spectral-spatial features with limited training data and is robust to rotation and affine transformation. The comparison experiments with five state-of-the-arts on two well-known datasets demonstrate the efficiency of the proposed method.

Keywords: Hyperspectral image classification · Capsule networks · Convolutional neural network · Multi-scale

1 Introduction

The hyperspectral images (HSIs) that are acquired by remote sensors have rich spectral information for objective detection and classification applications. Compared to the RGB image or infrared image, hyperspectral images contain more spectral channels and provide coarse-grained spatial context information [1]. As one of the tasks of hyperspectral image processing, classification has drawn broad attentions and wide applications such as monitoring of the global environment, management of agricultural development, national defense security, etc. This problem brings opportunities and challenges to the development of new data processing technologies [2].

In the literature, a variety of classifiers have been proposed for hyperspectral image classification [3], such as k-nearest neighbor (k-NN) [4], support vector machine (SVM) [5], k-means clustering [7], Gaussian process (GP) [8], random forest (RF) [9], extreme learning machine (ELM) [10]. The k-nearest neighbor (k-NN) [4] can be regarded as the simplest classifier that uses the Euclidean distance metric to test the similarity between testing samples and training samples. The support vector machine method [5] used kernel function to determine the boundary of high-dimensional space,

© Springer Nature Switzerland AG 2019
Z. Lin et al. (Eds.): PRCV 2019, LNCS 11858, pp. 749–760, 2019.
https://doi.org/10.1007/978-3-030-31723-2_64

so that it is less sensitive to high dimensions and Hughes phenomenon. Moreover, it can achieve good classification performance with limited training samples, which has once become a benchmark for HIS classification [6]. However, it is difficult to accurately distinguish different categories only through a single spectral dimension [11]. Therefore, in order to make use of spatial information, spectral-spatial techniques have been studied. For example, based on Markov Random Fields (MRFs) models, the spectral-spatial features [12, 13] has been successfully extracted, achieving better classification results than previous methods.

Recently, a method based on deep learning for hyperspectral feature extraction and classification—regular stacked auto-encoders (SAE) [14] was proposed. In [15], the spectral characteristics of HSIs were extracted using five-layer deep convolutional neural networks (CNNs). Then, in [16], a new pixel pair method was proposed to utilize deep CNN to learn pixel-pair features which is expected to have more discriminative power. The method based on deep learning also effectively utilizes 3D spectral-spatial information. The 3D CNNs can obtain better results than the 1D CNN that only considered spectral information and the 2D CNN that only considers spatial information [17, 18]. However, the hyperspectral image classification still faces two challenges. First, the ability to detect relationship between features of the traditional CNNs-based approach is quite limited. Second, the availability of training samples is limited, making the deep neural network face serious over-fitting problems [19]. Therefore, further improvement of classification accuracy requires changing the structure of the traditional CNNs. In order to improve the feature extraction ability of CNNs, multi-scale convolutional neural networks (MS-CNNs) [22] were developed for HSI classification. The multi-scale convolution kernel in MS-CNNs realizes parallel convolution, which makes it possible to extract multi-scale features. In addition, the parallel method can increase the width of the deep network, which has a positive effect on improving the representation ability of the model.

Recent proposed capsule network [20] encodes the input data into a movable vector rather than a scalar in the traditional sense. The length and direction of the vector can be used to represent the estimated probability between the predicted class and the real label. Based on capsule networks, [19, 21] proposed a new CNN architecture, which achieves high-precision HSI classification results while reducing network complexity. However, in [19, 21], the low-level feature is extracted by the traditional CNN structure that is not effective for the high-level feature extraction.

Based on the above ideas, this paper proposes a multi-scale convolutional capsule network for hyperspectral image classification. The proposed HSI classification model consists of several parts, namely a multi-scale convolutional layer (L1), a single-scale convolutional layer (L2), a PrimaryCaps layer (L3), a DigitCaps layer (L4), and a fully connected neural networks layer (L5). L1 and L2 are used to extract the basic spectral-spatial features of the input 3D data, thereby providing a high-level capsule networks. L3 converts the features from the previous layer into dynamic vectors by a convolution process for effective prediction of the output of the L4. L4 is classified by a vector of L3 output through a dynamic routing and the non-linear squashing function. The fully connected neural network layer L5 is used to reconstruct the input data, and the loss of the reconstruction can be used as a regularization term for the total loss. The above process can take into account both the physical location of the data, the characteristics of the spectral dimensions of the data, and the changes in the data that occur during the process. The experimental results show that the proposed method has the potential to effectively extract high-resolution spectral-spatial features with limited training data, and has certain advantages over 3D CNNs classifiers and other related advanced classification methods.

The remainder of the paper is organized as follows. Section 2 reviews the multi-scale CNN model and the capsule network model structure. Section 3 describes the proposed network structure in this paper. Section 4 is compared with four existing HSI classification methods and compared with a non-multi-scale capsule networks model. Finally, Sect. 5 concludes the paper and puts forward some opinions and suggestions for the future research direction.

2 Related Work

This section reviews the structure of the multi-scale CNN and the capsule network.

2.1 Multi-scale CNN

Compared to traditional machine learning algorithms, CNN has shown better performance in image classification tasks. Available studies have shown that the 3D CNN considering both spatial and spectral dimensions outperform the 1D and 2D CNN [18]. The CNN structure with multi-scale convolution kernel for hyperspectral image classification has been proven that it can achieve better classification results [22], and the framework is shown in Fig. 1. The parallel convolutions, which increase the width and depth of the network model, can improve the feature representation ability of the deep learning model and effectively extract the hierarchical features.

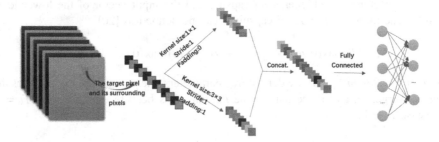

Fig. 1. Multi-scale convolutional neural network for HSI classification

2.2 Capsule Network

Capsule network [20] is a new deep learning architecture that attempts to overcome the limitations and shortcomings of CNNs, such as the lack of explicit entity concepts and the loss of valuable information in the Max-pooling. A capsule-based representation method not only captures the features, but also the underlying relationships between these features. Therefore, in this case, the capsule network is more robust to affine transformations and achieves good results with less training samples.

A typical capsule network is a multi-layer capsule system with discriminative capabilities during training. It consists of four parts, a convolutional layer, a PrimaryCaps layer, a DigitalCaps layer, and a fully connected layer. The capsule converts the input data into a vector output. The length of the vector indicates the probability of its existence, and the direction indicates the attribute it has. The output vector of capsule j is calculated by a non-linear squashing function in the network [20], i.e.

$$v_j = \frac{\|s_j\|^2}{\varepsilon + \|s_j\|^2} \frac{s_j}{\|s_j\|} \tag{1}$$

where ε is a fixed size determined value, s_j is obtained by Eq. (2)

$$s_j = \sum_i c_{ij} W_{ij} u_i \tag{2}$$

where u_i is the output of the previous layer, W_{ij} represent the weights of the prediction vectors of the capsule of the next layer, and the coefficient c_{ij} are determined by the dynamic routing process,

$$c_{ij} = \frac{\exp(b_{ij})}{\sum_k \exp(b_{ik})} \tag{3}$$

where b_{ij} are the log prior probabilities that capsule i should be coupled to capsule j. The dynamic routing is accomplished during the iteration process. A lower level capsule sends its output to a higher level capsule with a larger scalar product between the output vector of the higher level capsule and the input vector of the lower level capsule. The marginal loss L_k of capsule k can be defined as [20],

$$L_k = T_k \max(0, m^+ - \|v_k\|)^2 + \lambda(1 - T_k)\max(0, \|v_k\| - m^-)^2 \tag{4}$$

where $m^+ = 0.9, m^- = 0.1$ are default free parameters, the parameters λ guarantees the final convergence, and if the data of the kth class has been recognized, then $T_k = 1$, otherwise $T_k = 0$.

3 Proposed Approach

This section proposes a capsule network based on the multi-scale convolution for hyperspectral image classification.

3.1   Network Design

To extract the multi-scale features with the capsule network and keep the reliability of the network, we develop a multi-scale convolutional capsule network which is composed of 5 layers. Figure 2 shows the proposed network architecture.

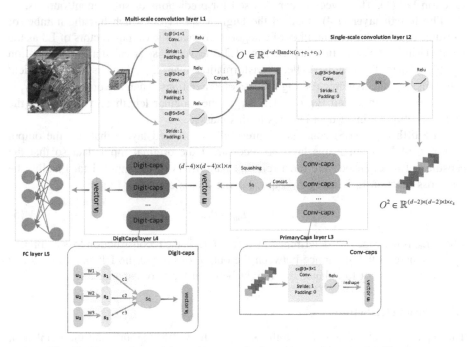

Fig. 2. Proposed networks architecture for hyperspectral image classification

The first layer (L1) is the multi-scale convolution process, which is located at the beginning of the network model. The convolution layer extracts the patch $P_{ij} \in \mathbb{R}^{d \times d \times \text{Band} \times 1}$ from the HSI data cube. It is transferred to the parallel convolution process where the sizes of 3D convolution kernel are $1 \times 1 \times 1, 3 \times 3 \times 3, 5 \times 5 \times 5$ and steps are set to 1, and then activated by the Relu function for multi-scale feature extraction. The number of channels of the three types of convolution kernels are c_1, c_2, and c_3 respectively. When the convolution process of the three types completes, the feature maps obtained by the convolution process are connected. Therefore, the output of the first layer is denoted as $O^1 \in \mathbb{R}^{d \times d \times \text{Band} \times (c_1 + c_2 + c_3)}$.

The second layer (L2) is a single-scale convolutional network. This layer takes the output $O^1 \in \mathbb{R}^{d \times d \times \text{Band} \times (c_1 + c_2 + c_3)}$ of L1 as the input. The convolution kernel size is $3 \times 3 \times \text{Band}$, the step size is 1, and the channel number is c_4. Batch normalization is used for regularization before the activation function to accelerate the convergence of the final model. It is then activated using the Relu function. The output of the second layer is denoted as $O^2 \in \mathbb{R}^{(d-2) \times (d-2) \times 1 \times c_4}$.

The third layer (L3) is the PrimaryCaps layer with a $3 \times 3 \times 1$ sized convolution kernel and n channels, where the step size is 1. The convolution process in this layer is repeated m times and the final result is saved into the vector. Therefore, after the main capsule layer, the output $O^2 \in \mathbb{R}^{(d-2) \times (d-2) \times 1 \times c_4}$ of L2 is converted into $(d-4) \times (d-4) \times 1 \times n$ vectors with m dimensions. They are then activated with the squashing function Eq. (1). These vectors can be used for predictions of subsequent outputs.

The fourth layer (L4) is called the DigitalCaps layer, which has the number of capsules equal to the total number of categories. It takes the output vectors of L3 as the input. Using the vector $\mathbf{u_i}$ obtained from L3, the vector $\mathbf{s_j}$ is calculated by equation Eq. (2), where W_{ij} can be called transformation matrix, and c_{ij} is the coefficient determined by the dynamic routing process of T iterations. Then the output vector $\mathbf{v_j}$ is computed through $\mathbf{s_j}$ and Eq. (1). The larger the modular length of vector $\mathbf{v_j}$ is, the more possibly the input data belongs to this class.

The fifth layer (L5) consists of three fully connected layers that use the output vector v_j of L4 DigitalCaps layer to reconstruct the original input data so that the capsule networks encode the most relevant parameters of the input data. Finally, the total loss function L_t is given by Eq. (5) using Adam optimizer [25].

$$L_t = L_m + \theta L_r \tag{5}$$

where L_m is the edge loss determined by Eq. (4), L_r is the reconstruction loss computed by the square of the difference between the output of L5 and the L1 input, and θ is a regularization factor to balance the weight between the two loss metrics.

3.2 Parameter Setting

The input data cube size is 7 (length) $\times$ 7 (width) $\times$ 100 (depth), and the number of training batches is 128. The number of channels c_1, c_2, and c_3 of the three convolution kernels in L1 are all set to 4, and convolution is performed using padding. The number of L2 convolution kernel channels is 128, the step size is 1, and the convolution mode does not use padding. The number of convolution kernel channels in L3 is 32, the number of convolutions m is set to 8, and the step size is 1. The convolution mode does not use padding. The number of capsules in L4 is set to the total number of classes, and the number of iterations of dynamic routing T is 3. The fifth layer has three layers of fully connected neural networks, where the first layer has 329 neurons, the activation function is Relu, and the dropout ratio is 0.9, the second layer has 192 neurons, the activation function is Relu, and the dropout ratio is 0.9, the third layer has $7 \times 7 \times 100$ neurons, and the activation function is sigmoid. The final total loss function θ takes a value of 0.06 and the learning rate is 1e−3.

4   Experiments

In this section, to evaluate the proposed network framework we conduct experiment on Indian Pines [23] (see Tables 1) and University of Pavia [24] (see Tables 2) datasets and compare with five existing mainstream deep learning methods, including CNNs

[15], 3DCNNs [18], MSCNNs [22], DDMSCNNs [22], CAPs [19]. The networks are written in the TensorFlow architecture. All experiments are executed on i7-8700 CPU and GTX1060 GPU.

Table 1. The number of training and testing samples for the Indian Pines dataset

#	Class	Train	Test
1	Alfalfa	23	23
2	Corn-notill	200	1228
3	Corn-min	200	630
4	Corn	118	119
5	Grass/Pasture	200	283
6	Grass/Trees	200	530
7	Grass/Pasture-mowed	14	14
8	Hay-windrowed	200	278
9	Oats	10	10
10	Soybeans-notill	200	772
11	Soybeans-min	200	2255
12	Soybeans-clean	200	393
13	Wheat	102	103
14	Woods	200	1065
15	Building-Grass-Trees-Drives	193	193
16	Stone-steel Towers	46	47
–	Total	2309	7940

4.1 Datasets

Indian Pines. The dataset covers different agricultural fields in northwestern Indiana, USA, and was collected by the AVIRIS sensor in 1992. The image contains 145×145 pixels with a spatial resolution of 20 m/pixel (mpp) for a total of 224 spectral bands with wavelengths ranging from 400 to 2500 nm. The dataset contains a total of 16 mutually exclusive classes, the number of training and testing samples for the Indian Pines dataset is shown in Table 1.

University of Pavia. The dataset is collected by the ROSIS sensor (2001) at the University of Pavia in northern Italy. The image, after rejecting multiple noise-contaminated bands, contains 103 spectral bands (from 0.43 m to 0.86 m), including 610×340 pixels and a spatial resolution of 1.3 mpp. It contains 9 mutually exclusive classes. The number of training and testing samples for the University of Pavia dataset is shown in Table 2.

Results and Discussion
Our experiment takes 50% of the samples in each class as training data, and when each type of training data is greater than 200, only 200 of them are taken (see Tables 1 and 2). The last item to be compared is based on a non-multi-scale capsule network. The detailed classification results of Indian Pines are shown in Table 3. The results of the University of Pavia classification are shown in Table 4.

Table 2. The number of training and testing samples for the University of Pavia dataset

#	Class	Train	Test
1	Asphalt	200	6431
2	Meadows	200	18449
3	Gravel	200	1899
4	Trees	200	2864
5	Sheets	200	1145
6	Baresoil	200	4829
7	Bitumen	200	1130
8	Bricks	200	3482
9	Shadows	200	747
–	Total	1800	40976

Table 3. Classification results for the Indian Pines dataset

Class	CNNs [15]	3DCNNs [18]	3DMSCNNs [22]	DDMSCNNs [22]	CAPs [19]	MSCAPs
1	91.30	100.0	95.65	–	100.0	**100.0**
2	80.04	92.67	89.08	98.06	89.65	**99.18**
3	77.46	96.19	95.87	**99.74**	76.34	98.88
4	79.83	99.15	92.43	–	100.0	**100.0**
5	94.34	99.29	**100.0**	100.0	94.34	93.28
6	97.73	97.16	98.11	–	99.62	**100.0**
7	78.57	100.0	100.0	–	100.0	**100.0**
8	98.20	100.0	**100.0**	100.0	99.28	98.92
9	60.00	100.0	100.0	–	90.00	**100.0**
10	88.47	98.05	95.59	**98.78**	98.05	97.79
11	70.86	86.16	88.55	94.31	98.62	**99.06**
12	85.49	97.20	96.18	99.36	99.49	**99.23**
13	100.0	100.0	100.0	–	100.0	**100.0**
14	88.92	96.80	95.68	100.0	99.62	**99.90**
15	76.16	**100.0**	96.89	–	99.48	98.96
16	87.23	100.0	100.0	–	97.87	**100.0**
OA	82.04	93.65	93.21	97.62	95.66	**99.04**
AA	77.58	91.99	93.77	98.78	97.11	**99.46**
Kappa	79.24	92.62	92.08	97.08	94.90	**98.87**

From Tables 3 and 4, The evaluation criteria include the overall accuracy (OA) of all test samples, the average accuracy (AA) of each class, and the kappa coefficient (Kappa) to measure data consistency. We can see that compared with the CNNs, 3DCNNs, 3DMSCNNs, DDMSCNNs and CAPs, the proposed method has quantitative and qualitative advantages. This is the fact that the generalization of the network is enhanced, because the corresponding spectral-spatial feature complements the important information about the transformation of the feature data as a set of instantiation parameters, ultimately allowing the HSI data to be characterized at a higher level of abstraction. Unlike other deep models such as CNNs, 3DCNNs and CAPs the

Table 4. Classification results for the University of Pavia dataset

Class	CNNs [15]	3DCNNs [18]	3DMSCNNs [22]	DDMSCNNs [22]	CAPs [19]	MSCAPs
1	88.38	96.00	98.59	98.56	99.16	**99.78**
2	91.27	94.87	98.84	98.92	99.66	**99.88**
3	85.88	96.20	95.57	95.00	**99.78**	97.57
4	97.25	97.62	98.76	98.80	96.26	**99.26**
5	99.91	100.0	100.0	100.0	100.0	**100.0**
6	96.41	95.83	99.81	99.11	100.0	**100.0**
7	93.62	98.67	99.15	99.20	99.46	**99.55**
8	87.45	94.11	**97.62**	94.40	97.47	96.84
9	99.57	**100.0**	**100.0**	**100.0**	99.19	99.59
OA	92.27	95.69	98.72	98.37	99.20	**99.35**
AA	93.36	94.57	98.70	98.22	98.92	**99.36**
Kappa	93.16	94.25	98.27	97.81	98.92	**99.13**

components of the multi-scale convolutional capsule network proposed in this paper are intended to reveal typical spectral-spatial features and their corresponding instantiation parameters. These features allow HSI data to be described at a higher level of abstraction while reducing the over-fitting inherent in complex and deep networks. However, in some categories with a large number of samples, the capsule networks do not have a significant advantage over traditional CNNs. Figures 3 and 4 show the classification maps obtained by CNNs, 3DCNNs, 3DMSCNNs, CAPs and MSCAPs on the Indian Pines dataset and the University of Pavia dataset. It can be concluded that our proposed MSCAPs outperform the others.

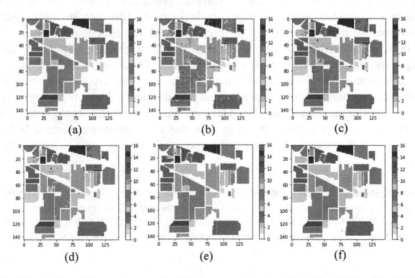

Fig. 3. The Indian Pines dataset classification maps: (a) GT, (b) CNNs, (c) 3DCNNs, (d) 3DMSCNNs, (e) CAPs, (f) MSCAPs

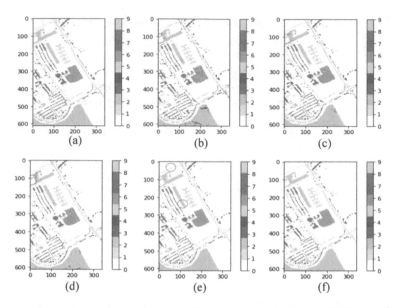

Fig. 4. The University of Pavia dataset classification maps: (a) GT, (b) CNNs, (c) 3DCNNs, (d) 3DMSCNNs, (e) CAPs, (f) MSCAPs

5   Conclusions

This paper proposes a multi-scale convolutional capsule network for hyperspectral image classification. The deep learning model is a five-layer structure for extracting information from the low-level features to high-level features to their relationships. Our approach is able to handle the inherent complexity of the HSI datasets itself, which is derived from the high resolution of the spectrum itself. The experimental results show that the proposed method has certain competitive advantages. Specifically, the model manages spectral-spatial features at a higher level of abstraction, extracting more relevant and complete HSI datasets information. The network structure can essentially model complex connections to better express HSI data and achieve high classification performance with limited training data. However, the multi-scale convolutional capsule network has a relatively slow operation time due to its many parameters. In future research, we will attempt to improve the speed of training while achieving better results.

Acknowledgment. The authors would like to thank the anonymous referees for their fruitful comments and corrections which have helped improve the paper. The research is supported by the National Natural Science Foundation of China (Nos.61502003, 61472002, 61671018 and 61860206004), Natural Science Foundation of Anhui Province (Nos. 1608085QF133).

References

1. Chang, C.: Hyperspectral Imaging: Techniques for Spectral Detection and Classification. Springer, Heidelberg (2003). https://doi.org/10.1007/978-1-4419-9170-6
2. Landgrebe, D.: Hyperspectral image data analysis. IEEE Signal Process. Mag. **19**(1), 17–28 (2002)
3. Ghamisi, P., Plaza, J., Chen, Y.: Advanced spectral classifiers for hyperspectral images: a review. IEEE Geosci. Remote Sens. Mag. **5**(1), 8–32 (2017)
4. Blanzieri, E., Melgani, F.: Nearest neighbor classification of remote sensing images with the maximal margin principle. IEEE Trans. Geosci. Remote Sens. **46**(6), 1804–1811 (2008)
5. Gualtieri, J.A., Cromp, R.F.: Support vector machines for hyperspectral remote sensing classification. In: 27th AIPR Workshop: Advances in Computer-Assisted Recognition, vol. 3584, pp. 221–233. International Society for Optics and Photonics (1999)
6. Melgani, F., Bruzzone, L.: Classification of hyperspectral remote sensing images with support vector machines. IEEE Trans. Geosci. Remote Sens. **42**(8), 1778–1790 (2004)
7. Haut, J.M., Paoletti, M., Plaza, J.: Cloud implementation of the K-means algorithm for hyperspectral image analysis. J. Supercomput. **73**(1), 514–529 (2017)
8. Bazi, Y., Melgani, F.: Gaussian process approach to remote sensing image classification. IEEE Trans. Geosci. Remote Sens. **48**(1), 186–197 (2010)
9. Ham, J., Chen, Y., Crawford, M.M.: Investigation of the random forest framework for classification of hyperspectral data. IEEE Trans. Geosci. Remote Sens. **43**(3), 492–501 (2005)
10. Haut, J.M., Paoletti, M.E., Plaza, J.: Fast dimensionality reduction and classification of hyperspectral images with extreme learning machines. J. Real-Time Image Proc. **15**(3), 439–462 (2018)
11. Liu, B., Yu, X., Zhang, P.: Supervised deep feature extraction for hyperspectral image classification. IEEE Trans. Geosci. Remote Sens. **56**(4), 1909–1921 (2018)
12. Tarabalka, Y., Fauvel, M., Chanussot, J.: SVM-and MRF-based method for accurate classification of hyperspectral images. IEEE Geosci. Remote Sens. Lett. **7**(4), 736–740 (2010)
13. Li, J., Bioucas-Dias, J.M., Plaza, A.: Spectral–spatial hyperspectral image segmentation using subspace multinomial logistic regression and Markov random fields. IEEE Trans. Geosci. Remote Sens. **50**(3), 809–823 (2012)
14. Chen, Y., Lin, Z., Zhao, X.: Deep learning-based classification of hyperspectral data. IEEE J. Sel. Top. Appl. Earth Obs. Remote Sens. **7**(6), 2094–2107 (2014)
15. Hu, W., Huang, Y., Wei, L.: Deep convolutional neural networks for hyperspectral image classification. J. Sens. (2015)
16. Li, W., Wu, G., Zhang, F.: Hyperspectral image classification using deep pixel-pair features. IEEE Trans. Geosci. Remote Sens. **55**(2), 844–853 (2017)
17. Chen, Y., Jiang, H., Li, C.: Deep feature extraction and classification of hyperspectral images based on convolutional neural networks. IEEE Trans. Geosci. Remote Sens. **54**(10), 6232–6251 (2016)
18. Li, Y., Zhang, H., Shen, Q.: Spectral–spatial classification of hyperspectral imagery with 3D convolutional neural network. Remote Sens. **9**(1), 67 (2017)
19. Paoletti, M.E., Haut, J.M., Fernandez-Beltran, R.: Capsule networks for hyperspectral image classification. IEEE Trans. Geosci. Remote Sens. **57**, 2145–2160 (2018)
20. Sabour, S., Frosst, N., Hinton, G.E.: Dynamic routing between capsules. In: Advances in Neural Information Processing Systems, pp. 3856–3866 (2017)

21. Deng, F., Pu, S., Chen, X.: Hyperspectral image classification with capsule network using limited training samples. Sensors **18**(9), 3153 (2018)
22. Gong, Z., Zhong, P., Yu, Y.: A CNN with multiscale convolution and diversified metric for hyperspectral image classification. IEEE Trans. Geosci. Remote Sens. **57**, 3599–3618 (2019)
23. Green, R.O., Eastwood, M.L., Sarture, C.M.: Imaging spectroscopy and the airborne visible/infrared imaging spectrometer (AVIRIS). Remote Sens. Environ. **65**(3), 227–248 (1998)
24. Kunkel, B., Blechinger, F., Lutz, R., Doerffer, R., Van der Piepen, H., Schroder, M.: ROSIS (Reflective Optics System Imaging Spectrometer) - a candidate instrument for polar platform missions. Optoelectron. Technol. Remote Sens. Space **868**, 134–142 (1988)
25. Kingma, D.P., Ba, J.: Adam: a method for stochastic optimization. arXiv preprint arXiv: 1412.6980 (2014)

Dark Channel Prior Guided Conditional Generative Adversarial Network for Single Image Dehazing

Yan Zhao Su[✉], Zhi Gao Cui, Ai Hua Li, Tao Wang, and Ke Jiang

Xi'an Research Institute of High-Tech, Xi'an 710025, China
syzlhh@163.com

Abstract. Single image dehazing is a challenging while important problem as the existence of haze hinders most high-level computer vision tasks. Previous methods solve this problem using various hand-crafted priors or by CNN learning on synthetic data sets. In practice, many CNN based methods estimate the transmission maps and atmospheric lights without considering the pre-defined priors, and always need huge data to train the model. In this work, we propose Dark Channel Prior Guided Conditional Generative Adversarial Network, an end-to-end model that generates realistic haze-free images using hazy image input and dehaze image based on dark channel prior. A Siamese like encoder is proposed to extracted the feature, and multi-scale features are enhanced by feature aggregation block for decoding. Our algorithm can efficiently combine the prior-based and CNN based image dehazing method. Experimental results on synthetic datasets and real-world images demonstrate our model can generate more perceptually appealing dehazing results, and provide superior performance compared with the state-of-the-art methods.

Keywords: Single image dehazing · Conditional Generative Adversarial Network · Dark Channel Prior

1 Introduction

Images are often degraded under bad weather condition such as haze, snow, rain drop and so on. When capture the image in the haze condition, the reflected lights of the object are absorbed or scattered by the particles in the atmosphere. Image dehazing aims to recovery the visual quality of the hazy images or improve performance of further computer vision algorithms [1]. However, Single image dehazing is an ill-posed inverse problem that requires to recover the unknown haze-free image, atmospheric light and medium transmission from a single hazy image [2].

Many algorithms were proposed by the computer vision community in recent years, which can be divided into two category, model-based methods or learning-based methods. Traditional model-based methods mainly relied on the hand-crafted prior information, such as dark channel priors [3], color attenuation prior [4], haze-line prior [5]. These model-based methods are effective in single image dehazing due to the

© Springer Nature Switzerland AG 2019
Z. Lin et al. (Eds.): PRCV 2019, LNCS 11858, pp. 761–771, 2019.
https://doi.org/10.1007/978-3-030-31723-2_65

investigations of prior knowledge and understandings of the physical mechanism for hazes. However, these priors are mainly based on human observations and would not always hold for diverse real-world images. Learning-based methods estimation the parameters from the training data. Many Deep learning based single image dehazing methods were proposed to estimation the transmission map [6, 7], the atmosphere or both of them [8]. These methods have shown promising results for single image dehazing. However, the results of these methods are deteriorated by the inaccuracy of estimation images. Another deep learning-based method formulate the dehazing problem as image translation, and can directly recover the haze-free image without explicitly estimation transmission or atmosphere. However, these methods usually take CNNs to learn a mapping function from input hazy images to the hazy-free images, without considering haze-related priors to constrain the mapping space compared with the traditional methods. And to learn the mapping function, many hazy and hazy-free images needed to synthesis according to the atmospheric scattering model [9].

In this paper, we formulate the single image dehazing as conditional image generation, and propose a novel conditional generative adversarial network (cGAN) guided by the dark channel prior. Different from the energy minimization method [10], We only integrate the dehazing image which is conducted by dark channel prior with the hazy image. And Our idea is also different from multi-image fusion mechanism, and the initially dehazing image was only regarded as an additional condition to guide the GAN to generate hazy-free image. On the one hand, the artifacts of traditional prior-based method can be removed by the CNN. On the other hand, with the guidance of dark channel prior dehazing image, the cGAN can learn effective mapping function which is well adopted to indoor and outdoor scenes.

Comparative experiments have been conducted to validate that guiding with the partially correct dehazing image can provide much better results than the original cGAN. In addition, we have conducted extensive experimental studies on both synthetic and real-world hazy image data. Our experimental results have verified the effectiveness of the proposed DCP guided cGAN and shown that our approach performs favorably against the state-of-the-arts both in indoor and outdoor scenes.

2 Related Work

The haze generation process can be described by the widely used atmosphere scattering model. To recover the dehaze image, two parameters medium transmission map and global atmospheric light need to be estimated. Most of the dehazing methods concentrated on the estimation of medium transmission map. Fattal [11] proposes to infer the transmission by estimating the albedo of the scene using independent component analysis, under the assumption that the transmission and surface shading are locally uncorrelated. However, the assumption will become invalid in dense hazy area or low signal-to-noise ratio area. He et al. [3] propose dark channel prior (DCP) to estimate transmission based on the statistics of thousands of images that the local minimum of color channels of haze-free images is close to zero. The DCP is effective for most outdoor images but usually fails for those containing white scenery such as white walls or clouds in sky region. Zhu et al. [4] propose a color attenuation prior and estimate the scene depth by learning the linear model in a supervised manner. Instead of using local priors, Berman et al. [12] propose a non-local color prior, with the observation that a haze-free image can be well approximated by a few hundred distinct colors. However, these priors-based dehazing methods are not always hold for diverse real-world images, and the global atmospheric light is not effectively estimated.

Recently, Deep Learning have also been used for image recovering problems, and many learning-based single image dehazing approaches has been proposed. Some methods estimated the transmission with stacked CNN [6] or multi Scale CNN [7]. However, these methods estimate the global atmosphere with traditional methods. Li et al. [13] proposed a light-weight CNN to dehaze image by estimating only one variable K(x). Zhang et al. [8] propose jointly learning the transmission, atmosphere light, and the dehazing image all together by embedding the atmospheric scattering model into the network. Du et al. [14] propose to reformulate the image dehazing problem as image denoise, and remove haze from a single image by a deep residue learning (DRL) network. Ren et al. [15] propose to recover the hazy-free image by gated fusion multi-derived images from hazy images.

The GAN framework was proposed to generate realistic-looking images from random noise via an adversarial learning mechanism [16]. By optimizing a minimax two-player game, the generator can generate high quality image with the help of the discriminator. Inspired by this framework, many Gan-based dehazing methods were proposed. Zhu et al. [17] recover the hazy-free image by the composition of the transmission and global atmosphere estimation in GAN framework. Yang.et al. [18] propose a Disentangled Dehazing Network to generate realistic haze-free images using only unpaired supervision. Li et al. [19] propose a method to recover the images directly under the framework of conditional GAN (cGAN). Different from these works, we propose to dehaze image by using conditional GAN framework with the guidance of Dark Channel Prior.

3 Proposed Method

To generate clear images from hazy inputs, we modify the conditional GAN framework by utilizing the guidance of the DCP based dehazing result. With the partially correct guidance, our network can generate satisfactory hazy-free images. Figure 1 shows the overall representation of DCP guided cGAN dehazing architecture. The model consists of a Siamese like generator module with feature aggregation and a multiscale discriminator module. In the following, we detail the architecture.

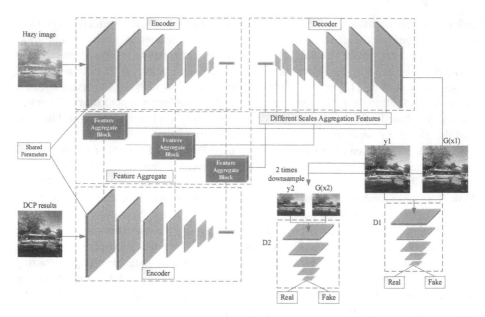

Fig. 1. The architecture of the DCP guided single image dehazing model

3.1 Siamese like Generator

The Encoder-Decoder Architecture. The Siamese like generator module is consist of an encoder and decoder, as shown in the Fig. 1. The encoder includes eight convolution blocks with the form of Convolution-Batch Norm-Relu, which maps the input high resolution image to high level semantic space, and the decoder is symmetric to the encoder, which using deconvolution to recover the high-resolution results from semantic level. We argued that the DCP based dehazing result can be treated as an intermediate state of the clean image, and some useful information can be distilled to guide the image generation. However, the prior based dehazing result usually contains some artifacts. To avoid the negative effect, we extract the features of the hazy images and DCP based dehazing result at the same time by sharing the parameters of the encoder. And the features are aggregated in different scales by feature aggregation block. On the other hand, the DCP based dehazing result can be treated as another kind of image degradation, which can regularize the generator to recover the clean images with multi-task learning method. Then the enhanced features are fed to the decoder by skip-connection to generate the hazy-free image progressively.

Feature Aggregation Block. In order to aggregation feature which is positive to the image dehazing, we propose a feature aggregation block to gather different scale features of the hazy image and DCP based dehazing image. As shown in Fig. 2, the block includes concatenate and a residual block which contains 1×1 Convolution-Instance Norm-Relu, 3×3 Convolution-Instance Norm-Relu and a skip connection. From the feature concatenation, more feature information is provided, though the feature is redundancy. Then, the residual block can extract much more important information from the redundancy features. And after the feature aggregation, the generator can recover the hazy-free images under the guidance of DCP based dehazing results without any harmful.

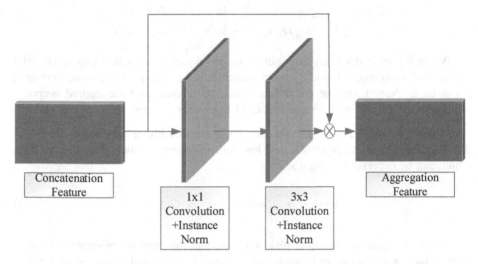

Fig. 2. The feature aggregation block

3.2   Multi-scale Discriminator

To enhance the details of the image generation, we adopt a multi-scale discriminator like the pix2pixHD [20]. The multi-scale discriminator module contains two scale discriminator which named D1 and D2. D1 and D2 have the same architecture, and the output of the Siamese like generator is directly sent to D1, the 2 times down sampled output is sent to D2. With the supervision of the two-scale discriminators, the generator can recover more details in coarse-to-fine manner. On the one hand, D2 guides the generator to produce a global pseudo realistic image on a coarse scale. On the other hand, D1 guides the generator to reconstruct some details in a high-resolution scale and prevent the halo artifacts of generated images.

3.3   Overall Loss Function

In order to optimization the proposed method, we utilize three loss functions as Eq. (1), the conditional GAN loss L_{cGAN}, the dark channel prior loss L_d, and the sum of pixel-wise L_1 loss. The adversarial loss and the dark channel prior loss are used to make the generator to recover the structure of the clean images. And the pixel-wise loss is used to reinforce the contrast of generated image and encourage less blurring.

$$L = L_{cGAN} + \lambda L_d + \lambda L_1 \tag{1}$$

The Conditional GAN Loss. The single image dehazing can be formulated as an image translation problem, which means that the generator tries to translation the hazy image to a clean image, and the discriminator aims to distinguish the image is real or fake. And the objective of a conditional GAN can be expressed as

$$
\begin{aligned}
L_{cGAN} = & \mathrm{E}_{x,y_1}[\log D_1(x,y_1)] + \mathrm{E}_x[\log(1 - D_1(x, G(x)))] \\
& + \mathrm{E}_{x,y_2}[\log D_2(x,y_2)] + \mathrm{E}_x[\log(1 - D_2(x, G(x)))]
\end{aligned}
\tag{2}
$$

Where the generator G try to minimize to this objective and against the adversarial two scale discriminator D_1 and D_2 try to maximize it. In the Eq. (2), the condition input x can be an hazy image or the concatenation of images, and the desired output y represents the ground truth image, and $G(x)$ represents a generated hazy-free image.

The Dark Channel Prior Loss. To make the generated image much more similar to the real clean image, we propose a new loss function named as dark channel prior loss, which can be expressed as Eq. (3).

$$
L_d = \frac{1}{N} \sum_i |Dark(y) - Dark(G(x))|
\tag{3}
$$

Where N represents the total pixel number, and the $Dark(*)$ represents the dark image function, the details of this function can refer to [3]. The dark image is treated as statistics representation of an image, and the dark image of the generated image should be same to the clean image in theoretically.

The Pixel-Wise L1 Loss. The mean of the absolute distance between the haze-free image y and final output $G(x)$ is regarded as the pixel-wise L1 loss, which is defined as

$$
L_1 = \frac{1}{N} \sum_i |y - G(x)|
\tag{4}
$$

4   Experiments

We evaluate the proposed algorithm on both synthetic dataset and real-world hazy images. To demonstrate the effectiveness of the proposed method, we compare our proposed method with five state-of-the-art methods: DCP [3], DehazeNet [7], AOD-Net [13], GFN [15], and DCPDN [8]. For the fairness of comparison, the source codes of the compared methods are presented publicly by the authors. In addition, we do an ablation study to demonstrate the effectiveness of our DCP guided cGAN for single image dehazing.

4.1   Dataset

For the training of the proposed method, we adopt to the Indoor Training Set (ITS) of the new proposed large dataset RESIDE [9]. And we test the performance of the model on the Synthetic Objective Testing Set (SOTS) part. The ITS is synthesized with only indoor images with depth information, which contains 13990 hazy images. And the SOTS contain both indoor and outdoor images, with 500 and 492 hazy images respectively. We can test the domain adaption ability in this dataset.

4.2 Implementation Details

During training all of the ITS are using as the training dataset, which is also used as training dataset for the compared methods. In our network, the patch size is set as 256×256. We use ADAM [21] optimizer with a batch size 1 for training, and set a learning rate as 0.0002, the exponential decay rates as 0.5 and 0.99 respectively. The hyper-parameter of loss function is set as $\lambda = 100$. We implement our model with the TensorFlow framework and a GTX 1080 Ti GPU. And we can process a 640×480 image within 0.04 s. To evaluate the performance of our method, we adopt two metrics: the Peak Signal to Noise Ratio (PSNR) and the Structural Similarity index (SSIM).

4.3 Ablation Study

To better demonstrate the effectiveness of the architecture of our method, we conduct an ablation study by considering the combination of four factors: cGAN, DCP dehazing results (DCP), Siamese Encoder and feature aggregation block(SEF), and the dark loss (DL). We construct the following variants with different component combinations: (1) cGAN: only pix2pix [22] is used; (2) cGAN+DCP: the DCP dehazing results and the hazy image are concatenated to pass to the pix2pix; (3) cGAN+DCP+SEF: combined the concatenated inputs to the Siamese Encoder and enhanced the feature with multi-scale feature aggregation block; (4) cGAN+DCP+SEF+DL: with additional dark channel prior loss for the training of the network. The results are given in Table 1. It demonstrates that the proposed method achieves the best performance of image dehazing in PSNR and SSIM compared with pix2pix [22], the improvement gains in PSNR and SSIM are 1.07 dB and 0.039 respectively. And with the DCP dehazing results, we can get much better results just by concatenation inputs to the pix2pix. Adding the Siamese Encoder and feature aggregation block, an apparently improvement is provided. With the dark channel prior loss, the network can train more stably, and provide with a little gain.

Table 1. Comparison of variants with different components on the outdoor dataset of SOTS.

Method	PSNR	SSIM
cGAN	20.88	0.856
cGAN+DCP	21.56	0.873
cGAN+DCP+SEF	22.03	0.885
cGAN+DCP+SEF+DL	22.05	0.884
Ours	22.15	0.895

4.4   Comparisons with State-of-the-Art Methods

Results on Synthesis Dataset. The comparison results are shown in Table 2, in which the digital values are the averages of the results on SOTS in terms of PSNR and SSIM. It demonstrates that our method achieves the best performance of image dehazing in terms of both PSNR and SSIM on the indoor dataset of SOTS, and it achieves the same SSIM, but gain with 0.77 dB in PSNR compared with the second-place method GFN [15].

On the outdoor dataset of SOTS, our method achieves the best performance in SSIM, ranks the second among the compared methods in PSNR. The GFN results decrease both in PSNR and SSIM in outdoor scene. Our method gets a better domain adaption ability than other methods with the guidance of DCP dehazing results.

Table 2. Comparison results of the state-of-the-art dehazing methods on SOTS.

Method		DCP	DehazeNet	AOD-NET	DCPDN	GFN	Ours
Indoor	PSNR	17.08	21.14	19.06	16.85	22.30	23.07
	SSIM	0.813	0.847	0.850	0.819	0.880	0.880
Outdoor	PSNR	19.56	22.46	20.29	19.96	21.55	22.15
	SSIM	0.821	0.851	0.877	0.846	0.844	0.895

Results on Real-World Images. Figure 3 shows the comparison results of visual effects on real hazy images. It is observed that: (1) Though the proposed method is trained on synthesis data, it still achieves desirable dehazing results on the real-world dataset, which shows the robustness of proposed method. (2) Compared with DCP [3], which results in color distortion in the sky area and suffers from blur, our method can remove the negative effect of DCP dehazing results. (3) Compared with other learning-based methods, Dehaze Net [7] and AOD-Net [13] cannot remove haze effectively. DCPDN [8] and GFN [15] cannot remove haze effectively in heavily hazy scene. And our method achieves much better visual effect.

Hazy
Inputs

DCP[3]

Deha-
zeNet[7]

AOD-
NET[13]

DCPDN[8]

GFN[15]

Ours

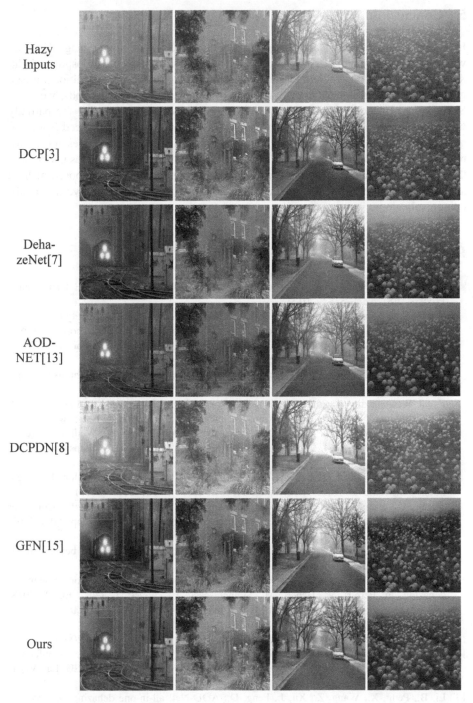

Fig. 3. Comparison of the state-of-the-art dehazing methods on the real-world images.

5   Conclusion

In this paper, we propose Dark Channel Prior guided cGAN for single image dehazing which does not rely on the estimations of the transmission map and atmospheric light. And we transform the problem of image dehazing to the problem of conditional image generation. Combined with prior-based and CNN-based dehazing methods, we use a Siamese like Encoder and feature aggregation block to efficiently using the partially correct DCP dehazing results, following with the decoding of the enhanced feature to generate hazy-free image. And the multi-scale discriminator only guides the multi-resolution output of the generator to recover more details. Experimental results on both the synthesis dataset and the real-world dataset demonstrate that the proposed method achieves the best performance of image dehazing in both the quantitative and qualitative evaluations.

References

1. Ancuti, C.O., Ancuti, C.: Single image dehazing by multi-scale fusion. IEEE Trans. Image Process. **2**(8), 3271–3282 (2013)
2. Tan, R.T.: Visibility in bad weather from a single image. In: Computer Society Conference on Computer Vision and Pattern Recognition (CVPR), pp. 1–8. IEEE, Anchorage (2008)
3. He, K., Sun, J., Tang, X.: Single image haze removal using dark channel prior. IEEE Trans. Pattern Anal. Mach. Intell. **33**(12), 2341–2353 (2011)
4. Zhu, Q., Mai, J., Shao, L.: A fast single image haze removal algorithm using color attenuation prior. IEEE Trans. Image Process. **24**(11), 3522–3533 (2015)
5. Fattal, R.: Dehazing using color-lines. ACM Trans. Graph. **34**(1), 1–14 (2014)
6. Ren, W., Liu, S., Zhang, H., Pan, J., Cao, X., Yang, M.H.: Single image dehazing via multi-scale convolutional neural networks. In: Leibe, B., Matas, J., Sebe, N., Welling, M. (eds.) ECCV 2016. LNCS, vol. 9906, pp. 154–169. Springer, Cham (2016). https://doi.org/10.1007/978-3-319-46475-6_10
7. Cai, B., Xu, X., Jia, K., Qing, C., Tao, D.: Dehazenet: An end-to-end system for single image haze removal. IEEE Trans. Image Process. **25**(11), 5187–5198 (2016)
8. Zhang, H., Pattel, V.M.: Densely connected pyramid dehazing network. In: Computer Society Conference on Computer Vision and Pattern Recognition (CVPR), pp. 3194–3203. IEEE, Salt Lake City (2018)
9. Li, B., Ren, W., Fu, D., et al.: Benchmarking single-image dehazing and beyond. IEEE Trans. Image Process. **28**(1), 492–505 (2019)
10. Yang, D., Sun, J.: Proximal dehaze-net: a prior learning-based deep network for single image dehazing. In: Ferrari, V., Hebert, M., Sminchisescu, C., Weiss, Y. (eds.) ECCV 2018. LNCS, vol. 11211, pp. 729–746. Springer, Cham (2018). https://doi.org/10.1007/978-3-030-01234-2_43
11. Fattal, R.: Single image dehazing. ACM Trans. Graph. (TOG) **27**(3), 1–8 (2008)
12. Berman, D., Avidan, S., et al.: Non-local image dehazing. In: Computer Society Conference on Computer Vision and Pattern Recognition (CVPR), pp. 1674–1682. IEEE, Las Vegas (2016)
13. Li, B., Peng, X., Wang, Z., Xu, J., Feng, D.: AOD-Net: all-in-one dehazing network. In: IEEE International Conference on Computer Vision (ICCV), pp. 4770–4778. IEEE, Venice (2017)

14. Du, Y., Li, X.: Recursive deep residual learning for single image dehazing. In: Computer Society Conference on Computer Vision and Pattern Recognition (CVPR), pp. 730–737. IEEE, Salt Lake City (2018)

15. Ren, W., et al.: Gated fusion network for single image dehazing. In: Computer Society Conference on Computer Vision and Pattern Recognition (CVPR), pp. 3253–3261. IEEE, Salt Lake City (2018)

16. Goodfellow, I., et al.: Generative adversarial nets. In: 27th International Conference on Neural Information Processing Systems, pp. 2672–2680. MIT Press (2014)

17. Zhu, H., Peng, X., Chandrasekhar, V., et al.: DehazeGAN: when image dehazing meets differential programming. In: 27th International Joint Conference on Artificial Intelligence, pp. 1234–1240. AAAI Press (2018)

18. Yang, X., Xu, Z., Luo, J.: Towards perceptual image dehazing by physics-based disentanglement and adversarial training. In: Thirty-Second AAAI Conference on Artificial Intelligence (2018)

19. Li, R., Pan, J., Li, Z., Tang, J.: Single image dehazing via conditional generative adversarial network. In: Computer Society Conference on Computer Vision and Pattern Recognition (CVPR), pp. 8202–8211. IEEE, Salt Lake City (2018)

20. Wang, T., Liu, M., Zhu, J., Tao, A., Kautz, J., Catanzaro, B.: High-resolution image synthesis and semantic manipulation with conditional GANs. In: Computer Society Conference on Computer Vision and Pattern Recognition (CVPR), pp. 8798–8807. IEEE, Salt Lake City (2018)

21. Kingma, D., Ba, J.: Adam: a method for stochastic optimization. In: 3rd International Conference on Learning Representations (ICLR), San Diego, CA, USA (2015)

22. Isola, P., Zhu, J.-Y., Zhou, T., Efros, A.A.: Image-to-image translation with conditional adversarial networks. In: Computer Society Conference on Computer Vision and Pattern Recognition (CVPR), pp. 1125–1134. IEEE, Honolulu (2017)

A Fast Region Growing Based Superpixel Segmentation for Hyperspectral Image Classification

Qianqian Xu, Peng Fu$^{(\boxtimes)}$, Quansen Sun, and Tao Wang

School of Computer Science and Engineering,
Nanjing University of Science and Technology, Nanjing 210094, China
fupeng@njust.edu.cn

Abstract. In recent studies, superpixel segmentation has been integrated into hyperspectral (HS) image classification methods. However, the existing superpixel-based classification methods usually suffer from two serious problems. First, the accuracy and efficiency of current superpixel segmentation approaches cannot meet the demands of practical applications for HS images; second, conventional superpixel-based classification methods generally consider each generated superpixel as a unit for the image classification, which may help to reduce the computing time but result in a significant decrease of the classification accuracy. To solve the problems, we propose a fast region growing based superpixel segmentation (FRGSS) algorithm and a novel texture-adaptive superpixel integration strategy (TASIS) for the HS image classification. Experimental results on real Airborne Visible/Infrared Imaging Spectrometer (AVIRIS) HS images demonstrate that the proposed FRGSS outperforms the state-of-the-art superpixel algorithm. In addition, the superiority of the TASIS is verified compared to the pixel-wise and the conventional superpixel-based classification methods.

Keywords: Superpixel segmentation · Hyperspectral image classification · Region growing · Adaptive integration strategy

1 Introduction

Hyperspectral (HS) image classification is of growing interest as a key technique to Earth remote sensing. The ground object classification of HS images is applied in many application fields, such as environment monitoring [1], urban mapping [2], and precision agriculture [3].

By using the spectral information of HS images, a large number of techniques have been introduced for the image classification in the last few decades. Typical methods include multinomial logistic regression (MLR) [4], random forests (RF) [5], sparse representation (SR) [6], and the support vector machine (SVM) [7]. With the development of HS remote sensors, the spatial resolution of HS images has been

---

Q. Xu—Student

© Springer Nature Switzerland AG 2019
Z. Lin et al. (Eds.): PRCV 2019, LNCS 11858, pp. 772–782, 2019.
https://doi.org/10.1007/978-3-030-31723-2_66

significantly increased. As a result, many researchers attempt to exploit the spatial information in classification methods, where the superpixel technique has been widely used to extract spatial information in HS images [8–10]. Superpixels are the regions that composed by pixels which color and texture characteristics are similar. Algorithms for generating superpixels can be roughly divided into graph-based [11–15] and gradient ascent [16–20] methods. Among the existing superpixel algorithms, Achanta et al. [21] proposed a linear iterative clustering algorithm (SLIC) which has been widely utilized for the simple operation and decent segmentation results. In [22], the author improved the SLIC with a simple non-iterative clustering (SNIC) technique, where the accuracy and efficiency of the superpixel segmentation method has been greatly improved.

As introduced above, superpixel segmentation has been exploited in HS images classification methods, which may improve the classification results in some aspects. However, there are still two main challenges in the current superpixel-based HS image classification methods: (1) most of the existing superpixel algorithms are designed for the 2-dimension natural images, where the performance of these methods may decrease for the 3-dimension HS images; (2) conventional superpixel-based classification methods generally regard each segmented superpixel as a unit for the image classification, which may improve the algorithm efficiency but usually suffer from a decrease of the classification accuracy. To address the challenges, we propose a fast region growing based superpixel segmentation (FRGSS) algorithm and a new texture-adaptive superpixel integration strategy (TASIS) for the HS image classification in this paper. In the proposed FRGSS, the superpixels are generated by the region growing approach based on a spectral-spatial combined distance. Compared to the most current superpixel algorithms, the superpixel segmentation is faster with FRGSS as it eliminates the iteration process. Moreover, a distance map is established to reduce the traversal times of the unlabeled pixels, which may further speed up the superpixel generating process. Completely different from the traditional superpixel-based classification methods, the proposed TASIS superpixel integration strategy can help to mine the spatial features of HS images more efficiently and thus improve the pixel-wise classification results (Fig. 1).

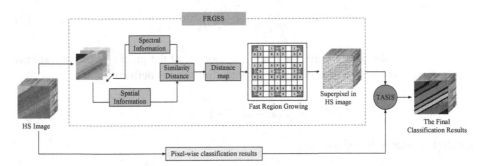

Fig. 1. Framework of the proposed method

2 Proposed Method

In this section, the proposed method for HS images classification is presented. Our method consists of two major steps: including a fast region growing based superpixel segmentation and a novel texture-adaptive superpixel integration strategy.

2.1 FRGSS for HS Images Superpixel Segmentation

For a given HS image, the FRGSS is adopted for the superpixel segmentation. First, K centers $C[k] = \{\mathbf{x}_k,\ \mathbf{s}_k\}$ are sampled on a regular grid region, which are represented by K elements as

$$e_k = \left\{\mathbf{x}_k,\ \mathbf{s}_k, k, d_{k,k}\right\}, \tag{1}$$

where $\mathbf{x}_k = [x_k\, y_k]^T$ represents the pixel location in spatial space; $\mathbf{s}_k = [s_{1_k}\, s_{2_k}\, s_{3_k}]^T$ are spectral values of first three principal components obtained by the principal component analysis (PCA); k denotes the kth center; $d_{k,k}$ represents the distance between pixel $\mathbf{x}_k$ and label k, is set to zero.

Based on the initialized centers, the superpixels are generated with a region growing algorithm. In the step, a sortable queue Q is created to determine the label of each pixel. The queue is arranged in ascending order of the distance between the pixel and the label. We push these centers elements into Q, while Q is not empty, the queue leader element a_k is popped always. Simultaneously, the unlabeled pixel is labeled to unique label k. The spatial and spectral values of the kth superpixel are the mean values of all pixels in the superpixel, which are updated with the determination of pixel labels. In addition, the four or eight neighbor unlabeled pixels of the outlier element should be judged whether they can enter the queue by calculating the spectral similarity and spatial similarity with region k. The metric uses Euclidean distance (ED) to compute and takes advantage of the spectral and spatial information of HS images. Create a new element $a_j = \left\{\mathbf{x}_j,\ \mathbf{s}_j, k, d_{j,k}\right\}$ that represents one of the pixels in the neighborhood region k, the similarity between the pixel $\mathbf{x}_j$ and kth superpixel is defined as:

$$d_{j,k} = \sqrt{d_{1_{j,k}}^2 + \left(\frac{d_{2_{j,k}}}{S}\right)^2 \times m^2}, \tag{2}$$

where m is introduced to weight the relative important of the pixel spectral and spatial similarities. S is the size of superpixel. Spatial similarity is defined as:

$$d_{1_{j,k}} = \sqrt{\left(x_j - x_k\right)^2 + \left(y_j - y_k\right)^2}, \tag{3}$$

spectral similarity is defined as:

$$d_{2_{j,k}} = \sqrt{\left(s_{1_j} - s_{1_k}\right)^2 + \left(s_{2_j} - s_{2_k}\right)^2 + \left(s_{3_j} - s_{3_k}\right)^2}. \tag{4}$$

During the enqueuer operation, unlabeled pixels can be traversed by multiple regions. For example, pixel $\mathbf{x}_j$ may be detected by region k_1 first and is listed as element a_j. Since the growth trend of region k_2 is faster than that of region k_1, $\mathbf{x}_j$ is detected by region k_2 again. Each pixel is queued when it is detected by a region, which wastes a lot of time. In order to deal with this problem, we introduce a distance map D to prevent the pixels from performing multiple unnecessary enqueuer operations. D indicates the closest distance between the pixel and the region. The simple rule is that when d_{j,k_1} is smaller than $D(\mathbf{x}_j)$, the pixel is pushed into queue and updated with d_{j,k_1} to $D(\mathbf{x}_j)$. It significantly reduces the times of pushing and popping pixels the queue, thus further improves the efficiency of the FRGSS superpixel segmentation algorithm. The pseudo-code of the proposed FRGSS algorithm is presented in Algorithm 1.

Algorithm 1 FRGSS algorithm

Input: A HS image, K cluster centers $C[k] = \{\mathbf{x}_k, \mathbf{s}_k\}$, a predefined color parameter m

Output: Labels matrix L

Initialization: $Q = \{\phi\}$, indicating a sortable queue;

$D(i) = \infty$, indicating the closest distance of each pixel with class;

$L(i) = -1$, indicating the segmentation class of each pixel

  # Comments

$e_k = \{\mathbf{x}_k, \mathbf{s}_k, k, d_{k,k}\}$ # create K centers elements

$Q = \{e_k\}$ # add all centers elements into Q

While Q is not empty **do**

$a_k - Q.pop$ # pop out a pixel from Q

if $L(\mathbf{x}_k) < 0$ **then**

  $L(\mathbf{x}_k) = k$

  $\mathbf{A} = Unlabeld(a_k)$ # select all unlabeled connected neighbors of a_k

  for each pixel $\mathbf{x}_j$ in $\mathbf{A}$ **do**

    $a_j = \{\mathbf{x}_j, \mathbf{s}_j, k, d_{j,k}\}$ # create new element

    if $d_{j,k} < D(\mathbf{x}_j)$ **then**

      $Q = \{a_j\}$ # add element into Q

      $D(\mathbf{x}_j) = d_{j,k}$ # update $D(\mathbf{x}_j)$

    end if

  end for

end if

end while

Return L

2.2   TASIS for HS Images Classification

The traditional superpixel-based classification methods usually take each generated superpixel as a unit for the image classification, which may help to reduce the calculation time but lead to a significant reduction in classification accuracy. In order to improve the HS images classification by using the results of superpixel segmentation, we propose a texture-adaptive superpixel integration strategy. It is worth noting that the texture complexities are various in real HS images. The texture complexity inside different superpixels will affect the classification effect. As a result, the texture factor is considered in the proposed TASIS of HS remote sensing images, the complexity of textures can be denoted by some measures, such as variance, fractal model, gradient and so on. Taking into account time-consuming problem, we utilize variance to display the texture complexity of each superpixel. For superpixels with different texture degrees, we define an adaptive threshold to integrate the classification results and segmentation results. The texture adaptive threshold of each superpixel is given by:

$$\delta_k = \frac{v_k}{\max(\mathbf{v})}, \tag{5}$$

where v_k is the variance of kth superpixel, $\max(\mathbf{v})$ is the maximum variance of all superpixels. In a superpixel, the proportion of the largest class is calculated. If the proportion is greater than the texture adaptive threshold of the superpixel, the labels of all pixels in the whole superpixel are set as the label of this class. Otherwise the superpixel texture is complex, the adaptive threshold is too large to change the superpixel labels.

3   Experimental Results

In this section, we present the experimental results by the proposed HS images classification method on a real Airborne Visible/Infrared Imaging Spectrometer (AVIRIS) HS image. First, the results of the FRGSS model and other state-of-the-art superpixel segmentation approaches are analyzed. Next, the effectiveness of the TASIS strategy is evaluated by embedding the FRGSS superpixel segmentation results to the traditional pixel-based classification methods.

The real hyperspectral data set is collected by the AVIRIS sensor over Salinas Valley, California. The scene is a small sub-scene of the Salinas image, denoted Salinas-A. The image size is $83 \times 86 \times 224$ and it is characterized by high spatial resolution which 3.7-m pixels. In the experiments, 20 spectral bands (i.e., the 108th to 112th, 154th to 167th, and 224th bands) are discarded because of water absorption and the number of spectral bands was reduced to 204. Figure 2(a) and (b) show the color composite of Salinas-A image and the corresponding reference data. All the experiments are performed on an Intel Core i3 CPU @ 3.10 GHz.

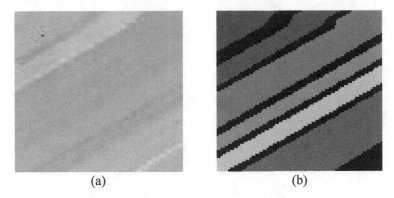

(a)   (b)

Fig. 2. Color composite of Salinas-A image and the corresponding reference data. (Color figure online)

3.1   Performance of the FRGSS Superpixel Segmentation

In order to demonstrate the effectiveness and superiority of FRGSS superpixel segmentation algorithm, we compare the proposed algorithm and a state-of-the-art approach SNIC on the Salinas-A image, where the performances of the superpixel segmentation are evaluated by using three widely used parametric metrics including under segmentation (US), boundary recall (BR), and time cost (TIME). In our algorithm, the parameter m is set to 20 according to the segmentation performance. Table 1 lists the superpixel segmentation results of FRGSS and SNIC for different number of superpixels. As reported in Table 1, several conclusions can be summarized as follows.

(1) SNIC and FRGSS segmentation results are generally positively correlated with the number of superpixels.
(2) The US and BR of FRGSS are close to SNIC, but it is basically more accurate than SNIC.
(3) FRGSS algorithm is always faster than SNIC algorithm. The speed has increased by almost a third. The segmentation speed is greatly improved while the precision is guaranteed.

Table 1. The segmentation result of SNIC and FRGSS

NUM	SNIC			FRGSS		
	US	BR	TIME	US	BR	TIME
20	**0.4631**	**0.5845**	0.0031	**0.4631**	**0.5845**	**0.0022**
30	0.3744	**0.6443**	0.0037	**0.3741**	**0.6443**	**0.0022**
50	0.2938	**0.7289**	0.0040	**0.2936**	**0.7289**	**0.0023**
100	0.2124	0.8216	0.0039	**0.2119**	**0.8237**	**0.0026**
200	**0.1536**	**0.9134**	0.0044	**0.1536**	**0.9134**	**0.0030**
300	**0.1208**	**0.9526**	0.0046	0.1210	**0.9526**	**0.0035**

For a more clearly visual comparison, the superpixel segmentation results with SNIC and FRGSS are presented in Fig. 3 (a) and (b), respectively. From Fig. 3 we can see that the superpixels generated by FRGSS exhibit better boundary adherence.

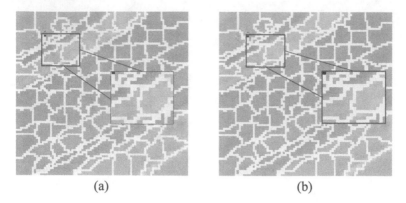

(a)   (b)

Fig. 3. Segmentation results of SNIC and FRGSS methods for the Salinas-A image.

3.2 Performance of the TASIS Classification Strategy

In this part, we present the classification results with TASIS method on the Salinas-A image. We evaluate the proposed method by using four objective metrics including overall accuracy (OA), average accuracy (AA), Kappa coefficient (Kappa), and time cost (Time).

The superpixels generated by FRGSS are used as the preprocessing step for HS image classification, where the number of superpixels may affect the accuracy of HS image classification. Figure 4 shows that the accuracies of classification varies with the increase of the number of superpixels. We can observe that when the number of superpixels is 100, the classification accuracies are the highest. The reason is that when the number of superpixels is less, the size of each superpixel is larger, thus each superpixel may contain multiple classes. On the contrary, more segmented superpixels can help to reduce the class number in each superpixel, but suffer from less spatial information obtained and more time consuming. To balance the complexity and the estimation performance, the number of superpixels is set to 100 in all the experiments.

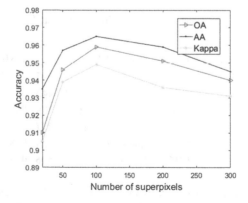

Fig. 4. The accuracy of classification with the number of superpixel increases.

To evaluate the performance of the TASIS classification strategy, we compare the pixel-wise classification method (PWCM), conventional superpixel-based method (CSBM) and the TASIS classification strategy. In this experiment, the widely used classification approach SVM is adopted where the Radial basis function (RBF) kernel is selected, the conventional superpixel-based method takes superpixel as a unit where the parameters are set in accordance with the literature [23].

As reported in Table 2, compared with the PWCM, the CSBM help to reduce the computing time but result in the decrease of the classification accuracy. Our proposed method improves accuracy in almost every category. Although a little time is sacrificed, the accuracies of classification are greatly improved.

Table 2. The classification results of the PWCM, CSBM and FRGSS-TASIS

Class	PWCM	CSBM	FRGSS-TASIS
Weeks_1	99.48	93.02	**100**
Corn	68.87	87.90	**88.01**
Lettuce 4wk	85.55	50	**92.53**
Lettuce 5wk	**100**	86.22	**100**
Lettuce 6wk	**99.85**	82.85	99.55
Lettuce 7wk	96.99	80.23	**98.99**
AA (Mean in %)	91.79	80.04	**96.51**
OA (Mean in %)	90.01	81.47	**95.92**
Kappa	0.876	0.767	**0.949**
Time(s)	1.24	**0.66**	1.24 + 0.54

To illustrative the improvement results of classification, Fig. 5(a) and (b) show the maps of PWCM and FRGSS-TASIS classification, which magnified regions are showed in Fig. 5(c) and (d), respectively. It is clear that many mislabeling pixels are fixed to the correct category in magnified regions. It is worth noting that there are still some incorrect classified pixels as a superpixel may contain too many wrong classes, which can be improved by using more advanced pixel-wise classification approaches.

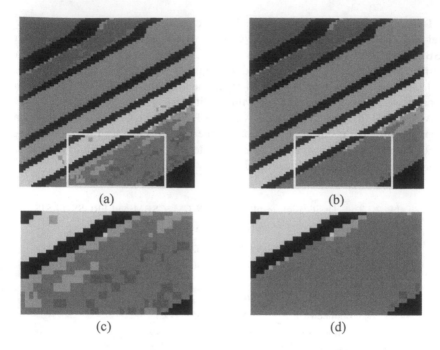

Fig. 5. Classification results of PWCM and FRGSS-TASIS methods for the Salinas-A image.

4   Conclusion

In this paper, we have proposed a fast region growing based superpixel segmentation (FRGSS) algorithm and a new texture-adaptive superpixel integration strategy (TASIS) for the HS image classification. The FRGSS method effectively reduces the traversal times of the unlabeled pixels when generating superpixels in a HS image. In contrast with the conventional superpixel based classification methods, TASIS sacrifices a little time but greatly improves the classification accuracy. In the experiment, compared with pixel-based and traditional superpixel-based classification methods, the proposed method exhibits higher accuracies in a real HS image. In recent years, amount of HS image classification methods have been developed by using deep learning techniques, in the future work, we will apply FRGSS-TASIS to these advanced methods for HS images classification.

Acknowledgements. This work was in part supported by the National Natural Science Foundation of China under Grant no. 61801222 and no. 61673220, and in part supported by the Fundamental Research Funds for the Central Universities under Grant no. 30919011230, and in part supported by the Jiangsu Planned Projects for Postdoctoral Research Funds.

References

1. Cheng, G., Li, Z., Han, J., Yao, X., Guo, L.: Exploring hierarchical convolutional features for hyperspectral image classification. IEEE Trans. Geosci. Remote Sens. **99**, 1–11 (2018)
2. Fang, L., He, N., Li, S., Ghamisi, P., Benediktsson, J.A.: Extinction profiles fusion for hyperspectral images classification. IEEE Trans. Geosci. Remote Sens. **56**(3), 1803–1815 (2018)
3. Haut, J.M., Paoletti, M.E., Plaza, J., Li, J., Plaza, A.: Active learning with convolutional neural networks for hyperspectral image classification using a new bayesian approach. IEEE Trans. Geosci. Remote Sens. **99**, 1–22 (2018)
4. Li, J., Bioucas-Dias, J.M., Plaza, A.: Semisupervised hyperspectral image segmentation using multinomial logistic regression with active learning. IEEE Trans. Geosci. Remote Sens. **48**(11), 4085–4098 (2010)
5. Dalponte, M., Orka, H.O., Gobakken, T., Gianelle, D., Nasset, E.: Tree species classification in boreal forests with hyperspectral data. IEEE Trans. Geosci. Remote Sens. **51**(5), 2632–2645 (2013)
6. Chen, Y., Nasrabadi, N.M., Tran, T.D.: Hyperspectral image classification via kernel sparse representation. IEEE Trans. Geosci. Remote Sens. **51**(1), 217–231 (2013)
7. Melgani, F., Bruzzone, L.: Classification of hyperspectral remote sensing images with support vector machines. IEEE Trans. Geosci. Remote Sens. **42**(8), 1778–1790 (2004)
8. Fang, L., Li, S., Duan, W., Ren, J., Benediktsson, J.A.: Classification of hyperspectral images by exploiting spectral–spatial information of superpixel via multiple kernels. IEEE Trans. Geosci. Remote Sens. **53**(12), 6663–6674 (2015)
9. Fang, L., Li, S., Kang, X., Benediktsson, J.A.: Spectral–spatial classification of hyperspectral images with a superpixel-based discriminative sparse model. IEEE Trans. Geosci. Remote Sens. **53**(8), 4186–4201 (2015)
10. Jia, S., Deng, B., Zhu, J., Jia, X., Li, Q.: Local binary pattern-based hyperspectral image classification with superpixel guidance. IEEE Trans. Geosci. Remote Sens. **56**(2), 749–759 (2018)
11. Felzenszwalb, P.F., Huttenlocher, D.P.: Efficient graph based image segmentation. Int. J. Comput. Vis. **59**(2), 167–181 (2004). https://doi.org/10.1023/B:VISI.0000022288.19776.77
12. Liu, M.Y., Tuzel, O., Ramalingam, S., Chellappa, R.: Entropy rate superpixel segmentation. In: IEEE Conference on Computer Vision and Pattern Recognition (CVPR), pp. 2097–2104 (2011)
13. Moore, A.P., Prince, S.J., Warrell, J., Mohammed, U., Jones, G.: Superpixel lattices. In: IEEE Conference on Computer Vision and Pattern Recognition (CVPR), pp. 1–8 (2008)
14. Shi, J., Malik, J.: Normalized cuts and image segmentation. IEEE Trans. Pattern Anal. Mach. Intell. **22**(8), 888–905 (2000)
15. Zhang, Y., Hartley, R., Mashford, J., Burn, S.: Superpixels via pseudo-boolean optimization. In: 2011 International Conference on Computer Vision, pp. 1387–1394 (2011)
16. Comaniciu, D., Meer, P.: Mean shift: a robust approach toward feature space analysis. IEEE Trans. Pattern Anal. Mach. Intell. **24**(5), 603–619 (2002)
17. Levinshtein, A., Stere, A., Kutulakos, K.N., Fleet, D.J., Dickinson, S.J., Siddiqi, K.: TurboPixels: fast superpixels using geometric flows. IEEE Trans. Pattern Anal. Mach. Intell. **31**(12), 2290–2297 (2009)
18. Vedaldi, A., Soatto, S.: Quick shift and kernel methods for mode seeking. In: European Conference on Computer Vision, pp. 705–718 (2008)

19. Vincent, L., Soille, P.: Watersheds in digital spaces: an efficient algorithm based on immersion simulations. IEEE Trans. Pattern Anal. Mach. Intell. **6**, 583–598 (1991)
20. Fu, P., Li, C., Cai, W., Sun, Q.: A spatially cohesive superpixel model for image noise level estimation. Neurocomputing **266**, 420–432 (2017)
21. Achanta, R., Shaji, A., Smith, K., Lucchi, A., Fua, P., Süsstrunk, S.: SLIC superpixels compared to state-of-the-art superpixel methods. IEEE Trans. Pattern Anal. Mach. Intell. **34**(11), 2274–2282 (2012)
22. Achanta, R., Susstrunk, S.: Superpixels and polygons using simple non-iterative clustering. In: IEEE Conference on Computer Vision and Pattern Recognition, pp. 4651–4660 (2017)
23. Chung, H., Lu, G., Tian, Z., Wang, D., Chen, Z.G., Fei, B.: Superpixel-based spectral classification for the detection of head and neck cancer with hyperspectral imaging. In: Medical Imaging 2016: Biomedical Applications in Molecular, Structural, and Functional Imaging, p. 978813 (2016)

Complexity Reduction for Depth Map Coding in 3D-HEVC

Shifang Yu[1], Guojun Dai[1], Hua Zhang[1,2(✉)], and Hongfei Huang[1]

[1] School of Computer Science and Technology, Hangzhou Dianzi University,
Hangzhou, China
zhangh@hdu.edu.cn

[2] Key Laboratory of Network Multimedia Technology of Zhejiang Province,
Zhejiang University, Hangzhou, China

Abstract. 3D-HEVC is an emerging coding standard for the compression of multi-view video plus depth data. In 3D-HEVC, Depth Modeling Modes (DMMs) searching and coding unit (CU) partition consume a large proportion of the 3D-HEVC encoding complexity. This paper proposes techniques to speed up 3D-HEVC depth intra mode decision and early terminated depth CU partition. The feature of the smooth pixel block can directly skip the DMM without segmentation. The method of this paper is to determine whether the pixel block is smooth in advance. This technique takes advantage of the fact that after the smooth pixel block is subjected to wavelet transform (WT), the high-frequency coefficient of the new matrix are all zeros. If not, then judge whether the variance of the pixel values on the four sides of the pixel block is less than a given threshold. Experimental results show that the proposed algorithm can achieve on average 23.3% time reduction, with a distinguished BD-rate decrease of 1.3% on synthesized views.

Keywords: 3D-HEV · Depth coding · Intra mode · CU · Wavelet transform

1 Introduction

3D-HEVC [1] is the first coding standard that manages both texture and depth video, aiming at providing free view-point videos through depth image base rendering (DIBR) technique [2]. For the depth video, the depth map images are characterized by large homogeneous areas and sharp edges [3]. To represent the depth information in a better way, two depth modeling modes (DMMs), named Wedgelet Partition mode (DMM1) and Contour Partition mode (DMM4) [4],

This work is supported by the National Natural Science Foundation of China (No. 61471150, No. 61501402, No. U1509216), the Key Program of Zhejiang Provincial Natural Science Foundation of China (No. LZ14F020003). Thanks for support and assistance from Key Laboratory of Network Multimedia Technology of Zhejiang Province. Student paper.

© Springer Nature Switzerland AG 2019
Z. Lin et al. (Eds.): PRCV 2019, LNCS 11858, pp. 783–793, 2019.
https://doi.org/10.1007/978-3-030-31723-2_67

have been added into the intra 3D-HEVC coding. DMMs could greatly benefit the depth coding, but they also bring lots of computational complexities [3].

For 3D-HEVC encoder, most of computational time is spent on CU split decision, because the brute-force search for rate-distortion optimization (RDO) [5]. As the extension of HEVC, 3D-HEVC also adopts the quad-tree structure coding which supports the CU varying from 64*64 to 8*8 without any optimization. The traditional process of CU decision adopts an exhaustion method which results with very high computational complexities.

To solve these problems, many complexity reduction approaches have been proposed for 3D-HEVC encoder. In [6,7], Gu et al. used the evaluation cost of intra traditional mode as the skip signal to avoid some DMMs calculation. Park et al. [8], proposed an algorithm which performs a simple edge classification in the Hadamard transform to omit unnecessary DMMs. In [9], Silva et al. proposed an algorithm to reduce the number of modes which would be evaluated in the mode decision. All these methods focus on the mode decision of DMMs.

The process of CU decision has been optimized by many fast algorithms in conventional HEVC [10,11], In [5], a deep learning approach is used to decide whether CU is split into finer partition. Ruiz et al. [12] proposed an algorithm to speed up the process by using data mining. These approaches explore some intermediate features to predetermine the CU partition before checking all possible quad-tree patterns. This paper proposes methods to accelerate the intra encoding of depth video, including fast depth map intra mode decision and early terminated depth CU partition. The solution is based on an adaptive approaches that a smooth CU after wavalet transforming (WT), its high frequency coefficient are all zeros. If not, then judge whether the variance of the pixel values on four sides of the pixel block is smaller than a given threshold. As a result, 23.3% encoding time is reduced with a distinguished BD-rate decrease of 1.3% on synthesized views.

2   3D-HEVC Intra Depth Coding

2.1   Fast DMMs Selection

Depth Modling Mode is a new type of pattern of intra prediction which is used to code areas with obvious transitional depth values. There are 37 optional intra prediction modes for 3D-HEVC, including 35 traditional HEVC intra prediction models and two DMMs. When encoding depth map, firstly, 35 traditional HEVC intra models would be selected roughly. Equation 1 is adopted to select N patterns whose $H - cost$ is cheap as most possible patterns (MPMs) and add them to the selection list. Secondly, add two DMMs into selection list. Finally, the Rate Distortion Optimization (RDO) is calculated for all the prediction modes in the selection list, and only one with the lowest distortion cost will be chosen as the best.

$$H - cost = SATD + \lambda * R \qquad (1)$$

$SATD$ is the sum of absolute values of predict unit (PU) residual information after Hadamard transformation, λ denoted the Lagrange factor, R represents the number of bits required for encoding. Combining the DMMs with traditional HEVC could effectively decrease internal boundary ring effect and improve the encoding quality of depth map. Meanwhile, it also vastly increases the calculation complexity of coding. Due to the fact that the new type of pattern results in a increasing number of selective modes which may waste much more time in mode judging. Table 1 represents the optimal intra prediction modes of PUs. It contains 98.21% conventional modes and 1.79% DMMs on average. It means that most of DMMs are unnecessary for depth coding [4]. Therefore, the coding process can be accelerated by optimizing the pattern decision process. The fast depth map intra mode decision of this work aims at reducing the number of candidate intra patterns.

Table 1. The optimal intra prediction modes of PUs

Sequence	Conventional modes	Contour	Wedgelets
Balloons	98.77%	0.52%	0.71%
Kendo	99.10%	0.37%	0.53%
Newspaper_CC	97.41%	0.93%	1.66%
GT_Fly	97.48%	2.07%	0.45%
Poznan_Hall2	99.74%	0.12%	0.14%
Poznan_Street	99.16%	0.43%	0.41%
Undo_Dancer	99.06%	0.44%	0.50%
Shark	94.96%	4.20%	0.84%
Average	**98.21%**	**1.14%**	**0.65%**

2.2 CU Partition

CU partition [13] is the core process of 3D-HEVC. It is a key contribution to improve the efficiency of 3D video coding but it is also one of the major time-consuming to 3D-HEVC standard. The default sizes of the maximum CU(CTU) is 64*64, the minimum is 8*8. The size of LCU can be determined by the encoder. Compared with the previous video coding standard, the size of LCU can be undivided, as a CU directly, or it can be further recursively divided into multiple CUs using a brute-force RDO search, which includes a topdown checking process and a bottom-up comparison process. Figure 1 illustrates the RD cost checking and comparison between a parent CU and its sub-CUs. In the checking process, the encoder checks the RD cost of the whole CTU, followed by checking its sub-CUs, till reaching the minimum CU size. In Fig. 1, the RD cost of a parent CU is denoted as R^{pa}, and the RD costs of its sub-CUs are denoted as R_m^{sub}, where

$m \in \{1, 2, 3, 4\}$ is the index of each sub-CU. Afterwards, based on the RD costs of CUs and sub-CUs, the comparison process is conducted to determine whether a parent CU should be split. As shown in Fig. 1(b), if $\sum_{m=1}^{4} R_m^{\text{sub}} < R^{\text{pa}}$, the parent CU needs to be split; otherwise, it is not split [5].

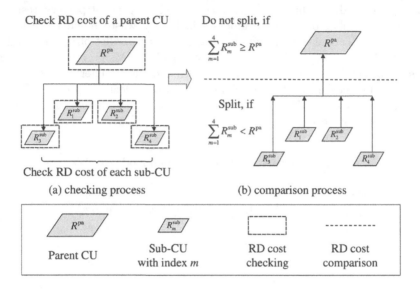

Fig. 1. Image division structure diagram

3   Proposed Fast Algorithm

Considering the observation presented in the previous section, a fast intra encoding in depth video decision scheme for the 3D-HEVC is proposed in this work. The proposed scheme is divided into two main parts:fast depth map intra mode decision and early terminated CU spilt decision.

3.1   Fast Depth Map Intra Mode Decision

Wavelet transform [14] is usually used in signal and image process, especially lossy compression, which has a strong concentration on energy distribution. An image will obtain low frequency region LL and high frequency HL, LH, and HH after wavelet transforming, as presented in Fig. 2. If an image has the same pixel value, its high frequency region values of wavelet matrix are all zeros. Figure 3(a)(b) show a PU of 8*8 size with the same pixels and its wavelet matrix, respectively.

As we all know, depth map has a large range of smooth area and poignant edge. DMMs is only applied to the PUs with poignant edge when we conducte

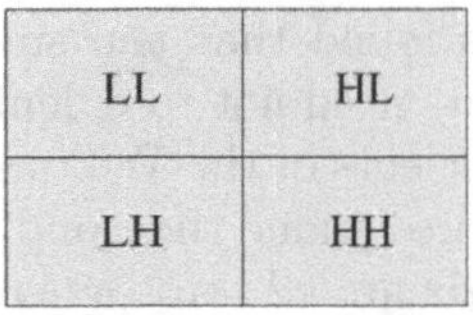

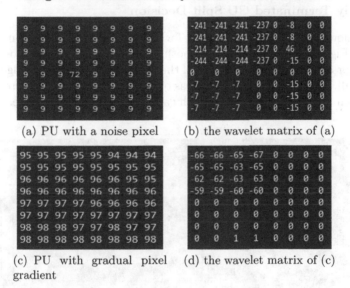

LL	HL
LH	HH

Fig. 2. Frequency distribution of image wavelet transform

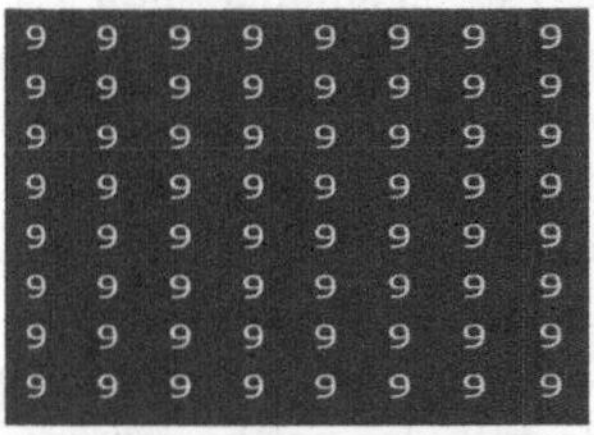

(a) PU with the same pixels    (b) the wavelet matrix of (a)

Fig. 3. PU with the same pixels and its WT matrix

(a) PU with a noise pixel   (b) the wavelet matrix of (a)

(c) PU with gradual pixel   (d) the wavelet matrix of (c)
gradient

Fig. 4. PUs and their WT matrixs

intra prediction for depth map. If current PU only has a smooth region, it is unnecessary to add DMMs into the selection list as alternative modes. Thus, this work will observe whether the values of wavelet matrix of high frequency region are all zeros after WT of depth PU, in order to judge whether this PU is smooth or not. If it is smooth, remove DMMs from the selection list. In the algorithm, the condition which is used to judge the smooth of depth PUs is that the Sum of high frequency coefficient is 0.

Through experiments, it is found that the smooth PUs with several noisy points or gradual pixel gradients need not to calculate DMMs. For PUs in these cases, the high-frequency coefficients of the WT matrix are not all zeros, as presenting in Fig. 4(a–d). Therefore, under the condition that the high-frequency coefficients of the wavelet matrix are all zeros, current PU can only be judged as absolutely smooth, rather relatively smooth. Hence, we compute the variance of the pixel values on the four sides of the current PU, denoted it as Var and compare the Var with a given threshold T_{cu}. If Var is smaller than T_{cu}, we believe that the current depth PU is relatively homogeneous. Fig. 6(a) presents the operation flow of the proposed fast depth map intra mode decision scheme. Firstly, select MPMs from 35 Intra Prediction Mode using the Eq. 1. Secondly, compute the Sum of the high-frequency coefficients of the current PU WT matrix. If Sum is 0, DMMs will not be required, if it is not 0, then compute the variance of the pixel values on the four sides of the current PU, denoted as Var, if Var is smaller than the given threshold T_{cu}, DMMs will also not be required, otherwise, DMMs should be added into the candidate list.

3.2   Early Terminated CU Split Decision

It is well known that large CU is suitable for locally homogeneous region. As can be seen from Fig. 5, the CU size of the smooth area is relatively large, most of which are 64*64 or 32*32, while the CU size of the area in which contains edge information is small. Therefore, for smooth areas of depth map, the decision process at a larger depth level can be skipped, which can save a lot of coding time.

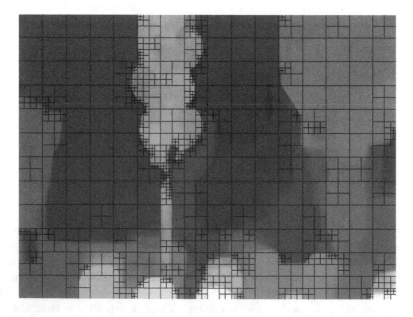

Fig. 5. CU partition of a depth map

In order to terminate the CU segmentation in advance, this paper judges whether the current CU is smooth or not. The condition of judging whether the CU is smooth is the same as that of judging whether the PU is smooth or not. Figure 6(b) presents the flowchart of the proposed early terminated CU split decision scheme. Firstly, compute the Sum of the high-frequency coefficients of the current CU WT matrix. If the current CU doesn't meet the condition that the Sum not equals to zero, the current CU doesn't have to be split. If Sum equals to zero, compute the variance of the pixel values on the four sides of the current CU, denotes as Var, if Var is bigger than the given threshold T_{cu}, the current CU does have to be split, otherwise the current CU doesn't have to be split.

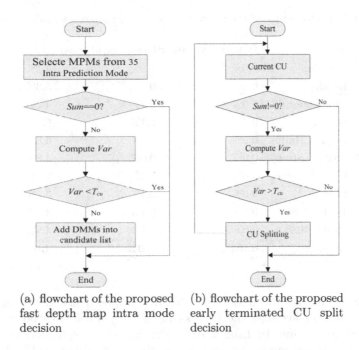

(a) flowchart of the proposed fast depth map intra mode decision

(b) flowchart of the proposed early terminated CU split decision

Fig. 6. Flowcharts of the proposed algorithms.

4   Experiment Results

In the experiment, the two solutions proposed use the reference software HTM13.0 [4] following the common test condition (CTC) [15]. All test sequences are coded using all intra configuration for three-view cases. Three test sequences (Balloons, Kendo, Newspaper_CC) are with 1024×768 resolution and five test sequences (GT_Fly, Poznan_Hall2, Poznan_Street, Undo_Dancer, Shark) are with 1080P resolution. The texture images use the QPs at 25, 30, 35 and 40. The depth maps use the QPs at 34, 39, 42 and 45. Other encoding parameters are kept the same as the CTC. Coding efficiency loss is evaluated by Bjontegaard delta bierate (BD-rate) [18], and a negative percentage indicates the rate savings that the proposed algorithm can bring. Conversely, the positive percentage represents the loss of coding performance. And the time saved by the entire coding which derives from Eq. (2) is used to measure the complexity reduction.

$$\Delta T = (T_{org} - T_{prop})/T_{prop} * 100\% \tag{2}$$

T_{org} represents the encoding time of the anchor (HTM-13.0) and T_{prop} represents the encoding time of the proposed algorithm.

Table 2. Performance of the proposed fast depth map intra mode decision

Sequence	BD-rate (video)	BD-rate (synthesis)	ΔT
Balloons	0.0%	0.0%	4.1%
Kendo	0.0%	−0.4%	5.3%
Newspaper_CC	0.0%	−0.1%	4.2%
GT_Fly	0.0%	0.1%	0.7%
Poznan_Hall2	0.0%	0.2%	6.6%
Poznan_Street	0.0%	0.0%	4.8%
Undo_Dancer	0.0%	0.1%	8.8%
Shark	0.0%	0.1%	3.7%
1024 × 768	0.0%	−0.1%	4.2%
1920 × 1088	0.0%	0.1%	4.9%
Average	**0.0%**	**0.0%**	**4.6%**

Table 2 summaries the performance of the proposed fast depth map intra mode decision. On average, the time saving is only 4.6% with no increase of bitrate in depth coding. In Table 3, early terminated CU split decision reduces 22.5% computational complexity on average while increasing by 0.1% of BD-rate in depth coding. The reasons why the same judgement condition in two decisions leads to different results are as follows: 1. The recursive process of the quad-tree CU partition which takes up the largest proportion of the encoding time (at least 80% in the reference software HM [17]). 2. CU partition precedes the intra mode prediction. If the CU is smooth, the corresponding PU is also probably smooth.

Table 4 shows the experimental results of coding performance and complexity reduction for the algorithm which combines fast depth map intra mode decision with early terminated CU split decision compared with HTM13.0. From Table 4, we observe that the proposed algorithm achieves an average of 23.3% saved time for total video coding, with a distinguished BD-rate decrease of 1.3% on synthesized views. Specifically, for sequences like Kendo, Undo_Dancer, and GT_

Table 3. Performance of the proposed early terminated CU split decision

Sequence	BD-rate (video)	BD-rate (synthesis)	ΔT
Balloons	0.0%	0.0%	17.9%
Kendo	0.0%	0.1%	22.2%
Newspaper_CC	0.0%	0.0%	9.6%
GT_Fly	0.0%	0.0%	10.8%
Poznan_Hall2	0.0%	0.3%	40.2%
Poznan_Street	0.0%	−0.1%	13.9%
Undo_Dancer	0.0%	0.0%	33.1%
Shark	0.0%	0.7%	32.4%
1024 × 768	0.0%	0.0%	16.6%
1920 × 1088	0.0%	0.2%	26.1%
Average	**0.0%**	**0.1%**	**22.5%**

Table 4. The proposed algorithms in terms of BD-rate and time reduction

Sequence	BD-rate (video)	BD-rate (synthesis)	ΔT
Balloons	0.0%	0.1%	21.7%
Kendo	0.0%	−2.4%	25.3%
Newspaper_CC	0.0%	0.1%	9.5%
GT_Fly	0.0%	−6.5%	12.5%
Poznan_Hall2	0.0%	0.6%	42%
Poznan_Street	0.0%	0.2%	13.1%
Undo_Dancer	0.0%	−2.9%	38.8%
Shark	0.0%	0.7%	23.5%
1024 × 768	0.0%	−0.7%	18.9%
1920 × 1088	0.0%	−1.3%	26%
Average	**0.0%**	**−1.3%**	**23.3%**

Fly, the BD-rate turns to negative, indicating that an RD performance gain has been achieved by early coding unit splitting termination for depth. Because these sequences have ground-truth depth maps with clean edges, it is easier to predict the CU partition structure than those camera-captured sequences, whose depth maps estimated by stereo matching for which contain many artifacts. It does not make any impact on the texture videos compression (BD-rate(video)), since the algorithm only works for depth map compression. It only affects the depth map and synthesized views. Table 5 compares the proposed algorithm with the state-of-art for depth map coding. The BD-Rate is measured on the synthesized views. Most researches on depth map achieve 21.8%–37.65% time reduction but at the cost of BD-rate increase. Our decision can save 23.3% coding runtime while maintaining a distinguished BD-rate decrease of 1.3% on synthesized views.

Table 5. Comparison result

	HTM (version)	BD-rate (synthesis)	ΔT
Gu's [6]	HTM7.0	0.24%	21.84%
Gu's [7]	HTM7.0	0.30%	34.4%
Park's [8]	HTM9.1	0.13%	22.19%
Sliva's [9]	HTM9.3	0.26%	9.2%
Peng's [2]	HTM13.0	0.8%	37.6%
Proposed	**HTM13.0**	**−1.3%**	**23.3%**

5   Conclution

In this paper, an effective and efficient technique is proposed to reduce the complexity of depth coding in 3D-HEVC. Smooth pixel blocks of the depth map can skip DMMs and unnecessary splitting. We firstly expore the characteristics of the pixel block after wavelet transforming in order to determine an absolutely smooth area of depth map. Then we judge whether the variance of the pixel values on the four sides of the pixel block is smaller than a given threshold to determine relatively smooth areas of the depth map. The final algorithm combines two decisions including fast depth map intra mode decision and early terminated CU split decision. Experimental result shows that the proposed methods can reduce computational time by 23.3% with a distinguished BD-rate decrease of 1.3% on synthesized views.

References

1. Tech, G., Chen, Y., Muller, K., Ohm, J., Vetro, A., Wang, Y.: Overview of the multiview and 3D extensions of high efficiency video coding. IEEE Trans. Circ. Syst. Video Technol. **26**(1), 35–49 (2016)
2. Peng, K.K., Chiang, J.C., Lie, W.N.: Low complexity depth intra coding combining fast intra mode and fast CU size decision in 3D-HEVC. In: IEEE International Conference on Image Processing (2016)
3. Guo, R., Gang, H., Li, Y., et al.: Fast algorithm for prediction unit and mode decisions of intra depth coding in 3D-HEVC. In: IEEE International Conference on Image Processing (2016)
4. Chen, Y., Tech, G., Wegner, K., Yea, S.: Test model 11 of 3D-HEVC and MVHEVC.JCT-3V Document, JCT3V-J1003, Geneva, CH (2015)
5. Mai, X., Li, T., Wang, Z., et al.: Reducing complexity of HEVC: a deep learning approach. IEEE Trans. Image Process. **27**(10), 5044–5059 (2018)
6. Gu, Z., Zheng, J., Ling, N., Zhang, P.: Simplified depth intra mode selection for 3D video compression. In: IEEE International Symposium on Circuits Systems, pp. 1110–1113, 1–5 June 2014
7. Gu, Z., Zheng, J., Ling, N., et al.: Fast bi-partition mode selection for 3D HEVC depth intra coding. In: IEEE International Conference on Multimedia & Expo. IEEE (2014)

8. Park, C.-S.: Edge-based intramode selection for depth-map coding in 3D-HEVC. Image Process. IEEE Trans. Image Process. **24**(1), 155–162 (2015)
9. da Silva, T.L., Agostini, L.V., da Silva Cruz, L.A.: Complexity reduction of depth intra coding for 3D video extension of HEVC. In: Visual Communications and Image Processing Conference 2014 IEEE, pp. 229–232, 7–10 December 2014
10. Liu, Z., Yu, X., Gao, Y., Chen, S., Ji, X., Wang, D.: CU partition mode decision for HEVC hardwired intra encoder using convolution neural network. IEEE Trans. Image Process. A Publ. IEEE Signal Process. Soc. **25**(11), 5088–5103 (2016)
11. Zhang, T., Sun, M.T., Zhao, D., Gao, W.: Fast intra mode and CU size decision for HEVC. IEEE Trans. Circ. Syst. Video Technol. **27**(8), 1714–1726 (2016)
12. Ruiz, D., Fernandez-Escribano, G., et al.: Fast CU partitioning algorithm for HEVC intra coding using data mining. Multimedia Tools Appl. **76**(1), 861–894 (2017). https://doi.org/10.1007/s11042-015-3014-6
13. Sullivan, G.J., Ohm, J.-R., Han, W.-J., Wiegand, T.: Overview of the high efficiency video coding (HEVC) standard. IEEE Trans. Circ. Syst. Video Technol. **22**(12), 1649–1668 (2012)
14. Antonini, M., Barlaud, M., Mathieu, P., Daubechies, I.: Image coding using wavelet transform. IEEE Trans. Image Process. **1**(2), 205–220 (1992)
15. Muller, K., Ohm, J., Vetro, A.: Common test conditions of 3dv core experiments document jct3v-g1100 itu-t sg 16 wp 3 and iso/iec jtc1/sc 29/wg 11. January (2014)
16. JCT-VC. (2014). HM Software. https://hevc.hhi.fraunhofer.de/svn/svnHEVC Software/tags/HM-16.5/. 05 November 2016
17. Katayama, T., Song, T., Shi, W., Jiang, X., Shimamoto, T.: Fast edge detection and early depth decision for intra coding of 3D-HEVC. Int. J. Adv. Comput. Electroni. Eng. **2**(7), 11–20 (2017)
18. Bjontegaard, G.: Calculation of average PSNR differences between RD-Curves. ITU-T VCEG-M33 (2001)

Super Resolution via Residual Restructured Dense Network

Yifeng Wang$^{(\boxtimes)}$ (ID), Yaru Rong (ID), Haihong Zheng (ID),
and Aoli Liu (ID)

School of Computer Science and Technology, Xidian University,
Xi'an 71000, China
yfwang@xidian.edu.cn

Abstract. Recently, Convolutional Neural Networks (CNN) have made an impressive breakthrough in single image super-resolution (SISR). By utilizing the advantages of densely connected neural network and classical residual network, we propose a deep convolutional network named residual restructured dense network (RRDN). By combining dense concatenation and residual skip connection, we design residual restructured dense block (RRDBlock), which extracts long and short memory features with different receptive fields and helps the network reuse effective features. Moreover, direct paths from the previous layers to the subsequent layers helps RRDN mitigate the problems of gradient vanishing and instability during training. We evaluate the proposed method using four standard benchmark datasets and the results show that RRDN achieves high reconstruction performance.

Keywords: Super resolution · Residual skip connection · Dense concatenation

1 Introduction

Single image super resolution (SISR) [1] reconstructs a high-resolution (HR) image from a low-resolution (LR) image. HR images contain important features such as edge and texture, which can provide key information for later high-visual image processing, such as iris recognition, ultrasound imaging and medical image processing. Recently, many SISR methods based on deep convolutional neural network (CNN) have acquired high quality HR images.

Kim et al. [2] construct a deep convolutional network (VDSR) with 20 weight layers for residual learning, and the reconstruction performance achieves a significant improvement. The deep recursive residual network (DRRN) [3] with 52 convolutional layers uses global and local residual learning to mitigate the difficulty of training, and it combines recursive learning to control the model parameters. Tai et al. [4] propose a deep persistent memory network (MemNet) that introduces a memory block consisting of a recursive unit and a gate unit to explore persistent features. One commonality of the works above is that they only use high-level features to reconstruct HR images but ignore using features of different layers together. In addition, they need pre-interpolated LR images as input, which increases computational complexity and also loses some pixel-level information.

© Springer Nature Switzerland AG 2019
Z. Lin et al. (Eds.): PRCV 2019, LNCS 11858, pp. 794–805, 2019.
https://doi.org/10.1007/978-3-030-31723-2_68

To solve these problems, SRResNet [5] with 37 convolutional layers is designed based on ResNet [6] and combines sub-pixel convolutional layers [12] to complete image up-sampling. Although SRResNet introduces residual learning, features of local convolutional layers cannot reach the subsequent layers directly, so not all layers' information is fully utilized. SRDenseNet [7] adopts the dense concatenations [8] to build direct short paths between input/output and each layer, alleviating the vanishing-gradient problem. However, SRDenseNet ignores the residual information between layers, which eventually leads to greater redundancy.

To address these drawbacks, we propose a novel network called residual restructured dense network (RRDN), which takes the LR image as input and uses deconvolution [11] to speed up the reconstruction. We propose residual restructured dense block (RRDBlock) with bottleneck layer and local residual learning as the main module of RRDN. In RRDBlock, contiguous memory (CM) mechanism persistently deliver information from previous layers to later layers, bottleneck layer allows to explore and transport locally dense features, and local skip connection with local dense concatenation (LSC with LDC) effectively learns residual information between high-level features and low-level features local. As a result, RRDN can make full use of features to reconstruct HR image. As far as peak signal-to-noise ratio (PSNR) and structural similarity index (SSIM) are concerned, experiments on four standard benchmark datasets indicate that the network achieves better reconstruction accuracy.

2 Related Work

2.1 ResNet

Residual learning is the core idea of ResNet, which aims at mitigating the difficulty of training deep networks. Experiments demonstrate that it is challenging to stack multiple convolutional layers to learn the identity mapping in deep networks. To solve this issue, ResNet learns the difference between the input and output of multiple convolutional layers, and the sum of input and residual mapping is equivalent to the identity mapping. Formally, residual learning can be expressed as:

$$H(W;x) = x + F(W;x) \tag{1}$$

where, x indicates the input of residual learning, $H(W;x)$ indicates the identity mapping, and $F(W;x)$ indicates the residual mapping. $+$ indicates element-wise addition.

Bottleneck block is proposed to build a deeper residual network. The middle 3×3 convolutional layer is used to learn the residual mapping function. The 1×1 convolutional layer at the start and end are used to reduce and increase the number of channels, letting the middle 3×3 convolution work on fewer inputs and further reduce the amount of network parameters. ResNet is a modular architecture stacked by multiple residual learning modules.

2.2   DenseNet

Dense concatenations establish direct short paths between any layer and all subsequent layers. Information can be transmitted directly to the network's head or tail, thus enhancing the flow of signals and mitigating the gradient disappearance or explosions, which can help build a deeper network. The output of each layer that is densely cascaded can be formulated as:

$$x_n = H_n([x_0, x_1, \ldots, x_{n-1}]) \tag{2}$$

where, x_n indicates the output feature-maps of the n-th layer, $[x_0, x_1, \ldots, x_{n-1}]$ indicates the concatenation of feature-maps from the 0-th to $(n-1)$-th layer. H_n indicates the composite function of the n-th layer, mainly including convolution, activation operation and batch normalization.

Growth rate regulates the number of new features that each layer contributes to the whole network. Assuming that k indicates the number of output feature-maps of each layer, then the number of input feature-maps of the n-th layer is $(k*(n-1))$. In the case where the number of layer n is determined, smaller k guarantees that each layer has smaller inputs. So that each layer of the network learns only a very small number of features, then the number of features obtained by dense cascading will not explode, which significantly reduces the parameters quantity.

3   Residual Restructured Dense Network

In order to take full advantage of features extracted from the preceding layers and to reconstruct HR image with features of different receptive fields, We design Residual Restructured Dense Block (RRDBlock) with Bottleneck Layer and local residual learning as the building module of our proposed network, RRDN.

3.1   Bottleneck Layer

As shown in Fig. 1, each of our Bottleneck Layer consists of two units: dense features collection (DFC) unit and features integration and learning (FIL) unit.

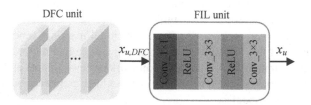

Fig. 1. Architecture of Bottleneck Layer

DFC aims at collecting features with different receptive field size, to ensure long-term memory of the effective features, and to further improve the flow of information through direct short connections between the previous and latter layers in network. We cascade the output of all Bottleneck Layers before current Bottleneck Layer, and define it as DFC of the u-th Bottleneck Layer, which is formulated as:

$$x_{u,DFC} = [x_0, x_1, \ldots, x_{u-1}] \tag{3}$$

where, $[x_0, x_1, \ldots, x_{u-1}]$ indicates the concatenation of output feature-maps from the 0-th to the $(u-1)$-th Bottleneck Layer, $x_{u,\,DFC}$ indicates DFC of the u-th Bottleneck Layer.

FIL is designed according to the bottleneck structure of ResNet, and aims at improving the bottleneck layer of DenseNet, but abandons all batch normalization layers. In detail, the FIL unit includes a 1×1 convolutional layer (C_1), an active layer, a 3×3 convolutional layer (C_2), an active layer, and a 3×3 convolutional layer (C_3) from left to right. The output of FIL or the u-th Bottleneck Layer is formulated as:

$$x_u = H_u(x_{u,DFC}) \tag{4}$$

$$x_u = \omega_{u,3} \cdot \sigma(\omega_{u,2} \cdot \sigma(\omega_{u,1} \cdot x_{u,DFC})) \tag{5}$$

where, H_u indicates the composite function of the u-th Bottleneck Layer, including convolution operations and activation functions. Equation 5 is an expanded description of Eq. 4, where $\omega_{u,1}$, $\omega_{u,2}$ and $\omega_{u,3}$ indicate weight parameters of C_1, C_2 and C_3 in the u-th Bottleneck Layer, respectively. σ indicates the nonlinear activation function ReLU.

Assuming that C_3 produces k outputs, then the u-th Bottleneck Layer accepts $(k_0 + k*(u-1))$ input feature-maps, where k_0 represents the number of input channels of the first Bottleneck Layer, and k represents the growth rate in DenseNet. In each Bottleneck Layer, C_1 reduces the number of input feature-maps and controls the parameter quantity of network; C_2 explores more new features; C_3 determines how many local features are transmitted to whole network. So we let C_1, C_2 and C_3 output 2 k, 4 k and k features, respectively.

3.2   Residual Restructured Dense Block(RRDBlock)

To increase the diversity of local features and ensure a small growth rate of features, we introduce the Bottleneck Layer and LSC with LDC to restructure DenseNet block into RRDBlock.

RRDBlock collects features of different levels by dense concatenations while mining more new features. Each RRDBlock is composed of U Bottleneck Layers. For simplicity, Fig. 2 shows an RRDBlock with four Bottleneck Layers.

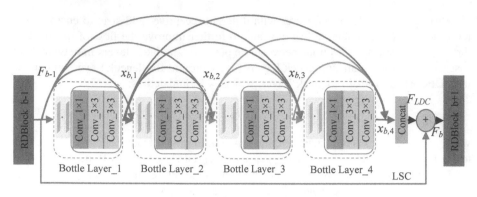

Fig. 2. Architecture of RRDBlock

In a RRDBlock, the input of the u-th Bottleneck Layer (i.e. the u-th DFC unit, see Eq. 3) $x_{b,u,DFC}$ can be re-represented as Eq. 6.

$$x_{b,u,DFC} = \left[F_{b-1}, x_{b,1}, \ldots, x_{b,u-1}\right] \tag{6}$$

where, F_{b-1} indicates the outputs of the $(b-1)$-th RRDBlock, $[F_{b-1}, x_{b,1}, \ldots, x_{b,u-1}]$ indicates the concatenation of outputs of the $(b-1)$-th RRDBlock and outputs of the 1-th to $(u-1)$-th Bottleneck Layers in the b-th RRDBlock.

The DFC unit in each Bottleneck Layer can also be regarded as a **contiguous memory** (CM) mechanism for feature information, which is realized by transferring the state of the previous RRDBlock to each Bottleneck Layer in the current RRDBlock. The outputs of the preceding RRDBlock have direct paths to each Bottleneck Layer in the subsequent RRDBlock, and the red lines in Fig. 2 indicates that features can be passed directly between the two above without replication. So, following forward propagation, features can flow in the network efficiently.

Local skip connection with local dense concatenation (LSC with LDC) mainly consists of two parts: LDC and LSC, which can improve the flow of information and the network reconstruction performance. Local dense concatenation (LDC) is implemented by paralleling the output of each Bottleneck Layer by channel (the Concat Layer in Fig. 2). LDC establishes direct paths in each Bottleneck Layer of the current RRDBlock and the subsequent RRDBlock, that helps local feature information arrive to the end of the network.

To satisfy local residual learning, we let LDC only cascade the output of each Bottleneck Layer in a RRDBlock. The densely cascaded local feature F_{LDC} can be formulated as:

$$F_{LDC} = \left[x_{b,1}, \ldots, x_{b,U}\right] \tag{7}$$

where, $[x_{b,1}, \ldots, x_{b,U}]$ indicates the concatenation of output features from each Bottleneck Layer in the b-th RRDBlock, U indicates the number of Bottleneck layers in a RRDBlock.

Local skip connection (LSC) is introduced based on LDC, which helps the network adaptively select the common features with long-term memory (F_{b-1}) and the local dense features of the current RRDBlock (F_{LDC}).

Finally, the output of the b-th RRDBlock F_b is formulated as:

$$F_b = F_{b-1} + F_{LDC} \tag{8}$$

This can be seen as a residual learning (+) with a dense operation part (F_{LDC}).

3.3   Residual Restructured Dense Network(RRDN)

We cascade several RRDBlocks as the core module of RRDN to enrich the variety of global features that are ultimately used for reconstruction. The framework of RRDN is shown in Fig. 3. It is mainly divided into four parts: low-level features extraction block (LFEBlock), residual restructured dense blocks (RRDBlocks), features fusion block (FFBlock) and reconstruction block (RecBlock). X_{LR} and Y_{HR} represent LR input image and HR output image of network respectively, Y_T indicates the truth HR images.

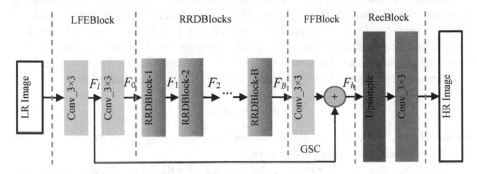

Fig. 3. Architecture of RRDN

Firstly, we stack two consecutive 3×3 convolutional layers in LFEBlock to extract rich low-level features from LR images, which is formulated as:

$$\begin{aligned} F_0 &= H_{LEFBlock}(X_{LR}) \\ &= \omega_0 \cdot (\omega_l \cdot X_{LR}) \\ &= \omega_0 \cdot F_l \end{aligned} \tag{9}$$

where, F_l indicates output of the first convolution in LFEBlock, F_0 indicates the output of LFEBlock, $H_{LEFBlock}$ indicates the low-level feature extraction functions, ω_l and ω_0 indicates the weights of two convolutions, respectively.

Secondly, we stack B RRDBlocks, which helps RRDN learn higher-level feature. The output of RRDBlocks F_B is formulated as:

$$F_B = H_{RRDBlock-B}(\dots(H_{RRDBlock-b}(\dots(H_{RRDBlock-1}(F_0))\dots))\dots) \qquad (10)$$

where, $H_{RRDBlock-b}$ indicates the composite function of the b-th RRDBlock.

Next, we build FFBlock to reinforce long-term memory on common features. More concretely, we first stack a 3×3 convolutional layer to enhance the local dense feature information. Then, we introduce global skip connection (GSC) between low-level features and high-level features in LR feature space to learn difference between the two. The output of FFBlock F_h is formulated as:

$$F_h = F_l + H_{FConv}(F_B) \qquad (11)$$

where, F_l indicates low-level features of the first convolutional layer in LFEBlock, F_h indicates the fusion high-level features in LR feature space, H_{FConv} indicates the composite function of FFBlock, that is a 3×3 convolution operation.

Lastly, we stack an up-sampling layer and a convolutional layer in the RecBlock to reconstruct the HR estimation. For up-sampling layer, we adopt deconvolution to transform the LR feature space into the HR feature space. In detail, the $\times 2$ and $\times 3$ models use a deconvolution with 128 filters of size 5×5; the $\times 4$ model uses two consecutive deconvolution operations, each operation has 128 filters of size 5×5. After the feature space transformation, the 3×3 convolution layer outputs one reconstructed HR image. The final output of RRDN Y_{HR} is formulated as:

$$Y_{HR} = H_R(H_{DeConv}(F_h)) \qquad (12)$$

where, H_{DeConv} indicates the deconvolution of up-sampling layer, H_R indicates the 3×3 convolution of reconstruction layer.

RRDN has three key parameters: the number of RRDBlocks (denotes as B), the number of Bottleneck Layers in one RRDBlock (denotes as U), and the growth rate (denotes as k), where B and U control the depth of RRDN, and U and k control the width of RRDN. Each RRDBlock is composed of U Bottleneck Layers, and one Bottleneck Layer produces k output feature-maps, so each RRDBlock produces $(U*k)$ output feature-maps. For LSC, in addition to the convolutional layers in RRDBlocks and RecBlock, we let the other layers produce $(U*k)$ output feature-maps. In this paper, we call RRDN $\{B = 4, U = 4, k = 16\}$ the standard RRDN.

4   Experiments

4.1   Settings

Datasets and Preprocess. For training, we use DIV2K [9] dataset composed of 1000 h images. For testing, we utilize four standard benchmark datasets: Set5 [13], Set14 [14], BSD100 [15] and Urban100 [16]. We apply data augment (90 rotation and horizontal flip) on DIV2K. Then we preprocess the training dataset. Firstly, we transform HR image from RGB space into YCbCr space, and only process the Y-channel image during training. Secondly, we down-sample the Y-channel HR image by bicubic interpolation, to generate LR image with corresponding scaling factor. Next, we crop LR image to no-overlapping 41 *41 size patches, and obtain corresponding HR patches for different scaling factors.

Training Setting. Weight parameters are initialized by MSRA [10] and bias parameters are set to zero. We optimize RRDN with Adam [17] algorithm by minimizing mean square error (MSE), and we set momentum to 0.9, weight decay to 0.0001, mini-batch size to 64. RRDN is trained on NVidia GeForce GTX 1070 GPU during 100 epochs. We set the initial learning rate to 0.0001, and reduce it by a factor of 10 every 50 epochs. Note, we first train ×4 model in Caffe platform. After the model converges, we use the optimal parameters to initialize other models and fine-tune others in 50 epochs with learning rate of 5×10^{-5}.

4.2 Ablation Investigation

Table 1 shows the ablation investigation of continuous memory (CM) and local skip connection with local dense concatenation (LSC with LDC).

Table 1. Ablation investigation of CM and LSC with LDC

	The combination of CM and LSC with LDC			
CM	×	×	✓	✓
LSC with LDC	×	✓	×	✓
PSNR (dB)	31.58	31.75	31.78	31.91

Based on the standard RRDN, RRDN_Base (the first combination in Table 1) is obtained without CM and LSC with LDC, and performs relatively poorly (PSNR = 31.58 dB). This is mainly due to the difficulty of deep network training, meanwhile gradient and feature information cannot flow in the network in time.

We then add LSC with LDC and CM to RRDN_Base respectively, and get two networks RRDN_LSC_with_LDC and RRDN_CM (the second and third combination in Table 1). Experimental results show that the two network performance is increased by 0.17 dB and 0.20 dB respectively. This is mainly because each component can efficiently improve the flow of features and gradient, and avoid the disappearance of information, thus ensuring the stability of training deeper network.

We further add two components (i.e. RRDBlock) to RRDN_Base, resulting in RRDN_CM_LSC_with_LSC (the last combination in Table 1). It can be seen that two components perform better than only one component; the average PSNR is increased by 0.13 dB. RRDN_CM_LSC_with_LSC gets the best reconstructed performance, so, the contribution of RRDBlock is obvious.

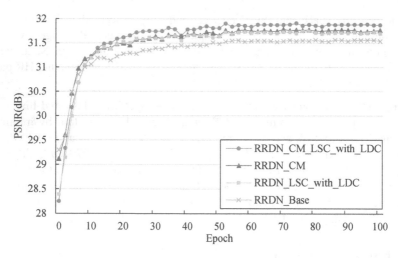

Fig. 4. Convergence analysis on CM and LSC with LDC. The curves for each combination are based on the PSNR on Set5 with scaling factor ×4 in 100 epochs.

The convergence process of these four combinations is shown in Fig. 4, we can see the effectiveness of the proposed RRDBlock.

4.3   Comparison with State-of-the-Art Models

We compare the proposed method with other SR methods, including bicubic, VDSR, DRRN and MemNet quantitatively and qualitatively.

Table 2 shows the quantitative results on the four benchmark datasets in terms of PSNR and SSIM. We can see that, RRDN always outperforms the comparison algorithms by a considerable margin under all scale factors. Especially on the recent difficult Urban100 dataset, RRDN achieves the improvement margin of 0.56, 0.32, and 0.30 dB on scale factor ×2, ×3 and ×4 respectively, compared with MemNet.

Table 2. Benchmark results. Average PSNR/SSIMs for scale factor ×2, ×3 and ×4 on datasets Set5, Set14, BSD100 and Urban100.

Dataset	Scale	Bicubic PSNR/SSIM	VDSR PSNR/SSIM	DRRN PSNR/SSIM	MemNet PSNR/SSIM	RRDN PSNR/SSIM
Set5	×2	33.66/0.9299	37.53/0.9587	37.73/0.9591	37.78/0.9597	**37.92/0.9598**
	×3	30.39/0.8682	33.66/0.9213	34.03/0.9244	34.09/0.9248	**34.20/0.9252**
	×4	28.42/0.8104	31.35/0.8838	31.68/0.8888	31.74/0.8893	**31.91/0.8905**
Set14	×2	30.24/0.8688	33.03/0.9124	33.23/0.9136	33.28/0.9142	**33.48/0.9162**
	×3	27.55/0.7742	29.77/0.8314	29.96/0.8349	30.00/0.8350	**30.15/0.8380**
	×4	26.00/0.7027	28.01/0.7674	28.21/0.7720	28.26/0.7723	**28.37/0.7749**
BSD100	×2	29.56/0.8431	31.90/0.8960	32.05/0.8973	32.08/0.8978	**32.15/0.8991**
	×3	27.21/0.7385	28.82/0.7976	28.95/0.8004	28.96/0.8001	**29.00/0.8026**
	×4	25.96/0.6674	27.29/0.7251	27.38/0.7284	27.40/0.7281	**27.48/0.7310**
Urban100	×2	26.88/0.8403	30.76/0.9140	31.23/0.9188	31.31/0.9195	**31.87/0.9257**
	×3	24.46/0.7349	27.14/0.8279	27.53/0.8378	27.56/0.8376	**27.88/0.8457**
	×4	23.14/0.6577	25.18/0.7524	25.44/0.7638	25.50/0.7630	**25.80/0.7752**

Figure 5 illustrates the qualitative results. Image "barbara" has serious distortion due to loss of high frequency information, which can be seen from other comparison algorithms. Only RRDN captures clear texture, and its reconstructed effect is almost the same as HR ground truth. From image "78004", we can see that RRDN not only obtains clearer outline, but also avoids image distortion largely, while other algorithms have different degrees of image distortion. In image "img_072", only RRDN solves image blurring problems and get a clearer structure. Image "8023" of all comparison algorithms have serious artifacts, while RRDN eliminates partial artifacts and restores HR image closer to the original one.

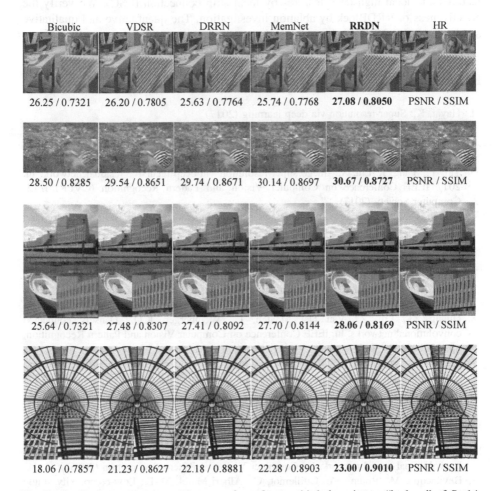

Bicubic	VDSR	DRRN	MemNet	**RRDN**	HR
26.25 / 0.7321	26.20 / 0.7805	25.63 / 0.7764	25.74 / 0.7768	**27.08 / 0.8050**	PSNR / SSIM
28.50 / 0.8285	29.54 / 0.8651	29.74 / 0.8671	30.14 / 0.8697	**30.67 / 0.8727**	PSNR / SSIM
25.64 / 0.7321	27.48 / 0.8307	27.41 / 0.8092	27.70 / 0.8144	**28.06 / 0.8169**	PSNR / SSIM
18.06 / 0.7857	21.23 / 0.8627	22.18 / 0.8881	22.28 / 0.8903	**23.00 / 0.9010**	PSNR / SSIM

Fig. 5. Qualitative comparison. The rows from first to third show image "barbara" of Set14, image "8023" of BSD100 and image "78004" of BSD100 with scale factor ×3, respectively. The last row shows image "img_072" of Urban100 with scale factor ×4.

5 Conclusion

In this paper, we propose a residual restructured dense network (RRDN), where residual restructured dense block (RRDBlock) serves as the core module. We cascade several RRDBlocks to enrich the diversity of features that the network eventually learns. RRDN allows direct connection paths between the preceding RRDBlock and all Bottleneck Layers of the current RRDBlock, which improves the flow of information. In addition, RRDBlock guarantees the utilization of different-level features by local dense concatenation (LDC), and learns the residual coefficients between local low-level features and local high-level features by local skip connection (LSC). We verify the effectiveness of RRDBlock by ablation investigation. The quantitative and qualitative results show that RRDN achieves superior reconstruction performance.

References

1. Hayat, K.: Super-resolution via deep learning (2017)
2. Kim, J., Kwon Lee, J., Mu Lee, K.: Accurate image super-resolution using very deep convolutional networks. In: IEEE Conference on Computer Vision and Pattern Recognition, pp. 1646–1654 (2016)
3. Tai, Y., Yang, J., Liu, X.: Image super-resolution via deep recursive residual network. In: 2017 IEEE Conference on Computer Vision and Pattern Recognition (CVPR) IEEE Computer Society (2017)
4. Tai, Y., Yang, J., Liu, X., et al.: MemNet: a persistent memory network for image restoration (2017)
5. Ledig, C., et al.: Photo-realistic single image super-resolution using a generative adversarial network (2016)
6. He, K., Zhang, X., Ren, S., et al.: Deep residual learning for image recognition (2015)
7. Tong, T., et al.: Image super-resolution using dense skip connections. In: 2017 IEEE International Conference on Computer Vision (ICCV) IEEE Computer Society (2017)
8. Huang, G., Liu, Z., Van Der Maaten, L., Weinberger, K.Q.: Densely connected convolutional networks. In: IEEE Conference on Computer Vision and Pattern Recognition, pp. 2261–2269 (2017)
9. Timofte, R., et al.: NTIRE 2017 challenge on single image super-resolution: methods and results. In: IEEE Conference on Computer Vision & Pattern Recognition Workshops (2017)
10. He, K., Zhang, X., Ren, S., et al.: Delving deep into rectifiers: surpassing human-level performance on ImageNet classification (2015)
11. Xu, L., Ren, J.S.J., Liu, C., et al.: Deep convolutional neural network for image deconvolution, vol. 2, pp. 1790–1798 (2014)
12. Shi, W., et al.: Real-time single image and video super-resolution using an efficient sub-pixel convolutional neural network. In: Computer Vision & Pattern Recognition (2016)
13. Bevilacqua, M., Roumy, A., Guillemot, C., Alberi-Morel, M.-L.: Low-complexity single image super-resolution based on nonnegative neighbor embedding (2012)
14. Wang, Z., Liu, D., Yang, J., Han, W., Huang, T.: Deep networks for image super-resolution with sparse prior, pp. 370–378 (2015)

15. Martin, D., Fowlkes, C., Tal, D., Malik, J.: A database of human segmented natural images and its application to evaluating segmentation algorithms and measuring ecological statistics. In: Proceedings of 8th IEEE Conference Computer Vision, vol. 2, pp. 416–423, July 2001
16. Huang, J.-B., Singh, A., Ahuja, N.: Single image super-resolution from transformed self-exemplars. In: IEEE Conference on Computer Vision and Pattern Recognition, pp. 5197–5206 (2015)
17. Kingma, D., Ba, J.: Adam: a method for stochastic optimization. computer science (2014)

Author Index